TOWARDS THE PROSPERITY OF INTERNATIONAL LAW STUDIES

(SIX VOLUMES)

走向繁荣的国际法学

（全六卷）

2009 ~ 2019

SYMPOSIUM IN CELEBRATION OF
THE 10TH ANNIVERSARY OF
THE CASS INSTITUTE OF INTERNATIONAL LAW

【English Volume】

General Editor-in-Chief
Mo Jihong

Editor-in-Chief
Liao Fan
Ren Hongda

社会科学文献出版社
SOCIAL SCIENCES ACADEMIC PRESS (CHINA)

Group photo of Chen Guoping, Secretary of the Joint Party Committee of the Institute of Law and the Institute of International Law, and Deputy Director of the Institute of Law; Chen Su, Director of the Institute of Law; Mo Jihong, Director of the Institute of International Law; Zhou Hanhua, Deputy Director of the Institute of Law; and Liu Huawen, Deputy Director of the Institute of International Law

Group photo of Chen Guoping, Secretary of the Joint Party Committee of the Institute of Law and the Institute of International Law, and Deputy Director of the Institute of Law; Mo Jihong, Director of the Institute of International Law; and Liu Huawen, Deputy Director of the Institute of International Law

November 20, 2009, Ceremony for the renaming of the CASS Center for International Law into the CASS Institute of International Law (from left: Wang Keju, Jiang Xihui, Tao Zhenghua, Liu Nanlai, Wang Weiguang, Chen Zexian, Chen Su, Wang Suyue, Feng Jun, Zhao Jianwen, Zhang Wenguang, Sun Shiyan, Liu Huawen)

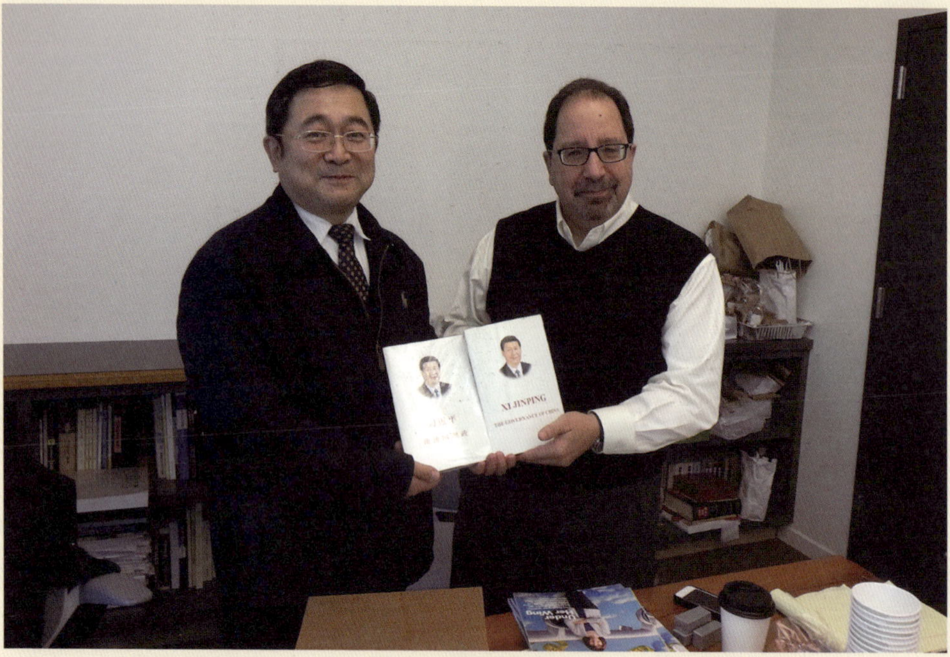

February 6, 2015, at the US-Asia Law Institute of the NYU School of Law, Professor Mo Jihong presented the Executive Director Ira Belkin the Chinese and English versions of the book *Xi Jinping: The Governance of China*

February 8-11, 2019, Director Mo Jihong attended the 1st LAWASIA Human Rights Conference in New Delhi, India

December 4, 2018, Director Mo Jihong delivered a speech at the CCTV Rule of Law Figures of 2018 Awards Ceremony

March 1, 2017, the then Vice Foreign Minister Liu Zhenmin presented Professor Liu Huawen the certificate of the Member of the Advisory Committee on International Law, Ministry of Foreign Affairs, China

In turn: group photos of the Department of Public International Law, Department of Private International Law, Department of International Economic Law, Department of International Human Rights Law, and Editorial Department of *Chinese Review of International Law*

May 5, 2019, members of the CASS "Belt and Road Legal Risk Prevention and Legal Mechanism Building " (*herein* "Belt and Road") research project visited Macau SAR, China

May 20, 2019, members of the CASS "Belt and Road" research project visited the ruins of the Chinese Embassy in the Former Yugoslavia

June 27, 2019, members of the CASS "Belt and Road" research project visited the National Institute of Justice of the Ministry of Justice of the Laos

June 24, 2019, members of the CASS "Belt and Road" research project visited the Institute of Chinese Studies, Vietnamese Academy of Social Sciences

July 29, 2019, Deputy Director Liu Huawen attended the Colloquium on International Law in the Changing World: The Role of Developing Countries sponsored by the Ministry of Foreign Affairs and Chinese Society of International Law

June 5, 2019, Deputy Director Liu Huawen attended the CASS High-end Think Tank Forum on the Problems and Solutions regarding the Sino-US Trade Friction

September 1, 2015, Chen Zexian and Liu Huawen attended the Colloquium on the Ways of Enhancing and Ensuring Compliance with International Humanitarian Law sponsored by the ICRC and the Institute of International Law

August 25, 2017, Liu Huawen and Dai Ruijun had a group photo with the ICJ Judge Xue Hanqin (middle) at the 6th Biennial Conference of the AsianSIL in Seoul, Korea

June 16, 2016, Mo Jihong, Liao Fan and Dai Ruijun attended the Sino-Brazilian Comparative Law Seminar in San Paulo, Brazil

August 7, 2019, Assistant Minister Li Chenggang of the Ministry of Commerce signed the Singapore Convention on Mediation on behalf of the Chinese government. The Institute of International Law delegation attended the signing ceremony in Singapore upon invitation (from left: Sun Nanxiang, Fu Panfeng, Mao Xiaofei, Li Chenggang, Huang Jin, Liu Jingdong)

August 7, 2019, the Institute of International Law delegation had a group photo with the UNCITRAL Secretary Anna Joubin-Bret (from left: Fu Panfeng, Liu Jingdong, Anna Joubin-Bret, Mao Xiaofei, Sun Nanxiang)

April 18, 2019, Professor Liao Fan presided a session at the Colloquium on the Future of Globalization and the Sino-Europe/Sino-Italy Cooperation at the Luigi Sturzo Institute in Rome, Italy

Forward

Promoting the Continuous Prosperity of International Law Studies in China

With the establishment of the Central Government of the People's Republic of China on October 1,1949,the Chinese people ended the near 100-year history of being oppressed and enslaved in a semi-colonial and semi-feudal society and stood up tall among the nations of the world. In the past 70 years,they have,under the strong leadership of the Communist Party of China and the Chinese Government,continuously summarized experiences,overcome difficulties,realized breakthroughs and developments,and made tremendous achievements in socialist construction. Especially during the 40 years of reform and opening-up,China has realized economic take-off and social progress,and gained unprecedented international standing and influence. The Eighteenth National Congress of the Communist Party of China in 2012 marked a new era of socialism with Chinese characteristics. China has realized the development process from "standing up" to "getting rich",and ultimately to "becoming strong",and is moving ever closer to the center of the world stage and to the realization of the Chinese Dream of the rejuvenation of the Chinese nation.

The establishment and the 70-year development of the People's Republic of China has created favorable political,economic,social and historical conditions for the development of international law studies in China. The older generation of international law scholars,represented by Professor Zhou Gengsheng,Professor Chen Tiqiang,Professor Li Haopei,Professor Wang Tieya and Professor Han Depei, have made outstanding contributions to and laid the foundation for the startup and the development of the theoretical research, the teaching, as well as the practical work of international law in the People's Republic of China.

On December 13, 1978, Comrade Deng Xiaoping gave a speech entitled "Emancipate the Mind, Seek Truth from Facts and Unite as One in Looking to the Future" at the Central Working Conference held in preparation for the Third Plenary Session of the Eleventh Central Committee of the Chinese Communist Party. In the speech, he clearly pointed out that: "We should intensify our study of international law." This speech, like a spring breeze and a clarion call, greatly inspired the Chinese international law scholars and ushered in the spring of international law studies in China. In February 1980, the Chinese Society of International Law was established and Professor Huan Xiang, the then Vice President of Chinese Academy of Social Sciences, became the first president of the Society.

Chinese Academy of Social Sciences is a stronghold of international research in China. In 1959, the year following the establishment of the Institute of Law under the Division of Philosophy and Social Sciences of Chinese Academy of Sciences, the Research Group of International Law was established under the Institute of Law. In May 1977, with the approval of the Central Committee of the Communist Party of China, the Chinese Academy of Social Sciences (CASS) was formally established on the basis of the Division of Philosophy and Social Sciences of the Chinese Academy of Sciences. And in September 1978, the Research Group of International Law was restructured to become the Department of International Law under the CASS Institute of Law.

The year 2002 was an extraordinary year in the development process of China: it was in this year that China deepened the reform and opening-up, formally joined the WTO, and ratified the International Covenant on Economic, Social and Cultural Rights—an important component of the International Bill of Human Rights. It was also in this year that, with the efforts made by Professor Li Tieying, the then President of CASS, and the approval of the Office of Central Institutional Organization Commission of the Communist Party of China, the Center for International Law was established on the basis of the Department of International

Law of the CASS Institute of Law, as an independent research institution directly under CASS, in parallel with CASS Institute of Law. The establishment of the Center further strengthened and promoted the international law research at CASS. In September 2009, exactly ten years ago, the CASS Center for International Law was officially renamed the CASS Institute of International Law with the approval of the Office of Central Institutional Organization Commission of the Communist Party of China.

The first director of the Institute was Professor Chen Zexian. Professor Chen Su, the current director of CASS Institute of Law and a CASS member, had been the acting director of the CASS Institute of International Law between September 2017 and November 2018; and Professor Mo Jihong became the current director of the Institute in November 2018. The Institute was born in a time when China was making historical breakthroughs in economic development and social progress, greatly boosting its position in international community, and continuously expanding its international influence, with a mission entrusted by the Communist Party of China and the Chinese Government: to promote the development and prosperity of international law studies in China.

In the past ten years, the CASS Institute of International Law has kept in close contact with the Ministry of Foreign Affairs, the Ministry of Commerce and other relevant government departments and worked together with the Chinese Society of International Law and other national-level international law research organizations and academic institutions in actively promoting the prosperity of the international law studies in China. By relying on its discipline and talent advantages, the Institute has set up the following subordinate bodies under it: four research departments, namely the departments of public international law, private international law, international economic law and international human rights law; three Research centers, namely the Center for Oceans Law and Maritime Law, the Center for Competition Law, and the Center for International Criminal Law; and one research base—the "Belt and Road" Judicial Research Base established in cooperation with the Supreme People's Court of China. Meanwhile, by relying on its master's, doctoral and post-doctoral programs, the Institute has also strengthened the instruction of and supervision over master and doctoral candidates and post-doctoral researchers.

The *Chinese Review of International Law*(*CRIL*), inaugurated in 2014, is the first Chinese language periodical of international law in China with an official registration number for publications and the CASS Institute of International Law is its main sponsor and chief editorial unit. Today, *CRIL* is in a leading position in China in terms of reprint rate among academic periodicals in the field of international law and has become an important platform of academic demonstration and exchange in the Chinese international law circle. Since 2004, the Institute of International Law has hosted the annual "International Law Forum" for 15 consecutive years. As a well-known brand of CASS international seminar, the Forum has attracted the attention of and been active participated by international law scholars both at home and abroad. Under the care and encouragement by the older generation of scholars of the Institute, such as Professor Liu Nanlai, Professor Wang Keju, Professor Tao Zhenghua, and Professor Lin Xin, many young and middle-aged scholars of the Institute are becoming academic backbones of the Chinese international law circle.

This symposium, published on the occasion of the 10th anniversary of the establishment of CASS Institute of International Law, contains carefully selected research achievements by scholars of the Institute, including many influential papers published in *CRIL*. By reviewing the journey taken by the Institute since its establishment and displaying its current styles and features, it is a brief summarization of the development of the Institute, as well as a demonstration of the firm determination of the Institute to make even more splendid achievements in the future.

As China is making more and greater achievements in the construction of the "Belt and Road" around the world and winning increasingly extensive international support for and positive response to its proposition of "building a community with shared future for mankind", the Institute of International Law is faced with many new opportunities as well as new challenges. In the future, the scholars of the Institute will remain true to their original aspiration and keep their mission firmly in mind, and seize every minute to work closely together with their colleagues in the international law circle for promoting the continuous prosperity of the international law studies in China.

Mo Jihong

August 20, 2019

Contents

中国社会科学院国际法研究所概况

一 历史沿革

中国社会科学院国际法研究所是中国国际法学研究的重镇。她的前身是中国社会科学院国际法研究中心、中国社会科学院法学研究所国际法研究室和最早时的中国科学院法学研究所国际法组。

1959 年，在中国科学院哲学社会科学部建立法学研究所的第二年，法学研究所成立了国际法组。1977 年 5 月，经党中央批准，中国社会科学院在中国科学院哲学社会科学部基础上正式组建。1978 年 9 月，中国社会科学院法学研究所国际法组改建为国际法研究室。2002 年 10 月，经中央机构编制委员会办公室批准，在国际法研究室基础上成立国际法研究中心，作为与法学研究所平行的院属所级机构。2009 年 9 月，经中央机构编制委员会办公室批准，国际法研究中心正式更名为国际法研究所，陈泽宪研究员担任首任所长。2017 年 9 月至 2018 年 11 月，由法学研究所所长陈甦研究员代行所长职责。2018 年 11 月至今，莫纪宏研究员担任所长；2019 年 4 月，柳华文研究员被任命为副所长。

二 机构及人员概况

国际法研究所下设“四室一部一处”，即国际公法、国际私法、国际经济法、国际人权法四个研究室，《国际法研究》编辑部和科研处事处。

2014 年创刊的《国际法研究》是中国第一本获得正式刊号的国际法专业原创中文期刊，国际法研究所是其主要主办单位，出版单位为社会科学文献出版社。依托学科和人才优势，国际法研究所还设有竞争法研究中心、国际刑法研究中心、海洋法治研究中心等非实体研究中心，以及最高人民法院“一带一路”司法研究基地。国际法研究所设有国际法专业的博士点和硕士点，目前国际公法、国际私法、国际经济法、国际人权法四个研究方向均可招收博士、硕士研究生和指导博士后研究人员。

国际法研究所目前受聘在岗职工共计 35 人，其中研究员 9 名，副研究员 10 名；博士研究生导师 4 名，硕士研究生导师 14 名。

国际法研究所的研究人员在国内外均拥有很高知名度和广泛影响力。在国际层面，莫纪宏研究员任国际宪法学协会终身名誉主席，刘楠来荣誉学部委员任海牙常设仲裁法院仲裁员，陈泽宪研究员任国际刑法学协会中国分会副主席，柳华文研究员任亚洲国际法学会执委、荷兰跨文化人权研究院执委，孙世彦研究员任《红十字国际评论》编委会委员，王翰灵副研究员曾任联合国法律办公室海洋事务与海洋法司顾问，并长期提任联合国海洋争端解决机制渔业特别仲裁员。

在国内，莫纪宏研究员被评为中国法学会“全国十大杰出青年法学家”，入选人力资源和社会保障部“国家百千万人才工程”，并被授予“有突出贡献中青年专家”荣誉称号，系中宣部文化名家暨四个一批人才、第三批国家“万人计划”哲学社会科学领军人物，为中国法学会学术委员会委员、最高人民检察院专家咨询委员，兼任中国宪法学研究会常务副会长、北京市法学会立法学研究会会长等。刘楠来荣誉学部委员担任外交部第一至第三届国际法咨询委员会顾问。柳华文研究员系外交部第二届、第三届国际法咨询委员会委员，北京国际法学会副会长，中国行为法学会软法研究会副会长，中国国际法学会《中国国际法年刊》主编，云南省法治政府建设专家。刘敬东研究员系中国法学会世界贸易法研究会副会长，中国法学会“百名法学家报告团”成员，曾挂职最高人民法院民四庭副庭长，现任最高人民法院特邀咨询员、最高人民法院国际商事专家委员会首批专家。廖凡研究员系中国国际经济贸易法学研究会国际金融法专业委员会副主任委员、最高人民法院涉外商事海事审判专家库首批专家、新华社首批特约观察员。张文广副研究员系最高人民法院涉外商事海事审判专家库首批专家、最高人民法院国际海事司法上海基地特邀咨询员。此外，莫纪宏研究员、刘楠来研究员、王可菊研究员、陶正华研究员、陈泽宪研究员、沈涓研究员、柳华文研究员系享受国务院政府特殊津贴专家。

三 学科贡献

国际法研究所长期以来扎实推进学科建设，科研实力和综合影响力居于国内领先地位。本所国际公法优势学科依托国际公法和国际人权法两个研究室，研究涵盖国际法基础理论、国际海洋法、人权法、条约法、国际组织法等多个专业方向。国际经济法重点学科依托国际经济法研究室，研究涵盖国际贸易法、国际金融法、国际投资法、国际环境法、海商法等多个专业方向。国际私法学科依托国际私法研究室，研究涵盖冲突法、国际民事诉讼、国际商事仲裁等多个专业方向。自成立至今，各学科均形成了规范完备的学科体系和科学合理的研究梯队。

作为国际法研究所的前身，法学研究所国际法组和国际法研究室是改革开放后国内最早恢复国际法专业研究的团队之一，为中国国际法学的奠基作出了重要贡献。在国际法基本理论方面，早在20世纪60年代，本所学者就出版了两部代表性译著：彼・斯・罗马什金等主编，刘楠来、魏家驹等译的《国家和法的理论》（法律出版社，1964）和格・伊・童金著，王可菊等译的《国际法理论问题》（世界知识出版社，1965）。他们首次向国内学界介绍了苏联的国际法基本理论和与国际法发展动向相关的代表性成果，是国际法基本理论在中国的早期引入者。

海洋法领域。1973年12月第三次联合国海洋法会议在美国纽约拉开序幕，本所国际公法学者全程跟踪会议进程，积极参与有关部门组织的讨论，为与会中国代表团建言献策，成为我国海洋法研究领域的主要先行者。苏联学者拉扎列夫著，吴云琪、刘楠来、王可菊译的《现代国际海洋法》（天津人民出版社，1981），是国内最早介绍国际海洋法发展的成果。刘楠来、王可菊与柳子亚、虞源澄、倪轩等合著的《国际海洋法》（法律出版社，1986）是当时国内最全面系统的研究国际海洋法的专著，联合国出版的《海洋法公报》将该书列为国际海洋法领域的重要中文著作。此后，刘楠来等合译的《各国专属经济区和大陆架法规选编》（法律出版社，1988）更是被政府机关和各大院校普遍作为参考资料。2008 年 9 月，王翰灵副研究员牵头成立了国际法研究中心（2009 年后改为国际法研究所）海洋法与海洋事务研究中心；2015 年 10 月，该中心成为中国社会科学院院属中心；2019 年 8 月，该中心更名为海洋法治研究中心。王翰灵副研究员参编联合国海洋管理英文教材《海洋活动管理的生态系统方法》（联合国出版，2011）。

航空法领域。1961 年、1963 年和 1971 年，国际社会先后通过东京、海牙和蒙特利尔等三个“反劫机”公约，中国是上述三个公约的缔约国。1983 年卓长仁等将民航 296 号班机劫持到韩国，引起举国上下震动，各方面对如何才能把他们引渡回国加以惩处十分关注，而当时国内却没有这方面的完整理论。1985 年赵维田的专著《论三个反劫机公约》（群众出版社，1985）开创了国内研究航空刑法的先河，弥补了国内劫持航空器国际犯罪研究的空白。此后，赵维田又相继在我国台湾地区和大陆出版了两版《国际航空法》。此书是国内首部系统研究国际航空法学各个分支领域的学术著作，标志着国内学者开始构建航空法理论体系。

国际刑法领域。20 世纪 80 年代，国际刑法作为一个独立的法律部门和独立的法律学科，其地位尚有争议。在林欣的《国际法中的刑事管辖权》（法律出版社，1988）出版之前，国内既没有国际刑法的系统性研究成果，也鲜见就国际刑法开展专门研究的成果。林欣的著作一定意义上填补了我国国际法研究领域的学科空白，堪称国际刑法研究的奠基之作。

人权法领域。中国社会科学院是在社科领域较早开展人权研究的学术机构之一。1991 年 6 月，法学研究所主持召开全国第一个人权理论研讨会。同年，由法学研究所副所长刘海年任团长，信春鹰、李林、林地等参加的首个人权考察团赴北美考察，在国际上引起广泛关注。1991 年，中国社会科学院人权研究中心成立，成为中国大陆成立的第一家人权研究机构，由王家福、刘海年研究员担任联合主任。中心依托法学研究所和国际法研究所的研究力量，在开展人权理论与实践研究、促进人权教育和人权国际交流方面一直发挥着积极、重要的作用。莫纪宏研究员现任该中心主任，柳华文研究员任执行主任。为加强国际人权法学科研究，国际法研究所于 2009 年成立国际人权法研究室，集中了一批以人权法为主要研究领域的优秀学者。目前人权研究已经形成特色鲜明、成果丰硕、国际法与国内法相结合、理论与实践相结合、老中青队伍有机结合的良好局面。

国际经济法作为国际法专业的一个新兴分支，在法学研究所国际法研究室时期并未作为一门独立的学科而存在，但这并没有影响前辈学人对国际经济法学理论和实践的不懈探索。他们在国际经济法重大理论问题上勇于突破，锐意创新，对中国国际经济法学的形成和发展作出了重要而独特的贡献，也诞生了一大批在国内外享有盛誉的知名专家，包括芮沐（研究领域为国际公法、国际经济法，曾任法学研究所副所长）、盛愉（研究领域为国际公法、国际经济法，曾任法学研究所副所长）、徐鹤皋（研究领域为国际私法、国际经济法，曾任法学研究所国际法研究室主任，后任司法部中国法律事务中心主任）、李泽锐（研究领域为国际经济法）、任继圣（研究领域为国际私法、国际经济法，曾任法学研究所国际法研究室副主任，后任司法部中国法律事务中心主任）、魏家驹（研究领域为国际私法、海商法）、姚壮（研究领域为国际私法、海商法，后调入外交学院）、陶正华（研究领域为国际公法、国际经济法，曾任法学研究所国际法研究室主任）等，可谓群星璀璨。

中国的国际私法学科也经历了一个从无到有的过程。1949 年之后，虽有大学开设国际私法课程，但授课内容援用当时苏联的国际私法体系，学习和研究国际私法时参考的也是苏联国际私法学者的著作，中国还没有自己学者编写的教材。1981 年，姚壮和任继圣共同编写了中华人民共和国第一部国际私法教材《国际私法基础》（中国社会科学出版社，1981）并发表多篇学术论文，是中华人民共和国国际私法研究的先驱。香港、澳门回归后，中国区际法律冲突问题日益增多，沈涓的专著《中国区际冲突法研究》（中国政法大学出版社，1999）通过分析现代中国区际法律冲突的状况和调整法律冲突的障碍，提出了若干调整区际法律冲突的方法，对中国未来建立自己的区际冲突法律体系具有较大的启发意义。

四　科研成果

在过去的 60 年间，国际法研究所紧跟我国建设发展和改革开放实践，本着“科研强所”、“人才强所”、“教学强所”、“管理强所”四大战略和“走出去”、“请进来”的基本思路，在国际法各学科领域进行了广泛、深入的研究，取得了全面、丰硕的成果。

截至2018年底，国际法研究所已出版学术著作170余部，译著40余部；发表学术论文1000余篇，译文300余篇。此外，国际法研究所研究人员还承担了大量的立法、司法论证和咨询任务，向中央领导机关、有关政府部门以及有关决策机构报送立法建议、研究报告或法律意见书300余篇，受到高度重视和广泛好评。国际法研究所研究人员作为专家提供论证咨询的议题涉及国际条约、协定的制定和修改，涉外法律法规的起草和修订，重大国际政治、外交和法律事件的预案或对策研究，中国提交国际人权机构的审议报告，重大国际经济案件的应对和处理等。为充分发挥本所作为党和政府在民主法治、人权建设、对外交流方面重要思想库和智囊团的作用，国际法研究所研究人员积极通过中国社会科学院《要报》渠道建言献策，多份内部报告获得中央主要负责同志、党和国家领导人批示。

五　课题项目

国际法研究所还完成和承担了大量重大、重点课题项目。国际法研究所目前有3项国家社科基金项目在研，包括刘敬东主持的“海外利益法律保护的中国模式研究”项目、戴瑞君主持的“国际条约在中国法律体系中的地位分析与制度设计研究”项目和孙南翔主持的“国际裁决的合宪性问题研究”项目。

2018年以来，国际法研究所立项课题25项，结项课题17项，目前在研课题共计34项。具体完成中央有关部门交办重要课题6项。

自2012年中国社会科学院哲学社会科学创新工程启动以来，国际法研究所积极参加，成效显著。目前共设4个研究类创新项目，即“构建人类命运共同体、促进全球治理体系变革的国际法保障研究”项目、“‘一带一路’建设中的国际经济法律问题研究”项目、“国际经济法治危机及对策研究”项目和“中国《涉外民事关系法律适用法》的实施及发展”项目，全面涵盖我国当前国际法治建设的重大主题。

2019年，国际法研究所承接了中国社会科学院院领导交办委托的重大项目“‘一带一路’沿线国家法律风险防范与法律机制构建调研”。该项目以习近平新时代中国特色社会主义思想为指导，从国际法和国别法两个视角，对“一带一路”沿线国家分阶段、分步骤开展实地调研。调研活动重点关注“一带一路”沿线国家法律制度和法治水平、“一带一路”相关政策措施的实施效果、中国企业面临的障碍和风险以及“一带一路”争端解决机制的建立和完善等方面，力争形成具有实践指导意义和参考价值的扎实成果。

六 学术活动及交流

国际法研究所与国内外高校、研究机构和实务部门不断建立和发展良好合作关系。在国际交流方面，先后派出访问学者和进修生 160 余人次，接待来访外国学者 300 余人次，主办或联合举办国际学术会议 70 余次。从 20 世纪 80 年代至今，本所研究人员先后赴美国哥伦比亚大学、美国丹佛大学、美国兰德公司、美国科罗拉多州最高法院、英国牛津大学、英国皇家国际事务研究所、荷兰人权研究所、丹麦人权研究所、挪威人权研究所、瑞典隆德大学罗尔·瓦伦堡人权和人道法研究所、德国马克斯·普朗克比较公法与国际法研究所等国外著名高校、研究机构和实务部门进行学术访问。

自 2004 年以来，国际法研究所连续主办了 15 届“国际法论坛”。作为对国际法学科“全覆盖”的国际性会议，论坛主题广泛涉及同时期国际法领域的重大理论和现实问题，已经成为国际法研究所的“拳头产品”和知名品牌，为国内外国际法学者交流思想、探讨学术提供了重要平台。2010 年起，国际法论坛纳入中国社会科学院学部主办的“中国社会科学论坛”系列，在新的高度继续发展。2019 年是国际法研究所正式挂牌 10 周年，国际法研究所将以国际法论坛的成功经验为基础，组织举办四个重要的国际学术会议，包括金砖国家国际法治论坛、中国—拉美国家国际法治论坛、“一带一路”国际法治论坛和人类命运共同体国际法治论坛，以论坛带动各界对国际法治重大问题的关注，以论坛推进多边学术合作与交流。

以正式挂牌建所 10 周年为契机，国际法研究所将继续按照中央“三个定位”要求，坚守思想阵地，加强智库建设，聚焦创新工作，完善绩效考核，努力打造面向世界的学术平台，继续招纳国内外高层次人才。我们将倾全所之力，推出一批反映当代国际法学研究水准的高质量系列学术著作，夯实本所作为国际法研究国家队的学科基础和人才基础，不断扩大本所的国内外学术影响力，努力提升中国国际法学理论研究成果在国际学术界的话语权。我们将持续追踪国际法前沿动态，反映国际法实践的新问题和新趋势，为中国和国际社会的国际法理论与实务研究提供一个重要的交流平台。我们愿与所有从事国际法科研、教学、实务的同仁一道，为推动中国国际法事业和中国特色社会主义法治建设进程而不懈奋斗。

Introduction to the Institute of International Law, Chinese Academy of Social Sciences

I Historical Evolution

The Institute of International Law, Chinese Academy of Social Sciences (CASS) is an important entity in international law studies in China. Its predecessor, originally, was the Research Group of International Law and the Research Department of International Law of the Institute of Law, CASS, and then the Center for International Law of CASS.

In 1959, the year following the establishment of the Institute of Law under the Division of Philosophy and Social Sciences of the Chinese Academy of Sciences, the Research Group of International Law was established under the CASS Institute of Law. In May 1977, with the approval of the Central Committee of the Communist Party of China, the Chinese Academy of Social Sciences (CASS) was formally established on the basis of the Division of Philosophy and Social Sciences of the Chinese Academy of Sciences. In September 1978, the Research Group of International Law of CASS Institute of Law was restructured to form the Department of International Law. In October 2002, the Center for International Law was established on the basis of the Department of International Law with the approval of the Chinese government as an independent research institution directly under CASS, in parallel with the Institute of Law. In September 2009, with the approval of the Chinese government, the Center for International Law was renamed the Institute of International Law, and Professor Chen Zexian served as the first director of the Institute. From September 2017 to November 2018, Professor Chen Su, the director of Institute of Law, served as the acting director of the Institute of International Law. In November 2018, Professor Mo Jihong became the director of the Institute of International Law. In April 2019, Professor Liu Huawen was appointed as the deputy director of the Institute of International Law.

Ⅱ Overview of Structure and Staff

The Institute of International Law has four research departments, one editorial office and one administrative department, i. e., the departments of public international law, private international law, international economic law and international human rights law, respectively, the editorial office of *Chinese Review of International Law*, and the department of research administration and international cooperation. The *Chinese Review of International Law*, inaugurated in 2014, is the first Chinese periodical of international law in China with an official registration number for publications. The Institute of International Law is responsible for its editorial work, and the Social Sciences Academic Press for its publication. The Institute of International Law has also established the Center for Competition Law, the Center for International Criminal Law, the Center for Oceans Law and Maritime Law and the "Belt and Road" Judicial Research Base in cooperation with the Supreme People's Court of China (SPC). The Institute of International Law has master's, doctoral and post-doctoral programs in the fields of public international law, private international law, international economic law and international human rights law, respectively.

The Institute of International Law currently has 35 full time staff members, including 9 research fellows (equivalent to full professor), 10 associate research fellows (equivalent to associate professor), amongst which 4 research fellows are qualified to supervise doctoral programs and 14 research fellows/associate research fellows are qualified to supervise master's programs.

The researchers of the Institute of International Law have a high reputation and wide influence both at home and abroad. At the international level, Prof. Mo Jihong is the (Lifetime) Honorary President of the International Association of

Constitutional Law; Prof. Liu Nanlai is an arbitrator of the Permanent Court of Arbitration in The Hague; Prof. Chen Zexian is the Vice President of the Society of International Criminal Law; Prof. Liu Huawen is a member of the Executive Council of the Asian Society of International Law and the Co-director of the Cross-cultural Human Rights Center in the Netherlands; Prof. Sun Shiyan is a member of the editorial boards of the *International Review of the Red Cross* and the *Chinese Journal of International Law*; Prof. Wang Hanling served as a consultant to the Division for Ocean Affairs and the Law of the Sea of the United Nations Legal Office, and as a special arbitration expert for international fisheries for many years.

At the national level, Prof. Mo Jihong was awarded the honorary title as one of the "National Top Ten Outstanding Young Jurists" by China Law Society; selected for the "National Talents Project" and awarded the honorary title as one of the "Young and Middle-aged Experts with Outstanding Contributions" by the Ministry of Human Resources and Social Security of China, as one of the "Cultural Masters" in the "Four Batches of Talents Project" and as one of the fourth batch of "Philosophy and Social Science Leaders" for the "National Ten Thousand Talents Plan" by the Publicity Department of the Communist Party of China Central Committee; he is also a member of the Academic Committee of China Law Society, a member of the Supreme People's Procuratorate Expert Advisory Committee, the Executive Vice President of the Chinese Association of Constitutional Law, and the President of the Association of Legislative Studies of the Beijing Law Society. Prof. Liu Nanlai, an honorary CASS academician, has been a consultant to the first, second and third International Law Advisory Committee of the Ministry of Foreign Affairs of China. Prof. Liu Huawen has been a member of the second and third International Law Advisory Committee of the Ministry of Foreign Affairs of China; he is also the Vice President of the Beijing Society of International Law, the Vice President of the Soft Law Research Society of the Chinese Society of Behavioral Law, the editor-in-chief of the *Chinese Yearbook of International Law*, published by the China Society of International Law, and an adviser on the construction of the rule of law to the Government of Yunnan Province. Prof. Liu Jingdong is the Vice President of WTO Law Research Society of China Law Society, a member of the"Reporting Group of 100 Jurists"of China Law Society, a deputy division chief of No. 4 Civil Division of the Supreme People's Court from 2015 to 2017, a special consultant to the Supreme People's Court and a member of the first International Commercial Expert Committee of SPC. Professor Liao Fan is the Deputy Head of the Committee of International Financial Law of the China Society of International Economic and Trade Law, a member of the Expert Group for the Adjudication of Foreign-related Commercial and Maritime Cases of the Supreme People's Court, and a special observer of the Xinhua News Agency. Prof. Zhang Wenguang was appointed by the Supreme People's Court as an expert(of the First Batch) on foreign-related commercial and maritime trials in 2015, and a special advisor to the Shanghai International Maritime Judicial Base of the Supreme People's Court in 2018. Furthermore, Profs. Mo Jihong, Liu Nanlai, Wang Keju, Tao Zhenghua, Chen Zexian, Shen Juan and Liu Huawen have been the recipients of the Special Government Allowance from the State Council.

Ⅲ Academic Achievements and Contributions

The Institute of International Law has always been firmly promoting the building of academic programs, and is in a leading position in China in research capacity and comprehensive influence. The program of public international law, which has been designated as a leading program by CASS and structured on the basis of the two research departments of public international law and international human rights law, covers such specialized areas as the fundamental theories of international law, international law of the sea, human rights law, treaty law, and the law international organizations. The program of international economic law, which has been designated as a key program by CASS and structured on the basis of the research department of international economic law, covers such specialized areas as international trade law, international financial law, international investment law, international environmental law, and maritime law. The program of private international law, structured on the basis of the department of private international law, covers such specialized areas as international conflict of law, international civil litigation, and international commercial arbitration. Since the foundation of the Institute of International Law, all the academic programs have established a well-structured academic system and a highly capable and solid team of researchers.

The Research Group of International Law/the Department of International Law of the Institute of Law, CASS, as the predecessors of the Center for International Law/Institute of International Law of CASS, have been one of the earliest organizations to resume academic research on international law in China since the reform and opening-up, and had made significant contributions to the establishment of international legal scholarship in China. With respect to the research on fundamental theories of international law, as early as in the 1960s, scholars working at the Research Group of International Law had translated and published two representative works of international law: *The Theory of State and Law* edited by Petr Semenovich Romashkinet et al. (translated by Profs. Liu Nanlai and Wei Jiaju et al., and published by the Law Press · China in 1964); and Grigorij I. Tunkin's *Theory of International Law* (translated by Wang Keju et al., and published by the World Affairs Press in 1965). These translated books introduce the fundamental theories of international law of the former Soviet Union and its representative achievements relating to the developments of international law to the Chinese academia, and serve as the pioneer in introducing researches on the fundamental theories of international law into China.

In the field of the law of the sea, since the Third United Nations Conference on the Law of the Sea started in December 1973, the international law scholars of the Institute of Law had closely followed the process of the conference, actively participated in the relevant discussions, and contributed opinions and suggestions to the Chinese delegation, thus becoming the main pioneers in the field of the law of the sea studies in China. Profs. Wu Yunqi, Liu Nanlai and Wang Keju translated the Soviet scholar Lazarev's *The Modern International Law of the Sea* (Tianjin People's Publishing House, 1981), which was the earliest introductory work to the development of the international law of the sea in China. In 1986, Profs. Liu Nanlai and Wang Keju, in cooperation with scholars from other institutions, co-authored the book *International Law of the Sea* (Law Press · China, 1986) to make a comprehensive and systematic exposition of issues related to the international law of the sea, which became the most comprehensive and systematic volume on the international law of the sea in China at that time, and was listed in *The Law of the Sea Bulletin* published by the United Nations as an important Chinese works in the field of international law of the sea. *Selected Laws and Regulations on Exclusive Economic Zones and Continental Shelf of Different Countries* (Law Press China, 1988), translated and compiled by Prof. Liu Nanlai et. al. , has also been widely used by Chinese authorities and universities as an important reference material. In 2008, Prof. Wang Hanling played a leading role in establishing the Center for the Law of the Sea and Ocean Affairs of then the Center for International Law, which became a research center directly under the leadership of CASS in 2015, and was renamed the Center for Oceans Law and Maritime Law in 2019. Prof. Wang Hanling also participated in the compilation work of the United Nations' textbook *Ecosystem Approaches to the Management of Ocean* (United Nations, 2011).

In the field of aviation law, the international community successively adopted three conventions against hijacking of aircrafts in Tokyo in 1961, The Hague in 1963 and Montreal in 1971, to all of which China is a state party. In 1983, Zhuo Changren and others hijacked Flight CA296 to South Korea. The event shocked the whole country and raised the question of how to bring the highjackers back to China to face trial and punishment. However, there was no adequate understanding of and research on this issue at that time in China. In 1985, Prof. Zhao Weitian published the book *On Three Anti-hijacking Conventions* (Mass Publishing House, 1985), initiating the study on criminal matters relating to aviation law in China and thus filled the gaps in the research on the crimes of aircraft hijacking in the country. Prof. Zhao Weitian subsequently published two editions of *International Aviation Law* in Taiwan and Mainland China, respectively, which was the first academic works systematically covering various branches of international aviation law, thus marking the beginning of the construction of the theoretical system of aviation law by Chinese scholars.

In the 1980s, when it was still disputed whether international criminal law was a separate field of legal studies or an independent branch of international law, there was no systematic research on international criminal law, nor any noticeable research outcome on specific topics in this area in China, until Prof. Lin Xin published the book *Criminal Jurisdiction in International Law* (Law Press China, 1988). This book has in a sense filled a gap in the studies of international law in China, and therefore can be fairly regarded as the foundation work on international criminal law in China.

In the field of human rights law, CASS was one of the first academic institutions to carry out human rights research in China. In 1991, the CASS Institute of Law convened the first nationwide seminar on human rights theories, and dispatched the first academic delegation of human rights scholars to North America, with Prof. Liu Hainian, then Deputy Director of the Institute of Law, as the head, and Profs. Xin Chunying, Li Lin and Lin Di as members. Their visit attracted wide international attention. In 1991, the CASS Center for Human Rights Studies was established, with Profs. Wang Jiafu and Liu Hainian as co-directors, which was the first human rights research institution in Mainland China.

Benefiting from the research capacity of the CASS Institute of Law and CASS Institute of International Law, the CASS Center for Human Rights Studies has been playing an active and important role in carrying out researches on theoretical and practical issues of human rights, and promoting human rights education and international exchanges on human rights. Prof. Mo Jihong is the current Director of the Center, and Prof. Liu Huawen is the Executive Director. In order to strengthen the research on international human rights law, the Institute of International Law established the Department of International Human Rights Law in 2009, bringing together a group of outstanding scholars in the field of human rights law. The studies on human rights law at the Institute of International Law have combined academic research and practical work, and international law and domestic law, and have a highly regarded status in China.

As a new branch of study in the field of international law, international economic law did not exist as an independent program during the period of Department of International Law of the CASS Institute of Law. However, this did not prevent the first generation of international economic law scholars in the Department from vigorously exploring the theories and practice of international economic law. They had made great and unique contributions to the formation and development of the discipline of international economic law in China by conducting groundbreaking and innovative researches on major theoretical issues of international economic law. There had been a number of renowned experts with domestic and international reputations, including Prof. Rui Mu and Prof. Sheng Yu, who had been the deputy director of the Institute of Law and did research in the fields of public international law and international economic law; Prof. Xu Hegao, who was the head of the Research Department of International Law, subsequently transferred to the Ministry of Justice to undertake the directorship of China Legal Affairs Center, and did research in the fields of private international law and international economic law; Prof. Li Zerui, who specialized in the research on international economic law; Prof. Ren Jisheng, who was the deputy head of the Research Department of International Law, subsequently transferred to the Ministry of Justice to undertake the directorship of China Legal Affairs Center, and did research in the fields of private international law and international economic law; Prof. Wei Jiaju, who did research in the fields of private international law and maritime law; Prof. Yao Zhuang, who did research in the fields of private international law and maritime law; Prof. Tao Zhenghua, who was the head of the Research Department of International Law, and did research in the fields of pubic international law and international economic law.

The discipline of private international law in China has also undergone a process of starting from scratch. After the founding of the People's Republic of China in 1949, some Chinese universities offered courses of private international law, the contents of which were based on the private international law system of the Soviet Union at that time. The studies of private international law in China were also based on the textbooks and reference materials from the Soviet Union, without any book written by Chinese scholars in this field. In 1981, Profs. Yao Zhuang and Ren Jisheng co-authored the first textbook of private international law in China, *Foundation of Private International Law* (China Social Sciences Press, 1981) and published a number of articles in this field, thus becoming the pioneers of the study of private international law in China. After China resumed its sovereignty over Hong Kong and Macao, problems of inter-regional conflict of laws within China have been increasing. Prof. Shen Juan's monograph *Research on China's Inter-regional Conflict of Law* (China University of Political Science and Law Press, 1999) analyzes the situation of inter-regional conflict of laws in China and puts forward some thoughts regarding the regulation of those inter-regional conflict of laws, thereby making contributions to the establishment of a Chinese system of inter-regional conflict of laws in the future.

Ⅳ Publications and Other Research Achievements

Ever since they were still the Research Group of International Law of the Institute of Law, the Researchers staff of the Institute of International Law have endeavored to conduct in-depth research and publish high-quality works in the field of international law. Especially in the era of Reform and Opening-up, the Institute of International Law and its predecessor, the Department of International Law of the Institute of Law, have persistently made extensive and in-depth studies in various fields of international law, and produced fruitful research outcomes.

By the end of 2018, the Institute of International Law had published more than 170 books and 40 translated books, more than 1000 research articles and 300 translated articles. In addition, the researchers of the Institute of International Law have also undertaken a large number of analytical and advisory work with respect to the legislative and judicial practice in China. They have submitted over 300 proposals, reports or legal opinions regarding various legal issues to the central government of China, relevant government agencies and decision-making bodies, which have been highly valued and widely praised, some of them have been recognized by the leaders of the Chinese government and the Communist Party of China as significant to the legal and other related works in China. The proposals, reports or legal opinions provided by the researchers of the Institute of International Law in their capacity of experts have covered such topics as the formulation and revision of international treaties and agreements, the drafting and revision of laws and regulations related to foreign affairs, emergency plans for or responses to major international political, diplomatic and legal events, reports submitted by China to international human rights bodies for consideration, and the handling of major international economic cases. Therefore, in addition to its role as a major research institution of international law in China, the Institute of International Law has also played the role of a think tank to the Chinese government and various authorities in the fields of construction of democracy and rule of law, protection and promotion of human rights, conduct of foreign affairs as well as in the field of international law in its broadest sense.

V Research Projects

The Institute of International Law has also undertaken and completed a large number of research projects. In 2018, the Institute had completed 17 research projects, established and secured funding for 25 research projects, and had 34 research projects in progress, including three projects funded by the highest level of funding in China, the National Social Sciences Foundation of China—"The Chinese Model of Legal Protection of Interests Overseas", led by Prof. Liu Jingdong, "International Treaties in Chinese Domestic Legal System: Analysis of Status and Design of Institutions", led by Prof. Dai Ruijun, and "The Compatibility of International Rulings with the Constitution", led by Prof. Sun Nanxiang.

Since the launch of the CASS "Philosophy and Social Sciences Innovation Project" in 2012, the Institute of International Law has actively participated in, benefited from, and contributed to the Innovation Project, with remarkable accomplishments. The Institute now has four research projects founded by the Innovation Project, i. e., "International Law Guarantee of Building a Community with Shared Future for Mankind and Promoting the Transformation of the Global Governance System", "International Economic Legal Issues in the Construction of the 'Belt and Road'", "The Rule of Law Crisis in International Economy and the Responding Strategies" and "Implementation and Development of *The Law on the Application of Law for Foreign-related Civil Relations of PRC*". These research projects comprehensively cover the major legal issues in relations to China's involvement in the global governance and conduct of foreign affairs on the basis of rule of law. The "Leading Program" of public international law and the "Key Program" of international economic law, both designated by CASS, and the publication of *Chinese Review of International Law*, are also covered and sponsored by the Innovation Project.

In the context of China's "Belt and Road" Initiative, the Institute of International Law has been entrusted a major project by the leadership of CASS in 2019, "The Survey on Legal Risk Prevention and Legal Mechanism Building in Countries along the 'Belt and Road'", which will conduct field research in the countries along the "Belt and Road", from the perspectives of both international law and domestic law, and focus on the legal systems and level of rule of law in relevant countries, the effect of implementation of relevant policies and measures of the Initiative, obstacles and risks faced by Chinese enterprises, and the establishment and improvement of the dispute settlement mechanism for the Initiative, with a view to providing practical guide to the Initiative.

Ⅵ International Cooperation

The Institute of International Law has established and kept frequent communications and close relations with universities, research institutions as well international and domestic practicing bodies all over the world. In the past four decades, the Institute and its predecessors have sent more than 160 person-times to study or conduct research at well-known academic institutions, think tanks or practicing bodies in many countries, and received 300 person-times visits from other countries and international organizations. The Institute has also organized or co-hosted more than 70 international seminars and symposiums.

Since 2004, the Institute of International Law has hosted the "International Law Forum" for 15 consecutive times. As an international conference covering various areas of international law, the Forum has extensively addressed major theoretical and practical international law issues of the relevant years. It has become a well-known brand of the Institute by providing an important platform for international law scholars at home and abroad to exchange ideas and explore academic issues. Since 2010, the Forum has been incorporated in the series of "China Social Sciences Forum" sponsored by CASS, and has continued to develop at a new height.

The year 2019 marks the 10th anniversary of the official establishment of the Institute of International Law, and the Institute will organize four important international conferences based on the successful experience of the "International Law Forum", including the BRICS Forum on the International Rule of Law, the Sino-Latin America Forum on the International Rule of Law, the Belt and Road Forum on the International Rule of Law, the Community of Shared Future for Mankind and International Rule of Law Forum, with a view to drawing the attention of persons from all walks of life to major issues of international rule of law, and promoting multilateral academic cooperation and exchanges.

Taking the 10th anniversary of its official establishment as an opportunity, the Institute will continue to strengthen the construction of think tanks, focus on innovation, improve performance appraisal, strive to build a world-oriented academic platform, and continue to recruit high-level talents at home and abroad. The Institute will make every effort to launch a series of high-quality academic works reflecting the research level of contemporary international law, consolidate the academic foundation and capacity building of the Institute as the national team of international law research, constantly expand its academic influence at home and abroad, and strive to enhance the discourse power of the research results of China's international law theory in the world. The Institute will continue to closely follow the latest developments in international law, reflect upon new problems and trends in international law practice, and provide an important platform for the exchange of international law theory and practice between China and the international community. The Institute is willing to work tirelessly with all colleagues engaged in the research, teaching and practice of international law in order to promote the cause of international law in China and the process of building the socialist rule of law with Chinese characteristics.

Introduction to the Department of Public International Law

Ⅰ Historical Evolution

In 1958, the Institute of Law was established under the Division of Philosophy and Social Sciences of Chinese Academy of Sciences. The International Law Group was set up as the Fourth Research Group under the Institute of Law in the following year. In 1978, the Institute of Law was transferred to the Chinese Academy of Social Sciences (CASS) and the International Law Group was reorganized into the International Law Research Department of the Institute of Law. In October 2002, the Center for International Law Studies was officially established on the basis of the Research Department of International Law. Then in 2004, three research departments of public international law, private international law and international economic law were founded. The Research Center for Law of the Sea and Ocean Affairs was established by relying on personnel specialized in the law of the sea research in the Department of Public International Law.

In September 2009, the Center for International Law Studies of CASS was renamed the Institute of International Law of CASS, and the Department of International Human Rights Law was added to the existing three research departments. The Department of Public International Law has become one of the four departments, parallel with the departments of International Economic Law, Private International Law and International Human Rights Law, in the Institute of International Law of CASS. In October 2015, with the approval of the leadership of the

CASS, the Research Center for Law of the Sea and Ocean Affairs was upgraded from an institute-level research center to an academy-level research center. The Department of Public International Law has one doctoral program(in public international law) and one master's program(in public international law).

Ⅱ Composition of Personnel

From the establishment of the International Law Group in 1959 until the establishment of the International Law Studies Center in 2002, researchers engaged in public international law research and those engaged in the research of other aspects of international law all belonged to the International Law Group and the subsequent Department of International Law of CASS Law Institute. When the International Law Group was established in 1959, its members included Wang Keju, Liu Zhen, Xia Guoqiang and Wu Jianfan(part-time), and Ma Xiangcong, Ye Weijun and Wang Cunxue were transferred in 1960. In 1961, the Institute of Law decided that Zhang Youyu would also be the head of the International Law Group, with Xie Tieguang as the acting head, Ma Jun(Institute of Foreign Affairs) as the part-time deputy head, and Wang Keju as the secretary of the Group.

At the end of 1977, the researchers of the Institute of Law were regrouped according to their specialties. In addition to the members of the original fourth group, namely Wang Keju, Ye Weijun and Wang Cunxue, members of the International Law Group also included Xu Hegao, Wei Jiaju, Wu Yunqi, Liu Nanlai and Shen Xiaoming, who were transferred from other groups of the Law Institute, and Yao Zhuang, Ren Jisheng and Wang Sunhuan, who were transferred from other institutions. Xu Hegao and Liu Nanlai were put in temporary charge of the new International Law Group. In September 1978, the International Law Group was reorganized into the International Law Research Department of CASS Law Institute, with Xu Hegao as its head, and Liu Nanlai and Ren Jisheng as its deputy heads. From 1984 to 1993, Liu Nanlai served as the head of the International Law Research Department, and Zheng Chengsi as deputy head. From 1978 to 1993, Zheng Chengsi(1979), Sheng Yu(1979), Zhao Weitian(1980), Li Zerui(1980), Yu Hua, Zeng Jianfan(1981), Lin Xin(1981), Tao Zhenghua(1982), Zhu Xiaoqing(1984),

Zhu Wenying, Ma Shouren, Zhang Wei, Zhao Lixin (1987), Yang Lijun (1987), Tao Xiuming (1992) and others were successively transferred to the International Law Research Department. From February 1994 to December 2003, Tao Zhenghua was the head of the International Law Research Department (Department of Public International Law), while Yang Lijun and Shen Juan successively served as deputy heads.

In October 2002, after the International Law Research Department was reorganized into the International Law Research Center, former members of the department were reorganized into three departments, namely public international law, private international law and international economic law, according to their professional directions. The Department of Public International Law is composed of personnel mainly engaged in public international law research and has become a professional department engaged in public international law research and teaching. Since November 2004, Sun Shiyan has been appointed the head and Zhu Xiaoqing the deputy head of the Department. At the same time, Sun Shiyan and Zhu Xiaoqing are respectively the head and deputy head of the preparatory group of the Department of Public International Law of the International Law Research Center. From 1993 to August 2009, Guo Qiang, Zhang Ruosi, Liu Huawen (2000), Shen Minrong (2001), Lin Changyuan, Wang Hanling (2004), Sun Shiyan (2006) and Zhao Jianwen (2008) were transferred to the Department in succession and Dai Ruijun was employed by the institute after her graduation in 2006.

After the establishment of Institute of International Law of CASS in 2009, Sun Shiyan served as the head of the Department of Public International Law (2009 - 2015) and Zhu Xiaoqing served as the deputy head (2009 - 2014). From January 2016 to now, Jiang Xiaohong has served as the head of the Department. Since 2009, Li Zan (2010), Hao Luyi (2012), Zhang Weihua (2016) and Ma Jinxing (2018) have successively been transferred to the Department. As of January 2019, the Department of Public International Law has a total of six in-service researchers, including Jiang Xiaohong, Wang Hanling, Li Zan, Hao Luyi, Zhang Weihua and Ma Jinxing. Among them there are one research fellow, three associate research fellows and two assistant research fellows, and Zhu Xiaoqing has been rehired by the Department after her retirement.

In addition, three senior research fellows, Liu Nanlai, Wang Keju and Tao Zhenghua, have participated in the research work of public international law after retirement. Among them, Prof. Liu Nanlai enjoyed special government allowances of the State Council in 1992 and was elected honorary member of the CASS in 2006. He was a member of the National Expert Group on Marine Resources Research, Development and Protection, a member of the National Philosophy and Social Science Planning (Evaluation) Law Group, a vice president of the Chinese Society of International Law, and the editor-in-chief of the *Chinese Yearbook of International Law*, among other titles and positions. He has participated in the draft of such laws and regulations as "the Law on Territorial Sea and Contiguous Zone", "the Law on Exclusive Economic Zone and Continental Shelf", and "the Law on the Administration of Sea Areas". In 2011, he served as a member of the National Senior Advisory Committee for the Development of Maritime Undertaking, and in 2015, he served as a consultant to the International Law Advisory Committee of the Ministry of Foreign Affairs. Prof. Wang Keju enjoyed special government allowances of the State Council in 1992. She was once a member of the Council of Chinese Society of International Law and the Chinese Society for the Law of the Sea, a member of the editorial board of the *China Yearbook of International Law*, and a vice president of the Beijing Society of International Law. She was once also a member of drafting group on the Law on Exclusive Economic Zone (EEZ) and Continental Shelf, a consultant of the China Legal Advisory Center, and an editor-in-chief of the Part on International Law in "the Law Volume of Encyclopedia of China" (2004). Prof. Tao Zhenghua was a part-time professor at the Institute of International Law of Wuhan University, an executive member of the Council of the Chinese Society of International Law, an arbitrator at China International Economic and Trade Arbitration Commission, a deputy editor-in-chief and the sole contributor to the discipline of public international law of the "Dictionary of Law". He has also enjoyed special government allowances of the State Council.

Two researchers have positions in international organizations. In May 2009, Liu Nanlai was appointed by the Chinese government as an arbitrator of the Permanent Court of Arbitration (PCA) in The Hague. In 2006, Wang Hanling was nominated by the Chinese government, in accordance with Article 2 of Annex Ⅷ of the United Nations Convention on the Law of the Sea(UNCLOS) , as a special arbitration expert for international fisheries of the UN, and served as a consultant to the Division for Ocean Affairs and the Law of the Sea of the United Nations Legal Office from 2006 to 2007.

Ⅲ Major Academic Achievements

The International Law Group of the Institute of Law of the Division of Philosophy and Social Sciences of the Chinese Academy of Sciences was one of the earliest institutions engaged in international law research after the founding of the People's Republic of China. Since its establishment, scholars of public international law have made rich research achievements, published many monographs and a large number of academic papers. Their researches cover various branches of international law, and are in the leading position in China with remarkable achievements. Meanwhile, the Institute has undertaken a large number of legislative, monographic study and legal consultation tasks, carried out research on plans and countermeasures for major international events, submitted legislative proposals, research reports or legal opinions to central authorities, relevant government departments and units, and obtained written comments from the Party and State leaders such as Xi Jinping, Hu Jintao et al. .

1. The Period from the Establishment of International Law Group in 1959 to the Establishment of International Law Research Department in 1978

In the process of abolishing the old legal system and creating a new legal system in People's Republic of China, international law scholars began to explore and apply the Marxist standpoints, outlooks and methods to study legal issues on the basis of absorbing the theories of state and law of the former Soviet Union, which laid a preliminary foundation for the development of Marxist jurisprudence in China. Restricted by historical conditions, the research work on international law at that time was mainly to translate and introduce the theories of state and law and the theories and materials of international law of the former Soviet Union, and to elaborate and analyze the relevant expositions of classical Marxist writers or Party and State leaders.

During this period, the translations of public international law scholars mainly included *The Theory of State and Law* (edited by Bis Romashkin et al. , translated by Liu Nanlai, Wei Jiaju and others, and published by Law Press China in 1964), and *Theoretical Issues of International Law* (edited by Geii Tongkin, translated by Wang Keju et al. , and published by World Affairs Press in 1965). In addition, Wu Yunqi published *The Imperialist State is a Tool for the Cruel Dictatorship of the Monopolizing Bourgeois—Refuting the Fallacy of Modern Yugoslav Revisionists That Distorts the Essence of the Imperialist State* [Chinese Journal of Law, 4(1962)], which used State Theory of Marxism-Leninism to expose and criticize the fact that the modern capitalist state was essentially a tool for exercising dictatorship over the working people. Generally speaking, the representative research results in the field of public international law during this period had distinctive characteristics of the times, and the theoretical research on the transplanted Soviet international law research results reflected the influence of Soviet international law theory on Chinese scholars at that time.

Since the "Cultural Revolution" began in 1966, the work of the Law Institute of the Division of Philosophy and Social Sciences of the Chinese Academy of Sciences had come to a standstill. Most of the staff went to Henan cadre schools to take part in hard labor and returned to Beijing in 1972. Since 1974, the research on public international law had been gradually resumed.

2. The Period from the Establishment of the Research Department of International Law in 1978 to the Establishment of the Center for International Law Studies in 2002

From 1978 to 2002, the research achievements in public international law kept emerging. Especially after the establishment of the Department of Public International Law, the research on public international law had become more and more sophisticated, and scholars had "done intensive work" in their respective fields of study or certain branches of international law. During this period, scholars in the Research Department of International Law mainly engaged in the following aspects of research work.

2.1 The Relationship between Domestic Law and International Treaties

From the beginning of the reform and opening-up in 1978 to the end of the 20th Century, the number of international treaties concluded by China had been increasing, and the relationship between international treaties and domestic law had become the focus of academic circles. Scholars from the Research Department of International Law of CASS Institute of Law started theoretical research on this issue at an early stage and actively participated in the formulation and revision of the Law of the People's Republic of China on the Procedure for the Conclusion of Treaties.

In December 1999, the "Sino-German Seminar on the Relationship between International Treaties and Domestic Laws", sponsored by Institute of Law of CASS and funded by the German Konrad-Adenauer Stiftung (KAS) was successfully held in Shanghai. This was the first academic seminar on the relationship between international treaties and domestic laws held in China. After the seminar, on the basis of the collected papers by Chinese scholars, a book titled *The Relationship between International Treaties and Domestic Laws* (edited by Zhu Xiaoqing and Huang Lie) was published by World Affairs Press in September 2000. The book included articles by scholars from the Research Department of International Law, such as Liu Nanlai, Tao Zhenghua, Zhu Xiaoqing and Sun Shiyan, as well as articles by scholars from other colleges and universities and other research institutes. Thanks to the participation of experts in the constitutional and jurisprudential circles, the research results contained in this book explore the relationship between international treaties and domestic laws from a multi-disciplinary perspective, and provide an opportunity to further clarify the relationship between international treaties and domestic laws of China. After its publication, this book became one of the classic works on the relationship between international treaties and domestic law in China. The content of the book is still cited and quoted by many scholars even today. It can be said that the research result is a summary of representative domestic academic researches on the relationship between international treaties and domestic laws in the 1990s.

Since then, scholars have deepened their research on the relationship between international treaties and domestic laws. Zhu Xiaoqing's "International Treaties as Components of China's Legal System" [*International Law Review*, 1 (2001)] holds that international treaties are an indispensable part of Chinese legal system, the ratification of international treaties is a national legislative activity, and international treaties are one of the sources of Chinese law. Since there is no explicit provision in Constitution of China, it is difficult to truly resolve the problem of relationship between international treaties and domestic laws or the Chinese legal system, which led to many difficulties in judicial practice. Since "the domestic application of international law to a large extent involves the domestic distribution of power", whether or not the relationship between the two is constitutionally stipulated, it has become a matter to be considered carefully by the Chinese government.

2.2 International Human Rights Law

Since the founding of the People's Republic of China, China has always recognized and respected the protection and promotion of human rights as one of the purposes and principles of the United Nations. After resuming its legitimate seat in the United Nations in 1971, China has actively participated in the United Nations' human rights affairs. By the end of 1991, China had ratified eight international human rights conventions formulated under the auspices of the United Nations. Since the early 1980s, international public law scholars in the Research Department of International Law have begun to translate international human rights materials, introduce the researches of foreign scholars and discuss issues related to international human rights law.

Ren Yunzheng's translation of "Marxist – Leninist View of Human Rights and Contemporary Ideological Struggle" [*Global Legal Review*, 6 (1980)] is the first systematic introduction to domestic scholars of the Marxist – Leninist view of human rights put forward by Soviet scholars, enabling domestic scholars to understand human rights instead of criticizing human rights as bourgeois theory. Louis Henkin's "American Constitutional Rights and Human Rights" [*Global Law Review*, 6 (1981)], selected and translated by Li Zerui, introduced to domestic scholars the researches of American scholars comparing constitutional rights and human rights, international human rights and American constitutional rights. Li Zerui published "On the Re-emergence of the Concept of Joint Relations—A Noteworthy Trend of Western International Legal Thoughts" [*Chinese Journal of Law*, 6(1985)], which systematically introduced and analyzed the view of "third generation human rights", composed of "joint relations' rights" proposed by Karel Vasak. Liu Nanlai's "The Birth and Significance of the Universal Declaration of Human Rights" (*People's Daily*, December 8, 1988) explained the background, main content and significance of the Universal Declaration of Human Rights.

After 1989, some Western countries attacked China on the pretext of human rights issues. However, domestic scholars had great differences in their understanding of human rights. Many people mistakenly believed that human rights are bourgeois things and should be criticized. Under such circumstances, Jiang Zemin, then the Secretary General of the CPC Central Committee, gave the instruction that "human rights issues should no longer be evaded, but should be studied". In order to implement this instruction, scholars of public international law have published a large number of high-quality research results. These results can be divided into two categories: one is the objective introduction of human rights theories of western and developing countries. Wang Keju's "Contemporary Western Scholars' Views on Human Rights and Sovereignty" [*CASS Journal of Foreign Law*, 3(1997)] systematically introduces the views of western scholars on the impact of human rights on national sovereignty, the questions of whether human rights can become a pretext for interference and whether human rights are matters under domestic jurisdiction, as well as the status of individuals in international law and the legal effect of international human rights documents. Written by R. J. Vincent and translated by Zhu Xiaoqing, *Human Rights and International Relations* (World Affairs Press, 1997) elaborated on the theory of human rights, explored the role of human rights in international relations, and proposed the ways in which western countries should deal with human rights issues in their policies. The above results provided reference for Chinese scholars at that time to understand, question and refute western human rights theories.

Developing Countries and Human Rights(Sichuan People's Publishing House, 1994), edited by Liu Nanlai, is a systematic collection of the provisions on human rights in the constitutions of developing countries, the information about the ratification of international human rights conventions, regional international human rights documents in Asia, Africa and Latin America, and the human rights theories put forward by scholars and diplomats from developing countries. With detailed information and objective content, the book has become the must-read material for domestic scholars studying the human rights of developing countries in the 1990s.

The other category is the systematic study of international human rights issues. Liu Nanlai and Tao Zhenghua's *Universality and Particularity of Human Rights*(Social Sciences Academic Press, 1996) and the subsequent *Human Rights: Chinese and Dutch Perspectives*(Martinus Nijhoff Pub., 1996) pointed out that safeguarding and respecting the rights and dignity of everyone as an individual are the general requirements of human rights and the universality of human rights, while in countries with different levels of development in the contemporary world, in different cultural environments and in different ethnic and religious areas, the concrete human rights people strive for and the content and nature of the human rights actually enjoyed by each person are necessarily different. There are obvious differences between developing countries, including China, and western developed countries in the criteria for measuring the human rights situation and in the goals of improvement of the human rights situation. Zhu Xiaoqing's "On the Implementation Measures of the United Nations' International Protection of Human Rights" [*Chinese Journal of Law*, 4(1994)] analyzes the implementation measures of the United Nations' international protection of human rights in theory and practice, points out the difficulties in the actual operation of the implementation measures of the international protection of human rights, and proposes that the future international human rights protection mechanism and system will be a highly effective, coordinated and unified mechanism and system consisting of implementation measures with better functions of monitoring and prevention, mediation and action, and protection and promotion.

2.3 International Criminal Law

After the World War Ⅱ, international criminal law, as a new branch of international law, has developed rapidly. At the "International Seminar on the Teaching of Criminal Law", organized by the International Institute of Advanced Criminal Sciences in Syracuse, Italy in 1986, most scholars believed that international criminal law had met all the conditions for being an independent discipline. Against this background, scholars of public international law in the International Law Research Department launched the study of international criminal law in due course.

Lin Xin's *Criminal Jurisdiction in International Law* (Law Press China, 1988) gives a comprehensive and detailed discussion on the issue of criminal jurisdiction in international law, leading to a thorough study of theoretical issues of international criminal law. He published "On the New Development of International Criminal Law Issues" [*Chinese Journal of Law*, 4 (1992)] which, in light of the discussions at the International Law Commission and the criminal legislation of foreign countries, explored the new development of such issues as the prohibition of illegal trade in narcotic drugs, extraterritorial criminal jurisdiction and extradition during the period from the 1980s to the early 1990s. In 1996, Lin Xin led the research work of the National Social Science Fund Project *Research on International Criminal Law*. The book *Research on International Criminal Law*, edited by Lin Xin and published in April 2000, makes a comprehensive and systematic exposition on the history and definition of international criminal law, international criminal responsibility, international criminal jurisdiction, various international crimes, the international criminal court, the principle of *aut dedere aut judicare* and other issues of international criminal law, thereby laying a foundation for international criminal law researches carried out by domestic scholars afterwards.

2.4 International Law of the Sea

In December 1973, the Third United Nations Conference on the Law of the Sea was held in New York. It was the first important international legislative conference that China participated in after the restoration of its legitimate seat at the United Nations, and, as such, had attracted the attention of the whole country. Researchers in public international law from the International Law Group and later the International Law Research Department volunteered to participate in the research and discussion on issues related to the Third Conference on the Law of the Sea, which was warmly welcomed by relevant government departments.

At the same time, information and theoretical research work on the international law of the sea has been carried out. Corresponding academic achievements included, e. g. , the translation and publication by Wu Yunqi, Liu Nanlai and Wang Keju of *Modern International Law of the Sea* by Soviet scholar Lazarev (Tianjin People's Publishing House, 1981). In 1986, Liu Nanlai and Wang Keju, together with Zhou Ziya, Chen Zhenguo, Yang Zhixiong from Shanghai Academy of Social Sciences, Yu Yuancheng and Ni Xuan from State Oceanic Administration, co-authored *The International Law of the Sea* (Ocean Press, 1986), which was the most comprehensive, systematic and well-documented monograph on the international law of the sea in China and contributed to the foundation of the discipline of the law of the sea in China. At that time, the State Marine Administration listed it as an important reference book for its desk work. The Law of the Sea Bulletin published by the United Nations listed it as an important Chinese work in the field of international law of the sea. *Selected Laws and Regulations on Exclusive Economic Zones and Continental Shelf of Different Countries* (Law Press China, 1988) jointly translated by Liu Nanlai and others are also widely used by government agencies and universities.

2. 5 International Aviation Law

In 1961, 1963 and 1971, the international community successively adopted three "anti-hijacking" conventions, namely the Tokyo, Hague and Montreal conventions, to all of which China is a contracting party. In 1983, Zhuo Changren and others hijacked the China Airline Flight No. 296 to South Korea. The incident shocked the whole country and raised the question of how to bring the highjackers back to China to face trial and punishment. Zhao Weitian was one of the earliest domestic scholars to study the anti-hijacking issue. His book *On the Three Anti-hijacking Conventions* (Masses Publishing House, 1985) filled the gap in the domestic research on international crime of hijacking of aircraft. It is also China's earliest monograph on aviation law and played a leading role in the research of aviation law and international criminal law in China. Zhao Weitian has published *International Aviation Law* in Taiwan (Taiwan Buffalo Press, 1991) and the Mainland

(Social Sciences Academic Press, 2000). As the first academic work in China that systematically covers all branches of international aviation law, it has been highly praised by the academic and aviation circles, deeply influenced the research on international aviation law across Taiwan, and marked the beginning of the construction of the theoretical system of international aviation law by domestic scholars.

2.6 International Environmental Law

In 1980, Sheng Yu published the "Preliminary Discussion on Nuclear Law" [*Chinese Journal of Law*, 6 (1980)], in which she clearly pointed out that China needs to adopt a set of legal norms on the development, use, and management of nuclear energy, and on the related protective measures and compensation system, which is the basic content of modern nuclear law. Legal norms on the military use of nuclear energy and those on the civilian use of nuclear energy together constitute the whole body of the nuclear law. In 1981, Sheng Yu published the article "Environmental Strategy and International Environmental Law" [*China Environmental Science*, 3 (1981)]. Sheng Yu and Wei Jiaju co-authored the book *A Brief Discussion on New Fields of International Law* (Jilin People's Publishing House, 1984), in which there is a special chapter that briefly discusses the background, formation process, main content and basic principles of international environmental law. Sheng Yu and Zhou Gang's *Introduction to Modern International Law of Water Resources* (Law Press China, 1987) is the earliest book on international water law in China. It uses the logic of international law to analyze international water law's subject, research object and origin, discusses the historical development process of international water law and various legal systems and organizations of international waters, and explains the basic characteristics, theories and principles of international law of water resources. In the 1990s, China's research on international environmental law had been further strengthened. *An Introduction to International Environmental Law* (Social Science Academic Press, 1994), edited by Ma Xiangcong and others, is one of the earliest works systematically studying international environmental law in China. It has played a positive role in theoretically supporting national environmental diplomacy, and in improving and perfecting

China's environmental rule of law.

To sum up, despite the breakdown of the Sino-Soviet relations since the mid-1960s, the theory and practice of public international law in China basically continued the tradition of the 1950s, and the framework of international law established under the guidance of Marxism – Leninism and on the basis of the Soviet Union's international law theory had not changed substantially. However, on specific issues, Chinese scholars of public international law had shown obviously different views from those of Soviet scholars. In late 1980s, Chinese scholars of public international law had keenly captured the problems of public international law from the regional and global problems or events at that time, paying close attention to the new trends in the development of public international law, publishing a series of cutting-edge research results with theoretical depth, thus playing a leading role in the research of public international law in China.

3. The Period from the Establishment of the Center for International Law Studies in 2002 to Now

The highly complex and specialized issues of today's international society demand the academic community to carry out refined research on these issues. Shortly after the establishment of the Center for International Law Studies in 2002, the Public International Law Department was set up to gather the strength and improve the quality of the theoretical research on public international law. The Department became a part of the Institute of International Law of CASS after the latter was established in 2009. The representative research results in this period show the following three characteristics: firstly, focusing on the research of basic theories, increasing the depth of theoretical research, and constantly innovating; secondly, basing on the branches of disciplines, gradually refining the research on public international law issues and strengthening theoretical research; thirdly, focusing on national development strategies and global issues, and analyzing relevant international law issues from a broader perspective, with research results being rich in Chinese characteristics and problem awareness. Representative achievements in this period include the followings.

3.1 Basic Theories of International Law

Tao Zhenghua pointed out in his article "Four Issues to be Studied in International Law" [*Chinese Journal of Law*, 2 (2004)] that, as a result of the multi-polarization pattern of international politics and the trend towards economic globalization in the 21st century, international law is faced with major challenges, changes and developments in all aspects. China is playing a more and more important role and having great influence in the international political and economic relations nowadays. Against this background, the research on international law should focus on the following four aspects: the principle of national sovereignty in the 21st century, the international protection of human rights, ways of establishing a new international political and economic order, and the principles and systems for settling international disputes. With respect to the views derogating or denying the value and role of international law, Liu Nanlai pointed out in his article "Safeguarding the Solemnity of International Law" (*People's Daily*, August 15, 2016) that, although some countries have violated international law for their own interests, the binding force and enforceability of international law cannot be denied. The destructive use of international law by a country in pursuit of its own interests will not be accepted and recognized by the international community.

3.2 Branches of International Law

During this period, scholars of the Department of Public International Law have made great achievements in the fields of international organization law, international human rights law, international law of the sea, international criminal law and European Union law. Li Zan's *Jurisdictional Immunity of International Organizations* (China Social Sciences Press, 2013) studies the jurisdictional immunity of international organizations, that is, whether international organizations enjoy immunity in domestic courts and how to realize such immunity. The book mainly expounds this issue from the perspective of the legality and legitimacy of jurisdictional immunity of international organizations: legality refers to the legal source of the jurisdictional immunity of international organizations whereas legitimacy refers to the balance between international organizations and their member states through the functional restrictions, mandatory waivers and optional dispute settlement mechanisms of their jurisdictional immunity.

In the field of international human rights law, Sun Shiyan's book *The Obligations of States Parties under the International Covenant on Civil and Political Rights* (Social Sciences Academic Press, 2012) combines empirical and theoretical researches, and relies on a large number of materials and documents to conduct a comprehensive study on the obligations of States Parties under the International Covenant on Civil and Political Rights. The purpose of the book is to deepen Chinese scholars' understanding of the Covenant by studying the obligations of States Parties under the Covenant, thus providing a theoretical basis for the study of specific contents of the Covenant. Jiang Xiaohong's article "The Nexus between Trade and Human Rights—An Analysis of the Human Rights Goal in EU Trade Law" [*Chinese Journal of European Studies*, 5 (2016)] reveals many problems and challenges in the establishment and implementation of human rights goals in EU trade law, such as legitimacy, consistency, effectiveness and credibility. She points out that these problems and challenges have proved once again from another perspective that international cooperation is the best and acceptable way to promote international human rights protection.

In the field of international law of sea, Wang Hanling's article "Mechanism for Settling Fishery Disputes for Straddling and Highly Migratory Fish Stocks" (*Chinese Yearbook of International Law*, 2008) makes a comparative analysis of the dispute settlement procedures under UNCLOS and the "Agreement for the Implementation of the Provisions of the UNCLOS Relating to the Conservation and Management of Straddling Fish Stocks and Highly Migratory Fish Stocks", and clarifies their complex interrelationships, procedures for settling disputes and the concepts they contain. Zhang Weihua's article "On the Legal Status and Freedom of Overfly in the Airspace over the EEZ" [*Global Legal Review*, 1 (2015)] has made an in-depth study on this topic, holding that the freedom of overfly in the airspace over the exclusive economic zone is a kind of freedom of high sea, and it virtually has nothing to do with the sovereign rights and jurisdiction of coastal states in the exclusive economic zone, from which the Defense Identification Zone (DIZ) outside territorial seas cannot find legal grounds. In fact, the DIZ is an exercise of the right of self-preservation by a coastal state. With respect to the maritime disputes between China and its maritime neighbors, Wang Hanling has published a series of articles, including "China Has Sufficient Legal Basis for Sovereignty over Diaoyu Islands" (*Legal Daily*, June 10, 2005), "What kind of 'South China Sea Order' does the United States Wants to Create" (*Guangming Daily*, July 12, 2016), "Bilateral Negotiations Are the Right Way to Resolve the Dispute between China and the Philippines in South China Sea" (*China National Defense News*, June 10, 2016), etc., which have openly responded to relevant international law disputes. In his article "Review of the Award on the Legal Statue of Maritime Features in South China Sea Arbitration" [*Chinese Review of International Law*, 1 (2017)], Ma Jinxing analyzes the Arbitral Award on the Legal Statue of Maritime Features in South China Sea Arbitration, and concludes that the essence of this issue is territorial sovereignty and maritime delimitation disputes between China and the Philippines. He points out that the Tribunal misinterpreted China's diplomatic position, showed intense subjective tendency in the interpretation of Art. 121(3) of UNCLOS, tried to create rights and obligation for parties on the basis of presumed intention, deviated from the principles of *in dubio mitius* and evolutive interpretation of treaties, made legislation in the name of interpretation of law, and departed from purpose of treaty interpretation. During the factual proof, the relative evidences, which were selected from historical fragments by the tribunal, lacked legitimacy, authenticity and relevancy, and therefore cannot support the legality and validity of the award.

In 2002, the International Criminal Court was formally established with the entry into force of the "Rome Statute of the International Criminal Court" (hereinafter referred to as "the Statute"). Although China has not yet signed the Statute, it has been paying close attention to the development of the International Criminal Court with a positive attitude. Yang Lijun's article "On the Normative Role of Complementarity in the Rome Statute of the International Criminal Court (ICC) over the National Legislation" [*International Law Review of Wuhan University*, 1 (2006)] makes a detailed analysis of the "principle of complementarity" stipulated in the Statute, pointing out that the principle of complementarity has a major role in supervising over the implementation of the substantive law of the Statute by states parties; the Statute may also have an indirect or direct impact on non-parties in the implementation of substantive international criminal law. The substantive law of the International Criminal Court has the status of customary international law and therefore has an indirect impact on all countries.

After years of development, international public law scholars of the Institute have achieved fruitful results in the field of EU law research. Their research covers various aspects, including EU trade law, EU human rights mechanism, EU women's rights protection, and EU immigration law etc.. Zhu Xiaoqing's book *European Protection Mechanism for Human Rights* (Law Press China, 2003) is a comprehensive and systematic study on the European human rights protection mechanism with the European Convention on Human Rights as the core and the European Union's human rights protection mechanism. Hao Luyi's book *The Study on EU Legal System of Protection of Women's Labor Rights* (China Social Sciences Press, 2013) studies the protection of women's labor rights under the framework of international law. On the basis of defining the concept, content and principles of women's labor rights protection, it explores the EU's legal system of protection of women's rights in employment and in cross-border migration at the level of regional international organization. After reviewing the EU's legal systems on equal pay for equal work, equal treatment of men and women, coordination of work and family life, and protection of women's social rights in the employment of women's labor force and in cross-border migration, it points out that the EU adopts a gradual legislative mechanism for formulating the relevant laws, regulations and measures on the equality of men and women, and revises and develops the legal norms in small and gentle steps, finally establishing a relatively perfect and scientific legal system. Jiang Xiaohong's book *European Union Trade Law and Sino-EU Trade* (China Social Sciences Press, 2014) takes World Trade Organization's legal system and EU's legal system as the background, and uses case studies, comparative studies, historical analysis and other methods to systematically build the overall framework of EU trade law from two aspects of autonomous legislation and contractual arrangements and practice, to comprehensively introduce and analyze EU trade law, to sort out the main contents of EU trade law, to analyze the main rules of EU trade law, especially those applicable to China, and to explain its theoretical meaning and practical operation.

3.3 The "Belt and Road" Initiative and the Building of Community with Shared Future for Mankind

Wang Hanling points out in his article "Maritime Silk Road Needs International Legal Environment" (*People's Daily*, February 15, 2015) that the common interests linked by 21st Century Maritime Silk Road and its regional economic integration will surely promote the integration and unification of regional legal systems. The construction of 21st Century Maritime Silk Road needs a complete set of international and domestic legal systems involving the construction of maritime transportation infrastructure, international finance, shipping, economy and trade, and even maritime safety. Li Zan's article "Doctrine of International Law and Ways of Building a Community with Shared Future for Mankind" [*Chinese Review of International Law*, 6 (2016)] conducts an in-depth study on this issue. He believes that in the process of globalization, the common interest of international society will be continuously strengthened and become the material basis of the construction of a community with shared future for mankind. The doctrine of International-Community-Orientation, which is based on but transcends state sovereignty, is the thinking basis. Its moral basis is realizing the justice of international society and striking a balance between formal justice and substantive justice. In order to reduce the legal obstacles to communications among countries, the trend towards the convergence of law is developing and becomes the domestic law approach to the building of a community with shared future for mankind. International law and international organizations have promoted and maintained the peace of world, but have failed to realize the perpetual peace of the world. The international law should attach more importance to the building of the inner peace of human beings as a more important means to realizing the perpetual peace of the world. This is the international law approach to the construction of a community with shared future for mankind. The peaceful rise of China based on the traditional Chinese culture and basic principles of international law is China's unique contribution to the construction of a community with shared future for mankind.

In addition to the representative achievements of the above historical periods, the scholars of the Department of Public International Law have undertaken the compilation of a large number of reference books and teaching materials. In the process of writing the *Dictionary of Law* (Shanghai Lexicographical Publishing House, 1980), Yao Zhuang served as a standing member of the editorial board and a main contributor, while Wang Keju and Wei Jiaju served as members of the editorial board and main contributors. Later, Wang Keju has successively been a reviewer of or contributor to the "Law Volume" and "Military Volume" of *Encyclopedia of China* (Encyclopedia of China Publishing House, 1984 & 1989), the "International Military Charter" fascicle of *China Military Encyclopedia*, and the *International Law Volume of Encyclopedia of Chinese Law* (edited by Wang Tieya, China Procuratorial Press, 1996). Zhu Xiaoqing is a contributor to *International Instruments of Human Rights and International Institutions of Human Rights* (Social Science Academic Press, 1993) and the *Dictionary of Human Rights* (Wuhan University Press, 1993). In the process of compiling the *Great Dictionary of Law* (edited by Zeng Qingmin, Shanghai Lexicographical Publishing House, 1998), Tao Zhenghua served as deputy editor-in-chief and, editor-in-chief of the part on public international law. In the process of compiling the *Encyclopedia of China's Human Rights* (Encyclopedia of China Publishing House, 1998), edited by Wang Jiafu and Liu Hainian, Wang Keju and Liu Nanlai served as deputy editors-in-chief and contributors, while Zhu Xiaoqing and Yang Lijun served as contributors. Tao Zhenghua served as a contributor to the part on international law during the compilation of the *China Practical Cyclopedia* (Encyclopedia of China Publishing House, 2000). In the process of compiling the *Law Dictionary* (Law Press China, 2003) edited by Law Dictionary Compilation Committee of CASS Institute of Law, Tao Zhenghua served as a member of the editorial board, and Wang Keju, Liu Nanlai, Zhao Weitian, Lin Xin, Yang Lijun, Zhu Xiaoqing and Liu Wenhua wrote entries on international law.

In addition, Zhu Xiaoqing, as editor-in-chief, has successively published the general teaching material *International Law* (Social Sciences Academic Press,

2005) for postgraduate students of Juris Master and the major textbook *International Law* (China Social Sciences Press, 2012) for postgraduate students of the Graduate School of CASS.

Ⅳ Major Academic Activities

Since the International Law Group was established in 1959, scholars of public international law have served the country's foreign exchange activities and legal construction. Through organizing or participating in various forms of activities, such as those of China Law Society, China Society of International Law and Beijing Society of International Law, they have continuously strengthened the communication and exchange with other domestic practical departments, research institutions and international law scholars in institutions of higher learning to promote the research, practice, dissemination and development of international law in China. In 1980, the Chinese Society of International Law was established. The Vice President of the CASS, Huan Xiang, served as the first president, and Xu Hegao served as the secretary-general of the Society. The office of the Society was set up in the International Law Research Department (later moved to the Institute of Foreign Affairs) and its members were responsible for the editing and publication of the *China Yearbook of International Law* (founded in 1982). In addition, Sheng Yu, Liu Nanlai, Wang Kejü, Tao Zhenghua, Zhu Xiaoqing, Sun Shiyan, and Jiang Xiaohong have served as Vice President of China Law society, Vice President of the China Society of International Law, Vice President and member of the council of the Beijing Society of International Law, respectively.

For a long time, the Department of Public International Law has established and developed good cooperative relations with state organs, domestic and foreign institutions of higher learning and research institutions, international organizations as well as with domestic and foreign colleges. From the 1980s to the present, some scholars have visited Columbia University, University of Denver, Rand Corporation, Colorado Supreme Court, Netherlands Institute for Human Rights, Danish Institute for Human Rights, Norwegian Institute for Human Rights, Raoul Wallenberg Institute of Human Rights and Humanitarian Law in Lund University, Chatham House, Max Planck Institute for Comparative Public Law and International Law in Germany and other institutions for academic exchange activities.

In the past two decades, members of the Department of Public International Law have participated in foreign (academic) exchange activities and government official activities, including the Sino-German Seminar on the Relationship between International Treaties and Domestic Laws(Shanghai, 1999), the UN Committee on the Elimination of Racial Discrimination meeting considering China's 10th to 13th Periodic Reports on the Implementation of the "International Convention on the Elimination of All Forms of Racial Discrimination" (Geneva, 2009), and the China – EU Human Rights Dialogue(Ireland, 2012), Asia – Pacific and Marine Security Research Roundtable (Beijing, 2013), China – Vietnam People's Forum (Hanoi, 2014), the Second ASEAN Regional Seminar on the "United Nations Convention on the Law of the Sea" (Manila, 2014), Bangkok Asia – Pacific Security Conference (Bangkok, 2014), the Fourth Eurasian Anti-Corruption Forum (Moscow, 2015), Advanced Seminar on Oceans and the "United Nations Convention on the Law of the Sea" (Hạ Long Bay, 2015), China Institute of International Studies and the Brookings Institution Dialogue Conference (Washington, 2015), International Seminar on International Cooperation in the Field of Human Rights and China's Perspective(Beijing, 2016), Annual Meeting of University of Virginia Center for Law of the Sea and Ocean Policy (Beijing, 2018), Beijing Human Rights Forums and other international(academic) exchange activities.

V Summary and Outlook

The Department of Public International Law not only boasts a number of renowned scholars and masterpieces at home and abroad, but also participates in legislative and judicial work and national human rights dialogues and exchanges at the entrustment and invitation of relevant departments of the government. It also plays an important role in domestic and overseas academic exchanges.

The Report of the 19th National Congress of the CPC made a major political judgment that socialism with Chinese characteristics has entered a new era, determined the goals and strategic arrangements for the new era, and made a comprehensive plan for the promotion of the great cause of socialism with Chinese characteristics and the implementation of the new great project of Party building in the new era. The new era has created unprecedented opportunities and conditions for international law scholars to study international law, and has also raised higher expectations and demands on international law scholars. Take the right path, no followers will lose. Focusing on the strategic layout of promoting the construction of "the Belt and Road" Initiative and speeding up the construction of China into marine power, public international law scholars will continue to serve the strategic needs of the country's economic and social development and will fulfill their commitments by keeping forging ahead, push forward the development of public international law, and contribute to the prosperity of international law study in China.

Ⅵ Curriculum Vitae of Personnel

Jiang Xiaohong

A Basic Information

Jiang Xiaohong is a research fellow at CASS Institute of International Law and a Professor at the University of CASS. She graduated from China University of Political Science and Law with a bachelor's degree in law in 1992, from the Leiden University (the Netherlands) with the "LL. M. in European Community Law" in 1999 and from the Graduate School of CASS with a doctoral degree in law in 2004.

Prof. Jiang worked at the Institute of Law, CASS from 1992 to 2005. She has been working at CASS Institute of International Law since 2005. Since she got the LL. M. from Leiden Law School, she has been specialized in the study of European Union Law. She is a member of the Executive Board of China Association for EU Law. Her academic interests include international trade law and international investment law, especially in the fields of trade remedy law, fair competition, trade and human rights, international investment and sustainable development, and WTO reform.

Prof. Jiang has advised many Chinese Ministerial bodies in matters relating to outbound investment, trade disputes and treaty negotiations. In addition, she lectured on trade remedy law and international trade law for Chinese enterprises and industry associations. She was a visiting scholar in Lund University (Sweden), Leiden University(the Netherlands) and Columbia University(U. S. A).

Prof. Jiang has published widely in the fields of European Union law and international economic law. In 2004, she published her monograph *EC Anti-dumping Law and Sino-EC Trade*. It is one of the earliest systematic study of the EC anti-dumping law in China. The study on this topic is still in urgent need in theory and in practice. In 2014, she published another monograph *European Union Trade Law and Sino-EU Trade*. The book examines the main contents of the EU trade law under the two pillars of the EU autonomous legislations and contractual arrangements, focusing on the rules applicable to China. On the basis of the *EC Anti-dumping Law and Sino-EC Trade*, the book emphasizes the new development of EU trade remedy law. The book also covers the key legal issues in the relations between China and EU, such as the non-market economy status, raw material friction, trade remedy disputes and Bilateral Investment Treaty negotiation.

Prof. Jiang published many articles in the above-mentioned fields. As a member of CASS Think Tank, she has submitted many reports on legal issues between China and the EU to the Chinese government.

B Main Publications

1. "The Entanglement and Balance between Trade Policy and Security Policy

of European Union: The New Development of EU's Legislation on the Dual-use Export Controls", *Journal of the Party School of the Central Committee of the C. P. C*, 6(2015).

2. "The Nexus between Trade and Human Rights: An Analysis of the Human Rights Goal in EU Trade Law", *Chinese Journal of European Studies*, 5(2016).

3. "The Calculation Methodology of Dumping after China's Non-market Economy Treatment", *Chinese Review of International Law*, I4(2017).

4. "Community with a Shared future for Mankind and International Rule of Law", in Chen Su(ed.), *New Development of Rule of Law in China*, China Social sciences Press, 2018.

5. "Research on the New Development of International Investment Law: from the Perspective of How International Investment Treaty Promotes Sustainable Development", *Hebei Law Science*, 3(2019).

Wang Hanling

A Basic Information

Wang Hanling is a research fellow of international law and the founding director of the National Center for Ocean Affairs and the Law of the Sea, Chinese Academy of Social Sciences.

He is an adjunct professor at Shanghai Ocean University and other universities; a research fellow at the China Center for Collaborative Studies of the South China Sea at Nanjing University (funded by the Ministry of Education of China), the Center for Ocean Development of China; a member of the Doctoral Supervisory Committee of the Schulich School of Law, Dalhousie University, Canada, and a member of the China Center (Research Group of Maritime Affairs and the Law of the Sea), University of Macerata, Italy.

He got his Ph. D. in Law from Chinese Academy of Social Sciences, Master of Law degree from Sichuan University School of Law, and M. Sc. in Maritime Law and Policy from World Maritime University in Sweden, worked as a researcher at University of Lapland Law School in Finland, a postdoctoral fellow at Dalhousie University of Canada, and a visiting research fellow at the Center for International Law and East Asian Institute of National University of Singapore, University of Colorado and University of Denver, the USA.

Dr. Wang's research interests include public international law, the law of the sea, fisheries law and international environmental law. He has published widely in Chinese and English, and submitted numerous consulting reports to the Chinese central government. He has been invited to speak and lecture on ocean law and policy at numerous international conferences, institutes and embassies as well as military academies in the US, Canada and Indonesia. He is frequently interviewed by China Global Television Network (CGTN) and other media.

He was nominated by the Chinese central government as an expert for Special Arbitration under Article 2, Annex Ⅷ of the United Nations Convention on the Law of the Sea, and served as a consultant to the Division for Ocean Affairs and the Law of the Sea (DOALOS) of the Office of Legal Affairs of the United Nations. He was one of the four international experts appointed by DOALOS to coauthor *Eco-system Approaches to the Management of Ocean-Related Activities*, which was published by the United Nations in 2011.

B Representative Publications

1. *Ecosystem Approaches to the Management of Ocean-Related Activities*, UN, 2011 (Co-author).

2. "Le Droit De la Mer Face Aux" Méditerranées: "Quelle contribution de la Méditerranée et des mers semi-fermées au droit international de la mer?", *Editoriale Scientifica*, 2016 (Co-author).

3. "Ecosystem Management and Its Application to Large Marine Ecosystems: Science, Law, and Politics", *Ocean Development & International Law*, Vol. 35, 2004, pp. 41-74.

4. "An Evaluation of the Modular Approach to the Assessment and Management of Large Marine Ecosystems", *Ocean Development & International Law*, Vol. 35, 2004, pp. 267-286.

5. "China's Position on India's Bid for Permanent Membership of the UN Security Council", East Asian Institute (EAI), National University of Singapore, 2011.

6. "China's Diplomacy and Stand on Implementing the Declaration on the Conduct of Parties in the South China Sea", East Asian Institute (EAI), National University of Singapore, 2011.

7. "China Faces Unprecedented Challenges on the South China Sea Issue", East Asian Institute (EAI), National University of Singapore, 2011.

Li Zan

A Basic Information

Li Zan, Ph. D., Associate Professor, graduated from Law School of Peking University, and got his doctoral degree in 2010. He is an associate research fellow at the Department of Public International Law, Institute of International Law, Chinese Academy of Social Sciences(CASS) since 2013.

Professor Li's research and teaching focus on the theory of public international law, the law of international organizations, cultures and international law, international human rights protection of the elderly and the old-age care in China. He has authored or edited more than 20 academic publications in international law, including 6 books and 14 articles. His representative works include *The Jurisdictional Immunity of International Organizations*(2013), *The Application of International Treaties in Hong Kong*(2010), etc..

B Main Academic Viewpoints

1. Jurisdictional Immunity of International Organizations before Domestic Courts: Restriction and Balance. As international organizations(IOs) becoming increasingly active and their functions constantly expanding, they continue to wrestle internally with the questions of when they have immunity and how to realize it in domestic judicial proceedings. The subject of immunity of IOs has been on the agenda of ILC for 30 years as part of the study of "relations between states and international organizations", but in 1992, ILC decided to put aside the consideration of the topic. In recent years, some scholars and ILC members began to rethink and call for continued deep study of IO jurisdictional immunity. This study discusses the jurisdictional immunity of IOs, namely whether IOs have immunity and how to realize it in domestic judicial proceedings.

The study concentrates on the legality and legitimacy of IO jurisdictional immunity and proceeds in four parts: (i) defining the existing legal sources of IO jurisdictional immunity; (ii) exploring the functional limitations on such immunity; and (iii) analyzing the limitations on such immunity that exist via waivers of immunity and (iv) alternative dispute settlement mechanisms.

This study seeks to review IO jurisdictional immunity thoroughly to fill existing gaps in scholarly attention and to assist practitioners who must regulate IO immunity via treaty or domestic legislation. To do so, this study makes two claims. First, it argues that IO jurisdictional immunity is a restrictive right of IOs. In doing so, it rejects as superfluous the view of scholars who insist that IOs deserve absolute jurisdictional immunity. This study finds this restrictive right to immunity is needed in order for IOs to function independently in the course of implementing their purposes without interference from member states. This "functional necessity test" for IO jurisdictional immunity can identify when immunity is required based on whether it would maintain an IO's independence and protect its effective functioning. But this functional necessity for immunity is not unlimited, even if IOs themselves might desire absolute immunity. Just as states may be over-strict in denying IO's jurisdictional immunity, IO immunity itself should be tailored to avoid overly interfering with the operation of a state's legal system. Second, assuming functional necessity dictates a restrictive IO right to jurisdictional immunity, this study discusses in detail two modes for limiting IO immunity: the existence of compulsory waivers of immunity and remedial arrangements for private party claims via alternative dispute settlement mechanisms. Taken together, IO functional immunity, compulsory waivers of immunity, and alternative dispute settlement mechanisms provide an immunity regime that will protect the effective functioning of IOs without causing unreasonable damage to the sovereignty of states. The restriction and balance of IO jurisdictional immunity connect and influence each other. The restriction of IO jurisdictional immunity is useful and helpful to realize the balance of IO jurisdictional immunity, which is the reason and result of restricting the IO jurisdictional immunity.

2. Doctrine of International Law and Ways to Construct a community with shared future for mankind. International law is needed in the construction of a community with shared future for mankind. In the process of globalization, the common interest of international society is continuously strengthened and become the material basis of the construction of a community with shared future for mankind. The doctrine of International-Community-Orientation, which is based on but transcends sovereignty, is the ideological basis. The moral basis is the need to realize the international social justice and strike a balance between formal justice

and substantive justice. In order to reduce the obstacles to communications among countries, the laws in different countries are developing towards convergence and becoming the domestic approach to the construction of a community with shared future for mankind. International law and international organizations have promoted and maintained the peace of world, but have failed to realize the perpetual peace of the world. The international law should attach more importance to the construction of inner peace of human beings, which is a new approach to the perpetual peace of the world and a community with shared future for mankind. The peaceful rise of China based on the traditional Chinese culture and primary principles of international law is the unique contribution made by China to the construction of a community with shared future for mankind.

Hao Luyi

A Basic Information

Hao Luyi is an associate research fellow at CASS Institute of International Law, an editor of *Chinese Review of International Law*, and a member of the Gender and Law Research Center of CASS Institute of Law. She has been a visiting scholar at Columbia University in the city of New York.

Hao Luyi has a B. A. from Shandong University, the LL. M. from Nottingham University of UK and a Ph. D. in international law from East China University of Political Science and Law. She was also a Post-doctoral researcher at CASS Institute of Law.

B Main Academic Viewpoints

Hao Luyi's main research areas are public international law and international migration law. Her published works include: *Study on the EU Legal System of International Migration* (People's Publishing House, 2011); *Study on the Legal System for the Protection of Women's Labor Rights in the EU* (China Social Sciences Press, 2013); "The Changed or Unchanged Issues of the International Refugee Legal System" [*Northern Legal Science*, 1 (2018)]; "The Human Rights Approach to Global Migration Governance" [*Journal of Shenzhen University* (*Humanities & Social Sciences*)]; "Analysis of EU Immigration Law, Historical Evolution, Realistic Dilemma and Development Trend" (*Global Law Review*, 2016); "Human Rights in Extradition" (*Chinese Review of International Law*, 2015); and "The Protection of the Rights of Domestic Workers" (*Hebei Law Science*, 2014).

Hao Luyi has paid more attentions on the relationships between individuals and the states in the perspective of international public law, making an in-depth exploration on the theory and practice of human rights protection and national security involved in the field of immigration and refugees. Her academic views are as follows.

Her research is trying to explore the meaning and path of the global migration governance. The human rights approach to global migration governance is not to rebuild a new system of international human rights legal norms, but to integrate, on the basis of existing human rights normative frameworks, international human rights concepts and standards such as the principle of non-discrimination, empowerment and inclusion, oversight and accountability and so on. The integration of the human rights protection responsibilities and obligations of States, such as the original countries of migrants, transit and destination countries, provides practical guidance and concrete paths to guarantee the human rights and fundamental freedoms of all migrants.

Regarding to the area of refugees, her research emphasizes the importance of effective compliance with and effective implementation of the 1951 Refugees Convention and its Protocol at the international level in the context of the international refugee regime. Her research proposed a global approach to international cooperation on refugee governance, centered on safeguarding the rights of refugees, addressing the root causes of refugees and effectively sharing responsibilities.

Her research tracks the issue of immigration and refugees in the process of EU integration from an empirical point of view. The fundamental contradiction between the common governance of EU integration and the diversified demand of sovereign countries restricts the integrated structure and function of EU immigration law, which not only brings significant limitations to the decision-making and legislation in the field of external migration, but also sows the root cause of the realistic predicament and development hidden danger of the EU immigration legal system. In the long run, the issue of immigration has become a substantial "challenge" to the EU integration process in the EU, which has been internalized by the apparent "crisis", making it an important factor in determining the fate of the EU.

Zhang Weihua

A Basic Information

Zhang Weihua is an assistant research fellow at CASS Institute of International Law. He received his Bachelor of Law(Economic Law) degree from Zhengzhou University in 1998, his Master of International Law degree from Zhengzhou University in 2004, and a Ph. D. in International Law from China University of Political Science and Law in 2008. Mr. Zhang has published widely in the field of international humanitarian law, international law of the sea, and aviation law.

B Main Academic Viewpoints

1. The use of policy-oriented jurisprudence to analyze the legal system of diplomatic protection reveals that the actual operation of the diplomatic protection law is regarded as a part of the global process of authoritative decision. Participants in the process of diplomatic protection(claimant states, respondent states, individuals and companies, international tribunals and arbitral tribunals, and other international organizations) play different roles in diplomatic protection, including intelligence, promotion or recommendation, prescription, invocation, application, termination and appraisal, etc.. Traditional legal schools are unable to correctly apprise the status of ideas in law, some of them overemphasizing the importance of perspectives, and ignoring practical operations of law, while some others isolating perspectives from the concept of law. Policy-oriented schools regard both perspectives and operations as the essential characters of law. Perspectives of human rights have profoundly affected the authoritative decision-making process of diplomatic protection. Any state has to decide the specific strategy to be used in the process of diplomatic protection, including diplomatic methods and judicial procedures. All the means and methods to be used should be peaceful, and any use of force should pass the examination of the right to self-defense.

2. A Community with a Shared Future for Mankind is a theoretical innovation made by China for the establishment of a fair and equitable international order. Just as any other community, a Community with a Shared Future needs common values to bring its members together. To build a new model of relations featuring win-win cooperation, a Community with a Shared Future should attach great

importance to the overall interests of mankind and take the protection of human dignity and human rights as its highest purpose and objective and human rights and freedoms as its common values. On the other hand, to build a Community with a Shared Future, we should reconstruct the concept and system of human rights from the perspective of developing countries, instead of from the perspective of Western powers.

3. China's historical rights to the waters within the South Sea have been resource-based, and China has never imposed any restrictions on the freedom of navigation in that sea. China's historical rights to the South Sea are based on its territorial sovereignty over the South Sea Islands and its historical activities thereof, the essential elements of which are the special geographical features of the South Sea and China's economic needs for the resources thereof. China's long-term navigation activities in the South China Sea do not generate exclusive rights. The South China Sea has also been governed by the United Nations Convention on the Law of the Sea, just as any other areas world oceans and seas. Different regime of navigation should apply to different areas of the South Sea, such as territorial seas, EEZs, internal waters, etc..

4. The United Nations Convention on the Law of the Sea(UNCLOS) has evaded the issue of the legal status of EEZ. Both the claim that the EEZ still belongs to the high seas and the claim that it is a self-contained zone violate the provision of UNCLOS. The legal system of EEZ under UNCLOS has been a compromise among contracting Parties, and the Convention fails to give a clear answer to the question of whether the EEZ is a part of the High Seas, or to provide a definition on the EEZ. What it does is to stipulate that "the Exclusive Economic Zone is an area subject to the specific legal regime established by this part, under which the rights and jurisdiction of the coast State and the rights and freedoms of the other States are governed by the relevant provisions of this Convention". Therefore, the legal status of the EEZ is actually defined through the precise definition of the legal characters of the rights, freedoms and obligations of the coastal State or other States. According to the Convention, the rights and jurisdictions of the coastal State are rights of sovereignty, while the freedoms of the other States are freedoms

of high sea.

5. Problems arising from the freedom of navigation in EEZ should be resolved in accordance with the relevant provisions of the United Nations Convention on the Law of the Sea(UNCLOS) and may not be inferred from the fact that the exclusive economic zone belongs to "international waters" or "national jurisdictions". The regime of EEZ under UNCLOS is a delicate balance between the sovereign rights and jurisdiction of the coastal State and the rights and freedoms of other States. Any issue concerning EEZ should be resolved in accordance with Part V of UNCLOS. Neither "international waters" nor "national waters" have emerged in UNCLOS. Any question of freedom of navigation should be resolved in accordance with the relevant provisions of UNCLOS(especially Article 58).

C Main Publications

1. *New Theory of Diplomatic Protection Law*, China University of Political Science and Law Press, 2012.

2. "The Origins and Evolution of the 1977 Additional Protocols to the 1949 Geneva Conventions", *Human Rights*, 6(2018).

3. "The Human Rights Dimension in Building a Community with a Shared Future for Mankind", *Human Rights*, 5(2017).

4. "Suggestions on Revising Civil Aviation Law(Draft Articles): From Perspective of International Civil Aviation Security Conventions", *Journal of Beijing University of Aeronautics and Astronautics*(*Social Science Edition*), 1(2017).

5. "Freedom of Navigation in the South China Sea Waters", *Journal of Hainan University*(*Humanities & Social Science*), 6(2016).

6. "1949 Geneva Conventions, the Compilation and Development of Basic Standards of Humanitarian Law", *Human Rights*, 5(2016).

7. "On the Obligation of 'Due Regard' in the Exclusive Economic Zone", *Chinese Review of International Law*, 5(2015).

8. "On the Legal Status and Freedom of Overflight over the Exclusive Economic Zone", *Global Law Review*, 1(2015).

9. "The Doctrine of 'Clean-hands' in Diplomatic Protection", *Chinese Yearbook of International Law*, 2009.

Ma Jinxing

A Basic Information

Ma Jinxing is an assistant research fellow at CASS Institute of International Law. He obtained his LL. B. and Ph. D. from Dalian Maritime University(DMU) in China, and his LL. M. from Saarland University(UdS) in Germany. From 2015 to 2018, he worked as a postdoctoral researcher at CASS Institute of Law. His research interests include Maritime Territorial & Delimitation Disputes, Maritime Traffic Safety and Law Enforcement, Marine Environmental Protection, Historical Rights, Enforcement Mechanism of IMO Conventions, Marine Police and Legislation, Integrated Management of Coastal and Marine Areas, etc. .

He has published about 20 articles (including translation) in authoritative journals; his recent works have been published at *International Review of the Red Cross*(2016), *Chinese Review of International Law*(2017), and *Journal of East Asia & International Law*(2018). Some of his papers are included in *China Social Science Excellence* (*CSSE*). He finished the first Chinese translation of *German Commercial Code*(HGB) Part V "Maritime Act" after its restatement in 2013.

In recent 5 years, he has submitted more than 40 internal research reports, all of which have been adopted by Central Governmental departments, some have obtained written approvals from leaders of the Central Government and awarded prizes by CASS. He has finished the research project (Class I) "Study on Legal Countermeasures for Regulating the Utilization of Uninhabited Islands" (2016M590174) with the support of China Post-doctoral Science Foundation, and participated in many research programs, such as National Social Science Foundation Programs, Major Research Projects of Philosophy and Social Sciences of Ministry of Education, MOT and NOS programs, and so on.

His main researches involve the following four subjects: (i) maritime territorial & boundary delimitation disputes, including the Diaoyu Islands issues between China and Japan, South China Sea disputes between China and neighboring countries, Territorial Sea and Exclusive Economic Zone delimitation, etc.. (ii) marine environment, which involves the Particularly Sensitive Sea Area in IMO Convention, the prevention and control of pollution from ships, and the protection of the environment in armed conflicts at sea. (iii) Maritime Traffic Safety Maintenance, involving Ship's Routing, Collision and Navigation Rules, etc.. (iv) National Marine Legislation & policies, including the Basic Law of Marine Issues, Island Legislation and Marine Legal System.

B Main Academic Viewpoints

1. The Effect of Island Occupation in China – Japan dispute over Diaoyu Islands. Occupation is the common claim made by China and Japan in the dispute over Diaoyu Islands, other viewpoints of China and Japan over Diaoyu Islands are all based on the claim of occupation. Based on historical facts and international law, this article puts forward the idea that China is the sole legitimate owner of the Diaoyu Islands and Japan's claim on territorial sovereignty over the Diaoyu Islands based on occupation is deceptive. China's claims over the Diaoyu Islands, based on occupation and efficiency control, are reasonable and lawful. A critical date exists in the dispute between China and Japan, and Japanese and American infringing behaviors after the critical date do not have the effect of obtaining the territorial sovereignty over the Diaoyu Islands in meaning of international law. Territorial sovereignty over the Diaoyu Islands was returned back to China after World War

Ⅱ, and China gives no tacit consent to Japan's claims.

2. Compulsory Dispute Settlement Mechanism and the South China Sea Arbitration Case. Compulsory arbitration procedure is an unique compulsory dispute settlement mechanism under UNCLOS. Philippines' submission of the dispute about the International Arbitration Tribunal evaded the limitations on the applicability of the procedure. As a result, China's rejection to the arbitration only means a preliminary objection to the jurisdiction of the tribunal but cannot cease the procedure. With regard to the development of the compulsory arbitration, China should adhere to its claims for sovereignty over the islands in the South China Sea and regions within the "Nine-dashed line", and declare that the tribunal has no jurisdiction over the dispute. China should intensify the actual control of the disputed regions between China and Philippines by building marine structures and setting up the ADIZ, so as to uphold its inherent interests on the South China Sea.

3. Maritime Safety Investigation is an important measure to improve the safety of marine navigation. Under the influence of the emphasis on territorial jurisdiction, there exists an imbalance between coastal state jurisdiction and flag state jurisdiction in marine safety investigation. The implementation of IMO Maritime Safety Investigation Rule and its amendments accelerated the uniform trend of International Maritime Safety Investigation Legislations, expanded state participation in the investigation, and strengthened the flag state obligations and the protection of seafarers' human rights.

4. Navigation safety control and the building of "21st Century Maritime Silk Road" (21st CMSR). The safety of maritime navigation, which is the basis for the building of 21st CMSR, has territorial characteristics. The national jurisdiction is the basis of the right of coastal states to ensure the safety of navigation in the South China Sea (SCS). The existing coordination mechanism in SCS belongs to soft law. In addition, the existing maritime disputes make it more difficult to safeguard the safe navigation in SCS. Under the initiative of building 21st CMSR, China and other SCS costal countries should work together to solve the dilemma of jurisdiction coordination, conditionally recognize the living space of state jurisdiction in the disputed sea areas, follow the restrictive provisions in international conven-

tions, reasonably apply the principle of priority and closest connection of personal jurisdiction, and safeguard navigation safety in SCS through joint application.

5. The restrictions on the use of force at sea exist in different branches of international law: the law of the sea and environmental law, which are mainly applicable during the peace time, and international humanitarian law (IHL), which is applicable in times of armed conflict. Different rules from these areas must be compared and analyzed to determine the common principles applicable to restricting the use of force at sea for environmental protection. Taking into account the particular problems in protecting the marine environment in the context of the use of force, the law of the sea and international environmental law could be applied to restrict means and methods of using force at sea during armed conflict, and the interpretation of the principle of precaution should be able to fill the gaps in international law. The detailed concepts and approaches in the law of the sea and environmental law may address some of the lacunae of IHL in marine environmental protection during armed conflict.

C Introductions to Representative Works

1. "Review of the Award on the Legal Statue of Maritime Features in South China Sea Arbitration", *Chinese Review of International Law*, 1 (2017).

Legal statue of maritime features is one of the core issues in the South China Sea Arbitration Case, and the essence of such issue is territorial sovereignty and maritime delimitation disputes between China and the Philippines. Basing itself on the interception of some facts and evidences, the Tribunal distorted the China's diplomatic position, and showed intense subjective tendency in the interpretation of Art. 121 (3) UNCLOS, tried to create rights and obligation for parties on the basis of presumed intentions, deviated from *in dubio mitius* and evolutive interpretation of treaties, and made legislation in the name of interpretation of law, thus departing from purpose of treaty interpretation. During the factual proof, the relative evidences, which were selected from historical fragments by the tribunal, lacked of legitimacy, authenticity and relevancy, and therefore the legality and validity of the award cannot be supported.

2. "On Application of Particularly Sensitive Sea Area System—In the View of Ecological Environment Governance in South China Sea", *Pacific Journal*, 5(2016).

Particularly Sensitive Sea Area system(PSSAs), as one of Marine Protection Areas regimes led by IMO, different from other relative Marine Protection Areas regimes, is based on wide national practices. South China Sea meets PSSA standards. In order to hold international discourse power in regional environment management and accumulate political mutual trust, China should combine the bilateral and multilateral approaches under the regional cooperation system established by relevant international conventions and take part in the application for the designation of South China Sea as PSSA, then adopt the protection measures in accordance with IMO legal documents and punish the violations in accordance with the relevant domestic laws.

D Main Publications

1. "China's Responses to the South China Sea Arbitration: from the Perspective of Treaty Interpretation on the Status of Maritime Features", *Journal of East Asia & International Law*, 1(2018)(in English).

2. "Review of Issues Relating to the Legal Statue of Maritime Features in South China Sea Arbitration", *Chinese Review of International Law*, 1(2017)(in Chinese).

3. "Restrictions on the Use of Force at Sea: an Environmental Protection Perspective", *International Review of Red Cross*, 902(2016)(co-authored with Sun Shiyan)(in English).

4. "Confliction and Coordination of Maritime Jurisdiction over Navigation in South China Sea", *Social Science Journal*, 6(2016)(in Chinese).

5. "The Application of Particularly Sensitive Sea Area System in South China Sea", *Pacific Journal*, 5(2016)(in Chinese).

6. "Development of International Legislation on Maritime Safety Investigation and Its Implication for China", *Journal of Ocean University of China* (Social Sciences edition), 5(2016)(in Chinese).

7. "Compulsory Dispute Settlement Mechanism under UNCLOS and China's

Response: from China – Philippines South China Sea Arbitration Case Perspectives", *Law Science Magazine*, 2 (2015) (in Chinese).

8. "On the Ocean Legislation in China", *Journal of Social Science*, 7 (2014) (co-authored with Li Zhiwen) (in Chinese).

9. "Study on the Effect of Island Occupation in View of International Law Principle", *Law Science Magazine*, 12 (2013) (co-authored with Li Zhiwen) (in Chinese).

Introduction to the Department of Private International Law

I Historical Evolution

In 1958, the Institute of Law was established under the Department of Philosophy and Social Sciences of the Chinese Academy of Sciences. In 1959, the Fourth Research Group, namely the International Law Research Group, was established under the Institute of Law. For a long time, although there were more than a dozen researchers in the International Law Research Group, there were no people specializing in private international law research. In May 1977, the Chinese Academy of Social Sciences was established on the basis of the former Department of Philosophy and Social Sciences of the Chinese Academy of Sciences and the Institute of Law became a research institute under the Chinese Academy of Social Sciences. In 1978, the International Law Research Group was reorganized into the Department of International Law under the CASS Law Institute, consisting of three international law research fields: public international law, private international law and international economic law. Since then, Yao Zhuang, Ren Jisheng and Lin Xin have been transferred to the Institute of Law, and the Department of International Law began to be equipped with personnel engaged in private international law research. At the end of 1999, Shen Juan joined the Department of International Law and was engaged in the research of private international law. At this time, Yao Zhuang and Ren Jisheng had left the Law Institute, and Lin Xin had retired.

In 2002, Liu Xinyan joined the Department of International Law. In the same year, the Chinese Academy of Social Sciences established the Center for International Law Research, and all personnel of the Department of International Law of the Institute of Law joined the Center for International Law Research. After a period of preparation, the Center for International Law established in 2004 the Department of Public International Law, the Department of Private International Law and the Department of International Economic Law. Since then, the Department of Private International Law has become an independent research branch. At that time, members of the department included Shen Juan and Liu Xinyan, and Shen Juan was the head of the department. In 2005, Liu Xinyan left the Center for International Law Research, leaving the Department with only one research fellow. In 2007, Xie Xinsheng joined the department. In 2009, Li Qingming joined the department. In the same year, the Center for International Law Research was renamed the Institute of International Law. In 2012, Xie Xinsheng left the Institute of International Law. At the end of 2014, Shen Juan retired from the post as the head of the department, and Li Qingming became the deputy head of the department. In 2017, Fu Panfeng joined the department. As of April 2019, the Department of Private International Law of the Institute of International Law of the Chinese Academy of Social Sciences had three research fellows: Professor Shen Juan, Associate Professor Li Qingming and Assistant Professor Fu Panfeng.

Ⅱ Composition of Personnel

Over the past 60 years, research fellows from the Department of Private International Law and those doing private international law studies at the Chinese Academy of Social Sciences have experienced a process of development that started from scratch. Several generations of private international law researchers have joined in, enabling the creation and continuation of the Department of Private International Law. Their rich research results have laid the foundation for the academic prestige of the Department of Private International Law both at home and abroad.

In the early years of the People's Republic of China, although universities in China did offer courses of private international law, the content of the courses was dominated by Soviet Union's notion of private international law. The works of Soviet private international law scholars were also taken as the sole reference for the study and research of private international law. There was no textbook written by Chinese scholars at that time. It was not until early 1980s that China's modern private international law began to revive.

In 1980, Yao Zhuang and Ren Jisheng co-authored the first textbook on private international law in People's Republic of China, and published many academic papers. For example, Yao Zhuang and Ren Jisheng co-authored the paper "On the Adjustment Targets and Norms of Private International Law". Yao Zhuang published the paper "On the Distinction between the Adjustment Targets of Private International Law and Those of International Economic Law". Ren Jisheng published the paper "On the Development Trend of Private International Law". Their papers laid the theoretical foundation for the "big private international law" theory when the basic issues of the targets of adjustment, nature and norms of private international law were under heated discussion by Chinese scholars at the time. They have made important contributions to the clarification of the scopes of research and teaching of private international law and international economic law and also pointed out the direction for the study of private international law at the time. Their research opened the door for the revival of China's private international law research, and also paved the way for the study of basic theoretical issues of private international law as a research discipline. They have become pioneers in the study of private international law not only at the Institute of International Law but also in the whole People's Republic of China.

Lin Xin played a pivotal role in the development of private international law as a research discipline. After Yao Zhuang and Ren Jisheng left the Institute of Law, Lin Xin became the only scholar engaged in private international law research for a period of time and achieved fruitful research results.

In the field of private international law, Lin Xin published two monographs—*The Study of Issues of Private International Law Theory* and *Private International*

Law—and such papers as "On the New Development of Law Application in the Field of Private International Law and the related Chinese Practice", "New Viewpoints of International Law and Private International Law Theory" and "Jurisdiction in International Civil Litigation and China's Civil Procedure Law". In addition to private international law, Lin Xin has also conducted in-depth research on international criminal law. He has published such monographs as *Criminal Jurisdiction in International Law* and *New Interpretation of International Criminal Law* and such academic papers as "New Development of the Principle of Double Criminality in International Criminal Law" and "New Trends of Extradition and Asylum".

Shen Juan has been a researcher of the Institute of International Law for more than 20 years. She has served as the head of the Department of Private International Law for 10 years. She plays a leading role in the teaching and research of private international law at the Institute of International Law and has made important contributions to the development of private international law in China. Shen Juan is a prolific scholar during her long career of research and teaching of private international law. She has published 3 monographs—*Research on Inter-Regional Conflict Law in China*, *Explanation of the Theory of Contract Law* and *Conflict Law and Its Value Orientation* (Revised Edition), and edited such books as *New Developments in Private International Law*, *The Road to the Prosperity of Private International Law*, *Research on International Law*, and *Private International Law*. She has also edited conference proceedings and textbooks designed for graduate students. She has published more than 40 papers including "The Latitude and Limitation of the Forum Law—On the Attitudes of China's Private International Law", "Rational Choice of Applicable Law of Succession between Unitary System and Scission System—A Commentary on Article 3 of the Law of the Application of the Foreign-Related Civil Relations of P. R. China", "An Explanation of the Validity of Agreement on the Choice of Law", "The Concept of Inter-regional Conflict Law", "The Principle of the Closest Connection in Development", "The Improvement and Development of the Rules on the Conflict of Law", "Putting aside Minor Differences to Seek the Common Ground, Stones from Other Hills to Polish the Jade of This One: A Comparative Study of the Hague Convention on Jurisdiction and Recognition and Enforcement of Foreign Judgments in Civil and Commercial Matters(Draft) and Relevant Chinese Laws", "An Opportunity of the Times and a Rational Choice: Reflections on the China's Legislation Concerning the Method to Ascertain the Applicable Law for Contracts", "The Criteria to Determine the Most Significant Relationship", "New Developments in the Recognition and Enforcement of Judgments in Civil and Commercial Matters between the Mainland and Hong Kong, Macau—A Tentative Analysis of Two Arrangements between the Three Places", "Improving China's Judicial and Arbitration System Concerning Foreign-Related Economic Dispute Resolution", "Judges' Awareness of the Result-Oriented Choice of Law When Exercising Their Discretion", "Recent Trends of Development of Private International Law", "Development of Contract-Related Private International Law in Asia", "Further Discussion on the Drafts of the Hague Convention on Jurisdiction and Recognition and Enforcement of Foreign Judgments in Civil and Commercial Matters and Considerations from Chinese Perspective" and "Analysis of the Abuse of Procedural Rights in International Civil Procedure".

Xie Xinsheng joined the Department of Private International Law at a time when the department was extremely shorthanded. His joining the Department added to the research strength of the department and promoted further development of private international law as a discipline. His research combines theory and practice and has achieved excellent results. He has published a monograph entitled *The Applicable Procedural Law in the International Commercial Arbitration*. He has also published more than 20 papers, including "The Solution to the Disputes Related to the International Seabed Shipwreck Relics—From the Perspective of the US Odyssey Case", "Extraterritorial Execution of Chinese Judgments Absent a Treaty or Reciprocity—From the Perspective of the First Case of Enforcement by US Courts of a Chinese Civil and Commercial Judgment", "A Critique of the Proposal to Abolish the Setting-aside of International Commercial Arbitration Awards", "An Analysis of the Applicable Law on Agency", "Foreign-Related Civil Jurisdiction Based on Agreement from the Perspective of Ecommerce: Centering on the Amendment and Improvement of Article 244 of China's Civil Procedure

Law", "The Rules of Law Application for Maritime Liens", "Three Issues of the Relationship between Conflict Laws and Substantive Laws in Civil Code", "The Application of International Law in International Commercial Arbitration" and "The Road to the Procedural Autonomy of International Commercial Arbitration".

Li Qingming's joining the Department of Private International Law once again strengthened the research team at the department. He is well versed in private international law and has a very high level of professionalism. Over the past 10 years since he joined the department, he has made great progresses in his research and has gradually become the backbone of the department. He is the author of the book *A Study of the Alien Tort Claims Act of U. S. A.* and the translator of the book *The New Role of Comity in Private Procedural International Law*. He is also a co-author of the book *Private International Law Judicial Practice in China* (2001 - 2010). He has contributed to many books, such as *Contemporary Research on International Law*, *Chinese Model of Legal Education*, *New Development of Private International Law*, *International Law in Transformation: Frontiers and Hot Issues*, *Research on Jurisdiction Issues in Foreign-Related Civil Litigation*. He has published around 30 papers, including "On the State Immunity of Chinese State-Owned Enterprises in the Civil Procedures of the United States Courts", "Jurisdiction Issues in Confirming Foreign Arbitral Awards in the Federal Courts of the United States: Study of Two Cases Involving the Chinese Government", "Immunity from Execution of State Property of People's Republic of China in the United States—Taking Walters v. Industrial and Commercial Bank of China, Ltd., et al. as an Example", "State Immunity and the Right to Resort to the Court", "On Using Extraterritorial Civil Judgments as Evidence in Civil Procedure in China" and "Legal Issues Arising out of Arbitration Seated in Mainland China but Administered by Overseas Arbitration Institutions".

Fu Panfeng is the youngest researcher at the Department of Private International Law. His joining made the department as robust a team as ever before. He is diligent and professional. He has a good command of English and French, and has already achieved considerable research results, showing that he has great research potential. He has published a book entitled *Research on the French International Commercial Arbitration System* and many papers, such as "Ethical Dilemma Facing Unilateral Appointment of Arbitrators and the Way to Break through It—A Discussion Centering around Paulsson's Proposal", "The Unending Debate: Recognition and Enforcement of Annulled International Commercial Arbitral Awards", "The Test for the Application of the Doctrine of Res Judicata in Investor-State Arbitration—From a Formalistic to a Substantive Approach", "The Emergency Arbitrator in ICC Arbitration Rules", "On Multi-party Arbitration: Its Institutional Construction and Practical Difficulties", "Res Judicata of International Commercial Arbitration Awards", "Judicial Experience in Handling Res Judicata Issues Arising from International Commercial Arbitration Awards in Common Law Countries: Taking Associated Electric v. European Re as an Example", "The Application Dilemma of the Doctrine of Most Significant Relationship and Its Solution: an Examination Based on the Judicial Practice in Foreign-Related Civil and Commercial Matters in China", "Annual Review on Commercial Arbitration in China (2016)", "Chinese Courts' Approach to Non-signatory Issues in Arbitration: a Case Study". He has also published many translated works, such as "Should the Setting Aside of Arbitral Awards be Abolished", "Past, Present and Future Perspectives of Arbitration", "Recognition and Enforcement of Foreign Awards under the New York Convention in Australia and New Zealand", "The Conducting of International Commercial Arbitration Proceedings", "Party Autonomy and Case Management: Experiences and Suggestions of an Arbitrator", "Commercial and Investment Arbitration: How Different Are They Today", "Arbitrability, Due Process, and Public Policy under Article V of the New York Convention-Belgian and French Perspectives", "International Arbitration in a Global Economy: The Challenges of the Future" and "The ILA Report on Lis Pendens and Res Judicata in Arbitration".

Ⅲ Curriculum Vitae of Personnel

Shen Juan

A Basic Information

Prof. Shen Juan was born in Wuhan. She is a research fellow(second-grade), professor and supervisor of Ph. D. student at the Department of Private International Law of CASS Institute of International Law.

Prof. Shen graduate from the Department of Law of China University of Political Sciences and Law with a bachelor's degree in law in 1983. She taught at the Department of Economic Law and Department of International Economic Law of Zhongnan College of Political Sciences and Law from August 1983 to September 1995. In July 1995, she graduated from the Law School of Wuhan University with a doctor's degree in law. From October 1995 to October 1997, she taught at and was the vice director of the Institute of Comparative Law of Zhongnan College of

Political Sciences and Law. From November 1997 to December 1999, she was a postdoctoral research fellow at CASS Institute of Law. From January 2001 to September 2002, she worked at the Department of International Law of CASS Institute of Law as a full-time research fellow. From 2002 until now, she worked at the CASS Research Center of International Law which became the Institute of International Law of CASS in 2009.

Prof. Shen became an associate research fellow in November 1994, a research fellow in August 2000, and a second-grade research fellow in September 2016.

Her main research fields are private international law, inter-regional conflicts of law and international civil litigation.

From September 2003, she has been serving as the vice-president of the China Society of Private International Law. She has been a council member of the Chinese Judicial Studies Association from July 2015. In 2007, she received special government allowance from the State Council. In January 2018, she was elected as a member of Beijing People's Political Consultative Conference. From May 2018, she serves as a council member of Chinese Society of International Law.

B Academic Exchange Experiences

From 2002 to 2003, Prof. Shen was invited to Seoul National University as a visiting scholar. During this visit, she built good academic relationship with Korea Private International Law Association. She participated in the annual meeting of the Korea Private International Law Association and various academic seminars. She gave academic lectures at Seoul National University and Korea University several times. Meanwhile, she translated into Chinese the Korean Private International Law Rules and made them known to the Chinese Private International Law Community. Her visit to South Korea has made considerable contributions to the academic exchange between China and South Korea.

In 2005 and 2006, she went twice to Japan to participate in the "Tripartite Private International Law Seminar of China, Japan and South Korea" and visited Waseda University, Hitotsubashi University and Tohoku University.

In 2006, she paid an academic visit to Leiden University during which period she also visited Amsterdam University and Utrecht University and did academic exchange with senior Dutch private international law scholars.

In 2007, she was invited to Hsuan Chuang University (Taiwan) to give lectures to undergraduate and graduate students at the law school. During her visit, she made deep academic exchange and built extensive connections with private international law scholars in Taiwan.

In 2010, she paid an academic visit to King's College London to learned about the arrangement and the content of conflict of laws courses in British universities and exchanged opinions with British scholars doing research on conflict of laws. She also visited Oxford University and Cambridge University.

C Research Projects

1. CASS Major Research Project: WTO Dispute Resolution System and International Law.

2. CASS Major Research Project: Research on the Theory of Chinese Legislation on Private International Law.

3. CASS Major Research Project: Treaty-Making Power and the Revision of the Treaty-Making Procedural Law.

4. CASS National Conditions Investigation Project: Trial of Civil and Commercial Cases Involving a Foreign Country, Hong Kong, Macau and Taiwan in Chinese Courts.

5. CASS National Conditions Investigation Project: Recognition and Enforcement of Chinese Courts' Judgments in Foreign Countries.

6. CASS Special Investigation Project on Hong Kong: Research on the Laws of HKSAR and the Legal System with Chinese Characteristics—From the Perspective of Judicial Assistance between Mainland China and Hong Kong in Civil and Commercial Matters.

7. CASS "Great Wall Scholarship" Project: the Chinese Law on Choice of Law for Foreign-related Civil Relationships and Its Implementation.

8. CASS Innovation Project: The Implementation and Development of the Chinese Law on Choice of Law for Foreign-related Civil Relationships.

D Teaching Achievements

Prof. Shen has been teaching for 36 years. Her students include undergraduate, graduate and Ph. D. students. She has also cooperated with and supervised several postdoctoral researchers. Up till now, she has independently supervised 21 masters of law students, 13 Ph. D. students and 7 postdoctoral researchers.

E Main Academic Viewpoints

Over the past 30 years, Prof. Shen has published extensively on private international law. She has established herself as one of the most distinguished scholars of private international law. The following are some of the academic viewpoints that she has put forward in her recent publications.

1. Regarding the Value Orientation of Conflict Laws

Conflictlaws not only are the substantive laws that adjust international relationship or the principles that resolve conflict of laws, but also embody the rational values and moral orientation pursued by mankind, that is, to achieve harmony and coordination among human beings through the approach and process of conflict resolution. Therefore, conflict laws are not only laws that resolve conflict of laws or transcend jurisdictional interests, but also a vehicle used to lead human beings to goodness and international society to harmony and mutual assistance. This is a viewpoint put forward by Prof. Shen in 1993 that laid a jurisprudential foundation for the ideal of "a community with shared future for mankind".

2. Regarding the Theory of Applicable Law of Contract

The principle of party autonomy is in line with the theory of freedom of contract and the spirit of autonomy in private law. It can not only fulfill the will of the parties, but also ensure the certainty, predictability and consistency of the process of law application, thus ensuring smooth and orderly international contractual relationship in civil and commercial matters. Therefore, the theory of the applicable law of contract should equip the parties with the right to choose the applicable law to the widest extent, and in the case where the parties have chosen a law, parties' choice should be given legal effect as far as possible. The doctrine of the most significant relationship does not aim to abandon the system of traditional conflict rules, but to introduce a mechanism for the exercise of discretion by judges while inheriting the traditional conflict rules system, and to reform the rigid and mechanical system of the traditional conflict rules with its unique flexibility. The theory of the most significant relationship underlines the congenital deficiency of the pre-established conflict rules and encourages the use of judge's discretionary power to overcome such deficiency. This is where the theory of the most significant relationship is better than traditional theories. If this theory is considered to only encourage judges to use their discretionary power and to add flexibility to the determination of the applicable law of contract regardless of the stability of the process of law application, putting this theory into practice would undermine the certainty, predictability and consistency of the process of law application. It will also undermine the smooth and orderly international contractual relationship in civil and commercial matters. Therefore, it is a misinterpretation of the essence of the theory, a reduction of the practical significance of the theory and a limitation on the functions of the theory.

3. Regarding the Validity of Agreement on the Choice of Law

Although the validity of agreement on the choice of law has a direct influence on party autonomy, few studies have been conducted on this issue. Currently, there are two different opinions on the validity of agreement on the choice of law in private international law: the application of the law chosen by the parties and the application of the law of the court. Professor Shen points out that there are many weaknesses in the method of application of the law chosen by the parties for the confirmation of the validity of agreement on the choice of law, such as logical contradiction and inapplicability in areas other than contract law; the content of an agreement on the choice of law should be the rules on the choice of law and the confirmation of the validity of an agreement on the choice of law is the application of the rules on the choice of law; the principle of party autonomy not only gives the parties the right of the choice of law but also sets a limit to such autonomy; the confirmation of the validity of an agreement on the choice of law through the application of the law chosen by the parties in areas other than contract law is even more unreasonable; in such areas, the application of the law of the court is a more reasonable and feasible approach.

4. Regarding the Draft Hague Convention on Jurisdiction and Recognition and Enforcement of Foreign Judgments in Civil and Commercial Matters

The Hague Convention on Jurisdiction and Recognition and Enforcement of Foreign Judgments in Civil and Commercial Matters(hereinafter referred to as "the Convention") has been in the process of preparation for almost 20 years. Disputes over many problems among different countries delayed the completion of this project. Although many drafts of the Convention have taken civil and commercial matters as the targets of their application, these drafts keep enlarging the scope of civil and commercial matters excluded from the application of the Convention and referring these matters to other Hague Conventions. These exclusions will certainly break the integrity and comprehensiveness of the Convention, increase the difficulties for all countries to join the Hague procedural Conventions, and severely affect the effectiveness of the application of the Convention. The latest draft of the Convention even abandoned the arrangement of direct jurisdiction, thus not only once again breaking the integrity of the Convention without eliminating the conflicts of jurisdiction between countries, but also depriving the Convention of specific standards for judging the legitimacy of jurisdiction in the recognition and enforcement of foreign judgments. As to the reasons for the refusal to recognize and enforce foreign judgments, the draft should pay special attention to and amend the inconsistency between criterions on the examination of the legitimacy of jurisdiction and those on the finality and enforceability of judgments, which will lead to a disharmony between the effectiveness of jurisdiction and the effectiveness of judgments.

5. The Role of the Forum Law in Private International Law

In private international law, the concept of the forum law can be represented in a variety of way, each of which has different characteristics. When expressed as mandatory rules of a state, forum law has the effect to exclude the application of foreign law. Abusive application of such rules should be contained. When expressed as rules on conflict of law of a state, forum law is equated to unilateral rules of law application. By limiting the number of such unilateral rules, the return of territoriality of law application as well as the damage to the universality of law choice can be avoided. If the forum law is interpreted as rules on the conflict of law of the forum state, then it follows that the court at the forum has the advantage to exert its judicial jurisdiction. In this case, when choice of the forum law has the effect of improperly expanding the application scope of the law of the forum state, its application should be restrained. When the choice of the forum law can bring a better result to the parties, its application should be encouraged. The law of the place of real estate is a special expression of the forum law and, in this respect, the necessity to restrain the application of the forum law should be embodied in the field of inheritance. Legislative jurisdiction and judicial convenience are not rational reasons for choosing to apply the forum law. The close connection between the forum law and the legal relationship in a particular case as well as the special needs of the parties are the criteria to take into consideration when deciding whether the forum law should be applied.

F Awards

1. Her monograph *Research on Inter-Regional Conflict Law in China* was awarded "the Prize for Excellent Research Result" by CASS Institute of Law in 2001.

2. Her monograph *Conflict Law and Its Value Orientation* (Revised Edition) was awarded "the Second Prize for Excellent Research Result" by CASS Institute of Law in 2003.

3. Her monograph *Conflict Law and Its Value Orientation* (Revised Edition) was awarded "Third Prize for Excellent Research Result" by Chinese Academy of Social Sciences in 2004.

4. Her monograph *Explanation of the Theory of Contract Law* won the "Silver Tripod Award for Excellent Legal Research Work by Young Chinese Scholars" in 2005.

5. Her paper "An Opportunity of the Times and a Rational Choice: Reflections on China's Legislation Concerning the Method to Ascertain the Applicable Law for Contracts" was awarded the Third Prize for Excellent Research Results by Chinese Academy of Social Sciences in 2011.

6. Her monograph *Explanation of the Theory of Contract Law* was awarded the Second Prize for Excellent Post-doctoral Legal Research Results in 2013.

7. Her paper "Judges' Awareness of the Result-Oriented Choice of Law When Exercising Their Discretion" was awarded the Prize for Excellent Research Results by CASS Institute of International Law in 2015.

8. Her monograph *New Developments in Private International Law* was awarded the Prize for Excellent Monograph by CASS Institute of International Law in 2015.

9. Her paper "Judges' Awareness of the Result-Oriented Choice of Law When Exercising Their Discretion" was awarded "The Third Prize for Excellent Research Results" by Chinese Academy of Social Sciences in 2016.

G Main Publications

Monographs

1. *Conflict Law and Its Value Orientation*, China University of Political Science and Law Press, 1993.

2. *Research on Inter-regional Conflict Law in China*, China University of Political Science and Law Press, 1999.

3. *Explanation of the Theory of Contract Law*, Law Press China, 2000.

4. *Conflict Law and Its Value Orientation* (Revised Edition), China University of Political Science and Law Press, 2002.

5. *Private International Law: Textbook for Master's Students Masters of Law*, Social Sciences Academic Press, 2006.

6. *Research on International Law*, Chinese People's Public Security University Press, 2016.

7. *New Developments in Private International Law*, China Social Sciences Press, 2010.

8. *Research on International Law*, Chinese People's Public Security University Press, Vol. 5, 2012.

9. *Research on International Law*, Social Sciences Academic Press, Vol. 9, 2013.

10. *New Developments in Private International Law*, China Social Sciences Press, 2015.

11. *Road to the Invigoration of Private International Law*, Social Sciences Academic Press, 2019.

Papers

1. "The Status Quo and Prospect of the Interregional Conflict Law of the Mainland and Taiwan", *Journal of Zhongnan University of Political Science and Law*, 2(1992).

2. "The Origins, Orientation and Realization of Conflict Law Value", *Journal of Comparative Law*, 2(1992).

3. "A Historical Research on Interregional Conflict Law in China", *Studies in Law and Business*, 2(1996).

4. "The Doctrine of the Most Significant Relationship in Development", in *Contemporary Issues on Private International Law*, Wuhan University Press, 1996.

5. "Coordination of Interregional Civil Procedure in China", in *Chinese Yearbook of Private International Law and Comparative Law*, Law Press China, 1999.

6. "The Concept of Interregional Conflict Law", *Chinese Journal of Law*, 5 (1999).

7. "The Improvement and Development of the Conflict of Law Rules", *Tribune of Political Science and Law*, 6(1999).

8. "The Determination and Restriction of Party Autonomy in Contracts", *Tsinghua Law Review*, 3(2000).

9. "Putting aside Minor Differences to Seek the Common Ground, Stones from Other Hills to Polish the Jade of this One: A Comparative Study of the Hague Convention on Jurisdiction and Recognition and Enforcement of Foreign Judgments in Civil and Commercial Matters (Draft) and Chinese Relevant Laws", in *Chi-nese Yearbook of Private International Law and Comparative Law*, Law Press China, 2001.

10. "Legislation and Practice of Jurisdiction over Foreign-related Civil and Commercial Cases in China", in *The Present Situation and Problems of Civil Procedure Law in China*, Korea Legislation Research Institute, June 2003.

11. "An Overview of Private International Law in China", *Research on Private International Law, Korean Society of Private International Law*, 9(2003).

12. "The Legislation Problems of Private International Law in China", *Chinese Journal of Law*, 2(2004).

13. "The Present Situation of the Legislation of Private International Law in China", in *Research on Chinese Law*, Vol. 4, the Korean – Chinese Society of Law, 2004.

14. "The Overview of the Legislation of Korea's Private International Law in 2001", February 2005. available at: http://www. iolaw. org. cn/.

15. "Research on Korea's Private International Law and Comparison with China's Private International Law", in Law School of Hsuan Chuang University, *A Collection of Papers of the Cross-strait Seminar on Private International Law*, Great Press Taiwan, 2005.

16. "The Comparative Research on Private International Law of China and Japan", in *Waseda Proceedings of Comparative Law*, *Institute of Comparative Law of Waseda University*, Vol. 8, 2005.

17. "An Opportunity of the Times and a Rational Choice: Reflections on the China's Legislation Concerning the Method to Ascertain the Applicable Law for Contracts", in *Research on International Law*, Vol. 1, Chinese People's Public Security University Press, 2006.

18. "The Explanation of the Concept 'Proper Law of Contract' in Private International Law", in Institute of International Law, Chinese Academy of Social Sciences (ed.), *A Collection of Academic Papers Dedicated to the 30th Anniversary of the Founding of CASS*, Local Records Publishing House, 2007.

19. "The Criteria to Determine the Most Significant Relationship", in Chen Su (ed.), *A Collection of Academic Papers Dedicated to the 50th Anniversary of the Founding of the Institute of Law*, *Chinese Academy of Social Sciences*, China Social Sciences Press, 2008.

20. "New Developments Concerning Recognition and Enforcement of Judgments in Civil and Commercial Matters between the Mainland and Hong Kong, Macau—A Tentative Analysis of Two Arrangements between the Three Places", in *Research on International Law*, Vol. 3, Chinese People's Public Security University Press, 2009.

21. "Improving China's Judicial and Arbitration System Concerning Foreign-Related Economic Dispute Resolution", in Chen Sue (ed.), *China's Construction*

of the Rule of Law in the Context of Globalization, Economy & Management Publishing House, 2010, Chapter 11.

22. "The Theory of the Most Significant Relationship", in Chen Zexian (ed.), *Development of the International Law Studies in China*, China Social Sciences Press, 2010, Chapter 14.

23. "Development of the Theory of Interregional Conflict Law in China", in Chen Zexian (ed.), *Development of the International Law Studies in China*, China Social Sciences Press, 2010, Chapter 17.

24. "Judges' Awareness of the Result-Oriented Choice of Law When Exercising Their Discretion", in *Research on International Law*, Vol. 4, Chinese People's Public Security University Press, 2011.

25. "Recent Trends of Development of Private International Law", in Zhu Xiaoqing (ed.), *International Law on the Move: Current Issues and New Perspectives*, China Social Sciences Press, 2012.

26. "Report on the Settlement of Civil and Commercial Cases Related to Foreign Countries and to Hong Kong, Taiwan and Macao in Chinese Courts", in *Research on International Law*, Vol. 8, Social Sciences Academic Press, 2013.

27. "Development of Contract-Related Private International Law in Asia", in Kong Qingjiang (ed.), *International Law Review*, Vol. 4, Tsinghua University Press, 2013.

28. "The Latitude and Limitation of the Forum Law—On the Attitudes of China's Private International Law", *Tsinghua University Law Journal*, 4 (2013).

29. "Rational Choice of Applicable Law of Succession between Unitary System and Scission System—A Commentary on Article 3 of the Law of the Application of the Foreign-related Civil Relations of P. R. China", *Chinese Review of International Law*, 1 (2014).

30. "An Explanation of the Validity of Agreement on the Choice of Law", *Chinese Journal of Law*, 6 (2015).

31. "Further Discussion on the Drafts of the Hague Convention on Jurisdiction and Recognition and Enforcement of Foreign Judgments in Civil and Commercial Matters and Considerations from Chinese Perspective", *Chinese Review of In-*

ternational Law,6(2016). Reprinted in *International Law*, *China Social Science Excellence*,D416,2017(5). Reprinted by *Chinese Social Sciences Network* at: http://www.cssn.cn/,2017.8.31.

32. "The Developments, Current Issues and Difficulties of Private International Law",exclusives on http://www.iolaw.org.cn/,2017.5.

33. "Analysis of the Abuse of Procedural Rights in International Civil Procedure",*Chinese Review of International Law*,6(2017).

34. "Legislative Achievements of Chinese Private International Law over the Past 40 Years Since China's Opening up", *Chinese Social Sciences Today*, 26th Dec. 2018, simultaneously published at the website of *Chinese Social Sciences* (26th Dec. 2018).

Translated Works

"Private International Law of the Republic of Korea 2001", a 9000 - word translation, in *Chinese Yearbook of Private International Law and Comparative Law*, Law Press China, 2003.

Li Qingming

A Basic Information

Li Qingming is an associate research fellow and the deputy head of the Department of Private International Law, Institute of International Law, Chinese Academy of Social Sciences and a part-time editor of the *Chinese Review of International Law*.

He graduated from the Law School of Wuhan University with a Bachelor of Law in 2004, an LL. M. in 2006 and a Ph. D. in Law in 2009. He was a visiting scholar at Colombia Law School from September 2010 to September 2011. His main research areas are private international law, international civil litigation and commercial arbitration. He is the author of the book *A Study of the Alien Tort Claims Act of U. S. A.* (Wuhan University Press, 2010) and the translator of the book *The New Role of Comity in Private Procedural International Law* (China Social Sciences Press, 2011). He has published over 30 articles in various Chinese and foreign academic journals.

B Main Academic Viewpoints

Professor Li is the first Chinese scholar who has systematically studied international human rights civil litigation in the United States of America. In the book *A Study of the Alien Tort Claims Act of U. S. A.*, he expressed the following opinions: (1) the revival of the ATCA in 1980s was closely related to the upsurge of the civil rights movement in the United States, as well as the explosion of international civil litigation. (2) The jurisdiction of the ATCA is not the universal civil jurisdiction, but exercised according to the domestic law of the United States, and the cases are actually associated with the United States. (3) After the plaintiffs have brought the civil action according to the ATCA, the defendant may put forward many defenses such as *forum non conveniens*, exhaustion of local remedy, state immunity, the acts of state doctrine, international comity, the political question doctrine, and thus many cases are dismissed. (4) The practice of holding individuals accountable for their conducts of violation of international law has not been generally accepted by nations except the United States. The prosperity of the alien tort litigation in the United States is rooted in the United States' unique legal system, and it is difficult for other countries to transplant, copy and use for reference.

He has published four articles on state immunity. He argues that the courts have no competence to attach the property of the instrumentality of a foreign state (including the state-owned enterprise) to execute the judgment against the foreign state. Both Chinese government and Chinese state-owned enterprises are independent bodies, and thus the federal courts of the United States of America shall dismiss the cases of recognition and enforcement of foreign arbitral awards involving the Chinese government and Chinese state-owned enterprises in which the independent legal status of the Chinese government and Chinese state-owned enterprises may be mixed up. When being sued in a United States court, a Chinese state-owned enterprise should appear in court to specially object the court's subject-matter jurisdiction and personal jurisdiction over the case, so as to avoid a default judgment by the court. When Chinese state-owned enterprises are sued in the United States, their claiming state immunity will not lead to the confusion with the state responsibility, nor the enforcement against other state-owned enterprises' property.

He also argues that the right of access to court may be limited by the principle of state immunity. The purpose of state immunity granted to foreign countries to limit the right of access to the court is legitimate and in compliance with international law. As to the principle of proportionality, the restrictive rules in the U. N. Convention on Jurisdictional Immunities of States and Their Property is playing an increasingly important role, especially in cases involving employment contract, personal injury, the protection of the complainant's right to access to court, in which it is necessary to limit the invocation of state exemption. The decisions of the European Court of Human Rights have a profound impact on State parties' domestic law and practice, which in turn influence the decisions of the European Court of Human Rights, and the relationship between right of access to court and state immunity may change and develop in the future. Of course, as to the relationship between jus cogens and state immunity, the European Court of Human Rights tends to recognize that the granting of state immunity by State parties' domestic courts to foreign states does not violate the principle of proportionality or Article 6(1) of the European Convention on Human Rights.

He argues that using the extraterritorial civil judgments as evidence does not harm the sovereignty of China, nor does it bring injustice to the parties. On the contrary, it contributes to increasing judicial efficiency, saving judicial resources and reducing unnecessary conflicts of judgments. The parties who have applied to use extraterritorial civil judgments as evidence should prove the authenticity and validity of the judgments, and the other party may also put forward other facts and evidences to refute the facts established by the judgments. Chinese courts should not regard the facts established by extraterritorial civil judgments as proof of facts without evidence, but just a kind of evidence, and should make the judgment for the case in question based on the whole facts and forum's law.

He has published an article on international commercial arbitration, in which he argues that an award made by an overseas arbitration institution which administers the arbitration in the Mainland of China is not a "non-domestic award". The problems of how to support and supervise such arbitration and by what criteria to determine the recognition and enforcement of the award are still to be solved. The fact that parties from the Mainland of China are increasingly participating in overseas arbitration, coupled with the need to develop the foreign-related legal service industry and to promote the international and public credibility of China's arbitration, necessitates the permission of overseas arbitration institutions to administer arbitration in the Mainland of China. It is thus imperative that the "Arbitration Law of the People's Republic of China" be revised to stipulate that the nationality of the arbitration award is to be determined by the seat of arbitration, and to treat any arbitration seated in the Mainland of China equally, be it under the administration of overseas arbitration institutions or arbitration commissions established under the Arbitration Law of the People's Republic of China.

C Main Publications

1. *A Study of the Alien Tort Claims Act of U. S. A.*, Wuhan University Press, 2010.

2. *The New Role of Comity in Private Procedural International Law*, transla-

ted work, China Social Sciences Press, 2011.

3. "On the State Immunity of Chinese State-Owned Enterprises in the Civil Procedures of the United States Courts", *Jiangxi Social Sciences*, 11 (2018).

4. "On Using Extraterritorial Civil Judgments as Evidence in Civil Procedure in China", *Chinese Review of International Law*, 3 (2017).

5. "Legal Issues Arising out of Arbitration Seated in the Mainland of China but Administered by Overseas Arbitration Institutions", *Global Law Review*, 3 (2016).

6. "Jurisdiction Issues in Confirming Foreign Arbitral Awards in the Federal Courts of the United States: Study of Two Cases Involving the Chinese Government", *Chinese Review of International Law*, 3 (2015).

7. "Immunity from Execution of State Property of People's Republic of China in the United States—Taking Walters v. Industrial and Commercial Bank of China, Ltd., et al. as an Example", *Wuhan University Journal (Philosophy & Social Sciences)*, 3 (2013).

8. "State Immunity and Violation of Human Rights", *Global Law Review*, 6 (2012).

9. "On the Jurisdiction over the Cases under the *Alien Tort Statute* of U. S. A.", *American Studies Quarterly*, 1 (2012).

10. "Chinese Judicial Practice in Private International Law: 2006" (co-author), *Chinese Journal of International Law*, 3 (2009).

11. "On the Qualification Standard in the Private International Law", *Cross-Strait Law Review*, 20 (2008).

12. "A Chinese Student's Perspective of Clinic-Why Clinic?", *Horitsu Jiho*, 3 (2007).

13. "A Review of Judicial Practice of Chinese Courts in 2005" (co-author), *Chinese Yearbook of Private International Law and Comparative Law*, 9 (2006).

14. "Private International Law Towards Maturation", *International Law Review of Wuhan University*, 4 (2006).

15. "An Introduction to the Due Process of Arbitration Procedure", *Commercial Arbitration*, 1 (2006).

16. "A Review of Judicial Practice of Chinese Courts in 2004" (co-author), *Chinese Yearbook of Private International Law and Comparative Law*, 8 (2005).

Fu Panfeng

A Basic Information

Dr. Fu Panfeng was born in Miluo, Hunan Province in 1987. He is currently an assistant research fellow at the Department of Private International Law of the Institute of International Law of Chinese Academy of Social Sciences. He specializes in private international law, arbitration law and comparative law with a particular academic focus on international dispute resolution, international commercial arbitration, investor-state arbitration and international sports arbitration. He is a member of China Society of Private International Law and China Academy of Arbitration Law.

Dr. Fu graduated from the Southwest University of Political Sciences and Law in 2009 with a bachelor's degree of law. He went to the Law School of Wuhan University to pursue his graduate studies and earned a master's degree of law in 2011 and a doctor's degree of law in 2015. Besides, while doing his doctoral research at Wuhan University, he had the opportunity to be funded by China Scholarship Council to study at University of Montreal as a visiting scholar for a year. After graduating from Wuhan University, he joined the Institute of Law of Chinese Academy of Social Sciences as a post-doctoral researcher. He became a full-time researcher at the Institute of International Law of Chinese Academy of Social Sciences in 2017. He used to be an editor of the *Wuhan University International Law Review* and the *Chinese Yearbook of Private International Law and Comparative Law*. He has published over 20 papers in such Chinese law journals as Modern Law Science and Journal of Comparative Law. He has been in charge of two prominent research projects: a first-class research project funded by China Postdoctoral Science Foundation and a key research project sponsored by Beijing Arbitration Commission.

B Major Awards

1. The Prize for Excellent Postdoctoral Research Report awarded Chinese Academy of Social Sciences.

2. The Second-Prize for Excellent Academic Achievement awarded by China Society of Private International Law in 2016.

3. The Second-Prize for Excellent Academic Achievement awarded by China Society of Private International Law in 2018.

C Research Projects

1. A first-class research project funded by China Postdoctoral Science Foundation.

2. A key research project sponsored by Beijing Arbitration Commission (2016).

3. An ordinary research project sponsored by Beijing Arbitration Commission (2014).

D Academic Viewpoints

Most of Dr. Fu's academic contributions are related to international arbitration. Over the past several years, he has conducted in-depth research on such issues as the moral dilemma of the unilateral appointment of arbitrators, the enforcement of annulled arbitral awards and the application of res judicata doctrine in investor-state arbitration. He has also done a comprehensive research on French arbitration law. His main academic viewpoints are summed up as follows.

1. The Solutions to the Moral Dilemma of the Unilateral Appointment of Arbitrators

To address the ethical dilemma facing unilateral appointment of arbitrators, Paulsson proposed to abolish the unilateral appointment and to appoint arbitrators by a neutral institution, which caused drastic reaction from the international arbitration community. On the one hand, unilateral appointment brings parties closer to the arbitral proceedings, thus reinforcing party's trust in arbitration and its legitimacy as a dispute resolution mechanism outside national court system. On the other hand, unilateral appointment causes serious ethical problems such as arbitrator's inclination to act as a party's counsel, which hinders normal delivery of justice and damages arbitration's positive image. In an era in which arbitration is more and more diversified, any one-size-fits-all solution could backfire. For unilateral appointment to break out the dilemma, commercial and investor-state arbitration should be treated separately. For investor-state arbitration, it is feasible to abolish unilateral appointment, with the problem being how to find a neutral appointing institution. For commercial arbitration, it is not feasible to abolish unilateral appointment, but necessary measures should be taken to avoid or reduce the negative effects caused by unilateral appointment. Meanwhile, the practice of sole arbitrator should be advocated. It also bears noting that special mechanism should be brought in when the gap of the actual status between the two parties is huge, so as to ensure the impartiality of the arbitral tribunal.

2. Res Judicata as Applied in International Investment Arbitration: From a Formalistic Approach to a Substantive Approach

Investor-state arbitration has been suffering from severecriticism for frequent inconsistencies between arbitral awards. The Doctrine of Res Judicata, however, can serve as an effective means to ensure consistency between a former arbitral award and a latter one under specific circumstances. With respect to its application, the traditional triple identity test is widely recognized by both the common law and the civil law systems. But if arbitral tribunals interpret this test mechanically, the Doctrine of Res Judicata risks never having the chance to be applied, thus is unable to avoid double adjudication on the same issue or claim in closely related arbitrations. Through a substantive analysis of the parties, the cause of action and the claim and through the softening of the requirement for identity of each element, unreasonable inference in the arbitral tribunal's adjudicating process could be avoided and a balance could be achieved between the consideration for due process and the application of the Doctrine of Res Judicata.

3. Putting the Enforcement of Annulled Arbitral Awards in Perspective

The past 30 years of international commercial arbitration practice has witnessed frequent recognition and enforcement of arbitral awards annulled at the seat of arbitration. The French courts' approach as seen in the cases of Hilmarton and Putrabali, is most representative. This has continuously caused heated debates in the international arbitration community. The focus of the debates is whether the discretion exists for courts to recognize and enforce arbitral awards annulled at the seat. Opposite conclusions can be drawn depending on how the legislative purpose of the New York Convention is to be interpreted and how the present status and future trend of modern international arbitration is to be identified. It is suggested, however, that a positive realistic approach be taken. That is, the answer is yes, but the discretion should be exercised prudently. Chinese courts have not yet been faced with such cases until now. China has made it clear upon ratifying the New York Convention that Chinese courts shall dismiss the application for recognition and enforcement of an award when the party against whom it is invoked furnishes proof that the award has been set aside at the seat. In the future, it is necessary for China to fine-tune its position to the effect that Chinese courts shall only refuse to recognize and enforce arbitral awards that have been set aside at the seat for the internationally accepted grounds contained in the UNCITRAL Model Law. Otherwise, Chinese courts will reserve the right to utilize such discretion as to recognize and enforce awards annulled at the seat.

4. China is Advised to Learn from France and Establish a Dualistic Legislation Model on Commercial Arbitration When Revising the 1994 Arbitration Law

France is a typical country that takes a dualistic approach to legislation on commercial arbitration. The 2011 French Arbitration Law is divided into two parts: domestic arbitration and international arbitration. The dualistic model stems from the fact that French legislators wanted to provide different legal frameworks for domestic arbitration and international arbitration with regard to such aspects as the arbitration agreement, the number of arbitrators for an arbitral tribunal, the confidentiality requirement, the arbitral opinions, and the setting aside and the enforcement of arbitral awards. Under this model, the characterization of the "internationality" of arbitration is a very important practical issue. To deal with this issue, France takes an objective test based on economic considerations. This test is rather tolerant in that it confers on courts the discretion to decide, in light of specific circumstances, whether or not a given arbitration is an international arbitration. When China amends its arbitration law in the future, it should learn from France and establish a clearly dualistic legislation model on commercial arbitration. With regard to the characterization of "internationality", French judicial practice is also of reference value to some extent.

E Main Publications

1. *A Study of the French International Arbitration Legal System*, China of Social Sciences Press, 2018.

2. "Ethical Dilemma Facing Unilateral Appointment of Arbitrators and the Way to Break through It—A Discussion Centering around Paulsson's Proposal", *Contemporary Law Review*, 3(2017).

3. "The Unending Debate: Recognition and Enforcement of Annulled International Commercial Arbitral Awards", *Modern Law Review*, 1(2017).

4. "The Test for Application of the Doctrine of Res Judicata in Investor-State Arbitration—From a Formalistic Approach to a Substantive Approach", *Journal of Comparative Law*, 4(2016).

5. "The Emergency Arbitrator in ICC Arbitration Rules", *Beijing Arbitration Quarterly*, 91 (2015).

6. "On Multi-Party Arbitration: Its Institutional Construction and Practical Difficulties", *Beijing Arbitration Quarterly*, 87 (2014).

7. "Judicial Experience in Handling Res Judicata Issues Arising from International Commercial Arbitration Awards in Common Law Countries: Taking Associated Electric v. European Re as an Example", *Arbitration Study*, 20 (2012).

8. "The Application Dilemma of the Doctrine of Most Significant Relationship and the Solution: An Examination Based on the Judicial Practice in Foreign-related Civil and Commercial Matters in China", *Chinese Yearbook of Private International Law and Comparative Law*, 15 (2012).

9. *Annual Review on Commercial Arbitration in China* (2016), Wolters Kluwer, 2016 (co-authored with Song Lianbin and Helena Chen).

10. "Chinese Courts' Approach to Non-signatory Issues in Arbitration: A Case Study", *Arbitration Study*, 43 (2017).

Selected Translation Works

1. "Should the Setting Aside of Arbitral Awards Be Abolished", *Beijing Arbitration Quarterly*, 103 (2018).

2. "Past, Present and Future Perspectives of Arbitration", *Beijing Arbitration Quarterly*, 96 (2016).

3. "Recognition and Enforcement of Foreign Awards under the New York Convention in Australia and New Zealand", *Commercial Arbitration*, 13 (2016).

4. "The Conducting of International Commercial Arbitration Proceedings", *Arbitration Study*, 38 (2015).

5. "Party Autonomy and Case Management: Experiences and Suggestions of an Arbitrator", *Arbitration Study*, 36 (2014).

6. "Commercial and Investment Arbitration: How Different Are They Today", *Arbitration Study*, 36 (2014).

7. "Arbitrability, Due Process, and Public Policy under Article V of the New York Convention-Belgian and French Perspectives", *Arbitration Study*, 35 (2014).

8. "International Arbitration in a Global Economy: The Challenges of the Future", *Arbitration Study*, 32(2013).

9. "The ILA Report on Lis Pendens and Res Judicata in Arbitration", *Beijing Arbitration Quarterly*, 76(2011).

Introduction to the Department of International Economic Law

Ⅰ Overview

The Department of International Economic Law is a professional entity engaged in International Economic Law research at the Institute of International Law of the Chinese Academy of Social Sciences (CASS). The mission of the Department is to conduct in-depth research in the development of international economic order and international rule-based system.

The Department was established in 2007. As of April 2019, it has 8 full-time researchers, who provide high quality publications and policy recommendations on a full range of international economic law issues, particularly those relating to international trade law, world trade organization law, arbitration law, international commercial law, international investment law, international financial law, international competition law, maritime law, and international environmental law.

In recent years, researchers of the Department have published more than 10 monographs on international economic law, as well as numerous academic articles on Chinese influential journals and SSCI journals, such as *Chinese Journal of Law*, *Global Law Review*, and *Journal of World Trade.* Additionally, they have undertaken dozens of national research projects since 2007 and submitted a large number of advisory opinions to the Chinese central governments, which have been highly valued by Chinese authorities and the public.

Ⅱ A Brief History

In 1958, the Institute of Law was established under the Department of Philosophy and Social Sciences of the Chinese Academy of Sciences. In 1959, the Fourth Research Group, namely the International Law Research Group, was established under the Institute of Law.

In May 1977, the Chinese Academy of Social Sciences was established on the basis of the former Department of Philosophy and Social Sciences of the Chinese Academy of Sciences. The Institute of Law became a research institute of the Chinese Academy of Social Sciences. Since then, several international economic law scholars, including Xu Hegao, Wei jiaju, Yao Zhuang and Ren Jisheng, have been transferred to the Institute of Law.

In 1978, the International Law Research Group was reorganized into the Department of International Law, consisting of three international law branches: public international law, private international law and international economic law. Xu Hegao was the director of Department of International Law from 1978 to 1984. Later, Sheng Yu, Zhao Weitian, Li Zerui and Tao Zhenghua joined the Department.

From 1994 to 2007, Tao Zhenghua was the head of the Department. During this period, Zhang Ruosi, Zhang Wenguang, Huang Jin, Li Hui, Liu Jingdong, Liao fan, Mao Xiaofei, Zhong Ruihua joined the Department, which began to be equipped with a full staff engaged in international economic law research.

In 2007, the Institute of International Law was established under the Chinese Academy of Social Sciences, and all personnel of the Department of International Law of the Institute of Law joined the Institute of International Law. The institute of International Law is divided into the Department of Public International Law, the Department of Private International Law and the Department of International Economic Law.

From 2007 to 2014, Huang Dongli was the head of the Department of International Economic Law, and Liu Jingdong, Zhang Wenguang had successively become the deputy head of the Department. During this period, He Jingjing joined the department.

Since 2014, Liu Jingdong has been the head of the Department of International Economic Law, and Huang Jin became the deputy head of the Department. During this period, Sun Nanxiang and Ren Hongda joined the Department. Tian Fu became one of the members of the CASS Innovation Project of International Economic Law under the guidance by Liu Jingdong.

As of April 2019, the Department has eight full-time researchers: Research Fellow Liu Jingdong, Research Fellow Liao Fan, Associate Research Fellow Huang Jin, Associate Research Fellow Zhang Wenguang, Associate Research Fellow He Jingjing, Assistant Research Fellow Mao Xiaofei, Assistant Research Fellow Sun Nanxiang, and Assistant Research Fellow Ren Hongda.

Ⅲ Major Academic Achievements

Over the past 60 years, researchers at the Chinese Academy of Social Sciences have conducted in-depth research in International Economic Law. Their rich research results have laid the foundation for the academic prestige of the Department of International Economic Law domestically and globally. For the purpose of demonstrating the academic achievements of the Department, several excerpts of influential articles on international economic law published by the researchers of the Department are shown below.

In 1984, Professor Xu Hegao published an insightful article entitled "Legal Issues in Foreign-related Economic Work", in which he stated that, "the most fundamental thing when solving the foreign-related economic disputes is to consciously adhere to three principles, that is, independence, equality and mutual benefit, and to follow international customs and practices". Furthermore, he said that, "disputes between Chinese and foreign parties in economic domain can generally be resolved through friendly consultations and mediation. With an arbitration agreement, either party may also submit the dispute to arbitration for settlement. If there is no arbitration agreement, the dispute can be settled by domestic courts through judicial proceedings. In recent years, the number of foreign-related economic disputes resolved by the courts has increased significantly over the past. Therefore, the jurisdiction over such disputes is a matter worthy of attention in China".

In 1985, Professor Tao Zhenghua pointed out that China should strengthen the international law research during the period of Reform and Opening-up. In the article entitled "Opening-up Policy Demands the Research in International Law", he said, "the implementation of the opening-up policy and the expansion of economic cooperation globally raised numerous new issues for international law academia. Therefore, as China's international law scholars, we should pay more attention to the following topics: the fundamental principles of international economic relations; the economic rights and obligations of states; the establishment of a new international economic order; and the legal characteristics of international economic activities".

In 2002, a Chinese pioneer in WTO law research, Professor Zhao Weitian published a famous article entitled "New Development of the Rule of Non-discrimination of WTO", in which he elaborated that, "[i]n the multilateral trading system, the rule of non-discrimination includes such aspects as the most-favored nation status and the national treatment. Both of them belong to the relations of rights and obligations established by agreement. The related provisions in the 'Protocol for China's Entry into the WTO' have gone beyond the structure and content of most-favored nation status and the national treatment or non-discrimination of the WTO, and achieved some new developments. Meanwhile, there are some shades of meaning between the provisions of the Protocol and those in the WTO. The new developments brought about by the Protocol fully embody the trends of our times, which have some deeper origins".

In 2005, Professor Huang Dongli pointed out in her article "Legal Interpretation of Paragraph 242 of the Report of the Working Party on the Accession of China Under the World Trade Organization Legal Framework" that, "[w]ith respect to the procedural rules in Paragraph 242, investigation rules in Article 3 of the Agreement on Safeguards of the WTO are applied to domestic legislations or regulations under Paragraph 242. Also, a WTO member cannot authorize its competent authority to impose quantitative restriction measures on imports covered in a request for consultations immediately upon making the request". Additionally, she added that "Given the significant position of China in the textile and clothing trade, proper interpretation and application of Paragraph 242 in accordance with the treaty interpretation rules of public international law and the WTO practice on treaty interpretation will bring certainty to the textiles and clothing trade. China's textiles and clothing exports not only benefit China, but also contribute to the world economy and development. Accordingly, it is important to establish clearer rules on the application of Paragraph 242".

In 2011, Professor Liao Fan published the article "Regulation of Financial Conglomerates in China: From De Facto to De Jure", which he stated that, "[f]inancial operations and the regulation thereof have undergone drastic changes in China in the past few decades. Among these changes, the emergence and development of various financial conglomerates are quite noteworthy. At present, such financial conglomerates mainly exist in a *de facto* sense, due to the lack of corresponding specific laws and regulations. The regulatory structure is also immature in this respect. In particular, no meaningful coordination mechanism exists among different sectorial regulatory authorities, and the division of supervisory responsibilities in relation to financial conglomerates remains to be clarified". Therefore, he suggested that, "an effective coordination mechanism based on separated, functional regulation, with the central bank as the leading coordinator, is a more realistic and potentially better choice for China".

In 2014, Professor Liu Jingdong published an influential article entitled "Accession Protocols: Legal Status in the WTO Legal System", in which he insisted that "[a]ccession protocols are unique legal instruments in the World Trade Organization (WTO) legal system. With the increasing numbers of new members joining the WTO, the number of accession protocols is also on the rise. However, due to the ambiguous legal status of the accession protocols in the WTO legal system, disputes relating to the understanding and application of the provisions in accession protocols occur frequently". He explained that, "[b]ecause accession protocols concern the fundamental trade interests of new members, their status in the WTO legal system is of great importance. The WTO Ministerial Conference and General Council should therefore fulfil their statutory duties in such a way as to mitigate potential challenges posed by the possible legal uncertainty of accession protocols in pursuing the aims of the multilateral trading system, in adhering to and promoting WTO principles and rules as well as the basic principles of international law and in particular situating accession protocols appropriately within the overall WTO legal framework".

Ⅳ Curriculum Vitae of Personnel

Liu Jingdong

A Basic Information

Liu Jingdong, Ph. D. in Law, Head of International Economic Law Department of CASS Institute of International Law; Professor of International Law; Vice-Chief Justice of No. 4 Civil Division of the Supreme People's Court of China (April, 2015 – December, 2017); Vice President of WTO Law Research Society under China Law Society and a standing member of Council of China's Arbitration Law Society. He is a special consultant of the Supreme People's Court of China, a member of first-International Commercial Expert Committee of China International Commerce Court (CICC), and an arbitrator at China International Economic and Trade Arbitration Commission.

B Educational Experiences

1986 – 1990: Law Faculty, China University of Political Sciences and Law,

Bachelor of Law.

1990 – 1993: Graduate School, Chinese University of Political Sciences and Law, majoring in International law; LL. M.

1998 – 2001: Graduate School, Chinese University of Political Sciences and Law, majoring in International economic law; LL. D.

2003 – 2005: Post-Doctoral Researcher, Law Institute of Chinese Academy of Social Sciences.

2008 – 2009: Visiting Scholar, Columbia Law School, U. S..

2010: Visiting Scholar, Zurich University, Switzerland.

C Academic Achievements

Professor Liu has been engaged in the research on international law, international economic law and international commercial law for a long time and published many books, such as *Legal Issues of International Financial Leasing*, *The Interpretation of Articles of the Protocol of China's Accession to WTO* and so on. He has also published many articles in *Chinese Journal of Law*, *Chinese Review of International Law*, *Journal of World Trade*, etc.. He has won the Prize for Excellent Research Paper by China Society of International Law in 2012, the Second and the First Prizes for Outstanding Research Paper by WTO Law Research Society of China Law Society in 2014 and 2015. In ICCA Convention of 2016, Professor Liu gave a speech on the Mauritius Convention as the head of the delegation of the Supreme People's Court of China.

D Introductions to Major Academic Works

1. Bringing the New Mode of Global Economic Governance under the Rule of Law

There are many indications that global economic governance is faced with increasingly urgent tasks, and the traditional model of governance and the process of the rule of law are being challenged by the historical changes of the balance of world economic powers. In order to promote the process of global economic governance and the rule of law, the principle of equality and mutual respect, the common interest principle, and the principle of promoting cooperation and broad consensus should be established as new legal principles. The principle of quality and mutual respect is the basis of the legitimacy of the global economic governance, which requires all members of the international community to enjoy equal participation in international exchanges and decision-making and mutual respect for their respective positions. The common interest principle is the core objective of the global economic governance, which requires realizing the interest of all countries through global economic governance, rather than the self-interest a country of group of countries, nor the self-interest of the developed countries. The principle of promoting cooperation and broad consensus is the guiding principle of global economic governance. Economic globalization needs the cooperation among countries and a broad consensus is the only way to solve the various problems and challenges faced by globalization. Global economic governance needs not only to reform the existing model and built a new one, but also to seek the new path of the rule of law. An "International Economic Charter" should be formulated to meet the new requirements of international economy, a new International Economic Organization with the highest authority should be established to integrate the existing international economic organizations, and a complete set of Economic Dispute Settlement Mechanism should be built on the basis of the dispute settlement mechanism of WTO to further enhance the stability and predictability of the international economic relations and governance.

2. Research on the Construction of the Rule of Law System of the "Belt and Road"

At present, the "Belt and Road" initiative has become the major impetus for global economic development, and its system and developing mode are the focus of the world attention and viewed as an important part of global economy governance. Historical experiences and lessons tell us that the "Belt and Road" construction cannot deviate from the rule of law, and the long-term, steady and healthy development of the "Belt and Road" initiative can be guaranteed only if the road of rule of law has been chosen. The construction of rule of law system of the "Belt and Road" should follow the basic principles of equality and mutual benefit, rule-oriented and sustainable development, and focus on the two areas of international law and domestic law: on the one hand, it should innovate present international economic and trade law system on the basis of integrating modern international law and the new development of international economic law with the characteristics of the "Belt and Road"; on the other hand, it should constantly improve and perfect China's foreign economic and trade law system and the foreign-related civil and commercial law system on the basis of learning from advanced legal experiences of other countries. Fair and efficient dispute settlement system is vital for the rule of law. China should build a multi-level, integral economic trade dispute settlement mechanism by combining the international and domestic systems, abiding by the principles of settling disputes through equal consultation and negotiation, utilizing modern international law and generally-accepted international commercial rules, and pushing the judicial corporation among the countries joining in the "Belt and Road", so as to create a steady and predictable legal environment for the "Belt and Road" and set an example for global economic governance in the new century.

3. Legal Status of Accession Protocols in the WTO Legal System

Accession protocols are unique legal instruments in the WTO legal system. With the increasing number of new members joining the WTO, the number of accession protocols is also on the rise. However, due to the ambiguous legal status of the accession protocols in the WTO legal system, disputes over the understanding and application of the provisions in accession protocols are frequently taking place. Because accession protocols concern the fundamental trade interests of new members, their status in the WTO legal system is of great importance. The WTO Ministerial Conference and General Council should therefore fulfil their statutory duties in such a way as to mitigate potential challenges posed by the possible legal uncertainty of accession protocols in pursuing the aims of the multilateral trading system, in adhering to and promoting WTO principles and rules as well as the basic principles of international law, and in situating accession protocols appropriately within the overall WTO legal framework. Specifically, this article proposes that the WTO Ministerial Conference and General Council should properly address the relationship between accession protocols and the Marrakesh Agreement Establishing the World Trade Organization and its annexes. Such action will help safeguard the legal rights and interests of new WTO members.

4. Thoughts on the Reform of WTO

Faced with the historical changes of international relations and current international financial crisis, the WTO should reform its system to adapt to the new situation, so as to promote international trade development and prosperity in the new century. Although there are many different ideas and schemes about the reform, the international community has reached a broad consensus on the WTO reform: the WTO system is not adapted to the characteristics of new international relations, its institutional defects have already seriously impeded the WTO from performing its function as a multilateral trade system. However, there still are differences between developed and developing members and among scholars over the guiding ideology of the reform. In light of the current situation and feasibility and on the basis of extensive solicitation of opinions, the WTO should carry out the necessary reforms on the three basic systems, namely the functions and powers of the director general and the Secretariat, transparency, and the decision-making mechanism, as soon as possible.

Liao Fan

A Basic Information

Liao Fan is a senior research fellow and professor at CASS Institute of International Law, and the head of the Department for Research Coordination and International Cooperation of the Institute. He is the lead research fellow of the CASS innovation project "International Economic Law Issues in the BRI Implementation" and council director of Chinese Society of International Economic Law. Before taking the present post, he was a visiting scholar at Columbia University. He is an arbitrator at China International Economic and Trade Arbitration Commission (CIETAC) and Shenzhen Court of International Arbitration(SCIA), and a specialist mediator at Singapore International Mediation Center(SIMC).

Professor Liao Fan has led or participated in numerous research projects sponsored by the World Bank, National Development and Reform Commission, Ministry of Foreign Affairs, Ministry of Commerce, People's Bank of China, China Banking and Insurance Regulatory Commission, China Securities Regulatory Commission, China Law Society and CASS. He holds a B. A. in Law from China Youth University of Political Studies, an LL. M. from Southern Methodist University in the US, and a Ph. D. in Law from Peking University. His major fields of research include fundamental theory of international law, international economic law and banking and financial law. He has published three monographs and one co-authored book, as well as numerous articles, essays and comments on leading law journals and newspapers, such as *Chinese Journal of Law*, *China Legal Science*, *People's Daily* and *European Business Organization Law Review*.

Professor Liao Fan is one of the leading scholars at CASS Institute of International Law as well a leading scholar in the field of international economic law and in particular international financial law. He is among the most-cited Chinese international law scholars of his age. He frequently participates in the decision-making consultations and expert meetings of the relevant ministries and judicial organs. He has written a wide range of internal reports, several of which received official comments from the Party and State leaders. In virtue of his legal expertise and English language skill, he is very active in the English language media, participating for example in scores of live interviews on the China Global Television Network

(CGTN,formerly the CCTV's English Channel).

B Educational and Work Experiences

Since 2013:Research Fellow and Head of the Department of Research Coordination and International Cooperation,CASS Institute of International Law.

2007 –2013:Associate Research Fellow and Deputy Head of the Department of Research Coordination and International Cooperation,CASS Institute of International Law.

2006 –2007:Visiting Scholar at Columbia University.

2005 –2007:Assistant Research Fellow at the CASS Institute of International Law.

2005:Ph. D. in Law,Peking University.

2002:LL. M. ,Southern Methodist University,USA.

1999:B. A. in Law,China Youth University of Political Studies.

C Academic and Professional Affiliations

Council Director,Chinese Society of International Economic Law.

Council Director,Chinese Society of International Economic and Trade Law.

Deputy Head,Committee of International Financial Law,China Society of International Economic and Trade Law.

Standing Council Director,Beijing Society of Financial Services Law.

Standing Council Director,Beijing Society of Internet Finance Law.

Arbitrator,China International Economic and Trade Arbitration Commission.

Arbitrator,Shenzhen Court of International Arbitration/Shenzhen Arbitration Commission.

Specialist Mediator,Singapore International Mediation Center.

Member of the Expert Group for the Adjudication of Foreign-related Commercial and Maritime Cases,the Supreme People's Court.

D Representative Academic Viewpoints

1. On the global agenda and China's position as to the reform of the WTO(2019)

The WTO is facing an unprecedented crisis and it has become a consensus that the organization must be reformed. However, the involved parties are divided over the basic principles, contents and priorities of the reform. Proposals that have been submitted so far generally support increasing the flexibility of the organization's negotiation mechanism, thus breaking the multilateral negotiation deadlocks caused by the consensus requirement, and support making new trade rules, enhancing fair trade and eliminating investment barriers; they also support improving the review and surveillance functions of the WTO to ensure better compliance of the transparency and notification obligations by its members; in terms of dispute resolution, they support timely revision of relevant protocols and breaking the deadlock in the designation of appellate body members to ensure the normal functioning of the organization. For China, the key is to clearly understand its basic position and core concerns and present more specific reform proposals on the basis of the current Position Paper, so as to more actively participate in and push forward the reform process.

2. On the status quo and problems of the cross-border financial regulatory cooperation and possible solutions thereto(2018)

There are two ways of cross-border financial regulation cooperation: the bilateral one and the multilateral one. The former, represented by the US Cross-border securities regulatory cooperation, is carried out by means of memorandum of understanding, regulatory dialogue, technological aids and so on. The latter, according to participants and cooperation modes, may be further classified into the international organization mode, the informal country bloc mode and the inter-governmental network mode. The main problems and obstacles of the cross-border financial regulation include as follows: the international financial regulatory rules led by soft laws lack "hard effect"; the international financial regulatory standards implementation and supervision mechanisms are seriously insufficient, and the crisis-driven regulation cooperation lacks persistence and stability. The long-term aim of improving cross-border financial regulation is to establish a global financial regulatory (cooperation) organization on basis of a multiple agreement and capable of formulating, implementing and supervising the enforcement of binding international rules. The current solution is to take full advantage of the existing international organizations and mechanisms and systematically consolidate the effect of rules of relevant soft laws, thus strengthening their force, enforcement and implementation effect.

3. On the interpretation and construction of a Community with Shared Future for Mankind against the background of global governance (2018)

A Community with Shared Future for Mankind is a new global governance program that China contributes to the international community in the new era. In the origin of thought, a Community with Shared Future for Mankind is rooted in the idea of cosmopolitanism with the unanimous pursuit of universal harmony in the world and the Chinese traditional culture, and the Marxist community with the ultimate goal of building a "union of free men". In the concept inheritance, the community of a shared future is in line with the Five Principles of Peaceful Coexistence, the establishment of a new international order, the third-generation human rights, the principle of common inheritance of human property and other theories, principles and propositions. The concept of a Community with Shared Future for Mankind provides a new possibility for the combination of the interests and value, realism and idealism in international relations and international order, which can be understood and interpreted from the three dimensions of interest community, value community and responsibility community. A Community with Shared Future for Mankind should be promoted and constructed from the two levels of deepening the opening-up to the outside world and providing the "Chinese Solution", and adhering to the common discussion and construction and forming the "Common Solution".

4. On the reflection of and outlook for Chinese international economic law research (2018)

The "prosperity" of contemporary Chinese international economic law research is, to a great extent, superficial or even false, which reflects an overall anxiety for quick success and lack of taste and calmness. Major problems and shortcomings in such research include the weakness in the study of basic theories; the lack of issue awareness, approach consciousness, academic focus, clear orientation, proper balance, independent character and distinctive personality; and the lack of a reasonable and scientific academic environment and evaluation mechanism. In future, efforts should be made to further strengthen the study of basic theories and construct international economic theories with Chinese characteristics; to raise the overall taste and level of the research for it to go from "prosperity" to standardization; and to improve the academic environment and evaluation mechanism, so as to create a more researcher-friendly environment and atmosphere.

5. On the status and role of soft law in global financial governance (2016)

International financial soft law refers to the norms and rules governing international financial relations which have no legally binding force but which nevertheless may have practical effects, especially the various international financial standards formulated by international standard-setting bodies. The limited role played by the existing treaty rules, the complexity and volatility of financial regulatory practice, the sensitiveness of issues related to national sovereignty, and the lack of an effective dispute settlement mechanism in the international financial sector, all lead to the necessity of soft law in global financial governance. Soft law has a dual role in global financial governance: first, as a transfer station or interim period towards "hard law", and second and more importantly, as a set of rules having independent value and contributing to global financial governance in its own right. To a large extent, soft law plays a more substantial role in global financial governance than in hard law, and global financial governance might even be characterized as "rule of soft law".

6. On the definition and scope of "financial consumers" (2012)

It is imperative to shape the concept of "financial consumer" in China today, since there exists uncertainty when the traditional concept of consumer is applied in financial area and insufficiency of protection provided by current financial laws and regulations. A careful study of relevant legislations in the United States and United Kingdom indicates that the definition and scope of the concept of financial consumer is more of a product of practical evolution than of a result of theoretical deduction, and is inseparably linked to the model and system of financial regulation. Proceeding from actual conditions in China, a feasible approach may be adopted as follows. With regard to financial consumers, the concept may be defined in a broad way, thus enabling it to cover the whole financial service area. With regard to protection of consumers, the principle of minimum coordination should be observed, thus only providing for a general framework and leaving the drafting of detailed rules for implementation to industrial regulation departments based on their respective industrial characteristics and needs of regulation. Meanwhile, the existing concept of securities investor and the correspondent system of protection of investors should be maintained, so as to bring into coexistence and co-operation of the two concepts of financial consumer and securities investor and two systems of protection of financial consumers.

7. On the proper regulation of financial conglomerates in China (2011)

Financial operations and the regulation thereof have undergone drastic changes in China in the past few decades. Among these changes, the emergence and development of various financial conglomerates are quite noteworthy. At present, such financial conglomerates mainly exist in a de facto sense, due to the lack of corresponding specific laws and regulations. The regulatory structure is also immature in this respect. In particular, no meaningful coordination mechanism exists among different sectorial regulatory authorities, and the division of supervisory responsibilities in relation to financial conglomerates remains to be clarified. Different factors taken into account, it is submitted that a single mega-regulator is not desirable for the time being, while an effective coordination mechanism based on separated, functional regulation, with the central bank as the leading coordinator, is a more realistic and potentially better choice for China.

8. On the difficulties facing the international monetary system and the possible solutions thereto (2008)

The current international monetary system with the International Monetary Fund (IMF) at the core historically originated from the political compromise between major powers, more specifically the U. S. and U. K. This has left the system with inborn deficiencies in terms of effectiveness and enforceability. Moreover, with the evolution of the world economy, developing countries, especially those dynamic emerging markets such as the BRICs, have come to challenge the representativeness of this system dominated by wealthy developed countries. The unexpected global financial crisis further disclosed the underlying problems of the existing system.

From the viewpoint of China as a unique actor in the IMF, the author summarizes the four major problems facing today's IMF, i. e. , strayed institutional role, one-sided policy supervision, imbalanced governance structure, and paralyzed dispute resolution. Some reform measures have already been taken or on the way, but they are inadequate for a meaningful change of the status quo. The author argues that further efforts should be made in terms of reshaping the institutional role, strengthening bilateral supervision, improving governance structure and promoting dispute resolution. The dual goal of the reform should be on the one hand to readjust the functions of the IMF, in order to enhance the effectiveness of its operation, and on the other hand to rebalance its power structure, so as to promote the democratization of its governance.

Given that any reform can only be realized by means of revising the relevant legal instruments, and given that the revision of the Articles of Agreement themselves is extremely difficult, the author suggests to begin with lower instruments such as Rules and Regulations and Decisions, and also to make fuller use of the interpretation power conferred on the Board of Governors and the Executive Board by the Articles of Agreement.

E Main Publications

Monographs

1. *New Development of the Study of International Financial Law*, China Social Sciences Press, 2013.

2. *Legal Issues Regarding the Reform of the International Monetary and Financial System*, Social Sciences Academic Press, 2012.

3. *Legal Issues Regarding the Securities Customer Property Risk*, Peking University Press, 2005.

Co-authored Books

1. *The Practical Development and Institutional Innovation of the Shanghai Pilot Free Trade Zone*, China Social Sciences Press, 2017.

2. *The Changing International Law: Hotspots and Frontier*, China Social Sciences Press, 2012.

3. *Research on Contemporary Chinese International Law*, China Social Sciences Press, 2010.

4. *International Economic Law*, Social Sciences Academic Press (China), 2006.

Articles

1. "The Reform of the WTO: Global Agenda and China's Position", *International Economic Review*, 2 (2019).

2. "The American Unilateralism and Possible Responses from the Perspective of the USMCA", *Journal of Latin American Studies*, 1 (2019).

3. "Cross-border Financial Regulatory Cooperation: Status Quo, Problems and Solutions", *Political Science and Law*, 12 (2018).

4. "The Implication of Human Rights and Sovereignty in the Context of a Community with Shared Future for Mankind", *Jilin University Journal Social Sciences Edition*, 6 (2018).

5. "The Interpretation and Construction of a Community with Shared Future for Mankind against the Background of Global Governance", *China Legal Science*, 5 (2018).

6. "From 'Prosperity' to Standardization: Reflection on and Outlook for Chinese International Economic Law Research", *Tribune of Political Science and Law*, 5 (2018).

7. "China's Rule of Law in Internet Finance 2017", in *Blue Book of Rule of Law*, Social Sciences Academic Press (China), March 2018.

8. "Regulation of Government Subsidies: International Rule and China's Response", *Political Science and Law*, 12 (2017).

9. "New Development of the ISDS Mechanism", *Jiangxi Social Sciences*, 10 (2017).

10. "The 'Conditionality' of the AIIB Lending from a Comparative Law Perspective", *Law Science Magazine*, 6 (2016).

11. "The Status and Role of Soft Law in Global Financial Governance", *Journal of Xiamen University (Arts & Social Sciences)*, 2 (2016).

12. "Quenching Thirst with Poison? Local Government Financing Vehicles-Past, Present, and Future", in Benjamin L. Liebman & Curtis J. Milhaupt (ed.), *Regulating the Visible Hand: the Institutional Implications of Chinese State Capitalism*, Oxford University Press, 2016.

13. "Legal Solutions to the Prevention of the Local Governmental Debt Risk", *Social Sciences in Guangdong*, 4(2018).

14. "Theoretical Breakthrough and Mechanical Innovation: Recent Development in UK's Protection of Financial Consumers", *Social Sciences*, August 2013.

15. "Development and Trend in the Supervision of Global SIFIs", *Journal of International Economic Law*, 1(2013).

16. "The Definition and Scope of the Concept of 'Financial Consumer'", *Global Law Review*, 4(2012).

17. "Regulation of Financial Conglomerates in China: from *De facto* to *De jure*", *European Business Organization Law Review*, 2(2011).

18. "Reform of the Voting Power and Governance Structure in the IMF: Review and Comments", *Chinese Yearbook of International Law* (2010), July 2011.

19. "Evolution and Prospect of East-Asian Monetary Cooperation: A CMIM-focused Analysis", *Chinese International Law Review*, Volume 4, April 2011.

20. "International Monetary System: Difficulties and Way Out", *Chinese Journal of Law*, 4(2010).

21. "Economic Globalization and the New Trends in International Economic Law: How Should China React", *Tsinghua Law Review*, 6(2009).

22. "Competition, Conflict and Coordination of Financial Supervision", *Journal of Peking University*, 3(2008).

23. "EU's Supervision of Financial Conglomerates: from the Perspective of the Financial Directive", *Chinese International Law Review*, 2(2008).

24. "Towards a Fairer International Trade System: Rethinking of the WTO Principle of Reciprocity", *International Trade*, 6(2007).

25. "The Financial Contract Exception in the New Bankruptcy Act of the US: Introduction and Comments", *Securities Market Harold*, 5(2007).

26. "Introduction to and Comments on the Enforcement Mechanism of the

HK Securities and Futures Commission", *Global Law Review*, 3(2007).

27. "Theories and Practices of Reverse Piercing of the Corporate Veil in U. S. : A Case-based Analysis", *Peking University Law Review*, 2(2007).

28. "On the Model and Coordination Mechanism for the Regulation of the Cross-sector Financial Operation in China", *Securities Market Harold*, 11(2006).

29. "Some Comments on the Orientation, Functions and Operation of the Securities Investor Protection Fund", *Financial Law Forum*, 8(2005).

30. "Balance on the Wire: Evolution of the Disclosure Framework in U. S. Securities Regulation", *Law Science*, 4(2003).

Huang Jin

A Basic Information

Huang Jin is an associate research fellow and associate professor at CASS Institute of International Law, the deputy head of the Department for International Economic Law of the Institute and the deputy director of Center for Competition Law of the Institute. He was a visiting scholar at Waseda University of Japan, Columbia Law School in the United States and Leiden Law School in the Netherlands. He is a notable expert in the fields of international economic law, competition law, internet competition, international investment law, foreign investment and overseas investment, company law, consumer protection and international trade.

Prior to joining the Institute, he served as a law clerk at the Third Civil Division of Beijing Higher People's Court. He received a Bachelor of Economics from Dalian Maritime University and Ph. D. in Law from Graduate School of Chinese Academy of Social Sciences.

He has led or participated in numerous research projects sponsored by National Development and Reform Commission, Ministry of Commerce, Ministry of Transportation and Cyberspace Administration of China. He frequently participates in decision-making consultations and expert meetings of the relevant ministries and judicial organs. He has written a wide range of internal reports, several of which received official comments from the Party and State leaders. In virtue of his legal expertise, he is very active in the media, including CCTV and CGTN.

Huang Jin is a council director of Beijing Society of Financial Services Law and an expert member of Liaowang Institute, Xinhua News Agency.

He has published one monograph and one co-authored book, as well as numerous articles, essays and comments in law journals and newspapers such as *Chinese Review of International Law*, *Insurance Studies*, *People's Daily* and *Economic Information Daily*.

B Representative Academic Viewpoints

1. Identification of Foreign Investors in China's National Security Review System: with a Comment on the Draft Foreign Investment Law (2016)

In this article, he points out that the complexities of national security review demand Chinese investment regulatory authorities to establish a more complete and effective regulatory system; and it is of great importance to identify foreign investors within the framework of this regulatory system, not only because it can be helpful to clarify the notification obligation for foreign investors but also accelerate the review process of foreign investment security by national security review authority; the draft foreign investment law establishes for the first time the identification system for foreign investors; compared with the identification systems for foreign investors in German, Japanese and U. S. investment laws and regulations, the draft foreign investment law still needs to be developed and improved.

2. Merger Control Law: From the Perspective of US and EU(2013)

In this book, he points out that the important role of merger control system in protecting market competition and consumer interests is generally accepted by market economy countries. Nowadays more than 100 countries have passed antimonopoly laws. Among them, more than 60 countries have introduced merger control system into their antimonopoly laws. There is a consensus among these countries that mergers may lead to reduced output, higher prices and impaired consumer welfare. Taking the merger control system as the research object, the book focuses on the legal issues involved, chooses the jurisdictions of the United States and the European Union which are most concerned by the Chinese academic circles, and, in light of the relevant opinions of the International Competition Network Working Group, carries out comparative analysis on the legal issues of the merger control system, such as procedures, substantive norms, jurisdiction and international cooperation, and at the same time discusses ways of improving Chinese merger control system.

C Main Publications

Monograph

Mergers Control Law from the Perspective of US and EU, China Social Sciences Press, 2013.

Co-authored Books

1. *The Practical Development and Institutional Innovation of the Shanghai Pilot Free Trade Zone*, China Social Sciences Press, 2017.

2. *The Changing International Law: Hotspots and Frontier*, China Social Sciences Press, 2012.

3. *Research on Contemporary Chinese International Law*, China Social Sciences Press, 2010.

4. *International Law*, Social Sciences Academic Press (China), 2005.

Articles

1. "Legislative Suggestions on Regulating Multinational Corporations, Mergers and Acquisitions of Chinese Enterprises", *China Reform*, 4 (2004).

2. "Mergers and Acquisitions of Multinational Corporations and Antimonopoly System", *Journal of the Chinese Academy of Social Sciences*, 7 (2005).

3. "Research on Non-Competition Provisions Related to Mergers and Acquisitions Based on the Antimonopoly Legal System", in *Research on the Anti-monopoly Examination Related Legal System of Chinese Enterprises' Mergers and Acquisitions*, Beijing University Press, April 2008.

4. "Chinese Merger Control System from the perspective of Coca-Cola's Purchase of Huiyuan Juice Case", *Journal of the Chinese Academy of Social Sciences*, October 2008.

5. "Remedies for Merger Control in American Antitrust Law", in *International Law Studies*, Volume 2, People's Public Security University Press, November 2008.

6. "The Challenge Faced by China's Insurance Industry Association after the Adoption of China's Antimonopoly Law—Based on Chongqing Insurance Association Case", *Insurance Studies*, 12 (2008).

7. "Foreign Anti-dumping Faced by Chinese Enterprises", in *Blue Book of Rule of Law*, Social Sciences Academic Press (China), March 2011.

8. "Antitrust Enforcement in China 2012", in *Blue Book of Rule of Law*, Social Sciences Academic Press (China), January 2011.

9. "Bilateral Law Enforcement Cooperation between the EU and the United States in the field of Merger Control", *Chinese Review of International Law Research*, 4 (2014).

10. "The 'Belt and Road' and the Rule of Law", *People's Rule of Law*, 11 (2015).

11. "Identification of Foreign Investors in China's National Security Review System: with a Comment on the Draft Foreign Investment Law", *Journal of Graduate School of Social Sciences*, 3 (2016).

12. "Chinese National Security Review System in the Free Trade Pilot Zone",

People's Rule of Law, 12(2016).

13. "Development and Prospect of China's Foreign Investment Access", in *Blue Book of Rule of Law*, Social Sciences Academic Press (China), March 2017.

14. "Rule of Law and Development of China's Free Trade Pilot Zones", in *Blue Book of Rule of Law*, Social Sciences Academic Press (China), December 2017.

15. "Merger Review and Belt and Road—A Case Study of the Approval of Maersk's Acquisition of Hamburg South America", *People's Rule of Law*, 2(2018).

16. "Research on Non-Competition Provisions Related to Mergers and Acquisitions—Based on the Antimonopoly Legal System", in *Research on the Anti-monopoly Examination Related Legal System of Chinese Enterprises' Mergers and Acquisitions*, Beijing University Press, April 2008.

17. "Suggestions on Investment Opening and Market Regulatory Policy in Free Trade Pilot Zones", in *Blue Book of Rule of Law*, Social Sciences Academic Press (China), June 2018.

18. "Cooperation and Development of Maritime Law between Panama and China", *China Shipping Gazette*, 36(2018).

Zhang Wenguang

A Basic Information

Zhang Wenguang is an associate research fellow and associate professor at CASS Institute of International Law. He is Director of the CASS Center for Oceans Law and Maritime Law, and Deputy Director and General Secretary of the "Belt and Road" Research Base of the Supreme People's Court of PRC. After joining Chinese Academy of Social Sciences, he conducted post-doctoral research activities in Columbia Law School of the United States and Tsinghua University, and worked as a visiting scholar in the Supreme People's Court of PRC. From 2004 to 2014, he worked as the deputy head of the Department for International Economic Law of the Institute.

He is a notable expert in the fields of maritime law, contract law, insurance law, and international economic law. He has published two monographs and three co-authored books, as well as more than 40 articles, essays and comments on law journals and newspapers.

B Introductions to Major Academic Works

Building International Maritime Judicial Center against the Background of the "Belt and Road" Initiative

The "Belt and Road" Initiative provides the shipping industry a historical opportunity for development, and demands higher service from maritime judiciary. After firmly establishing itself as the maritime judicial center of Asian-Pacific region, China now aims at building itself into an international maritime judicial center. There are three reasons for China to build itself into an international maritime judicial center: Firstly, to serve and safeguard the national strategies, including but not limited to, constructing the "Belt and Road", the maritime power, the shipping power, etc.. Secondly, creating a rule of law and internationalized business environment. Thirdly, participating in the formulation of international rules. Now, China has the economic strength of becoming international judicial center, but also faces competitions from the historical international maritime judicial center—London, and emerging international judicial center—Singapore. To be an international maritime judicial center, China has to perfect ocean-related laws and regulations, reform maritime judicial regime, promote maritime judicial credibility, expand international judicial cooperation, and support the development of maritime arbitration.

He Jingjing

A Basic Information

Dr. He Jingjing gained her Master and Ph. D. degrees from University of Bristol in 2004 and 2011. She was a visiting Ph. D. at Cambridge University from 2009 to 2010. From 2011 to 2013, she worked as a postdoc researcher at CASS Institute of Law. She was a visiting scholar at the University of Helsinki in 2013 and at University of Turin in 2015, and an Edwards Fellow at Columbia Law School from 2016 to 2017. She is currently an associate research fellow at the Department of International Economic Law, CASS Institute of International Law. Dr. He Jingjing also works as an Assistant Chief of Tribunal of Financial Street at Xicheng of the People's Court of Xicheng District of Beijing Municipality. She is the Deputy General Secretary of the "Belt and Road" Research Base of the Supreme People's Court of PRC, a member of User Council of Singapore International Arbitration Center (SIAC), an associate professor at the University of Chinese Academy of

Social Sciences and a part-time editor of *Journal of People Rule of Law*. Her research areas include international arbitration and mediation, international economic law, international environmental law and environmental law.

B Introductions to Major Academic Works

From Kyoto Protocol to Paris Agreement: the Start of a New Climate Governance Age

The successful completion of the COP 21 UN Climate Change Conference marked the start of a new climate governance age. Given the limits of Kyoto Protocol, its successor, Paris Agreement, represents historical progress and necessity. Paris Agreement and Kyoto Protocol are different in many fundamental ways, ranging from governance mechanism, legal form, key principles, compliance mechanism to market mechanism. The flexibility of Paris Agreement in terms of Intended Nationally Determined Contributions helps to attract worldwide participation and contributes to narrowing the gaps between developed and developing countries. However, the lack of a strong compliance mechanism increases the risks of treaty non-compliance. How to build a transparent compliance framework in order to realize the twin goals of flexibility and effectiveness, and how to reduce the compliance costs to enhance compliance willingness are among the key challenges to be addressed in the Post-Paris-Climate-Agreement age.

C Research Activities and Academic Achievements

1. One joint paper entitled "China's Regional Emissions" (with Y. Huang) is published by *Nature Climate Change*, Vol. 1, October 2011.

2. One joint paper entitled "The Role of Climate Finance in the Age of Green Economy" (with Y. Huang) is published by *The World Financial Review*, November – December, 2012.

3. One joint paper entitled "The Decarbonization of China's Agriculture" (with Y. Huang) is under review by *Greenhouse Gases: Science and Technology* and also included as a UNU_WIDER working paper WP2012/074, August 2012.

4. One joint paper entitled "Has the Clean Development Mechanism Assisted Sustainable Development?" (with Y. Huang and F. Tarp) is published by *Natural*

Resources Forum—A United Nations Sustainable Development Journal, Volume 38, Issue 4, Pages 248 – 260, November 2014.

5. One joint paper entitled "Is the Clean Development Mechanism Effective for Emission Reductions?" (with Y. Huang and F. Tarp) is published by *Greenhouse Gases: Science and Technology*, Volume 4, Issue 6, Pages 750 – 760, December 2014. Also included as UNU-WIDER working paper WP2012/073, August 2012.

6. One joint UNU-WIDER *Environment & Climate Change* project commissioned paper "Foreign Aid for Climate Change Related Capacity Building" (with Z. Chen) is published as UNU-WIDER working paper WP2013/046, April 2013.

7. One paper entitled "On China's Path towards Carbon Tax Legislation: A Legal Perspective" is published in *Chinese Review of International Law* (Chinese Academic Journal), Vol. 8, May 2013.

8. One paper entitled "Legal Thoughts on Establishing China's Carbon Emission Trading Law" is published by *Journal of China's Soft Sciences* (Chinese Academic Journal), September 2013.

9. One paper entitled "On the Legislation of China's Low Carbon Agriculture—A Comparative Approach" is published by *Journal of China's Soft Sciences* (Chinese Academic Journal), December 2014. This paper won the third prize in the Ninth China Law Society Forum entitled "Deepening of Legal Reform and Rule of Law", organized by China Law Society in 2014.

10. One Paper entitled "The Human Rights Dimension of Climate Change" is published by *Journal of Human Rights*, Vol. 5, 2015.

11. One paper entitled "From Kyoto Protocol to Paris Climate Change Agreement: the Start of an Era of Global Climate Governance" is published by *Chinese Review of International Law* (Chinese Academic Journal), May 2016.

12. One paper entitled "The Human Rights Dimension of Paris Agreement" is published by *Journal of Human Rights*, December 2017.

13. One paper entitled "The Dispute Resolution Mechanism for the Belt and Road Initiative" is published by *Chinese Social Sciences Paper*, December 2018.

14. One book entitled *The Role of Public Brokerage in Managing Interorganizational Network* is published by VDM Publishing House, Germany, January

2011.

15. One book entitled *On the Legislation of China's Low Carbon Development in the Framework of International Climate Change Law* is published by the China Social Sciences Press, China, December 2014.

16. Translated Books include *Research on the Laws of Contemporary China Volume* 1 1949 – 1978, *Research on the Laws of Contemporary China Volume* 2 1978 – 1992, and *Research on the Laws of Contemporary China Volume* 3 1992 – 2009, published by Paths International Ltd. & China Social Sciences Press in August 2018.

17. Book Chapter entitled "Foreign Aid for Climate Change Capacity Building" was published in Jan. 2018 in the book *Aid Effectiveness for Environmental Sustainability* by Palgrave Macmillan.

18. Presented joint paper "The Decarbonization of PRC's Agriculture" at the 2nd 2013 Asian Development Review Conference organized by the Asian Development Bank, August 2013, Manila, Philippines.

19. Joint paper "Is the Clean Development Mechanism Effective for Emission Reductions?" (with Y. Huang & F. Tarp) was presented at XXXIV Annual Meeting of the Finnish Economic Association, February 2012, Vaasa, Finland.

20. Presented a conference paper entitled "Exploring Public Brokerage Effects in the Context of Public-led Networks" at UK Social Network Conference, July 2007 (Queen Mary, University of London).

21. Attended the UNU-WIDER Conference on Climate Change and Development Policy in September 2012, Helsinki, Finland.

22. Attended the National Climate Change Legislation and Policy Seminar organized by the Law Faculty of University of Helsinki, in May 2013, Helsinki, Finland.

23. Presented a paper entitled "China's Legislation on Low Carbon Agriculture" at the 5th China Postdoc Forum of Law, Beijing, in October 2014.

24. Presented a paper entitled "Post-Kyoto International Climate Change Agreement" at the 11th International Forum of International Law, Beijing, in November 2014.

25. Attended the UNFCCC Climate Change Conference in Paris, December 2014.

Tian Fu

A Basic Information

Tian Fu, Han ethnicity, a native of Renhuai City, Guizhou Province, was born in July 1982. Currently he is an associate research fellow at CASS Institute of International Law and a supervisor of master's students at CASS Graduate School. He is specialized in jurisprudence and philosophy of law. His academic focus is on the areas of natural law and procuratorial theory.

Tian is a graduate of China University of Political Science and Law, where he earned a Bachelor of Law degree, a Master of Law degree and a Doctor of Law degree from 1999 to 2010. He did postdoctoral research at the CASS Institute of Law from 2010 to 2012. He has been working at CASS Institute of International Law since 2012. He became an associate research fellow in 2016 and a supervisor of master's students at CASS Graduate in 2017.

Tian is a council member of the Research Committee of Jurisprudence of the China Law Society.

B Major Academic Viewpoints

The jurisprudential mechanism for producing guiding knowledge should be abandoned

From the holistic view of knowledge production mechanism, Chinese textbooks of jurisprudence have failed to look beyond the framework of the textbooks in Soviet Union in which the research objects of jurisprudence and those of branch laws are different. Besides, it is believed that jurisprudence is the discipline that provides "guidance" for branch laws, hence its operation mechanism for the production of "guiding" knowledge. Such operation mechanism has two dimensions: the obverse dimension and the reverse dimension. The obverse dimension means jurisprudence that produces "guiding" knowledge for branch laws while the reverse dimension means branch laws that facilitate jurisprudence to produce "guiding" knowledge. The legal relation theory typically corresponds to the obverse dimension while the legal act theory corresponds to the reverse dimension accordingly. However, the mechanism for producing "guiding" knowledge is found to be invalid at the level of operation mechanism. Furthermore, the production mechanism should be abandoned because it is false both at the level of basic principle and at the level of theoretical foundation.

C Main Publications

Books

A Study on Finnis' Natural Law Theory, Publishing House of Local Records, 2015.

Articles

1. "The Mechanism for Jurisprudence to Produce Guiding Knowledge and Its Predicament: from the Perspective of Textbooks", *Northern Legal Science*, 6(2014).

2. "A Historical Analysis of the Institution of Independent Exercise of Judicial Power in China", *Global Law Review*, 2(2016).

3. "From Coercive Justice to Authoritative Justice: A Paradigm Shift in Justice of China", *Studies in Law and Business*, 6(2017).

4. "A New Interpretation of the People's Procuratorates' Nature", *Law and*

Social Development,6(2018).

5. "Supervision and Public Prosecution: A Sino-Soviet Comparison", *Tsinghua University Law Journal*,1(2019).

Mao Xiaofei

A Basic Information

After acquiring her Bachelor degree in English at Beijing Broadcasting Institute(now Communication University of China) in 1995, Mao Xiaofei first worked for "Economic Half-Hour"at the Chinese Central Television Station(CCTV)as a journalist. In 1997, she began a five-year master program specialized in political science and law at Johann Wolfgang Goethe University(Frankfurt a. M.) in Germany. She was called to the Department of International Economic Law of CASS Institute of International Law in 2004. She specializes in international antitrust Law, international dispute settlement, German law as well as European law Studies. She has been invited to Germany by Freie Universitaet Berlin(FU)and Technische Universitaet Berlin(TU)as a part-time lecturer to teach Chinese law since 2009.

B Research Activities and Achievements

Mao Xiaofei has participated in various research projects and legislative activities both inside and outside the institute, in particular, the drafting of the Antimonopoly Law of the People's Republic of China in 2007. She conducted a thorough investigation into the monopoly situation of Chinese salt industry and submitted research reports to the Chinese government, which greatly contributed to the significant reform of salt industry in 2016. The monopoly regime of the salt industry was abolished at last. Since 2017, she has focused on the research of international dispute settlement, including international arbitration, and initiated the CASS Arbitration Roundtable.

She published dozens of articles and papers in key domestic and international academic journals such as *International Law Studies*, *Journal of Law Application*, *Chinese Journal of European Studies*, *Jiangxi Social Sciences*, *Zeitschrift für Wettbewerbsrecht* (*ZweR*), *Gewerblicher Rechtsschutz und Urheberrecht-Internationaler Teil* (*GRUR Int.*), etc..

Further, she submitted policy recommendations to the *Internal Reference* at *People's Daily*, *Journal of Administration in Industry and Commerce* at State Administration for Market Regulation (SAMR) and *Leaders' Reference* at the Chinese Academy of Social Sciences, etc.. She also wrote comments and reviews for such prominent newspapers in China as *People's Daily*, *Guangming Daily*, *Economic Daily*, *Legal Daily* and *The Beijing News*, etc..

Her co-translated work *The International Law*, written by Prof. Graf von Vitztum and other German International Law scholars, has become a standard reference book for the research and study of international law in China.

She has attended many important domestic and international conferences on international law and delivered keynote speeches at these conferences.

C Major Publications and Viewpoints

1. "The Unique Model of Chamber for International Commercial Disputes in Germany—An Analysis of the Draft Law of the Establishment of Chamber for International Commercial Disputes in the Federal Republic of Germany", *International Law Studies*, Vol. 2018/06, pp. 97 –109.

In this article, she pointed out that the establishment of International Commercial Court has become a "new ecology" in the field of international commercial disputes settlement. In April 2018, the German Bundestag promulgated the Draft

Law on the Establishment of Chamber for International Commercial Disputes, aiming at setting up court chambers specialized in international commercial disputes settlement and adopting English as the language of trial in the German court system. The establishment of Chamber for International Commercial Disputes will lead to significant changes to the current German Code on Court Constitution and the Civil Procedure Law. From the perspective of international comparison, the German model is pretty different from the well-known international commercial courts. It is the mixture of the tradition of Chamber for Commercial Disputes and the modernity of international commercial disputes settlement in Germany.

2. "Constitutional Constraints on the Right to Decide External Financial Aid—Constitutional Review of Euro Zone Aid Bill by the German Federal Constitutional Court", *Chinese Journal of European Studies*, Vol. 2/2013, pp. 135 – 151.

In this article, she pointed out that, by signing the collective financial bailout programs reached by the Euro countries, international commitments have been incorporated into Germany's domestic laws, which caused constitutional complaints filed by the opponents at the German Federal Constitutional Court for judicial review. The Court reiterated in its decisions that the Federal Parliament is the only constitutional body in Germany entitled to make decisions on foreign aid, which may impose burdens upon the national fiscal policy, and that it deals with an unalienable constitutional power of the Federal Parliament protected by the free and equal right of election by citizens as well as the democratic principles enshrined in the Basic Law. Even when participating in the collective bail out operations to solve the sovereign debt crisis in the Euro Zone, it must be ensured that the competence of the German Parliament not be deprived and constitutional constraints complied with in terms of limited individual authorization, retention of congressional supervision as well as due process.

3. "An Analysis of Civil Remedies in the Chinese Antimonopoly Law for Consumer Protection", *Journal of Law Application*, Vol. 2/2013, pp. 47 – 54.

In this article, she reiterated that the ultimate goal of the Chinese Antimonopoly Law is to protect consumer interest by maintaining effective market competition. It has become an essential part of the modern enforcement mechanism of antitrust law in the civil litigation for the purpose of restricting monopolistic behavior. The private enforcement of antitrust law, which is conducive to initiating civil lawsuits and obtaining compensations by consumers, has also emerged. However, there are still no adequate mechanism for private enforcement of Antimonopoly Law in China. The ambiguous understanding of litigious right of consumers, the suppression of class action, the burden of proof and the inappropriate damage reliefs for consumers have made the private enforcement of anti-monopoly law difficult, which has a grim prospect in the protection of consumer rights and interests.

D Main Publications

Book

Mao Xiaofei(ed.), *Selected Antimonopoly Cases and Analysis on the Chinese Administrative Antimonopoly Enforcement*, Law Press China, 2007.

Articles Published in Chinese

1. "The Unique Model of Chamber for International Commercial Disputes in Germany—An Analysis of the Draft Law of the Establishment of Chamber for International Commercial Disputes in the Federal Republic of Germany", *International Law Studies*, 6(2018).

2. "The Dilemma of Applying Competition Law in Regulating Transnational Tax Avoidance and Its Solutions", *Jiangxi Social Sciences*, 11(2017).

3. "Innovation of China's Commercial Arbitration System against the Background of the 'Belt and Road' Initiative", *People's Rule of Law*, 2(2018).

4. "An Analysis of Civil Remedies in the Chinese Antimonopoly Law on Consumer Protection", *Journal of Law Application*, 2(2013).

5. "Constitutional Constraints on the Right to Decide External Financial Aid—Constitutional Review of Euro Zone Aid Bills by the German Federal Constitutional Court", *Chinese Journal of European Studies*, 2(2013).

6. "Revising the Measures for the Exclusive Dealing of Table Salt: Discarding Monopoly", *Insider Information on Economic Reform*, (34)2008.

7. MAO Xiaofei/ HU Jian, "A Reflection on the Drafting of the Anti-monop-

oly Law", *Journal of the Eastern China University of Political Science and Law*, 2 (2008).

8. "An Analysis of the Case of Restricting Competition by Gas Companies in Ninghai County", *Journal of Administration in Industry and Commerce*, 14(2006).

9. "A Conceptual Change in the Chinese Anti-monopoly Administration: From 'Public Undertaking' to 'Undertaking with a Market Dominant Position'", *Journal of Administration in Industry and Commerce*, 3(2006).

Articles Published in German and English

1. "Eine neue Epoche füer die private Durchsetzung des Kartellrechts in China?", *ZweR*(*Zeitschrift füer Wettbewerbsrecht*), 3(2012).

2. "Das chinesische Antimonopolgesetz im Lichte des deutschen Kartellrechts", *ZWeR*, 1(2008).

3. MAO Xiaofei/Tobias Glass, "Das neue Antimonopolgesetz der Volksrepublik China", *GRUR Int.* (*Gewerblicher Rechtsschutz und Urheberrecht-Internationaler Teil*), 57(2008).

4. "Das Kartellrecht in China, *GRUR Int.* (*Gewerblicher Rechtsschutz und Urheberrecht-Internationaler Teil*)", 57(2007).

5. "An Overview of the Antimonopoly Practice in the People's Republic of China", in Hassan Qaqaya/Goerge Lipimile(ed.), *The Effects of Anti-competitive Business Practices on Developing Countries and Their Development prospects*, UNTAC, 2008.

Newspaper Articles

1. "Creating a New Era of Rule of Law in Arbitration", *Guangming Daily*, March 31, 2019.

2. "Collective Collection of Fuel Surcharge is Suspicious", *Legal Daily*, June 14, 2018.

3. "Time to Establish a Fair Competition Regime", *Chinese Economic Weekly*, October 30, 2016.

4. "Eliminate the Economic Barriers and Promote the Supply-side Reform in Salt Industry", *Chinese Food Safety Daily*, October 1, 2017.

5. "The Open System of Evidence in Deciding Monopoly Issues", *New Bei-*

jing Daily, March 28,2009.

6. "Only Detailed Explanations for the Prohibition of M&A Can Eliminate Misunderstandings", *New Beijing Daily*, March 20,2009.

7. "Consumers Should Not Pay for the Industrial Self-discipline", *New Beijing Daily*, July 29,2008.

Sun Nanxiang

A Basic Information

Dr. Sun Nanxiang is an assistant research fellow at CASS Institute of International Law. His major is international economic law and cyber law. From September 2006 to June 2016, he studied at Southwest University of Political Science and Law and obtained a bachelor's degree in international economics and trade (2010), a master's degree in international law (2013), and a Ph. D. in international law (2016). He joined the Institute in July 2016.

Dr. Sun is the deputy director of the Editorial Office of the *Blue Book on Cyber Law*, council director of the Cyber and Information Law Society under the *Chi-*

na Society of Law, council director of *Beijing Society of Internet Finance Law*, a senior researcher at the Digital Economy and Law Center of the University of International Business and Economics, one of Top 100 Young Legal Scholars selected by Beijing Law Society, and a specialist commentator at Legal Daily Network.

Dr. Sun has published more than 30 academic papers in Chinese's SSCI and SSCI journals, as well as 10 commentaries in newspapers and media, such as *People's Daily*. He also submitted nearly 20 reports to China's central government.

Dr. Sun has conducted academic research at the Max Planck Institute, the World Trade Institute, and the University of Technology in Sydney. He has also participated in several academic activities in the United States, Canada, and HKSAR.

Dr. Sun has recently presided over such national projects as the National Social Science Fund, the Chinese Ministry of Justice Research projects. He has also undertaken the International Research and Exchange Program of the Chinese Academy of Social Sciences, the Collaborative Research Project between the Chinese Academy of Social Sciences and the Australian Academy of Social Sciences, and the Youth Research Project of the Chinese Academy of Social Sciences.

B Major Academic Viewpoints

1. Legal Issues Concerning Internet Regulation in the International Trade Regime

Since the beginning of the 21st century, with the development of communication and network technologies, such as Internet, cloud computing and the Internet of Things, the cyberspace has been regarded as the fifth human domain. While Internet technology is conceptually neutral, it could be used as a basic communication medium that transmits illegal information and data, which would pose serious threats to individual rights, public morality, public order and national security. Therefore, cyberspace cannot be exempt from the governance by sovereign States. However, all the internet regulatory measures, which are in the form of domestic regulations and aim to protect individual rights, collective rights and national interests, have extraterritorial effects to some extent and would pose a threat to free trade. As global trade rules, the WTO Agreement can be applied to the Internet trade-related issues. In view of this situation and on the basis of recognizing the WTO Agreement application, this book probes the following legal issues: first, whether Internet regulations could constitute trade barriers; second, what kinds of trade barriers posed by Internet regulations can exist in reality; and third, how to invoke the exception clauses to justify internet regulations.

2. The United States' Economic Unilateralism: Current Situation and Legal Issues

After Donald Trump became the U. S. President, the U. S. has not only hindered the operation of multilateral dispute settlement mechanism, but also advocated reciprocal treatment to replace non-discriminatory treatment doctrine and continued to strengthen the restraint on international law by domestic law. Those U. S. economic unilateral measures undermine the rule-oriented international economic order. The conflict between WTO agreement and current trade practices, the ineffectiveness of the dispute settlement mechanism, and the lack of consensus on the "market economy mode" are the reasons why the U. S. blocks WTO. In practice, U. S. economic unilateralism is threatening the function of multilateral mechanism and triggering an international rule of law crisis. In order to solve the challenges posed by the U. S. , the international community should introduce the majority vote system into the decision-making procedure, and strengthen the WTO's disciplines to regulate bilateral or regional trade agreements. As a responsible developing country, China should base itself on the fair competitive conditions to improve its market economy and also actively promote WTO reform from a multilateral perspective.

3. The Human Rights Attribute of the Internet Freedom and Its Application

In the New Millennium, the cyberspace has been transformed from a res nullius system to a human-centered system and a right-oriented regime. Internet freedom consists of free expression, Internet freedom of information, free communication, and the availability of Internet infrastructure. Internet freedom is not absolute. However, the restrictions on Internet freedom should meet at least three conditions: firstly, the restrictive measures should be expressly provided for by law; secondly, the measures should meet legitimate objectives; thirdly, the measures should pass the necessity test. China's Internet policy does not violate international human rights' obligations. It should be noted that the potential for human rights' achievement is endless. In future, the law of cyber-security should guarantee the reasonable legal remedies and offer diversified dispute settlements. China shall strengthen domestic and international Internet infrastructure and actively participate in the solution of the regional "digital divide", so as to build a cyber international community for all mankind.

4. Taking Internet Trade Freedom and Its Regulation Seriously: A Reflection from the Perspective of the WTO Law

"Internet Freedom" and "Internet regulation" are two core issues in the information age. In the WTO framework, Internet trade freedom includes free trade in information technology products, freedom of services, freedom of the media and information freedom. Undoubtedly, Internet trade freedom is not unlimited. The WTO law stipulates three types of non-trade concerns for domesticregulations, e. g. , national security exception, public morality and public order exceptions, and personal data protection exception. It should be noted that different non-trade concerns apply different standards and conditions. For instance, in order to successfully defend its violations, the measures should meet the requirements of the necessity test and be applied non-discriminately. During the process of promoting the "Internet plus" strategy, China could draw on the cyber freedom concept in the WTO law. Furthermore, as a responsible country, China should adopt measures to protect its national, public and private interests in cyberspace in accordance with the WTO law.

5. Piercing the Veil of National Security: Does China's Banking IT Security Regulation Violate the TBT Agreement?

The first decade of the 21st century has witnessed disputes between China and the Western world over regulation of IT products. Currently, China's banking IT security regulation has spurred a heated debate among international lawyers. More specifically, the critical issue is how to strike a balance between the wants of free trade and the needs of national security. Under WTO jurisprudence, China's banking IT security regulation would be a trade barrier to not only foreign IT products, but also other domestic products. However, China would defend its measures on the ground of national security in the TBT Agreement. Theoretically, China would not shoulder the responsibility of adopting the Common Criteria as a basis of technical regulations. It should be noted that the real risk of treaty violation is the de facto discrimination created by China's regulations. Multilateral or bilateral co-operation, or good practice guidance may be feasible and practical measures for addressing the issue of cyber security regulations.

C Main Publications

1. "The United States' Economic Unilateralism: Current Situation and Legal Issues", *Global Law Review*, 1 (2019).

2. "USMCA's Restraint on the Non-market Economy Countries and Its Legality", *Journal of Latin American Studies*, 1 (2019).

3. "On the Data Subject as a Consumer and the Relevant Data Protection Mechanism", *Political Science and Law*, 7 (2018).

4. "The Application of the Margin of Appreciation in International Adjudication and Its Further Implications", *Chinese Review of International Law*, 4 (2018).

5. "The Responsibility Distribution between the European Union and Its Member States in Investor-State Dispute Settlement", *Chinese Journal of European Studies*, 1 (2018).

6. "The Human Rights Attribute of the Internet Freedom and Its Application", *Science of Law*, 3 (2017).

7. "From Right Restriction to Empowerment: The Future of Internet Trade Law", *Contemporary Law Review*, 5 (2016).

8. "Taking Internet Trade Freedom and Its Regulation Seriously: A Reflection from the Perspective of WTO Law", *Peking University Law Journal*, 2 (2016).

9. "Piercing the Veil of National Security: Does China's Banking IT Security Regulation Violate the TBT Agreement?", *Asian Journal of WTO & International Health Law and Policy*, 2 (2016).

10. "The Research on Non-Governmental Obstacles in Foreign Investment and China's Strategy", *Modern Law Science*, 1 (2016).

Ren Hongda

A Basic Information

Dr. Ren Hongda is an assistant research fellow at the Department of International Economic Law, CASS Institute of International Law. Before that, he had studied at Beihang University in Beijing and the Friedrich Schiller University of Jena (Germany), where he had obtained a bachelor's degree in German literature, a bachelor's degree in law, a master's degree in law, and a doctoral degree in law. Currently, his research focuses on international investment law, cross-border mergers & acquisitions and foreign aid law. He has participated in some collective research projects and published some interesting articles in Chinese and foreign academic journals. He has also submitted some legislative proposals to the Chinese government and received positive feedbacks. Moreover, he has served as a research fellow at the "Belt and Road" Initiative Judicial Research Center of the Supreme People's Court and at the International Competition Law Research Center of CASS Institute of International Law.

B Academic Experience

1. Interdisciplinary Education

Dr. Ren is a native of Baoji City in Shaanxi Province. Based on his outstanding ability of foreign language in high school, he had chosen German Literature as his major in university. Thanks to the systematic training at Beihang University, he finished his graduation thesis, a literary analysis of the novel *Be Yourself*(*Werder, die du bist*) by the German feminist author Hedwig Dohm in the 19th century. In the form of a diary, this famous novel shows the flow of consciousness of a woman who is suspected of having a mental problem. As one can imagine, if we analyze it in a traditional way, we will almost never understand it. Moreover, the author played a word game in the novel's name: the feminine definite article " die " is clear. Therefore, he built a database with the corpus linguistic research method, in this way the objective evidence proves that " die " refers not only to women themselves, but also to the concept of the sprite and the soul in the novel. In other words, women should have independent thoughts and consciousness to change the unreasonable social order at that time. By virtue of its methodological innovation and a breakthrough in the conclusion, the thesis got the highest score of the undergraduate theses in the year, which is the first beneficial attempt of his research.

Thanks for the diversified design of lessons at Beijing University, which enabled him to complete a second bachelor's degree in law. In the Law School, he gradually realized the charm of rules and logic. Fortunately, he had participated in the Manfred-Lachs International Space Law Moot Court Competition, which generated in him a strong interest in international law. His undergraduate thesis " Analysis of the State Immunity from the Perspective of the Case of Augusto Pinochet" was highly recognized by the Law School, which encouraged him to a further legal research.

Based on a comprehensive ability of law and German, he had successfully applied for a major of private and public economic law at the University Jena, Germany. The full name of the University of Jena is Friedrich-Schiller-Universität

Jena. It has a history of 500 years and many well-known people, such as Johann Gottlieb Fichte, Georg Wilhelm Friedrich Hegel, Karl Marx, come from this university. After completing a large number of programs, his research interests focused on corporate governance. Based on the traditional dual management structure of German companies, his master's thesis "On the independence of independent supervisors" systematically analyzed and interpreted the independence of supervisors within the framework of German law and EU law.

A German supervisory board fully reflects its diversity. Its composition includes shareholder representatives, dispatchers of holding company, employee representatives, financial experts (companies limited by shares), audit committees (large companies) and independent supervisors (listed companies). But its diversity excludes the independence of some positions. Horizontally, the independent requirements of financial experts, auditors, and independent supervisors are scattered among different legal sequences, so there is a conceptual overlap and intersection. Vertically, EU law, German law, German "soft law" and judicial practice also have different requirements and understandings of independence itself. In his research, he combed the above concepts and legal consequences, emphasizing a respect for the self-identification of the supervisory committees of each company. In the end, his graduation thesis passed with distinction.

After his master's degree, he continued to work with Prof. Dr. Walter Bayer in a doctoral program. The title of his doctoral thesis is "Special Purpose Vehicles in the Context of Mergers & Acquisitions", which mainly focus on the legal reasons and obstacles for build complex holding structures via special purpose vehicles in the context of acquiring Chinese non-listed companies by international companies.

Due to the low transparency of the information about acquisitions of non-listed companies, the previous research mainly focuses on listed companies. This paper uses economics databases to analyze the M&A model and fills in a gap in methodology. Due to the innovation of this research, the article finally passed with distinction (in Latin: magna cum laude). In March 2017, the thesis was published with the subsidy from the prestigious law foundation "Johanna und Fritz Buch Gedaechtnis-Stiftung".

2. Diversified Work Experience

In the last two years, it seems that Dr. Ren has done another "Ph. D. research", which is not focused on a certain point, but involves many different fields. Besides his ordinary academic research, he also works at the Department of Research Coordination and International Cooperation of CASS Institute of International Law, where he has organized many international legal forums.

C Academic Activities

CASS Institute of International Law provides researchers a good platform for academic exchanges. On this platform, Dr. Ren has participated in more than 30 international and domestic academic conferences in recent years, and has conducted extensive and in-depth exchanges with experts and scholars from the executive departments of the Chinese government, well-known research institutions, international organizations, and embassies abroad, including the following academic activities sponsored by the CASS and organized by his department:

1. 27 – 28 October 2018, CASS Forum and the Fifteenth International Law Forum "Reform and Opening-Up in the New Era and International Law".

2. 2 – 3 December 2017, CASS Forum and the Fourteenth International Law Forum "International Law in a New Era: Change, Innovation, and Development".

D Academic Achievements

1. Publications

(1) "Chinese Outbound Foreign Investment and Host Country Policies", by Rainer Kulms, translated by REN Hongda, *Chinese Review of International Law*, 1 (2019).

Chinese investors are important players in the international market for takeovers. Host country politicians have come to greet these takeover activities with calls for rigid investment controls. By building on the *causes célèbres*, this paper addresses the most prevalent investment control law issues as they have emerged for U. S. and EU regulators.

(2) "The Application of Law of the Contractual Relations in Foreign-related

Share Deals", *Chinese Review of International Law*, 1(2018).

A strict system of administrative examination and approval of foreign direct investments (FDI) in China inclusive of a mandatory application of Chinese law to the relevant agreements has been set up for a long time. Currently very few studies have been carried out on these issues from the point of view of private law.

The application of law of share transfer contracts should be determined by *lexcontractus* which is mainly governed by Article 41 of *The Law on the Application of Law for Foreign-related Civil Relations of the People's Republic of China*, and in the framework of inbound acquisitions. Article 22 of the *Provisions on M&A of A Domestic Enterprise by Foreign Investors* does not have a priority. With regard to the application of law of the listed shares, characteristic performance should be excluded.

(3) *Special Purpose Vehicles bei Mergers & Acquisitions*, Jenaer Wissenschaftliche Verlagsgesellschaft, 2017, ISBN: 978 - 3 - 938057 - 57 - 5.

See the introduction in "Interdisciplinary Education" above.

2. Internal Reports

As a jurist, especially a research fellow of the Chinese Academy of Social Sciences, one should make an academic response to the important rule of law and legislative activities in China. At present, Dr. Ren's policy recommendations mainly focus on three aspects, namely international investment, international trade and foreign aid. Some of Dr. Ren's internal reports have received positive feedback from the State Council.

Introduction to the Department of International Human Rights Law

I　Overview

The Institute of Law of the Chinese Academy of Social Sciences is the earliest academic institution to carry out human rights research in China. As early as 1994, the Center for Human Rights Studies of the Chinese Academy of Social Sciences was established, which is the earliest human rights research institution in China. Since the establishment of the Center for International Law of the Chinese Academy of Social Sciences in 2002, international human rights law was also one of its important research fields. At that time, the researchers in this field mainly belonged to the Research Department of Public International Law. In 2009, when the Center for International Law was renamed the Institute of International Law, a separate Research Department of International Human Rights Law (IHRL) was also established.

When the IHRL Research Department was established, there were three researchers, namely Zhao Jianwen, Liu Huawen and Dai Ruijun, with Zhao Jianwen as the head of the department, and Chen Zexian, the director of the CASS Institute of International Law, was associated with the IHRL Research Department for the purpose of membership in a research department. In 2011, Qu Xiangfei joined the IHRL Research Department; in 2012, Liu Huawen was transferred to the Editorial Board of *Chinese Review of International Law* as the deputy editor-in-chief; in 2016, Zhao Jianwen retired, Sun Shiyan and Zhong Ruihua were transferred from the Research Department of Public International Law and the Research Department of International Economic Law, respectively; Sun Shiyan was appointed the acting head of the IHRL Research Department in 2016 and the head of the department in 2018.

Currently there are four full-time researchers at the IHRL Research Department: Research Fellow Sun Shiyan and Research Fellow Qu Xiangfei, Associate Research Fellow Dai Ruijun and Assistant Research Fellow Zhong Ruihua. Mo Jihong, the Director of the CASS Institute of International Law, and Liu Xiaomei, Deputy Head Librarian of the CASS Law Library, are associated with the IHRL Research Department for the purpose of membership in a research department. All members of the IHRL Research Department have long-term experience of visiting and working abroad, and maintain long-term and close contacts with foreign human rights academic institutions. In addition to conducting research and teaching in the field of international human rights law, the IHRL Research Department has also participated extensively in China's international human rights activities, including the preparation of reports submitted by China to United Nations human rights bodies and the considerations of these reports by United Nations human rights bodies in various ways.

Ⅱ Major Research Works

The main research area of the IHRL Research Department is international human rights law. However, this is a broad cross-disciplinary area. In addition to the study of international human rights law, it also includes the study from the perspective of international human rights law of other phenomena and problems that may be related to human rights in the field of international law. In the context of China, it also includes the study on the policies, laws and practices of China from the perspective of and with reference to international human rights law.

At the Institute of International Law, in addition to the fact that research stuff of the IHRL Research Department focus on human rights and related legal issues, researchers in other departments have also conducted extensive research on human rights topics. The papers in this volume on the subject of international human rights law include not only articles published by the researchers at the IHLR Research Department, but also those published by the research staff of other research departments of the Institute of International Law as well.

The research outcomes in the field of international human rights law include books(including monographs, translated works and collections of papers), journal articles, newspaper articles, compilations of materials, and a large number of internal reports. In terms of their contents, those outcomes can be divided into the following categories: fundamental theories of human rights; the theories, laws and practices of human rights in China; international human rights covenants and conventions; specific human rights and human rights of special groups; the relationship between human rights and other phenomena and problems in the field of international law; human rights issues in other regions and countries; and international humanitarian law—an area closely related to international human rights law. Although most of the papers in this volume are published in academic journals, they basically cover all the above-mentioned categories.

1. Fundamental Theories of Human Rights

The fundamental theories of human rights are the theoretical foundations of the whole system of human rights law, including international human rights law. the Department of IHRL attaches great importance to the study of fundamental theories of human rights, which is represented by Qu Xiangfei's monograph *How Far Is Human Rights from Us: The Concept of Human Rights and Its Evolution in Modern China* (Tsinghua University Press, 2015) and Mo Jihong's article "On the Amorality of Human Rights". In addition, the Department of IHRL has also extensively studied and published on such topics as the subjects of human rights(Qu Xiangfei), the relationship between human dignity and human rights (Liu Huawen and Qu Xiangfei), and the evolution history of human rights theory in China(Qu Xiangfei).

2. Human Rights Theories, Laws and Practices of China

The Department of IHRL attaches great importance to the study and publicity of the human rights theories, laws and practices of China, which is represented by

Liu Huawen's article "Forty Years of Reform and Opening-up and the Way of Human Rights Development in China", Liao Fan's article "The Human Rights and Sovereignty Implications of a Community with Shared Future for Mankind", Liu Xiaomei's article "Promoting the Building of a Community with Shared Future for Mankind through the Development of the Human Rights", Zhang Weihua's article "The Human Rights Dimension in the Building of a Community with Shared Future for Mankind", and Liu Huawen's monograph *The Road of Human Rights Development in China* (China Social Sciences Press, 2018). In addition, the Department of IHRL has also extensively studied and published on such topics as the mainstreaming and localization of human rights in China (Liu Huawen), the socialist concept of human rights with Chinese characteristics (Liu Huawen), human rights and the Chinese Dream (Liu Huawen), and the legislative and judicial protection of human rights in China (Liu Xiaomei).

3. International Human Rights Covenants and Conventions

International human rights covenants and conventions are the principal instrument that contain international human rights standards, and they are therefore the research focus of the Department of IHRL. There have been extensive studies and publications on the overall situation of international human rights legal system with international human rights covenants and conventions as the core, specific international human rights covenants and conventions, some aspects of those covenants and conventions, and the relations between those covenants and conventions and China.

In the field of international human rights law, an important issue is the overall situation of the United Nations human rights system. The research outcome in this respect is represented by Liu Huawen's article "United Nations and the International Protection of Human Rights", and his monograph *Core United Nations Human Rights Conventions and Mechanisms* (Hunan University Press, 2016). The influences and impacts of international human rights law on domestic law is also one of the research subjects, which is represented by Dai Ruijun's article "International Human Rights Law as Impetus for the Evolution of Fundamental Rights System".

The outcome of research on the International Covenant on Economic, Social and Cultural Rights (ICESCR) is represented by Liu Huawen's monograph *The Asymmetry of the State's Obligations under the International Covenant on Economic, Social and Cultural Rights* (Peking University Press, 2005; reprinted, Social Sciences Academic Press, 2019) and *Research on the Justiciabilities of Economic, Social and Cultural Rights*, edited by Liu Huawen (China Social Science Press, 2008). The outcome of research on the International Covenant on Civil and Political Rights (ICCPR) is represented by Zhu Xiaoqing and Liu Huawen's *The International Covenant on Civil and Political Rights and Its Implementation Mechanism* (China Social Sciences Press, 2003). In addition, Zhao Jianwen and Sun Shiyan have also studied and published extensively on such issues relating to ICCPR as obligations, derogations, reservations and relations with the domestic legal system. Sun Shiyan's research on the Chinese text(s) of the ICCPR (to a certain extent, also the ICESCR) has given rise to some international responses.

An important aspect of the study on international human rights covenants and conventions is the study of their implementation mechanisms, which is represented by Zhu Xiaoqing's article "The Implementation Mechanism of the International Covenant on Civil and Political Rights", Dai Ruijun's article "Strengthening UN Human Rights Treaty Body System: Latest Development of UN Human Rights Protection System". A representative study on the domestic implementation of international human rights covenants and conventions is Dai Ruijun's monograph *Domestic Implementation of International Human Rights Treaties: A Global Perspective* (Social Sciences Academic Press, 2013).

A focus of international human rights law research is the relationship between China and international human rights covenants and conventions, which is represented by Mo Jihong's monograph *International Covenants on Human Rights and China* (World Knowledge Press, 2005) and *International Covenant on Civil and Political Rights: Ratification and Implementation*, edited by Chen Zexian (China Social Sciences Press, 2008). With regard to the ratification of the ICCPR, Mo Jihong proposed to enact *Law of the People's Republic of China on Human Rights Protection* to integrate the universal human rights in the human rights covenants with the individual rights guaranteed by the Constitution and other laws and regulations of China. In the context of China's prospective ratification of the ICCPR, Sun Shiyan analyzed the issue of its understanding and interpretation; while Zhao Jianwen put forward an innovative proposal that China should accept the individual complaint mechanism contained in United Nations human rights treaties.

4. Specific Human Rights and Human Rights of Special Groups

The Department of IHRL attaches great importance to the study of specific human rights, especially in the light of international human rights law. With respect to civil and political rights, the representative work is Mo Jihong's monograph *Legal Limits of Freedom of Expression* (People's Public Security University of China Press, 1998) and Zhao Jianwen's article "Article 14 of the International Covenant on Civil and Political Rights: On the Right to Fair Trial". The Department of IHRL has also conducted in-depth research on the issue of death penalty, which is represented by Chen Zexian's article "On Strict Restriction of the Application of Death Penalty" and Sun Shiyan's articles "The International Trend towards the Abolition of the Death Penalty: Viewed from the Reports of the United Nations Secretary-General" and "The Publicity of the Information on the Death Penalty: The Requirements of the United Nations and Responses of China". With respect to economic, social and cultural rights, the representative work is Qu Xiangfei's article on the right to educations "A Tentative Exploration of the Right to Education", and her article on the right to health "Safeguarding the Right to Health in International Law Cases". With respect to the third-generation human rights, the representative work is Zhao Jianwen's articles on the right to self-determination and right to peace, and Liu Huawen's article on the right to development.

The Department of IHRL attaches particular importance to the study of human rights of special groups, in particular women's rights (and related gender issues and the issue of domestic violence), rights of the child and the rights of persons with disabilities. With respect to women's rights and gender equality, the representative work is Liu Huawen's article "Gender Equality: The Practice of the UN

Human Rights Treaty Bodies and Its Implications", and Li Xixia's article "The Protection of Women's Right to Health under International Human Rights Law". With respect to the rights of the child, the representative work is *The Rights of the Child and Their Legal Protection* edited by Liu Huawen (Shanghai People's Publishing House, 2009). Qu Xiangfei has conducted extensive and in-depth research on the rights of persons with disabilities, which is represented by her article "The Convention on the Rights of Persons with Disabilities and the Protection of the Rights of Persons with Disabilities"; and in particular, the study on the concept of "reasonable accommodation", which is represented by her article "Reasonable Accommodation in the Convention on the Rights of Persons with Disabilities: Benchmark of Consideration and Method of Protection". Liu Huawen has also studied the features of the protection of the rights of persons with disabilities in China. Research on the human rights of special groups also includes research on the rights of older persons and foreigners by Liu Huawen and Dai Ruijun. Zhong Ruihua's article "On the Nature of Consumers' Rights" includes an analysis of the nature of consumers' rights from the perspective of human rights.

5. The Relationship between Human Rights and other Phenomena and Problems in the Field of International Law

Human rights are not confined to the field of international human rights law; instead, they have interacted with phenomena and problems in other fields of international law. the Department of IHRL pays attention to these cross-cutting areas and conducts distinctive studies on such issues as human rights and trade, human rights and extradition, human rights and migration, human rights and climate change, and human rights and corruption. With respect to the relations between human rights and trade, the representative work is Liu Jingdong's articles "Human Rights in International Trade" and "Human Rights Protection or Trade Protection? A Theoretical thinking from the Perspective of Labor Rights", and Li Xixia has also conducted research on the relations between free trade zones/agreements and Labor standards. With respect to the relations between human rights and extradition, the representative work is Liu Huawen's article "The Significance and Implication of the First Case of Extradition of the Inter-American Court of Human

Rights" and Hao Luyi's article "An Exploration of Human Rights Issues in Extradition". With respect to the relations between human rights and migration, the representative work is Liu Huawen's monograph *Research on the United Nations Protocol against Human Trafficking from the Perspective of Human Rights Law* (Social Sciences Academic Press, 2010). The study on the relations between human rights and climate change is represented by He Jingjing's relevant articles. With respect to the relations between human rights and corruption, the representative work is Sun Shiyan's article "How Corruption Impairs Human Rights".

6. Human Rights Issues in Other Regions and Countries

The Department of IHRL also pays attention to human rights issues in other regions and countries. With respect to the research on regional human rights systems, the representative is Zhu Xiaoqing, one of the earliest scholars in China to study the European human rights system, whose publications include the monograph *Legal Protection Mechanism of Human Rights in Europe* (Law Press China, 2003) and the article "Evolution of the Legal Status of Human Rights in the Process of European Integration". Sun Shiyan also published one article on the doctrine of "margin of appreciation" in the European human rights system. As for the relations between international human rights law and other countries, the representative work is Li Qingming's article "International Human Rights Treaties and the Double Standards of American Courts". He also published a book on the US *Alien Tort Claim Act*, which includes the relations between that law and human rights.

7. International Humanitarian Law

International humanitarian law is different from but closely related to international human rights law. The representative work of the Department of the IHRL in this respect is Zhang Weihua's article "1949 Geneva Conventions: Codifications and Developments of Fundamental Standards of International Humanitarian Law" and the article co-authored by Ma Jinxing and Sun Shiyan, "Restrictions on the Use of Force at Sea: from an Environmental Protection Perspective".

8. Translation of Human Rights Literature

In addition to the articles and monographs introduced above, another important contribution of the Department of IHRL to the studies of human rights in China is the translation of human rights literature, which is represented by Sun Shiyan and Bi Xiaoqing's translation of Manfred Nowak's *CCPR Commentary*(first and revised second edition, SDX Joint Punishing Company, 2003 and 2008, respectively); Liu Huawen's translation of Manfred Nowak's *Introduction to the International Human Rights Regime* (Peking University Press, 2010); Sun Shiyan's translation of Ben Saul, David Kinley and Jacqueline Mowbray's *International Covenant on Economic, Social and Cultural Rights: Commentaries, Cases and Materials* (Law Press China, 2019). Many of these translated books are among the most frequently cited reference books in the field of human rights studies in China. Since 2019, the discipline of the IHRL has launched a series of translation, which will translate some commentaries on the core international human rights covenants and conventions so as to benefit the human rights academia in China.

Ⅲ Summary and Prospect

The Department of IHRL has three characteristics. Firstly, its research scope is very broad, covering almost all the fields related to international human rights law. Secondly, its research is very realistic. In addition to paying attention to the practice and development of international human rights law itself, it is particularly important to pay attention to the significance of international human rights law to the construction of the rule of law in China. Thirdly, its research is of introductory nature. International human rights law, whether as a legal area or a legal discipline, has not been known for a long time in China. Therefore, an important task of the Department of IHRL is to act as a "bridge" to help the domestic human rights and legal academia to understand the latest developments, both practical and academic, in the field of international human rights law.

In the new era, the Department of IHRL will continue to play the role as "bridges of human rights between the world and China". Firstly, it will continue to study the practice and development in the field of international human rights law itself, so that the domestic human rights and legal academia can learn the latest developments in this field at the international level. Secondly, it will continue to study the role and significance of international human rights law in the construction of the rule of law in China, make use of the resources available in international human rights law to further contribute to the cause of respecting and safeguarding human rights in China. Finally, and most importantly, it will move more from the Chinese side of the "bridge of human rights" to the world side, that is, to make efforts to achieve two points: one is to play more the role of showing the practice and research results of China in the field of human rights to the outside world; the other is to participate more in international human rights discussions and discourse construction, so as to make Chinese contributions to such discussions and construction.

Ⅳ Curriculum Vitae of Personnel

Mo Jihong

A Basic Information

Professor Mo Jihong, born on May 21, 1965, Han nationality, Jingjiang City, Jiangsu Province, and Ph. D. is currently the director and a research fellow of the CASS Institute of International Law, a supervisor of doctoral and master's students at CASS Graduate School, and a distinguished professor at the University of the Chinese Academy of Social Sciences. His majors are constitutional law, legislative studies, administrative law and international human rights law and his key research areas are constitutional philosophy, constitutional theory, constitutional supervision system and constitutional review theory, basic human rights theory, international human rights law implementation mechanism, the state of emergency system, and national security and public safety theory.

The main social positions and part-time jobs held by Professor Mo Jihong include: Honorary President of the International Association of Constitutional Law (Lifetime), an executive member of China Law Society, a member of the Academic Committee of China Law Society, an executive vice president of Chinese Association of Constitutional Law, President of the Association of Legislative Studies of Beijing Law Society, Vice President of the Association of Legislative Studies of China Law Society, Vice President of the Association of Lawyer Studies of China Law Society, etc..

Mo Jihong graduated from the Department of Law of Peking University in 1986. He obtained a master's degree in law and a J. D. from CASS Graduate School in 1989 and 1994, respectively. From 1989 to 1990, he worked at the Institute of Political Science of the Chinese Academy of Social Sciences. From 1991 to 2018, he worked at the Institute of Law of the Chinese Academy of Social Sciences. From 2018 to the present, he worked at the Institute of International Law of the Chinese Academy of Social Sciences. He became an associate research fellow in 1993, a research fellow in 2001, and a doctoral supervisor in the field of international human rights law in 2004. He was awarded the title of one of the "National Top Ten Outstanding Young Jurists" by China Law Society in 2004, selected for the "National Talents Project" by the Ministry of Human Resources and Social Security and awarded the honorary title of "Young and Middle-aged Expert with Outstanding Contributions" in 2013, received a special government allowance from the State Council in 2015, was awarded the honorary title of "Cultural Master and Talent" by the Central Propaganda Department and the honorary title of Leader in the Field of Philosophy and Social Science in 2017. He was a member of the Supreme

People's Procuratorate Expert Advisory Committee, a member of the Central Lecturers Group under the "Fifth-Five-year National Plan" and "Seventh-Five-year National Plan" for the Popularization Law, a member of the "100 Jurists Reporting Group" of China Law Society, a legal adviser to Beijing Municipal People's Congress Standing Committee, and a legal consultant to Beijing Municipal People's Government, a legal advisor on the publicity of ruling the city by law to the government of Beijing Municipality, a legal advisor to Guangdong Provincial Party Committee and the deputy secretary of the CPC Zhangye Municipal Committee of Gansu Province (a temporary leading post held from April 2017 to March 2018).

Professor Mo Jihong has been a visiting professor and visiting scholar at famous universities and research institutions abroad: he was a visiting researcher at the Faculty of Law of the University of Tokyo in 1995, at the Norwegian Institute of Human Rights in 1998, at Lund University in Sweden in 2001, and at the University of Fribourg in Switzerland in 2002.

Professor Mo Jihong's doctoral students in the direction of international human rights law who have already graduated were: Wang Zhenjun, Dai Ruijun, Wang Yi, Luo Yan, Xia Zuyi, Yu Haixia, Jiang Nancheng, Shao Yi, Wu Wenyang and his current doctoral students are Zhou Fanmiao, Huo Yaping andChu Xiaohua. Up to now, he has supervised nearly 20 postdoctoral researchers, 60 master students, 10 advanced students, and 2 undergraduate students in the direction of constitutional and administrative law.

B Research Activities and Contributions

In his research work of nearly 30 years, Professor Mo Jihong presided over and participated in many important research projects both in and outside of the Institute and the Academy, and actively participated in national legislative activities by taking part in the drafting, demonstration and advisory work of nearly 100 laws and regulations. Many of his important academic research results have won provincial and ministerial level awards. Many of his nearly 100 internal research reports have been received positive responses from Party and state leaders. He has won more than 60 awards for Excellent Countermeasure Information from the Chinese Academy of Social Sciences. Among his published articles, more than 350 have been collected in the database China Knowledge Network, nearly 10 reprinted in Xinhua Digest, and more than 20 reprinted in *China Social Science Excellence* published by Renmin University of China. His main research achievements include the following aspects:

1. Actively participating in or organizing the research work of key national projects and key projects of the Chinese Academy of Social Sciences. A number of relatively significant academic achievements have been made by Professor Mo in this respect. The followings are some of the more influential national key projects and key projects of the Academy of Social Sciences participated in or organized by Professor Mo:

(1) He has led and successfully completed the major project of the National Social Science Fund in 2007, "the Organic Unity of the Party's Leadership, the People Being the Masters of the Country and Governing the Country by Law".

(2) He is the leader of the key projects of the National Social Science Fund in 2017, "Civil Norms and Local Legislation", which is making effective progress.

(3) He has led the demonstration and drafting of the expert proposal draft of the Decision of the Fourth Plenary Session of the 18th CPC Central Committee, the result became an important reference material for the decision drafting group.

(4) He has participated in the research project on the Books Series *Comprehensively Deepening the Reform*, organized by the Chinese Academy of Social Sciences, and written and published one of the books in the series: *The Constitutional Foundation of the Rule of Law in China*.

(5) He has participated in the research project on Readers Series *Xi Jinping's Thought on Socialism with Chinese Characteristics in a New Era*, organized by the Chinese Academy of Social Sciences, and written and published one of the books in the series: *Ruling the Country by Law in a Comprehensive Way and Building the Rule of Law China*.

(6) He has led the 2015 CASS National Condition Survey Project "Research on the Current Situation of Law-based Administration of Religious Affairs in Ningxia Hui Autonomous Region", the 2017 CASS National Condition Survey Project "Studies on Local Rule of Law", and the 2018 National Condition Survey Pro-

ject"Construction of Ecological Civilization and Awareness of Ecological Rule of Law".

(7) He is the leader of the 2019 – 2022 large-scale CASS investigation project"the Prevention of Legal Risk and Construction of Legal Mechanism relating to the 'Belt and Road'"and so on.

2. Actively participating in national legislative activities. Many of his important legislative proposals have been adopted by legislative organs. Some of his works compiled and published in conjunction with legislative activities have become important reference materials for legislative activities:

(1) He has participated in the work of legislation on earthquake prevention and disaster reduction and the construction of legal system on earthquake disaster prevention and reduction. He has successively served as the deputy head of the legislative drafting group of the Regulations on Emergency Responses to Destructive Earthquake and as a member of the Drafting Group of the Law of the People's Republic of China on Protecting against and Mitigating Earthquake Disasters, as an adviser to the Drafting Group of the Provisions on Issuance of Earthquake Predictions, to the Drafting Group of the Regulations on the Management of Aseismatic Fortification Requirements, and to the Legislative Drafting Group of the Regulations on the Key Areas for Earthquake Surveillance and Protection. In order to cooperate with the earthquake prevention and disaster reduction legislation work, he compiled the book *Foreign Emergency Legal Systems* (Law Press China, 1994), which became an important basis for the establishment of the earthquake emergency response mechanism in the Law on Protecting Against and Mitigating Earthquake Disasters.

(2) He has participated in the legislative discussion and consultation work of the Martial Law, the National Defense Law, the Legislation Law, the Supervision Law, the Law on Civil Servants, the Organic Law of People's Procuratorates, the Organic Law of People's Courts, the Charity Law and other laws. His book *An Introduction to the Legal System of Martial Law* (Law Press China, 1996) became an important reference material in the drafting of the Martial Law and the National Defense Law.

(3) He participated in the drafting of the Emergency Response Law and was an important member of the Drafting Group of the National Security Law.

(4) He participated in the consultation and publicity work of the fourth and fifth revisions of the of the Constitution in 2004 and 2018, and many of his proposals on constitutional amendments had been adopted by the Constitutional Amendment Group.

(5) He has made a systematic summarization of his own experiences of participating in national and local legislative activities, which were published in the book *In Defense of Legislation*(Wuhan University Press, 2007).

3. Actively responding to the call of "premium projects" and "innovative projects" proposed by the Leading Party Group and the leaders of CASS. On the basis of combining theory with practice, especially his own practical experience of participating in national legislative activities, Professor Mo has submitted numerous internal reports on major issues of construction of the rule of law in China, many of which attracted the attention of Party and state leaders. More than 60 reports have received awards for excellent information or excellent countermeasures from the Chinese Academy of Social Sciences or other types of provincial and ministerial awards, and produced extensive social impacts. The followings are some examples:

(1) In 1999, in response to emergency incidents such as NATO's bombing of the Chinese Embassy in the former Yugoslavia and the "Falungong" incident and on the basis of his own long-term research on the legal system of the state of emergency, Professor Mo submitted to the Chinese government an internal report entitled "The Establishment of a National Emergency Response Mechanism", which was published in issue No. 558 of *Compilation of Situation Reports*, an internal reference material edited by the Editorial Board of the *People's Daily*. The internal report was highly valued by the party and state leaders.

(2) Main countermeasures reports that have received instructions from Party and state leaders and awarded first prize for excellent countermeasures information by the Chinese Academy of Social Sciences include: "Several Issues to be Paid Attention to in the Revision of the Representative Law", September 2011, special

prize; "Intensifying the Publicity of the Revision of the Election Law", September 2011, the first prize; "Several Theoretical Issues to Be Taken Seriously When Declaring the Formation of a Socialist Legal System with Chinese Characteristics", September 2011, the first prize; "The Need to Carry out Legal Remedial Work in the Aftermath of Election Bribery Incident in Hengyang City", June 2015, the first prize; "It Is not Advisable for the National People's Congress To Amend the Laws Adopted by the Standing Committee of the National People's Congress", June 2015, the first prize; "The Need for the Law of the People's Republic of China on National Medals and National Titles of Honor to Embody the Spirit of 'Scientific Legislation'", June 2016, the first prize; and "It Is not Appropriate to Use Legislative Means to Intervene in the Preservation of Religious Practices", June 2016, the first prize.

4. Strengthening the study of the basic constitutional theory. Professor Mo has published 12 monographs in this field. Among them, *Outline of the Constitutional Trial System* (People's Public Security University of China Press, 1998) is the first academic work to study the constitutional trial system in the Chinese constitutional academic circle. *The Legal Limits of the Freedom of Expression* (People's Public Security University China Press, 1998) comprehensively introduces the judgment of the Norwegian Supreme Court on the "Kjuus" case, systematically analyzes the function of the modern constitutional trial system in safeguarding basic human rights, and makes a useful attempt in studying cases of constitutional trial. *Constitutional Amendments: A Must Book for the Government and Citizens* (Chinese People's Public Security University Press, 1999) gives a detailed introduction to the background, content, meaning, and theoretical and practical values of the 1999 Constitutional Amendments and is the most comprehensive reference book on the 1982 Constitution and its amendments. *The Logical Basis of the Modern Constitution* (Law Press China, 2001) is the first academic book to apply the method of logics to explain the basic principles of the modern constitution, to position the constitution as a value law, to explore in detail the value characteristics of legitimacy, certainty, validity of the Constitution and to point out that the design of the constitutional system must be based on constitutional values. *The Extraordinary Rule of Law in the Period of*

SARS Outbreak(Law Press China,2003) introduces the legislative status of China's disaster law and the law on the state of emergency and the legal countermeasures against SARS. *The International Human Rights Covenants and China*(World Knowledge Press,2005) provides a comprehensive and systematic introduction to the basic human rights systems and its implementation mechanisms established by the International Covenant on Civil and Political Rights and the International Covenant on Economic,Social and Cultural Rights. *Doctrines of Constitutional Law in Practice* (Renmin University of China Press,2007) brings together the author's constitutional views and ideas resulting from his systematic theoretical thinking of constitutional issues in practice. *In Defense of Legislation* (Wuhan University Press, 2007) is a comprehensive and systematic collection of the legislative materials of the national and local legislation participated by the author,as well as expert legislative proposals on certain social issues drafted by the author on the basis legislative needs and techniques. *Doctrines of Constitutional Law*(China Social Sciences Press,2008) uses the methods of comparative constitutional law and normative constitutional law to summarize the constitutional system in the written constitutional texts of various countries in the world, and construct a brand-new system of constitutional doctrines. *The Constitutional Foundation of the Rule of Law in China*(Social Sciences Academic Press,2014) ,which is a part of the book series *Comprehensively Deepening the Reform*,comprehensive and systematically discusses,summarizes and analyzes various constitutional issues in the process of building the rule of law in China and puts forward the theoretical framework and main academic viewpoints of ruling the country by the Constitution. *The Rule of Law in China and Institutional Construction*(China Local Records Publishing House,2016) contains the author's academic thinking and recommendations on some major theoretical and practical issues in the construction of the rule of law in China.

C Main Academic Ideas and Viewpoints

Professor Mo Jihong's unique contributions to the improvement of the theoretical research of constitutional law and human rights law are embodied in the following academic views that have had a major impact in the academic circle:

1. The essence of ruling the country by law is ruling the country by the constitution

Professor Mo is the first person in the Chinese legal academic circle to put forward the idea that the essence of ruling the country by law is ruling the country by the constitution, which has been elaborated in a series of articles, including "Governing the Country according to the Constitution as an Important Guarantee for Governing the Country according to Law". He believes that the implementation of the spirit of "ruling the country by law" means not only that in a society ruled by law, all social relations must be evaluated by legal rules, so that "there is a law to follow", but more importantly, the premise of "ruling the country by law" should be guaranteed. Namely, the problems relating to the law itself must be solved by the means of the rule of law. The solution of the contradictions of the law itself must be achieved through the implementation of the constitution. If the core position of the constitution in ruling the country by law is not highlighted, ruling the country by law may evolve into the normalization of the rule of man or a new form of rule of man in practice.

2. The dualization of law and morality is the product of "rule of man"

Professor Mo first puts forward the view that the duality of morality and law as the product of "rule of man" in his article "Social Autonomy and Modern Constitutionalism" and some other articles. He believes that under the "rule of man", because the ruler is separated from the ruled, he acts according to his own will and makes laws to restrain the ruled. For the ruler, law and morality are united; but for the ruled, law and morality are separated. The law embodies the will of the ruler, which might not meet the demand of the ruled. The will of the ruled cannot become law. As a result, there is a subjective demand raised by the ruled on the ruler. Therefore, the purpose of morality is to restrain the ruler, not the ruled. Under the rule of man, there are two kinds of ruling ideas in society: one is the "rule of law" concept of the ruler, and the other is the "rule of virtue" concept of the ruled.

3. At the level of national law, constitutional rights have higher legal effect than universal human rights provided for in international human rights conventions

In the article "On the Relationship between Basic Human Rights in International Human Rights Conventions and Constitutional Rights in Domestic Constitutions", Professor Mo holds that, for state parties to an international human rights convention, the basis of their undertaking of obligations under international human rights conventions are the relevant provisions of the Vienna Convention on the Law of Treaties. That is to say, the universal human rights in an international human rights convention do not have direct legal binding force on state parties to the convention, but could have the international law effect on state parties by virtue of the international law nature of the international convention itself. Since most state parties to a convention must ratify the convention through a law adopted by the parliament, the legal effect of an international human rights convention under domestic law can only be equivalent to the laws enacted by the parliament. From the point of view of legal effect, universal human rights in international human rights conventions approved by the parliament can only be regarded as ordinary legal rights as far as their importance is concerned. The protection enjoyed by these rights under domestic law should not exceed that enjoyed by constitutional rights. Only through a specific procedure and by means of an amendment to the constitution, can the parliament upgrade the protection of universal human rights in the ratified international human rights conventions to the level of protection given to constitutional rights.

4. Human rights are the products of dialectical development of the rights system

In the article "Legal Limitation of Freedom of Expression" and other articles, Professor Mo puts forward for the first time the view that "human rights are the products of the dialectical development of the rights system". He believes that human rights and rights are two philosophical categories with independent values. The purpose of rights is to set a qualification to realize benefits, and the purpose of the rights system is to realize the benefits to a maximum extent. Human rights emphasize human dignity and human value. It is a concept generated in the development of the rights system. The purpose of human rights is to restrict the abuse of the rights system so as to prevent human beings themselves from being exchanged and distributed as a kind of interest. Therefore, the human rights system is a production of dialectical negation of the rights system aimed at correcting the shortcomings of the rights system in the realization of benefits and enabling it to better serve humanity.

5. Human rights have independent values different from those of morality

In his article "The Amorality of Human Rights" and other articles, Professor Mo points out from perspective of the public morality of law that the morality of human rights must be embodied in a legal system. Without legal judgment, the morality of human rights does not have the public attribute. Under a legal system, the choice of human rights value is not completely subject to the requirements of public morality, but also subject to such ontological and epistemological factors as the objectivity of the social reality, national interest, public interest, and the goal of freedom. Therefore, the legitimacy of human rights is not entirely derived from moral evaluation. Human rights also have the amoral attribute, which mainly stresses that the legitimacy of human rights should be examined from the perspectives of historical materialism and dialectics. Human rights have certain objectivity. They are restricted by social, economic and cultural conditions and are realized in realistic social relations. Human rights cannot be separated from moral evaluation. However, because of the conflict of interests behind human rights, the value choice of human rights is not completely subject to moral requirements. Human rights themselves are the products of history and are constantly developing in the process of social development. Therefore, in examining the legitimacy basis of human rights, attention should be paid to the dialectical unity between the morality and amorality of human rights. The moral foundation of human rights cannot simply stay at the level of the normative requirements of human rights. In examining human rights in the framework of social relations, it is necessary to pay attention to the actual situation and the extent of realization of the institutional guarantees of personality interest pursued by human rights. The over subjectification of the nature of human rights is not conducive to the development of the human rights cause.

6. Strengthening the constitutional review of laws, administrative regulations, autonomous regulations, separate regulations, and administrative rules

In order to comprehensively and systematically discuss the theory of constitutional review, Professor Mo has published a series of academic articles, in which he puts forward systematic academic suggestions on how to conduct scientific and effective constitutional review under the current Chinese legal system. In the article "On the Mechanism for the Constitutional Review of Laws", he proceeds from the principle of the unity of the legal system stipulated in Article 5 of the current Constitution and points out that laws, just as administrative regulations and local regulations, are the objects of constitutional review. However, the design of the system of constitutional review of laws is different from that of administrative regulations and local regulations in that the latter has clear procedures and mechanisms provided for in the Legislation Law, whereas the former lacks corresponding procedures and mechanisms. Starting from the basic characteristics and requirements of the people's congress system established by the current Chinese constitution, he points out that under the current legislative system, in which the National People's Congress and its Standing Committee exercise the state legislative power while at the same time can amend and interpret the Constitution, the law-making body itself is also the body carrying out constitutional review. Therefore, the western "antagonistic" or "confrontational" constitutional review methods are not compatible with the Chinese political system, in which the Communist Party of China exercises leadership over legislation. The only feasible solution is to give full play to the role of the NPC and its Standing Committee's own internal supervision mechanism, especially the role of the Constitution and Law Committee of the NPC in ensuring the constitutionality of laws. In the review of the constitutionality of laws, only the conclusions of "consistent" or "inconsistent" can be made. In the case of "inconsistency", the problem may be dealt with through an amendment to or interpretation of the constitution or the law under review, so as to ensure a high degree of consistency between laws and the Constitution and uphold the authority of the constitution and the legitimacy of laws. In the article "On the Mechanism for the Constitutional Review of Administrative Regulations", Professor Mo proceeds from the relevant provisions of the current Constitution, the Legislation Law and other laws and regulations to carry out a comprehensive and systematic analysis of the institutional design, operational mechanism and characteristics, and the result and effect of the mechanism for the constitutional review of administrative regulations within the framework of the current legal system, summarizes the main characteristics of the mechanism, and on the basis of the analysis of the *status quo* of the mechanism and in light of the actual condition of the current political and legal systems in China, points out some important theoretical and practical issues to be paid special attention to in establishing and improving the mechanism for the constitutional review of administrative regulations in China. He points out that, in order to effectively promote the construction of the mechanism for the constitutional review of administrative regulations in practice, it is necessary to proceed from the reality of China and focus on the consistency between the drafts of administrative regulations and the Constitution in the process of formulating administrative regulations, thereby enhancing legislative quality of administrative regulations. As for the external review of the constitutionality of administrative regulations, it is necessary to make proper institutional arrangements in accordance with the relevant provisions of the Legislation Law and the principle of the Party's leadership over legislation and in light of the characteristics of administrative regulations as the central regulations, so as to uphold the authority of administrative regulations as the central regulations and ensure the effective implementation of the Constitution. In the article "The Jurisprudence and Stratification of the Constitutional Review of Autonomous Regulations and the Separate Regulations", he proceeds from the institutional design that autonomous regulations and separate regulations are subject to the constitutional review by the Standing Committee of the National People's Congress, as provided for in the relevant provisions of the Legislation Law, analyzes the characteristics of the confirmation of legislative mechanism for the adoption of autonomous regulations and separate regulations by the Constitution, the Legislative Law, the Law on Regional National Autonomy and other laws, and points out that the constitutional review of autonomous regulations and separate regulations consists of two levels: at the first level is the constitutional review of the autonomous regulations and separate regulations adopted by autonomous regions; and at the second level is the constitutional review of the autonomous regulations and separate regulations adopted by autonomous prefectures and autonomous counties. Of the two levels of constitutional review, the former can only be carried out before the entry into force of the autonomous regulations and separate regulations whereas the latter should be carried out after the entry into force of the autonomous regulations and separate regulations. Professor Mo believes that the particularity of the procedures for the approval and coming into force of autonomous regulations and separate regulations stipulated in the Constitution and the Legislation Law has made it difficult to simply apply the principle of "the lower-level law being subject to the upper-level law" to the legislative supervision over the adoption of autonomous regulations and separate regulations. It is therefore necessary to strictly distinguish different levels of the legal effect of autonomous regulations and separate regulations and establish a corresponding hierarchical constitutional review mechanism. Since the Legislation Law provides for the system whereby the Standing Committee of the National People's Congress reviews the constitutionality of autonomous regulations and separate regulations of autonomous regions, including those approved by itself, the NPC Standing Committee may carry out self-supervision in practice. Therefore, in the practice of constitutional review, efforts should be made to promote the constitutional review of autonomous regulations and separate regulations, and to distinguish between different situations, so as to find specific solution suited to each situation. In the article "On the Mechanism for the Constitutional Review of Administrative Rules", the author proceeds from the relevant provisions of the Chinese Constitution, the Legislation Law and other laws and regulations, comprehensively and systematically summarizes the system and characteristics of constitutional review of administrative rules within the framework of China's current legal system, and clearly points out that constitutional review of administrative rules is a legislative supervision system that is already in existence in China and but needs to be further improved. Starting from the analysis of the three types of administrative rules, Professor Mo proposes that formal legal relations be established between the current Constitution and the rules of departments under the State Council, rules of local governments, and military rules through constitutional amendments or constitutional interpretations, so as to provide a jurisprudential basis for the formal constitutionality of the constitutional review of administrative rules. He also points out that currently a key system design is to bring administrative rules into the scope of constitutional review by the Standing Committee of the National People's Congress as stipulated in the Legislation Law, so as to ensure the authority of the constitutional review of administrative rules.

D Introductions to Representative Works

1. Book

The Logic Foundation of the Modern Constitution, Law Press China, December 2001.

In this book, Professor Mo used the analytical method of constitutional logic to express his own unique views on a series of basic frontier theoretical issues currently under discussion in the constitutional law circles in China. Specifically, the book has two important features: (1) It is innovative in methodology. The author proposes that constitution law belongs to the value phenomenon. Therefore, the basic method used in analyzing the constitutional phenomenon must reflect the basic characteristics of value, that is, the constitution should be placed in the logical chain of causality between means and purpose, and the basic characteristics of constitutional phenomena should be understood through the discussion of their basic value attributes, such as the legitimacy, rationality, certainty and validity of the constitution. The author uses the above-mentioned analytical methods throughout the book, aiming to discover the laws of value that have long been hidden behind the constitutional phenomenon because there has been no proper methodology to discover them. In the author's view, constitutional law science is the unity of history and logic. Constitutional logic is the highest embodiment of human reason, because its methodology is the most effective way to solve the most complex social problems. The establishment of constitutional logic is of great significance to advancing the development of logical forms and logical laws of moral logics. (2) Making new legal interpretations of some important constitutional theory issues. For example, in light of the Draft of Legislation Law, the author analyzes the essential boundaries between constitution-making powers and legislative powers, and points out that, by ignoring constitution-making powers in the construction of the constitutional system, we will not be able to overcome the various value contradictions arising from the lack of constitution-making powers. Constitution-making powers, sovereignty, referendum and social rights are all concepts of value. They exist to solve the problem of legitimacy of the constitution and are important constitutional categories that should not be abandoned at will. In addition, the author also proposes new constitutional categories that should be emphasized in the study of constitutional theory, such as international democratic principles, international rule of law principles, constitutional responsibilities, constitutional procedures, etc.. These new constitutional categories are conducive to and play a pioneering role in the development in depth and breadth of the study of constitutional theory.

2. Papers

(1) "An Examination of 'Ought to Be' —A Field of Vision of Constitutional Logic", *Social Sciences in China*, 6(2001).

In this paper, Professor Mo puts forward for the first time his own unique views on the issue of "ought to be", which has been long debated in the legal theoretical circle, from the perspective of epistemology. He uses the method of constitutional logic to explore the connotation of "ought to be" from the perspectives of ontology, epistemology and axiology, and points out that the logical form of "ought to be" in the sense of axiology has two fields of value: certainty and uncertainty. The "ought to be" in traditional jurisprudential theory is overly influenced by the subjectivity of the subject of value judgment. Therefore, it is expressed in an uncertain logical form and it is difficult to form a proposition of "ought to be" with universal value on such a basis. The "ought to be" as a certainty manifests itself in "have to be", which is based on epistemology. "Have to be" as a kind of capacity judgment is a category that has been forgotten by traditional legal philosophy. It can avoid the excessive uncertainty of "ought to be" caused by the "hypothesis" theory and therefore should be taken as a logical criterion for the examination of the "ought to be" with minimum certainty. In this paper, Professor Mo points out that the fundamental flaw of traditional legal theory in analyzing "factual problems" and "value problems" is confusing "factual problems" with "value problems" or not being able to tell the difference between the two. In order to realize the logical transition between "factual problems" and "value problems", it is necessary to introduce the analytical method of "capacity judgment" between "fact judgment" and "value judgment" on the basis of epistemology, and achieve the unity of the three analytical methods of ontology, epistemology and axiology. Based on the logical analysis of "ought to be", the author points out that the value attribute of the constitution consists of two aspects: the constitution "ought to be" and the "ought to be" of the constitution, with each of them belonging to a different category of value. The values of democracy and human rights belong to the constitution "ought to be". They are the sources of constitutional legitimacy, rather than entirely the products of "constitutionality". On this basis, the author distinguishes between the different functions of "pre-constitutional phenomenon" and "constitutional phenomenon" in the construction of the constitutional value system, and stresses that the core value of the modern constitution is a "law on the rule of law."

(2) "On Constitutional Principles", *China Legal Science*, 4(2001).

In this paper, Professor Mo makes a new exploration of the criteria for determining constitutional principles. He believes that the function of constitutional principles lies in "opposing the phenomenon of privilege", and the constitutional system must design corresponding measures for achieving this purpose. This is the logical starting point of the construction of the constitutional system, which may lead to two different constitutional principle systems interacting as both cause and effect: "teleological constitutional principles" and "instrumental constitutional principles". "Teleological constitutional principles" require that all constitutional systems must be designed to serve "the principle against special powers", "the principle against special rights" and "the principle against special advantages". Any constitutional system that does not meet these three requirements of "teleological constitutional principles" is not a legitimate constitutional system. The "instrumental constitutional principles" require that there is at least a logical possibility of preventing various phenomena of privilege in the design of the state power system, the civil rights system, and the system of relationship between state power and civil rights. "Instrumental constitutional principles" can be designed at two levels, namely the primary constitutional principles and the auxiliary constitutional principles. Primary constitutional principles are centered on the authority of the constitution, including the principle of popular sovereignty, the principle of supremacy of the constitution, the principle of surplus power and the principle of surplus rights. Auxiliary constitutional principles are centered on the authority of the laws enacted by the legislature, including the principle of the priority of law, the principle of law reservation, the principle of constitutional authorization, the principle of administration by law, and the principle of judicial final remedy for human rights.

E A List of Important Publications

Monographs

1. *Summary of the Constitutional Trial System*, China People's Public Security University Press, November 1998.

2. *The Legal Limits of Freedom of Expression* (translated work), the People's Public Security University Press, November 1998.

3. *Constitutional Amendments: A Must Book for the Government and Citizens—A Panoramic Analysis of the Constitutional Amendments of the People's Republic of China*, China People's Public Security University Press, April 1999.

4. *The Logic Foundation of the Modern Constitution*, Law Press China, December 2001.

5. *The Extraordinary Rule of Law in the Period of SARS Outbreak*, Law Press China, June 2003.

6. *International Human Rights Conventions and China*, World Knowledge Press, September 2005.

7. *Doctrines of Constitutional Law in Practice*, China Renmin University Press, February 2007.

8. *In Defense of Legislation*, Wuhan University Press, April 2007.

9. *Doctrines of Constitutional Law*, China Social Sciences Press, October 2008.

10. *The Constitutional Basis of the Rule of Law in China*, Social Sciences Academic Press, September 2014.

11. *The Rule of Law and Institutional Building in China*, Local Records Publishing House, January 2016.

Articles

1. "Several Dialysis of Legal Acts", *Journal of the Graduate School of the Chinese Academy of Social Sciences*, 3 (1988).

2. "The Process of Legal Evaluation and Its Standards", *Journal of the Graduate School of the Chinese Academy of Social Sciences*, 6 (1989).

3. "The Meaning and Significance of Legal Behavior", *Journal of Graduate School of the Chinese Academy of Social Sciences*, 6 (1991).

4. "Analysis of the Voters' Intentional Structure of Elections", *China Legal Science*, 3 (1992).

5. "Intensify Law Enforcement Supervision and Improve the Level of Law Enforcement Supervision", *Qiushi*, 7 (1996).

6. "Governing the Country according to the Constitution as an Important Guarantee for Governing the Country according to Law", in Wang Jiafu et. al. (eds.), *Governing the Country according to Law and Building a Socialist State under the Rule of Law*, China Legal Publishing House, August 1996.

7. "Governing the Country according to the Constitution Is the Core of Governing the Country according to Law", *Law Science Magazine*, 3 (1998).

8. "On the Relationship between International Human Rights Conventions and Domestic Constitutions", *China Legal Sciences*, 3 (1999).

9. "On the New Trends in the Relationship between International Law and Domestic Law", *World Economics and Politics*, 9 (2000).

10. "On the Final Judicial Remedy for Human Rights", *Jurist*, 3 (2001).

11. "On Constitutional Principles", *China Legal Sciences*, 4 (2001).

12. "An Examination of 'Ought to Be' —A Field of Vision of Constitutional Logic", *Social Sciences in China*, 6(2001).

13. "On the Constitutional Consciousness of Citizens", *Qiushi*, 6(2002).

14. "The Right to Appeal Is the First Institutional Human Right in a Modern Society Ruled by Law", *Law Science Magazine*, 4(2002).

15. "The Obligations under the Two International Human Rights Covenants and China", *World Economics and Politics*, 8(2002).

16. "The Connotation of the Constitutional Protection of the Right to Education", *The Jurist*, 3(2003).

17. "The Status and Characteristics of China's Emergency Legislation", *Legal Forum*, 4(2003).

18. "On the Constitutional Relationship", *Chinese Journal of Law*, 1(2003).

19. "Types and Functions of Constitutional Procedures", *Tribune of Political Science and Law*, 2(2003).

20. "The Significance of the Incorporation of the System of State of Emergency into the Constitution", *The Jurist*, 4(2004).

21. "Conceptual Analysis of the Human Rights System", *Law Science Magazine*, 1(2005).

22. "Unconstitutional Subject Theory", *Law Science Magazine*, 1(2006).

23. "Study on the Applicability of the Constitution in Judicial Trials", *North Legal Sciences*, 3(2007).

24. "On the Relationship between the Constitution and Other Legal Forms", *Journal of Shanghai University of Political Science and Law*, 6(2007).

25. "The Two Thinking Approaches to the Ratification of the International Covenant on Civil and Political Rights", *Journal of Capital Normal University (Social Science Edition)*, 6(2007).

26. "The Relationship between Constitutional Law and Public Law," *Journal of Jianghan University(Social Science Edition)*, 1(2008).

27. "On the Constitutional Protection of Social Rights", *Journal of Henan Provincial Political and Legal Cadre Management College*, 3(2008).

28. "Close Attention Should Be Paid to the Obligation of Safeguarding Basic

Rights", *Legal Science*, 4(2009).

29. "On the Technical Route of Legislation", *Guangdong Social Sciences*, 4(2009).

30. "The Lack of the Theory of Constitutional Application as Seen from Article 100 of the Chinese Constitution", *Social Science Front*, 9(2009).

31. "On the Effective Relationship between the Constitution and the Basic Law", *Henan Social Sciences*, 5(2010).

32. "Discussion on the Defects of China's Legislative Supervision System", *Journal of Jiangsu Administration Institute*, 4(2010).

33. "The Development of the Concept of 'Citizen' in the Text of the Chinese Constitution", *Human Rights*, 4(2010).

34. "On the Amorality of Human Rights", *Guangdong Social Sciences*, 2(2011).

35. "On the Evolution of the Status of the Ruling Party in the Constitutional Text of China", *Law Forum*, 4(2011).

36. "Comparison of the Characteristics of Constitutional Texts of Various Nations on the Eve of the Revolution of 1911", *Chinese Journal of Law*, 5(2011).

37. "Constitutional Protection of Cultural Rights", *Legal Forum*, 1(2012).

38. "Evaluation Methods and Impacts of Constitutional Implementation", *China Legal Science*, 4(2012).

39. "How Should We Amend the Constitution?", *Tsinghua Law Review*, 6(2012).

40. "The Status and Development of Constitutional Principles in the Theoretical System of Constitutional Studies", *Law Forum*, 6(2012).

41. "The Rule of Law and a Well-off Society", *China Legal Science*, 1(2013).

42. "To Face the 'Three Challenges': the Jurisprudential Analysis of Hengyang Election Bribery Incident", *Law Review*, 2(2014).

43. "Adhering to the Party's Leadership and Governing the Country by Law", *Chinese Journal of Law*, 6(2014).

44. "Institutional Building as the Key to Ruling the Country by Constitution", *Theoretical Horizon*, 3(2015).

45. "Formation and Characteristics of Xi Jinping's Thought of Constitutional Governance", *Law Science Magazine*, 5(2016).

46. "Emphasizing Practical Effect in the Construction of Intra-Party Regulation System of the CPC", *Eastern Legal Science*, 4(2017).

47. "Attention Should Be Paid to the Study of the Nature of Supervision Power in the Reform of National Supervision System", *Academic Journal of Zhongzhou*, 10(2017).

48. "On the Construction of a Mechanism for Strengthening Constitutional Review", *Guangdong Social Sciences*, 2(2018).

49. "On the Mechanism for the Constitutional Review of Administrative Regulations", *Journal of Jiangsu Administration College*, 3(2018).

50. "On the Mechanism for the Constitutional Review of Administrative Rules", *Journal of Jianghan University(Social Science Edition)*, 3(2018).

51. "40 Years of Construction of the Constitutional Review Mechanism in China", *Journal of Beijing Union University(Social Science Edition)*, 3(2018).

52. "Taking the Constitutional Amendment as an Opportunity to Promote the Governing the Country in Accordance with the Constitution", *Journal of Northwest University(Philosophy and Social Sciences)*, 4(2018).

53. "On the Application of the Constitutional Retention Principle in the Constitutional Review", *Law and Modernization*, 5(2018).

54. "On the Mechanism for the Constitutional Review of Laws", *Law Review*, 6(2018).

55. "Theoretical Value and Practical Significance of Xi Jinping's Important Discussions on Ruling the Country by Constitution and Exercising the Ruling Power in accordance with Constitution", *Governance Modernization Studies*, 2(2019).

56. "The Jurisprudence and Stratification of Constitutional Review of Autonomous Regulations and Separate Regulations", *Gansu Social Sciences*, 2(2019).

Sun Shiyan

A Basic Information

Sun Shiyan is a research fellow and the head of the Research Department of International Human Rights Law of CASS Institute of International Law and a professor at the Graduate School of the Chinese Academy of Social Sciences.

He obtained his LL. B and LL. M from Jilin University School of Law in 1991 and 1994, respectively, and a Ph. D. from the Graduate School of Chinese Academy of Social Sciences in 1999. He was an assistant professor, lecturer and associate professor at Jilin University School of Law from 1994 to 2003 and a researcher at the Center for Jurisprudence Research of Jilin University from 2000 to 2003. He was a visiting professor at the Raoul Wallenberg Institute of Human Rights and Humanitarian Law, Lund University, from 2003 to 2004. He started to work at the (then) Center for International Law Studies of the Chinese Academy of Social Sciences in April 2004 as an associate research fellow and the head of the Research Department of Public International Law. He became a full research fellow in 2012 and transferred to the Research Department of International Human Rights Law in 2016 as the acting head (2016 - 2018) and the head (2018) of the Department.

He was a visiting scholar at the Netherlands Institute of Human Rights, Utrecht University; Columbia University School of Law, USA; Norwegian Institute of Human Rights, University of Oslo; University of Toronto Law School, Canada; and the Royal Institute of International Affairs (Chatham House), UK and other academic institutions.

He is a member of the Chinese Society of International Law and the Chinese Society for Human Rights Studies. He serves as a deputy editor-in-chief of *Chinese Review of International Law*, and a member of the editorial board of *Chinese Yearbook of International Law*, *Chinese Journal of International Law* and *International Review of the Red Cross*.

B Main Academic Ideas and Viewpoints

His main research area is international human rights law. He has published more than 30 articles in Chinese, 5 articles in English, many books as authors, editor-in-chief or translators.

His work mainly focuses on the following topics.

1. Obligations of States imposed by international human rights law. His article "On the Obligations of the State under International Human Rights Law" was the first research done by Chinese scholars on the obligations of the State under international human rights law, suggesting that international human rights law impose four obligations upon States, namely, to recognize, respect, fulfill and promote, and protect human rights. "The Extraterritorial Application of the International Covenant on Civil and Political Rights" analyzes the extraterritorial obligations of States parties to the International Covenant on Civil and Political Rights (ICCPR) based on the practice of the Human Rights Committee. "The Continuing Applicability of International Human Rights Treaties" studies the issues of denunciation and succession of international human rights treaties and the special issues regarding the applicability of the two Human Rights Covenants to Hong Kong SAR and Macao SAR. The book *The Obligations of State Parties under the International Covenant on Civil and Political Rights* published in 2012 comprehensively explores the forms, nature, scope and domestic implementation of the obligations of States Parties under the ICCPR.

2. The International Covenant on Civil and Political Rights. In addition to the study of the obligations of States parties under the ICCPR, he also published many articles on the same Covenant, including "The Understanding and Interpretation of ICCPR in the Context of China's Ratification", *Chinese Journal of International Law*, 1 (2007); "The Universality and Relativity of Human Rights—From the Perspective of the International Covenant on Civil and Political Rights"; "The International Covenant on Civil and Political Rights and Domestic Legal System—Some Preliminary Observations"; "The First Instance Jurisdiction of the Supreme People's Court over Criminal Cases: from the Perspective of Article 14(5) of the International Covenant on Civil and Political Rights". In this respect, the most noteworthy work is about the Chinese text(s) of the ICCPR, on which he published "International Covenant on Civil and Political Rights: One Covenant, Two

Chinese Texts?", *Nordic Journal of International Law*, 2 (2006) and its corresponding version in Chinese. With respect to an article implying that China should be responsible for the emergence of the unauthentic Chinese texts of the two Human Rights Covenants, he responded with "The Problems of the Chinese Texts of the International Human Rights Covenants: A Revisit", *Chinese Journal of International Law*, 4 (2016) and its corresponding version in Chinese published on *Taiwan Human Rights Journal.*

3. Death penalty. His work on the issue of death penalty from the perspective of international human rights law includes: "'The Most Serious Crimes' and Death Penalty—The Definition of Death Penalty in International Law"; "The International Trend towards the Abolition of the Death Penalty: Viewed from the Reports of the United Nations Secretary-General"; "The Publicity of the Information on the Death Penalty: The Requirements of the United Nations and Responses of China"; and "Countries with Large Populations and the Death Penalty: Viewed from the Reports of the United Nations Secretary-General", in which he showed that, while most countries with large populations have not abolished the death penalty, they are nevertheless not "big countries in terms of the death penalty" with respect to the frequency of executions, the rate of execution or the number of the persons executed.

4. Human rights education. He was one of the earliest Chinese scholars to study the issues of human rights education, especially the teaching of human rights law in universities. In this respect, he published "A Preliminary Observation of Human Rights Law Teaching at Chinese Universities" and "Human Rights Education and Research in China: The Contribution of the Raoul Wallenberg Institute" in Jonas Grimheden and Rolf Ring, eds., *Human Rights Law: From Dissemination to Application—Essays in Honor of Göran Melander*, Martinus Nijhoff, 2006; co-edited *Selected Cases of Human Rights* with Professor Li Buyun and edited *Human Rights Law Teaching at Chinese Universities: Problems and Prospects*, which has been the only book in Chinese addressing the various aspects of teaching human rights law at Chinese universities.

5. Translation of human rights works. He co-translated Manfred Nowak's

U. N. Covenant on Civil and Political Rights: CCPR Commentary, the first edition in 2003 and the revised edition in 2008, which has become one of the most frequently cited human rights books in China. He also translated and published David Kinley's *Civilizing Globalization: Human Rights and the Global Economy*, and Ben Saul, David Kinley and Jacqueline Mowbray's *The International Covenant on Economic, Social and Cultural Rights: Commentary, Cases, and Materials.*

Qu Xiangfei

A Basic Information

Qu Xiangfei is a research fellow at CASS Institute of International Law. Beginning from August 2017 she also serves as the deputy head of the Department of Rights and Interest, All-China Women's Federation. She is a member of China Law Society, and an executive member of China Society of Jurisprudence.

She obtained her Ph. D. from Law School of Shandong University and conducted post-doctoral research at the Law School of Renmin University. Before she joined CASS, she was an associate professor at Law School of Shandong University. She also was a visiting scholar at Raoul Wallenberg Institute of Human Rights and Humanitarian Law/RWI, Sweden and a visiting scholar of CCSEP at the Law

School of Victoria University, Canada. She also conducted short time research in several foreign universities and international organizations.

B Main Research Works

Her main research areas include: Human Rights Philosophy, Human Rights History in the Republic of China and International Human Rights Law. In recent years, she has paid much attention to rights of persons with disability, gender equality, right to education and right to health.

In 2014 Tsinghua University Press published her book *How Far Is Human Rights Away from Us—The Concept of Human Rights and Its Evolution in Modern China*. In this book, she discussed and probed deeply into a series of essential issues of Human Rights, emphasized the universality of human rights, analyzed the congruent relationship between the subjects and the content of human rights, and elaborated the changes and challenges human rights had gone through in modern Chinese history from late Qing Dynasty to 1949. This book has earned a good reputation in China.

She also co-authored and co-edited several books and textbooks on human rights law and jurisprudence, and published more than 40 articles on human rights in Chinese core journals.

C Main Publications

1. "Reasonable Accommodation in the Convention on the Rights of Persons with Disabilities—Benchmark of Consideration and Method of Protection", *Tribune of Political Science and Law*, 2(2016).

2. "Human Beings, Citizens and World Citizens: Evolution of Subjects of Human Rights and Institutional Safeguards of Human Rights", *Tribune of Political Science and Law*, 4(2008).

3. "On the Origin and Development of the Concept of 'Reasonable Accommodation'", *Human Rights*, 6(2015).

4. "Human Dignity and Human Rights Protection", *Human Rights*, 3(2013).

5. "The Convention on the Rights of Persons with Disabilities and the Change of Chinese Disability Model", *Study and Exploration*, 4(2014).

6. "The Convention on the Rights of Persons with Disabilities and Protection of Persons with Disabilities in China", *Law Science*, 4(2013).

7. "Approaches to Removing Constitutional Barriers to Farmers' Right of Land Development", *Law Science*, 6(2012).

8. "Reflections on the Improvement of the Procedures of Expropriation of Rural Collective Land", *Study and Exploration*, 6(2012).

9. "Analysis of Rights of Corporate Legal Persons under the US Constitution", *Global Law Review*, 4(2011).

10. "Can the Human Rights Clause of the Chinese Constitution Be Interpreted from the International Human Rights Law Perspective?", in *Human Rights and Good Governance*(Volume I), Brill Publishers, 2016.

11. "The Constitutional Analysis of the 'Reporting on Its Work' by State Organs and that by the Supervisory Committee", *Journal of Beijing University*(*Humanities and Social Sciences*), 2(2017).

12. "Characteristics of Reasonable Accommodation and Its Application in Employment in China", *Human Rights*, 2(2018).

13. "Reasonable Accommodation and Its Application in Education in China", *Human Rights*, 2(2017).

14. "The Subjects of Human Rights", co-author, *China Legal Science*, 2(2001).

15. "Interpretation of Law (Conversation by Writing)", *Chinese Journal of Law*, 2(2001).

16. "A Useful Experiment in the Reform of Legal Education System: Borrowing from the Clinic Legal Education Mode", *Journal of Shandong University*, 6(2001).

17. "A Tentative Exploration of the Right to Education", *Journal of Political Science and Law*, 3(2002).

18. "Analysis of the Equal Right to Education", *Journal of Shandong University*, 5(2003).

19. "On the Subjects of Human Rights", in *Human Rights Studies*, Vol. 1, Shandong People's Publishing Press, 2001.

20. "On the Right to Dignity", in *Human Rights Studies*, Vol. 3, Shandong People's Publishing Press, 2003.

21. "A Criticism of Liberalist View on Human Rights Subjects", in *Human Rights Studies*, Vol. 4, Shandong People's Publishing Press, 2004.

22. "Legitimacy of Human Rights and Theory of Conscience", *Journal of Literature, History and Philosophy*, 3(2005).

23. "Safeguarding the Right to Health in International Law Cases", *Study and Exploration*, 2(2008).

24. "The Concept of Human Rights in China in the End of the 19th Century and the Beginning of the 20th Century", *The Jurist*, 4(2008).

25. "A Review of Major Human Rights Theories in China During the Past Thirty Years of Reform and Opening-up", in *Human Rights Studies*, Vol. 8, Shandong People's Publishing Press, 2008.

26. "On the Universality and Subjects of Human Rights", *Journal of Literature, History and Philosophy*, 4(2009).

27. "Protection of the Right to Health in Foreign Constitutional Cases", *Seeking Truth*, 4(2009).

28. "Constitutional Safeguards for the Rights of Fetus: German and U. S. Modes", *Global Law Review*, 6(2009).

29. "Citizen's Right to Have Access to Self-Service Dialysis", *Pacific Journal*, 8(2009).

30. "Safeguards for Citizen's Constitutional Rights and Institutional Development of Democracy", *Case Study*, 4(2009).

31. "Artificial Localization of Colleges Affiliated to Ministry of Education and the Equality of Right to Education", *Law Science*, 11(2009).

32. "Human Rights Belief: Reflections on Human Rights Education", *Journal of Guangzhou University*, 1(2010).

33. "Analysis of Xiamen PX Project Incident", in Hu Jingguang (ed.), *Analysis of Typical Constitutional Cases in China*, Renmin University of China Press, 2008.

34. "Major Doctrine of Human Rights Theory in the Past Thirty Years of Re-

form and Opening up", *Human Rights*, 4(2009).

35. "Safeguarding the Life and Dignity of Persons with Intellectual and Mental Disabilities", *Journal of Henan Administrative Institute of Politics and Law*, 2 (2010).

Liu Xiaomei

A Basic Information

Professor Liu Xiaomei, Ph. D. in Law, was born in Honghu City, Hubei Province in March 1977. Currently she is a research fellow at CASS Institute of International Law, a professor and supervisor of master's students at CASS Graduate School, a professor at University of Chinese Academy of Social Sciences; and the deputy head librarian of CASS Law Library. Her other full-time and part-time positions include: Deputy Secretary General of the Constitutional Law Research Committee of China Law Society; Deputy Secretary General of the Legislative Law Research Committee of Beijing Law Society; Specially-engaged Research Fellow at Ningxia Academy of Social Sciences; expert of All-China Women's Federation Expert Bank; a member of the Lecturers Group for the Implementation of the Seventh Five-year Plan for the Popularization of Law in Beijing; and a member of the Lecturers Group for the Implementation of the Seventh Five-year Plan for the Popularization of Law in Shanxi Province.

B Research Fields

Constitutional law, legislative law and administrative law, especially the people's congress system, legislative system, the capital city system, grassroots governance, human rights theory, and history of modern constitutional thoughts in China.

C Teaching Experience

Professor Liu mainly teaches constitutional law. She has been awarded the honorary title of one of the "Top Ten Teachers" in 2014, 2015 and 2018. She has been the supervisor of seven graduate students, four of them have already received their master's degree.

D Education and Past Work Experience

- Sept. 1995 – July 1999: Bachelor of Law, Faculty of Economic Law, Zhongnan University of Economics and Law.
- Aug. 1999 – Aug. 2001: teacher, the High School Affiliated to Zhongshan University.
- Sept. 2001 – July 2017: Mater of Law and Ph. D. in Law, China University of Political Science and Law.
- Aug. 2007 – Dec. 2009: Post-doctoral researcher, CASS Law Institute.
- Dec. 2009 – now: Researcher, CASS Institute of International Law.

E Main Research Activities and Research Results

In the past ten years, Professor Liu has been mainly engaged in the research on the theoretical basis and Chinese characteristics of constitutional law and the construction of the rule of law, closely followed the development in such key areas as the reform of the supervision system and state organs, construction of legislative systems and mechanisms, construction of the rule of law in the capital, and construction of the rule of law at the grassroots level. She has published four monographs and over 20 academic articles in these areas. She has also paid close attention to the practical issues relating to the construction of the rule of law in China, actively organized or participated in many state and provincial-level research projects and research projects sponsored by various state organs, conducted deep-going investigations on the rule of law practice, and written over 30 research reports and internal reports on related issues.

1. She has led or participated in numerous research projects, including the followings.

(1) Professor Liu Xiaomei has been in charge of two National Social Science Fund Projects: "Studies on the Mechanism for Citizens' Participation in Community Governance and Its Rule of Law Safeguards" (2010) and "Investigation on the Development of 100 Counties during the 40 Years since the Reform and Opening-up: the Tongzhou Project" (2018). The 2018 project was rated as excellent project and its result—the Research Report on High-Level Construction of City Sub-Center—is published in the book *Reform and Opening-up and the County-level Development in China: Part 1* (Social Sciences Academic Press, 2018).

(2) Ten other projects Led by Professor Liu Xiaomei

• "Studies on the Construction of Intelligent Court by the Administrative Trial Center of Shenzhen City", a research project commissioned by Yantian Court of Shenzhen City, 2019.

• "Studies on Index of Law-based Work Involving Complaints by Letters and Visits", a research project commissioned by the Office of Complaints by Letters and Visits of the Government of Beijing Municipality, 2018.

• "Post-legislative Assessment on Energy Conservation Regulations for State-funded Institutions", a project jointly commissioned by the Ministry of Justice and State Administration of Land and Resource, 2018.

• "Legislative Safeguard for the Determination and Realization of the Functions of the Capital", a research project sponsored by the State Governance Think Tank of CASS, 2018.

• "Studies on the Legislative Safeguarding of the Realization of the Functions of the Capital", a project sponsored by Beijing Law Society, 2017.

• "Studies on Legal Issues Relating to the Election at the Expiration of Terms of Office", a research project commissioned by the Party Committee of Shifang City, Sichuan Province, 2016.

• "Studies on Issues Relating to the Legislation on the Capital against the Background of Coordinated Development of Beijing-Tianjin-Hebei Region", a research project sponsored by Beijing Law Society, 2016.

• "Rule of Law Safeguards for the Grassroots Democratic Self-Governance", a research project sponsored by Beijing Law Society, 2015.

• "Studies on the Rule of Law Safeguard for the Realization of the Core Functions of the Capital", a research project commissioned by the Legislative Affairs Office of the Government of Beijing Municipality, 2014.

• "Studies on the Rule of Law Safeguard for Citizens' Participation in Public Affairs in Urban Communities", a research project funded by Youth Research Initiation Fund of CASS, 2010.

(3) She has also participated in over 20 other research projects. She was the person in charge of two sub-projects of major projects funded by the National Social Science Foundation: "The Organic Unity of Party's Leadership, the People Being Masters of the Country and Ruling the Country by Law" (2007) and "Folk Norms and Local Legislation" (2017) and three sub-projects under the CASS Project on the Investigation of National Conditions and other key projects of CASS: "Studies on Local Rule of Law" (2017); "Ruling the Country by Law and the Modernization of State Governance" (2017) and "Studies on the Integrated Construction of a Law-based State, a Law-based Government and a Law-based Society" (2018).

2. She has closely followed the practical problems and hot issues in the construction of the rule of law, carried out timely application and countermeasure studies, written nearly 20 internal reports, won one first prize (2016) and three third prizes (in 2016 and 2017) for excellent countermeasures proposals awarded by CASS; published two theoretical articles in the *People's Daily*. One of them, "the Chinese Road to a Strong Law-based State", was awarded the prize for excellent theoretical article by the Publicity Department of the Central Committee of the CPC; and written over a dozen research reports. One of which, entitle "Making the Civil Administration Index System More Scientific and Modernizing the State

Governance Capacity"(2015) won the third national prize for excellent research results in the field of civil administration policy.

3. She has paid special attention to the research on basic theories and so far, has published four monographs, two co-authored books, over 20 academic articles, and more than a dozen research reports. Her representative works include "Studies on Issues Relating to the Legislation on the Capital City against the Background of Coordinated Development of Beijing-Tianjin-Hebei Region", "The Rule of Law Dimension of Grassroots Self-governance", "Research Report on the Provincial-Level Local Legislation", "The State Supervision System and Mechanisms under the People's Congress System" and "Promoting the Building of a Community with Shared Future for Mankind through the Development of Human Rights", etc..

F Main Research Fields and Academic Viewpoints

1. Professor Liu has closely followed the development of the legislative system and practice in China, and carried out theoretical and empirical researches at the macroscopic, mesoscopic and microscopic levels of such issues as state legislative systems and mechanisms, provincial legislative practices, special legislation and the legislative safeguards for the construction of the rule of law at the grassroots level.

In the annual reports on legislation published in the Blue Book on the Rule of Law in China and the article "Legislative Reform and the Construction of the System of Law", she summarizes the achievements made, experiences gained and problems encountered by China in the construction of the rule of law during the 40 years of reform and opening-up, especially in recent years. In her monograph "Research Report on the Provincial-Level Local Legislation", she summarizes the general rules and characteristics of provincial-level local legislation on the basis of the big data analysis of 5637 pieces of provincial-level local legislation, and analyzes the dual function of provincial-level local legislation of implementing state laws and adopting local regulations and mechanisms for its realization under the "unified and hierarchical" legislative system.

In her monograph "The Rule of Law Dimension of Grassroots Self-governance", she reviews and studies the legal system of grassroots democracy and grassroots self-governance and holds that the current urban-rural dual electoral pattern created by the constitution, local organic laws and the organic laws of villagers' and residents' committees has very limited "spillover effect" on the construction of democratic political system in the country, whereas grassroots participation and grassroots self-governance have a greater role to play and therefore it is especially important to strengthen the research on and construction of the state and folk laws in this area.

Law on the capital city is a new research area. Since 2014, she has led four research projects relating to the law on the capital city commissioned by the Legislative Affairs Office of the Government of Beijing Municipality, Beijing Law Society and other organizations, and published the think tank Report "Studies on Issues Relating to the Legislation on the Capital City against the Background of Coordinated Development of Beijing-Tianjin-Hebei Region", and two research reports and two articles in Annual Reports from Research Projects Sponsored by Beijing Law Society (2017), Post-doctoral Symposium (2017), Reform and Opening-up and the County-level Development in China: Part Ⅰ (2018), and BFSU Legal Science (2019). In these reports, she defines the connotation of capital city and capital functions and puts forward proposals on the construction of corresponding power-responsibility relations and legal systems. Moreover, she has also carried out researches on such topics as intra-Party regulations, local environmental legislation, and embodiment of core values in legislation, and submitted many internal reports—some proposals in these reports have been adopted by Party or state leaders.

2. Professor Liu has also engaged in theoretical researches on the people's congress system and the system of representative government. To teach graduate course on "the people's congress system and the election system", she has carried out thorough researches on theories of representative government and on historical materials on the people's congress system, and have achieved some preliminary results in the research in these two areas. In her article "State Supervisory System and Mechanisms under the People's Congress System", she analyzes the dual supervision system that consists of the supervision over state organs and the supervi-

sion over civil servants from the perspective of the people's congress system and the theory of representative government, and puts forward the opinion that the supervision over supervisory committees by people's congresses should not take the form of simple work reporting. Instead, China should adopt a system whereby a supervisory committee reports their specific work to the standing committee of the people's congress at the same level, while at the same time continuously enriching and innovating the mode of supervision by adopting different supervisory mechanisms.

G Introductions to Representative Works

1. *The Rule of Law Dimension of Grassroots Self-Governance*, China Social Sciences Press, 2018.

Democracy is not only a value concept, but more importantly, also a political practice: it is only through the practice of democratic politics can we know what kind of democratic politics can be developed in Chinese society and how to further improve the existing democratic political system. This book, by looking back at history, observing the current reality, and analyzing the relevant theories, puts forward the following original suggestions on the research of grassroots governance: (1) Analyzing "the spillover effect" of urban-rural grassroots self-governance on democracy and its mode and scope of action on the basis of the "upward and downward" two-way approach to the construction of democratic politics, the "upward and downward" two-way promotion of grassroots governance, the mutual development of electoral democracy and participatory democracy and the dual pattern of rural villagers' self-governance and urban residents' self-governance. (2) Taking community participation as the test field and training ground for participatory democracy, carrying out empirical study and analysis of the sense of political efficacy of community participation. (3) Transcending the limitation of simple "rule of law safeguard" in research perspective and analyzing the multiple rule-of-law dimensions of grassroots governance system, namely: grassroots governance needs to be effectively safeguarded by the construction of the rule of law in the country while at the same time directly contributing to and promoting the construction of the rule of law in the country; it is the most important field of the construction of law-based society while at the same time providing solid basis and key elements for the construction of a law-based state and a law-based government; and it is subject to both the hard regulation by state laws and the soft constraint by such civil-society norms as village rules and folk laws. (4) Thoroughly reviewing the current laws and policies on grassroots self-governance, and putting forward concrete suggestions on improving the legal system of self-governance. This book expands the research horizon of and enriches the research results on grassroots democracy and social governance innovation.

2. "State Supervision System and Mechanisms under the People's Congress System", *Tribune of Political Science and Law*, 3(2018).

This article holds that, under the people's congress system and the principle governing the activities of state institutions, namely democratic centralism, the supervisory power performs the important modern governance function of "restraining power with power". The reform of the supervisory system, by integrating supervisory powers and reconstituting the state supervisory system and the constitutional power structure, has developed a dual supervisory system under the people's congress system in which the supervision over state organs and supervision over civil servants interlink and coordinate with each other while at the same time overlap and restrain each other. Under the "dual" supervisory system and the system of part-time deputies to people's congresses, the supervision over supervisory committees by people's congresses should not take the form of simple work reporting by supervisory committees to people's congresses. Instead, China should adopt a system whereby a supervisory committee submits special work reports to the standing committee of the people's congress at the same level, while at the same time continuously enriching and innovating the mode of supervision by adopting different supervision mechanisms. This article carries out insightful analysis of the reasonable mode of supervision over supervisory committees by people's congresses and their standing committees from the perspectives of the theory of representative government and the principle of democratic centralism, which is of important theoretical significance and reference value to the improvement of the state supervisory system and the people's congress system in China.

3. "Promoting the Building of a Community with Shared Future for Mankind through the Development of Human Rights", *Chinese Review of International Law*, 3(2018).

Since 2017, the idea of "building a community with shared future for mankind" has been written into the Report to the Nineteenth National Congress of the CPC, the Constitution of the CPC, the Preamble of the Chinese Constitution, as well as the resolutions of UN General Assembly, UN Security Council and UN Human Rights Council, thereby establishing the "big power diplomatic strategy" and highlighting the great contribution made by China to global governance. The concept, the connotation and the thought of "building a community with shared future for mankind" have been gradually developed by the CPC since its Eighteenth National Congress. However, the ideological resources and the practice of international cooperation go back to ancient times. The originality of this article lies in the following two aspects: firstly, it traces the ideological sources of "building a community with shared future for mankind" back to the common ideological resources of mankind, such as the Confucian idea of "the Great Harmony" in ancient China, the idea of city-state community in ancient Greece, the European theory of Utopian Socialism, the Kantian theory of cosmopolitanism, and the idea of "a community of free individuals" put forward by Karl Marx and Friedrich Engels in the Communist Manifesto, and reviews the effective practices and limitations of UN and regional human rights bodies and human rights protection systems established after the World War Ⅱ in protecting fundamental human rights, upholding world peace and constructing the post-war world order. Secondly, it points out that "building a community with shared future for mankind" also takes the joint creation of a better future for mankind as the basic objective and guaranteeing the full realization of human rights as the value basis and concrete approach. More specifically, it means taking the right of existence, the right to development and the right to pursue happiness as the primary human rights and promoting the development of the human rights cause in a new era and the establishment a more attainable, fairer and more just new world order.

H A List of Main Academic Achievements

Monographs

1. *The Rule of Law Dimension of Grassroots Self-Governance*, China Social Sciences Press, 2018.

2. *Studies on Issues Relating to the Legislation on the Capital City against the Background of Coordinated Development of Beijing-Tianjin-Hebei Region*, China Social Sciences Press, 2017.

3. *Research Report on Provincial-level Local Legislation: the Realization of the Dual Function of Local Legislation*, China Social Science Press, 2016.

4. *Introduction to Studies on Complaints by Letters and Visits*, co-author, China Democracy and Law Press China, 2012.

5. *The Rule of Law Textbook for Leading Cadres*, co-author, Party Building Books Publishing House, 2016.

6. *Theory and Practice of "the Overall View on Rule of Law Publicity and Education"*, co-author, Social Sciences Press, 2016.

Articles

1. "Institutional Reform and the Innovation of the Organizational Law System", *Journal of Northwest University (Philosophy and Social Sciences Edition)*, 3 (2019).

2. "Studies on the Functional Positioning of Beijing City Sub-Center and Its Legislative Safeguards", *BFSU Legal Science*, 1 (2019).

3. "State Supervision System and Mechanisms under the People's Congress System", *Tribune of Political Science and Law*, 3 (2018).

4. "Promoting the Building of a Community with Shared Future for Mankind through the Development of the Human Rights", *Chinese Review of International Law*, 3 (2018).

5. "Seeking the Positive Interaction between Online Public Opinions and Judicial Trial" (the second author), *People's Tribune*, 3 (2018).

6. "Legislative Reform and the Construction of the System of Law", in *The Rule of Law in China* (1978 – 2018), Social Sciences Academic Press, October 2018.

7. "A Brief Introduction to Foreign Legislation on Capital Cities and Capital Circles", in *Creating a New Situation of the Construction of the Rule of Law in China* (*The Sixth of Post-doctoral Symposium*), China Social Sciences Press, February 2018.

8. "Embodying the Requirements of Scientific, Democratic and Law-based Legislation", *China Discipline Inspection and Supervision Daily*, March 17, 2018.

9. "The CPC's Leadership Is the Most Essential Characteristic of Socialism with Chinese Characteristics", *China Discipline Inspection and Supervision Daily*, March 21, 2018.

10. "Providing Effective Constitutional Safeguards for the Great Rejuvenation of the Chinese Nation", *China Discipline Inspection and Supervision Daily*, March 28, 2018.

11. "Following the Chinese Road with More Consciousness and Self-Confidence", *People's Daily*, August 27, 2017.

12. "Spectacular Achievements Made by China in the Establishment of the New Internet + Party Building Mode" (the second author), *People's Tribune*, 1 (2017).

13. "Analysis of Xi Jinping's Thought on China's Road to the Rule of Law", *Legal Science Magazine*, 5 (2016).

14. "The National Security Law Fully Embodies the Principle of Human Rights Protection", *People · Rule of Law*, 8 (2016).

15. "The Chinese Road to a Strong Law-based State" (the second author), *People's Daily*, October 26, 2015.

16. "Human Rights Must Be Fully Respected and Safeguarded in Upholding National Security", *Guangming Daily*, July 18, 2015.

17. "Characteristics of the System of Judicial Safeguarding of Human Rights and Related Measures in China", *Journal of Law Application*, 11 (2014).

18. "The Fourth Plenary Session of the Eighteenth CPC Central Committee in the Eyes of Foreign Experts", *Guangming Daily*, November 10, 2014.

19. "Reflections on the Mechanism for Urban Community Participation", *Journal of Heilongjiang Administrative Cadre College of Politics and Law*, 5 (2014).

20. "A Preliminary Analysis of the Theory of Public Participation in Urban Community Governance", in *Ruling the Country by Law and Modernization of State Governance* (*The Fifth Post-Doctoral Symposium*), China Social Sciences Press, October 2014.

21. "The Formation and Evolution of Rights Outlook in Modern Chinese History", in *China Democracy Review*, Vol. 2, China Social Sciences Press, November 2013.

22. "Comparison of the Legislative Power of Representative Institutions in China and UK: an Examination from the Perspective of Democracy and the Rule of Law", in *New Understanding of the Rule of Law: a Comparative Study*, Social Sciences Academic Press, May 2011.

23. "On 'Being People-oriented' and Emergency Response" (the second author), *Legal System and Economy*, 2(2010).

24. "A Law-based Approaches to Citizens' Participation in Urban Community Governance", in *Studies on Constitutional Law*, Vol. 11, Heilongjiang University Press, 2010.

25. "Analysis of the Channels of Legislative Participation by Citizens in Urban Communities", *Law Science Magazine*, 10(2009).

26. "The Rhetoric of Constitutional Law: the Changing Status of the Citizen and Its Mode of Expression", *Journal of Jishou University* (*Social Sciences*), 5 (2009).

27. "Channels and Procedures of Legislative Participation by Citizens in Communities", in *Public Participation in the Legislative Process*, China Social Sciences Press, October 2009.

28. "The Rights Attribute of the Freedom of the Press", in *Studies in Constitutional Law* (Vol. 10), Sichuan University Press, August 2009.

29. "The Dilemma of Constitutional Values behind the 'Basic Law' System" (the second author), in *Chinese Yearbook of Constitutional Law* (2008), Law Press China, August 2009.

30. "The Relationship between the Individual and the Collective from the Confucian Perspective", *Post-doctoral Communication*, 1(2009).

31. "Studies on Major Theoretical and Practical Issues in the Legislation on the Safeguarding of Human Rights", *Academic Trends*, 25(2008).

32. "Studies on the Conflicts between Laws, Administrative Regulations and the Constitution"(the second author), in *Case Law Studies*(*Vol.* 1), The Masses Publishing House, December 2008.

33. "Theoretical Reflections on Citizens' Participation in Administrative Legislation", *Administrative Law Review*, 2(2007).

Research Reports

1. "Chinese Legislation in 2018", in *The Blue Book of the Rule of Law* (2018), Social Sciences Academic Press, February 2019.

2. "High-level Construction of City Sub-Centers", in *Reform and Opening-up and the County-level Development in China*: *Part* 1, Social Sciences Academic Press, December 2018.

3. "Chinese Legislation in 2017", in *The Blue Book of the Rule of Law* (2017), Social Sciences Academic Press, March 2018.

4. "Chinese Legislation in 2016", in *The Blue Book of the Rule of Law* (2016), Social Sciences Academic Press, March 2017.

5. "Chinese Legislation in 2014", in *The Blue Book of the Rule of Law* (2014), Social Sciences Academic Press, March 2015.

6. "Chinese Legislation in 2013", in *The Blue Book of the Rule of Law* (2013), Social Sciences Academic Press, March 2014.

7. "Strengthening and Perfecting the Legislation Made by People's Congresses and Improving the Quality of Legislation", in *Local Experiences of Construction of the Rule of Law in China*: *The Guangdong Sample*, Social Sciences Academic Press, September 2015.

8. "The Enrichment of the Connotation of the Disciplinary Inspection Work by the Constitution of CPC Adopted at the Sixteenth Party Congress", in *The Discipline in the Constitution of CPC*, Founder Press, July 2015.

9. "Government Legislation and the Regulation of Normative Documents", in *The Guangdong Experience in the Construction of a Law-based Government*, Social Sciences Academic Press, July 2014.

10. "Innovations on the People's Congress System in Guangdong Province", in *The Guangdong Experience in Promoting Reform and Opening-up by the Rule of Law*, Social Sciences Academic Press, November 2012.

Dai Ruijun

A Basic Information

Dr. Dai Ruijun is an associate research fellow at the Institute of International Law, Chinese Academy of Social Sciences (CASS); and associate professor and a supervisor of graduate students at the CASS Graduate School.

She obtained her LL. B from Beijing Jiaotong University in 2003, and her LL. M and Ph. D. from CASS Graduate School in 2006 and 2009, respectively. She was a visiting scholar at the Law School of Columbia University, USA; a visiting professor at the Law School of Helsinki University, Finland; and a visiting scholar at the Law Faculty of Oxford University, UK. She joined the Center for International Law Studies of CASS (predecessor of Institute of International Law of CASS) in 2006, and was transferred from the Research Department of Public International Law to the Research Department of International Human Rights Law in 2009. Since 2015, she has been a supervisor of master's students at CASS Graduate School, supervising graduate students in the field of public international law and international human rights law.

Dai Ruijun is a member of the Chinese Society of International Law and a member of the Research Society of Hong Kong Basic Law and Macau Basic Law. She serves as the Secretary-General of the Center for Gender and Law Studies of CASS Law Institute. She has been selected as one of the "100 Law Talents" by Beijing Society of Law, appointed as an expert on the development of women and children during the 13th Five-Year Plan Period of Beijing.

B Main Research Fields and Academic Viewpoints

Her main research areas are public international law and international human rights law, with focus on such issues as the relationship between international law and municipal law, the law of treaties, the basic theory and monitoring mechanism of international human rights law, gender equality and women's human rights, and the power of external affairs of Special Administrative Region. She has been the person in charge of the National Social Sciences Fund Project "Analysis of the status of international treaties in Chinese legal system and research on related institutional designs", the CASS key project "Domestic application of international human rights treaties", and the Basic Law project of Standing Committee of NPC "Power of External Affairs of the Special Administrative Region". She has published one academic monograph, one co-authored monograph, and nearly 30 academic articles.

She has travelled worldwide, and presented her papers on several influential international academic conferences such as the World Conference on Constitutional Law and the Biennial Conference of the Asian Society of International Law. She has actively participated in several legislative consultations, and submitted advisory opinions and suggestions on the draft State Reports of China under UN human rights treaties.

Her work mainly focuses on the following topics.

Monitoring Mechanism of International Human Rights Law. She has published a series of articles, such as "Reform of the Monitoring Mechanism for UN Human Rights Treaties" (2009), "Sovereignty, Human Rights and China: from the Perspective of UN Human Rights Protection Mechanism and Its Reform" (2012), "Strengthening UN Human Rights Treaty Body System: Latest Development of UN Human Rights Protection System" (2013) and "Follow-up Procedure for UN Human Rights Monitoring Mechanisms" (2014), tracking the reform process and effectiveness of the United Nations' Charter-based mechanism and treaty-based mechanism for human rights protection, and pointing out the contradiction between the motive of international human rights bodies to strengthen international human rights mechanism and their shortage of resources and backlog of work. She argued that the fundamental way out of the dilemma of international human rights mechanism is the improvement of domestic human rights protection system.

Relationship between International Law and Municipal Law. The paper "Taking International Law Seriously: An Empirical Investigation Based on Constitutional Texts of All Asian States" demonstrated a clear tendency among Asian constitutions: most countries choose to make definite commitment to their international obligations; and give primacy to international law, especially international human rights law, over national law. It provides positive reference for China to answer the question of the relationship between international law and domestic law in its constitution. The monograph *Domestic Implementation of International Human Rights Treaties: a Global Perspective* (Social Sciences Academic Press, 2013) proves the interaction between the acceptance of international human rights standards and domestic constitutional, legislative, judicial and administrative guarantees for human rights. "Impetus from International human rights Law for the Evolution of Fundamental Rights System" (2015) focuses on the evolvement of fundamental constitutional rights system, and illustrates the obvious impact of international human rights law on the evolution process of constitutions.

Special Administrative Region's Power of External Affairs. The core issue of the external affairs' power of SAR is the conclusion and application of international treaties. The article "Conclusion and Application of International Treaties in Special Administrative Regions of China" comprehensively analyzes the theoretical and practical issues relating to the concluding procedures, responsibility, scope of application, approaches to application and the legal status of international treaties in SAR. In light of the misunderstandings of some country about the SAR's external affairs, the article "Application of Bilateral Treaties Concluded by China in the Special Administrative Region: Comments on *Sanum v. Laos* Appeal Judgment" refutes the appeal judgment made by Singapore Supreme Court. Meanwhile, it points out that it is necessary for China to solve as soon as possible the problem of the third-party effect of the arrangement of SAR's external affairs.

Gender Equality and Women's Human Rights. Her works in this field include: "Promoting Domestic Implementation of CEDAW in China" (2007), "International Monitoring Mechanisms for Women's Social Rights" (2013), and "Who Pay the Bills for Women's Housework: Analysis from the Perspective of International Human Rights Law" (2014). Her translation of Freeman, Chinkin and Rudolf's work *The UN Convention on the Elimination of All Forms of Discrimination against Women: A Commentary* will be published in 2019 by Social Sciences Academic Press.

Zhong Ruihua

Dr. Zhong Ruihua is an assistant research fellow at the Department of International Human Rights Law, Institute of International Law of the Chinese Academy of Social Sciences(CASS).

She obtained her LL. B and LL. M from the China University of Political Science and Law in 1997 and 2000, respectively, and her Ph. D. from the Graduate School of Chinese Academy of Social Sciences in 2005. She started to work at the (then) Center for International Law Studies of the Chinese Academy of Social Sciences in 2005. She was a visiting scholar at Emory University School of Law and the University of California, Santa Barbara. Her main research areas are the study of law and religion, and consumer law. She has published more than 10 articles in Chinese and several books as authors or translators.

Introduction to the Editorial Department of *Chinese Review of International Law*

Ⅰ Overview

The Editorial Department of the bi-monthly law journal *Chinese Review of International Law* (the *Review*) is a subordinate department of the Institute of International Law of the Chinese Academy of Social Sciences (CASS). It was formally established in June 2012. The current Editor-in-Chief of the *Review* is Prof. Mo Jihong, Director of CASS Institute of International Law, and the Deputy Editors-in-Chief are Prof. Liu Huawen and Prof. Sun Shiyan.

Prof. Liu Huawen is the head of the Editorial Department and Associate Prof. Li Xixia is the deputy head of the Editorial Department. There are four members at the Editorial Department, namely, Prof. Liu Huawen, Associate Prof. Li Xixia, Assistant Prof. Luo Huanxin, and Assistant Prof. He Tiantian. In addition, Prof. Qu Xiangfei from the Department of International Human Rights Law, Associate Prof. Li Qingming from the Department of Private International Law, and Associate Prof. Hao Luyi from the Department of Public International Law are part-time editors of the *Review*.

The Editorial Department is responsible for realizing the purpose of the *Review* in compliance with relevant state policies and rules, strictly controlling the quality of the journal in the process of editing, proofreading, reviewing, etc., and establishing the journal's distinctive academic brand and the high reputation of CASS Institute of International Law. The purpose of the *Review Law* is to conduct in-depth, comprehensive and accurate research of international law; to reflect the latest developments and research results of the international legal theory and legal system at home and in the international society, and to create a high-end academic platform in the field of international law.

Ⅱ Creation of the *Review* and the Establishment of the Editorial Department

CASS Institute of International Law is a research institution specializing in international law. Its predecessor was the CASS Center for International Law Studies (October 2002 to September 2009), the International Law Department of CASS Institute of Law (September 1978 to September 2002) and the International Law Group (1959 – August 1978). The *Review* was first established as a book series published by CASS Center for International Law Studies. Its development and evolution results from the efforts of the Editorial Department of the *Review*.

Since the Institute of International Law became an independent institute under the Chinese Academy of Social Sciences in October 2002, it had made preparations to establish a new international law journal for original academic papers and to change the situation of lack of international law journal in Mainland China. In August 2006, the Center for International Law Studies established the *Review* as a book series and officially published the first volume, covering such fields as public international law, international economic law and private international law. Since then, until the approval of the publication of the *Review* as a journal in 2013 by the national authority, a total of 9 volumes of *Chinese Review of International Law* were published in 8 years, the executive editors-in-chief for these volumes are as follows: Shen Juan for Volume 1, Volume 5 and Volume 9, Sun Shiyan for Volumes 2, 6, and 7, Huang Dongli for Volumes 3 and 8, and Zhao Jianwen for Volume 4. The painstaking efforts of successive editors-in-chief and the editorial staff have accumulated valuable experiences for the development of *Chinese Review of International Law*.

In 2011, the Institute of International Law was approved as an innovative unit under the Innovation Project of the Chinese Academy of Social Sciences. Under this Project, *the Chinese Review of International Law* received special funding. With the strong support of the leadership from both the Institute and the CASS, in December 2013, the State Administration of Press, Publication, Radio, Film and Television officially approved the creation of the *Chinese Review of International Law* as a bi-monthly Chinese journal—6 issues a year, and each issue is published on the 15th of the odd-numbered month.

Ⅲ Works and Achievements of the Editorial Department

Since the publication of the journal, the Editorial Department has, under the guidance of the two levels of leadership, adhered to the governmental guidance, abided by the Copyright Law of the People's Republic of China, strictly followed the discipline of the journal, and successfully conducted the editorial work. Since the publication of the first issue of the *Chinese Review of International Law* in May 2014, it has been published on a bi-monthly basis. The *Review* has gained a good reputation in the field of international law and practice, and established itself as a rigorous, professional and in-depth academic journal brand:

1. Keeping high standards and quality

As the first original journal of international law in Chinese, the Editorial Department takes a professional, strict and prudent attitude towards the selection of papers and the editing work. To strictly abide by the rules on running the journal and upholding the image of the journal, it adheres to the anonymous review system, the three-review and three-proofreading system, the editor responsibility system and the collective review system. Authoritative experts are invited to participate in the review of manuscripts. In addition to the content of articles, the editors repeatedly check the format, concepts, terms and punctuation of each article, so as to lead the standardization of international law research, and advocate excellence in academics.

2. Reflecting representative studies in the field of international law

In editing this professional journal of international law, the Editorial Department pays special attention to the professional coverage and academic representation of the articles published. Taking the 6 issues published in 2017 as an example, they contain a total of 47 papers in the field of international law, including 26 in the field of public international law, 11 in the field of international economic law, and 10 in the field of private international law. The proportion is respectively 55%, 24% and 21%. Among the 26 papers in the field of public international law, 6 reflect China's propositions and Chinese scholars' views on hot issues in the field of human rights, 5 in the field of ocean law, 4 in the field of international humanitarian law, and 4 in the field of international criminal law. The 11 papers in the field of international economic law highlight China's "Belt and Road" Initiative, and international commercial arbitration and foreign investment in China. The 10 papers in the field of private international law are not limited to pure theoretical discussion, but also highlight the practical issues in foreign-related (international) civil and commercial litigation. By the end of 2017, the 47 articles published in the *Review* had about 1.23 million Chinese characters.

3. Setting up special columns to reflect the latest developments in the field of international law

The Editorial Department has successively set a series of columns to highlight the latest development in the frontiers of the international law and respond to the new theoretical and practical issues of international law.

For example, the special column "Experts' Review of the South China Sea Arbitration" was established in the second issue of 2016. At that time, the South China Sea Arbitration instituted unilaterally by the Philippines was at the stage of arbitrational review before the so-called award was made. It was a hot spot of international and domestic concern and an important theoretical and practical issue in international law. Three papers were published under this column in the second issue of 2016, and four were published in the third issue of 2016. Written by experts from academic and practical departments, they were the first series of papers in China to authoritatively and professionally interpret the South China Sea arbitration. Many articles in the column have been highly valued by the Ministry of Foreign Affairs and the State Oceanic Administration, and they have been promoted as the voice of Chinese international law scholars. A number of papers published in the column were included in the Special Issue of the Chinese Yearbook of International Law on the Jurisdiction of the South China Sea Arbitration Case published by the China Society of International Law. This column brings a good reputation to the *Review*.

Similarly, the *Review* has also launched the "International Human Rights Law Column" (No. 1, 2017), "Column on Victims' Participation in the International Criminal Court" (Nos. 2 to 4, 2017), "Commemorating the 40th Anniversary of the 1977 Additional Protocols to the 1949 Geneva Conventions" (No. 4, 2017), and "the Implementation of the 'Belt and Road' Initiative and the International Law" (No. 5, 2017).

In addition, the Editorial Department has published a series of papers that combine international law theory with Marxist theory. The papers in this area include: "On the Formulation of China's Judicial Participation in International Economic Rules" (No. 1, 2016), "The Socialist Outlook on Human Rights with Chinese Characteristics: Interpretation of the Letter of Congratulations from Xi Jinping to the '2015 Beijing Human Rights Forum'" (No. 5, 2016), "Principles and Paths of International Law for the Construction of a Community with Shared Future for Mankind" (No. 6, 2016), and "the Idea of a Community with Shared Future for Mankind and Its Theoretical Innovation on International Law: Comparative Analysis of Obligations *erga omnes*" (No. 2, 2018) and so on.

4. Gaining recognition and reputation

With the active efforts of colleagues in the Editorial Department, *Chinese Review of International Law* was selected as a statistical source journal by the 2017 "China Academic Journal Impact Factors Annual Report" after a comprehensive evaluation of many academic indicators. Its rank in "the Academic Journal Impact Factor Annual Report (Humanities and Social Sciences, 2017, published by China Knowledge Network, CNKI China)" is 38 out of 94. On November 16, 2018, *Chinese Review of International Law* was selected as "the core journal in Chinese humanities and social science journals based up the new comprehensive evaluation of AMI".

The articles published in the *Review* have achieved high reprintability and recognition in authoritative professional reprints. As of March 2018, the Renmin University's leading academic digest journal *International Law* had reprinted 46 papers from the *Chinese Review of International Law*. Another Chinese leading academic digest journal *China Social Science Abstracts* reprinted 6 articles. The Chinese national popular digest journal *Xinhua Digest* reprinted 2 papers.

In the "Reprinted Index Ranking and Analysis Report of 2017" issued in March 2018 and the "Report on the Development of Journals of Important Reprinted Sources of Newspapers and Periodicals" (2017 edition), the result of the *Chinese Review of International Law* in the "Legal Journal Ranking" is as follows: 21st in the number of full-text printed papers (11 papers), 15th (22%) in full-text reprint rate ranking indicator, and 18th in the comprehensive index ranking indicator (composite index 0.489706). The *Chinese Review of International Law* continues to be selected as a source of important reprint journals.

5. Making use of social media to promote publicity and exert influence

In order to publicize the *Chinese Review of International Law*, the Editorial Department participates in many academic conferences and other academic activities, and keeps pace with the times by making good use of various modern data bases and social media platforms.

On January 21, 2014, a microblog named the *Chinese Review of International Law* and registered on the Sina microblog platform was officially certificated. Since the beginning of May 2014, the full text of the papers of each issue of the *Review* has been promoted in the *China Law Network*, and has also been launched online by the Chinese Academy of Social Sciences Library on the *China National Knowledge Infrastructure* (CNKI). *China Social Science Network* and *China-foreign Jurisprudence Service Platform* (WELLS) have also reprinted the catalogue of the *Chinese Review of International Law* and some of its papers several times; *China Law Innovation Network* of the China Law Society publishes the abstracts of the articles in each issue of *Chinese Review of International Law*.

In April 2016, CASS Institute of International Law reached an agreement on the use of works with the National Philosophy and Social Science Academic Journal Database. In the same month, the WeChat subscription user named *Chinese Review of International Law* was opened. The official website of the Editorial Department also began to operate in full in 2017.

Ⅳ Academic Activities Organized by the Editorial Department

The Editorial Department has also organized seminars and colloquia to promote academic exchanges and thematic studies. The followings are some of these meetings.

1. The Colloquium on the Journal of *Chinese Review of International Law*

On February 26, 2014, the Colloquium on the Journal of *Chinese Review of International Law*, hosted by CASS Institute of International Law, was held in Beijing. The colloquium was attended by leaders from the Department of Treaty and Law and the Department of Boundary and Ocean Affairs of the Ministry of Foreign Affairs, the Oceanic Development Strategy Institute of the State Oceanic Administration, and other government organs, scholars from such academic organizations as China Society of International Law, China International Economic Law Society, Peking University, Renmin University of China, Beijing Normal University, University of International Business and Economics, China Foreign Affairs University, Xiamen University, as well as editors from such Chinese law journals as *China Legal Science*, *Chinese Journal of Law*, and *Global Law Review*. At the colloquium, the participants discussed the question of how to promote the work and the development of *Chinese Review of International Law*.

2. The Seminar on "Implementing the Spirits of the 19th CPC National Congress and Promoting the Prosperity of International Law in China"

On November 4, 2017, the Editorial Department of the Review held a seminar on "Implementing the Spirit of the 19th CPC National Congress and Promoting the Prosperity of International Law in China". The seminar was attended by experts from the Ministry of Foreign Affairs, the Ministry of National Defense, and the Ministry of Environmental Protection, scholars from University of International Relations, Xiamen University, Peking University, China Foreign Affairs University, China University of Political Science and Law, Beijing Institute of Technology, Dalian Maritime University, Ningxia University, and Wuhan University, as well as editors for the *Chinese Yearbook of International Law*, *Journal of Comparative Law*, *Political and Law Forum*, *Boundary and Ocean Research Journal*, *International Law Review of Wuhan University*, *South China Sea Law Journal*, *Pacific Journal*, *Peking University International Law* and *Comparative Law Review of Peking University* and other leading law journals in China. This seminar helped the Journal to join the efforts of the international law circle and law journals in China to promote Chinese international law studies.

3. The Seminar on the "Return of the State and the Reconstruction of the International Legal Order"

From April 28 to 29, 2018, the Editorial Department of the *Chinese Review of International Law* and the Law School of Xiamen University jointly hosted the seminar "The Return of the State and Reconstruction of the International Legal Order" in Xiamen. The editors of the *Review*, members of the International Law Innovation Team of Law School of Xiamen University, and scholars from East China University of Political Science and Law, Xi'an Jiaotong University, Southeast University, Suzhou University, Fuzhou University, Hebei University of Economics and Business, etc., attended the seminar and carried out in-depth exchanges and discussions on this topic.

V Prospects

While cheering its achievements, the Editorial Department also needs to sum up experience and faces up to the challenges and difficulties. Innovation knows no end and the road of development is long. All the staff members of the Editorial Department of *Chinese Review of International Law* are resolved to continue their efforts to ensure the quality of the *Review*, enhance its reputation and promote its development.

Ⅵ Curriculum Vitae of Personnel

Liu Huawen

A Basic Information

Liu Huawen, was born in Qixia City, Shandong Province in July, 1972. He is currently the Deputy Director and a research fellow of the Institute of International Law of the Chinese Academy of Social Sciences (CASS), a member of the Joint Committee of the Chinese Communist Party of the Institute of Law and Institute of International Law, a doctoral supervisor and at CASS Graduate School, the Executive Director of the CASS Center for Human Rights Studies; and a deputy editor-in-Chief and the editorial director of *Chinese Review of the International Law*. His key research area is international law, especially basic theories of international law, international human rights law, international treaty law, international organization law, settlement of international disputes, prohibition of trafficking in human beings, and international cooperation in the field of anti-corruption.

Liu Huawen is currently a member of the 3rd International Law Advisory Committee of the Chinese Ministry of Foreign Affairs, the Editor-in-chief of the *Chinese Yearbook of International Law*, a member of the Executive Council of the Asian Society of International Law, a co-director of the Cross-cultural Human Rights Center in the Netherlands, the Vice President of Beijing Society of International Law, the Vice President of the Soft Law Research Society of the Chinese Society of Behavioral Law, a council member of China Society of International Law, a council member of Chinese Society of the Law of the Sea, a council member of China Society for Human Rights Studies, a member of China Economic and Social Council, a council member of Youth Humanities and Social Sciences Research Center, CASS, and an expert on implementation of the National Development Program of Children, the Office of the National Committee for Women and Children's Work of State Council. He is a guest professor at the Human Rights School of China University of Political Science and Law, Human Rights Research School of the Southwest University of Political Science and Law, and China Women's College. He is an expert on the construction of the rule of law for the Government of Yunnan Province.

Liu Huawen graduated from the Law Faculty of Southwest University of Political Science and Law in 1995 with a bachelor's degree in law. In 1998, he graduated from Law School of Peking University with a master's degree in international law. In 2003, he graduated from Law School of Peking University with a doctorate degree in international law. From September 2000 to now, he has been working at the Chinese Academy of Social Sciences. From 2000 to 2002, he worked as an assistant research fellow at the Institute of Law. From 2002 to 2006, he worked at CASS Center for International Law Studies as an associate research fellow and the deputy head of the Research Coordination and International Cooperation Department. From 2006 to 2010, he worked at CASS Institute of Law as associate research fellow, deputy head and head of the Research Coordination and International Cooperation Department. He became a research fellow in 2011. In 2016, he became a supervisor of doctoral candidates in the field of international law. In 2016, he received Special Allowance from the State Council for his contribution in the field of social sciences. He was a member of the Second International Law Advisory Committee of the Ministry of Foreign Affairs, a member of the Review Committee of the Imported Online Games of the Ministry of Culture, a member of the Anti-Corruption and Transparency Council of the World Summit of the World Economic Forum, a member of the International Youth Research Expert Committee of the China Youth Research Association, and a legal expert of the Thematic Program Center, Beijing TV Station.

Professor Liu Huawen has been a visiting scholar at many foreign universities and institutions, including Raoul Wallenberg Institute of Human Rights and Humanitarian Law, the University of Lund; Sweden and Norwegian Center for Human Rights Studies, the University of Oslo, Norway(2002); Amsterdam Center for International Law, the University of Amsterdam, the Netherlands(2004); and the Norwegian Academy of Science and Literature(2009).

Professor Liu Huawen is currently teaching students international law in undergraduate, master's and doctoral programs.

B Research activities and contributions

In the past 20 years of research work, Professor Liu Huawen has been in charge or participated in many research projects, both within and outside CASS. As an expert, he has actively participated in the drafting of national legislation and policy documents in the field of international law and in international cooperation in the field of human rights, including human rights dialogues and seminars organized at the government level or at the non-governmental level, and human rights treaty procedures under the UN Human Rights mechanism. He participated the preparations for the first review of the Chinese implementation of the UN Convention against Corruption. He has won many ministerial-level awards for his important academic works. And he has published many Chinese or English papers and articles at home and abroad.

1. He has actively participated in and(or) led many key projects sponsored by the National Social Sciences Fund, the China Law Society and Chinese Academy of Social Sciences

(1) He is currently the person in charge of the sub-project "Research on China's Human Rights Assessment Indicator System" under the Major Project of

Theoretical Research and Construction of Marxism"Basic Theoretical Research on Major Human Rights Issues in China".

(2) He is current the person in charge of the project"Research on the Application of the Thought of a Community with Shared Future for Mankind in the Field of International Law", sponsored by the International Law Advisory Committee of the Ministry of Foreign Affairs.

(3) He is currently the person in charge of the CASS Innovation Project "Building a Community with Shared Future for Mankind and Promoting International Law Guarantee for the Reform of the Global Governance System".

(4) He is current participating in the large-scale CASS research project (2019 - 2022), "Legal Risk Prevention and Legal Mechanism Construction in the Implementation of the 'Belt and Road Initiative'".

(5) He was the person in charge of the major project"International Implementation of the Convention on the Rights of Persons with Disabilities and its Implications for China", sponsored by the China Federation of Disabled Persons (the project has already been completed).

(6) He was the person in charge of the project"Study of the Palermo Protocol of the United Nations Convention against Human Trafficking and Reform of Chinese Law", sponsored by the China Law Society (the project has already been completed).

(7) He was the person in charge of the project"Studies on Human Rights Public Diplomacy", sponsored by the China Society of Human Rights (the project has already been completed).

(8) He was the person in charge of the project"*Wong Ho Yong v. Peru Case* and Its Implications", sponsored by the China Study Center for Clean Governance, CASS (the project has already been completed).

(9) He was the person in charge of the project"the International Covenant on Economic, Social and Cultural Rights and the Implementation of the Millennium Goals in China and Italy", which was a cooperation project between CASS and the Research Council of Italy (the project has already been completed).

(10) He was the person in charge the project"The Study of the Justiciability

of Economic, Social and Cultural Rights", undertaken by the CASS Institute of Law as part of the technical cooperation between the Office of the UN High Commissioner for Human Rights and the Chinese Government(the project has already been completed).

2. He has actively participated in national legislative and policy making activities. Some of his important proposals have been adopted by the legislative or policy-making organs. He has participated as an expert in think-tank diplomacy, legal diplomacy, and other international law practices

(1) In 2006, he participated as an expert of the All-China Women's Federation in the revision of the Law on the Protection of Minors. He has also served as an expert at the Office of the National Committee on Women's and Children's Work of the State Council for a long time on the implementation of the China's Program on Children's Development(2011 – 2020), and participated in many related policy-or law-making activities organized by the Ministry of Civil Affairs, the Ministry of Education and other relevant state organs.

(2) He has repeatedly provided opinions and suggestions for the drafting of the Chinese State Party reports on the implementation of the UN human rights Conventions and the preparation of the State report according to the UN Human Rights Council's Universal Periodic Review procedure. He has participated in the drafting of some White Papers on Human Rights published by the State Council Information Office.

(3) On April 13, 2011, with the authorization of the State Council, the State Council Information Office released the first National Human Rights Action Plan (2009 – 2010). In 2008, Professor Liu Huawen participated as an expert in the drafting of the Plan. Later, he introduced and publicized the Plan to domestic and foreign institutions and the general public. He participated in the assessment and evaluation of the implementation of the Plan, including the preparation of the evaluation report, which was published later. He also participated in the drafting of the National Human Rights Action Plan(2012 – 2015) and other related work.

(4) In January 2012, his internal report on providing sign language translation in the live broadcast of the sessions of the National People's Congress and the

National Congress of Chinese People's Political Consultative Conference (the "Two Sessions") got positive response. The sign language interpretation was provided in the live broadcast of "Two Sessions" since March of that year.

(5) In 2012, China participated in the preparation of the first examination of the implementation of the UN Convention against Corruption in China. Liu Huawen provided expert opinions and suggestions. In 2014, he participated in the World Economic Forum Global Summit Transparency and Anti-Corruption Council meeting as a member of the Council.

(6) In 2014, with the approval of the Inter-American Court of Human Rights, he participated as an expert witness in the case before the Inter-American Court of Human Rights—*Wong Ho Yong v. Peru case*, and contributed to the international human rights case law that was conducive to the settlement of similar cases.

(7) He has participated many times in anti-trafficking legislation seminars and case analysis meetings organized by the relevant state and judicial organs, such as the Supreme People's Court and the Ministry of Public Security, and was invited to give lectures on the prevention of human trafficking at training classes for judges and representatives of women's federations at different levels.

(8) He has participated in all the meetings of the "Beijing Human Rights Forum" hosted by China Society for Human Rights Studies and China Human Rights Development Foundation since 2008 as well as the preparations for some of them.

(9) He has led the preparation and organization of China – EU non-government human rights judicial seminars hosted by CASS Institute of Law and CASS Center for Human Rights Studies. He has participated in many international human rights dialogues and seminars, such as China – EU, China – US, China – Australian and China – German human rights dialogues.

(10) In 2016, in response to the Philippine Government's unilateral filing of the South China Sea arbitration case, Liu Huawen participated as an expert in some important seminars on this issue both at home and abroad. On the eve of the release of the arbitral award, he attended the International Symposium on the South China Sea Arbitration held in the Hague and the International Symposium on Arbitration Case in the South China Sea held in Hong Kong. He led the editing

work of the special issue of the *Chinese Yearbook of International Law* on the Jurisdiction of the South China Sea Arbitration Case.

C Main Academic Viewpoints

1. International law and domestic law are two different legal systems. There are both connections and differences between the two. International law has its own features and operating rules. Chinese International law lawyers should know domestic law and study Chinese diplomatic history, history of international relations, diplomacy and international relations theories. International law researchers should have a national standpoint and a global perspective. If necessary, law and history research should be combined, and the political, economic, cultural, social, historical, military and other factors should be borne in mind as well.

2. Human dignity is the foundation of human rights law. Security, development and human rights are the three pillars of the reform and development of the UN. There has been a trend towards the mainstreaming of human rights in the international community. In China, the rule of law, development and human rights are the three basic dimensions of national development that are interrelated and mutually reinforcing. Everyone enjoys human rights and all human rights are a whole. Human rights should not be viewed in isolation or in a simple way. Human rights development needs to be based on national conditions and consistent with level of the rule of law and development. In the international community, China's initiative of "promoting development through cooperation and promoting human rights through development" is consistent with the UN's advocacy of the sustainable development agendas.

3. International human rights law is first and foremost a part of the international law. The exchange and cooperation between countries in the field of human rights on the basis of equality and mutual respect is in conformity with the nature of international human rights law. Human rights treaties have the problem of expressing high and plentiful substantive requirements but imposing single and weak procedural obligations. The realization of human rights standards mainly relies on the efforts of the domestic society. Clarifying the legitimacy of the international implementation mechanism is conducive to the reform of international organizations. It is necessary to distinguish between *lex ferenda* and *lex lata*, and steadily

promote the reform and development of the UN human rights regime.

4. There has been great development in the law of the sea in recent year, and the UN Convention on the Law of the Sea is far from meeting the practical needs of the international community. There are some issues not explicitly defined in the Convention that require the search for applicable norms of international law through the examination of general international law. Even so, the problem of lack of clarity of law in the field of the law of the sea is still outstanding. The development history of the law of the sea is a history of adaptation of the law of the sea to state practice, rather than that of the adaptation of state practice to the law of the sea. International law is the basis for national ocean practice. At the same time, states are the main entities formulating and implementing international law. The interpretation and application of the law of the sea should be cautious and rigorous, and not influenced by a few individual states, institutions or scholars.

5. International law is a body of legal norms applicable to the international society formed by sovereign states. The environment, development and operation of the application of the international law are very different from those of the application of domestic law in domestic society. We cannot simply use domestic law thinking to analyze international law problems. For example, the concepts and roles of soft law and non-governmental organizations are often topics in different fields in domestic and international law or in the context of domestic society and international society that should not be mixed up. Many myths and misunderstandings about international law issues in related fields are resulted from the lack of awareness of the boundaries between domestic law and international law. In international law, there are also issues of soft law phenomena and soft law governance that cannot be ignored, but should be given attention to and researched on.

D Introduction to representative works

Books

1. *The Asymmetry of the State's Obligations under the International Covenant on Economic, Social and Cultural Rights*, Peking University Press, 2005; Social Sciences Academic Press (China), 2019.

The International Covenant on Economic, Social and Cultural Rights is one of the "two human rights covenants" in the International Human Rights Charter. The Chinese government officially ratified the Covenant in 2001. This book summarizes the nature and characteristics of the state's legal obligations under the Covenant, clarifies the multi-level and rich nature of the state's substantive obligations and the unity and weakness of the state's procedural obligations, and analyzes the causes of the asymmetry between the two, the efforts made by the international community to change this asymmetry and the opportunities and challenges faced by it in the formulation and implementation of the Optional Protocol to the Covenant. It draws on the theory and practice of the auxiliary principle emphasized in the process of European integration, and makes a creative interpretation of the asymmetry of the state's obligations under the Covenant, pointing out its rationality and irrationality, and proposes solutions to this problem. Through the study of the asymmetry of state obligations under the International Covenant on Economic, Social and Cultural Rights, this book helps us to explore some regular understandings of the relationship between international human rights mechanisms and state sovereignty.

2. *Research on the UN Trafficking in Persons Protocol—From the Perspective of Human Rights Law*, Social Sciences Academic Press (China), 2011.

Human trafficking, which is an ancient crime, has revived today and the situation of the crime is serious. The author believes that the UN Trafficking in Persons Protocol is both a weapon against transnational organized crime and a basis for promoting human rights protection. In recent years, the UN has incorporated a human rights perspective into its anti-trafficking work. Based on the emphasis on human dignity, the Protocol redefines trafficking in persons and expands the crimes covered by the concept of trafficking in persons and their scope. On the basis of both prevention and combating crimes, the Protocol places special emphasis on the protection of victims and brings international legislation into a "trinity" model. The protocol was approved by the Chinese legislature and entered into force for China in 2010. To implement the protocol, it is necessary to base on national conditions, sum up experience, further improve domestic legislation, and establish and improve the anti-trafficking mechanism. The author emphasizes that carrying out social governance innovation and realizing the rule of law, including the rule of soft law, is a new trend in implementing international standards and strengthening anti-trafficking work.

Papers

1. "An International Law Analysis of the 1887 Sino-Portuguese Treaty", *China's Borderland History and Geography Studies*, 2(1999).

The 1887 Sino-Portuguese Treaty was the only international treaty in the modern history of China that stipulated the legal status of Macao. This article focuses on this treaty, compares academic arguments from the perspective of international law, and conducts jurisprudential analysis and evaluation: the treaty stipulated a special leasehold status for Macao; the dispute over Macao's demarcation did not affect the validity of the treaty itself, but Portugal's serious violations of the treaty did. Only then did the effectiveness of the treaty be shaken; the abolition of this treaty by the Chinese Government in 1928 was legally effective; the Macao issue was solved in the contemporary era and embodied a practice of international law in China. International law is a necessary condition for the success of diplomatic practice, but relying solely on international law cannot always resolve the disputes. Diplomatic activities may not only be considered from a legal perspective, but also influenced by the international environment, national ideologies, and political, economic and military factors.

2. "40 Years of Reform and Opening up and China's Human Rights Development Path", *World Economics and Politics*, 9(2018).

In the 40 years of reform and opening up, China has been the fastest-growing country in the field of human development, according to the assessment of the UN Development Program. China has consistently combined the principle of universality of human rights with the realities of the country and has embarked on a path of human rights development suited to its own national conditions. China has achieved economic development and social progress, and has taken the "Chinese Dream" as a symbol to push the development of human rights to a new era. 1978 was both the starting point of China's reform and opening up and the new original point of China's human rights protection. Since then, China has been strengthening its ties with the outside world and continuously deepened its understanding of the rule of law and human rights. It has strengthened the Constitutional guarantee of human rights by embodying the principle of safeguarding human rights into the Constitution. The legal system of human rights protection has been basically completed, continuous breakthroughs have been made in legislation, and the implementation of laws has been strengthened with innovations. China has responded actively to the UN's call for the drafting and implementation of the National Human Rights Action Plan, thus enabling the human rights cause in the country to enter into a period of planned and rapid development. China has proposed to build a new type of international relations and a community with shared future for mankind. It gradually deepens and strengthens international exchanges and cooperation in the field of human rights, and tries to make unique and constructive contributions and become participant and builder of and contributor to the international human rights governance.

E Main Publications

Books

1. *Asymmetry of the State's Obligations under the International Covenant on Economic, Social and Cultural Rights*, first edition, Peking University Press, September 2005; new edition, Social Sciences Academic Press (China), January 2019.

2. *Research on the United Nations Protocol against Human Trafficking from the Perspective of Human Rights Law*, Social Sciences Academic Press (China), November 2010.

3. *International Covenant on Civil and Political Rights and Its Implementation Mechanism* (co-authored with Zhu Xiaoqing), first edition, China Social Sciences Press, September 2003; new edition, Social Sciences Academic Press (China), January 2019.

4. *Research on the Justiciability of Economic, Social and Cultural Rights* (editor), China Social Sciences Press, January 2008.

5. *Children's Rights and Their Legal Protection* (editor), Shanghai People's Publishing House, October 2009.

6. *United Nations Core Human Rights Conventions and Their Implementation Mechanisms*, Hunan University Press, July 2016.

7. *International Cooperation and China's Perspectives in the Field of Human Rights* (Deputy Editor-in-Chief), China University of Political Science and Law Press, June 2017.

8. *China's Path of Human Rights Development*, China Social Science Press, December 2018.

Translation book

Manfred Nowak, translated by Liu Huawen into Chinese, *Introduction to the International Human Rights Regime*, Peking University Press, January 2008.

Papers and Articles

1. "The 40 Years of Reform and Opening up and China's Path of Human Rights Development", *World Economics and Politics*, 9 (2018).

2. "Basic Features of China's Cause of Protection of the Rights of the Persons with Disabilities", *Studies on the Persons with Disabilities*, 2 (2017).

3. "The Significance and Implication of the First Case of Extradition before the Inter-American Court of Human Rights", *Journal of Southeast University (Philosophy and Social Sciences)*, 6 (2016).

4. "On the Basis of Anti-Human Trafficking", *Jianghai Academic Journal*, 2 (2016).

5. "A Human Rights Outlook with Chinese Characteristics: An Interpretation of the Congratulatory from Xi Jinping's for 2015 Beijing Human Rights Forum", *Chinese International Law Review*, 5 (2016).

6. "The United Nations and the International Protection of Human Rights", *World Economics and Politics*, 4 (2015).

7. "Five Principles of Peaceful Coexistence: Basic Principles of International Law in the Past and for the Future", in *Chinese Yearbook of International Law* (2014), Law Press China, 2015.

8. "Research on the Implementation Mechanism of the United Nations Convention against Corruption", *Journal of the Contemporary Law*, 1 (2014).

9. "Establishment of 'the Abandoned Baby Island' and Protection of the Rig-

hts of Children" ,*Human Rights*,1(2014).

10. "Human Rights: Environmental Protection and the Right to Development" ,*Human Rights*,1(2013).

11. "Respecting and Protecting Human Rights and Realizing the Chinese Dream" ,*Human Rights*,2(2013).

12. "Preliminary Study on the Drafting of the UN Convention on the Rights of the Elderly" ,in *Chinese Yearbook of International Law*(2012),Law Press China,2013.

13. "On the Promotion of Human Rights by Law as a Whole" ,*Human Rights*, 5(2013).

14. "New Trends in the Protection of Children's Rights in China—Review of China's Development Program for Children (2011 - 2020)", *China Women's Movement*,3(2012).

15. "Soft Law, Human Rights and Social Construction", *Human Rights*, 2 (2012).

16. "Gender Equality:The Practice of the UN Human Rights Treaty Bodies and Its Implications" ,*Journal of Law*,8(2009).

17. "Development and Human Rights: Reflections on Ageing", *Human Rights*,2(2009).

18. "Correct Understanding of Human Rights as the Prerequisite for Human Rights Education" ,*Journal of Guangzhou University*(*Philosophy and Social Sciences Edition*),5(2010).

19. "The Enlightenment of the Logical Framework Methods on the Management of Social Science Projects" ,*Social Science Management Review*,3(2010).

20. "Interpretation of Human Rights from the Perspective of Dignity", *Human Rights*,1(2011).

21. "On the Post-financing System of Social Science Research" ,*Social Science Management Review*,2(2011).

22. "On the Mainstreaming and Localization of Human Rights in China", *Learning and Exploration*,4(2011).

23. "Starting from System Building:Child Rights Protection and the Non-dis-

crimination Principle in China", in Marit Skivenes and Karl Harald Søvig (Editors): *Child Rights and International Discrimination Law: Implementing Article 2 of the United Nations Convention on the Rights of the Child*, Routledge Research in International Law, 1st Edition, Routledge, February, 2019 (English).

24. "Children's Rights Protection Enters New Stage in China", *Human Rights*, 2 (2012) (English).

25. "Soft Law, Human Rights and Social Construction", *Human Rights*, 3 (2012) (English).

26. "Gender Equality and Human Rights: ICCPR and its Impacts in China", in Pauline Stolz, etc. (eds.), *Gender Equality, Citizenship & Human Rights: Controversies and Challenges in China and the Nordic Countries*, Routledge, 2010 (English).

27. "Can Rapid Economic Growth Benefit More? Review of the Medical Care Reform in Shenmu County in China", in *Journal of Asia Public Policy*, 3 (2010) (English).

28. "Focusing on the Role of Soft Law", *People's Daily*, September 16, 2013.

29. "The Human Rights Review Must Adhere to the Principles", *People's Daily*, September 25, 2013.

30. "Promoting the Rule of Law in China Must also Be People-oriented", *Legal Daily*, November 17, 2012.

31. "Territorial Asylum Is Violation of International Law: A Discussion with Mr. Shi Zhiyu", *Lianhe Zaobao* (Singapore), May 19, 2012.

32. "Basic Characteristics of China's Path to Safeguarding the Rights of Persons with Disabilities", *Guangming Daily*, December 5, 2016.

33. "A Comprehensive Push and a New Focus on Action—A New National Human Rights Action Plan That Keeps Pace with the Times", *Guangming Daily*, June 13, 2012.

34. "The Rule of Law, Development and Human Rights: Three Basic Dimensions of the China's Path", *Guangming Daily*, December 31, 2014.

35. "Forty Years of Reform and Opening up and the Road of Human Rights Development in China", *Guangming Daily*, December 14, 2018.

Li Xixia

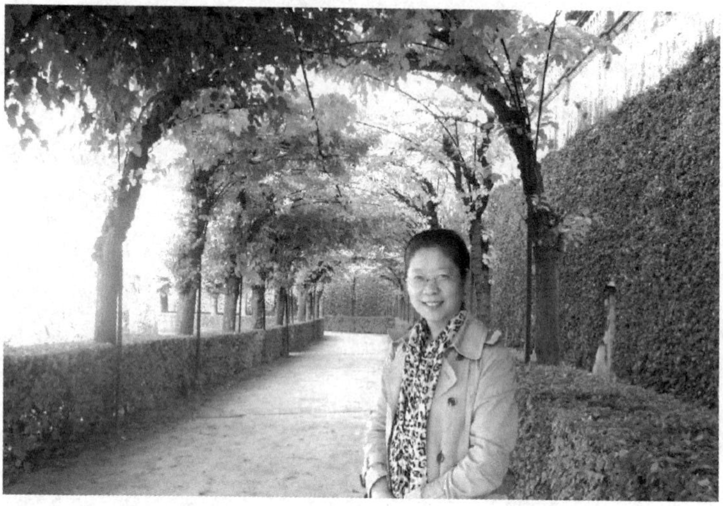

A Basic Information

Li Xixia is an associate research fellow at the CASS Institute of International Law, the deputy head and an editor of the Editorial Department for the *Chinese Review of International Law*. Her researches focus on international labor standards, human rights, women's social rights and social security law.

Li Xixia is also the vice-chairman of the 12th Special Working Committee on Social and Legal Affairs of Beijing Committee of Chinese Peasants and Workers Democratic Party, a member of Dongcheng District Committee of Chinese Peasants and Workers Democratic Party, a council member of the Social Law Studies Institute of China Law Society, and council member of the Chinese Society of International Law.

From 1983 to 1987, Li Xixia studied English Language and Literature at the Foreign Languages Department of Henan University and got a B. A. Degree in English; from 1987 to 1989, she studied Applied English Linguistics at the Foreign Languages Department of Xi'an Jiaotong University and got a Master's Graduate Diploma; from 2000 to 2003, she studied law at the Law Faculty of University of International Business and Economics and got a Master's Degree in Law; from 2008 to 2017, she undertook short-term research fellowships at University of Fribourg in Switzerland, University of Alberta in Canada, Stockholm University in Sweden and the National Autonomous University of Mexico, respectively.

She won the second prize for excellent countermeasure research report from Chinese Academy of Social Sciences in 2014, and the third prize for excellent research results for her book *Protection of Women's Social Rights: from International and Domestic Law Perspectives* from Wang Jinling Gender Research Foundation in 2016.

B Main Academic Ideas and Viewpoints

Among her major publications are research findings on international labor standards, women's social rights and maternity leave protection.

First of all, Professor Li suggests that labor standards acceptable to China be included in the Free Trade Agreements. Since the establishment of the World Trade Organization (WTO) on 1 January 1995, Free Trade Areas (FTAs) have been developing rapidly around the world. This development triggered a new round of reconstruction of regional trade rules, with the setting up of labor standards in FTAs as an important aspect. This is a departure from the current WTO rules and has established links between international trade and labor standards to varying degrees, which brought great challenges to the multilateral trade system and produced major impacts on international trade and labor market. Especially over the past 20 years, the three major economies, the EU, the United States and Canada, have incorporated labor standards into a series of free trade agreements, and have developed different models of regional labor rules, which have exerted impact on trade and investment in varying degrees and posed challenges that cannot be ignored and avoided by China. Under this context, how to deal with this challenge in the process of implementing China's Free Trade Area Strategy and "Belt and Road" initiative? Professor Li suggests that labor standards acceptable to China be included in FTAs so as to further advance the making of regional labor rules acceptable to China.

Secondly, women's social rights are important components of women's human rights, and they are recognized both at the international level and the domestic level. Because of the inherent differences in physical makeup and physiology between men and women, women have to perform the social function of childbearing. Compounding with cultural prejudice and traditional sex discrimination, this has posed more difficulties and greater challenges for women in the protection and realization of their social rights. Therefore, while providing equal protection for women's social rights, special protection should be emphasized in order to achieve substantive equality. The Chinese government has always attached great importance to the development of women and the equality of men and women. For the protection of women's social rights, China has developed a system of protection of women's social rights consisting of legislative, administrative and judicial measures.

Thirdly, maternity leave system is an important component of maternity protection system. Based on this maternity leave system, paternity leave and parental leave systems are developed by some foreign countries, which have greatly promoted gender equality in paid work and unpaid family housework and obviously improved level of maternity protection. At present, in order to cope with aging population, China adopts two-child policy as one of measures for encouraging childbirth. This requires the establishment of supporting systems, such as paternity leave and parental leave systems, for the promotion of maternity protection.

C Main Publications

1. *Labor Standards in Free Trade Agreement* (monograph), Social Sciences Academic Press (China), 2017 (author).

2. *Protection of Women's Social Rights: from International and Domestic Law Perspectives* (English Version), Paths International Ltd. (UK), 2016 (first editor-in-chief).

3. *Protection of Women's Social Rights: from International and Domestic Law Perspectives* (Chinese Version), Social Sciences Academic Press (China), 2013 (first editor-in-chief).

4. *On Minority Rights* (English Version), Paths International Ltd. (UK), 2012 (first editor-in-chief).

5. *A New Understanding of the Rule of Law: A Comparative Law Analysis*, Social Sciences Academic Press (China), 2011 (deputy editor-in-chief).

6. *On Minority Rights* (Chinese Version), Social Sciences Academic Press (China), 2010 (co-editor-in-chief).

7. *Social Security Law in Context*, Peking University Press, 2006 (first co-translator).

8. *The Reform of Social Insurance in China and the Development of Legal Systems*, Social Sciences Academic Press (China), 2005 (deputy editor-in-chief).

9. "Advancing Reform of Individual Account System of Employees Basic Medical Insurance in accordance with the Law", *Chinese Social Sciences Today*, April 3, 2019.

10. "Labor Standards in Canada's Free Trade Agreements and Their Implications", *Hebei Law Science*, 4 (2018).

11. "Implementing 'The Belt and Road Initiative' with the Help of International Law", *Chinese Social Sciences Today*, May 2, 2018.

12. "Labor Standards in the EU's Free Trade Agreements and Their Revelations", *Law Science*, 1 (2017).

13. "TPP Labor Standards, Their Impacts and China's Countermeasures", *Law Science Magazine*, 1 (2017).

14. "A Study of the Legal System against Discrimination against Women in Employment in China", *Journal of Human Right*, 1 (2017).

15. "Development of Maternity Leave Systems in Foreign Countries and Their Implications", *Journal of Beijing Union University*, 1 (2016).

16. "Development Trend of Labor Standards in Free Trade Agreements", *Global Law Review*, 1 (2015).

17. "The Decentralization of Labor Standards in the Process of Global Trade Liberalization", *Journal of Social Development*, 1 (2015).

18. "Constructing Labor Standards in Chinese Free Trade Agreements", *Journal of Human Right*, 6 (2014).

In addition, she also authored or translated a series of articles published in other journals and books.

Luo Huanxin

A Basic Information

Luo Huanxin, female, born in Hunan Province, is an associate research fellow at CASS Institute of International Law and an editor of the periodical *Chinese Review of International Law*.

Luo Huanxin's main research fields are the peaceful settlement of international disputes, law of the sea, and international law theory and culture. She got her bachelor degree in law from Xiangtan University in 2002 and her master degree and doctor degree in law from Peking University in 2008 and 2013, respectively. During recent years, she has been a visiting scholar at the University of Cambridge and Columbia University. She also got a training certificate in Venice Academy of Human Rights of EIUC in 2012, and a Diploma in Japanese Modern Research Center of Peking University in 2011. She passed the bar exam in 2002 and had the Lawyer's Practice Certificate in 2003. Besides, she is also an executive director of Institute for Marine Affairs of Liaoning Law Society, and the director of Marine Rights Protection and Law Enforcement Branch of Pacific Society of China. Since joining CASS Institute of International Law in 2013, she has been in charge of or participated in a number of research projects funded by National Social Science Funds or sponsored by one or more ministries and commissions under the State Council.

B Introductions to Representative Works

1. *Territorial Status of the Ryukyus and the Sovereignty of Diaoyu Islands in International Law*, China Social Sciences Press, 2015.

This book purports to doubt the legal grounds of Japan's claims over the Diaoyu Islands through questioning the legal status of the Ryukyus, and to clarify the relationships among the Ryukyus, Japan and the Diaoyu Islands from the international law perspective. This study is designed not to resolve the dispute, but to enrich the existing researches on the Diaoyu Islands by taking a specific Ryukyus' approach. The innovations of this book can be manifested in three aspects: First, it partly resolves the "conundrum" of Ryukyus' legal status, which seems to have perplexed the academic circle for a long time. Second, it fills in the blanks in monographs specializing in the sovereignty of the Diaoyu Islands in Chinese international law circle. Finally, this book combines historical approach with legal approach. Regarding the historical approach, parts of the maps and historical documents cited in the book are personally collected by the author. Also, for the convenience of further researches, some significant documents in English are laid in the footnotes or appendices. With respect to the legal approach, this book strictly adheres to the positive international law perspective, identifying the legal norms and sources in accordance with the criteria of treaties and customaries emanating from states' own free will.

2. "Title to Territory: Theoretical Meaning and Main Types in International Law", *Global Law Review*, 4(2015).

With the rapid development of international society, the doctrinal construction of "modes of acquisition of territory" has not been able to meet the need of relevant analysis in legal theory. In reality, the notion of "title to territory" is preferred in judicial practice of the International Court of Justice, which refers generally to the acts, facts, proofs or sources of right, that constitute the legal foundation of the establishment of a state's sovereign right over a territory. However, up to now, no systematic research has been carried out by Chinese scholars on this issue. At first, the five modes, i. e. occupation of *terra nullius*, etc., can be attributed to sources of territorial title as establishing territorial sovereignty in traditional way, although most of them are outdated. Second, state practice and case law evince that there are many other titles by which territorial sovereignty is established, including the following acts or facts: treaty, the creation of a new state, attribution by an organ or international organization having the capacity to dispose of a given territory, and unilateral acts of territorial renunciation/acquiescence by a state. Besides, effectivité cannot *per se* independently constitute the establishment of a title of sovereignty, but it should be noted that, in case of the territorial renunciation or acquiescence occurs, effectivités may play a significant role in territorial disputes and lead to the effect of transferring the sovereignty of a territory from one state to another.

3. "The Role and Function of States in the Process of International Law-Making—A Study of the Formation and Operation of International Law of the Sea", *Chinese Journal of Law*, 4(2018)

The modern international order is based on international law with the UN Charter as the core. Under Article 38 of the Statute of the International Court of Justice, new international law is made by states, primarily through treaty or customary international law. International law is a multidimensional and comprehensive process that reflects the complex game between international relations and politics, and a state is both the creator of the rules and the object of its restraint. The formation and operation of the international law of the sea profoundly reflects the ideas of western developed countries, which not only have natural advantages of cultural origin, but their theoretical preparation, consideration of political decisions and choice of rules in practice are well ahead of the developing countries, whose lack of fully understanding of their role and function in international law-making is the main reason for the gap between states. If China aims to build itself into a maritime power, the great significance of deep participation in international law-making should be emphasized.

C Main Publications

1. *Territorial Status of the Ryukyus and Sovereignty of Diaoyu Islands in International Law*, China Social Sciences Press, 2015.

2. "Territory Dispute between Russia and China: an International Law Perspective", *Oriental Law*, 2(2010).

3. "Limitation of International Court of Justice in Solving Territorial Disputes", *Journal of Shanghai University of Political Science & Law*, 1(2010).

4. "On the Issue of State Responsibility in the Diaoyu Island Incident", *Journal of Political Science and Law*, 6(2010).

5. "An Analysis of the Legitimacy of the US' Administration over the Ryukyus before 1972", *Collection of Weiming Japanese Studies*, 5(2012).

6. "A Summary of Forty Years' Studies on the Diaoyu Islands in China and Abroad", in *Annual Report on Research of Japan* 2013, Social Sciences Academic Press, 2013.

7. "The Issue of the Diaoyu Islands: Watch out for the Rashness and Craftiness of Japan", *China Legal Daily*, Aug. 7, 2012.

8. "Declaration of Sovereignty and International Law Confidence, a Comment on Hong Kong Citizens' Private Acts of Defending the Diaoyu Islands", *China Legal Daily*, Aug. 21, 2012.

9. "Margaret Thatcher: the Woman Who Saved the Great Britain", *China Legal Daily*, Apr. 16, 2013.

10. "The Diaoyu Islands as an Inherent Territory of China: Facts are Certain and Law is Clear", *China Legal Daily*, Sep. 25, 2012.

11. "The Status of the Ryukyus in International Law", *Chinese Review of International Law*, 1(2014).

12. "A Historical and Legal Investigation on the 'Residual Sovereignty' Involved in the Ryukyus Issues", *Japanese Studies*, 4(2014).

13. "Recognizing both Domestic and International Situations of China's Maritime Rights Protection", *Motherland*, Dec. 27, 2014.

14. "Title to Territory: Theoretical Meaning and Main Types in International Law", *Global Law Review*, 4(2015).

15. "A Preliminary Review of the AJIL's Agora Articles on South China Sea (in Chinese)", *Northern Legal Science*, 4(2016).

16. "The Illegality of Japan's Management of the Ryukyus after 1972", in *Chouhai Collected Marine Works*, Vol. 2, 2016.

17. "Illegal Disposal of Title to Land Territory in SCS Arbitration Award—On the Tribunal's Finding on the Status of Features", *Chinese Review of International Law*, 5(2016).

18. "Language Challenges in the South China Sea Dispute", *Comparative Jurist(Willian & Mary Law School)*, Oct. 26, 2016.

19. "Innovation of 'a Community with Shared Future for Mankind' in International Law—A Comparative Analysis of 'Obligations *Erga Omnes*'", *Chinese Review of International Law*, 2(2018).

20. "Innovation of 'a Community with Shared Future for Mankind' in International Law", *China Social Sciences Today*, Feb. 7, 2017.

21. "The South China Sea Arbitration Awards: A Critical Study", in *Chinese Society of International Law*, Foreign Languages Press, 2018 (article written in Chinese and English, co-author).

22. "Construction of a Maritime Power and the Great Significance of Participating in International Law-Making—A Study of the Formation and Operation of International Law of the Sea", *Chinese Journal of Law*, 4(2018).

He Tiantian

A Basic Information

He Tiantian graduated from Renmin University of China with a Ph. D. in International Law in 2015. She is currently an assistant research fellow at CASS Institute of International Law and an editor of *Chinese Review of International Law*. Her research interests include international dispute settlement, international criminal law, international humanitarian law, and the law of the sea. She was awarded the title of one of the "100 Potential Young Scholars of Law" by Beijing Law Society in 2018.

B Main Academic Viewpoints

In recent years, Dr. He has published several articles on the *South China Sea Arbitration Case* and some procedural and evidence issues in international dispute resolution and expressed the following views:

First, the South China Sea arbitral tribunal has no jurisdiction over the unilateral arbitration initiated by the Philippines. According to the awards, the arbitral tribunal improperly adopted and accepted the evidence provided by the Philippines. Second, with respect to procedural and evidentiary issues, the practice of international courts and tribunals has some similarities with the domestic ones while having its own characteristics. The evidentiary international practice is flexible, specific, and could be reviewed on a case-by-case basis.

C Main Publications

Book in Chinese

The War Crime of Child Recruitment: Analysis of the First Judgment of the International Criminal Court, Social Sciences Academic Publication, 2018.

Articles in Chinese

(1) "International Courts of Justice and Experts Evidence: From the Perspective of Case Concerning the Land and Maritime Boundary between Cameroon and Nigeria", *Chinese Review of International Law*, 30(2019).

(2) "Law Interacts with Science: Experts' Appointment in International Court of Justice", *Contemporary Law Review*, 1(2018).

(3) "Commentary on Award on Jurisdiction and Admissibility of the Philippines-instituted Arbitration under Annex Ⅶ to the UNCLOS: Fact-finding and Evidence-handling", *Chinese Review of International Law*, 21(2016).

(4) "International Law Analysis on the Philippines Submission of South China Sea Issue to International Arbitration", *Pacific Journal*, 12(2013).

Articles in English

(1) "Book Review: The Philosophy of International Law", *Chinese Journal of International Law*, 16(2017).

(2) "Book Review: James Gerard Devaney, Fact-Finding before the International Court of Justice", *Chinese Journal of International Law*, 17(2018).

(3) "Manila's Arbitration Has Evidence Problem", *China Daily*, May 6th, 2016;

(4) "Commentary on the Award on the Jurisdiction and Admissibility of the Philippines-instituted Arbitration Case under Annex Ⅶ to the UNCLOS: A Discussion on Fact-Finding and Evidence", *Chinese Journal of Global Governance*, 2(2016).

图书在版编目(CIP)数据

走向繁荣的国际法学：中国社会科学院国际法研究所十周年所庆纪念文集：全六卷／莫纪宏总主编．--北京：社会科学文献出版社，2019.9

ISBN 978-7-5201-5520-5

Ⅰ.①走… Ⅱ.①莫… Ⅲ.①国际法-法的理论-理论研究-文集 Ⅳ.①D990-53

中国版本图书馆CIP数据核字(2019)第188800号

走向繁荣的国际法学（全六卷）

——中国社会科学院国际法研究所十周年所庆纪念文集

总 主 编／莫纪宏

主　　编／柳华文　廖　凡　沈　涓　刘敬东　孙世彦　蒋小红 等

出 版 人／谢寿光

责任编辑／芮素平

文稿编辑／郭瑞萍　楼　霏　李娟娟　尹雪燕

出　　版／社会科学文献出版社·联合出版中心(010)59367281

地址：北京市北三环中路甲29号院华龙大厦　邮编：100029

网址：www.ssap.com.cn

发　　行／市场营销中心(010)59367081　59367083

印　　装／三河市东方印刷有限公司

规　　格／开 本：787mm×1092mm　1/16

印 张：88.25　插 页：4.5　字 数：1424千字

版　　次／2019年9月第1版　2019年9月第1次印刷

书　　号／ISBN 978-7-5201-5520-5

定　　价／980.00元(全六卷)

走向繁荣的国际法学

（全六卷）

TOWARDS THE PROSPERITY OF
INTERNATIONAL LAW STUDIES (SIX VOLUMES)

2009
~
2019

中国社会科学院国际法研究所十周年所庆纪念文集

【国际公法卷】

莫纪宏　总主编
蒋小红　马金星　主　编

社会科学文献出版社
SOCIAL SCIENCES ACADEMIC PRESS (CHINA)

国际公法研究室全家福（蒋小红、朱晓青、王翰灵、李赞、郝鲁怡、张卫华、马金星）

2017 年 12 月 2 日至 3 日，刘楠来荣誉学部委员出席中国社会科学论坛暨第十四届国际法论坛

2019 年 1 月 20 日，首届国际法热点问题研讨会（从左至右：莫纪宏所长、刘楠来荣誉学部委员、余永定学部委员）

国际公法学科相关研究人员（从左至右：李赞、王翰灵、李庆明、罗欢欣、蒋小红、柳华文、陈泽宪、朱晓青、李西霞、郝鲁怡、马金星、何田田、戴瑞君、张卫华）

2014 年 2 月 24 日，赵建文研究员应邀在全国人大外事委员会全体会议上作条约与国内法关系讲座

北京市国际法学会主办、中国社会科学院国际法研究所承办的“构建人类命运共同体与国际法学术研讨会暨北京国际法学会 2018 年学术年会”在北京召开

2015 年 4 月 14 日，参加外交部主办的“《联合国宪章》与战后国际秩序——纪念世界反法西斯战争胜利和联合国成立 70 周年”国际研讨会

2015 年 4 月 24 日，在参加于莫斯科举行的“第四届欧亚反腐败论坛”期间，访问俄罗斯联邦政府立法与比较法研究所

1998 年，蒋小红在荷兰留学时拜见王铁崖先生

2013 年 6 月 25 日，在国务院法制办国际司条约法规处就“条约在我国国内适用的有关法律问题”进行调研

2013 年 6 月 26 日，在全国人大外事委员会法案室条约处就“条约在我国国内适用的有关法律问题”进行调研

2019 年 5 月 25 日，“一带一路”项目调研团组在布达佩斯访问中国驻匈牙利大使馆商务处

2019 年 5 月 23 日，“一带一路”项目调研团组在塞尔维亚访问贝尔格莱德律师事务所

序

推动中国国际法学不断走向繁荣

1949 年 10 月 1 日，中华人民共和国中央人民政府宣告成立，结束了旧中国近百年半殖民地半封建受压迫受奴役的历史。中国人民从此站起来了！

在中国共产党和中国政府的坚强领导下，70 年来，中华人民共和国不断总结经验，克服困难，实现突破和发展，取得社会主义建设事业的伟大成就。特别是改革开放 40 年来，中国实现了经济腾飞和社会进步，中国的国际地位和影响力前所未有。2012 年党的十八大召开以来，中国特色社会主义进入新时代，中国人民实现了从站起来、富起来到强起来的发展过程，中国日益走近世界舞台的中央，中华民族比以往任何时候都更加接近实现中华民族伟大复兴的中国梦！

中华人民共和国的成立和 70 年来的发展历程，为中国国际法学的发展创造了良好的政治、经济、社会和历史条件。以周鲠生、陈体强、李浩培、王铁崖、韩德培等老一辈中国国际法学者为代表的中国国际法人为中国国际法理论研究和实践工作的起步和发展作出了卓越的贡献，为中国国际法学研究和教学做了大量奠基和铺路的工作。

1978 年 12 月 13 日，邓小平同志在党的十一届三中全会前召开的中央经济工作会议上发表了《解放思想，实事求是，团结一致向前看》的讲话，明确提出“要大力加强国际法的研究”。如春风，如号角，中国国际法研究获得极大的鼓舞。中国国际法学迎来了发展的春天。1980 年 2 月，中国国际法学会成立，中国社会科学院副院长宦乡担任首任会长。

中国社会科学院是中国国际法学的研究重镇。1959 年，也就是中国科

学院哲学社会科学部建立法学研究所之后的第二年，法学研究所成立了国际法组。1977 年 5 月，经党中央批准，中国社会科学院在中国科学院哲学社会科学部基础上正式组建。1978 年 9 月，中国社会科学院法学研究所国际法组改建为国际法研究室。

2002 年又是中国发展历程中一个不平凡的年份。这一年，中国改革开放渐入佳境，中国正式加入世界贸易组织；这一年，中国批准了作为“国际人权宪章”重要内容的联合国《经济、社会和文化权利国际公约》。也是这一年，在时任中国社会科学院院长李铁映的推动下，经中央机构编制委员会办公室批准，在国际法研究室基础上成立了国际法研究中心，使其成为与法学研究所平行的院属所局级机构。

国际法研究中心成立后，中国社会科学院国际法学研究获得进一步加强和推进。2009 年 9 月，经中央机构编制委员会办公室批准，国际法研究中心正式更名为国际法研究所。到今天，国际法研究所刚好成立 10 年了！

陈泽宪研究员任国际法研究所首任所长。2017 年 9 月至 2018 年 11 月，现任法学研究所所长、中国社会科学院学部委员陈甦研究员代行国际法研究所所长职责。2018 年 11 月，莫纪宏研究员开始担任国际法研究所所长。国际法研究所正是在国家经济发展和社会进步取得历史性突破，中国在国际社会地位极大提升、国际影响力不断扩大的背景下诞生的。它的成立和发展承载了党和国家繁荣和发展中国国际法学的使命。

10 年来，国际法研究所与外交部、商务部等相关政府部门密切联系，与中国国际法学会等全国性国际法研究学会、学术机构一道，积极进取，努力推动中国国际法学走向繁荣。依托学科和人才优势，国际法研究所设有国际公法、国际经济法、国际私法和国际人权法 4 个研究室，还设有海洋法治研究、竞争法研究和国际刑法研究领域的 3 个非实体中心以及最高人民法院“一带一路”司法研究基地。依托国际法研究所国际法专业的博士点和硕士点，博士、硕士研究生和博士后研究人员的指导工作也得到了加强。

2014 年创刊的《国际法研究》是中国第一本获得正式刊号的国际法专业原创中文期刊，国际法研究所是其主要主办单位和主编单位。该刊在国际法研究领域学术期刊的发文转载率方面处于全国领先地位，已经成为国际法学界重要的学术展示和交流平台。一年一度的国际法论坛已成功举办

15 届，成为中国社会科学院院级国际研讨会的学术品牌，吸引了国内外权威和知名专家的积极参与。在刘楠来、王可菊、陶正华、林欣等前辈国际法学家的关心和鼓舞下，国际法研究所一大批中青年国际法学者正在成为国际法学界的学术骨干。

值此国际法研究所 10 周年所庆之际，我们出版文集，选粹研究人员的研究成果，包括《国际法研究》发表过的有影响力的论文，回顾走过的历程，展示当下的风貌，既是国际法研究所成长道路上的一个小结，更是展现坚定的再创辉煌的决心。

中国倡导的“一带一路”建设正在世界范围内获得越来越多、越来越大的发展成就，推动构建人类命运共同体的中国主张日益获得国际社会的广泛支持和积极响应。

前路不乏机遇和挑战，中国社会科学院国际法研究所全体同仁必将以只争朝夕的精神，不忘初心、牢记使命，与全国国际法学同仁一道，推进中国国际法学不断走向繁荣！

莫纪宏

2019 年 8 月 20 日

目录
Contents

国际公法研究室简介

国际公法学科是中国社会科学院法学研究所和国际法研究所历史最悠久的学科之一。从1959年中国科学院法学研究所国际法组成立至今，国际公法学科的成长始终追随时代脚步和国家发展需求，在中国国际法学领域形成学科发展传承有序、学术研究方向齐全、各项科研成果领先和国内外影响力显著的鲜明特征。60年征程薪火相传，一代又一代国际公法学人砥砺前行，不断推进学科研究创新发展，为中国国际法学的繁荣贡献一份力量。

一 历史沿革

1958年，中国科学院哲学社会科学部建立法学研究所。1959年，法学研究所成立第四研究组，即国际法组。1978年，法学研究所改属中国社会科学院，国际法组改建为国际法研究室。2002年10月，中国社会科学院法学研究所国际法研究室改组为中国社会科学院国际法研究中心。2004年分设国际公法、国际私法及国际经济法三个研究室，并依托国际公法研究室专门从事海洋法研究的人员设立海洋法与海洋事务研究中心，国际公法研究室由原国际法研究室主要从事国际公法研究的人员组成。2009年9月，中国社会科学院国际法研究中心更名为中国社会科学院国际法研究所，在既有三个研究室的基础上增设国际人权法研究室，国际公法研究室成为国际法研究所内与国际经济法研究室、国际私法研究室和国际人权法研究室并列的四个研究室之一。2015年10月，海洋法与海洋事务研究中心由所级非实体研究中心升格为院级研究中心，2019年8月，中心更名为海洋法治研究中心。国际公法研究室设有法学博士点 1 个（国际法学专业国际公法学方向），硕士点 1 个（国际法学专业国际公法学方向）。

二 人员组成

1959 年国际法组成立至 2002 年国际法研究中心成立，从事国际公法研究的人员与从事国际法其他方向研究的人员同属于国际法组、国际法研究室。1959 年国际法组建立后，组成成员包括王可菊、刘珍、夏国强和吴建璠（兼）。1960 年调入马骧聪、叶维钧和王存学。1961 年法学研究所确定由张友渔兼任国际法组组长，由解铁光代管，马骏（外交学院）兼副组长，王可菊任组秘书。1977 年底，法学研究所研究人员按专业重新分组，国际法组除原四组的王可菊、叶维钧、王存学外，从其他组转来徐鹤皋、魏家驹、吴云琪、刘楠来和沈小明，并调入姚壮、任继圣、王孙奂，其中，徐鹤皋与刘楠来为临时负责人。1978 年 9 月，国际法组改组为国际法研究室，徐鹤皋任主任，刘楠来、任继圣任副主任。1984—1993 年，刘楠来任国际法研究室主任，郑成思任副主任。1978—1993 年，郑成思（1979）、盛愉（1979）、赵维田（1980）、李泽锐（1980）、于华、曾建凡（1981）、林欣（1981）、陶正华（1982）、朱晓青（1984）、朱文英、马守仁、张薇、赵李欣（1987）、杨力军（1987）、陶修明（1992）等陆续调入国际法研究室。1994 年 2 月至 2003 年 12 月，陶正华任国际法研究室（国际公法研究室）主任，杨力军、沈涓先后任副主任。

2002 年 10 月，国际法研究室改组为国际法研究中心，2004 年下设国际公法、国际私法及国际经济法三个研究室。国际公法研究室由主要从事国际公法研究的人员组成，成为从事国际公法研究与教学的专业部门。2004 年 11 月起，孙世彦受聘任国际公法研究室主任，朱晓青任副主任。1993 年至 2009 年 8 月，郭强、张若思、柳华文（2000）、沈敏荣（2001）、林长远、王翰灵（2004）、孙世彦（2006）、赵建文（2008）等陆续调入，戴瑞君毕业留所工作（2006）。

2009 年中国社会科学院国际法研究所成立后，孙世彦任国际公法研究室主任（2009—2015），朱晓青任副主任（2009—2014）。2016 年 1 月至今，蒋小红任国际公法研究室主任。2009 年至今，李赞（2010）、郝鲁怡（2012）、张卫华（2016）、马金星（2018）相继调入国际公法研究室。截至 2019 年 4 月，国际公法研究室共有在职研究人员 6 人，包括蒋小红、王翰灵、李赞、郝鲁怡、张卫华、马金星，其中研究员 1 人、副研究员 3 人、助理研究员 2 人。退休返聘人员 1 人，为朱晓青。另有刘楠来、王可菊、陶正华 3 位资深研究员参与国际公法科研工作。其中，刘楠来研究员 1992 年享受国务院政府特殊津贴，2006 年当选中国社会科学院荣誉学部委员，曾任全国海洋资源研究开发保护专家组成员、全国哲学社会科学规划（评审）法学组成员、中国国际法学会副会长、《中国国际法年刊》主编等；参与起草《领海及毗连区法》、《专属经济区和大陆架法》、《海域使用管理法》等法律法规；2011 年被聘为国家海洋事业发展高级咨询委员会委员，2015 年被聘为外交部国际法咨询委员会顾问。王可菊研究员 1992 年享受国务院政府特殊津贴，曾任中国国际法学会和中国海洋法学会理事、《中国国际法年刊》编委、北京市国际法学会副会长、中国专属经济区大陆架法起草小组成员、中国法律咨询中心咨询顾问、《中国大百科全书·法学卷》（2004 年版）国际法主编。陶正华研究员曾任武汉大学国际法研究所兼职教授、中国国际法学会常务理事、中国国际经济贸易仲裁委员会仲裁员、《法学大辞典》副主编、国际公法学科独任撰稿人，享受国务院政府特殊津贴。

两名研究人员在国际机构任职。2009 年 5 月，刘楠来由我国政府指定担任设在海牙的常设仲裁法院仲裁员。2006 年，王翰灵由中国政府按照《联合国海洋法公约》附件八第 2 条向联合国提名而担任国际渔业特别仲裁专家，并于 2006—2007 年担任联合国法律办公室海洋事务与海洋法司顾问。

三 重要科研成果

中国科学院哲学社会科学部法学研究所国际法组是中华人民共和国成立后最早从事国际法研究的机构之一。从成立至今，国际公法学者研究成果丰富，出版了多部专著，发表了大量学术论文，研究内容涵盖国际法各分支领域，处于国内领先水平，成就斐然。其间，还承担了大量的立法、专题研究以及法律咨询任务，并就重大国际事件开展预案及对策研究，向中央机关、政府有关部门以及有关单位报送立法建议、研究报告或法律意见书，并获得党和国家领导人的批示。

（一）1959 年国际法组成立至 1978 年国际法研究室成立

在中华人民共和国废除旧法制、创建新法制的过程中，国际法学者在吸收苏联国家和法的理论基础上，开始探索运用马克思主义的立场、观点、方法研究法律问题，为我国马克思主义法理学的发展奠定了基础。受历史条件的制约，当时国际法研究工作主要是翻译、介绍苏联国家和法的理论、国际法理论和资料，阐述、分析马克思主义经典作家或党和国家领导人的有关论述。这一时期，国际公法学者的译著主要包括《国家和法的理论》（彼・斯・罗马什金等主编，刘楠来、魏家驹等译，法律出版社，1964）、《国际法理论问题》（格・伊・童金著，王可菊等译，世界知识出版社，1965）。此外，吴云琪发表的《帝国主义国家是垄断资产阶级残暴专政的工具——驳斥南斯拉夫现代修正主义者歪曲帝国主义国家本质的谬论》（《法学研究》1962 年第 4 期），运用马克思列宁主义国家学说对现代资本主义国家在本质上都是对劳动人民实行专政的工具进行了揭露和批评。总体上看，这一时期国际公法学者的代表性研究成果有着鲜明的时代特征，理论研究移植苏联国际法的研究成果，反映了苏联国际法理论对当时中国学者的影响。

1966 年“文化大革命”开始后，中国科学院哲学社会科学部法学研究所的工作陷于停顿状态，绝大部分人员到河南干校参加劳动，1972 年陆续回到北京。1974 年开始，国际公法研究工作逐步得到恢复。

（二）1978 年国际法研究室成立至 2002 年国际法研究中心成立

1978—2002 年，国际公法研究成果不断涌现，国际公法研究越来越精细，学者在各自的学科领域或某一分支领域内“精耕细作”。这一时期，国际法研究室国际公法学者主要从事以下六方面的研究工作。

一是研讨国内法与国际条约之间的关系。1978 年改革开放至 20 世纪末，中国缔结参加的国际条约不断增多，国际条约与国内法的关系成为学术界关注的焦点问题。国际法研究室的学者较早开始对该问题进行理论研究，并积极参与《中华人民共和国缔结条约程序法》的制定及修改工作。1999 年 12 月由中国社会科学院法学研究所主办、德国阿登纳基金会（KAS）资助的“中德国际条约与国内法关系研讨会”在上海成功举办，这是首次在中国举办有关国际条约与国内法关系的学术研讨会。会后，在收集到的中国学者论文基础上，出版了《国际条约与国内法的关系》（朱晓青、黄列主编，世界知识版社，2000）一书，该书既收入了刘楠来、陶正华、朱晓青、孙世彦等国际法研究室学者的文章，也收入了其他高等院校、研究所等科研机构学者的文章。由于宪法和法理学界专家的参与，本书收入的研究成果从多学科、多角度探讨了国际条约与国内法的关系，并为进一步明确国际条约与中国国内法的关系提供了契机。该书成为国内学者研究国际条约与国内法关系的经典著作之一，书中的内容至今仍不断被学者援引和参考，可以说，该研究成果是对20世纪90年代国内关于国际条约与国内法关系学术研究的一次总结，也是这一时期国内法与国际条约关系研究的代表性成果。此后，学者对于国内法与国际条约关系的研讨愈加深入。朱晓青发表的《作为中国法律体系组成部分的国际条约》（载《依法治国与法律体系建构》，中国法制出版社，2001）认为，国际条约是中国法律体系不可或缺的一部分，国际条约的批准是国家的一项立法活动，国际条约是中国法律的渊源之一。由于我国宪法未作出明文规定，因而难以真正解决国际条约与国内法或中国法律体系的关系问题，这也使得司法实践中很难操作。由于“国际法的国内适用问题在很大程度上涉及国内的权力分配”，是否以宪法规定二者的关系成为国家审慎考虑的事项。

二是积极投入国际人权法的研究。中华人民共和国成立以来，我国一贯承认和尊重《联合国宪章》保护和促进人权的宗旨和原则，1971年恢复联合国合法席位后，积极参与联合国人权事务，至1991年底参加了联合国主持制定的八项国际人权公约。自20世纪80年代初，国际法研究室的国际公法学者便开始翻译国际人权资料，介绍域外学者的研究动态，讨论国际人权法相关问题。任允正翻译的《马克思列宁主义的人权观与当代意识形态斗争》（《环球法律评论》1980年第6期），首次向国内学者系统介绍了苏联学者提出的、以马列主义为基础的人权观，引导国内学者对于人权的认识，而不是一概将人权视为资产阶级理论加以批判。李泽锐摘译的路易斯·亨金（Louis Henkin）的《美国人的宪法权利与人权》（《环球法律评论》1981年第6期），是其向国内学者介绍美国学者在比较宪法权利与人权、国际人权与美国人宪法权利后得出的研究成果；他发表的《论连带关系概念的重新出现——一个值得注意的西方国际法学思想动向》（《法学研究》1985 年第 6 期），较为系统地介绍和分析了卡雷尔·瓦萨克提出的“连带关系权利”构成的“第三代人权”的观点。刘楠来的《〈世界人权宣言〉的诞生及其意义》（《人民日报》1988 年 12 月 8 日）对《世界人权宣言》的产生背景、主要内容及意义作出了阐释。1989 年后，一些西方国家借口人权问题对我国展开了广泛攻击，而国内学者在有关人权的认识上却存在很大分歧，有不少人错误地认为人权是资产阶级的东西，应当加以批判。在这种情况下，时任中共中央总书记的江泽民同志作了“人权问题不应再回避，要进行研究”的批示。为了贯彻落实这一批示，国际公法学者出版及发表了大量高质量的研究成果。这些成果可以分为两类。一类是客观介绍西方及发展中国家人权理论及学说。王可菊的《当代西方学者关于人权与主权的观点》（《外国法译评》1997 年第 3 期）针对人权对国家主权带来的影响、人权是否可以成为干涉的口实、人权是否属于国内管辖事项，以及个人在国际法上的地位和国际人权文件的法律效力等，系统介绍了西方学者的观点。文森特（R. J. Vincent）著、朱晓青等译的《人权与国际关系》（知识出版社，1997），详细阐述人权的理论，探讨人权在国际关系中的作用，并在最后提出西方各国应该在外交政策中怎样处理人权问题。上述成果为当时的中国学者了解、质疑及反驳西方人权理论，提供了参考。刘楠来主编的《发展中国家与人权》（四川人民出版社，1994）系统搜集了发展中国家宪法有关人权问题的规定、批准国际人权公约概况、亚非拉区域性国际人权文书，以及发展中国家学者和外交官论人权，资料翔实，内容客观，成为 20 世纪 90 年代国内学者研究发展中国家人权的必读资料。另一类是系统研究国际人权问题。刘楠来、陶正华主编的《人权的普遍性和特殊性》（社会科学文献出版社，1996），以及之后的 *Human Rights: Chinese and Dutch Perspectives*（Martinus Nijhoff Pub.，1996）指出，维护和尊重作为个体的每个人的权利和尊严是人权的一般性要求，是人权的普遍性。在当代世界不同发展程度的国家中、在不同的文化环境中、在不同的民族宗教地区中，人们为争取人权而奋斗的目标、每个人实际权利的内容和性质，都必然是不同的。包括中国在内的发展中国家与西方发达国家之间，在衡量人权状况的标准上，在为改善人权状况而提出的奋斗目标上，都有明显的区别。朱晓青的《论联合国人权国际保护的执行措施》

（《法学研究》1994 年第 4 期）从理论及实践方面分析了联合国人权国际保护的执行措施，指出了人权国际保护执行措施实际运作中的困难，并且提出未来的人权国际保护机制与体系将是由更具有监测与预防、调解与行动、保护与促进功能的执行措施构成的高效力的和协调统一的机制与体系。

三是大力开展国际刑法研究。第二次世界大战结束以后，国际刑法作为国际法的一个新兴分支，得到迅猛发展。在 1986 年国际刑事科学高级研究院于意大利锡拉丘萨市举行的国际刑法学教学讨论会上，大多数学者认为，国际刑法学已经具备了其作为独立学科的一切条件。在这一背景下，国际法研究室的国际公法学者适时展开了国际刑法研究。林欣撰写的《国际法中的刑事管辖权》（法律出版社，1988）对国际法中的刑事管辖权问题作了全面细致的论述，把国际刑法理论问题的研究引向深入。他发表的《论国际刑法问题的新发展》（《法学研究》1992 年第 4 期）结合国际法委员会的讨论、域外国家刑事立法等，对 20 世纪 80 年代至 90 年代初禁止非法买卖麻醉药品、域外刑事管辖权和引渡问题的新发展作了探讨。1996 年林欣领衔开展国家社会科学基金项目“国际刑法问题研究”的研究工作，2000 年 4 月出版《国际刑法问题研究》（林欣主编）一书，对国际刑法的历史、定义、刑事责任、刑事管辖权、各种国际犯罪、国际刑事法院或引渡或起诉原则等问题，作了全面系统的论述，是其后国内学者开展国际刑法研究的奠基之作。

四是积极开展国际海洋法的研究。1973 年 12 月第三次联合国海洋法会议在美国纽约拉开序幕，这是我国恢复联合国合法席位后参加的第一个意义重大的国际立法会议，受到了全国上下的关注。国际法组以及之后的国际法研究室的国际公法研究人员，急国家之所急，主动请缨参加第三次海洋法会议有关问题的研究讨论，受到有关政府部门的热烈欢迎。同时，展开了国际海洋法的资料和理论研究工作。吴云琪、刘楠来及王可菊合译出版了苏联学者拉扎列夫的《现代国际海洋法》（天津人民出版社，1981）。1986 年，刘楠来、王可菊与上海社会科学院周子亚、陈振国、杨志雄，国家海洋局虞源澄、倪轩等合著的《国际海洋法》（海洋出版社，1986），为当时国内最全面、系统的国际海洋法专著，为我国海洋法学科的奠基作出了贡献，当时国家海洋行政主管部门将其列为案头业务工作重要参考书，联合国出版的《海洋法公报》将该书列为国际海洋法领域的重要中文著作。刘楠来等合译的《各国专属经济区和大陆架法规选编》（法律出版社，1988）也被政府机关和各大院校普遍作为资料加以使用。

五是引领国内航空法的研究。1961 年、1963 年和 1971 年国际社会先后通过了东京、海牙和蒙特利尔等三个“反劫机”公约，中国是上述三个公约的缔约国。1983 年卓长仁等将民航 296 号班机劫持到韩国，举国震动，各方面十分关注把他们引渡回国惩处问题。赵维田是国内最早研究反劫机问题的学者之一，他于 1985 年出版的《论三个反劫机公约》（群众出版社，1985）填补了国内劫持航空器国际犯罪研究的空白，也是我国最早的航空法专著，在我国航空法和国际刑法研究领域起了引领作用。赵维田先后在我国台湾地区（水牛出版社，1991）和大陆（社会科学文献出版社，2000）两地出版的《国际航空法》，是国内第一部系统涵盖国际航空法各个分支领域的学术著作，获得了学术界和航空界的高度评价，深刻影响了海峡两岸国际航空法的研究，也标志着国内学者开始构建国际航空法理论体系。

六是较早关注国际环境及资源法发展。在国外，国际环境及资源法的研究始于 20 世纪 70 年代，在我国这一领域从 70 年代末开始才逐渐引起法学界的注意，1981 年国内有关刊物开始发表国际环境法研究成果。1980 年盛愉发表了《核法初论》（《法学研究》1980 年第 6 期），明确提出核能的开发、使用、管理、保护措施、赔偿制度等，需要有一套法规准则，这是现代核法的基本内容，军用核法准则与民用核法准则共同构成核法的整体。1981 年，盛愉发表了《环境战略与国际环境法》（《中国环境科学》1981 年第 3 期），盛愉、魏家驹合著的《国际法新领域简论》（吉林人民出版社，1984）设有专门一章对国际环境法的产生背景、形成过程、主要内容、基本原则等作了概要的论述。盛愉、周岗的《现代国际水法概论》（法律出版社，1987），是国内最早的国际水法著作，书中用国际法的逻辑分析国际水法的主体、研究对象、渊源，论述国际水法历史发展的过程和国际水域的各种法律制度及组织，阐释了现代国际水法的基本特点、理论和原则。进入 20 世纪 90 年代，我国国际环境法研究进一步加强，马骧聪等主编的《国际环境法导论》（社会科学文献出版社，1994）是国内最早系统研究国际环境法的著作之一，对于从理论上支持国家环境外交、健全和完善我国环境法治发挥了积极作用。

总结这一时期的研究成果可以看出，尽管中苏关系自20世纪60年代中叶以后公开破裂，但是，国际公法理论和实践基本上延续了20世纪50年代的传统，以马列主义为指导、以苏联国际法理论为基础确立的国际法的框架体系没有实质性的变化，但是在具体问题上，国际公法学者已表现出明显不同于苏联的观点。进入20世纪80年代后，国际公法学者从当时的区域性及全球性问题或事件之中，敏锐捕捉到了其中的国际公法问题，密切关注国际公法发展的新动向，出版及发表的一系列具有前沿性和理论深度的研究成果，引领国内在国际公法领域的研究。

（三）2002年国际法研究中心成立至今

当今国际社会各种问题的高度复杂化、专业化向学界提出了精细化研究的要求。2002年国际法研究中心成立，2004年组建了国际公法研究室，聚集国际公法研究力量，提升理论研究水平，并在2009年国际法研究所成立后得以延续。这一时期的代表性研究成果呈现三方面特征：一是聚焦基础理论研究，拓展理论研究深度，不断推陈出新；二是以学科分支为基础，有关国际公法问题的研究趋于精细化，理论研究纵深不断加强；三是聚焦国家发展战略和全球性问题，以更为宽广的视野审视相关国际法问题，研究成果富于中国特色与问题意识。这一时期的代表性成果包括以下方面。

第一，关注理论发展动态，聚焦基础理论研究。陶正华发表的《国际法要研究的四个问题》（《法学研究》2004年第2期）指出，21世纪国际政治多极化格局和经济全球化趋势使国际法在各个方面都面临重大挑战、变化和发展。中国在当今国际政治经济关系中正产生着越来越大的作用和影响，在此背景下，国际法的研究重点应聚焦在21世纪的国家主权原则、人权的国际保护、如何建立国际政治经济新秩序，以及解决国际争端的原则与制度四个方面。面对贬低或者否定国际法的价值和作用的观点，刘楠来发表的《维护国际法严肃性》（《人民日报》2016年8月15日）认为，尽管一些国家为了自身利益作出违反国际法的行为，但国际法的约束力和执行力是不能否定的。某个国家为了追求自己的私利而破坏性利用国际法的行为，是不会被国际社会接受和认可的。

第二，以学科分支为基础，积极拓展国际法分支领域研究。这一时期，国际公法学者在国际组织法、国际人权法、国际海洋法、国际刑法及欧盟法领域，均颇有建树。李赞的《国际组织的司法管辖豁免研究》（中国社会科学出版社，2013）就国际组织的司法管辖豁免，即国际组织在国内法院是否享有豁免和如何实现这种豁免的问题进行了研究。该成果主要从国际组织司法管辖豁免的合法性和正当性两方面加以论证。合法性指国际组织司法管辖豁免的法律渊源，正当性指国际组织通过其司法管辖豁免的职能性限制、强制性放弃和任择性争端解决机制以实现国际组织与成员国关系的平衡。

在国际人权法研究领域，孙世彦的《〈公民及政治权利国际公约〉缔约国的义务》（社会科学文献出版社，2012）采用实证研究和学理研究相结合的研究方法，运用大量的资料文献，对《公民及政治权利国际公约》缔约国的义务进行了全面研究，目的在于通过研究缔约国根据《公约》承担的义务，加深中国学者对《公约》的理解，从而为研究《公约》的具体内容提供理论基础。蒋小红的《贸易与人权的联结——试论欧盟对外贸易政策中的人权目标》（《欧洲研究》2016 年第 5 期）揭示了欧盟对外贸易政策中人权目标的设立和实施面临的合法性、一致性、有效性和公信力等诸多问题和挑战。她指出，这些问题和挑战也从另一个角度再次证明：国际合作是促进国际人权保护的最好的、令人接受的方式。

在国际海洋法研究方面，王翰灵的《跨界和高度洄游鱼类渔业争端的解决机制》（载《中国国际法年刊（2008）》，世界知识出版社，2009）对《联合国海洋法公约》和《执行 1982 年 12 月 10 日〈联合国海洋法公约〉有关养护和管理跨界鱼类种群和高度洄游鱼类种群的规定的协定》的争端解决程序进行比较分析，厘清了其复杂的相互关系、有关争端解决的程序及其包含的理念。张卫华的《论专属经济区上空的法律地位和飞越自由》（《环球法律评论》2015 年第 1 期）对这一议题作了深入研究，认为专属经济区上空的飞越自由是公海性的，而且与沿海国在专属经济区的主权权利和管辖权关涉不大。故此，防空识别区制度不可能从沿海国在专属经济区的主权权利和管辖权中找到法律依据，其实际上是国家行使自保权的行为。面对我国与周边海洋邻国存在海洋争端，王翰灵发表的《中国对钓鱼岛拥有主权法律依据充分》（《法制日报》2005 年 6 月 10 日）、《美国欲制造何种“南海秩序”》（《光明日报》2016 年 7 月 12 日）、《双边谈判才是解决中菲南海争议的正道》（《中国国防报》2016 年 6 月 10 日）等，公开回应了相关国际法争议问题。马金星的《南海仲裁案中有关岛礁法律地位问题的评介》（《国际法研究》2017 年第 1 期）对南海仲裁案裁决书第六部分作了系统分析，指出仲裁庭在自裁管辖权的基础上，对中国有关外交立场进行了曲解，阐释《联合国海洋法公约》第 121 条第 3 款含义时具有强烈的主观倾向，通过推定意图为缔约国创设权利和义务，偏离了有疑从轻解释和演变性解释的合理化路径，以“释法”之名行“立法”之实，背离了条约解释的目的。相关证据缺乏合法性、真实性和关联性，无法支撑其裁决的合法性和有效性。

2002 年，国际刑事法院随着《国际刑事法院罗马规约》（以下简称《规约》）的生效而正式建立。我国虽尚未签署《规约》，但一直以积极的态度关注着国际刑事法院的发展。杨力军的《论〈国际刑事法院罗马规约〉中的补充性原则对国内立法的规范作用》（《武大国际法评论》2006 年第 1 期）对《规约》规定的“补充性原则”作了具体分析，指出补充性原则对缔约国在履行《规约》实体法方面具有重大的督促和规范作用；《规约》在执行国际刑法实体法方面对非缔约国也会产生间接或直接的影响。国际刑事法院实体法规定具有习惯国际法地位，因此对所有国家都产生间接影响。

经过多年的发展，国际公法学者在欧盟法研究领域取得了丰硕的成果，研究内容涉及多个方面，包括欧盟贸易法、欧盟人权机制、欧盟妇女权益保护、欧盟移民法等。朱晓青的《欧洲人权法律保护机制研究》（法律出版社，2003）对《欧洲人权公约》为核心的欧洲人权法律保护机制，并结合欧洲联盟人权法律保护机制对欧洲人权法律保护机制，作了全面系统的研究。郝鲁怡的《欧盟妇女劳动权利保护的法律制度研究》（中国社会科学出版社，2013）在国际法框架下，对妇女劳动权利保护进行了研究，在界定妇女劳动权利保护概念、内容和原则基础上，特别考察了欧盟在区域性国际组织层面对妇女就业和跨国转移中权利保护的法律制度。在考察欧盟有关妇女劳动力就业与跨国转移中的同工同酬、男女平等待遇、协调工作与家庭生活，以及妇女社会权利保障权利方面的法律制度后，指出欧盟在制定调整男女平等之相关法律、法规与措施时，采取一种渐进式的立法机制，并通过小幅度、温和方式对法律规范予以修订和演变，最终建立起较为完善和科学的法律制度。蒋小红的《欧盟对外贸易法与中欧贸易》（中国社会科学出版社，2014）以WTO法律体系和欧盟法律体系为背景，运用案例研究、比较研究、历史分析等方法从自主性立法和契约性安排与实践两个方面系统搭建欧盟对外贸易法的整体框架，全面介绍和解析欧盟对外贸易法，梳理欧盟对外贸易法主要内容，分析欧盟对外贸易法中的主要规则，特别是重点分析了适用于中国的有关规则，阐释其理论含义和实践运作。

第三，在国际法领域推动“一带一路”建设、构建人类命运共同体。王翰灵发表的《海上丝路需要国际法治环境》（《人民日报》2015年2月15日）指出，由21世纪海上丝绸之路联结起来的共同利益及其区域经济一体化，必将促进区域法律制度的融合及统一。21世纪海上丝绸之路建设需要一套完备的国际、国内法律制度，涉及海上交通基础设施建设、国际金融、航运、经贸，乃至海洋安全等诸多领域。李赞的《建设人类命运共同体的国际法原理与路径》（《国际法研究》2016年第6期）对这一问题进行了深入研究。他从物质基础、思想基础、道德基础、国内法及国际法路径，对建设人类命运共同体进行了深入研究，认为国际法应更加重视人的内心和平的建设，从而实现世界的永久和平，这是人类命运共同体建设的国际法新途径，建立在传统文化和国际法基本原则基础之上的中国和平发展，是对人类命运共同体建设的独特贡献。

除以上各个历史时期代表性成果外，中国社会科学院的国际公法学者承担了大量工具书、教材的编写工作。《法学词典》（上海辞书出版社，1980，第1版）编写过程中，姚壮担任常务编委及主要撰稿人，王可菊、魏家驹作为编委及主要撰稿人参加词典撰写工作。之后，王可菊又先后担任《中国大百科全书》（中国大百科全书出版社，1984、1989）“法学卷”及“军事卷”、《中国军事百科全书》“国际军事约章”分册、《中华法学大辞典》“国际法卷”（王铁崖主编，中国检察出版社，1996）的审稿人或撰稿人。朱晓青担任《国际人权文件与国际人权机构》（社会科学文献出版社，1993）、《人权大辞典》（武汉大学出版社，1993）的撰稿人。《法学大辞典》（曾庆敏主编，上海辞书出版社，1998）编写过程中，陶正华任副主编兼国际公法学科主编和撰稿人。在王家福、刘海年主编的《中国人权百科全书》（1998）编写过程中，王可菊、刘楠来担任副主编和撰稿人，朱晓青与杨力军担任撰稿人。在《中国实用大百科辞典》（中国大百科全书出版社，2000）编写过程中，陶正华担任国际法学科撰稿人。在中国社会科学院法学研究所法律辞典编纂委员会主编的《法律辞典》（法律出版社，2003）编写过程中，陶正华担任编委，王可菊、刘楠来、赵维田、林欣、杨力军、朱晓青、柳华文等撰写国际法词条。

此外，朱晓青作为主编，先后出版了法律硕士专业学位研究生通用教材《国际法学》（社会科学文献出版社，2005）和中国社会科学院研究生重点教材《国际法学》（中国社会科学出版社，2012）。

四 重要的学术活动

1959 年国际法组成立至今，国际公法学者服务于国家对外交往活动和法制建设，通过组织或参与中国法学会、中国国际法学会、北京市国际法学会等多种形式的活动，不断加强与国内其他实务部门、研究机构、高等院校国际法学者的沟通与交流，促进国际法在中国的研究、实践、传播和发展。1980 年中国国际法学会成立，中国社会科学院副院长宦乡担任首届会长，徐鹤皋任秘书长，学会办公机构设立在国际法研究室（后迁至外交学院），研究室成员负责《中国国际法年刊》（1982 年创刊）的出版编辑工作。此外，盛愉、刘楠来、王可菊、陶正华、朱晓青、孙世彦、蒋小红等，分别担任过中国法学会副会长、中国国际法学会副会长、北京市国际法学会副会长及学会理事等。

长期以来，国际公法研究室与国家机关、国内外高等院校和研究机构、国际组织和国内外同行不断建立和发展良好的合作关系。从 20 世纪 80 年代至今，部分学者赴美国哥伦比亚大学、丹佛大学、兰德公司、科罗拉多州最高法院、荷兰人权研究所、丹麦人权研究所、挪威人权研究所、瑞典隆德大学罗尔·瓦伦堡人权和人道法研究所、英国皇家国际事务研究所、德国马克斯·普朗克比较公法与国际法研究所等机构，进行交流访学。

近 20 年来，国际公法研究室成员参与的对外（学术）交流活动和政府公务活动，包括中德国际条约与国内法关系研讨会（1999，上海）、联合国消除种族歧视委员会审议中国履行《消除一切形式种族歧视国际公约》第 10 至 13 次定期报告会议（2009，日内瓦）、中欧人权对话（2012，爱尔兰）、亚太及海洋安全研究圆桌座谈会（2013，北京）、中越人民论坛（2014，河内）、东盟地区第二届《联合国海洋法公约》研讨会（2014，马尼拉）、曼谷亚太安全会议（2014，曼谷）、第四届欧亚反腐败论坛（2015，莫斯科）、海洋问题与《联合国海洋法公约》高级研讨会（2015，下龙湾）、中国国际问题研究院与美国布鲁金斯学会对话会议（2015，华盛顿）、人权领域的国际合作与中国视角国际研讨会（2016，北京）、美国弗吉尼亚大学海洋法与海洋政策中心年会（2018，北京）、历届北京人权论坛等。

五　总结及展望

国际公法研究室不仅拥有一批享誉海内外的著名学者，出版、发表了一批精品名作，还应国家有关部门的委托和邀请，多次参与立法、司法工作和国家级人权对话和交流活动，在国内外学术交流中发挥着重要作用。

党的十九大报告作出中国特色社会主义进入了新时代的重大政治判断，确定新时代的奋斗目标和战略安排，对新时代推进中国特色社会主义伟大事业和党的建设新的伟大工程作出全面部署。“秉纲而目自张，执本而末自从”，新时代为国际法学人创造了前所未有的研究国际法的机遇和条件，也为国际法学人提出了更高的期望和要求。围绕推进“一带一路”建设、加快建设海洋强国等国家战略布局，国际公法学人将继续服务于国家经济社会发展的战略需要，不辱使命，砥砺前行，不断推进国际公法学科向前发展，为中国国际法学的繁荣贡献一份力量。

研究室成员简介

蒋小红

一　基本情况

江苏东海人。中国社会科学院国际法研究所研究员、中国社会科学院大学教授，硕士生导师。1992 年获中国政法大学法学学士学位；1999 年获荷兰莱顿大学欧盟法专业法学硕士学位；2004 年获中国社会科学院国际法专业法学博士学位。1992—2005 年，就职于中国社会科学院法学研究所，先后任助理研究员、副研究员、科研外事处副处长；2005 年至今，就职于中国社会科学院国际法研究所，先后任副研究员、科研外事处处长、研究员、国际公法研究室主任。

蒋小红研究员长期专注于欧盟法的研究，任中国欧盟法研究学会常务理事。她的研究领域还包括国际贸易救济法、国际投资法、国际竞争法、国际争端解决。近年来从事的研究主题涉及贸易与人权、国际投资与可持续发展、国际投资仲裁、中欧双边投资协定谈判等。

蒋小红研究员曾主持并完成中国社会科学院重点科研项目“贸易救济法的新发展”、中国社会科学院重大国情调研项目“滥用贸易救济措施给中国企业带来的影响”以及“国际贸易中的限制竞争行为及其规制”等中国社会科学院委托交办的项目。另外，她作为课题组主要成员参与并完成外交部、商务部、国家药监局等部门委托课题多项，涉及《缔结条约程序法》的修改、加入《WTO 政府采购协议》对我国相关部门的影响等问题的研究。

蒋小红研究员曾多次参与商务部、贸促会、行业协会组织的有关国际贸易和投资热点法律问题和贸易纠纷案件的讨论和咨询工作，并为相关的出口企业和行业协会讲授国际贸易法、欧盟对外贸易法等相关法律知识。通过这些活动，理论与实践相结合，为中国的出口企业实施“走出去”战略服务，发挥学者智囊的作用，为维护国家利益作出贡献。蒋小红研究员曾赴瑞典隆德大学、荷兰莱顿大学、美国哥伦比亚大学研修。

二 主要科研成果

（一）专著

1.《欧共体反倾销法与中欧贸易》

该书是中国国内较早系统研究欧盟反倾销法的论著之一。获得商务部 2006 年全国商务发展研究成果三等奖，2007 年中国社会科学院优秀科研成果三等奖。

本书以欧共体法律体系为背景，深入论述了欧共体反倾销法的历史发展轨迹、立法渊源、与反不正当竞争法和其他贸易保护措施法的关系、反倾销实体法和程序法等问题，特别是重点论述了对中国出口产品的反倾销政策，即反倾销法中的非市场经济问题。本书在全面理解欧共体反倾销规则和客观分析我国应对欧共体反倾销现状的基础上，探求我国合法、理性应对欧共体反倾销指控的法律对策并对未来如何减少和防止反倾销指控提出了建议。在贸易保护主义抬头的今天，贸易救济措施是保护国内产业的重要手段。本书仍然具有重要的理论和实践指导意义。

2.《欧盟对外贸易法与中欧贸易》

本书被推选为中国社会科学院国际法研究所 2014 年创新工程优秀专著。2018 年获得中国社会科学院国际法研究所优秀科研成果一等奖。

本书是目前国内较为系统地研究欧盟对外贸易法的专著，是《欧共体反倾销法与中欧贸易》的姊妹篇。作者认为，研究欧盟对外贸易法是研究欧盟法和国际法，特别是国际贸易法的一个极佳入口，也为欧盟法和国际法的交叉研究提供了一个良好范例。长期以来，欧盟法以欧洲经贸一体化为依托深入发展了现代国际法，对国际法的基础制度和部门法产生了重大的建构效应。欧盟对外贸易法的研究涉及国际贸易法、国际组织法、国际条约法、国际人权法等相关内容，将进一步促进对现代国际法的研究。

本书以欧盟对外贸易法为研究对象，以欧盟法律体系与 WTO 法律体系为研究背景，从自主性立法和契约性安排与实践两个方面，系统梳理了欧盟对外贸易法的主要内容，分析了欧盟对外贸易法中的主要规则，特别是重点分析了适用于中国的有关规则，阐释其理论含义和实践运作。在全面介绍和解析欧盟对外贸易法的基础上分析了发展中欧经贸关系所存在的法律问题并提出了建议和对策。在阐述欧盟对外贸易法的主要规则中，考虑到欧盟法具有显著的动态性和演进性的特点，特别是 2009 年底生效的《里斯本条约》给欧盟的对外贸易法律制度带来了显著影响，本书强调了欧盟对外贸易法的新发展，有助于全面掌握欧盟对外贸易法的最新动态。书中对一些热点问题，特别是涉及中国的贸易利益的问题，如非市场经济问题、普惠制问题、原材料摩擦问题、贸易救济纠纷问题、正在进行的中欧双边投资协定谈判问题，都作了深入研究并提出了相应对策。

（二）合著

1.《社会主义市场经济法律集注》，人民日报出版社，1994。

2.《中国人权建设》，四川人民出版社，1994。

3.《涉外经济贸易与投资》，中国法制出版社，1995。

4.《中日企业破产法律制度比较研究》，辽宁人民出版社，1996。

5.《结社：理论与实践》（译著），三联书店，2006。

6.《国际经济法学》，中国科学出版社，2007。

7. *Contemporary Chinese Law*，中国检察出版社，2009。

8.《国际商事仲裁》（译著），中国社会科学出版社，2009。

9.《欧洲法律之路》（译著），清华大学出版社，2010。

10.《国际法学》，中国社会科学出版社，2012。

11.《变化中的国际法：热点与前沿》，中国社会科学出版社，2012。

（三）论文

1.《欧共体非市场经济反倾销规则研究》，《外国法译评》2000 年第 4 期。

2.《GATT/WTO 在欧共体法律体系中的地位》，载《依法治国与法律体系构建》，中国法制出版社，2000。

3.《欧共体保障措施制度研究》，《北大国际法与比较法评论》第 1 卷，北京大学出版社，2002。

4.《英国对表达自由权的保护与限制》，《欧洲法通讯》第 5 辑，法律出版社，2003。

5.《欧共体反补贴立法与实践》，《法学评论》2003 年第 1 期。

6.《试论 WTO 反倾销协议的完善》，《环球法律评论》2004 年冬季号。

7.《更加透明、简化的毕业程序——欧盟普惠制立法的最新发展及影响》，《国际贸易》2006 年第 1 期。

8.《通过公益诉讼，推动社会变革》，《环球法律评论》2006 年第 3 期。

9.《欧盟对企业合并的法律监管》，《国际贸易》2006 年第 7 期。

10.《反倾销法中的公共利益问题考量》，《国际法研究》第 1 卷，中国人民公安大学出版社，2006。

11.《9·11 事件及其对国际法的挑战》（译文），《国际法研究》第 1 卷，中国人民公安大学出版社，2006。

12.《论反垄断法的私人实施机制》，载《反垄断立法热点问题》，社会科学文献出版社，2007（获得 2012 年国际法所优秀科研成果奖）。

13.《论 WTO 法在欧盟法律体系中的地位》，载《依法治国与法律体系构建》，社会科学文献出版社，2008。

14.《匈牙利公民社会组织考察》，《环球法律评论》2009年第4期。

15.《〈里斯本条约〉对欧盟对外贸易法律制度的影响》，《国际贸易》2010年第3期。

16.《欧盟扫除贸易壁垒的法律措施及对中国的启示》，《国际法研究》第6卷，社会科学文献出版社，2012。

17.《欧盟普惠制立法的最新发展及影响》，《国际贸易》2013年第3期。

18.《试析欧盟贸易救济立法的最新发展》，《欧洲研究》2013年第6期（被中国人民大学书报资料中心复印报刊资料《国际法学》2014年第4期全文转载）。

19.《欧盟贸易政策与安全政策的纠结与碰撞》，《中央党校学报》2015年第6期。

20.《解析欧盟对外贸易投资新政》，《中国社会科学报》2016年2月1日。

21.《刍议欧盟对外贸易法的主要特点》，《欧洲法律评论》第1卷，中国社会科学出版社，2016。

22.《中欧原材料纠纷的解决之道》，载《中欧双边投资协定谈判相关法律问题研究》，法律出版社，2016。

23.《贸易与人权的联结》，《欧洲研究》2016年第5期。

24.《中国“非市场经济待遇”之后倾销的计算方法》，《国际法研究》2017年第4期。

25.《试论欧盟对外贸易政策中的人权目标》，载《人权领域内的国际合作与中国视角》，中国政法大学出版社，2017。

26.《国际投资协定谈判与可持续发展》，《中国社会科学报》2018年11月28日。

27.《人类命运共同体与国际法治》，载《新时代法治发展的新面向》，中国社会科学出版社，2018。

28.《国际投资法的新发展——以国际投资条约如何促进可持续发展为视角》，《河北法学》2019年第3期。

王翰灵

一　基本情况

中国社会科学院国际法研究所国际公法研究室副研究员、法学系教授。主要研究领域是国际法基本理论、国际海洋法、渔业法、国际环境法及海洋事务。1998年中国社会科学院研究生院法学系国际法专业国际海洋法研究方向博士毕业，获法学博士学位。2002—2003年在加拿大达尔豪斯大学（Dalhousie University）从事国际海洋法专业博士后研究，师从已故世界著名海洋法律与政策专家、联合国顾问勃基斯教授等人。曾在四川大学、联合国国际海事组织所属的世界海事大学、芬兰的拉普兰大学（University of Lapland）从事学习和研究工作。2006年由中国政府提名而担任《联合国海洋法公约》争端解决机制特别仲裁专家（无限期）。2006—2007年担任联合国法律办公室海洋事务与海洋法司顾问。现任上海海洋大学等多所大学兼职教授，兼任中国海洋发展研究院研究员、南京大学中国南海研究协同创新中心研究员、意大利马切拉塔大学海洋法与海洋事务研究员。曾任新加坡国立大学国际法研究中心和东亚研究所访问研究员、美国科罗拉多大学和丹佛大学法学院访问学者。曾应邀到美国哈佛大学等多所国际著名大学讲学，并为美国海军战争学院、加拿大国防学院、印度尼西亚国防大学学员授课。撰写过研究报告和学术论文100多篇，其中多篇论文发表于美国国际海洋法专业权威英文期刊《海洋开发与国际法》（*Ocean Development & International Law*）和国内法学专业核心期刊。有的论文在国际上被全文转载，被美国、加拿大等国多所大学的海洋法和海洋管理研究生课程选为教材或阅读材料，并被广泛引用。有30多篇研究报告获得党和国家领导人批示，荣获中国社会科学院对策研究特等奖、一等奖等30多项学术奖励。承担中办、外交部、海洋与渔业部门等多项科研课题。多次作为中国代表团成员参加有关海洋问题的1.5轨和二轨国际对话会议。多次参加中美、亚欧海洋战略、海事安全对话，亚洲－北约对话，东盟地区论坛南海问题及海洋法会议，以及其他海洋问题国际会议。

二　主要科研成果

（一）合著

1. *Ecosystem Approaches to the Management of Ocean-Related Activities*, UN, 2011.

王翰灵参编的联合国海洋管理英文教材《有关海洋活动管理的生态系统方式》（*Ecosystem Approaches to the Management of Ocean-Related Activities*, 联合国出版，2011，共296页）从多学科、多层面对与海洋有关的人类活动管理的生态系统方式的各方面问题进行全面、系统而深入的阐述，是国际上关于此专题的开创性教材，由联合国出版并在世界各地推广应用，获得国际理论界和业界的认可。王翰灵是参编此教材的四位国际专家中唯一的发展中国家专家，其承担的研究和写作部分是导论及法律与政策等主要内容，其成果被联合国采用，为联合国的有关工作及国际上关于此领域的理论研究与实践作出了贡献。

2. Le Droit De la Mer Face Aux "Méditerranées": Quelle contribution de la Méditerranée et des mers semi-fermées au droit international de la mer? Editoriale Scientifica, 2016.

该书从海洋划界、海洋资源环境养护与管理等多方面论述了作为半闭海的地中海的有关海洋法理论与实践及其对有关国际实践的启示。王翰灵撰写的部分是关于海洋渔业资源的共同开发，特别是从《联合国海洋法公约》关于闭海和半闭海沿岸国在海洋生物资源的管理、养护、勘探和开发方面的合作义务的角度进行论述，对有关的国际案例进行了分析，并探讨了在南中国海进行渔业资源共同开发与养护管理的相关问题。

（二）代表性论文

1. "Ecosystem Management and Its Application to Large Marine Ecosystems: Science, Law, and Politics", *Ocean Development & International Law*, 35: 41 –74, 2004.

2. "An Evaluation of the Modular Approach to the Assessment and Management of Large Marine Ecosystems", *Ocean Development & International Law*, 35: 267 –286, 2004.

3.《跨界和高度洄游鱼类渔业争端解决机制》，《中国国际法年刊（2009）》，世界知识出版社，2010。

（三）公开发表的部分研究报告

1. "China's Position on India's Bid for Permanent Membership of the UN Security Council", East Asian Institute (EAI), National University of Singapore, 2011.

2. "China's Diplomacy and Stand on Implementing the Declaration on the Conduct of Parties in the South China Sea", East Asian Institute (EAI), National University of Singapore, 2011.

3. "China Faces Unprecedented Challenges on the South China Sea Issue", East Asian Institute (EAI), National University of Singapore, 2011.

李　赞

一　基本情况

湖南长沙人，北京大学法学博士（2010 年），中国社会科学院国际法研究所副研究员。

主要研究方向：国际法基本理论、国际组织法、国际老年人权保护和中国养老事业、文化与国际法。

二　主要代表性学术成果

（一）专著

1.《国际条约在香港的适用问题研究》（合著），中国民主法制出版社，2010。

2.《国际组织的司法管辖豁免研究》（独著），中国社会科学出版社，2013。

3.《国际经济一体化进程中的国内法与国际规则》（合著），武汉大学出版社，2016。

4.《爱与陪伴——老人临终关怀的理论和实务》（独著），辽宁人民出版社，2018。

（二）论文

1.《论联合国专家的地位的确定》（独著），载《中国国际法年刊（2010）》，世界知识出版社，2011。

2.《论国际组织高级职员的豁免——从国际货币基金组织总裁卡恩案说起》（独著），《环球法律评论》2011 年第 5 期。

3.《人类命运共同体建设的国际法原理与路径》（独著），《国际法研究》2016 年第 6 期。

三　主要学术成果介绍

1.《国际组织的司法管辖豁免研究》

国际组织活动日益频繁，功能日益扩大。在与有关国家和私人进行交往时，国际组织不得不经常面对自身是否享有司法管辖豁免和如何在国内法院实现这种豁免的问题。国际组织豁免问题曾作为“国家与国际组织关系”研究的一部分，停留在国际法委员会的日程上长达 30 年之久。但 1992 年国际法委员会决定暂时搁置对此问题的编纂工作。近年来不少国际法学者和部分国际法委员会委员开始重新考虑并呼吁继续展开和深化对国际组织司法管辖豁免问题的研究。鉴于此，作者对国际组织的司法管辖豁免问题进行了研究。

作者主要从国际组织司法管辖豁免的合法性和正当性两方面加以论证。合法性指国际组织司法管辖豁免的法律渊源，正当性指国际组织通过其司法管辖豁免的职能性限制、强制性放弃和任择性争端解决机制以实现国际组织与成员国关系的平衡。期望通过对国际组织司法管辖豁免问题进行比较深入的理论探讨，为该问题的学术研究、国际缔约，甚至有关国内立法有所助益。

通过对上述问题的探讨，作者试图得出如下两个结论。

第一，国际组织司法管辖豁免是一种受限制的权利。关于国际组织司法管辖豁免的性质，争论主要集中在绝对性与限制性上。世界上没有不受限制和约束的权利。国际组织的司法管辖豁免权也不能例外，它同样是一种受到限制或制约的权利。国际组织享有司法管辖豁免，是为了保证国际组织不受成员国干涉，以独立履行职能和实现其目的。在国家主权面前，司法管辖豁免是保护国际组织免受干涉的重要法律机制。对国际组织司法管辖豁免的限制，首先来自其建立在职能必要基础上的理论依据。从国际组织豁免的职能性特征来看，它是一种受到职能限制的豁免，并不是绝对的。其次，国际组织在一定条件下负有放弃豁免的义务，这是对国际组织司法管辖豁免的制度性约束。国际组织一旦放弃豁免，那么，组织及其人员将与其他私人一道，成为国内法院的审判对象。这将有力地约束组织及其人员的行为，严格要求其在职能必要的范围内行事。

第二，司法管辖豁免是国家与国际组织之间相互制约与平衡的机制。国家与国际组织是一种相互制约与平衡的关系。这种法律关系是通过私人权利与国际组织司法管辖豁免之间实现某种平衡的制度性安排而得以体现的。这种制度性安排包括豁免的强制性放弃和任择性争端解决机制。国际组织享有司法管辖豁免是一般原则。但实际上，为了平衡国际组织与国家之间的利益与权利的分配关系，司法管辖豁免总是存在很多制约。这些制约机制的存在，一方面是为了防止国际组织在享有司法管辖豁免以履行其职能时可能滥用其豁免，另一方面是为了防止国家在行使司法管辖权以限制国际组织的司法管辖豁免时矫枉过正。这是由国家与国际组织的现实关系决定的。在一个依然是由主权国家主导的国际社会里，既要保证国际组织有效履行职能，实现其宗旨与目标，又不能过分损害国家的主权，因此，保持国家与国际组织关系的平衡状态是维持和促进正常国际关系的重要环节。国际组织司法管辖豁免的限制与平衡是相互交织、相互影响的。对国际组织司法管辖豁免进行限制有助于实现组织与私人权利之间的平衡，实现国际组织与私人权利的平衡是对司法管辖豁免进行限制的理由和结果。

2.《人类命运共同体建设的国际法原理与路径》

这是第一篇比较全面和深入地从国际法视角来研究和阐述人类命运共同体的较有分量的学术论文。建设人类命运共同体作为新时期我国外交事务的重要指导思想，蕴含着深刻的国际法思想与内涵。全球化发展进程中，不断加强的国际社会共同利益，是人类命运共同体建设的物质基础。

基于主权又超越主权的国际社会本位理念，是人类命运共同体建设的思想基础。实现国际社会正义，达成形式正义与实质正义的平衡，是人类命运共同体建设的道德基础。为了减少世界各国交往的法律障碍，各国法律趋同化发展，是人类命运共同体建设的国内法路径。国际法律制度的建立和国际组织的发展，有力地促进和维护了世界和平，但未能实现永久和平。国际法应更加重视人的内心和平的建设，从而实现世界的永久和平，这是人类命运共同体建设的国际法新途径。建立在传统文化和国际法基本原则基础之上的中国和平发展，是对人类命运共同体建设的独特贡献。

郝鲁怡

一　基本情况

籍贯山东，中国社会科学院国际法研究所副研究员，硕士生导师，中国社会科学院法学研究所性别与法律中心成员，《国际法研究》责任编辑，美国哥伦比亚大学访问学者。

郝鲁怡毕业于山东大学法学院，获得学士学位。之后相继获得英国诺丁汉大学国际法专业硕士学位、华东政法大学国际法专业博士学位。2009年进入中国社会科学院法学研究所博士后流动站从事博士后研究工作，并于2012年开始在中国社会科学院国际法研究所国际公法研究室任职。

郝鲁怡主要从事国际法基础理论、国际移民与难民法、妇女权利问题以及欧盟移民法律制度等方面的研究，致力于研究国际法中的个人与国家的关系问题，特别对移民和难民领域所涉及的人权保护、国家安全等理论与实践问题开展了较为深入的探索。先后出版专著两部，在专业学术期刊发表学术论文20余篇，主持司法部、外交部、中国人权研究会、中国妇女研究会等多项课题。

二　主要学术观点

1. 探索全球移民治理人权方法的含义与路径

全球移民治理是引导国家与移民个人关系的一个重要概念，它提供了国家对外来移民的单方“管理”或“控制”政策与措施的一种制衡。全球移民治理人权方法并非重新构建一套新的国际人权法律规范体系，而是在现有人权规范框架的基础上，将非歧视原则、赋予与包容、监督与问责制等国际人权理念与标准相融合，将移民原籍国、过境国和目的地国等各国的人权保护责任与义务相融合，为保障所有移民的人权与基本自由提供实践指导与具体路径。

2. 移民与人权中的发展权密切相关

难民或寻求庇护者往往被描述为受暴力与迫害的无助和可怜的受害者，必须依靠慈善和人道援助生存，在接纳国没有地位也没有自力更生的能力。对个人的赋权理念正是立足于消弭对难民的这种刻板印象并且对抗因刻板印象带来的各种歧视。同时，确保移民或难民享有充分的发展权，通过发掘移民或难民的潜力与技能，使他们能够获得谋生机会，运用自己的技能以自主方式支持本人及其家庭的生活，促进移民或难民自力更生的信心与能力，并进而为移民社区作出贡献。保障移民或难民的尊严、权利，将遣返与赋权、发展与援助相结合，帮助移民在国外培育技能和能力使之获得就业或教育机会，为最终返回自己的国家创造条件，这是永久解决移民或难民问题的正确导向。

3. 切实遵行并有效执行1951年关于难民地位公约及议定书具有重要意义

以主权原则为基础的难民公约制度承载着国家间的法律承诺与共识，为国家接纳与保护难民的行为提供了一致、可靠的国际标准。任何重构或重新开放的讨论都可能破坏该项兼具持久性、稳定性的国际制度来之不易的成果，对已经确立的规则和原则造成冲击，进而动摇现有制度的根基。事实证明，背离1951年公约的行为既没有减少也未能阻止难民及其他被迫移民的数量与大规模流动，相反却导致对难民及被迫移民流入的管理不力、难民不当转移乃至国家、地区间的紧张局势。

4. 移民问题在欧盟已经由表象性"危机"内化为对欧盟一体化进程的实质性"挑战"，成为决定欧盟命运的重要因素

移民既是"关于人"也是"关于国家"的问题，欧盟移民问题由表象性危机到实质性挑战的内化嬗变深刻地揭示国际移民活动对于个人、国家、区域，乃至国际社会不同面向的影响与诉求冲突。欧盟一体化共性治理与主权国家多元化需求的根本矛盾制约着欧盟移民法的一体化结构与功能，不仅对其外部移民领域的决策与立法带来显著的局限性，也为欧盟移民法律制度的现实困境及发展隐患埋下根源。

三 代表作简介

1.《欧盟妇女劳动权利保护的法律制度研究》

本书从妇女劳动力就业和妇女劳动力转移两重视角对欧盟妇女劳动力就业和转移状况进行了详尽梳理，其中所运用的社会性别的分析方法，使得对问题的分析更为多面和透彻。在此基础上，深入探索了欧盟妇女劳动权利保护的法律制度，在欧盟类别多元的法律和政策之中精练出劳动权利保护的相关规范，从立法原理、价值考量、权利保护等诸多方面对法律制度进行了客观详尽的阐述。最后，对中国妇女劳动权利保护法律制度的现状及其不足作出比较分析，提出完善中国妇女劳动权利保护法律制度的构想。

2.《全球移民治理的人权方法——从碎片化到整合的艰难进程》

文章指出，尽管移民问题是全球性挑战，管理与控制移民的政策、规则多数却体现了国家的单边性质，而国际人权规范机制过于分散的状态，也在一定程度上阻碍了移民人权的普遍性核心价值的实现。全球移民治理的人权方法是将保障个人的人权与基本自由置于全球移民治理的中心，以

综合、平衡、连贯的方式处理国际移民问题，确认原籍国、过境国和目的地国对移民人权保护负有共同责任与义务，并强调监督与问责机制。人权方法遵循非歧视，赋权、参与和包容，监督与问责等基本原则，强调从关注移民的行为模式本身出发，通过跨国流动的成因与目的、跨国流动的特征与影响等因素探究人口跨国流动活动的本质，加强移民的权能以充分发挥移民的优势与促进社会包容及移民融合。此外，可持续发展、人的安全以及国际合作三重维度对动态地推进全球移民治理人权方法发挥着重要作用。

3.《解析欧盟移民法：历史演进、现实困境与发展趋势》

文章指出欧盟国际移民法律制度的发展同欧盟一体化进程如影随形，并凸显出与成员国国家利益不相融合的矛盾。欧盟国际移民法律制度从内部与外部的两重性上体现了一体化程度的巨大落差；外部边界控制制度的发展存在局限性；庇护制度对欧盟“团结”与人权价值造成冲击。尽管欧盟不断加大国家间合作与政策的协调，但收效甚微。欧盟亟待通过巩固团结和责任分担原则基础重塑一体化边界控制制度与共同庇护制度。

四 主要研究成果

（一）著作类

1.《欧盟国际移民法律制度研究》（专著），人民出版社，2011。

2.《中国社会科学院博士后论丛》第 8 卷（参著），中国社会科学出版社，2011。

3.《变动中的国际法：前沿与热点》（参著），社会科学文献出版社，2012。

4.《欧盟妇女劳动权利保护的法律制度研究》（专著），中国社会科学出版社，2013（本书获全国妇联 2014 年中国妇女研究优秀成果三等奖）。

5.《反就业歧视的机制与原理》（参著），法律出版社，2013。

6.《反歧视法讲义》（参著），法律出版社，2016。

（二）论文、译文类

1.《国际移民法律体系构建之初探》，《太平洋学报》2007 年第 7 期。

2.《人才跨国流动的法律保护——以欧盟与北美自由贸易区为视角》，《中国人才》2008 年第 8 期。

3.《论国际条约的解释规则》，《世界贸易组织动态与研究》2009 年第 4 期。

4.《欧盟短期入境的统一签证制度考察》，《山东大学学报》（哲学社会科学版）2009 年中青年学者专辑。

5.《国际法视野下南极领土主权之争》，载《浙工大法律评论》第 4 卷，中国检察出版社，2009。

6.《人口跨国流动中移民妇女劳动权利的保护》，载《国际法研究》第 7 卷，社会科学文献出版社，2012。

7.《非法移民及其遣返法律制度研究》，《河北法学》2013 年第 11 期。

8.《资产没收与分享制度——以美国法为视角》，载《国际法研究》第 9 卷，社会科学文献出版社，2013。

9.《跨国流动人口与妇女劳动力社会保障权利探析——欧盟法的考察》，载《社会法论丛》（2014 年卷总第 1 卷），社会科学文献出版社，2014。

10.《资产没收与分享制度》，载《国际法学论丛》第 9 卷，中国方正出版社，2014。

11.《家庭工人权利保障问题检视——国际人权普遍性原则与劳动权利保护的竞合方法》，《河北法学》2014 年第 11 期。

12.《引渡中的人权问题探究》，《国际法研究》2015 年第 5 期。

13.《欧盟妇女就业权利保护制度研究》，载《中欧双边投资协定谈判相关法律问题研究》，法律出版社，2016。

14.《解析欧盟移民法：历史演进、现实困境和发展趋势》，《环球法律评论》2016 年第 2 期。

15.《全球移民治理的人权方法》，载陈泽宪、柳华文主编《人权领域的国际合作与中国视角》，中国政法大学出版社，2017。

16.《金砖国家、国际合作和人权话语南方国家视角的思考》（译文），《国际法研究》2017 年第 1 期。

17.《全球移民治理的人权方法——从碎片化到整合的艰难进程》，《深圳大学学报》（人文社会科学版）2017 年第 4 期（人大复印报刊资料《国际法学》2017 年第 12 期全文转载）。

18.《国际难民制度的变与不变问题思考》，《北方法学》2018 年第 1 期。

张卫华

一 基本情况

河南平舆人，中国社会科学院国际法研究所助理研究员，法学博士。1998 年获得郑州大学法学学士学位（经济法专业）；2004 年获得郑州大学国际法学硕士学位；2008 年获得中国政法大学国际法学博士学位。2013—2015 年在中国社会科学院法学研究所从事博士后研究。主要研究方向：国际法基础理论、国际海洋法。

二 主要学术观点

1. 运用政策定向的法学方法对外交保护法律制度进行分析，揭示了外交保护法的实际运作过程

外交保护过程的参与者（求偿国、被告国、个人和公司、国际法庭和仲裁庭、国际组织）在外交保护中发挥着不同的功能和作用，包括情报、倡导、规定、援引、适用、终止和评估。传统法学流派往往不能正确评价理念在法律中的地位，而政策定向学派认为理念和运作都是法律不可或缺

的理念，而全球化的世界中南北两大阵营对于外交保护的不同理念，诞生了卡尔沃条款，而人权理念的诞生和发展，更加深刻地影响了外交保护的权威决策过程。国籍联系原则和用尽当地救济原则是求偿人进入外交保护进入权威场合，对另一个国家提出指控的条件，是否拥有“干净的手”将会影响到求偿人的资格。当事国根据自己控制的基础价值并结合具体案情来决定所要使用的具体策略，包括外交方法和司法程序，外交保护的手段和方法一般应当是和平的，武力的使用应当符合行使自卫权的标准。

2. 人类命运共同体应当把人权理念作为共同价值

人类命运共同体是我国在新形势下，提出的全面构建新型国际关系的重大理论创新。与任何其他共同体一样，人类命运共同体需要共同的价值体系作为连接的纽带和根基。由于人类命运共同体强调全人类的合作共赢，更加关注人类的整体利益，必然要求将维护人类的尊严和权利作为“共同体”的最高宗旨和目标，从而，人的权利和自由构成了人类命运共同体的共同价值体系。作为一种国际秩序和国际体系变革的中国方案，人类命运共同体是对发展中国家建立平等、公平和公正的国际秩序的努力和斗争的继承和发扬，在构建人类命运共同体的过程中，需要从发展中国家的角度，对人权概念和体系作出超越西方话语体系的新诠释。

3. 我国对南海断续线内水域的历史性权利是资源性的，我国从未对南海水域的航行自由施加限制

我国对南海水域的历史性权利基于我国对南海诸岛的领土主权和我国在南海的历史性活动，其核心要素是南海的特殊地理特征和我国对南海的资源的经济需求。我国在南海的长期航行活动并不产生排他性权利，南海在航行自由方面依据《联合国海洋法公约》，适用内水、领海、专属经济区等不同航行自由制度。

4.《联合国海洋法公约》回避了专属经济区的法律地位问题，不论是主张专属经济区仍然属于公海，还是自成一体的海域，都违背了《公约》的本意

1982 年《联合国海洋法公约》中规定的专属经济区制度是缔约国妥协的产物。《公约》排除了专属经济区属于领海的可能性，并给专属经济区下了一个功能性的定义，即通过精确界定沿海国和其他国家权利、自由和义务来实现对专属经济区的界定，但未对专属经济区是否属于公海作出明

确回答。因此，无论明确肯定或者否定专属经济区属于公海的一部分，都与《公约》的本意违背。

5. 专属经济区航行自由方面出现的问题，应当依据《联合国海洋法公约》的有关条款来解决，不能根据专属经济区属于“国际水域”或者“国家管辖水域”来推断

《联合国海洋法公约》的专属经济区制度是沿海国主权权利和管辖权与其他国家的权利和自由之间的精致平衡，任何有关专属经济区的问题都应当依照《公约》第五部分来解决。不论是“国际水域”还是“国家管辖水域”，均未在《公约》中出现。任何有关航行自由的问题，应当依照《公约》的有关条款（尤其是第58条）来解决。

三 代表作

（一）专著

《外交保护法新论》，中国政法大学出版社，2012。

（二）论文

1.《外交保护中“干净的手”理论》，载《中国国际法年刊（2009）》，世界知识出版社，2010。

2.《论专属经济区上空的法律地位和飞越自由》，《环球法律评论》2015年第1期。

3.《专属经济区中的“适当顾及”义务》，《国际法研究》2015年第5期（人大复印报刊资料《国际法学》全文转载）。

4.《1949年日内瓦四公约：国际人道法的基本标准的编纂和发展》，《人权》2016年第5期。

5.《我国南海水域的航行自由》，《海南大学学报》2016年第6期。

6.《对民用航空法修订征求意见稿的若干修改意见——以国际民用航空安保条约为视角》，《北京航空航天大学学报》（社会科学版）2017年第1期。

7.《构建人类命运共同体的人权之维》，《人权》2017年第5期。

8.《国际人道法的现代化——1977年两个议定书的起源和发展》，《人权》2018年第6期。

马金星

一　基本情况

天津市人，中国社会科学院国际法研究所助理研究员。2008 年、2015 年分别获得大连海事大学法学学士、法学博士学位，2010 年获得德国萨尔大学（UdS）法学硕士。2015—2018 年，在中国社会科学院法学研究所从事国际法方向博士后研究工作。2018 年进入中国社会科学院国际法研究所国际公法研究室，专业方向为国际法学。重点研究领域为海洋领土及海域划界争端、海上交通安全及海上执法、海洋环境保护、历史性权利、海事法实施机制、海洋政策及立法、海洋综合管理等。主要研究内容涉及四部分：一是海洋领土及海域划界争端，包括中日钓鱼岛问题、中国与南海周边国家海洋争端、领海及专属经济区划界等；二是海洋环境保护，涉及国际海事公约特别敏感海域、防治船舶污染，以及海上武装冲突中的环境保护问题；三是海上交通安全维护，涉及船舶定线制、避碰规则、通航规则等；四是海洋立法及海洋政策，包括海洋基本法立法、海岛立法、海洋法律体系构建等。

二　科研活动与贡献

从事科研工作以来，在《国际法研究》、《社会科学》、《法学杂志》、*International Committee of the Red Cross* 和 *Journal of East Asia & International Law* 等中外刊物发表论文近 20 篇，多篇中文成果被人大复印报刊资料《国际法学》转载。所译德国《商法典第五编·海商》，系该法重述后中国国内首部中译本。近五年来，被中央有关部门采纳的内部研究报告 40 余篇，其中部分研究报告获得中央领导批示，并获中国社会科学院优秀对策信息一等奖 1 次、三等奖 4 次。主持和完成中国博士后科学基金面上资助一等项目“无居民海岛使用管理法律对策研究”（2016M590174），参与国家社会科学基金项目、教育部哲学社会科学重大攻关项目、交通运输部软科学研究项目、国家海洋局科研项目等多项国家级、省部级科研项目研究工作。

三　主要学术观点

1. 中日钓鱼岛争端中的时际法问题

在中日钓鱼岛论争中，双方皆主张是通过“先占”取得钓鱼岛主权，中日其他主张均以先占取得为存在基础。结合历史文献和国际法中的时际法原则，指出中国是钓鱼岛唯一合法的所有者，日方所谓无主地先占取得钓鱼岛主权的主张具有欺骗性，中方基于“先占”和“有效控制”取得钓鱼岛主权具有合理性与合法性。中日钓鱼岛争端中存在“关键日期”，日本和美国在“关键日期”之后对钓鱼岛的侵害行为不发生国际法上的领土取得效力，二战后钓鱼岛主权依法回归中国，不存在所谓中国对日本“拥有”钓鱼岛的默认。

2. 强制性争端解决机制与南海仲裁案

强制仲裁程序是《联合国海洋法公约》特有的强制性争端解决机制。菲律宾针对中国南海问题提交的国际仲裁规避了《联合国海洋法公约》中的限制条件，中国不接受强制仲裁程序，只意味着对仲裁庭管辖权的初步反对，却不能阻止仲裁程序的进行。针对强制仲裁程序的发展趋向，中国应坚持主张对南海诸岛及“断续线”的权利主张，表明仲裁庭不具有管辖权，并通过建设海上构造物和防空识别区，强化对中菲争议区域的实际控制，维护我国在南海的固有权益。

3. 海事安全调查国际立法发展趋势

海事安全调查是改进海上航行安全的重要措施。在偏重属地管辖影响下，海事安全调查中的沿海国管辖与船旗国管辖存在失衡现象，IMO 海事安全调查国际规则及其修正案的生效实施，加速了海事安全调查国际立法的统一化进程，扩大了参与海事安全调查的国家范围，强化了海事安全调查中船旗国的义务和对海员人权的保护。

4. 航行安全保障与“21 世纪海上丝绸之路”建设

海上航行安全是共建“21 世纪海上丝绸之路”的基础，海上航行安全保障具有属地特征，国家管辖权是沿岸国参与南海航行安全保障的权源基础，中国与南海五国现存航行安全保障管辖权协调机制具有软法性特征，加之地区海洋争端的存在和当事国国内法的冲突，使航行安全维护的实效性更难以保证。在共建“21 世纪海上丝绸之路”的积极倡导下，中国与南海五国应协同破解管辖权协调困境，有条件地认可国家管辖权在争议海域的生存空间，遵循国际公约中限制性条款的规定，合理适用属人管辖优先与最密切联系原则，通过联合申请的方式维护南海航行安全。

5. 海上武装冲突中的环境保护问题

对在海上使用武力的限制存在于国际法的不同分支部门中，具体包括适用于和平时期的海洋法和环境法，以及适用于武装冲突时期的国际人道法。必须对这些领域的不同规则进行比较和分析，以确定适用于限制在海上使用武力以保护环境的共同原则。考虑到在使用武力的情况下保护海洋环境的特殊问题，海洋法和国际环境法可适用于限制武装冲突期间在海上使用武力的手段和方法，对预防原则的解释可以填补国际法的空白。海洋法和环境法中的具体概念及部分规定，可以弥补国际人道法在武装冲突中保护海洋环境时存在的一些法律空白。

四　代表作简介

1.《南海仲裁案裁决中有关岛礁法律地位问题的评介》

岛礁法律地位问题是南海仲裁案的核心仲裁事项之一，其本质是中国与菲律宾间的领土主权及海域划界争端。仲裁庭在自裁管辖权的基础上，对中国有关外交立场进行了曲解。仲裁庭在阐释《联合国海洋法公约》第

121 条第 3 款含义时具有强烈的主观倾向，通过推定意图为缔约国创设权利和义务，偏离了有疑从轻解释和演变性解释的合理化路径，以“释法”之名行“立法”之实，背离了条约解释的目的。在事实证明阶段，仲裁庭从历史片段中选取的有关南海岛礁的证据，缺乏合法性、真实性和关联性，无法支撑其裁决的合法性和有效性。

2.《论特别敏感海域制度在南海的适用》

特别敏感海域制度是 IMO 主导的海洋保护区制度，与其他海洋保护区制度具有差异性，在 IMO 框架内具有广泛的国家实践基础。南中国海符合特别敏感海域鉴定标准，从把握区域环境治理国际话语权及积累政治互信角度出发，我国应在相关国际公约确立的区域合作框架制度内，采取双边路径与多边路径相结合的方式，参与南中国海特别敏感海域申请指定，适用 IMO 法律文件框架内的管护措施，在实际管理中根据相关国内法对违法行为予以制裁。

五　学术作品目录

1.《我国海域物权生态化新探——理念、实践和进路》，《武汉大学学报》（哲学社会科学版）2013 年第 2 期（第二作者）。

2.《从时际法原则解析先占取得岛屿行为的效力》，《法学杂志》2013 年第 12 期（第二作者）。

3.《论我国海洋法立法》，《社会科学》2014 年第 7 期（第二作者）。

4.《在南海“断续线”水域内设置避航区的法律问题探讨》，《社会科学战线》2014 年第 9 期（第二作者）。

5.《〈海洋法公约〉中的强制性争端解决机制与中国应对——以中菲南海强制仲裁为切入点》，《法学杂志》2015 年第 2 期（独著）。

6.《论海事安全调查国际立法发展趋势及启示》，《中国海洋大学学报》2016 年第 5 期（独著）。

7.《论特别敏感海域制度在南海的适用》，《太平洋学报》2016 年第 5 期（独著）（人大复印报刊资料《国际法学》2016 年第 8 期、国务院发展研究中心“中国智库网”全文转载）。

8.《南海航行安全中国家管辖权的冲突与协调》，《社会科学辑刊》2016 年第 6 期（独著）。

9.《论沿海国海上执法中武力使用的合法性》，《河北法学》2016 年第 9 期（独著）（人大复印报刊资料《国际法学》2017 年第 2 期全文转载）。

10.《德国〈商法典第五编·海商〉》，载《东南法学》第 10 辑，东南大学出版社，2016（独著）。

11. "Restrictions on the Use of Force at Sea: An Environmental Protection Perspective", *International Committee of the Red Cross*, Vol. 98, No. 902, 2016（与孙世彦合著，第一作者）。

12.《南海仲裁案裁决中有关岛礁法律地位问题的评介》，《国际法研究》2017 年第 1 期（独著）。

13. "China's Responses on the South China Sea Arbitration: A Perspective of Treaty Interpretation on the Status of Maritime Features", *Journal of East Asia & International Law*, Vol. 11, No. 1, 2018（独著）。

略论人类命运共同体国际法的构建

刘楠来*

当今世界处于大发展大变革大调整时期。在世界多极化、经济全球化不断深入发展的大趋势中，人类社会也面临着外来入侵、恐怖主义、环境恶化、单边主义等众多挑战，这一世界今后朝着什么方向发展，还存在许多不确定性。在这一背景下，习近平主席顺应时代要求，站在人类社会发展的高度，提出了推动构建人类命运共同体的思想，为全球治理、人类社会的发展指明了方向，提出了中国方案，这是具有深远历史意义的。目前，构建人类命运共同体思想，在国内，已经写入了宪法，成了反映全国人民意志，需要聚集全国之力为之实现而竭尽努力的对外政策目标。在国际上，它得到了许多国家和国际组织的认同和支持，写进了联合国的多项文件，很大程度上达成了共识。构建人类命运共同体已经从人们的理念、方案，迅速地转入了付诸实施的阶段。

人类命运共同体的构建，需要以国际规则为基础。习近平主席在其有关人类命运共同体的论述中，十分重视国际法治在构建人类命运共同体中的地位和作用，他不止一次地强调，“法者，治之端也”，人类命运共同体的构建，应该遵循国际法。2014 年，他在纪念和平共处五项原则发表 60 周年的大会上说：“我们应该共同推动国际关系法治化。推动各方在国际关系中遵守国际法和公认的国际关系基本原则，用统一适用的规则来明是非、促和平、谋发展。”① 2017 年在联合国日内瓦总部发表的演讲中，他

---

* 刘楠来，中国社会科学院荣誉学部委员、国际法研究所研究员。

① 《弘扬和平共处五项原则　建设合作共赢美好世界》，载习近平《论坚持推动构建人类命运共同体》，中央文献出版社，2018，第 134 页。

更进一步地具体阐述了构建人类命运共同体应遵循的一些国际法原则："从三百六十多年前《威斯特伐利亚和约》确立的平等和主权原则，到一百五十多年前日内瓦公约确立的国际人道主义精神；从七十多年前联合国宪章明确的四大宗旨和七项原则，到六十多年前万隆会议倡导的和平共处五项原则……这些原则应该成为构建人类命运共同体的基本遵循。"① 习近平主席的这些论述，清楚地阐明了人类命运共同体的构建与国际法的内在关系，为我国提供了构建人类命运共同体国际法的指导思想。

历史唯物主义告诉我们，国际法与所有法律一样，是在人类社会出现了阶级和国家以后，为了用于调整国与国之间的关系而被创建出来的，它的存在是以国家的出现和国与国之间的关系形成为前提的。在中华文化"天下大同"和马克思主义"自由人联合体"概念下的人类命运共同体作为一种社会形态形成情况下，阶级和国家已不再存在，没有了国家，就没有了国与国之间的关系，没有国际关系，也就没有了国际法。在这一语境下，严格地说，是不会有什么人类命运共同体的国际法的。然而，十分明显的是，人类命运共同体的构建是一个漫长的历史过程，在这一过程中，人类命运共同体的构建，不能没有适应其需要的国际法来保驾护航。这样的国际法，我们或许可以简便地称之为人类命运共同体国际法；实际上是指构建人类命运共同体过程中实行的国际法，或者说，指的是为构建人类命运共同体而需要的国际法。

人类命运共同体国际法，是在人类社会进入构建人类命运共同体时代应运而生的。它仍然是"国家之间的法"，具有与以往各个历史时期的国际法共有的内容和特征，与此同时，也必然应有一些适应时代要求的新的内容和特征。习近平主席在上述纪念和平共处五项原则发表60周年的讲话中，在论述推动建设新型国际关系和美好世界问题时提出了"六个坚持"，即坚持主权平等、坚持共同安全、坚持共同发展、坚持合作共赢、坚持包容互鉴、坚持公平正义。② 这六个坚持，为构建人类命运共同体指明了方向和路径，也为构建人类命运共同体国际法绘制了蓝图，明确了基本的原

① 《共同构建人类命运共同体》，载习近平《论坚持推动构建人类命运共同体》，中央文献出版社，2018，第416页。

② 《弘扬和平共处五项原则　建设合作共赢美好世界》，载习近平《论坚持推动构建人类命运共同体》，中央文献出版社，2018，第130—133页。

则要求。这些基本的原则如下。

第一，人类命运共同体国际法应建立在主权平等的基础上，将尊重国家主权确立为适用于国际生活所有领域的最基本的原则。在人类命运共同体构建的历史进程中，主权独立的国家仍是国际社会的主要成员，在国际事务中扮演着主要角色，它们的主权应得到切实的尊重和维护，这是国际社会稳定发展的基本条件。国家不分大小、强弱、贫富，都是国际社会的平等成员，人类命运共同体国际法应确认并保证所有国家都有平等参与国际事务的权利，包括平等参与国际造法的权利，使它们的合法权益都得到平等的尊重和保护。每个国家都有选择自己的发展道路和制度的权利，一国的内政不容外来干涉。

第二，人类命运共同体国际法应以维持世界持久和平，保障各国及其人民安全为其宗旨和首要任务。侵略战争及恐怖主义等非传统安全威胁祸害人类至深，人类命运共同体国际法应宣告外来入侵、恐怖主义、种族灭绝等为反人类罪行，将禁止国家间使用武力、用和平方法解决国际争端、制度相同和制度不同国家和平共处等确立为各国必须遵行的基本原则。应建立集体安全体制，确保发生战争或其他安全威胁情况下能及时有效地得到制止和消除，特别是要为小国、弱国提供和平与安全的法律保障。

第三，人类命运共同体国际法应将维护国际社会共同利益和人类整体利益放在更加突出的位置，将促进各国共同发展作为一大宗旨和基本原则。以往以民族国家为本位，主要着眼国家利益的传统国际法已不能适应人类进步发展的需要，事实上，特别是第二次世界大战结束以来，在国际法的许多领域已经出现了以国际社会共同利益和人类整体利益为对象的国际法概念和制度，如“维持国际和平与安全”、“增进并激励对于全体人类之人权及基本自由之尊重”、“人类共同继承财产”、“共同而有区别原则”、“和平共处”、“对一切的义务”等。在走向人类命运共同体的时代，国际法应妥善处理国家利益与国际社会共同利益之间的关系，于维护国家权益的同时，更多地关注国际社会的共同利益和全人类的当前、长远利益，并为此目的，创建和完善有关的国际法原则和制度。发展是谋求社会进步的根本之道，人类命运共同体国际法应强调发展权是国家和个人的基本权利，在概念创新、制度设计、机制实施各个环节，保证各个国家不分大小、强弱、制度异同、发展程度差异，都能得到权利平等、机会平等，在共同繁荣的目标下，在经济、政治、社会、文化、生态环境等各个领域都能得到发展，将人类社会建设成为持久和平、普遍安全、共同繁荣、开放包容、清洁美丽的人类命运共同体。

第四，人类命运共同体国际法应将合作共赢确立为适用于政治、经济、社会、文化、军事、法律、生态环境、科学研究等国际生活一切领域的基本原则。国际合作是国家间的相互依存、共同发展的必然选择和应有行为方式。《联合国宪章》序言指出，为维护国际和平与安全，促进全球人民经济及社会之发展，“务必同心协力”。《宪章》还明确地将促成国际合作，以解决国际经济、社会、文化、人类福利等问题，列为联合国的宗旨之一。在走向人类命运共同体的时代，国际法应进一步强调国际合作的普遍适用性和作为国际法原则的性质。合作是方法，共赢是目的，人类命运共同体国际法不仅要促进和规范国际合作，而且要从制度上保证合作各方权责相当，都能从合作中获得利益，要消除歧视，防止不公平、不合理的安排，以致你输我赢、赢者通吃现象的发生。

第五，人类命运共同体国际法应尊重世界文明的多样性，对于不同国家、不同民族创造的优秀文明成果，特别是优秀法律理念、法律制度，应兼收并蓄，交流互补。如果说以《威斯特伐利亚和约》为起端的近代国际法主要是欧洲基督文明的产物，那么，《联合国宪章》序言关于联合国人民决心“力行容恕，彼此以善邻之道，和睦相处”的宣告，《国际法院规约》要求法院法官全体确能代表世界各大文化及各主要法系的规定，显示的是当代国际法力图体现世界文明的包容和大汇合。人类命运共同体国际法应发扬不同时期国际法尊崇世界文明的传统，在新的历史条件下，进一步地保证多种文明的和谐共生，反对对任何文明的贬低和践踏，在世界文明的交流互鉴中，发挥世界文明推动人类社会进步的基础引领作用。

第六，人类命运共同体国际法应以公平正义为基本价值取向，保证公平正义在现实的国际关系中真正地得到实现。公平正义是全人类的共同追求，也是包括国际法在内的一切法律应有的品质。人类命运共同体国际法要在公平正义的理论基础上，保证国际社会各方成员都能在国际事务中得到公平对待，包括都能平等地参与国际规则的制订和意志的充分表达，确立的国际法原则、规则和制度应当体现公平正义理念要求，真正做到国家不分大小、强弱，在法律面前一律平等，并有助于消除事实上的不平等。

人类命运共同体国际法还应以维护正常国际秩序、伸张国际正义为出发点，坚决反对霸权主义和强权政治。

人类命运共同体国际法的构建，是一个对以往的法律文化和国际规则继承和发展的过程，它不要求将现行的国际法推倒重来，另起炉灶。正如上面引用的习近平主席的有关讲话所表明的，现行国际法体系的许多原则、规则和制度，特别是《联合国宪章》的宗旨和原则、和平共处五项原则等，都是人类命运共同体国际法应有的重要组成部分，将继续为构建人类命运共同体这一历史任务发挥作用。尽管如此，与以往的国际法比较，人类命运共同体国际法毕竟是一个在使命和内容上都有许多不同，在一定程度上甚至有质的差异的国际规则体系，它的构建要求人们表现出极大的智慧和创造性，也离不开世界各国持久的共同努力。

中外许多国际法学者认为，国际法是一种特殊的法律体系，它与国内法不同，不是由某一国家的什么立法机关制定出来，强加给其他国家的，而是由各个国家通过协商谈判，达成协议，或表示同意而产生的，表现的不是一个国家的意志，而是多个国家的协调意志。人类命运共同体国际法具有国际法的一般特征。习近平主席在多个场合论述构建人类命运共同体问题时，一贯强调要实行共商、共建、共享。[①] 中国是构建人类命运共同体理念和方案的提出国，在构建人类命运共同体国际法的伟大工程中，理应从理论到实践积极发挥引领作用。但是独木不成林，我国要善于联合世界上一切认同和支持人类命运共同体理念的国家、国际组织和学术舆论界，努力形成共同的国际法立场，与他们一起共同推动人类命运共同体国际法的构建。

（本文系作者在北京国际法学会 2018 年学术年会的发言稿）

① 参见习近平《论坚持推动构建人类命运共同体》，中央文献出版社，2018，第 7、61—63、133—134、259—261 页。

WTO 规则在中国大陆法律体系框架下的适用

朱晓青[*]

世界贸易组织（WTO）是在国际条约的基础上建立的。《建立世界贸易组织协定》（以下简称《WTO 协定》）及其四个附件构成一个国际条约群。这就是说，WTO 规则的性质是国际条约，而不是国际习惯。亦即，WTO 规则是 WTO 全体成员协商达成，是各成员共同意志的结果；WTO 规则规定的权利和义务为约定产生。因此，通常认为，WTO 规则是现代国际法的重要组成部分，一般国际法原则同样适用于 WTO 规则。本文将从国际法的角度，对 WTO 规则在中国大陆法律体系框架下的适用及其相关问题作一些探讨。

一 《WTO 协定》第 16 条设定的成员方义务

作为人类历史上第一个“多边贸易体制”的条约文件，关贸总协定（GATT）在其“临时适用”的 46 年（1948—1994 年）间，取得了有目共睹的巨大成就。但是，GATT 又存在缺陷或“先天不足”。如：“祖父条款”的隐患；因不是国际组织而致的条约执行的困难；以及 GATT 规则不具有强制性所导致的混乱；等等。WTO 作为唯一安排国家间贸易规则的全

* 朱晓青，中国社会科学院国际法研究所研究员。

球性国际组织,[①] 它的法律体制在继承 GATT 规则的同时，弥补了 GATT 的不足。

WTO 规则的适用范围非常之广，涉及从货物贸易到服务贸易，从知识产权到投资，并包含一整套为 WTO 的多边贸易体制提供保障的国际司法机制——WTO 争端解决机制。WTO 规则对国际经济关系发展的影响，以及它与国际经济秩序稳定间的联系不言而喻。然而，由国际法的性质决定，WTO 规则维护国际经济秩序稳定的程度主要依赖于 WTO 的每一个成员在其国内法中忠实履行 WTO 规则所赋予的国际法律义务。否则，WTO 规则的效力是难以实现和发挥的。为此，每一个加入 WTO 的国家（包括单独关税区）都被责成接受构成 WTO 规则的《WTO 协定》及其附件。这一点在《WTO 协定》中得到了明确表述。该协定第 2 条规定："附件 1、附件 2 和附件 3 所列协定及相关法律文件（下称'多边贸易协定'）为本协定的组成部分，对所有成员具有约束力。"[②] 这无疑确定了 WTO 规则是具有强制约束力的规则的性质。

《WTO 协定》第 16 条还为加入 WTO 的每一个成员设定了一项至关重要的义务，即"每一成员应保证其法律、法规和行政程序与所附各协定对其规定的义务相一致"，并且"不得对本协定的任何条款提出保留"。从而不仅进一步确立了 WTO 规则对各成员的强制性法律约束力的地位，而且也奠定了"WTO 法律制度或规则优于各国国内法的宪法性原则"。[③] 根据第 16 条的规定，WTO 的成员承担使其国内立法、行政措施与 WTO 规则相符合的义务。由 WTO 规则的条约性质所决定，这是一项条约义务。因此，国际法所特有的"条约必须信守"（pacta sunt servanda）原则同样适用于 WTO 规则。

"条约必须信守"是国际法理论和实践所确认，并得到公认的一项重要的国际法原则。这项原则之所以成为国际法的重要原则，一个不可忽略的原因在于，国际法领域不存在统一的、超国家的、能够保证条约履行的

---

① 这一界定来自世界贸易组织网站 www. wto. org。《建立世界贸易组织协定》第 16 条的"解释性说明"规定："本协定和多边贸易协定中使用的'国家'一词应理解为包括任何 WTO 单独关税区成员。"

② 本文所涉及的 WTO 规则条款，均引自《世界贸易组织乌拉圭回合多边谈判结果法律文本》，对外贸易经济合作部国际经贸关系司译，法律出版社，2000。

③ 赵维田：《世贸组织（WTO）的法律制度》，吉林人民出版社，2000，第 31 页。

司法机关，因而，各国遵守国际条约的愿望逐渐导致了该原则的形成。“条约必须信守”原则的基本要素是善意履行条约。所谓善意履行条约，“就是诚实地和正直地履行条约，从而要求不仅按照条约的文字，而且也按照条约的精神履行条约，要求不仅不以任何行为破坏条约的宗旨和目的，而且予以不折不扣的履行”。①

信守条约义务的原则已载入了诸多国际文件中。例如，《联合国宪章》序言强调“尊重由条约与国际法其他渊源而起之义务，久而弗懈”。《宪章》第2条指出，“各会员国应一秉善意，履行其依本宪章所担负之义务”。《维也纳条约法公约》第26条规定：“凡有效之条约对其各当事国有拘束力，必须由各该国善意履行。”

从“善意”这一履行条约的基本要素出发，可以说，“条约必须信守”应该也包含一个道德命题，即约定必须遵守。因此，缔约国通常确信，应当信守其承诺，履行条约义务，否则将招致违法的谴责，甚至惩罚。

此外，国际法学界一般认为，条约必须信守原则是一项国际习惯法规则。从国际习惯法成立应具备的两个因素，即“通例”和“法律确信”来分析，条约必须信守原则的国际习惯法性质是显而易见的，因而可以说，“条约必须信守原则的拘束力，是国际习惯法所赋予的”。② 在条约必须信守原则之下，缔约国具有采取立法、司法、行政等措施履行条约义务的义不容辞的责任，并且，“一当事国不得援引其国内法规定为理由而不履行条约”（《维也纳条约法公约》第27条）。③

因此，为确保WTO规则的效力，在“条约必须信守”的原则之下，WTO各成员必须履行保证其法律、法规、行政程序均符合《WTO协定》的不可推卸的义务。但是，以何种方式来履行第16条规定的这项义务，也就是说，在WTO成员各自的法律体系框架下，采取何种方式使其国内法律、法规、行政程序与WTO规则相一致，以保证WTO规则在国内法中的充分适用，这应是各成员依其法律体系予以选择并决定的问题。

① 李浩培：《条约法概论》，法律出版社，1987，第329页。
② 李浩培：《条约法概论》，法律出版社，1987，第346页。
③ 法学教材编辑部：《国际法资料选编》，法律出版社，1982。

二 中国大陆法律体系框架下国际条约与国内法关系的现状及其对 WTO 规则适用的影响

从一国法律体系与国际条约间的相互作用和联系的角度来分析，WTO 每个成员的国内法律体系均在谈判、批准和实施三个阶段影响 WTO 体制。在谈判阶段，国家法律体系的构成决定着谁有权力代表每一个成员进行谈判。而通过对有关利益集团进入谈判程序的影响，这种决定又反过来影响该成员的谈判态度。在这一阶段，国家法律体系同样控制着谈判者提出建议和接受他方建议的谈判权力，从而影响每个成员谈判立场的可信度。在批准阶段，国家法律体系决定着谁有权力阻遏协议的结果或阻止它的实施。在实施阶段，国家法律体系对于国际义务被忠实履行的程度能够产生深刻影响。这里，关键问题就是国际义务在国内法中的地位及执行国内法的国内司法体制的构成。[①] 由于 WTO 规则已对中国大陆生效，目前我们面临的首要问题是 WTO 规则的实施问题。

（一）中国大陆法律体系的构成

何谓法律体系？按照《中国大百科全书 · 法学》的解释，“法律体系通常指由一个国家的全部现行法律规范分类组合为不同的法律部门而形成的有机联系的统一整体”。“在统一的法律体系中，各种法律规范，因其所调整的社会关系的性质不同，而划分为不同的法的部门，如宪法、行政法、刑法、刑事诉讼法、民法、经济法、婚姻法、民事诉讼法，等等”。[②] 中国大陆法学界的学者对于法律体系的界定多持这种观点。但也有学者认为，法律体系不仅指现行法律规范的部门划分及其整体性，还应关注法律体系本身是一个母系统，它由若干子系统组成的基本事实。[③] 依此种观点，在以成文法为法律渊源的中国，法律体系的构成，除了法律规范的部门划

① John H. Jackson and Alan O. Sykes, *Implementing the Uruguay Round* (Clarendon Press, 1997), p. 5.

② 《中国大百科全书 · 法学》，中国大百科全书出版社，1984，第 84 页。

③ 参见李林《中国特色社会主义法律体系的构成》，载刘海年、李林主编《依法治国与法律体系建构》，中国法制出版社，2001，第 5 页。

分以及划分后的整体性外，还应当包括法律的渊源体系、法律的构成体系、法律的规范体系和法律的效力体系等。就法律的效力体系而言，这种观点的持有者认为，法律效力是指法律约束力和法律强制性。根据宪法和有关法律，中国法律的效力体系主要是按照逻辑关系建构的，依据立法主体的权力位阶，形成了法律效力的位阶体系。而位阶则是指法律在一国法律体系中的不同地位和由这种地位构成的不同法律之间上下左右的相互关系。[①] 这种观点主张，国际条约是法律的直接渊源，故而构成中国法律体系的组成部分。

然而，国际条约与中国大陆法律体系之间是一种什么样的关系？也就是说，国际条约是不是中国大陆法律体系的组成部分？对这一问题的回答迄今是不统一的。在传统的国际法与国内法关系的一元论和二元论理论的支配下，大陆国际法学界对国际条约是不是中国法律体系的组成部分仍存在是与否的两种争论。[②]

（二）中国大陆法律体系框架下国际条约与国内法关系的现状

国际条约与国内法关系中最为重要的问题是国际条约在国内法中的适用，以及与此相关的国际条约在国内法律体系中的地位问题。之所以如此，原因在于这两个问题均与条约能否在缔约国得到忠实和有效实施密切相关。

---

① 法律的渊源体系是指由法律取得权威和效力的方式所决定的法律的存在方式。法律的渊源体系主要指直接法律渊源。法律的直接渊源则是指由一定权威机关按照法定程序制定的以规范性文件表现出来的法律，主要包括宪法、法律、行政法规、部委规章、地方性法规、民族自治条例和单行条例、条约等。法律的构成体系主要是指由法律的格式和体例所构成的布局合理、结构完整、逻辑严密、搭配得当的表现法律形式的有机整体。法律的规范体系是指由国家颁布的并受国家强制力保障实施的、有普遍约束力的行为规则。详见李林《中国特色社会主义法律体系的构成》，载刘海年、李林主编《依法治国与法律体系建构》，中国法制出版社，2001，第7—29页。

② 否定的观点其依据主要是：条约不是中国法律的渊源形式；从国内法角度看，制定法律和缔结条约属于两种不同的权限，前者属立法权，后者属缔约权，因此，国内立法和国际条约是两类法律规范。笔者持肯定的观点。主要依据在于：国际条约的批准是国家的一项立法活动；国际条约是中国法律的渊源之一；国际条约被直接纳入中国法律体系并成为其不可或缺的组成部分。可详见朱晓青《作为中国法律体系组成部分的国际条约》，载刘海年、李林主编《依法治国与法律体系建构》，中国法制出版社，2001，第531—536页。

1. 国际条约在中国大陆法律体系中的地位

所谓国际条约在中国大陆法律体系中的地位，即指国际条约与大陆法律间的相互关系。由于篇幅的限制，本文无意介入关于法律体系的概念讨论中。但是，此处将借用以上提及的关于中国法律体系构成中的“位阶”说，对国际条约在中国大陆法律体系中的地位问题进行分析，相信“位阶”说会对这一问题的论述和理解有所帮助。

按照“位阶”说，法律效力的大小，取决于每个具体法律在法律体系中的位阶；而因立法机构的不同，法律的位阶就不同，或说在法律体系中的地位就不同，当然，法律的效力也就不同。

根据《中华人民共和国宪法》（1999 年《宪法修正案》）第 58 条的规定，全国人民代表大会及其常务委员会为中国的国家立法机关。前者的立法权限是：修改宪法，以及制定和修改刑事、民事等基本法律。后者的立法权限是：制定和修改除应当由全国人民代表大会制定的法律以外的其他法律。[①] 再据《中华人民共和国立法法》的规定，国务院根据宪法和法律，制定行政法规（第 56 条）；省、自治区、直辖市和较大的市的人民代表大会及其常务委员会，在不同宪法、法律、行政法规相抵触的前提下，可以制定地方性法规（第 63 条）；国务院各部委、省级和较大的市人民政府可以根据法律，或行政法规，或地方性法规制定行政规章（第 71—73 条）。由此，大陆法律的“位阶”已一目了然。由全国人民代表大会制定的宪法在大陆法律体系中处于首位，具有最高法律效力，依次是基本法律——法律——行政法规——地方法规——行政规章（部门规章和地方政府规章）（第 78—82 条）。

在中国大陆的这种法律体系框架下，国际条约似也因具有立法权的批准机构的不同而处于不同的“位阶”，也就是处于不同的地位。然而，中国现行宪法、立法法等均未规定国际条约与国内法的关系。因此，目前大陆关于国际条约在中国大陆法律体系中的地位，是学界尤其是国际法学界根据现行法律的有关规定推断出来的。

根据《中华人民共和国缔结条约程序法》第 4 条的规定，中国与外国缔结条约可以中华人民共和国、中华人民共和国政府和中华人民共和国政

① 《宪法》第 62 及 67 条。

府部门的名义。在条约签署后，视缔结条约的名义不同，由不同的批准机构审批，并相应执行不同的审批程序。按照这一线索，从逻辑推论来分析，结论即：条约因其批准机构不同，在中国大陆法律体系中所处的地位也不同。从现行法律规定具体分析，依据之一：宪法第67条在关于全国人民代表大会常务委员会的立法权限中规定，常务委员会有权“决定同外国缔结的条约和重要协定的批准和废除”。[①] 又依宪法第64条，宪法的修改必须经全国人民代表大会以全体代表的三分之二以上的多数通过，方为有效。依宪法同条及立法法第22条，基本法律议案由全国人民代表大会以全体代表的过半数通过。而根据立法法第40条和全国人民代表大会组织法第31条的规定，法律议案由常务委员会全体组成人员的过半数通过。这就是说，待批准的条约和重要协定与制定法律的议案均由全国人民代表大会常务委员会批准，并以过半数通过。这就表明，这类条约和重要协定的地位应该低于宪法，与法律同等。[②] 依据之二：《缔结条约程序法》第8条规定，国务院核准除全国人民代表大会常务委员会批准的条约和重要协定之外的那些协定和其他具有条约性质的文件。据此推断，由国务院核准的协定和其他具有条约性质的文件，其地位应与国务院制定的行政法规同等。

但是，对于哪一类协定和具有条约性质的文件由国务院核准，现行法律并没有作出任何规定。换句话说，《缔结条约程序法》仅原则规定除全国人民代表大会常务委员会批准的条约和重要协定外，须经国务院核准的为“协定和其他具有条约性质的文件”（第8条）。其他法律也没有对条约、协定加以分类。由此导致一个不可忽略的问题：如果不能根据条约、协定的内容或内涵对它们进行分类，那么，随之而来的必然会是一种连锁反应，即因条约、协定的分类不明，而造成批准机构的难以确定，接着便是条约、协定的地位以致效力无从确定，条约、协定的适用也将产生问

---

① 根据《缔结条约程序法》第7条的规定，这类条约和重要协定是指：友好合作条约、和平条约等政治性条约；有关领土和划定边界的条约、协定；有关司法援助、引渡的条约、协定；同中华人民共和国法律有不同规定的条约、协定；缔约各方议定须经批准的条约、协定；其他须经批准的条约、协定。

② 从中国大陆法律体系来看，由全国人民代表大会制定的基本法律及由全国人民代表大会常务委员会制定的法律其地位还是有区别的，但是，现行宪法和立法法均未对它们孰高孰低予以规定。从现有的条款来分析，条约和重要协定所处的地位应与常务委员会批准的法律同等。

题。这最终将影响条约义务的充分履行。

2. 国际条约在中国大陆法律中的适用

对于国际条约在一国国内法或法律体系中如何适用，国际上并无统一的方式。在履行国际条约义务的前提下，一国对条约的适用方式有自主选择权。因此，实践中各国做法不同。适用方式的选择通常在一定程度上会受“一元论”和“二元论”的影响，因而，就有了实际中处理国际条约与国内法关系的不同方式，一般有条约的纳入（adoption）及转化（transformation）之分。但是，从各国司法实践考察，各法律体系很少固守任何完全单纯的纳入方式。如遵循一元论的国家，在其实践中也不都是绝对采用纳入方式，它们会视条约的具体内容，将其分为“自动执行”和“非自动执行”两类。典型的国家如美国。它将《WTO 协定》及人权条约归于“非自动执行”类，须经国内立法予以转化，才能在国内适用。而遵循二元论的国家在处理国际条约与国内法的关系时，会采取国际习惯法的纳入原则及国际条约的转化原则。如英国和意大利。[①]

由于在中国大陆法律体系框架下，国际条约与国内法的关系尚未从立法或法律上理清和明确，因此，就国际条约在国内法中的适用而言，目前至少存在四个不确定因素：一是国际条约是不是中国大陆法律体系的组成部分尚未确定；二是国际条约在中国大陆法律体系中的地位尚未确定；三是国际条约在中国国内法上的适用方式尚未确定；四是由前述不确定带来的国内法院可否援引国际条约作为其判案依据的不确定。在这种状况下，国际条约在中国大陆法律中的适用方式是学者们依据现行法律、司法解释、司法实践等推断而出的。并且许多学者认为，国际条约在中国大陆的

---

① 英国采取纳入方式接受国际习惯法为普通法的组成部分。通常引用来支持这种观点的判例是 1737 年的巴沃特诉巴比特案（Buvot v. Barbuit）及 1764 年的特里奎特诉巴思案（Triquet v. Bath）。前者清楚地表明了“国际法在其最大程度上是英国法的组成部分”的观点；后者涉及外交豁免权，它引用并重申了这种观点。对于国际条约，英国采取转化方式将其纳入国内法中。这就是说，在英国，国际条约不是自动执行的。除非国际条约经立法纳入英国法律，否则，国际条约不是英国法律的一部分。参见 D. J. Harris，*Cases and Materials on International Law*（5th edition）（Sweet & Maxwell，1998），pp. 74，78，83－86。意大利 1947 年宪法第 10 条规定，意大利法律制度应符合公认的国际法规范。这里的“公认的国际法规范”即指国际习惯法规则。而依该法第 80 条之规定，国际条约在意大利国内的效力必须有将条约纳入意大利法律的立法行为。可参见〔日〕木下太郎编《九国宪法选介》，康树华译，群众出版社，1981，第 96、111 页。

适用采取的是纳入方式，即条约具有直接适用性，不需要通过国内立法予以转化。① 然而，事实上，因缺乏作为国家根本法的宪法规定，以及立法实践中存在国际条约适用方式的不同例证，故迄今尚不能说在中国大陆法律体系下已形成或确立了国际条约在国内法中直接适用的普遍原则。②

（三）中国大陆法律体系框架下国际条约与国内法关系的现状对WTO规则适用的影响

从宏观分析，因WTO规则的国际条约性，所以，在处理WTO规则与中国大陆法律间的关系时，必然要受到中国大陆法律体系框架下国际条约与国内法关系现状的影响。如前分析，一方面，截至2003年中国大陆尚未通过宪法，或者退其次，通过宪法性文件对国际条约与国内法的关系作出规定，故而国际条约与国内法关系的不确定因素同样存在于作为国际条约的WTO规则与国内法的关系之中。因此，我们并不能确定WTO规则是不是中国大陆法律体系的组成部分，同样也不能确定WTO规则在中国大陆法律体系中的地位及适用方式，以及这些规则能否在大陆法院作为判案依

① 学者们在推断国际条约在中国国内法中的直接适用性时的依据：（1）现行法律的有关条款。主要如《民法》、《民事诉讼法》、《继承法》等中载有的关于国际条约与国内法关系的条款，即“中华人民共和国缔结或者参加的国际条约同本法有不同规定的，适用该国际条约的规定，但中华人民共和国声明保留的条款除外”。（2）司法解释。主要有中华人民共和国最高人民法院《关于执行我国加入的〈承认及执行外国仲裁裁决公约〉的通知》、《关于印发〈全国沿海地区涉外、涉港澳经济审判工作座谈会议纪要〉的通知》、《关于国际铁路货物联运货损赔偿适用法律问题的复函》等。（3）司法实践。法院审理的涉及刑事、民事、知识产权、海商事等方面的、直接适用国际条约的涉外案件。可参见朱晓青、黄列主编《国际条约与国内法的关系》，世界知识出版社，2000。

② 有学者认为，国际条约在中国国内法中的适用方式除直接适用或“纳入”外，也有“转化”适用。通常被作为典型例证的是：（1）在1975年和1979年先后加入《维也纳外交关系公约》和《维也纳领事关系公约》后，于1986年和1990年先后颁布了《中华人民共和国外交特权与豁免条例》及《中华人民共和国领事特权与豁免条例》。（2）为在国内实施《联合国海洋法公约》而于1992年和1998年先后颁布了《中华人民共和国领海及毗连区法》和《中华人民共和国专属经济区和大陆架法》。（3）对批准的国际人权公约采取转化方式适用。如通过《中华人民共和国妇女权益保障法》，该法将中国批准的《消除对妇女一切形式歧视公约》所确认的有关权利融入其中。再如《香港特别行政区基本法》第39条关于《公民权利和政治权利国际公约》、《经济、社会、文化权利国际公约》必须通过香港特别行政区的法律予以实施的规定。可参见朱晓青、黄列主编《国际条约与国内法的关系》所载刘楠来、梁淑英、韩燕煦文；以及朱晓青《〈公民权利和政治权利国际公约〉的实施机制》，《法学研究》2000年第2期。

据直接援引。另一方面，在中国大陆的立法实践中，的确有“纳入”与“转化”方式并用的端倪。但是，哪一类性质或内容的国际条约适用“纳入”方式，哪一类条约适用“转化”方式？由于我们没有对国际条约进行分类，以致难以确定在国内法中应以何种方式来适用性质、内容和作用各异的国际条约。这种现状势必影响 WTO 规则在中国大陆法律中的适用。

从微观分析，《中国加入工作组报告书》表示，《WTO 协定》是经全国人民代表大会常务委员会批准的“重要国际协定”。[①] 这似乎是对《WTO 协定》在中国大陆法律体系中的地位作了排序。其实不然。“报告书”并不是具有法律效力的法律文件。另外，条约批准程序的法律存在也并不等于条约地位的确定，《WTO 协定》的“重要国际协定”的地位还有待于法律或立法的确认。因此，无论从立法和司法实践上讲，WTO 规则在中国大陆法律体系中的地位仍然是不确定的；WTO 规则在中国大陆法律体系框架下的适用问题仍是我们面临的、亟待探讨和解决的问题。

三　中国大陆法律体系框架下 WTO 规则适用的难度

在信守条约义务的前提下，缔约国对国际条约在国内法上的适用方式拥有广泛的自主权。对于 WTO 规则的适用亦如此。因此，实践中 WTO 各成员方采取的适用 WTO 规则的方式不尽相同。以欧共体为例，一方面它采取一元论的主张，以欧共体法院/欧洲法院判例表明，GATT/WTO 规则构成欧共体法的组成部分，GATT/WTO 规则的效力优于欧共体成员国法。另一方面，它又否定 GATT/WTO 规则具有直接效力。在 1972 年“国际水果公司案”[②] 中，欧共体法院认为，在确定 GATT 在共同体法律体系中的效力时，

---

① 《中国加入世界贸易组织法律文件》，对外贸易经济合作部世界贸易组织司译，法律出版社，2002，第 775 页。

② Cases 21 - 24/72, International Fruit Company v. Produktschap voor Groenten en Fruit [1972] ECR 1219. 该案原告向荷兰法院起诉，称共同体限制苹果进口的保护性措施违背了 GATT 1947 的规定，要求撤销荷兰机构作出的驳回其从第三国进口苹果的进口许可证申请的决定。荷兰法院就此案询问欧共体法院：它对于针对国际法措施的共同体措施的效力是否拥有管辖权；遭指责的共同体条例是否违背了 GATT。参见 Paul Craig and Grainne de Burca, *EU Law: Text, Cases and Materials* (2nd edition) (Oxford University Press, 1998), pp. 179 - 180。

必须考虑 GATT 的精神、总体结构和措辞。欧共体法院指出，GATT 的规定具有极大的灵活性，因此，共同体内的个人不能在法院援引 GATT 的条款。法院同时指出，GATT 的规定仅对共同体有约束力。[①] 在 1994 年“香蕉案”[②] 中，欧共体法院/欧洲法院进一步确定了 GATT 无直接效力的原则。再以美国为例，美国法律将国际协定分为自动执行和非自动执行两类；并且其实践表明，国际条约不是自动执行的，需经国内立法的转化，才能在国内适用。根据 1994 年美国的《乌拉圭回合协议实施法》，GATT/WTO 协定被视为非自动执行条约，须经国内立法才能在美国国内适用。[③] 加拿大的做法与此类似。加拿大是一个主张二元论的国家，国际条约必须经转化才能在国内法中适用。因此，《WTO 协定》应由联邦政府制定实施法予以适用。[④] 事实上，WTO 规则的非直接适用似乎是大多数 WTO 成员所选择的适用方式。究其原因，主要在于：第一，WTO 规则的内容广泛、复杂，其中的一些规定较为原则，甚或极为灵活，或不明确，给直接适用带来难度；第二，直接适用涉及对 WTO 规则的解释问题，但成员方法院是否有权力对 WTO 规则进行解释，仍然是一个没有定论的问题；第三，成员方力图最大限度地保留其自主性，以便较灵活地平衡国际条约义务与国家利益。

中国已加入 WTO，势必应履行 WTO 规则所设定的条约义务，在国内法中适用 WTO 规则。因此，在中国大陆法律体系框架下采取何种方式适

---

① 参见 Paul Craig and Grainne de Burca, *EU Law: Text, Cases and Materials* (2nd edition) (Oxford University Press, 1998), pp. 180 - 181。

② Case C - 280/93, Germany v. Commission [1994] ECR I - 4873. 该案原告德国方的诉由是理事会 1993 年 2 月 13 日的第 404/93 号关于建立香蕉共同市场组织的条例违反了非歧视和比例性原则及 GATT 的规定，要求废止理事会条例。欧洲法院驳回了德国的诉讼。法院认为，GATT 规则仅在以下情况可能被援引：如果共同体意欲履行那种义务；或者，如果受到质疑的共同体措施明显涉及 GATT 规定。参见 Paul Craig and Grainne de Burca, *EU Law: Text, Cases and Materials* (2nd edition) (Oxford University Press, 1998), pp. 181, 183, 274。

③ David W. Leebron, "Implementation of the Uruguay Round Results in the United States", in John H. Jackson and Alan O. Sykes, *Implementing the Uruguay Round* (Clarendon Press, 1997), pp. 187 - 188. 还可参见曹建明主编《WTO 与中国的司法审判》，法律出版社，2001，第 242—243 页。

④ Debra P. Steger, "Canadian Implementation of the Agreement Establishing the World Trade Organization", in John H. Jackson and Alan O. Sykes, *Implementing the Uruguay Round* (Clarendon Press, 1997), p. 281.

用 WTO 规则就成为法律理论和司法实践上均需急迫解决的问题。当然，作为 WTO 的新成员，在 WTO 规则的适用方面，借鉴 WTO 其他成员的经验和做法，并且，不固守某种单一的适用方式，而是视 WTO 具体协定的内容，“纳入”与“转化”并用，这不失为一种可考虑的路径。但无论采取什么方式，在 WTO 规则的适用上，我们都面临诸多难点。这些难点大致有以下几种。

第一，来自 WTO 规则本身的难点。作为国际条约的 WTO 规则具有所有国际条约所特有的“弱点”，即它是各成员妥协的产物。这种妥协性反映在 WTO 规则中，突出的表现就是条款规定的模糊性。诸如 WTO 规则中使用的“接近”、“相同”、“相似”等词语。此外，WTO 规则还具有灵活性的特征，尤其是那些给予减损可能性的条款，以及在例外情况和要求成员方履行协定时采取措施的条款，其灵活性的特征就更为明显。条款中的表述如：“应采取所能采取的合理措施”、“适当的保护水平”、“适当的克制”、“酌情适用”、“必需的措施”、“力所能及的范围内”等。这种灵活性在给予成员方适用规则的空间或余地的同时，也埋下了争端隐患，由此成为 WTO 规则的适用难点。

第二，来自立法的难点。根据中国在《中华人民共和国加入议定书》中的承诺，中国将通过废止、停止或修改与 WTO 规则不一致的法律、法规及其他措施的方式，履行其在 WTO 规则下的条约义务。[①] 为履行此项承诺，截至 2003 年，中国大陆对法律进行了大规模的立、改、废工作。事实上，自 1999 年底以来，中国大陆就开始对有关法律、法规、行政规章进行清理、修改，并制定了立、改、废计划。据此，全国人民代表大会及其常务委员会首先对《中外合资经营企业法》、《中外合作经营企业法》、《外资企业法》、《海关法》、《商标法》、《专利法》、《著作权法》等 7 部法律进行了修改，完成了中国正式成为 WTO 成员之前修改法律的承诺。其余的将按照承诺，在过渡期按时完成。此外，根据承诺，国务院需要制定和修改的行政法规有 30 件，已经完成 25 件；并废止了 12 件行政法规，停止执行了 34 件有关的政策文件；国务院有关部委修改或废止的部门规章有

① 《中国加入世界贸易组织法律文件》，对外贸易经济合作部世界贸易组织司译，法律出版社，2002。

1000余件。[①] 在法律的立、改、废方面取得了实际成效及进展。但是，由于过去长期以来存在的“政出多门”的弊端，在地方法规和部门规章的清理方面，我们仍面临大量艰巨工作。

关于WTO规则在国内法中的适用方式，《中国加入工作组报告书》表示，“中国将通过修改其现行国内法和制定完全符合《WTO协定》的新法的途径，以有效和统一的方式实施《WTO协定》”。[②] 这就意味着，除修改法律外，中国大陆似将采取“转化”方式适用WTO规则。这样，我们将面临由“转化”方式带来的难点。简言之，“转化”即条约的缔约方根据一项已批准的国际条约所进行的国内再立法。众所周知，WTO规则由一系列协定构成，客观地讲，每一项协定均再进行国内立法，这无疑是一项巨大的工程。尽管，对于WTO规则的适用一般都有过渡期的宽限，这在适用时间上给予了成员方一个回旋余地，但这不能回避再次立法的巨大难度。此外，WTO规则是一套涉及范围广泛、内容宏大、制度复杂的法律体系，其中有一些条款或制度很难用国内的单项立法予以表述和处理，如GATT 1994及其若干谅解、WTO总体框架中的原则或制度等。这必然成为国内立法将遇到的障碍。

第三，来自司法的难点。一方面，有效司法的前提是熟悉WTO规则，这就对司法提出了两个基本要求：一是精确和权威的WTO规则中译本，二是司法工作的高标准。根据《乌拉圭回合多边贸易谈判结果最后文件》的规定，WTO各项协定的正式文本用英文、法文和西班牙文写成。但即使中文译本仅作为参考，依然需要精确和权威，否则，更会增加WTO规则在司法中适用的难度。而正是WTO规则的复杂与广泛，对司法工作及司法人员提出了更高标准。可以说，两个基本要求是大陆司法部门充分和有效实施WTO规则的基本保证。另一方面，对大陆司法部门来说，WTO规则是一套全新的法律体制，许多问题无现成答案可循，况且又处于国际条约的国内适用方面存在许多不确定因素的状况之下，这就要求以司法解释作为法律、法规的补充，并以此达到统一执法。因此，司法部门面临着来自司法解释的难度。

---

① 资料来源于《中国经济时报》2002年3月5日，第1版。

② 《中国加入世界贸易组织法律文件》，对外贸易经济合作部世界贸易组织司译，法律出版社，2002，第775页。

此外，因中国大陆、香港、澳门和台湾同为 WTO 的成员方，因而形成了目前一国四法域的特殊状况，这也给 WTO 规则的适用，尤其是给在四个区域间发生争端时 WTO 规则的适用带来了挑战。现今，建立大中华自由贸易区的呼声高涨。在这种未来可能的经济安排之下，如何解决所涉及的法律问题，包括争端解决问题，四地的法律工作者仍需加紧探讨，以应对加入 WTO 给各法律体系带来的挑战。

综上所述，中国大陆在国际条约与国内法的关系上，始终恪守“条约必须信守”原则，履行条约义务。但是，由于在国际条约的国内法适用问题上，目前中国大陆在立法上还没有确定的原则，以致在司法上仍显法律依据欠缺。因此，如何在立法上更为明确地确立国际条约与国内法的关系，以及明确国际条约在中国大陆法律中的适用原则，以便 WTO 规则在中国大陆法律体系框架下得到充分和有效实施，是大陆面临的、亟待解决的问题。

［本文原载于张宪初主编《世贸规则与两岸四地经贸法律关系》，商务印书馆（香港）有限公司，2003］

试论国际投资法的新发展

——以国际投资条约如何促进可持续发展为视角

蒋小红[*]

可持续发展的理念逐渐得到了国际社会的普遍认同，成为一项国际法原则。国际投资条约（主要是双边投资条约）中的许多规定与可持续发展目标相冲突，限制了东道国可持续发展目标的实现，特别是环境保护、劳工权利保护等公共政策目标的实现。目前，几乎每一个国家都至少是一个国际投资条约的缔约方。许多国家，包括中国，还在继续谈判新的国际投资条约。缔结的国际投资条约越多，就越有可能在不同的国际义务之间产生冲突。国际法的碎片化呈现出越发严重的态势。作为国际投资法载体的国际投资条约为实现可持续发展的目标，其作用何在？换言之，在国际投资条约中如何设置具体的规则和制度才有助于可持续发展目标的实现？本文将探求在国际投资规则变革和重塑进程中国际投资条约在促进和保护投资的同时如何促进可持续发展目标的实现。

一　多元、全方位的可持续发展理念

（一）可持续发展的内涵

正确地理解可持续发展的概念是探讨国际投资条约如何促进可持续发展目标这一问题的前提。在很多时候，可持续发展被理解为环境与资源的

* 蒋小红，中国社会科学院国际法研究所研究员。

可持续发展，但是其内涵远不止于此。对此我们应该有全面的认识。可持续发展的概念经历了长期的发展历程，其含义随着时间的推移而不断扩展和深化。

可持续发展的概念纳入国际视野最早出现在战后关于利用海洋渔业资源的问题中。在对海洋资源的利用过程中，人们逐渐认识到人类的经济活动不能超越环境的承受能力，人类的整体生活要与自然环境保持和谐。在这一阶段，可持续发展的概念强调环境与经济发展的关系。之后，人们认识到可持续发展不仅仅是一个经济发展与环境领域的问题。它还涉及社会治理的方方面面，如尊重人权、抵制腐败、追求一个公正和谐的社会等。例如，20 世纪 90 年代，人们认识到人是发展的中心，人权的要素被加入可持续发展的概念中。可见，可持续发展的概念外延不断外溢，扩展到了人类生活的更多方面，[①] 已经从持续利用自然资源的最初含义演变为以人为本且具有社会经济性质的概念。20 世纪 80 年代中期以来，世界各国和有关的国际组织从不同的属性对可持续发展这一概念作了几十种不同的界定。目前，对于可持续发展的概念最广为接受的界定是世界环境与发展委员会 1987 年出版的报告《我们共同的未来》中的定义："满足当代的需要，且不危及后代满足其需要的能力的发展。"[②] 从以上的论述中，我们可以看到可持续发展是一个多元的概念，具体包含三个支柱，即经济、环境和社会。[③] 这三个支柱相互联系，形成一个整体，共同构建了可持续发展的完整内涵。通过这一概念，经济目标和非经济目标实现了有机的融合。涉及这三个领域的政策必须相互促进，才能达到人类社会可持续发展的目标。

在理解这一概念时，值得注意的是，一方面，我们不能把可持续发展的概念仅仅片面地理解为生态的可持续性，另一方面，也不能将其理解为一个无所不包的概念，应当防止可持续发展内涵的泛化。正如一位学者所

---

① Nico Schrijver, *The Evolution of Sustainable Development in International Law: Inception, Meaning and Status* (Leiden/Boston: Martinus Nijhoff Publishers, 2008).

② *World Commission on Environment and Development*, *Our Common Future* (Oxford: Oxford University Press, 1987). 世界环境与发展委员会的主席为挪威前首相格罗·哈莱姆·布伦特兰，因此，该报告又称为布伦特兰报告。

③ 参见 2005 年世界首脑会议成果文件，联合国文件 A/RES/60/1，2005 年 10 月 24 日，第 48 段。

言，“当各个方面的问题都成为可持续发展问题时，就不存在可持续发展的问题了”。[①] 与以上概念仅限于权益的代际分配不同，发展中国家的学者提出可持续发展还要关注权益在当代不同国家、不同地区的人民之间的合理分配和平衡。[②] 的确，人类社会从未像今天这样相互依存，离开了全人类的共同发展，个别国家、个别地区无法单独实现可持续发展。全方位的可持续发展理念显示出了追求人类命运共同体的新主张。

（二）促进可持续发展成为一项国际法原则

可持续发展着眼于人类社会整体的可持续发展，已经成为一项国际法原则。与在构建国际政治和经济新秩序背景下发展中国家提出的发展权概念不同，可持续发展的概念在纳入国际日程后很快在国际社会达成了共识。尽管发达国家和发展中国家面临着不同的发展任务，但各国政府都认识到可持续发展的重要性和紧迫性，这种政治上的共识使得可持续发展的理念从最初的可持续使用自然资源逐渐向经贸法、投资法、人权法等领域延伸，正在形成一项具有实质指导意义的法律原则。目前，可持续发展的概念不仅被众多的国际条约所纳入，而且已经被国际司法机构或准司法机构，例如国际法院和 WTO 争端解决机制的判例所确认为一项基本原则。[③] 2012 年，联合国贸发会制定了《可持续发展的投资政策框架》，[④] 呼吁各国秉持可持续发展原则制定和实施国内、国际投资政策。2016 年中国杭州 G20 峰会制定了《二十国集团全球投资指导原则》。[⑤] 该原则明确规定“投资及对投资产生影响的政策应在国际、国内层面保持协调，以促进投资为

① 何志鹏：《国际经济法治：全球变革与中国立场》，高等教育出版社，2015，第 150 页。

② 吴岚：《国际投资法视域下的东道国公共利益规则》，中国法制出版社，2014，第 144 页。

③ 国际法院的法官在一份判决中指出：“可持续发展的原则是——现代国际法的组成部分，这不仅是因为其具有必然存在的逻辑，也在于全球已普遍、广泛地认可该原则。”参见 Separate Opinion of Vice-President Weeramantry in the Case Concerning the GabčÍkovo-NAGY-MAROS Project, Judgment, 25 September 1997, *ICJ Report* 1997, p. 88, at 95.

④ UNCTAD, “World Investment Report 2012 - Towards a New Generation of Investment Policies”, available at: https://unctad.org/en/PublicationsLibrary/wir2012overview_en.pdf，最后访问日期：2018 年 4 月 21 日。

⑤ 这是全球首个多边投资规则框架，填补了国际投资领域的空白，为下一步制定多边的国际投资协定奠定了基础。《人民日报》2016 年 9 月 7 日，第 21 版。

宗旨，与可持续发展和包容性增长的目标相一致”。① 可持续发展的目标被纳入了全球投资指导原则。这一原则为各国协调制定国内投资政策和签订对外投资协定提供了重要指导。

二 可持续发展被纳入国际投资条约的时代背景

（一）从新自由主义到嵌入式自由主义：国际投资法的范式转变

在国际投资法领域，不同的国际经济理论体系奠定了国际投资规则构建的主要模式。目前，双边投资条约（BIT）和区域性投资条约构成国际投资法的主要载体。② 20 世纪 50 年代发展起来的 BIT，起初主要是作为资本输出国的发达国家用来保护本国海外投资者的工具。直到 20 世纪末，BIT 也主要是发达国家与作为资本输入国的发展中国家之间缔结的。在国际投资领域，新自由主义一直占据着主导地位。新自由主义是在古典自由主义思想的基础上建立起来的一个新的理论体系。这一理论体系自 20 世纪 70 年代以来在国际经济政策上扮演着越来越重要的角色，在苏联解体和经济全球化的过程中得到广泛接受。③ 新自由主义主张自由市场、自由贸易和不受限制的资本流动，主张将政府的开支、税赋最小化，同时将政府的管制最小化，并将政府对经济的直接干预最小化。直至现在，由于国际投资法的改革正在进行，出于多种原因，传统的 BIT 不可能在短期内得到更新甚至废止，其仍然是主要的国际投资法文件。新自由主义的思潮在国际投资法领域展现得淋漓尽致。BIT 在国民待遇、最惠国待遇、公平公正待遇、征收及其补偿标准、资本自由汇兑转移等方面的规定都体现了新自由主义投资保护的思想。越来越多的 BIT 的调整范围已扩展到准入前阶段，强调外资准入前的自由化、透明度以及其他投资便利。愈来愈多的 BIT 纳入了投资者诉东道国争端解决条款，并且放弃国内救济的前置程序而允许投资者直接起诉东道国成为通行的做法。在数量不断增加的国际投资仲裁

---

① 《二十国集团全球投资指导原则》第 5 条。

② 本文所指的国际投资条约主要是指双边投资条约和区域性投资条约（包括自由贸易协定中的投资章节）。

③ 于同申：《20 世纪末新自由主义经济思潮的沉浮》，《中国人民大学学报》2003 年第 5 期。

案件中，仲裁员倾向于保护投资者的利益。客观地说，新自由主义的经济理论推动了国际投资自由化的发展，促进了东道国的经济发展。然而，新自由主义片面强调投资自由化和对投资者私人权利的保护，由此导致的对东道国国内监管权的限制引发了国际社会对新自由主义的国际投资法范式的广泛讨论。

鉴于新自由主义经济理论本身所固有的缺陷，国际社会开始强调用平衡的方法来处理投资自由化和投资保护与东道国的监管权之间的紧张关系。以欧美国家为主导的国际投资缔约实践引领着国际投资法范式的转变。一种新的被称为“嵌入式自由主义”[①] 的国际投资法范式正在成为主流。所谓“嵌入式自由主义”，简言之，是指具有国家干预性质的自由主义，由此而形成的多边国际经济机制则是指国家干预以确保国内经济稳定和社会安全的理念嵌入战后国际经济机制之中，从而使战后国际经济机制在主要具有自由主义的多边性质的同时又内含国家干预的成分，由此体现了共享社会目标。[②] 由欧美国家所倡导的嵌入式国际投资法范式越来越得到包括众多发展中国家的普遍认可。新自由主义不再成为主导国际投资条约制定的支配性力量。发展中国家和发达国家都开始注重政府的规制权，重视投资者和东道国规制权之间的平衡。维护国家安全、保护劳工权利和环境保护的有关公共利益的条款被纳入越来越多的 BIT 和区域性自由贸易协定中。这些条款赋予了东道国较为灵活的自主规范外资活动的监管空间。

国际投资法从新自由主义到嵌入式自由主义的转变为在投资协定中纳入可持续发展目标提供了契机。可持续发展的目标需要国家、个人和非政府组织的共同努力才能实现。但国家在其中肩负着最主要的责任。新自由主义的国际投资法范式片面地强调投资者的权利而忽略了国家的监管权力，这种不平衡使得国家无法获得追求可持续发展所必要的空间和途径。嵌入式自由主义的国际投资法范式反映了国际社会对于投资自由化和投资管制之间关系的认识趋于理性化。嵌入式自由主义的国际投资法范式代替新自由

① 嵌入式自由主义（Embedded Liberalism）是约翰·鲁杰（John G. Ruggie）对二战后国际经济机制总体特征的描述。参见舒建中《“嵌入式自由主义”与战后多边国际经济机制的演进》，《世界经济与政治论坛》2008 年第 1 期。

② 漆彤、余茜：《从新自由主义到嵌入式自由主义——论晚近国际投资法的范式转移》，《国际关系与国际法学刊》第 4 卷，厦门大学出版社，2014，第 207 页。

主义的国际投资法范式推动了在国际投资协定中纳入可持续发展的目标。

（二）从发展到可持续发展：国际投资法的新视野

国际投资最初由西方发达国家所主导，这些国家占据对外直接投资的绝大多数，国际投资条约主要在发达国家和发展中国家之间缔结。由于历史和现实的原因，在国际投资领域，长期存在发达国家与发展中国家之间在谈判地位、能力、谈判目标与效果、权力与利益等方面的不平等或不平衡现象。最初的投资协定本质上是第二次世界大战后产生的“南北矛盾”中发达资本输出国手中的一把利剑。其目的在于通过强化相关国际法原则和建立去政治化的投资者-东道国争端解决机制来保护资本输出国及其投资者的利益。先前的国际投资立法的焦点集中在南北关系上，表现在南北之间的对立和分歧。发达国家主张投资自由化和投资保护而发展中国家则试图在吸收外资的同时保留一定的对外资管控的权力，但现实却是发展中国家为了吸引外资以促进本国经济发展不得不放弃一定的对外资管控的权力。很长一段时间以来，对发展中国家来说，追求经济发展是缔结国际投资协定的最终目标。20 世纪 90 年代以来，国际投资格局发生了深刻的变化。联合国刚刚发布的《2018 世界投资报告》显示，发展中国家吸引了世界一半以上的投资流入量以及世界三分之一的投资流出量。发展中国家在国际投资尤其是对外直接投资中的崛起，意味着它们不再从资本输入国角度而开始从资本输入国的角度看待国际投资体制。包括美国和欧盟在内的发达经济体由于在仲裁案件中频繁被诉，也开始从作为资本输入国的防御利益，而不仅仅是作为资本输出国的角度来重新思考 BIT。[①] 发达国家和发展中国家在国际投资中的身份混同使得国际投资协定的内容出现趋同化。国际社会，无论是发达国家还是发展中国家都开始更加关注投资者和东道国之间的权利和义务的平衡问题。国际投资条约制定的时代背景已经发生了显著的变化，立法的焦点已经从以前的“南北冲突”发展到了“公私冲突”，[②] 最初的投资条约所体现的发展中国家与发达国家的对立已经不再那么泾渭分明。

---

① 王露阳：《ISDS 中投资者与东道国权益平衡性探究——美国路径转变及对中国的启示》，《河北法学》2016 年第 12 期。

② 单文华：《从“南北矛盾”到“公私冲突”：卡尔沃主义的复苏与国际投资法的新视野》，《西安交通大学学报》（社会科学版）2008 年第 4 期。

三 国际投资协定促进可持续发展的路径

在国际层面，把可持续发展的原则细化到各个具体的领域是国际法各个分支面临的一项迫切任务。这也是国际投资法面临的一个挑战。当然，国际投资协定的宗旨是保护和促进投资。把促进可持续发展的任务完全交由国际投资协定来完成是不现实的。但是，投资协定应当支持或者至少不应成为实现可持续发展的障碍。现有的 BIT 中的一些实体规则和程序规则与可持续发展的目标相冲突，阻碍了可持续发展目标的实现。当务之急是以可持续发展的理念和目标对国际投资规则进行批判和解构。

（一）国家规制权：为东道国实现可持续发展目标提供政策空间

在国际投资条约中，通过多种规则设置，东道国承担着对外资保护的义务。同时东道国还肩负着促进可持续发展的历史使命。回顾现有的国际投资缔约实践，我们可以看到现有的大量的 BIT 的许多规则并不是有助于促进可持续发展目标的实现。如何正确地处理投资保护和可持续发展的关系？毫无疑问，在实现经济、社会和环境可持续发展的过程中，一国政府承担着最重要的角色。要处理好以上两者之间的关系最重要的是要平衡处理投资者权益保护和东道国管理外资的权力之间的关系。平衡投资者权利和东道国权力的关系是现代国际投资法的一个重要特征。其中蕴含的一个关系是投资保护和可持续发展的关系。[①] 如前所述，国际投资政策正在经历着从放任的新自由主义到嵌入式自由主义、从南北矛盾向公私冲突的根本性范式转变。这一范式的转变为在投资协定中促进可持续发展目标的实现提供了新的路径。作为回应，国际投资协定应以一种平衡的制度来纠正现有的国际投资协定的缺陷。在这样的背景下，国家规制权（the right to regulate）的概念被强化。之所以说这一概念被强化而不是说产生，是因为东道国管理外资的权力是东道国作为一个主权国家所固有的管理外资活动

---

① Steffen Hindelang and Markus Krajfwski edited, *Shifting Paradigms in International Investment Law: More Balanced, Less Isolated, Increasing Diversified* (Oxford: Oxford University Press, 2016), p. 5.

的权力，是国家经济主权的应有之义。① 这一概念之所以被强调是因为在现有的国际投资条约中无论从规则的设定到仲裁机构对规则的解释都过多地保护投资者的利益而忽略了东道国对外资的合理的规制权，造成国际投资关系中最重要的一对关系，即投资者和东道国之间权利和义务关系失衡的状态。这是目前的国际投资法律制度受到众多批判的最重要的一个方面。② 另一方面，越来越多的国际投资协定赋予投资者直接利用投资者—东道国投资争端仲裁机制，穷尽东道国国内救济方式的前置条件逐渐被放弃，不仅众多的发展中国家被诉，美国等发达国家也频繁地成为被告，加上高昂的赔偿费用，这些因素都对国家规制权的行使产生了“寒蝉效应”，束缚了东道国为了实现可持续发展的目标而合理地行使对外资的规制权。2010 年 8 月，全球 50 多名知名学者签署了一份声明，表达了对国际投资条约有损公共福利的担忧。声明认为，国际投资条约抑制了政府回应人的发展和环境可持续性关切的行动能力。③ 为了纠偏这一失衡的关系，国家规制权的概念被提出来。可见，国家规制权并不是一个新产生的概念。

国家规制权这一概念在国际投资法的视野下具有特殊的含义。它是指允许东道国对外资的规制背离国际条约中承诺的对外资保护的义务而不对受到不利影响的外资赔偿的法律权利。④ 规制权的概念在国际投资条约中正式得到确认开始于 20 世纪初的美式 BIT 中。2002 年美国国会通过的《贸易促进授权法案》，要求美国将维持投资者与东道国之间的平衡作为缔

① 联合国大会第 29 届会议通过的《各国经济权利与义务宪章》第 2 条第 2 款规定，各国有权根据本国的法律和条例，对境内的外国资本实行管辖和管理；有权对境内跨国公司的经营活动加以监督、管理；有权采取各种措施，以确保跨国公司的经营活动切实遵守本国的法律、条例和规章制度，符合本国的经济政策和社会政策。

② Catgarine Titi, *The Right to Regulate in International Investment Law* (Nomos and Hart Publishing, 2014), pp. 28, 33 - 34; Razeen Sappideen, Ling Ling He, "Dispute Resolution in Investment Treaties: Balancing the Rights of Investors and Host States", *49 Journal of World Trade 1*, 2015, pp. 85 - 116.

③ "Public Statement on the International Investment Regime", available at: https://www.osgoode.yorku.ca/public-statement-international-investment-regime - 31 - august - 2010，最后访问日期：2018 年 6 月 24 日。

④ 根据投资者 - 东道国投资争端解决机制，仲裁庭虽无权要求废除东道国作出的不符合国际投资协定的立法、司法和行政决定，但可以裁定东道国因违反国际投资条约的义务给投资者造成的损失承担赔偿责任。Catharine Titi, *The Right to Regulate in International Investment Law* (Nomos and Hart Publishing, 2014), pp. 33 - 34.

约的重要目标之一加以考虑。2004年，规制权概念被明确地写入美国和加拿大的BIT范本[①]中。在这之后，更多国家的BIT范本中纳入了规制权的概念。[②] 在最近几年缔结的国际投资协定中，规制权条款似乎成了“标配”。例如，2015年9月欧盟委员会颁布的《跨大西洋贸易与投资伙伴关系协定》（*Transatlantic Trade and Investrnent Partnership*，TTIP）投资章草案将其主要挑战界定为达成投资者保护和保证欧盟及其成员国权利和公共利益进行规制能力的恰当平衡。在这些国际投资协定中，如何保障国家规制权的行使？太多的规制空间会损害国际义务的价值，太苛刻的义务又会过分限制国内规制的空间。如何找到一个以促进可持续发展为导向的平衡点是各国在缔结国际投资协定时面临的挑战。在新近缔结的国际投资协定中对规制权的规定不尽相同，但体现出趋同的趋势——增加规制空间，保持规制的灵活性。

1. 在国际投资条约的序言中明确提出规制权

回顾近年来的缔约实践，可以发现越来越多的在国际投资协定中明确地阐明可持续发展是协定的主要目标，明确地承认规制权。例如，《欧盟与加拿大全面经济贸易协定》（*Comprehensive Economic and Trade Agreement between Canada and EU*，CETA）[③] 在序言中写道：“承认本协定的规定维护缔约方在其领土内的规制权以及为了合法的政策目标，例如公共健康、安全、环境、公共道德以及促进和保护文化的多样性，各缔约方的灵活

---

① “Canada's New Model Foreign Investment Protection Agreement Adopted in 2004”，available at：http://www.international.gc.ca/trade-agreements-accords-commerciaux/assets/pdfs/2004 - FIPA-model-en.pdf，最后访问日期：2018年5月26日。

② 例如，德国、哥伦比亚、印度、埃及、印度尼西亚BIT范本。在这些国家的BIT范本的修改中，增加规制的灵活性是共同的特征。欧盟在2015年的投资政策文件“Investment in TTIP and beyond—the path for reform—Enhancing the right to regulate and moving from current ad hoc arbitration towards an Investment Court”，强调规制权成为欧盟缔结的新的协定的组成部分，把规制权作为欧盟投资政策领域需要重点加强的部分。

③ 由于这个条约是欧盟自《里斯本条约》取得对外直接投资专属权能以来缔结的首部包含投资章节的自由贸易协定，被学者们视为了解欧盟新一代双边投资条约范本的窗口。参见August Reinisch，“Putting the Pieces Together…an EU Model BIT?”，15 *Journal of World Investment & Trade* 679，2014，pp. 681 - 682；“Consolidated CETA Text”，published on 26 September 2014，available at：http://trade.ec.europa.eu/doclib/docs/2014/september/tradoc_152806.pdf，最后访问日期：2018年5月6日。

性。”[①] 欧盟在2015年提出的《跨大西洋贸易与投资伙伴协定》文本草案的投资一章中有着文字上完全相同的规定。印度的2015年BIT范本也在其序言中有着类似的规定：“重申缔约方在其领土内根据其法律和政策对投资的规制权，包括改变投资条件的权利。”巴西在其2015年的投资合作和便利化协定范本的序言中直指规制权的本质：“确保规制的自主权和政策空间。”虽然条约序言并不能创设有拘束力的条约义务，但是其阐明缔约的目的和目标，并提供缔约的相关背景，这些都有助于条约的解释。当发生投资争端时，仲裁庭有义务根据《维也纳条约法公约》的规定[②]参考缔约目标和背景来解释相关的投资保护规则，在东道国的政府规制权和私人财产保护之间寻求一个平衡。这类宣言式的条款越来越多地进入国际投资协定，除了在条约解释中能够起到一定的作用，因条约序言处于总领条约的地位，对条约的具体条款的制定也会有影响，从而，对缔约方的具体权利和义务都有指引作用。[③] 从这些范本中，我们也可以看到，规制权概念尽管是由发达国家首先倡导提出的，但发展中国家也开始注重政府的规制权，表现出对这一概念的共同接受。

2. 明晰投资者权利和国家规制权的界限

国际投资法律制度，经过多年的发展，已经就条约的核心内容——投资者的保护义务达成了共识，包括国民待遇、最惠国待遇、公平公正待遇、征收和补偿、对资金转移的限制等方面。但是，在这些内容的具体规定方面，仍然存在概念界定不清晰问题，造成投资者权益保护和国家规制权之间的边界模糊，从而导致许多国际投资争端。可持续发展的理念不仅应体现在国际投资协定的序言中，也要贯穿于条约的每一个条款的制定中。近年来，大多数的国际投资协定的实体性条款已经被重新拟定，以便明晰投资者权利和国家规制权的界限，更好地平衡两者的利益。CETA在

---

① “Consolidated CETA Text”, published on 26 September 2014, available at: http://trade. ec. europa. eu/doclib/docs/2014/september/tradoc_152806. pdf，最后访问日期：2018年5月6日。

② Art. 31 (1) and (2) VCLT reads “1. A treaty shall be interpreted in good faith in accordance with the ordinary meaning to be given to the terms of the treaty in their context and in the light of its object and purpose. 2. The context for the purpose of the interpretation of a treaty shall comprise, in addition to the text, including its preamble and annexes: [⋯]”.

③ 韩秀丽：《中国海外投资的环境保护问题研究》，法律出版社，2013，第55页。

这一领域起着先锋的作用，特别是在与国家规制权紧密联系的公平公正待遇、间接征收等概念的界定上作出了创新，引领着国际投资法的改革，受到了学者们的关注。[①] 这样的改革，为东道国行使规制权提供了明确的法律依据，使得条约的规定更具有可预见性，也有助于减少仲裁员的自由裁量，使得东道国在作出有关环境保护、劳工保护等与可持续发展有关的公共决策时不必担心有可能违反了公平公正待遇、间接征收的规定而畏手畏脚。

3. 通过保留和例外条款缩小东道国的义务范围

如前所述，传统的国家投资条约通过赋予投资者各种权利的规定对东道国施加了种种义务。这些义务对东道国的规制权产生了一定的限制。许多国家新的 BIT 范本以及最近的缔约实践都表明，东道国可以通过保留和例外条款对这些义务作出限制，从而给东道国更多的空间来实现公共政策的目标。国际投资条约中的保留和例外条款成为维护东道国利益的最后一道阀门。（1）保留。通过保留，可以限制公约的适用范围，例如可以排除某些产业适用公约。CETA 就明确规定视听或文化产业不在条约保护的范围。（2）例外条款。国际投资协定中的例外条款是指协定中关于某些情况下特定的规则不予适用或部分适用的规定，从而限定了国家加入国际协定后承担义务的程度。例外条款包括一般例外条款，如安全例外，以及具体条款的例外，如最惠国待遇的例外。CETA 规定了模仿 GATT 1994 第 20 条那样的一般例外。这些规定相比序言中仅有宣示性意义的规制权的一般表述更具有确定的条约效力。相比国际贸易协定中的例外条款，国际投资协定中的例外条款是晚近才出现的现象，但例外条款正在成为国际投资条约的普遍实践。[②] 这主要是为了在投资者权利和东道国对外资的监管权力之间寻求平衡。通过这些保留和例外规定，对投资者的权利保护范围进行限制，为东道国促进可持续发展而采取的必要的管理措施提供了合法性。

---

① 石静霞、孙英哲：《国际投资协定新发展及中国借鉴——基于 CETA 投资章节的分析》，《国际法研究》2018 年第 2 期；Caroline Henckels，“Protecting Regulatory Autonomy through Greater Precision in Investment Treaties：The TPP，CETA，and TTIP”，*19 Journal of International Economic Law 1*，2016，pp. 27－50。

② 刘艳：《论发展权在国际投资协定中的实现》，武汉大学出版社，2016，第 204 页。

（二）规定投资母国和投资者的义务

在国际投资法律关系中存在三个法律关系主体，即投资者、投资母国和东道国。传统的国际投资条约主要是通过规定投资者的权利和东道国的义务来促进投资，主要规范的是投资者和东道国之间的关系，较少涉及投资者的义务，更不用说要承担起进行负责任的投资的义务。这一部分的内容主要由各国的国内法来调整。在讨论可持续发展问题时，涉及很多还没有达成共识的问题，但有一点是可以确定的，即在追求可持续发展目标的征途中，尽管国家是最主要的责任承担者，但国家并不是唯一的行动主体，私人主体、非政府组织都是重要的参与者。在国际投资法领域，企业，特别是跨国公司作为国际投资的最主要的主体，都要承担相应的责任。[①] 遗憾的是，除了最近缔结的双边投资协定外，绝大多数的国际投资协定对于外国投资者在其所投资的东道国应该承担的促进可持续发展的义务都保持了沉默。[②] 国际投资法，由 3000 多个国际投资条约为基础而构建的国际法机制，在很多方面遭到了很多的批评。其中一个方面就是国际投资条约为投资者创设了权利而没有施加义务。[③] 东道国国民，无论是个人还是社会群体在受到跨国投资者人权、环境等方面的侵害时，无法借助国际投资条约寻求国际法上的救济。

关于投资者促进可持续发展的义务方面，国际法的其他分支也存在一些固有的缺陷。国际法并没有规定一些有效的方法让那些侵犯环境保护、人权、劳工保护的投资者承担责任。例如，国际人权法就没有对投资者施加直接的义务，而是要求缔约国采取各种措施确保在其管辖范围内私人主体，包括投资者，不侵犯个人人权。被投资者或投资行为侵犯人权的受害者只能在东道国国内寻求救济。如果不能得到救济，只能到国际人权法庭

---

① ［澳］戴维·金利：《全球化走向文明：人权和全球经济》，孙世彦译，中国政法大学出版社，2013，第 163—187 页。

② Gordon, K., J. Pohl and M. Bouchard, "Investment Treaty Law, Sustainable Development and Responsible Business Conduct: A Fact Finding Survey", OECD Working Papers on International Investment 2014/01 (OECD Publishing, 2014), p. 5, available at: http://dx. doi. org/10. 1787/5jz0xvgx1zlt-en，最后访问日期：2018 年 5 月 11 日。

③ Marc Jacob, "International Investment Agreement and Human Rights", INEF Research Paper Series Human Rights, Corporate Responsibility and Sustainable Development, March, 2010, p. 21.

去起诉东道国。

针对以上问题，国际投资条约可以包含促进可持续和负责任投资(Sustainable and Responsible Investing)[①] 内容的专门条款，要求投资者承担相应的义务。例如，可以要求投资者遵守国际上普遍认可的企业社会责任的标准[②]；规定投资者必须遵守东道国的法律，遵守国际上认可的国际人权标准和国际核心劳工标准等。[③] 随着对国际法性质和功能认识的不断发展，国际条约已经突破了仅在国家之间创设权利和义务的传统模式，开始对私人主体创设义务和责任。[④] 在国际投资法领域，2007 年缔结的《东南非共同市场投资条约》就对投资者施加了各种义务，以在缔约国和投资者的权利和义务之间寻求一个平衡。[⑤] 许多资本来源地国家出于国际和国内各方面的压力，被要求其投资企业在国外承担起促进环境保护、保护劳工权益、抵制腐败等可持续发展的义务。但因对海外的投资者域外适用国内法会招致干涉别国主权，甚至是有新殖民主义的嫌疑，这一方法并不总是令人欢迎的。通过在国际投资协定中直接规定投资者的义务则可以解决这一问题，并且为东道国和受害人提起国际层面的救济提供了前提条件。目前，在国际投资协定中直接规定投资者责任的实践还处于初步尝试阶段。近年来，已有一些国际投资协定纳入了公司社会责任问题。对这一问题的

① 可持续和负责任的投资，与此概念含义相近的概念是社会责任投资（Socially Responsible Investing）。是指在追求投资财务回报的同时，结合社会、环境、伦理或道德、公司治理、人权等因素追求投资非财务回报，是旨在利用投资促进经济和社会可持续发展的一种投资理念或投资方式。参见张庆麟主编《公共利益视野下的国际投资协定新发展》，中国社会科学出版社，2014，第 154 页。

② Joshua Waleson, "Corporate Social Responsibility in EU Comprehensive Free Trade Agreements: Towards Sustainable Trade and Investment", *42 Legal Issues of Economic Integration 2*, 2015, pp. 143 – 174. Van der Zee, "Eva. Incorporating the OECD Guidelines in International Investment Agreements: Turning a Soft Law Obligation into Hard Law?", *40 Legal Issues of Economic Integration 1*, 2013, pp. 33 – 72.

③ Emily Hush, "Where No Man Has Gone before: The Future of Sustainable Development in the Comprehensive Economic and Trade Agreement and New Generation Free Trade Agreement", *43 Columbia Journal of Environmental Law 1*, 2018, pp. 157.

④ 例如，《国际刑事法院罗马规约》规定了追究实施灭绝种族罪、危害人类罪、战争罪和侵略罪的国际犯罪的个人刑事责任。

⑤ 《东南非共同市场投资条约》第 11 条。参见 Peter Muchlinski, "The COMESA Common Investment Area: Substantive Standards and Problems in Dispute Settlement", *Soas School of Law Legal Studies Research Paper Series*, Research Paper No. 11/2010, available at: https:// www. soas. ac. uk/law/researchpapers，最后访问日期：2018 年 8 月 10 日。

重视实际上代表了国际投资条约新的发展方向。[①]

与东道国对投资者的规制相比，投资母国因对投资者的属人管辖，在促进可持续发展方面也可以发挥重要的作用。国际投资协定可以要求母国的国内法和国际法之间进行有效的衔接。母国可以要求海外投资者的活动与其条约中的促进可持续发展义务及国内法中有关的可持续发展政策相符。此外，东道国对投资者权利的保护规定可以补充为要求投资母国提供技术性援助、分享相关的信息以支持东道国建立一个透明的、有效的对外资的规制，并可以辅之以建立东道国和投资母国之间长期合作的制度性安排。

（三）改革投资者－东道国争端解决机制：实现可持续发展目标的程序性保障

缔结国际投资条约不仅要仔细斟酌与可持续发展有关的实体规则，也要精心设置程序规则，这样体现可持续发展的实体性规则才能得到正确的解释和适用，得到程序性保障。

赋予私人当事方在国际仲裁中就投资争端起诉一个主权国家被认为是一场国际法的“无声革命”，[②] 投资者和国家之间的争端解决方式在国际法中的这种独特性使它一直以来争议不断。虽然大多数的国际投资协定都有这方面的规定，但是差别很大，规定的具体程度、适用的性质、投资者使用的范围等规定都有所不同。[③] 随着20世纪90年代后国际投资自由化的迅猛发展，越来越多的国家接受美式BIT和《北美自由贸易协定》的立法模式，采纳了直通车性质的争端解决机制。这一类的投资条约没有为投资者将争议提交国际仲裁设置实质性的限制，使投资者不受约束地针对主权国家提起国际仲裁成为可能。可以说，现代国际投资条约已经使投资者获

---

① 例如，2011年4月6日，欧洲议会通过一项决议呼吁在欧盟未来缔结的每一个包含投资章节的自由贸易协定中都要包含公司社会责任条款。参见The European Parliament Adopted Its Resolution on the Future International Investment Policy，INI/2010/2203。

② 〔尼泊尔〕苏里亚·P·苏贝迪：《国际投资法：政策与原则的协调》，张磊译，法律出版社，2015，第26页。

③ David Gaukrodger and Kathryn Gordon，“Investor State Dispute Settlement：A Scoping Paper for the Investment Policy Community”，OECD Working Paper on International Investment，No. 2012/3 (OECD Publishing，2012)，p. 64.

得了参与国际和国内交往的各类私方主体在国际贸易体制、国际人权体制和其他国际法律体制中无法获得的挑战国际公权力的权利。

在仲裁案件中，仲裁员如何解释国际投资规则，仅仅限于缔约方在投资条约中承诺的义务吗？还是裁判的理由还要基于更为广泛的涉及可持续发展的其他国际条约？根据《维也纳条约法公约》的规定，[①] 国际法庭和仲裁庭在适用或解释 BIT 或 FTA 时有义务考虑东道国在其他条约下所承担的义务，包括与环境保护、人权或者维护公共道德有关的国际条约。这说明，国际投资法规范不应该在与其他国际规则相绝缘的情况下运行。国际常设仲裁院也认为：在解释 BIT 或 FTA 等条约的规定时，应当考虑国际法中任何相关的规则，包括在当事方之间可以被适用的一般国际习惯法。[②] 基于这样的认识，条约的解释者，包括仲裁员在解释国际投资条约时要考虑到所涉及的所有条约的规则和国际法原则、国际习惯法。遗憾的，在仲裁实践中，仲裁机构的解释限制了东道国制定有可能对投资者不利的政策的能力，这些政策很可能是保护环境、人权等的政策。仲裁员在解释投资条约时，并没有给予人权以及公民的其他权利相对于对投资者的保护义务的优先考虑。例如，当被告的东道国以履行对投资者的保护与其承担的公民人权保护义务相冲突作为辩护理由时，仲裁庭拒绝了优先考虑人权保护的主张。[③] 这意味着当东道国在考虑制定一项促进可持续发展的法律措施，而该法律措施很可能会损害投资者的利益时，东道国不得不履行对投资者的义务而不管这样做是否会使促进可持续发展的制度变得更没有效力。换言之，在目前国际投资法的争端解决谈判桌上，个人的权利（除去投资者）和公共利益被忽视。目前的国际投资仲裁机制在合法性、公信力等方面受到了来自各方的质疑。

在目前这种状况下，国际投资法律制度要引导和鼓励仲裁庭对国家在促进可持续发展方面给予更多的注意，为此要改革投资仲裁机制中制约可持续发展目标实现的因素。首先，在仲裁员的选任上要考虑公法的知识背

---

① Art. 31（3）（C）of the Vienna Convention on the law of Treaties, 1969.

② *Saluka Investment BV（the Netherlands）v. the Czech Republic*, A Partial Award of 22 May 2006, para 254.

③ *Siemens A. G. v. The Argentine Republic*, ICSID case No. ARB/02/8（Award, 6 Feb. 2007）, at paras. 75, 79.

景要求。例如，TTIP 投资章草案提出了应当利用投资法院取代临时仲裁。在法官的任职资格上明确要求法官应具备国际公法领域的知识。这是一个在国际公法框架下运行的国际投资仲裁机制的必然要求。[①] 这实际上也是对投资者权益和东道国规制权之间失衡的纠偏。当评估一项涉及可持续发展的投资措施时，仲裁员仅仅具备国际投资法的知识显然是不够的。其次，要加强缔约国对投资协定解释权的控制。[②] 当发生投资争端时，仲裁庭对投资协定的规定进行解释。在实践中，仲裁庭常被指责扩大解释或对相同或类似的规定作出不一致的裁决，造成东道国的规制权和私人权益保护之间失衡的状态。[③] 授权仲裁庭解决东道国和投资者之间的纠纷并不意味着割断缔约方与条约的关系。相反，根据国际法，缔约方有权对投资协定的含义作最终的解释。很遗憾的是，目前，在缔结的众多国际投资条约中，缔约方还没有充分地使用这一权力。在缔结国际投资协定时，可以成立由各个缔约方代表组成的投资协定委员会，负责监督投资协定的实施情况，特别是监督发生投资争议时仲裁庭审理案件的情况，包括仲裁庭对投资协定具体规定的解释，防止仲裁庭的解释违背东道国合理管制外资的权利。如果委员会发现，不同的仲裁庭对某一个规定，例如公平公正待遇或者是间接征收的解释相互矛盾，就可以发布一个联合解释。根据《维也纳条约法公约》的规定[④]，仲裁庭有义务在解释投资条约时考虑到这一联合解释。此外，还可以在仲裁程序中建立一个“初步提交程序”，允许仲裁庭就条约的条款要求委员会作出权威性的解释，以此来作为裁定案件的基础。通过这些程序的设置来强化缔约方作为投资协定“监护者”的角色定位，防止投资协定中涉及公共利益的内容被错误地解释。另一方面，当国内的投资政策发生调整时，这一制度可以发挥“安全阀”的作用，减少或避免被众多的投资者所指控。

鉴于在国际投资条约中纳入可持续发展问题是一个新的尝试，对于双

---

① Stephan W. Schill, “The Public Law Challenge: Killing or Rethinking International Investment Law”, Columbia DFI Perspectives No. 58 (New York: Vale Columbia Center on Sustainable International Investment, 2012).

② August Reinisch and Lukas Stifter, “European Investment Policy and ISDS”, p. 8., available at: http://ssrn.com/abstract=2564018，最后访问日期：2018 年 8 月 19 日。

③ 张生：《国际投资仲裁中的条约解释研究》，法律出版社，2016，第 142—172 页。

④ Art. 31 (3) (A) of the Vienna Convention on the law of Treaties, 1969.

边投资条约中直接规定可持续发展问题的实体规则，例如劳工保护问题，是否适用一般的投资争端解决程序还处在探讨中。实践中，可参考自由贸易协定中对该问题的处理方式。主要有两种模式。（1）较为温和的欧盟模式。欧盟在2008年以前，有关社会问题的争议只能由缔约方政府协商解决。新一代的贸易协定则规定，在政府协商后如果仍然得不到解决，可以提交到专家小组。对于专家小组作出的最后的报告，缔约双方应该履行。劳工争议明确地被排除在条约一般性的争端解决程序外。[①] 贸易协定中的可持续发展章节没有规定可以对那些严重的系统性地违反有关的国际公约的情况进行制裁。例如，在实践中，加拿大通常采取缔结附属协议的方式，建立单独的劳工争议解决机制，以避免与贸易适用同一争端解决机制。[②]（2）激进的美国模式。贸易协定中的劳工、环境保护争议被纳入贸易协定中的一般争端解决机制，针对严重的系统性地违反贸易协定中规定的劳工保护和环境保护义务可以采取制裁（包括贸易制裁和金钱制裁）这一更为有效的威慑措施；引入个人申诉机制。相比以“制裁”为主要特征的美国模式，欧盟模式强调以积极鼓励的态度，通过政府间合作的方式，借助贸易工具来实现可持续发展的目标。这个模式较为灵活，适当地考虑到缔约对方的需求和能力，相比美国模式，更容易被缔约方所接受。

（四）对外资进行可持续性影响评估

传统上，许多国际投资协定仅调整外资准入后的权利义务关系。例如，长期以来，我国对外缔结的投资协定都限于投资保护、投资促进和投资便利化领域，尚未涉及投资自由化问题，也就是说这些投资协定都不包括市场准入问题。但随着投资自由化的深入发展，这一状况发生了变化。在2013年7月12日结束的第五轮中美战略与经济对话中，我国同意以准入前国民待遇和负面清单为基础与美国进行BIT谈判。这是我国第一次在BIT谈判中作出这样的立场。目前正在进行的中欧BIT谈判也改变了过去

① 2017年7月，欧盟委员会发布了题为《欧盟自由贸易协定中的贸易与可持续发展章节》的文件，正式启动了对现有模式进行改革的讨论。以欧洲议会为代表的激进派主张贸易协定中的劳工、环境保护争议纳入贸易协定中的一般争端解决机制。

② 李西霞：《加拿大自由贸易协定劳工标准及其启示》，《河北法学》2018第4期。

与欧洲国家缔结的BIT不涵盖准入前待遇的状况。外资获得准入前的国民待遇使得外资权利的范围扩大了，另一方面，外资在准入阶段也应该承担相应的义务。将对外资进行可持续影响评估作为允许外资进入的前提条件，不仅是投资者履行负责任投资的义务，也是东道国行使规制权的表现。对东道国来说，通过可持续影响评估有助于获得高质量的投资，对投资者来说则可以为未来的投资成功奠定一个良好的基础。

资本的逐利性决定了外资并不必然与可持续发展的目标相一致。在国际投资协定中纳入对外资的可持续性影响评估是保证两者相互一致的重要途径，也是东道国履行可持续发展义务的重要工具。外资可持续性影响的评估主要分为环境影响评估、社会影响评估和人权影响评估。环境影响评估和社会影响评估已经较为成熟，人权影响评估则刚刚起步。目前，在投资协定中纳入可持续影响评估机制还很少见。环境影响评估已经出现在许多国家的立法中，也被许多国际条约和软法文件所提及。[①] 这说明各国已经承认，它可以成为实现可持续发展政策的有效工具。虽然在国际投资条约中还没有纳入环境评估的规定，但它已被纳入其他国际条约的实践表明这一方式可以被移植到国际投资条约中。如何对外资进行可持续性影响评估是一项技术操作性非常强的工作，需要进一步探讨。

四 简要的结语：中国的立场

伴随着国际贸易和投资格局的发展变化，国际经贸投资规则正经历着重大的变革。以国际投资条约为载体的国际投资规则借此历史契机，从实体规则到投资争端解决机制程序性规则都正处在改革和重塑的进程中。在这一进程中，国际投资规则呈现出许多新的发展特点，其中一个特点就是国际投资规则逐渐摒弃原有的偏重投资保护的理念，纳入可持续发展的目

① 例如，欧盟的法律规定缔结一项国际投资协定需要作可持续性影响评估。2017年11月，欧盟发布了《关于欧洲联盟与中华人民共和国投资协议的可持续性影响评估》（Sustainability Impact Assessment in Support of an Investment Agreement between the European Union and the People's Republic of China），available at：www.trade-sia.com/china/wp-content/uploads/sites/9/2014/12/SIA-EU-China-Investment-Agreement-final-report.pdf，最后访问日期：2018年6月1日。

标，在提升对投资者利益保护的同时，注重环境、人权和社会利益的平衡保护。

在国际投资的缔约过程以及实践中，应该重视可持续发展这一目标的价值指引作用，国际投资法追求的目标、采取的手段都应着眼于可持续发展。国际社会在缔结国际投资协定时应体现可持续发展这一主旨，从序言到定义、从实体规则到程序规则、从核心投资规范到相关社会条款，都融入可持续发展的理念。在国际投资条约的具体规则实施的全过程中也应当充分重视可持续发展各个方面的规范与要求。无论是从国际投资条约的缔结层面还是实施层面，都应增加可持续发展在国际投资条约中的考量。如前文所述，国际投资条约中的许多规定虽不能直接促进可持续发展，其规定却可能会严重制约可持续发展目标的实现。因此，国际投资条约要从制度设计上消除不利于可持续发展目标实现的各种因素。修改目前的国际投资条约的某些具体规定以增加政府规制外资的空间以及增加可持续影响评估程序、对投资者施加保护环境、保护劳工权利、禁止贿赂等义务是值得探索的路径。当然，这些修改和变革是否能真正产生积极的效果还有待进一步的观察。总体的方向是实现投资者、东道国、投资母国权利和义务的平衡，通过平衡来实现可持续发展的目标。

如今，国际投资格局已经发生了重大变化，中国不仅是引资大国，同时也已成为对外投资大国，保持着世界第二大对外投资国的地位。这种身份的变化决定了我国在国际投资缔约中立场的转变。我国的对外开放不仅需要外国投资，更需要可持续发展友好型的高质量的投资。我国应秉持“可持续发展”、“人类命运共同体”理念，以东道国和投资母国的双重身份来谈判具体的投资规则，寻求东道国对外资的合理规制与维护投资者利益之间的适当平衡，从而兼顾利用外资和保护外资的需要。

随着中国经济实力和综合国力的提升，中国参与国际经济秩序重构的内在要求日益强烈。目前，全球主要经济体正在为克服国际投资碎片化，引领国际投资保护标准的走向，并最终形成有利于自己竞争的国家投资法律框架而积极进行投资协定谈判。2016 年 1 月 1 日，联合国《2030 年可持续发展议程》正式生效。我国高度重视落实 2030 年可持续发展议程，率先发布了国别方案和进展报告。我国作为全球投资大国和对全球可持续发展有重大影响的国家，应该抓住国际投资规则变革与重塑的历史机遇，更加积极主动地参与投资与可持续发展规则的制定，对既有的国际投资法律制度进行主动塑造，将可持续发展的理念嵌入国际投资条约的缔结中并真正履行这些体现可持续发展理念的规则，从而在新型国际经贸秩序建设中发挥积极作用。当然，需要注意的是，要做到既顺应世界可持续发展规则的大势，又不能作出超越我国社会经济发展水平和自身能力的承诺。

（本文原载于《河北法学》2019 年第 3 期）

《联合国海洋法公约》 公海渔业法律制度的主要缺陷及其影响

王翰灵*

1982 年《联合国海洋法公约》（以下简称《公约》）规定的公海渔业法律制度在 20 世纪 90 年代中期经历了较大的发展变化。当前，国际海洋法律制度，尤其是有关国家管辖以外的海域的法律制度仍在不断发生变化。回顾《公约》的一些主要原则和制度的来龙去脉，探讨其深层次的内在矛盾及发展变化规律，对我们深入理解和把握海洋法的有关原则和制度及其发展趋向是有现实意义的。本文分析《公约》公海渔业法律制度存在的主要缺陷及其对公海渔业和相关制度发展的影响。

一 《公约》之公海渔业法律制度框架

《公约》关于公海渔业的规定主要载于第七部分，尤其是第二节。根据《公约》第 87 条，所有国家均享有在公海捕鱼的自由。这一自由受到有关公海生物资源养护和管理规定，尤其是下述第 116 条规定的限制。第 63 条第 2 款和第 64 至 67 条的规定虽然出现在《公约》关于专属经济区部分，但对公海生物资源的养护和管理却有着重要影响。

根据第 117 条和第 118 条，所有国家均有义务为其国民采取养护公海生物资源的必要措施。各国有相互合作以养护和管理公海生物资源的一般义务；凡其国民开发“相同生物资源，或在同一区域内开发不同生物资

* 王翰灵，中国社会科学院国际法所副研究员。

源”的国家，负有特殊义务，进行谈判，以期采取养护有关生物资源的必要措施，以及在适当情形下，设立分区域或区域渔业组织。

《公约》第119条列举了在对公海生物资源决定可捕量和制订其他养护措施时，应该考虑的各种因素。这种措施的制订应“根据有关国家可得到的最可靠的科学证据，并在包括发展中国家的特殊要求在内的多种有关环境和经济因素的限制下，使捕捞的鱼种的数量维持在或恢复到能够生产最高持续产量的水平，并考虑到捕捞方式、种群的相互依存以及任何一般建议的国际最低标准，不论是分区域、区域或全球性的”。①

在采取措施时，各国有义务考虑与所捕捞鱼种有关联或依赖该鱼种而生存的鱼种所受的影响。《公约》还规定通过各主管国际组织，不论是分区域、区域或全球性的，并在所有有关国家的参加下，经常提供和交换可获得的科学情报、渔获量和渔捞努力量统计，以及其他有关养护鱼的种群的资料。②

此外，《公约》第十五部分有关公海渔业争端解决的规定也是公海渔业法律制度一个不可缺少的组成部分。

二 《公约》公海渔业制度的主要缺陷

《公约》之公海渔业制度至少存在以下几个主要方面的缺陷和不足。

（一）专属经济区与海洋生态系统不协调，跨界种群问题突出

1982年《公约》创立专属经济区制度，标志着国际渔业法上的革命。③200海里界线将专属经济区和公海截然分开。在此界线以内的专属经济区里，沿海国对渔业资源及其捕捞活动享有排他性的管辖权，除受到养护和给其他国家分配剩余量的一般义务约束以外。也就是说，沿海国对专属经济区内的渔业所作出的决定是权威性的，这些决定不仅对其国民产生拘束

---

① 《联合国海洋法公约》第119条第1款（a）项。

② 《联合国海洋法公约》第119条第1款（b）项、第2款。

③ Lawrence Juda, “The 1995 United Nations Agreement on Straddling Fish Stocks and Highly Migratory Fish Stocks: A Critique”, *Ocean Development and International law*, Vol. 28, 1997, p. 147.

力，而且对所有其他国家的国民同样产生拘束力。在200海里界线以外的公海上，所有国家都享有捕鱼自由权，只受到包括养护义务在内的一些限制。

专属经济区的产生对世界渔业管理的影响是巨大的。据估计，世界海洋总渔获量的90%以上来自专属经济区。[①] 这样一来世界渔业问题似乎已由此而得到解决了，因为世界上绝大多数的鱼类已处于国家管辖之下。这种看法很快就被证明是简单和幼稚的。在《公约》通过的十余年里，世界渔业，特别是公海渔业中存在的严重问题就暴露出来了。对鱼类来说，《公约》规定的200海里界线没有任何意义，因为它们不知道人类通过艰苦的外交谈判后给它们划定了一条管辖界线。它们继续按照生物和自然规律，如海水的温度和食物供给等到处游动、求生，固执地穿梭于各国的专属经济区和公海之间。这样就出现了专属经济区与生态系统管理不协调的矛盾。[②] 事实上，200海里界线是人为的政治界线，而不是生物学上的分界线。200海里界线运作的理想状态是，所有的鱼都表现出与人类合作的态度，都老老实实地只待在某一个国家的专属经济区里或只待在公海上。然而，现实并非如此。200海里界线是死的，鱼是活的，鱼类的洄游习性决定了专属经济区制度存在先天性的不足。建立专属经济区的一个结果是允许沿海国控制在该区域的捕捞量，根据《公约》和有关的国家实践，这主要通过限制外国在专属经济区的捕捞来实现。然而，鱼类的高度流动性潜在地削弱了专属经济区的这种管理制度。在某种情况下，它可能使沿海国对专属经济区的渔业管理措施和成果付诸东流。对于跨界和高度洄游鱼类，这种现象普遍存在。在世界许多地区，200海里范围与鱼类种群洄游的自然范围是不一致的。许多沿海国在专属经济区内采取的养护和管理措施被在邻接专属经济区的公海的外国渔船的捕鱼活动所抵消。从沿海国的角度来看，不仅其在专属经济区内的养护措施有被邻接区域内的外国渔船的捕捞活动破坏的潜在危险，而且沿海国专属经济区渔业管理所产生的经济利益可能也会被这些外国渔船捞走。事实上，在专属经济区制度建立以

---

① David A. Balton, "Strengthening the Law of the Sea: The New Agreement on Straddling Fish Stocks and Highly Migratory Fish Stocks", *Ocean Development and International Law*, Vol. 27, 1996, p. 127.

② 关于这个问题的深入论述，参见 Hanling Wang, "Ecosystem Management and Its Application to Large Marine Ecosystems: Science, Law, and Politics", *Ocean Development and International Law*, Vol. 35, No. 1, 2004。

后，被从沿海国专属经济区排斥出来的外国渔船有的返回本国水域，而有的则继续在专属经济区的邻接公海区域捕鱼。[①] 由于大量的远洋捕鱼船队从国家管辖区域转移到公海，造成了公海捕鱼活动的增多，再加上捕鱼工具和方法上的技术进步，世界许多地方的鱼类种群不断减少和枯竭。[②] 据粮农组织估计，在广泛建立专属经济区以前，200 海里以外的总的海洋渔获量占世界总渔获量的 5%，而此后这个数字上升至 8% –10%。[③]

应当承认，《公约》并非没有预见到上述问题，否则便没有关于跨界种群及高度洄游鱼种等特定鱼种的第 63 条至 67 条的规定。但由于第三次联合国海洋法会议对公海渔业问题不够重视，再加上沿海国和公海捕鱼国之间的利益关系难以调和，就造成了有关跨界种群和高度洄游鱼种规定的简单化和原则化。可以说，《公约》没有给如何解决既出现在专属经济区又出现在公海的所谓的跨界鱼类种群和高度洄游鱼类种群这样一些有价值的鱼类种群问题提供具体的指导。在缺乏明确、具体的法律规范的情况下，一些公海捕鱼国忽视国际社会关于对由于环境减损和过度渔捞而处境危险的某些鱼类种群采取更有力的养护措施的要求，而一些沿海国则试图将其对渔业资源的管辖延伸至《公约》规定的 200 海里界线以外，整个《公约》所依托的微妙的利益平衡面临着遭到破坏的危险。《公约》关于国际海底开发制度的问题于 1994 年得以解决后，[④] 有关跨界和高度洄游鱼类种群问题的矛盾成了现代海洋法中的最不稳定的因素。[⑤]

（二）对公海捕鱼自由权缺乏有效的约束机制

专属经济区制度的确立，结束了 200 海里海域范围内的捕鱼自由。然

---

① UN Press Release, Sea/1381, 12 July 1993, p. 1.

② Satya Nandan and Shabtai Rosenne, United Nations Convention on the Law of the Sea 1982: A Commentary, The Hague-London-Boston, 1995, Vol. III, p. 38.

③ Some High Seas Fisheries Aspects Relating to Straddling Fish Stocks and Highly Migratory Fish Stocks, FAO Fisheries Circular No. 879, Rome, 1994, p. 1.

④ 1994 年 7 月 28 日，经联合国秘书长主持的多次协商，《关于执行 1982 年 12 月 10 日〈联合国海洋法公约〉第十一部分的协定》获得通过，解决了西方主要工业国家因对《公约》国际海底区域开发制度的规定持有强烈的保留态度而迟迟未批准《公约》的问题。

⑤ David A. Balton, "Strengthening the Law of the Sea: The New Agreement on Straddling Fish Stocks and Highly Migratory Fish Stocks", *Ocean Development and International Law*, Vol. 27, 1996, p. 126.

而，200 海里以外的公海渔业制度仍是以公海捕鱼自由原则为基础。《公约》关于公海渔业制度的基本框架大体上沿袭了以传统的公海捕鱼自由原则为核心的日内瓦海洋法公约公海渔业法律制度。对于公海捕鱼自由，《公约》一方面确认这是所有国家都享有的一种权利，另一方面对这种权利设定了一定的限制条件。第 87 条第 2 款规定，所有国家在行使公海捕鱼自由权时须“适当顾及”其他国家行使公海自由的利益。第 116 条规定，公海捕鱼权受以下三个方面的限制：（1）条约义务，这一般指捕鱼国与其他国家通过签订条约，对其在某个公海区域的捕鱼权进行限制，或者捕鱼国承诺放弃公海捕鱼自由权；（2）除其他外，第 63 条第 2 款至第 67 条规定的沿海国的权利、义务和利益，这里指的是有关特定鱼种的权利和利益，分别涉及跨界鱼类种群、高度洄游鱼类、溯河产卵种群、降河产卵鱼种和海洋哺乳动物；（3）《公约》关于公海生物资源养护和管理的各项规定，这指的是《公约》第七部分第 2 节的各项规定，主要涉及养护和合作义务。《公约》虽然对公海捕鱼自由权规定了这样的限制，但它并未对这种限制的性质和适用的方法作出具体、明确的规定。也就是说，它没有说明公海捕鱼权如何被限制，或对捕鱼权的限制如何适用于公海捕鱼国。比如，《公约》规定公海捕鱼权受到沿海国的权利、义务和利益的限制，但它并没有对具体情况下捕鱼国和沿海国之间的这种权利和利益的顺序作出适当安排，致使这些权利之间潜伏着冲突，而《公约》并未提供一个解决这种冲突的具体办法。沿海国的权利仅限于 200 海里界线以内，难以约束 200 海里以外的公海捕鱼权。《公约》第 117 条和第 118 条虽然为公海捕鱼国设定了养护义务和合作义务，但这些义务都被规定得过于原则化、抽象化，对其所包含的具体内容，理论界缺乏统一的认识，在实践中就更缺乏可操作性了。况且，在缺乏有效监督和控制机制的公海渔业环境中，这些养护义务和合作义务主要靠捕鱼国及渔民以自律的方式来履行。在实践中，有些国家不愿或没有能力对本国渔民的公海捕鱼活动进行严格监督、限制和处罚；而对于渔民来说，正如约翰斯顿（Douglas M. Johnston）所指出的，“认为渔民会自愿地和有见识地参与养护的想法是不现实的。养护政策在理论上的正当性是难以把握的，要在短期内有效地说服渔民减少捕捞努力量或使用大网眼的网具以使更多的小鱼能够逃生是为了他们自己及其子孙后代的利益往往是不容易的”。[①] 因此，可想而知，《公约》规定的这些原则性的养护和合作义务对公海捕鱼活动的约束是非常有限的，甚至可以说是无效的。总而言之，《公约》有关规定的这种模糊性削弱了对公海捕鱼自由的约束机制，在一些情况下甚至使公海捕鱼处于一种不受约束的状态。经验证明，对权利缺乏有效的约束必然导致权利的滥用。德国国际法学家闵希指出，公海自由往往由于滥用权利而受到损害，无节制的捕捞就是一个典型的例子。[②]

1995年，联合国粮农组织报告说，自从对渔业数据进行收集以来，世界海洋渔获量在1989年达到高峰之后首次开始下跌。当时，大约70%的海洋鱼类种群就已完全遭到严重开发、过度开发、枯竭或恢复缓慢。[③] 有价值的跨界种群（如西北大西洋的鳕鱼和白令海的绿鳕）衰退，而一些高度洄游鱼种（如大西洋西部的金枪鱼）处于萧条状态。导致这种状况的原因可能是多方面的，但对捕鱼不加以适当、有效的限制无疑是直接的原因。实践证明，对捕鱼权，尤其是公海捕鱼权缺乏有效的约束机制将产生灾难性的后果。

（三）缺乏有效的公海执法机制

《公约》继续承认捕鱼自由原则在公海渔业法律制度中的首要地位。要使公海捕鱼自由原则得以顺利运作，就需要有一个前提条件，或者说保障因素，那就是渔船在公海上航行及作业不受任意干涉或阻碍。舍此便无捕鱼自由可言。与公海捕鱼自由原则相适应，《公约》沿袭了传统海洋法中的船旗国专属管辖原则。《公约》第92条规定，除国际条约或本《公约》明文规定的例外情形外，船舶在公海上应受船旗国的专属管辖。这项规定当然适用于在公海上的渔船。它排除和否定了除船旗国以外的其他任何国家对在公海上的渔船的不当干预。与此相应，《公约》对公海执法问题保持沉默。换句话说，《公约》没有关于公海执法的规定。而《公约》

---

① 参见 Douglas M. Johnston, *The International Law of Fisheries: A Framework For Policy-Oriented Inquiries* (Dordrecht: Martinus Nijhoff Publishers, 1987), p. 43。

② 参见〔德〕英戈·冯·闵希《国际法教程》，林荣远等译，世界知识出版社，1997，第332页。

③ FAO, The State of World Fisheries and Aquaculture, 1995.

第 66 条则推定不存在公海执法权。该条规定，溯河产卵鱼种的鱼源国对在公海上捕捞源自其河流的这些鱼种的外国渔船享有管理权，但又要求对这些渔船的执法应由鱼源国和有关国家协议进行。这等于不承认鱼源国有对在公海上捕捞溯河产卵鱼种的外国渔船采取单方执法行动的权利。第 116 条对公海捕鱼权规定了一些限制，但也没有关于执法的规定。对此，柏克（William T. Burke）教授曾指出，第 116 条是令人难以理解的。它规定公海捕鱼权受到，除其他外，第 63 条第 2 款和第 64 至 67 条规定的沿海国的权利、义务和利益的限制。不幸的是，这种使公海权利受到沿海国权利限制的执法意义没有得到进一步阐述，使正常的公海自由不受干涉的含义继续适用，即使公海权受到另一个国家的权利的限制。[①] 他认为，缺乏有效的公海执法可能是国际渔业法决策方面的主要的、突出的问题。关于适用于公海捕鱼本身的一般原则的协议已经比较普遍，却没有类似的关于公海捕鱼国对沿海国负有的具体义务的协议。公海捕鱼受到沿海国权利、义务和利益限制的一般原则已得到承认，而且在《公约》中已作了规定，但其含义并未在其他任何协议中得以阐述。不过即使有这样一种协议，在目前缺乏健全的公海执法制度的情况下，其履行也是困难的。[②] 公海执法的主要障碍是，根据现代国际法，公海上的船只免受船旗国以外的任何国家的干涉。[③]

柏克教授还指出，《公约》在渔业管理方面有两个最主要的问题没有解决，其中一个就是公海渔业的无效管理（另一个问题是新近受到沿海国管辖的渔业未能产生预期的效益）。他认为，国家管辖以外的渔业继续处于无效的管理状态，部分是因为缺乏决策的体制结构，部分是因为各种切身利益不可调和。这个问题在《公约》建立了新的国际海洋法制度后仍未得到解决，事实上在某种程度上是由这种新制度而产生的。它也是由捕鱼

---

① 参见 William T. Burke, *The New International Law of Fisheries*：*UNCLOS 1982 and Beyond*（Oxford：Clarendon Press，1994），p. 336。

② 参见 William T. Burke, *The New International Law of Fisheries*：*UNCLOS 1982 and Beyond*（Oxford：Clarendon Press，1994），p. 345。

③ 参见 William T. Burke, *The New International Law of Fisheries*：*UNCLOS 1982 and Beyond*（Oxford：Clarendon Press，1994），p. 310。

自由造成的。[①]

对公海上的渔船实行船旗国专属管辖原则而缺乏相应的公海执法机制，这确实是《公约》公海渔业制度的一个主要缺陷。在国际渔业实践中，这种制度性的缺陷已经造成了严重弊端。在船旗国对在公海悬挂其旗帜的渔船不愿或没有能力行使管辖的情况下，公海捕鱼就处于一种几乎完全不受约束的状态，其后果是可想而知的。船旗国专属管辖的另一个消极影响就是造成一些渔船通过更换旗帜来规避管辖的现象。这种现象普遍存在，已经成为国际渔业管理中的一大难题。

以上概括的三个方面的主要缺陷并未能涵盖《公约》公海渔业制度存在的所有问题，但所提到的这几个方面的缺陷都是根本性的。

三 《公约》公海渔业制度缺陷对公海渔业的影响

《公约》公海渔业制度的上述缺陷和不足使其在实际运作过程中出现了许多问题，在公海渔业的养护和管理中未能充分发挥应有的作用，给公海渔业带来了不利的影响。《公约》通过后的20世纪八九十年代，世界海洋渔业出现了一种极为矛盾的现象：一方面是渔业资源日益衰退；另一方面是公海捕捞努力量逐日增长。在这种情况下，国际渔业纠纷不断发生。例如，西班牙和法国渔民在比斯开湾发生冲突；苏联及其继承者俄罗斯威胁要对在鄂霍茨克公海的外国渔船采取军事行动；哥斯达黎加逮捕只通过其专属经济区而不携带渔具的四艘美国船只。[②] 美国和苏联面对白令海峡鳕鱼种群的衰退，也感到在白令公海（Donut Hole）地区的相当小的“公海口袋”阻止来自日本、中国、韩国和波兰的船只的过度渔捞的国内压力。有的提议利用《公约》的争端解决规则来解决，[③] 而有的提议则寻求

① 参见 William T. Burke, *The New International Law of Fisheries: UNCLOS 1982 and Beyond* (Oxford: Clarendon Press, 1994), p. 348。

② David A. Balton, “Strengthening the Law of the Sea: The New Agreement on Straddling Fish Stocks and Highly Migratory Fish Stocks”, *Ocean Development and International Law*, Vol. 27, 1996, p. 131.

③ E. Miles and W. T. Burke, “Pressures on the United Nations Convention on the Law of the Sea of 1982 Arising from New Fisheries Conflicts: The Problem of Straddling Stocks”, *Ocean Development and International Law*, Vol. 20, 1989, p. 20.

依靠《公约》关于闭海和半闭海的几项简洁的规定来解决。[①]

面对这种国际渔业形势，一些沿海国宣称，在北大西洋、太平洋和白令海出现的困难和冲突是由于《公约》关于跨界种群的规定的缺陷和沿海国与在专属经济区邻接海域捕鱼的国家之间的权利分配不明确造成的。[②]尽管第三次联合国海洋法会议拒绝承认沿海国在其专属经济区以外地区的特殊利益，以加拿大和阿根廷为首的一些拥有宽大陆架的国家仍坚持这种主张。在实践中，一些沿海国要求对 200 海里以外的海域实行单方控制。比如拥有近海跨界鱼类种群和高度洄游鱼种的几个拉美国家和加拿大就要求将其管辖扩大到 200 海里以外。[③] 这些主张和做法引起了国际争议，有的已经引起了国际争端。其中智利提出的存在海（Mar Presencial 或 presential sea）概念及主张和由于加拿大将其渔业管辖权延伸至 200 海里以外而引发的与欧盟之间的争端就是两个典型的例子。

存在海的理论是 1990 年 5 月由智利海军总司令布思奇（Jorge Martinez Busch）提出的。根据存在海的理论及智利的有关立法，存在海是位于智利专属经济区外部界线和经过复活岛大陆架两端的经线之间的公海，它从智利和秘鲁的海上分界线延伸至南极，在太平洋东南部占据一片总面积约为 19967337 平方公里的宽阔的梯形海域。布思奇认为，对于其他国家在存在海中从事的活动，智利都应该实际地在场观察或参加并在《联合国海洋法公约》规定的公海的法律地位范围内进行活动。它构成智利提防国家利益受到损害和抵抗对其发展和安全的直接或间接威胁的一种办法。他还强调需要建立与存在海的经济利用之间的联系，这意味着对资源的合理开发和在该地区建立控制捕鱼活动的机制。布思奇认为，沿海国对其存在海享有“主权的胚胎”（embryo of sovereignty）。他宣称沿海国对邻接其专属经济区的公海部分应享有一定程度的主权。他将这种主权说成是“维持生计

---

① L. Miovski, “Solutions in the Convention on the Law of the Sea to Overfishing in the Central Bering Sea: Analysis of the Convention, Highlighting the Provisions Concerning Fisheries and Enclosed and Semi-Enclosed Seas”, *San Diego L. Rev.*, Vol. 26, 1989, p. 525.

② Edward S. Miles and William T. Burke, “Pressure on the United Nations Convention on the Law of the Sea of 1982 Arising from New Fisheries Conflicts: The Problem of Straddling Stocks”, *Ocean Development and International Law*, Vol. 20, 1989, pp. 343 - 357.

③ E. Meltzer, “Global Overview of Straddling and Highly Migratory Fish Stocks: The Non-Sustainable Nature of High Sea Fisheries”, *Ocean Development & International Law*, Vol. 25, 1994, pp. 255, 264.

的主权”（sovereignty of subsistence），而这部分的公海则是其他国家的活动对沿海国的专属经济区和领海造成一些影响的空间。

存在海理论提出后在智利国内赢得了许多支持者，他们有的为该主张寻找理论依据，有的对该理论进一步加以阐释。例如，有的人从战略需要方面为存在海的主张寻找理论依据，指出，因为只有主要的海洋国家拥有技术能力开发公海资源，只有它们能够从执行《公约》的管理规定中得到好处。这样将存在由主要海洋国家填补的权力真空，如果智利想维护其在未来国际秩序中的地位，它就必须采取行动填补在太平洋东南部的这样一个真空，在开发和管理公海渔业、海洋科研及开发海底矿物中发挥积极的作用。

关于存在海概念所包含的内容，维昆纳［Orrego Vicu（a）］解释为以下几个方面。首先，沿海国参加和监督其他国家在公海上从事的活动。这并不是把任何国家从这些地区排斥出去，而是确保有关沿海国的积极参与。存在海的概念也不包含沿海国的专属权利，或划分法律意义上的新的海洋边界；沿海国参与其他国家所从事的这种活动不能理解为沿海国对这种活动的强行干预，而只是保证其在这些公海地区的积极行动的权利。这个概念明确维护《公约》规定的公海的法律地位，而无意否认公海的这种法律地位。因此，它是完全符合当代国际海洋法的。其次，存在海概念鼓励沿海国在公海上从事经济活动以促进其国内经济的发展，并避免在这些公海上进行的其他活动对这种发展造成直接或间接有害的影响。存在海包含竞争的合法形式，同时要求发展更为积极的合作形式和其他措施，以防止对沿海国利益的不利影响。在诸如跨界种群、高度洄游鱼种、鲑鱼饲养和鲑鱼野生种群、海洋污染以及其他许多事项方面，这种情况已得到承认，在不久的将来还将以种种方式加以完善。存在海概念不包含管辖内容或主张，但如果国际合作机制不存在或无效，它可以最终含有管辖的意义。例如，当无人对公海地区进行管理时沿海国对其采取养护措施的情况就是这样。最后，存在海概念与广泛的国家安全观念有关，它不是一种严格的军事意义上的国家安全，而是关于包含经济方面，尤其是指专属经济区和领海的国家利益的保护。它也涉及沿海国对国家管辖以外的大陆架及其海底的利益，它无损于国际制度，但要确保以适当的方式体现沿海国的利益。

在法律依据上，存在海的理论认为，《公约》规定的公海制度不太明确，这给公海捕鱼国在适用中留有较大的决定权。一方面有关沿海国的管辖在很大程度上被认为是一种国家实践。但另一方面，沿海国一般对公海上的活动缺乏管辖权，这导致了远洋捕鱼国获得并维持在公海上的实质上比沿海国优先的权利。在法律上，所有国家在原则上都可以享有开发公海生物资源的相同的平等的权利，但事实上只有拥有远洋捕鱼船队的国家捕捞这些渔业资源而不必让其他国家分享这种利益。此外，远洋捕鱼国在捕鱼技术和科研方面占有优势，这便于其提高捕捞能力，增加渔获量，但也容易造成对公海生物资源养护和管理措施的损害和破坏。而且，远洋捕鱼国由于拥有以上优势，在有关公海生物资源的养护和管理的谈判中也往往处于有利地位。总之，《公约》并未给邻接沿海国专属经济区的公海带来公正而平等的秩序。

从《公约》的有关规定来看，它为存在海理论辩护的底线是明确的：它规定各国有为养护海洋生物资源制订措施的权利和义务。尽管如此，执行这些重要义务的办法并没有明确、具体的规定，因而是含糊不清、模棱两可的。因此，养护措施留给各国，实际上主要是由远洋捕鱼国根据意愿而定。捕鱼国制定的公海养护措施总是有利于其经济利益的。这也是提出存在海理论的理由。提出存在海概念的动机主要是经济。一方面是为了减少外国人在公海上的捕鱼活动对智利专属经济区造成的不利影响；另一方面是智利想通过对太平洋东南沿海的开发来振兴国内经济，其中一个重要的方面就是公海渔业。存在海所包含的一个新内容就是利用跨界种群问题，在使其他远洋捕鱼国受损的情况下为智利国内日益扩大的捕鱼船队保留海洋空间。①

虽然存在海的主张遭到了一些国家政府和学者的反对，但是，它还是被智利政府采纳为一项国家政策，并通过立法的形式体现出来。1991 年，

---

① 参见 Jos A. De Yturriage, *The International Regime of Fisheries*: *From UNCLOS 1982 to the Presential Sea* (Martinus Nijhoff Publishers, 1997), pp. 228 – 232; Francisco Orrego Vicu (a), "Toward an Effective Management of High Seas Fisheries and the Settlement of the Pending Issues of the Law of the Sea", *Ocean Development and International Law*, Vol. 24, 1996, pp. 87 – 89; Christopher C. Joyner and Peter N Decola, "Chile's Presential Sea Proposal: Implications for Straddling Stocks and the International Law of Fisheries", *Ocean Development and International Law*, Vol. 24, 1996, pp. 107 – 111。

智利修改了其 1989 年的《渔业与水产法》，在立法上采纳了存在海的概念。该法没有规定智利对存在海的具体权利，但包含了对邻接其专属经济区的公海的生物资源、渔业、水产等的养护。智利在 1991 年 8 月 12 日修改的另一项渔业法令中规定，智利政府有权对既出现在其专属经济区又出现在公海的跨界和高度洄游种群、溯河产卵种群制定养护和管理措施，并对来自这些地区的渔获或产品的上岸进行管理。它规定，如有理由怀疑外国渔船所从事的捕鱼活动有害于渔业资源或智利在其专属经济区内的渔业资源的开发，可以禁止该渔船的渔获上岸或口岸服务，等等。此外，智利还在其他的法律中采纳了存在海的理论。[①] 值得注意的是，智利的存在海主张及其有关的立法已对其邻国阿根廷造成影响。虽然阿根廷没有明确地在其立法中采用存在海的概念，但它已经以与智利相对应和同步的方式作出反应，在 1991 年及其以后的几项国内立法中规定了对专属经济区以外的公海区域的生物资源的养护和管理的内容。[②]

总之，从存在海产生的原因、内容和目的等几个方面来看，它都与跨界种群的问题有关。它一方面反映了《公约》的有关规定存在缺陷和不足；另一方面，正如有的学者所指出的，存在海的产生代表了沿海国采取单方面行动保护专属经济区近海渔业的一种尝试，它通过在邻接公海地区建立广阔的缓冲区，以有利于智利的方式解决智利的跨界种群的问题。[③]

在西北大西洋，跨界种群的问题也导致了加拿大通过国内立法，将其管辖权扩大到专属经济区以外，并因而引起了与捕鱼国的冲突。该地区的渔业处于西北大西洋渔业组织（NAFO）的管制之下。该组织成立于 1978 年，有 14 个成员国，包括加拿大、欧盟、日本、俄罗斯、波兰等。其宗旨是致力于渔业资源的最适度利用、合理管理和养护。然而，由于过度渔捞，再加上加拿大 200 海里专属渔区内管理不善，对 NAFO 成员国及非成员国在管制区内的捕鱼活动管制不严或不加管制，NAFO 成员国使用反对

---

① 参见 Jos A. De Yturriage, *The International Regime of Fisheries*: *From* UNCLOS 1982 to the Presential Sea,（Martinus Nijhoff Publishers, 1997）, pp. 233 – 235。

② 参见 Jos A. De Yturriage, *The International Regime of Fisheries*: *From UNCLOS 1982 to the Presential Sea*（Martinus Nijhoff Publishers, 1997）, pp. 235 – 238。

③ 参见 Joyner and DeCola, Chile's Presential Sea Proposal: Implications for Straddling Stocks and the International Law of Fisheries, *Ocean Development and International Law*, Vol. 24, 1996, pp. 110, 115。

程序否决养护和管理提案等原因，NAFO 对其管制区内的跨界种群的养护和管理效力相当低。在 NAFO 内部，加拿大和欧盟之间在养护和管理措施，特别是配额方面经常发生纠纷，而欧盟动辄行使否决权，使 NAFO 的决策机制陷于瘫痪。由于在配额问题上未能达成协议，双方曾多次单方面决定配额。1986 年两个重要的远洋渔业国西班牙和葡萄牙加入欧盟之后，上述矛盾进一步加剧。在 1983 年 8 月西班牙加入 NAFO 以前，其渔民就在 NAFO 管制区内从事未受管制的捕鱼活动。加入 NAFO 之后，其捕捞量仍有超过配额的现象。1990 年，西班牙和葡萄牙开始在纽芬兰大浅滩的“鼻子”（nose）和“尾巴”（tail）海域大量捕捞庸鲽。当年，这两个国家的渔船就捕捞了 32200 吨的庸鲽。1992—1994 年，庸鲽总渔获量的四分之三被欧盟的渔船捕获。尽管如此，直至 1995 年 1 月，庸鲽才受到 NAFO 的配额管理。1994 年 2 月，加拿大和 NAFO 科学理事会对格陵兰庸鲽的调查研究结果均表明，该鱼种已大幅衰减，需要采取严格而有力的养护措施。当年，加拿大大幅削减庸鲽捕捞量，并要求欧盟采取同样措施。然而，双方在配额问题上再度发生纠纷，欧盟再次行使否决权，并单方面决定配额。对于欧盟的这种单方面行动，加拿大采取了两项对抗措施：一是对格陵兰庸鲽采取为期 60 天的暂禁；二是在 1995 年 3 月 3 日修改其《沿岸渔业保护法》，宣布西班牙和葡萄牙渔船在加拿大 200 海里专属渔区以外的大西洋沿岸纽芬兰大浅滩捕捞格陵兰庸鲽为非法。3 月 5 日，加拿大通过电台对欧盟渔船发出警告。3 月 7 日加拿大渔业与海洋部部长托宾（Tobin）告诫欧盟渔船在 3 月 8 日以前从大浅滩的“鼻子”和“尾巴”撤走，否则将有被捕的危险。3 月 9 日，加拿大官员在鸣枪警告之后，登临并逮捕了正在距加拿大海岸 218 海里的大浅滩“鼻子”捕鱼的西班牙渔船“埃斯塔”（Estai）。3 月 26 日，加拿大海岸警卫队又剪断西班牙另一艘拖网渔船的网具，并试图登临两艘渔船。对此，西班牙政府也不甘示弱，先后派出两艘海军护卫舰到有争议的地区保护其渔船作业。3 月 28 日，西班牙政府向国际法院起诉加拿大。为此，欧盟和加拿大就北大西洋的捕鱼权问题进行了谈判，并于 1995 年 4 月 20 日达成一项协定。该协定提高了欧盟的庸鲽配额；加拿大同意修改其《沿岸渔业保护法》中的有关规定；加强管制区内的渔业养护和管理；加拿大还同意撤回对埃斯塔渔船的起诉并将 500000 加元的保证金返还给该船船长。这样，加拿大和西班牙及欧盟之间的庸鲽之战暂告一个段落。然而，这一争端所暴露出来的问题及其对国际法及国际海洋法所产生的影响是发人深省的。就这一点而言，所涉及的问题是多方面的，其中至少有以下几点值得注意。

首先，加拿大和欧盟之间的争端典型地代表了沿海国和远洋捕鱼国之间的利益冲突。可以说，西北大西洋渔业组织的历史就是加拿大和欧共体（欧盟）关于跨界种群管理措施冲突的历史。这种冲突的原因是多方面的。就法律制度方面的原因而言，其根源在于《公约》关于跨界种群问题的规定存在缺陷和不足，因而未能有效地养护和管理这些种群。

其次，这一争端是由于 NAFO 本身未能解决的内部矛盾而在其成员国之间发生的，而 NAFO 被公认为是世界上最先进的区域渔业组织之一，这说明现存的区域渔业管理组织仍存在严重弊端，在国际渔业资源养护和管理方面尚未能充分发挥其应有的作用，因而有待进一步加强。

最后，埃斯塔事件是在联合国跨界和高度洄游鱼类会议进行到关键阶段时发生的，它是加拿大旨在影响这个会议的结果而采取的策略的一部分。[①] 该会议通过了 1995 年《执行 1982 年 12 月 10 日〈联合国海洋法公约〉有关养护和管理跨界鱼类种群和高度洄游鱼类种群的规定的协定》（以下简称《协定》）。[②] 从《协定》的有关内容来看，特别是在关于邻接公海地区跨界种群的养护和管理制度方面，作为沿海国的加拿大在很大程度上实现了自己的目的。因此，在许多方面，《协定》被认为是加拿大和欧盟之间渔业争端的结局。[③]

四 结论

《公约》之公海渔业制度至少存在三个主要方面的缺陷和不足：（1）专属经济区与海洋生态系统不重合、不谐调，导致跨界种群的养护和管理效

---

① 参见 Yann-Huei Song, "The Canada-European Union Turbot Dispute in the Northwest Atlantic: An Application of the Incident Approach", *Ocean Development and International Law*, Vol. 28, No. 3, 1997, p. 296。

② 1995 年 8 月 4 日通过，2001 年 12 月 11 日生效。

③ 参见 Michael Sean Sullivan, "The Case in International Law for Canada's Extension of Fisheries Jurisdiction Beyond 200 Miles", *Ocean Development & International Law*, Vol. 28, 1997, p. 242。

果不彰；（2）对公海捕鱼自由权缺乏有效的约束机制；（3）缺乏有效的公海执法机制。这些缺陷在很大程度上导致了专属经济区养护利益与公海捕鱼利益之间的冲突，以及世界海洋渔业资源的日益衰退，同时也促使一些沿海国将自己的管辖权向公海延伸。《公约》关于公海渔业的规定实际上在 1975 年第三次联合国海洋法会议的谈判过程中就已确定下来，直至 1982 年 12 月《公约》通过，几乎没有改变。《公约》通过以后，有关情况发生了很大的变化。20 世纪 70 年代制定的有关制度不能适应公海渔业迅速发展的形势。出于弥补《公约》公海渔业制度的缺陷，加强公海渔业管理的目的，20 世纪 90 年代以来，一系列的国际法律文件应运而生，其中包括上述《协定》和 1993 年的《促进公海上渔船遵守国际养护和管理措施的协定》等。公海渔业法律制度由此进入了一个新的调整期。

（本文部分内容原载于《变化中的国际法：热点与前沿》，中国社会科学出版社，2012，第 126—142 页，收入本书时略作修改）

国际法的和平软肋

——从康德的《永久和平论》说起

李　赞*

对和平的追求，是人类最久远的梦想。20 世纪，在经历了两次惨不堪言的世界大战之后，人类开始认真地反思和实践关于实现和平的构想。一战后成立的国际联盟，没能阻止第二次世界大战的发生，自己也在战火硝烟中灰飞烟灭。在二战的废墟上建立的联合国，在过去的半个多世纪里，确实对于阻止世界大战的发生起了重要作用。但是，事实告诉人们，战争一刻也没有停止。人们一般认为，国际联盟和联合国的先后建立，是将 200 多年前康德的永久和平思想付诸实践的正式努力。但也许是康德永久和平论的局限性在实践中的投射，人类为世界和平的努力总是在一次又一次的战火中遭受失败的检验。这当然不是康德的错。国际法是以维护和平与促进发展为根本价值取向的国际法律体系。实现和平的使命是国际法赖以存在的重要基础。在战争与冲突的硝烟此起彼伏的现实面前，人们有理由怀疑和质问：国际法本身是否存在妨碍和平实现的软肋？

一　康德永久和平思想的偏颇

康德曾提出了“永久和平论”。在其名著《永久和平论》① 中，康德首先列举了国与国之间永久和平的先决条款，包括：凡缔结和平条约而其

---

* 李赞，中国社会科学院国际法研究所副研究员。

① 康德：《永久和平论》，何兆武译，上海世纪出版集团，2005。

中秘密保留导致未来战争的材料的，均不得视为真正有效；没有一个自身独立的国家，无论大小，可以由于继承、交换、购买或赠送而被另一个国家所取得；常备军应该及时地全部加以废除；任何国债均不得着眼于国家的对外战争而制定；任何国家均不得以武力干涉其他国家的体制和政权；任何国家在与其他国家作战时，均不得容许在未来和平中使双方的互相信任成为不可能的那类敌对行动，如派遣暗杀者、放毒者、破坏降约以及在交战国中教唆叛国投敌等。康德认为，走向各国之间永久和平的正式条款包括：每个国家的公民体制都应该是共和制；国际权利应该以自由国家的联盟制度为基础；世界公民权利应限于以普遍的友好为其条件。康德的思想在今天的国际法上几乎都已得到体现，变成了国际法治的现实。当今世界上大量国际组织的存在，正是他“自由国家联盟”的构想变成现实的明证。

康德的永久和平理论一般被认为是20世纪一战后的国际联盟和二战后的联合国成立的思想与理论基础。从其永久和平论中我们可以看出，康德的所谓永久和平是建立在主权国家基础之上的一个和平机制。不论是他的“没有一个自身独立的国家，无论大小，可以由于继承、交换、购买或赠送而被另一个国家所取得”，还是他的“国际权利应该以自由国家的联盟制度为基础”，都是建立在对国家主权的充分尊重基础之上的。建立国家联合是为了互相维持并保障国家自由，而非树立类似国家权力的东西于国家之上。[①] 康德一开始就将自己紧紧地限定在国与国之间的永久和平上，这种限定的实质就是以国家的主权概念为前提，国家主权就是康德所讲的国家的国际权利，它构成最底线。既然国家主权丝毫不能动摇，那么在理论上正确的世界共和国这一积极的观念就只能被抛弃掉。在康德看来，国家主权是先天应然之物，它本身是完备的封闭的自足的。[②] 因此，国家与自由联盟这两者之间的分裂与矛盾显而易见。

康德发表“永久和平论”之后，在德国引发了一场激烈的辩论。康德在柯尼斯堡时的学生根茨（Friedrich von Gentz）在1800年发表了《论持久和平》的论文，这篇论文对康德的永久和平论说了一些恭维话之后，论

---

① 陈佳慧：《和平理念与人权保障》，《月旦法学杂志》第132期（2006年）。

② 周凡：《康德的和平构想：自由国家的联盟制度》，《浙江社会科学》2003年第6期。

述了人的冲突本性，认为持久的和平是不可能实现的。① 虽然根茨永久和平不能实现的观点未免过于悲观，但他正确地认识到了康德永久和平论中对人的内在心理因素的忽视。国内也有学者对康德的永久和平论无视国际伦理提出了不满。康德在其“永久和平论”中说：世界公民权利应限于以普遍的友好为其条件，但同时又强调，这并不是一个仁爱问题，而是一个权利问题。显而易见，康德把仁爱问题，即伦理问题排斥在永久和平的主题之外。这样极端的权利论，固然是十分深刻的，但又是极端形式主义的。② 这里的所谓伦理问题，就是着重于人的内心世界而言的。

康德的永久和平思想至少表现出了两方面的局限性。一方面是主权与自由国家联盟之间的内在矛盾性，自由国家联盟难以克服强调主权带来的消极影响，无法真正实现主权国家之间的永久和平状态。另一方面是对人的内在心理因素的忽视，这确实构成他在理论上的软肋，与他几乎同时代的学者早已发现了这一点，今天也有越来越多的学者有了清醒的认识。也许是康德永久和平思想在近代国际法律实践中的运用，国际法也宿命般地出现了重视国际法律制度与国际组织建设的倾向，而对人类内心和平建设的重视严重不足。

二　从国际法视角剖析妨碍和平的原因

（一）人类不和平的心理因素：思想与利益的冲突

冲突，表现于人类的语言文字和行动，而实际上深刻地存在于人的内心。内心的冲突有两种，即思想的不同和对利益的争夺。国际法的发展历程，其实就是一部运用法律手段解决上述两种冲突的人类史。

人类由于认识的有限性，往往对事物的认识不完整，不能把握真正的事理，容易以偏概全、以末为本、以非为是，一切如盲人摸象。人类习惯以自己所见为正确，固执己见和排斥异见。人类常以成见和偏见为真理，

---

① 〔意大利〕玛丽娅·格拉齐亚·梅吉奥妮：《欧洲统一，贤哲之梦——欧洲统一思想史》，陈宝顺、沈亦缘译，世界知识出版社，2004，第25页。

② 吴根友：《墨家“兼爱”思想与二十一世纪的国际伦理——兼论康德的和平思想》，《新东方》1998年第1期。

而论争不断，乃至兵戎相见，生灵涂炭。十字军东征、欧洲三十年战争、伊斯兰圣战、两次世界大战、社会主义和资本主义两大阵营的长期征伐，无不是打着征服异教甚至解放全人类的堂皇口号，以己之非，强人所难。所以，康德也不得不承认：大自然采用了两种手段使得各个民族隔离开来而不至于混合，即语言的不同和宗教的不同；它们确实导致了互相敌视的倾向和战争的借口……①

人类思想的冲突，也就是当今世界所常见的文明和意识形态的冲突。人类意见的分歧和内心固有的歧见和偏执，导致出现了基于宗教、种族、肤色、性别的歧视等。人类逐渐意识到了这种思想冲突引起的不平等与不和平，为了解决这些问题，国际社会先后通过一系列的国际法律文件和制度来消除歧视。于是便有了《禁奴公约》、《消除对妇女一切形式歧视公约》、《消除基于宗教或信仰原因的一切形式的不容忍和歧视宣言》、《消除一切形式种族歧视公约》等国际法律制度的制定和实施。

人类对利益的争夺是导致冲突与不和平的又一个重要原因。权力、名誉、生命、地位、金钱、资源等都是人类所贪求的。根据自己的主观标准，对上述事物引起爱欲而恋恋不舍。没有得到的，一心一意去追求；得到了的，希望无限增多；拥有的，希望永远拥有。由于大家都以爱欲而想占有，不断地占有，于是必然引起冲突而成为不息的斗争乃至战争。

在人类国家的发展史上，掠夺他国的人口、土地、资源、武器甚至为了国王或领导人的荣誉和私利发动战争者，不计其数。由于世界人口的急剧增长、人类生存环境的恶化和各种资源的有限性，各国展开了争夺资源以维持本国生存与发展甚至维持本国奢侈消费的战争。中东的石油，是直接导致两次美国与伊拉克之间开战的诱因之一，对中亚地区丰富资源的觊觎又何尝不是美国在阿富汗作战的真正目的之一呢？正如托马斯·霍布斯（Thomas Hobbes）在回顾充满血腥的英国内战后所总结的："人类普遍存在一种欲望，即对权力的追逐永无休止，直至死亡。"②

正因为有大国强国对小国弱国的凌辱，《联合国宪章》才有必要对各国主权平等原则作出明确规定，并且联合国大会又在《关于各国依联合国

---

① 康德：《永久和平论》，何兆武译，上海世纪出版集团，2005，第37页。

② 托马斯·霍布斯、F. J. E. 伍德布莱治编《选择》，转引自〔美〕大卫·巴拉什，查尔斯·韦伯《积极和平——和平与冲突研究》，刘成等译，南京出版社，2007，第125页。

宪章建立友好关系及合作之国际法原则之宣言》等国际法律文件中一再重申这些看似普遍已被接受的原则。正因为有一国对另一国的掠夺，发达国家对发展中国家的剥削，所以联合国大会才需要通过《各国经济权利和义务宪章》来保护所有国家，特别是发展中国家的权利，否则就不可能建立公正的秩序和稳定的世界。宪章的目的就在于建立一个以公平、主权平等和发达国家与发展中国家利益相互依存为基础的国际经济关系新制度。正因为有人无视和侮蔑对他人的人权并已发展为野蛮的暴行，这些暴行玷污了人类的良心，为使人类不致迫不得已铤而走险对暴政和压迫进行反抗，才有必要使人权受法治的保护，联合国才有必要通过《世界人权宣言》，并连续通过《经济、社会和文化权利国际公约》和《公民权利和政治权利国际公约》，并作持续不懈的努力。正因为有资方对劳方的压迫和盘剥，才有国际劳工组织及一系列劳工权利公约的产生。如此等等，不一而足。

（二）人类不和平的外在因素：不公平、不公正的国际法律秩序

人们具有不同的思想和文化，具有不同的意识形态和宗教信仰，本来是十分正常的事情，但问题就在于有些国家执着于将自己的一切强加于他国，而不能做到“和而不同”。世界各国的和平共处需要有一套具有普遍约束力的国际法律制度，而且这套法律制度必须基于平等和公平的原则，确保各国的信守。

在国际法的发展史上，战争曾经是推行国家政策的合法手段，为弱肉强食大开绿灯。也曾出现过领事裁判权等严重损害小国弱国的制度，所以一再地引起反抗和斗争，最后国际法只能放弃这些不合理的制度而更趋合理化。

今日的国际社会在《联合国宪章》精神的指引下，能够获得更长时间的和平与发展。但由于现有体制依然是在战胜国的主导下建立起来的，而且囿于国际社会大国强国主宰世界事务的现实，不得不作出很多妥协，依然保留了很多不平等、不公正的痕迹，无法达到世界的真正永久和平。对东西方文化的差距、南北经济的失衡、发达国家与不发达国家之间的巨大鸿沟等，目前国际上还没有一个真正能有效解决的机制或途径。不论是朝韩的停战协定，还是联合国五大国的双重否决权，抑或是世界银行的加权表决制，都包含不公平、不合理的因素，并没有实现真正意义上的主权平

等，还保留有康德在《永久和平论》中所说的“导致未来战争的材料”。[①]目前很多国际法律制度和国际组织机制都似乎只是暂时地解决现实的国际政治问题，并不能引导走向一个真正永久和平的未来。

更何况世界上还有许多国家并未实现真正的国内民主、法治、人权与和平，国内危机四伏，问题重重，当国内的不和平达到一定的程度便极有可能表现于外，通过对外战争或其他暴力手段达到转移国内人民视线、转移国内矛盾的目的。

三 当代国际法对和平的确信

人类在遭遇两次惨不堪言的世界大战之后，内心对和平的诉求和渴望可谓达到了极点。《联合国宪章》序言云：“我联合国人民，同兹决心，欲免后世再遭今代人类两度惨不堪言之战祸，……并为达此目的，力行容恕，彼此以善邻之道，和睦相处，……用是发愤立志，务当同心协力，以竟阙功。”宪章序言中的“容恕”、“发愤”、“同心”等措辞字字表明，创建联合国的各国实在是意识到了战祸的惨烈、人类的遭罪，才从内心发出要建立国际组织，维护世界和平，并促进社会进步及较善之民生。《联合国宪章》在第 13 条中亦要求“大会应发动研究，并作成建议，以促进政治上之国际合作，并提倡国际法之逐渐发展与编纂。” “研究”与“建议”、“促进”与“提倡”的用语，昭示着对和平之国际法思想与理念的传播和教育，从人类的心灵上唤起对和平的热爱和追求。各种国际法律文件和宣言均使用“深信”、“信念”、“念及”、“鉴于”、“察悉”、“考虑到”、“铭记着”、“认识到”等描述内心感受和欲望的词汇，来表明对和平的渴求。

1948 年的《美洲国家组织宪章》第 5 条丑项也明确规定：人民的教育应指向正义、自由及和平。联合国大会 1965 年通过的《在青年中促进各国人民之间和平、互尊和了解的理想的宣言》，其原则一就是：青年之教养应培养其和平、公道、自由、互相尊重及彼此了解之精神，以期促进全人类及所有国家之平等权利、经济及社会进步、裁军及国际和平与安全之

① 康德：《永久和平论》，何兆武译，上海世纪出版集团，2005，第 5 页。

维持。尤其是联合国大会1978年12月15日33/73号决议通过的《为各社会共享和平生活做好准备的宣言》，更是明确指出："认识到战争发端于人心，故此必须在心中念念不忘保卫和平。"这可谓是对着重内因的内心和平的极佳诠释。

在推进人类内因为重的内心和平建设方面，联合国教科文组织可谓居功至伟。联合国教科文组织在其组织法中明确规定：因为战争是在人的心中开始的，所以，保护和平必须建于人的心中。而且，如果希望和平能持久，则必须以全人类智慧上和精神上的团结为基础。其组织法还明确说明，广泛传播文化和教育人类崇尚正义、自由与和平，是保持人类尊严所必要，并为所有国家必须以一种互相协助和共同关切的精神去执行的神圣义务。

随后，联合国教科文组织在其一系列的宣言和国际文件当中一再重申和阐述内心和平建设的重要性。1966年联合国教科文组织第十四届会议通过《国际文化合作原则宣言》，其第7条第2款表示，在文化合作上，应着重足以创造一种友好与和平气氛的思想和价值。在态度上和在意见的表达上，应当避免任何敌意的痕迹。在1978年的第二十届会议上，联合国教科文组织大会通过了《关于新闻工具有助于加强和平与国际了解、促进人权、反对种族主义、种族隔离及战争煽动的基本原则宣言》。该宣言第4条规定：新闻工具在以和平、正义、自由、相互尊重和了解的精神教育青年方面应发挥主要作用，以促进人权、全人类与各民族间的权利平等和经济与社会进步。第7条规定：新闻工具应更广泛地传播有关联合国各机构据以通过决议的各项普遍接受的目标与原则之新闻，这就会为加强和平与国际了解、促进人权和建立更加公正和平等的国际经济秩序而作出有效的贡献。联合国教科文组织作为世界上全面负责教育、科学、文化事业的最大国际组织，以在人类的内心建立和平的信念，进而促进和实现全人类和平为己任。

在国际人权法律文书中，思想、良心、宗教和信仰自由，意见、表达和信息自由是受到保护的基本人权。联合国《公民权利和政治权利国际公约》第18条和第19条对此作出了规定。但是，该公约第20条明确规定了禁止进行战争宣传和鼓吹仇恨。该条第1款规定：任何鼓吹战争的宣传，应以法律加以禁止。第2款规定：任何鼓吹民族、种族或宗教仇恨的主张，构成煽动歧视、敌视或强暴者，应以法律加以禁止。因为，进行战争宣传和鼓吹仇恨将导致人们内心的严重不平，彻底破坏人们内心的宁静与平衡。一旦人们在内心接受这样的宣传和鼓动，将会反应在其行动上，将战争和仇恨付诸行动，给他人造成极大的灾难和痛苦。禁止战争宣传和鼓吹种族或类似仇恨比该公约中的任何其他规定都更多地表明了对于国家社会主义（即纳粹主义）的恐怖影响的反应。[①] 这是人类反复经历战争与仇恨所造成的浩劫而获得的宝贵认识，国际人权法将这种认识以法律的形式加以固定化，使其成为世界各国和人民遵守的基本行为准则。

以上国际文件表明，整个国际社会确实已经清醒地认识到了光有维护与促进和平的国际组织与国际法规则，尚不足以实现真正持久的和平，唯有逐步实现人类内心的和平，从精神上彻底认识到战争的罪恶、在任何时候和任何情况下都彻底拒绝诉诸战争的手段，世界的永久和平才有可能实现。但是，现有国际法和国际组织机制对于建设人类内心和平的努力明显不足。因此，通过国际法律制度和国际组织机制，进行和平精神的教育与宣扬，实现人类内心和平，进而实现全人类的永久和平。

上述国际法律文件中，《联合国宪章》、《美洲国家组织宪章》、《公民权利和政治权利国际公约》等是具有法律效力的国际文件，联合国大会及联合国教科文组织大会通过的各种宣言和决议虽然不具有法律效力，但具有政治和道义上的力量，而且，通过各种国际文件的反复重申和宣言，可能使其具有了习惯国际法的效果。

四　克服实现内心和平的障碍

人们普遍认为，和平必须从每个个体开始，然后向外扩展。在某种程度上，如果每个人都在他们自己的生活中追求和平，世界将变得更加美好，暴力更少。个人转化涉及达到个人内心和平的问题，尽管这点很重要，然而个人转化仅仅是必要平衡中的一部分；不仅应该追求内心和平，

① 〔奥〕曼弗雷德·诺瓦克：《〈公民权利和政治权利国际公约〉评注》，孙世彦、毕小青译，生活·读书·新知三联书店，2008，第488页。

而且应该追求外在和平，并拓展到有点丑陋的真实世界中。[1] 这就意味着，现代国际法律制度和组织架构从外在的方面对于缔造和维护世界和平是必要的，但是不充分的，还需要更加重视人的内心和平的引导和建设。人对内心和平的追求又必须被现实世界的政治所接受，并发挥出作用。虽然人们不难认识到国际法在实现世界和平问题上确实存在软肋，即对人类内心和平建设的忽视，但是，在推动建设人类内心和平的现实面前，人们往往容易出现争论，甚至悲观的情绪。

个人转化是实现公正而持久和平的先决条件，但不是它的唯一前提。不是说每个人都必须转化，对于大多数成功的社会运动来说，只需要一定数量的人全力以赴就可以了，这个数字大约是不到 10% 的人。无论如何，和平的最大障碍很有可能不是世界性问题的不可驾驭性，而是这些问题在心理上和政治上的隐蔽性。许多西方发达国家的人虽然觉察到这些问题，但是他们对这些问题的反应要么是绝望，要么是弄巧成拙的暴力行为。

建设和平的主要障碍并不是实现和平过程中的实际困难，而是有一种和平不能成功的感觉，即许多人不能或者拒绝把和平想象成可以实现的现实前景。对于和平可以实现所表示出来的普遍怀疑是和平成为现实的一个主要障碍。在采取任何行动之前，必须首先进行想象。当然，有效想象以及个人对目标进行构想的重要不能被高估。这是一种思维方式，它能够对可能以及应该出现的情况进行想象，因而有助于人们发掘出潜力并展开行动。这些想象产生能量，并能抢先一步与不太严重的后果妥协。这样的想象通常被斥为不切实际的幻想，通常唤醒那种反应的思维状态是我们这个社会的一种负担。这种思维状态通过事先把运动的目标看成不可实现的幻想，抑制了运动朝着可能被普遍认为有效而且重要的目标迈进。因此，为了实现世界向和平的转变，人们必须相信和平的可能性，否则他们所进行的任何努力都有可能陷入无意义的境地。人们必须开始想象世界是和平的。

实现和平从“硬件”来说，只是处于第二位的问题，可以通过对生态和社会结构的操纵加以解决。正如前面所论述到的当代国际法律制度和国

---

① 〔美〕大卫·巴拉什、查尔斯·韦伯：《积极和平——和平与冲突研究》，刘成等译，南京出版社，2007，第 550 页。

际组织机制，是实现和平的所谓“硬件”，它们是通过外在的法律制度和组织机制规范各个国际法律行为体的行动，预防和阻遏损害和平事件的发生。但是，实现和平，首先是人的“软件”问题，涉及人们的思维方式以及人们对实现和平的顽固拒绝。希望也存在于这里，因为人类族群中潜藏着巨大的潜力，不仅可以删除我们计划中的“缺陷”，而且可以在我们重建世界家园时重塑我们的生命。刘易斯·芒福德（Lewis Mumford）曾说：人类的每一次转化都建立在新的理论和意识形态基础上，或者说建立在重新描绘宇宙和人的本性的基础上。……我们正站在一个新时代的边缘。……在把人类的自我转化带入第二个台阶之后，世界文化会产生一种新的精神能量的释放，它将揭开新潜能的面纱，如今难以发现自身的这些潜能和一个世纪前物理学难以发现镭一样，虽然它们都一直存在。①

需要注意的是，在参与和平斗争的过程中，一种冲突将不可避免，即个人从道德上对非暴力的责任与无情的现实世界之间的冲突。在这个无情的现实世界中，如果要发生有意义的变化，自由、平等和解放可能就会以非暴力的手段与当局发生冲突。

五　履行国际法的新使命以实现永久和平

康德之后的罗尔斯和哈贝马斯，不论是建立万民法所彰显出来的社会公平与正义，还是追求实现人权的背后所隐藏的对人性的尊重与满足，理论上确实存在一种从外缘为重的和平理念到兼重内因的内心和平的回归。在国际法律文件与制度建设的实践上，也确实存在强化人类和平建设的痕迹和趋向。

联合国、欧洲联盟等国际组织在促进和维护和平方面的实践，不论是其成功的经验，还是其局限性和失败的例证，都为永久和平理念作了初步却重要的背书。应该说这是人类在历经战争浩劫之后进行反思的结果。正如一位学者所说的：反思是建立在理性的基础上对历史的思考，是对历史谬误认知的矫正和对有历史价值的思想的认可。虽然反思的对象是历史，

① 〔美〕大卫·巴拉什、查尔斯·韦伯：《积极和平——和平与冲突研究》，刘成等译，南京出版社，2007，第551—561页。

但是反思这一行为本身却具有一种启蒙性。[①] 确实，人类在不断向前行走的同时，不得不总是要回过头去搜寻历史的遗珍，以作为前进道路上的精神力量和方向指引。人类最终要实现最真实、最彻底、最长久、最完美的和平。人类的智慧体现在不断试错之后，能够纠错并找到正确的出路。

当代国际法和国际组织制度更多的是体现在对人类社会的政治、经济、文化、人权、法治等方面的制度设计和建设上，是着重于外缘为重的世界和平的建设方面。这当然是整个人类社会最终走向真正永久和平的必经之道。但要实现真正永久和平的终极目标，则还需要加强内因为重的内心和平的建设，这是国际法的和平软肋所在，而这恰恰是更艰巨的任务和更难实现的目标。古人云：千里之行始于足下。既然人类思慕和渴望永久和平的实现，那人类的智慧和理性一定能够战胜路途遥远和艰难所带来的畏难情绪和恐惧心理。在既有的国际法治基础上，强化内因为重的内心和平的宣传和建设，改善国际法律制度和组织上存在的不平等、不公平、不合理的残留，让人类内心的和平建设与外在制度与机制的和平建设成为飞向真正永久和平目标的双翼。康德曾经正确地指出："和平是必须被建立起来的。"[②] 永久和平，只能从人的内心开始。国际法应该在进一步加强和完善现有国际法制度和国际组织建设的基础上，更加重视人类内心和平的宣传和建设。这是国际法的新使命。建设真正的永久和平，实现人类久违的梦想，从心开始。

（本文原载于《时代法学》2013 年第 4 期）

① 汤侠：《对刘宾雁及其作品的审思》，《文学教育》2009 年第 12 期。

② 康德：《永久和平论》，何兆武译，上海世纪出版集团，2005，第 13 页。

国际难民制度“变”与“不变”的问题思考

——兼论国际难民事务的中国立场

郝鲁怡*

引 言

现代国际难民制度的核心是1951年《关于难民地位的公约》（以下简称“1951年公约”）与1967年《关于难民地位的公约议定书》（以下简称“议定书”），迄今为止，已有148个国家加入上述一项或全部两项法律文件。

1951年公约与议定书通过的半个多世纪以来，全球的难民形势旷日持久且复杂多变，国际难民制度正经历如何充分地反映难民现实、全面地考虑难民困境以及永久地解决难民问题等巨大考验。① 难民问题一方面关涉国家控制外国人进入其领土的固有的主权权利，另一方面牵连国家对生命和自由受到威胁的难民给予保护的义务。国际难民制度需要调和国家主权与个人权利之间相互竞争的异质价值，既凸显了其固有张力与复杂性，也构成不断前行的动力。②

---

* 郝鲁怡，中国社会科学院国际法研究所副研究员。

① Alexander Betts and Jean-Francois Durieux, “Convention Plus as a Norm-Setting Exercise”, (2007) 20 *Journal of Refugee Studies* 509, p. 512.

② Vincent Chetail, “Are Refugee Rights Human Rights? An Unorthodox Questioning of the Relations between Refugee Law and Human Rights Law”, in Ruth Rubio-Marin (ed.,), *Human Rights and Immigration* (Oxford: Oxford University Press, 2014), p. 33.

国际难民制度“变”与“不变”的问题是回应现实需求的思考，目的不是要改写国际难民法，而是旨在促进现有制度的切实遵行与有效执行，并以此为基础，凝聚国际社会力量寻求应对难民问题的综合路径。①

一 主权原则是建构国际难民制度的基础

1951 年公约通过明确接纳国（或目的地国）与难民之间的法律关联来兑现难民保护的承诺，② 所以国际难民制度语境的设定围绕于难民在接纳国的抵境阶段，集中调整接纳国与难民之间的二元结构关系。接纳国在本国领土上承认和保护外国人时形成对国家主权的坚守，使主权原则普遍立场成为建构 1951 年公约的基础。③

（一）国家接纳难民的择选性与个体化特征

1951 年公约第 1 条为难民定义条款，开宗明义地确立缔约国接纳难民的法定条件。其内容赓续国际社会保护难民的传统，涵括了法律因素、社会因素和个体因素。

——法律因素，此项条件源于国际联盟时期施行的南森护照制度，旨在保护因失去代表法律身份的国籍而无法获原籍国保护的无国籍者。④

——社会因素，此项条件源于第二次世界大战期间有关难民问题的国际协定，⑤ 旨在保护受特定政治或社会事件影响的个人。⑥

——个体因素，此项条件源于 1947 年联合国成立的国际难民组织

① James Hathaway, “Why Refugee Law Still Matters”, (2007) 8 (1) *Melbourne Journal of International Law* 88, p. 91.

② 〔美〕詹姆斯·C. 哈撒韦：《国际法上的难民权利》，黄云松译，中国社会科学出版社，2017，第 11 页。

③ Colin Harvey and Satvinder Juss, “Critical Reflections on Refugee Law”, (2013) 20 *International Journal Minority and Group Rights* 143, p. 143.

④ Karen Musalo, Jennifer Moore and Richard A. Boswell, *Refugee Law and Policy: A Comparative and International Approach* (Durham: Carolina Academic Press, 2th ed., 2002), p. 25.

⑤ 如 1938 年《关于来自德国难民的地位公约》，规定了两类难民：一是因当时德国纳粹法令与社会政策受到影响的德国犹太人；二是因政治原因离开德国的人。

⑥ Louise W. Holborn, “The Legal Status of Political Refugees, 1920 - 1938”, (1938) 32 *American Journal of International Law* 680, pp. 693 - 695.

（International Refugee Organization）规约的难民定义，[①] 广泛地保护“因第二次世界大战处于原籍国或原定居国之外，不能或不愿意受原籍国或原定居国保护的个人”。[②] 这一个体因素极大地泛化了难民范畴，使保护机制事实上沦为为寻求自由的个人提供便利的一种手段，在当时受到各国普遍抵制而最终导致国际难民组织运行失败。

1951 年公约直接承继了法律因素，并将社会因素的范畴明确为种族、宗教、国籍、社会团体与政治见解原因等，同时对个体因素的主观、随意性给予限定，规定为“有正当理由因畏惧迫害”而不能或不愿受原籍国保护的个人。其中，“畏惧迫害”带有对个人的心理状态的主观评估，并且“畏惧迫害”要有“充分理由”，须由申请人提供客观证据来证明其主观心理的充分合理。[③]

1951 年公约的难民定义为保护难民设立统一的最低标准，避免各国在决定接纳哪些人给予保护时出现“竞相垫底”（race to the bottom）的状况。[④] 作为一国接纳与实施保护对象的难民是该国依据主观与客观并存的法定条件进行身份甄别的结果，属于非常狭窄范畴的一类特殊人员，带有显著的择选性与个体化的构成特征。

由此得见，国家接纳难民并非不加区别地涵盖因失去原籍国保护而陷入困境的广泛意义上的群体，也排除不可预知的新群体，彰显了国家主权普遍立场的一种预先协调结果。[⑤] 在原籍国未能履行对本国公民保护义务的特定情况下，由其他国家根据主权原则无可争议地对经择选的个体化对

---

① 国际难民组织规约的难民定义非常宽泛，将难民分为六类：（1）纳粹、法西斯或类似政权的受害者；（2）西班牙法西斯政权的受害者；（3）基于种族、宗教、国籍和政治观点原因在二战前被视作难民；（4）因第二次世界大战爆发而处于原籍国或原定居国之外，不能或不愿意受原籍国或原定居国保护的个人；（5）未经安置的受纳粹迫害的犹太人或无国籍人；（6）处于原籍国之处的战争孤儿。

② Karen Musalo, Jennifer Moore and Richard A. Boswell, *Refugee Law and Policy: a Comparative and International Approach* (Durham: Carolina Academic Press, 2002), pp. 25 – 26.

③ Jacqueline Bhabha, "Internationalist Gatekeeper?: The Tension between Asylum Advocacy and Human Rights", (2002) 15 *Harvard Human Rights Journal* 155, p. 155.

④ Guy S. Goodwin-Gill and Jane McAdam, *The Refugee in International Law* (New York, Oxford University Press, 3rd ed., 2007), p. 16.

⑤ Vincent Chetail, "Are Refugee Rights Human Rights? An Unorthodox Questioning of the Relations between Refugee Law and Human Rights Law", in Ruth Rubio-Marin (ed.,), *Human Rights and Immigration* (Oxford: Oxford University Press, 2014), p. 24.

象行使替代保护的职能。

(二) 国家接纳与保护难民的权利和义务

基于主权原则，国家享有保护难民的权利而非承担保护难民的义务，相对应，难民自身不享有当然获得受外国保护的积极权利，两者的权利结构呈现不对等性。有学者主张，这种权利结构与国内法的“信托关系”的内在机理相暗合。国家是难民制度法律关系的主体，难民不属于法律关系的主体而类似信托中的“受益人”。国家对置于其管辖内的难民单方面行使公共权力与酌处权，有权决定并影响难民的待遇或实际利益。而难民作为受益人由于不享有对应权利处于相对被动与脆弱的境地。①

国家的权利首先表现为对难民身份进行甄别与择选的自由裁量权。1951 年公约并未规定承认与接纳难民的统一的程序性规范，而将判断个人是否符合难民定义条件，包括是否“畏惧迫害”以及判定“畏惧”是否成立等权利“下放”至各缔约国，由各国制定国内法律标准自行酌处。

实践中，由于衡量个人是否有资格获得难民地位的标准和程序在不同国家大相径庭，所以即便难民定义为国家择选难民的实质条件提供了统一标准，具有立法形式上的普遍性，但是因不同国家行使自由裁量权乃至甄别标准的适用呈现以主权国家为单位的碎片化。其次，国家的权利还体现在国家给予难民的法律地位以及福利、待遇的自由裁量权。对于难民的法律地位，1951 年公约仅规定缔约国应当为难民同化或入籍提供便利，未要求将难民接受为永久居民或赋予其与本国公民相同的法律地位，所以难民的法律地位在接纳国具有临时性特点。② 联合国第一任难民高级专员歌德哈特（Heuven-Goedhart）就曾提及：难民地位不是永久的。③

任何法律主体享有的权利都不是绝对、不受限制的。国家对难民的权利亦如此。1951 年公约第 33 条规定国家负有不可推回的义务，是对国家接纳外国人的自由裁量权的一个重要但有资格的限制，为难民提供了更广

---

① Evan Fox-Decent and Evan J. Criddle, “The Fiduciary Constitution of Human Rights”, (2009) 15 *Legal Theory* 301, p. 301, p. 315.

② 参见《关于难民地位的公约》第 34 条。

③ UN General Assembly, *Conference of Plenipotentiaries on the Status of Refugees and Stateless Persons: Summary Record of the Second Meeting*, UN Doc. A/CONF. 2/SR. 2, 20 July, 1951.

泛的保护，在一定程度上调和了不对等性。

第一，不可推回义务的适用具有统一性。不可推回义务为一国驱逐或遣返难民设定了统一的禁止门槛，即当个人生命与自由因法定情形遭受威胁时不得将其推回，有效地限制了国家拒绝接纳外国人并将之遣返的自由裁量权。因为国家承担不可推回义务与“下放”至各国国内的难民审核程序相脱离，所以不再享有本国国内法所赋予的无条件和不受控制的酌处权，对于不具有获得外国接纳与保护积极权利的难民而言，具有深远的保障意义。

第二，国家不可推回义务的受益者不仅仅是难民。联合国难民署主张：不可推回义务不仅适用于被承认的难民，而且也适用于那些没有正式获得难民地位的人员。[①] 即使是还未获得难民地位的寻求庇护者，无论其入境行为是合法还是非法，只要其处于某一外国领土之内，该国就负有义务不得将其推回生命与自由可能受威胁的原籍国或第三国，所以不可推回义务为陷入困境而不得已违反目的地国入境法律的寻求庇护者提供了一种有限豁免与合理保障。

第三，受不可推回义务约束的国家行为具有广泛性。不可推回义务取决于个人的生命或自由是否因特定情形受到威胁，与国家“推回”行为的性质和形式无关。[②] 受不可推回义务约束的国家行为可以广泛地涵盖使难民或寻求庇护者可能陷入危险的各类强制措施，包括驱逐、遣返、拒绝入境、引渡等。

实践中，各国越来越倾向实施抵境前的域外拦截以规避不可推回义务，而这种做法是否违反不可推回义务目前存在学理争议。[③] 笔者认为，国际难民法及其不可推回义务以主权原则为基础，因而与国家领土紧密相关、不可分离，其效力范畴不及于领土之外。只是这一做法凸显了难民公

---

① UNHCR, *Advisory Opinion on the Extraterritorial Application of Non-Refoulement Obligations under the 1951 Convention relating to the Status of Refugees and its 1967 Protocol*, 26 January, 2007, para. 6, http://unhcr.org/4d9486929.pdf，最后访问日期：2018 年 3 月 25 日。

② Colin Harvey and Satvinder Juss, "Critical Reflections on Refugee Law", (2013) 20 *International Journal Minority and Group Rights* 143, p. 146.

③ 〔美〕詹姆斯·C. 哈撒韦：《国际法上的难民权利》，黄云松译，中国社会科学出版社，2017，第 138 页。

约制度的两难境地，这可能是1952年公约试图兼顾维护国家主权与保护个人两个并行出发点而付出的代价。①

（三）难民在接纳国的待遇

1951年公约文本的表述为，“缔约国应当给予难民相应待遇”，而不是“难民应当享有权利”，显然依旧是国家视角的赋权模式。

接纳国给予难民的待遇遵循递增原则，具有循序渐进特点，由基本待遇和附加待遇叠加组成。前者是指个人无论基于何种方式入境，一旦获得难民地位一律享有的基本保障，不带有任何进一步的资格要求。例如，第3条的不受歧视待遇，第13条动产与不动产的取得，第16条出席法院，第22条公共教育，等等。附加待遇则是指难民在接纳国具备合法停留（lawful stay）或居留（residence）两项附加条件后所享有的额外优待。例如，第17条至第19条的就业、自营业及自由职业，第21条房屋管制，第23条公共救济，第24条劳动立法与社会安全，等等。附加待遇取决于难民与所在国的领土关系的密切程度，在接纳国处于合法停留或在接纳国境内居留时间越长，应享待遇的范围相应越宽泛。

综上，边界保留着最终的国家价值，即便对难民而言，人的价值渗透也取决于（国家）同意。② 归根结底，对难民的承认与接纳倚重一国的意愿与能力，否则等于让各国签署空头支票。国际难民制度代表各种利益冲突达成的妥协与折中，反映了实用主义的价值，只有从主权原则出发，才能最大限度地弥合各国分歧而获得普遍接受，并继续保持稳固。同时，也只有依据主权原则，一国才能够自行对个人因特定原因不能或不愿受原籍国保护的情境作出判断，进行难民地位甄别，并且不受其他国家干涉地对择选的难民行使替代保护职能。

---

① Vincent Chetail, “Are Refugee Rights Human Rights? An Unorthodox Questioning of the Relations between Refugee Law and Human Rights Law”, in Ruth Rubio-Marin (ed.), *Human Rights and Immigration* (Oxford: Oxford University Press, 2014), pp. 31 – 32.

② 〔美〕路易斯·亨金：《国际法：政治与价值》，张乃根等译，中国政法大学出版社，2005，第288页。

二 国际人权法对国际难民制度的渗透及影响

（一）国际人权标准丰富了难民定义的内涵

1951 年公约难民定义中“畏惧迫害”个体因素具有主观性质，使“迫害”成为诠释难民定义的一个难以琢磨、颇具争议的概念，直接影响了难民法定条件的实践应用。这一局限性因纳入国际人权客观标准作为参照系而得到纠正。有学者主张，迫害应当被定义为与《世界人权宣言》原则不相符的严厉措施和任意性制裁。① 还有更多的观点不断将迫害行为统摄在违反人权的具体行为当中。例如，主张对基本人权的持续或系统性侵犯应当纳入迫害的范畴；② 再如，任意、严重违反《世界人权宣言》或核心人权标准应被视为迫害行为等。③ 联合国难民署亦申明，严重违反人权的行为构成迫害。④ 目前，尽管迫害的概念尚未在国际层面达成一致，人权标准至少已成为界定迫害的重要参考因素，为确定谁是难民提供了一个相对客观、更可预测的法律基准。⑤

国际人权法不同领域的发展也广泛地影响着阐释“迫害”的方法，尤其是纳入与性别有关的人权标准以及对儿童权利的保护。性别视角可以影响或决定个人所遭受的迫害或伤害的类型及其产生的原因。如果 1951 年公约的缔约国同时也是《公民权利和政治权利国际公约》或《消除对妇女一切形式歧视公约》的缔约国，那么缔约国有义务将后两项公约中对性别平等和妇女保护的承诺与对 1951 年公约中难民定义的解释相结合，如此以

---

① Jacques Vernant, *The Refugee in the Post-war World* (New Haven: Yale University Press, 1953), p. 8.

② Marissa Jackson, "Closing the Gap: Towards a Rights-Based Approach to Refugee Law", 2011 (4) *Northwestern Interdisciplinary Law Review* 147, p. 171.

③ David Weissbrodt, *The Human Rights of Non-Citizens* (New York: Oxford University Press Inc., 2008), p. 108.

④ UNCHR, *Handbook on Procedures and Criteria for Determining Refugee Status Under the 1951 Convention and the 1967 Protocol Relating to the Status of Refugees*, UN Doc HCR/1P/4/Eng/REV. 3, 2011, para. 51.

⑤ Marissa Jackson, "Closing the Gap: Towards A Rights-Based Approach to Refugee Law", 2011 (4) *Northwestern Interdisciplinary Law Reviews* 147, p. 167.

来，针对妇女的一些特殊伤害显然应当被列入难民定义的迫害范畴。此外，2009 年联合国难民署颁行《关于儿童庇护申请指南》，提出以儿童敏感方式（child-sensitive manner）来处理儿童难民的法律地位问题，特别关注到儿童可能经历针对儿童才特有的迫害形式。[①] 适用该方法来解释迫害，则应当包括对儿童特有权利的侵犯，例如针对儿童的身心暴力、虐待和剥削等。

（二）国家不可推回义务的效力得到强化

随着国际人权法蓬勃发展，国家的不可推回义务为多项国际人权条约所重申。例如，1984 年《禁止酷刑和其他残忍、不人道或有辱人格的待遇或处罚公约》第 3 条规定：如有充分理由相信任何人在另一国家有遭受酷刑的危险，任何缔约国不得将该人驱逐、遣返或引渡至该国。《美洲人权公约》规定，如果外国人的生命权或自由权在一个国家遭到被侵犯的危险，则不得将该人驱逐或送至该国。《欧洲人权公约》第 3 条保障个人享有禁止酷刑、非人道或有辱人格待遇的权利也已经与缔约国的不可推回义务结合在一起。

有别于国际难民制度，国际人权法体现了国家与个人权利义务的相互对等关系——个人享有法律规定的各项基本权利，而国家承担保障个人各项权利的义务，不仅包括承担不侵犯人权的消极义务，而且还负有确保个人有效享有相应基本权利而防止侵权行为的积极义务。在国际人权法领域，国家的不可推回义务与个人的积极权利相结合，使前者的法律效力得到显著强化。如果说 1951 年公约的不可推回义务的适用还存在个别例外，包括国家安全与个人严重犯罪，[②] 那么，国际人权法的不可推回义务无例外地保护所有的个人（包括难民）免受酷刑、非人道或有辱人格行为的侵犯，则具有效力上的绝对性。甚至有观点主张，不可推回原则已经演变为具有普遍约束力的习惯国际法。[③] 只是这一观点在目前尚无明确的依据予

---

① *Guidelines on International Protection*: *Child Asylum Claims under Articles 1 (A) 2 and (1) F of the Convention and/or 1967 Protocol Relating to the Status of Refugees*, 22 December 2009, UN Doc. HCR/GIP/09/08, para. 13.

② 1951 年公约第 33 条第 2 款。

③ 1951 年公约的各缔约国曾公开承认不可推回原则的适用性已深植于习惯国际法。

以支持。①

（三）扩展了难民保护途径

受国际人权标准普遍性与包容性影响，各国逐渐承认除了1951年公约难民定义之外的其他人亦需要获得国际保护，进而发展了新的保护形式：补充保护和临时保护。②

补充保护是向不属于1951年公约范畴的“事实难民”（de facto refugees）免受武装冲突、普遍暴力、酷刑等侵害所提供的保护，主要以联合国决议以及区域组织立法为法律依据。联合国难民署确认，补充保护是对现实需要作出务实反应的积极途径，鼓励各国以补充形式保护不符合难民定义的特定个人。③ 在区域组织层面，2004年，欧盟创设了新的国际保护（international protection）机制概念，涵盖1951年公约保护与附属保护（subsidiary protection）。前者对符合1951年公约的难民提供保护；后者为公约难民之外的更广泛范畴个人提供补充性保护。④ 有些学者质疑这一机制在试图强化个人权利保护的同时破坏了1951年公约的统一执行标准，甚至带有取代或重新商榷1951年公约的目的。⑤

临时保护是针对特定局势或事件所导致的大规模流离失所群体提供最低限度援助的临时措施，虽然是人道主义的产物，但与国际人权标准密切关联。联合国难民署提出，要在不可推回原则下，对寻求庇护者的大规模

---

① “Declaration of States Parties to the 1951 Convention and or/its 1967 Protocol relating to the Status of Refugee”, UN Doc. HCR/MMSP/2001/09, Dec. 13, 2001, para. 4，转引自〔美〕詹姆斯·C. 哈撒韦《国际法上的难民权利》，黄云松译，中国社会科学出版社，2017，第159页，注释2。

② Vincent Chetail, “Are Refugee Rights Human Rights? An Unorthodox Questioning of the Relations between Refugee Law and Human Rights Law”, in Ruth Rubio-Marin (ed.), *Human Rights and Immigration* (Oxford: Oxford University Press, 2014), p. 37.

③ UNHCR, *Note on International Protection*, UN Doc. A/AC. 96/830 (7 Sept. 1994), para. 52.

④ “Directive 2011/95/EU of The European Parliament and of the Council of 13 December 2011 on Standards for the Qualification of Third-country Nationals or Stateless Persons as Beneficiaries of International Protection, and for the Content of the Protection Granted (Recast)”, *Official Journal of the European Union*, 2011 L 337/9, article 1, article 2.

⑤ 参见 Jane McAdam, *Complementary Protection in International Refugee Law* (Oxford: Oxford University Press, 2007), pp. 90 - 93; David Weissbrodt, *The Human Rights of Non-Citizens* (New York: Oxford University Press Inc., 2008), p. 178。

迁移活动作出紧急反应与提供基本最低待遇。

1951 年公约保护、补充保护和临时保护三项机制在保护对象、法律依据以及保护程度等各方面具有不同特征（见表 1）。

表 1

保护机制	保护对象	法律依据	个人待遇
难民保护	难民公约界定的个人	1951 年公约与议定书	法定难民地位待遇
补充保护	难民公约范畴之外的个人	国际人权法	低于难民地位待遇
临时保护	流离失所者群体	国际人道法	最基本待遇

可以说，国际人权法中通过保护形式的拓展将游离于公约保护机制之外的个人纳入保护范畴，对国际难民制度适应不断变化的人口跨国迁移现实具有重要意义。然而，后两种保护形式也带有一定的争议与局限性。例如，欧盟国际保护机制在试图加强个人保护的同时，对于如何确保 1951 公约制度适用的一致性带来挑战。而临时保护由于缺乏统一、正式的国家行动支持，某些地区的难民营存续多年而久拖不决。

（四）驱逐与遣返程序中的个人权利保障

寻求庇护者在等待审查程序或等待遣返中往往被剥夺人身自由而身处困境，国际人权法首先为剥夺人身自由的个人提供程序性保障。欧洲人权法院要求：“只有在对有关人员采取适当的保障措施时，才可以接受拘禁。……不能剥夺寻求庇护者获得难民地位有效途径的权利。”① 任何拘禁都必须符合法律的规定和授权，而不得仅仅单纯以拘留决定的形式作出。任何人在被逮捕时有权被告知原因和罪名；任何被逮捕或拘禁的个人有权在法庭进行诉讼，法庭须决定其拘禁的合法性，否则应当将其释放。②

其次，国际人权法还提供禁止对个人实行任意性拘禁的实质性保障。相称性原则是衡量是否构成任意性拘禁的基本条件。对申请庇护个人的拘禁不能是系统的或强制性的，必须根据每个案件的具体情况进行评估。拘

① *Amuur v. France*, ECHR (1996) Reports 1996 – III, para. 43.

② Sumbul Rizvi, “International Dimensions of Refugee Law”, (2004) 4 *Indian Society of International Law Year Book of International Humanitarian and Refugee Law* 103, pp. 113 – 114.

禁理由应在整个拘留期间持续存在，否则剥夺自由将不是正当的。同时，拘留不应超过国家可提供适当理由的期限。相称性原则还要求各国审查是否可以利用其他不影响个人自由和安全权利的替代措施而非拘禁手段来实现其目标，如实行报告义务、提供担保人等。[①]

人权的普遍性与包容性为巩固和加强难民权利的保护提供了更广泛的法律基础，通过方法与路径的调适对突破国际难民制度的固有局限具有深远意义。与此同时，国际人权法对国际难民制度的渗透及影响也引发了1951年公约是否已不合时宜而应当为国际人权法所取代的争议，将两者的关系问题推至理论前沿。

笔者认为，国际难民制度调整国家关系，难民并非法律关系的主体，只是国家共同行为的受益人，因而与个人作为主体的国际人权法在精髓与实质上都截然不同，[②] 国际人权法不能撼动国际难民制度作为主权原则的产物并取而代之。[③] 在实践中，将不同法律制度相互混淆是十分危险的，会导致各方主体与责任含糊不清及冲突，最终反而阻滞了迫切需要的保护。[④] 如果每个人都是难民，也就没有人是难民了，国际难民制度本身也将因失去其特殊、必要的内核而面临分崩瓦解的危险。

三　难民现实对接纳国与难民传统二元结构的冲击

当前，大规模流离失所者与难民潮基于暴力冲突、自然灾害、战争、侵犯人权等多元化根源而产生，并在整个世界范围内嬗变与扩展，对接纳

---

① Vincent Chetail, "Are Refugee Rights Human Rights? An Unorthodox Questioning of the Relations between Refugee Law and Human Rights Law", in Ruth Rubio-Marin (ed.,), *Human Rights and Immigration* (Oxford: Oxford University Press, 2014), p. 55.

② 〔美〕詹姆斯·C. 哈撒韦：《国际法上的难民权利》，黄云松译，中国社会科学出版社，2017，第5页。

③ Guy S. Goodwin-Gill, "The Continuing Relevance of International Refugee Law in a Globalized World", (2015) 10 *Intercultural Human Rights Law Reviews* 25, p. 30.

④ Anna Lise Purkey, "Questioning Governance in Protracted Refugee Situations: The Fiduciary Nature of the State-Refugee Relationship", (2014) 25 (4) *International Journal of Refugee Law* 693, p. 694.

国与难民之间单向的二元结构主体关系造成冲击，引发冲突和矛盾。[①]

（一）外部冲突：多重性因素干扰国家接纳难民的意愿

国际难民制度在本质上使接纳国得以有选择性地对特定个人提供保护，其运行在很大程度上取决于国家与个人接纳与被接纳的互动“收益”，在实践中具象为两者的“趋同利益”，包括政治因素、价值观与意识形态的认同等。[②] 有学者就指出，在冷战时期，西方国家将难民的选择优先置于迎合西方国家意识形态与共同价值而迁移的个人，使难民制度实质沦为冷战政治的工具与棋子。[③]

当前，造成大规模难民潮与流离失所者的社会与政治事件呈现多元化，接纳国与难民个人之间共同利益的交汇点变得模糊，直接影响了国家接纳难民的主观意愿。与此同时，对大规模外来者的恐惧心理、种族歧视、仇外、责任分担失败等诸多外部干扰却日益兴盛，成为主导接纳国与难民二元关系的显性甚至主流因素，进一步造成各国遵守或充分执行 1951 年公约的政治意愿难以协调。

（二）内在矛盾：单一、近距离原则不利于国家接纳难民的责任分担

接纳难民的责任承担与责任分担有所不同。前者指某一国家作为单一接纳国承担审查及接收难民的法律责任，而责任分担则指其他国家不带有法律任务的自愿为接纳国分担难民责任。

接纳国与难民之间的二元法律责任建立在“近距离原则”基础上，即通常由难民首先抵达的目的地国对入境人员进行难民地位审查与甄别。在地理位置上更接近难民或难民最早入境的国家往往成为担负保护难民的法律责任和不可推回法律义务的单一接纳国，那么，非接纳国的所有其他国

---

① Nergis Canefe, “The Fragmented Nature of the International Refugee Regime and its Consequences: a Comparative Analysis of the Applications of the 1951 Convention”, in James C. Simeon (ed.,) *Critical Issues in International Refugee Law* (Cambridge: Cambridge University Press, 2010), p. 205.

② Guy S. Goodwin-Gill and Jane McAdam, *The Refugee in International Law* (New York: Oxford University Press, 3rd ed., 2007), p. 16.

③ James C. Hathaway, “The Law of Refugee Status”, in B. S. Chimini (ed.,) *International Refugee Law: A Reader* (New Delhi: Sage Publications, 2000), p. 352.

家因不产生接纳难民的法律责任，实施援助或保护行为就属于自愿的、人道主义的责任分担。[①] 这意味着，接纳国对难民的法律责任的分配与实际承担实质取决于难民入境的地理位置，与该国是否有能力承担责任无直接关系。

与之对应，国家对难民的非法律责任的分担则在一定程度上取决于距离，并且会受到距离的制约以及影响国家决定应该和需要做什么。[②] 当一国缺少接纳能力而其他国家又不愿意分担责任，或者没有可靠途径向其邻国、国际组织及整个国际社会寻求援助时，只能选择最简单粗暴的方式，严控或关闭本国边界甚至进行域外拦截，以避免成为接纳国单独承担难民保护的法律责任和不可推回的法律义务。这种单一、近距离的接纳难民法律责任范式与大规模难民潮给特定国家造成不堪重负现实之间存在内在张力，展现了制度层面应对难民问题的局限性与不可持续性。[③]

囿于接纳国与难民之间的二元结构关系，错综复杂的冲突与矛盾因缺少疏导路径难以得到释放而不断激化，从中也为寻求解决方案提供一种反向的思考。大规模流离失所者或难民的流动行为涉及原籍国、过境国、目的地国（或接纳国）等多个国家，须构建从消除难民产生根源、接纳与安置难民以及难民自愿遣返各阶段入手，广泛动员不同国家参与其中的多边框架。

四　国际难民制度的优化进路思考

2016 年联合国《关于难民与移民问题纽约宣言》（以下简称《纽约宣言》）重申了“缔约国充分和有效执行两项文书的重要性及其体现的价值”，使国家切实遵行并有效执行 1951 年公约在国际层面达成共识。[④] 同

---

① Alexander Aleinikoff, “Reflections on the Worldwide Refugee ‘Crisis’”, (2017) 21 *UCLA Journal of International Law and Foreign Affairs* 1, p. 4.

② 参见〔澳〕彼得·辛格《如何看待全球化》，沈沉译，北京联合出版公司，2017，第 187 页。

③ Andreas Zimmermann (ed.), *The 1951 Convention Relating to the Status of Refugees and its 1967 Protocol* (New York: Oxford University Press Inc., 2011), p. 7.

④ United Nations, New York Declaration for Refugees and Migrants, 2016, UN Doc A/71/L. 1, para. 65.

时，优化外围措施、凝聚国际社会力量比以往任何时候都迫切。[①]

在法律层面，国际难民法、国际人权法与国际人道法为加强难民保护提供了“硬性”法律框架，通过功能互补与理念融合，以期强化对国家的监督与问责、提升向难民的赋权与保障、拓展国际机构的行动空间。在实践层面，推动“软法”意义上的国际合作，超越国家分野、整合多方资源，动员广泛的利益攸关方参与分担难民责任。[②]

（一）国际难民法、国际人权法、国际人道法的功能互补与理念融合

1. 强化对国家的监督与问责

依据 1951 年公约，对国家的监督与问责有两项途径。其一，诉诸争端解决机制。第 38 条规定涉及公约的争端与解释由国际法院管辖，国家有权就任何其他缔约国违法行为诉诸国际法院。但是，实践中，尚没有一个缔约国援引该机制来实施有效监督，凸显出传统的国家间争端解决机制在保护个人权利方面固有的局限性。[③] 其二，第 35 条赋予联合国难民署监督缔约国尊重与执行公约的职责。然而经联合国大会的多项决议确认，联合国难民署逐渐演变为提供人道主义援助的最前沿行动机构，需要与各国开展密切合作，反而阻碍了其原本更重要的监督国家履行公约的立场。[④]

国际人权条约机构能够对国家保障难民个人权利行使重要的监督与问责以弥补难民公约的不足。

第一，根据国家违反人权义务行为的个人申诉机制，难民可就国家在难民地位审查国内程序中侵犯其基本权利或国家违反不可推回义务等向相关人权机构提出申诉。

第二，实施国家报告定期审议机制，人权条约机构通过审议国家报告来评估该国对难民和寻求庇护者的人权保障情况。联合国于 1999 年通过决议还

---

① Volker Tiurk, “Prospects for Responsibility Sharing in the Refugee Context”, (2016) 4 *Journal on Migrationand Human Security* 45, p. 46.

② Alexander Betts (ed.), *Global Migration Governance* (Oxford: Oxford University Press, 2011), p. 233.

③ James C. Hathaway, *The Rights of Refugees under International Law* (Cambridge: Cambridge University Press, 2005), p. 995.

④ Vincent Chetail, “Are Refugee Rights Human Rights? An Unorthodox Questioning of the Relations between Refugee Law and Human Rights Law”, in Ruth Rubio-Marin (ed.), *Human Rights and Immigration* (Oxford: Oxford University Press, 2014), p. 64.

设立了移民人权问题特别报告员一职，职责涉及接收包括难民在内的移民信息，预防侵犯人权的国家行为发生，并就消除这些行为的措施提供建议。[①]

第三，司法机构的问责。近年来，国际人权条约机构与区域司法机构（欧洲人权法院）的判例裁断对确定寻求庇护者的脆弱性、检审与纠正国家侵犯难民或寻求庇护者的人权行为以及维护不得推回原则等发挥了重要的问责作用。

2. 赋权个人与保障发展权

难民权利涉及公共利益并且与发展具有内在联系。长期以来，难民或寻求庇护者往往被描述为受暴力与迫害的无助和可怜的受害者，必须依靠慈善和人道援助来生存，在接纳国没有地位也没有自力更生的能力。

对个人的赋权理念正是立足于消弭对难民的这种刻板印象并且对抗因刻板印象所带来的各种歧视。通过发掘难民的潜力与技能，充分展示其代表自己或他人行事的自愿与自主能动性，促进难民自力更生的信心与能力。同时，确保难民享有充分的发展权，能够获得谋生机会、运用自己的技能以自主方式支持本人及其家庭的生活，并进而为难民社区作出贡献。保障难民的尊严、权利，将遣返与赋权、发展与援助相结合，帮助难民在国外培育技能和能力使之获得就业或教育机会，为最终返回自己的国家创造条件，这是永久解决难民问题的正确导向。[②]

3. 拓展联合国难民署的行动空间

联合国大会赋予难民署向难民与流离失所者提供安全保障与援助的人道主义职能。然而，一些武装冲突无视人道主义原则，针对联合国难民署的保护行为诉诸犯罪活动或恐怖主义活动，例如武力攻击或对难民营和定居点的难民实施暴力行为，极大限制了难民署人道主义行动的空间，使难民及流离失所者的困境进一步恶化。

而国际人道法有助于平衡军事必要性与保障作为平民的难民安全之间的关系。联合国大会重申了难民高级专员的活动纯属人道主义和非政治性质，并谴责所有侵犯难民和寻求庇护者权利和安全的行为，特别是士兵针对难民营以及难民实施的暴行。联合国难民署执行委员会也提出关于禁止

---

① 联合国大会决议：《保护移徙者》，UN Doc. A/RES/54/166，第5段。

② Alexander Aleinikoff, "Reflections on the Worldwide Refugee 'Crisis'", (2017) 21 *UCLA Journal of International Law and Foreign Affairs* 1, p. 8.

对难民营和定居点进行武装和军事攻击的原则草案，并且多次敦促各国提供人道主义安全干预，专门涉及公共安全、刑事调查和对弱势群体的特殊保障。[①] 各国有责任与联合国难民署合作，加强国际人道法对难民安全的保障。

（二）推动“软法”意义上的国际合作，动员各方广泛参与难民责任分担

1951 年公约序言强调了国际合作的重要性。在各国不愿意加深难民保护承诺大背景之下，[②] 软法性质的国际合作占据应对与协调复杂难民问题的“天然优势”。[③] 要促成更广泛、灵活基础上的国际合作以及责任分担取决于外在与内在的动机。

首先，只有在合作收益（外部性问题）很大的情况下，国际法才会出色地运行。[④] 那么，努力降低难民的全球性不利影响、化解国家间及地区紧张关系的显性“收益”无疑将是带动难民领域国际合作的外部动因。

其次，全球化进程促使国际体系的相互依赖性不断增强，构成各国在诸多重大全球性议题上开展自愿合作进而分担责任的内在动机，譬如环境、反恐、跨国人口流动等领域。大规模流离失所者与难民这一长期存续并愈演愈烈的全球性难题需要人类共同面对，没有哪个国家能够单独应对挑战。

有鉴于此，《纽约宣言》申明要在“国际合作以及责任分担基础”上提供难民问题的全面响应框架，并拟议制定难民全球契约。[⑤] 联合国难民署于 2018 年 1 月 31 日发布《难民全球契约》“零草案”（zero draft），强调了构建更具可预测性的国家及其他利益攸关方的责任分担机制。[⑥]《难民全球契约》业已成为现阶段以联合国为主导、在难民领域最富有建设性的

---

① Pablo Antonio Fernindez-Sinchez, “The Interplay between International Humanitarian Law and Refugee Law”, (2010) 1 *International Humanitarian Legal Studies* 329, pp. 377 – 379.

② International Organization for Migration, *World Migration Report 2018* (Geneva: International Organization for Migration, 2017), p. 34.

③ Agnes Hurwitz, “Norm-Making in International Refugee Law”, (2012) 106 *American Society of International Law Proceedings* 430, pp. 432 – 433.

④ 参见〔美〕艾伦·赛克斯《国际法何时能发挥作用》，历咏译，载何志鹏、历咏、孙劼等《国际法的未来》，法律出版社，2017，第 213 页。

⑤ United Nations, New York Declaration for Refugees and Migrants, 2016, UN Doc A/71/L. 1, Annex I, para. 1, para. 19.

⑥ UNHCR, “*The Global Compact on Refugees, Zero Draft*”, p. 1, para. 1, http://www.unhcr.org/Zero-Draft.pdf，最后访问日期：2018 年 3 月 15 日。

国际合作路径。

根据《难民全球契约》“零草案”，国际合作与责任分担行动不仅调动国家间相互协助的积极性，而且发挥其他行动者如国际组织、非政府组织、区域性机构和民间社会的重要作用，最大限度地动员各利益攸关方参与其中，以期提供集保护、援助与支持三位一体的难民问题全面响应框架。①

具体而言，各国及利益攸关方的责任分担可涵盖以下内容：（1）有能力的国家之间进行合作，将难民实际接纳或安置于本国领土之内；（2）各国、国际组织、私营部门伙伴、其他合作伙伴等联合规划及合作，对难民流动的治理提供技术援助；（3）各国、国际组织机构、多边捐助方等视情提供经济、财政等人道主义援助；（4）参与责任分担的国家、国际组织机构牵头商定安置难民与寻求庇护者的共同框架协定等。②

总体上，《纽约宣言》和《难民全球契约》虽然尚未完全为解决难民问题搭建起国际合作的法律性框架，但是两份国际文件无疑彰显了这一领域的法治化方向，引领国际社会广泛参与并为之努力。国际社会面临的挑战是如何从原则走向实践，使概念性的责任分担成为具体的实际承诺以促进公平有效的责任分担。

五　国际难民问题的中国立场

中国的边界地缘复杂、周边各国发展不均衡，有必要对难民问题进行深入研究，切实参与全球移民与难民的治理与合作，倡导中国立场，贡献中国方案。

第一，习近平主席提出构建人类命运共同体重要思想，推动相互依赖、利益交融、休戚相关的全球治理模式，为着力解决包含难民问题在内的棘手的国际问题指明了国际合作的新方向。

（1）中国政府积极维护国际和平与稳定，坚定支持共同发展，高度重

① UNHCR，“*The Global Compact on Refugees*，*Zero Draft*”，p. 2，para. 3，http://www.unhcr.org/Zero-Draft.pdf，最后访问日期：2018 年 3 月 15 日。

② Jeannie Rose C. Field，“Bridging the Gap between Refugee Rights and Reality：a Proposal for Developing International Duties in the Refugee Context”，(2010) 22 (4) *International Journal of Refugee Law* 512，p. 533，pp. 546 - 547.

视并深入参与解决难民问题，向有关国家和国际机构提供人道主义援助。[①]

（2）倡导可持续发展原则，将保障发展权与国家可持续目标相结合改善民生，营造难民回归的和平与发展环境。[②]

（3）坚持公平原则。一些西方国家肆意违反《联合国宪章》干预其他国家的内政，激化了有关国家的国内政治矛盾，造成社会动荡殃及个人被迫逃离家园沦为流离失所者。对此，应当呼吁从公平原则出发，要求引发难民与流离失所者产生根源的国家分担更多责任。

（4）充分考虑接纳国能力原则。在难民重新接纳或再分配合作时，应当充分考虑国家的人口、难民接纳与安置能力，切实防止责任分担演变为难民责任的二次转移。

第二，作为1951年公约及其议定书的缔约国，中国应当始终坚持国际难民制度的主权原则。以主权原则为基础的难民公约制度承载着国家间的法律承诺与共识，为国家接纳与保护难民的行为提供了一致、可靠的国际标准。[③]

任何重构或重新开放的讨论都可能破坏该项兼具持久性、稳定性的国际制度来之不易的成果，对已经确立的规则和原则造成冲击，进而动摇现有制度的根基。事实证明，背离1951年公约的行为既没有减少也未能阻止难民及其他被迫移民的数量与大规模流动，相反却导致对难民及被迫移民流入的管理不力、难民不当转移乃至国家、地区间的紧张局势。[④] 中国历来主张“移民不是难民”，有必要对移民与难民加以区分并给予区别对待，切实维护1951年公约与议定书在统一标准下得到有效适用与执行。

（本文原载于《北方法学》2019年第1期）

---

① 《和平、发展与合作是解决地中海难民问题的根本》，人民网，http://world.people.com.cn/n1/2017/0408/c1002－29196924.html，最后访问日期：2018年3月25日。

② 《王毅谈黎巴嫩难民问题称难民不是移民应营造难民回归的环境》，人民网，http://world.people.com.cn/n1/2017/0625/c1002－29360663.html，最后访问日期：2018年3月25日。

③ Guy S. Goodwin-Gill，“The Continuing Relevance of International Refugee Law in a Globalized World”，（2015）10 *Intercultural Human RightsLaw Reviews* 25，p. 26.

④ Colin Harvey and Satvinder Juss，“Critical Reflections on Refugee Law”，（2013）20 *International Journal Minority and Group Rights* 143，p. 146.

试论外交保护中“干净的手理论”

张卫华 *

对海外公民的外交保护（diplomatic protection）在国家和国际法的历史中是一个比较“现代”的概念，① 国际常设法院在马夫罗马蒂斯巴勒斯坦特许权案（Mavrommatis Palestine Concessions Case）的判决中强调外交保护的习惯法渊源已经确定。该判决中说：“当一个国家的国民因为另一个国家违反国际法的行为受到损害时，如果其国民无法通过平常的渠道获得赔偿（satisfaction），该国有权保护其国民，这是国际法的一项基本原则。”②外交保护是一个国家代表个人（通常是其公民）对抗违反国际法的另一个国家而实施的保护。③

在外交保护制度中，常常需要考虑个人角色，也就是个人和他所受的损害之间是否有关系，这就是所谓的“干净的手理论”（clean hands doctrine），它是指在确定东道国（host state）的责任时，个人的表现也应在考虑之列，（实际）受害人的过错（fault）可被援引以免除或者减轻东道国的责任。④ 把干净的手理论适用于外交保护，在国际法律团体（international legal community）中，特别是国际法委员会中，是一个有着很大争议的

---

* 张卫华，中国社会科学院国际法研究所助理研究员。

① Edwin Borchard, The Diplomatic Protection of Citizen Abroad, New York, 1915, p. 3.

② *Case of the Mavrommatis Palestine Concessions* (Greece v. U. K.), P. I. C. J., *Series A*, No. 2, judgment of 30 August 1924, p. 12.

③ *Black's Law Dictionary* (8th ed., 2004), p. 490.

④ *Preliminary Report on Diplomatic Protection*, UN. Int'l L Comm'n, 50th Sess., U. N. Doc. A/CN. 4/484 (1998), para. 25.

话题。[①] 本文将对外交保护过程中的干净的手理论进行深入分析，探讨干净的手理论的概念和其在外交保护中的功能，从而对这一理论有一个清晰的认识。

一 干净的手理论的内涵

干净的手理论在国际法中并没有一个清晰的定义，它的含义通常通过各种各样的法谚和格言表达出来。这个原则和公平、善意等概念密切相关，在18世纪学者的著作中就有所表述。理查德·弗朗西斯（Richard Francis）说：“做了不公平的事情的人不应当得到公平。”[②] 一般认为按照干净的手理论，故意的不法行为不产生诉讼权利（ex dolo malo non oritur action）。类似的格言还有“任何人不得因其不当行为而获益”（mullus commodum capere potest de injuria sua propria）。很早就有学者指出：“许多国际求偿被根据下述衡平法格言驳回：原告来到法庭时他的手必须是干净的，如果原告是个实施了不法行为的人，他就不能得到救济。”[③] 在最一般意义上，干净的手原则被理解为要求，主张公平救济或者提出公平辩护的一方当事人，其自身行为符合公平原则。[④] 杰拉尔德·菲茨莫里斯（Gerald Fitzmaurice）爵士认为：“‘来向公平（equity）寻求救济的人，两手必须干干净净’。因此，犯有不法行为的国家可能被剥夺投诉其他国家的相应非法行为而需具备的出庭资格，特别是其他国家的不法行为是该国不法行为造成的结果，或者是为了针对该国不法行为而实施的——简而言之是由它所引起的。”[⑤]

这些格言和学者的论述描述了干净的手理论的基本含义，使我们对它有了一个初步的了解，然而，国际法庭在涉及该理论时总是直接引用格

---

① Aleksandr Shapovalov, “Should a Requirement of Clean Hands Be a Prerequisite to the Exercise of Diplomatic Protection? Human Rights Implications of the International Law Commission's Debate”, *American University International Law Review* (2005), p. 830 & n. 2.

② Richard Francis, *Maxims of Equity* (1727), p. 5.

③ E. Borchard, *The Diplomatic Protection of Citizen Abroad* (New York, 1915), p. 718 & n. 2.

④ *Black's Law Dictionary*, p. 268 (8th ed., 2004).

⑤ *Sixth Report on Diplomatic Protection*, UN. Int'l L Comm'n, 57th Sess., U. N. Doc. A/CN. 4/546 (2004), para. 2.

言，没有对它进行科学分析，使得我们对这一理论的轮廓仍然不是很清晰。为了更为深入地分析干净的手理论的含义，我们将把它和相近的概念进行比较。

在国际法和国内法中，与“干净的手”相似的概念主要有自身过失理论（contributory negligence doctrine）和自负风险（assumption of the risk, also named assumption of risk）。自身过失理论是指“如果原告所遭受的损害部分是由原告的过失造成的，则原告完全不能获得救济”。[①] 但是《布莱克法律词典》同时指出，大多数国家已经废除了这种理论，而代之以比较过错理论（comparative negligence）。[②] 这种国内法的变化是出于公平的考虑，同样也给国际法中的争端解决带来了启示，那些主张“干净的手理论完全阻止外交保护”的学者不应当忽视这种变化，当然这是我们下文中所要讨论的问题，这里不作展开。

比较过失理论是指：“按照损害产生中原告的过失程度相应的按比例减少对原告的救济，而不是完全不予救济。”[③] 在“Poggioli Case”中，原告要求委内瑞拉政府作出赔偿，因为委内瑞拉政府没有对给他造成巨大财产损失的强盗和暴徒进行逮捕和起诉。[④] 委内瑞拉政府争辩说：“作为辩护，（原告）是高利贷者，诱骗他们的邻居签订了大量对自己不利的合同，所有的一切都是由于对这些高利贷者的仇恨造成的，而不是委内瑞拉官员的行为，因此，政府不应承担责任。”[⑤] 法庭拒绝了这种辩解，判决委内瑞拉赔偿原告的部分损失。[⑥] 但是，无法确定仲裁员是否认为原告的行为导致了损害的发生，从而只判决委内瑞拉赔偿部分损失。

自负风险是指“预期的原告承担损失、伤害或者损害的风险的行为或事件”（The act or an instance of a prospective plaintiff's taking on risk of loss,

① *Black's Law Dictionary* (8th ed., 2004), p. 353.

② *Black's Law Dictionary* (8th ed., 2004), p. 353.

③ *Black's Law Dictionary* (8th ed., 2004), p. 300.

④ *Poggiolicase* (Italy v. Venez.), J. Ralston, *Venezuelan Arbitrations of 1903*, p. 847, 10 R. Int'l Arb. Awards, p. 669.

⑤ *Poggiolicase* (Italy v. Venez.), J. Ralston, *Venezuelan Arbitrations of 1903*, p. 847, 10 R. Int'l Arb. Awards p. 865, 10 R. Int'l Arb. Awards, p. 686.

⑥ David J. Bederman, "Contributory Fault and State Responsibility", *Virginia Journal of International Law* (Winter, 1990), p. 347.

injury or damage)。[1] 自负风险本来是一种积极辩护理由，但是现在完全或部分地被自身过失所代替了。[2] 在“Upton Case”中，仲裁员认为：“（原告的损失）是由于这个国家的混乱局势造成的，归因于委内瑞拉的内战，而不是委内瑞拉政府或者其官员特别针对原告或者其财产的行为导致的。在这种情况下，原告的特权与豁免与居住在这个国家的其他人没有任何不同。原告在进入一个外国时，就自愿承担了居住在那里的风险和利益。”[3]

自身过失的概念强调受害人自己的行为“引起”或者“导致”他的损害发生，[4] 而自负风险则侧重于受害人将自己置于危险的境地，从而受到了伤害。稍加分析就可以发现，自负风险的行为人其主观上也是有过失的，他没有尽到应有的谨慎义务，至少也是一种疏忽，因此，自负风险也可以用自身过失理论进行解释，所以自身过失和自负风险都有被比较过失理论取代的趋势也就不足为奇了。与自身过失、比较过失和自负风险不同，干净的手理论在定义中不侧重考虑受害人的主观心理状态，也就是说，它只要求受害人的手是“干净的”，当然，这绝不是说受害人的主观过失是不相关的。我们认为，干净的手理论可以涵盖自身过失理论和自负风险，后两个概念对干净的手理论从受害人主观心理态度的角度作了区分，对于我们理解干净的手理论有很大的帮助。事实上，在外交保护的案例中，国际法庭几乎不考虑它们之间的区别。

例如，在本·蒂利特案（The Ben Tillett Case）中，仲裁员甚至未提到任何和干净的手理论有关的事情。本·蒂利特是大不列颠国民，劳工联盟运动的激进分子。1896 年 8 月 21 日，他到比利时参加一个码头工人会议。当局在他到达比利时的当天逮捕了他，随后拘押了他数个小时，然后把他驱逐回大不列颠。大不列颠代表其国民提出比利时违反了它自己的法律，并索赔 75000 法郎。该案在谈判失败后进入仲裁，英国最终输了这个案子。

---

① *Black's Law Dictionary* (8th ed., 2004), p. 134.

② *Black's Law Dictionary* (8th ed., 2004), p. 134.

③ *Upton Case* (U. S. v. Venez.), in J. Ralston, *Venezuelan Arbitrations of 1903*, p. 172, 174, 9 R. Int'l Arb. Awards, pp. 234, 236.

④ David J. Bederman, "Contributory Fault and State Responsibility", *Virginia Journal of International Law* (Winter, 1990), p. 339.

有利于比利时的主要论辩是该国实施的行为不是国际不法行为。①

约翰·杜加尔德先生认为此案和干净的手理论没有任何关系，其裁决中没有提到任何和干净的手理论有关的术语。② 但是该案事实上是涉及干净的手理论的。仲裁员之所以认为比利时的行为符合国际法，就是因为本·蒂利特的行为违反了比利时法律，也就是说他的手是不干净的。Dominique Carreau 认为本·蒂利特没有干净的手，因为他违反了比利时法律，所以仲裁员拒绝了英国的求偿要求。③ 他同时把该案作为“国家为其行使或要求为其行使外交保护的个人本身不必有‘可以被指责的行为’”的例证。④

二 干净的手理论适用的范围

干净的手理论的适用范围在国际法委员会中也是一个有争论的问题。有的委员认为干净的手理论不适用于不涉及国家为保护其国民而发生的国际关系，⑤ 它只在外交保护中发生作用。⑥ 在国际法委员会，这一立场的最有力支持者是阿兰·佩利特（Alain Pellet）先生，⑦ 他认为：“‘干净的手’这个模糊的概念与国家间关系情况中的一般善意原则没有很大区别，不产

---

① Antoine Pillet & Paul Fauchille, “Revue Générale de Droit International Public 46 – 55 (1899), quote from Aleksandr Shapovalov, Should a Requirement of Clean Hands Be a Prerequisite to the Exercise of Diplomatic Protection? Human Rights Implications of the International Law Commission's Debate”, *American University International Law Review* (2005), p. 856.

② *Sixth Report on Diplomatic Protection*, UN. Int'l L Comm'n, 57th Sess., U. N. Doc. A/CN. 4/546 (2004), para. 11.

③ Aleksandr Shapovalov, “Should a Requirement of Clean Hands Be a Prerequisite to the Exercise of Diplomatic Protection? Human Rights Implications of the International Law Commission's Debate”, *American University International Law Review* (2005), p. 856 & note 115.

④ Dominique Carreau, *Droit International*, 7th ed. (2001), pp. 467 and 468, quote form *Sixth Report on Diplomatic Protection*, UN. Int'l L Comm'n, 57th Sess., U. N. Doc. A/CN. 4/546 (2004), para. 11.

⑤ *Provisional Summary Record of the 2792rd Meeting*, pp. 17 – 18, U. N. Int'l L. Comm'n, 56th U. N. Doc. A/CN. 4/SR. 2793. *Provisional Summary Record of the 2793rd Meeting*, p. 3, U. N. Int'l L. Comm'n, 56th U. N. Doc. A/CN. 4/SR. 2793.

⑥ *Provisional Summary Record of the 2793rd Meeting*, U. N. Int'l L. Comm'n, 56th U. N. Doc. A/CN. 4/SR. 2793, p. 4.

⑦ Aleksandr Shapovalov, “Should a Requirement of Clean Hands Be a Prerequisite to the Exercise of Diplomatic Protection? Human Rights Implications of the International Law Commission's Debate”, *American University International Law Review* (2005), p. 831.

生自动的后果，而且对国际责任的一般规则几乎没有实际影响。然而，在涉及国家与个人关系的外交保护情况中，此概念有了新的含义：它变得有作用了，在此若没有‘干净的手’，外交保护就无法行使。如果享有外交保护的私人个人侵犯了保护国（此处似乎应为东道国）的国内法——应当指出在涉及国家间关系的案件中国内法毫无作用——或国际法，那么在一般的求偿过程中，被要求行使保护的国家不再能这样做。”①

相反，有的委员认为干净的手理论适用于与外交保护无关的、直接发生在国家与国家之间的国际争端，这个时候所指的是原告国家的手是否干净。约翰·杜加尔德先生认为“……支持干净的手理论不适用于涉及直接国家间关系的争端的观点是很困难的。各国经常在直接发生在国家间的求偿中提出干净的手理论，而国际法院不曾在任何案件中说过该原则与国家间的求偿不相干。”②

在“Nicaragua case”（尼加拉瓜案）中，施韦贝尔（Schwebel）法官认为干净的手理论应对尼加拉瓜适用：“尼加拉瓜没有带着干净的手来到法院。相反，尼加拉瓜作为侵略者（aggressor），间接地，但最终要对萨尔瓦多境内大量人员的死亡和大面积破坏负责，这显然远超过尼加拉瓜所蒙受的损害，因此尼加拉瓜的手可憎的肮脏。而且，尼加拉瓜因向法院撒谎增加了它的过错。因此，由于它在萨尔瓦多进行非法武装干预，并由于它在有关干涉事实方面通过让其部长们作伪证，故意努力误导法院，所以尼加拉瓜针对美国提出的求偿不应被受理。”③ 施韦贝尔法官为了支持他的推理，引用了常设国际法院和国际法院的许多判决。所有被引用的案件均可被认为是直接发生在国家间的案件。④

在南斯拉夫针对北大西洋公约组织成员国提交的关于“使用武力的合法性”案件的临时措施和法院管辖阶段的口头辩论中，有几个被告国认为南斯拉夫所请求的禁令不应得到同意，因为南斯拉夫来到法院没有带着干

---

① *Provisional Summary Record of the 2793rd Meeting*, U. N. Int'l L. Comm'n, 56thU. N. Doc. A/CN. 4/SR. 2793, p. 4.

② *Sixth Report on Diplomatic Protection*, UN. Int'l L Comm'n, 57th Sess., U. N. Doc. A/CN. 4/546 (2004), para. 6.

③ 1986 *I. C. J. Reports* 392, para. 268.

④ *Sixth Report on Diplomatic Protection*, UN. Int'l L Comm'n, 57th Sess., U. N. Doc. A/CN. 4/546 (2004), para. 5.

净的手。[①] 在逮捕证案（Arrest Warrant Case）中，比利时专案法官范·登·温加尔特（van den Wyngaert）认为："刚果没有带着干净的手来到法院。刚果谴责比利时对本应由刚果自己负责的国际罪行的指控进行调查和起诉，是出于恶意。"[②] 在石油平台案（Oil Platform Case）中，美国提出伊朗有违法行为，伊朗认为美国的这种主张可以归入"干净的手"之类。[③]

我们可以看出，干净的手理论在国际争端中的适用是大量存在的，如上所述，不仅国际法庭从来没有否认干净的手理论的存在，而且很多国家也往往提出干净的手理论作为辩护理由。事实上，干净的手理论不仅存在于国家之间发生的争端，而且存在于国家间因为行使外交保护而引起的争端。

阿兰·佩利特认为干净的手理论"在国家之间的关系中和善意原则并没有太大的不同，并且在国际责任一般规则上并没有自动效果，也几乎没有实际效果"。[④] 考虑到阿兰·佩利特主张干净的手理论在国家之间的争端中没有意义，他的观点好像暗示善意原则在国家之间的争端中也不能适用。[⑤] 这一立场显然是不正确的，因为除了否认干净的手理论在国际法中的作用外，他还主张了善意原则在国家间争端中毫无用武之地，而善意原则是公认的一般法律原则，它的作用是毋庸置疑的。

另外一种观点正确地认为"干净的手理论在涉及外交保护的要求中没有特殊地位"。[⑥] 外交保护当前在国际法中被视为将个人的诉求引入国家间领域的一条途径，它的概念中暗含着如下观点："一旦一个国家在一个国际法庭中代表其国民进行诉讼，在国际法庭的眼中，该国家是唯一的原告。"[⑦] 所以外交保护的行使一旦导致国家之间的争端，和其他国家争端在

---

① *Sixth Report on Diplomatic Protection*, UN. Int'l L Comm'n, 57th Sess., U. N. Doc. A/CN. 4/546 (2004), para. 5.

② Arrest Warrant Case, 2002 I. C. J. Reports, para. 35.

③ Case Concerning the Oil Platforms, 2003 I. C. J. Reports, paras. 27 – 30.

④ Provisional Summary Record of the 2793rd Meeting, supra note 24, p. 4.

⑤ Aleksandr Shapovalov, "Should a Requirement of Clean Hands Be a Prerequisite to the Exercise of Diplomatic Protection? Human Rights Implications of the International Law Commission's Debate", *American University International Law Review* (2005), p. 838.

⑥ *Sixth Report on Diplomatic Protection*, UN. Int'l L Comm'n, 57th Sess., U. N. Doc. A/CN. 4/546 (2004), para. 9.

⑦ Case of the Mavrommatis Palestine Concessions (Greece v. U. K.), supra note 2.

性质上就没有什么不同了。作为一种抗辩理由，干净的手理论在国际争端中的适用并没有什么特殊之处，它毫无疑问可以适用于包括外交保护在内的各种国际争端，而在每个具体的争端中干净的手理论作为辩护理由是否成立，需要作个案分析，而不能事先预设结论。我们需要认真考虑的不是干净的手理论可以适用于哪一类国际争端，而是它在外交保护中究竟起什么作用。

三 干净的手理论在外交保护中的作用

Aleksandr Shapovalov 提出我们在外交保护中有三种途径看到干净的手理论，[①] 这给出了一个很好的分析基础。他所说的第一种途径是：“如果一个国家用类似的方式对外国公民采取行动，干净的手理论能够排除它行使外交保护。”[②] 美国在拉格兰德案（La Grand Case）中对德国的抗辩似乎可以归入此类。在该案中，美国提出德国的起诉不应被受理，因为它试图对美国适用与德国自己的实践不同的标准，德国并未证明它的刑事司法程序规定在违反领事通知义务时应当取消刑事判决，德国在类似案件中的做法只不过是赔礼道歉。美国坚持认为对美国适用德国似乎并未接受的规则，违反基本司法原则和当事人之间的公平。[③]

第二种途径是：“当保护国在涉及其国民的特定案件中有非法行为，造成它的手不干净的时候，这个理论可以排除外交保护。”[④] 逮捕证案中刚果的行为似乎可以归入这种类型，但是刚果在起诉中避开了这一不利的处境，它坚持认为对比利时进行起诉不是由于保护自己的国民，它抓住外交

---

① Aleksandr Shapovalov, “Should a Requirement of Clean Hands Be a Prerequisite to the Exercise of Diplomatic Protection? Human Rights Implications of the International Law Commission's Debate”, *American University International Law Review* (2005), p. 835.

② Aleksandr Shapovalov, “Should a Requirement of Clean Hands Be a Prerequisite to the Exercise of Diplomatic Protection? Human Rights Implications of the International Law Commission's Debate”, *American University International Law Review* (2005), p. 836.

③ La Grand Case, I. C. J. Reports, paras. 61 -63.

④ Aleksandr Shapovalov, “Should a Requirement of Clean Hands Be a Prerequisite to the Exercise of Diplomatic Protection? Human Rights Implications of the International Law Commission's Debate”, *American University International Law Review* (2005), p. 836.

部长的豁免权不可侵犯，主张刚果国家本身直接受到了伤害。[①] 刚果否认它是在行使外交保护，这应当被看作一种诉讼策略，它选择了一个最有利的诉讼理由，但是从客观的角度分析，本案中外交保护也是可以作为诉讼理由的，如果刚果这样做了，那么它的行为就是我们现在所说的这种情况了。

第三种途径："如果声称受到侵害的国民所受到的侵害是他自己的不法行为的结果，可认为干净的手理论排除一个国家行使外交保护。"[②] 第三种解释正是国际法委员会中所争论的，也是本文所要讨论的。这种情况下，干净的手理论中的"干净的手"指的是受到侵害的国民的"手"，并且，他的"不干净的手"和他所受到的侵害之间有联系，也就是说在某种程度上侵害可以"归因于"他的手不干净。

国际法委员会中主张在外交保护的条款草案中列入干净的手理论的委员，并不仅仅把干净的手理论看作普通的抗辩理由，他们"援引干净的手理论，是为了使提出外交保护的请求不被受理"。[③] 也就是说，在外交保护情况中，如果一国设法保护的国民是因其自己的错误行为而受到伤害，那么援引这个理论是为了阻止该国行使外交保护。[④] 特别报告员约翰·杜加尔德先生反对这种观点，他认为："如果这个理论适用于关于外交保护的求偿，看来，在涉及减轻或免除责任的案件实质阶段才提出，而不是在受理阶段提出，是比较合适的。"[⑤]

争论的实质在于：干净的手理论是行使外交保护的前提条件，必须在案件的受理阶段提出，还是一个普通的抗辩理由，最好是在案件的实质阶段提出？

有几位学者认为干净的手理论是一个可受理性的问题，同样，可以提

---

① Arrest Warrant Case, 2002 I. C. J. Reports, paras. 37 – 40.

② Aleksandr Shapovalov, "Should a Requirement of Clean Hands Be a Prerequisite to the Exercise of Diplomatic Protection? Human Rights Implications of the International Law Commission's Debate", *American University International Law Review* (2005) 5, p. 836.

③ Provisional Summary Record of the 2793rd Meeting, supra note 24, p. 4.

④ *Sixth Report on Diplomatic Protection*, UN. Int'l L Comm'n, 57th Sess., U. N. Doc. A/CN. 4/546 (2004), para. 2.

⑤ *Sixth Report on Diplomatic Protection*, UN. Int'l L Comm'n, 57th Sess., U. N. Doc. A/CN. 4/546 (2004), para. 16.

出该理论作为对行使外交保护的拒绝。[①] 这种干净的手理论导致诉求不可受理的观点，在我们前面提到的施韦贝尔法官在“有关尼加拉瓜的军事和准军事行动案”的异议意见中，和范·登·温加尔特法官在“有关2000年4月11日逮捕证案”的异议意见中得到了支持。伊恩·布朗利把干净的手理论看作众多“可接受性问题和‘实体’事项问题难以区分的事例”之一。[②] 对于干净的手是可采纳性的一个条件，还是在实质问题审查阶段提出的实体法事项，在国际法委员会并没有一个一致意见。饶有兴趣的是，阿兰·佩里特，这个干净的手理论在国际法委员会的强烈支持者，承认国家间争端中：“没有一个法庭曾经因此得出（干净的手理论）自动导致一个诉求不可接受。”[③]

实际上，阿兰·佩里特的观点是矛盾的，干净的手理论作为一个可受理性的条件是站不住脚的。正如埃德温·博查德（Edwin Borchard）所主张的那样，甚至在违反刑法的情况下，“也不是绝对不能行使外交保护，但是一般而言它被局限于确保公正的审判和适用普通罚金或者试图减轻任意性措施的严厉性。”[④] 埃德温·博查德支持违反东道国法律（即不干净的手）不能自动导致外交保护不能行使，而仅仅是外国人的国籍国在考虑是否给予外交保护时受到了限制。简而言之，干净的手理论是一个国家决定是否行使外交保护时的一个考虑因素，更为明确的是，它是国家决定不行使外交保护时的一条途径。[⑤]

对此，约翰·杜加尔德先生作了最好的论述，他说：“如果一名外国人在外国因某种不法行为被认为有罪，并根据该国正当法律程序被剥夺自由或财产，那么其国籍国不能介入进行保护。事实上，在这种情况中国籍国介入是错误的，因为在多数情况中不存在国际不法行为。在这个意义上，‘干净的手’理论起到阻止外交保护的作用。然而，如果被告国因为

---

① Aleksandr Shapovalov, “Should a Requirement of Clean Hands Be a Prerequisite to the Exercise of Diplomatic Protection? Human Rights Implications of the International Law Commission's Debate”, *American University International Law Review* (2005), p. 842 & note 46.

② Ian Brownlie, *Principles of Public International Law* (5th ed., 1998), p. 508.

③ Provisional Summary Record of the 2793rd Meeting, supra note 24, p. 3.

④ Edwin Borchard, *The Diplomatic Protection of Citizen Abroad* (New York, 1915), p. 734.

⑤ Aleksandr Shapovalov, “Should a Requirement of Clean Hands Be a Prerequisite to the Exercise of Diplomatic Protection? Human Rights Implications of the International Law Commission's Debate”, *American University International Law Review* (2005), p. 851.

外国人的不法行为而对他实施了国际不法行为——例如，被怀疑犯有刑事罪行的外国人遭到酷刑或不公平审判，那么这种情况便具有了一种不同的性质。在这种情况下，国籍国可以针对该国际不法行为代表其国民行使外交保护"。[①] 杜加尔德先生认为："在后一种情况中，因为出现了违反国际法的情况，不能对受害的个人适用干净的手理论。第一，由于提出的要求现在具有了国际性，是国家对国家的求偿；第二，由于该个人不具备国际法律人格，因此不能（国际刑法领域除外）对违反国际法负责。简而言之，由于对一国民的伤害即是对国家本身的伤害的拟制，代表遭受国际不法行为侵害的国民提出的求偿便成为一项国际求偿，而且只能针对保护国的行为提出干净的手理论，而不能针对受害个人的错误行为，尽管这种错误行为可能早于该国际不法行为。"[②]

从杜加尔德先生的上述推理可以得出干净的手理论在涉及外交保护的求偿中没有特殊地位。"如果个人在东道国实施了不法行为，并根据正当法律程序受到审判和处罚，那么就不存在国际不法行为，因而干净的手理论也就毫不相干。但是，从另一方面看，如果该国民的国内法上的错误行为导致了被告国在处理该错误行为时犯下了国际法上的错误，同时，如果受害国民的代表国籍国为他提的外交保护，该求偿便成为一种国际性求偿。此时只能针对原告国自己的行为提出干净的手理论。"[③] 杜加尔德先生认为拉戈兰德案和埃夫纳案（Avena case）都证明了这一点。在这两起案件中，外国国民犯下了严重罪行，对其审判和惩罚是正当的。但是在两起案件中，美国在对他们进行起诉时没有准许他们会见领事，违反了国际法。美国在任何阶段都没有主张这两个外国国民的严重罪行使得他们的手是不干净的，从而阻止德国和墨西哥各自根据《维也纳领事关系公约》来保护他们。相反，在这两起案件中，美国认为原告国自己的手不干净，因

① *Sixth Report on Diplomatic Protection*, UN. Int'l L Comm'n, 57th Sess., U. N. Doc. A/CN. 4/546 (2004), para. 8.

② *Sixth Report on Diplomatic Protection*, UN. Int'l L Comm'n, 57th Sess., U. N. Doc. A/CN. 4/546 (2004), para. 8.

③ *Sixth Report on Diplomatic Protection*, UN. Int'l L Comm'n, 57th Sess., U. N. Doc. A/CN. 4/546 (2004), para. 9.

为它们没有按照它们要求美国的方式适用《维也纳公约》。[①]

结 论

干净的手理论在国际法中并没有明确的定义，它存在于各种各样的法律格言中。在国际争端中经常会提到干净的手理论，它不仅适用于外交保护，还适用于国家之间直接发生的争端，也就是说，它在由于行使外交保护而引发的国际争端中并没有特殊的地位。因此，特别报告员杜加尔德先生认为不应把它列入有关外交保护的条款草案。在国际争端中，干净的手理论只是一个普通的辩护理由，应当在案件审理的实质阶段予以考虑，而不是案件是否可以受理的前提，不能作为排除外交保护的条件。在案件的实质问题审理阶段，干净的手理论将会影响损失的分担和赔偿金额的确定，也就是说它可能会减轻，甚至免除被告国的赔偿责任。

（本文原载于《中国国际法年刊（2009）》，世界知识出版社，2010）

① *Sixth Report on Diplomatic Protection*, UN. Int'l L Comm'n, 57th Sess., U. N. Doc. A/CN. 4/546 (2004), para. 9.

论琉球在国际法上的地位

罗欢欣*

引　言

近年来，钓鱼岛争端持续升温，琉球地位问题日益受到关注。其中，舆论与媒体关注的时间点可以追溯到2005年。该年8月，商务部国际贸易经济合作研究院研究员唐淳风在接受中国评论通讯社专访时将东海问题与琉球问题联系起来，他指出，“日本挑战东海、钓鱼岛，要争的是琉球……中国应该据理争回琉球；争回琉球，就不再有钓鱼岛、东海问题了”。① 同月，北京大学历史系教授徐勇在《世界知识》杂志发表短评文章《琉球谜案》，提到“琉球王国变成日本的‘冲绳县’，是军国主义侵略的结果；战后日本从美国手中接收琉球群岛，同样缺乏国际法依据”，“从主权归属的合法性考察，‘琉球地位并未确定’”。② 2010年9月7日，中日在钓鱼岛海域的撞船事件发生后，《环球时报》连载了几篇质疑琉球地位的文章。③ 之后，香港的诸多媒体也提出了钓鱼岛问题应与琉球主权联系起来探讨。④

---

* 罗欢欣，中国社会科学院国际法研究所副研究员。

① 林泉忠：《钓鱼台怒涛中的琉球地位新议：五年来“收回琉球”论的来龙去脉》，香港《明报月刊》2011年2月号。

② 徐勇：《琉球谜案》，《世界知识》2005年第15期。

③ 唐淳风：《日本没有资格与中国谈钓鱼岛》，《环球时报》2010年9月19日，第8版；唐淳风：《应支持琉球独立运动》，《环球时报》2010年10月8日，第11版；陈德恭、金德湘：《日本对琉球无合法主权》，《环球时报》2010年10月8日，第14版。

④ 例如，香港中国评论新闻网2010年10月20日报道：《日本没有资格谈钓鱼岛》，中国评论新闻网，http://www.crntt.com/crn-webapp/search/searchZpyk.jsp?sw=琉球&pg=4，最后访问日期：2013年5月8日；香港凤凰卫视在同月也制作了专题节目：《石齐平：中国应同提对台湾、琉球及钓鱼岛主权》，凤凰资讯台，http://news.ifeng.com/mainland/special/zrczdydxz/content-0/detail_2010_10/05/2703558_0.shtml，最后访问日期：2014年2月18日。

传媒报道凸显了人们对琉球问题的关切。然而，琉球的地位在法律层面究竟如何？“琉球地位未确定”这样的假设与追问在国际法上是否成立？已有研究成果中，从历史、政治或国际关系的角度分别探讨琉球与钓鱼岛问题的著作、文章不在少数，[①] 但从国际法的角度专门分析琉球地位或涉及琉球地位的文章，直到2012年6月以后才开始出现。[②] 并且，这些已发表的成果对琉球地位问题的分析尚欠深入，特别是对战后琉球问题的演变过程缺乏较清晰的梳理，对琉球问题产生的一些关键环节缺乏关注与探讨。琉球问题作为一个重大现实案例，其法律分析不能脱离事实基础。为此，针对已有研究的不足，本文不但在历史（主要是国际关系史）层面进行了较多的资料收集、整理与提炼工作，在国际法的理论论证层面，也起到了一定程度的疏遗补漏效果。

一 琉球的基本情况及问题的产生

（一）琉球的名称与来历

琉球（英译有 Ryukyu，LooChoo，Lewchew，Liukiu 等）[③] 是历史上琉

---

① 参见罗欢欣《海内外钓鱼岛研究四十年：比较与述评》，载《日本研究报告2013》，社会科学文献出版社，2013，第128—156页。

② 其中代表性的学者及其著作有：梁淑英《国际法视角下的琉球地位》，《法学杂志》2013年第4期；管建强《国际法视角下的中日钓鱼岛领土主权纷争》，《中国社会科学》2012年第12期；刘丹《琉球托管的国际法研究——兼论钓鱼岛的主权归属问题》，《太平洋学报》2012年第12期；罗欢欣《论1972年前美国“统治”冲绳的法律依据》，载《未名日本论丛》第6辑，社会科学文献出版社，2011，第220—233页，并且，罗欢欣的博士论文为《国际法上的琉球地位与钓鱼岛主权》（2013年5月答辩提交，中国社会科学出版社，2015）。这里未将中国台湾地区学界计算在内。关于中国台湾学者的研究，或者想要全面了解相关的已有研究的状况，可以参见罗欢欣《海内外钓鱼岛研究四十年：比较与述评》，载《日本研究报告2013》，社会科学文献出版社，2013，第128—156页。

③ 现在琉球的英文译法基本上统一为“Ryukyu”。之前的历史地图中，多用 LooChoo，LuChoo，LooChu，LiuKiu，Lewchew 等，这些词语的来源都是汉语中“琉球”一词的中文发音。战后美国军用文书及地图中多用 LooChoo 标注琉球，有时也对以上拼法互换使用。琉球名字的译法之差别在帕特里克·贝尔维尔编纂的琉球资料汇编中有清楚反映。参见 Patric Beillevairee，(ed.,) *Ryukyu Studies to* 1854：*Western Encounter*（UK：Curzon press，2000）。琉球自原中国藩属之琉球王国演变而来，目前成为日本所控制下的“冲绳县”，其界限一度含糊，逐渐从广义的琉球演变为狭义的琉球——“冲绳县”。因二战后盟国在处理琉球群岛的领土问题上，琉球的范围存在演变，因而在此过程中，本文所称的琉球也泛指北部、中部与南部的整个琉球群岛，或是南西诸岛这样的抽象概念的简称，具体依据上下文来确定。下文不再标注。

球王国的简称，也是地理上的琉球群岛的简称。琉球群岛又有广义和狭义之分。琉球群岛从广义上讲是西太平洋的一长段岛链，位于中国台湾岛与日本九州岛之间，呈东北—西南走向，从北到南，共分为北部、中部与南部三段。最北部为大隅诸岛（ōsumi）、吐噶喇列岛（Tokara）和奄美诸岛（Amami），中部主要是冲绳诸岛（Okinawa），南部即先岛诸岛（Sakishima）直到最南端的与那国岛（Yonaguni），这三段岛链加起来统称为琉球群岛。此外，还有大东群岛（Daitō），距离冲绳本岛有349公里，在明治时期以前一直是无人岛，与琉球群岛一起，被日本统称为南西诸岛（Nansei islands/shoto）。而在英语中，南西诸岛与琉球群岛被一律简称为琉球（Ryukyu）。因北部的大隅诸岛、吐噶喇列岛与奄美诸岛（又被统称为萨南诸岛 Satsunan Islands）都属于日本鹿儿岛县（Kagoshima Prefecture），被认为不属于传统琉球王国的范围，故狭义的琉球群岛仅指目前的日本“冲绳县”区域，主要包括中部的冲绳诸岛和南部的先岛诸岛，先岛诸岛又具体分为宫古（Miyako）和八重山（Yaeyama）诸岛，目前的琉球（冲绳）面积大概2270平方公里，人口137万左右。①

在中国古籍上，琉球之名，多至十几二十几个，有邪久、掖久、益救、瀛洲、夷洲、沃焦、焦侥、周饶、恶焦、流求、流鬼、恶石等，亦称侏儒国、毛人国。② 琉球国史《中山世鉴》记称：“当初，未（有）琉球之名。数万年后，隋炀帝令羽骑校尉朱宽，访求异俗，始至此国。地界万涛间，远而望之，蟠旋蜿蜒，若虬浮水中，故因以名琉虬也。”③ 不管怎样，关于中国与琉球的关系，即使从隋朝算起至今也有千年左右。④ 还有一些历史学家认为，从近年琉球出土的文物来看，中国人发现琉球，应该有两千年以上。⑤ 早在公元12世纪，琉球群岛上就建立了封建国家。明朝洪武五年（1372年），明太祖正式发布诏谕遣使前往琉球。从此，琉球正式与中国建立“臣属关系”。琉球国王累世接受中国皇帝册封，派遣使节

---

① Public Relations Division, Executive Office of the Governor, Okinawa Prefectural Government, Outline of Okinawa Prefecture 2008 (Okinawa: Senden Inc., 2008), p. 1.

② 杨仲揆：《中国·琉球·钓鱼岛》，香港友联研究所，1972，第2页。

③ 转引自米庆余《琉球历史研究》，天津人民出版社，1998，第2页。

④ 古代琉球，“国无典籍”，有关记述最先出现在中国《隋书·流求传》中。转引自米庆余《琉球历史研究》，天津人民出版社，1998，第1页。

⑤ 参见杨仲揆《中国·琉球·钓鱼岛》，香港友联研究所，1972，第4—5页。

向中国皇帝称臣纳贡，举国奉行中国年号、正朔，接受中国政治文化和社会经济等全方位的影响。中国与琉球维持宗藩关系达500余年。但中国封建朝廷并不干涉琉球内政，许其自治，琉球“自为一国”。[①]

（二）琉球地位成为问题的源起

日本古籍中对于琉球的记载，始自清康熙五十八年（1719年）新井白石所著之《南岛志》。该书引述中国的《隋书·流求传》末段“大业元年，……三年，隋炀帝令羽骑尉朱宽入海，求仿异俗……因到流求国，言不相通，掠一人而返。明年，帝复令宽慰抚之，流求不从，宽取其布甲而还。时倭国使来朝，见之曰，此夷邪久国人所用也。”[②] 新井白石试图以此说明日本（时名倭国）与琉球来往已久。中国历史学家认为，这是因为日本“古无信史，往往附会我国史籍，或加以演绎、或进行伪造，以证明日本与琉球的关系久远”。[③] 实际上，日本与琉球真正发生联系是在1868年明治维新以后。明治维新使日本经济得到迅速发展，从而逐步确立军国主义路线，大力推行扩张政策。时值中国清政府内忧外患之际，中国周边领土便成了日本对外扩张的主要对象。[④] 1879年（明治十二年）3—4月，日本天皇政府派出一支450人的军队和160人的警察队伍，前去镇压已有200年历史不设军队的琉球，把琉球王强行移居到东京，并废除藩政，改成了天皇政府直辖的冲绳县（Okinawa Prefecture），这就是历史上的“琉球处分”。[⑤] 此后，清政府立刻向日本提出了抗议，并在美国前总统格兰特（Ulysses Simpson Grant）的调停下与日本进行过多次谈判，并在1880年与日本达成“分岛加约”的方案，即中岛（冲绳岛）以北归属日本，南岛（宫古、八重山）归属中国，同时修改日清通商条约，增添了允许日本人

---

① 参见鞠德源《日本国窃土源流——钓鱼列屿主权辩》，首都师范大学出版社，2001，第72页、第326页；米庆余《琉球历史研究》，天津人民出版社，1998，第1页。

② 转引自杨仲揆《中国·琉球·钓鱼岛》，香港友联研究所，1972，第6页。

③ 杨仲揆：《中国·琉球·钓鱼岛》，香港友联研究所，1972，第7页。

④ 日本在1874年2月至12月侵略台湾；在1875年5月，与俄罗斯签订千岛、桦太交换条约；1876年10月，日本通告世界各国，小笠原诸岛由日本政府管辖等。参见〔日〕井上清《钓鱼岛：历史与主权》，贾俊琪、于伟译，中国社会科学出版社，1997，第48—49页。

⑤ 〔日〕井上清：《钓鱼岛：历史与主权》，贾俊琪、于伟译，中国社会科学出版社，1997，第46页。“琉球处分”也叫“琉球处置”，狭义上指1879年对琉球的废藩置县，广义上泛指整个过程。〔日〕新崎盛辉：《现代日本与冲绳》，《开放时代》2009年第3期。

进入中国内地从事贸易的条款。[①]“分岛加约”案尽管没有最后签约，但双方对约文文本的合意反映了日本的主权意识在当时其实并不及于琉球全境，或者说只对琉球北部有行使主权的意愿。

之后，中国对于日本在琉球的主权状况采取了不予承认的态度。譬如，1934 年 4 月，在江西省抚州，迫于全国上下对其“攘外必先安内”政策的强烈不满，蒋介石发表了题为“日本之声明与吾人救国要道”的讲演，进一步表明了自己的态度：“日本将我们当作朝鲜、台湾这些地方一样”，“中国又受到了一个最大的侮辱”，“不仅是东北四省的失地我们要收复”，而且，“台湾、琉球这些地方都是我们的旧有领土，一尺一寸都要从我们手里收回”。[②] 宋子文担任外交部长时，于 1942 年 11 月 3 日首次召开的中外记者招待会上，关于“战后领土”方面，曾明确表示，“……中国应收回东北四省，琉球及台湾等地”。[③] 由此可知，“琉球处分”的效力之争是琉球地位成为问题的开端。直到 2012 年，琉球人在向联合国大会人权理事会控诉日本时，还提出 1879 年日本将琉球王国改为冲绳县违反了《维也纳条约法公约》第 51 条的规定，形成对一国代表之强迫或威胁，应无法律效果。[④]

（三）二战期间琉球受到严重的“差别待遇”

第二次世界大战（以下简称二战）期间，琉球人民受伤害至深，牺牲惨烈，“琉球战役”被称为“太平洋最血腥的战役”。[⑤] 早在 1942 年，在

---

① 关于中日谈判“分岛加约”案，学界所知者不多，史料仅见于《清光绪朝中日交涉史料》卷二和王弢夫编的《清季外交史料》卷二十一和二十五所载《琉案专约底稿》和《加约底稿》，以及南北洋大臣审议琉球案所上的奏折等件。参见鞠德源《日本国窃土源流——钓鱼列屿主权辩》，首都师范大学出版社，2001，第 96 页。另外，日本学者西里喜行最近的著作中也提到了“分岛加约”案。参见〔日〕西里喜行《清末中琉日关系史研究》，胡连成等译，社会科学文献出版社，2010，第 299—300 页。

② 陈志奇编《中华民国外交史料汇编》（八），中国台湾地区台北渤海堂文化公司，1996，第 3349 页。

③ “中央执行委员会”秘书处图书室编《资料剪辑》第 13 号，1943 年 5 月 17 日。转引自中国台湾地区“中国国民党中央委员会党史委员会”编《抗战时期收复台湾之重要言论》，“中国国民党党史委员会”，1990，第 99 页。

④ The Association of the Indigenous Peoples in the Ryukyus（AIPR），*Japan：Violation of human rights of indigenous peoples of Ryukyus in Okinawa*，UN Doc. A/HRC/20/NGO/20/Rev. 1.

⑤ Miyume Tanji，*Myth，Protest and Struggle in Okinawa*（Abingdon：Routledge，2006），p. 36.

"南海诸岛"[①] 受到美国军队的猛烈攻击后，日本军队在撤退中杀死了大量的平民，包括很多琉球人。[②] 对于日本统治者来说，冲绳防卫军（Okinawa Defense Troops）的使命不过是延缓盟军对日本的攻击。所以，冲绳本地的安危从一开始就不是优先考虑的对象。[③] 在整个战争中，琉球的防御受到极度忽视，日本统治者根本没有针对美国的登陆制定共同的计划或整体的抵抗战略。[④] 1944 年 10 月，整个那霸城市的 90% 就在美国 B－29 战斗机的空袭中毁于一旦。[⑤]

日本在名义上将琉球视为其帝国领土，但 1945 年的战争表明日本军队根本没有将琉球人视作日本人。[⑥] 在冲绳战场上，日本军人强奸、怀疑和滥杀平民，以及在投降前后逼迫琉球人集体自杀，使琉球民众受到美国与日本军队的双重伤害，他们用"前有狼，后有虎"来形容当时的绝望境地。[⑦] 在庆良间（Kerama）岛上，日本仅部署了小部分兵力，而部队指挥官却命令 700 余岛民自杀，以保障"军队的战斗行动不受非战斗人员打扰"。[⑧] 村民们被强迫用自己的家用物品，如斧子、剃刀、锄头、鼠药等杀

---

① 就是日本在战前管理的原德属太平洋岛屿，当时被日本视作殖民地而称其为南海诸岛（South Sea Islands），具体包括马里亚纳（Mariana）、帕劳（Palau）、加罗林（Caroline）和马绍尔（Marshall）。这些岛屿在战后由联合国安理会通过决议成为战略托管地。后文会提及。

② Takashi Arashiro, *Kotogakko Ryukyu Okinawa-shi* (Okinawan History Textbook for High Schools) (Naha: Toyo Kikaku, 1997), p. 203.

③ George Kerr, *Okinawa: The History of an Island People* (Tokyo: Charles E. Tuttle, 1958), p. 466. 同时参见 Masahide Ota, *Okinawa: Senso to Heiwa* (*Okinawa, War and Peace*) (Tokyo: Asahi Shimbunsha, 1996), p. 77。

④ Miyume Tanji, *Myth, Protest and Struggle in Okinawa* (Abingdon: Routledge, 2006), p. 36. Takashi Arashiro, *Kotogakko Ryukyu Okinawa-shi* (Okinawan History Textbook for High Schools) (Naha: Toyo Kikaku, 1997), p. 203. George Kerr, *Okinawa: The History of an Island People* (Tokyo: Charles E. Tuttle, 1958), p. 466. 同时参见 Masahide Ota, *Okinawa: Senso to Heiwa* (*Okinawa, War and Peace*) (Tokyo: Asahi Shimbunsha, 1996), p. 77。

⑤ Takashi Arashiro, Kotogakko Ryukyu Okinawa-shi (Okinawan History Textbook for High Schools) (Naha: Toyo Kikaku, 1997), p. 203.

⑥ Matthew Allen, *Identity and Resistance in Okinawa* (New York: Rowman & Littlefield publisher, 2002), p. 33.

⑦ Michael S. Molasky, *The American Occupation of Japan and Okinawa* (*Literature and Memory*) (London: Routledge, 1999), pp. 15－17; Matthew Allen, *Identity and Resistance in Okinawa* (New York: Rowman & Littlefield publisher, 2002), pp. 38－45.

⑧ Masahide Ota, *Okinawa: Senso to Heiwa* (*Okinawa, War and Peace*) (Tokyo: Asahi Shimbunsha, 1996), p. 92.

死家人、邻居，最后自杀。然而，幸存的日本兵却在村民们死后向美国军队投降。[1] 美军于1945年4月登陆冲绳主岛后，琉球居民们便躲进家族坟墓、应急洞穴中避难。5月后，绝望的日本官兵们也躲进了这些坟墓与洞穴。日本官兵们不但优先享用仅有的食物，还通常将居民们赶到狭小的、最不安全的区域，甚至为了防止他们所躲藏的区域被发现，而用刺刀杀死哭叫的小孩，或是强迫父母们将三岁以下的小孩掐死。[2] 此外，日本兵还强征琉球妇女作"慰安妇"（Comfort Women）。当时的群岛军部共设有130处"安慰点"（Comfort Station）。[3] 在"冲绳战役"中，琉球非战斗平民的死亡人数比美军与日本军队合起来的死亡人数还多，[4] 平民死亡率是军队战士死亡率的两倍。[5] 可见，日本在殖民统治期间，亦是以严重差异于日本本土的待遇来对待琉球的，这些事实均可以视作琉球在二战后的安排中被继续区别对待的由来。

二 二战后琉球的"分离性处理"与其法律地位未定

（一）琉球受"分离性处理"的基本情况

战败后的日本随即被盟军占领，并接受盟军最高司令官总司令部（GHQ/SCAP，以下简称"最高司令部"）的管理。实施占领的盟国以美国为首，美国远东军司令麦克阿瑟（Douglas MacArthur）兼任盟军最高司令部总司令官。1945年8月16日，联合战争计划委员会（JWPC）曾经通过385/1号文件将日本的占领区域分为两部分，其中北海道（Kokkaido）和

---

① 参见 Masahide Ota, *Okinawa: Senso to Heiwa* (*Okinawa, War and Peace*)（Tokyo: Asahi Shimbunsha, 1996），pp. 39 - 96。

② Miyume Tanji, *Myth, Protest and Struggle in Okinawa*（Abingdon: Routledge, 2006），p. 39.

③ Takazato Suzuyo, *Beigun Hanzai to Okinawa Josei*（*US Crimes and Okinawan Women*）（Tokyo: Shuukan Kinyobi, 1998），pp. 9 - 26.

④ Edward Robert D. Eldridge, *The Origins of the Bilateral Okinawa Problem: Okinawa in Postwar U. S. - Japan Relations, 1945 - 1952*（New York: Garland publishing Inc., 2001），p. xviii.

⑤ Matthew Allen, *Identity and Resistance in Okinawa*（New York: Rowman & Littlefield publisher, 2002），p. 33. 作者在该书中用的冲绳（Okinawa）一词，笔者为了行文方便将冲绳改写为琉球，下文不再标注。

日本东北部（Tohoku）交由苏联领导的军队。[①] 然而，随着冷战的爆发，以及防止重蹈德国占领区各自为政的局面，该决议又经后面的 SWNCC70/5 号文件取消。于是，在占领队伍中，除了英国派出不多的部队参加了在本州西部区域的军事占领外，[②] 中国和苏联都没有派兵参加，对日占领的实施主要由美国包揽。[③] 1947 年 6 月 19 日的《远东委员会对投降后日本之基本政策的决议》第二部分专门规定了盟军的权力："对日本进行的军事占领"；"该占领具有代表参战各国之行动的性质，由美国指派之最高统帅指挥，各国部队参加占领"；"天皇及日本政府之权力，将隶属于最高统帅。最高统帅具有实施投降条款、执行占领及管制日本各种政策之一切权力"。[④]

按照战前制定的日本投降后基本政策，最高司令部对日本本土实行间接统治，即保留天皇制度体系，对当地民众通过日本政府实施间接控制（indirect control）。[⑤] 然而，与"间接统治"完全不同，琉球一开始就被盟军实施了"分离性处理"：天皇制在琉球并不适用，而是由美军代表盟国直接进行军事统治。天皇是日本政权的象征，所以，对于琉球的单独安排也就意味着在法律意义上，日本的政权所及领土已经不再适用于琉球，琉球在战后即成为"从敌国剥离的领土"。1946 年 1 月 29 日发布的《关于若干外廓地区在政治上行政上自日本分离之备忘录》（SCAPIN 677）对日本领土进行了明确定义后指令："即日起日本帝国政府对日本以外的区域或此区域内的任何政府官员、职员或个人，停止实施一切政府的、行政的权

---

① Ultimate occupation of Japan and Japanese Territory（Aug, 16 1945），JWPC 385/1，Record Group 218，National Archives II，College Park，Maryland. 同时参见 Makoto Iokibe（ed.），*The Occupation of Japan*，*Part I*：*US Planning Documents*，*1942 – 1945*（Bethesda：Congressional Information Service，1987），p. 276。

② 英国派出的军队主要是澳大利亚人。参见 Theodore Cohen，*Remaking Japan*：*The American Occupation as New Deal*（New York：Free Press，1987），pp. 58 – 61。

③ 1945 年 12 月底中苏英美四个盟国在东京也建立过一个"盟国理事会"（Allied Council），同时在华盛顿建立了一个由中国、苏联、英国、美国、法国、荷兰、澳大利亚、加拿大、新西兰、印度和菲律宾 11 个战胜国组成的"远东委员会"，但是这些机构都没有发挥作用，麦克阿瑟对它们也不认同。Kenneth G. Henshall，*A history of Japan*：*From Stone Age to Superpower*（London：Palgrave Macmillan，3rd ed.，2012），p. 143.

④ 关捷等主编《中日关系全书》，辽海出版社，1998，第 1507—1511 页。

⑤ "US Initial Post-Surrender Policy for Japan"，SWNCC 150/4，Record Group 218，National Archives II，College Park，Maryland.

力或实施这些权力的企图”，[①] 即琉球被视作日本以外区域（area outside of Japan）。与最高司令部间接管理下的日本不同，琉球被留在了美军的“直接统治”之下。[②]

按照战后计划委员会（PWC）的计划，所谓间接管理便是保留日本的天皇及相应的官僚机构，只是国会、参议会成员、部长与副部长等原高级官员的职务暂停。[③] 同时，按照《波茨坦公告》第10条、第11条：“日本政府应当将阻止日本人民民主的复兴与增强的所有障碍予以消除”，“日本最后参加国际贸易关系当可准许”。对于间接管理的地区，日本有责任进行民主改革和重建和平经济。但是，此时的琉球已经不被视作日本领土，所以，这些对日本政府民主管理与经济发展方面的期待和安排都不适用于琉球。[④]

而美军的“直接统治”则意味着，与盟军占领的日本本土相比，琉球的统治更没有组织性和管理性。[⑤] 占领琉球的第一年，统治琉球的机构经常在美国的陆军与海军之间变动，直到1946年7月才确定下来，而作为专门统治琉球的军政府——琉球群岛美国民政府（USCAR）直到1950年才正式设立。[⑥] 占领之初，美军将居民赶入收容所，以暴力强制手段接收了广大的军用地并无偿使用。[⑦] 1948年5月琉球银行成立，股份的51%被美军掌控，直到琉球“复归”日本时，美军拥有的股份才向居民开放，改组

---

① “Memorandum for Imperial Japanese Government on Governmental and Administrative Separation of Certain Outlying Areas from Japan”, in Fukunagea Fumio (ed.), *GHQ Minseikyoku Shiryo*, Vol. 2, *Occupation Reforms: Election Law and Political Funds Law* (Tokyo: Maruzen, 1997), pp. 141 - 142.

② 冲绳与总务部知事公室基地对策室：《冲绳——美军基地》，http://pief.okinawa.jp/kiti-taisaku/D-mokuji.html，最后访问日期：2011年8月23日。

③ Makoto Iokibe (ed.), Translated and Annotated by Robert D. Eldridge, *The Diplomatic History of Postwar Japan* (London: Routledge, 2011), p. 20.

④ Makoto Iokibe (ed.), Translated and Annotated by Robert D. Eldridge, *The Diplomatic History of Postwar Japan* (London: Routledge, 2011), pp. 19 - 22.

⑤ Michael S. Molasky, *The American Occupation of Japan and Okinawa* (*Literature and Memory*) (London: Routledge, 1999), p. 15.

⑥ Makoto Iokibe (ed.), Translated and Annotated by Robert D. Eldridge, *The Diplomatic History of Postwar Japan* (London: Routledge, 2011), p. 20.

⑦ “到了1952年才公布了军用地租借契约的方法、租借时间、使用费用等第91号法令。1953年又进一步施行了第109号法令——《土地征用令》。”也就是说，在1951年的《旧金山和约》生效之前，1945—1952年美国军事统治期间，琉球的土地是被美国军队无偿使用的。参见〔日〕新崎盛晖《冲绳现代史》，胡冬竹译，三联书店，2010，第83—84页。

为普通银行。[①] 美军曾在奄美、琉球、宫古、八重山四个群岛上分别设置了居民自己的群岛政府，但1952年4月撤销了当地政府，在美国民政府下设置了统一的琉球政府。琉球政府虽然采取了三权分立的形式，但其权限极为有限。琉球政府行政主席由美民政副长官（后来的高等专务官）任命，不得不直接或间接听从美军的指示。琉球立法院虽然由居民直接选出的议员构成，但实际上选举会受到美军的干涉，而且立法活动被限制在和布告、命令（实质上就是美军的命令）不相抵触的范围之内。[②]

“琉球居民”的法律地位又如何呢？琉球居民进出琉球列岛必须申请美国民政府发行的渡航证明书，而美国民政府经常不作任何说明就停止护照的发放。护照发放的停止是美国民政府控制政治活动、言论自由最有效的手段。甚至于发生过东京大学的学生回琉球过完暑假，无法取得护照（签证）只能退学的事。另外，1945—1958年琉球通用的货币是一种被称为B币的军票。[③] 1950年，美国民政府还公布了琉球独立国国旗，只是没有普及使用。[④] 而在美国军政府统治期间，琉球的船舶旗也是独立的。[⑤] 1947年，麦克阿瑟建议对日本的占领可以结束了，因为最高司令部的目标已经大部分实现，但是琉球必须继续留在美军控制之下，因为琉球人不是日本人。[⑥]

（二）琉球受“分离性处理”的法律性质

“分离性处理”的合法性取决于它是否具有明确的国际法依据，事实

---

① 参见〔日〕新崎盛晖《冲绳现代史》，胡冬竹译，三联书店，2010，第28页。

② 〔日〕新崎盛辉：《现代日本与冲绳》，《开放时代》2009年第3期，第32页。

③ 〔日〕新崎盛辉：《现代日本与冲绳》，《开放时代》2009年第3期，第33页。

④ 沖縄民政府の旗。将来の沖縄中央政府の旗となる計画もあったが後に放棄され使われなくなった，Flag of the Independent State of Okinawa. The proposed flag representing Okinawa, announced on January 1950. Never widely used. http://en. wikipedia. org/wiki/United_States_Civil_Administration_of_the_Ryukyu_Islands，最后访问日期：2012年7月9日。

⑤ Flag of US Occupied Ryukyu Islands | Source = self-made, Category: Flags of Japan, civil ensign of Ryukyu, http://www. worldstatesmen. org/Japan. htm | Date = May 21, 2007 | Author = Scott Alter (User: Scottalter)}} {{PD-self}}，最后访问日期：2012年9月12日。

⑥ “Ashida Declares Japan Decrees no Territory, Denies Press Reports”, *Pacific Stars and Strips*, July 3, 1947. 同时参见“MacArthur Foresees Japan Peace Within 18 months”, *Pacific Stars and Stripes*, June 29, 1947; Michael S. Molasky, *The American Occupation of Japan and Okinawa* (*Literature and Memory*) (London: Routledge, 1999), p. 20. 日本也是从这一年开始积极展开与美国的媾和协商，但直到1951年才正式达成和平条约。

上，盟军占领文件中所提及的权力来源正是其法律依据的表述。1945 年 11 月，《为占领和控制投降后之日本对盟军最高司令官基本指令》第 2 条规定："你（即盟军总司令，笔者注）在日本所拥有的权力与权威的基础来自美国总统所签署的《盟军司令委任令》、《日本投降书》、《日本天皇的执行令》……而这些文件又都建立在 1945 年 7 月 26 日的《波茨坦公告》等文件的基础上。"① 指令是由美国国家陆海军协调委员会（SWNCC）和参谋长联席会议（JCS）向时任盟军最高司令官的麦克阿瑟下达的，因为麦的身份具有双重性，他同时也是美国远东军总司令，所以对他的指令中同时出现了国际法与国内法文件。其中只有《日本投降书》、《波茨坦公告》与《开罗宣言》属于国际法渊源。

1.《日本投降书》

日本的投降文件实际上包含一系列文书，包括：日本天皇 1945 年 8 月 15 日发布的停战投降诏书，同日日本政府致中美英苏政府的投降电文，以及在各降区日本向受降将领呈递的投降书等。1945 年 9 月 2 日，各作战盟国及日本代表在停泊于东京湾的美国战舰密苏里号上举行正式的受降仪式，作为战败国的日本的签字代表有新任外相重光葵和陆军参谋长梅津美治郎，而作为战胜国的中国、美国、英国、苏联、澳大利亚、法国、新西兰、荷兰等国代表都在投降书上签字。所以，我们通常所说的《日本投降书》主要是指这一份正式签署的文件。鉴于这一份文件的多边性、公示性和代表之权威性，它毫无疑问具有国际条约的性质，产生条约国际法的效力。

一个条约在法律上成立，因而发生拘束各该当事国的法律效果，该条约的规定即成为各当事国的法律，各当事国必须予以善意履行。② 日本在其正式签署的投降书中明确承诺接受中、美、英发布的《波茨坦公告》（苏联后来加入）的条款。因此，《波茨坦公告》条款被明纳入了投降书之中，成为投降书内容的一部分。日本在投降书中同时承诺，"日本所支配

① "Basic Initial Post-Surrender Directive to Supreme Commander for the Allied Powers for the Occupation and Control of Japan", November 1, 1945. GHQ/SCAP Records, Top Secret Records of Various Sections. Administrative Division Box No. GS - 1 (11) "1) Relaxation of Purge Restrictions, 2) De-Purging of Japanese Ex-Officers" <Sheet No. TS00304 - 00306>, RG331, National Archives & Records Administration.

② 李浩培：《条约法概论》，法律出版社，1987，第 205 页。

下的一切军队，悉对（中、美、英、苏）盟国无条件投降”，并且“服从盟国最高司令官及其指示，对日本国政府之各机关所课之一切要求，应予以应诺”等，这便是日本无条件投降的确认。据此，日本有义务全面履行投降书中的承诺，而各盟国亦享有投降书上约定的各项权利。

当然，除了以上多边条约的约束外，在中日两国之间，日本还有义务遵守其单方面向中国递交的投降书或正式通电电文之内容，因为在实在国际法上，国家的单方行为也是国际义务的来源，国家的正式声明、通告都是一种单方行为。对此，国际法委员会工作报告明确予以确认，① 国际法院在“法国核试验案”中也明确予以认可。② 所以，以下正式通告亦可以说是日本国际义务的来源，譬如，日本政府在 1945 年 8 月 15 日致中、美、英、苏政府的投降电文如下：

> 一、关于日本接受波茨坦宣言之各项规定事，天皇陛下业已颁布赦令。
>
> 二、天皇陛下准备授权，并保证日本政府及日本大本营，签订实行波茨坦宣言各项规定之必需条件。
>
> 天皇陛下并准备对日本所有海陆空军当局，及在各地受其管辖之所有部队，停止积极行动，交出军械，并颁发盟军统帅部所需执行上述条件之各项命令。③

日本发布的投降电文与其正式签署的投降书的内容一致，反复强调了对《波茨坦公告》条款的认可与遵行。从国家单方行为的角度，日本应该履行自身的承诺。

---

① 2006 年国际法委员会工作报告认为，国家正式的单边行为或声明会产生国际法上的义务。UN ILC Unilateral Acts of States：Report of the Working Group：Conclusions of the International Law Commission Relating to Unilateral Acts of States（20 July 2006），*ILC Conclusions*，p. 3. 另参见 UN ILC Guiding Principles Applicable to Unilateral Declarations of States Capable of Creating Legal Obligations（1 May – 9 June and 3 July – 11 August 2006），*ILC Guiding Principles*，p. 368。

② *Nuclear Tests Case*（*Australia v. France*），ICJ Reports，1974，para. 43.

③ 中国第二历史档案馆编《第二次世界大战中国战区受降纪实——国民政府国防部史政局及战史编纂委员会档案》，中共党史资料出版社，1989，第 57 页。

2.《波茨坦公告》和《开罗宣言》

《开罗宣言》是中、美、英等二战主要盟国于1943年在开罗召开会议后所发表的宣言（苏联为之后声明加入的盟国)。《波茨坦公告》最初由中、美、英三国在1945年7月26日于波茨坦召开会议后所发表（苏联在之后声明加入)。关于《波茨坦公告》和《开罗宣言》是否为条约的问题存在争论，一些学者认为，《波茨坦公告》与《开罗宣言》没有经历签署、批准等正式的条约缔结程序，因而在国际法上不具有法律效力。[①] 然而，这样的说法明显不成立。

首先，按照习惯国际法，国际法对于条约的形式并没有实质的要求，根据缔约方自己的意见，只要取得一致同意，一项条约甚至可以见于换文或会议记录中。[②]《维也纳条约法公约》虽然作了“书面协定”的定义，但它在第3条又规定，这一限制并不影响“非书面协定”的法律效力。[③] 同时，对于条约是否需要批准等程序性问题，《维也纳条约法公约》在第14条、第15条、第16条都规定了要以缔约国的同意为准。也即，只要缔约国认为不需要经过批准等程序，或者没有作特别要求，都不影响符合缔约国意志的条约生效。《开罗宣言》与《波茨坦公告》是作战盟国真实意思的表示，各国在战争时期及战争胜利以后都一再地声明认可和遵行，其作为条约的有效性是有充分理由的。

其次，《日本投降书》中明确约定了“遵从《波茨坦公告》条款”，而《波茨坦公告》又明确规定“《开罗宣言》必须实施”，所以，这两个条约实际上又已经被纳入投降书的内容，成为投降书的组成部分。换个角度说，假如《波茨坦公告》条款不加以遵从和实施，投降书的签订还有什么意义呢，《波茨坦公告》不但是投降书的内容，而且是核心内容，代表了各国联合作战的根本目的。

再者，国家首脑是国家权威的最高代表和象征，《开罗宣言》与《波

① 譬如，林田富《再论钓鱼岛列屿主权争议》，五南图书出版股份有限公司，2002，第51页，及其引注所称其他学者亦有类似观点。

② Case Concerning Martime Delimitation and Territorial Questions (Qatar V. Bahrain), ICJ Reports, 1994, pp. 120 - 122.

③《维也纳条约法公约》第3条（甲）：本公约不适用于国家与其他国际法主体间所缔结之国际协定或此种其他国际法主体间之国际协定或非书面国际协定，此一事实并不影响：此类协定之法律效力。

茨坦公告》作为中国、美国和英国等国家的首脑公开的、权威的、集体的承诺，其内容本身产生了明确的国际法义务，是国际法的义务渊源。其效力依据就和前面提及的日本天皇的投降通告一样，国家有义务按照其发布的公告内容信守承诺。对此，《奥本海国际法》中亦将《波茨坦公告》作为一个典型的因签字而具有法律效力的国家单方声明的例证。[①]

综上，《开罗宣言》与《波茨坦公告》不但在条约国际法和国家单方行为上具有效力，在内容上亦得到《日本投降书》的确认和保证。同时，所谓“无条件”就是接受战胜国的一切条件。因而在条约解释上，即便存在不明朗或分歧，也必然应该作有利于战胜国而不是有利于侵略国的解释。对此，《维也纳条约法公约》第75条所规定的“侵略国问题”可以佐证，该条特别指出：“本公约之规定不妨碍因依照联合国宪章对侵略国之侵略行为所采取措施而可能引起之该国任何条约义务。”

（三）“分离性处理”与琉球法律地位未确定

1. 琉球不属于《波茨坦公告》中的“其他小岛”

如前所述，盟军占领日本和对琉球实施“分离性处理”，均以《开罗宣言》、《波茨坦公告》和《日本投降书》所形成的权利义务为基础，而这三个文件属于国际法的渊源，使琉球的“分离性处理”具备国际法上的合法性。接下来，受到这种“分离性处理”后的琉球的法律地位又如何呢？这实际上又涉及对《波茨坦公告》之领土条款的解释问题。之所以涉及条约解释，是因为按照《波茨坦公告》，“日本之主权必将限于本州、北海道、九州、四国及吾人所决定之其他小岛之内”，那么琉球是否在“吾人所决定之其他小岛”的范围内呢？

条约解释是国际法上很重要的一个问题。特别是由于条约规定所用的文字有时难免存在或多或少含糊暧昧的缺点，从而引起条约当事国的争论。[②]《维也纳条约法公约》第31条规定：“条约应依其用语按其上下文并参照条约之目的及宗旨所具有之通常意义，善意解释之”，此解释通则亦

---

① Robert Jennings, Arthur Watts, (ed.), *Oppenheim's International Law* (Burnt Mill: Longman, 1992), p. 873.

② 李浩培：《条约法概论》，法律出版社，1987，第405页。

为国际法委员会和国际法院所认可，具有习惯国际法的性质。[①] 首先，琉球群岛包含大小岛屿几百个，其中最大的岛屿冲绳有1200余平方公里，人口100多万，是除日本的本州、北海道、九州、四国以外的第五大岛屿。如果从字面意义上看，琉球作为一个全长1000多公里的岛群，难以被视作“小岛”。事实上，以《波茨坦公告》的文字含义为基础，美国军方以及政府方面对“其他小岛”问题有过明确的讨论与解释。

陆海军协调委员会（SWNCC）成立于1944年11月，下辖一个远东支部（Subcommittee on the Far East，简称SFE或是SWNCCFE），以专门处理领土调整（Territorial Adjustment）问题，具体以“处分从日本剥离出来的领土（Disposition of Areas to be Removed from Japan's Sovereignty）”为议题。[②] 按照该委员会及其报告讨论的会议纪要，对于《波茨坦公告》所述之“吾人所决定之其他小岛”中的小岛是否含琉球群岛，最早在美国军部与国务院之间发生了争议。对此，早在1944年12月20日召开的一次会议上，担任远东支部负责人的布莱克斯利（Blackslees）提出，琉球或冲绳是包含在“波茨坦公告中所说‘吾人所决定之其他小岛’中的‘小岛’之内的”。[③] 然而，布莱克斯利的说法未被文件确认，而且很快被二战胜利（1945年）后的文件所否定。

首先，在1945年9月6日，驻日盟军最高司令部颁布“投降后美国初期对日政策”，对日本的领土专门规定为，“日本主权将被限定在‘本州、北海道、九州、四国’，以及按照《开罗宣言》等美国是或可能要成为缔约国的其他协定所规定的周边其他小岛之内”。[④] 虽没有具体规定“其他小岛”的范围，但明确说明以《开罗宣言》为依据。1945年10月25日，美国参谋长联席会议（JCS）在其570/40号文件中将琉球划为首要基地区域（primary base areas）时认为：“所有从日本分离出来的委托统治岛屿和太

---

① 李浩培：《条约法概论》，法律出版社，1987，第425—427页。

② Political-military Problems in the Pacific (Jan. 31, 1945), SWNCC 16, in Makoto Iokibe, (ed.), *The Occupation of Japan Part 2: U. S. And Allied Policy 1945 - 1952* (Bethesda: Congressional Information Service, 1989), microfiche 2 - A - 6.

③ Minutes of Inter-Divisional Area Committee on the Far East, Meeting No. 243 (Oct. 12, 1944), in Makoto Iokibe, (ed.), *Nichibei Senso to Sengo Nihon* (*The Japan-US War and Postwar Japan*) (Osaka: Shoseki, 1989). microfiche 2 - B - 130.

④ II Holborn, War and Peace Aims of the United Nations (1948), p. 135.

平洋中心岛屿，包括琉球和小笠原群岛，将放于美国专有的战略控制之下”，此规定暗示琉球属于“从日本分离出来的领土”。[①] 1945 年 11 月 1 日，盟军最高司令部颁布《为占领和控制投降后之日本对盟军最高司令官基本指令》，其第 1 条（b）款再次规定，“本指令中所述的日本，其定义包含：4 个主岛：北海道（旧称虾夷）、本州、九州、四国，以及邻近的包括对马岛在内的 1000 个附属小岛屿”。[②] 仍然只是暗示未提到的其他岛屿可能从日本分离，而没有对琉球是否属于“其他小岛”进行专门说明。但是，到了 1946 年 1 月 29 日，驻日盟军最高司令部发布《关于若干外廓地区在政治上行政上自日本分离之备忘录》，其中对日本的定义是：日本由四个本岛（北海道、本州、九州、四国）和约 1000 个较小的邻接岛屿所组成，包括对马岛及北纬 30 度以北的琉球（南西）岛屿。[③] 至此，日本领土与琉球以北纬 30 度为界得到清楚划分，即以北的琉球群岛为日本，以南的琉球群岛则不再属于日本（或者说已经从日本分离），此时，北纬 30 度被视作日本的“一条实际边界线”（a real boundary）。[④]

琉球并不包含在“吾人所决定之其他小岛”之内，这一观点在 1947 年美国国务院的 PPS/28 号文件（凯南报告）中进一步得到认可。该文件规定：

---

① All Japanese Mandate Islands and Central Pacific Islands detached from Japan, including the Bonins and Ryukyus, will be brought under exclusive United States strategic control, JCS 570/40, Section 9, CCS 360 (12 – 9 – 42), JCS 1942 – 1945, RG 218, National Archives & Records Administration.

② November 1, 1945. GHQ/SCAP Records, Top Secret Records of Various Sections. Administrative Division Box No. GS – 1 (11) “1) Relaxation of Purge Restrictions, 2) De-Purging of Japanese Ex-Officers” <Sheet No. TS00304 – 00306>, RG331, U. S. National Archives & Records Administration. 同时参见 I Documents & State Papers, Department of State, No. 1, April 1948, pp. 32 – 33. For the texts of “the reply of the Secretary of State on 11 August 1945 to the Japanese communication of 10 August 1945, and the final Japanese communication on 14 August 1945”, 参见 XIII Bulletin, Department of State, No. 320, Aug. 12, 1945, pp. 205 – 206; No. 321, Aug. 19, 1945, pp. 255 – 256。

③ “Memorandum for the Imperial Japanese Government from General Headquarters, SCAP,” 29 January 1946, in SCAP, Political Reorientation of Japan, p. 477. 同时参见 Appendices, Political Reorientation of Japan, September 1945 to September 1948, Report of Government Section, Supreme Commander for the Allied Powers, p. 477。

④ Robert D. Eldridge, the Return of the Amami Islands: The Reversion Movement and US-Japan Relations, Levingt on Books, 2004, p. 5.

> 琉球群岛在今天的地位是完全不确定的（completely indefinite）。技术上作为日本的一部分，它的地位在《波茨坦公告》中没有确定，该公告将日本的领土限制在四个主岛以及“我们决定的其他小岛”之内。这个附带的“我们”，在这里明显指该文件的签字方美国、中国和英国。不管这一条款的最后解释是什么，我们有理由认为，冲绳以及琉球岛链的中部和南部不是属于这些“小岛”的范畴，对于最高司令部所提之南部30度边界线的接受，构成了一种默示的国际认可（tacit international recognition），即该线以南的琉球已经不再被视作日本的一部分（the Ryukyu south of that boundary were no longer to be considered a part of Japan）。①

美国军方和政府方面关于战后日本领土处置相关的文件中，不少都明确反映出琉球不应包含在日本领土的范围之中，譬如，美军政策参谋处（Policy Planning Staff）在1947年所作的PPS10/1地图就给琉球全境作了单独划界处理。② 值得一提的是，按“北纬30度”划界的理由是认为“北纬30度以北”的区域在历史上不属于琉球，而是日本九州岛鹿儿县的一部分。譬如，在1946年1月31日的JCS 570/50号文件中，南西诸岛也以北纬31度为界。后来，军部一名哈佛大学毕业的日本专家赖肖尔（Edwin O. Reischauer，后为美国驻日本大使）认为应该以北纬28度东经40度为界，该线以北属于日本本土（Mainland），以南才是琉球。③ 经过讨论，到了1946年3月，盟军最高司令部同意改为以北纬30度为界，并要求保持与1946年1月29日指令的一致性。这样，北纬30度到31度之间的鹿儿岛（Kagoshima）区域就被归入日本的本土。④ 基于同样的理由，后又将北纬30度线调整为29度线。为了区分方便，美国内部文件还以“北部琉

---

① Miyazato Seigen, *Amerika no Taigai Seisaku Kettei Katei*（*The Process of American Foreign Policy-Making*）（Tokyo：Sanichi Shobo，1981），p. 222.

② *Special Recommendation on Ultimate Disposition of the Ryukyus*（*Oct. 15，1947*），PPS/10/1（New York：Garland Publishing，1983），pp. 116－117.

③ Edwin O. Reischauer，*My Life Between Japan and America*（New York：Weatherhill，1986），p. 107.

④ “Memo from Government Section to Chief of Staff on Military Government of Ryukyu Islands（April 1946）”，Staff Study on Military Government of Ryukyu Island，March 27，1946，Fukunaga（ed.），*GHQ Minseikyoku Shiryo*，pp. 216－218.

球”（Northern Ryukyu）和“南部琉球”（Southern Ryukyu）概念来区分。[①] 这便是《旧金山和约》中的“北纬 29 度”界限之形成，其理由是认为“北部琉球”并不是传统意义上的琉球，而是日本鹿儿岛县的领土范围，“南部琉球”才是真正应该脱离日本的琉球。[②]

有必要指出，日本对于盟军发布的以上命令及解释是清楚的。日本曾在 1947 年试图说服盟军最高司令长官麦克阿瑟，但以失败告终。1947 年 3 月，日本为展开进一步的领土协商计划而制定了一份针对琉球的 29 页的报告，以试图澄清日本的领土边界，提出《波茨坦公告》中的“吾人所决定之其他小岛”过于模糊。报告名称为《邻近日本的小岛》（Minor Islands Adjacent to Japan Proper），主要目的在解释琉球以及其他南西诸岛，其中附加了五份地图，从各个历史阶段分别说明琉球与日本的地理、历史、政治与种族等方面的联系，突出强调了琉球人与日本人的平等与相似等因素，而弱化了琉球与中国的联系及当时琉球人作为“二等公民”的真实地位。[③] 这份报告相当于日本政府觊觎琉球主权的理论准备。

接着，1947 年 6 月 4 日，日本召开首次新闻发布会，希望尽早召开和平会议。次日，日本新任外长芦田（Ashida）趁机宣布“冲绳对于日本的经济并不是很重要，但从感情因素出发，国家期望归还（return）这些岛屿”。[④]

---

① “The Problem of Administering the Northern and Southern Ryukyu（Jan. 15 1946）”, in Committee Members for the Watkins Paper Publication（ed.）, *Papers of James T. Watkins IV: Historical Records of Postwar Okinawa: The Beginning of US Occupation Policy*（Ginowan: Ryokyurindo Shoten, Vol. 25, 1993）, p. 41.

② 1953 年，又是基于同样的理由，奄美大岛“返还”给了日本，被划入日本的鹿儿岛县。所以，现在日本的“冲绳县”不包括奄美大岛，只有冲绳诸岛及先岛群岛（含宫古和八重山）。目前，同样也有学者质疑奄美大岛返还的合法性，认为奄美大岛的地位应该由国际社会重新决定。限于篇幅，本文不展开讨论。

③ Minor Islands Adjacent to Japan Proper: Part II, Ryukyu and Other Nansei Islands, March 1947, Flash Number 1, Microfilm Reel Number B－0012, Beijawa ni Teishutsu Shiryo（Eibun）（Dai Ikkan）, Materials Submitted to the United States（English Copies）（First Roll）, Tainichi Kowa ni Kansuru Honpo no Junbi Taisaku Kankei（File on Preparatory Meawures by our Country Relating to the Peace Treaty）, DRO-MOFA, 0066－0083, Asakai gave this study to Archeson in early July 1947.

④ “Okinawa to Chishima no Ichibu Henkan no Kibo（Desire for the Return of Okinawa and a Part of the Kuriles）”, *Asahi Shimbun*, Saturday, June 7, 1947；同时参见 Tom Lambert, “Okinawa, Kuriles Asked by Japan”, Ashida Declares, *Pacific Stars and Stripes*, Friday, June 6, 1947, at B2。

此番言论遭到了麦克阿瑟的强烈反对，麦克阿瑟一再表态说“琉球人不是日本人”。[①] 并且，芦田的言论在一定程度上也激怒了其他各国。记录反映，当时不只美国，其他国家对于日本的领土言论也反应强烈，所以芦田事后承认自己“在领土问题上说得太多了”。[②] 此后日本吸取经验教训，在1947年9月13日举行的铃木与艾克尔伯格（Suzuki Eichelberger）讨论和平条约及安保问题的会议中，“铃木向艾克尔伯格提出的讨论前提是冲绳与小笠原是日本以外的领土。”[③]

2. 战时占领期间琉球地位未定

接下来，琉球作为“从敌国剥离的领土”脱离日本以后，其自身的主权地位又如何呢？一方面，美军“直接统治”但不拥有琉球的主权是基于其在《开罗宣言》中关于“领土不扩大”的承诺。同时，美军的这种直接统治在性质上属于战时占领，在国际法上，占领事实本身不能获得领土主权，不属于国际法上的领土取得方式。[④] 所以，琉球从此成为地位未确定的领土。

《奥本海国际法》认为，占领是作战的一个目的。如果交战国成功地占领了敌国领土的全部或者一部分，它就实现了战争的一个重要目的。这时，它不但可以将敌国领土的资源用于军事目的，而且可以暂时保持敌国领土作为自己军事胜利的保证，因而使敌人认识到有接受媾和条件的必

---

① “MarcArthur Foresees Japan Peace Within 18 Months”, *Pacific Stars and Strips*, June 29, 1947, at B4.

② “Probably talked too much about the territorial problem”, Hitoshi Ashida, edited by Shindo Eiichi ans Shimokobe Motoharu), Ashida Hitoshi Nikki (The Diary of Ashida Hitoshi). Tokoyo: Iwanami Shoten, 1986. vol. 2, 5. 同时参见 Ashida Declares Japan Desires No Territory, Denied Press Reports, *Pacific Stars and Stripes*, July 3, 1947, at B2。

③ Kumao Nishimura, Senryo Zenki no Tainichi Kowa Mondai-Muttsu no Dentatsu (The Problem of the Peace Treaty with Japan-Six Attempts at Communication), Fainansu (Finance), in Michael M. Yoshitsu, *Japan and the San Francisco Peace Treaty Settlement* (New York: Columbia University Press, 1983), p. 80.

④ 传统国际法认为，领土主权的获得有5种模式，即先占（或占领）、添附、时效、割让和征服。五种领土取得模式中，征服（conquest）在法律文献中已经不被认为是一种有效权利了。而有效占领（effective occupation）必须与前期的历史阶段联系起来，因为“无主地”已经被认为基本不再存在。除时效是具有争议的以外，在国际法上还产生了一些其他有争议的领土取得方式，如历史性权利巩固（Historical Consolidation of Title）、有效控制（Effectivités）、人民自决权等。

要。国际法关于作战的规则在占领问题上比任何其他部门都进步。[①] 占领者绝不能仅因占领领土的事实而获得对该领土的主权，它实际上对该地区暂时行使军事权力。国际法对于占领国不仅赋予权利，并且也课以义务。占领国在军事占领期间，还应该遵守关于战时占领的国际法规则，如关于战争法与人道法的海牙体系与日内瓦体系。[②] 同时，占领不能与侵略混为一谈。占领是对敌国领土的暂时占有，入侵则以保有该领土为目的。[③] 以美国为首的盟军对于琉球的“直接管理”只是暂时的军事占领，不能获得琉球的领土主权。

从国际法上说，对特定领土的处理尚不能确定是否为最终方案，或者在其最终地位的解决方案出来之前进行共同统治（condominium）的领土是地位未定的领土。[④] 琉球显然符合这样的状况。在 1945 年日本投降、琉球从“敌国剥离”以后，琉球的领土地位无论在理论上（依国际法律文件的规定），还是在实践中（盟军的占领），都处于一种待定的状态。就是说，琉球虽然已经从“敌国剥离”，但它的实际地位还未决定，盟军的军事占领只是一个暂时安排。

三 《旧金山和约》与琉球的法律地位未定

（一）对日媾和的政治与法律背景

琉球作为从敌国剥离的领土，尽管在日本投降后已从日本分离并被美军政府单独占领，但美军政府并不以获得主权为目的，因而琉球的领土归属及法律地位此时没有确定。同时，日本在二战结束后即被盟军占领并进入战时占领阶段，从法律上讲，日本与盟国的战争状态并没有结束。所

① 〔英〕劳特派特修订《奥本海国际法》（下卷第一分册），王铁崖、陈体强译，商务印书馆，1989，第 321 页。

② 调整作战手段、方法、行为关系，以及对平民、受难者和伤病者、战俘等进行保护的制度与规则，分别由在海牙与日内瓦签订的系列条约构成，故称为海牙体系与日内瓦体系。

③ 〔英〕劳特派特修订《奥本海国际法》（下卷第一分册），王铁崖、陈体强译，商务印书馆，1989，第 322 页。

④ *The Lighthouses Arbitration*, ILR 23 (1956), pp. 664 – 666, 668 – 669; Robert Jennings, Arthur Watts, (ed.), *Oppenheim's International Law* (Burnt Mill: Longman, 1992), pp. 566 – 567.

以，通过订立和平条约结束与日本的战争状态并对未决事项加以确认是一件必要的事情。

1945 年通过的《联合国宪章》倡导深刻吸取世界大战的教训，“欲免后世再遭今代人类两度身历惨不堪言之战祸”，然而，世界很快又陷入冷战和局部战争。1950 年 6 月朝鲜战争爆发后，琉球群岛中的冲绳迅速成为美军最重要的作战基地。同时，日本之于美国的战略价值也大大提升。美国在 1950 年后任命原共和党外交事务发言人杜勒斯（Dulles）为国务卿顾问，最后的对日和约草案就是由杜所起草。

1951 年 9 月 4—8 日，对日媾和会议在美国旧金山举行，故该会议通过的和约又简称为《旧金山和约》。旧金山会议是一个实现美国片面战略利益的媾和会议。美国当时的想法是：“美国总不能强迫和会中的任何国家在和约上签字，不过这个国家也不能阻止其他国家在条约上签字。显然，这些规定是针对苏联等少数主张对日采取更强硬政策的国家，以防止这些国家干扰对日媾和的进程。”① 所以，中国实施对日抗战长达 14 年之久，却被完全排除在了旧金山会议之外，并且参加会议的苏联、波兰、捷克斯洛伐克都未在和约上签字。印度、缅甸、南斯拉夫因反对美国的媾和政策也拒绝参加旧金山会议。最后，参会的 52 个国家里面只有 48 个国家签字，而中、苏、英、美 4 个主要作战盟国里面就有 2 个（中国与苏联）不是和约的签字国。②

“条约不及第三国”是一项基本的法理。对此，国际法学家安齐洛蒂（Anzilotti）亦说道：“很少有国际法原则是像它一样确定和得到普遍承认的”。③ 仲裁员胡伯（Huber）于 1928 年 4 月 4 日在“帕尔马斯岛案”的裁决中亦明确提到：“很明显，不论对于该条约的正确解释怎样，该条约不能解释为对独立的第三国的权利进行处分。”④ 就一个条约而言，第三国是指非该约当事国的国家。因此，一个国家如果并未参与条约的谈判和缔结，当然是第三国。即使参加了该约的谈判，如果该国并未签署该约，或

① 于群：《美国对日政策研究》，东北师范大学出版社，1996，第 55 页。

② U. S. Treaties and Other International Agreements, 3. 3 U. S. T. 1952, p. 3169.

③ 转引自李浩培《条约法概论》，法律出版社，1987，第 476 页。

④ Island of Palmas (or Miangas) (United States/Netherlands), Reports of International Arbitral Awards 1928, p. 15.

者签署而在需要作出批准、接受或核准的情况下并未作出，它仍然是第三国。[①] 按照这些国际法理论与实践，中国政府有充分的理由反对《旧金山和约》不利于中国的安排（譬如剥夺权利、设定义务），而有利于或无关于中国的条款，只要不侵害国际社会的整体利益，可以不简单地主张无效。当然，从争端的角度，有利还是不利只是个假设问题。为此，本文撇开和约的效力不谈，暂且立足于《旧金山和约》本身的条款，看看该和约对琉球地位的处理到底是什么。

（二）和约第3条规定琉球为"潜在的托管领土"

《旧金山和约》的内容涉及国家和领土地位、撤军、安全、对外关系、财产赔偿等各个方面，其第3条是和约中有关"琉球"地位的唯一条款，该条规定：

> 日本对于美国向联合国提出将北纬29度以南之南西诸岛（包括琉球群岛与大东岛）、孀妇岩岛以南之南方诸岛（包括小笠原群岛、西之鸟与硫黄列岛）及冲之鸟岛与南鸟岛置于联合国托管制度之下，而以美国为唯一管理当局之任何提议，将予同意。在提出此种建议，并对此种建议采取肯定措施以前，美国将有权对此等岛屿之领土及其居民，包括其领海，行使一切及任何行政、立法与司法权力。[②]

国内学界的已有研究中，一些学者翻译时对原文进行随意变动或缩

① 李浩培：《条约法概论》，法律出版社，1987，第474页。

② "Japan will concur in any proposal of the United States to the United Nations to place under its trusteeship system, with the United States as the sole administering authority, Nansei Shoto south of 29deg. north latitude (including the Ryukyu Islands and the Daito Islands), Nanpo Shoto south of Sofu Gan (including the Bonin Islands, Rosario Island and the Volcano Islands) and Parece Vela and Marcus Island. Pending the making of such a proposal and affirmative action thereon, the United States will have the right to exercise all and any powers of administration, legislation and jurisdiction over the territory and inhabitants of these islands, including their territorial waters", Treaty of Peace with Japan: Signed Sept. 8, 1951; proclaimed Apr. 28, 1952. Declaration by Japan, and exchange of notes signed Sept. 8, 1951. U. S. T 1955, 1952 vol. 3 Part 3, p. 3169.

减，造成了条文原意被曲解，法律概念被混淆的现象。[①] 在国际法上，对于条约的理解有分歧的，有必要加以解释。对于条约解释的规则，本文在前面解释《波茨坦公告》时也已经提及。我们来分析《旧金山和约》第3条的原文。从字面的通常意义来全面理解这句话，不难发现该条实际是个并列句，首末句的信息综合起来，对于琉球地位的安排是：置于联合国托管制度之下（美国为唯一管理当局），而提交托管前，由美国行使“施政权”。

怎么理解“联合国托管”？联合国托管制度是《联合国宪章》所制定的一套国际领土监督与管理机制，正式取得托管领土的地位还需要经过特定的程序，并接受联合国相应机构的监督。作为一套相对完善的体系，联合国托管具体分为普通托管和战略托管两种类型，[②] 战略托管下的领土又称为战略防区。普通托管领土必须经过联合国大会的核准（第85条）；如果是战略防区，需要经过安理会的核准（第83条）。即，根据《联合国宪章》，普通托管领土和战略防区是有明显区别的。战略托管作为一种战略防区，出于防卫和安全的战略上需要，使得有必要将联合国大会对于一般托管领土所行使的职权交由安理会来行使。[③] 并且，不管是普通托管还是战略托管，都应该专门签订托管协议，“由直接关系各国……予以议定”（第79条）。再次，托管领土应该接受联合国相应机构的监督。1945年6月26日，联合国专门成立了托管理事会（TC），负责对置于国际托管制度下的领土实行管理，行使联合国关于除指定为战略防区之外的托管领土的职能。所以，对于普通托管领土，管理国需要定期向托管理事会提交报告。托管理事会一般每年5—6月举行一次会议，审议管理国所提交的报

---

① 譬如，刘少东在其出版的著作中对该条的翻译如下：“日本将北纬29度以南的西南群岛（包括琉球群岛以及大东群岛）、南方群岛（包括小笠原群岛、西之岛以及火山列岛）以及冲鸟岛和南鸟岛置于作为唯一施政者的联合国的托管统治制度之下，日本完全同意美利坚合众国对联合国的提案。在该提案付诸实施及通过以前，联合国对包括领水域在内的群岛以及居民，具有行政、立法及司法上的一切权利及部分行使权”，这一译法和原文意思相差甚远。刘少东：《日美冲绳问题起源研究（1942—1952）》，世界知识出版社，2011，第200页。类似情况还出现在其他作者的论文中，笔者不一一列举。

② 或者也将普通托管称为非战略托管。

③ 〔英〕詹宁斯、瓦茨修订《奥本海国际法》，王铁崖等译，中国大百科全书出版社，1995，第191—192页。

告，并且会同管理国接受和审查托管地居民的请愿书，定期派出视察团视察托管地情况等。托管理事会以简单多数进行表决，但其决议须经联合国大会通过才能生效。而战略防区直接由安理会负责监督。因此，托管理事会、联合国大会与安理会是联合国制度下的托管领土的监督机关。

怎么理解“美国为唯一管理当局”呢？对此，宪章亦明文规定，对于托管领土的管理必须是一个或几个国家，或者是联合国本身。根据《联合国宪章》第 87 条，大会在原则上与托管理事会共同行使对托管领土行政管理的监督。尤其是，管理当局应该接受联合国的监督并提交年度报告。[①]所以，托管领土的管理当局是指基于宪章的规定与托管协议的约定，并由联合国大会或安理会核准，具体对托管领土行使管理（包括立法、行政与司法权）的一个或几个国家，或者联合国，或者其他国际组织。因此，“美国为唯一管理当局”意指：在琉球经大会或安理会核准被置于联合国托管制度之下后，仅由美国这一个国家作为具体的管理当局。但是，不管是一个国家，或是几个国家，或是由国际组织作为管理当局，都有义务向联合国的托管理事会，或大会，或安理会提交年度报告。

又怎么理解“在联合国托管的措施作出以前美国行使一切行政、立法与司法权”呢？行政、立法与司法权统称为“管理权”或“施政权”，不同于主权。在国际法上，主权与管理权是有区别的。根据《国际联盟盟约》第 22 条（委任统治）或者《联合国宪章》第 12 章（托管）的规定，国家分别按照委任统治协议或托管协议行使委任统治或管理托管领土时，无须获得相关领土的主权，也就是说，在这种情况下，主权与管理权是分离的。一国可以将其特定领土上的权利之运行赋予另一个国家，而保留其主权。领土的主权权利与管理权利之间的区别在于权利持有人是否能够处分所涉领土。[②] 因此，约文所述美国行使的“立法、行政与司法权”只是一种管理权，美国不能行使放弃、变更和转让领土等涉及处分琉球的权

---

① 联合国托管主要由托管理事会监督，另外安理会和联合国大会按各自的程序也分别有监督的职能。其中，联合国托管理事会的年度报告是固定的，每年都需要有。凡经过联合国程序合法托管的领土，其年度报告在联合国文件资料库有完整保存和记载。联合国网页 http://search.un.org/search? q = trusteeship + report，最后访问日期：2012 年 12 月 10 日。

② Marcelo G Kohen, Territory, Acquisition, *Max Planck Encyclopedia of Public International Law*, last updated March 2011, paras. 5 – 6.

利。同时，“在联合国托管的措施作出以前”是一个时间状语，用以限制美国拥有“管理权”的时间。

因此，综合《旧金山和约》的文本含义与《联合国宪章》的相关规定，可以归纳出48个签字国通过《旧金山和约》第3条之约定，对1952年后琉球的地位安排是：日本同意，琉球作为普通托管领土或者战略托管领土，经过联合国大会或者安理会批准并置于联合国托管理事会、大会以及安理会的监督之下后，由美国作为唯一管理当局。而在此托管程序开始及完成之前，琉球暂时由美国“施政”。所以，一旦琉球完成联合国托管的程序，则正式成为托管领土，而在此之间，则是由美国临时施政的“潜在托管领土”。对此，起草《旧金山和约》的杜勒斯在其发表的有关“剩余主权”的讲话中，亦同时指出，琉球为“作为第二次世界大战的结果而将‘从敌国割离的领土’（第77条）。毫无疑问，将来的托管协议将决定这些居民与日本相关的公民身份”。[①] 可见，所谓的“剩余主权”论并不能够悖于和约第3条关于联合国托管的要求。

（三）琉球至今未实现联合国托管，其地位仍未确定

1. 美国一直未将琉球提交联合国托管

《马普国际法大百科全书》在介绍联合国托管制度这一词条时，将《旧金山和约》第3条项下的琉球视为“从敌国分离的潜在的托管领土”，[②] 并指出这项义务没有得到履行（this commitment was not implemented）。[③] 按照前文对《旧金山和约》第3条的解释，该条赋予美国占领和管理冲绳的权利是带有限制条件的，即其出发点和归宿是将琉球提交联合国托管。然而，美国的实际做法是将它们排除在了联合国托管制度的安排之外。在1952—1972年美国施政的20余年里，没有进行任何将琉球置于联合国托管制度之下的行为。

---

① Record of Proceedings, September 4 - 8, 1951, Japan, San. Francisco, California, *1951 Department of State publication 4392*, pp. 73, 77 - 79, 84 - 86.

② Andriy Melnyk, United Nations Trusteeship System, *Max Planck Encyclopedia of Public International Law*, para. 12.

③ Andriy Melnyk, United Nations Trusteeship System, *Max Planck Encyclopedia of Public International Law*, para. 12.

这里需要澄清一个事实，我国有些学者混淆了一份联合国文件，他们误以为1947年安理会关于核准托管太平洋岛屿的决议就是对琉球托管的核准，从而认为联合国从此赋予了美国在琉球的托管权。[①] 事实上，1947年7月交由美国托管的太平洋岛屿托管地是联合国唯一战略托管地，包括马里亚纳（Mariana）、帕劳（Palau）、加罗林（Caroline）和马绍尔（Marshall）四个政治实体。[②] 虽然都位于太平洋海域，美国是唯一管理国，容易让人误以为上述岛屿包括琉球在内，但是实际上与琉球无关。[③] 关于这个事实，《奥本海国际法》中早就有记载，该书中提到“这里的委任统治地实际上是指日本接手的原属德国领有的南洋诸岛。琉球并不是日本的委任统治地，仍然成了太平洋岛屿托管领土的例外性处理”。[④]

《旧金山和约》第3条项下的“琉球与大东群岛区域”与原德属的“太平洋岛屿区域”本来都应该正式成为联合国托管的区域。然而，事实情况是，马里亚纳和帕劳等“太平洋岛屿区域”正式通过联合国安理会决议成为《联合国宪章》第82条、第83条规定下的战略托管地（美国作为唯一管理当局管治），并且在联合国安理会的监督下，这些岛屿最终通过民族自决权实现完全自治、自由联合或独立。[⑤]

---

① 譬如，张毅在其文章中称：“故此，1947年4月，联合国通过《关于前日本委任统治岛屿的协定》，琉球群岛随同钓鱼岛列屿等岛屿列为托管地，划归美国管理。”张毅：《琉球群岛法律地位的国际法分析——兼论东海划界问题的新思维》，《北京科技大学学报》（社会科学版）2010年第3期。类似错误还出现在其他作者的论文中，笔者不一一列出。

② 《1995—1996世界知识年鉴》，世界知识出版社，第18页。此内容还可以参见联合国托管理事会官方主页：http://www.un.org/zh/mainbodies/trusteeship，最后访问日期：2012年6月8日。

③ 参见Carnegie Endowment for International Peace Division of Intercourse and Education Publication and Editorial Offices, *International Conciliation-Documents Collection 1952*, pp. 433-434。

④ 参见〔英〕詹宁斯、瓦茨修订《奥本海国际法》，王铁崖等译，中国大百科全书出版社，1995，第［428］目注释。

⑤ 1990年12月22日，联合国安理会通过第683号决议［UNSC Resolution 683（1990）of 22 December 1990］，终止了该托管区域三块领土的托管协议：密克罗尼西亚、马绍尔群岛和北马里亚纳群岛。其中，密克罗尼西亚成为联邦；马绍尔群岛成为共和国，实现了与美国自由联合的完全自治；北马里亚纳群岛也作为一个充分自治的联邦与美国实现政治联合。1994年11月10日，联合国安理会通过第956号决议［UNSC by Resolution 956（1994）of 10 November 1994］，结束了帕劳的战略托管地位，帕劳亦成为一个独立的国家，与美国实行自由联合。

而在“琉球区域”，美国持续的单边“施政”行为使“联合国托管”之约定形同虚设，带有以谋取单方利益为目的，恶意地歪曲或局部履行的性质。在国际法上，善意是缔约国履行条约的首要标准。善意与恶意相对，恶意履行就是不正当地歪曲地履行，善意履行就是公正地、适当地、诚实地履行。善意履行不以获取单方面的利益为目的，更不以牺牲甚至榨取缔约他方的利益为目的。善意履行还必须以善意解释条约作为前提，而恶意的解释必然导致非善意履行的结果。[①] 对此，《联合国宪章》在序言中申明“尊重由条约与国际法其他渊源而起之义务，久而弗懈”。宪章第2条第2项又规定，“各会员国应一秉善意，履行其依宪章所担负之义务，以保证全体会员国由加入本组织而发生之权益”。《维也纳条约法公约》第26条更是规定，“凡有效之条约对其各当事国有拘束力，必须由各该国善意履行”。古典国际法学家真提利斯曾举出一个因恶意解释条约而导致非善意履行的著名实例：罗马皇帝瓦勒里安在许诺向其敌国安提阿归还所有船舶的半数后，竟将其许诺歪曲解释为归还每一船舶剖成两半后的一半。[②]

在现代国际法规则确立之前，一国武装力量在另一国的存在被认为要么是战争期间的军事占领，要么是殖民主义的统治。[③] 1972年之前在琉球成立的抗议政党曾称美国在琉球实施的是“殖民地政策”。[④] 1950年12月4日，中华人民共和国外交部部长周恩来发表《关于对日和约问题的声明》，较早地对美国在对日媾和中的动机提出质疑：“……美国政府此种野心，纯为假借联合国名义，实行对琉球群岛和小笠原群岛的长期占领，在远东建立侵略的军事基地。”[⑤] 从《旧金山和约》的后续发展来看，美国确实存在假借联合国托管之名，而行单边占领之实的情况。

2. 非法的《琉球与大东群岛协定》亦不涉及琉球的主权地位变更

1971年6月17日，美国与日本签订《日本和美国关于琉球群岛与大

---

① 万鄂湘、石磊等：《国际条约法》，武汉大学出版社，1998，第167页。

② 〔意〕真提利斯：《论战争法三卷》，转引自李浩培《条约法概论》，法律出版社，1987，第329页。

③ John Woodliffe, *The Peacetime Use of Foreign Military Installations under Modern International Law* (Springer: Martinus Nijhoff Publishers, 1992), p. 15.

④ 〔日〕新崎盛晖：《冲绳现代史》，胡冬竹译，三联书店，2010，第86页。

⑤ 田恒主编《战后中日关系文献集》，中国社会科学出版社，1996，第90页。

东群岛的协定》（简称为《琉球与大东群岛协定》）。[①] 依据该协定，美国擅自将琉球（并将中国的钓鱼岛列屿非法地纳入其中）交由日本“管理”。根据《琉球与大东群岛协定》第1条：“对于以下第2段所定义的琉球与大东群岛，美国让渡其在1951年9月8日于旧金山签订的对日和约第3条项下的所有权利与利益给日本，自本条约生效之日起，由日本承担全部的权限与责任，以实施对所涉岛屿领土及其居民的一切以及任何行政、立法及司法权。”[②]

首先，从内容上看，《琉球与大东群岛协定》只是一种“施政权”（行政、立法与司法权）的“放弃与让渡”，而不涉及主权地位的变化。这一点与美国政府在《琉球与大东群岛协定》受到中国强烈反对后的表态相一致。1971年10月，美国政府表示：“把原从日本取得的对这些岛屿的施政权归还给日本，毫不损害有关主权的主张。美国既不能给日本增加在他们将这些岛屿施政权移交给我们之前所拥有的法律权利，也不能因为归还给日本施政权而削弱其他要求者的权利。……对此等岛屿的任何争议的要求均为当事者所应彼此解决的事项。”[③]

其次，从性质上看，该协定明确提到了“和约第3条项下的所有权利与利益让渡给”日本的说法，涉及将和约项下的“管理国”予以变更的情况，是一种对和约权利义务的处分，构成对《旧金山和约》第3条的修订或变更。然而，对于由48个国家签字的多边和平条约，又如何可以由美国和日本这两个国家私自处分呢？在国际法上，条约的修订是指条约当事国对已生效的条约在其有效期内增加、删除或变更其某些条款规定的行为。[④]

---

① 《琉球与大东群岛协定》签订后，美日政府及传媒往往将该协定简称为“冲绳返还协定”（Okinawa Reversion Treaty）。然而，除了签订该条约的美日双方领导人在其个人发言、新闻发布会或是媒体报道中用过“Reversion of Okinawa”这样的字眼外，《琉球与大东群岛协定》的正文中并无返还或复归（reversion）的任何字眼，所涉领土的名称也未直接使用冲绳（Okinawa）而是用的琉球（Ryukyu）。鉴于“冲绳返还协定”在名称上就容易让人误以为涉及“冲绳主权返还”的问题，故本文不采用此简称。

② Agreement Between Japan and the United States of America Concerning the Ryukyu Islands and the Daito Islands, 23.1 U.S.T. 1972, June 17, 1971, p. 447 – 574.

③ United States Senate, Committee on Foreign Relations, *Okinawa Reversion Treaty. Hearings*, 92*nd Congress*, *first session*, Ex. J. 92 – 1, October 27 – 29, 1971 (Washington: U.S. GPO, 1971), p. 11.

④ 万鄂湘、石磊等：《国际条约法》，武汉大学出版社，1998，第268页。

传统国际法遵从绝对主权原则，如果对已经生效的条约进行修订，必须经该条约的全体当事国的共同同意。譬如，1871 年《伦敦宣言》中提出："国际法的一个主要原则是，只有通过友好协商，经过各缔约国的同意，一个国家才能解除一个条约义务或改变其约款。"① 随着国际法的发展，现在的习惯法规则虽没有要求全体当事国同意那么严格，但必须遵守按照《维也纳条约法公约》所体现的"修正条约之通则"："条约得以当事国之协议修正之，除条约可能另有规定外，此种协议适用第二编（即条约的缔结与生效——笔者注）所订之规则"（第 39 条），"在全体当事国间修正多边条约之任何提议必须通知全体缔约国，各该缔约国均应有权参加"（第 40 条）。在《旧金山和约》中，并没有专门约定条约的修正问题，但其第 7 章第 23 条明确要求需要包括美国在内的多数国批准才能生效。因此，参照条约法公约所规定的条约修正通则，《旧金山和约》之条款的修正应该适用其缔结与生效的要求——多数国同意并批准，并通知全体缔约国参加协商。当然，条约法公约也未排除多边条约在若干当事国间进行某些修正，但有着严格的要求（第 41 条）：

> 多边条约两个以上当事国得于下列情形下缔结协定仅在彼此间修改条约：（甲）条约内规定有作此种修改之可能者；或（乙）有关之修改非为条约所禁止，且：（一）不影响其他当事国享有条约上之权利或履行其义务者；（二）不关涉任何如予损抑即与有效实行整个条约之目的及宗旨不合之规定者。

然而，从《旧金山和约》的宗旨与目的来看，其第 3 条之规定显然属于和约的集体决定事项，不应该由美国和日本两个当事国私自处分。

事实上，和平条约的目的主要在于处理战争与领土问题，所以更严格要求大国的行动一致。在国际实践中，多边和平条约一直是处理领土问题的常见形式。诚然，在欧洲历史上，超级大国的意愿对于和平条约的缔结和欧洲领土的处分起着关键作用，但是，这些实践也反映了，早在 19 世

① David Bederman, "the 1871 London Declaration, Rebus Sic Stantibus and a Primitivist View of the Law of Nations", (1988) 82 *American Journal of International Law* 1, pp. 1－40.

纪，通过和平条约实施的领土处分，要求大国行动一致的同时意味着拒绝某个大国单方面地进行更改。[①] 19世纪以来，和平会议、缔结多边条约对于欧洲国家间结束战争、处分领土起着重要作用。著名的和平会议、和约或国际安排有：1815年的维也纳和会，[②] 1815—1848年的欧洲同盟，[③] 1856年的巴黎条约，[④] 1878年的柏林会议，1897—1913年的克里特（Crete）政府，[⑤] 1906年的阿尔赫拉斯法案，[⑥] 1913年的伦敦和约和阿尔巴尼亚的诞生[⑦]等。正是通过这些会议与条约的实践，才产生了国家同意原则。整体上说，在这些领土或国家的处理当中，都经过了所涉当事国（或类国家实体）的同意。

在一些领土处理的案例中，当超级大国实施的行动没有经过小国家的同意时，其行动的有效性就会受到质疑。譬如，1927年产生了加拉兹和布勒伊拉间的多瑙河欧洲管理委员会管辖权案。[⑧] 欧洲多瑙河委员会根据1856年的巴黎条约而建立。根据1878年的柏林条约，它的管辖权扩展到了罗马尼亚的加拉兹。此时，罗马尼亚被视为已从奥斯曼帝国独立出来（尽管土耳其是，但罗马尼亚不是柏林条约的缔约国）。之后，根据1883年的伦敦协定，委员会将管辖权进一步扩展到布勒伊拉，而罗马尼亚也没有签署这个条约，或参加起草会议。[⑨] 但是，1919年的凡尔赛和约第346条在确认战前的事实地位，以及在1921年7月的多瑙河定义章程中，罗马尼亚是当事国之一。[⑩] 于是，国际常设法院认为，委员会对于布勒伊拉管辖权的扩展是基于1919年以及1921年条约的解释，它并不认为1883年的

---

① James R. Crawford, *The Creation of States in International Law* (Oxford: Oxford University Press, 2007), p. 505.

② Schroeder, The Transformation of European Politics 1763 - 1848, pp. 517 - 582.

③ Schroeder, The Transformation of European Politics 1763 - 1848, pp. 583 - 894.

④ British Declaration of the Causes of War against Russia, 28 March 1854, 46 BFSP, p. 33.

⑤ PICJ ser. C no. 82, p. 82 - 131, Chapter 8.

⑥ *Act of Algeciras*, 7 April 1906, 99 BFSP 141, Chapter 7.

⑦ Méir Ydit, Internationalised Territories: A Study in the Historical Development of a Modern Notion in International Law and International Relations (1815 - 1960) (Leyden: L & Université de Fribourg, 1961), pp. 29 - 33.

⑧ Jurisdiction of the European Commission of the Danube between Galatz and Braila, PICJ ser B 1927, no. 14.

⑨ PICJ ser. B 1927, no. 14. p. 11.

⑩ 114 BFSP 535, Arts V, VI.

伦敦条约本身对罗马尼亚具有法律效力。尽管从1883年开始，委员会事实上在加拉兹到布勒伊拉区域实施了一些权利，不管这些权利实施的法律基础是什么，这并不能证明罗马尼亚对伦敦条约存在默示认可，在没有其同意的情况下，这些权利也不能约束罗马尼亚。[①] 据此，可以得出结论：早在19世纪国际先例就不支持超级大国在领土事务处理上主张法律霸权主义（Legal hegemony）。[②]

二战后成立的远东委员会议事程序所要求的多数同意加四大国一致原则，也体现了在战后问题处理上主张多边性、反对个别国家霸权主义的要求。1945年12月16日至26日，苏联、英国和美国的外交部长在莫斯科会面，于12月27日签订关于成立远东委员会（Far Eastern Commission）和盟国理事会（Allied Council）的协议，约定并经中国同意后，成立远东委员会和盟国理事会。远东委员会由中国、苏联、英国、美国、法国、荷兰、澳大利亚、加拿大、新西兰、印度和菲律宾组成。其职能主要在于根据《日本投降书》条款制定政策、方针和标准，使之切实施行，同时按照任何成员国的请求，对盟军最高司令部颁布的任何指令，或对最高司令部采取的任何涉及委员会管辖范围的行动进行审议。其中美国政府的职能还包括按照委员会的决议准备政策指令，并通过其合适的政府代理机构向最高司令部进行传达，最高司令部有义务履行这些表达远东委员会决议的指令。协议同时规定远东委员会的议事程序为不少于全体代表投票的多数同意，并且应当包括中国、苏联、英国与美国四大国的同意在内。[③]

1950年美国抓紧对日媾和时，在其对远东委员会的陈述中，亦表明了对国际多边处理机制的尊重与承诺。是年11月24日，美国国务院新闻发布会公开了其出席远东委员会的一份纪要，陈述了美国在对日媾和上的基本方针。其第3项专门提到处理领土问题的原则为：

3. 领土。日本必须：a）承认朝鲜（Korea）的独立；b）同意对

① PICJ ser. B 1927, no. 14. p. 27.

② James R. Crawford, The Creation of States in International Law, p. 505.

③ U. S. TIAS 1555; 60 Stat. 1899, 1901 - 1905; 20 UNTS 259, 276 - 280, 282 - 286; *A Decade of American Foreign Policy: Basic Documents, 1941 - 49* (1950), S. Doc. 123, 81st Cong., 1st sess., pp. 58 - 59, 60 - 61, 62 - 63.

琉球和小笠原群岛实行联合国托管，以美国为管理当局；[①] c）接受英国、苏联、中国与美国在将来对台湾、澎湖列岛、南萨哈林和库页岛地位的决定，如果在和约生效后一年以内没有决定时将由联合国大会决定……。[②]

因此，从对《旧金山和约》内容变更的角度，我们有理由指出，美日私自缔结的《琉球与大东群岛协定》侵害了其他缔约国的同意权与监督权，违反了和约的多边处理机制，当属非法和无效。

最后，如果只从美国放弃这样的单方行为的角度，国际法上虽然不禁止委任统治、托管或非自治领土之管理权的拥有者放弃对这类处于国际地位之下的领土的管理，但这种放弃并不导致这类领土成为“无主地”，其将来的地位由对这类领土承担监督职能的有权机构来决定。[③] 一方面，因为琉球还没有经过联合国大会或安理会的批准程序，还没有正式置于联合国托管制度之下，美国的“施政”还不是以“托管制度下的管理当局”的名义，所以，《琉球与大东群岛协定》之性质亦不能说是托管管理权的放弃或让渡。另一方面，作为一个管理权利（临时）享有者，美国也许可以放弃对琉球（仅作为非自治领土）的管理权，但却不能放弃后让渡给日本，因为日本显然不是“承担监督职能的有权机构”。

综上，对琉球地位的处理，要在国际法上成就其合法性，或者说，让琉球的主权地位得到合法有效的确定，有必要严格遵循《联合国宪章》的规定，回到和平条约的多边处理机制，或者联合国大会、安理会的集体处理机制上来，以尊重战后盟国的平等意志和琉球作为“潜在托管领土”本身的权利。

结　论

琉球在历史上本是中国的藩属国，1879 年日本实施“琉球处分”，单

① 这里进一步证明了和平条约对琉球的处理为“联合国托管”。

② XXIII Bulletin, Department of State, No. 596, Dec. 4, 1950, p. 881.

③ Marcelo G. Kohen Mamadou Hébié, Territory, Acquisition, *Max Planck Encyclopedia of Public International Law*, para. 6.

方面设置冲绳县。此后，清政府与日本展开持久谈判，在国际社会的关注下，双方达成了“分岛加约”案的合意，但没有正式签约。“琉球处分”的效力之争是琉球地位成为问题的最早源起。

第二次世界大战期间，琉球居民被日本政府“不视作日本人”，伤亡最惨重。1945 年日本战败后，对日占领期间，琉球继续被实施区别待遇：以美国为主的盟军对它实行“分离性处理”和直接统治。按照盟军最高司令部的相关指令以及远东委员会等机构的决议和规定，琉球的这种“分离性处理”明确以《开罗宣言》、《波茨坦公告》和《日本投降书》为依据，琉球从“敌国剥离”，不被视作日本领土。日本的主权领土仅限于“本州、北海道、九州、四国及吾人所决定之其他小岛之内”，而琉球不在“吾人所决定之其他小岛”的范围内。

1951 年签订的《旧金山和约》虽然有对琉球的处理，但该和约的效力存在争议。并且，即便是按照和约内容的规定，这种处理以将琉球“置于联合国托管制度下”为目的，美国的“施政”（全面行使立法、行政和司法权）只是一种提交托管之前的临时安排。也即，《旧金山和约》第 3 条项下的琉球是“潜在的托管领土”。如果将 1972 年视作美国对琉球施政期的截止，那么，1952—1972 年，美国在琉球持续的单边“施政”，根本未将琉球“提交联合国托管”的予以实施，构成对和约的“非善意履行”，或者，对联合国托管义务的“没有履行”。不但如此，美日还在 1971 年私自签订《琉球与大东群岛协定》，美国将其在《旧金山和约》第 3 条项下的施政权“让与给日本”，构成对和约履行的擅自变更，侵害了其他缔约国的同意权与监督权，违反了和约的多边处理机制，也忽视了琉球作为“潜在托管领土”本身的地位，是超级大国在领土事务处理上实行法律霸权主义的体现。

因此，《琉球与大东群岛协定》自始至终都是非法、无效的。从这个角度来说，日本对琉球不但没有主权依据，就从美国“施政权让与”的角度讲，日本目前对琉球的管理亦缺乏合法依据。关于钓鱼岛争端，日本提出钓鱼岛列屿是琉球的一部分，并在琉球的框架下主张对钓鱼岛列屿的主权。然而，通过本文的分析，我们有充分理由指出，琉球的地位在国际法上并没有确定。

当然，可能会有观点提出，日本从 1972 年至今管理着“琉球”40 余年，领土的“时效取得”是否可以作为其主权依据呢？时效是在非无主地领土上确立主权的方式，其适用的对象是非法获得的或是在有关情况下不能证明取得的合法性的领土。[①] 一国在占有他国的某块土地后，因为在相当长时期内不受干扰地占有，可能基于时效而取得该土地的领土主权。但是，因为时效取得适用于主权不明或没有合法主权依据的情况，所以它在国际法上作为一种领土取得方法在早期就存在争议。[②] 首先，按照“非法行为不产生合法权利”的一般法理，时效被认为不能成为所涉领土在该情况下转移给另一国家的基础。其次，在国际法上并没有任何确切的时间标准认为经过多长时间后能够据此获得主权。更重要的是，建立在时效取得基础上的主张在事实上都有反效果（counter-effect），因为它意味着认可领土的原始权利属于另一个国家。所以，国家的实践表明，各国都很谨慎地不依赖于时效取得作为它们主张领土权利的主要基础。[③] 在国际司法判例中，至今还没有一个案例所认定的领土主权是单纯通过时效取得的，相关认定多与领土放弃、默认、禁止反言规则密不可分。事实上，日本也没有明确提出过其通过时效取得琉球或冲绳的主权。[④] 既然日本对琉球都没有合法的主权依据，那么它对钓鱼岛列屿提出的主权主张不过是一个伪命题。

（本文原载于《国际法研究》2014 年第 1 期）

① 〔英〕马尔科姆·N. 肖：《国际法》（第 6 版），白桂梅等译，北京大学出版社，2011，第 397 页。

② Marcelo G. Kohen，Mamadou Hébié，Territory Acquisition，*Max Planck Encyclopedia of Public International Law*，2012，para. 17.

③ Marcelo G. Kohen，Mamadou Hébié，Territory Acquisition，*Max Planck Encyclopedia of Public International Law*，2012，para. 21.

④ 限于篇幅，本文对此不再展开探讨。

南海仲裁案裁决中有关岛礁法律地位问题的评介

马金星*

2013 年 1 月 22 日，菲律宾依据《联合国海洋法公约》（以下简称《公约》）第 15 部分以及附件七的规定，就中国与菲律宾之间有关南海问题的争端，单方面发起对中国的国际仲裁（以下简称“南海仲裁案”）。2016 年 7 月 12 日，仲裁庭作出最终裁决（以下简称《裁决书》），① 其中第 6 部分涉及岛礁法律地位问题。② 仲裁庭将满足《公约》第 121 条第 1 款标准的地物统称为“高潮地物”（high-tide features），不能维持人类居住或其本身经济生活（第 121 条第 3 款）的高潮地物为“岩礁”（rocks），反之，则为“全效岛屿”（fully entitled islands）。③ 仲裁庭认为，黄岩岛、赤瓜礁、华阳礁、西门礁和永暑礁是不享有专属经济区和大陆架的岩礁；美济礁、仁爱礁、渚碧礁和东门礁属于低潮高地；南薰礁（南）属于低潮高地，南薰礁（北）属于岩礁。南沙群岛无一海洋地物能够产生专属经济区

---

* 马金星，中国社会科学院国际法研究所助理研究员。

① In the Matter of the South China Sea Arbitration before an Arbitral Tribunal Constituted under Annex VII to the 1982 United Nations Convention on the Law of the Sea between the Republic of the Philippines and the People's Republic of China（PCA Case No. 2013 – 19），AWARD（hereinafter as “AWARD”），Permanent Court of Arbitration，https://www.pcacases.com/pcadocs/PH-CN%20 – %2020160712%20 – %20Award.pdf，pp. 472 – 474，para. 1203，最后访问日期：2016 年 11 月 28 日。

② 本文除引用仲裁庭表述外，依我国惯常表达，依然将菲律宾第 3 项至第 7 项仲裁请求及《裁决书》第六部分涉及的南海地物（Maritime features），统称为岛礁。

③ AWARD，p. 119，para. 280.

和大陆架，且不能够作为一个整体主张海洋权利。[①] 就岛礁法律地位问题而言，上述裁决几乎完全支持了菲律宾第3项至第7项仲裁请求。[②] 就《裁决书》第6部分内容而言，争端构成、条约解释和证据证明三部分鼎足而立，是支撑其有关岛礁法律地位认定的支柱，只有上述三部分同时有效成立，才足以支持裁决的合法性。本文以南海仲裁案裁决的逻辑进路为主线，对《裁决书》第6部分展开专门研究，对其认定的岛礁法律地位争端构成提出质疑，分析《裁决书》中涉及岛礁法律地位的条约解释内容，指明仲裁庭所认定的证据存在的瑕疵与缺陷。

一 《裁决书》中涉及岛礁法律地位仲裁请求的内容概要

仲裁庭在《裁决书》中，首先回顾和总结了2015年《管辖权及可受理性裁决》[③] 对南海岛礁法律地位仲裁请求在管辖权及可受理性上的认定，[④] 继而从条约解释入手，区分《公约》定义的低潮高地和岛屿，[⑤] 对《公约》第121条第3款进行解释，并得出“不能维持人类居住或其本身的经济生活的岩礁”的判断标准，然后依据解释确立的标准及相关证据，逐一认定黄岩岛、赤瓜礁等地物的法律地位。

---

① AWARD, pp. 471 - 474, para. 1203.

② 菲律宾第6项仲裁请求为“南薰礁和西门礁（包括东门礁）”是低潮高地，《裁决书》对南薰礁作了分割处理，将西门礁认定为岩礁。参见 AWARD, p. 472, para. 1203。

③ 参见 In the Matter of the South China Sea Arbitration before an Arbitral Tribunal Constituted under Annex VII to the 1982 United Nations Convention on the Law of the Sea between the Republic of the Philippines and the People's Republic of China（PCA Case No. 2013 - 19）, Award on Jurisdiction and Admissibility（hereinafter as “Award on Jurisdiction and Admissibility”）, Permanent Court of Arbitration, https://www.pcacases.com/web/sendAttach/1506，最后访问日期：2016年11月27日。

④ 针对菲律宾第3项至第7项仲裁请求，仲裁庭在2015年《管辖权及可受理性裁决》第413段，先行裁决对菲律宾第3、4、6、7项诉求具有管辖权，对菲律宾第5项诉求是否有管辖权的决定将涉及不具有完全初步性质的实体问题审查，因此保留其对第5项诉求管辖权的审查至实体问题仲裁阶段。之后，在2016年《裁决书》中明确对菲律宾第5项诉求具有管辖权。参见 Award on Jurisdiction and Admissibility, p. 149, para. 413; AWARD, p. 471, para. 1202。

⑤ 《联合国海洋法公约》第13条、第121条第1款。

（一）解释《公约》第13条和第121条

条约解释是《裁决书》第6部分法理论证的核心。《公约》第13条和第121条第1款在表达结构上类同，而第121条第3款关于岛屿海洋权利的规定又是涉及南海岛礁法律地位判定乃至《公约》第8部分岛屿制度的核心。仲裁庭在《裁决书》第6部分中首先借助对潮汐标准的认定，将《公约》第13条定义的低潮高地和第121条第1款定义的岛屿区分开来，然后，重点对第121条第3款作了解读，逐一解释了该款中岩礁（rocks）、不能（cannot）、维持（sustain）、人类居住（human inhabitation）、或者（or）、自身经济生活（economic life of their own）六个术语。仲裁庭认为，构成"岩礁"的自然成分不限于岩石，但是必须是自然形成的物质。[①]"不能"表示的是一种能力，尽管人类居住和经济生活的历史证据可能与确立地物的能力有关，如果某处靠近有人类居住活动陆块的地物从未被人类居住过，或从来没有维持过经济生活，那么该处地物就是无人类居住的。相反，正面例证是，人类有史以来就居住在该地物上，或地物上一直有经济活动，方能构成地物能力的相关证据。[②]"维持"有基础、时间和质量三个层面的含义，基础层面是指支持或提供必需品，时间层面指不应当是一次性或一时的，质量层面指根据适当的标准，必须保持人类生存且健康地"持续渡过一个时期"。[③]居住不仅仅是简单的存在，"人类居住"标准要求主体已经选择以定居方式存在且居住在地物上，而非短暂的存在，并且地物上存在满足人类居住的所有基本要件，能够支持、保持以及提供食物、饮水及遮蔽条件。尽管《公约》未对居住人数进行规定，仲裁庭认为单独个体显然不能满足上述要求，居住的人数要求应当是一群或一个团体的人，[④]南沙诸岛上驻军及政府人员的生活补给均来源于大陆，是基于领土争端的存在而非为了定居而居住，故不属于"人类居住"。[⑤]仲裁庭认为经济活动是由人实施的，人类很少居住在没有经济活动或生计来源

① AWARD, pp. 205 - 206, para. 480.
② AWARD, pp. 206 - 207, paras. 483 - 484.
③ AWARD, pp. 207 - 208, para. 487.
④ AWARD, p. 208, paras. 489 - 491.
⑤ AWARD, p. 252, para. 618.

的地方是可能的，不认为《公约》第121条第3款因为“或”字，而存在两类判断海洋地物权利的标准。因此，《公约》条款中“或”字前后的两个概念是联系在一起的。[①] 维持“自身经济生活”的资源必须是当地的，而不是依赖外来资源或纯采掘业的经济活动，那些源自潜在专属经济区或大陆架的经济活动必须被排除。[②]

概言之，仲裁庭重申《公约》基于岛礁的自然状态对其进行的归类。仲裁庭在解释《公约》第121条第3款时，始终围绕一个中心思想，即“防止微不足道的岛礁产生大面积的海洋权利，而侵犯有人定居的领土的权利，或者侵犯公海以及作为人类的共同继承财产保留的海床的区域”，[③] 岛礁可主张的海洋权利取决于其在自然状态下维持稳定人类社群活动，或者不依赖于外来资源或纯采掘业的经济活动的客观承载力。

（二）审查运用相关证据及事实

仲裁庭对菲律宾提交的相关地图、图表、潮位资料、卫星图像、照片、历史、人类学、地理以及水文信息证据，[④] 作了甄别和筛选。仲裁庭认为，“卫星图片无法识别较小地物或低潮高地的惯常形态，有关南海岛礁法律地位的更有力的证据为海图、调查记录和航行指南”；[⑤] “由于中国岛礁建设和政治情势对个案观察的限制，对菲律宾仲裁请求中的海洋地物进行直接观察，已无可能”。[⑥] “鉴于岩礁和凝结在礁盘上的大块珊瑚岩石具有高度的持久性，并且可以合理地预期基本保持不变，甚至超过百年，历史上的直接观测并非毫无价值”。[⑦] 作为首要情形，仲裁庭认为，更重要的是着眼于测量的时机，而非海图的出版，并将适宜作为证据的地图比例尺限定为1∶250万。[⑧]

---

① AWARD, p. 210, paras. 495 – 496.

② AWARD, pp. 211 – 212, paras. 500 – 503.

③ 参见2016年7月12日南海仲裁案新闻稿（菲律宾共和国V. 中华人民共和国），常设仲裁院（PCA）网，https://www.pcacases.com/web/view/7，最后访问日期：2016年12月26日。

④ Award on Jurisdiction and Admissibility, pp. 131 – 132, para. 373.

⑤ AWARD, p. 140, para. 327.

⑥ AWARD, p. 138, para. 321.

⑦ AWARD, p. 140, para. 327.

⑧ AWARD, p. 141, para. 329.

倚重英国与日本对南沙群岛的军事测量资料。仲裁庭提出，第一次对南海岛礁持续性测量活动发生于1862—1868年，由英国海军实施。之后，在20世纪20年代和30年代，英国及日本海军对南沙群岛进行了持续的军事测量活动，尽管这些信息都是在第二次世界大战（以下简称“二战”）之后，才被公之于众的。① 法国和美国海军在20世纪30年代同样实施了上述测量活动，但程度逊于英国及日本，南海周边国家则是在晚近时期，才开始在各自近岸海域开展测量活动。② 相当一部分不同国家出版的南海海图，或多或少存在互相复制的情况。现有海图中被合并或直接复制的信息，经常不表明其引用状况。③ 甚至有晚近出版的海图，依然大量追踪（trace）英国、日本19世纪60年代或20世纪30年代的军事测量数据。④ 事实上，大部分近期出版的海图，对特定的南海地物，没有或者仅更新少量信息。⑤ 仲裁庭在评价《航行指南》与军事测量的关系时指出，英国20世纪30年代再版的南海《航行指南》，是在皇家海军“步兵号”（HMS Rifleman）测量形成的第1版《中国海指南》基础上，增补或修正形成的。除美国外，其他国家的《航行指南》似乎都援用上述英国版本的内容。而美国早先的关于南海《航行指南》的内容，似乎来自日本和中国方面的信息。因此，仲裁庭已独立地寻求来自英国和日本的测量材料，并据此得出相关结论。⑥

援引学术文献等资料进行补充说明。仲裁庭在《裁决书》第6部分B项反复引用汉考克斯（David Hancox）和普雷斯科特（Victor Prescott）的论文和专著，证明其他国家《航行指南》大量直接援用英国、日本军事测量数据的情况，在第6部分C项引用日本人平塚均⑦、藤岛范孝⑧、

① AWARD, p. 141, para. 329.

② AWARD, p. 141, para. 329.

③ AWARD, p. 141, para. 330.

④ AWARD, p. 141, para. 330.

⑤ AWARD, pp. 141 - 142, paras. 329 - 330.

⑥ AWARD, p. 142, para. 331.

⑦ 参见 Hitoshi Hiratsuka, “The Extended Base for the Expansion of the Fishery Business to Southern Area: New Southern Archipelagoon Site Survey Report”, *Taiwan Times*, May 1939; AWARD, p. 239, para. 582。

⑧ 参见 Noritaka Fujishima, “Discussions on the Names of Islands in the Southern China Sea”, (1994) 9 *The Hokkaido General Education Review of Komazawa University*; AWARD, p. 244, para. 595。

山本运一[①]、台湾学者黄增泉等人[②]的学术论文或调查报告，日本前海军中佐小仓卯之助的文稿[③]，以及1933—1939年大阪《朝日新闻》和1945年5月4日《纽约时报》的新闻报道[④]，分析了黄岩岛和南沙岛礁的植被与生物环境条件、淡水、土壤及农业潜力、以往渔民活动的记录、商业活动的记录，与前述《航行指南》和军事测量资料的记载进行对比分析。

二　对南海仲裁案中岛礁法律地位争端构成的质疑

南海仲裁案中，菲律宾所诉有关岛礁法律地位的争议本质是领土主权争端。仲裁庭对既往国际司法实践有关争端（dispute）的定义或解释的援引，具有强烈的主观色彩。菲律宾和仲裁庭对中国相关外交立场作了曲解，以此推理得出中国具有针对南海个别岛礁法律地位的主张，以断定中菲两国就岛礁法律地位存在《公约》第288条所述争端。因此，中菲两国间就岛礁法律地位仲裁事项是否存在争端，以及该仲裁事项是否因涉及海域划界而被2006年中国依据《公约》规定作出的声明（以下简称“2006年声明”）[⑤]，排除于强制争端解决程序适用范围，是分析争端构成问题的重点。

（一）曲解中国有关岛礁法律地位的照会立场

援引外交照会辨别中国对相关南海岛礁法律地位的立场。菲律宾和仲裁庭援引2009年《中国反对日本以冲之鸟礁主张专属经济区和大陆架的

---

① Yun-ichi Yamamoto, “The Brief History of the Sinnan Islands”, (1939) 7 *Science of Taiwan* 3; AWARD, p. 242, para. 588.

② 参见 AWARD, p. 188, paras. 428 - 430。

③ 参见小仓卯之助《暴风之岛》，小仓久仁子、桥本博编，小仓中佐遗稿刊行会，1940，第188、194页。参见 AWARD, pp. 239, 241, paras. 583, 586。

④ 参见 AWARD, pp. 241, 244, 248, 249, paras. 586, 594, 607, 609。

⑤ 2006年8月25日，中国向联合国秘书长提交声明，就《公约》第298条第1款（a）、（b）和（c）项所述的任何争端，不接受《公约》第15部分第2节规定的任何国际司法或仲裁管辖。该声明已经将涉及海域划界等《公约》第298条第1款（a）、（b）和（c）项所述的任何争端，排除适用强制仲裁程序。

照会》[①]、《建议在第19次缔约国会议议程内列入一个补充项目的照会》[②]，2011年《就有关南海问题致联合国秘书长的照会》[③] 和2015年《中国驻马尼拉大使馆给菲律宾外交部的照会》[④]，并参照中国国内法和2014年《中华人民共和国政府关于菲律宾共和国所提南海仲裁案管辖权问题的立场文件》（以下简称《立场文件》）[⑤]，认为不能接受中国将南沙群岛作为一个封闭的或被直线基线环绕的群岛，[⑥] 中国基于南沙群岛的200海里主张与关于《公约》第121条第3款的立场相悖。[⑦] 菲律宾和仲裁庭将各岛礁分别描述为孤立的礁石，否定这些岛礁之间、岛礁与毗邻海域之间的整体性，是对中国立场的曲解。

第一，中国以群岛立场概括性主张南海诸岛的海洋权利早于《公约》的制定和生效。在民国时期，中国政府就以群岛立场对南海诸岛主张海洋权利；[⑧] 1949年至今，中国政府有关南海问题的立场和声明均将东沙、西沙、中沙和南沙群岛作为整体主张海洋权利，并且从未对南海诸岛中的某个特定岛礁，单独主张过领海、专属经济区和大陆架。即使是菲律宾、越

---

① Note Verbale from the Permanent Mission of the People's Republic of China to the Secretary-General of the United Nations, No. CML/2/2009 (6 Feb. 2009), p. 1.

② Note Verbale from the Permanent Mission of the People's Republic of China to the United Nations to the Secretary-General of the United Nations (21 May 2009), reprinted in UN Convention on the Law of the Sea, Meeting of States Parties, Proposal for the inclusion of a supplementary item in the agenda of the nineteenth Meeting of States Parties, UN Doc. SPLOS/196, 22 May 2009.

③ Note Verbale from the Permanent Mission of the People's Republic of China to the Secretary-General of the United Nations, No. CML/8/2011 (14 Apr. 2011), p. 2. MP, Vol. VI, Annex 201. Hearing on the Merits and Remaining Issues of Jurisdiction and Admissibility 25th November 2015, Award on Jurisdiction and Admissibility (hereinafter as Hearing on the Merits 25th November 2015), Permanent Court of Arbitration, https://pcacases.com/web/sendAttach/1548（最后访问日期：2016年12月28日），p. 104, paras. 9 - 12。

④ Note Verbale from the Embassy of the People's Republic of China in Manila to the Department of Foreign Affairs, Republic of the Philippines, No. 15 (PG) - 214, 28 June 2015.

⑤ 参见《中华人民共和国政府关于菲律宾共和国所提南海仲裁案管辖权问题的立场文件》第3段，新华网，http://news.xinhuanet.com/mil/2014 - 12/07/c_127283404.htm，最后访问日期：2016年12月26日。

⑥ AWARD, pp. 235 - 236, paras. 571, 573.

⑦ Hearing on the Merits 25th November 2015, pp. 104 - 105, para. 23; AWARD, pp. 198 - 199, para. 153, paras. 453 - 458.

⑧ 参见吴士存主编《南海问题文献汇编》，海南出版社，2001，第13页、第22页。

南对南沙岛礁的主权声索，也分别是以“卡拉延岛群”、“长沙群岛”① 的立场主张的。对于中国将南沙群岛作为一个整体主张海洋权利，菲律宾曾明确予以承认，② 但仍把中国的主张解释为是对南沙群岛中的每一个岛礁均主张领海、专属经济区和大陆架，且未向仲裁庭提交任何证据。《公约》在定义相关概念时，严格区分“为本公约的目的”③ 和“为本部分的目的”④，一方面，第46条第2款是“为本公约的目的”定义“群岛”⑤，说明该概念具有普适性，中国以“群岛”主张对南沙岛礁享有的权利具有法律基础。另一方面，《公约》区分群岛国制度与岛屿制度，大陆国家拥有洋中群岛是客观现实，并非所有洋中群岛都构成群岛国，非群岛国家是否可以适用群岛制度，在第三次联合国海洋法会议上就已提出，但并未妥善解决。⑥ 仲裁庭以《公约》中未规定大陆国家洋中群岛制度及中国不是群岛国，否定中国以群岛立场概括性主张南海诸岛海洋权利，⑦ 不仅是将《公约》作为国际海洋法制度的全部，更是无视《公约》序言中所述“确认本公约未予规定的事项，应继续以一般国际法的规则和原则为准据”的

① 越南的立场主张存在摇摆。菲律宾在庭审答辩中指出，越南在南海争议地物的海洋权利的问题上与菲方立场一致，即南海争议岛礁均无法产生专属经济区或大陆架的权利，并列举了相应证据。越南在2015年7月23日针对南海仲裁案的声明中，明确表态：“越南认为，菲律宾在仲裁程序中所提的地物均无法享有其专属经济区或大陆架，或产生12海里以外的海洋权利，因为这些地物属于低潮高地或《公约》第121条第3款意义上的‘不能维持人类居住或其本身经济生活的岩礁’。”但是，越南1977年《领海、毗连区、专属经济区和大陆架》、1979年及1982年白皮书、1988年关于“黄沙群岛和长沙群岛与国际法”文件中，均主张“长沙群岛”（南沙群岛）拥有专属经济区和大陆架。参见 Written Responses of The Philippines to the Tribunal's 13 July 2015 Questions Vol. 1, Award on Jurisdiction and Admissibility (hereinafter as Written Responses of The Philippines 13 July 2015), Permanent Court of Arbitration, https://pcacases.com/web/sendAttach/1847（最后访问日期：2016年12月28日），p. 25, para. IV. 3; Hearing on the Merits 25th November 2015, p. 104, paras. 6 - 22。

② 参见 Written Responses of The Philippines 13 July 2015, pp. 1 - 2, paras. I. 1 - I. 3。

③ 《联合国海洋法公约》中“为本公约的目的”（for the purposes of this Convention）定义的概念包括：区域、海洋环境污染等（第1条）、海湾（第10条）、军舰（第29条）、群岛及群岛国（第46条）等。

④ 《联合国海洋法公约》中“为本部分的目的”（for the purposes of this Part）定义的概念包括：地理不利国（第70条第2款）、资源、矿物（第133条）等。

⑤ 《联合国海洋法公约》第46条第2款。

⑥ 参见傅崐成、郑凡《群岛的整体性与航行自由——关于中国在南海适用群岛制度的思考》，《上海交通大学学报》（哲学社会科学版）2015年第6期。

⑦ AWARD, pp. 236 - 237, paras. 573, 575.

规定，[①] 篡改中菲两国有关岛礁争端的性质。[②] 仲裁庭的做法是力图将有关岛礁法律地位问题引入《公约》第121条框架内，为其确立条约解释的合法性铺路。

第二，中国对日本冲之鸟礁的照会不适用于南沙群岛。仲裁庭在《裁决书》中援引上述2009年、2011年照会，[③] 说明中国对待“岩礁”的态度，不仅存在以具体事例补充解释《公约》第121条第3款的企图，而且也试图在某种程度上利用“禁止反言原则”回击中国对南海仲裁案的立场。但冲之鸟礁与南沙群岛在地物形态上不具有可比性，2009年及2011年照会与中国对南沙群岛的权利主张不具有相关性。冲之鸟礁是大洋上孤立的岩礁，高潮时仅两块约16厘米和6厘米的岩石露出海面，面积不足10平方米，[④] 而南沙群岛是由以双子群礁、中业群礁等为主体构成的群岛。无论是从岛礁数量、面积、上面的植被，还是从经济活动、权利主张等方面对比，冲之鸟礁与南沙群岛都不是同一类型的海洋地物，菲律宾作此种援引属于混淆概念。且日本是基于大洋上的孤立岩礁主张其海洋权利，中国是以作为整体的南沙群岛主张其海洋权利，二者存在本质差别。《公约》第121条规定的是岛屿而非群岛的概念及海洋权利，中国在照会文本中已清楚表明其针对《公约》第121条第3款的规定所阐述的立场，故2009年、2011年照会与“禁止反言原则”也无真正的相关性。

（二）中菲两国就岛礁法律地位问题不存在争端

仲裁庭主张“国际法确立了争端的概念，并将其纳入《公约》第288条，符合争端的概念是仲裁庭行使管辖权的最低要求”。[⑤] 依据仲裁庭主张及《公约》第288条，识别南海仲裁案中岛礁法律地位争端构成时，先要解决国际法确立的争端概念与《公约》第288条所述争端的关系，之后才

---

① 《联合国海洋法公约》序言第8段。

② 参见《中华人民共和国政府关于菲律宾共和国所提南海仲裁案管辖权问题的立场文件》第22段，新华网，http://news.xinhuanet.com/mil/2014-12/07/c_127283404.htm，最后访问日期：2016年12月27日。

③ 参见AWARD，pp. 196-199，paras. 449-458。

④ 参见薛洪涛《国际法专家解析日本“以礁变岛”于法无据原因》，《法制日报》2012年5月18日，第4版。

⑤ Award on Jurisdiction and Admissibility，p. 57，para. 148.

需要判断中菲两国就岛礁法律地位问题是否存在《公约》第 288 条所述争端。

第一，国际法中不存在一个被广泛认可的争端概念。仲裁庭分别援引“1924 年马弗罗马蒂斯巴勒斯坦特许权案”（以下简称“特许权案”）、“保加利亚、匈牙利和罗马尼亚关于和平协议的解释咨询意见”、“西南非洲案”和“《消除一切形式种族歧视国际公约》适用案”中，关于“争端”的定义或解释，作为国际法确立的争端概念。[①] 事实上，早有国际法学者指出，这些同一时期出现的有关争端的定义或解释，不是过宽就是过窄。[②] 在上述案件之外，诸如“东帝汶案”[③]、“得克萨斯海外石油公司和加利福尼亚亚洲石油公司诉阿拉伯利比亚民众国政府案”[④] 等国际司法或仲裁案件中，也存在大量关于争端的阐释。因而，国际法中是否确立了一个普遍接受的争端概念，本身就存在疑问，更遑论将争端概念纳入《公约》第 288 条。从《管辖权及可受理性裁决》案例援引的角度看，仲裁庭既未说明为何只选取上述四个案件关于争端的定义及解释，也未说明为何上述四个案件有关争端的界定或解释，就足以构成“国际法确立的争端概念”的合理理由。从定义阐释角度看，“特许权案”定义的争端含义最为宽泛，仲裁庭似乎有意选择一个宽泛的争端概念，并以此概念为基础，根据南海仲裁案需求，援引其他国际司法或仲裁中的争端解释，对其加以裁剪或补充，如此“塑造”出的争端概念，实难称之为“国际法确立的争端概念”。

第二，中菲之间就南海岛礁地物法律地位不存在针对性的反对。当事方之间就同一事项持有相反的态度或观点，是证明法律争端存在的前提要件。为此，当事国在发起国际司法或仲裁程序前，“必须足够清楚地提到相关条约的主题事项，以让对方识别出就该事项存在或可能存在争端”。[⑤]

---

① Award on Jurisdiction and Admissibility, p. 57, para. 148.

② 参见 G. Hafner, “the Physiognomy of Disputes and the Appropriate Means to Resolve Them”, (1995) *Proceedings of the United Nations Congress on Public International Law* 559, p. 560。

③ 参见 Case Concerning East Timor (Portugal v. Australia), Judgment, I. C. J. Reports 1995, paras. 21, 22。

④ 参见 Texaco Overseas Petroleum Company and California Asiatic Oil Company v. Libyan Arab Republic, Preliminary Award of 27 November 1975, (1979) 53 I. L. R. 389, p. 416。

⑤ 参见 Case Concerning Application of the International Convention on the Elimination of All Forms of Racial Discrimination (Georgia v. Russian), Preliminary objections, Judgment, I. C. J. Reports 2011, pp. 18 – 19, para. 30。

之后，“只要一方的权利主张受到另一方的积极反对”[①] 即表明存在争端，当事国单方面主张不足以证明争端的存在。因而，要证明中国与菲律宾之间就第3项至第7项仲裁请求存在有关《公约》解释和适用的争端，菲律宾和仲裁庭必须基于事实证明，菲律宾在提起仲裁前曾向中国提出过上述主张，而中国就此表示过反对、否认或反驳。在《裁决书》中，仲裁庭仅通过类推方式，对中国涉及黄岩岛、太平岛法律地位的主张作了说明，援引1997年5月22日中国外交部关于黄岩岛的声明指出，“该声明提到了‘专属经济区重叠’而不是‘专属经济区和领海重叠’，而黄岩岛位于所有中国主张的高潮地物200海里范围外，故所提‘专属经济区重叠’显示中国认为黄岩岛是可以拥有专属经济区的‘岛屿’”。[②] 仲裁庭上述论断属于“类推”而非“解释”，充其量只是说明，此类声明并不排除中国基于黄岩岛主张200海里专属经济区的意图，并未从正面回答中国到底有无此种意图，以确定争端的存在。除此之外，仲裁庭承认中国将南沙群岛作为整体主张权利，未如上述声明般特别地对美济礁、永暑礁等岛礁法律地位逐一表明立场，[③] 故对于菲律宾第4项至第7项仲裁请求，也不存在“一方的主张被另一方有针对性地反对”。[④]

第三，不恰当地援引国际司法判例作为确立管辖权的依据。仲裁庭在处理中菲两国领土主权争端对岛礁法律地位仲裁事项管辖权的影响时，援引了国际法院“在德黑兰的美国外交和领事人员案”中的判决，即没有理由“只因为争端存在其他方面，不论其多重要，而不考虑争端的某一方面”，[⑤] 国际法院在该判词后作了进一步阐释，“然而，之前从来没有这样的观点被提出，即因为提交法院的法律争端仅仅是政治争端的一个方面，法院就拒绝为当事方（国）解决其之间的法律问题”。[⑥] “法院作为司法

---

① 参见 South West Africa（Ethiopia v. South Africa/Liberia v. South Africa），Preliminary Objections，Judgment，I. C. J. Reports 1962，p. 13；Case Concerning East Timor（Portugal v. Australia），Judgment，I. C. J. Reports 1995，p. 14，para. 22。

② AWARD，pp. 130，195，paras. 298，446.

③ AWARD，pp. 130，195，196，202，203，paras. 298，446，449，472.

④ 参见 The South West Africa Cases（Ethiopia v. South Africa/Liberia v. South Africa），Preliminary Objections，Judgment，I. C. J. Reports 1962，p. 13。

⑤ Award on Jurisdiction and Admissibility，p. 59，para. 152.

⑥ 参见 United States Diplomatic and Consular Staff in Tehran（United States v. Iran），Judgment，I. C. J. Reports 1980，pp. 3，19－20，para. 36。

机构，只关注是否存在一个能够通过适用国际法原则和规则加以解决的法律争端。求助法院的目的是和平解决争端，法院的判决是法律宣告，它不能以政治动机来确认自身之宣告，从而导致该国在特殊时期内或特殊情形下来选择司法解决方法”。[①] 国际法院在之后的“边境及跨境武装行动案”[②]、“对尼加拉瓜进行军事和准军事行动案”[③]、“以色列隔离墙案”[④]等案件中，对上述判决的援引，也是建立在区分政治争端与法律争端基础上的。但上述四个案件都是因为当事国一方具体的国家行为引发的争端，国际法院所指“争端的某一方面”的真实含义应是“政治争端的法律方面”，具体而言是国家政治行为中的可裁决部分，并非泛泛地扩大到任何争端及其任何方面。[⑤] 这里暂不去讨论在混合争端中领土主权争端和《公约》所规定事项争端之间的附带性或辅助性关系，[⑥] 仅从援引内容与仲裁事项的对应而言，南海仲裁案的诱因是领土主权争端而非具体的国家行为，仲裁庭截取国际法院判决的只言片语，刻意回避判决上下文内容，将政治争端替换为领土主权争端，将法律方面替换为海洋地物法律地位及其权利方面，无疑是在断章取义，曲解国际法院上述判决。

（三）岛礁法律地位问题涉及海域划界不适用强制仲裁程序

2015 年仲裁庭在《管辖权及可受理性裁决》中，认为中国 2006 年声明是试图适用《公约》第 298 条强制争端解决程序的例外情况的例证。但是，除了这些例外情况，第 309 条规定“除非本公约其他条款明文规定，否则不得作出任何保留或例外”。相应地，《公约》缔约国不得随意选择其

---

① 参见 United States Diplomatic and Consular Staff in Tehran（United States v. Iran），Judgment，I. C. J. Reports 1980，pp. 20 – 21，para. 36。

② 参见 Border and Transborder Armed Actions（Nicaragua v. Hondura），Judgment，I. C. J. Reports 1988，p. 93。

③ 参见 Case Concerning Military and Paramilitary Activities in and against Nicaragua（Nicaragua v. United States），Judgment，I. C. J. Reports 1984，p. 293。

④ 参见 Legal Consequences of the Construction of a Wall in the Occupied Palestinian Territory，Advisory Opinion，I. C. J. Reports 2004，p. 136。

⑤ 参见 *Antonio Cassese*，*Legal Restraints on the Use of Force 40 Years after the U. N. Charter*（Hague：Brill Academic Pub.，1986），p. 329。

⑥ 参见陈喜峰《争端的构成和本质：“南海仲裁案”第 1 项诉求及其管辖权裁决评析》，《国际法研究》2016 年第 2 期。

希望接受或拒绝的部分”。[1] 在仲裁庭的逻辑中，中国2006年声明属于对《公约》的“保留”（Reservation），而《公约》第309条明确规定“除非本公约其他条款明示许可，对本公约不得作出保留或例外”，所以，中国2006年声明不能排除适用强制仲裁程序。事实上，《公约》第309条和第310条分别规定了“保留和例外”、“声明和说明”，[2] 从措辞看，《公约》严格区别“保留”和“声明”，对“保留”采取以禁止为原则、以允许为例外的态度，但明确允许一国在签署、批准或加入《公约》时，作出不论如何措辞或用何种名称的声明（Declaration）或说明。中国2006年声明文本表述中明确使用的是“声明”，而《公约》第298条允许一国就本条所列争端作出书面声明（declare in writing），不接受第2节规定的一种或一种以上的程序。中国2006年声明清楚地指明是根据《公约》第298条作出的，声明的内容也是关于《公约》第298条第1款（a）、（b）和（c）项所述的争端。即使按照仲裁庭上述逻辑将中国2006年声明认定为“保留和例外”，其也是在《公约》第309条“除非本公约其他条款明文规定”的基础上作出的。

仲裁庭对中国2006年声明的解释与既往国际司法实践不符。早在1923年“东卡雷里亚地位案”（Status of Eastern Carelia）判决中，常设国际法院已明确表示，“国际法已确立国家未经其本身同意，不能被迫将其与他国之纠纷提交调停或仲裁或其他种类之和平解决方式”。[3] 中国作出2006年声明既是《公约》赋予的权利，也表明针对《公约》第298条第1款（a）、（b）和（c）项所述的争端不接受强制仲裁的态度。解释此类声明与条约解释存在差异，对此，国际法院在“渔业管辖权案”中认为：“一国接受国际法院强制管辖的声明是主权国家的单方行为，其解释规则与1969年《维也纳条约法公约》确立的解释规则不同。国际法院以往的案件中已经详细论述过解释声明和保留的适当规则。依据这些规则，国际法院将考虑接受国当时的本意，以自然合理的方式，对接受国际法院强制管辖的声明和保留进行解释。保留国的本意不仅可以从相关条款的内容中

① 参见 Award on Jurisdiction and Admissibility, p. 37, para. 107。

② 参见《联合国海洋法公约》第310条。

③ 参见 Status of Eastern Carelia (USSR v. Finland), Advisory Opinion, Permanent Court of International Justice 1923, Part IV, p. 27。

推断出来，同时还可以通过参考条款的上下文、考察保留国起草时的背景和所追求的目的得出。”[①] 在该案投赞成票法官的个别意见中，科罗马法官指出：“法院审理争端的管辖权来自法院规约和政府声明中的授权同意，而不是来自其可能适用的法律。”[②] 小田滋法官在“伊朗石油平台案”的异议意见中，认为“法院不应该解释某些条款以寻求管辖权，而应弄清由破坏石油平台而引起的争议是否在条约范围内，未拒绝伊朗的诉讼请求，可能会导致这样一个情况，即每一个国家都可以借口因任何条约的违反而将其他国家送上法庭，尽管另一个国家否认该争议属于条约管辖范围”。[③] 在“边境及跨境武装行动案”个别意见中，小田滋法官同样指出，“强调当事国接受法院管辖权的意图至关重要”，认为“该意图永远是法院受理案件的必要条件”。[④] 可见，仲裁庭在解释中国 2006 年声明及评估其效力时，不是没有认识到中国 2006 年声明的真实意图，而是有意以条约解释的方法扩大对案件的管辖权。

南海岛礁法律地位仲裁请求构成中菲两国海域划界不可分割的组成部分。中国在《立场文件》中主张，即使菲律宾提出的仲裁事项涉及有关《公约》解释或适用的问题，也构成海域划界不可分割的组成部分，已被中国 2006 年声明所排除，不得提交仲裁。[⑤] 仲裁庭在《裁决书》中回顾了中国《立场文件》所表达的观点，[⑥] 但坚持《管辖权及可受理性裁决》中的观点，认为菲律宾所提第 3 至 7 项诉求不是涉及海洋划界的争端，第 298 条未限制仲裁庭的管辖权。[⑦] 对于一个争端是否因涉及（concerning）另一个争端，而被当事国声明或保留排除的问题，同样出现在国际法院审

---

① 参见 The Fisheries Jurisdiction Case（Spain v. Canada），Judgment，I. C. J. Reports 1998，pp. 23－28，paras. 39－56。

② 参见 The Fisheries Jurisdiction Case（Spain v. Canada），Judgment，I. C. J. Reports 1998，Separate Opinion of Judge Koroma，p. 59，para. 4。

③ 参见 Oil Platforms（Islamic Republic of Iran v. United States of America），Judgment，I. C. J. Reports 1996，Dissenting Opinion of Judge Oda，p. 101，para. 26。

④ 参见 Border and Transborder Armed Actions（Nicaragua v. Honduras），Judgment，I. C. J. Reports 1988，Separate Opinion of Judge Oda，p. 60，para. 16。

⑤ 参见《中华人民共和国政府关于菲律宾共和国所提南海仲裁案管辖权问题的立场文件》第 58－59 段，新华网，http://news.xinhuanet.com/mil/2014－12/07/c_127283404.htm，最后访问日期：2016 年 12 月 27 日。

⑥ AWARD，p. 58，para. 153.

⑦ Award on Jurisdiction and Admissibility，pp. 141－143，paras. 400－404.

理的“渔业管辖权案”中。对此，国际法院在解释排除其管辖的“源起或涉及”（disputes arising out of or concerning）该问题保护和管理措施以及它们的实施时，认为“保留并没有降低排除争端的‘事由’的标准，保留中‘源自或涉及……争端’排除的不仅仅是那些直接‘实质问题’（Subject-Matter）为争端的措施及其实施的争端，还排除了‘涉及’（concerning）这些措施的争端，甚至更广的包括那些‘源起’（arising out of）这些措施的争端。也就是说，如果没有这些措施，该类争端就不会产生，这就是这一用语的含义”。① 在南海仲裁案中，对于岛礁法律地位的认定，必然牵涉当事国在未划界海域可主张海洋权利的否定或肯定，仲裁庭对《公约》第298条作出窄化其适用范围、变更其实质内容的限制性解释，否定中国2006年声明的效力，与国际法院上述判决不符。

综上，在承认岛礁领土为一国所有、领土相向国家尚未划定海洋边界的情况下，径行裁决岛礁法律地位及其海洋权利，不仅有悖于国家主权原则，也变相划定了当事国之间的海洋边界。换言之，即使有关岛礁法律地位仲裁事项，涉及《公约》解释或适用，也构成中菲两国海域划界不可分割的组成部分，② 被中国2006年声明排除于强制争端解决程序适用范围。

三 南海仲裁案涉及岛礁法律地位条约解释的分析

南海仲裁案中，仲裁庭一反既往的国际司法与仲裁实践，有意避开直接解释与适用《公约》第121条第3款，从条约解释的路径出发，声称应用《维也纳条约法公约》第31条、第32条来加以解释，然后从文本解释、目的解释和缔约准备三个方面，对《公约》第121条第3款进行解释并得出结论，认为没有证据表明存在基于国家实践形成的协议对该条款的解释与仲裁庭的解释不同。③

---

① 参见 Fisheries Jurisdiction Case（Spain v. Canada），Judgment，I. C. J. Reports 1998，pp. 458 - 459，paras. 61 - 62。

② 参见《中华人民共和国政府关于菲律宾共和国所提南海仲裁案管辖权问题的立场文件》第3段，新华网，http://news.xinhuanet.com/mil/2014 - 12/07/c_127283404.htm，最后访问日期：2016年12月27日。

③ AWARD，p. 232，para. 553.

（一）曲解《公约》第121条第3款含义的表现

仲裁庭对《公约》第121条第3款中六个术语采取了严格解释的倾向，对《公约》第121条第3款术语的解释屡有“出人意料”之处，甚至“客观地解释”出了《公约》缔约国未曾讨论过的标准，推定出缔约国不曾形成的共同意图。

第一，《公约》第121条第3款界定的标准被引向苛责。总体上看，由此带来如下问题。

一是文本解释未能将条款的含义引向清晰化。仲裁庭在解释“岩礁”时，援引《公约》第121条第1款岛屿中“自然形成的陆地区域”的标准，一概认定自然形成的岛屿不得存在地质或地形上的塑造，[①] 然而，维持“人类居住”和“自身经济生活”本身就需要对居住地进行改造。在解释“不能”时延续了菲律宾在庭审答辩中的逻辑，[②] 缺少时间延续性，未讨论未来的情形，而这恰是第121条第3款模糊措辞难以解释适用的重要原因之一。[③] 对“维持”的解释缺少可执行性标准，持续渡过一个时期是一年、十年，还是一百年？适当标准的具体参数是什么？仲裁庭都没有给予回答。在解释“人类居住”标准时对主体范围进行了限缩，将驻守在南沙岛礁上的军人和政府人员排除在“人类”之外却未能给出国际法依据，[④] 刻意强调补给的外来输入性，而回避了环境承载力与岛上人员数量在比例上的客观联系。在解释“自身经济生活”时，仲裁庭仅从逻辑角度将“从可能的专属经济区或大陆架衍生的经济活动必然被排除在外”，[⑤] 却无视古今众多洋中岛屿居民以外海捕鱼作为维持生计的最主要活动的现实，这些居民在从事生计活动时无一不是从自身历史传统和惯常生活习惯出发，而不会考虑从离岸12海外取得渔获是否属于“自身经济生活”的范畴。关于“人类居住”与“自身经济生活”关系的讨论（即“或”一词），实际

① AWARD, p. 206, para. 481.

② Hearing on the Merits 25th November 2015, p. 70, paras. 7 – 26.

③ 参见中国法学会菲律宾南海仲裁案研究小组《关于中菲“南海仲裁案”中岛礁法律地位仲裁事项的初步研究报告》，中国法学会网，www. chinalaw. org. cn/Column/Column_View. aspx? ColumnID = 893&InfoID = 19914，最后访问日期：2016年12月27日。

④ AWARD, p. 252, para. 618.

⑤ AWARD, p. 212, para. 501.

上从《公约》第121条第3款起草伊始就已经在学术界存在,[①] 仲裁庭在《裁决书》中的分析并无新意，只不过是借南海仲裁案确立一种观点的权威性而已。

二是仲裁庭对《公约》第121条第3款的解释涉嫌造法。包括仲裁案中菲方专家证人在内的众多国际法学者均认为，仅基于文本而建立起对《公约》第121条的确切解释，已经被贴上了“几乎不可能”的标签。[②] 仲裁庭除了在“岩礁”解释中援引国际法院在尼加拉瓜诉哥伦比亚“领土和海洋争端案”的判决作为支撑外，在其他术语解释中，仲裁庭一方面用《牛津英语词典》和《简明牛津英语词典》中的语义解释厘清该条款用语的通常意义,[③] 俨然将字典作为《公约》的组成部分;[④] 另一方面在解释中不仅夹杂着仲裁员个人的观点，而且还包括对存在争议学术观点单方面截取及编纂，未给出包括习惯国际法在内的任何法律例证。

第二，目的解释不足以反映缔约国对《公约》第121条第3款的共同意图。仲裁庭将“《公约》第121条第3款和专属经济区目的之间的联系”[⑤] 作为目的解释的内容之一，回顾了专属经济区制度在《公约》中确立的过程，认为第121条第3款起草者关注的“人类居住”，指的是从专属经济区获得利益的那部分人口的“居住”。[⑥] 根据《维也纳条约法公约》

---

① 参见 Erik Franckx, “The Regime of Islands and Rocks”, Malgosia Fitzmaurice, in Norman A. Martínez Gutiérrezthe (eds.), *IMLI Manual on International Maritime Law* (Oxford: Oxford University Press, 2014), pp. 105 – 124。

② Clive H. Schofield, “The Trouble with Islands: The Definition and Role of Islands and Rocks in Maritime Boundary Delimitation”, in S-Y Hong, J. M. Van Dyke (eds.), *Maritime Boundary Disputes, Settlement Processes, and the Law of the Sea* (Hague: Martinus Nijhoff, 2009), pp. 19, 27; A. G. Oude Elferink, “Clarifying Article 121 (3) of the Law of the Sea Convention: The Limits Set by the Nature of International Legal Processes”, (1998) 6 *Boundary and Security Bulletin*, pp. 58 – 59。

③ AWARD, pp. 207 – 208, 211, paras. 485 – 488. 499.

④ 也有观点认为援引词典解释条约文本通常含义无可厚非。例如，世界贸易组织（WTO）上诉机构前主席詹姆斯·巴库斯（James Bacchus）认为，《牛津英语词典》正是发现条约用语“通常意义”的最佳处所，因为“就英语单词而言，没有比《牛津英语词典》定义得更好的了”。参见 James Bacchus, “The Appeals of Trade: The Making of an Old GATT Hand”, World Trade Law Net, http://www.worldtradelaw.net/document.php?id=articles/bacchusgatthand.pdf，最后访问日期：2016年11月26日。

⑤ AWARD, p. 215, paras. 512 – 514.

⑥ AWARD, p. 218, para. 520.

第 31 条和第 32 条，条约解释的目的是确定缔约方的共同意图而非某国或某些国家团体的个别意图，[①] 确定专属经济区制度的目的与岛礁的权利范围，应当如解释《公约》其他条文一样涉及确定缔约国的共同意图。况且，国际法院在“卡塔尔诉巴林案”中业已强调“无论地物有多小，岛屿应当像陆地那样形成同样的海洋权利”，[②] 因而，从专属经济区获得利益角度对人类居住及非居住行为划出一条边界，本身就非常主观。尽管，仲裁庭引用了 1973 年秘鲁代表在海床洋底委员会上的发言、新加坡大使在第三次海洋法会议期间的总结发言加以证实，[③] 然而，不得不承认的是，“目的解释方法（intention approach）太过主观，整体解释方法（integration approach）更有助于条约含义的明确。《维也纳条约法公约》第 31 条第 2 段所规定的条约解释规则就是对‘整体解释方法’的阐释”。[④] 而且，因为相关规范的谈判过程更为复杂，试图厘清这种可能存在于文本之外的缔约国意图，可能具有更大的困难。[⑤]

第三，缔约准备对于理清《公约》第 121 条第 3 款含义作用有限。由于《公约》第 121 条第 3 款文本的模糊性，借助于缔约前的准备确定该条款的含义，其作用十分有限。[⑥] 国际法院法官阿吉博拉在利比亚诉乍得“领土争端案”中认为，“《维也纳条约法公约》第 32 条对条约签订前的准备工作及缔约环境在条约解释中的作用进行了规定，将其作为使条约条款含义进一步明晰的补充资料。但在实际的条约解释中，我对准备资料的作用表示怀疑。大量的准备材料（如谈判文件、报告、会议辩论及地图等）

---

① China-Measures Affecting Trading Rights and Distribution Services for Certain Publications and Audiovisual Entertainment Products, WT/DS363/AB/R, 21 December 2009, p. 164, para. 405.

② Maritime Delimitation and Territorial Questions between Qatar and Bahrain (Qatar v. Bahrain), Judgment, I. C. J. Reports 2001, p. 61, para. 185.

③ AWARD, p. 216, para. 514.

④ 参见 Territorial Dispute (Libyan Arab Jamahiriya v. Chad), Judgment, I. C. J. Reports 1994, Separate Opinion of Judge Ajibola, pp. 64 – 69, paras. 59 – 78。

⑤ 房东：《对“文本”的扬弃：WTO 条约解释方法的一种修正——以服务贸易具体承诺表的解释为分析起点》，《法律科学》2011 年第 3 期。

⑥ 参见 David Anderson, “Islands and Rocks in the Modern Law of the Sea”, in Myron H. Nordquist, C. H. Schofield (eds.), *The Law of the Sea Convention*: *US Accession and Globalization* (Hague: Martinus Nijhoff, 2012), pp. 307 – 321。

本身就容易导致解释上的冲突”。[①] 仲裁庭在《裁决书》对缔约准备的梳理，似乎也没有得出更多有助于解释《公约》第121条第3款的肯定性结论，反而证明在该条款制定期间存在大量不同立场，以至于除了模糊条文表述以实现妥协外，无法进一步就区别岛屿和岩礁的面积、人口等具体标准形成共同的意图。事实上，仲裁庭也未找到充分的证据证明这种共同意图是真实的、客观存在的。

（二）在推定意图与有疑从轻解释之间未实现平衡

有疑从轻（in dubio mitius）解释属于条约解释习惯规则。[②] 即如果一项规定的含义含糊，应该采纳那种使负担义务方较少负担，或对当事国的属地或属人最高权较少干涉，或对当事方较少限制的含义。[③] 1925年，常设国际法院在《洛桑条约》解释案咨询意见中即采纳有疑从轻解释原则，主张对限制主权予以严格解释。[④] 南海仲裁案中仲裁庭所作解释与上述国际司法裁决相距甚远。

第一，缔约国针对《公约》第121条第3款不存在共同意图。条约解释方法的基础是，条约文本必须假定为缔约国意图的权威表述，……将其用语的通常意义、条约的背景、其目的和宗旨、国际法一般规则，连同缔约国的作准解释，作为解释条约的主要标准。[⑤] 推定意图是通过应用《维也纳条约法公约》第31条、第32条承认的各种解释资料所确定的当事国的意图，[⑥]

---

① 参见 Territorial Dispute (Libyan Arab Jamahiriya v. Chad), Judgment, I. C. J. Reports 1994, Separate Opinion of Judge Ajibola, p. 72, para. 88。

② Ian Brownlie, *Principles of Public International Law* (Oxford: Oxford University Press, 4th ed., 1990), p. 631.

③ 参见 Lassa Oppenheim, International Law: A Treatise (Vol. 1) (London: Longmans, Green and Co., 1905), p. 561; Ian Brownlie, *Principles of Public International Law* (Oxford: Oxford University Press, 4th ed., 1990), p. 631。

④ 参见 Permanent Court of International Justice, Interpretation of Article 3, Para. 2 of the Treaty of Lausanne, Advisory Opinion, P. C. I. J. 1925, Series B No. 12, p. 25；张卫彬《国际法院解释领土条约的路径、方法及拓展》，《法学研究》2015年第2期。

⑤ 参见 Yearbook of the International Law Commission, Documents of the first part of the seventeenth session including the report of the Commission to the General Assembly, 1964, vol. II, pp. 204 - 205, para. 15。

⑥ 参见 Report of the International Law Commission, Subsequent agreements and subsequent practice in relation to the interpretation of treaties, A/68/10 (2013), p. 27。

推定意图的前提是缔约国存在一个潜在的“共同意图”，并可以从公约条款用语的通常意义等方面，抽象出来。如果缔约国在缔约期间本就缺失共同意图，通过解释的方法创设缔约国“共同意图”，实则是单方面增加或减少《公约》缔约国的权利和义务。然而，推定意图并非一个单独可确定的最初意愿，准备工作并非确定当事国推定意图的主要基础，而是如《维也纳条约法公约》第 32 条所示，仅仅是补充解释资料。[①] 况且，《公约》缔约准备材料已经清晰地表明，缔约国之间有关第 121 条第 3 款的含义从未形成过共同意图，更遑论其目的和宗旨，以至于这种异议延续至今，既无国际法院判决予以澄清，也无可以依赖的国家实践。[②] 在缺少缔约国的作准解释，无法从第 121 条第 3 款用语的通常意义、条约背景及国际法一般规则，推知缔约国共同意图的情况下，[③] 仲裁庭没有承认缔约国共同意图存在空白，而是迂回利用《公约》第 5 部分（专属经济区）缔约准备工作，推定和填补缔约国在《公约》第 8 部分存在的共同意图，这种方式不仅无视《公约》缔约期间的客观事实，也是在借用条约解释之名为缔约国创设权利和义务。

第二，有疑从轻解释是共同意图缺失情形下条约解释的合理化选择。适用有疑从轻解释原则的前提，是承认其属于条约解释习惯规则，而非普遍适用的一般规则。对此，有学者质疑“在解释中强调该原则将造成条约分裂，即使条约在不同情况下适用不同国家时具有不同含义”。[④] 但是不同岛礁的水文、生态、经济生活等情况本来就千差万别，在《公约》制定期间不同国家对第 121 条也是观点各异，即使在《维也纳条约法公约》第 31 条、第 32 条限制下，条约解释本身依然具有相当大的灵活性，不存在唯一标准，仲裁庭选择何种解释方法应属其自由裁量范围。然而，条约解释目的之一是使约文含义明晰化、当事国争端缓和化，面对菲律宾的仲裁请求，仲裁庭只能在“继续解释”或“拒绝解释”中二选其一。囿于“不得拒

① 参见 Report of the International Law Commission, Subsequent agreements and subsequent practice in relation to the interpretation of treaties, A/68/10（2013）, p. 27。

② AWARD, pp. 225－226, paras. 534－535.

③ AWARD, p. 215, para. 512.

④ 参见〔美〕约翰·H·杰克逊《国家主权与 WTO——变化中的国际法基础》，赵龙跃、左海聪、盛建明译，社会科学文献出版社，2009，第 215—216 页。

绝裁判”原则和《管辖权及可受理性裁决》，拒绝解释《公约》第121条第3款显然行不通，推定共同意图又涉嫌为缔约国创设权利和义务。故此，解释该条款的唯一路径只能是承认缔约国共同意图存在空白，适用有疑从轻解释原则。然而，仲裁庭在《裁决书》中对《公约》第121条第3款解释恰恰相反，不仅推定得出一个莫须有的共同意图，而且严格限制了该条款的适用。

（三）对条约术语的时间演变特征未作出合理化解释

根据解释之时存有的解释资料确定当事国意图时，必须回答当事国签订条约中的“术语”（term）含义是否可随时间演变。[①] 即条约是应当根据其缔结时的情况和法律来解释，还是应当根据使用之时的情况和法律来解释。[②] 术语并不限于具体措辞（如商业、领土地位或投资），而是还可能包含更为相互关联和相互交叉的概念，如“依法”、“必须”等。[③] 国际法院在解释条约术语时存在两种倾向：一种是偏向于“当时意义”解释；另一种更偏向于“演变性”解释，采用演变解释办法的国际司法和仲裁机构，均采用逐案处理的方式，通过《维也纳条约法公约》第31条和第32条提到的各种条约解释资料，确定是否应当赋予条约术语以能够跟随时间演变的含义。[④] 对于以上两种解释倾向，纪尧姆专案法官在“航行权和相关权利争端案”中总结指出，更倾向于“当时意义”解释的法院裁决，大多涉及相当具体的条约术语（如分水岭、主航道或河流最深线、地名、河口）。[⑤] 而演变性

---

① 参见 Report of the International Law Commission, Subsequent agreements and subsequent practice in relation to the interpretation of treaties, A/68/10（2013）, p. 27。

② 参见 M. Fitzmaurice, “Dynamic（Evolutive）Interpretation of Treaties Part I”,（2008）21 *Hague Yearbook of International Law*, pp. 101ff.。

③ 参见 Report of the International Law Commission, Subsequent agreements and subsequent practice in relation to the interpretation of treaties, A/68/10（2013）, p. 30。

④ 参见 Report of the International Law Commission, Subsequent agreements and subsequent practice in relation to the interpretation of treaties, A/68/10（2013）, p. 25。

⑤ 参见 Dispute regarding Navigational and Related Rights（Costa Rica v. Nicaragua）, Judgment, I. C. J. Reports 2009, Declaration of Judge ad hoc Guillaume, pp. 294 – 300, paras. 9 – 18; Report of the International LawCommission, *Discussion on the Study on the interpretation oftreaties in the light of “any relevant rules of international law applicable in the relations between the parties”（article 31（3）（c）of the Vienna Convention on the Law of Treaties）, in the context of general developments in international law and concerns of the international community*, A/60/10（2005）, para. 479。

解释的案件涉及更一般的术语，如“现代世界的艰难条件”或“这些人民的福祉和发展”等。①

应区分对待《公约》第121条第3款术语的解释。《公约》第121条第3款中的“岩礁”显然属于纪尧姆法官所指具体的条约术语，“不能”、“维持”、“人类居住”和“自身经济生活”会随着人类社会的发展与科学技术的进步呈现出不同的形式与内容，属于一般术语。在《公约》长期有效的前提下，则需要通过在个案的基础上考虑某些标准，在使用各种解释资料中得出此种演变解释。②“航行权和相关权利争端案”中，国际法院在解释1858年条约中“商业”（comercio）一词时，认为“在一些情况下，当事国缔结条约的意图是……赋予所用术语……一种能够演变的含义或内容，而非一旦设定即永不改变的含义或内容”，以便“为国际法的发展留出余地”。③ 国际法院在认定“商业”（comercio）作为一般术语后，指出“当事国必然意识到其含义……很可能随时间演变”，意识到“缔结的条约要持续很长时间”，并得出结论认为“必须推定当事国……意图使”该术语“具有演变的含义”。④ 在“美国海虾海龟案”中，世界贸易组织上诉机构认为，“第20条（g）项中‘自然资源’这一通用术语不是‘静止’的，而‘根据定义是发展的’”。⑤ 可见，对于条约中的一般术语作演变性解释，在国际司法及仲裁中存在共识，并非不具有代表性的个案情况。反观南海仲裁案，仲裁庭偏倚“当时意义”解释，以19世纪60年代、20世纪30至40年代的个别记载判断南海岛礁当前状况，就是选择了与国际司法实践相背离的条约解释方向，因而无法期待其得出一个合理、合法的结论。

---

① 参见《国际联盟盟约》第22条。

② 参见 Report of the Study Group of the International Law Commission Finalized by Martti Koskenniemi, *Fragmentation of International Law: Difficulties Arising from the Diversification and Expansion of International Law*, A/CN. 4/L. 682 and Corr. 1 (2006), para. 478。

③ Dispute Regarding Navigational and Related Rights (Costa Rica v. Nicaragua), Judgment, I. C. J. Reports 2009, p. 213, at p. 242, para. 64.

④ Dispute regarding Navigational and Related Rights (Costa Rica v. Nicaragua), Judgment, I. C. J. Reports2009, p. 243, paras. 66 – 68.

⑤ United States-Import Prohibition of Certain Shrimp and Shrimp Products, WT/DS58/AB/R, 12 October 1998, pp. 48 – 49, para. 130.

四 南海仲裁案涉及岛礁法律地位引用证据的剖析

南海仲裁案中仲裁庭在评估证据的可靠性及证明价值基础上，主要依据军事测量数据、航行指南及海图、学术文献及新闻报道，适用国际法相关规则证明南海岛礁的历史及事实状况，并结合解释《公约》第121条第3款后确立的标准，判断相关岛礁的法律地位。

（一）秘密军事测量所得证据不具有合法性

仲裁庭在引用英国、日本军事测量数据时，虽承认这些信息是在二战后被公之于众，[①] 但径行越过了对证据合法性的判定。由此即会产生疑问，通过侵犯主权行为获取的信息是否可以作为仲裁证据，以及默认和禁止反言是否会支持证据的合法性。

第一，合法性是适用证据的首要前提。合法性，是指证据形式合法，且取得方式、手段及程序必须符合法律规定，证据的合法性直接影响其可采性（admissible）。国际法中并没有系统的证据合法性判定及排除规则，通常经由个案审查的方式判定证据合法性，提出证据可采性的限制条件。在“科孚海峡案”中，针对英国主张1946年11月12日和13日的扫雷行为是基于其与苏联、美国和法国的协议，以及搜集水雷是为了保存证据，[②] 国际法院以14票对2票判决英国上述行为侵犯了阿尔巴尼亚的主权，认为“对领土主权的互相尊重是独立国家间国际关系的主要基础”，“为确保对国际法的尊重，作为国际法的执行机关，国际法院必须宣告英国海军的行为构成对阿尔巴尼亚主权的侵犯”。[③] 在该案中，国际法院并未直接审查搜集水雷行为与证据合法性之间的关系，而是从国家主权角度，否定了英国取证行为的合法性，间接地否定了其证据的合法性和可采性。由此可见，

---

① AWARD, p. 141, para. 329.

② 英国海军在阿尔巴尼亚水域的行为有两次：一次发生在1946年10月22日英国军舰因触碰水雷导致爆炸；另一次发生在1946年11月12日和13日在该海峡进行扫雷。参见Corfu Channel Case (UK v. Albania), Merits (including the text of the declaration of Judges Basdevant and Zoričić), I. C. J. Reports 1949, p. 6。

③ 参见Corfu Channel Case (UK v. Albania), Merits (including the text of the declaration of Judges Basdevant and Zoričić), I. C. J. Reports 1949, pp. 34 – 35。

侵犯他国主权获得的证据或许具有真实性和关联性，但依然需要排除其证明效力。

第二，南海岛礁相关信息是通过秘密军事测量取得的。仲裁庭认为，早期对南海进行军事测量的国家主要有英国、日本、法国和美国，其中，第一次对南海岛礁持续性军事测量活动发生于1862—1868年，由英国海军实施。[①] 之后，在20世纪20至30年代，英国、日本海军对南沙群岛进行了持续测量活动，上述大部分测量信息是在二战之后才被公众知晓的，[②] 这一事实在被仲裁庭援引的《南沙群岛秘密水文测量》中也得到了证实。[③] 且不论《裁决书》和《南沙群岛秘密水文测量》认定的南海水文测量历史事实是否狭隘，[④] 仅就裁决认定的事实而言，可以得出如下结论。一是，测量是在南海岛礁附近及以上进行的。如《裁决书》认定英国海军曾于1866年、1932年两次测量黄岩岛，[⑤] 1864年至1865年、1938年两次测量华阳礁等。[⑥] 二是，未说明测量行为是否得到中国政府许可。1840年后伴随国际法传入中国，当时的中国政府对水文测量与国家主权之间的关系已有明确认识。如1883年，德国军舰非法测量我西沙、南沙群岛，在清政府提出抗议后，德国停止了非法活动，[⑦] 1933年“九小岛事件”的肇事船舶也是法国西贡当局的军舰和测量船。[⑧] 而且外国军舰测量中国水道，也有事先告之中国政府并获得同意的事例。[⑨] 如1906年英国军舰测绘福建沿

---

① 1862年前，英国航海者和水文地理学者已开始对南沙岛礁进行水文测量。参见房建昌《近代南海诸岛海图史略——以英国海军海图官局及日本、美国、法国和德国近代测绘南沙群岛为中心（1685—1949年）》，《海南大学学报》（人文社会科学版）2013年第4期。

② AWARD, p. 141, para. 329.

③ 参见 David Hancox, Victor Prescott, *Secret Hydrographic Surveys in the Spratly Islands* (Philadelphia: Coronet Books Inc., 1999), pp. 154 - 155。

④ 1935年4月，中华民国海军海道测量局完成实地测量后，水陆地图审查委员会会刊第2期专门绘制《中国南海各岛屿图》。参见毛剑杰《纸上谈疆：南海断续的国界线是如何形成的?》，人民网，http://history.people.com.cn/GB/205396/15093538.html，最后访问日期：2016年12月27日。

⑤ AWARD, p. 143, para. 333.

⑥ AWARD, p. 144, para. 335.

⑦ 郭渊：《晚清政府的海洋主张与对南海权益的维护》，《中国边疆史地研究》2007年第3期。

⑧ 参见吴士存主编《南海问题文献汇编》，海南出版社，2001，第8—12页。

⑨ 参见房建昌《近代南海诸岛海图史略——以英国海军海图官局及日本、美国、法国和德国近代测绘南沙群岛为中心（1685—1949年）》，《海南大学学报》（人文社会科学版）2013年第4期。

海，已经报明外务部同意，次年英国军舰测量广东归善亦得到粤督同意，但大量的测量活动没有告知中国政府。[①] 可见，仲裁庭突出英国、日本对南海岛礁军事测量的“原创性”和“持续性”，本就是对历史事实的片面截取，刻意回避了中国政府对特定国家非法测量行为的抗议。

第三，违背国际法规则取得的证据应予排除。19 世纪 60 年代南海尚无领土争端，20 世纪三四十年代中国与日本正处于交战状态，秘密军事测量行为是否违反国际法，应从三方面厘定。一是，时际法原则是判断秘密军事测量合法性的标尺。即根据不同时期的法律与历史事实，适用不同类型的法律，特别是那些当时有效的法律原则与概念，借以解决法律因溯及既往所产生的争议。[②] 英国、日本有关南海岛礁军事测量发生在百年之前、公布于二战之后，当事国行为的合法性受行为当时有效的法律支配，依照这一原则，该行为的合法存续也必须与法律演进要求的情况相一致。[③] 英国、日本对南海的军事测量活动是在中国领土上进行的，依照与之同时的法律来判定，测量行为受到领土主权的限制。从前述中国政府对外国军舰非法测量行为的抗议及国际法院“科孚海峡案”的判决看，即使在 19 世纪 60 年代和 20 世纪 30 年代，该测量行为也是非法的。其二，日本军事测量行为属于侵略行为。《裁决书》援引 20 世纪 30 年代日本在南海实施测量获取的数据时，除两处引文标明数据信息来源于日本帝国海军 1938 年测绘海图外，其他均未标注具体测量或出版时间，[④] 汉考克斯和普雷斯科特指出，该测量用于舰队停泊和军事用途，而且这些 1938 年出版的日本海图，直到二战后才对非日本军事使用者（non-Japanesemilitary users）公开，[⑤] 由此证明，日本在南海的测量行为是其侵略行为的一部分，属于国

① 参见刘利民《近代中国水道测量事业的民族化进程述论——以海道测量局为中心的考察》，《晋阳学刊》2016 年第 3 期。

② 参见 Clive Parry，John P. Grant，*Encyclopaedic Dictionary of International Law*（London：Ocean Pub.，1986），p. 190。

③ 参见 Reports of International Arbitral Awards Volume II，*Island of Palmas Case 1928*，United Nations（2006），pp. 829 – 850。

④ 参见 AWARD，p. 136，para. 315，at p. 157，para. 361.

⑤ David Hancox，Victor Prescott，“A Geographical Description of the Spratly Islands and an Account of Hydrographic Surveys Amongst Those Islands”，International Boundaries Research Unit，(1995) 1 *Maritime Briefing* 6，p. 37.

际罪行。[①] 三是，默认和禁止反言不适用于判断秘密军事测量行为的合法性。英国、日本海军对南沙群岛的秘密测量信息是在二战之后才被公众知晓的，尽管当时中国在测量技术方面落后于英国、日本，但是在国际法领域从未对他国非法测量南海岛礁的行为采取默许。在20世纪70年代南海争端公开化之前，包括英国、日本等国家一方面承认中国对南沙群岛的主权，另一方面采取秘密方式测量中国领土，本身就是对禁止反言的违反。毋庸讳言，时间不会“洗白”证据的非法性，强权也非公理，秘密军事测量取得的证据不仅不能支持仲裁裁决的合法性，也违反了既有的国际法判决。

（二）《航行指南》及海图资料不属于同时期证据

在尼加拉瓜诉哥伦比亚“领土和海洋争端案”中，国际法院在考察奎塔苏埃诺礁是否存在高潮时高于水面自然形成的陆地时，没有采纳多年（某些情形下是数十年）的测量结果，不认为此类海图有对证明上述地物的情况有什么证明价值（probative value）。国际法院指出，此类海图是用以说明在奎塔苏埃诺礁航行的危险，而非区分高潮时哪些地物高于水面，哪些低于水面。与之相关的是同时期证据（contemporary evidence），到目前为止，最为重要的是史密斯博士（Robert Smith）编写的《关于奎塔苏埃诺礁的专家报告》，该报告是在对奎塔苏埃诺礁实际观测及对这些情况的科学评估基础上形成的，尽管如此，国际法院仍认为必须谨慎对待报告结论。[②] 南海仲裁案中仲裁庭称“已经注意到上述判明，但认为对其理解应基于该判决部分上下文”，并逆向推理《公约》第5条[③]认为，“该条设想了一种状况，即能够期待通过当事国良好的测量和绘制，一国可以给出其海岸线的信息。由于远海地物很少被声索国仔细测量，故经修订的海图可以校正错误或引入新的信息，《航行指南》可以作为问题地物（features in question）直接观察的替代来源”。[④] 本文认为，仲裁庭该论断不成立。

---

① 参见朱文奇《东京审判与追究侵略之罪责》，《中国法学》2015年第4期。

② Territorial and Maritime Dispute (Nicaragua v. Colombia), Judgment, I. C. J. Reports2012, p. 644, paras. 35 – 36.

③ 《联合国海洋法公约》第5条：“除本公约另有规定外，测算领海宽度的正常基线是沿海国官方承认的大比例尺海图所标明的沿岸低潮线。”参见 AWARD, p. 142, para. 331。

④ AWARD, p. 142, paras. 331 – 332.

第一，《公约》第5条的规定与判断南海岛礁形态无关。《公约》第5条规定的是沿岸低潮线可以作为领海基线，而非大比例尺海图所标明的信息可以作为判断沿海国地物形态的依据。即使在该条款框架下，从海图上读取沿海国岛礁的形态信息，也需受到限制：一是应当依据沿海国官方承认的大比例尺海图，而非任意大比例尺海图；二是读取信息的对象仅指向沿海国大陆“沿岸”；三是不属于该条“除外”规定，即第6条（礁石）、第7条（直线基线）、第9条（河口）、第10条（海湾）、第11条（港口）和第13条（低潮高地）。[①] 仲裁庭在《裁决书》中未说明其所选定的1：250万比例尺是否为中国承认的“大比例尺”，也未说明其所依据的他国大比例尺海图是否为中国官方承认的海图。即便承认仲裁庭逆向推理的合理性，对于“位于环礁上的岛屿或有岸礁环列的岛屿”[②] 水文及形态信息的推知，也应当援引《公约》第6条的规定。因此，无论是从法律依据，还是从水文测量与海图之间的信息反馈关系看，仲裁庭对《公约》第5条的援引都无法为其进一步利用航行指南及海图资料奠定证据基础。

第二，同时期证据在判断南海岛礁形态中同样适用。国际法院在尼加拉瓜诉哥伦比亚案同时期证据判决部分，再次肯定“即使最小的岛屿也能够划定12海里领海”，[③] 并指出所述证据必须有效满足检验地物高潮时高于水面。[④] 国际法院一方面承认国际法没有规定岛礁的面积下限，另一方面认为《关于奎塔苏埃诺礁的专家报告》中的潮汐模型推算，对于计算奎塔苏埃诺礁这种的浅水区地物是存在争议的，不能有效证明这些微小海洋地物一直高于水面几厘米。[⑤] 南海仲裁案中，仲裁庭显然注意到了上述判

---

① 参见 A. G. Oude Elferink，D. R. Rothwell（eds.），*The Law of the Sea and Polar Maritime Delimitation and Jurisdiction*（Hague：Martinus Nijhoff，2001），pp. 34，56－68。

② 《联合国海洋法公约》第6条：“在位于环礁上的岛屿或有岸礁环列的岛屿的情形下，测算领海宽度的基线是沿海国官方承认的海图上以适当标记显示的礁石的向海低潮线。”

③ 参见 Maritime Delimitation and Territorial Questions between Qatar and Bahrain（Qatar v. Bahrain），Merits，I. C. J. Reports 2001，pp. 101－102，para. 205；Territorial and Maritime Dispute between Nicaragua and Honduras in the Caribbean Sea（Nicaragua v. Honduras），Judgment，I. C. J. Reports 2007（II），p. 751，para. 302。

④ Territorial and Maritime Dispute（Nicaragua v. Colombia），Judgment，I. C. J. Reports 2012，p. 644，para. 36.

⑤ Territorial and Maritime Dispute（Nicaragua v. Colombia），Judgment，I. C. J. Reports 2012，p. 645，para. 38.

决暗含的时间标准，在面对繁杂、差异甚至是相互矛盾的证据时，仲裁庭并未充分行使调查、获取补充证据的权力，或者进行有效的甄别，而是采取回避和以偏概全的态度，希望利用证据的时间跨度，弥补因缺少同时期观测导致的证据真实性质疑，却无法回避那些过时文献所提到的岛礁特征，至今已经不复存在或位置不够精确。正如弗兰克法官在"利吉丹岛和西巴坦岛案"中指出的，"撇开案件输赢不谈，法院未能广泛地阐明所涉的法律问题，而是将精力放在决定一些模糊证据的细微的事实评价问题之上，这将造成国际法律体制的迷失"。①

第三，不同时期的南海岛礁证据内容存在差异。《裁决书》援引了英国海军 1864 年测量南沙群岛和 1926 年测量双子群礁的报告，称南沙群岛潮高是 1.6 米，高高潮（Higher High Water）和低低潮（Lower Low Water）之间的潮差是 0.91 米。1966 年英国海军对双子群礁的测量结果显示其高高潮和低低潮之间的潮差是 0.81 米，潮高是 1.4 米。② 仲裁庭对于证据的选择是不能支持其结论的。

首先，南海岛礁的形态处于发展中。南沙岛礁为发育中的珊瑚礁，有地质资料显示，南海底部的地壳在近地质时期处于缓慢上升状态，南海诸岛平均每年升高约 1 厘米，所以南海中不断有新的地物出现。20 世纪 80 年代的观测资料显示，西沙群岛的东新沙洲、西南沙洲和全富岛等就是近期露出水面的。③ 因此，用百年之前的测量结果证南海岛礁当前的水文及形态信息，必不足取。其次，《航行指南》及海图不是判断岛礁地理及水文信息的可靠依据。海图是用以说明在岛礁附近海域航行的危险，而非区分高潮时哪些地物高于水面，哪些低于水面。④ 由于各国求值方法有别，因此采用的深度基准面也不相同，得出的水文数据差值大小也各异。因此，海图深度基准面是一种数值表示，⑤ 其意义是为航海安全提供最小的

① Sovereignty over Pulau Ligitan and Pulau Sipadan (Indonesia v. Malaysia), Judgment, I. C. J. Reports 2002, dissenting opinion of Judge Ad Hoc Franck, p. 692, para. 3.

② AWARD, p. 135, para. 314.

③ 广东地名委员会编《南海诸岛地名资料汇编》，广东省地图出版社，1987，第 144 页。

④ 参见 Territorial and Maritime Dispute (Nicaragua v. Colombia), Judgment, I. C. J. Reports 2012, p. 644, para. 35。

⑤ 参见暴景阳等《中国沿岸主要验潮站海图深度基准面的计算与分析》，《武汉大学学报》（信息科学版）2006 年第 3 期。

静水深，而非对岛礁周边海域作出精确的水文描述。正如一个法庭所言，“大量的证据不会构成证明，就像一百个兔子不会变成马一样”，[①] 在错误的路径上选择了错误的证据，再多的证据也不能支持仲裁结论的合法性。最后，英国海军的测量结果不具有准确性。南沙海区以东北—西南对角线为界，西北半部为正规日潮区，最大可能潮差小于1米；东南半部为不正规日潮区，向岸潮差逐渐增大，如仙娥礁的最大可能潮差大于2.5米。[②]《裁决书》援引1864年测量结果概指南沙群岛，但没有说明具体的测量位置，在逐一分析华阳礁、永暑礁等地物时鲜有提及单个岛礁周边的潮汐状况。[③] 双子群礁位于南沙群岛西北端最外延，菲律宾第3至7项仲裁请求没有涉及该群礁内的地物，该群礁与美济礁、仁爱礁也不属于同一潮区。仲裁庭所谓“南海潮差相对较小，选择不同的高程基准（vertical datum）在大多数情况下对认定地物地位没有差别”的说法，[④] 是以偏概全，与国际法院在尼加拉瓜诉哥伦比亚案中谨慎对待水文数据的判决，背道而驰。

（三）学术文献及新闻报道的证据证明力有限

国际司法及仲裁机构对学术文献及新闻报道的证明力予以限制。国际法院在“对尼加拉瓜进行军事和准军事行动案”中，针对美国与尼加拉瓜均提出了大量书籍和新闻报道作为案件证据，认为即使这些材料满足非常高的客观标准，也不能作为确认事实的证明，但在某些情况下，它能补强事实的存在，且可以作为其他来源的证据说明性材料。[⑤] 因而，学术文献及新闻报道的证明力有限。

学术文献及新闻报道仅能对其他证据构建的证据链予以补充。仲裁庭在《裁决书》第6部分C项未给出筛选学术文献及新闻报道的证据标准，1940年出版的《暴风之岛》是由小仓久仁子、桥本博在小仓卯之助遗稿基

---

① 参见 Maritime Delimitation and Territorial Questions（Qatar v. Bahrain），Judgment，I. C. J. Reports 1994，Joint dissenting opinion of Judges Bedjaoui，Ranjeva and Koroma，p. 172，para. 82。

② 参见南沙海域环境质量研究专题组《南沙群岛及其邻近海域环境质量研究》，海洋出版社，1996，第10页。

③ AWARD，pp. 144－174，paras. 336－384.

④ AWARD，p. 134，para. 313.

⑤ Case Concerning Military and Paramilitary Activities in and against Nicaragua（Nicaragua v. United States），Merits，I. C. J. Reports 1986，p. 40，para. 62.

础上编辑而成的，遗稿记录的是小仓卯之助1919年在太平岛的活动，[①] 故《暴风之岛》类型上应属于回忆录，有必要对其证据资格及内容的真实性提出质疑。仲裁庭只选择了1933—1939年大阪《朝日新闻》、《每日新闻》和1945年5月4日《纽约时报》的新闻报道，既未给出筛选标准，也未对上述报道的真实性与可靠性作出充分说明。有关南海岛礁存在大量中文报道，裁决南海岛礁问题，却撇开中文资讯而转求他国报道，仲裁庭援引证据的标准无法令人信服。

刻意挑选证据为证明而证明。仲裁庭援引1947年席连之《广东南沙群岛土壤纪要》有关太平岛土壤及植被状况的记录，认为“接受太平岛可以种植瓜果和蔬菜的事实，但认为太平岛土壤的耕作能力有限，岛上农业不能有效支持一定数量的人口”。[②] 面积狭小的洋中岛是否能够进行农业活动，并支持一定数量的人口？在席文同期刊物另一篇关于南海永兴岛的调查报告中，就可以窥见：“并非此群岛土壤，不能种植，而实为各岛面积过小，且与内地交通联系困难，况广东南部及海南岛一带，荒地甚多，若能绥靖地方，以谋开发，正未可限量，此时似不必舍近而求远”；“区内可植陆稻，每年稻作，如能供给充足肥料，且可种植三季，惟一般言之，仍以种两季为宜，该恐地力消耗过促，易化石田”。[③] 永兴岛与太平岛均属于珊瑚岛，表层土壤构成相似，岛上之所以没有持续的农业活动，并非其自然条件达不到农作要求，而是没有必要“舍近求远”到远离大陆的地方进行耕作。历史上关于南海岛礁的记载浩如烟海，依据同一期刊物的不同文献就可以得出不同结论，由此，至少说明仲裁庭利用学术文献考证岛礁信息得出的结论不具有可靠性。

五 结语

综上所述，《公约》只是国际海洋法制度的一部分而非全部。仲裁庭否定南海各类岛礁之间、岛礁与相连海域及其他自然地物之间，在地理、

---

① 参见小仓卯之助《暴风之岛》，小仓久仁子、桥本博编，小仓中佐遗稿刊行会，1940，第1—3页。

② AWARD, p. 245, para. 596.

③ 陆发熹：《广东西沙群岛之土壤及鸟粪磷矿》，《土壤》（季刊）1947年第3期。

经济和政治上的整体性，无视南海诸群岛在历史上已被视为整体，曲解中国相关外交照会，对《公约》的解释以“释法”之名行“立法”之实。仲裁庭在《裁决书》中曲解《公约》第121条第3款应有的含义，背离条约解释是以约文含义明晰化、当事国争端缓和化为目的的初衷，无视国家实践是推动《公约》制度内容形成和发展的原动力。仲裁庭依赖于从历史片段及证据解释中所得出的间接证据，对南海岛礁的自然及地理信息进行推理证明，未兼顾证据的合法性、真实性和关联性，并且与国际法院的判例存在诸多抵触之处。南海仲裁案中仲裁庭有关岛礁法律地位的裁决，不仅侵犯了中国依据《公约》自主选择争端解决方式的权利，破坏《公约》的整体性和权威性，更是对《公约》第15部分确立的争端解决制度的挑战，损害了包括中国在内的《公约》缔约国的合法权益。

（本文原载于《国际法研究》2017年第1期）

徘徊在法律与科学之间

——国际法院的专家指定

何田田*

2016 年是联合国的主要司法机关国际法院成立 70 周年。国际法院院长罗尼·亚伯拉罕（Ronny Abraham）在向联合国大会第 71 届会议提交法院的年度报告时提及，国际法院（以下简称“法院”）应该庆贺过去 70 年对于法治所取得的成就，但是法院也不得不注意其面临的挑战，非常有必要采用新的工作方法，以应对案件数量和案件复杂度的日益增加。罗尼·亚伯拉罕向大会保证，[①] 法院“将继续利用一切可行之法，发挥好其作为联合国主要司法机关的作用”。[②] 以“一切可行之法”应对日益复杂的案件，在 2016 年度法院的工作中，就有这么一个突出例子：在“加勒比海和太平洋划界案（哥斯达黎加诉尼加拉瓜）”中，法院行使了其在《国际法院规约》（以下简称《规约》）第 50 条下指定专家的权力。这是法院 70

---

* 何田田，中国社会科学院国际法研究所助理研究员。

① “The President of the International Court of Justice Assures the General Assembly that the Court ‘will continue to use all the resources at its disposal to fulfil its role as principal judicial organ of the United Nations’”, Press Release, 28/10/2016, p. 1, International Court of Justice, http://www.icj-cij.org/presscom/files/0/19270.pdf，最后访问日期：2017 年 11 月 7 日。

② “The President of the International Court of Justice assures the General Assembly that the Court ‘will continue to use all the resources at its disposal to fulfil its role as principal judicial organ of the United Nations’”, Press Release, 28/10/2016, p. 2, International Court of Justice, http://www.icj-cij.org/presscom/files/0/19270.pdf，最后访问日期：2017 年 11 月 7 日。

年以来第二次主动运用此权力，打破了其在此问题上一直谨慎的局面。[①]

面对这一背景，结合近年来法院的司法实践，可以引出以下三个值得深思的问题。一是法院现在面临的案件事实日趋复杂，法律以外的专业程度逐渐提高，是否已经到了必须由专家提供意见的阶段？二是为什么法院70年以来对于行使指定专家的权力，抱着如此谨慎和“不愿意”的态度？这就引出了本文所要关注的核心问题即第三个问题，就是法院在后续的案件中，必然会面临一些科学难题，例如“转基因食品是否安全”、“海平面潮汐基准”、“环境是否已经造成污染”等目前并不存在确切的科学结论的问题，这个时候应该以什么样的方式予以对待？为了分别回应上述三个问题，本文主体也对应分为三部分，最后一部分是结论。

一 法院的“难题”：涉及科技事实案件的增多

在2006—2016年这十年期间，法院越来越多地遇到了涉及科学与技术事实密集型的争端，专家证据在解决这些争端中发挥了重要的作用。同时，案件各方当事国也越来越依赖专家证言或其他类似的证据提供方式。[②]

这类专家证据，从定义上来说，就是为帮助法院认定案件所需事实，那些熟悉特定知识领域的个人，通过实际经验或仔细研究，就某个问题形成的意见或结论。“某个问题”既可能是简单的，也可能是复杂的，但这个问题并不在法院或法官的知识领域之内，例如划界案件中争端地区的特定地理地貌状况。但是，不同的专家对某个问题的意见也可能不是完全一致的，某个问题所涉及的科技领域又可能是多维度的，但法院又需要这些科学、技术或其他专业的知识以帮助理解事实。如何去处理这些问题，在某种程度上，已经是今天的法院所面临的一个最大困难。

法院已经发现自己在这个问题上处于两难境地：一方面是涉及科学与

---

① “The President of the International Court of Justice Assures the General Assembly that the Court ‘will continue to use all the resources at its disposal to fulfil its role as principal judicial organ of the United Nations’”, Press Release, 28/10/2016, p. 1, International Court of Justice, http://www.icj-cij.org/presscom/files/0/19270.pdf，最后访问日期：2017年11月7日。

② Loretta Malintoppi, “Fact Finding and Evidence Before the International Court of Justice (Notably in Scientific-Related Disputes)”, *Journal of International Dispute Settlement* 7 (2016): 421.

技术事实密集型的争端在持续增多，不得不“求教”于其他专业领域的知识；另一方面又需要在明显不同但都有效的科学或技术意见中有所取舍地认定事实，还要确保法律适用的准确性与争端解决任务的顺利完成。

法院这70年以来所积累的经验，基本侧重于解决法律问题，这也是法院成立时的国际社会所赋予它的重要职能。在“乌拉圭河纸浆厂案（阿根廷诉乌拉圭）”中，法院有这样一段其对待复杂证据的经典论述：“法院需要注意的是，尽管提交给法院的事实信息数量多且复杂，但法院有责任，在仔细考虑双方提出的所有证据以后，确定相关的证据材料，评估其证明价值，并从中得出结论。因此，根据惯例，法院将根据向其提出的证据，对事实作出自己的认定，然后适用相关的国际法规则。”① 可见，认定当事国所称的事实，评估证据的相关性及其证明力，再据此解释和适用法律，一直是法院多年以来主要的司法任务。

但是，近十年来，情况有所改变。争端当事国开始向法院提交“大量复杂的技术、科学或者专业资料”。② 以2006年5月阿根廷在法院对乌拉圭提起的诉讼为例。阿根廷认为乌拉圭“批准、建设并运营乌拉圭河沿岸的两个纸浆厂”，违反了防止污染和保护水生环境的义务。双方为证明环境是否受到纸浆厂建设影响，提交了大量数据、技术和研究报告，例如阿根廷提交了Latinoconsult S. A. 公司、阿根廷独立环境科学小组（Independent Argentinian Environmental Scientific Team，IAEST）、帝国理工与医学科学院（Imperial College of Science，Technology and Medicine，London）专家、加拿大海特菲尔德（Hatfield）咨询公司专家、国际金融公司所委托的俄克拉荷马咨询公司（EcoMetrix，一家专门从事环境和工业事务的咨询公司）的各种技术报告。③ 乌拉圭同样提交了大量材料，例如其环境理事会（National Directorate for the Environment of the Uruguayan Government，DINAMA）编制的数据和环境影响评估报告等。④ 这些报告本身的观点就互相冲突，

---

① Pulp Mills on the River Uruguay（Argentina v. Uruguay），Judgement，I. C. J. Reports 2010，para 168.

② Chester Brown，*A Common Law of International Adjudication*（Oxford：Oxford University Press，2007），p. 112.

③ *Pulp Mills on the River Uruguay*，Memorial of Argentina（15 January 2007），p. 151，para. 7. 5.

④ Pulp Mills on the River Uruguay（Argentina v. Uruguay），Judgement，I. C. J. Reports 2010，para. 226.

双方对报告的解释也截然相反。[①]

法院采取了什么样的方式处理如此专业的报告？法院首先认为，为确定纸浆厂排放的污水与河流环境的关系，它将“主要权衡和评估”（principally weigh and evaluate）会对河水质量造成影响的物质及其数据，这些物质包括溶解氧、总磷（以及由磷酸盐引起的富营养化的相关物质）、酚类物质、壬基苯酚和壬基苯酚乙氧基化物、二噁英和呋喃。这些物质及其数据本身就是一系列的技术问题，[②] 包括河流中壬基苯酚浓度是否已经升高（壬基苯酚乙氧基化物降解为壬基苯酚的可能性），水体富营养化所引起的藻类迅速繁殖的原因，[③] 河流中磷的浓度，[④] 以及河流的地貌和流体动力学特征（即纸浆厂的选址、河流的方向和速度决定污染物的扩散和稀释）。[⑤] 在经过对数据本身的考察后，法院多次认为阿根廷没有清楚的（clear evidence）[⑥] 或充分的证据（insufficient evidence）[⑦] 支持其主张。也就是说，在所审查的每一个技术问题上，法院认为阿根廷没有满足法院所需要的证明标准（standard of proof）。[⑧]

法院的做法，尤其是对壬基苯酚相关证据处理的方式，鲜明地体现了其坚持传统方法和守旧的态度。作为一个司法机构，不求助于专家评估，法院的法官能完全理解上述物质及其变量问题吗？奥恩·肖卡特·哈苏奈

---

① Pulp Mills on the River Uruguay（Argentina v. Uruguay），Judgement，I. C. J. Reports 2010，para. 166.

② Pulp Mills on the River Uruguay（Argentina v. Uruguay），Judgement，I. C. J. Reports 2010，para. 237.

③ Pulp Mills on the River Uruguay（Argentina v. Uruguay），Judgement，I. C. J. Reports 2010，para. 241.

④ Pulp Mills on the River Uruguay（Argentina v. Uruguay），Judgement，I. C. J. Reports 2010，paras. 240 – 250.

⑤ Pulp Mills on the River Uruguay（Argentina v. Uruguay），Judgement，I. C. J. Reports 2010，para. 212.

⑥ Pulp Mills on the River Uruguay（Argentina v. Uruguay），Judgement，I. C. J. Reports 2010，paras. 257，259，262，264.

⑦ Pulp Mills on the River Uruguay（Argentina v. Uruguay），Judgement，I. C. J. Reports 2010，paras. 254，262.

⑧ Pulp Mills on the River Uruguay（Argentina v. Uruguay），Judgement，I. C. J. Reports 2010，para. 239（regarding dissolved oxygen in the river），para. 247（phosphorous discharge），para. 250（algal bloom），para. 254（phenolic substances），para. 257（presence of polyphenols），para. 259（dioxins and furans），para. 262（effects on biodiversity），and para. 264（air pollution）.

（Awn Shawkat Al-Khasawneh）法官和西玛（Simma）法官在他们的联合反对意见中措辞激烈地批评了大多数人，认为法院被要求“评估证据的相关性并衡量其重要性”，然而“法院本身不具备充分资格评估和衡量各方提交的复杂科学证据”。他们认为，法院错失了充分处理科学问题的一个机会，并称法院这样的一种处理方式，只会增加国际社会对法院作为一个司法机关，是不是能处理如此复杂科学问题的疑惑；法院应该作出的“最有说服力”的选择是根据《规约》第50条任命专家，“在一个涉及如此高密度科学事实的案件中，法院为了作出合理且有说服力的决定，必须要有来自专家的意见”。①

如此高科技密集度的案件在法院中并不是孤例，相反，同类型的案件接踵而来。

日本在法院的第一案——“南极捕鲸案”，由于法院更深入地参与到一系列科学问题中，在国际社会中引起了广泛的关注。该案是2010年5月由澳大利亚提起，新西兰参加，诉请法院裁决，日本凭借其特许南极捕鲸第二阶段研究方案（以下简称JARPA Ⅱ）的名义推行大规模捕获、击杀和加工处理鲸鱼的活动，违反了日本在《国际捕鲸管制公约》及其他国际法规则中的义务。由此，法院要解决的核心问题是JARPA Ⅱ是否符合《国际捕鲸管制公约》第8条中的“为科学研究的目的”。早在案件裁决前，属于国际捕鲸委员会下设的科学委员会的科学家们就认为，日本活动的目标是基于“几个不成立的或不正确的假设”，这些假设包括不同种类的鲸鱼是相互竞争的、小须鲸是所在生态系统的顶级捕食者、小须鲸的减少将导致蓝鲸的增加、蓝鲸的数量都是由小须鲸和座头鲸的数量所决定的。科学家认为，这些假设的验证就需要南极海洋生物资源养护委员会（CCAMLR，Convention for the Conservation of Antarctic Marine Living Resources）的专门知识来评估。②

从本案争端当事国所提交的诉状（1251页）和辩诉状（1757页）的篇幅及其具体内容来看，法院确实处理了大量涉及科学的证据。法院为了

① Pulp Mills on the River Uruguay（Argentina v. Uruguay），Judgement，I. C. J. Reports 2010，Joint dissenting opinion Judges Al-Khasawneh and Simma，para. 111.

② Caroline E. Foster，“New Clothes for the Emperor? Consultation of Experts by the International Court of Justice”，*Journal of International Dispute Settlement* 5（2014）：148 - 149.

确定 JARPA Ⅱ 方案设计和实施（特别是方案中所采用的致死性取样手段）对于实现既定研究目标来说是否合理，进而确定是否“为科学研究的目的”，考查了大量的因素。例如法院在作“手段对于研究目标实现的合理性”的分析时，审查了大量资料以确定 JARPA Ⅱ 使用致死性采样方法的决定过程，方案使用的致死性方法的规模（包括 JARPA 和 JARPA Ⅱ 样本量的比较、3 个特定种群样本量大小的决定和实际捕捉的样本大小的比较）、方案开放式的时间表、方案迄今为止取得的科学成果以及与其他研究机构的合作程度等。① 本案中法院的处理方式，在法院的历史中，可以说是前所未有的，以至于有法官在其个别意见中认为法院在判决中过多地关注了科学问题，而偏离了司法的职能。②

“盖巴斯科夫—拉基马洛大坝案（匈牙利/斯洛伐克）”、“空中喷洒除草剂案（厄瓜多尔诉哥伦比亚）”，以及“加勒比海和太平洋划界案”等案件，同样是科技事实密集型的案件。法院在事实认定时，遇到了大量的科学和技术问题，以致不得不确定“生态必要性”（ecological necessity），③ 除草剂草甘膦的有害性或者加勒比海的地形地貌，不得不同时面对包括地震学、水文学、水文生物学、水化学、泥沙学、河流形态学、土壤科学、林业、生物学、生态学和环境影响评估（EIA）方法等广泛的技术和科学专业领域的问题。④

这样一些科学技术密集型的案件，又由于科学信息在现实世界本身所具有的不确定性，对法院确实构成了多重挑战。⑤ 正如哈苏纳和西玛法官在“乌拉圭河纸浆厂案”中所认为的，在这些高度复杂事实的案件中，专家的使用对于法院确立“当事方主张事实的真实性或虚假性”是必要的。⑥

---

① *Whaling in the Antarctic*（*Australia v. Japan*：*New Zealand intervening*），Judgment，I. C. J. Reports 2014，paras. 128 - 222；也可参见何田田《国际法院“南大洋捕鲸”案评析》，《国际法研究》2015 年第 1 期。

② *Whaling in the Antarctic*，Separate opinion of Judge Xue，para. 2.

③ Gabčíkovo-Nagymaros Project（Hungary/Slovakia），Judgment，I. C. J. Reports 1997，para. 35.

④ Riddell Anna and Plant Brendan，*Evidence Before the International Court of Justice*（London：British Institute of International and Comparative Law，2009），p. 347.

⑤ 参见 Makane Moïse Mbengue，“Scientific Fact-finding by International Courts and Tribunals”，*Journal of International Dispute Settlement* 3（2012）：514 - 518。

⑥ Pulp Mills on the River Uruguay（Argentina v. Uruguay），Judgement，I. C. J. Reports 2010，para. 113.

同样，优素福法官（Judge Abdulqawi A. Yusuf）主张法院应该利用《规约》第50条下的专家以帮助法院更深入理解缔约方提交的证据。[①] 这里又引出一个问题，如此专业的领域，法院的法官们为什么在这么多年来就极少行使《规约》第50条所赋予的指定专家的权力呢？

二 法院的“难处”：指定专家的参与

法院能行使指定专家权力的直接依据是《规约》的第50条，“法院得随时选择任何个人、团体、局所、委员会或其他组织，委以调查或鉴定之责。”[②] 与此相关的还有《规约》第48条，“法院为进行办理案件应颁发命令；对于当事国每造，应决定其必须终结辩论之方式及时间；对于证据之搜集，应为一切之措施”，以及《国际法院规则》（以下简称《规则》）的配套规定。

这里需要明确的是，《规约》第50条中法院可以随时选择的专家范围包括“任何个人、团体、局所、委员会或其他组织”。在实践中，下文也将会提及，目前法院的实践是仅限于个人，尚未有其他组织或委员会受到法院的委托。选择个人，还是选择其他机构作为第50条下的“专家”不在本文的讨论范围内，但目前已经有学者明确提出选择个人可能是更为适当的方式。[③] 另一方面，条文中也明确提及了“调查”或“鉴定”两种主动咨询专家的方式。但在法院的实践中，要求专家进行“调查”或“鉴定”的区别并没有那么泾渭分明，无论是进行“调查”或“鉴定”，都需要条款中提及的专家或专业组织的专门知识。[④]

《规约》第50条中提及的专家与当事方的专家既有联系也有区别。两

---

① Pulp Mills on the River Uruguay（Argentina v. Uruguay），Judgement，I. C. J. Reports 2010，para. 216.

② “The Court may，at any time，entrust any individual，body，bureau，commission，or other organization that it may select，with the task of carrying out an enquiry or giving an expert opinion.”

③ Caroline E. Foster，“New Clothes for the Emperor? Consultation of Experts by the International Court of Justice”，*Journal of International Dispute Settlement* 5（2014）：139.

④ 参见 Christan J. Tams，“Article 50”，in Andreas Zimmermann et al.（eds.），*The Statute of the International Court of Justice：A Commentary*，2nd edition（Oxford：Oxford University Press，2012），pp. 1293 – 1295。

种类型的专家共通的地方在于“帮助法院（或法庭）确立或者澄清事实问题”。[①] 克里斯托弗·格林伍德（Christopher Greenwood）法官在纪念法院成立70周年的论文中也持相同的看法：“专家的职责，无论是法院指定的，还是当事方自行任命的，都是以客观中立的方式向这个领域的‘外行’解释或阐明问题的。但是，专家并不能代替法院作出决定。”[②] 而互相区别的地方在于当事方的专家一般与其聘请国是“志同道合”或“沆瀣一气”的，[③] 当事方专家的观点一般是用于支持其聘请国所声称的事实与诉求的；但指定专家不一样，指定专家是帮助法院在作出判决的过程中厘清相关事实，[④] 因而指定专家的意见或报告一般会具有比当事方专家更高的证明作用。[⑤]

但是，国际法院在实践中极少地行使这一项权力。前文提及，在最近的“加勒比海和太平洋划界案”中，法院根据第50条，行使了其历史上第二次指定专家的权力。而第一次行使该权力是60多年前，用于法院刚成立不久时的“科孚海峡案（阿尔巴尼亚诉英国）”中。

在“科孚海峡案”中，法院为了确定案件中的一个关键问题，即阿尔巴尼亚是否知道其领海布有水雷，任命了三位专家组成专家委员会，[⑥] 对双方之间的争议事实进行独立研究，[⑦] 尤其是“考虑到萨兰达（Saranda）地区的警戒措施，阿尔巴尼亚当局有没有意识到埋雷的可能性”。[⑧] 法院在

---

① Gillian White, “The Use of Experts by the International Court”, in Lowe, V./Fitzmaurice, M., (ed.), *Fifty Years of the International Court of Justice, Essays in Honour of Sir Robert Jennings* (Cambridge: Cambridge University Press, 1996), pp. 528 - 540.

② Amelia Keene (ed.), “Outcome Paper for the Seminar on the International Court of Justice at 70: In Retrospect and in Prospect”, *Journal of International Dispute Settlement* 7 (2016): 254 - 255.

③ Joost Pauwelyn, “The Use of Experts in WTO Dispute Settlement”, *The International and Comparative Law Quarterly* 51 (2002): 325, 334, 称当事方的专家为“雇用的枪支”(hired gun)，这个比喻与说法后来被多次引用。

④ Application for Revision and Interpretation of the Judgment of 24 February 1982 in the Case concerning the Continental Shelf (Tunisia/Libyan Arab Jamahiriya) (Tunisia v. Libyan Arab Jamahiriya), Judgment, I. C. J. Reports 1985, p. 228, para. 65.

⑤ Daniel Peat, “The Use of Court-appointed Experts by the International Court of Justice”, *British Yearbook of International Law* 84 (2013): 271 - 303.

⑥ 三位专家分别为挪威皇家海军司令官 Commodore J. Bull，瑞典皇家海军司令官 Commodore S. A. Forshell，以及荷兰皇家海军中尉指挥官 Commander S. J. W. Elfferich。

⑦ *Corfu Channel Case*, Order of 19 November 1949, I. C. J. Reports 1947, p. 126.

⑧ *Corfu Channel Case*, Judgment of 9 April 1949, I. C. J. Reports 1949, p. 21.

专家们提交了第一份报告后,[1] 要求这些专家到阿尔巴尼亚的萨兰达进行实地考察（site visit)，作出更有说服力的观察。[2] 基于实地考察的结果，专家们在一个月以后，再次提交了第二份报告。[3] 他们认为，只要阿尔巴尼亚在海峡各个巡视点有正常的放哨、瞭望及配备有望远镜，那么阿尔巴尼亚对布雷活动必须是有所了解的。[4] 这是“无可争议的”（indisputable）事实。由于专家们作了实地调查，法院在判决中给予了这些专家意见非常高的证明力,[5] 并最终认定阿尔巴尼亚必须为此负责任。[6] 随后，法院再次委托荷兰皇家海军的两名成员，对英国军舰所受损害作专家评估,[7] 由此产生的报告大部分支持了英国的主张。在这两种情况下，专家都没有直接参与法院的审议，都只是以提交报告的形式，将其调查结果详细交由法院审议。

可以说，“科孚海峡案”的专家指定是比较成功的，因而经常得到学者文章的援引、论述，被称为“《规约》第 50 条的优秀案例”。[8] 有学者认为，“科孚海峡案”中的法院之所以最后认定了阿尔巴尼亚的国家责任，但此种认定主要是基于证据链,[9] 并不是仅依赖于专家观点的,[10] 指定专家的报告在这里发挥的只是一个协助法官认识事实的作用，但这个作用是不

---

① *Corfu Channel Case*, Judgment of 9 April 1949, I. C. J. Reports 1949, p. 142 (Annex 2).

② *Corfu Channel Case*, Decision of the Court Regarding an Enquiry on the Spot in Order of 19 November 1949, I. C. J. Reports 1949, p. 151.

③ *Corfu Channel Case*, "Experts' Report Dated February 8th, 1949, On the Investigations and Tests at Sibenik and Saranda", in Order of 19 November 1949, I. C. J. Reports 1949, p. 152.

④ "If minelaying were conducted from the South, the lookouts at Cape Kiephali and St. George's Monastery would have seen the operations; if conducted from the North, the lookout at Cape Kiephali would have seen the operations", *Corfu Channel Case*, Judgment of 9 April 1949, I. C. J. Reports 1949, p. 22.

⑤ *Corfu Channel Case*, Judgment of 9 April 1949, I. C. J. Reports 1949, p. 21.

⑥ *Corfu Channel Case*, Judgment of 9 April 1949, I. C. J. Reports 1949, p. 23.

⑦ *Corfu Channel Case*, Order of November 19th, I. C. J. Reports 1949, pp. 237, 238.

⑧ Daniel Peat, "The Use of Court-appointed Experts by the International Court of Justice", *British Yearbook of International Law* 84 (2013): 208.

⑨ 参见 Michael P. Scharf and Margaux Dayt, "The International Court of Justice's Treatment of Circumstantial Evidence and Adverse Inferences", *Chicago Journal of International Law* 13 (2012)。

⑩ 参见 Gillian White, *The Use of Experts by International Tribunals* (Syracuse, NY: Syracuse University Press, 1965), pp. 107 - 113; 同时参见 Riddell Anna and Plant Brendan, *Evidence Before the International Court of Justice* (London: British Institute of International and Comparative Law, 2009): 63 - 64。

可忽略的。

既然根据《规约》和《规则》，法院是可以行使指定专家的权力的，甚至是不需要当事方同意就可以行使的，但为何法院仅在成立后的第一个案件中（“科孚海峡案”）指定过专家，而此后的60余年，这个条款一直处于隐藏、不受注意的状态？

事实上，这60余年来，法院也在其他案件中收到了当事国指定专家的要求，但是法院均拒绝行使此权力。例如在“尼加拉瓜境内针对尼加拉瓜的军事与准军事活动案（尼加拉瓜诉美国）”中，尼加拉瓜称，由于美国在实体阶段不到庭，也要求法院指定专家以帮助认定事实，但法院拒绝了这样的请求。法院称，它注意到在本案中已经有一定数量的证据了，[①] 如果要指定专家，法院将会遇到困难。法院认为，这种权力的行使可能并不是切实可行的。[②] 另外，在“陆地、岛屿和海洋边界争端案（萨尔瓦多/洪都拉斯）”中，萨尔瓦多在口头听证阶段也要求法庭安排专家就争议事项进行调查或提出专家意见。但是法庭认为，没有必要行使其主动获取证据的此项权力，也没有必要安排调查或指定专家。[③]

法院的法官们对此纷纷表达过异议意见或批评意见，都希望法院能行使第50条的权力，通过寻求专家的帮助，运用《规约》下此项重要的“工具”，以帮助认定事实。早在常设法院时，安切洛蒂法官（Judge Anzilotti）就指出，法院这项权力的基础除了第50条以外，还得到一般法律原则的支持。在任何情况下，法院都有权行使此命令。[④] 顾维钧法官在1962年“柏威夏寺案（柬埔寨诉泰国）”中就提出，本案中很多问题都带有技术性质，呼吁法院指定专家提供可靠的答案。顾法官认为，根据《规约》第50条，法院本应在专家意见中得到良好的启发，如同在“科孚海峡案”一样，指定专家进行现场调查，并请专家提出报告，这样的报告将极大地

① Military and Paramilitary Activities in and against Nicaragua（Nicaragua v. USA），Merits，Judgment，I. C. J. Reports 1986，para. 62.

② Military and Paramilitary Activities in and against Nicaragua（Nicaragua v. USA），Merits，Judgment，I. C. J. Reports 1986，para. 61.

③ Land，Island and Maritime Frontier Dispute（El Salvador/Honduras：Nicaragua intervening），Judgment of 11 September 1992，I. C. J. Reports 1992，p. 362，para. 22；p. 400，para. 65.

④ 参见 Gillian White，*The Use of Experts by International Tribunals*（Syracuse，NY：Syracuse University Press，1965），p. 73。

协助法院在法律上解决技术性的问题，以认定案件中的相关事实。就目前而言，由于没法得到这些技术问题的答案，而且这些答案又至关重要，因此没法作出令自己满意的结论。[①] 小田滋（Shigeru Oda）法官则在1999年“卡西基里和色杜杜岛案（博茨瓦纳/纳米比亚）”中注意到了法院拒绝使用《规约》第50条下的权力，他在个别意见中指出，确定主航道标准是个法律问题，但把这些标准适用到本案中特定地理状况就是另一回事了。法院可以去主动获取解决问题的客观科学知识，却没有选择这样做，只根据双方书面与口头阶段的材料与意见，就作出了决定。[②]

由此看来，法院内部已经有多次这样的声音了；对于一些法官来说，早就已经觉察到有行使此项权力的需要，但法院却在整体上拒绝行动。当中的原因没法得知，但有学者推测，法院如此谨慎，可能是担心某些案件中的专家并不能给出让法院满意的决定；或者是《规约》和《规则》中对于指定专家的相关配套规定与程序并不充分，法院无法就此项权力的行使达成一致意见；甚至有学者提出，由于指定专家意见的证明力一般比较高，如果法院不遵照自己指定专家意见，是需要解释原因的；[③] 也就是说，一旦指定了专家，法院就可能感觉其司法权受到了限制，很难再去作出一个与专家不一致的决定，而法院一直以来对于自身认定事实和适用法律的司法权力有着非常清晰的认识。

三 法律VS科学

法院的现状与所处的“两难处境”不容忽视，如果法院希望未来能继续保持其在解决国家间争端的良好作用，必须要直面这些挑战，并开始把资源

---

① *Temple of Preah Vihear* (*Cambodia v. Thailand*), Judgment of 15 June 1962, Dissenting Opinion of Judge Wellington Koo, I. C. J. Reports 1962, p. 100, para. 55.

② *Kasikili/Sedudu Island* (*Botswana/Namibia*), Judgment of 13 December 1999, Separate opinion of Judge Oda, I. C. J. Reports 1999, pp. 1118 – 1119, para. 6.

③ Markus Benzing, "Evidentiary Issues", in Andreas Zimmermann et al (eds.), *The Statute of the International Court of Justice: A Commentary*, 2nd edition (Oxford: Oxford University Press, 2012), p. 1255, MN 78; Riddell Anna and Plant Brendan, *Evidence Before the International Court of Justice* (London: British Institute of International and Comparative Law, 2009): 320.

与注意力转向如何认定日益复杂的事实问题，以形成解决此类科学技术证据公开、公平且合理的处理方式。只有这样，国家才能有信心，继续把一些涉及高科技事实的争端提交给法院，形成良性循环，促进国际法治的实现。

事实上，如本文开篇的新近案件，法院已经又一次行使其指定专家的权力，也表现出其处理科学问题与专业知识的方法与程序了。但国际法的理论与实践均存在一些对指定专家模糊不清的认识与理解。因此，本文提出，国际法院应改进其指定专家的程序与做法，认真考虑法律与科学之间关系的时机已经到来。

（一）尊重科学，承认法院自身的局限

让不懂某些专业知识的法官去取舍专业性很强的科学结论，这实际上是司法权的一种错位。法院的法官们可以确保其遵守《规约》与《规则》下的法定程序，确保其适用法律的准确与公开，但当涉及科学或专门技术时，法官们却没法保证其认定事实的准确性，也就不能保证法院所作的判决是公正的。本文认为，这样一些集科学性、技术性和学术性于一体的科学问题，由于科学的特点以及社会发展的一些局限性，本身就有不完善之处，法院的判例也已经表明，对于同一个科学问题，当事方的专家各有不同见解，互不相让是很常见的；特别到了法院或法庭面前，当事国的律师及其聘请的专家一般只陈述对己方有利的部分，而法院的法官作为非专业人士，是难以准确判断科技事项结论的正确性的。这是法院的局限性。

就以“盖巴斯科夫——拉基马洛大坝案（匈牙利/斯洛伐克）”为例，匈牙利力求证明其不遵守与斯洛伐克缔结的关于建立水坝系统的条约的理由之一是，如果它确实按计划进行了工程，该地区的环境，特别是饮用水资源会遭受严重的风险。在诉讼中，匈牙利和斯洛伐克均提出了“令人印象深刻的科学材料”（impressive amount of scientificmaterial）。法院坦言，双方都为其各自的立场提供了科学依据，但这些材料对于法院本身构成了巨大的挑战。甚至连匈牙利的律师也指出，这并不容易，不仅要求法官理解这件事的科学复杂性，而且要确定每一方提交的科学材料的相对合理性。[①] 法院

---

① JE Vinuales, “Legal Techniques for Dealing with Scientific Uncertainty in International Law”, *Vanderbilt Journal of Transnational Law* 43 (2010): 477.

在判决中承认，它没有必要确定这些观点哪一个在科学上是更好的。[①] 且不论法院这种做法在该案中是否合理，本文认为，法院的此种方式是不妥的，不应该再延续至后续的案子当中。当事方已经提交了大量的、互相矛盾的科学证据，法院的工作之一就是要对这些科学观点作出应有的判断。这也是后来在“乌拉圭河纸浆厂案”中，法官们提出法院应该寻求独立的专门科学知识，以帮助法院的原因。[②] 在这些与环境相关的争端中，法院必须评估一方的某些行为是否已经对环境产生了影响，这就不得不依赖于以专家报告为载体的科学和技术知识。

在涉及科学事实的案件中，无论是法官或当事国的代理人在法律领域均属专业人士，但他们在遇到非法律领域的其他专业问题时，是缺乏必要的知识储备与判断能力的，寻求专家的辅助或协助就显得非常必要。本文认为，当科学问题变得越来越与案件事实相关时，如果法院再对科学证据保持沉默，必定会影响最后司法判决的合法性和合理性。这些与案件密切相关的科学问题不解决，单凭法官的法律知识，已经不再足以证明判决的价值了。一个合法与合理的判决，必须是科学知识和法律知识在程序与实体中的结合。当然，在司法过程中，尊重案件中所出现的科学与技术问题，承认法院司法功能的局限性，就必然触摸到了问题的关键之处，即如果法院更多地利用第 50 条指定专家，那么就有专家“越俎代庖”的风险。[③] 也就是说，实际上，可能会使得专家意见代替了法官的判断，以决定某个条约的条款是否被违反，这是当事国最不愿意看到的情况。那么专家的指定如何合法合理，指定专家的意见应该赋予何种证据价值？这些挑战一直困扰着法院，也可能成为法院一直不愿意在程序中指定专家的重要原因。

（二）指定专家意见的合法运用：指定程序必须公开且透明

为应对争端的日益专业化，专家的指定将是不可避免的。《规约》和

① Gabčíkovo-Nagymaros Project (Hungary/Slovakia), Judgment, I. C. J. Reports 1997, p. 7.

② *Pulp Mills on the River Uruguay* (*Argentina v. Uruguay*), Judgement, Joint dissenting opinion Judges Al-Khasawneh and Simma, Declaration of Judge Yusuf, Separate Opinion of Judge Cancado Trindade, Dissenting Opinion of Judgead hoc Vinuesa.

③ Gillian White, *The Use of Experts by International Tribunals* (Syracuse, NY: Syracuse University Press, 1965), pp. 11 – 12.

《规则》已经在这方面有一定的设计与考虑，但对于具体如何指定依然是不清晰的。因此，法院在选择自己专家的相关程序上，仍有相当多的空白与模糊之处。这些空白与模糊之处，法院可以从别的争端解决机构中借鉴。

例如，在世界贸易组织（以下简称WTO）的争端解决机制中，专家小组非常注重如何选择双方都能接受的专家。在“欧共体关于肉类及肉类制品的措施案”中，专家小组指定的专家名单来自食品法典委员会秘书处和国际癌症研究机构；[①] 在“日本农业产品案”中，指定专家是从国际植保公约秘书处的专家名单中选择而来的；[②] 在“欧盟生物科技产品案”中，专家小组指定的专家的选择名单是由《生物多样性公约》、食品法典委员会、联合国粮食及农业组织、《国际植物保护公约》、世界动物卫生组织和世界卫生组织的秘书处提供的。[③] 可见，WTO 争端解决机构中的专家小组采用了这样一种做法，即向国际专门机构请求列出可能在案件中任命为专家的候选人名单。这样，各专门机构就会间接地参与到案件当中，协助WTO，同时以机构作为中立第三方参与提名的过程，增强了对所选专家的权威性、独立性与中立性。本文认为，法院要充分利用指定专家意见在判案中应有作用的前提，首先就应该有一套指定专家的明确程序规定，依照目前《规约》、《规则》中的相关规定以及一般程序法原则，指定的程序必须做到公开、透明与合理。以下的指定步骤有其必要性与重要意义。

第一，当法院认为有必要指定专家，获取专家意见时，应首先听取当事方对法院这一意向的意见，包括指定的必要性、指定的方式、指定的人数以及诉讼过程中所需要遵循的其他程序。这样将会最大程度保证诉讼程序的顺利进行，能有效避免后续程序中当事方再提出对专家的质疑。

第二，在征得当事方的意见后，法院发布指定命令，明确界定专家的任务，以及需要专家发表意见或建议的主题或问题。法院对专家的问题，

---

① World Trade Organization, *EC Measures Concerning Meat and Meat Products (Hormones) Complaint by the United States*, Report of the Panel, WT/DS26/R/USA, 18 August 1997, paras. 6.5, 6.6.

② World Trade Organization, *Japan—Measures Affecting Agricultural Products*, Report of the Panel, WT/DS76/R, 27 October 1998, para. 6.2.

③ 参见 Caroline E. Foster, *Science and the Precautionary Principle in International Courts and Tribunals: Expert Evidence, Burden of Proof and Finality* (Cambridge: Cambridge University Press, 2011), p. 171。

无论是书面或口头问题，必须记录。

以上两个程序对于法院是相当重要的，有利于案件程序的平稳推进。在 WTO 的实践中，就存在质疑专家中立性的先例，虽然这个挑战与质疑并没有影响争端的结果，[①] 但足以看出以上程序的重要性。

第三，指定专家以后，法院应要求每名指定专家在接受任务前宣誓。根据《规则》第 64 条第 2 款，无论是当事方的专家还是法院指定的专家，[②] 都要求庄严宣誓或声明。但实践中，法院指定的专家的宣誓或声明与当事人的专家宣誓，措辞上会有所不同。在法院的“科孚海峡案”中，专家是公开地作了宣誓的。宣誓与声明的程序作用是不可忽略的，这对专家的中立性、客观性和责任感都有一定的保障。

在文章开篇所提及的“加勒比海和太平洋海洋划界争端案”中，法院就已开始使用此种做法，但依然存在改进的地方。

2014 年 4 月，哥斯达黎加递交请求书，就“加勒比海和太平洋海洋划界争端”对尼加拉瓜提起诉讼，请求法院确定分属哥斯达黎加和尼加拉瓜的加勒比海和太平洋所有海洋区域之间单一海洋边界的完整走向及其准确坐标。考虑到两国在重要问题上有不一致的看法，法院发布命令，决定就哥斯达黎加和尼加拉瓜边界附近的一段加勒比海岸的状况征求专家意见。命令中要求专家通过实地考察，取得所有加勒比海海洋边界线起点的两点间[③]的海岸事实状况，[④] 并就此提出建议，并回答法院提出的 4 个问题。[⑤]

---

① 参见 Caroline E. Foster, *Science and the Precautionary Principle in International Courts and Tribunals: Expert Evidence, Burden of Proof and Finality* (Cambridge: Cambridge University Press, 2011), pp. 174 - 175。

② “(b) every expert shall make the following declaration before making any statement: I solemnly declare upon my honour and conscience that I will speak the truth, the whole truth and nothing but the truth, and that my statement will be in accordance with my sincere belief.”

③ 即哥斯达黎加与尼加拉瓜在诉状中各自建议的点之间，即圣胡安河河口右岸（the point located on the right bank of the San Juan River at its mout）与最接近 Punta de Castilla（the land point closest to Punta de Castilla）陆地界点之间。

④ *Maritime Delimitation in the Caribbean Sea and the Pacific Ocean* (*Costa Rica v. Nicaragua*), Order of 31 May 2016 (The Court to arrange for an expert opinion), para. 4, http://www.icj-cij.org/docket/files/157/19030.pdf，最后访问日期：2017 年 11 月 7 日。

⑤ *Maritime Delimitation in the Caribbean Sea and the Pacific Ocean* (*Costa Rica v. Nicaragua*), Order of 31 May 2016 (The Court to arrange for an expert opinion), paras. 6, 10. http://www.icj-cij.org/docket/files/157/19030.pdf，最后访问日期：2017 年 11 月 7 日。

根据2016年5月31日的命令，法院院长于2016年6月16日再次发布命令，任命了两名相关专家。在这两位专家的指定过程中，哥斯达黎加非常支持，对两位专家没有任何异议，并愿意向专家提供任何协助；[①] 尼加拉瓜则认为不需要指定专家进行现场考察，但也没有提出正式的反对，并表示支持法院的工作。[②]

在上述各部分的程序中，本文认为法院在此案中指定专家的做法已经符合第二步的相关程序了，但当中最关键而且目前还是最不透明的是第一步，即专家是如何产生的，如何选择的。专家是不是当事方协议的？或者专业机构所推荐的？在《规约》和《规则》中，并没有为指定专家规定任何程序。法院需要为甄选和任命专家设计一个健全且透明的程序，这样才能在诉讼中与诉讼后应对任何可能的程序挑战。WTO的经验是有价值的，法院可以借鉴使用以确定在此问题上的最佳方法。[③]

（三）指定专家意见的合理运用：专家意见的辅助性

在寻求专家意见的案件中，由法院，而非专家决定案件的裁判，这是一个重要的基本原则。[④] 本文认为，专家意见的合理运用是个案中检验法律与科学关系的“试金石”。

指定专家意见需得到合理运用，包括以下三层含义：专家的任务仅是提供信息，法院或法庭基于这些信息作判断；专家需要与法院及其他各方充分且公开地互动；专家意见在最终认定事实上的定位是“辅助性”。

第一，指定专家的任务仅是向法院提供信息。专业问题需要专家意

---

① *Maritime Delimitation in the Caribbean Sea and the Pacific Ocean*（*Costa Rica v. Nicaragua*），Order of 31 May 2016（The Court to arrange for an expert opinion），para. 5，http://www.icj-cij.org/docket/files/157/19030.pdf，最后访问日期：2017年11月7日。

② *Maritime Delimitation in the Caribbean Sea and the Pacific Ocean*，Order of 16 June 2016（Appointment of experts），International Court of Justice，http://www.icj-cij.org/docket/files/157/19054.pdf.pdf，最后访问日期：2017年11月7日。

③ Caroline E. Foster，*Science and the Precautionary Principle in International Courts and Tribunals：ExpertEvidence，Burden of Proof and Finality*（Cambridge：Cambridge University Press，2011），pp. 171 – 175.

④ Gillian White，*The Use of Experts by International Tribunals*（Syracuse，NY：Syracuse University Press，1965），p. 164.

见，但并不是案件中的所有专业问题都需要专家意见，对哪些是“专业问题”法院应在适当的程序阶段予以明确和限定。在当事方之间的争端中，可能存在许多复杂的专业性问题，有些对于解决争端是无关的，是不需要法院在案件中处理的。如在法院的“南极捕鲸案”中，澳大利亚提出了“科学研究”定义的解释，并提出了几个要件。法院认为，虽然“科学研究”是法院需要解释和适用的《国际捕鲸管制公约》第 8 条措辞的一部分，但法院认为在该案中不需要，而且也没能力、没必要去决定“科学研究”的含义。①

同样可以从 WTO 的案例上看到一些有价值的做法。根据《实施动植物卫生检疫措施的协议》第 5 条的规定，成员在对其动植物卫生检疫措施进行风险评估时，应考虑现有的科学依据（例如：有关的工序和生产方法；有关的检验、抽样和测试方法；某些病害或虫害的流行；病虫害非疫区的存在；有关的生态和环境条件；检疫或其他处理方法；等等）。WTO 上诉机构在“新西兰诉澳大利亚苹果限制措施案”中认为，专家小组的任务是审查 WTO 成员的风险评估，而不是用自己的科学判断来替代风险评估人的科学判断。因此，专家不需要确定风险评估是否正确，而是“确定该风险评估是否基于合逻辑的推理以及得到承认的科学证据的支持，是否客观合理”。②

WTO 上诉机构的这一观点很好地说明了国际裁判机构在适用法律过程中所要求的科学内容。裁判者的作用是根据所有现有的科学证据和专家意见，考虑一方主张是否满足法律的要求。这个例子还表明，裁判机构并不需要去决定一些与法律适用无关的但当事方有争议的科学事项。裁判者要决定的是，法律的要求是否基于现有的科学证据得到了满足。因此，在法院的“南极捕鲸案”中，如前撰述，法院根本就不需要去确定科学委员会科学家们所提出的几个科学假设是否正确。

---

① Francesca Romanin Jacur, “Remarks on the Role of Ex Curia Scientific Experts in International Environmental Disputes”, in Nerina Boschiero and others, *International Courts and the Development of International Law-Essays in Honour of Tullio Treves* (The Hague: TMC Asser Press 2013), pp. 180 – 181.

② World Trade Organization, *Australia-Measures Affecting the Importation of Apples from New Zealand*, Appellate Body Report, WT/DS367/AB/R, 29 November 2010, para. 213.

第二，指定专家需要与法院及其他各方充分公开地互动。专家与法院等各方的动态互动过程，是检验“试金石”的重要步骤。

法院在此问题上也是有过成功先例的，就是其第一个指定专家的“科孚海峡案”。法院在该案中处理证据的能力得到了持续的称道，这与法院和各方、指定专家之间良好的合作与互动密不可分。如果没有阿尔巴尼亚、英国、南斯拉夫以及专家所在国的充分合作，事实认定问题得到较为满意的解决是不可能的。①

另外，根据实践经验，当事国及其聘请的专家的陈述往往会给出互不相同的意见。法院因此可以行使其指定专家的权力，更多地就指定专家的意见与报告进行参考。但指定专家的报告与意见要发挥一定的证明力，同样应该像当事方的专家一样，在口头等阶段接受法院和当事国各方的提问或质询。《规则》中有一些关于专家的质证与认证的规定，例如《规则》第 67 条规定，每个专家意见应通知各当事方，并应有机会对其作出评论。另外，根据《规则》第 65 条，只要有需要，专家将参加口头诉讼程序，并回答当事双方提出的问题。法院保留在其认为必要时向专家提出更多问题的权利。无论是大陆法系国家的直接言词原则，还是英美法系国家的反对传闻证据规则，都要求专家需就有关问题出庭接受质询。法院作为两大法系综合的体现，更应重视此程序。指定的专家报告是否能够客观地反映所要解决问题的真实状态，专家所采用的方法是否科学，所出具的意见和报告是否有科学依据，这些都可以通过互动、合作、质询等各种形式，审查专家报告的证明力；如果仅凭书面审查，是难以发挥其作为认定事实重要依据的作用的。

值得强调的是，保持专家与各方互动的公开、完整与准确的记录同样是一个非常重要的要素。无论哪种形式的合作、书面或口头磋商、辩论与质疑，完整与准确的记录都有程序上的重要意义。

第三，专家意见在最终认定事实上的定位是“辅助性”。法院任命的专家在案件中的参与必然会引起法律与科学关系的讨论。由于专家意见

① Gillian White, “The Use of Experts by the International Court”, in Lowe, V./Fitzmaurice, M., (ed.), *Fifty Years of the International Court of Justice*, *Essays in Honour of Sir Robert Jennings* (Cambridge: Cambridge University Press, 1996), pp. 528, 530.

对案件法律层面的影响，科学专业问题相关争议的存在将特别容易使法官偏离“试金石”。哈苏奈法官和西玛法官在关于“乌拉圭河纸浆厂案”中评论说：“在如本案的科学问题上，合理的法律决定必须由法官在指定专家意见的基础上作出，最后必须由法院来确定其已履行相关的司法职能，例如解释法律概念、对事实问题的法律分类以及分配和评估证明责任等。”[①]

需要明确的是，专家意见只能针对事实问题而不是法律问题作出，方能避免法院一直以来可能存在的担忧，即通过指定专家，把法院的司法功能间接地授予庭外者。在 WTO 的裁判实践中，专家的任务仅限于帮助“理解和评估当事方所提交的证据和诉求”的定位是较为明显的。同时，专家没有权力“回答法律问题，确定一个缔约方是否违反 WTO 协定”。明确要求专家们在他们的书面和口头证词中避免对法律问题表达意见，[②] 如果专家们发表了法律意见，或者其意见超越了其“辅助性”的地位，那么专家报告的证明力将会受到严重的影响。

结　语

无论是国内法院还是国际性裁判机构，在司法实践中都会遇到一些相似的问题，这其中就包括对专家指定、专家报告、专业资料等的处理与认定。当今案件事实越来越专业和复杂，同时这些科学技术性的证据在案件中又是认定事实、作出裁判的重要甚至关键依据，指定自己的专家以协助法院已成必要。本文在回顾法院成立 70 年来指定专家和涉及科技证据处理案例的基础上，提出法院要维持其在国际社会中争端解决机构的权威地位，就不应该再在此问题上“犹豫不前”了。

同时，指定专家以及对专家意见的运用，本身就具有两面性，如一把

① *Pulp Mills on the River Uruguay* (*Argentina v. Uruguay*), Judgement, Joint dissenting opinion Judges Al-Khasawneh and Simma, para. 12.

② Caroline E. Foster, *Science and the Precautionary Principle in International Courts and Tribunals*: *Expert Evidence*, *Burden of Proof and Finality* (Cambridge: Cambridge University Press, 2011), p. 78.

双刃剑，如果不能够深刻把握好其中的特点与定位，就有可能使法院一直不愿意使用的担忧变成现实。本文指出，法院现行的专家指定制度是不完善的，应设计公平透明的指定程序，在专家意见的证明力上需要用“试金石”检验其作用。处理好专家的指定、相关的审查与采纳采信机制，弥补或解决法官专业知识之不足，才能促进国家争端的有效解决。

（本文原载于《当代法学》2018 年第 1 期）

走向繁荣的国际法学

（全六卷）

TOWARDS THE PROSPERITY OF
INTERNATIONAL LAW STUDIES (SIX VOLUMES)

2009
~
2019

中国社会科学院国际法研究所十周年所庆纪念文集

【国际私法卷】

莫纪宏　总主编
沈　涓　傅攀峰　主　编

社会科学文献出版社
SOCIAL SCIENCES ACADEMIC PRESS (CHINA)

国际私法研究室成员合影

2019 年 4 月 10 日，2019 年度第二届国际法热点问题研讨会，最高人民法院罗东川副院长出席会议并致辞

2018 年 1 月 22 日，沈涓参加第十三届北京市政协会议

2015 年 7 月，沈涓参加中华司法研究会首届高峰论坛

2017 年 12 月 2 日至 3 日，沈涓出席中国社会科学论坛暨第十四届国际法论坛

2017 年 5 月 11 日，沈涓在中国社会科学院建院 40 周年系列学术报告会上作专题报告

2005 年 7 月，沈涓参加中国台湾地区马汉宝教授在国际法研究所的讲座

2005 年 12 月，沈涓参加中国台湾地区赖来焜教授在国际法研究所的讲座

2005 年 9 月，陈泽宪、沈涓等在日本访学期间参观日本最高法院

2010 年 11 月，沈涓参加中国社会科学论坛暨第七届国际法论坛期间与日本木棚照一教授合影

2006 年 8 月，沈涓在荷兰访学期间参观联合国国际法院

2006 年 8 月，沈涓在荷兰莱顿大学访学

2007 年 10 月，沈涓在中国台湾地区玄奘大学讲学

2010 年 4 月，沈涓在英国牛津大学访学

2018 年 10 月 27 日至 28 日，李庆明出席中国社会科学论坛暨第十五届国际法论坛

2018 年 12 月 19 日，李庆明应邀在外交学院作讲座

2017 年 12 月 2 日至 3 日，傅攀峰出席中国社会科学论坛暨第十四届国际法论坛

傅攀峰与国际仲裁员、法国 Emmanuel Gaillard 教授合影

序

推动中国国际法学不断走向繁荣

1949 年 10 月 1 日，中华人民共和国中央人民政府宣告成立，结束了旧中国近百年半殖民地半封建受压迫受奴役的历史。中国人民从此站起来了！

在中国共产党和中国政府的坚强领导下，70 年来，中华人民共和国不断总结经验，克服困难，实现突破和发展，取得社会主义建设事业的伟大成就。特别是改革开放 40 年来，中国实现了经济腾飞和社会进步，中国的国际地位和影响力前所未有。2012 年党的十八大召开以来，中国特色社会主义进入新时代，中国人民实现了从站起来、富起来到强起来的发展过程，中国日益走近世界舞台的中央，中华民族比以往任何时候都更加接近实现中华民族伟大复兴的中国梦！

中华人民共和国的成立和 70 年来的发展历程，为中国国际法学的发展创造了良好的政治、经济、社会和历史条件。以周鲠生、陈体强、李浩培、王铁崖、韩德培等老一辈中国国际法学者为代表的中国国际法人为中国国际法理论研究和实践工作的起步和发展作出了卓越的贡献，为中国国际法学研究和教学做了大量奠基和铺路的工作。

1978 年 12 月 13 日，邓小平同志在党的十一届三中全会前召开的中央经济工作会议上发表了《解放思想，实事求是，团结一致向前看》的讲话，明确提出“要大力加强国际法的研究”。如春风，如号角，中国国际法研究获得极大的鼓舞。中国国际法学迎来了发展的春天。1980 年 2 月，中国国际法学会成立，中国社会科学院副院长宦乡担任首任会长。

中国社会科学院是中国国际法学的研究重镇。1959 年，也就是中国科

学院哲学社会科学部建立法学研究所之后的第二年，法学研究所成立了国际法组。1977 年 5 月，经党中央批准，中国社会科学院在中国科学院哲学社会科学部基础上正式组建。1978 年 9 月，中国社会科学院法学研究所国际法组改建为国际法研究室。

2002 年又是中国发展历程中一个不平凡的年份。这一年，中国改革开放渐入佳境，中国正式加入世界贸易组织；这一年，中国批准了作为“国际人权宪章”重要内容的联合国《经济、社会和文化权利国际公约》。也是这一年，在时任中国社会科学院院长李铁映的推动下，经中央机构编制委员会办公室批准，在国际法研究室基础上成立了国际法研究中心，使其成为与法学研究所平行的院属所局级机构。

国际法研究中心成立后，中国社会科学院国际法学研究获得进一步加强和推进。2009 年 9 月，经中央机构编制委员会办公室批准，国际法研究中心正式更名为国际法研究所。到今天，国际法研究所刚好成立 10 年了！

陈泽宪研究员任国际法研究所首任所长。2017 年 9 月至 2018 年 11 月，现任法学研究所所长、中国社会科学院学部委员陈甦研究员代行国际法研究所所长职责。2018 年 11 月，莫纪宏研究员开始担任国际法研究所所长。国际法研究所正是在国家经济发展和社会进步取得历史性突破，中国在国际社会地位极大提升、国际影响力不断扩大的背景下诞生的。它的成立和发展承载了党和国家繁荣和发展中国国际法学的使命。

10 年来，国际法研究所与外交部、商务部等相关政府部门密切联系，与中国国际法学会等全国性国际法研究学会、学术机构一道，积极进取，努力推动中国国际法学走向繁荣。依托学科和人才优势，国际法研究所设有国际公法、国际经济法、国际私法和国际人权法 4 个研究室，还设有海洋法治研究、竞争法研究和国际刑法研究领域的 3 个非实体中心以及最高人民法院“一带一路”司法研究基地。依托国际法研究所国际法专业的博士点和硕士点，博士、硕士研究生和博士后研究人员的指导工作也得到了加强。

2014 年创刊的《国际法研究》是中国第一本获得正式刊号的国际法专业原创中文期刊，国际法研究所是其主要主办单位和主编单位。该刊在国际法研究领域学术期刊的发文转载率方面处于全国领先地位，已经成为国际法学界重要的学术展示和交流平台。一年一度的国际法论坛已成功举办

15 届，成为中国社会科学院院级国际研讨会的学术品牌，吸引了国内外权威和知名专家的积极参与。在刘楠来、王可菊、陶正华、林欣等前辈国际法学家的关心和鼓舞下，国际法研究所一大批中青年国际法学者正在成为国际法学界的学术骨干。

值此国际法研究所 10 周年所庆之际，我们出版文集，选粹研究人员的研究成果，包括《国际法研究》发表过的有影响力的论文，回顾走过的历程，展示当下的风貌，既是国际法研究所成长道路上的一个小结，更是展现坚定的再创辉煌的决心。

中国倡导的“一带一路”建设正在世界范围内获得越来越多、越来越大的发展成就，推动构建人类命运共同体的中国主张日益获得国际社会的广泛支持和积极响应。

前路不乏机遇和挑战，中国社会科学院国际法研究所全体同仁必将以只争朝夕的精神，不忘初心、牢记使命，与全国国际法学同仁一道，推进中国国际法学不断走向繁荣！

莫纪宏

2019 年 8 月 20 日

目录

Contents

国际私法研究室简介

一　研究室概况

1958年，中国科学院哲学社会科学部成立法学研究所。1959年，法学研究所成立第四研究组，即国际法研究组。在相当长一段时间内，国际法研究组虽有十多位研究人员，但没有专门从事国际私法研究的人员。1977年5月，以中国科学院哲学社会科学部为主体成立了中国社会科学院，法学研究所成为中国社会科学院的一个研究所。1978年，国际法研究组改建为国际法研究室，包括国际公法、国际私法和国际经济法三个国际法专业。此后，姚壮、任继圣和林欣先后调入法学研究所，国际法研究室才有了从事国际私法专业的研究人员。1999年底，沈涓进入国际法研究室，从事国际私法专业研究。此时，姚壮、任继圣已调离法学研究所，林欣已退休。2002年，刘欣燕进入国际法研究室。同年，中国社会科学院成立国际法研究中心，法学研究所国际法研究室全体人员进入国际法研究中心。经过一段时间的筹备，2004年，国际法研究中心成立了国际公法研究室、国际私法研究室和国际经济法研究室。自此，国际私法专业研究室成为一个独立的研究室，当时成员有沈涓和刘欣燕，沈涓任研究室主任。2005年，刘欣燕调离国际法研究中心，国际私法研究室仅有沈涓一位研究人员。2007年，谢新胜进入国际私法研究室。2009年，李庆明进入国际私法研究室。同年，国际法研究中心更名为国际法研究所。2012年，谢新胜调离国际法研究所。2014年底，沈涓卸任研究室主任一职，李庆明任研究室副主任。2017年，傅攀峰进入国际私法研究室。至2019年4月，中国社会科学院国际法研究所国际私法研究室有沈涓研究员、李庆明副研究员和傅攀峰助理研究员三人。

60 年来，中国社会科学院的国际私法研究室和国际私法专业的研究人员都经历了从无到有的发展历程，几代国际私法研究者的先后加入，使国际私法研究室得以创立和延续，他们取得的丰富研究成果奠定了国际私法研究室在国内外具有影响的学术地位。

二 研究室成员代表作

中华人民共和国成立之初，虽有大学开设国际私法课程，但授课内容援用当时苏联的国际私法体系，学习和研究国际私法时参考的也是苏联国际私法学者的著作，还没有我们自己的学者编写的教材。20 世纪 80 年代初期，中国现代国际私法开始复兴。

1980 年，姚壮和任继圣共同编写了中华人民共和国第一本国际私法教材，并发表多篇学术论文，如姚壮和任继圣合作发表的论文《论国际私法的调整对象和规范》、姚壮发表的论文《试论国际私法与国际经济法调整对象的区分问题》、任继圣发表的论文《论国际私法的发展趋势》。他们的论文在国内国际私法学界关于国际私法调整对象、性质和规范组成等基本问题的讨论中奠定了“大国际私法”说的理论基础，在当时国际私法和国际经济法各自的学科研究范围和教学中的课程讲授范围的厘清上有重要贡献，也为当时的国内国际私法研究指明了方向和路径。他们的研究开启了中国国际私法研究的复兴之门，也开启了国际私法学科基本理论问题的研究之路。他们不仅成为国际法研究所国际私法研究的先驱，也是中华人民共和国国际私法研究的先驱。

林欣在国际私法学科发展中承担了承上启下的使命，在姚壮和任继圣调离后，林欣在一段时间内成为国际法研究所唯一从事国际私法研究的专业人员，并取得丰硕的研究成果。在国际私法领域的研究中，林欣出版专著《国际私法理论诸问题研究》、《国际私法》等，发表论文《论国际私法中法律适用问题的新发展与我国的实践》、《国际法和国际私法理论若干新观点》、《国际民事诉讼中的管辖权与我国民事诉讼法》等。除了国际私法学科，林欣在国际刑法领域也有深入研究，获得丰富成果，出版专著《国际法中的刑事管辖权》、《国际刑法新论》等，发表论文《国际刑法中双重犯罪原则的新发展》、《论引渡与庇护制度的新动向》等。

沈涓进入国际法研究所从事国际私法专业的研究已20余年，曾担任国际私法研究室主任10年，是国际法研究所国际私法学科的骨干和带头人，为国际私法学科的发展作出了重要贡献。沈涓在长期的国际私法研究和教学中取得了丰富的研究成果，出版专著《中国区际冲突法研究》、《合同准据法理论的解释》、《冲突法及其价值导向》（修订本）等，主编《国际私法学的新发展》、《国际私法的振扬之路》、《国际法研究》（第一卷、第五卷、第九卷）、《国际私法》等多部专著、论文集和法律硕士研究生教材，发表论文40余篇，包括《法院地法的纵与限——兼论中国国际私法的态度》、《继承准据法确定中区别制与同一制的理性抉择——兼评〈涉外民事关系法律适用法〉第31条》、《法律选择协议效力的法律适用辩释》、《区际冲突法的概念》、《论发展中的最密切联系原则》、《冲突法规则的完善与发展》、《存异以求同　他石可攻玉——海牙〈民商事管辖权和外国判决公约〉（草案）与中国相关法律之比较研究》、《时代的契机　理智的选择——关于中国国际私法中确定合同准据法立法的几点思考》、《最密切联系的判断标准》、《内地与港澳之间民商判决承认与执行新进展——浅析三地之间的两个〈安排〉》、《完善涉外经济纠纷解决机制的中国司法与仲裁制度》、《法官裁量对结果选择的实现之认识》、《国际私法晚近发展趋势》、《亚洲国际私法在合同领域的发展》、《再论海牙〈民商事管辖权和外国判决的承认与执行公约〉草案及中国的考量》、《国际民事诉讼中滥用诉权问题浅析》等。

谢新胜进入国际私法研究室时正是国际私法学科人员极度短缺之际，他的加盟为研究室补进了新生源泉，加强了专业研究的力量，推进了学科的进一步发展。他注重理论与实践的结合，取得了一系列质量较高的成果。他出版了专著《国际商事仲裁程序法适用研究》，发表了论文20余篇，包括《国际海底沉船文物打捞争议的解决路径——以美国“奥德赛”案的审理为视角》、《条约与互惠缺失时中国判决的域外执行——以美国法院执行中国民商事判决第一案为视角》、《国际商事仲裁裁决撤销制度“废弃论”之批判》、《代理的法律适用规则探析》、《电子商务视角下的涉外民事协议管辖制度——以我国〈民事诉讼法〉第244条的修改和完善为中心》、《船舶优先权的法律适用规则》、《民法典中冲突法与实体法关系三题》、《论国际法在国际商事仲裁程序中的适用》、《论国际商事仲裁实现程序自治的路径》等。

李庆明进入国际私法研究室又一次壮大了学科研究队伍，他有扎实的专业知识积累和良好的专业素养，10余年间在专业研究上取得了很大进步，逐渐成为研究室的中坚力量。他出版了专著《美国外国人侵权请求法研究》、译著《国际私法程序中礼让的新作用》、合作著作《中国国际私法司法实践研究（2001—2010）》，参编著作《当代国际法研究》、《法学教育的中国模式》、《国际私法学的新发展》、《变动中的国际法：前沿与热点》、《涉外民事诉讼管辖权问题研究》等多部，发表了论文30余篇，包括《论中国国有企业在美国民事诉讼中的国家豁免》、《美国联邦法院确认外国仲裁裁决的管辖权问题——以涉及中国政府的两个案件为例》、《中国国家财产在美国的执行豁免——以沃尔斯特夫妇诉中国工商银行为例》、《国家豁免与诉诸法院之权利》、《论域外民事判决作为我国民事诉讼中的证据》、《境外仲裁机构在中国内地仲裁的法律问题研究》等。

傅攀峰是国际私法研究室最年轻的研究人员，他的加盟使研究室恢复了曾经的兴旺景象。他勤奋认真，专业知识坚实，具有较高的英文和法文水平，至今已取得较丰富的研究成果，显示了很大的研究潜力。他出版了专著《法国国际商事仲裁制度研究》，发表了论文《单边仲裁员委任机制的道德困境及其突围》、《未竟的争鸣：被撤销的国际商事仲裁裁决的承认与执行》、《国际投资仲裁中既判力原则的适用标准——从形式主义走向实质主义》、《论ICC仲裁规则中的紧急仲裁员制度》、《论“多方当事人仲裁”的制度建构与实践困境》、《论国际商事仲裁裁决的既判力》、《普通法系国际商事仲裁裁决既判力问题的处理经验及其启示——以Associated Electric v. European Re案为例》、《“最密切联系原则”的适用困境及其解决之道——基于我国涉外民商事审判实践的考察》、“Annual Review on Commercial Arbitration in China”(2016)、“Chinese Courts' Approach to Non-signatory Issues in Arbitration：A Case Study”等，发表了译文《仲裁裁决撤销制度应被废除吗?》、《纵观仲裁：过去·现在·未来》、《〈纽约公约〉项下外国仲裁裁决的承认与执行——澳大利亚与新西兰的实践》、《国际商事仲裁中庭审的开展》、《当事人意思自治与案件管理：来自一位仲裁员的几点经验》、《商事仲裁与投资仲裁：当今两者差异几何》、《〈纽约公约〉第5条下的可仲裁性、正当程序以及公共政策——以法国与比利时为视角》、《经济全球化背景下的国际仲裁——未来的挑战》、《国际法协会关于仲裁中平行诉讼与既判力的报告》等。

研究室成员简介

沈　涓

一　基本情况

汉族，湖北武汉人。中国社会科学院国际法研究所国际私法研究室二级研究员，教授，博士生导师。

1983 年 7 月毕业于中国政法大学法律系，获法学学士学位。1983 年 8 月至 1995 年 9 月任教于中南政法学院经济法系、国际经济法系。1995 年 7 月毕业于武汉大学法学院，获法学博士学位。1995 年 10 月至 1997 年 10 月任教于中南政法学院比较法研究所，任副所长。1997 年 11 月至 1999 年 12 月于中国社会科学院法学研究所从事博士后研究工作。2000 年 1 月至 2002 年 9 月，于中国社会科学院法学研究所国际法研究室从事科研工作。2002 年 10 月至今，于中国社会科学院国际法研究中心（2009 年更名为国际法研究所）国际私法研究室从事科研工作。

1994 年 11 月被评为副教授。2000 年 8 月被评为研究员、教授。2002 年 5 月被评为博士生导师。2016 年 9 月被评为二级研究员。

主要研究领域为国际私法、区际冲突法、国际民事诉讼法。

2003 年 9 月起任中国国际私法学会副会长。2015 年 7 月起任中华司法研究会理事。2018 年 5 月起任中国国际法学会理事。2007 年起享受国务院政府特殊津贴。2018 年 1 月当选为北京市第十三届政协委员。

二　访学经历

2002 至 2003 年于韩国国立汉城大学作学术访问，其间与韩国国际私法学会建立了良好的学术交流关系，多次参与韩国国际私法学会的年会及各类学术研讨会，并多次在国立汉城大学、高丽大学等韩国著名大学作学术讲座，同时，将韩国 2001 年新的国际私法法规翻译成中文，介绍到中国国际私法学界。在韩国的学术访问对促进中韩国际私法学术交流作出了一定贡献。2005 年和 2006 年两次赴日本参加“中、日、韩三国国际私法研讨会”，并访问日本早稻田大学、一桥大学和东北大学。2006 年于荷兰莱顿大学作学术访问，与荷兰国际私法学界资深学者进行了交流，并访问了阿姆斯特丹大学、乌特勒支大学、海牙国际法院等机构。2007 年赴我国台湾地区玄奘大学讲学，为法律学院研究生和本科生讲授“国际私法专题”，并与台湾地区国际私法学界建立了广泛联系，进行了深入的学术交流。2010 年赴英国伦敦大学国王学院作学术访问，了解了英国大学中冲突法课程的设置和讲授内容，与英国冲突法学者进行了学术交流，并访问了牛津大学、剑桥大学。

三　主要成果

（一）专著

1.《冲突法及其价值导向》，中国政法大学出版社，1993。

2.《中国区际冲突法研究》（中青年法学文库），中国政法大学出版社，1999。

3.《合同准据法理论的解释》，法律出版社，2000。

4.《冲突法及其价值导向》（修订本），中国政法大学出版社，2002。

5.《国际私法》（主编），法律硕士研究生教材，社会科学文献出版社，2006。

6.《国际法研究（第一卷）》（主编），中国人民公安大学出版社，2006。

7.《国际私法学的新发展》（主编），中国社会科学出版社，2010。

8.《国际法研究（第五卷）》（主编），中国人民公安大学出版社，2012。

9.《国际法研究（第九卷）》（主编），社会科学文献出版社，2013。

10.《国际私法学的新发展》（主编），中国社会科学出版社，2015。

11.《国际私法的振扬之路》（主编），社会科学文献出版社，2019。

（二）论文

1.《论调整大陆、台湾区际法律冲突的现状与前景》，《中南政法学院学报》1992 年第 2 期。

2.《冲突法价值的起源、导向及实现》，《比较法研究》1992 年第 2 期。

3.《中国区际冲突法的历史研究》，《法商研究》1996 年第 2 期。

4.《论发展中的最密切联系原则》，载《当代国际私法问题》（论文集），武汉大学出版社，1996。

5.《中国区际民事诉讼程序的协调》，载《中国国际私法与比较法年刊（1999）》，法律出版社，1999。

6.《区际冲突法的概念》，《法学研究》1999 年第 5 期。

7.《冲突法规则的完善与发展》，《政法论坛》1999 年第 6 期。

8.《合同当事人意思自治的确定和限制》，载《清华法律评论》第 3 辑，清华大学出版社，2000。

9.《存异以求同　他石可攻玉——海牙〈民商事管辖权和外国判决公约〉（草案）与中国相关法律之比较研究》，载《中国国际私法与比较法年刊（2001)》，法律出版社，2001。

10.《中国涉外民商事案件管辖权的立法及实践》，载韩国法制研究院《中国民事诉讼法的现状和问题》，2003。

11.《中国国际私法概况》，载韩国国际私法学会《国际私法研究》第9号，芝山，2003。

12.《中国国际私法立法问题》，《法学研究》2004年第2期。

13.《中国国际私法立法现状》，载（韩国）韩中法学会《中国法研究》第4辑，2004。

14.《韩国2001年国际私法立法概况》，中国法学网，2005。

15.《韩国国际私法研究及与中国国际私法之比较》，载玄奘大学法律学院《两岸国际私法研讨会论文集》，伟大出版社，2005。

16.《中日国际私法之比较》，载早稻田大学比较法研究所《早稻田大学比较法研究所演讲记录集》，2005年第8卷。

17.《时代的契机理智的选择——关于中国国际私法中确定合同准据法立法的几点思考》，载《国际法研究（第一卷)》，中国人民公安大学出版社，2006。

18.《国际私法中“合同自体法”概念的解析》，载中国社会科学院国际法研究中心编《纪念中国社会科学院建院三十周年学术论文集·国际法研究中心卷》，方志出版社，2007。

19.《最密切联系的判断标准》，载陈甦主编《法苑撷英——纪念中国社会科学院法学研究所建所50周年文集》，中国社会科学出版社，2008。

20.《内地与港澳之间民商判决承认与执行新进展——浅析三地之间的两个〈安排〉》，载《国际法研究（第三卷)》，中国人民公安大学出版社，2009。

21.《完善涉外经济纠纷解决机制的中国司法与仲裁制度》，载陈甦主编《全球化背景下的中国法治建设》，经济管理出版社，2010。

22.《最密切联系理论》，载陈泽宪主编《当代中国国际法研究》，中国社会科学出版社，2010。

23.《中国区际冲突法理论的发展》，载陈泽宪主编《当代中国国际法研究》，中国社会科学出版社，2010。

24.《法官裁量对结果选择的实现之认识》，载《国际法研究（第四卷)》，中国人民公安大学出版社，2011。

25.《国际私法晚近发展趋势》，载朱晓青主编《变化中的国际法：热点与前沿》，中国社会科学出版社，2012。

26.《中国法院审理涉外（涉港澳台）民商案件情况》，载《国际法研究（第八卷)》，社会科学文献出版社，2013。

27.《亚洲国际私法在合同领域的发展》，载孔庆江主编《国际法评论》第 4 卷，清华大学出版社，2013。

28.《法院地法的纵与限——兼论中国国际私法的态度》，《清华法学》2013 年第 4 期。

29.《继承准据法确定中区别制与同一制的理性抉择——兼评〈涉外民事关系法律适用法〉第 31 条》，《国际法研究》2014 年第 1 期。

30.《法律选择协议效力的法律适用辩释》，《法学研究》2015 年第 6 期。

31.《再论海牙〈民商事管辖权和外国判决的承认与执行公约〉草案及中国的考量》，《国际法研究》2016 年第 6 期（中国人民大学书报资料中心复印报刊资料 D416《国际法学》2017 年第 5 期全文转载；中国社会科学网全文转载，2017 年 8 月 31 日)。

32.《国际私法学科的发展及热点、难点问题》，中国法学网首发，2017 年 5 月。

33.《国际民事诉讼中滥用诉权问题浅析》，《国际法研究》2017 年第 6 期。

34.《改革开放 40 年中国国际私法的立法成就》，《中国社会科学报》2018 年 12 月 26 日（中国社会科学网全文转载，2018 年 12 月 26 日)。

（三）译文

《韩国 2001 年修正国际私法》，载《中国国际私法与比较法年刊(2003)》，法律出版社，2003。

四　获奖情况

1. 专著《中国区际冲突法研究》获 2001 年中国社会科学院法学研究所“优秀科研成果奖”。

2. 专著《冲突法及其价值导向》（修订本）获 2003 年中国社会科学院法学研究所“优秀科研成果二等奖”。

3. 专著《冲突法及其价值导向》（修订本）获 2004 年中国社会科学院“第五届优秀科研成果三等奖”。

4. 专著《合同准据法理论的解释》2005 年获第一届中国青年法律学术奖“法鼎奖”之“银鼎奖”。

5. 论文《时代的契机理智的选择——关于中国国际私法中确定合同准据法立法的几点思考》获 2011 年中国社会科学院“第七届优秀科研成果三等奖”。

6. 专著《合同准据法理论的解释》2013 年获第一届法学博士后科研成果奖专著类二等奖。

7. 论文《法官裁量对结果选择的实现之认识》获 2015 年中国社会科学院国际法研究所优秀成果一等奖。

8. 专著《国际私法学的新发展》获 2015 年中国社会科学院国际法研究所优秀专著。

9. 论文《法官裁量对结果选择的实现之认识》获 2016 年中国社会科学院“第九届优秀科研成果三等奖”。

五　主持课题

中国社会科学院重大课题：WTO 争端解决制度与国际法

中国社会科学院重点课题：中国国际私法立法理论研究

中国社会科学院重点课题：缔约权与缔约程序法的修改

中国社会科学院国情调研项目：中国法院审理涉外涉港澳台民商案件情况

中国社会科学院国情调研项目：中国法院判决在外国的承认与执行

中国社会科学院香港专题调研项目：香港特别行政区法律与中国特色法律体系研究——以内地与香港区际民商事司法协助安排的落实为视角

中国社会科学院“长城学者资助项目”：中国《涉外民事关系法律适用法》及其实施

中国社会科学院创新工程项目：中国《涉外民事关系法律适用法》的实施及发展

六　教学成果

沈涓从事国际私法专业教学 36 年，授课对象包括本科生、硕士生、博士生，以及合作指导博士后研究人员。至今已独立指导硕士生21人、博士生13人、博士后研究人员7人。

七 主要学术观点

1. 关于冲突法的价值导向

冲突法不仅是调整国际关系的实体法或解决法律冲突的原则，更内含了人类索求的理性价值和道德取向，这就是通过解决冲突的方式和过程实现人类整体的和谐、协调。因此，冲突法不只是解决法律冲突和超法域利益冲突的法律，也是弘扬人类向善精神和引导国际社会走向和谐、互助的秩序载体。这一观点于1993年提出，其时已经为当代提出的构建人类命运共同体提供了法理依据。

2. 关于合同准据法理论

当事人意思自治原则是符合契约自由和私法自治精神的理论，它既能实现当事人的意愿，又能保证法律适用的确定性、可预见性和一致性，从而保障国际合同关系的顺畅和有序。因此，合同准据法理论应在尽可能大的范围内和程度上赋予当事人选择合同准据法的权利，并且，在当事人选择了法律的情况下，应尽量给予当事人的意向以法律效力。最密切联系原则并非以抛弃法律选择规则体系为目的，而是在承继传统规则体系基础上，引进法官自由裁量机制，以其特有的灵活性改革传统规则体系的僵化和机械。最密切联系理论优于传统理论之处正在于对弥补预制规则先天不足的重视，并运用法官自由裁量方法有效克除了预制规则的缺陷。如果认为最密切联系理论只鼓励法官的自由裁量，为确定合同准据法的方法补充灵活性，而不顾法律适用的稳定性，适用这一理论将会破坏法律适用的确定性、可预见性和一致性，也将破坏国际合同关系的顺畅和有序，这便曲解了最密切联系理论的精髓，降低了这一理论的意义，也限制了这一理论的作用。

3. 关于法律选择协议效力的法律适用

在意思自治原则下，当事人选择法律的合意是否有效，直接关系到意思自治的实现，但现有研究较少涉及这一问题。目前国际私法学界存在当事人选法协议效力适用当事人所选之法或适用法院地法两种主张的分歧。适用当事人所选之法确定选法协议效力的主张和规定存在逻辑矛盾等诸多弱点，特别是存在合同之外领域无法采行的重大缺陷。选法协议的内容是法律选择规则，确定选法协议效力是法律选择规则的适用过程。意思自治原则体系既包括赋予当事人选择法律的权利，也包括限制当事人意思自治的条件。合同领域之外的法律关系适用当事人选择的法律确定选法协议效力存在更大不合理性。适用法院地法确定选法协议效力才是更合理、更可行的方法。

4. 关于海牙《民商事管辖权和外国判决的承认与执行公约》草案

海牙《民商事管辖权和外国判决的承认与执行公约》的制定已近20年，各国对诸多问题的争执使公约的制定至今未能完成。公约多个草案虽将公约的适用对象定位于民事和商事关系，但又不断扩大被公约排除适用的民商事项范围，将这些事项交由其他相关公约调整，这无疑会破坏公约的完整性和全面性，增加各国加入海牙程序性公约的困难，严重影响公约的适用效力。新近的公约草案舍弃了直接管辖权的设置，不仅又一次破坏了公约的完整性，而且未能消除各国管辖权的冲突，也使公约缺失了在承认和执行外国判决时判断管辖权正当性的明确标准。在拒绝承认和执行外国判决的理由方面，公约草案有必要重视并修正审查管辖权正当性与判决终局性和可执行力的依据的不一致，这种不一致将导致管辖权效力和判决效力之间的不和谐。

5. 关于法院地法在国际私法中的角色

法院地法在国际私法中呈现多种表述，每一种表述都有不同特性。表述为内国强制性规则的法院地法具有对外国法的排他性，需要克制对适用这类规则范围的不当宽纵。将法院地法表述为内国法的冲突规范通常是单边规范，限制这种单边规范的数量，可避免对法律适用属地主义的回归和法律选择普遍性的破坏。将法院地法直接表述为法院地法的冲突规范体现的是司法管辖权的优势，这时，选择法院地法仅为不当扩大内国法的适用范围时，当限；选择法院地法若为尽可能使法律适用结果有利于当事人时，可纵。不动产所在地法是法院地法的一种特殊表述，在此方面，对法院地法“限”的必要应该体现在继承领域。选择适用法院地法，实现立法管辖权和司法的便利不是理性的理由，法院地法和法律关系之间的密切联系和当事人利益的特殊需要才是考量法院地法是否应该被选择适用的标准。

李庆明

一 基本情况

2009 年 7 月至今就职于中国社会科学院国际法研究所，现任国际私法研究室副主任、副研究员，兼任《国际法研究》编辑。2010 年 9 月至 2011 年 9 月，作为访问学者在哥伦比亚大学法学院访学。

2000 年 9 月至 2009 年 6 月就读于武汉大学法学院，先后获法学学士（2004 年）、硕士（2006 年）、博士学位（2009 年）。

二 主要成果

（一）著译作

1.《美国外国人侵权请求法研究》（专著），武汉大学出版社，2010。

2.《国际私法程序中礼让的新作用》（译著），中国社会科学出版社，2011。

（二）论文

1.《仲裁的最低正当程序简析》，《商事仲裁》2006年第1期。

2.《走向成熟的国际私法》，《武大国际法评论》第4卷，武汉大学出版社，2006。

3.《2004年中国国际私法司法实践述评》（与黄进教授、杜焕芳合著），载《中国国际私法与比较法年刊》第8卷，法律出版社，2006。该文同时收录于孙南申、杜涛主编《当代国际私法研究——21世纪的中国与国际私法》，上海人民出版社，2006。

4.《2005年中国国际私法司法实践述评》（与黄进教授、杜焕芳合著），载《中国国际私法与比较法年刊》第9卷，法律出版社，2007。

5.《中国诊所式法学教育的现状与问题——学生的视角》，日本《法律时报》2007年第79卷第2号。

6.《论国际私法中定性的标准》，《月旦民商法杂志》2008年第20期。

7. "Chinese Judicial Practice in Private International Law: 2006" (co-author), *Chinese Journal of International Law*, Vol. 8, Issue 3, 2009.

8.《美国〈外国人侵权请求法〉诉讼中的管辖权》，《美国研究》2012年第1期（人大复印报刊资料《国际法学》2012年第8期全文转载）。

9.《国家豁免与诉诸法院之权利》，《环球法律评论》2012年第6期。

10.《中国国家财产在美国的执行豁免——以沃尔斯特夫妇诉中国工商银行为例》，《武汉大学学报》（哲学社会科学版）2013年第4期。

11.《美国联邦法院确认外国仲裁裁决的管辖权问题——以涉及中国政府的两个案件为例》，《国际法研究》2015年第3期（人大复印报刊资料《国际法学》2016年第1期全文转载）。

12.《境外仲裁机构在中国内地仲裁的法律问题》，《环球法律评论》2016年第3期。

13.《论域外民事判决作为我国民事诉讼中的证据》，《国际法研究》2017年第5期（人大复印报刊资料《国际法学》2018年第2期全文转载）。

14.《论中国国有企业在美国民事诉讼中的国家豁免》，《江西社会科学》2018年第11期（人大复印报刊资料《国际法学》2019年第3期全文转载）。

三 主要学术观点

1. 美国国际人权民事诉讼

李庆明是国内第一个系统研究美国国际人权民事诉讼的学者。《美国外国人侵权请求法研究》一书讨论了美国国际人权民事诉讼的管辖权基础、历史进程、法律选择、面临的抗辩与障碍等问题。该书认为，作为美国国际人权民事诉讼法律基础的《外国人侵权请求法》在20世纪80年代的复兴，与美国国内的民权运动高涨以及国际民事诉讼爆炸密不可分；《外国人侵权请求法》中的管辖权并不是普遍民事管辖权，而是受到不方便法院、用尽当地救济、国家豁免、国家行为理论、国际礼让、政治行为理论等的制约；美国的外国人侵权请求诉讼的繁荣，根源于美国独特的法律制度，难以为其他国家所移植、复制和借鉴。

2. 国家豁免

在国家豁免问题上，李庆明认为美国和中国均有反对中国国有企业主张国家豁免的声音，但从已有的经验和教训来看，如在美国被起诉，中国国有企业和政府还是应积极应诉，出庭抗辩美国法院缺乏事项管辖权和对人管辖权。因美国法律和法院均首先推定外国国有企业具有独立人格，中国国有企业出庭抗辩管辖权，主张主权豁免，并不会导致揭开公司面纱，以至于各国有企业和中国政府之间承担连带责任。李庆明还讨论了国家豁免与诉诸法院之权利，认为国家豁免虽然限制了诉诸法院之权利，但目的合法且符合比例原则，一国授予外国国家在本国法院享有国家豁免并非对人权的不当限制。

3. 中国国际私法

李庆明研究中国国际私法的司法实践问题，从涉外民事判决书中分析我国法院审理涉外案件时如何适用管辖权规则、法律选择规则、外国法查明规则和证据认定规则等，认为我国法院优先适用法院地法，有出于司法任务简单化的考虑，也有外国法查明制度等配套制度不健全的因素。考虑到我国承认（认可）和执行域外民事判决的实践不多，可以将域外民事判决作为证据。

4. 国际仲裁

在仲裁领域，李庆明认为境外仲裁机构在中国内地作出的裁决并非

“非内国裁决”，有必要及时修改《仲裁法》，明确将仲裁地作为认定裁决国籍的标准，并同等对待境外仲裁机构与我国涉外仲裁机构在中国内地进行的仲裁。

四　主持课题

国家社科基金 2012 年度青年项目“国际人权民事诉讼中的国家豁免问题研究”。

中国社会科学院 2012 年度重点课题“中国政府在美国诉讼的对策”等项目。

傅攀峰

一　基本情况

汉族，1987 年生，湖南汨罗人，法学博士。现任中国社会科学国际法研究所国际私法研究室助理研究员。专业方向为国际私法、仲裁法学、比较法。研究领域是国际争议解决机制、国际商事仲裁、国际投资仲裁、国际体育仲裁。目前担任的主要社会职务和兼职有中国国际私法研究会理事、中国仲裁法学研究会成员。

2009 年毕业于西南政法大学，获法学学士学位。2009 年至 2015 年就读于武汉大学法学院，获法学硕士学位与法学博士学位。2013 年至 2014 年获国家留学基金委资助在加拿大蒙特利尔大学法学院以联合培养博士生身份访学。2015 年至 2017 年在中国社会科学院法学研究所从事国际私法方向博士后研究工作。曾担任《武大国际法评论》、《中国国际私法与比较法年刊》编辑。曾在《现代法学》、《比较法研究》等核心期刊上发表文章 20 多篇。

二　学术成果

（一）专著

《法国国际商事仲裁制度研究》，中国社会科学出版社，2018。

（二）论文

1.《普通法系国际商事仲裁裁决既判力问题的处理经验及其启示——以 Associated Electric v. European Re 案为例》，《仲裁研究》第 30 辑，法律出版社，2012。

2.《“最密切联系原则”的适用困境及其解决之道——基于我国涉外民商事审判实践的考察》，载《中国国际私法与比较法年刊》（第 15 卷），北京大学出版社，2013。

3.《论国际商事仲裁裁决的既判力》，《武大国际法评论》第 16 卷第 1 期，武汉大学出版社，2013。

4.《论“多方当事人仲裁”的制度建构与实践困境》，《北京仲裁》第 87 辑，中国法制出版社，2014。

5.《论 ICC 仲裁规则中的紧急仲裁员制度》，《北京仲裁》第 91 辑，中国法制出版社，2015。

6.《国际投资仲裁中既判力原则的适用标准——从形式主义走向实质主义》，《比较法研究》2016 年第 4 期。

7. “Annual Review on Commercial Arbitration in China”, Wolters Kluwer, 2016, co-authored with SONG Lianbin and Helena Chen.

8.《未竟的争鸣：被撤销的国际商事仲裁裁决的承认与执行》，《现代法学》2017 年第 1 期。

9.《单边仲裁单边仲裁员委任机制的道德困境及其突围》，《当代法学》2017 年第 3 期。

10. "Reversal of Tide：2016 Successful Cases in Challenging Arbitral Awards"，*APRAG Newsletter*，July-December 2017 Issue，co-authored with David Fong.

11. "Chinese Courts' Approach to Non-signatory Issues in Arbitration：A Case Study"，*Arbitration Study* 43 （2017）.

12.《法国仲裁制度的发展历程——从文艺复兴时期谈起》，《北京仲裁》第 104 辑，中国法制出版社，2018。

13.《国际投资仲裁的中国参与》，《中国社会科学报》（法学理论版）2018 年 9 月 12 日。

14.《临时仲裁司法协助制度的本土建构》，《法制日报》2018 年 11 月 5 日。

15.《法国商事仲裁二元立法模式及其启示》，《国际法研究》2019 年第 1 期。

三　学术观点

1. 单边仲裁员委任机制道德困境的突破路径

傅攀峰深入研究争议中的单边仲裁员委任机制，并认为，虽然单边仲裁员委任机制拉近了当事人与仲裁程序之间的距离，增强了人们对仲裁的信任，巩固了仲裁作为一种诉讼外纠纷解决模式的合法性，但此种委任机制带来了诸如仲裁员代理人化等严重的道德问题，阻碍了正义的正常输送，破坏了仲裁的正面形象。当今，仲裁的类型日趋细化，任何一刀切的解决方案，都可能适得其反。在经济领域，欲使单边仲裁员委任机制从困境中成功突围，有必要对投资仲裁与商事仲裁加以区分。对于投资仲裁，废除单边仲裁员委任机制具有可行性，但关键问题在于如何确保委任机构的中立性。对于商事仲裁，废除单边仲裁员委任机制不具有可行性，但应采取必要措施以规避或降低此种委任机制给案件带来的负面影响。与此同时，应大力倡导独任仲裁员机制的运用；在双方当事人实际地位悬殊之时，有必要引入特殊机制，以保障仲裁庭的公正性。

2. 既判力在国际投资仲裁中的适用标准从形式主义走向实质主义

国际投资仲裁因裁决不一致现象频繁而饱受批评，傅攀峰认为，在特定情形下，适用既判力原则是一条确保前后裁决一致的有效途径。在既判力原则的适用标准上，传统的三重因素一致标准乃为两大法系所公认。然而，倘若投资仲裁庭对这一标准作机械解释，既判力原则将面临无法得到适用的僵局，进而无法避免后诉仲裁庭对前诉仲裁庭已裁断的同一请求或同一争点作重复裁断。通过对当事人、诉因以及请求这三重因素中的每一重因素作实质分析，适当软化三重因素一致性的要求，可避免诸多不合理的实践推论，从而达到平衡正当程序考量与满足既判力原则适用的双重目的。

3. *辩证看待被撤销的仲裁裁决的承认与执行*

晚近30年的国际商事仲裁实践中，被仲裁地撤销的仲裁裁决在他国获得承认与执行的案例屡次出现。以 Hilmarton 案、Putrabali 案等为代表，法国法院的实践最具代表性。这种司法态度持续地引起了人们的争议。争议的焦点在于，承认与执行被撤销的裁决的自由裁量权是否存在？傅攀峰认为，对此，从裁决撤销制度的意义以及《纽约公约》相关条款的解读出发，可得出截然相反的结论。结合《纽约公约》的立法宗旨以及当代国际仲裁的现状与发展趋势，对于这一问题，人们宜采取积极的现实主义态度：回答应为肯定，操作则当谨慎。目前中国法院尚未面临相关类似案件。中国加入《纽约公约》时即已表明，被执行人证明裁决存在已被仲裁地撤销的情形时，人民法院应当裁定驳回申请，拒绝承认及执行。未来中国有必要明确：只有仲裁地法院根据《示范法》所确立的国际通行标准撤销的仲裁裁决，中国法院才应当拒绝承认及执行，否则，中国法院将保留承认与执行被撤销的仲裁裁决的自由裁量权。

4. *《仲裁法》修订应借鉴法国采用二元立法模式*

法国是对商事仲裁采取二元立法模式的典型国家，其现行《法国仲裁法（2011）》分为“国内仲裁篇”与“国际仲裁篇”。法国商事仲裁二元立法模式本质上源于，在涉及仲裁协议、仲裁庭人数、保密要求、裁决意见、裁决撤销以及裁决执行等诸多问题上，立法者欲为国内仲裁与国际仲裁作出不同的制度安排。此种立法模式下，对仲裁“国际性”进行识别是一个十分重要的实践问题。对此，法国采取的是基于经济因素考量的客观标准。这一标准具有极强的开放性，因其赋予法院根据具体情形界定案件是否为国际仲裁的自由裁量空间。傅攀峰认为，中国未来修订仲裁法时，有必要借鉴法国，确立清晰的二元立法模式。在仲裁“国际性”的识别问题上，亦可在一定程度上借鉴法国的司法实践。

四　主要荣誉

1. 第一届“北仲杯”全国高校商事仲裁征文比赛一等奖（2013 年）
2. 中国国际私法优秀学术成果奖二等奖（2016 年）
3. 第四届“中伦杯”全国国际商事仲裁征文大赛一等奖（2016 年）
4. 第五届“中伦杯”全国国际商事仲裁征文大赛一等奖（2017 年）
5. 第六届“中伦杯”全国国际商事仲裁征文大赛一等奖（2018 年）
6. 中国国际私法优秀学术成果奖二等奖（2018 年）
7. 中国社会科学院法学研究所优秀博士后研究报告奖（2018 年）

五　科研项目

1. 主持 2014 年度北京仲裁委员会科研基金一般项目
2. 主持 2016 年度北京仲裁委员会科研基金重点项目
3. 主持 2016 年中国博士后基金第 60 批面上资助（一等）项目

试论国际私法与国际经济法调整对象的区分问题

姚　壮*

一　问题的提出

关于国际私法调整的对象问题，本来就在国际私法学者之间存在意见分歧，这种分歧可以归纳为两种不同的主张：一些学者认为，国际私法调整的对象是涉外民事法律关系中的法律冲突，而不是涉外民事法律关系本身；① 另一些学者则认为，国际私法调整的对象是涉外民事法律关系，尽管用以调整这种涉外民事法律关系的规范和方法可以有所不同，但是它们都被包括在国际私法之内。② 这两种不同主张之间的争论，在国际范围和国内范围内都是存在的，而且已经争论了好几十年，看来也不大可能在短

---

* 姚壮，1975 年 11 月来中国社会科学院法学研究所工作，20 世纪 80 年代初调入外交学院。

① 持这种观点的有李浩培、董立坤同志。李在司法部第二期全国法律专业师资进修班《国际私法》课程讲授中，给国际私法下的定义是："国际私法是关于在各国民法不一致的情况下，在解决含有涉外因素的民法关系时，规定应适用哪一国家的法律的法律部门。"（参见《国际私法讲义》上册，上海华东政法学院出版，1982，第 2 页）董在《论国际私法的范围》（《法学研究》1982 年第 2 期）一文中给国际私法下的定义是："国际私法是对于涉外的民事法律关系适用法律及如何适用法律的法。"

② 持这种观点的有任继圣、钱骅、袁成第、姚壮等同志。姚、任在合著的《国际私法基础》（中国社会科学出版社，1981）中说："国际私法是专门调整涉外民事法律关系的规范的总称。"钱在 1983 年中国政法大学出版的《国际私法讲义》中说："国际私法室调整国际交往中所产生的民事法律关系的国际法的一个部门。"袁在 1984 年 10 月西南政法学院出版的《国际私法教程》一书中说："国际私法是以间接或直接手段调整涉外民事法律关系的国际法性质的一个法的部门。"

时期内得出一个为大家所一致同意的结论。

但是需要指出，关于国际私法调整对象的争论，在第二次世界大战后，特别是在20世纪60年代以前，还只是局限在国际私法本身，即局限在国际私法究竟是冲突法还是既包括冲突规范又包括实体规范这些问题。可是这一情况到60年代以后就起了变化。从世界范围来说，第二次世界大战以后，特别是60年代以来，随着国际经济贸易关系的发展及国家对经济生活干预的加强，出现了一个新的法律部门——国际经济法。关于国际经济法的性质、范围、调整对象及其与邻近部门法的关系等问题在国内外法学界中从一开始就有争论。学者们观点分歧，难以统一。这些问题虽不属本文研究的范围，但是作为国际私法专业的工作者，我们对其中的一个问题，即国际经济法与国际私法的关系，或者说国际经济法所调整的对象与国际私法所调整的对象有何异同的问题，却不能不表示应有的关注并给予一个初步的回答。

不同的国际经济法的概念直接导引出在国际经济法与国际私法关系问题上的不同观点，就是说，各种不同理解的国际经济法，与国际私法之间有着各不相同的关系。为了说明这一问题，有必要对国际经济法在调整对象、主体、规范组成等问题上的一些主要分歧之点，作些扼要的介绍。

首先，我们是从这样一个前提出发的，即承认国际经济法是一个独立的法律部门。[①] 因为如果否认国际经济法是一个独立的法律部门，那么与国际私法之间的关系也无从谈起，很明显，和一个根本不存在的东西是没有什么关系可谈的。

既然国际经济法是一个独立的法律部门，那么它究竟是怎样的一种法律呢？对此，国内外学者们的观点基本上可以归纳为三种：（1）国际经济法只是把国际公法的一些基本原则、制度适用于国际经济事务而已；（2）国际经济法是国际公法的一个分支，除具有国际公法的一般特征外，还具有它自身的某些特点；（3）国际经济法既包括国际经济制度和机构的公法方面的法律，也包括一国涉外经济方面的法律，总之，国际经济法调整国际范围内一切超越国境而发生的经济关系。简言之，持前两种观点的学者或者把国际经济法看作国际公法的具体运用，或者把国际经济法看作国际法

① 直至今日，无论是在国内还是在国外，都有人否认国际经济法是一个独立的法律部门。

的一个独立分支，我们姑且把他们合称为国际经济法学中的“经济国际法”学派，持第三种观点的学者，则一般被称为国际经济法学中的“跨国法”学派。持经济国际法学派观点的学者，在国外有韦尔、施瓦曾伯格、金泽良雄等，在国内有王铁崖、黄秉坤、汪暄、史久镛等。这些学者认为，国际经济法调整的对象是国家间的经济关系，主要调整国际投资、国际货物、服务和资本交易，国际技术转让，以及与这些活动密切相关的国际货币、金融和财政制度。它的主体是国家，渊源是国际条约，一国的涉外经济法律是国内法，不包括在国际经济法之内。[①] 持跨国法学派观点的学者，在国外有杰塞普、弗莱曼、洛温菲尔、樱井雅夫等，在国内有姚梅镇、刘丁、袁海涛等。这些学者认为，国际经济法调整的对象是国际范围内一切超越国境而发生的经济关系，包括国际贸易、国际金融、税收、外汇管理，甚至“传统的国际公法、国际私法、关于国家契约的法律及国际行政法等等”，亦“构成跨国法这一独立法学部门的各个分支”。[②] 它的主体不仅有国家，而且包括法人（跨国公司）和自然人；国际经济法的渊源不仅有国际条约，也包括一国的国内立法。[③]

本文一开始谈到在国际私法调整对象问题上有两种不同的理解，刚才又提到学者们对国际经济法有几种不同的观点。我们可以看出，由于对这两个部门法的调整对象有不同见解，因而在国际私法与国际经济法调整的对象问题上存在两种不同的情况。一种情况是，把国际私法理解为冲突法，其调整对象为涉外民事法律关系中的法律冲突；同时把国际经济法理解为经济国际法，其调整对象是以国家为主体的国家之间的经济关系。这样，这两个法律部门的调整对象倒是不会发生“重叠”问题，即不会发生国际私法与国际经济法同时调整某一类法律关系的现象。而在这种场合下却可能发生另一方面的问题，那就是某类法律关系既不为国际私法所调整，又不为国际经济法所调整：某些调整涉外民商关系的法律规范既不属于国际私法范围，也不属于国际经济法范围，从而处于“真空”地带或

---

① 史久镛：《论国际经济法的概念和范围》，载《中国国际法年刊（1983）》，中国对外翻译出版公司，1983，第359—372页。

② 杰塞普：《跨国法》（英文版），1956。

③ 姚梅镇：《国际经济法是一个独立的法学部门》，载《中国国际法年刊（1983）》，中国对外翻译出版公司，1983，第375—385页。

“空白”状态。以国际条约或国内立法中一些直接规定涉外民事法律关系当事人双方权利义务的实体规范为例，就可以清楚地看出这一点。因为在上述情况下，这类规范既不包括在冲突法之内，也不是经济国际法的组成部分。另一种情况是，把国际私法理解为调整涉外民事法律关系的规范的总称（即既包括冲突规范又包括实体规范），同时把国际经济法理解为调整国际范围内一切超越国境而发生的经济关系的法律规范的总和，这样一来，国际经济法与国际私法在调整对象上就可能出现重合的现象。某些超越国境而发生的经济关系，就可能同时成为国际经济法与国际私法调整对象，因为某些超越国境而发生的经济法关系就是涉外民法关系的一部分，根据一般的理解，民法关系的内涵，较经济法关系的内涵更广，后者实为前者的一部分，国内大部分民法学者持这种观点。[①] 本文写作的目的就是试图解决国际经济法与国际私法在调整对象上的“空白”和“重叠”问题，恰当地区分这两个法律部门的范围。

二 区分的依据及理由

毋庸讳言，笔者对国际私法的观点一向被一些学者称为“大国际私法”[②] 观点，因此，在区分国际私法与国际经济法的调整对象时，也是从这一根本观点出发的。在区分这两个法律部门的调整对象时，需要从理论上解决如下两个问题：（1）国际经济法究竟是“经济国际法”还是“跨国法”？（2）如对国际经济法持“跨国法”的观点，那么又如何来区分它和国际私法所调整的不同对象？笔者认为，前一问题是首要的，后一问题是第二位的，如果对国际经济法持“经济国际法”的观点，那么从“大国际私法”的角度出发，它们两者在调整对象上就既不会发生“重叠”的现象，也不会留下什么“真空”的地带。

笔者认为，国际经济法就是经济国际法。为了说明这一点，我们不妨从它产生的历史背景谈起。大家知道，国际经济法的产生与国内经济法的

---

① 参见《中国大百科全书》（法学卷），中国大百科全书出版社，1984，第412—416页。

② 唐表明：《当前国际私法研究中的几个理论问题》，载《中国国际法年刊（1984）》，中国对外翻译出版公司，1984，第247—256页。

产生有着共同的经济根源。就国内经济法的产生而言，它首先是在资本主义国家出现的。建筑在私有财产神圣不可侵犯的资本主义私有制基础上的资产阶级国家，在自由资本主义时期，在经济上实行放任主义的政策，国家原则上不干预私人之间的经济活动，所以在当时并没有现在所说的那种经济法。但是随着资本主义从自由竞争发展到垄断阶段——帝国主义阶段，由于垄断资本与国家政权的接近与结合，国家政权对私人之间经济活动的干预逐渐加强。特别是在发生经济危机或国民经济遭受战争破坏之后，生产下降，竞争激烈，资本主义自身具有的那种调节作用，已经不能完全解决问题了。于是就由资本主义国家出面，颁布一些立法（如反托拉斯法等）来直接干预私人之间的经济活动，对经济进行统治，以调整整个国民经济的关系。这些立法就是现在被人们称为“经济法”的法律。经济法这一名词之所以最早出现于德国，正是反映了19世纪末期以来生产的集中和垄断最早出现在德国这一历史事实。由此可见，国家在颁布经济法的时候，就是既作为经济法的制定者（立法者），又作为这种法律关系的参与者——主体之一的资格出现的。国际经济法的产生与发展也有类似的情况。大家知道，第二次世界大战期间及战后，资本主义国家生产大幅度下降，失业人口激增，一些国家为了刺激生产，增加出口贸易和创造就业机会，纷纷采取关税壁垒及进口配额制等措施来进行“经济战”。第二次世界大战后，美国与西欧国家之间的一场有名的“冻鸡战”即属一例。它是国家直接干预国际经济关系的表现，可见无论是国内经济法还是国际经济法的产生，都是国家直接干预经济的结果。在这些场合，国家不仅是这些法律的制定者或参与制定者（对国际条约而言），而且是这种法律关系的主体之一——权利义务的承担者。再如，1984年秋季美国政府坚持要在当年9月7日起对我国实行限制纺织品进口的新规定，这个法令调整的是美国与向美国出口纺织品的有关国家之间的关系，而不是调整美国纺织品进口商和有关国家的纺织品出口商之间的关系。附带指出，这个美国国内法的规定，按照我们的看法，根本不能算作国际经济法的规范，它只是一国的涉外经济法规，但如按照跨国法的观点，则属国际经济法规范。这个法令对某一个美国纺织品进口商和另一个其他国家的纺织品出口商之间的关系来说，并不起直接调整的作用，它只能通过各自的国家来约束本国的出口商或进口商。国际上通行的配额制度所起的作用也是这样的。它只是规定了某种商品向某一国输入的总的限制，并没有限制两国商人在一笔具体交易上的数量。出口商人能在一笔交易中出口多少商品，直接取决于它的国家在总的配额内能分配给他多少商品，而不是由配额制本身来决定。可见配额制是通过有关国家对配额的再分配而影响或调整这种超越一国范围的经济关系的。调整这种既不由传统的国际公法，也不由“大国际私法”来调整的法律关系的法律，就是我们所说的国际经济法，或叫经济国际法。总之，国内经济法和国际经济法都是从国家对经济活动的直接干预中产生的，国家一开始就以立法者和该法律关系的主体之一（权利义务的担当者）的双重资格出现的。所以经济法最初具有行政法的性质，它是从行政法中脱胎、分离出来的。

在这里，还需要顺便谈谈整个国际私法与国际经济法的关系问题。在这个问题上有两种论点值得商榷。

一种论点是，从国际私法是冲突法的观点出发，认为“两者所调整的法律行为的主体及其关系基本相同。但其最主要的区别是：国际经济法是直接调整国际经济关系中的权利义务关系，属于实体法规范。而国际私法则是间接调整涉外民事法律关系，其作用主要是解决法律冲突及法律适用问题，虽然也涉及实体法部分，但主要是从解决法律冲突的角度出发。离开冲突规范，就无所谓国际私法”。[①] 关于国际私法就是冲突法的观点，笔者在以前发表的文章与小册子中已多次作过评述，此处不再重复。这里只想补充指出一点，就是正如有的国际私法学者在论述国际经济法与国际私法的关系时所说的那样，既然允许国际经济法舍弃（或突破）传统的法学分科的严格界限，坚持实证的、综合的研究方法，广义地理解国际经济法活动的含义及范围，创造出一门完全新的法律学科——国际经济法，那么为什么又不允许国际私法也突破传统的冲突法的框框，把调整当事人权利义务的实体规范列入国际私法呢？[②] 难道这种实体规范的出现不正是“国际私法发展的自然进程”、“国际私法发展日趋完善的一个合乎逻辑的阶段”[③]

① 姚梅镇：《国际经济法是一个独立的法学部门》，载《中国国际法年刊（1983）》，中国对外翻译出版公司，1983，第375—385页。

② 韩德培同志在为姚梅镇同志撰写的《中国大百科全书》（法学卷）国际经济法条目释文致编辑部的修改意见中就提出了这一看法。

③ 韩德培、李双元：《应该重视对冲突法的研究》，《武汉大学学报》1983年第6期。

吗？笔者完全同意这一论点。

另一种观点是，有人说，持“大国际私法”观点的同志在“打着国际私法的招牌，讲述国际经济法的内容”。笔者对此也不能完全表示同意。直率些说，持这种观点的同志缺乏国际私法学的历史知识，特别是缺乏对我国国际私法学发展状况的了解。大家知道，国际私法作为一门独立的法律学科，已有100多年至200年的历史了，而国际经济法，正如前面已经提到的，从其产生到现在，充其量不过40多年或稍长一些的历史。应该说它还是一门非常年轻的学科，它的许多问题都存在争论，还没有形成一个比较固定、完整的体系。至于我国的具体情况，则经济法或国际经济法的历史就更短了，经济法或国际经济法这两个名词，直到1976年粉碎“四人帮”，我国采取对外开放政策，加强法制建设，制定和公布了一系列法律、条例之后，才逐渐为人们所知道，在有关法律院系中才或先或后地设置国际经济法的课程。与此相反，国际私法作为一门独立的学科，不仅在旧中国有，在新中国也有，而且获得了突破性的发展。这可从中华人民共和国成立后在有关高等院校中一直设有国际私法课程这一事实中得到佐证。大家也都知道，从20世纪50年代初期直到“文化大革命”前的1965年为止，在有关高等院校中始终设有国际私法这门课程，而它的体系与内容又基本上与法学教材编辑部所审订并于1983年出版的全国统编教材《国际私法》一书相一致。这种情况难道能够证明“大国际私法”是在讲述国际经济法的内容吗？毋庸置疑，无论是国际私法或国际贸易法，还是国际商法，它们的历史都要比国际经济法的历史早得多。事实上，跨国法观点的国际经济法现在所讲述的某些内容，倒是以前国际私法或其他学科所涉及的范围，这些内容在国际经济法产生以前就已经为有关学科所论述了，怎么可能发生早前存在的学科去讲述那些当时尚未产生的学科所包括的内容呢？如果反过来说，现在的国际经济法（应指跨国法）是在讲述国际私法以前曾讲述的某些内容，难道不是更符合历史事实与逻辑吗？这里我们讲的是事实，而不是否认国际经济法的独立存在。我们承认国际经济法是一个独立的法律部门，但是我们也不愿看到国际经济法反过来把国际私法“吃掉”。

如果既主张国际经济法是“跨国法”，而对国际私法又持“大国际私法”的观点，那么如何来区分这两个法律部门所调整的不同的对象呢？

依个人所见，可用一个根本的依据和一个辅助的依据来区分国际私法和国际经济法所调整的不同对象。

区分不同法律部门的根本依据是某一法律部门所调整的法律关系的性质。由于法律关系性质的不同，才使调整这一类法律关系的规范与调整另一类法律关系的规范区别开来，各自构成一个独立的法律部门。这种区分是符合马列主义关于特殊的矛盾构成一事物区别于他事物的特殊的本质，和科学研究的区分就是根据科学对象所具有的特殊的矛盾性这一教导的。[①]依据这一根本的标志，国际私法调整的是涉外民事法律关系，国际经济法调整的是超越一国范围的经济法律关系。依个人的见解，涉外民事法律关系所涉及的范围比国际经济法律关系所涉及的范围要更广些，在涉外民事法律关系与国际经济法律关系中，两者有相异的部分，如涉外婚姻关系、涉外继承关系及与保护个人权利有关的涉外身份关系等，这些都是涉外民事法律关系而非国际经济法律关系，照例由国际私法来调整，而且事实上也没有人主张这类法律关系要由国际经济法来调整。其次是那些既为“大国际私法”又为国际经济法（跨国法）所调整的涉外财产关系（亦可被称作国际经济关系），如国际货物买卖、运输、支付、投资、税收、外汇管理等关系，究竟由哪个法律部门来调整呢？区分这些调整对象时，因为它们都具有涉外财产关系的共性，所以单用财产关系或经济关系这一特征来区分就显得不够了，此时需要借助于辅助性的依据——根据法律关系的主体的不同来区分不同的调整对象。当然这一辅助性依据不是区分不同法律部门的根本标准，但有时在区分不同的法律部门时仍不失为一种辅助的手段。例如，民法与刑法的区分，它们的不同主要取决于它们所调整的法律关系的不同性质，但是有时主体在区分这两个法律部门时也起一定的作用。大家知道，民法的主体可以是自然人和法人，有时可能是国家，但我国刑法的主体就只能是个人而不可能是法人或其他组织，我们还没有听说过我国法人犯罪而受到刑罚的。可见法律关系的主体在决定法律关系的性质时也起一定的作用。根据这两个标准，在具有涉外因素的财产关系（经济关系）中，如果双方当事人都是法人或自然人，或一方为自然人另一方为法人，则这种关系就由国际私法来调整，因为这种关系在国际经济法产生以前就已存在，并且一直由国际私法或其他法律部门调整着。如果在这

① 《毛泽东选集》第1卷。

种涉外经济关系中双方当事人都是国家，那么这种关系就由国际经济法来调整，而不再由国际私法来调整。试以国际贸易中的货物买卖关系为例说明之：如果甲国的一个进口商与乙国的一个出口商订立一个具体的买卖合同，那么这种买卖的合同关系就由国际私法来调整，因为这种法律的主体，也就是这一法律关系的权利与义务的承担者都是法人而不是国家。如果国际货物买卖的行为首先是通过国家之间缔结对外贸易机构交货共同条件议定书的方式进行，那么这种国际条约的当事人就是国家而不是一国从事外贸业务的某一机构，如某进出口公司，因为国际条约义务的承担者只能是国家而不可能是法人。至于有关国家的对外贸易机构，根据两国签订的议定书的有关规定，签订某一具体货物的买卖合同，这种合同关系的主体则是从事进出口业务的两国的对外贸易机构本身，而不是国家，因为只有这些对外贸易机构才直接对该项买卖合同的履行负责。因此，在前一场合，有关交货共同条件议定书的问题，由国际经济法来调整；在后一场合，有关具体买卖合同的问题，由国际私法来调整。

依据这样两个标准来区分国际私法与国际经济法所调整的对象后，可能还有一种涉外财产（或国际经济）关系没有被包括进去，这就是以国家为一方当事人，和以法人或自然人为另一方当事人的关系应由哪一法律部门来调整？依个人看法，这个问题应取决于作为此类法律关系主体的国家究竟以何种身份或资格出现。如果国家在这一法律关系中是以民法主体的资格出现（如作为公民遗产的继承人），则由国际私法来调整。如果国家以主权者的资格出现，那么这种关系就由国际经济法来调整。例如，某些发展中国家以国家（主权者）的名义与外国公司或企业签订关于开采本国自然资源的协议或合同，由于签订这种协议或合同而产生的法律关系，在确定这种法律关系的准据法时，就不适用国际私法中在解决合同准据法时所通行的意思自治原则，即由双方当事人来共同选择应予适用的法律，而应根据国际法中的国家主权原则，适用这个发展中国家的法律。

三　简单的结论

国际经济法是在国家对一国的涉外经济活动直接进行干预的情况下产生的，在国际经济法中，国家既作为这种法律的参与制定者，同时又作为这种法律的主体之一。如果国际经济法中不存在国家作为这种法律关系的主体之一这一事实，那么国际经济法就不成其为国际经济法，而是别的法律部门了。所以国际经济法调整的对象是以国家为主体的国家之间的经济法律关系，国际私法调整的对象主要是以公民（包括法人）为主体的具有涉外（或国际）因素的财产关系和人身非财产关系，两者在调整对象的关系上，既不发生“重叠”，也没有出现“空白”的现象。

最后，笔者也清楚地认识到，如何区分国际私法和国际经济法的调整对象，是一个理论性很强、涉及面很广的复杂问题，它还直接涉及在高等院校中这两门课程的设置与体系。这一问题的正确的、合理的解决，需要全国国际法学界较长时期的共同努力。笔者在这里提出的一孔之见，远非成熟的想法，只是解决这个问题的一种初步尝试与探索，期望能够引起国际法学界的重视，共同把我国的国际私法学和国际经济法学推向一个新的发展阶段。

（本文原载于《外交学院学报》1985 年第 3 期）

论国际私法的发展趋势

任继圣*

在我国进行社会主义现代化的建设过程中，我国与外国的经济和文化交往势必不断扩大，随之产生大量的涉外财产关系，以及与财产密切相连的其他权利关系。前者如对外贸易的货物买卖、运输、保险关系，对外投资、借贷关系，后者如对外的专利权关系，涉外婚姻、家庭关系，等等。这些关系统称为涉外民事法律关系。国际私法就是专门调整这种关系的法律部门。了解这个法律部门的发展变化，有利于更好地使用它为我国对外经济与文化交往服务。

国际私法是资本主义国际经济交往的产物，13 世纪时，在现今的意大利北部，存在许多城市国家，它们之间商业交往频繁，随之产生了较多的涉外民事法律关系，为适应这种发展，专门调整这种关系的“国际私法”开始形成。19 世纪中叶以后，由于国际经济和文化交往进一步加速向前发展，国际私法也有着较大的发展和变化。第二次世界大战以后，发展变化的速度加快，为我国和国际上的研究者所注目。有的外国学者在这种发展面前改变了传统的观念，本来认为国际私法不应包括条约中所订立的、调整涉外民事法律关系双方权利与义务的实体法规范，现在改变了观点，认为应该包括。有的外国学者提出，国际私法发展的现阶段，是现代国际私法的开始阶段，如捷克斯洛伐克学者克伦斯基。我国的研究者也就国际私法的发展问题，进行了认真的讨论。应如何看待国际私法的发展趋势，是

---

* 任继圣，1975 年 11 月来中国社会科学院法学研究所工作，曾任国际法研究室副主任，20 世纪 80 年代初调入司法部担任中国法律事务中心主任。

讨论中的一个关键问题。笔者认为，19 世纪中叶以后，国际私法的发展趋势主要表现为以下三个方面。

第一，涉外民事法律关系的范围不断扩大，国际私法所适用的范围也随之扩大。

19 世纪后半叶，国际经济关系中的一个特点是，资本主义的商品输出逐步向资本输出发展，伴随资本输出而出现的，是工、商业公司和银行的国际活动增多，不同国家的法人、自然人之间的交往频繁，涉外民事法律的关系也随之经历了一个大发展。到 19 世纪末，它已涉及当时国际经济、文化交往和社会生活的各个主要方面。在普通法国家，英国王室法律顾问、法学博士 A. V. 戴西教授所著的《冲突法》一书中，总结了英国的司法实践，抽出 204 条处理涉外民事法律关系的规则，所涉及关系的范围包括：自然人的身份、能力、住所、国籍，法人的国籍、住所、能力、破产、结婚、离婚、家庭、遗嘱、继承，侵权行为，多种合同关系及涉外民事案件诉讼程序上的问题。这些关系所涉及的范围，比 19 世纪初《法国民法典》的规定广泛得多。以涉外合同关系为例，1804 年的《法国民法典》只规定在外国订立的合同不得用在法国的不动产设立抵押权。戴西的《冲突法》在合同问题上则涉及动产、不动产、买卖、租赁、运输、共同海损理算、票据、利息等关系，以及合同中的代理、效力、履行、解释、解除等问题。在大陆法系国家，与戴西《冲突法》出版的同年，公布了《德国民法典施行法》，用法律条文总括记录了当时发生的涉外民事法律关系的大部分。由于当时"铁血宰相"俾斯麦的阻挠，这个单行法没有包括涉外债权关系和物权关系。两年后，1898 年日本公布的《法例》弥补了《德国民法典施行法》中的缺欠。《法例》第 7—12 条，就涉外合同、物权和债权等关系的法律适用作了规定。这个单行法规中反映的涉外民事法律关系的范围，已超过 19 世纪中叶以前的有关立法。除上述著作和立法所涉及的涉外民事法律关系之外，属于涉外民事法律关系范围的涉外专利权、商标权和著作权关系发展较快，因而出现了专门调整这些关系的国际公约。总括起来，在原来已存在的关系的基础上，到 19 世纪末在国际私法领域内，又发展了以下三个方面的涉外民事法律关系：（1）由于法人在国际交往中作用的增大，法人的国籍、地位和能力问题，以及涉外的代理和破产关系，也随之发展；（2）由于银行在国际交往中作用的增大，涉外信贷和票据关系随之发展；（3）由于国际文化与科学技术交往的发展，涉外著作权、专利权和商标权关系随之发展起来。

进入 20 世纪后，涉外民事法律关系在 19 世纪的基础上，继续向广度和深度发展，开创了新的局面。向广度发展包括两层含义：一是这种关系所涉及的地区，不仅包括西方国家和经济发达的国家，而且较多地涉及了东方和广大第三世界国家的自然人和法人，甚至有时国家本身也作为国际私法关系中的关系主体出现；二是这种关系的数量一直在不断增加。向深度发展就是，在第二次世界大战以后，由于生产力的发展，国家之间在商品生产过程中的合作关系加强，生产的国际化促使涉外民事法律关系在已有的领域内出现了更新的关系。如在涉外法人问题上出现了现代的合资经营关系、跨国公司问题；在涉外工业产权中兴起了国际技术转让及许可证协议关系；在涉外合同关系中发展了现代的来料（来样）加工、补偿贸易、涉外劳务和承揽等关系。另外，在涉外侵权关系中增加了污染的民事责任等。

在我国，100 多年来，先是由于清朝统治者实行了闭关锁国政策，后是因为外国人在旧中国享有各种特权，我国与外国的经济与文化交往关系不能正常开展，限制了涉外民事法律关系的正常发展。中华人民共和国成立以后，取消了帝国主义的特权，我国人民掌握了自己的对外贸易、运输、保险，开展与各国人民的交往，现在又通过各种形式利用外国资本，吸收先进的外国技术，与外国进行广泛的文化交流。因此，与我国有关的各种类型的涉外民事法律关系，得到了正常的发展。

20 世纪，特别是第二次世界大战以后，涉外民事法律关系所涉及的范围急速扩大。一些相关国际条约和某些国家的专门立法中，反映了这种扩大情况。如 1928 年在第六次泛美会议上通过的《国际私法典》中，已就民商法中的 50 多种涉外关系的法律适用作了规定。中华人民共和国成立以后，我国与外国所签订的双边条约及我国所参加的国际公约也广泛地涉及了与我国有关的各种涉外民事法律关系，它主要包括：在对外贸易买卖、运输、支付及保险中发生的涉外民事法律关系，中、外自然人（或法人）之间的债、家庭、继承关系，中、外合资经营企业中的各种关系，知识产权国际保护中的各种关系，以及涉外污染中的民事责任关系，等等。有的国家，在其国内立法中，较为突出地反映了涉外民事法律关系所涉及范围的扩大。如1975年12月5日德意志民主共和国公布的《关于国际民事、家庭和劳动关系以及国际经济合同适用法律条例》（简称《法律适用条例》），就58种涉外民事法律关系的法律适用作了规定。

世界上多数国家在国际经济、文化和生活方面的涉外民事法律关系频繁地发生，专门调整这种关系的法律得以广泛适用。涉外民事法律关系所涉及范围的扩大，使国际私法适用范围随之扩大。这两种扩大，又必然会引起国际私法规范在数量、种类、形式和内容上的变化和发展。

第二，国际私法规范的种类逐渐增加，作为国际私法渊源的条约和惯例的作用逐步增大。

专门调整涉外民事法律关系的规范曾经历了一个漫长的发展阶段。19世纪初，1804年的《法国民法典》第一次比较系统地总结了过去的实践，为适应当时涉外民事法律关系发展的需要，规定了三种专门调整涉外民事法律关系的规范。这就是：（1）关于给予外国人民事权利的规范；（2）指示适用某国法律的冲突规范；（3）关于涉外民事案件诉讼问题的规范。虽然该法典对这三种规范的内容都规定得比较简单，但规定这几种规范的事实，却说明了在当时历史发展的条件下，需要从这三个方面对涉外民事法律关系加以专门规定。给予外国人民事权利的规范，是发生涉外民事法律关系的法律前提。涉外民事案件诉讼问题的规范，是处理涉外民事法律关系程序上的专门规定。冲突规范指明了某涉外民事法律关系当事人的权利和义务应适用何国法律。当时，这三种规范组成了专门调整涉外民事法规的整体。其中的冲突规范规定了与涉外民事法律关系有关的国家法律效力的范围，对调整这种关系起主要作用。因此，在《法国民法典》所规定的各种国际私法规范中，冲突规范是主要的。在19世纪初，用法律规定哪些涉外民事法律关系应适用本国法，哪些应适用外国法，是个进步。它以法律明文规定，突破了任何涉外民事法律关系都得依所在地国家法律的国界，适应了当时国际交往的要求，并能促进这种交往的发展。由此，《法国民法典》中的有关规定，为19世纪欧洲大陆国家及某些南美国家的一系列立法所接受。19世纪中叶发展起来的美英国际私法，也都接受了欧洲大陆的办法，把解决法律适用问题，作为处理涉外民事法律关系的中心。从历史的发展来看，这是当时实际可行的办法，为此冲突规范合乎规律地成了处理涉外民事法律关系的主要规范。在这个基础上，把“冲突法”看作"国际私法"同义语的习惯逐渐形成。

冲突规范在法律上具有三个特点。其一，与实体法规范相比，它过于简单，不构成法律关系当事人作为或不作为的准则，依其本身不能直接预见法律关系的行为后果，缺乏法律所应具有的预见性和明确性。其二，在长期使用中逐渐形成了与冲突规范相联系的各种制度，这就是反致、转致、识别、外国法内容的确定、公共秩序保留等。这些制度的实质是，利用冲突规范过于简单的特点，从各个不同角度来限制其效力，极大地削弱了冲突规范的稳定性。其三，适用冲突规范的结果，总是导致适用某一个国内的实体法来处理涉外民事法律关系，而任何一国的一般国内实体法，都是根据其国内的政治经济条件和法律传统制定的，不会专门针对涉外民事法律关系制定。因此，冲突规范所指示适用的国内法，对涉外民事关系来说，往往针对性不强。冲突规范所具有的这些法律特点，在某些涉外民事关系随着国际交往的发展而进一步发展的情况下，就难以适应并促进这种关系的发展。19 世纪末 20 世纪初，在知识产权的国际保护及国际贸易中所产生的某些涉外债务关系方面，所面临的就是这个现实。

当时，历史的发展向专门调整涉外民事法律关系的法律部门——国际私法提出了问题，而解决这个问题的办法，就是在国家之间制定直接确定涉外民事法律关系双方当事人权利与义务关系的统一实体法规范，简称统一实体法规范。当然，由于国家间的利益矛盾，各国经济、政治制度和法律传统不同，在制定统一实体法规范过程中会存在严重的斗争。但是既然存在频繁的交往，并由此而产生众多的涉外民事法律关系，就存在共同点，为适应历史的要求把这种交往继续下去，就能把共同点用条约具体地规定下来。斗争只能影响这种规范的内容，或延缓其制定进程，不能阻止其发展趋势。实际上，对国际海上运输、买卖等领域内发生的某些涉外民事法律关系，人们早就越过冲突规范，而适用直接确定双方权利与义务关系的国际惯例。现在的问题是要以法律形式确认和发展它，历史的实践充分证实了这点。1883 年出现了《关于保护工业产权的巴黎公约》，1886 年达成了《关于保护文学和艺术作品的伯尔尼公约》，1891 年订立了《关于商标注册的马德里协定》。虽然这些公约只在一些个别问题上作了统一实体法的规定，但它们是先声，是开拓者。紧接着而来的，是 20 世纪初在海上运输方面的载有统一实体法规范的国际公约，如 1910 年的《统一船舶碰撞若干规则公约》及《统一海上救助若干规则公约》。第一次世界大战以后，统一实体法的活动进一步发展。1924 年在国际联盟主持下建立了一个政府间的国际组织，罗马“统一私法国际研究所”为专门从事统一实体法活动的国际组织。1924 年通过了《统一提单的若干法律规定的公约》（简称《海牙规则》），1929 年制定了《统一国际航空运输某些规则的公约》（简称《华沙公约》），1930 年签订了《统一本票、汇票法公约》（简称《日内瓦公约》）。与此同时，一些国际组织所编制的、属于国际惯例性质的统一实体法规则也先后问世。如经 1890 年、1903 年、1924 年三次修改的《约克－安特卫普共同海损规则》，1932 年制定的《C. I. F. 华沙－牛津规则》，1936 年制定的《国际贸易术语解释通则》等。两次世界大战以后，由于世界上国家间政治和经济关系的变化，特别是 20 世纪 60 年代以后，由于科学技术进步的速度加快，生产力社会化的程度随之加深，资本和生产国际化发展很快，国家之间的经济交往越来越频繁，在经济上相互制约的关系大为发展，发展中国家要求在这种交往与制约关系中，建立新的国际经济和法律秩序。这些国际条件，推动了统一实体法规范的制定进入一个新的发展时期。它分为三个方面进行：（1）一些国家之间订立了载有统一实体法规范的双边条约；（2）一些经济共同体之内签订了地区性的统一实体法公约；（3）世界性的国际组织推动了统一实体法规范公约的制定。这三方面的活动都是有成效的。以世界性的国际组织来说，在罗马“统一私法国际研究所”的推动下，1964 年在海牙通过了《国际货物买卖统一法公约》及《国际货物买卖合同成立统一法公约》。1966 年第 21 届联合国大会决定成立“联合国国际贸易法律委员会”，1968 年开始工作，在该委员会的努力下，1974 年通过了《国际货物买卖时效公约》，1978 年通过了《海上货物运输公约》（简称《汉堡规则》），1989 年 4 月签订了《国际货物销售合同公约》。此外，还有许多世界性的载有统一实体法规范的公约在制定或修改中。现在，统一实体法规范已在调整涉外知识产权关系中，以及涉外的债的某些关系中占有重要地位。它已在国际私法中确立，成为国际私法规范的一个组成部分。各主权国家都在不同范围内、不同程度上卷入了统一实体法的活动。

统一实体法规范发展的必然结果是，作为国际私法渊源的国际条约（双边或多边的）数量很快增加，实际作用大为增长。在实践中，对在国际运输、买卖领域内的一些涉外民事法律关系，20 世纪初一国还可以据其所适用的冲突规范的规定，引用某一个国家法律处理，而不考虑统一实体法的规定。但在现在，这种办法是难以妥善解决问题的。由于统一实体法规范作用的增大，影响一些国家参照统一实体法规范的内容，通过国内立法形式，直接就某些涉外民事法律关系双方的权利与义务作出规定，形成了国际私法中的另一种实体法规范，它正在发展中。

与统一实体法规范发展的同时，通过条约形式统一冲突规范、外国人民事权利规范，以及涉外案件诉讼和仲裁程序规范的实践也在不断发展。这样就更加重了条约在国际私法渊源中的分量。如在统一冲突规范方面，早在 1902 年与 1905 年，就在海牙签订了几个关于婚姻、家庭问题的法律适用的公约，1928 年以条约形式制定了《国际私法典》，它是一部内容为冲突规范的法典。1951 年将早已存在的国际私法会议，改为一个常设的政府间国际组织，专门从事推进统一冲突规范工作。在它的推进下，已在婚姻、家庭、对外贸易买卖等法律适用方面，制定了一些公约。在统一程序规范方面，主要是关于统一仲裁程序发展很快，它的发展推动了仲裁方法在涉外民事案件的使用。现在不仅对国际贸易与航海中的涉外民事案件经常采用仲裁程序，而且仲裁方法已逐步扩大到用来解决知识产权、合资企业、外国投资、对外开发资源等关系中所发生的争议。因此，涉外仲裁程序规范已构成处理涉外民事案件程序的一个不可缺少的部分，自然应包括在国际私法规范的组成之内。

总括起来，从专门处理涉外民事法律关系出发，现在的国际私法规范不仅应包括关于外国人民事权利的规范、冲突规范、涉外民事案件诉讼和仲裁程序规范，也应包括条约中的统一实体法规范，以及国内法中专用于（或直接用于）确定涉外民事法律关系双方的权利与义务的实体法规范。这是历史发展的必然结果。

第三，在国际私法规范发展的基础上，逐渐形成新的法律部门。

涉外民事法律关系中包括各种不同的权利与义务关系，涉及范围很广，这些关系有它们的共性，在共性下又各有其特性。当某种涉外民事法律关系和调整这种关系的规范迅速发展时，这种关系所属的特性突出，就会逐渐脱离曾经孕育着它的国际私法母体，形成新的法律部门。20 世纪以来，在涉外民事法律关系中，与外贸有关的债的关系的发展，在广度、深度和速度上，超过了其他种类的涉外民事法律关系，调整这种关系的统一实体法规范，相应地也得到了较大的发展。在此基础上，逐渐形成一个新的法律部门，这就是在20世纪60年代初提出的国际贸易法。1962年在伦敦召开了国际法律科学协会，英国国际私法学者，伦敦大学教授施密托夫提出一个题为《国际贸易法的产生、形成及作用》的报告，就这个新的法律部门的形成作了理论上的叙述。1968年联合国国际贸易法律委员会开始工作，使国际贸易法进入了有计划制定阶段。近十几年来，这个新的法律部门发展的速度加快，取得了相当的成绩，现在以统一实体法为主体的国际贸易法体系已经形成。国际贸易法的出现是个进步，它是具有自己完整体系的新法律部门，其内容远远超过现在国际私法中所涉及的国际贸易中的法律问题。然而，即使如此，在现阶段并不能排斥在国际私法体系中包括涉外的债、外国人地位、涉外诉讼及仲裁程序等问题有关的各种规范。犹如高能物理学已经形成，但并不排斥在普通物理学体系中包括基本粒子问题。海洋法形成后，并不排斥在国际公法体系中包括领海、经济区、大陆架等问题。

随着我国对外关系的不断发展，为我所用的直接调整涉外民事法律关系的各种规范，也须相应地发展，才能使之有效地为实践服务。因此，当前我们的任务应该是，加速总结中华人民共和国成立以来的经验，参照国际上的做法，及早用订立国内立法、签订国际条约、采纳国际惯例等办法，制定各种调整涉外民事法律关系的专用法律规范，以适应需要。这样，才能做到利用国际私法发展的规律，使国际私法更好地为促进我国的四个现代化服务。

（本文原载于《法学研究》1981年第4期）

论国际私法中法律适用问题的新发展与我国的实践

林　欣*

法律适用问题在国际私法中占有重要地位。它是指一个具有涉外因素的民商事案件应该适用哪一个国家的法律来确定当事人的权利与义务，从而解决他们之间的争议。现在国际经济和贸易关系越来越发展迅速，各国之间人员来往越来越频繁。在这种情况下，各国之间具有涉外因素的民商事纠纷也日益增多。各国在解决这些纠纷的实践中，发展了国际私法中的法律适用问题。现就侵权行为、合同（契约）和婚姻家庭关系的法律适用的新发展与我国的实践作一论述。

一　侵权行为

对具有涉外因素的侵权行为案件的法律适用问题，从前有两种主张：一种主张适用侵权行为地法，另一种主张适用法院地法。

主张适用侵权行为地法的法学家，如英国的威斯特勒克认为，被告人的侵权行为扰乱了当地国家的社会秩序，因此这个国家的法律是处理这类案件最有权威的法律。①

主张适用法院地法的法学家，如19世纪德国著名的法学家萨维尼认为，侵权行为的责任与刑事责任有相似之处，而行使刑事管辖权只适用本

---

* 林欣，1981年10月来中国社会科学院法学研究所工作，曾任研究员，现已离休。

① 戴赛、莫里斯：《法律的冲突》第2卷，1980，伦敦，英文第10版，第928—929页。

国的刑法，不适用外国的刑法。因此对侵权行为应该适用法院地法。[①] 后来，萨维尼的主张遭到一些法学家的反对，他们认为民事侵权行为与刑事犯罪有重大的区别，对民事侵权行为不能机械地采用行使刑事管辖权的法律适用原则。

这样，过去各国对具有涉外因素的侵权行为的法律适用便形成了如下原则：适用侵权行为地法，如果这种法律违反法院地的公共秩序，则适用法院地法。

至于什么是侵权行为地，当侵权行为和损害不在同一个国家或者同一个法域发生时，就有两种不同的理解。一种理解，如德国、奥地利和苏联等国把侵权行为实施地视为侵权行为地。1978 年的奥地利国际私法法规第 48 条第 1 款规定："非合同的损害求偿权，依造成此种损害的行为实施地国家的法律。"另一种理解，如美国把损害发生地视为侵权行为地。美国第一部《冲突法重述》（1934 年）第 377 节关于侵权行为过错地点规定："过错地点是指行为人需要对其侵权行为负责的最后事件发生地。"该重述解释说，最后事件发生的州就是损害发生的州。[②]

据《美国比较法杂志》介绍，其他许多国家，如意大利、法国、西班牙、荷兰、芬兰、波兰和南非等国所说的侵权行为地法，究竟是指侵权行为实施地法还是指损害发生地法则不明确。[③]

现在在欧洲有一个发展趋势，那就是把侵权行为实施地和损害发生地都视为侵权行为地。欧洲共同体法院在 1976 年 11 月 30 日的判决中指出，侵权行为的损害事件发生地，或是损害发生的地点，或是引起损害事件的地点。[④] 1983 年英国在修订其最高法院规则第 11 号法令规则时，明确了侵权行为的含义。旧的规则只规定，关于在管辖区内发生的侵权行为的诉讼，英格兰法院有裁量管辖权。新的规则则规定，有关侵权行为的诉讼（损害发生在管辖区内，或者行为发生在管辖区内），英格兰法院有裁量管辖权。[⑤] 这就是说，损害发生地或者侵权行为实施地都是侵权行为地。从

① 麦克洛德：《法律的冲突》，1983，加拿大 · 阿尔伯塔，英文版，第 528 页。
② 里斯 · 罗森堡：《法律的冲突：判例与资料》，1978，纽约，英文第 7 版，第 423 页。
③ 《美国比较法杂志》1990 年第 3 期。
④ 《共同市场法律评论》（英文），1983 年 10 月号，第 543 页。
⑤ 诺斯、福西特：《切希尔与诺斯国际私法》，1992，伦敦，英文第 12 版，第 190—203 页。

发展的趋势来看，把侵权行为实施地和损害发生地都视为侵权行为地的观点将获得普遍承认。

原来美国对具有涉外因素（即州际或国际）的侵权行为案件都适用损害地法，如果这种法律不违反法院地的公共秩序的话。后来，由于汽车和航空运输事业的迅速发展，具有涉外因素的侵权行为案件日益增多。在汽车和航空运输中发生的侵权行为案件，其损害地往往带有偶然性，许多案件与损害地没有直接关系，有些则难以确定损害地。如果法院机械地适用损害地法，而不考虑其他有关的各种因素，就可能作出不一定合理的判决。

从 1963 年起，美国各州相继放弃了损害地法原则，转而采用最重要关系原则或称利益分析原则。这种改变的转折点是 1963 年纽约州上诉法院的一个判例（巴勃科克诉杰克逊）。该案的原告人是被告人（车主兼司机）的客人，双方都是纽约州的居民。他们从纽约开车去加拿大度周末，在安大略省，由于被告人的过失，汽车出了事故，使原告人受了重伤。当时安大略省的客人条例规定，如果是免费载乘客，汽车出了事故，使乘客的人身或财产受到损害，车主或司机免除责任。纽约州的法律则没有这样的规定。如果此案适用损害地法，那么被告人就不需要赔偿损害。但在判决中，纽约州上诉法院没有适用损害地法，而适用了纽约州的法律。法院认为双方当事人都是纽约州的居民；旅行从纽约州开始，又在纽约州结束；汽车是在纽约州登记并保险的；所以纽约州与此案具有最重要的关系。①

最重要关系原则来源于美国法学会提出的第二部《冲突法重述》（1953 年提出试行初稿，1971 年定稿公布）。第二部《冲突法重述》总结了第一部《冲突法重述》公布以来美国国际私法理论和实践的发展。在法律适用方面，第二部《冲突法重述》以最重要关系原则取代了第一部《冲突法重述》的以既得权学说为基础的一些原则。在侵权行为的法律适用方面，即以最重要关系原则取代了损害地法原则。第二部《冲突法重述》第 145 节规定：

（1）当事人对侵权行为中的问题的权利与责任，由同此事及当事人关系最重要的州的法律决定。

---

① 马丁：《法律的冲突：判例和资料》，1984，波士顿，英文第 2 版，第 176—179 页。

（2）在确定问题应适用何种法律时，应考虑的联系是：

（a）损害发生地；

（b）引起损害的行为的发生地；

（c）当事人的住所、居所、国籍、公司的地点和各当事人的营业地点；

（d）各当事人之间关系集中的地点。

要按与特定问题的相对重要性来估价这些联系。

实践表明，最重要关系原则使美国法院对法律适用具有更大的灵活性。在侵权行为的法律适用方面，以最重要关系原则取代损害地法原则，实际上是以灵活性取代了确定性，这种改变同法律的特性是不符合的。我们知道，法律要求确定性，以便当事人能预见其权利与义务。

为了使侵权行为的法律适用具有一定的确定性，1972 年纽约州上诉法院在诺伊迈尔诉屈尔纳一案的判决中规定了以下三项规则。

（1）当客人—乘客和主人—司机住在同一个州，汽车也在该州登记，主人对客人应负的照顾责任，由该州的法律决定。

（2）当司机的行为发生在他的住所地州，而该州不认为他要对该行为负责，即使按照受害人的住所地州的侵权行为法认为他要负责，他也不该负责。反之，当客人在他的住所地州受伤，而该州的法律允许赔偿，进入该州的司机，除非有特殊情况，不得以他本州的法律为自己辩护。

（3）当乘客和司机住在不同的州时，一般适用事故发生地州的法律；如果能证明适用其他的法律能增进实体法的目的而不损害多州制度的顺利运作，或者产生很大的诉讼不确定性，也可以适用其他的法律。①

1985 年纽约州上诉法院在舒尔茨诉美国童子军公司一案的判决中，还把侵权的行为事项的适用法律与损害赔偿事项的适用法律加以区分。② 一般来说，侵权的行为事项适用行为实施地法；损害赔偿则适用另一种法律，比如说适用当事人双方的共同住所地法，如果他们住在同一个州的话。

紧跟纽约州的实践，路易斯安那州于 1992 年通过了该州的冲突法法典。该法典关于侵权行为适用法律的规定就是纽约州上诉法院上述两个判例的综合。该法典也把侵权的行为事项的适用法律与损害赔偿事项的适用

---

① ［美］《东北地区判例法报告》第 2 编第 286 卷，第 457—458 页。

② ［美］《东北地区判例法报告》第 2 编第 480 卷，第 679 页。

法律加以区分。

关于侵权的行为事项的适用法律，路易斯安那州冲突法法典第 43 条规定：

（1）适用行为实施地州的法律，如果损害也发生在该州，或者损害发生在另外的州，而该另外州的法律没有规定更高的行为标准。

（2）适用损害发生地州的法律，如果加害人可预见其损害将在那个州发生的话。

（3）第 2 款不适用于行为实施地和加害人的住所地是同一个州，或者加害人同行为实施地州有密切联系，他虽然不住在行为实施地州。

关于损害赔偿事项的适用法律，路易斯安那州冲突法法典第 44 条规定：

（1）当损害发生时，被损害人和加害人住在同一个州，适用该共同住所地州的法律。

（2）当损害发生时，被损害人和加害人住在不同的州：

（a）行为和损害发生在同一个州，适用该州的法律；

（b）行为和损害发生在不同的州，也适用损害发生地州的法律，如果被损害人的住所在那个州，同时该州的法律比行为实施地州的法律为被损害人规定了更高的财务保护。

关于侵权行为的法律适用问题，在美国除纽约州和路易斯安那州采用较具确定性的规则外，其他各州可分两种情况。一种是加利福尼亚州，它从 1978 年开始采用“比较损害法”（comparative impairment approach）来决定侵权行为的适用法律。采用比较损害法确定的适用法律，实际上类似纽约州上诉法院的诺伊迈尔案的规则。另一种是其他州仍然采用第二部《冲突法重述》中规定的最重要关系原则，但在实践中，绝大多数判例也采用了纽约州的诺伊迈尔案的规则，尽管许多判例解释的理由仍然采用最重要关系的说法。美国伊利诺斯大学教授彼得·海研究了这些州仍然采用最重要关系原则的 16 个判例以后，他发现除一个判例外，其余 15 个判例都采用了纽约州的诺伊迈尔案的规则。[①] 由此可见，在美国，关于侵权行为法律适用问题的新趋势是从灵活性向确定性方向发展。

美国采用的具有灵活性，但是缺乏确定性的关于侵权行为的法律适用

---

① 〔美〕《国际律师》杂志 1993 年第 2 期。

原则——最重要关系原则，对欧洲大陆民法法系国家的影响很小。这些欧洲国家仍然采用原有的较具确定性的规则。欧洲大陆国家在这方面的新发展是，1987 年通过的瑞士国际私法法规允许当事人双方同意法院地法为侵权行为的准据法。该法规第 132 条规定："当事人双方可于损害事件发生后的任何时候，同意适用法院地法。"否则，适用加害人和受害人的共同惯常居所地法，如果他们在同一个国家有惯常居所的话。如果他们的惯常居所不在同一个国家，则适用侵权行为发生地法。如果结果在另一个国家发生，并且加害人能预见损害将在该国发生，则适用该国的法律（第 133 条）。

我国关于涉外侵权行为适用法律的规定也采用较具确定性的规则。我国《民法通则》第 146 条规定："侵权行为的损害赔偿，适用侵权行为地法律。当事人双方国籍相同或者在同一国家有住所的，也可以适用当事人本国法律或者住所地法律。"关于侵权行为地法律的确定，我国最高人民法院 1988 年发布的《关于贯彻执行〈中华人民共和国民法通则〉若干问题的意见（试行）》第 187 条规定："侵权行为地的法律包括侵权行为实施地法律和侵权结果发生地法律。如果两者不一致时，人民法院可以选择适用。"我国的这些规定符合国际私法法律适用问题新发展的潮流。

二 合同（契约）

美国的最重要关系原则在侵权行为的法律适用方面对欧洲大陆国家的影响不大，然而这个原则在合同（契约）的法律适用方面则对欧洲大陆国家产生了很大的影响。

涉外合同应适用的法律，一般为当事人所选择的法律。如果当事人没有选择适用的法律，或者他们所选择的法律没有被有关的国家认可，过去各国的做法差别较大。有些国家根据自己的法律确定应适用的法律。有些国家则根据与合同有关的情况，如合同使用的文字，合同订立地、履行地，当事人的住所地、国籍，约定支付的货币所属国等，选择其中某一因素，推定适用的法律。这种推定，法官的主观因素很大，推定的结果有时与合同的客观情况相去甚远，颇不合理。

对此，美国第二部《冲突法重述》（第188节）采用最重要关系原则加以解决。它规定：如果当事人没有有效地选择所适用的法律，那么当事人对合同中问题的权利与义务，由同此交易和当事人具有最重要关系的州的法律决定。在确定问题应适用的法律时，应考虑的联系包括：

（1）合同订立地；

（2）合同谈判地；

（3）合同履行地；

（4）合同标的物所在地；以及

（5）当事人的住所、居所、国籍、公司所在地和当事人的营业地。

要按与特定问题的相对重要性来估价这些联系。

该重述还规定，除关于土地权益的合同以外，如果合同的谈判地和履行地是在同一个州，那么合同的适用法律为该州的法律。

美国关于涉外合同的最重要关系原则被许多欧洲大陆国家采纳，只是名称有所不同，欧洲共同体和德国、瑞士等国叫作“最密切联系”原则，奥地利则称为“最强联系”原则。

最重要关系原则有一个特点，那就是灵活性有余，确定性不足。这个特点不符合法律的要求。为了弥补这个缺点，欧洲国家采用了根据当事人承担履行具有特性的义务，确定各种合同应适用的法律。这些欧洲国家的法律把它称为特性履行（characteristic performance）。

根据特性履行来确定涉外合同的准据法，是受到德国著名法学家萨维尼观点的影响。他于1849年出版了《现代罗马法制度》一书，该书第8卷是论述国际私法的。他在这一卷中提出合同的履行是当事人的希望所在的观点，认为合同履行地比缔结地（订立地）与当事人的利益有更密切的关系，所以主张合同履行地法优先主义。萨维尼的观点在德国、奥地利和瑞士等国有很大的影响。

欧洲共同体于1980年6月19日在罗马签订的《关于合同义务的法律适用公约》就是以特性履行来补充最密切联系原则，从而使涉外合同的准据法较具确定性。该公约规定，合同应适用当事人选择的法律（第3条第1款）。如果当事人没有选择适用的法律，那么合同应适用与其具有最密切联系的国家的法律（第4条第1款）。

对于什么是与合同具有最密切联系的国家，该公约第4条就不同种类的合同作了明确规定。

该条第2款规定，除本条第5款另有规定外，应推定，在合同订立时，承担履行该合同具有特性的义务的当事人一方有其惯常居所的国家，或如为法人团体或非法人团体，则有其中央管理机构的国家，为与合同有最密切联系的国家。然而，如合同系在当事人进行与其职业或专业有关的活动过程中订立的，则与之有最密切联系的国家应为主营业所所在的国家，或如根据合同的条款，合同的履行地是主营业所所在地以外的其他营业所所在地，则应为其他营业所所在的国家。

该条第3款规定，如果合同的标的物是有关不动产的权利，或者是使用不动产的权利，应推定与合同有最密切联系的国家为不动产所在地国家，本条第2款的规定，不适用之。

该条第4款规定，货运合同不适用本条第2款进行推定。在此种合同中，如在合同订立时，承运人的主营业所所在国，也是装货地或卸货地所在国，或者也是托运人的主营业所所在国，应推定这个国家为与该合同有最密切联系的国家。

该条第5款规定，如果特性履行不能确定，则第2款不得适用；如果从总的情况来看，合同与另一个国家具有更密切的联系，则上述第2款、第3款和第4款的规定均不适用。

1978年的奥地利国际私法法规，1986年的德国民法施行法（国际私法法规是它的一个组成部分）和1987年的瑞士国际私法法规关于当事人没有选择适用法律的涉外合同准据法的规定，都是以特性履行来补充最密切联系原则，从而使涉外合同的准据法较具确定性。

从以上的分析可以看出，关于涉外合同法律适用问题的新趋势，也是由灵活性向确定性方向发展。

我国《民法通则》和《涉外经济合同法》规定，涉外合同的当事人可以选择处理合同争议所适用的法律，法律另有规定的除外；涉外合同的当事人没有选择的，适用与合同有最密切联系的国家的法律（《民法通则》第145条，《涉外经济合同法》第5条）。

至于什么法律是与合同有最密切联系的国家的法律，我国立法未作任何规定。这比美国第二部《冲突法重述》中的规定更缺乏确定性。这样的规定实在使人无所适从。为了弥补这个缺点，我国最高人民法院于1987年发布了《关于适用〈涉外经济合同法〉若干问题的解答》（以下简称《解答》）。该《解答》第二节（关于处理涉外经济合同争议的法律适用问题）第6条规定，如果当事人未选择合同所适用的法律时，对于下列涉外经济合同，人民法院按照最密切联系原则确定所应适用的法律，在通常情况下是：

（1）国际货物买卖合同，适用合同订立时卖方营业所所在地的法律。如果合同是在买方营业所所在地谈判并订立的，或者合同主要是依买方确定的条件并应买方发出的招标订立的，或者合同明确规定卖方须在买方营业所所在地履行交货义务的，则适用合同订立时买方营业所所在地的法律。

（2）银行贷款或者担保合同，适用贷款银行或者担保银行所在地的法律。

（3）保险合同，适用保险人营业所所在地的法律。

（4）加工承揽合同，适用加工承揽人营业所所在地的法律。

（5）技术转让合同，适用受让人营业所所在地的法律。

（6）工程承包合同，适用工程所在地的法律。

（7）科技咨询或者设计合同，适用委托人营业所所在地的法律。

（8）劳务合同，适用劳务实施地的法律。

（9）成套设备供应合同，适用设备安装运转地的法律。

（10）代理合同，适用代理人营业所所在地的法律。

（11）关于不动产租赁、买卖或者抵押的合同，适用不动产所在地的法律。

（12）动产租赁合同，适用出租人营业所所在地的法律。

（13）仓储保管合同，适用仓储保管人营业所所在地的法律。

但是，合同明显地与另一国家或者地区的法律具有更密切的关系，人民法院应以另一国家或者地区的法律作为处理合同争议的依据。

该《解答》还规定，当事人有一个以上的营业所的，应以与合同有最密切关系的营业所为准。当事人没有营业所的，以其住所或者居所为准。

将来在修订我国有关国际私法问题的立法时，应该将最高人民法院的《解答》和实践经验加以总结，在立法中明确规定具有最密切联系的国家的法律的具体内容。

三　婚姻家庭关系

家庭是社会的基础。婚姻是维系和组成家庭的纽带。由于人类文明的提高、社会的进步及国际交往的频繁，婚姻家庭状况也随之发生变化。这种变化必然要反映到国际私法的领域中来，并促进婚姻家庭关系法律适用问题的发展。这种新发展主要表现在以下几个方面。

（一）男女平等的原则被引进冲突法的领域

社会主义国家的法律一向规定男女平等的原则。我国《婚姻法》规定，我国“实行婚姻自由、一夫一妻、男女平等的婚姻制度”（第2条）；“夫妻在家庭中地位平等”（第9条）；“夫妻双方都有各用自己姓名的权利”（第10条）；“子女可以随父姓，也可以随母姓”（第16条）。

但是，许多资本主义国家的法律长期存在重男轻女的规定，特别是在冲突法的领域中。现在这些国家也逐步地把男女平等的原则引进冲突法。德国和日本就是突出的例子。

根据德国旧《民法施行法》（1896年批准，1900年生效）的规定，夫妻关系适用夫之本国法，如夫妻财产制，依夫之本国法（第15条）；离婚，依起诉时夫之本国法（第17条）。德国新《民法施行法》（1986年生效）则规定：婚姻的一般效力适用配偶双方国籍所属国法律，或者配偶双方共同惯常居所所在国法律（第14条）；夫妻关系适用支配婚姻一般效力的法律（第15条）离婚，适用离婚请求提出时，支配婚姻一般效力的法律（第17条）。

日本旧《法例》（1898年公布，同年施行）在第二次世界大战以后虽然经过两次修改，但是男女不平等的原则始终没有改变。旧《法例》规定：婚姻的效力，依丈夫本国法（第14条）；夫妻财产制，依结婚当时丈夫本国法（第15条）；离婚，依其原因事实发生时丈夫本国法（第16条）。日本新《法例》（1990年1月1日生效）对婚姻的效力、夫妻财产制和离婚，则根据男女平等的原则采用三步法：第一步，适用配偶双方的共同国籍所属国法律；如果他们没有共同的国籍所属国，则第二步，适用配偶双方的共同惯常居所所在国法律；如果他们没有共同的惯常居所，则第三步，适用与夫妻双方有最密切联系地的法律（第14—16条）。

（二）注意保护儿童的合法利益

保护儿童的合法利益已成为国际私法发展的又一个新趋势。德国新《民法施行法》增加了保护儿童合法利益的条款，该法关于婚生子女的第19条中规定：如果子女的最大利益受到损害时，应根据子女惯常居所所在国法律采取保护措施（第19条第3款）。但是该法对非婚生子女则没有这样的规定。

对非婚生子女的问题，社会主义国家的法律远比资本主义国家的先进。我国《婚姻法》明确规定："非婚生子女享有与婚生子女同等的权利，任何不人得加以危害和歧视。"（第19条）不过德国新《民法施行法》对非婚生子女准正的条件比旧《民法施行法》有所放宽。它规定：通过后来结婚准正非婚生子女，适用支配婚姻一般效力的法律；如果配偶国籍不同，但根据其中一国法律该子女可得准正，则他便获准正（第21条第1款）。

日本新《法例》对儿童是否婚生比旧《法例》也放宽了要求。旧《法例》规定：儿童是否婚生，依其出生时母之丈夫本国法，如母之丈夫在儿童出生前死亡，依其丈夫最后所属国法（第17条）。新《法例》则规定：儿童是否婚生，适用父或母之国籍所属国法；在儿童出生时，父或母之国籍所属国中有一国之法律承认该儿童为婚生，则该儿童为婚生（第17条）。

关于父母与子女之间的关系，日本旧《法例》规定，依父之本国法；如无父时，依母之本国法（第20条）。新《法例》则考虑到适用子女方面的法律。它规定：父母与子女之间的关系，适用父母与子女的共同国籍所属国法律；如果他们没有共同的国籍所属国，则适用父母与子女的共同惯常居所所在国法律；如果他们没有共同的惯常居所，则适用与他们有密切联系地的法律（第21条）。这个规定也包含保护儿童合法利益的意思。

（三）防止跛足婚姻的新措施

涉外婚姻成立及其效力的最古老的准据法是婚姻举行地法，亦称婚姻缔结地法。那时候，对涉外婚姻成立的要件不分实质要件与形式要件，认为在举行地有效的婚姻到处有效，在举行地无效的婚姻到处无效。这种制度的优点是简便易行。它的缺点是当事人容易规避其本国法或住所地法的禁止性规定，到那些没有这些禁止性规定的国家去结婚。

为了克服这个缺点，后来一些欧洲大陆民法法系国家就把涉外婚姻成立的要件分为实质要件与形式要件，规定实质要件适用当事人的本国法，形式要件适用婚姻举行地法。实质要件一般是指男女双方的结婚能力，即是否达到法定的结婚年龄，双方当事人之间的关系是否属于禁止结婚的范围，双方当事人是否患有禁止结婚的疾病等。形式要件一般是指当事人双方到婚姻登记机关进行登记并领取结婚证书，或者需要有正式的仪式，需要有适当的人主持结婚仪式等。

英国原来对涉外婚姻的成立要件也不分实质要件与形式要件，一律适用婚姻举行地法。从 1858 年开始，它才作了区分，前者适用当事人的住所地法，后者适用婚姻举行地法。

这种制度的优点是使当事人无法规避其本国法或住所地法的禁止性规定。但是它也有缺点。由于各国对实质要件与形式要件有不同的识别，有些问题在一个国家被认为是实质要件，而在另一个国家则被认为是形式要件。例如，关于未成年人结婚的问题，英国的婚姻法规定，未成年人结婚，须征得其父母的同意。法国民法典第 148 条规定，未成年人非经其父母同意，不得结婚。看起来英、法两国法律对这个问题的规定是一致的。但是按照各自的法律进行识别，其结果则相差甚远。按照英国法识别，这是婚姻形式问题，适用婚姻举行地法。按照法国法识别，这是婚姻实质要件问题，适用当事人的本国法。同时各国对住所的定义及住所的设立与变更又有不同的规定。这样，这种制度就容易产生跛足婚姻，即在一个国家有效而在另一个国家无效的婚姻。由于跛足婚姻的存在，就可能出现一个人可以同在不同国家的两个以上的配偶维持着所谓的“一夫一妻”制婚姻的奇怪现象。[①]

美国和许多拉丁美洲国家，在解决涉外婚姻成立要件及其效力的法律冲突时，仍然采用婚姻缔结地法制度，因为这些国家都有大量的外国移民，采用婚姻缔结地法，能为外来移民提供方便，从而吸收他们前来这些国家参加开发和建设。

为了防止当事人规避其住所地法的禁止性规定，美国于 1912 年颁布了

---

① 沃尔夫：《国际私法》，1988，法律出版社，中文版，第 495—496 页。

《统一防止婚姻规避法》（只有一小部分州采用它作为法律）和其他各州的一些法律规定，如果男女双方的住所都在其他州，而根据住所地法，他们的婚姻是无效的或者是可以撤销的，那么他们就不能在这个州缔结婚姻，即使缔结了也是无效的。

美国第二部《冲突法重述》第283节（婚姻的效力）总结了美国全面的实践经验。该节规定，婚姻符合缔结地州的要件，在任何地方都被认为有效，除非它违反了另一个州的强硬的公共政策，而这个州同夫妻双方和该婚姻具有最重要的关系。在这里，婚姻成立的要件，没有区分实质要件和形式要件，一律适用婚姻缔结地法。至于具有最重要关系的州，据美国法学家里斯等解释，是指结婚时夫妻双方中有一方的住所在那个州，并且结婚后双方立即到那个州去居住。①

阿根廷、哥伦比亚、玻利维亚、秘鲁、乌拉圭和巴拉圭六国于1940年3月19日在蒙得维的亚签订了《关于国际民法的条约》。该条约对涉外婚姻的规定，一方面采用婚姻缔结地法制度，另一方面又注意克服其缺点。该条约第13条规定：自然人的结婚能力、结婚方式、结婚的事实及其有效性，依行为实施地法；但是有下列任何情况之一者，缔约国没有义务承认其婚姻：

（1）婚姻当事人一方不足婚龄，男方最低婚龄为14岁，女方为12岁；

（2）直系血亲或姻亲关系，不论是否婚生；

（3）婚生或非婚生的兄弟姐妹之间的亲属关系；

（4）以与未亡配偶结婚为目的，作为主犯或同谋者，杀死一方当事人的配偶的事实；

（5）未经合法解除先前婚姻。

为了防止跛足婚姻的产生，海牙国际私法会议吸取了美国和拉丁美洲国家的实践经验，于1978年3月14日通过了《结婚仪式和承认婚姻有效公约》。该公约对涉外婚姻成立的要件及其效力均适用婚姻举行地法。该公约第2条和第3条是确定婚姻成立的要件的。第2条规定，婚姻的形式要件，依结婚仪式举行地国的法律。第3条规定，缔结婚姻必须：

（1）未来的配偶双方符合婚礼举行地国国内法的实质要件，并且配偶

① 〔美〕《冲突法重述》（第二部）第2卷，1971，美国·圣保罗，英文版，第238页。

一方具有该国国籍或在该国设有惯常居所；或者

（2）未来的配偶各自符合婚礼举行地国法律选择规则所规定的国内法的实质要件。

关于婚姻的效力，该公约第9条规定，依婚礼举行地国法律缔结的有效婚姻，或者后来依该国法律成为有效的婚姻，各缔约国均应认为有效。

该公约同时对防止这种婚姻制度的缺点作了明确规定（第11条）：缔约国只有在结婚当时依其法律有下列情况之一者，得拒绝承认其婚姻效力：

（1）配偶之一方已婚；

（2）配偶之间是直系血亲或养父母子女，或是嫡亲及因收养而成为兄弟姐妹；

（3）配偶一方未达结婚的最低年龄，又未获得必要的特许；

（4）配偶一方在智力上缺乏同意的能力；

（5）配偶一方并未自愿应允结婚。

但对第1款所规定的情况，如果后来由于解除或取消前一婚姻而有效时，不得拒绝承认。

我国对涉外婚姻成立的要件也不分实质要件与形式要件，一律适用婚姻缔结地法。该法同时是涉外婚姻效力的准据法。我国《民法通则》第147条规定："中华人民共和国公民和外国人结婚适用婚姻缔结地法律。"这种制度的优点是简单易行，方便婚姻当事人，又可防止跛足婚姻的产生。它也有缺点，如可能发生重婚，因为现在世界上还有实行一夫多妻制的地方。我国立法对这种制度的缺点则未作任何防止性的规定。这是一个不足之处。另一个不足之处是只规定我国公民和外国人结婚的情况，至于男女双方都是我国公民在外国结婚，以及男女双方都是外国人在我国结婚的情况则未作规定。这也不适应对外开放的需要，因为在对外开放的条件下，这种情况是经常发生的。今后我国的立法应该借鉴国际上的实践经验，对这些不足之处作出规定，以完善我国的国际私法立法。

（本文原载于《法学研究》1994年第3期）

法律选择协议效力的法律适用辩释

沈　涓*

意思自治原则是国际私法中确定准据法的一项重要原则，已为几乎所有国家的国际私法的理论、立法和司法所接受和采行，其核心是冲突规则赋予当事人合意选择适用于他们之间法律关系的准据法的权利。这项原则的实现基于两个前提条件，即当事人选择法律的意思表示和意思表示的有效。这两个前提既关及意思自治原则的实现，也关及当事人所选择的法律的有效适用，进而关及当事人利益期望的实现。对意思自治原则的适用，国内外多从当事人选择法律的方式、时间、范围等方面进行研究，少有以当事人选择法律的意思表示的效力的法律适用为研究对象的成果。

有关法律选择合意效力的法律适用的讨论，应以这一问题所涉概念和性质为始。当事人选择法律的合意究竟应称为或视为法律选择条款、法律选择协议还是法律选择合同，影响对这一问题的认识和结论。当然，讨论的重点无疑是法律选择合意效力的法律适用问题。在各国国际私法中，对法律选择合意的效力应适用何法，存在多种主张：当事人选择的法律、法院地法、当事人没有选择法律时应适用的法律、当事人法律选择合意达成地法、法官裁量适用的法律、依最密切联系原则所确定的法律等。① 其中，以前两种主张居多，立法上和理论上主张适用当事人选择的法律的占绝大

---

* 沈涓，1999 年 12 月来中国社会科学院法学研究所工作，曾任国际私法研究室主任，现任中国社会科学院国际法研究所研究员。

① 参见孙维星《涉外合同中法律选择条款的法律适用》，《法制与社会》2007 年第 7 期。

多数，但学术讨论中有少数观点主张适用法院地法。[①]

在现有研究成果中，适用当事人选择的法律来确定当事人选择法律合意的效力的主张虽呈压倒多数之势，但论者均未予严密论证，在学术讨论中留下了不少漏洞和弱点，并影响立法和司法。本文试图从当事人选择法律合意的概念和性质、选法合意法律适用的合理性、选法合意法律适用的可行性等多个方面，对当事人选择法律合意效力的法律适用问题进行尽可能深入和全面的理解，提出并论证当事人选择法律合意的效力应适用法院地法的主张。

一 概念和性质之辩

（一）当事人选择法律合意的概念

对当事人选择法律的合意，有的学者称其为法律选择条款，[②] 有的学者称其为法律选择协议，[③] 还有的学者称其为法律选择合同。[④] 持这三种概念的学者一致认为，无论称其为条款还是协议或是合同，当事人选择法律的合意都是一种合同或具有合同的性质。[⑤] 对当事人选择法律合意的这种界定，是他们认为当事人选择法律合意的效力应该适用合同准据法的基础。由此可见，对当事人选择法律合意概念的界定直接决定了合意效力的法律适用。

一部法学辞书对“合同”概念的界定是：“广义泛指产生一定权利、义务的协议，狭义专指双方或多方当事人关于建立、变更或消灭民事法律关系的协议。特征：（1）是双方法律行为；（2）双方当事人须意思表示一致；（3）以建立、消灭或变更一定的法律关系为目的；（4）具有合法性。

---

① 参见秦瑞亭《提单法律选择条款探微》，《中国海商法研究》2013 年第 3 期；李春《涉外民商合同关系中的法律选择协议》，《人民法院报》2004 年 8 月 11 日，第 3 版。

② 参见孙维星《涉外合同中法律选择条款的法律适用》，《法制与社会》2007 年第 7 期。

③ 参见李良鸿、郑发国《法律选择协议相关问题研究》，《浙江万里学院学报》2006 年第 4 期。

④ 参见秦瑞亭《提单法律选择条款探微》，《中国海商法研究》2013 年第 3 期。

⑤ 参见孙维星《涉外合同中法律选择条款的法律适用》，《法制与社会》2007 年第 7 期；李良鸿、郑发国《法律选择协议相关问题研究》，《浙江万里学院学报》2006 年第 4 期；秦瑞亭《提单法律选择条款探微》，《中国海商法研究》2013 年第 3 期。

合同一经成立即具有法律效力，当事人一方或双方未按合同履行义务，应受到法律制裁。”①

另一部法学辞书对“合同”概念也作了类似界定：“……作为法律概念的合同，有广义与狭义之分。狭义合同概念专指以发生债权债务为内容的合意；而广义合同概念指以发生私法上效果为目的的一切合意……合同具有如下特征：(1）合同是一种民事法律行为。合同以意思表示为要素，并按意思表示的内容赋予法律效果，属民事法律行为，而非事实行为。(2）合同是两方以上当事人的意思表示一致的民事法律行为……（3）合同是以设立、变更、终止债权债务关系为目的的民事法律行为。(4）合同是当事人各方在平等自愿基础上产生的民事法律行为。”②

在民法学者的论著中，对合同概念的通常表述是：合同是一种民事法律行为；合同是一种双方或多方或共同的民事法律行为；合同是以在当事人之间设立、变更、终止财产性民事权利义务关系为目的的协议；所谓财产性民事权利义务关系，既可以是债权关系，也可以是物权关系。③

1999 年合同法第 2 条第 1 款规定：“本法所称合同是平等主体的自然人、法人、其他组织之间设立、变更、终止民事权利义务关系的协议。”

比较上述辞书、专著和合同法对合同概念的界定和规定，可以清楚地看到，当事人选择法律的合意并不完全符合合同的概念。除了当事人意思表示一致之外，二者最大也是最本质的差异有两点：一是当事人选择法律的合意内容仅仅是指定法律关系应适用的民事实体法，表达当事人希望由该民事实体法来确定他们之间民事权利义务关系的意愿，而不是直接设立、变更、终止民事权利义务关系。二是当事人选择法律的合意达成之后，一方违反合意通常不会产生承担违约责任，甚至受到法律制裁的严重后果。可见，对民事法律关系而言，合同具有确定权利义务关系的实体属性，而当事人选择法律的合意并不具有同样的实体属性，也不具有与合同同等程度的对当事人法律上的约束效力。

如果一定要认为当事人的选法合意是一种合同，那么根据上述相关界

---

① 邹瑜、顾明主编《法学大辞典》，中国政法大学出版社，1991，第 600 页以下。

② 中国社会科学院法学研究所《法律辞典》编委会编《法律辞典》，法律出版社，2003，第 638 页以下。

③ 参见马俊驹、余延满《民法原论》，法律出版社，2007，第 502 页。

定和规定，它至少不是狭义上的合同，充其量是广义上的合同，即以发生私法上效果为目的的合意或协议。上述两部辞书对合意也作出了解释：合意，又称“协议”，指当事人双方或多方意思表示达成一致;[①] 或者，合意指两个或两个以上的人就某些事项的意思表示达成一致。[②] 从这样的解释可以认识到，合意或协议的重点在于意思表示的明确性和一致性，其内容不必是明确的法律关系权利义务。国际私法中当事人选择法律的合意比较符合合意或协议的这些特征。

综上，本文认为，当事人选择法律的合意应该被称为也被视为法律选择协议（以下简称选法协议），无论这种协议是以合同中的条款形式存在，还是以合同之外独立的协议形式存在，都不应被视为狭义上的合同，更不应按照合同的标准寻求其效力的法律适用。努力厘清当事人选择法律的合意及其载体应该被称为协议还是被称为合同这一概念上的差异，是因为这是所有在选法协议效力应该适用的法律的认定上产生歧义的根源。

（二）当事人选法协议的性质

清楚区分当事人选法协议和合同的差异，以寻找选法协议效力法律适用的正确方向，除对二者概念进行界定之外，还须明确二者的性质。

如前所述，当事人选法协议与当事人双方缔结的主要合同有本质差别。当事人之间缔结的主要合同以确定双方权利义务为内容，根据国际私法中的意思自治原则，其有效性应该由当事人为合同选择的准据法确定。但当事人之间的选法协议是以法律选择为内容，无论是列入实体性合同的法律选择条款，还是专门就法律选择问题作出的单独协议，其中的诸如“合同受某国法律支配”或“双方同意产生争议时依据某国法律解决”等表述，实际上相当于当事人所创设的法律选择规则，其作用是选择准据法。

选法协议既然不具有实体性合同的性质，且其中内容属于法律选择规则，不属于实体规则，那么在区分了二者的性质之后，就可以得出以下理解。

第一，在国际私法中，根据意思自治原则，当事人并不具有选择一国

① 参见邹瑜、顾明主编《法学大辞典》，中国政法大学出版社，1991，第601页。

② 参见中国社会科学院法学研究所《法律辞典》编委会编《法律辞典》，法律出版社，2003，第646页。

法律中法律选择规则的权利。选法协议既然不属于实体性合同，一国确定选法协议效力的规则亦不属于确定法律关系当事人权利义务的实体规则，那么那些确定选法协议效力的规则也就不属于可由当事人选择适用的法律范畴。相应的，根据意思自治原则，当事人只具有选择实体法的权利，所选之法只能确定法律关系本身的实体问题，而不能确定法律选择问题。

第二，由于选法协议不具有确定当事人权利义务的实体内容，也就不需要寻找一个实体法来判断选法协议的效力，而是需要寻找一个确定法律选择效力的国际私法规则作为依据。另外，当事人缔结的选法协议性质上独立于主合同，确定选法协议的准据法不必与确定主合同的准据法捆绑在一起。

第三，有观点主张当事人选法协议是一种合同，具有实体属性，因此其效力须从实体法意义上考查，如当事人须有缔结协议的能力，意思表示须明确、一致，选择法律不得违反相关法律的规定，协议应具备法律要求的形式，协议应符合要约和承诺阶段的要求等。[①] 实际上，这些考查项目并不全是实体法意义上的。例如，当事人须有缔结协议的能力同样也是国际私法在确定人的行为效力时的考查项目之一，并且各国普遍制定了当事人行为能力的法律适用规则。意思表示须明确、一致及选择法律不得违反相关法律同样是国际私法上衡量当事人选择法律的意思表示效力的条件，并非只是实体法上的标准。至于协议形式，当事人达成选法协议的形式固然有合同条款和单独协议这样的书面形式，但有时也有口头的表达形式或直接援引法律的事实形式，对此法律并未作强制性的要求。

第四，从关联性考量，选法协议的内容是法律选择，当事人之间缔结的主合同的内容是确定双方权利义务，二者既不相似，也无关联。如果依合同准据法确定选法协议的效力，显然不符合最密切联系原则，法律选择和法律适用的合理性值得怀疑。

第五，当事人选择合同准据法时着眼于合同关系中权利的实现和义务的履行，并不会基于选法协议的效力来考虑法律选择。也就是说，当事人所选择的合同准据法对合同关系或许是合适的法律，但对选法协议效力而

---

① 参见李良鸿、郑发国《法律选择协议相关问题研究》，《浙江万里学院学报》2006 年第 4 期。

言却不一定是合适的法律，甚至有可能合同准据法并不是他们希望适用于他们之间选法协议效力的法律。

基于上述理解，可以进一步认识到，当事人选法协议的性质是法律选择规则。当事人创设的这种法律选择规则只是表达了他们希望适用某国法律来确定他们之间权利义务关系的意愿，并不足以最终确定合同应该适用他们所选择的法律。他们选择法律的意愿是否能够实现，还有赖于法院对他们所作选择的效力的认可。这一认可的过程仍然属于法律选择过程，而不是实体争议处理过程。在法院对当事人选法协议的效力予以确认之前，当事人所选之法还不是合同准据法，这一所选之法并不能被视为合同准据法而作为判断选法协议效力的依据。既然判断选法协议是否有效仍然属于法律选择的活动过程，那么判断的依据只能是法院地法。

由此可见，将选法协议效力的确定这样一个国际私法范畴内的法律选择问题认为是确定合同的成立和效力这样的实体合同法范畴的问题，并主张在立法或司法上推定进而确定选法协议效力应该适用合同准据法，是对选法协议性质的误解，很可能在选法协议效力的法律适用方面既不能成就意思自治原则的功效，也不能成就最密切联系原则的功效。

如果说，当事人表达选择法律的意思常常借助于合同条款或单独协议，从而使人很容易将这种合意形式视为合同，那么在实践中存在的一些情况或许可以帮助他们看清楚当事人选择法律合意的多样性或非合同性。

2013 年《最高人民法院关于适用〈中华人民共和国涉外民事关系法律适用法〉若干问题的解释（一）》［以下简称《涉外民事关系法律适用法司法解释（一）》］第 8 条第 2 款规定："各方当事人援引相同国家的法律且未提出法律适用异议的，人民法院可以认定当事人已经就涉外民事关系适用的法律作出了选择。" 2007 年《最高人民法院关于审理涉外民事或商事合同纠纷案件法律适用若干问题的规定》第 4 条第 2 款也有类似规定："当事人未选择合同争议应适用的法律，但均援引同一国家或者地区的法律且未提出法律适用异议的，应当视为当事人已经就合同争议应适用的法律作出选择。" 这两个司法解释所描述的情形在实践中确实存在，[①] 即当事

① 参见徐伟功《法律选择中的意思自治原则在我国的运用》，《法学》2013 年第 9 期。

人双方在争议产生之前没有达成选择法律的协议，在争议审理期间双方都引用了相同法律，这种行为可被视为双方达成了选择法律的合意。在这种情形下，虽然法院认定当事人达成了法律选择合意，但显然很难将这种达成合意理解为当事人之间缔结了一项合同，也很难按照一般合同的效力要素去判断这一选择的效力。

当事人双方选择法律的合意并非在缔结合同或成立法律关系时达成，而是在将争议诉诸法院之后才达成，此种情形在合同案件中存在。在侵权案件中，当事人在诉讼过程中达成法律选择合意更是唯一的意思自治方式，因为侵权关系双方当事人不可能在争议产生之前就法律选择达成合意。当事人在诉讼过程中就法律选择达成合意，常常不是以缔结合同或协议的方式，更多的是如上述两个司法解释所预设的情形，各方当事人援引相同国家的法律且未提出法律适用异议，或一方当事人援引一国法律，另一方当事人未提出异议。实践中，更多的情形是，法官就法律选择意愿口头询问双方当事人，若双方首肯，即达成合意。[①] 很显然，在上述情形中，当事人选择法律的意愿是否真实和一致容易直接为法官探知，对合意效力的确定，也完全没有考虑法院地法以外法律的适用。如果将上述情形下的当事人法律选择合意视为一种合同，并适用当事人所选择的法律来确定合意的效力，可以想象，这在司法实践中几乎是不可能的，也是完全没有必要的。

相似的情形还有合同对某国法律或国际公约和国际惯例的纳入[②]效力的确定：当事人虽然没有明确选择某国法律或某个国际公约和惯例作为法律关系准据法，但他们将某一国法律条文或某一国际公约条款和惯例直接纳入合同，作为合同条款，这种纳入能否作为当事人对法律关系准据法的选择，其效力也须确认。

对此，各国立法和司法态度不一致。[③]《涉外民事关系法律适用法司法

---

① 参见沈涓《中国法院审理涉外（涉港澳台）民商案件情况》，载黄东黎主编《国际法研究》第 8 卷，社会科学文献出版社，2013，第 350 页以下。

② 参见 Cheshire and North, *Private International Law*, 10th ed., Butterworths, 1979, pp. 202 – 203; *Collins, Dicey and Morris on the Conflict of Laws*, 11th ed., Stevens and Sons, 1987, pp. 1178 – 1180; Morris, *The Conflict of Laws*, 2nd ed., Stevens and Sons, 1980, p. 218。

③ 参见沈涓《合同准据法理论的解释》，法律出版社，2000，第 31 页以下。

解释（一）》第9条规定：“当事人在合同中援引尚未对中华人民共和国生效的国际条约的，人民法院可以根据该国际条约的内容确定当事人之间的权利义务，但违反中华人民共和国社会公共利益或中华人民共和国法律、行政法规强制性规定的除外。”虽然这条的指向是尚未对我国生效的国际条约，但既然当事人援引尚未对我国生效的国际条约都可以被视为当事人对准据法作出了选择，那么当事人援引已经对我国生效的国际条约当然就更应该被视为当事人作出了法律选择。

分析这种情形，可以认为，与上述各方当事人援引相同法律的情形类似，这两种情形都是缺乏当事人对法律的明确和直接的指定，但都通过援用法律的方式表达了当事人希望适用某特定法律的意愿，因而应该被视为当事人对准据法作出了选择。纳入方式既不同于在合同中设立法律选择条款，也不同于合同之外专门订立法律选择协议，而是直接将作为合同准据法的法律条文列为合同条款，当事人以此种方式表达了选择合同准据法的合意。虽然这些被纳入的法律条文以合同条款的形式存在，但是它们能否作为合同准据法，还须由相关法律确定。也就是说，在此种情形下，当事人将法律条文纳入合同的合意的成立和效力独立于合同的成立和效力，只有相关法律确认这种纳入方式可以作为当事人选择法律的方式，当事人所纳入的法律条文才能作为合同准据法适用。中国和其他国家都有成例表明，判断被纳入的法律能否作为合同准据法的依据是法院地法。①

值得注意的是，有人认为，上述各方当事人援引相同法律或在合同中纳入某国法律或国际公约或国际惯例的内容，应该被视为当事人对法律关系准据法的默示选择。② 对此，本文认为，各方当事人援引相同法律或将相关法律纳入合同的方式也应该被视为对法律的明示选择。理由是，第一，较之选法协议指定某一法律而没有提示出该法律内容，当事人以这两种方式提供了特定法律的具体内容，其意思表示的明确程度有过之而无不

① 参见林准主编《国际私法案例选编》，法律出版社，1996，第68页以下；参见 Cheshire and North, *Private International Law*, 10th ed., Butterworths, 1979, p. 1181 et seq。

② 参见刘仁山《国际合同法律适用中“意思自治原则”的晚近发展：〈海牙国际合同法律选择原则〉述评》，《环球法律评论》2013年第6期；刘仁山、黄志慧《国际民商事合同中的默示选法问题研究》，《现代法学》2014年第5期。

及。第二，我国法律和司法解释都强调，当事人选择法律的意思必须明示，[①] 不认可以默示方式选择法律。因此，既然司法解释已确定各方当事人援引相同法律和当事人将相关规则纳入合同条款都是对准据法作出选择的方式，那么也就是将这两种方式都视为明示选择法律的方式，否则就与已有司法解释不相符合。[②]

分辨当事人选法协议的概念和性质，是为了寻找合理和可行的选法协议效力的法律选择和法律适用方向。将选法协议确认为狭义的合同，便会忽视其非合同性和非实体性，忽视实践中当事人所采用的诸多以简单意思表示达成合意的选择法律的非合同方式，以及以直接提出他们希望适用的法律的具体内容的行为表示合意的方式，忽视选法协议的非实体性的法律选择规则的本质，最终落入选择未被确定适用效力的当事人所选之法的逻辑陷坑中，并导致选法协议法律适用上的不合理和不可行。

二　合理性之辩

以当事人选法协议的概念和性质为基础，本文将进一步论证选法协议效力适用法院地法的合理性。这是本文重要的目的。

（一）适用当事人选择之法的逻辑错误

无论如何论证当事人选法协议的效力应适用当事人所选择的法律这一主张的正确性，不可不说的是，论证者始终无法对这一主张中存在的逻辑错误作出合理解说。这一点已经成为此主张的最大弊害和弱点。

确定当事人选法协议的效力是为了确定所选之法的适用效力，在选法协议效力被确定之前，此法不具有适用于任何问题的效力。以一个未被确定适用效力的法去确定选法协议的效力，缺乏依据和说服力，更何况是确定赋予自身准据法效力的当事人意思自治的效力。

① 参见2010年《涉外民事关系法律适用法》第3条；2007年《最高人民法院关于审理涉外民事或商事合同纠纷案件法律适用若干问题的规定》第3条。

② 参见最高人民法院民四庭负责人就《关于适用〈中华人民共和国涉外民事关系法律适用法〉若干问题的解释（一）》答记者问，2013年4月23日，http://www.court.gov.cn/shenpan-xiangqing-5275.html，最后访问日期：2015年10月10日。

虽然所有主张选法协议效力应适用当事人选择的法律的人都不得不承认这一主张存在逻辑上的问题，但又都囿于选法协议是合同的认识，而坚持既是合同其效力就应该适用当事人选择的法律这一通则，难以接受选法协议效力应适用法院地法的主张，[①] 于是刻意对逻辑问题视而不见，或认为逻辑问题之弊不足以危害适用当事人选择的法律确定选法协议效力的结果，而将当事人选择的法律作为“假设（putative）有效的法律”[②] 适用于确定选法协议的效力。殊不知，正是这个逻辑弊端使选法协议效力适用当事人选择的法律这一主张严重缺乏说服力，进而将确定选法协议效力的法律适用问题的意义全然抹杀。

造成这样的效果的原因其实众所周知。确定选法协议效力的唯一目的是确定当事人选择的法律是否具有调整法律关系的准据法效力，这就意味着在选法协议效力被确定之前，当事人选择的法律的准据法效力还未被确定，只有在选法协议被确定为有效后，当事人选择的法律才具有准据法效力。如果预先“假设”当事人选择的法律已经具有准据法效力，可以适用于确定选法协议的效力（且不论选法协议的效力是否应由法律关系准据法来确定），那么就已经事实上赋予了当事人选择的法律以准据法效力，又何必多此一举要去确定选法协议的效力呢？何不直接认定当事人选择的法律无论如何都是有效的，可以直接适用于法律关系中权利义务的确定？更何况，对准据法效力的确定问题基于“假设”而求解，也十分有损法律选择和法律适用的严肃性和严谨性。

（二）意思自治原则体系的自洽完整性

意思自治原则是确定法律选择和法律适用的一项重要原则，自产生以来，在不断发展中已形成一个较丰富和较完善的体系，为各国国际私法采

---

① 参见许军珂《国际私法中的意思自治》，法律出版社，2007，第 145 页；肖永平《国际私法原理》，法律出版社，2003，第 177 页；韩德培主编《国际私法新论》，武汉大学出版社，1997，第 296 页。

② 参见 2008 年欧盟《关于合同之债法律适用的第 593/2008 号规则》（罗马 I 规则）第 10 条第 1 款，载《外国国际私法立法精选》，邹国勇译注，中国政法大学出版社，2011，第 338 页；Peter Stone，*EU International Law*，2nd ed.，Edward Elgar Publishing Limited，2010，p. 324；Cheshire，North & Fawcett，*Private International Law*，14th ed.，Oxford University Press，2008，pp. 744 - 745。

行。这项原则的核心是，法律赋予当事人作出法律选择的权利，当事人依此享有创设法律选择规则的权利。如2010年《涉外民事关系法律适用法》第3条规定："当事人依照法律规定可以明示选择涉外民事关系适用的法律。"有了这一规定的授权，当事人便可以明示方式达成选择法律的合意。

但意思自治原则体系中不仅包括赋予当事人选择法律的权利，也包括对当事人意思自治的限制，以及判断当事人选法协议效力的标准。一国国际私法在赋予当事人选择法律的权利时，都会对当事人选择法律时所涉问题作出相应的规定，这些问题主要有选择法律和变更选择时间（缔结合同时、缔结合同后、行为成立后、判决作出前）、方式（明示、默示）、范围（与法院地国之间的联系、实体法或冲突规范）、限制（不得排除国内法中强制性规定的适用、不得违反公共秩序、不得以欺诈及胁迫等方法达成协议）等。如《涉外民事关系法律适用法司法解释（一）》第6—10条分别对当事人选择法律和变更选择的范围、方式、时间及不能排除我国强制性规定的限制作出了规定。这些对意思自治的确认和限制的规定主要就是用于确定当事人选择法律的效力，当事人选择法律时，只有符合这些规定所要求的条件和限制，其选择法律的意思表示才具有确定法律关系准据法的效力。

有关当事人选法协议效力的规则与赋予当事人选法权利的规则共同构成当事人意思自治原则的规则体系，这已在各国间形成共识。[①] 很显然，那些判断当事人选法协议效力的规则存在于各国国际私法中，而不是存在于各国民法中。因此，第一，确定当事人选法协议效力的规则属于国际私法规则，而非民法规则，确定选法协议效力时应该适用的是国际私法规则，而不必在其他法律诸如民法领域中寻找依据和判断标准。第二，权利的赋予和行使权利的条件及限制应该是同源的完整体系，即意思自治原则体系具有自洽完整性，如果由一国的国际私法规则赋予当事人选法的权利，却由另一国法律——国际私法和民法——来确定行使这种权利的条件及限制，这样，既使赋予权利的效力不完整，也使权利的行使和限制的规定不统一，且实践中的可行性也可质疑。

---

① 参见吕岩峰《当事人意思自治原则内涵探析——再论当事人意思自治原则》，《吉林大学社会科学学报》1998年第1期。

（三）法官适用法律选择规则的职权范围

对当事人选择法律的合意的效力的认定，实际上是法官适用法律选择规则确定法律关系准据法的过程。因此，确定选法协议效力是法官确定准据法过程中的一个环节，是法官依职权而为司法行为的过程。

国际私法的主要效能是确定法律关系准据法，这一目的的实现依赖法官的司法活动。在法官为确定法律关系准据法的司法活动时，法律选择规则即冲突规则是准则。除以法律选择规则为内容的国际公约之外，法律选择规则主要存在于作为国内法的各国国际私法之中，其功能是为内国法院审理涉外民事案件时提供确定准据法的依据。

法律关系适用当事人选择的法律是一项遵循意思自治原则的法律选择规则，但这项法律选择规则并不是一项功能健全的法律选择规则，因为这项规则并没有明确指定法律关系应适用的特定实体法。准确地说，这项法律选择规则只是一项授权规则，即将选择法律的权利授予法律关系当事人，由他们指定准据法。这时，法官将确定准据法的司法职权的一部分让渡给了当事人，法官仅承担确认当事人选择法律的合意的效力这部分职权。

由此可见，在意思自治原则体系下，国际私法规则同样地赋予了当事人和法官一定的选择法律的权利或权力，但二者的范围和行使力度并不相同：当事人的权利范围仅在选择法律，并不适用法律，因为当事人不是真正的司法者。所以，表达选择法律的意愿就是当事人实现意思自治的全部活动范围，其意思自治的最终实现，还须依赖法官对当事人自己所选之法的适用。这种适用包括确定当事人意思自治的效力和以当事人所选之法最终确定当事人之间的权利义务关系。

这表明，当事人表达选法意愿的自由和法官依据内国国际私法规则对当事人选法自由的效力的确认共同构成准据法的选择过程，当事人和法官的共同作为才是法律选择的一个完整过程。可见，当事人选择法律的权利由法院地冲突规则赋予，不是由当事人所选择的实体法赋予。如果当事人选法意愿的效力不是依法院地国法律来确认，而是依据当事人所选之法来确认，一方面，剥夺了法官的那一部分选法权力，也中断了选择和确定准据法的完整过程；另一方面，在实践中，这种情形也难以想象和难以操作。

如前所述，赋予当事人选择法律权利的规则只是意思自治原则体系的一部分规则，另一部分规则是确定当事人选择法律的意思表示的效力的规则，包括意思自治须满足的条件和应受到的限制，这两部分规则是意思自治原则体系内不可分割的整体。这种整体性既体现在规则的构成上，也体现在依据的来源上：既然赋予当事人选择法律的权利的规则与意思自治的条件和限制的规则共同构成意思自治原则体系，那么法官确认意思自治效力的依据也应该取自同一个体系。所以，在审理涉外民事争议时，法官既然根据内国法律选择规则确认了当事人选择法律的权利，在确定当事人选法协议的效力以最终确定准据法的过程中，法官也只应该适用内国国际私法规则。

从另一方面看，如果由当事人所选之法而非法院地法中的相关规则来确定选法协议的效力，那么各国国际私法中有关确定选法协议效力的规则就都没有正面或直接被适用的可能。因为在选法协议效力适用当事人选择的法律的主张下，一国只有在内国实体法被当事人选择作为法律关系准据法时，内国确定选法协议效力的规则才能被适用于确定协议效力。这就意味着，各国国际私法立法中设立的有关确定当事人选法协议效力的规则都不是给内国法官作为判断选法协议效力的依据的，而是准备好给外国法官作为判断依据的。而内国法官确定当事人选法协议效力时都必须适用某一外国确定选法协议效力的规则，这样的结论未免荒唐。当然，在实际案件中也许有这样的情况，即当事人选择了法院地实体法为法律关系准据法，从而使其确定选法协议效力的规则被适用于确定协议效力，即便如此，也并非在确定协议效力方面适用了法院地法，而仍然是对协议效力适用了当事人选择的法律。

（四）区分选法协议效力确定准据法的不必要性

有观点认为，选法协议效力应由两部分法律确定：将选法协议视为合同，合同本身是否合法，由法院地的冲突法决定；该合同的成立和效力，受该合同的准据法支配。[①] 在一些国际私法公约和外国国际私法中，很少专门规定选法协议本身的合法性适用法院地法，但确实存在当事人选择法

① 参见秦瑞亭《提单法律选择条款探微》，《中国海商法研究》2013 年第 3 期。

律合意的成立和效力受当事人所选之法支配的规定。①

对选法协议的合法性的考查主要涉及当事人选择法律的时间、范围、方式等，属于赋予当事人选择法律的权利时的条件或限制，这几方面问题固然应适用法院地国冲突规则。而当事人选择法律合意的成立和效力涉及哪些问题，现有答案却有些混乱，有的认为有关当事人选择法律合意的自愿性和真实性，② 有的认为有关要约和承诺、欺诈和胁迫、形式有效性、人的缔约能力等。③

事实上，在确定当事人选法合意的效力方面，除对法律选择的时间、范围、方式等作出规定外，合意的自愿性和真实性又何尝不是冲突规则设立的当事人选择法律的条件呢？2007 年《最高人民法院关于审理涉外民事或商事合同纠纷案件法律适用若干问题的规定》第 3 条和第 4 条规定了当事人选择法律或变更选择必须是协商一致且明示的，这体现了国际私法规则对合意的自愿性和真实性的要求。美国国际私法也认为，如果合同一方当事人对法律选择条款所作的同意，是通过不适当的方式如谎报、胁迫、过度影响或错误获得的，那么该条款无效。④

无论是国际私法的理论、立法还是实践，合意的自愿和真实都被奉为意思自治原则的核心价值，既然国际私法采行意思自治原则，允许当事人选择法律，那么合意的自愿和真实也就同样是国际私法规则衡量选法协议效力的重要要求。可见，合意的自愿和真实既具有实体法属性，也是国际私法中意思自治原则体系的内容。国际私法规则对合意的自愿性和真实性也设立了判断标准，如是否协商一致、是否存在欺诈和胁迫等，在这一点

---

① 参见 2008 年欧盟《关于合同之债法律适用的第 593/2008 号规则》（罗马 I 规则）第 3 条第 5 款、第 10 条、第 11 条、第 13 条，载《外国国际私法立法精选》，邹国勇译注，中国政法大学出版社，2011，第 334 页以下；2015 年《海牙国际商事合同法律选择原则》第 6 条第 1 款，http://www.hcch.net/index_en.php? act = conventions.text & cid = 135，最后访问日期：2015 年 10 月 13 日；1987 年瑞士关于国际私法的联邦法（2010 年修订）第 116 条第 2 款，载《外国国际私法立法精选》，邹国勇译注，中国政法大学出版社，2011，第 166 页。

② 参见秦瑞亭《提单法律选择条款探微》，《中国海商法研究》2013 年第 3 期。

③ 参见 Peter Stone, *EU International Law*, 2nd ed., Edward Elgar Publishing Limited, 2010, p. 305; Cheshire, North & Fawcett, *Private International Law*, 14th ed., Oxford University Press, 2008, p. 744 et seq。

④ 参见 American Law Institute, *Restatement of the Law of Conflict of Laws*, Second, 1971, Volume1, p. 562。

上完全没有必要求助于实体法。

至于要约和承诺、合意的形式、人的缔约能力等，虽然属于实体性问题，但在国际私法中并非全部被置于法律关系准据法的支配之下。合意的形式通常受制于行为地法，人的缔约能力通常适用属人法或行为地法。事实上，只有将当事人的选法协议视为狭义合同，才有必要考查要约和承诺及形式等方面是否适用当事人选择的合同准据法。在一些情况下，当事人以简单的口头同意或援引相同法律的行为就达成了选择法律的合意，要约和承诺的过程简单明了，形式更是随意，无须按照实体法对要约和承诺以及形式的要求来判断当事人合意的成立与效力，故而也没有适用实体法的必要。

由此可见，实践中常常是只适用法院地国际私法规则来判断当事人选择法律的效力，而不必同时适用实体法律关系的准据法。

除了从这样的事实中得出上述结论，或许还可以从法院地国确定选法协议效力的规则的非任意性来获得支持。

《涉外民事关系法律适用法司法解释（一）》第6条规定："中华人民共和国法律没有明确规定当事人可以选择涉外民事关系适用的法律，当事人选择适用法律的，人民法院应认定该选择无效。"这项规定表明：在某项民事争议的审理中，当事人的选法协议是否有效，首先要看我国法律是否允许当事人在此领域选择准据法，也就是说，判断当事人选法协议效力的首要标准就是我国法律的规定，而不是当事人所选之法的规定。在我国法律没有赋予当事人选择准据法的权利的情况下，当事人达成了选择准据法的协议，即使依据当事人所选之法选法协议是有效的，我国法院仍然会确认当事人的选法协议无效。这种规定足以表明，确定当事人选法协议效力的依据是法院地法，而不是当事人所选之法。

当法院地国存在判断选法协议效力的规定，但同时又规定选法协议效力不适用法院地法而适用当事人所选之法时，实际上就存在内国法和外国法之间的冲突，实践中法院就很有可能会面对这种冲突。而事实是，面对这样的冲突，任何一个国家的法院都会遵照内国法的规定，而不论该协议在法律关系准据法上是否有效。这再次证明，一国确定选法协议效力的规则的适用是非任意的。

（五）意思自治的实现

有一种观点认为，如果适用法院地法确定选法协议的效力，就会使合同准据法确定中的意思自治成为空话。① 在这种观点看来，没有适用当事人选择的法律确定选法协议的效力，就是没有实现意思自治。这种认识存在误解，需要进一步辩释。

第一，确定选法协议的效力是确定当事人所选之法是否可以作为合同准据法，而不是确定当事人是否具有自己选择合同准据法的权利，即使最终当事人所选择的法律被认为不能作为合同准据法得到适用，也并不意味着对当事人自由选择合同准据法的权利的否定。所以，即使适用法院地法来确定选法协议的效力，且最终选法协议有可能被确定为无效，也不应认为这会使当事人的意思自治成为空话。

第二，无论是民商法还是国际私法，都没有赋予当事人绝对的意思自治，即使在合同法允许当事人依自由意志确定合同实体内容的前提下，合同法也仍然对当事人的意志有若干限制，合同的效力也仍然需要由法律而不是由当事人意志来确定。例如，我国合同法第三章规定了“合同的效力”，从多个方面确定了合同有效成立的条件以及合同无效的情形。面对这样的规定，没有人会认为合同法对当事人确定合同内容的意思自治的限制及对意思自治效力的确定会使当事人的意思自治成为空话。而在国际私法中，适用法院地法来确定当事人选择实体法的效力，并不涉及当事人在法律关系的实体问题上的意思自治，为什么就被认为会使当事人选择法律的意思自治成为空话呢？

第三，这种认识除了走入逻辑上自相矛盾的困境，可能还存在一种误解，那就是认为由于法律关系的权利义务内容和法律关系准据法的选择都遵行了意思自治原则，因此，确定当事人选法协议的效力也应该遵行意思自治原则，适用当事人所选之法。对此，有必要重新认识。首先，选法协议不确定法律关系的权利义务内容，只确定法律选择，所以选法协议的效力不应适用实体法，既然如此，就不一定要与法律关系的实体准据法相连

① 参见许军珂《国际私法中的意思自治》，法律出版社，2007，第 144 页；肖永平、胡永庆《法律选择中的当事人意思自治》，《法律科学》1997 年第 5 期；李广辉《论国际私法中的意思自治原则》，《河南大学学报》（社会科学版）2001 年第 1 期。

结。其次，法律选择的意思自治是由契约自由精神延伸而来，虽然法律选择的意思自治和法律关系内容的意思自治都遵循了相同的精神，但实质作用已大不相同。在法律选择方面，对最初的意思自治的本质已有了很大改变，从当事人决定法律关系内容变为当事人决定无关法律关系内容的法律选择，就已是名大于实了，如果再将意思自治原则延伸至确定选法协议的效力，则距意思自治原则初衷愈远，甚至有些牵强。

第四，那么是否可以考虑同样由当事人选择确定选法协议效力的准据法呢？这一探索也不值得鼓励。在国际私法的理论和立法上，似乎没有这样的原则或规定：选法协议的效力适用当事人为选法协议效力选择的准据法，那就意味着，国际私法在选法协议效力的法律选择和法律适用方面并没有确立意思自治原则。这正如前面已经论证的，确定选法协议效力的规则并非任意性规则，可由当事人选择，这也又一次证明了选法协议与合同的差别。而且，如果设置“选法协议效力适用当事人专门为选法协议效力所选择的法律”这样的法律选择规则，也会使选法协议效力的法律选择和法律适用进入无限循环过程，终究是没有了局，更无济于难题的解决。

另有一种类似观点认为，当事人选择了合同准据法，就期望以合同准据法确定选法协议的效力，所以，适用法院地法而不是当事人选择的合同准据法，不符合当事人的期望。[①] 这种认识或许有失主观。

第一，如果当事人没有约定其选法协议的效力判定适用他们所选择的法律，认为当事人有这样的期望就只是一种推测。

第二，立法和实践不可能无条件地满足当事人的所有期望，这一点从法律对当事人意思自治的多种限制就可以看出。例如，当事人想让他们之间的法律关系适用他们所选择的法律的期望，就常常因一国强制性规定的适用而落空。类似情形还有消费合同和劳动合同领域当事人选择法律的期望因法律对消费者和劳动者的特殊保护而不得实现。

第三，在此方面，需要分辨的是，在确定选法协议效力的法律适用方面究竟是应该更多考虑当事人利益还是法院地国利益。其中关键之处在于，将此问题视为合同准据法的确定还是法律选择规则的适用。如果将选

---

① 参见高宏贵、赖世旭《涉外经济合同法律适用中的意思自治原则》，《华中师范大学学报》（哲学社会科学版）1994 年第 3 期。

法协议效力等同于合同效力对待，在确定其准据法时自然应该更多考虑当事人利益；但如果将确定选法协议效力视为法律选择规则的适用，就应该更多考虑法院地国的利益，因为这关系法院地国所制定的赋予和限制当事人意思自治的法律规则效力的实现。

三 可行性之辩

选法协议效力的确定不是一个纯理论问题，而是存在于实践中的问题。对于选法协议效力的法律适用，除了从合理性角度讨论，还有必要从可行性角度讨论。

（一）适用外国国际私法规则之不可行性

国际私法的理论、立法和实践都表明，采行意思自治原则的范围一般是实体法选择和法院管辖权选择，而不包括冲突规则选择，即根据意思自治原则，当事人只能选择可以确定他们之间权利义务的实体法和受理他们之间争议的法院，而不能选择确定法律适用的冲突规则。如前所述，有关确定选法协议效力的规则通常属于国际私法规则，不属于实体规则。如果以当事人所选之法来确定选法协议效力，这个所选之“法”只能是该法中相关国际私法规则。但在国际私法中，除了接受反致和转致的情况，一国法院一般不会适用另一国的国际私法规则。对此，一些国际私法公约和国内法都主张在合同领域或当事人有权选择法律的情况下排除反致。如 1896 年德国民法典施行法第 4 条第 2 款规定：“当事人可以选择某一国法律时，则只能选择该国的实体规定。”① 这表明，在实践中，一国法院在审理合同

① 参见《外国国际私法立法精选》，邹国勇译注，中国政法大学出版社，2011，第 4 页。另见 2008 年欧盟《关于合同之债法律适用的第 593/2008 号规则》（罗马 I 规则）第 20 条，载《外国国际私法立法精选》，邹国勇译注，中国政法大学出版社，2011，第 340 页；2015 年《海牙国际商事合同法律选择原则》第 8 条，http://www.hcch.net/index_en.php?act=conventions.text&cid=135，最后访问日期：2015 年 10 月 13 日；1995 年意大利国际私法制度改革法第 13 条第 2 款，载中国国际私法学会《中国国际私法与比较法年刊（1999）》（第 2 卷），法律出版社，1999，第 540 页；2001 年韩国修正国际私法第 9 条第 2 款，载中国国际私法学会《中国国际私法与比较法年刊（2003）》（第 6 卷），法律出版社，2003，第 637 页；2005 年保加利亚关于国际私法的法典第 40 条第 2 款，参见《外国国际私法立法精选》，邹国勇译注，中国政法大学出版社，2011，第 223 页。

领域纠纷时是不可能考虑外国国际私法规则的适用的。如果立法上规定当事人选法协议的效力适用当事人所选择的法律中的国际私法规则，不仅与立法中合同领域排除反致的规定相抵触，而且实践中也会因为立法上的冲突而不可行。

在国际私法中，只有存在反致现象时，才考虑外国冲突规则的适用。但对比确定选法协议效力时考虑当事人所选法律中的国际私法规则，反致的情形并不能与之相提并论。

第一，虽然有一些国家的国际私法规定可以接受反致，但也有一些国家的国际私法明确规定不接受反致和转致，即不适用外国冲突规则。可见，即使国际私法中存在反致制度，也并非所有国家都会接受反致和转致而考虑外国冲突规范在内国的适用。既然接受反致、适用外国国际私法规则没有成为普遍规则，那么适用当事人所选之法中的国际私法规则来确定选法协议的效力，也不可能成为普遍规则。

第二，如前所述，由内国国际私法赋予当事人选择法律的权利，却适用外国国际私法中确定选法协议效力的规则，会造成意思自治原则体系中权利的赋予与权利的限制相分离，也会造成内国国际私法和外国国际私法在认定选法协议效力方面的冲突。反致制度不以意思自治原则为基础，除了赋予法官依法决定接受或不接受反致的权力，不需要对法官选择法律的权力作出限制，也就不会导致选法权利的赋予和限制的分离。

第三，就法院地国而言，在当事人选择外国法作为法律关系准据法时，适用当事人所选之法确定选法协议的效力，具有适用外国法（国际私法规则）的消极意义；而在存在反致现象的情形下，接受反致具有适用内国法（实体法）的积极意义。

（二）合同领域之外选法协议效力的法律适用

在国际私法发展史上，意思自治原则起源于契约领域，并在此领域得到成长至成熟。但时至今日，意思自治原则早已有了向其他领域渗透并被采纳的成果，这些领域包括侵权、婚姻家庭、遗嘱继承甚至动产物权。据此，关于意思自治效力的法律适用的讨论就不应仅限于合同领域。

除了协议离婚和夫妻财产契约，侵权、遗嘱继承和动产物权等领域都不以合同为基础。如果在合同领域主张将当事人选法协议视为一种合同，认为其效力的法律适用应同于主合同的法律适用，那么在合同之外的其他领域，仍然主张选法协议的效力应适用当事人为他们之间的法律关系所选择的准据法，就会缺乏可行性。因为在这些领域，当事人之间的关系并非合同关系，当事人选择的法律也并非合同准据法，该法律并不用来确定合同效力，也没有可以用于确定合同效力的内容，所以，即使将选法协议视为合同，也无法和当事人之间这些合同之外的法律关系合并，共同适用当事人所选之法。

可见，如果在合同之外的法律关系中，一定要求当事人选法协议的效力适用当事人所选之法，就必须对当事人选择的法律的范围作广义上的理解，即当事人所选择的法律既包括调整他们之间法律关系的法律，也包括调整合同效力的法律。例如，我国《涉外民事关系法律适用法》第 37 条规定："当事人可以协议选择动产物权适用的法律。"如果根据"选法协议的效力适用当事人选择的法律"这样的规则，就会发现法律适用的结果将会是以调整动产物权的实体法来确定选法协议的效力，这样的法律选择结果显然十分荒唐，也只能是落空。如果一定坚持适用当事人选择的法律来确定选法协议的效力，就只能对"当事人协议选择的动产物权适用的法律"作扩大解释，即这一"动产物权适用的法律"必须既包括可以用于调整动产物权关系的实体法，也包括可以用于调整选法协议效力的实体法，无疑这样的理解会因其过于牵强而显得十分不理性。而且，事实上这种扩大解释的荒谬之处更在于，这一经过扩大解释而用于确定选法协议效力的实体法根本就不是当事人所选择的法律。这样的扩大解释已经违背了意思自治原则的宗旨。根据这样的解释去选择和适用法律，实践中也不可能是一个切实可行的方法。

如果为了有一个说得通的理由，便说"选法协议效力适用当事人选择的法律"这一规则只适用于合同领域，其他领域的选法协议应适用法院地法或其他法律，这样的态度同样缺乏理性，因为它使国际私法中意思自治原则的适用出现了不统一。

（三）当事人选择之法适用可行性的反驳

在主张选法协议效力适用当事人选择的法律的观点中，适用当事人选择的法律被认为比适用法院地法和其他相关法律都具有更大可行性。[①] 事

① 参见许军珂《国际私法中的意思自治》，法律出版社，2007，第 145 页。

实并非如此。

第一，在当事人选择的法律是法院地法时，对法院而言，适用当事人选择的法律就是适用内国法，其可行性自然很高。但在当事人选择外国法时，法院就必须适用外国法来确定选法协议的效力。虽然在实现意思自治原则的过程中，法官可能常常要面对适用外国法的情形，由此遭遇的查知外国法的困难也是追求法律适用合理性所必须承担的，但在实践中，法院适用外国法的困难程度远远超过适用内国法，这是不难想象的。在各国审理涉外民商案件时，查知和适用外国法甚至成为顺利解决争议的最大障碍。[①] 因此，各国法院都有共同心理，在不影响法律适用合理性情况下，尽可能适用内国法，这样可以免去查证外国法的困难，提高争议解决效率。所以，不顾及法律适用的合理性和可行性，认为在确定选法协议效力方面适用当事人所选之法较适用法院地法更可行，显然不够客观。

第二，如前所述，在合同以外的领域，如侵权、动产物权、协议离婚、遗嘱继承等领域，当事人为法律关系所选择的法律不具有确定选法协议效力的内容，如果法院仍然遵守“选法协议效力适用当事人选择的法律”的规则，就必须在当事人选择的法律中寻找可以确定选法协议效力的规定。这样，一方面会给法院造成更多一层查证和适用外国法的困难，另一方面也严重违背了意思自治原则的宗旨。可见，在合同以外领域适用当事人所选之法确定选法协议效力的做法，其合理性和可行性无论如何不会高于适用法院地法。

（四）原告挑选法院的担忧

主张选法协议效力适用当事人选择的法律的论者还提出一个理由：如果适用法院地法确定选法协议的效力，会促使原告挑选其法律能够确定选法协议有效的国家的法院起诉，这种挑选法院的行为会对被告产生不公平的后果。[②] 这种担忧似乎没有必要。

根据自己的利益需求来决定选择在哪个国家的法院起诉，本就是原告

① 参见沈涓《中国法院审理涉外（涉港澳台）民商案件情况》，载黄东黎主编《国际法研究》第 8 卷，社会科学文献出版社，2013，第 345 页以下。

② 参见许军珂《国际私法中的意思自治》，法律出版社，2007，第 145 页；韩德培主编《国际私法新论》，武汉大学出版社，1997，第 296 页。

的自由和权利，他没有义务顾及被告的利益需求而选择在对被告有利的国家法院起诉。更何况，原告的起诉并不能最终确定管辖权，受诉法院是否对案件实行管辖，还必须由该受诉法院的相关法律确定。如果受诉法院根据内国相关法律，认为不应或不能对案件实行管辖，那么它将拒绝受理原告的诉求。这时，即使原告选择在该法院起诉是因为可以期望适用该法院地法确定选法协议的效力，也会因为受诉法院的拒绝而不能得逞。如果受诉法院依法确定了对案件的管辖权，就表明管辖权的正当性与原告的期望一致，原告挑选法院的意愿就无可厚非。可见，无论原告选择起诉法院的意图善或不善，对法院管辖权的确定及法律选择和适用都不具有决定性影响，法院管辖权对被告是否公平并不由原告决定，原告挑选法院理应不受质疑。

（五）当事人对选法协议效力和合同效力的合理预期

在主张选法协议效力适用当事人选择的法律的观点看来，还有一个理由可以支持这一主张，即当事人选择了某国法律，就是希望依据该法律来确定合同效力和选法协议效力，因此，他们在选择了准据法之后就可以预见选法协议效力和合同效力的结果，如果适用法院地法确定选法协议效力，就会因为无法在缔结合同时预知未来受理争议解决的法院而无法预见选法协议效力和合同效力的结果。由此得出的结论是：只有适用当事人选择的法律而不是法院地法来确定选法协议的效力才是可行的。[①] 这样的理由和结论或许因为理解的偏差而说服力不足。

第一，对法律选择和法律适用结果预见性低是国际私法的固有缺陷，根源于国际私法规则不直接确定法律关系中的权利义务。无论依据什么样的原则和规则调整法律冲突，对涉外或国际民商关系而言，国际私法规则或原则都不能使当事人明确预见他们之间法律关系的结果。提高预见性只是国际私法追求的目标，而不是国际私法规则适用的必然效果。

第二，如果说适用法院地法确定选法协议效力缺乏对结果的预见性，

① 参见许军珂《国际私法中的意思自治》，法律出版社，2007，第 145 页；韩德培主编《国际私法新论》，武汉大学出版社，1997，第 296 页；肖永平《国际私法原理》，法律出版社，2003，第 177 页；李良鸿、郑发国《法律选择协议相关问题研究》，《浙江万里学院学报》2006 年第 4 期；孙维星《涉外合同中法律选择条款的法律适用》，《法制与社会》2007 年第 7 期。

那么，也许还可以考虑另一种影响法律适用结果预见性的情况，即法官裁量。现代国际私法为提高法律选择的灵活性和法律适用的合理性，都赋予法官较大裁量权，这种选择法律和适用法律的权力要远大于当事人选择法律的权利。虽然现代国际私法立法和司法都主张限制法官裁量权的滥用，为法官裁量设置了合理和有效的标准，但法官裁量仍然在现代国际私法实践中发挥着重大作用。同时，法官裁量也成为当事人预见法律适用结果的较大障碍，因为灵活性是法官裁量的核心价值，虽有成规，但法官裁量的特殊作用在于选择法律时因人而异、因事而异。值得注意的是，法官裁量制度现在受到越来越多的重视和采行，这种趋势并没有因为这项制度影响了法律适用结果的可预见性而减缓。可见，相比法律选择和法律适用的合理性和有效性，法律适用结果的可预见性的需求更小。

第三，认为适用法院地法确定选法协议效力缺乏对结果的预见性，主要是认为无法预知最终会由何国法院受理案件，即无法预见选法协议效力最终会适用哪一国法律。但这一后果的危害性也许并非如想象中那么严重。首先，在很多情况下，当事人在选择了法律关系准据法的同时，也作出了法院管辖权选择，双方在法律关系开始时就已经明知法院地法的指向，在“选法协议效力适用法院地法”规则下，当事人自然可以预知法律适用的结果。其次，各国可以取得共识，将“选法协议效力适用法院地法”演变成通则，就如“合同适用当事人选择的法律”已被演变为通则一样。在当事人了解并遵行“合同适用当事人选择的法律”规则时，同时也能了解“选法协议效力适用法院地法”这一规则，便可促使当事人在法律关系开始时就一并达成法律选择和管辖权选择两方面协议，以提高对选法协议效力和法律关系法律适用结果的预见性。

在对与法律选择和法律适用的可行性可能相关的几方面问题进行辩释后，可以认为，声称选法协议效力适用当事人选择的法律较之适用法院地法更具可行性，显然不够客观，也不够理性。相应的，适用法院地法确定当事人选法协议的效力，符合选法协议是法律选择规则的本质的认定，可以避免不适当适用外国法的情况，也解决了合同领域之外的其他领域无法适用当事人选择的法律来确定选法协议效力的难题，无疑更具可行性。

（本文原载于《法学研究》2015 年第 6 期）

国际商事仲裁裁决撤销制度“废弃论”之批判

谢新胜*

一　问题的提出

有学者认为，在国际商事仲裁中，由于仲裁地的选择往往具有偶然性，与当事人的实际关系不大，仲裁地法院对仲裁裁决本身并没有多少实际利益，而且仲裁裁决的撤销制度方便当事人拖延仲裁执行的时间，损害了仲裁的优越性，更违背当事人意思自治原则。因而，撤销裁决本身没有任何法律后果，裁决的撤销制度也就没有存在的必要。仲裁地法院没有必要非得对仲裁程序进行干预。只有在仲裁裁决的执行阶段，法院的司法监督才是必要的。因为仲裁程序的最终目标是仲裁裁决得到履行或为法院所承认与执行。当事人的利益体现在仲裁裁决的执行上。只有在执行阶段，用国内立法对仲裁加以控制才是与仲裁程序相关的一个因素。① 一言以蔽之，由于国际商事仲裁裁决撤销制度（以下简称仲裁裁决撤销制度）相对国际商事仲裁裁决承认与执行制度（以下简称仲裁裁决承认与执行制度）而言没有任何优势，在理论上仲裁不受仲裁地法院的司法监督，实践中已

---

* 谢新胜，2007 年 7 月来中国社会科学院法学研究所工作，曾任副研究员，2012 年 7 月调离。

① 参见 J. Paulson, Arbitration Unbound: Award Detached from the Law of Its Country of Origin International and Comparative Law Quarterly, 1981 (2)；郭玉军、陈芝兰《论国际商事仲裁中的“非国内化”理论》，《法制与社会发展》2003 年第 1 期。

被撤销的仲裁裁决仍然可以获得法院的承认与执行，仲裁地法院对仲裁裁决的司法监督已显得无足轻重，完全可以由仲裁裁决执行阶段的司法监督所取代，因此仲裁裁决撤销制度没有独特功能，理应废弃。

笔者认为，上述这种针对仲裁裁决撤销制度的“废弃论”（以下简称“废弃论”）只看见了仲裁裁决撤销制度的弊端，没有看见其存在的基本意义，而且对仲裁的当事人意思自治原则存在重大误解在实践中是有害的，值得商榷。

二 “废弃论”的理论批判：从功能到原则

（一）仲裁裁决撤销制度的独特功能：主动救济

虽然仲裁制度是以当事人意思自治原则为核心的一种争议解决方式，但国家的司法干预是仲裁裁决得以履行的后盾，毕竟并非所有败诉方均能自觉履行仲裁裁决，难免会有当事人对仲裁裁决不服，期望寻求司法救济。从这个意义上说，对仲裁裁决的司法监督不可或缺。仲裁裁决承认与执行制度和仲裁裁决撤销制度是法院对仲裁裁决进行司法监督的两种基本方式。然而，在“废弃论”者看来，仲裁裁决承认与执行制度的功能可以完全取代仲裁裁决撤销制度的功能，仲裁裁决撤销制度没有必要存在。

殊不知，仲裁裁决承认与执行制度在仲裁败诉方不自动履行仲裁裁决义务时只能为胜诉方提供不充分的司法救济，并不能替代仲裁裁决撤销制度为双方当事人提供主动救济。由于申请执行仲裁裁决的当事人必然是仲裁胜诉方，因此对败诉方而言，法院不予执行仲裁裁决是一种被动救济，且只有在胜诉方提出执行申请而且法院受理后才能启动。对此，国际上并没有什么争议，但在国内仲裁界，曾有学者认为当事人可以独立发起仲裁裁决的不予执行程序。实际上，只有一方当事人提出仲裁裁决执行程序，另一方当事人才能向法院主张不予执行仲裁裁决。如果没有仲裁裁决的执行申请作为前提，就谈不上仲裁裁决的不予执行。例如，《中华人民共和国仲裁法》（以下简称《仲裁法》）第 62 条规定：“当事人应当履行裁决，一方当事人不履行的，另一方当事人可以依照民事诉讼法的有关规定向人民法院申请执行，受申请的人民法院应当执行。”紧接着第 63 条规定：

“被申请人提出证据证明裁决有民事诉讼法第217条第2款规定的情形之一的，经人民法院组成合议庭审查核实，裁定不予执行。”从逻辑上看，申请人申请执行仲裁程序在先，被申请人提出不予执行的抗辩在后，秩序不可紊乱。《最高人民法院关于适用〈中华人民共和国仲裁法〉若干问题的解释》第26条规定得更为清晰：“当事人向人民法院申请撤销仲裁裁决被驳回后，又在执行程序中以相同理由提出不予执行抗辩的，人民法院不予支持。”这一条规定清楚地说明当事人提出不予执行仲裁裁决的抗辩只能在仲裁裁决执行程序中提出，如果胜诉方不提起仲裁裁决的执行程序，所谓仲裁裁决的不予执行就只能是无源之水、无本之木。

相对于仲裁裁决不予执行程序的被动性，仲裁裁决撤销程序则能主动为仲裁双方当事人提供救济：胜诉方在仲裁请求没有得到充分支持时，可以启动仲裁裁决撤销程序；败诉方则可因其仲裁败诉或仲裁庭裁决有误，同样提出撤销仲裁裁决的申请。一旦废弃仲裁裁决撤销制度，对胜诉方而言，如果对仲裁裁决作出的赔偿数额不满，则将无法寻求司法救济。因为胜诉方一旦提起仲裁裁决的执行程序，就应视其为认同仲裁裁决的结果，执行法院只能执行仲裁裁决，不可能给予其更多的司法救济；若胜诉方不提起仲裁裁决的执行程序，他可能连仲裁裁决所赋予的“不充分”利益也无法实现。对败诉方而言，一旦废弃仲裁裁决撤销制度，他将无法主动寻求使仲裁裁决归于无效的途径，而只能被动受制于胜诉方在任何时间、任何地点发起的执行仲裁裁决程序。这就使败诉方与胜诉方之间的法律关系处于无法预料的不稳定状态，不利于保护败诉方的利益。这种弊端在败诉方财产分布在数个国家时表现得尤其明显。因为只要胜诉方不断地挑选执行法院并提出执行申请，败诉方就不得不断地以同一理由提出抗辩，完全跟着胜诉方的指挥棒起舞。只要有一国法院支持了胜诉方的仲裁裁决执行申请，其他国家法院的不予执行决定即纯属具文。“法国南方铁路电气公司诉南斯拉夫案”就是一个典型例子。虽然该案仲裁裁决早于1956年就作出了，但直到1986年当事人还在申请仲裁裁决的执行，其原因就在于被申请人在多国拥有财产。而仲裁裁决被仲裁地国瑞士认为不是依瑞士法作出的，因而不是瑞士的裁决，而是无国籍裁决，没有一个国家的法院有权撤销该裁决。[①] 可见，胜诉方即使在一国申请

① 参见宋连斌《国际商事仲裁管辖权研究》，法律出版社，2000，第246页。

执行仲裁裁决失败，他在其他国家仍可试图实现裁决利益，败诉方则对此无能为力。之所以出现这种情况，其根本原因即在于仲裁裁决承认与执行制度缺乏为当事人提供主动救济的功能。因此，无视仲裁裁决撤销制度所具有的独特的为当事人提供主动救济的功能，废除仲裁裁决撤销制度，既可能使胜诉方在胜诉的情况下“有口难言”，也可能导致败诉方受制于胜诉方申请执行仲裁裁决权利的行使，纯属“两面不讨好”的不智举措。

（二）当事人意思自治原则的体现：法律意义上的仲裁地法院对仲裁裁决的司法监督

“废弃论”的另一个论据在于，仲裁地的选择具有偶然性，难以反映当事人的真实意思，从而使仲裁地法院对仲裁裁决的司法监督缺乏足够的合法性与合理性。[①] 因为仲裁作为解决争议的手段，通常无须法院的介入与干预。如果当事人或案件与仲裁地无关，仲裁地就没有理由要求仲裁程序适用仲裁地的强制性规定，仲裁地法院也没必要必须对仲裁程序进行干预。[②] 总而言之，仲裁裁决不受仲裁地法院的控制，否则即有违反仲裁之当事人意思自治原则之嫌。

然而，仲裁地有地理意义上的仲裁地与法律意义上的仲裁地之分。现代国际商事仲裁中的仲裁地概念应为法律意义上的仲裁地。地理意义上的仲裁地通常是纯属偶然或出于中立的考虑而确定的，往往由其他一些因素如平等、适当、方便、裁决的执行等所决定，而非出于适用仲裁地的仲裁法或受仲裁地司法监督的考虑。法律意义上的仲裁地则通常是由当事人在仲裁协议中作出的专门约定，或当事人约定适用的仲裁规则作出的专门规定，它的确定是极为慎重的。在国际商事仲裁实践中，当仲裁地被确定后，仲裁庭可以选择在仲裁地点以外的国家和地区的任何适当的地点开庭审理仲裁案件，或者进行合议，甚至作出裁决。这些开庭审理地、合议地及仲裁裁决作出地即为地理意义上的仲裁地。由于较少体现当事人的意

---

① 参见郭玉军、陈芝兰《论国际商事仲裁中的“非国内化”理论》，《法制与社会发展》2003年第1期。

② 参见郭玉军、陈芝兰《论国际商事仲裁中的“非国内化”理论》，《法制与社会发展》2003年第1期。

思且偶然性较大，由此地理意义上的仲裁地法院撤销仲裁裁决当然不甚合理；而法律意义上的仲裁地是当事人意思自治的结果，选择仲裁地是当事人选择仲裁程序法的主要途径，也表明当事人有意将他们之间的仲裁置于仲裁地的法律监督与支持之下。[①] 简言之，仲裁裁决是受到法律意义上仲裁地监督的，仲裁地法院撤销仲裁裁决并不缺乏法律依据，也不违反当事人意思自治原则。例如，1996 年《英国仲裁法》第 3 条就规定："本编所称之'仲裁地'指通过下述方式之一指定的法律意义上的仲裁地：（a）仲裁协议的当事人选定，或（b）经全体当事人授权决定仲裁地之仲裁机构、其他机构或个人决定，或（c）经当事人授权的仲裁庭决定，或未作上述指定时，经考虑当事人的协议及所有相关因素后予以确定。"第 53 条规定："除非当事人有约定……裁决……视为根据第 3 条规定所确定的'仲裁地'作出。"由此可见，1996 年《英国仲裁法》对仲裁地的确定并不考虑仲裁进行的实际地点，而完全取决于当事人的直接或间接意思，仲裁地在英国的仲裁裁决受 1996 年《英国仲裁法》的支配。

法律意义上的仲裁地概念不仅为素以仲裁法属地色彩浓厚的 1996 年《英国仲裁法》接受，也广为其他国家仲裁立法所接受。例如，《瑞典仲裁法》第 47 条规定："本法中的仲裁地在瑞典是指仲裁协议约定仲裁在瑞典进行或仲裁庭或被授权之仲裁员决定仲裁地在瑞典，或者对方当事人同意此点。在其他情形下，仲裁地不在瑞典。"《荷兰民事诉讼法》第 1037 条规定："仲裁地由当事人间的仲裁协议决定，或没有约定，由仲裁庭决定。"《保加利亚国际商事仲裁法》第 1 条规定："本法适用于根据仲裁协议仲裁地点在保加利亚人民共和国境内进行的国际商事仲裁。"《比利时司法法典》第 1693 条规定："当事人的协议确定仲裁程序规则和仲裁地；如其在仲裁庭规定的期限内未达成协议，应由仲裁庭确定；如当事人和仲裁员均未确定仲裁地，裁决载明之裁决作出地应视为仲裁地。"可见，法律意义上的仲裁地正是当事人实现仲裁程序自治的主要途径，现代仲裁法的程序自治也多是通过选择仲裁地进而选择仲裁地程序法对仲裁裁决实施包括撤销在内的司法干预来实现的，仲裁地对仲裁裁决的控制自然顺理成

---

① 参见赵秀文《论法律意义上的仲裁地点及其确定》，《时代法学》2005 年第 1 期。

章。[1] 这种法律意义上仲裁地的适用并不减损国际商事仲裁当事人意思自治原则的核心价值，因为仲裁“当事人可以自由采纳其希望的几乎任何程序规则，仲裁地法律越来越倾向于支持仲裁程序并尽可能少地干预仲裁程序”。[2] 例如，1996 年《英国仲裁法》第 4 条、1998 年《德国民事诉讼法典》第 1042 条第 3 款、《联合国国际商事仲裁示范法》第 19 条都规定在不违反立法强制性规则的情况下，当事各方可就仲裁庭进行仲裁所应遵循的程序自由地达成协议，从而赋予当事人在仲裁程序塑造方面广泛、充分的自治权。

对于法律意义上的仲裁地取代地理意义上的仲裁地的情形，早有权威学者归纳道：“在人们说伦敦、巴黎或日内瓦是仲裁地时，并不仅仅是在提及某一个地理位置。人们指的是，仲裁是在英国、法国或瑞士的仲裁法律框架内进行。”[3] 从这个角度看，国际商事仲裁不可能与仲裁地的利益无关，而且这种利益关系正是通过当事人对仲裁地选择的意思自治来实现的。虽然在理论上，不少学者出于批驳“仲裁国内化理论”的需要，对仲裁地法的适用多少有贬抑的倾向，似乎实现仲裁的当事人意思自治就非要与适用仲裁地法势不两立。然而，现代仲裁立法和司法实践的发展表明，传统地理意义上的仲裁地已不再是仲裁地法得以适用的主要连接因素，法律意义上仲裁地概念已广泛渗入当事人的主观态度，在很大程度上使客观连接点的稳定性与主观连接点的灵活性得以有效平衡，法律意义上的仲裁地作为决定仲裁程序法适用的连接因素在仲裁立法中的作用并未显著降低。

三 “废弃论”的实践批判：导致败诉方丧失向司法寻求公正的机会

“废弃论”的一个恶果是可能导致国际商事仲裁的当事人在败诉后无

---

① 参见 Georgios Petrochios, *Procedure Law in International Arbitration*, Oxford University Press 2003, p. 118。

② 参见〔英〕艾伦·雷德芬等《国际商事仲裁法律与实践》，林一飞、宋连斌译，北京大学出版社，2005，第 91 页。

③ 参见〔英〕艾伦·雷德芬等《国际商事仲裁法律与实践》，林一飞、宋连斌译，北京大学出版社，2005，第 98 页。

法寻求对仲裁裁决的司法审查，从而丧失向司法寻求公证的机会。根据仲裁标的之性质和内容，仲裁请求也有给付请求与确认请求的区别。仲裁标的之性质和内容反映或决定了仲裁申请人请求仲裁庭给予保护的具体形式。具体来说，申请人提起给付请求旨在获得给付裁决，提起确认请求旨在获得确认裁决。然而在确认请求中，仲裁裁决的履行并不需要依靠法院对仲裁裁决的承认与执行，只要仲裁庭确认了胜诉方的请求，胜诉方就可以合法的私力实现裁决结果，无须再提起执行仲裁裁决的申请。因此，在胜诉方未向法院提起执行仲裁裁决申请的情形下，败诉方相当于丧失了主张仲裁裁决不可执行的机会，即无法寻求被动救济。由于法院对仲裁裁决的司法审查是通过仲裁裁决的承认与执行程序或仲裁裁决的撤销程序来实现的，因此败诉方在不可能提出仲裁裁决不予执行的抗辩时，如果不承认仲裁地法院撤销仲裁裁决的效力并废弃仲裁裁决撤销制度，那么无异于使其彻底丧失抗辩仲裁裁决效力的机会。广为关注的“百事仲裁案”[①] 是这一情形的最佳注脚。

在“百事仲裁案”中，四川韵律公司（以下简称四川韵律）与美国百事公司于 1993 年确定合作关系并设立四川百事公司（以下简称四川百事），2002 年 8 月 2 日美国百事公司和百事（中国）投资有限公司（以下简称百事中国）以四川韵律和四川百事严重违反合同、侵犯其合法权益为由，向瑞典斯德哥尔摩商会（以下简称瑞典商会）仲裁院提起仲裁申请，请求裁决终止上述四公司分别签署的《中美合作四川百事可乐饮料有限公司合作经营合同》、《商标许可合同》和《浓缩液供应协议》并解散合作公司四川百事。瑞典商会仲裁院受理了这一仲裁申请，并于 2003 年 8 月 7 日作出初步裁决，裁定瑞典商会仲裁院对以美国百事公司为一方当事人、四川韵律为另一方当事人的有关合作经营合同的案件不具有管辖权，对以百事中国为一方当事人、四川百事为另一方当事人的有关《商标许可合同》和《浓缩液供应合协议》的案件有管辖权。该案经仲裁庭审理于 2005 年 1 月 26 日作出裁决。仲裁庭以四川百事“不配合检查”和“跨区销售”为由，裁决终止《商标许可合同》和《浓缩液供应协议》，并全部驳回四

① 参见邹晓乔《浅析四川百事合作经营合同仲裁案中的几个法律问题》，《北京仲裁》2006 年第 1 期。

川百事的反请求。仲裁裁决作出后，百事中国自行终止了《商标许可合同》和《浓缩液供应协议》，四川百事陷于停产状态。仲裁庭对该案作出裁决后，四川百事对仲裁裁决在合并仲裁及仲裁员公正性等方面提出质疑，并在四川省国有资产监督管理委员会的支持下，向四川省成都市中级人民法院提出撤销仲裁裁决的申请。

需要说明的是，对仲裁裁决的撤销而言，一国法院仅对在本国作出的仲裁裁决或以本国法律为仲裁程序准据法的仲裁裁决才享有撤销权。这既符合《承认及执行外国仲裁裁决公约》的规定，也是一条普遍的国际准则。既然中国不是“百事仲裁案”的仲裁地，中国仲裁法也未支配“百事仲裁案”的仲裁程序，那么中国法院就无权撤销仲裁地在瑞典的仲裁裁决。至于向中国法院申请不予承认与执行仲裁裁决，作为权利的确认请求也同样无法操作。因为对于仲裁裁决，胜诉方在胜诉后即意味着自己的权利得到确认，其对权利的实现处于主导地位，完全可以自己执行仲裁裁决，而无须法院公权力的介入。只有在败诉方部分或全部不履行裁决义务时，胜诉方才须申请执行地法院予以承认和强制执行仲裁裁决。在“百事仲裁案”中，百事中国终止浓缩液供应的行为就是一种私力执行裁决的行为，此时并不涉及中国法院对仲裁裁决的承认和执行问题。然而，四川百事只有在胜诉方提起申请承认与执行仲裁裁决的前提下，才能被动地要求执行地法院不予执行仲裁裁决，否则其没有机会提起不予执行仲裁裁决的抗辩。从这个角度看，由于“百事仲裁案”的胜诉方未向法院申请仲裁裁决的承认与执行，因此四川百事即使在仲裁中遭受不公正待遇，也无法从执行地法院对仲裁裁决的司法监督中获得任何司法救济。而如果依照“弃废论”，由于作为胜诉方的百事中国完全依靠私力救济即可获得仲裁裁决的结果，其不会在任何国家申请承认与执行该案仲裁裁决，因此四川百事没有机会主张不予执行该案仲裁裁决。再加上向仲裁地法院主动提起撤销仲裁裁决已不可能，即使蒙受不白之冤，四川百事的司法救济之路已被彻底堵死。由此不难发现，执行地法院对仲裁裁决的司法监督无法取代仲裁地法院对仲裁裁决的司法监督，其对仲裁裁决的执行审查也达不到撤销审查那样的效果。“废弃论”在某种程度上也就等于拒绝为败诉方提供司法救济，使败诉方失去向司法寻求公正的机会。

四 “废弃论”的比较法批判：已被撤销的仲裁裁决难以得到法院的承认与执行

“废弃论”的另一个论据在于，由于国际上已经出现被撤销的国际商事仲裁裁决仍获得法院承认与执行的案例，因此仲裁裁决撤销制度就没有存在的必要。① 在“废弃论”者看来，由于仲裁地法院撤销仲裁裁决并不妨碍其他国家法院对该仲裁裁决的承认与执行，因此仲裁裁决撤销制度在根本上不能产生什么效果，仲裁地法院对仲裁裁决的司法监督自然形同虚设，最终废弃仲裁裁决撤销制度也就顺理成章。② 这一判断是否符合国际商事仲裁在各国的基本实践，需要进行全面的考察。

（一）法国实践：自相矛盾

不可否认，法国不仅是执行已被撤销国际商事仲裁裁决的先行者，而且是真正在立法和司法实践中全面贯彻这一仲裁理念的国家。《法国民事诉讼法典》第1502条规定：“法国法院仅因以下原因方能拒绝承认与执行一项外国仲裁裁决：仲裁员作出裁决时没有仲裁协议或虽有仲裁协议但该仲裁协议无效或失效；仲裁庭的组成或独任仲裁员的指定不合规定；仲裁员所作裁决超越权限；仲裁员未遵守正当程序；承认与执行仲裁裁决违反国际公共政策。”由此可见，法国法律在面对一项承认与执行外国仲裁裁决的请求时，并不理会仲裁地国对仲裁裁决效力的界定。

基于《法国民事诉讼法典》第1502条的规定，法国法院在执行已被他国法院撤销的仲裁裁决时，屡有惊人之举，目前已在1993年“波兰远洋运输公司诉乔娜斯丽案”、③ 1993年“优利克斯福公司诉热斯农公司案”④ 及1997年“希尔马顿公司诉奥姆排水技术公司案”⑤（以下简称

---

① 参见J. Paulsson，Arbitration Unbound：Award Detached from the Law of Its Country of Origin International and Comparative Law Quarterly，1981（2）。

② 参见江仁所《论已撤销国际商事仲裁裁决的承认和执行》，硕士学位论文，华东政法大学国际法学院，2005，第76页。

③ 参见 *Polish Ocean Line v. Jolasy*，Cass Civ lre 10 March 1993（1993）120 JDI 360。

④ 参见 *Unichps v. Gesnouin*，Paris 12 February 1993，［1993］Rev. Arb 255。

⑤ 参见赵秀文《国际商事仲裁及其适用法律研究》，北京大学出版社，2002，第217页。

“希尔马顿公司案”）等几个案件中执行了已被撤销的仲裁裁决，其中“希尔马顿公司案”最为著名。在“希尔马顿公司案”中，希尔马顿公司主动将其与奥姆技术排水公司的咨询合同争议提交国际商会仲裁院依国际商会仲裁规则仲裁，但仲裁庭随即裁决希尔马顿公司败诉。希尔马顿公司对此不服，随后向瑞士日内瓦上诉法院申请撤销仲裁裁决。经过瑞士日内瓦上诉法院与瑞士最高法院的两审裁判，仲裁裁决最终得以撤销。尽管该案仲裁裁决已被瑞士法院撤销，但奥姆排水技术公司仍向法国法院申请承认与执行该仲裁裁决，对此法国巴黎初审法院作出执行仲裁裁决的判决。于是，希尔马顿公司又上诉至法国巴黎上诉法院，法国巴黎上诉法院维持了法国巴黎初审法院作出的执行仲裁裁决的判决；最后经法国最高法院终审，执行仲裁裁决的原判得到维持。在法国法院看来，国际商会仲裁院对“希尔马顿公司案”作出的仲裁裁决是国际裁决，它并未融入仲裁地国的法律秩序。[①] 因此，尽管仲裁裁决被仲裁地法院撤销，但效力仍然存在。令人难以理解的是，“希尔马顿公司案”在仲裁裁决经瑞士法院撤销后又依瑞士法进行了重新仲裁。这一次希尔马顿公司胜诉，后来法国法院又执行了希尔马顿公司胜诉的仲裁裁决。

如此一来，针对同一案件，完全矛盾的两个仲裁裁决在法国都得到了执行。对于法国的这种实践，德国学者范·登·伯格教授不无辛辣地讽刺道：“如果一项仲裁裁决在仲裁地被撤销的话，当事人或许可以到法国有意外的收获。”[②] 之所以这样说，是因为法国法院认为“国际商事仲裁裁决因为其国际性，虽不能融入仲裁地国国内法律秩序，却可融入执行国的法律秩序”。[③] 依此逻辑适用法国法并以法国为仲裁地的国际商事仲裁裁决[④]也同样不属于法国法律秩序的范畴。然而，值得注意的是，尽管法国不认可仲裁地法院撤销仲裁裁决的效力，但法国法律并未废弃仲裁裁决撤销制度。《法国民事诉讼法典》第 1504 条、第 1506 条不厌其烦地对仲裁裁决撤销制度作了具体规定。法国如此规定本身就是希望他国法院在承认和执

---

① 参见赵秀文《国际商事仲裁及其适用法律研究》，北京大学出版社，2002，第 217 页。

② Christopher R. Drahozal, “Enforcing Vacated International Arbitration Awards: An Economic Approach”, *American Review of International Arbitration* 2000 (2).

③ 参见 Georgios Petrochios, *Procedure Law in International Arbitration*, Oxford University Press 2003, p. 118。

④ 《法国民事诉讼法典》第 1494 条规定了一项仲裁裁决为“国际仲裁”裁决的标准。

行仲裁裁决时，考虑法国法院对仲裁裁决的司法审查。所以说，法国在撤销仲裁裁决的立法与司法实践上是矛盾的，它使仲裁裁决具有相当的不稳定性。因为在仲裁裁决被撤销后，当事人仍可到其他国家申请仲裁裁决的承认与执行，直到成功为止，这就使仲裁地法院对仲裁裁决的司法审查变得毫无意义。不仅如此，在此规定之下，仲裁裁决一旦被撤销，如果仲裁地法院指令重新仲裁，并且仲裁裁决与原有仲裁裁决结果相反，则相互矛盾的仲裁裁决在相同国家可以并行获得承认与执行。这种荒唐的结果无疑有违公平、正义的司法理念。

（二）美国实践：拒绝执行已被撤销的仲裁裁决

美国早在1998年“克罗依马罗依公司案”[①]中就有执行已被撤销的仲裁裁决的先例。不过，在其后的司法实践中，在“克罗依马罗依公司案”中形成的先例并未得到遵循。即使对于“克罗依马罗依公司案”，批评者也认为，法院执行已被撤销的仲裁裁决可能导致不同法院对相同的事项和相同当事人之间的仲裁裁决作出相互抵触的裁决，进而违反国际商事仲裁程序所试图建立的统一性；其所产生的负面影响是人们对美国法院执行外国仲裁裁决的政策日趋怀疑，并形成这样的印象——美国法院对外国仲裁裁决实行不稳定的“挑拣政策”。[②] 或许是受这些批评的影响，美国法院在接下来的判例中采取了与“克罗依马罗依公司案”不同的做法。

在1999年“贝克公司案”[③]中，贝克公司因对方当事人违反合同而将争议提交仲裁地在尼日利亚的仲裁庭解决，而后仲裁庭裁决贝克公司胜诉。但是，败诉方向尼日利亚法院申请撤销仲裁裁决并得到法院支持。于是，贝克公司转而到美国申请执行仲裁裁决。最终，美国联邦第二巡回法院裁定，贝克公司没有充分理由拒绝承认尼日利亚法院撤销仲裁裁决的效力。

在2007年“特莫里奥公司诉爱特兰提科电气化公司案”[④]（以下简称“特莫里奥公司案”）中，爱特兰提科电气化公司与特莫里奥公司订立了一

---

① 参见 *Chromally Aeroservice v. Egypt*, 939 F. Supp. 907（DDC 1996）。

② 参见赵秀文《国际商事仲裁及其适用法律研究》，北京大学出版社，2002，第243页。

③ 参见 *Baker Marine（Njg.）Ltd. v. Chevron（Nig.）Ltd.*, 191 F. 3rd 194（2d Cir. 1999）。

④ 参见 *Term Rio S. A. v. Eletrana S. P.*, 487 F. 3rd 928（C. A. D. C. 2007）。

项电力买卖合同。后双方因买方爱特兰提科电气化公司违反合同义务引起争议，卖方特莫里奥公司根据电力买卖合同中的仲裁条款提起仲裁。最后仲裁庭裁决特莫里奥公司胜诉，要求爱特兰提科电气化公司赔偿超过6000万英镑的损失。对此，爱特兰提科电气化公司向哥伦比亚一家法院申请撤销仲裁裁决。哥伦比亚最高行政法院以当事人合同中的仲裁条款违反了哥伦比亚法为由，撤销了仲裁裁决。之后特莫里奥公司向美国联邦华盛顿地区法院申请要求执行仲裁裁决。美国联邦华盛顿地区法院驳回了特莫里奥公司的执行申请。而后特莫里奥公司上诉至美国联邦上诉法院华盛顿巡回法院，该法院维持了美国联邦华盛顿地区法院的判决并指出：仲裁裁决被仲裁地法院依法撤销的，根据《美国联邦仲裁法》或《承认及执行外国仲裁裁决公约》的规定，特莫里奥公司的执行申请不能得到支持，否则败诉方将非常可能遭遇胜诉方在一个又一个国家提起的申请仲裁裁决执行的诉讼，直到有国家准允这一执行申请。[①]

美国是判例法国家，法院审判一般遵循先例，但“贝克公司案”和“特莫里奥公司案”并未遵循“克罗依马罗依公司案”所确立的先例。这虽然不能说明美国法院完全推翻了“克罗依马罗依公司案”的先例，但至少可以表示美国法院倾向于对“克罗依马罗依公司案”判决的效力作出限制，只是将“克罗依马罗依公司案”作为一种严格的例外，其中维护美国的利益成为美国法院考虑的重要因素。

（三）其他国家实践：基本排除已被撤销的仲裁裁决的可执行性

我国对于已被撤销的国际商事仲裁裁决是否可以执行的问题，态度非常鲜明。根据最高人民法院《关于执行我国加入的〈承认及执行外国仲裁裁决公约〉的通知》的规定，在《承认及执行外国仲裁裁决公约》范围内的裁决，如果被执行人有证据证明仲裁裁决具有《承认及执行外国仲裁裁决公约》第5条第1款中的5种情形之一，法院“应当”裁定驳回申请，拒绝承认和执行。因此，如果仲裁裁决已被仲裁地法院撤销，我国法院将拒绝承认与执行。此外，根据1998年《德国民事诉讼法典》第1061条的

---

① 参见〔西班牙〕帕德罗·马丁内兹－弗拉加《国际商事仲裁——美国学说发展与证据开示》，蒋小红、谢新胜等译，中国社会科学出版社，2009，第137—149页。

规定，外国仲裁裁决的承认与执行的条件应完全与《承认及执行外国仲裁裁决公约》保持一致，而且即使仲裁裁决被德国法院宣告执行后在外国被撤销，当事人仍可向法院提出撤销其所作出的执行仲裁裁决的裁定。可见，已被撤销的仲裁裁决在德国不能得到执行。英国目前还没有承认与执行已被撤销的国际商事仲裁裁决的案例。一般认为，英国法从不承认仲裁程序可以脱离任何国家的法律制度而独立存在，也就是说，仲裁裁决不可能是浮动裁决。在英国法看来，仲裁程序法一般为仲裁地国的法律，当事人对仲裁地的选择极为重要。它意味着仲裁应当遵守该地的法律，而仲裁地法院也有权对在当地进行的仲裁进行司法监督。[①] 可以说，英国法认为国际商事仲裁应完全融入仲裁地的法律秩序并受仲裁地法律支配。由此可以推论，在英国，仲裁地法院对仲裁裁决的司法监督是必要的，仲裁地法院撤销仲裁裁决的行为将得到英国法院的尊重。由此不难发现，在大多数国家，基本排除已被撤销的仲裁裁决的可执行性。

五　结语：仲裁裁决撤销制度在坚持中完善

不可否认，在某些情况下，少数当事人可能利用法院对仲裁裁决的司法监督恶意拖延裁决执行时间，甚至使仲裁裁决无法在他国得以顺利执行。但是，这仅是改善仲裁裁决撤销制度的理由，而非对其“一棍子打死”的借口。事实上，针对仲裁裁决撤销制度带来的程序拖延问题，晚近一些国家的仲裁法在仲裁裁决撤销制度上作了不少修改，使撤销仲裁裁决的理由受到更多限制，完善了仲裁裁决撤销制度。例如，有的国家通过提高仲裁裁决审级的办法来预防当事人动辄提起仲裁裁决撤销申请，如1987年《瑞士联邦国际私法法典》规定，撤销仲裁裁决的申请只能向联邦最高法院提出，由此提高了受理撤销仲裁裁决之诉法院的审级，增加了当事人申请撤销仲裁裁决的难度和成本。[②] 又如，还有的国家在仲裁裁决撤销制度中明确规定“禁止反言”规则，规定当事人在仲裁过程中对仲裁协议的

① 参见赵秀文《国际商事仲裁及其适用法律研究》，北京大学出版社，2002，第110页。

② 参见〔英〕艾伦·雷德芬等《国际商事仲裁法律与实践》，林一飞、宋连斌译，北京大学出版社，2005，第123页。

形式、仲裁庭的组成、管辖权及仲裁程序等方面提出了异议且法院对此作出初步决定或者法院对仲裁庭的初步决定已进行过复审，那么在后来的法院撤销仲裁裁决程序中，当事人不能再以相同的理由向法院申请撤销仲裁裁决。[①]“禁止反言”规则在国际仲裁立法中广泛存在，如《国际商事仲裁示范法》第4条、1996年《英国仲裁法》第73条、1998年《德国民事诉讼法典》第1072条等都有此规定。一般来说，仲裁程序开始后，有权审查仲裁庭裁定的法院就是仲裁地法院。因此，仲裁程序中如已存在仲裁地法院所作的裁定，仲裁裁决作出后当事人以同一理由要求仲裁地法院撤销仲裁裁决是没有道理的，通常是一种恶意拖延仲裁执行的行为。因为同一国法院正常情况下不可能撤销已生效的法院裁定，或者作出相互矛盾的裁定。[②] 我国的仲裁立法也吸收了这一先进立法经验，《最高人民法院适用〈中华人民共和国仲裁法〉若干问题的解释》第27条规定：“当事人在仲裁程序中未对仲裁协议的效力提出异议，在仲裁裁决作出后以仲裁协议无效为由主张撤销仲裁裁决或者提出不予执行抗辩的，人民法院不予支持。”第26条则规定：“当事人向人民法院申请撤销仲裁裁决被驳回后，又在执行程序中以相同理由提出不予执行抗辩的，人民法院不予支持。”这一规定一方面禁止当事人以未在仲裁程序中提出的理由作为撤销仲裁裁决的诉由，另一方面则将法院对仲裁裁决的双重监督程序予以简化。如果当事人在仲裁裁决撤销程序中败诉，则其不得以相同理由进行不予承认与执行仲裁裁决的抗辩，这在一定程度上防止了当事人滥用仲裁裁决撤销程序拖延仲裁裁决的执行。再如，还有部分国家的立法则允许当事人通过意思自治的方式在不违反仲裁地强制性规则的情况下排除仲裁裁决撤销程序，如《瑞士联邦国际私法法典》第192条第1款就允许当事人通过协议排除瑞士法院对适用瑞士仲裁法的仲裁裁决撤销之权力等。

此外，还应注意的是，仲裁裁决撤销制度应遵循国际公共秩序，违反国际公共秩序的仲裁裁决撤销程序可能被他国法院认定为无效。在国际社会中，有些国际规则是保护国际社会的共同利益和维持国际社会所公认的公共道德标准的强行规则，仲裁地法院在撤销国际商事仲裁裁决时若违反

---

① 参见 Wilken and Villiers, *The Law of Waiver*, *Variation and Estoppel*, 2nd ed. , Oxford University Press 2003, p. 9。

② 参见宋连斌《国际商事仲裁管辖权研究》，法律出版社，2000，第246页。

这些强行规则，将构成对国际公共秩序的侵犯。例如，《公民与政治权利公约》第14条第1款规定："无论刑事指控抑或民事裁判，所有人应受合格法院之公平、公开、独立及毫无偏袒的审判。"《欧洲人权公约》第6条和《美洲人权公约》第8条也有类似规定。目前已有不少国家将"公平、公开以及独立的审判"作为仲裁地法院撤销国际商事仲裁裁决时应遵循的原则。值得注意的是，有极个别国家法律规定仲裁员不得为女性，否则构成仲裁裁决法定撤销理由。[①] 这明显违反有关性别歧视的国际公共秩序，不会被广泛认同。

在不违反仲裁地强制性规则和国际公共秩序的情况下，国际商事仲裁程序向更自由、更灵活的方向发展并非意味着废弃仲裁裁决撤销制度。从仲裁裁决撤销制度存废的现实来看，世界上还没有哪个国家，包括一向以仲裁"非国内化"策源地自居的法国，完全废除仲裁裁决撤销制度。如果真像主张仲裁"非国内化"的学者所论，仲裁应摆脱任何国家仲裁程序法的支配，那么法国仲裁裁决撤销制度是否为国内程序法对仲裁裁决的控制呢？如果仲裁"非国内化"了，那么这种司法控制的法律基础何在，是否与其原有主张相矛盾呢？实际上，由于仲裁裁决撤销制度对保护仲裁当事人的利益有不可替代的作用，理性的立法者不可能完全废弃仲裁裁决撤销制度，而是采取措施不断地对其进行完善。

（本文原载于《法商研究》2010年第4期）

① 参见 Hamid G. Gharavi Salas，"The 1997 Iranian Law on International Commercial Arbitration: The UNCITRAL Model Law"，*International Arbitration*，Vol. 15，No. 1 1999。

境外仲裁机构在中国内地仲裁的法律问题

李庆明*

一　问题的提出

境外仲裁机构在中国内地仲裁，[①] 是在构建开放型经济新体制、服务我国外交工作大局和国家重大发展战略的背景下，自由贸易试验区（以下简称自贸区）建设、“一带一路”建设和涉外法律服务业发展均有所涉及的重要问题。在法律上，其涉及《中华人民共和国仲裁法》（以下简称《仲裁法》）、《中华人民共和国民事诉讼法》（2012 年修正，以下简称《民事诉讼法》）等的解释、适用和进一步修改；在政策上，其涉及仲裁市场开放问题，还涉及中央全面深化改革领导小组第二十四次会议通过的《关于发展涉外法律服务业的意见》的执行问题。有鉴于此，本文拟结合我国

* 李庆明，2009 年 7 月来中国社会科学院国际法研究所工作，现任副研究员、国际私法研究室副主任。

① 仲裁地（seat of arbitration）在我国法律上并没有得到明确界定，一般认为指的是将仲裁和特定法律制度联系起来的地点。仲裁地决定仲裁程序法以及裁决的国籍（参见谢新胜《国际商事仲裁程序法的适用》，中国检察出版社，2009，第 147 页）。本文所讨论的是境外仲裁机构在仲裁程序和仲裁裁决中将“仲裁地”认定为中国内地的情形，不讨论仅在中国内地开庭；而将仲裁地认定为境外的情形。因我国特殊的国情，我国内地（大陆）与我国香港、澳门、台湾地区实际上构成四个法域，除统一适用的涉及国防、外交等领域的法律制度外，每个法域在民商法等许多领域都实行不同的法律制度。如无特别说明，本文中“境外仲裁机构”包括外国仲裁机构和我国港澳台地区的仲裁机构；“中国内地”和“我国”则仅指中国内地，不包括中国港澳台地区。

的立法、案例、政策和学者学说，对境外仲裁机构在中国内地仲裁的法律问题加以探讨。

目前，支持国际知名商事争议解决机构入驻中国（上海）自由贸易试验区（以下简称上海自贸区）已经被国务院上升到“推动权益保护制度创新”的层面。2015 年 4 月 8 日，国务院批准《进一步深化中国（上海）自由贸易试验区改革开放方案》（以下简称《方案》），《方案》第 11 点“推动权益保护制度创新”明确指出：“进一步对接国际商事争议解决规则，优化自贸试验区仲裁规则，支持国际知名商事争议解决机构入驻，提高商事纠纷仲裁国际化程度。探索建立全国性的自贸试验区仲裁法律服务联盟和亚太仲裁机构交流合作机制，加快打造面向全球的亚太仲裁中心。”《方案》出台后，境外仲裁机构不断在上海自贸区设立代表处或办公室。2015 年 11 月 19 日，中国香港国际仲裁中心在上海自贸区设立代表处；2016 年 2 月 24 日，国际商会仲裁院在上海自贸区设立仲裁办公室；2016 年 3 月 3 日，新加坡国际仲裁中心在上海自贸区设立代表处。

最高人民法院近年来开始转变立场，支持当事人约定由国际商会仲裁院在中国内地仲裁的仲裁协议的效力，[①] 并且探讨是否需要在时机成熟时进一步确认境外仲裁机构在自贸区仲裁的效力。同时，最高人民法院也可能要面临这样一个问题，即是否承认把“在中国仲裁”的仲裁协议下的“仲裁地”认定为香港的国际商会仲裁院裁决。

境外仲裁机构在中国内地仲裁主要有两种形式：第一，境外仲裁机构在中国内地设立分支机构，以商业存在的形式提供仲裁服务；第二，境外仲裁机构未在中国内地设立分支机构，但将仲裁地设定为中国内地。对于是否允许及在多大程度上允许境外仲裁机构在中国内地仲裁，学术界和媒

---

① 参见《最高人民法院关于宁波市北仑利成润滑油有限公司与法莫万驰公司买卖合同纠纷一案仲裁条款效力问题请示的复函》。《仲裁法》第 16 条第 1 款规定：“仲裁协议包括合同中订立的仲裁条款和以其他书面方式在纠纷发生前或者纠纷发生后达成的请求仲裁的协议。”本文不作区分，除所引案例、文件原文中使用“仲裁条款”外，其他地方统一使用“仲裁协议”。

体从 2004 年起开始了激烈的讨论。[①] 目前，境外仲裁机构在中国内地设立分支机构，也希望将来能管理在中国内地的仲裁案件和仲裁程序，将仲裁地设定为中国内地。因此，本文不区分境外仲裁机构是否在中国内地设立分支机构，而是统一论述其能否将中国内地作为仲裁地来管理仲裁案件和仲裁程序，在仲裁程序中能否得到我国法院的支持或受到监督，以及作出的裁决能否得到我国法院的承认与执行。

二　近 20 年来境外仲裁机构在中国内地仲裁的典型案例

境外仲裁机构在中国内地仲裁的问题，首先涉及的是相关仲裁协议的效力问题，而其中涉及国际商会仲裁院的案件最具代表性。1996—2016 年 20 年间，围绕境外仲裁机构在中国内地仲裁的仲裁协议的效力和裁决的执行，产生了很多有争议的案例。在这 20 年间，最高人民法院的立场也在不断转变，从最早承认境外仲裁机构在中国内地仲裁，到后来否认境外仲裁机构在中国内地仲裁，近年来又开始趋向于承认境外仲裁机构在中国内地仲裁。而在此期间，以厦门市中级人民法院、宁波市中级人民法院为代表的地方法院又不受最高人民法院的影响，承认过约定适用《国际商会仲裁规则》在中国内地仲裁的仲裁协议的效力。总体而言，虽然曾经有过混乱，但承认境外仲裁机构在中国内地仲裁是目前的趋势。

---

① 王生长、赵秀文等人支持放开中国的仲裁服务市场，允许国际商会等境外仲裁机构在我国仲裁［参见王生长《国际商会仲裁院能否在中国内地进行仲裁》，《仲裁与法律》2003 年第 6 期（总第 89 期），法律出版社，2004，第 29—35 页；赵秀文《中国仲裁市场对外开放研究》，《政法论坛》2009 年第 11 期］。康明则持反对态度［参见康明《我国商事仲裁服务市场对外开放问题初探——兼与生长同志商榷》，《仲裁与法律》2003 年第 6 期（总第 89 期），法律出版社，2004，第 36—70 页］。宋连斌等则从我国加入《纽约公约》时的保留等论述现在允许境外仲裁机构在我国仲裁的法律困境（参见宋连斌、王珺《国际商会在中国内地仲裁：准入、裁决国籍及执行——由宁波中院的一份裁定谈起》，《西北大学学报》（哲学社会科学版）2011 年第 3 期）。在海外发表的一些英文论文也注意到境外仲裁机构在中国仲裁的困境［参见 Fan Kun, "Prospects of Foreign Arbitration Institutions Administering Arbitration in China", *Journal of International Arbitration* 28 (2011): 343 - 353］。

（一）最高人民法院不认可境外仲裁机构在中国内地仲裁的案例

1996年12月，在“诺和诺德案”中，最高人民法院认定，当事人约定适用《国际商会仲裁规则》在英国仲裁的仲裁协议因无明确的仲裁机构而无法执行。[①] 此案之后，在国内外影响最大的是2004年“旭普林案”，国内外学术界和实务界就境外仲裁机构能否在中国内地仲裁展开了激烈的讨论。在“旭普林案”中，最高人民法院认为适用《国际商会仲裁规则》在上海进行仲裁的仲裁协议无效。[②] 据此，无锡高新技术产业开发区人民法院裁定涉案仲裁协议无效。[③] 旭普林公司一直在国际商会仲裁院推进仲裁，并在获得胜诉裁决后向江苏省无锡市中级人民法院申请强制执行该裁决。无锡市中级人民法院则以裁决所依据的仲裁协议已被我国法院认定无效为由拒绝承认该裁决。[④]

在此之后，2006年“达利特案”延续了“旭普林案”的逻辑，认定仅约定适用《国际商会仲裁规则》、仲裁地点在北京的仲裁协议无效。[⑤] 2009年“夏新电子案”也同样认定仅约定适用《国际商会仲裁规则》、仲裁地点包括厦门的仲裁协议无效。[⑥] 2011年的“江苏外贸公司案”中，[⑦] 合同中文本约定由设在中国北京的国际商会仲裁委员会仲裁，英文本约定依据《国际商会仲裁规则》在北京仲裁，最高人民法院最终以双方当事人不能就仲裁机构达成一致为由认定所涉仲裁协议无效。

---

① 《最高人民法院关于海南省高级人民法院审理诺和诺德股份有限公司与海南际中医药科技开发公司经销协议纠纷案的报告的复函》，法经〔1996〕449号。

② 《最高人民法院关于德国旭普林国际有限责任公司与无锡沃可通用工程橡胶有限公司申请确认仲裁协议效力一案的请示的复函》，〔2003〕民四他字第23号。

③ 德国旭普林国际有限责任公司与无锡沃可通用工程橡胶有限公司申请确认仲裁协议效力案，无锡高新技术产业开发区人民法院〔2004〕新民二初字第154号裁定书。

④ 德国旭普林国际有限责任公司申请承认和执行国外仲裁裁决案，江苏省无锡市中级人民法院〔2004〕锡民三仲字第1号裁定书。

⑤ 《最高人民法院关于仲裁条款效力请示的复函》，〔2006〕民四他字第6号；河北省高级人民法院〔2006〕冀民三初字第2-1号裁定书；最高人民法院〔2007〕民四终字第15号裁定书。

⑥ 《最高人民法院关于夏新电子股份有限公司与比利时产品有限公司确认经销协议仲裁条款效力的请示的复函》，〔2009〕民四他字第5号。

⑦ 《最高人民法院关于Salzgitter Mannesmann International GmbH与江苏省对外经贸股份有限公司之间仲裁协议效力的复函》，〔2011〕民四他字第32号。

在2012年的“泰州浩普投资公司案”中，[①] 当事人约定“仲裁应按国际商会的调解和仲裁规则进行。如果一方提出仲裁，仲裁地由另一方选择”。最高人民法院认为，当事人并未申请仲裁，不存在另一方选择仲裁地问题；该仲裁协议并未约定仲裁机构，且依据《国际商会仲裁规则》也不能确定仲裁机构，当事人事后亦未能达成补充协议，故认定该仲裁协议无效。

（二）最高人民法院认可境外仲裁机构在中国内地仲裁的案例

1996年5月，最高人民法院认可了厦门维哥木制品有限公司与台湾富源企业有限公司购销合同中的约定适用《国际商会仲裁规则》的仲裁协议的效力。[②]“旭普林案”后，国际商会于2012年修改了其1998年仲裁规则，修改后的第1条第2款规定国际商会仲裁院是唯一经授权对《国际商会仲裁规则》项下仲裁活动实施管理的机构，并在第6条第2款规定“当事人同意按照仲裁规则进行仲裁，即接受由仲裁院对该仲裁进行管理”。2013年2月发布的“龙利得案”认可了国际商会仲裁院在上海仲裁的仲裁协议的效力。[③] 最高人民法院认为，本案当事人约定适用《国际商会仲裁规则》但未同时约定其他仲裁机构进行仲裁，应当认为当事人的约定属于“按照约定的仲裁规则能够确定仲裁机构”的情形，国际商会仲裁院对当事人之间的合同争议具有管辖权。2013年12月发布的“北仑利成案”认可了“在北京适用《国际商会仲裁规则》进行仲裁”的仲裁协议的效力。[④] 最高人民法院认为，根据2012年生效的《国际商会仲裁规则》，当事人同意按照该规则进行仲裁，即接受由仲裁院对该仲裁进行管理。

（三）地方法院认可境外仲裁机构在中国内地仲裁的案例

2004年12月，在厦门象屿集团有限公司与米歇尔贸易公司确认仲裁

---

① 《最高人民法院关于泰州浩普投资公司与WICOR HOLDING AG（瑞士魏克公司）申请确认仲裁协议一案的请示的复函》，〔2012〕民四他字第6号。

② 《最高人民法院关于厦门维哥木制品有限公司与台湾富源企业有限公司购销合同纠纷管辖权异议案的复函》，法函〔1996〕78号。

③ 《最高人民法院关于申请人安徽省龙利得包装印刷有限公司与被申请人BP Agnati S. R. L申请确认仲裁协议效力案的请示的复函》，〔2013〕民四他字第13号。

④ 《最高人民法院关于宁波市北仑利成润滑油有限公司与法莫万驰公司买卖合同纠纷一案仲裁条款效力问题请示的复函》，〔2013〕民四他字第74号。

条款效力案中，厦门市中级人民法院认可了约定适用《国际商会仲裁规则》、仲裁地点为中国北京的仲裁条款的效力。[①] 2009 年 4 月，在 DUFERCOS. A（德高钢铁公司）申请承认与执行 ICC 第 14006/MS/JB/JEM 号仲裁裁决案（以下简称“德高钢铁公司案”）中，宁波市中级人民法院裁定执行国际商会仲裁院在北京作出的仲裁裁决，理由是该裁决构成《纽约公约》第 1 条第 1 款的非内国裁决。

三　境外仲裁机构在中国内地仲裁的障碍

“旭普林案”和“德高钢铁公司案”都曾引发业界对境外仲裁机构在中国内地仲裁所涉及的一系列问题的思考。这些问题主要包括：境外仲裁机构是否能在中国内地仲裁？如果能，其所作裁决的性质如何？此种裁决应否得到承认与执行？2013 年的“龙利得案”和“北仑利成案”让很多人看到了曙光，认为境外仲裁机构进入中国内地仲裁市场的时机已经成熟。[②] 2015 年和 2016 年，中国香港国际仲裁中心、新加坡国际仲裁中心和国际商会仲裁院在上海自贸区设立代表处或办公室，进一步引发了理论界和实务界对境外仲裁机构进入中国内地仲裁市场及中国仲裁国际化的激烈讨论。

（一）境外仲裁机构的市场准入问题

有学者认为境外仲裁机构不能在中国内地进行仲裁，主要理由是国际商事仲裁是商事性的法律服务而非公共服务，因此境外仲裁机构在中国内

① 福建省厦门市中级人民法院〔2004〕厦民认字第 81 号裁定书。

② 原来有观点认为，《仲裁法》中缺乏临时仲裁的规定，成了国际商会真正实现中国仲裁的“死穴”（参见王婧《外国仲裁机构或将撕开中国仲裁市场一角?》，《法制日报》2009 年 6 月 25 日）。陶景洲等人也认为，《仲裁法》第 10 条、第 16 条和第 18 条等条款关于仲裁委员会的规定阻碍了外国仲裁机构在中国内地仲裁［参见 Tao Jingzhou & Clarisse von Wunschheim, “Article 16 and 18 of the PRC Arbitration Law: The Great Wall of China for Foreign Arbitration Institutions”, *Arbitration International* 23（2007）: 311］。“龙利得案”之后，有人认为最高人民法院的复函为国际仲裁机构进入中国提供了新的机会，但还有很多问题有待解决［参见 Wei Sun, “SPC Instruction Provides New Opportunities for International Arbitral Institutions to Expand into China”, *Journal of International Arbitration* 31（2014）: 683 - 700］。

地进行仲裁属于国际服务贸易活动，在国际法层面应当受到《服务贸易总协定》等的调整，而我国并未承诺开放境外仲裁机构在中国内地从事商事仲裁服务贸易。[①] 曾经担任中国国际经济贸易仲裁委员会副秘书长的康明也认为，中国加入世界贸易组织议定书附件 9 中的法律服务内容列明了外国律师事务所进入中国提供相关法律服务的内容，其中并未提及商事仲裁服务事项，故境外仲裁机构不得在中国内地仲裁。[②] 但笔者认为，上述观点有待商榷。正如有学者指出的那样，国际性仲裁机构服务未被列入我国加入世界贸易组织承诺表的根源在于，它并不属于跨国服务贸易的范畴；秉持开放的态度，国际商会仲裁院在中国内地仲裁既可以节省我国当事人出境的时间和费用，也可使更多中国籍仲裁员参与知名国际仲裁机构的仲裁活动。[③]

《涉外民事关系法律适用法》第 14 条规定："法人及其分支机构的民事权利能力、民事行为能力、组织机构、股东权利义务等事项，适用登记地法律。法人的主营业地与登记地不一致的，可以适用主营业地法律。法人的经常居所地，为其主营业地。"境外仲裁机构能否在中国内地提供仲裁服务，首先应适用境外仲裁机构成立地的法律来判断其权利能力和行为能力。既然境外仲裁机构已经在境外注册，按其属人法具有权利能力和行为能力，仲裁服务又不属于受限制的特殊行业，那么就不应限制境外仲裁机构在中国内地提供仲裁服务。

（二）境外仲裁机构与《仲裁法》上的仲裁委员会

有学者认为，在国内法层面，正因为《仲裁法》对仲裁委员会有诸多要求，因而境外仲裁机构不是"仲裁委员会"，从而根据《仲裁法》第 16 条，将争议提交境外仲裁机构仲裁的仲裁协议无效。因此，根据我国《仲裁法》和《民事诉讼法》的规定，境外仲裁机构不得在我国内地进行国际商事仲裁。[④]

---

① 参见李健《外国仲裁机构在中国内地仲裁不可行》，《法学》2008 年第 12 期，第 134 页。

② 参见康明《我国商事仲裁服务市场对外开放问题初探——兼与生长同志商榷》，《仲裁与法律》2003 年第 6 期（总第 89 期），法律出版社，2004，第 49 页。

③ 参见宋连斌、王珺《国际商会在中国内地仲裁：准入、裁决国籍及执行——由宁波中院的一份裁定谈起》，《西北大学学报》（哲学社会科学版）2011 年第 3 期。

④ 参见李健《外国仲裁机构在中国内地仲裁不可行》，《法学》2008 年第 12 期。

"龙利得案"明确了境外仲裁机构属于《仲裁法》第16条规定的"仲裁委员会"，解决了境外仲裁机构在中国内地仲裁的仲裁协议的合法性争议。最高人民法院认为，涉外仲裁协议约定因合同而发生的纠纷由国际商会仲裁院进行仲裁，同时约定"管辖地应为中国上海"；根据《仲裁法》第16条，涉案仲裁协议有请求仲裁的意思表示，约定了仲裁事项，并选定了明确具体的仲裁机构，应认定为有效。

不过，就境外仲裁机构与《仲裁法》上的仲裁委员会的关系问题，最高人民法院有时又作出其他令人迷惑的解释。例如，在"神华公司案"中,[①] 最高人民法院没有指明境外仲裁机构是否属于《仲裁法》第16条上的仲裁委员会，但认为《仲裁法》第20条所指的仲裁委员会系依据《仲裁法》第10条和第66条设立的仲裁委员会，并不包括外国仲裁机构。故针对《仲裁法》第20条作出解释的《最高人民法院关于适用〈中华人民共和国仲裁法〉若干问题的解释》第13条的规定并不适用于外国仲裁机构对仲裁协议效力作出认定的情形。

《仲裁法》1994年通过时，我国社会主义市场经济体制刚刚起步，对外开放和国际化的广度和深度远未达到现在的程度；而且根据时任全国人大法工委主任顾昂然的说明，《仲裁法》总的精神是将仲裁委员会与行政机关分开,[②] 解决的是部分仲裁委员会不独立而附属于行政机关的问题。虽然当时已经提出"发展社会主义市场经济和开展国际经济贸易往来"和"借鉴国外仲裁制度的有益经验和国际通行做法"，并制定了统一的《仲裁法》，但因各种因素所限，对"仲裁委员会"的规定的确没有考虑到境外仲裁机构开展仲裁的问题。时至今日，如果狭隘地解释"仲裁委员会"，认定境外仲裁机构不属于《仲裁法》上的"仲裁委员会"，不承认境外仲裁机构在中国内地的仲裁，最终损害的将是我国当事人乃至国家的长远利益。

---

① 《最高人民法院关于神华煤炭运销公司与马瑞尼克船务公司确认之诉仲裁条款问题的请示的复函》，〔2013〕民四他字第4号。

② 参见全国人大常委会法制工作委员会主任顾昂然1994年6月28日在第八届全国人民代表大会常务委员会第八次会议上关于《中华人民共和国仲裁法（草案）》的说明，http://www.npc.gov.cn/wxzl/gongbao/2001-01/02/content_5003212.htm。本文网络资料的最后访问日期均为2016年5月20日。

（三）境外仲裁机构中的外国仲裁机构在中国内地作出的裁决是否构成“非内国裁决”

1. 裁决的分类及其意义

我国并未如《纽约公约》一样根据裁决作出地（仲裁地）来认定仲裁裁决的国籍，而是采用“仲裁机构所在地”的标准，将裁决分为《纽约公约》裁决、国内仲裁裁决、涉外仲裁裁决及港澳台地区的仲裁裁决。在此基础上，对不同种类仲裁裁决的承认与执行作出不同的安排，采取不同的审查标准和执行依据。

《纽约公约》规定了外国仲裁裁决和非内国仲裁裁决的承认与执行，我国在加入《纽约公约》时对非内国裁决进行了保留。根据我国相关法律规定，如果认定一项裁决构成外国仲裁裁决，且该国为《纽约公约》成员国，则适用《纽约公约》来承认与执行。如果认定一项裁决是内国仲裁裁决，则还需要区分其是没有涉外因素的国内仲裁裁决，还是具有涉外因素的涉外仲裁裁决。对于国内仲裁裁决，应适用《民事诉讼法》第 237 条确定的审查标准，即人民法院不仅可以对裁决根据的仲裁协议、涉及的程序事项进行审查，还可以对裁决的实体进行审查，例如裁决所根据的证据系伪造的，对方当事人向仲裁机构隐瞒了足以影响公正裁决的证据，仲裁员在仲裁该案时有贪污受贿、徇私舞弊、枉法裁决行为等；对于涉外仲裁裁决，则应适用《民事诉讼法》第 274 条的标准，即被申请人只能就仲裁协议的效力瑕疵、仲裁程序瑕疵等理由而申请不予执行，人民法院不得审查裁决的实体问题。

总之，对于《纽约公约》下的外国仲裁裁决和我国的涉外仲裁裁决，我国法院在承认与执行程序中只能进行程序审查，不得进行实体审查。相反，对于国内仲裁裁决，《民事诉讼法》第 237 条授权法院对仲裁裁决的程序和实体都进行审查。由此，认定外国仲裁机构在中国所作裁决的性质就成为首要的问题。时任最高人民法院副院长的万鄂湘曾经指出：“国外的仲裁机构在中国内地裁决的案件，是属于国外裁决还是国内裁决，目前还没有明确规定，这将必然导致裁决执行时的麻烦。”①

---

① 万鄂湘：《〈纽约公约〉在中国的司法实践》，《法律适用》2009 年第 3 期。

2. “非内国裁决”的界定及其承认与执行

在“德高钢铁公司案”中，宁波市中级人民法院将国际商会仲裁院在北京作出的裁决视为《纽约公约》上的“非内国裁决”，并最终依据《纽约公约》予以承认和执行。自此，理论界和实务界就对外国仲裁机构在中国内地作出的裁决是否构成“非内国裁决”展开了争论。实际上，在“旭普林案”中，无锡市中级人民法院首次提出“非内国裁决”问题，[①] 只是当初理论界和实务界都只重视国际商会在中国上海仲裁的仲裁协议的效力问题，而忽略了法院所提及的“非内国裁决”问题，直至“德高钢铁公司案”才误以为该案是第一次提出“非内国裁决”的问题。[②]

关于外国仲裁机构在中国内地作出的裁决的性质，有学者主张其既不是本国裁决，也不是外国裁决或者无国籍裁决，而是“非内国裁决”。[③] 有人认为，按照《纽约公约》的精神及我国加入公约时对公约适用范围所作的保留，该仲裁裁决属于我国仲裁裁决；但按照我国《民事诉讼法》（1991 年）第 269 条确立的以仲裁机构所在地决定国际商事仲裁裁决的国籍的规定，以及最高人民法院 2004 年对“天利公司案”的复函[④]及其他司法机构的实践，[⑤] 显然应

---

① 无锡市中级人民法院（2004）锡民三仲字第 1 号裁定书指出：“本案系承认和执行国外仲裁裁决案……本案被申请承认和执行的仲裁裁决系国际商会仲裁院作出，通过其总部秘书处盖章确认，应被视为非内国裁决。且双方当事人对适用《1958 年纽约公约》均无异议，因此本案应当适用《1958 年纽约公约》。”当然，该裁定书一方面认定本案系承认和执行外国仲裁裁决，另一方面却又认为所涉裁决为“非内国裁决”，在逻辑上存在不一致之处。

② 最高人民法院民四庭杨弘磊法官相对较早地注意到了“旭普林案”中的“非内国裁决”问题。参见杨弘磊《中国内地法院〈纽约公约〉项下外国仲裁裁决司法审查之新近实践述评》，《武大国际法评论》（第十三卷），武汉大学出版社，2012，第 334 页。

③ 参见赵秀文《从相关案例看 ICC 仲裁院裁决在我国的承认与执行》，《法学》2010 年第 3 期，第 77 页；刘晓红《非内国仲裁裁决的理论与实证分析》，《法学杂志》2013 年第 5 期，第 84 页；吕炳斌《论外国仲裁机构到我国境内仲裁的问题——兼析我国加入〈纽约公约〉时的保留》，《法治研究》2010 年第 10 期。与赵秀文主张我国法院应承认和执行“非内国裁决”不同，吕炳斌虽然也认为国际商会仲裁院在中国内地的裁决为“非内国裁决”，但认为我国法院没有义务予以承认和执行。

④ 《最高人民法院关于不予执行国际商会仲裁院 10334/AMW/BWD/TE 最终裁决一案的请示的复函》，〔2004〕民四他字第 6 号。最高人民法院认为国际商会仲裁院是在法国设立的仲裁机构，其在香港作出的裁决是法国裁决。

⑤ 例如，在 TH & T 国际公司与成都华龙汽车配件有限公司申请承认和执行国际商会国际仲裁院裁决案中，四川省成都市中级人民法院〔2002〕成民初字第 531 号裁定书就认定国际商会仲裁院在美国洛杉矶作出的裁决是法国裁决，并基于中法两国都是《纽约公约》缔约国而承认了该裁决。

被视为外国仲裁裁决。[①]

2009 年《最高人民法院关于香港仲裁裁决在内地执行的有关问题的通知》（以下简称《通知》）首次明确以仲裁地来确认仲裁裁决的国籍，规定当事人向人民法院申请执行在香港特别行政区作出的临时仲裁裁决、国际商会仲裁院等国外仲裁机构在香港特别行政区作出的仲裁裁决的，人民法院应当按照《关于内地与香港特别行政区相互执行仲裁裁决的安排》的规定进行审查。但《通知》只是就涉及在香港作出的裁决的性质的一个通知，最高人民法院并未明确声明将仲裁地作为认定裁决的性质的标准，也未明确无论是由境内仲裁机构还是由境外仲裁机构作出的，只要是在中国内地作出的仲裁裁决，均构成中国仲裁裁决，而在境外作出的仲裁裁决，均构成外国仲裁裁决。《民事诉讼法》（2012 年修正）第 283 条[②]也仍然保留了《民事诉讼法》（1991 年）第 269 条的内容，继续以仲裁机构所在地决定仲裁裁决的地域性质。

从仲裁协议的法律适用来看，仲裁地越来越受到重视。《最高人民法院关于适用〈中华人民共和国仲裁法〉若干问题的解释》第 16 条规定了在当事人没有选择时，仲裁地法律可以作为涉外仲裁协议的效力审查的准据法。《涉外民事关系法律适用法》第 18 条将仲裁机构所在地法和仲裁地法作为仲裁协议适用的法律的并列选择，规定："当事人可以协议选择仲裁协议适用的法律。当事人没有选择的，适用仲裁机构所在地法律或者仲裁地法律。"在司法实践中，《通知》发布之后，最高人民法院事实上将仲裁地作为认定外国仲裁裁决的标准。例如，2010 年 10 月 12 日发布的《最高人民法院关于申请人 DMT 有限公司（法国）与被申请人潮州市华业包装材料有限公司、被申请人潮安县华业包装材料有限公司申请承认和执行外国仲裁裁决一案请示的复函》就将国际商会仲裁院在新加坡作出的仲裁

---

① 参见王天红《论国际商事仲裁裁决国籍的确定》，《人民司法》2006 年第 9 期。康明也认为应当以仲裁机构所在地来判决仲裁裁决的国籍，而不论仲裁机构在何地作出裁决。参见康明《我国商事仲裁服务市场对外开放问题初探——兼与生长同志商榷》，载《仲裁与法律》2003 年第 6 期，法律出版社，2004，第 57 页。

② 该条规定："国外仲裁机构的裁决，需要中华人民共和国人民法院承认和执行的，应当由当事人直接向被执行人住所地或者其财产所在地的中级人民法院申请，人民法院应当依照中华人民共和国缔结或者参加的国际条约，或者按照互惠原则办理。"

裁决视为新加坡裁决，而不再视为法国裁决。

笔者认为，从我国立法机关在加入《纽约公约》时所作的互惠保留以及最高人民法院的意见来看，认定国际商会仲裁院在中国作出的仲裁裁决构成“非内国裁决”没有法律依据。1986 年 12 月 2 日发布的《全国人民代表大会常务委员会关于我国加入〈承认及执行外国仲裁裁决公约〉的决定》声明：“中华人民共和国只在互惠的基础上对在另一缔约国领土内作出的仲裁裁决的承认和执行适用该公约。”1987 年 4 月 10 日发布的《最高人民法院关于执行我国加入的〈承认及执行外国仲裁裁决公约〉的通知》第 1 条也再次明确指出：“根据我国加入该公约时所作的互惠保留声明，我国对在另一缔约国领土内作出的仲裁裁决的承认和执行适用该公约。”在“德高钢铁公司案”中，宁波市中级人民法院虽然认定国际商会仲裁院的裁决为“非内国裁决”而予以承认与执行，但并未在裁定书中详细说明，也未逐级通过浙江省高级人民法院转至最高人民法院请示，最高人民法院也就并未就此作出批复，不能代表最高人民法院的意见。“龙利得案”虽然认可国际商会仲裁院在中国仲裁的仲裁协议的效力，但最高人民法院并未就合肥市中级人民法院提出的裁决构成国内裁决这一观点表态。

有人认为，《纽约公约》关于互惠保留的规定与《纽约公约》规定的外国仲裁裁决界定标准是两个不同的概念：互惠保留是对缔约国义务的免除，是针对《纽约公约》的非缔约国而言的，而对“非内国裁决”标准的认定应属于申请承认及执行地所在国的一项权利。① 这种观点完全是对条约保留之效果的误解。正确的理解是，我国在加入《纽约公约》时声明作出互惠保留，即意味着排除了对“非内国裁决”的执行。

总之，我国《民事诉讼法》（2012 年修正）、《仲裁法》均未就“非内国裁决”作出规定，我国全国人大常委会在加入《纽约公约》时已经声明对《纽约公约》上的“非内国裁决”的规定作出了保留，最高人民法院在 1987 年 4 月 10 日发布的《最高人民法院关于执行我国加入的〈承认及执

---

① 参见李迅《中国承认与执行外国仲裁裁决的发展展望——从第一例承认与执行在中国做出的外国仲裁裁决谈起》，《仲裁研究》2010 年第 2 期。

行外国仲裁裁决公约〉的通知》也作出了同样的声明，依据条约保留的效果，则《纽约公约》上的“非内国裁决”的规定对我国不发生法律效力，故国际商会仲裁院在中国作出的仲裁裁决不属于《纽约公约》上的“非内国裁决”，我国法院不得依据《纽约公约》来承认和执行“非内国裁决”。“德高钢铁公司案”的裁定明显违反我国的法律法规及我国在加入《纽约公约》时作出的保留声明，不能作为先例援引。

（四）境外仲裁机构在中国内地作出的裁决的承认与执行

境外仲裁机构在中国内地作出的裁决，能否在中国内地得到承认与执行，关键在于对其性质的认定，即该裁决是构成《纽约公约》上的外国裁决或非内国裁决，还是构成我国的涉外裁决。

目前，理论界和实务界越来越倾向于以仲裁地而非仲裁机构所在地来作为裁决国籍的判断标准。也就是说，将境外仲裁机构在中国内地作出的裁决，视为我国的涉外裁决，并按照我国《民事诉讼法》第 274 条的规定来审查是否应当承认与执行。

在华南国际经济贸易仲裁委员会（深圳国际仲裁院）主办的华南企业法律论坛 2015 年年会暨“中国金融机构资产管理业务的发展与法律问题”研讨会上，最高人民法院法官高晓力在演讲中指出：“至于外界所说的是不是中国法院认可 ICC 可以到中国来进行仲裁，我个人认为这涉及仲裁服务市场准入问题，并非中国法院可以决定的事情，目前我们走到这一步仅仅是认定仲裁条款有效还是无效，但是在此之后，仲裁裁决作出之后是否能够在中国法院得到承认和执行，是需要继续讨论的……个人观点是倾向于把它认为是中国涉外的裁决，即根据中国法律规定进行相应的司法审查。”[①] 目前“龙利得案”的裁决尚未作出，待该裁决作出后，我国法院是依据《纽约公约》将其作为外国裁决或者非内国裁决，还是依据《民事诉讼法》将其作为涉外裁决予以承认与执行，我们拭目以待。当然，如果在此之前我国修订了《民事诉讼法》或《仲裁法》，对境外仲裁机构在中国内地所作裁决的性质予以明确，那就更加理想了。

---

① 参见最高人民法院第一巡回法庭主审法官高晓力《中国国际商事仲裁司法审查的最新发展》，“华南国际经济贸易仲裁委员会”微信公众号，2016 年 4 月 20 日。

四 关于放开境外仲裁机构在中国内地仲裁限制的思考

（一）中国内地当事人日益广泛参与境外仲裁要求允许境外仲裁机构在中国内地仲裁

中国目前已经成为贸易大国、对外承包工程大国、吸引外资大国，而且正在成为海外投资大国，中国内地当事人越来越多地主动或被动参与境外仲裁机构的仲裁。随着中国对外开放和国际化程度越来越高，国际经济、贸易、投资纠纷也日益增长。仲裁因其独特的优势而成为越来越多当事人的选择。在中国内地当事人不断参与境外仲裁的背景下，不允许境外仲裁机构在中国内地仲裁，对境外仲裁机构并不造成多大的损害，最终损害的是参与仲裁的中国内地当事人的利益：他们为此不得不远赴境外参与仲裁，增加许多无谓的成本和风险。相反，允许境外仲裁机构在中国内地仲裁，将大大减少我国当事人的各种成本和支出。

（二）发展涉外法律服务业要求允许境外仲裁机构在中国内地仲裁

在构建开放型经济新体制、服务我国外交工作大局和国家重大发展战略的背景下，大力发展涉外法律服务业已经受到中央高度关注。允许境外仲裁机构在中国内地仲裁，有助于我国涉外法律服务业的发展，也是对中央全面深化改革领导小组第二十四次会议通过的《关于发展涉外法律服务业的意见》的具体落实。涉外仲裁机构在中国内地仲裁，本身就是我国服务业开放的证明，将促使我国涉外法律服务机构在良性竞争中稳步提高。我国的各种专业性人才通过代理案件、被指定为仲裁员等各种方式参与境外仲裁机构在中国内地的仲裁实践，有助于发展壮大涉外法律服务队伍人才。

（三）打消境外法院、机构和当事人对我国的偏见要求允许境外仲裁机构在中国内地仲裁

由于我国法院对境外仲裁机构在中国内地仲裁的实践并不总是一致，

境外法院和当事人对我国仲裁业及人民法院的裁判水准都形成偏见。在争议发生之前，境外当事人要求选择境外仲裁机构在境外仲裁；即使经过中国内地当事人及其代理律师的努力，合同中最终约定境外仲裁机构在中国内地仲裁，在争议发生后，境外当事人也往往寻找各种理由拒绝在中国内地仲裁，转而在境外开始仲裁或诉讼程序。这种做法还每每得到境外仲裁机构和法院的支持，主要理由正是中国不允许境外仲裁机构在中国内地仲裁。因此，允许境外仲裁机构在中国内地仲裁，有助于改变境外法院、机构和当事人对我国的偏见，减少歪曲我国司法形象及恶意解释与适用我国法律法规的情形。

（四）提升中国仲裁的国际性和公信力要求允许境外仲裁机构在中国内地仲裁

目前，我国正在积极建设面向全球的亚太仲裁中心和国际海事司法中心，而这离不开商事海事纠纷仲裁国际化的推进。伦敦、巴黎等国际知名仲裁中心都是允许全球仲裁机构提供仲裁服务，甚至允许临时仲裁。不断提升和扩大中国仲裁品牌的公信力和影响力，不仅需要仲裁机构吸纳优秀人才、完善仲裁规则、创新服务能力，还需要人民法院依法履行支持和监督仲裁的司法职能，继续完善仲裁司法审查制度，保障和促进中国仲裁业的发展，共同为纠纷的多元解决营造良好的法治环境。① 为更好地促进中国仲裁的国际化、提升中国仲裁的公信力，必须尽量减少与国际仲裁普遍实践不一致的、限制我国仲裁事业发展的机制，进一步开放我国仲裁市场，允许境外仲裁机构在中国内地提供仲裁服务，允许全球各种仲裁规则在中国适用。

进而言之，基于境外仲裁机构已经在中国内地仲裁的历史和现实，只要其裁决不向我国法院申请承认与执行，而是向境外法院申请承认与执行，我国实际上无法干预境外仲裁机构在中国内地进行仲裁。换言之，我国法院相当于主动放弃了对境外仲裁机构在中国内地仲裁的监督。而境外法院会认为此类裁决是中国裁决，并据此拒绝受理败诉当事人撤销裁决的

---

① 参见沈红雨《贺荣在2015年“中国仲裁高峰论坛”上强调继续完善仲裁司法审查制度促进仲裁公信力提升》，《人民法院报》2015年9月26日。

申请。如此一来，败诉当事人既不能在我国法院，也不能在境外法院申请撤销该裁决，这既对败诉当事人一方不公平，也有损我国支持仲裁的形象和国家长远利益。

五　结语

外国仲裁机构在中国内地仲裁不但是一个理论问题，而且是当前一个重要的实践问题，关涉自贸区、亚太仲裁中心和国际海事司法中心建设，也影响我国法律服务业的进一步发展。新的时代背景呼吁放开对境外仲裁机构在中国内地仲裁的限制，解决境外仲裁机构在中国内地仲裁面临的一些实际障碍，如仲裁地的认定、裁决国籍的判断标准、裁决的承认与执行等。鉴于《涉外民事关系法律适用法》已经将仲裁地作为认定仲裁协议的准据法，最高人民法院和各级人民法院也已在司法实践中将仲裁地作为认定外国仲裁裁决和我国香港地区裁决的标准，有必要及时修改《仲裁法》，明确将仲裁地作为认定裁决国籍的标准。

若将仲裁地作为认定裁决国籍的标准，则无论是境内仲裁机构还是境外仲裁机构在中国内地对涉外案件提供仲裁服务、作出裁决，均应视为中国涉外仲裁裁决，按照涉外仲裁裁决的标准，依据《仲裁法》第 70 条和《民事诉讼法》第 274 条予以支持、监督、承认和执行。相应的，无论是境内还是境外仲裁机构在中国内地之外提供仲裁服务、作出裁决，均应视为境外仲裁裁决，具体又可分为外国仲裁裁决和区际仲裁裁决。对于外国仲裁裁决，按照《纽约公约》和互惠原则及《民事诉讼法》第 283 条予以承认与执行；对于区际仲裁裁决，则按照最高人民法院就港澳台地区作出的区际安排[①]予以认可和执行。

（本文原载于《环球法律评论》2016 年第 3 期）

---

① 这些安排主要包括《最高人民法院关于内地与香港特别行政区相互执行仲裁裁决的安排》（法释〔2000〕3 号）、《最高人民法院关于香港仲裁裁决在内地执行的有关问题的通知》（法〔2009〕415 号）、《最高人民法院关于内地与澳门特别行政区相互认可和执行仲裁裁决的安排》（法释〔2007〕17 号）和《最高人民法院关于认可和执行台湾地区仲裁裁决的规定》（法释〔2015〕14 号）。

未竟的争鸣：被撤销的国际商事仲裁裁决的承认与执行

傅攀峰*

一　问题的产生

作为一种备受商界人士青睐的纠纷解决机制，国际商事仲裁在解决国际民商事纠纷上，享有近乎垄断的地位。[①] 一方面，随着经济全球化的蓬勃发展，来自不同国家或地区的商人们都希望以独立于各自法院系统的中立纠纷解决机制解决他们之间的争议；另一方面，相对民事判决，仲裁裁决在全球范围内更容易得到执行，而这显然得归功于1958年《纽约公约》（全称《承认与执行外国仲裁裁决公约》）。[②]《纽约公约》被誉为商事领域有史以来最成功的国际立法典范之一，对当代国际商事仲裁起到不可估量

* 傅攀峰，2017年12月来中国社会科学院国际法研究所工作，现任助理研究员。

① 根据伦敦玛丽皇后大学2015年的调查报告，90%的受访者表示，国际仲裁是他们更倾向于选择的纠纷解决机制。参见 http://www.arbitration.qmul.ac.uk/research/2015/，最后访问日期：2015年11月10日。J. Paulsson 亦曾指出，相对其在一国领域内所起的作用，在国际商事交往中，仲裁已发展成为一种具有垄断地位的纠纷解决机制，因而发出“国际仲裁不是仲裁，而是垄断”的观点。参见 Jan Paulsson，“International Arbitration is Not Arbitration”，*Stockholm International Arbitration Review* 2008：2，pp. 1 - 20。

② 截至2016年8月27日，全球已有157个国家成为《纽约公约》的成员国，涵盖所有在全球商贸交往中占有重要地位的国家，基于此点考量，本文的考察对象限于《纽约公约》成员国。参见 http://www.newyorkconvention.org/contracting-states，最后访问日期：2016年8月27日。

的支撑作用。《纽约公约》对缔约国拒绝承认与执行在另一缔约国所作出的仲裁裁决在条件上作了严格限制，而且取消了 1927 年《日内瓦公约》的双重执行令制度（double exequatur），① 极大地促进了仲裁裁决在全球范围内的自由流动。

然而，在内容上，《纽约公约》仅对裁决执行地拒绝承认与执行外国仲裁裁决的条件作了限制性规定，没有亦无法对裁决来源地的裁决撤销制度作安排。因此，在现实上，国际商事仲裁裁决所受之“双重监督”依然存在：② 一方面，裁决来源地享有对撤裁之诉的排他管辖权，此即所谓“初级管辖权”（primary jurisdiction）；另一方面，裁决请求执行地亦须对是否承认与执行某项来自国外的仲裁裁决作审查，此即所谓“次级管辖权”（secondary jurisdiction）。③ 由此，当裁决的撤销与执行在地域上产生分离之时，撤裁之诉与执行之诉在结果上的搭配会出现四种情形（见表 1）。

表 1　撤裁之诉与执行之诉的结果

所涉地域	裁决来源地（撤裁之诉）	请求执行地（执行之诉）
诉之结果	未被撤销	获得执行
	未被撤销	被拒绝执行

① 在《纽约公约》之前的《日内瓦公约》时代，一项外国仲裁裁决要在裁决作出地之外的另一国获得执行，需要经过两道“坎”，即不仅需要获得执行地法院的准许，还需要获得裁决作出地法院的准许，此即所谓双重执行令制度。《日内瓦公约》第 1 条第 4 项规定：“（为获得承认或执行）裁决须（shall）在其所作出地国已为终局（final），如果裁决存在被抗辩、上诉或诉至最高院（在存在此种程序的国家）的可能或被证明针对该裁决的效力提出质疑的程序正在进行中，那么，裁决将不会被认为是终局的。”

② 需要注意的是，在国际投资仲裁领域，裁决可划分为 ICSID 裁决与非 ICSID 裁决，两者之间的一个重大差别在于，根据《华盛顿公约》，ICSID 裁决只接受 ICSID 特设仲裁庭（ad hoc tribunal）的内部机制审查，不受任何公约成员国的外部监督与控制，而公约成员国皆负有执行未被特设仲裁庭撤销的裁决的强制性义务。故此，ICSID 裁决不受《纽约公约》项下国际商事仲裁裁决所受之“双重监督”的约束，非 ICSID 裁决的执行实际上一般亦是遵照《纽约公约》而落实，因而亦须接受“双重监督”的约束。

③ 参见 W. Michael Reisman and Brian Richardson, “Tribunals and Courts: An Interpretation of the Architecture of International Commercial Arbitration”, in Albert Jan van den Berg（ed.）, *Arbitration: The Next Fifty Years*, ICCA Congress Series, No. 16（Kluwer Law International 2012）, p. 25。

续表

所涉地域	裁决来源地（撤裁之诉）	请求执行地（执行之诉）
诉之结果	被撤销	被拒绝执行
	被撤销	获得执行

此处须注意，撤裁之诉的提起及其结果并非必然先于执行之诉。例如，在近年著名的Dallah案①中，涉案裁决是在法国作出的，在裁决仍处于巴黎上诉法院撤裁之诉的审理期间，Dallah向英国法院申请执行涉案裁决，英国法院适用了法国法律，认为仲裁庭错误地认定其对案件具有管辖权，从而作出了拒绝执行涉案裁决的决定；几个月后，巴黎上诉法院却得出了截然相反的结论，认为仲裁庭认定其对案件具有管辖权并没问题，从而作出了驳回当事人撤裁申请的决定。不过，由于类似Dallah案的情况甚为罕见，且本文聚焦裁决被撤销的事实对其承认与执行的影响，因此，本文的研究范围限定于撤裁之诉的提起及其结果先于执行之诉的情形。

虽然在国际商事仲裁中，撤裁之诉与执行之诉在结果上的搭配存在上述四种情形，但这绝非意味着其中每一种情形皆合乎业界所有人士同一程度之预期。未被裁决来源地撤销的裁决最终获得请求执行地的执行，以及被裁决来源地撤销的裁决最终被请求执行地拒绝执行，此两种情形，实践中占绝大多数，亦不与《纽约公约》的精神相违背，不存在争议。未被裁决来源地撤销的裁决最终却被请求执行地拒绝执行，这种情形实践中虽不占多数，但时不时会出现。《纽约公约》的立法宗旨就是要限制这种情形产生的随意性，因而将请求执行地拒绝承认与执行一项未被裁决来源地撤销的裁决的理由严格限定在其文本下的第5条。只有一项裁决存在《纽约公约》第5条下的情形之一，请求执行地法院才可作出拒绝承认与执行该项裁决的决定。故此，这种情形本身不具有争议，争议往往需要根据个案的特殊情况而定，其主要聚焦请求执行地的法院是否合理地解释与适用《纽约公约》第5条，并郑重对待外国仲裁裁决的承认与

① 关于Dallah案之评述，参见Gary Born，Michael Jorek，Dallah and the New York Convention，Available，http://kluwerarbitrationblog.com/2011/04/07/dallah-and-the-new-york-convention/。

执行，不随意拒绝承认与执行一项未被裁决来源地撤销的裁决。①

以上三种情形，皆为《纽约公约》立法所允许，实践中亦不乏其例，乃正常情形。然而，极具争议的一种情形是，被裁决来源地撤销的裁决，在请求执行地却依然获得执行。此种情形，在晚近三十年的国际商事仲裁实践中，屡次出现，持续地引起人们的热议。支持与反对此种实践的人士，似乎都能从《纽约公约》中找到充分的依据。某种意义上，这与《纽约公约》对此种情形预估不足而语焉不详不无关系。这也一度成为某些人士建议对《纽约公约》作修订的重要理由。对《纽约公约》进行修订，固然能为实践提供明确的指引，平息理论上的纷争。然而，目前《纽约公约》整体上仍运行良好，对其作修订需要在全球范围内凝聚各国之共识，难度非常大，而且亦存在越修订问题越多的风险。② 在这种条件下，如何理性地认识此种极具争议的非主流实践，如何客观地评价学界在这个问题上的理论争鸣，如何对此种实践在未来的发展及中国法院应有的司法态度

---

① 在解释与适用《纽约公约》第5条时，会产生一个很重要的问题，即该条规定是否已将当事人阻止一项外国仲裁裁决承认与执行的抗辩理由项穷举，换而言之，请求执行地法院能否援用该条所列之理由项外的理由，作出拒绝承认与执行一项外国仲裁裁决的决定。这个问题即所谓“剩余自由裁量权”（residual discretion）问题。以澳大利亚为例，昆士兰州最高法院在 *Resort Condominiums v. Bolwell* 案（Resort 案）中作出的判决引发了学者们的大量讨论。在该案中，法院表示，在澳大利亚，执行法院在《纽约公约》所列明的理由项外仍享有拒绝承认与执行《纽约公约》项下裁决的一般自由裁量权。不过，学者们的一致看法是，此种剩余自由裁量权并不存在，因为《纽约公约》第5条将承认与执行外国裁决的抗辩理由项已作穷举，且不可被执行地法律下的其他理由增补，此乃《纽约公约》第5条起草者当时清晰的意图，美国（*Parsons & Whittemore Overseas Co.，Inc. v. Société Générale de l'Industrie du papier*）与英国［*Rosseel N. V. v. Oriental Commercial & Shipping Co.，（U. K.）Ltd.*］的权威判决亦支持此种观点。对此，澳大利亚著名仲裁员 Michael Pryles 和墨尔本大学教授 Richard Garnett 对 Resort 案判决提出了严厉批评，并明确地指出，《纽约公约》第5条下的抗辩理由项之所以是穷举的，乃因为《纽约公约》旨在通过压缩主权国家的法院与法律阻碍外国裁决的承认与执行的范围，达到鼓励并促进裁决得到公约缔约国的承认与执行的目的。由此，在外国裁决的承认与执行问题上，立法者希望《纽约公约》的实施能得到统一，而主权国家国内法中古怪的法律原则侵入外国裁决的执行过程，可能会破坏对《纽约公约》作统一解释并以开明的方式将其执行的政策目标。参见 Richard Garnett，“Michael Pryles，Recognition and Enforcement of Foreign Awards under the New York Convetion in Australia and New Zealand”，*Journal of International Arbitration* 25（6），2008。

② 参见 Neil Kaplan，If it Ain't Broke，Don't Change It，Arbitration（Chartered Institute of Arbitrators）80（2），2014，pp. 172－175。

作出前瞻性的预估与建议，则是十分值得探讨的问题。

二 争议中的实践：执行被撤之裁的典型案例

近30年来，在某些国家，特别是法国，出现了当地法院承认并执行已被撤销了的仲裁裁决的案例。根据 Francisco González de Cossío 的新近研究①，目前至少存在10起涉及被撤销的裁决的执行问题的案例，它们分别是：Norsolor 案②、Hilmarton 案③、Chromalloy 案④、Baker Marine 案⑤、Karaha Bodas 案⑥、Termorio 案⑦、Putrabali 案⑧、Yukos 案⑨、Castillo Bozo 案⑩、Commisa 案⑪。以上除 Baker Marine 案与 Termorio 案之外，其他8起案件，涉案裁决最终获得了执行地法院的承认与执行。下文选取其中4例著名案件，对其案情与判决意见作一简介。

---

① 参见 Francisco González de Cossío，"Enforcement of Annulled Awards：Towards a Better Analytical Approach"，*Arbitration International* 32（1），2016，pp. 17－27。

② *Société Pablak Ticaret Limited Sirketi v. Norsolor SA*，French Courde Cassation，9 November 1984.

③ *Société Hilmarton Ltd v. Société Omnium de Traitement et de Valorisation*（*OTV*），French Cour de Cassation，23 March 1994.

④ *Chromalloy Aeroservices*，*a Division of Chromalloy Gas Turbine Corporation v. Arab Republic of Egypt*，District Court，District of Columbia，31 July 1996（939 F Supp 907）.

⑤ *Baker Marine*（*Nig.*）*Ltd v. Chevron*（*Nig.*）*Ltd et al.*，Second Circuit Court of Appeals，United States of America，12 August 1999（191 F 3d 194）.

⑥ *Karaha Bodas Co. LLC Plaintiff v. Perusahaan Pertambangan Minyak Dan Gas Bumi Negara*，*Perusahaan Pertambangan Minyak Dan Gas Bumi Negara*，Fifth Circuit Court of Appeals，UnitedStates of America，23 March 2004（364 F 3d 274）.

⑦ *Termorio SA ESP and Lease Co. Group*，*LLC v. Electranta SP*，*et al.*，Court of Appeals of the United States，District of Columbia，25 May 2007（487 F. 3d 928，376 USApp. DC 242）.

⑧ *Société PT Putrabali Adyamulia v. Société Rena Holding et Société Moguntia Est Epices*，French Cour de Cassation，29 June 2007.

⑨ *Yukos Capital SARL v. Oao Rosneft*，Third Court of Appeals，civil section，Amsterdam，28 April 2009.

⑩ *Juan Jose Castillo Bozo v. Leopoldo Castillo Bozo and Gabriel Castillo Bozo*，District Court of the United States，South Florida's District，23 May 2013（1：12－cv－24174－KMW）.

⑪ *Corporación Mexicana de Mantenimiento Integral*，*S. De R. L de C. V v. Pemex-Exploración y Producción*，No. 10 Civ. 206（AKH），2013 WL 4517225（S. D. N. Y. Aug. 27，2013）.

（1）Hilmarton 案

法国的 OTV 公司委托英国的 Hilmarton 公司提供咨询意见与协调，以使前者在阿尔及利亚签订并履行与其业务相关的合同。纠纷发生后，Hilmarton 公司根据双方签订的仲裁协议向 ICC 国际仲裁院提起了仲裁，以追回 OTV 公司尚欠之余款。1988 年 8 月，仲裁庭在日内瓦作出了裁决，驳回了 Hilmarton 公司的请求。后来，该裁决被仲裁地瑞士的法院所撤销。然而，法国巴黎大审法院（Tribunal de grande instance）却宣布该裁决在法国能够获得执行。Hilmarton 公司随即向巴黎上诉法院（Cour d'appel de Paris）提起上诉，巴黎上诉法院作出了支持原审法院的裁定。

上诉程序中，Hilmarton 公司认为，根据《纽约公约》第 5 条第 1 款 e 项，既然裁决已被仲裁地瑞士法院撤销，法国法院就应该拒绝承认与执行这项裁决。同时，其进一步辩称，巴黎上诉法院的裁判意见也违反了《法国民事诉讼法典》第 1498 条①与第 1502 条②的规定。该案后来诉至法国最高法院（Cour de cassation），后者在 1994 年 3 月作出的裁定中肯定了巴黎上诉法院的意见，其认为，根据《纽约公约》第 7 条③，OTV 公司可以援引与外国仲裁裁决承认与执行有关的法国法律规则，特别是《法国民事诉讼法典》第 1502 条，因为该条并没有包含与《纽约公约》第 5 条第 1 款 e 项列出的拒绝承认与执行外国仲裁裁决相同的理由，并指出，涉案裁决乃是一项并未被纳入瑞士法律秩序之下的国际裁决，因此，即使其已被撤销，其效力依然存在，而且将其在法国执行不违反国际公共政策。

（2）Chromalloy 案

美国的 Chromalloy 公司与埃及政府于 1988 年签订了一份军事采购合

① 《法国民事诉讼法典》（2011 年修订前之“仲裁篇”）第 1498 条规定：“如果援引裁决的当事人能证明裁决存在且承认该裁决不会明显违反国际公共政策，该裁决应予以承认。基于同样的条件，该裁决由执行法官宣告能够获得执行。”

② 《法国民事诉讼法典》（2011 年修订前之“仲裁篇”）第 1502 条规定：“当事人可对准予承认或执行一项国际仲裁裁决的法院裁定提起上诉，但仅限于下列情形：（1）仲裁员是在不存在仲裁协议或者以无效或已过期的仲裁协议作为依据的情形下进行仲裁的；（2）仲裁庭的组成或者独任仲裁员的委任不符合相关规则；（3）仲裁员在其权限范围之外进行仲裁；（4）正当程序未得到尊重；（5）承认或执行该项裁决有违国际公共政策。”

③ 根据《纽约公约》第 7 条第 1 款，该公约之规定不影响缔约国间所订关于承认及执行仲裁裁决之多边或双边协定之效力，亦不剥夺任何利害关系人可依援引裁决地所在国之法律或条约所认许之方式，在其许可范围内，援用仲裁裁决之任何权利。

同。1991 年 12 月埃及终止了该项合同，并通知了 Chromalloy 公司。Chromalloy 公司表示反对埃及取消合同的行为，并根据合同中的仲裁条款提起了仲裁，1994 年 8 月仲裁庭作出了有利于 Chromalloy 公司的裁决。

1994 年 10 月 28 日，Chromalloy 公司向美国哥伦比亚特区地方法院（下称 DC 地方法院）申请执行该项裁决。埃及方面则随后于 1994 年 11 月 13 日向开罗上诉法院提起上诉，请求撤销该项裁决。1995 年 3 月 1 日，埃及方面请求 DC 地方法院暂停审理 Chromalloy 公司的裁决执行申请，并于 1995 年 5 月 5 日，请求 DC 地方法院驳回 Chromalloy 公司的裁决执行申请。1995 年 12 月 5 日，开罗上诉法院作出了撤销该项裁决的裁定。

然而，1996 年 7 月 31 日，DC 地方法院准予了 Chromalloy 公司请求执行该项裁决的申请，驳回了埃及方面的请求。在确认 Chromalloy 公司已遵循《纽约公约》第 4 条所规定的形式要求后，DC 地方法院注意到，根据《纽约公约》第 5 条第 1 款 e 项，其对是否拒绝执行已被“裁决作出地国或裁决所引法律之所属国具有管辖权限的机构撤销的裁决”拥有自由裁量权。其还注意到，该公约第 7 条第 1 项要求“该公约之规定……不剥夺任何利害关系人可依援引裁决地所在国之法律或条约所认许之方式，在其许可范围内，援用仲裁裁决之任何权利”。由此，DC 地方法院在其结论中认为，其拥有根据美国法律来审理 Chromalloy 公司之执行申请的权力，并认定该项裁决对于美国法律而言是一项合格的裁决。

值得注意的是，Chromalloy 公司同时向法国法院提起了请求执行该项裁决的申请。1995 年 5 月 4 日，巴黎大审法院作出了执行该项裁决的决定。埃及随后向巴黎上诉法院提起了上诉。1997 年 1 月 14 日，巴黎上诉法院作出的裁定维持了原审法院的决定，其表示，尽管裁决已经被埃及法院撤销，但其效力依然存在，且将其在法国执行不违反国际公共政策。

（3）Putrabali 案

印尼的 Putrabali 公司与法国的 Est Epices 公司（后来变成 Rena Holding 公司）订有白色辣椒买卖合同，并约定，根据 IGPA 仲裁规则以仲裁的方式解决纠纷。后来 Putrabali 公司运送的一批货物在海难中全部损毁，Rena Holding 公司因此拒绝付款，Putrabali 公司向位于伦敦的 IGPA 提起了仲裁。2001 年 4 月 10 日，仲裁庭作出的裁决（第一项裁决）认定 Rena Holding 公司拒绝付款的行为是有充分的理由作支撑的。根据英国 1996 年《仲裁法》，Putrabali 公司针对裁决中的一个法律问题向伦敦高等法院提起上诉，后者将裁决部分撤销，并认为 Rena Holding 公司拒绝付款的行为构成违约。后来该争议又重新回到仲裁庭。2003 年 8 月 21 日，仲裁庭作出了第二项裁决，支持了 Putrabali 公司的请求，并令 Rena Holding 公司支付合同价款。

为使第一项裁决能在法国得到执行，Rena Holding 公司向巴黎大审法院提出了执行请求。即使第一项裁决已被伦敦高等法院撤销，而且仲裁庭因此已作出了第二项裁决，在 2003 年 9 月 30 日，巴黎大审法院仍然作出了准予执行第一项裁决的决定。Putrabali 公司向巴黎上诉法院提起上诉，声称 Rena Holding 公司谋求在法国执行第一项裁决的行为无异于欺诈。2005 年 3 月 31 日，巴黎上诉法院作出了驳回 Putrabali 公司的上诉申请的裁定，理由在于，一项仲裁裁决在外国被撤销的事实并不阻碍相关当事人请求法国法院将其执行，并且执行第一项裁决也不会违背国际公共政策。

与此同时，Putrabali 公司成功地向巴黎大审法院申请获得了要求执行第二项裁决的决定。然而，2005 年 11 月 17 日，巴黎上诉法院推翻了巴黎大审法院的决定，其认为，由于第二项裁决与第一项裁决处理的是相同当事人之间的相同争议，而第一项裁决已获准执行，因此，第二项裁决不能在法国获得执行。

案件后来上诉至法国最高法院，针对以上两种情况，后者作出了两项裁定。首先，法国最高法院认可了巴黎上诉法院于 2005 年 3 月 31 日作出的裁定。法国最高法院认为，一项国际仲裁裁决，因其不锚定于任何国家法律秩序之下，乃一项蕴含国际正义的决定，其有效性必须由裁决执行地国的准据规则来确定。法国最高法院还作了以下补充，即 Rena Holding 公司可以向法国寻求执行第一项裁决，并且可以援用法国关于国际仲裁的法律规则，因为后者并未将裁决已被仲裁地法院所撤销列为一项拒绝承认与执行裁决的理由。其次，法国最高法院同样也认可了巴黎上诉法院于 2005 年 11 月 17 日作出的裁定，其认为，巴黎上诉法院 3 月 31 日作出的承认及执行第一项裁决的决定已产生既判力，从而能够阻止第二项裁决的执行。

（4）Yukos 案

Yukos Capital 是一家卢森堡的金融公司，从属于 Yukos 集团。在 2003 年和 2004 年，该公司向 Yukos Oil Company 的全资子公司 Yuganskneftegaz（下称 YNG 公司）借出四项贷款。后来 YNG 公司在一项极具争议的拍卖中被出售，处于俄罗斯国家石油公司 Rosneft 的控制之下。YNG 公司因此而没履行其欠 Yukos Capital 贷款的还款责任。2005 年 12 月，Yukos Capital 向“莫斯科商会国际商事仲裁院”[①] 提起了仲裁，请求 Rosneft 向其归还以上贷款及其利息。在 2006 年 12 月 19 日作出的四项裁决中，仲裁庭裁定支持 Yukos Capital 的大多数请求。当 Yukos Capital 随后在荷兰申请执行以上裁决之时，Rosneft 向俄罗斯的法院提出申请撤销裁决的申请。2007 年 5 月 18 日和 23 日，莫斯科商事法院作出了撤销上述裁决的决定，该决定得到了上面两级上诉法院的支持。

在荷兰的执行程序中，Rosneft 辩称由于裁决已被俄罗斯的法院撤销，且俄罗斯与荷兰都为《纽约公约》成员国，根据公约第 5 条，如果一方当事人证明裁决已被裁决作出地国具有管辖权的法院所撤销，那么，经该方当事人的请求，该裁决可以被拒绝承认与执行。Yukos Capital 对裁决已被俄罗斯法院撤销及其对此具有管辖权并无争议，但 Yukos Capital 认为由于俄罗斯法院在关于 Yukos 的一系列问题上既不公正又不独立，因此俄罗斯法院撤销裁决的决定不应成为执行地法院拒绝执行涉案裁决的理由。

阿姆斯特丹地方法院认为，例外的情形可以为准许执行已被撤销的裁决提供论据。不过，其同时指出，就目前的案件而言，Yukos Capital 并未充分展示出此种例外情形的存在。根据《纽约公约》第 5 条第 1 款 e 项所列之理由项，阿姆斯特丹地方法院于 2008 年 2 月 28 日作出了拒绝 Yukos Capital 请求执行涉案裁决的申请的决定。

Yukos Capital 向阿姆斯特丹上诉法院提起了上诉，而后者作出的裁定推翻了阿姆斯特丹地方法院作出的拒绝准许执行涉案裁决的决定，认为《纽约公约》并没有对荷兰法院应否拒绝承认被俄罗斯法院撤销了的仲裁裁决提供答案，这个问题应由荷兰国际私法来回答。根据阿姆斯特丹上诉法院的推理，如果撤销仲裁裁决的外国法院判决在荷兰无法获得承认，那么对于此种判决，荷兰法院应采取不予理会的态度。对于该案，阿姆斯特丹上诉法院在其结论中表示，由于俄罗斯法官所作出的撤销仲裁裁决的判决很可能是须被认定为缺乏公正与独立的司法的产物，因此，前述法院判决不能在荷兰获得承认，这意味着，在考虑 Yukos Capital 所提起的执行涉

---

① International Court of Commercial Arbitration of the Moscow Chamber of Commerce.

案裁决之申请时，俄罗斯法院撤销仲裁裁决的情形须被忽略。Rosneft 后来将案件上诉至荷兰最高法院，后者于 2009 年 6 月 25 日作出裁定，认为 Rosneft 向其提出的上诉申请不具备可受理性。[①]

三 争议的焦点：承认与执行被撤之裁的自由裁量权是否存在

需要指出的是，上述案例仅代表极少数法院在承认与执行被仲裁地撤销的裁决上的实践。事实上，大多数情况下，被仲裁地撤销的裁决往往都被请求执行地法院拒绝承认与执行。[②] 而某些国家的法院在这一问题上存在前后不一致的态度。以美国为例，虽然其在 Chromalloy 案中承认与执行了被埃及法院撤销了的仲裁裁决，但在其他类似案件中，该国法院又因外国仲裁裁决已被仲裁地所撤销而拒绝承认与执行之。[③] 不过，法国法院在这方面的司法态度却有高度的连贯性，从 20 世纪 80 年代的 Norsolor 案，到 90 年代的 Hilmarton 案，再到 21 世纪的 Putrabali 案，法国法院长期以来对被仲裁地撤销了的仲裁裁决的承认与执行采取的是一种极为宽容的态度。

到目前为止，被仲裁地撤销了的仲裁裁决能否获得承认与执行，仍是一个仁者见仁、智者见智的问题。过去 30 多年里，国际仲裁界对这一问题争论不休。根据张潇剑教授的研究，对这一问题的回答，理论上已形成以

---

① 荷兰最高法院在其作出的裁定中清楚地表明，在荷兰申请执行《纽约公约》项下的仲裁裁决的程序相对较为简单。如果申请人的执行申请被初审法院拒绝，其有权将初审法院的裁定诉至上诉法院；如果上诉法院同样作出拒绝执行的裁定，其还可以继续诉至最高法院。但是，如果初审法院或上诉法院作出了准许执行外国仲裁裁决之裁定，那么，不考虑特殊情况的话，另一方无权再作上诉，申请人可在获取执行准许后即刻推进执行裁决。

② Albert Jan van den Berg，Enforcement of Arbitral Awards Annulled in Russia：Case Comment on Court of Appeal of Amsterdam（April 28，2009），*Journal of International Arbitration*，Vol. 27，No. 2，pp. 183 – 185.

③ 相关案例参见 *Baker Marine*（*Nig.*）*Ltd v. Chevron*（*Nig.*）*Ltd et al.*，Second Circuit Court of Appeals，United States of America，August 12，1999；*Martin I. Spier v. Calzaturificio Tecnica S. P. A.*，US District Court，Southern District of New York，Oct. 22 and Nov. 29，1999；*Termo Rio S. A. E. S. P. et al. v. Electranta S. P. et al.*，US Court of Appeals，District of Columbia，May 25，2007。

下几种模式：传统模式[①]、法国模式[②]、克罗马罗依模式[③]、地方撤裁标准模式[④]和礼让模式[⑤]。这五种模式分别从不同的角度，对被撤销了的仲裁裁决能否获得承认与执行作出了解读，丰富了人们对这一问题的认识。然而，应当指出，被撤销了的仲裁裁决能否获得承认与执行，隐藏了一个更深的问题，即承认与执行被撤销了的仲裁裁决的自由裁量权是否存在。对这个问题的回答，在技术上可能存在前述五种模式中的某些模式（如法国模式与克罗马罗依模式）之间的差别，但在立场上，只能是肯定或否定。如何看待承认与执行被撤销的裁决的自由裁量权，必然涉及人们对裁决撤销制度与裁决执行制度的理解，而后者实际上又涉及人们对《纽约公约》相关条款的解读。下文将重点从裁决撤销制度的认识与《纽约公约》相关条款的解读两方面，来考察正、反两方的观点。

（一）肯定的观点

肯定的观点认为，是否应拒绝承认与执行已被仲裁地撤销的裁决，执行地法院对此拥有自由裁量权。此种观点为法国法院的相关司法实践所推崇，法国及法语界的不少学者对此种司法态度亦颇为赞赏。[⑥] E. Gailllard

---

① 根据传统模式，一项被撤销的仲裁裁决系属无效，并且不能在其他司法管辖范围内获得承认与执行，德国的实践亦属此列。参见张潇剑《被撤销之国际商事仲裁裁决的承认与执行》，《中外法学》2006 年第 3 期。

② 根据法国模式，如果一项仲裁裁决符合法国法上规定的承认与执行标准，即使它为裁决来源地法院所撤销，仍然可以在法国得到承认与执行。参见张潇剑《被撤销之国际商事仲裁裁决的承认与执行》，《中外法学》2006 年第 3 期。

③ 根据克罗马罗依模式，如果一项仲裁裁决符合美国法上规定的承认与执行标准，且双方当事人在其仲裁协议中共同约定了不对仲裁裁决提起上诉，那么虽然该项仲裁裁决已被裁决来源地法院所撤销，它仍然可以在美国获得承认与执行。参见张潇剑《被撤销之国际商事仲裁裁决的承认与执行》，《中外法学》2006 年第 3 期。

④ 根据地方撤裁标准模式，如果撤销仲裁裁决并非基于国际普遍认可的理由，而是基于地方撤销标准，那么被撤销的仲裁裁决可以得到其他国家的承认与执行。这是国际著名仲裁员 J. Paulsson 所提出的观点。参见张潇剑《被撤销之国际商事仲裁裁决的承认与执行》，《中外法学》2006 年第 3 期。

⑤ 根据礼让模式，请求执行地法院应当认同裁决来源地法院撤销裁决的决定，亦即拒绝承认与执行一项已被撤销的仲裁裁决，除非裁决来源地法院作出撤销决定时存在程序不公的行为或者违反了基本正义的理念。这一观点由国际著名仲裁员 W. Park 教授所提出。参见张潇剑《被撤销之国际商事仲裁裁决的承认与执行》，《中外法学》2006 年第 3 期。

⑥ 持此种观点的知名人士包括 Ph. Fouchard、B. Goldman、E. Gaillard、D. Hascher、P. Khan、C. Jarrosson、E. Loquin 等。

指出，在诸如法国等大陆法国家，人们对仲裁有这样的一种认识，这种认识曾被 B. Goldman 与 P. Lalive 等作系统化的阐释，即仲裁地只不过是当事人为方便起见而作出的选择，仲裁庭不需要仅仅因为仲裁地设在某一特定国家而像该国法院一样开展程序，仲裁员的权力亦非源自仲裁地所在国，而是源自所有在某种条件下承认仲裁协议及仲裁裁决有效性的法律秩序的总和，此亦即为何人们常说仲裁员不从属于任何属地司法系统的原因。[①] 一方面，很难想象被一国上诉法院撤销的该国下级法院的判决能在他国获得执行；然而，另一方面，如果仲裁地并非仲裁与国家法律秩序的唯一联系点，那么执行一项在他国已被撤销的仲裁裁决完全是合适的，因为对于执行地法，仲裁地法并不具有优先性。[②] 不难得知，根据此种观点，被仲裁地撤销的裁决的效力问题将变成一个国际私法上的问题。换言之，执行地法院在受理已被撤销的裁决之执行申请时，需要运用国际私法中的方法，以判断仲裁地与仲裁是否存在紧密的联系，或者仲裁地与仲裁之间是不是仅存在偶然的联系。虽然仲裁的开展及其相关活动时常在仲裁地进行，而且不少国家甚至努力将本国的城市打造成具有吸引力的仲裁地，从而间接地增进该国的经济利益，[③] 但只要裁决不在仲裁地寻求执行，那么仲裁地所在国对裁决作审查一般就不具有实质性的利益。

基于此，某些国家在 20 世纪 80 年代初就已开始在本国国际商事仲裁立法中作出了将裁决撤销制度相对化的尝试。典型之例莫过于瑞士。1982 年的《瑞士联邦国际私法》草案包含这样一条规定：对于在瑞士作出的裁决，若裁决双方都不是瑞士人，那么双方可自由约定放弃针对裁决提起撤裁之诉的权利。这种意定型“弃权条款”的目的在于，尽可能地确保仲裁的最大效率，并避免瑞士法院承受因受理与瑞士不存在任何实际关联、旨在拖延裁决执行的裁决撤销申请而带来的负担。1985 年修订的比利时仲裁

---

① E. Gaillard, The Enforcement of Awards Set Aside in the Country Of Origin, ICSID Review 14 (1) (1999), p. 18.

② E. Gaillard, The Enforcement of Awards Set Aside in the Country Of Origin, ICSID Review 14 (1) (1999), p. 19.

③ 对此，法国曾在 2011 年发布了一份加强巴黎在地域上的法律竞争力的报告（业界称之为“Prada 报告”），其中首要的方面乃是巩固巴黎在国际仲裁领域作为重要仲裁地的地位。另一个典型之例则是新加坡，新加坡国际仲裁中心（SIAC）近年取得瞩目的发展及新加坡现今已经发展成为全球最受欢迎的仲裁地之一被认为离不开新加坡政府的大力支持。

法则行得更远，其补充了一项强制性规定，效力在于：如果在比利时进行的仲裁不牵涉来自比利时的当事人，那么当事人不可向比利时法院提起撤销涉案仲裁裁决的申请。换言之，在此种制度安排下，只要在比利时发生的仲裁不涉及比利时人，不论当事人愿意与否，裁决作出后，都不可向比利时法院申请撤销涉案裁决。不过，后来在1998年再次修订仲裁法时，比利时悄悄地废除了该项规定，转而采纳前述瑞士的意定型“弃权条款”。

上述将裁决撤销制度相对化的立法尝试，目的在于避免与仲裁地无任何联系的当事人仅为达到拖延裁决执行的目的故意申请撤销裁决，以此提升仲裁的效率，进而提升该国在国际商事仲裁领域作为仲裁地的竞争力。支持此种立法安排的人士一般都认为，与仲裁地不存在紧密关系的仲裁裁决应留待裁决执行地法院来监督。相反，不作任何区分地让裁决置于仲裁地的绝对控制之下，不仅会纵容当事人通过提起撤销裁决的申请，故意拖延执行裁决，而且还会导致这样的风险，即仲裁地可能会运用当地相当奇特甚至狭隘的裁决撤销标准将裁决撤销，而在这种情况下，执行地亦不得不服从仲裁地法院的撤裁决定，如此，《纽约公约》真正的立法目的会大打折扣。[①]

J. Paulsson曾将裁决撤销标准区分为“当地标准”与“国际标准”。他认为，仲裁地法院已将裁决撤销的这一事实，不应当成为裁决在其他国家顺利获得执行的障碍，除非撤销裁决的决定是根据国际公认的理由所作出的。[②] 在他看来，裁决撤销的国际标准在范围上从属于《纽约公约》第5条第1款的前4项与《联合国国际贸易法委员会国际商事仲裁示范法》（简称《示范法》）第36条第1款a项所列出的理由，任何其他理由都属于裁决撤销的当地标准，依当地标准撤销裁决的结果，仅在当地具有法律效力。[③] 例如，有的法院可能会因为裁决书未获所有仲裁员签名而被撤销，奥地利直到1983年即是如此，而这显然与国际商事仲裁在裁决撤销标准方面的发展潮流相左，亦与现代仲裁规则存在冲突，因为后者通常都会明

---

① 当然，在上述将裁决撤销制度相对化的国家，即瑞士、法国、瑞典等国，此种情况基本不会发生，它们都是传统的仲裁强国，素以对仲裁友好著称。

② 参见 J. Paulsson，“Enforcing Arbitral Awards Notwithstanding Local Standard Annulments”，*Asia Pac. L. Rev.* 6（2），1998，pp. 1－2。

③ 参见 J. Paulsson，“Enforcing Arbitral Awards Notwithstanding Local Standard Annulments”，*Asia Pac. L. Rev.* 6（2），1998，p. 25。

确，即使某位仲裁员拒绝合作，仲裁庭依然可作出有效裁决。[①] 在 Paulsson 看来，若赋予基于这种情形而撤销仲裁裁决的结果以普遍效力，从而拒绝承认与执行之，则显然会违背《纽约公约》的立法宗旨，因为《纽约公约》旨在确保仲裁裁决能够在全球范围内获得执行，除非抵制裁决执行的一方当事人能够证明，涉案仲裁存在根本性问题，如仲裁庭超裁、仲裁庭组庭不当，以及未给予当事人陈述意见的机会。[②] 由此，他认为，对于一项已被撤销的仲裁裁决，执行地法院应考虑到裁决被撤销所基于的具体理由，如果裁决被撤销是基于当地标准，那么执行地法院可运用其自由裁量权，对裁决被撤销的事实置之不理。由于涉案裁决可能将在其管辖领域执行，事关重大，因此，如何判断裁决被撤销乃基于当地标准而非国际标准，执行地法院拥有不亚于仲裁地法院的权力，它可以自主判断仲裁地法院作出的撤销裁决的决定具有多大程度的说服力，而不至视其自动具有拘束力。[③]

在承认与执行被撤销的裁决问题上，Paulsson 甚至认为，执行地法院自由裁量权的行使不应仅局限于裁决乃基于当地标准被撤销之情形，还可延伸至裁决乃基于国际标准被撤销之情形。[④] 首先，仲裁地法院作出撤销裁决的决定时，可能以国际标准之名，行当地标准之实。其次，《纽约公约》第 5 条在内容上显得有些苛刻与过时，当今某些国家的仲裁法对承认与执行外国仲裁裁决采取了非常宽容的态度，即使裁决是按照国际标准被撤销的，亦未必不可能在这些国家获得承认与执行，而这也是《纽约公约》第 7 条第 1 款所允许的。该条款常被称作“更惠权条款”（more-favorable-right provision），其内容是，如果一国法律对承认与执行一项外国仲裁裁决存在比相关公约（如《纽约公约》）更优惠的条件，那么该国法院应适用本国的法律来对待外国仲裁裁决在该国的执行申请。

---

① 参见 J. Paulsson，“Enforcing Arbitral Awards Notwithstanding Local Standard Annulments”，*Asia Pac. L. Rev.* 6（2），1998，p. 2。

② 参见 J. Paulsson，“Enforcing Arbitral Awards Notwithstanding Local Standard Annulments”，*Asia Pac. L. Rev.* 6（2），1998，p. 2。

③ 参见 J. Paulsson，“Enforcing Arbitral Awards Notwithstanding Local Standard Annulments”，*Asia Pac. L. Rev.* 6（2），1998，p. 26。

④ 参见 J. Paulsson，“Enforcing Arbitral Awards Notwithstanding Local Standard Annulments”，*Asia Pac. L. Rev.* 6（2），1998，p. 26。

另外，《纽约公约》第5条的一项措辞，为执行地法院行使自由裁量权打开了一扇窗。这就是著名的“可能”与“必须”之争。英文版的《纽约公约》对拒绝承认与执行一项裁决的条件使用了“may”一词（recognition and enforcement of the award may be refused...），中文、俄文与西班牙文三个版本都与该措辞保持一致，而法文版本则使用了“seront”的表达，这是法语中的将来直陈式语态，意为“必须”。然而，颇具讽刺意味的是，法国法院乃是支持执行地法院对是否承认与执行已被撤销的裁决拥有自由裁量权的典型代表。对此，Paulsson认为，法语版本与其他四个语言版本在表达上的细微差异并不能改变《纽约公约》赋予执行地法院自由裁量权的本质，而且《纽约公约》的宗旨就是促进仲裁裁决的国际承认与执行，这点在《纽约公约》第7条上体现得尤为突出。①

（二）否定的观点

否定的观点认为，是否应拒绝承认与执行已被仲裁地撤销的裁决，执行地法院对此不具有自由裁量权。换言之，如果裁决已被仲裁地法院撤销，执行地法院必须拒绝承认与执行之。乍看，此一观点与“支持仲裁”的精神似乎相左，难以得到国际仲裁界的赞同。然而，实际情况恰好相反，因为就连《纽约公约》最重要的起草参与人P. Sanders及以研究《纽约公约》著称的A. J. van den Berg都持此种观点。②

在签订完《纽约公约》从纽约回荷兰后不久，针对被仲裁地撤销的裁决的执行问题，P. Sanders曾有过以下表述：“（对于被仲裁地撤销的裁决）由于已经不存在任何仲裁裁决，且执行一项已经不存在了的仲裁裁决乃为不可能之事，或者甚至会与执行地的公共政策相抵触，因此执行地的法院将会拒绝执行。”③ A. J. van den Berg指出：“拒绝执行一项仲裁裁决仅具有

---

① 参见J. Paulsson, “May or Must Under the New York Convention”, *Arbitration International* 14（2），1998，p. 229。

② 持此种观点的知名人士包括J-F. Poudret、P. Sanders、E. Schwartz、A. J. van den Berg、B. Oppetit、B. Leurent、H. Gharavi等。

③ 参见P. Sanders, “New York Convention on the Recognition and Enforcement of Foreign Arbitral Awards”, *Netherlands Int'l L. Rev.* 43，55（1959），转引自A. J. van den Berg, “Enforcement of Arbitral Awards Anulled in Russia: Case Comment on Court of Appeal of Amsterdam（April 28，2009）”, *Journal of International Arbitration* 27（2），2010，p. 187。

属地效力（即大多情况下其效力限于作出拒绝执行该项裁决的法院所在国），对于同样的裁决，其他国家可作出相反的决定，准予该项裁决在其境内获得执行。相反，撤销一项仲裁裁决则具有普遍效力（erga omnes effect），一旦某项裁决在裁决作出地国被撤销，那么该项裁决则丧失了在《纽约公约》成员国获得承认与执行的资格。由此，裁决的撤销制度能提供法律确定性（legal certainty）。”①

在对上文曾介绍的 Yukos 案进行分析时，A. J. van den Berg 认为，《纽约公约》并没有为被撤销的裁决获得承认与执行提供可能性，但 1961 年《欧洲国际商事仲裁公约》却提供了此种可能，因为不同于《纽约公约》，《欧洲国际商事仲裁公约》并没有与《纽约公约》第 5 条第 1 款 e 项相对应的条款，② 而且在撤销裁决事宜上，该公约第 9 条第 2 款还特别针对《纽约公约》第 5 条第 1 款 e 项的适用作出了限制。然而，问题是荷兰并非《欧洲国际商事仲裁公约》的成员国，因此，荷兰法院不能援引该公约的相关规定。基于此，A. J. van den Berg 认为，如果不存在类似《欧洲国际商事仲裁公约》第 9 条第 2 款的规则可供援引，执行地国单纯基于《纽约公约》的相关规定承认与执行被仲裁地撤销的裁决，便是于法无据。③

---

① Albert Jan van den Berg, "Enforcement of Arbitral Awards Annulled in Russia: Case Comment on Court of Appeal of Amsterdam (April 28, 2009)", *Journal of International Arbitration* 27 (2), 2010, p. 182.

② 1961 年《欧洲国际商事仲裁公约》第 9 条专门对“仲裁裁决的撤销”作出规定，其内容如下：（一）一缔约国撤销按本公约作出的仲裁裁决，只有在下列情况下，才构成另一缔约国拒绝承认和执行裁决的理由，即裁决是由在该国或按该国法律作出裁决的国家撤销的，并且具有下述理由之一：1. 仲裁协议的当事人，按对其适用的法律，不具有行为能力；或者按当事人所依据的法律，协议是无效的，如协议中未规定此项法律，依裁决地国家的法律规定，这项协议无效；2. 请求撤销裁决的当事人，没有得到关于仲裁员任命或仲裁程序的正式通知，或者因其他原因未能陈述其意见；3. 裁决涉及仲裁申请中没有提及的或不属于仲裁申请项目的一种争议，或者裁决中包含超出仲裁申请范围的裁决事项；如果仲裁申请范围内的裁决事项可以同仲裁申请范围外的裁决事项分开，则申请范围内的裁决事项可以不予撤销；4. 仲裁机构的组成和仲裁程序不是按照当事人的协议办理的，或者如无此项协议，不是按照本公约第 4 条的规定办理的。（二）缔约国同时是 1958 年 6 月 10 日《关于承认和执行外国仲裁裁决的纽约公约》的参加国时，在缔约国的关系中，仅在出现本条第 1 款规定撤销裁决的情形下，《纽约公约》第 5 条第 1 款 e 项才能被适用。

③ 参见 Albert Jan van den Berg, "Enforcement of Arbitral Awards Annulled in Russia: Case Comment on Court of Appeal of Amsterdam (April 28, 2009)", *Journal of International Arbitration* 27 (2), 2010, p. 198。

至于 Paulsson 所提到的仲裁地法院可能采用当地标准而非国际标准审查仲裁裁决的情况，van den Berg 指出："基于所谓狭隘理由而撤销仲裁裁决的案例可以说是屈指可数，有必要因此而使《纽约公约》的解释变得模糊、不确定吗？在我看来，这是为使《纽约公约》的解释具有确定性与可预见性而应付出的一个小小代价。"①

另外，对于某些国家将裁决撤销制度相对化的立法，van den Berg 认为，这种相对化的立法在实践中并未起到太多的正面作用。上文曾提到比利时在 1985 年的仲裁立法中规定，如果在比利时发生的仲裁不牵涉来自比利时的当事人，那么当事人不可向比利时法院提起撤销裁决的申请。这项规定当时似乎仅由比利时参议院的某位议员促成，比利时仲裁界为此感到极为惊讶。后来，这项安排所带来的实际效果却与那位议员所期待的全然相反，当事人不再将比利时约定为仲裁地，比利时同时被一些仲裁机构列入仲裁地黑名单。于是，后来比利时在 1998 年重新修订仲裁法时废除了这项制度。② 瑞士的裁决撤销相对化尝试并没有比利时当时那么激进，然而，瑞士不少评论家开始对《瑞士联邦国际私法》第 192 条项下的弃权条款的运用及其优势提出了质疑，并且建议当事人不要在合同中植入一条弃权性约定，因为在他们看来，向瑞士联邦法院提起撤裁之诉具有很高的效率与满意度。原因有三：其一，瑞士已将撤裁理由降至最低；其二，当事人在瑞士提起撤裁之诉，并不会对裁决的执行产生中断效应；其三，瑞士法院会在 6 个月之内针对撤裁申请作出裁定。在此种背景下，当事人很难利用撤裁救济手段达到实现拖延裁决执行的目的。③ van den Berg 指出："现实中，当事人明确约定排除撤裁之诉的情形事实上极为罕见，这似乎表明了，实践中，人们并不愿放弃通过在裁决来源地国提起撤裁之诉以阻止有瑕疵嫌疑的裁决获得执行的普遍性救济手段。"④

---

① Albert Jan van den Berg, "Should the Setting Aside of the Arbitral Award be Abolished", *ICSID Review* 29 (2), 2014, p. 286.

② 参见 Albert Jan van den Berg, "Should the Setting Aside of the Arbitral Award be Abolished", *ICSID Review* 29 (2), 2014, p. 276。

③ 参见 Albert Jan van den Berg, "Should the Setting Aside of the Arbitral Award be Abolished", *ICSID Review* 29 (2), 2014, p. 277。

④ 参见 Albert Jan van den Berg, "Should the Setting Aside of the Arbitral Award be Abolished", *ICSID Review* 29 (2), 2014, p. 277。

关于《纽约公约》第5条下的“可以”与“必须”之争，在van den Berg看来，与某些评论者所声称的相反，《纽约公约》的起草者们当时并非有意选择“may”一词，在关于其第5条第1款e项的适用上，《纽约公约》的“谈判记录”（travaux préparatoires）也没有对“may”与“shall”两词之选择作讨论。实际上，van den Berg认为《纽约公约》中的“may”一词应作“shall”理解，即在当事人证明案件存在《纽约公约》第5条以穷举的方式列出的具体情形的条件下，对于是否应承认与执行相关裁决，裁决执行地不具有剩余自由裁量权。他认为，即使裁决执行地法院将“may”解释为赋予其对是否应承认与执行相关裁决拥有剩余自由裁量权，其仅能在以下两种情形下使用此种自由裁量：（1）案件在《纽约公约》第5条所列举的理由项上仅存在细微情形；（2）当事人并未在仲裁程序中及时指出可构成拒绝执行裁决的理由的情形。[①] 他还指出，在已发布的超过1500件的相关案例中，人们都无法发现任何法院将剩余自由裁量权适用《纽约公约》第5条第1款e项的情形。法国法院的方法，在其看来，主要是基于《纽约公约》第7条第1款的规定，而非基于“可能”一词之表达。[②]

（三）对上述观点分歧之评价

首先，批评者所提出的“撤销一项仲裁裁决则具有普遍效力”的观点是颇值得商榷的。因为接受“撤销一项仲裁裁决则具有普遍效力”的观点，即意味着接受仲裁裁决的终局效力依赖仲裁地主权者的评价，逻辑结果便是，仲裁只不过是仲裁地司法体系的附庸，这与当代国际仲裁实践中仲裁地虚位化的发展趋势格格不入。[③] 当今，仲裁地实际上已经发展成为一种“法律拟制”，因为仲裁程序（主要是庭审）的实际开展地与仲裁地之间并非必须存在实际关联。实践中，当事人主要从中立性的角度选择“仲裁地”，换言之，“仲裁地”与任何一方当事人不能关系过密，以致可

---

① 参见Albert Jan van den Berg，“Enforcement of Arbitral Awards Annulled in Russia：Case Comment on Court of Appeal of Amsterdam（April 28，2009）”，*Journal of International Arbitration* 27（2），2010，p. 186。

② 参见Albert Jan van den Berg，“Should the Setting Aside of the Arbitral Award be Abolished”，*ICSID Review* 29（2），2014，pp. 278，281 - 282。

③ 参见Gabrielle Kaufmann-Kohler，“Globalization of Arbitral Procedure”，*Vanderbilt Journal of Transnational Law*，36（2003），pp. 1318 - 1320。

能影响仲裁地法院公正地行使裁决监督权；相反，仲裁程序的开展地则可能恰恰与一方当事人具有紧密的关系，目的在于让仲裁程序以更高效的方式推进。此种背景下，全球各国不少城市不断塑造其友好的仲裁形象，以期在当今日趋激烈的仲裁地竞争中脱颖而出[①]。仲裁地虚位化的发展趋势实际表明，在无法使仲裁裁决绝对摆脱国家法院控制的条件下，当事人希望选择对仲裁开放、友好，且具有公正品质与较高专业水平的仲裁地来对裁决行使监督权，即使其所选择的仲裁地与仲裁本身不存在联系。如果遵循仲裁地虚位化的发展逻辑，那么不论仲裁地位于什么国家，无论其对仲裁是否友好，仲裁地法院撤销裁决的决定，不应该是当然地对所有潜在裁决执行地国产生绝对的约束力。不过，潜在裁决执行地国可依照仲裁地对仲裁的友好程度及其在全球的受欢迎度来判定仲裁地法院作出撤销裁决的决定的可信任度与参考价值，仅此而已。另外，即使仲裁地确然与所发生的仲裁有这样或那样的联系，也不能改变这种事实，即仲裁的发生乃基于体现当事人自由意思的仲裁协议，而仲裁的这种契约基础才是仲裁裁决终局效力的根基之所在，[②] 而且，在广泛的社会层面，商界人士都希望仲裁此种私人性质的纠纷解决机制的结果能够被赋予终局效力。批评者们认为撤销一项仲裁裁决具有普遍效力能为裁决撤销制度提供法律上的确定性，这看似不无道理，因为如此一来，被撤销的仲裁裁决无论在什么国家都无法得到执行，从而避免出现裁决在某一潜在执行地无法得到执行而在另一潜在执行地却获得执行的冲突情形。然而，此种理由过于追求确定性与一致性，亦即过于追求裁决撤销制度在形式上的合理性，而忽略了基于个案对裁决撤销结果的本身作实质分析。

与批评者们不同，此种新方法的支持者们，他们注重从实质的角度分析仲裁地与案件本身的联系，而且还注意到仲裁地撤裁理由是否存在荒谬或明显不合理的情形等问题，因而始终对仲裁地的撤裁行为保持怀疑的态度。在支持者们看来，如果仲裁地与案件不具有任何实质联系，而在这种条件下，涉案仲裁裁决被仲裁地法院撤销，那么潜在执行地法院完全有理由忽视撤裁事实，自主决定是否应继续承认与执行涉案裁决。即使仲裁地

① 目前全球公认的最受欢迎的仲裁地包括伦敦、巴黎、日内瓦、新加坡、中国香港等地。

② 参见 Karl-Heinz Böckstiegel, Party Autonomy and Case Management—Experiences and Suggestions of an Arbitrator, 11 Schieds (2013, no. 1), pp. 1-5。

与案件存在实际联系，支持者们也注意到，仲裁地法院的撤裁理由不一定具有合理性，倘若因仲裁地法院基于明显不合理乃至荒谬的原因将裁决撤销，而该裁决因此无法在任何潜在执行地获得执行，这将对胜诉当事人极为不公。显然，支持者们对于国际商事仲裁裁决的承认与执行持相当自由与开放的态度。然而，人们也须充分意识到以下这一点，即仲裁在许多时候离不开仲裁地所提供的各种协助，如果激励鼓吹此种新方法，乃至鼓吹废除撤裁制度，那么这极有可能挫伤不少国家对仲裁的支持与热情，而且从现实来看，采纳这种新方法的国家极为有限，大部分国家都认为被仲裁地撤销的裁决无法获得承认与执行。

四 前瞻：被撤之裁的承认与执行迈向多元化及中国法院的因应

由此，人们需要在支持者与批评者的观点之间找到一个现实的平衡。《纽约公约》对《日内瓦公约》最大的突破在于其摒弃了后者的“双重执行令”制度，裁决的执行不需要在裁决作出地事先获得批准。然而，若将被仲裁地撤销的裁决视为已失去普遍效力的裁决，这无疑将变相复苏显然已过时的“双重执行令”制度。另外，《纽约公约》又理解并明确肯定仲裁地对裁决的监督与控制权限，以使该公约能在最大限度上获得全球各国的加入与支持。

因此，结合《纽约公约》的立法宗旨及当代国际仲裁的现状与发展趋势，对于“被仲裁地撤销的裁决能否在请求执行地获得执行”这一问题，人们宜采取积极的现实主义态度。所谓积极，即意味着前述相关国家的法院处理前述四个案件的新方法在具体情形下应被得到支持与借鉴。但当今各国仲裁制度及其实践的现实差异又决定了现阶段不宜鼓吹此种新方法，因为目前世界上绝大多数国家远未达到可以放弃裁决撤销制度，且无视仲裁地撤销仲裁裁决的事实，自由决定应否执行已被撤销的仲裁裁决的阶段。新方法与传统方法并存，这并非坏事，至于此种新方法未来是否会“遍地开花”，抑或仍停留在“平静的湖面上偶尔溅起几朵浪花”的阶段，则有待未来国际商事仲裁的充分发展方能揭晓。但无论怎样，这都应当是一个自然的演变过程。

在被仲裁地法院撤销的裁决能否获得执行的问题上，前面介绍的Hilmarton案、Chromalloy案、Putrabali案与Yukos案引来业界人士的广泛关注，因为根据传统的理念与主流的实践，执行国应当拒绝承认与执行被仲裁地撤销了的裁决，而这些案例却突破了传统，为国际商事仲裁裁决的承认与执行带来了新的实践方法。然而，正如前文所述，此种新方法引起了极大的争议，支持者与批评者的数量都相当可观，且不乏在国际仲裁界颇具影响力的人物。在可预见的未来，这一争议必然将延续下去。对于被仲裁地撤销的裁决的承认与执行，各国法院的实践将向多元化的方向进一步发展。这种多元化既是横向的，也是纵向的。横向上，不同国家，乃至同一国家内部的不同法院，在这个问题上的司法态度依然存在分歧；纵向上，在不同时期不同的案件中，同一国家，如美国，在这个问题上的司法态度会存在差异。不管怎样，有一点是可以肯定的，即对这个问题的回答将越来越取决于个案的具体情形。

另外，对于已被仲裁地撤销的裁决，中国法院是不是根据《纽约公约》第5条第1款e项的规定，将其当然视为不具有可执行性？目前尚未发现对这一问题作出直接回应的案件。不过，1987年中国加入《纽约公约》之时，最高人民法院曾颁布《关于执行我国加入的〈纽约公约〉的通知》(以下简称《通知》)。《通知》一共5条，其中第4条规定："我国有管辖权的人民法院接到一方当事人的申请后，应对申请承认及执行的仲裁裁决进行审查，如果认为不具有《1958年纽约公约》第五条第一、二两项所列的情形，应当裁定承认其效力，并且依照民事诉讼法（试行）规定的程序执行；如果认定具有第五条第二项所列的情形之一的，或者根据被执行人提供的证据证明具有第五条第一项所列的情形之一的，应当裁定驳回申请，拒绝承认及执行。"据此，《纽约公约》第5条第1款e项下裁决已被仲裁地法院撤销的情形，构成"应当"拒绝承认及执行的情形。换言之，只要被执行人证明裁决具有此种情形，中国法院就必须拒绝承认与执行之，没有任何行使自由裁量权的余地。最高人民法院当年发布的这一《通知》，符合国际上主流的解读与实践，时至今日，亦并非不合理。不过，自《通知》发出后，国际仲裁界关于被撤销的裁决的承认与执行的个别实践及理论探讨陡然剧增，这一问题已成为当今国际仲裁界一个常论常新、犹未了结的争论。

2010年时任最高人民法院副院长的万鄂湘教授等曾撰文指出：“《纽约公约》第五条规定了被请求承认与执行国‘可以’拒绝承认与执行的情形。须注意，第五条规定的拒绝事由使得被请求承认与执行国‘可以’拒绝，而非‘必须’或‘应当’拒绝，因此，不排除虽然存在这些情形，但被请求承认与执行国仍然予以承认与执行的情况。”① 按照此种理解，即使裁决出现《纽约公约》第5条第1款e项的情形，即裁决尚无拘束力、被撤销或停止执行，被请求承认与执行国并无义务拒绝将其承认与执行。在邦基农贸新加坡私人有限公司申请承认和执行英国仲裁裁决一案②，广东省高级人民法院认为，“英国伦敦FOSFA协会仲裁员R. W. ROOKES与W. PLUG作出的第3920号裁决尚未生效，对被申请人尚无拘束力，根据《纽约公约》第5条第1款第（戊）项的规定，应拒绝承认和执行该仲裁裁决”。该案上报至最高人民法院，在其复函中，虽然最高人民法院也认定人民法院应当拒绝承认与执行本案仲裁裁决，然而并未采纳广东省高级人民法院的理由。裁决尚无拘束力与裁决已被撤销这两种情况，虽然有较大的差别，但两者亦有相通点。首先，两者都并列置于《纽约公约》第5条第1款e项之下；其次，裁决已被仲裁地撤销通常被认为将导致裁决丧失拘束力。最高人民法院在邦基农贸案中并没有回答裁决尚无拘束力是否必然导致裁决应被拒绝承认与执行，人们更无从推断其对于裁决被仲裁地撤销后当事人仍向中国法院申请承认与执行的态度。

考虑到未来很可能会出现当事人，特别是中方当事人，向中国法院申请承认与执行已被外国法院撤销了的裁决，中国法院有必要对这个问题再行评估。无论是采取支持还是反对执行地法院对此拥有自由裁量权的司法态度，对中国而言，都是有利亦有弊。如果中国法院支持执行地法院对此拥有自由裁量权，那么，一方面，这能彰显中国法院对国际商事仲裁裁决承认与执行的特别支持，无形中会在国际仲裁界产生积极的信号，进而提升中国法院在国际商事仲裁领域的友好形象。须知，目前活跃于国际仲裁界且具有重要公共影响力的著名人士，如J. Paulsson、E. Gaillard、G. Born

① 万鄂湘、夏晓红：《中国法院不予承认以及执行某些外国仲裁裁决的原因——〈纽约公约〉相关案例分析》，载《武大国际法评论》（第十三卷），武汉大学出版社，2010，第10页。

② 参见《最高人民法院关于邦基农贸新加坡私人有限公司申请承认和执行英国仲裁裁决一案的请示的复函》，民四他字〔2006〕第41号。

都极力支持此种司法态度。另一方面，从利益的角度出发，在中方当事人的海外胜诉裁决被当地法院轻率撤销的情况下，如果其选择向中国法院申请承认与执行该裁决，且裁决涉及金额巨大，为保护中方当事人的合法利益，中国法院可以考虑依然承认与执行该裁决。[①] 不过，这种司法态度的弊端也是比较明显的。首先，它并非目前世界各国对待被撤销的仲裁裁决的主流态度；其次，承认与执行被撤销的裁决可能会损害中国与撤销裁决的仲裁地所在国的关系，特别是与其在司法领域的合作关系；最后，这种司法态度一定程度上会造成国际商事仲裁领域裁决监督权分配的混乱，因为国际上普遍认为，仲裁地法院拥有行使裁决监督权的正当权利，承认与执行已被仲裁地撤销了的裁决，必然会弱化仲裁地对裁决监督的意义，亦不利于中国法院对在其境内（即以中国为仲裁地）作出的国际商事仲裁裁决进行有效监督。

权衡利弊，对于被仲裁地撤销的裁决的承认与执行，中国法院有必要建立一套基于个案的审查机制。[②] 理想的状况应该是，仲裁地法院严格按照《示范法》确立的标准撤销的仲裁裁决，中国法院应当拒绝承认与执行之。否则，中国法院应保留承认与执行被仲裁地撤销的裁决的自由裁量权。为谨慎起见，应将此种自由裁量权集中授予最高人民法院行使。换言之，中、高级人民法院无权单独决定承认与执行已被仲裁地撤销的裁决，当其决定拒绝承认与执行此种裁决之时，经层报，最终由最高人民法院严格根据个案的具体情况决定是否应该依然承认与执行此种裁决。这既能确保此种自由裁量权不被滥用，又能彰显中国法院支持国际商事仲裁发展的开放态度。它有利于保护个案中胜诉方当事人的权利，而且会获得国际商事仲裁界大多数人士的赞赏，中国仲裁的对外形象也会获得相应的提升。

（本文原载于《现代法学》2017 年第 1 期）

---

① 赵秀文教授曾指出："对于美国和法国的某些做法，我们也可以在适当的情况下借鉴：当仲裁地国撤销国际仲裁裁决的理由在我国仲裁法上并不存在时，为了保护我国当事人的合法权益，我们也可以考虑承认与执行该被外国法院撤销了的裁决。但这只能在非常特殊的情况下加以适用，即在撤销裁决的理由不符合一般国际惯例的情况下适用。"（赵秀文：《从克罗马罗依案看国际仲裁裁决的撤销与执行》，《法商研究》2002 年第 5 期）

② 此处只考虑裁决被仲裁地法院撤销的情况。对于裁决被非仲裁地法院撤销的案件，由于极为罕见，且明显不合理，故不予考虑。

走向繁荣的国际法学

（全六卷）

TOWARDS THE PROSPERITY OF
INTERNATIONAL LAW STUDIES (SIX VOLUMES)

2009
~
2019

中国社会科学院国际法研究所十周年所庆纪念文集

【国际经济法卷】

莫纪宏　总主编
刘敬东　孙南翔　主　编

社会科学文献出版社
SOCIAL SCIENCES ACADEMIC PRESS (CHINA)

国际经济法研究室全家福

国际经济法老中青学者在一起

2019 年 3 月 7 日，中国驻塞尔维亚前大使李满长在国际法研究所作专题报告

2019 年 5 月 30 日，“‘一带一路’法律风险防范与法律机制构建”项目调研团组访问中国驻波兰大使馆

2019 年 5 月 22 日，国际商事仲裁理事会（ICCA）主席 Kaufmann-Kohler 女士访问国际法研究所

2018 年 9 月 19 日，国际经济法研究室在北京举办“联合国商事仲裁示范法与中国仲裁法的发展”会议（第四届中国社会科学仲裁论坛）

2018 年 8 月，国际经济法研究室同事探讨国际经济法新形势

2012 年，刘敬东研究员访问纽约联合国总部

2019 年 8 月 7 日，商务部部长助理李成钢代表中国政府签署《联合国调解协议公约》，国际法研究所代表团应邀赴新加坡参加签署仪式（从左至右：孙南翔、傅攀峰、毛晓飞、李成钢、黄进、刘敬东）

2018 年 4 月 8 日，国际法研究所举办“中美经贸关系法律问题”研讨会，讨论中美经贸法律问题

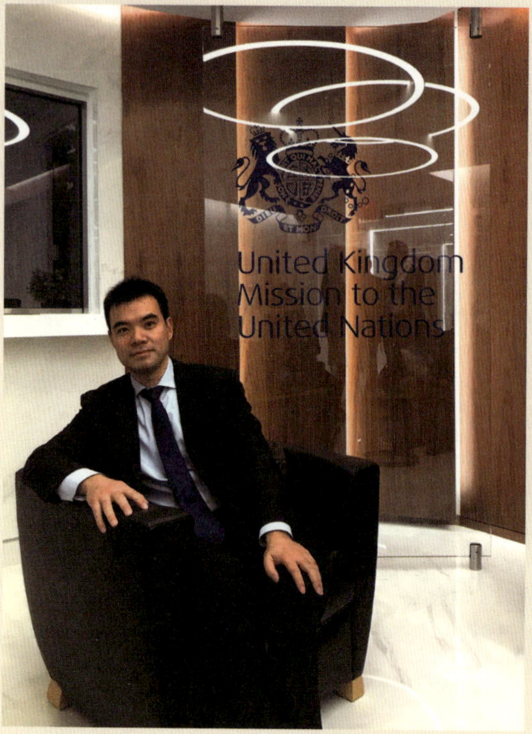

2018 年 11 月 13 日，廖凡研究员在美国纽约访问英国驻联合国使团

2018 年 11 月 10 日，廖凡研究员访问哥伦比亚大学法学院，与中国法研究中心主任李本教授合影

2018 年 9 月 17 日，廖凡研究员在彼得森国际经济研究所参加“全球经济中的中美经贸关系”研讨会

2018 年 10 月 27 日至 28 日，中国社会科学论坛暨第十五届国际法论坛在京召开

2018 年 9 月 27 日，黄晋副研究员参加北京市财政局举办的“规范性文件公平竞争审查”研讨会并发言

2018 年 11 月 11 日，黄晋副研究员参加“改革开放 40 年中国竞争法治建设和发展”研讨会并发言

2019 年 6 月 22 日，张文广副研究员参加 2019 中国海事司法与仲裁高峰论坛

序

推动中国国际法学不断走向繁荣

1949年10月1日，中华人民共和国中央人民政府宣告成立，结束了旧中国近百年半殖民地半封建受压迫受奴役的历史。中国人民从此站起来了！

在中国共产党和中国政府的坚强领导下，70年来，中华人民共和国不断总结经验，克服困难，实现突破和发展，取得社会主义建设事业的伟大成就。特别是改革开放40年来，中国实现了经济腾飞和社会进步，中国的国际地位和影响力前所未有。2012年党的十八大召开以来，中国特色社会主义进入新时代，中国人民实现了从站起来、富起来到强起来的发展过程，中国日益走近世界舞台的中央，中华民族比以往任何时候都更加接近实现中华民族伟大复兴的中国梦！

中华人民共和国的成立和70年来的发展历程，为中国国际法学的发展创造了良好的政治、经济、社会和历史条件。以周鲠生、陈体强、李浩培、王铁崖、韩德培等老一辈中国国际法学者为代表的中国国际法人为中国国际法理论研究和实践工作的起步和发展作出了卓越的贡献，为中国国际法学研究和教学做了大量奠基和铺路的工作。

1978年12月13日，邓小平同志在党的十一届三中全会前召开的中央经济工作会议上发表了《解放思想，实事求是，团结一致向前看》的讲话，明确提出"要大力加强国际法的研究"。如春风，如号角，中国国际法研究获得极大的鼓舞。中国国际法学迎来了发展的春天。1980年2月，中国国际法学会成立，中国社会科学院副院长宦乡担任首任会长。

中国社会科学院是中国国际法学的研究重镇。1959年，也就是中国科学院哲学社会科学部建立法学研究所之后的第二年，法学研究所成立了国际法组。1977 年 5 月，经党中央批准，中国社会科学院在中国科学院哲学社会科学部基础上正式组建。1978 年 9 月，中国社会科学院法学研究所国际法组改建为国际法研究室。

2002 年又是中国发展历程中一个不平凡的年份。这一年，中国改革开放渐入佳境，中国正式加入世界贸易组织；这一年，中国批准了作为“国际人权宪章”重要内容的联合国《经济、社会和文化权利国际公约》。也是这一年，在时任中国社会科学院院长李铁映的推动下，经中央机构编制委员会办公室批准，在国际法研究室基础上成立了国际法研究中心，使其成为与法学研究所平行的院属所局级机构。

国际法研究中心成立后，中国社会科学院国际法学研究获得进一步加强和推进。2009 年 9 月，经中央机构编制委员会办公室批准，国际法研究中心正式更名为国际法研究所。到今天，国际法研究所刚好成立 10 年了！

陈泽宪研究员任国际法研究所首任所长。2017 年 9 月至 2018 年 11 月，现任法学研究所所长、中国社会科学院学部委员陈甦研究员代行国际法研究所所长职责。2018 年 11 月，莫纪宏研究员开始担任国际法研究所所长。国际法研究所正是在国家经济发展和社会进步取得历史性突破，中国在国际社会地位极大提升、国际影响力不断扩大的背景下诞生的。它的成立和发展承载了党和国家繁荣和发展中国国际法学的使命。

10 年来，国际法研究所与外交部、商务部等相关政府部门密切联系，与中国国际法学会等全国性国际法研究学会、学术机构一道，积极进取，努力推动中国国际法学走向繁荣。依托学科和人才优势，国际法研究所设有国际公法、国际经济法、国际私法和国际人权法 4 个研究室，还设有海洋法治研究、竞争法研究和国际刑法研究领域的 3 个非实体中心以及最高人民法院“一带一路”司法研究基地。依托国际法研究所国际法专业的博士点和硕士点，博士、硕士研究生和博士后研究人员的指导工作也得到了加强。

2014 年创刊的《国际法研究》是中国第一本获得正式刊号的国际法专业原创中文期刊，国际法研究所是其主要主办单位和主编单位。该刊在国际法研究领域学术期刊的发文转载率方面处于全国领先地位，已经成为国际法学界重要的学术展示和交流平台。一年一度的国际法论坛已成功举办

15 届，成为中国社会科学院院级国际研讨会的学术品牌，吸引了国内外权威和知名专家的积极参与。在刘楠来、王可菊、陶正华、林欣等前辈国际法学家的关心和鼓舞下，国际法研究所一大批中青年国际法学者正在成为国际法学界的学术骨干。

值此国际法研究所 10 周年所庆之际，我们出版文集，选粹研究人员的研究成果，包括《国际法研究》发表过的有影响力的论文，回顾走过的历程，展示当下的风貌，既是国际法研究所成长道路上的一个小结，更是展现坚定的再创辉煌的决心。

中国倡导的“一带一路”建设正在世界范围内获得越来越多、越来越大的发展成就，推动构建人类命运共同体的中国主张日益获得国际社会的广泛支持和积极响应。

前路不乏机遇和挑战，中国社会科学院国际法研究所全体同仁必将以只争朝夕的精神，不忘初心、牢记使命，与全国国际法学同仁一道，推进中国国际法学不断走向繁荣！

莫纪宏

2019 年 8 月 20 日

目录

Contents

国际经济法研究室简介

一　历史沿革及人员组成

1958 年，中国科学院哲学社会科学部建立法学研究所。1959 年，法学研究所成立第四研究组，即国际法组。当时成员有王可菊、刘珍、夏国强和吴建璠（兼），刘、夏不久即调离。1960 年调入马骧聪、叶维钧和王存学。1961 年所里确定，张友渔兼第四研究组组长，由解铁光代管，王可菊任组秘书，外交学院马骏兼副组长。

1977 年年底，法学研究所研究人员按专业重新分组。国际法组除原第四研究组的王可菊、叶维钧、王存学外，从其他组转来徐鹤皋、魏家驹、吴云琪、刘楠来和沈小明，并调入姚壮、任继圣、王孙奂，召集人为徐鹤皋和刘楠来。后王存学转入民法研究室。

1978 年 9 月，国际法组改建为国际法研究室，徐鹤皋任主任，刘楠来、任继圣为副主任。此后陆续调入郑成思、盛愉、赵维田、李泽锐、于华、陶正华、林欣、曾建凡、朱晓青、朱文英、马守仁、张薇、赵李欣、杨力军、李顺德等人。

1984—1993 年，刘楠来任国际法研究室主任，郑成思为副主任。1994 年法学研究所建立知识产权研究室，郑成思、李顺德等转入该室。

1994—2004 年，陶正华任国际法研究室主任，杨力军、沈涓先后任副主任。在此期间，张若思、张文广、黄晋、李辉、刘敬东、廖凡、毛晓飞、钟瑞华等国际经济法学者陆续调入。

2002 年，在法学研究所国际法研究室基础上，正式成立中国社会科学院国际法研究中心。2004 年，国际法研究中心设立国际公法、国际私法及国际经济法三个研究室。2009 年，经中央机构编制委员会办公室批准，国际法研究中心更名为国际法研究所。2004—2014 年，黄东黎任国际经济法研究室主任，刘敬东、张文广先后任副主任。在此期间，何晶晶等人陆续调入。

2014 年至今，刘敬东任国际经济法研究室主任，黄晋任副主任。在此期间，孙南翔、任宏达等人陆续调入，田夫进入国际经济法学科创新工程。

二　学术名家

国际经济法是法学研究所的重要专业方向，建所之初作为国际法专业的一个分支，国际经济法学研究隶属法学研究所国际法研究室。尽管在那个时代国际经济法研究尚未作为一门独立的法学学科而存在，只是散见于国际公法和国际私法两个学科之中，但这丝毫未影响法学研究所国际法前辈们对国际经济法学理论和实践的深刻探索。特别是在改革开放后，法学研究所的国际经济法学研究更是开全国之先河，在涉及国家对外开放的重大法学理论领域勇于突破，锐意创新，对中国国际经济法学科的形成及发展作出了重要而独特的贡献，法学研究所也诞生了一大批享有盛誉的国际经济法学家，可谓大家云集、群星璀璨，他们是（排名不分先后）：

芮沐（研究领域为国际公法、国际经济法，曾任法学研究所副所长）、徐鹤皋（研究领域为国际私法、国际经济法、海商法，曾任国际法研究室主任，后任司法部中国法律事务中心主任）、李泽锐［研究领域为国际经济法（国际货币金融法）］、任继圣（研究领域为国际私法、国际经济法，曾任国际法研究室副主任，后任司法部中国法律事务中心主任，一级律师）、魏家驹（研究领域为国际私法、海商法）、姚壮（研究领域为国际私法、海商法，后调外交学院任教授）、陶正华（研究领域为国际公法、国际经济法，曾任国际法研究室主任）、赵维田［研究领域为国际公法（国际航空法）、国际经济法（WTO 法律制度）］、盛愉［研究领域为国际公法（国际水法）、国际经济法（国际货币金融法），曾任法学研究所副所长］。

2004 年国际经济法研究室成立后，黄东黎（研究领域为国际经济法，曾任国际经济法研究室主任）、张若思（研究领域为国际经济法）、杨联明

（研究领域为国际经济法）、李辉（研究领域为国际经济法）等同仁先后调离，他们同样给我们留下了十分宝贵的学术财富，为国际法研究所国际经济法学科建设作出了重要贡献。

三　代表作品

1. 盛愉：《国际货币法概论》，法律出版社，1985。

2. 赵维田：《最惠国与多边贸易体制》，中国社会科学出版社，1996。

3. 李泽锐：《国际货币金融法概论》，经济管理出版社，1997。

4. 赵维田：《世贸组织（WTO）的法律制度》，吉林人民出版社，2000。

5. 姚壮、任继圣：《论国际私法的对象和规范》，《法学研究》1980 年第 3 期。

6. 任继圣：《论国际私法的发展趋势》，《法学研究》1981 年第 4 期。

7. 魏家驹：《略论联合国国际货物多式联运公约》，《法学研究》1981 年第 6 期。

8. 芮沐：《关于国际经济法的几个问题》，《国外法学》（现《中外法学》）1983 年第 1 期。

9. 李泽锐：《略论国际经济软法与建立国际经济新秩序的斗争》，《法学研究》1983 年第 6 期。

10. 盛愉：《论国际法的发展及其预测》，《中国法学》1984 年第 2 期。

11. 徐鹤皋：《对外经济工作中的若干法律问题》，《法学杂志》1984 年第 3 期。

12. 陶正华：《对外开放要加强国际法研究》，《法学研究》1985 年第 1 期。

13. 赵维田：《论 GATT/WTO 解决争端机制》，《法学研究》1997 年第 3 期。

14. 张若思：《WTO 协定在欧共体及其成员国的适用》，《北大国际法与比较法评论》第 2 卷第 1 辑，北京大学出版社，2003。

15. 李辉：《WTO 转基因农产品贸易争端与欧盟转基因产品管制立法评析》，《环球法律评论》2007 年第 2 期。

16. 钟瑞华：《从绝对权利到风险管理——美国的德莱尼条款之争及其

启示》，《中外法学》2009 年第 4 期。

17. 廖凡：《国际货币体制的困境与出路》，《法学研究》2010 年第 4 期。

18. 黄东黎：《入世十年与中国法治》，《法治研究》2011 年第 3 期。

19. 刘敬东：《全球经济治理的新模式及其法治化路径》，《法学研究》2012 年第 4 期。

20. 毛晓飞：《对外财政援助决定权的宪法制约——德国联邦宪法法院对欧元区援助法案的违宪审查》，《欧洲研究》2013 年第 2 期。

21. 黄晋：《欧盟与美国在合并控制领域的双边执法合作》，《国际法研究》2014 年第 4 期。

22. 孙南翔：《从限权到赋权：面向未来的互联网贸易规则》，《当代法学》2016 年第 5 期。

23. 何晶晶：《从〈京都议定书〉到〈巴黎协定〉：开启新的气候变化治理时代》，《国际法研究》2016 年第 3 期。

24. 张文广：《“一带一路”背景下的国际海事司法中心建设》，《国际法研究》2017 年第 5 期。

25. 任宏达：《涉外股权收购合同关系的法律适用》，《国际法研究》2018 年第 1 期。

四　重要科研成果

1. 发时代之先声，积极探索国际经济法基本理论

在国际经济法基本理论层面，国际经济法研究室老一辈学者敢于立时代之潮头，发时代之先声，撰写并发表了大量开启国内国际经济法学科理论研究先河的学术论著。

（1）国际经济法的研究应重视国内法

在《关于国际经济法的几个问题》中，芮沐研究员一针见血地指出：“国际经济关系是在各国自己的经济制度和经济发展的基础上联结起来的。因此，国内法实际上往往决定着国际法。例如，一个国家在国内法律上是否容许或鼓励外国资本的输入，输入后给予什么样的法律地位，应该为它规定什么样的经营方式，这些法律在很大程度上影响着投资国（或其他国

际主体）和接受投资国即东道国之间或东道国和投资国（或其他国际主体）之间的经济关系及其规范措施。同样是一国的原材料生产和制成品生产以及这些方面的国内法律的管理控制制度也对国际经济关系发生着上层建筑所发生的影响。这种情况同用传统的国际法只在国际层面上解决问题的情况不一样，这给国际经济法又增加了一层复杂性。”

芮沐研究员进一步强调：“国际法不是一个抽象概念。没有什么天赐的、永存的或通用的国际法。就其现状讲，特别在国际经济领域，情况比较复杂。这里只存在一些在不同历史时期，在不同性质或类型的国家之间，通过斗争或妥协或沿用习惯做法而形成的得到大多数国家或一部分国家同意或不同意，并在不同程度上得到它们遵守或不遵守、用于调整它们相互间关系的国际规范和行动规则。特别在国际经济关系里，国际法同各国的国内法交错地发生相互影响和作用。研究这些情况，就成为国际经济法学科的一个重要课题。”

（2）对外经济工作中应坚持独立自主、平等互利和参照国际惯例

徐鹤皋先生在《对外经济工作中的若干法律问题》中提出：“在对外经济工作中，正确处理有关的法律问题，最根本的是要自觉坚持和正确掌握对涉外经济法律工作有重大指导意义的三项原则，即独立自主、平等互利和参照国际惯例。”他认为：“在对外经济贸易中，中外当事人之间发生争议，一般可以通过双方友好协商解决。在有仲裁协议的条件下，当事人任何一方也可将争议提交仲裁解决。如无仲裁协议，则可通过诉讼程序，由法院解决争议。最近几年，由法院解决对外经济争议的情况比过去大大增多。因此，争议案件的司法管辖权，是一个值得重视的问题。”

由此，徐鹤皋先生针对对外经济合作的争议解决进行了研究。他指出：“应该看到，一项仲裁协议的达成，并不单凭当事人一方的主观愿望，而必须经过双方的共同协商。根据谈判的具体情况和各个合同的不同条件，也可以一致同意选择被告所在国仲裁机构、第三国仲裁机构，或者组织临时仲裁庭进行仲裁。在适用仲裁规则方面，可以采用一些变通的办法。只要符合平等互利的原则，这些做法都是可以考虑和采用的。在对外经济合同中，由当事人双方协商，约定选择合同适用的法律，规定法律适用的条款，这在国际上也是常见的。因为任何一个合同，以及合同所确定的当事人双方的权利义务关系，总是要受一定国家的法律所管辖。对外经

济合同经常涉及不同国家的法律制度，因此在合同中规定法律适用条款，明确合同适用的法律，可以使合同当事人预见到各自享有的合同权利，将受到什么样的法律保障，使双方能更自觉地按合同的规定来调整相互的权利和义务关系，以避免或减少在履行合同时发生的争议；即使发生争议，双方也可依照所适用的法律去解决。而且，有了法律适用条款，对于需要通过仲裁或者提请法院处理的争议，也便于仲裁员或审判员考虑可以适用的法律。这个经双方当事人协议选择的法律，可能是我国的法律，也可能是对方国家的法律，或者是第三国的法律。这要根据合同的性质和内容由双方协商决定。我们的原则应该是，凡必须适用我国法律的合同，不得选择适用外国的法律；凡可以由当事人双方协议选择所适用的法律的合同，应允许当事人加以选择。对适用外国法律一概采取否定的态度，对于发展我国对外经济合作和交往，不一定是有利的，有时也是行不通的。”

最后，徐鹤皋先生强调：“对外经济合同在法律上只能对签订合同的各方有约束力，这是一个基本的法律原则。任何一个合同，其主要作用在于规定和调整合同当事人各方之间的权利和义务关系；合同的任何一方都无权把应由另一方承担的义务和责任强加给合同当事人以外的第三方。很显然，在我国国营公司和企业同外国公司和企业之间订立经济合同时，当事人只能是签订合同的中外公司和企业，把中华人民共和国或中国政府置于中国国营公司和企业同等的地位，一并视为合同当事人的一方，企图使之共同承担合同所规定的义务和法律责任，这是违反一般法律原则的。”

（3）对外开放应加强国际法研究

在20世纪80年代中叶，陶正华先生已提出“对外开放要加强国际法研究”。他指出：“当今世界面临着两大问题，一是维护和平，一是促进发展。这两大问题的解决，需要在国际范围内进行政治、外交、经济、文化等各个方面的合作和斗争。而国际法则为调整和处理当代的各种国际关系和国际问题规定了应遵循的原则和规范。在当前，加强国际法的研究，深入阐述和广泛宣传现代国际法的基本原则和规章、制度，有助于揭露和批判帝国主义、霸权主义和殖民主义国家违反、践踏国际法的各种行径，提高各国人民的觉悟，促使各国政府按照国际法的原则处理相互间的关系，从而达到维护和平与促进发展的目标。”

由此，陶正华先生建议道：“实行对外开放，扩大与世界各国的经济技术合作和交流，给我国的国际法研究工作提出了许多新的课题。为了适应对外开放的迫切需要，当前应该着重研究和探讨以下几个方面的问题：第一，国际经济关系的基本原则。第二，国家的经济权利和义务。第三，建立国际经济新秩序问题。第四，国际经济活动的主要法律形式和法律问题。

但是，与当前国际形势和国际法的发展，特别是与我国对外开放迅速扩大的形势相比，我国的国际法研究工作还是很不适应的。为了开创国际研究的新局面，更好地为我国对外开放服务，当前必须认真解决好下面几个问题：第一，以马克思列宁主义、毛泽东思想指导国际法研究。第二，坚持理论联系实际，加强国际法的基础理论研究、应用研究和普及工作。第三，抓紧研究和总结我国国际法的理论和实践。第四，深入了解和研究国外关于国际经济民事法律关系的理论和实践。第五，逐步解决国际法研究中的人员、组织和资料等问题。”

（4）建立具有中国特色的国际法学迎接21世纪国际法发展的新局面

在《论国际法的发展及其预测》中，盛愉先生直言：“国际法在发展。在国际社会的一切领域，每个国家的活动和相互之间的关系都需要遵循一定的国际法规。一个新的国际法律秩序正在出现，成为现代世界的一个重要现象。如何解释这个现象，并预测它的发展方向，使国际法更有效地维护各国的合法利益，促进建立公正、进步的国际秩序，这是研究国际法的根本目的。长期的国际实践证明：在世界历史过程中，国际法的发展有它自身的规律，用历史唯物主义的方法分析国际法的规律性特点，将可以清楚地看出它的发展方向。”

根据对国际法发展的预测，各国将从世界形势和本国具体情况出发，选择和确定重点研究课题，以参加这些方面的国际立法和法规修订工作。因此，盛愉先生建议，“我们的选择似可侧重以下方面：

其一，有关建立国际新经济秩序和发展我国对外经济合作中的法律问题，是有重要现实意义的课题。这两个方面有共通的，也有不同的内容，涉及的范围极广，可以将国际新经济秩序的主要法律问题与我国在对外经济关系中需要解决的重大理论和实际问题结合起来。在理论方面，着重研究与新经济秩序相适应的国际法律秩序和制定新的重要法规同时也要研究指导我国在对外经济活动方面的国际实践的理论和指导思想，在实际问题方面，例如结合国际金融体制和法规的改革，研究我国的涉外货币金融立法，在参与制定国际贸易法的过程中，完善我国的对外贸易立法。可以将我们对解决有关建立新经济秩序中的法律问题与解决我国经济开放政策中的法律问题有机地结合起来。此外，关于技术转让、利用外资、保护资源及环境、国际债务以及域外管辖、非关税壁垒措施等问题，都可以结合国际国内的立法进行研究。在这方面，国际合同的性质及解决合同纠纷所适用的法律是亟待解决的重要理论和实践问题，需要逐渐形成统一的法规，以利于发展国际经济合作。另一个需要注意的新课题是区域一体化所带来的一系列法律问题，重点应预测拟议中的太平洋经济体系同我国的法律关系。对这些课题进行研究并提出积极的对策，不但对第三世界国家是重大支持，而且直接关系到我国的切身利益，是迫切需要优先解决的法律问题。

其二，文化交流与合作的发展，包括科学技术方面，在国际关系中将占更加重要的地位。在这方面有版权、广播电视、卫星遥感技术合作以及各种科学考察合作和随之而来的很多复杂的法律问题。

正在兴起的新的技术革命对于国际法提出了很多新的课题。国际技术关系中已经和正在制定的各类法规，有可能形成国际法的一些新分支，许多学者已就信息革命对国际法的影响提出了一些预测性的论点，但还属于探讨阶段。从20世纪60年代起，电子技术已日益扩大应用于法学，有利于大量法律资料的储存、检索和广泛利用。70年代新技术对法学的影响已更加明显，法学与新技术结合而出现了一批新的学科，特别是提出了很多新的法律问题。进入80年代，研究新技术革命对法学所产生的全面影响已提上日程。一方面是新技术在法学方面的扩大应用，正在形成国际性计算机网络，另一方面是新技术进入生产和生活领域引起的结构和各种关系的变化，要求有相应的法律调整机制。在国际法方面，信息的国际化和知识资源的国际开发都已提出一些新的课题。跨国信息中心的出现已形成新的国际关系，需要确定跨国信息中心和网络的法律地位以及各有关方面的权利和义务的内容，特别需要研究这些变革对国际法律秩序和发展中国家的影响，以迎接这一新的历史性变革的挑战。

其三，在国际范围人员流动方面，外国人的法律地位和待遇是国际法学界长期有争议的理论和实际问题。这个问题以及我国在国外大批工人的法律地位问题都亟须研究并争取尽快达成国际协议。在国际社会关系中发生的民事纠纷包括交通事故、财产纠纷等问题，和犯罪活动如各种恐怖活动、劫持、走私、贩毒等，都会大量出现。促进国际合作需要妥善解决各种纠纷，特别是打击犯罪活动已是一个世界性的重要问题。因此，研究司法协助和冲突规范的新领域、新内容和新形式已提上日程。

此外，我国还有边界问题，包括海上划界以及其他一些历史上遗留下来的问题，并且正在同世界各地区的国家广泛发展各种关系。我国是一个发展中的社会主义国家，代表了中华文化和发展中的社会主义法系，对建立国际法律新秩序，促进国际法的进步发展，负有重大的国际责任。通过总结我国的国际实践和系统阐述我国倡导的和平共处五项原则、反霸权原则等国际法的重要原则，加强研究国际法发展中的重大理论和实践问题，将促进建立具有我国特色的国际法学，并以新的贡献迎接21世纪国际法发展的新局面。”

2. 奏时代之强音，深入研究全球经贸治理新变革

60年来，国际经济政治形势发生重大变化。国际经济法研究室的同事刻苦钻研，在历次全球经贸治理重大变革的结点上，均发出中国理论界的强音，阐述全球治理的中国观点、中国方案。

（1）充分认识国际经济软法在建立国际经济新秩序中的作用

改革开放初期，李泽锐先生撰写了《略论国际经济软法与建立国际经济新秩序的斗争》的文章。他指出：“软法是过渡性、暂时性的规则，有些规则并非一软到底，而是可以转变成硬法的。转变的方法主要有二：一是一国把软法引进国内法，则可使软法具有硬法的地位。自然，引进什么软法需要作趋利避害的选择，不可不慎。二是使软法成为国际习惯法，一方面，软法配合软程序对问题的解决，可以视为根据妥协精神或公平原则作出的裁决，假如此裁决在一些案件中作为判例而被援引，则此软法规则便有成为习惯国际法的趋势，另一方面，软法也可以按照通常形成习惯法的程序成为习惯法。”

李泽锐先生进一步指出：“目前国际社会中最大量也是最重要的‘软法’，是联合国大会制定的关于第三世界国家发展权的国际经济法。我们主观上坚决反对说这些新的国际经济法是软法，但客观上它们的确又缺乏拘束力，所以，根据新的国际经济法建立的新的国际经济秩序，目前只能说隐约出现了一个轮廓，实际尚未建立起来，因此，包括我国在内的第三世界国

家目前才竭力敦促举行全球谈判或南北对话，达成协议，以便建立新的国际经济秩序。但是，要达成协议是困难的，因为西方学者已经建议，‘宜用制定软法的方法来克服南北对话中的僵局，而且对第三世界国家来说，这应该是可以接受的最可行的解决办法’，这等于说西方决心只能制定软法。是否有别的办法呢？我国执行开放政策，我国的方针是立足于自力更生。自力更生也是争取软法变硬法的最好保证：第三世界国家加强它们之间的经济合作，实行集体的自力更生，就能从有力的地位出发同发达国家谈判，争取建立以平等互利为基础的新的国际经济秩序。

从研究国际经济软法中可以看出，发达国家和它们的学者对第三世界国家进行着争取国际立法权的极其激烈的斗争，制定国际经济软法正是它们进行这一斗争的重要手段。第三世界国家看来很有必要研究软法，以便在今后的国际立法中有意识地避免制定这类软规则，有意识地利用软规则的某种效力为发展自己的经济服务，有意识地运用制定软规则的方法‘以其人之道还治其人之身’。”

（2）在国际经济关系新变化过程中实现全球经济治理法治化

进入 21 世纪以来，刘敬东研究员在《全球经济治理的新模式及其法治化路径》中指出：“传统全球经济治理模式不能反映当前经济关系的新变化，正面临着缺乏民主性与合法性的危机，必须加以改革。应当在平等及相互尊重、实现共同利益和促进合作与广泛共识的原则下，扩大新兴经济体和广大发展中国家参与治理。各国可以考虑制定《国际经济宪章》、在 G20 的基础上设立具有最高权威的国际经济组织，以及以 WTO 为蓝本建立一整套争端解决机制，以此来加强全球经济治理的法治化。”因此，他建议，在制定《国际经济宪章》并成立“国际经济合作组织”的同时，还应当借鉴 WTO 构建国际经济争端解决机制确保全球经济治理的有效性和执行力。

在应对争端层面，刘敬东研究员提出：“WTO 争端解决机制的成功在国际法领域可谓独树一帜，堪称国际社会解决经济争端的典范。WTO《争端解决规则与程序的谅解》（DSU）保证了 WTO 规则的严肃性和执行力，就连美国、欧盟这样实力雄厚的成员方也不得不屈服于 WTO 的裁决。全球经济治理的法治化离不开强有力的争端解决机制。新成立的‘国际经济合作组织’应当在建立伊始以 WTO 为蓝本设计争端解决机制的框架，以强有力的法律手段监督执行国际经济重大决策。相对于WTO争端解决机制的成功，现有国际经济组织中的IMF、世界银行等明显缺乏执行力，最重要的原因就是缺少强有力的争端解决机制。诚然，在新成立的‘国际经济合作组织’中建立争端解决机制会面临不少困难，但有效的争端解决机制对于全球经济治理的有效性以及法治化进程不可或缺，在各国达成共识之前，可探讨扩大WTO现有争端解决机制的管辖范围，将全球经济决策、可持续发展议题纳入其中，与此同时，改变WTO专家组、上诉机构组成人员结构，适当吸收金融、环境等领域专家，保证裁决的公信力，通过WTO权威而高效的争端解决机制保障全球经济治理中重大决策的执行。”

最后，刘敬东研究员强调：“国际经济关系发生的历史性变化正催生着全球经济治理的新模式，各国应充分意识到，扩大发展中国家的参与权和决策权是改革全球经济治理模式、克服‘合法性’危机的核心，在继承现有体制科学、合理的法律原则基础上，应确立新的治理模式和国际经济法原则，并通过制定反映新的国际经济关系现实的《国际经济宪章》、建立‘国际经济合作组织’、构建国际经济争端解决机制的路径推动全球经济治理法治化进程。”

3. 开研究之先河，大力推动中国学界对世界贸易组织法的研究

20世纪80年代初，中国开始筹备复关谈判。作为国际经济法理论研究的重镇，中国社会科学院学者率先在国内开启世界贸易组织法的相关研究，奠定了中国世界贸易组织法理论和实践发展的基石。赵维田先生更被尊称为中国的“杰克逊”（GATT之父、美国著名国际法学家）。

（1）认真对待世界贸易组织法争端解决机制的守成与创新

GATT的解决争端机制经过不断法典化和法院化，终于瓜熟蒂落，在乌拉圭回合谈判中结出了硕果。可以说，与乌拉圭回合对国际贸易（包括服务贸易、知识产权与投资）制定的一整套实体法规则（即“各涵盖协议”）相配合，《WTO谅解》提供了一套相当完备的司法机制，形成了整个WTO多边贸易体制振翅飞翔的两翼。

赵维田先生在《论GATT/WTO解决争端机制》指出：“国内最近一本书中说，‘（WTO）谅解书将大大加强世界贸易组织解决争端机制的作用，可以说是这一机制的一次革命——从论坛和调解委员会变成法院或仲裁庭的革命。’这是值得探讨和商榷的。现在要讨论的是WTO解决争端机制是

不是对 GATT 体制的‘一次革命’。不论从理论或原则上，还是从实际上，似乎都不是这样。我认为正确的表述应该是‘继承与发展，包括某些突破性发展’。”

赵维田先生进一步阐述道：“从理论或原则上说，WTO 协定第 16 条第 1 款明文规定：‘除本协定或各多边贸易协议另有规定者外，WTO 要接受 1947 年关贸总协定缔约方全体与 1947 年关贸总协定框架内所设各机构所遵循的各决议、程序和习惯做法的指导。’该条款明确表达了从总体上继承 GATT 体制与规则的意思。据统计，所含 GATT 的决议达 200 多个，其中当然包括表述改善 GATT 解决争端程序规则的决议在内，例如 1979 年‘东京回合谅解’。而所说‘程序与习惯做法’，自然应理解为包括专家组断案在内。而在《WTO 谅解》这个具体规定解决争端规则的文件中，第 3 条第 1 款也明确表述说，‘各成员方确认他们恪守 1947 年关贸总协定第 22 条和第 23 条前此处理争端所适用的原则，以及其中经诠释与修改的规则与程序’。从实际内容上说，《WTO 谅解》也是具体承袭接受了 GATT 机制包括专家组断案在内的几乎全套衣钵。当然，《WTO 谅解》的规则在 GATT 基础上有不少发展，有些发展是突破性的。这些突破性发展主要表现为：专家组审案的‘强制管辖权’、司法独立的尝试以及严格规定了程序各环节的时间限制等。”

针对 WTO 创造的强制管辖权，赵维田先生指出：“《WTO 谅解》取得的一项最重大成果，是确立了‘解决争端机关’（DSB）对案件的强制审理权。这是对传统国际法里‘不得强迫任何国家违反其本身意志来进行诉讼’规则的重要突破。现在除海洋法庭外，一般国际组织包括联合国国际法院在内，司法诉讼是经争端当事国‘自愿同意’，国际法院才有权受理的。如前述，GATT 专家组断案‘法院化’面临的重大关口，就是专家组审理案件需经争端当事方的同意，审理报告要经 GATT 理事会以‘共识’通过，即给败诉方以否决权。如果说 GATT 前 40 年专家组竭力征得双方同意，使报告遭否决得以避免的话，那么 90 年代在审理反倾销与反补贴类案件中，遭败诉方否决的情况已屡有发生。因此，要求取消否决的呼声日高。”

（2）入世十年推动中国法治建设进程

2011 年，黄东黎研究员撰文阐述入世十年与中国法治的关系。她指出："加入世界贸易组织是中国法治建设历史上的一个重大事件。本文旨在梳理中国从复关到入世以及入世至今24年来，中国政府所作的努力以及世界贸易组织的规则和机制对中国经济和政治法治建设起到的推动和促进作用。历史证明，现实的需要往往比理想更能促进一个国家的法治建设。希望加入世界贸易组织成为中国因现实而非理想的需要最终走向法治的一个路径。

加入世界贸易组织，意味着中国以国际义务的形式表示遵循西方标准的政治透明度和程序公正。这恐怕是入世对中国政治法治建设所产生的最大的影响。此外，议定书承诺施行市场经济制度，使中国成为当今世界唯一一个以国际条约的方式确定国家经济制度的国家。国际义务的制约阻断了中国政治对经济制度的干预，反过来经济法治建设也使得政治法治建设不可避免。入世对中国政治法治建设的促进作用，具体体现在政府职能的转换以及依法行政两个方面。此外，世界贸易组织的争端解决机制将持续推进中国的政治法治建设。"

4. 研国家之所需，引领国际经济法学科全面发展新气象

除传统的国际经济法研究对象外，国际经济法学科有一支实力雄厚的研究团队，对国际经济法学科多领域进行深入的研究，并为国家方针政策的制定提供了大量的智力支持。

（1）开拓国内海商法研究

在国内海商法研究领域，魏家驹先生在1981年撰文以《国际货物多式联运公约》为主对国际货物相关的条约和协定进行深入研究。他指出："战后以来，随着国际政治、经济力量对比的改变，科学技术的迅速发展，各种单式运输公约也在不断发展，不断修订，使承运人和托运人之间的权利义务关系更趋于合理，法律规范更加准确。各个单式运输公约的制度也在互相渗透，互相影响，逐渐在国际运输中形成一些带有共同性的法律规范。当然，由于运输方式不同，运输工具有别，历史背景互异，在许多方面差别还是很大的。《国际货物多式联运公约》根据自身特点吸收了各个单式运输公约的最新成就。"

魏家驹先生进一步指出："所谓私法性质的国际条约和公法性质的国际条约，过去从来是不能沟通的，这一传统观念现在已在《国际货物多式联运公约》中打破了，公约按照实际情况，订入必要的公法规范，仅用一

条海关过境条款加上不长的附件，就概括了一个实同层床叠屋的海关过境条约，节省了为制订又一个海关过境条约的全部劳力，这是一个多么值得称赞和重视的发展。”

（2）深化国际金融法研究

在国际金融领域，廖凡研究员以《国际货币体制的困境与出路》强调：“以国际货币基金组织（IMF）为核心的现行国际货币体制渊源于大国之间的政治妥协，在约束性和执行力方面存在先天不足。世界经济格局的演变导致该体制的代表性受到质疑，全球金融危机进一步揭示出其所面临的困境，主要表现为机构职能误入歧途、政策监督顾此失彼、治理结构力量失衡和争端解决有心无力。有鉴于此，应当在近期已有改革举措的基础上，在重塑机构职能、加强双边监督、完善治理结构和促进争端解决等方面寻找出路。”

廖凡研究员阐述道：“可以说，在经过三分之二个世纪的发展之后，IMF 及其代表的国际货币体制已经走到了十字路口和转折关头，改革完善还是推倒重来，是各国面临的共同抉择。从目前情况看，维持 IMF 在国际货币体制中的核心地位，在此基础上对其进行全面而深入的实质性改革，是更为可取的现实选择。而综上所述，改革的基本目标和方向，一是梳理和重塑 IMF 相关职能，增强其对外运作的有效性；二是调整和平衡 IMF 权力结构，促进其内部治理的民主化。需要指出的是，无论改革如何进行，最终都需要通过 IMF 法律体系中相关规范的修订和变动来实现。IMF 法律体系不仅包括作为主体的《基金协定》，还包括理事会制定的章程和执行董事会制定的规则与条例，它们都对 IMF 及其成员国具有法律约束力。此外，理事会和执行董事会通过的决定也是具有约束力的法律文件。由于《基金协定》的修订极为困难，因此在不违反《基金协定》条款的前提下以规则与条例、决定等下位规范的形式先期落实某些改革举措，无疑是值得考虑的策略。此外，利用《基金协定》第 29 条赋予理事会和执行董事会的解释权，对《基金协定》相关条款作出更具开放性的解释，也是可能的途径。进而言之，IMF 部分成员国之间签订的区域货币一体化协定或其他相关协定，在一定意义上也可以视为这一进程的一部分，其价值正如区域自由贸易协定之于 WTO 多边协定的发展。”

最后，廖凡研究员建议：“可以考虑利用已被证实富有成效的 WTO 争端解决机制，将与贸易有关的货币领域争端渐进纳入其管辖范围，通过案例的累积逐步确立和强化相关争议事项的可诉性，从而为国际货币体制带来新的动力和活力。的确，长久以来由美欧发达国家所主宰的国际货币体制，在全球金融危机中前所未有地凸显出发展中国家，特别是以中国为代表的新兴市场国家的重要性。对于中国而言，IMF 及其所代表的国际货币体制的改革既是挑战，更是机遇。只要正视现实，厘清定位，找准方向，中国完全可以在 IMF 改革以及未来的国际货币新体制中发挥更加积极的作用。”

（3）加强国际经济法与国际私法的交叉性研究

在国际民商事领域，任继圣先生指出：“在我国进行社会主义现代化的建设过程中，势必不断扩大我国与外国之间的经济和文化交往，随着发生大量的涉外财产关系，以及与财产密切相连的其他权利关系。前者如对外贸易的货物买卖、运输、保险关系，对外投资、借贷关系，后者如对外的专利权关系，涉外婚姻、家庭关系，等等。这些关系统称为涉外民事法律关系。”他认为，了解相关法律部门的发展变化，有利于更好地使用它为我国的对外经济与文化交往服务。

因此，任继圣先生建议：“随着我国对外关系的日益不断发展，为我所用的直接调整涉外民事法律关系的各种规范，也需相应地发展，才能使之有效地为实践服务。因此，当前我们的任务应该是，加速总结中华人民共和国成立以来的经验，参照国际上的做法，及早用订立国内立法，签订国际条约，采纳国际惯例等办法，制定各种调整涉外民事法律关系的专用法律规范，以适应需要。这样，才能做到利用国际私法发展的规律，使国际私法更好地为促进我国的四个现代化服务。”

五　重要学术活动

1. “国际金融危机对我国金融法制建设影响”国情调研

2009 年 11 月 17 日，国际法研究所研究员陶正华，副研究员刘敬东、廖凡赴光大银行总行法律部开展了国情调研，此次调研的主题是“国际金融危机对我国金融法制建设影响”。调研期间，光大银行法律部负责人和工作人员详细介绍了国际金融危机发生后，中国银行业面临的困难和应对措施，特别介绍了雷曼事件对我国银行业的影响，以及各方为挽回损失正在采取的积极措施。此外，他们还就我国金融法制建设提出了很多有价值的建议，更就物权法有关质押的规定、《贷款通则》的修订等问题提出了具体建议。

2. “国际经济规则新趋势：中国视角”研讨会

2013 年 8 月 17 日，由中国社会科学院国际法研究所“变化中的国际经济规则与中国经济安全创新工程”主办的“国际经济规则新趋势：中国视角”研讨会在所内举行。来自中国社会科学院国际法研究所、北京大学、清华大学等 20 多家政府机关、高等院校、研究机构以及律师事务所的近 50 位代表参加了本次会议。与会学者认为，经济全球化首先是规则的全球化，只有接受并运用这套规则才能参与到全球化的过程中，才能更加顺畅地容纳到世界经济体制中。对于国际经济规则，首先是一个学习、运用和改变的过程。在透彻、深入理解规则的基础上，巧妙、灵活地运用规则，以改变现在我国面对某些问题时的被动局面；指出从规则相互影响的角度来讲，中国可能是世界上最大的规则“逆差国”，在参与国际全球化的过程中，中国总是在学习、接受国际经济规则，而很少对于国际经济规则的制定有自己的发言权，更不用说从中国向世界的规则体制当中输出规则。因此，理论界和实践界的专家学者们应该推动全社会尤其是决策层对于经济全球化规则性的重要性的认识。

3. 最高人民法院“一带一路”司法研究中心研究基地年度座谈会

2017 年 4 月 7 日，由最高人民法院“一带一路”司法研究中心主办，最高人民法院“一带一路”司法研究基地（中国社会科学院法学研究所、国际法研究所）承办的最高人民法院“一带一路”司法研究中心研究基地年度座谈会在中国社会科学院法学研究所、国际法研究所成功举行。来自最高人民法院及中国社会科学院法学研究所和国际法研究所等 15 家研究基地的 40 余名法官、司法工作人员及专家学者参加了此次座谈会。本次座谈会紧扣实务要点，发挥基地的智库作用，发挥基地学术优势，加强基础理论研究，落实各项管理规则，加大沟通合作力度。本次会议重点研究关于国际争端解决机制，重点服务于海洋强国战略，大力推动长江经济带司法保护程度，有力促进自贸实验区法治建设的深入发展并加大仲裁事业发展。

4. “WTO 法研究的中国视角”研讨会暨张月姣大法官新书发布会

2017 年 10 月 28 日，由中国社会科学院重点建设学科、国际法研究所国际经济法研究室主办的“WTO 法研究的中国视角”研讨会暨张月姣大法官《亲历世界贸易组织上诉机构》新书发布会在北京隆重举行。来自商务部、最高人民法院、中国社会科学院等单位的有关领导和专家学者近 50 人参加了此次盛会。与会人员指出，今天会议取得巨大成功。当前，我们面临一个非常美好的时代，大量的国际经济法概念和术语进入党的十九大报告，诸多新的课题和问题亟待研究。中青年国际法学者及实务界应不断将中国国际法理论推向新高度。

5. “中美经贸关系法律问题”研讨会

2018 年 4 月 8 日，由中国法学会世界贸易组织法研究会、中国社会科学院国际法研究所共同主办的“中美经贸关系法律问题”研讨会在京召开。最高人民法院、外交部、商务部、中国法学会、中国贸促会、中国社会科学院等单位的专家学者共计 50 余人参加了此次会议。与会专家学者一致认为，中美经贸合作是中美关系的稳定器和压舱石，中美经贸关系的本质是互利共赢，美国和中国都是经济全球化的受益者，中国不想打贸易战，但也不怕打贸易战。当前，中美经贸关系正面临新的挑战，美国的单边贸易政策不仅公然违反世界贸易组织协定规则，损害中国和其他国家的合法利益，更破坏了国际法治秩序，在世界范围内产生恶劣影响。法学理论界和实务界将从道义上、法律上积极发声，捍卫中国的合法利益，维护以规则为基础的国际贸易多边机制。

六　总结与展望

国际经济法是调整国际经济关系的国际法律制度，包括国际贸易法、国际投资法、国际金融法、国际竞争法、海商法等诸多门类，是国际法的重要组成部分。随着我国改革开放事业的不断深入，我国与世界各国的经济联系日益密切，贸易、投资、海商等国际经济活动十分活跃，国际经济法对我国推动形成全面开放新格局、维护国家经济利益的重要性凸显，国际经济法学已成为我国法学研究领域中一个极为重要的学科。

目前，国际法研究所国际经济法研究室的主要研究已涵盖国际贸易法、世界贸易组织法、国际商法、国际投资法、国际金融法、国际竞争法、海商法、国际环境法等广泛领域。近年来，本室研究人员已出版国际经济法学专著十余部，翻译国外学术著作多部，在《法学研究》、《环球法律评论》、《政法论坛》、《法学》、《清华法学》、《法学杂志》等国内法学核心期刊发表学术论文数十篇，在 *Journal of World Trade* 等国际著名学术杂志发表多篇英文论文，上述学术作品在国内外均产生了重要学术影响。同时，本室研究人员相继承担了国家社科基金课题，商务部重大课题，中国社会科学院重大课题、重点课题、国情调研课题、青年课题等数十项研究课题，为中央有关部门提供了大量决策咨询意见和建议，获得中央领导及相关部门高度重视。

在继往开来的新时代，国际经济法学科将以“国际经济法重点学科”建设为契机，以“中国社会科学院创新工程”为依托，致力于研究具有重大现实意义和理论价值的国际经济法问题。国际经济法研究室全体科研人员将继续努力钻研国际经济法理论，力争出版或发表数量更多、质量更好、影响力更高的专著、论文、研究报告等，为我国国际经济法学科的发展作出新的更大贡献。

研究室成员简介

刘敬东

一　基本情况

黑龙江省哈尔滨市人，法学博士，现任中国社会科学院国际法研究所国际经济法研究室主任、研究员，中国社会科学院研究生院教授，博士生导师。中国法学会 WTO 法研究会副会长、中国仲裁法学会常务理事。最高人民法院第四届特约咨询员、最高人民法院民四庭副庭长（2015 年 4 月至 2017 年 12 月）、最高人民法院首批国际商事专家委员会专家。对外经贸大学兼职博士生导师、上海海事大学兼职教授、中国国际经济贸易仲裁委员会仲裁员。

二 学术背景

1986—1990 年就读于中国政法大学法律系法学专业，1993 年，在中国政法大学研究生院获法学硕士学位，2001 年，在中国政法大学研究生院获国际法学博士学位，2003—2005 年进入中国社会科学院法学研究所博士后流动站学习、工作。2008 年美国哥伦比亚大学、2010 年 10 月瑞士苏黎世大学访问学者。

三 学术成果

近年来，先后出版《国际融资租赁交易中的法律问题》、《中国入世议定书解读》、《WTO 法律制度中的善意原则》、《人权与 WTO 法律制度》、《WTO 体制中的贸易与环境法律问题》等学术专著，以及译著《WTO 的未来》、《贸易政策审议——WTO 秘书处关于中华人民共和国的报告》，主编《反倾销案件司法审查制度研究》、《WTO：解释条约的习惯规则》（与赵维田教授合作）等著作。并在《法学研究》、《政法论坛》、《中国法律》（香港）、《国际贸易》、《中国国际法年刊》、《国际经济法学刊》以及 *Journal of World Trade* 等中外核心法律期刊发表大量学术论文，为《人民日报》、《经济参考报》、《中国社会科学报》、《法制日报》撰写多篇文章和评论。曾荣获中国国际法学会 2012 年度“航天科工”论文奖、2014 年中国法学会第七届 WTO 法与中国论坛优秀论文二等奖、2015 年中国法学会第八届 WTO 法与中国论坛优秀论文一等奖。

曾主持原对外经贸部重点科研课题“反倾销案件的司法审查制度研究”，承担国家商务部“WTO 反倾销裁决执行情况研究报告”、“中国贸易救济措施十周年报告”两项重大课题，完成中国社会科学院重大课题“WTO 体制下贸易与环境法律关系研究”及两项重点课题“WTO 法律制度中的善意原则”和“人权与 WTO 法律制度的关系研究”，2013 年主持国家社科基金课题“海外利益保护的中国模式研究”。

四 代表作介绍

（一）全球经济治理新模式的法治化路径

传统全球经济治理模式不能反映当前国际经济关系的变化，既缺乏民主性，也不适应经济全球化带来的新挑战，必须加以改革。各国可以考虑制定《国际经济合作宪章》，确立平等及相互尊重、实现共同利益和促进合作与广泛共识的法律原则；扩大新兴经济体和广大发展中国家参与治理，在G20机制的基础上设立具有最高权威的“国际经济合作组织”；以WTO争端解决机制为蓝本建立一整套国际经济争端解决机制，从而实现全球经济治理的法治化。

（二）“一带一路”法治化体系构建研究

当前，“一带一路”建设已成为全球经济发展的重要推动力，其制度建设和发展模式为世界瞩目，被视为全球经济治理的重要组成部分。历史经验和教训告诉我们，“一带一路”推进过程离不开法治的保障，只有选择法治化发展道路、构建科学的法治化体系，实现国内法治与国际法治的良性互动，才能确保“一带一路”建设的长期、稳定、健康发展。“一带一路”法治化体系构建，应遵循平等互利、规则导向以及可持续发展的基本原则，着眼于国际法和国内法两大领域：一方面，融合现代国际法、吸纳国际经贸规则发展的最新成果，结合“一带一路”建设特点，创新现有国际经贸法律体系；另一方面，借鉴各国先进法律经验，不断改进并完善我国对外经贸法律制度以及涉外民商事法律制度。公正、高效的争端解决机制对“一带一路”法治化体系不可或缺，应本着平等协商、谈判解决争端、坚持运用现代国际法规则及公认的国际商事规则、推动“一带一路”国家之间司法合作的基本原则，构建一套多层次、立体化、国际机制与国内机制相结合的经贸争端解决机制，从而为“一带一路”建设打造稳定性、可预见性的法治环境，为21世纪的全球经济治理树立典范。

（三）论“加入议定书”在WTO法律体系中的定位

“加入议定书”是WTO法律体系中一类独特的法律文件。随着新成员的不断加入，“加入议定书”的数量逐渐增多。由于WTO对“加入议定书”的定位模糊，涉及“加入议定书”条款解释和适用的争端频发。“加入议定书”在WTO法律体系中的定位问题，关乎各方重大贸易利益，重要而复杂。WTO部长会议和总理事会应当履行法定职责，充分尊重多边贸易体制的目标和宗旨，遵循WTO法律原则、规则以及国际法基本原则，将“加入议定书”置于WTO法律体系的整体框架内，妥善处理“加入议定书”与《建立 WTO 协定》及其附件之间的法律关系，平等保障新成员方应享有的 WTO 普遍性权利。

（四）浅析 WTO 未来之路——WTO 改革动向及思考

面对国际关系的历史性变化以及当前国际金融危机，WTO 理应改革自身体制适应新的形势，推动国际贸易在 21 世纪的发展和繁荣。尽管改革思路和方案内容不同，但对于 WTO 改革的必要性，国际上有广泛的共识：WTO 体制已不适应新的国际关系特点，自身存在的制度性缺陷已严重阻碍 WTO 发挥多边贸易体制功能。但对于 WTO 改革的指导思想，发展中成员与发达成员之间、学者之间尚有争论。结合当前形势以及可行性考虑，WTO 应当在广泛征求意见的基础上，围绕总干事以及秘书处的职权、透明度、现行决策机制这三项基本制度尽快开展必要的改革。

廖　凡

一　基本情况

四川省资中县人，现任中国社会科学院国际法研究所研究员、科研外事处处长。他是中国社会科学院创新工程项目“‘一带一路’建设中的国际经济法律问题”首席研究员。他主持和参与世界银行、国家发展改革委员会、外交部、商务部、中国人民银行、中国银行保险监督管理委员会、中国证券监督管理委员会、中国法学会、中国社会科学院等部门和机构的多项重大、重点课题。他的主要研究领域包括国际法基础理论、国际经济法和金融证券法。他迄今为止出版专著4部（含合著1部），在《法学研究》、《中国法学》、《人民日报》、《欧洲商事组织法评论》等国内外刊物和媒体发表学术论文、译文、评论100余篇，其中多篇被《新华文摘》、《中国社会科学文摘》、《高等学校文科学术文摘》、人大复印报刊资料转载。

二　教育及工作经历

1995—1999年，在中国青年政治学院学习，获法学学士学位。

1999—2005年，在北京大学法学院学习（硕博连读），获法学博士学位。

2001—2002年，在美国南方卫理公会大学（SMU）法学院学习，获法学硕士学位。

2005—2007年，中国社会科学院国际法研究所助理研究员。

2006—2007年，美国哥伦比亚大学访问学者。

2007—2013年，中国社会科学院国际法研究所副研究员。

2013年至今，中国社会科学院国际法研究所研究员。

三　主要学术兼职

中国国际经济法学会理事

中国国际经济贸易法学研究会理事

中国国际经济贸易法学研究会国际金融法专业委员会副主任委员

北京市金融服务法学研究会常务理事

北京市法学会互联网金融法治研究会常务理事

中国国际经济贸易仲裁委员会仲裁员

深圳国际仲裁院（深圳仲裁委员会）仲裁员

新加坡国际调解中心专家调解员

最高人民法院涉外商事海事审判专家库专家

四　学术地位及社会影响

廖凡研究员是国际法研究所中青年科研骨干和学科带头人，科研能力突出，科研成果丰硕。他在国际经济法领域的研究处于国内领先水平，论文引证率在中青年国际法学者中名列前茅。他发表的《国际货币体制的困境与出路》、《金融消费者的概念与范围》、《论软法在全球金融治理中的地位和作用》、《全球治理背景下人类命运共同体的阐释与构建》等论文代表了国内相关领域研究的水平，在学术界和实务界均有广泛影响和良好口碑。他经常参与有关部委和司法机构的决策咨询和专家论证，利用专业知识和经验积极建言献策。他撰写的内部研究报告多次获得中央主要领导同志和其他国家领导人批示，有效发挥了决策影响力。他曾在美国长期进修和访学，外语水平和国际交流能力突出。他利用专业强、外语好的优势，数十次接受原中央电视台英语频道、现中国国际电视台相关栏目的现场采访，阐释法治实践问题，宣传中国法治理念，社会反响良好。

五 代表性学术观点

（一）关于金融监管竞争、冲突与协调（2008）

如何应对因金融创新和混业发展而加剧的金融监管竞争与冲突，构建适应我国国情的混业经营监管体制，是当前金融监管中的一个突出课题。监管竞争有其自身价值，而应对监管冲突也需注意其深层背景。金融集团的发展强化了监管竞争与冲突，也使得监管协调更为必要。综合监管与功能监管基础上的伞形监管是金融监管协调的两种路径，从我国的现实情况出发，借鉴伞形监管经验，建立分业监管基础上的协调机制，是更为可取的选择。

（二）关于国际货币体制面临的现实困境与解决途径（2010）

以国际货币基金组织为核心的现行国际货币体制渊源于大国之间的政治妥协，在约束性和执行力方面存在先天不足。世界经济格局的演变导致该体制的代表性受到质疑，全球金融危机进一步揭示出其所面临的困境，主要表现为机构职能误入歧途、政策监督顾此失彼、治理结构力量失衡、争端解决有心无力。有鉴于此，应当在近期已有改革举措的基础上，在重塑机构职能、加强双边监督、完善治理结构、促进争端解决四个方面寻找出路。

（三）关于“金融消费者”的概念与范围（2012）

传统消费者概念适用于金融领域时存在的不确定性，以及现有金融行业立法在保护性上的不足，使得在我国构建金融消费者概念具有现实必要性。代表性的国外立法实践表明，金融消费者的概念和范围主要是实践塑造而非理论推演的产物，与金融监管模式和监管体制有着不可分割的内在联系。从我国现实情况出发，较为可行的做法是对金融消费者进行宽松的界定，使其涵盖整个金融服务领域，而在消费者保护制度方面则遵循最低限度协调原则，只作总体性、原则性的规定，由行业监管部门基于行业特点和监管需要制定实施细则；与此同时，保留和延续既有的证券投资者概念和投资者保护制度，实现金融消费者和投资者这两个概念、两套制度的并存和并用。

（四）关于“软法”在全球金融治理中的地位、作用和影响（2016）

国际金融软法是用以规范国际金融关系，虽不具有法律约束力但在实践中具有某种实际效果的规范性文件的总称，突出表现为国际金融标准制定机构制定和发布的各类国际金融标准。既有条约规则作用有限、金融监管实践复杂多变、关涉敏感主权问题、缺乏争端解决机制，是软法在全球金融治理中扮演重要角色的原因。软法在全球金融治理中的价值，既体现为“中转”价值，即作为向“硬法”演进或转化过程中的过渡阶段，更表现为独立价值，即凭借自身特点和优势长期稳定存在并独立发挥作用。在相当程度上，软法在当前全球金融治理中发挥着比硬法更为重要的作用，使得全球金融治理呈现“软法之治”的面貌。

（五）关于中国国际经济法学研究的现状、反思与展望（2018）

作为一门与改革开放大体同步的新兴学科，中国国际经济法学在过去40年中取得了长足进步，已经初步构建起较为完整的学科体系，并在各分支学科进行了范围广泛的研究，产出了数量可观的研究成果。但是，当前中国国际经济法学研究的“繁荣”在很大程度上是一种“表面繁荣”乃至“虚假繁荣”，折射出整体性的急功近利和无序浮躁。存在的问题和不足主要表现在：学科“支强干弱”，基本理论研究依旧薄弱；相关研究缺乏问题意识、方法自觉和学术定力，缺乏清晰定位和恰当平衡，缺少独立品格和鲜明个性；学术环境和评价机制不尽合理和科学。展望未来，应当继续加强基本理论研究，构建具有中国特色的国际经济法理论；提升学科的整体品位和规范性，从“繁荣”走向规范；改善学术环境和评价机制，创造更加宽松友好的研究环境和氛围。

（六）关于全球治理背景下人类命运共同体的阐释与构建（2018）

人类命运共同体是中国在新时代向国际社会贡献的全球治理新方案。在思想渊源上，人类命运共同体植根于以世界大同为一致追求的世界主义理念和中华传统文化，以及以“自由人的联合体”为终极目标的马克思主义共同体思想。在理念传承上，人类命运共同体与和平共处五项原则、建立国际新秩序主张、第三代人权、人类共同继承财产原则等理论、原则和主张一脉相承。人类命运共同体理念为糅合国际关系和国际秩序中的利益与价值、现实主义与理想主义这两个维度提供了一种新的可能性，可以从利益共同体、价值共同体和责任共同体这三个维度加以理解和阐释。应当从深化对外开放提供“中国方案”、坚持共商共建形成“共同方案”这两个层面，推动构建人类命运共同体。

（七）关于跨境金融监管合作的现状、问题与出路（2018）

跨境金融监管合作包括双边和多边两种途径。双边途径以美国跨境证券监管合作为代表，主要通过谅解备忘录、监管对话和技术援助等方式开展。多边途径根据参与主体及合作方式的不同，又可以进一步划分为国际组织模式、非正式国家集团模式和跨政府网络模式。以软法为主导的国际金融监管规则缺乏“硬约束”、国际金融监管标准的实施和监督机制严重不足、危机驱动型的监管合作缺乏持久性和稳定性，是跨境金融监管合作的主要问题和障碍所在。完善跨境金融监管的远景目标是建立一个以多边条约为基础，能够制定、实施和监督执行有约束力国际规则的全球金融监管（合作）组织；近期对策则是充分利用现有国际机构和机制，系统性地“硬化”相关软法性规则，加强其约束性、执行力和实施效果。

（八）关于世界贸易组织改革的全球方案与中国立场（2019）

世界贸易组织（WTO）正面临前所未有的生存危机，改革已经成为共识。但关于 WTO 改革的基本原则、具体内容和优先顺序，各方立场和意见则不尽相同，阵营划分也难以一概而论。综合现有的主要改革方案，大体而言，在谈判机制方面主张增加谈判机制灵活性，打破“协商一致”造成的多边谈判僵局；在实体规则方面主张制定贸易新规，强化贸易公平，消除投资障碍；在纪律约束方面主张更好地发挥 WTO 的审查和监督功能，加强对成员方遵守透明度和通报义务的约束；在争端解决方面主张尽快修改相关协定，打破上诉机构法官遴选僵局，确保 WTO 正常运转。对于中国而言，关键在于“以我为主”，明确自身基本立场与核心关切，并在现有《立场文件》基础上，出台具体改革方案，更加积极主动地参与乃至推动 WTO 改革进程。

六 主要科研成果

（一）独著

1.《证券客户资产风险法律问题研究》，北京大学出版社，2005。

2.《国际货币金融体制改革的法律问题》，社会科学文献出版社，2012。

3.《国际金融法学的新发展》，中国社会科学出版社，2013。

（二）合著

《上海自贸试验区建设推进与制度创新》（第一作者），中国社会科学出版社，2017。

（三）参编

1.《国际经济法》（黄东黎主编），社会科学文献出版社，2006。

2.《当代中国国际法研究》（陈泽宪主编），中国社会科学出版社，2010。

3.《变化中的国际法：热点与前沿》（朱晓青主编），中国社会科学出版社，2012。

（四）代表性学术论文

1.《钢丝上的平衡：美国证券信息披露体系的演变》，《法学》2003 年第 4 期。

2.《美国非公司型有限责任企业初探》，《法学》2003 年第 9 期。

3.《论证券公司破产清算的特别程序：以中美比较为视角》，《法学》2006 年第 7 期。

4.《间接持有证券的权益性质与法律适用初探》，《环球法律评论》2006 年第 6 期。

5.《美国反向刺破公司面纱的理论与实践：基于案例的考察》，《北大法律评论》第 8 卷第 2 辑，北京大学出版社，2007。

6.《竞争、冲突与协调：金融混业监管模式的选择》，《北京大学学报》（哲学社会科学版）2008 年第 3 期。

7.《论欧盟对金融集团的监管：以〈金融集团指令〉为中心》，《国际法研究》第 2 卷，中国人民公安大学出版社，2008。

8.《经济全球化与国际经济法的新趋势》，《清华法学》2009 年第 6 期。

9.《国际货币体制的困境与出路》，《法学研究》2010 年第 4 期。

10.《国际货币基金组织投票权与治理结构改革述评》，《中国国际法年刊 2010》，世界知识出版社，2011。

11. "Regulation of Financial Conglomerates in China：from *De facto to De jure*", *European Business Organization Law Review*, Volume 12, Issue 2, July 2011.

12.《英国金融监管体制改革的最新发展及其启示》，《金融监管研究》2012 年第 2 期。

13.《金融消费者的概念与范围：一个比较法的视角》，《环球法律评论》2012 年第 4 期。

14.《系统重要性金融机构国际监管的发展与趋势》，《国际经济法学刊》第 20 卷第 1 期，北京大学出版社，2013。

15.《美国海外金融账户和资产报告规则的演进与发展》，《环球法律评论》2015 年第 5 期。

16.《论软法在全球金融治理中的地位和作用》，《厦门大学学报》（哲学社会科学版）2016 年第 2 期。

17.《比较视野下的亚投行贷款条件研究》，《法学杂志》2016 年第 6 期。

18.《投资者—国家争端解决机制的新发展》，《江西社会科学》2017 年第 10 期。

19.《2017 年的中国互联网金融法治》，《中国法治发展报告 No. 16（2018）》，社会科学文献出版社，2018。

20.《从“繁荣”到规范：中国国际经济法学研究的反思与展望》，《政法论坛》2018 年第 5 期。

21.《全球治理背景下人类命运共同体的阐释与构建》，《中国法学》2018 年第 5 期。

22.《人类命运共同体的人权与主权内涵》,《吉林大学社会科学学报》2018 年第 6 期。

23.《跨境金融监管合作:现状、问题与法制出路》,《政治与法律》2018 年第 12 期。

24.《从〈美墨加协定〉看美式单边主义及其应对》,《拉丁美洲研究》2019 年第 1 期。

25.《世界贸易组织改革:全球方案与中国立场》,《国际经济评论》2019 年第 2 期。

(五)代表性报纸文章

1.《华盛顿共识、新自由主义与国际货币基金组织》,《法制日报》2008 年 12 月 14 日,第 10 版。

2.《推动金融体系改革的现实举措》,《人民日报》2009 年 7 月 13 日,第 13 版。

3.《功能监管与机构监管应"双剑合璧"》,《经济日报》2012 年 2 月 13 日,第 6 版。

4.《中国企业"走出去"要重视国际经济软法》,《经济参考报》2013 年 1 月 8 日,第 8 版。

5.《〈外国投资法〉宜完善审查机构设计》,《经济参考报》2015 年 1 月 28 日,第 6 版。

6.《自贸区建设要与顶层设计相协调》,《经济参考报》2015 年 2 月 13 日,第 8 版。

7.《企业走向"一带一路"中的风险应对》,《经济参考报》2016 年 6 月 22 日,第 6 版。

8.《为全球治理体系变革提供新动力》,《人民日报》2018 年 5 月 21 日,第 7 版。

9.《与全球化和多边主义同行》,《人民日报》(海外版)2018 年 9 月 11 日,第 6 版。

10.《〈外商投资法〉的四个特色和创新》,《经济参考报》2019 年 3 月 20 日,第 8 版。

黄　晋

一　基本情况

湖南常德人，经济学学士、法学博士。现为中国社会科学院国际法研究所国际经济法研究室副主任、副研究员，中国社会科学院研究生院法学系副教授、硕士生导师，中国社会科学院国际法研究所竞争法中心副主任兼秘书长。专业方向为国际经济法学。重点研究领域是国际经济法、竞争法、互联网竞争、国际投资法、外商投资与海外投资、公司法、消费者保护、国际贸易等。

目前担任的主要社会职务和兼职有：北京市金融服务法学研究会理事、新华社“瞭望智库”首批入驻专家。

二　教育及工作经历

1999 年在大连海事大学商务学院获得经济学学士，2002 年在大连海事大学法学院获得法学硕士学位，2007 年在中国社会科学院研究生院获得法学博士学位。2002 年至今在中国社会科学院法学研究所、中国社会科学院国际法研究所工作。

曾长期在国外著名大学和研究机构担任客座教授和访问学者。2004 年在日本早稻田大学比较法研究所访问研究，2005 年在美国哥伦比亚大学法学院做访问学者，2007 年在荷兰莱顿大学做访问学者。

三　学术地位及社会影响

主持和参加了中国社会科学院、商务部、交通部、国家发展和改革委员会、国家互联网信息办公室、市场监督管理总局等单位的 30 余项课题的研究工作，多次参与法规、规章的论证和咨询工作，撰写的多篇内部研究报告得到党和国家领导人批示的肯定，先后获得 2 项中国社会科学院优秀对策信息奖三等奖。

四　代表作介绍

《合并控制法：以美国和欧盟为视角》

本书指出，合并控制制度在保护市场竞争和消费者利益方面的重要作用为市场经济国家所普遍接受。当前，已经有 100 多个国家通过了反垄断法。其中，60 多个国家在其反垄断法中引入了合并控制制度。这些国家存在这样的共识，即合并有可能引起产出减少、价格提高以及消费者福利受损。专著以合并控制制度为研究对象，着力探讨所涉及的法律问题，选择美国、欧盟这两个学界最为关注的司法管辖区，结合国际竞争网络工作组的相关意见，就合并控制制度的程序、实体规范、管辖权和国际合作等法律问题进行专题分析，同时探讨了完善中国合并控制制度的相关内容。

五　主要研究成果

（一）独著

《合并控制法：以美国和欧盟为视角》，社会科学文献出版社，2013。

（二）合著

《上海自贸试验区建设推进与制度创新》，中国社会科学出版社，2017。

（三）参编/译

1.《国际法学》（参编），社会科学文献出版社，2005。

2.《中华人民共和国反垄断法详解》（参编），知识产权出版社，2008。

3.《中国企业并购反垄断审查相关法律制度研究》（参编），北京大学出版社，2008。

4.《国际商事仲裁》（合译），中国社会科学出版社，2009。

5.《当代中国国际法研究》（参编），中国社会科学出版社，2010。

6.《美国反托拉斯手册》（合译），知识产权出版社，2012。

7.《合并与收购：理解反垄断问题》（第三版）（独译），北京大学出版社，2012。

8.《经济学分析方法在欧盟企业并购反垄断审查中的适用》（合译），法律出版社，2017。

（四）论文

1.《与合并有关的不竞争条款问题研究——以反垄断法律制度为基础》，载《中国企业并购反垄断审查相关法律制度研究》，北京大学出版社，2008。

2.《美国反托拉斯法中的合并控制救济》，载《国际法研究》第 2 卷，中国人民公安大学出版社，2008。

3.《我国保险行业协会在反垄断法通过后面临的挑战——重庆市保险协会案启示》，《保险研究》2008 年第 12 期。

4.《国外反倾销与中国企业应诉》，载《中国法治发展报告 No. 9（2011）》，社会科学文献出版社，2011。

5.《中国反垄断执法》，载《中国法治发展报告 No. 10（2012）》，社会科学文献出版社，2012。

6.《欧盟与美国在合并控制领域的双边执法合作》，《国际法研究》2014 年第 4 期。

7.《以法治保障对外投资和贸易　助力“一带一路”战略》，《人民法治》2015 年第 11 期。

8.《国家安全审查制度中的外国投资者识别——兼评〈外国投资法（草案征求意见稿）〉》，《中国社会科学院研究生院学报》2016 年第 3 期。

9.《完善自贸试验区国家安全审查制度》，《人民法治》2016 年第 12 期。

10.《中国外资准入管理的发展与展望》，载《中国法治发展报告 No. 15（2017）》，社会科学文献出版社，2017。

11.《法治保障自由贸易试验区发展》，载《中国地方法治发展报告

No. 3（2017）》，社会科学文献出版社，2017。

12.《经营者集中反垄断审查为“一带一路”建设发展助力——以商务部附条件批准马士基收购汉堡南美案为例》，《人民法治》2018年第2期。

13.《关于自由贸易试验区投资开放与市场监管政策的思考与建议》，载《中国法治发展报告No.16（2018）》，社会科学文献出版社，2018。

14.《中国与巴拿马开启海事合作新篇章》，《中国航务周刊》2018年第36期。

（五）代表性报纸文章

1.《规范跨国公司并购我国企业的立法建议》，《中国改革报》2004年第4期。

2.《跨国公司的并购与反垄断》，《中国社会科学报》2005年1月25日。

3.《理性看待外资并购——浅谈可口可乐收购汇源果汁案》，《中国社会科学报》2008年10月16日。

4.《腾讯与360之争的资本非理性》，《法治周末》2010年11月10日。

5.《制定〈边界法〉有利于边疆的建设和保护》，《经济参考报》2012年8月28日。

6.《广药与加多宝应停止不正当竞争》，《经济参考报》2013年7月3日。

7.《强生案推动中国私人反垄断诉讼》，《经济参考报》2013年8月14日。

8.《腾讯-360终极诉讼战解读》，《经济参考报》2013年12月11日。

9.《三一重工在美诉讼赢了什么》，《经济参考报》2014年8月5日。

10.《外资安全审查需精准界定控制权》，《中国社会科学报》2015年12月9日。

11.《三部公平竞争法律亟待修改完善》，《经济参考报》2015年12月22日。

12.《滴滴收购优步的交易应该受到限制》，《经济参考报》2016年8月16日。

13.《马士基收购汉堡南美有助一带一路》，《经济参考报》2017年12月26日。

14.《规范互联网平台竞争行为》，《人民日报》2018年4月19日。

张文广

一 基本情况

河南南阳人。2002 年 6 月起在中国社会科学院工作；曾先后在哥伦比亚大学和清华大学从事博士后研究工作，也曾为最高人民法院法律研修学者；2004 年 6 月至 2014 年 12 月担任中国社会科学院国际法研究所国际经济法研究室副主任；现为中国社会科学院国际法研究所副研究员，海洋法治研究中心主任，最高人民法院“一带一路”司法研究基地副主任兼秘书长，最高人民法院涉外商事海事审判专家库首批专家，最高人民法院国际海事司法上海基地特邀研究员，长江海商法学会副会长，中国法学会保险法学研究会理事。

主要研究方向为海商法、合同法、保险法、国际经济法。出版独著 2 本，合著 3 本，在《国际法研究》、《环球法律评论》、《中国海商法研究》、《法律适用》、《中国审判》、《人民法治》、《经济参考报》、《人民法院报》、《中国航务周刊》、《航运交易公报》、《中国水运报》等报刊上发表文章 40 余篇。

二　教育背景

2003—2009 年，中国社会科学院研究生院民商法博士。

2006—2007 年，美国哥伦比亚大学，法学硕士（LLM）。

1995—2002 年，大连海事大学国际航运管理学士、国际经济法硕士。

三　工作经历

2002 年 6 月—2004 年 6 月，中国社会科学院法学研究所，助理研究员。

2004 年 6 月—2014 年 12 月，中国社会科学院国际法研究所中心/国际经济法研究室副主任。

2004 年 8 月—2005 年 8 月，哥伦比亚大学访问学者。

2007 年 5 月—2008 年 5 月，美国哥伦比亚大学法学院博士后研究人员。

2010 年 9 月—2012 年 12 月，清华大学法学院博士后研究人员。

2013 年 6 月至今，中国社会科学院国际法研究所副研究员。

五　代表作介绍

《“一带一路”倡议背景下的国际海事司法中心建设》

“一带一路”建设给海运业发展提供了历史机遇，同时对海事司法提出了更高要求。在牢固确立亚太地区海事司法中心后，中国将目光投向国际海事司法中心建设。服务和保障海洋强国、“一带一路”、海运强国等国家战略实施，营造法治化、国际化营商环境，参与国际规则制定等是中国建设国际海事司法中心的主要原因。中国初步具备成为国际海事司法中心的硬实力，但也面临软实力不足及来自传统国际海事纠纷解决中心伦敦和新兴国际海事纠纷解决中心新加坡的竞争。中国应统筹推进国际海事司法中心建设，完善涉海法律制度，改革中国海事司法机制，提升海事司法公信力，扩大国际司法协助范围，加强国际海事司法研究基地建设，支持海事仲裁发展，努力实现从海事司法大国向海事司法强国的转变。

五　学术项目

1. 中国社会科学院重点课题“《鹿特丹规则》研究”，主持人。课题研究成果体现为《海运承运人责任制度研究》，为中国社会科学院创新工程学术出版资助项目。

2. 中国社会科学院重点课题“《鹿特丹规则》对我国进出口贸易的影响”，主持人。

3. 中国社会科学院国情调研项目“海洋石油污染及其法律对策”，主持人。成果载《中国法治发展报告 No. 11（2013）》，社会科学文献出版社，2013。

4. 中国社会科学院重大项目“上海自贸试验区建设推进与制度创新”，课题组成员。

5. 最高人民法院研修课题“我国海洋维权司法对策研究”。

何晶晶

一 基本情况

江苏兴化人。2004—2011 年在英国布里斯托大学（University of Bristol）获得硕士和博士学位，2009—2010 年在剑桥大学（University of Cambridge）做访问博士生一年，2011—2013 年在中国社会科学院国际法研究所做博士后，并曾于 2013 年在芬兰赫尔辛基大学（University of Helsinki）法学院做访问学者，2015 年在意大利都灵大学（University of Turin）做访问学者，2016—2017 年在美国哥伦比亚大学法学院做 Edwards Fellow 访问学者。现为中国社会科学院国际法研究所国际经济法研究室的副研究员，西城区法院金融街法庭庭长助理，最高人民法院“一带一路”司法基地副秘书长，新加坡国际仲裁中心 User Council Committee 理事，中国社会科学院大学（研究生院）副教授，兼任《人民法治》理论部编辑，主要研究领域为涉外法律争端解决特别是国际仲裁与国际调解、国际经济法、国际环境法和环境法等。

二 代表作介绍

《从〈京都议定书〉到〈巴黎协定〉：开启新的气候变化治理时代》

联合国巴黎气候变化大会成功落幕，正式宣告一个气候变化治理时代被另一个时代所代替。鉴于《京都议定书》的明显不足，《巴黎协定》取代《京都议定书》具有历史的必然性和进步性。无论从治理机制、法律形式、法律基本原则、法律履约机制还是市场机制等方面，《巴黎协定》都与《京都议定书》有本质的区别。《巴黎协定》的灵活性制度设计虽然在最大程度上吸引了各个国家广泛参与和支持，淡化了发展中国家与发达国家间的对立，却又由于强制履约机制的缺失而使得国际条约履约充满风险和不确定性。如何通过构建有效的履约透明度框架实现条约的灵活性和有效性双重目标，如何通过降低履约成本提升履约积极性，是国际社会在“后《巴黎协定》时代”亟待解决的棘手问题。

三 学术成果

（一）著作

1. The Role of Public Brokerage in Managing Interorganisational Network（《政府在企业网络的管理中所起的作用》），被德国的 VDM 出版社（VDM publishing House，Germany）2011 年 1 月出版。

2.《国际气候变化法框架下的中国低碳发展立法初探》，中国社会科学出版社，2014。

3. 2018 年 1 月作为学术著作 *Aid Effectiveness For Environmental Sustainability* 的一章“Foreign aid for climate change capacity building”（“对外援助对气候变化应对能力的作用”）由麦克米兰（Palgrave Macmillan）出版社出版。

4. 2018 年 8 月由 Paths International Ltd. 和中国社会科学出版社共同出版三本译著《当代中国法学研究 1949—1978 上编》，《当代中国法学研究 1978—1992 中编》，《当代中国法学研究 1992—2009 下编》。

（二）论文

1. “China’s Regional Emission”（《中国的地区碳排放》，合著），SSCI 和 SCI 国际权威杂志 *Nature Climate Change*《自然》子刊《自然——气候变化》2011 年 10 月刊。

2. “The Decarbonization of China’s Agriculture”（《中国农业的低碳化发展》，第一作者），于 2012 年 8 月被联合国世界发展经济学研究院收录，文章出版序列号 WP2012/074，ISBN 978 - 92 - 9230 - 537 - 6，文章网上链接：http://www.wider.unu.edu/publications/working-papers/2012/en_GB/wp2012 - 074/。

3. 英文文章“The Role of Climate Finance in the Age of Green Economy”（《气候融资在绿色经济时代的作用》，合著），英文杂志 *The World Financial Review* 2012 年 11 月—12 月刊。

4. 2012 年 3 月—2013 年 3 月，参加并完成联合国世界发展经济学研究院的气候变化项目，已完成英文合著的联合国资助项目研究报告文章（UN commissioned paper）“Foreign Aid for Climate Change Capacity Building”（《对外援助对气候变化应对能力的作用》），此文章于 2013 年 4 月被联合国世界发展经济学研究院收录，文章出版序列号 WP 2013/046，ISBN 978 - 92 - 9230 - 623 - 6，文章网上链接：http://www.wider.unu.edu/publications/working-papers/2013/en_GB/wp2013 - 046/。

5.《构建中国碳排放权交易法初探》，《中国软科学》2013 年第 9 期。

6.《“十面霾伏”下的有中国特色碳税之路的法律思考》，载《国际法研究》第 8 卷，社会科学文献出版社，2013。

7. “Has the Clean Development Mechanism assisted sustainable development”（《清洁发展机制是否促进可持续发展?》，第一作者），发表于 SSCI 杂志 *Natural Resources Forum—A United Nations Sustainable Development Journal*, Volume 38, Issue 4, Pages 248 - 260, November 2014（2014 年 11 月），杂志影响因子（Impact Factor）：1.3。

8. 英文文章“Is the Clean Development Mechanism Effective for Emission

Reductions?”（第一作者），发表于 SCI 杂志 *Greenhouse Gases：Science and Technology*，*Volume* 4，Issue 6，Pages 750－760，December 2014（2014 年 12 月），杂志影响因子（Impact Factor）：3.067。

9.《构建中国低碳农业法思考：中西比较视角》，载第五届中国法学博士后论坛论文集《依法治国与推进国家治理现代化》，中国社会科学出版社，2014。

10.《构建中国低碳农业法思考——中西比较视角》，《中国软科学》2014 年第 12 期，该文获得 2014 年中国法学会主办的第九届中国法学家论坛三等奖。

11.《气候变化的人权法维度》，《人权》2015 年第 5 期，该文被人大复印报刊资料《国际法学》2016 年第 4 期全文转载。

12.《做好环境法治保障　打造“绿色丝绸之路”》，《人民法治》2015 年第 11 期。

13.《2015 年环境公益诉讼司法实践》，载《中国法治发展报告 No. 14（2016）》，社会科学文献出版社，2016。

14.《从〈京都议定书〉到〈巴黎协定〉：开启新的气候变化治理时代》，《国际法研究》2016 年第 3 期。

15.《〈巴黎协定〉的人权纬度》，《人权》2017 年第 12 期。

（三）研究报告

1. 2015 年主持并完成外交部应对气候变化谈判国别研究项目，并完成 7 万字项目研究报告。

2. 2018 年参与完成贸促会法律部的国际调解项目，并完成项目报告。

四　主要学术活动

1. 2007 年 7 月，参加在英国伦敦大学皇后玛丽学院（Queen Mary，University of London）举办的英国社会网络学学术年会（UK Social Network Conference），并在会议上讲演英文独著文章“Exploring Public Brokerage Effects in the Context of Public-led Networks”（《政府在企业网络的管理中所起的作用》）。

2. 2012 年 2 月，参加在芬兰瓦萨举办的第 34 届芬兰经济协会年会（XXXIV Annual Meeting of the Finnish Economic Association，Vaasa，Finland），

并在会议上提交英文合著文章“Is the Clean Development Mechanism Effective for Emission Reductions?”（《清洁发展机制是否促进碳减排？》）。

3. 2012 年 9 月，参加在芬兰举办的联合国世界发展经济学研究院的气候变化与发展政策大会（UNU-WIDER Conference on Climate Change and Development Policy）。

4. 2013 年 5 月，参加由芬兰赫尔辛基大学法学院举办的国家应对气候变化法案和政策研讨会“National Climate Change Legislation and Policy Seminar”。

5. 2013 年 8 月，应邀参加由亚洲开发银行（Asian Development Bank）在菲律宾举办的“亚洲发展回顾大会”（Asian Development Review Conference），并在会议上讲演英文合著文章“The Decarbonization of China's Agriculture”（《中国农业的低碳化发展》）。

6. 2014 年 10 月，参加第五届中国法学博士后论坛“依法治国与推进国家治理现代化”（北京），并作英文主题发言。

7. 2014 年 11 月，参加第十一届国际法论坛（北京），并在大会上作题为“京都议定书替代条约”的英文主题发言。

8. 2015 年 12 月，在法国巴黎参加联合国巴黎气候变化大会。

田　夫

一 基本情况

贵州省仁怀市人，现为中国社会科学院国际法研究所副研究员，中国社会科学院研究生院硕士生导师，专业方向为法理学，重点研究领域是自然法、检察理论等。

1999—2010 年，求学于中国政法大学，先后获得法学学士、硕士、博士学位。2010—2012 年，于中国社会科学院法学研究所从事博士后研究工作。2012 年至今在中国社会科学院国际法研究所工作。2016 年晋升为副研究员，2017 年被聘为中国社会科学院研究生院法理学方向硕士生指导教师。中国法学会法理学研究会理事。成果获最高人民检察院“2015 年度检察理论研究优秀成果二等奖”、中国社会科学院皮书学术评审委员会第八届“优秀皮书报告奖”一等奖。

二 主要学术观点

（一）法理学“指导”型知识生产机制应当被抛弃

从知识生产机制的整体视角来看，中国法理学教材还没有走出苏式法理学的框架。苏式法理学教材的“指导”型知识生产机制基于法理学与部门法学具有不同的研究对象这一基本原理，认为法理学是部门法学的指导性学科，并由此决定了“指导”型知识生产机制的运行机制。运行机制包含正面向度和反面向度两个方面，正面向度指的是法理学针对部门法学生产“指导”型知识，反面向度指的是部门法学帮助法理学生产“指导”型知识，法律关系理论和法律行为理论分别典型地对应着这两个方面。然而，对上述理论的检讨表明，“指导”型知识生产机制在运行机制层面是无效的，进一步地，该机制在基本原理层面及其理论基础层面也是错误的，因而应当被抛弃。

（二）中国司法理论经历了从强制型司法到权威型司法的范式转变

1949 年以来，中国司法经历了某种范式性的转变。法理学教材中的法律适用理论为这种转变奠定了最一般的理论基础，进而可以将中国司法理论的转变概括为从强制型司法到权威型司法的转变。强制型司法的母体是 20 世纪 40 年代和 50 年代苏联的法律适用理论，中国法理学在继承这一理论母体的基础上，形成了强制型司法，它具有强制性、工具性和阶级性。

从20世纪80年代下半期到90年代中期，强制型司法逐渐演变为权威型司法。权威型司法具有权威性、目的性和专业性。当前，权威型司法仍面临一些需要解答的问题，因而也存在进一步完善的空间。

（三）检察工作在未来应当形成“双面监督”的格局

1979年以来，中国检察制度走上独立发展之路：检察院不再是实行垂直领导制和一般监督制的苏式法律监督机关，而成长为实行法律监督的中式法律监督机关；相应地，法律监督概念的教义化进程开启并发展，逐渐获得了法纪监督、侦查监督、监所监督、审判监督、执行监督、民事调解监督等内容。2014年以来，十八届四中全会和六中全会分别提出建立检察机关提起公益诉讼制度和改革国家监察体制，检察制度发生重大变化，法律监督理论体系也被相应调整：法纪监督不复存在，行政公益诉讼监督被纳入其中。由于检察院主要是一个刑事司法机关，所以，未来应重在坚持：对刑事诉讼，依法进行程度较强的法律监督，对职务犯罪调查，依法进行程度适当的监督，形成“双面监督”的格局。

三 主要学术成果

（一）专著

《菲尼斯自然法理论研究》，方志出版社，2015。

（二）论文

1.《法理学“指导”型知识生产机制及其困难——从法理学教材出发》，《北方法学》2014年第6期。

2.《依法独立行使检察权制度的宪法涵义——兼论重建检察机关垂直领导制》，《法制与社会发展》2015年第2期。

3.《中国独立行使审判权制度的历史考察》，《环球法律评论》2016年第2期。

4.《从强制型到权威型：中国司法的范式转变——以法理学教材为主线》，《法商研究》2017年第6期。

5.《检察院性质新解》，《法制与社会发展》2018年第6期。

6.《监督与公诉的关系——以苏中比较为中心》，《清华法学》2019年第1期。

毛晓飞

一　基本情况

1995年毕业于北京广播学院（现中国传媒大学）英语专业。其后在中央电视台经济部《经济半小时》栏目担任记者。1997年进入德国法兰克福歌德大学攻读五年制的硕士学位，主修政治与法律。2004年毕业回国后进入中国社会科学院国际法研究所国际经济法研究室工作，主要从事国际竞争法、国际争端解决机制以及德国法和欧盟法的研究与教学工作。2009年起受聘于德国柏林自由大学和柏林工业大学，兼职教授中国法。

二　学术活动

在职期间参与了所内外重大课题的研究，参与了国家的立法活动，特别是2007年《中华人民共和国反垄断法》的立法，深入调查了中国盐业垄断状况，撰写调研报告并促成2016年中国盐业体制的重大改革。2017年开始从事国际争端解决和国际仲裁研究，并创办社科仲裁圆桌。

在中外核心学术期刊《国际法研究》、《法律适用》、《欧洲研究》、《江西省社会科学》以及德国《竞争法杂志》和《工业产权保护与版权杂志（国际）》等发表专业论文数十篇。为人民日报《内部参考》、国家市场监督管理总局《工商行政管理》以及中国社会科学院《领导参阅》等撰写多份政策建议。在《人民日报》、《光明日报》、《经济日报》、《法制日报》、《新京报》等国内重要报刊发表时评文章。

合作翻译魏智通等著《国际法》一书，由法律出版社出版，成为国际法教学与研究的重要参考书。

在职期间，她还多次参加国内外重要国际法学术会议并发表主题演讲。

三 代表作介绍

（一）《独特的德国国际商事法庭模式》

设立国际商事法庭成为当下国际商事纠纷解决领域中的一种“新生态”。2018 年 4 月德国联邦众议院公布了《引入国际商事法庭的立法草案》，希冀在德全境州中级法院引入国际商事法庭并以英语作为审判语言。引入国际商事法庭将对德国现行《法院组织法》和《民事诉讼法》作出制度性改变。从国际比较的视角来看，其与广为悉知的国际商事法庭皆有不同，是德国商事法庭传统性与国际商事纠纷解决现代性的结合。

（二）《对外财政援助决定权的宪法制约——德国联邦宪法法院对欧元区援助法案的违宪审查》

德国联邦宪法法院对有关欧元区援助法案的司法判决表明，联邦议会是德国唯一有权决定通过国家财政实施对外援助的机构；国家财政决定权是基于宪法规定的自由平等公民选举权和民主原则的不可随意转让的一项权力，它属于议会。即使在参与为解决欧元区成员国主权债务危机的集体性救助行动时，也必须保证联邦议会的权力不被完全剥夺，尤其要符合有限的单项授权、议会保留监督权以及正当程序的宪法约束等原则。

（三）《析我国反垄断民事救济中的消费者利益保护机制》

反垄断法通过维护市场有效竞争来达到保护消费者利益的最终目的。

通过民事诉讼途经由消费者直接向法院主张权利救济并以此遏制垄断行为，已成为现代反垄断法实施机制的一个重要组成部分。有利于消费者提起民事诉讼和获得损害赔偿的司法救济制度也应运而生，然而，我国现存的垄断民事纠纷解决机制中尚欠缺与之匹配的方案。对消费者起诉资格的模糊认识、对适宜处理“小额多数”群体性诉讼的压制以及消费者所长期面临的举证困难和损害赔偿的不足使得反垄断法的私人执行在消费者权益保护方面依旧前景暗淡。

四　主要学术成果

（一）著作

《反垄断典型案例及中国反垄断执法调查》（编著），法律出版社，2007。

（二）中文论文

1.《谈反垄断执法的观念转变：从“公用企业”走向“占有市场支配地位的经营者”》，《工商行政管理》2006 年第 3 期。

2.《宁海县煤气公司等限制竞争案评析》，《工商行政管理》2006 年第 14 期。

3.《反垄断立法的回顾与展望》（合著），《华东政法大学学报》2008 年第 2 期。

4.《修改〈食盐专营办法〉破除垄断》，《改革内参》2008 年第 34 期。

5.《对外财政援助决定权的宪法制约——德国联邦宪法法院对欧元区援助法案的违宪审查》，《欧洲研究》2013 年第 2 期。

6.《析我国反垄断民事救济中的消费者利益保护机制》，《法律适用》2013 年第 2 期。

7.《规制跨国避税的竞争法困局及其解决路径》，《江西社会科学》2017 年第 11 期。

8.《“一带一路”倡议背景下我国商事仲裁制度的革新》，《人民法治》2018 年第 2 期。

9.《独特的德国国际商事法庭模式》，《国际法研究》2018 年第 6 期。

（三）英语与德文论文

1.〔英〕“An Overview of the Antimonopoly Practice in the People’s Republic of China", in Hassan Qaqaya/GoergeLipimile (ed.), *The Effects of Anti-competitive Business Practices on Developing Countries and Their Development prospects*, UNTAC, 2008〔《中华人民共和国反垄断法实践概述》, Hassan Qaqaya/GoergeLipimile（主编),《发展中国家的反竞争性商业行为及发展前景》, 联合国贸发组织, 2008〕。

2.〔德〕Das Kartellrecht in China, GRUR Int. 57/2007, pp. 576 - 587（《中国的卡特尔法》,《工业产权保护与版权杂志（国际)》2007 年第 57 期, 第 576—587 页）。

3.〔德〕Das chinesische Antimonopolgesetz im Lichte des deutschen Kartellrechts, ZWeR 1/2008, S. 88 - 108（《德国卡特尔法视角下的中国反垄断法》,《竞争法杂志》2008 年第 1 期, 第 88—108 页）。

4.〔德〕Das neue Antimonopolgesetz der Volksrepublik China, MAO Xiaofei/Tobias Glass, GRUR Int. (Gewerblicher Rechtsschutz und Urheberrecht-Internationaler Teil), 57/2008, pp. 105 - 112（《中国的新反垄断法》,《工业产权保护与版权杂志（国际)》2008 年第 57 期, 第 105—112 页）。

5.〔德〕Eine neue Epoche füer die private Durchsetzung des Kartellrechts in China?, ZweR (Zeitschrift füer Wettbewerbsrecht) 3/2012, S. 349ff（《中国反垄断法私人执行的新时代?》,《竞争法杂志》2012 年第 3 期, 第 349—362 页）。

（四）主要报纸文章

1.《消费者不能为行业自律埋单》,《新京报》2008 年 7 月 29 日。

2.《禁止并购详细解释才能消除误解》,《新京报》2009 年 3 月 20 日。

3.《裁决垄断事务应"心证公开"》,《新京报》2009 年 3 月 28 日。

4.《建立公平竞争制度时不我待》,《中国经济周刊》2016 年 10 月 30 日。

5.《消除诸侯经济藩篱，推进盐业的供给侧改革》,《中国食品安全报》2017 年 1 月 10 日。

6.《集体征收燃油附加费值得商榷》,《法制日报》2018 年 6 月 14 日。

7.《开创仲裁法治的新时代》,《光明日报》2019 年 3 月 31 日。

孙南翔

一 基本情况

福建漳州人，法学博士，主要从事国际经济法、网络法研究。2006年9月至2016年6月于西南政法大学求学，先后获得国际经济与贸易学士学位（2010年）、国际法专业硕士学位（2013年）、国际法专业博士学位（2016年）。自2016年7月起，为中国社会科学院国际法研究所国际经济法研究室助理研究员。

孙南翔助理研究员系中国法学会网络与信息法学研究会理事、北京市法学会互联网金融法治研究会理事、网络法治蓝皮书工作室副主任、中国社会科学院文化法制研究中心研究员、对外经贸大学数字经济与法律创新研究中心研究员、北京市法学会百名法学英才、法制网特约评论员等。

孙南翔助理研究员先后在《中外法学》、《现代法学》、《法律科学》、《环球法律评论》、《政治与法律》等CSSCI刊物发表学术论文近30篇，在*Asian Journal of WTO & International Health Law and Policy*等SSCI期刊与外文期刊上发表论文 3 篇，在《人民日报》、《中国社会科学报》、《法制日报》等报刊与媒体发表近 10 篇评论，共有 5 篇研究成果为人大复印报刊资料所转载，1 篇研究成果为《法学文摘》所转载，并向中央和国家机关提交近 20 篇内部报告。

孙南翔助理研究员曾赴德国马克斯·普朗克研究所、瑞士世界贸易研究所、悉尼科技大学等机构开展学术研究，并多次赴美国、加拿大、中国香港特区参加学术活动。其主持国家社科基金、司法部、中国法学会等国家与省部级项目，并承担中国社会科学院《国际电信联盟》国际调研与交流项目、中国社会科学院与澳大利亚社会科学院合作研究项目、中国社会科学院青年调研项目等。

二 代表作介绍

（一）《互联网规制的国际贸易法律问题研究》

本书指出，互联网自由和规制规则是新一代国际经贸谈判的核心内容。多边经贸体系中的互联网规则涉及货物、服务、知识产权等领域，其核心在于平衡国家安全、公共利益与个人自由。中国互联网规制并不违反 WTO 协定和国际人权协定。同时，本书指出，为把握互联网时代的新贸易增长点，我国应尽早建立起一套系统的、完整的、分层次的互联网规制法律体系。

（二）《美国经贸单边主义：形式、动因与法律应对》

本文认为，自特朗普执政以来，美国通过阻碍多边争端解决机制运转、以互惠待遇取代非歧视原则、强化国内法对国际法约束等单边主义行为，加速破坏以规则为导向的现行国际经贸体制。多边经贸协定文本与实践发展脱节、争端解决机制缺乏有效性、成员方对市场经济模式的理解缺乏共识，是美国经贸单边主义兴起的动因。美国经贸单边主义威胁多边机制正常运转，引发国际法治危机。为应对此种单边主义行为，世贸组织成员应有效发挥多数票决制度的功能，并强化多边规则对双边或区域协定的纪律约束。作为负责任大国，中国应坚持以完善公平竞争条件为基础发展市场经济，并以多边主义方法推动世贸组织改革。

（三）《论互联网自由的人权属性及其适用》

本文认为，互联网自由包括互联网表达自由、互联网信息获得自由、互联网基础设施和设备的可获得性以及互联网通讯自由。然而，互联网自由是相对的。对互联网自由的限制应至少满足三个条件：一是限制措施为法律所明确规定；二是措施满足合法性目标；三是措施具有必要性。我国应在法律上明确信息利益主体的救济机制和争议解决方法，增强国内外互联网基础设施和设备的可获得性，解决区域性的“数字鸿沟”难题，以此打造全人类的网络空间命运共同体。

（四）《认真对待“互联网贸易自由”与“互联网规制”——基于WTO协定的体系性考察》

本文认为，“互联网自由”与“互联网规制”是信息时代的两项核心议题。在WTO框架下，互联网贸易自由包括信息技术产品贸易自由、服务贸易自由、网络分销媒介自由以及与贸易相关的信息自由。然而，互联网贸易自由并非绝对的。通过对非贸易关切的考量，WTO协定赋予成员方实施互联网规制措施的权力，其中包括国家安全例外、公共道德与公共秩序例外、个人数据保护例外。根据条约解释的方法，不同的例外条款具有不同的适用标准与条件。在从网络大国迈向网络强国的过程中，我国应明确互联网贸易自由的基本价值导向，以此推进“互联网+”战略；同时，作为一个负责任的大国，我国应以符合WTO协定的方式保护网络空间的国家利益、公共利益与个人利益。

（五）掀开国家安全的面纱：中国银行业信息技术安全法规违反TBT协定吗？

本文认为，在互联网贸易日益自由化和便利化之际，与信息技术产品相关的国家安全隐患愈发引起各国关注。在国际法层面，TBT协定是解决WTO成员技术法规和技术标准的核心法律规范。其要求WTO成员技术法规的采用、制定和适用不应构成超过实现国家安全目标所必要的贸易障碍，并且除非国际标准对实现合法目标是无效或不适当，否则成员方应将其作为国内技术法规的基础。实际上，中国银行业信息技术安全法规并不违反TBT协定，同时中国也能够利用国家安全例外作为其抗辩的理由。当然，在修改或更新信息技术产品法规时，中国应力求实现程序正义。

三 主要学术成果

（一）著作

1.《互联网规制的国际贸易法律问题研究》（独著），法律出版社，2017。

2.《网络行动国际法塔林手册2.0版》（参译），社会科学文献出版社，2017。

3.《涉外投资法律实务》（参编），厦门大学出版社，2017。

（二）论文

1.《追溯与寻明：国际法视角下的碳排放权单位》，《西南政法大学学报》2012年第3期。

2.《民事抗诉再审制度理论审视与实效分析——以当事人穷尽上诉救济之建构为视角》，《法律适用》2012年第7期。

3.《GATT 1994下的透明度规则研究——论GATT 1994第10条第3款a项的适用》，载《武大国际法评论》第15卷第2期，武汉大学出版社，2012。

4. "The Arbitration Law in Myanmar and China's Experience"，《中国—东盟法律评论》2013年第1期。

5.《国际商事仲裁员资格特征研究——兼评我国贸仲委聘任仲裁员之实践》，载《国际经济法学刊》2013年第1期，北京大学出版社，2013。

6.《中国—东盟自由贸易区规则改进路径研究综述》，《广西社会科学》2014年第1期。

7.《WTO体制下国内治理的"正当程序"规则研究》，载《国际经济法学刊》2014年第1期，北京大学出版社，2014。

8.《跨区域贸易安排的勃兴与中国的因应》，《汕头大学学报》（人文社会科学版）2015年第2期。

9.《论数据主权：基于网络空间博弈与合作的考察》，《太平洋学报》2015年第2期。

10.《私法自由的归来："非国家法"在冲突法中的适用之探》，载《民商法论丛》第57卷，法律出版社，2015。

11.《"一带一路"战略与多元化纠纷解决机制的构建》，《中国审判》

2015 年第 7 期。

12.《我国海外突发事件应急机制的构建探析》，《学术探索》2015 年第 8 期。

13.《文化与 FTAs：文化贸易规则的制度实践》，《国际商务（对外经济贸易大学学报）》2015 年第 4 期。

14.《超越先例作用力：基于 WTO 争端解决实践的研究》，载《武大国际法评论》第 18 卷第 1 期，武汉大学出版社，2015。

15.《论“发展的条约解释”及其在世贸组织争端解决中的适用》，《环球法律评论》2015 年第 5 期，本文被人大复印报刊资料《国际法学》2016 年第 1 期全文转载。

16.《走向命运共同体：网络空间治理的中国方案》，《学术前沿》2016 年第 2 期。

17.《从限权到赋权：面向未来的互联网贸易规则》，《当代法学》2016 年第 5 期。

18.《企业海外投资的非政府性障碍及中国的对策研究》，《现代法学》2016 年第 1 期。

19.《认真对待“互联网贸易自由”与“互联网规制”——基于 WTO 协定的体系性考察》，《中外法学》2016 年第 2 期，本文被人大复印报刊资料《国际法学》2016 年第 8 期全文转载。

20. “Piercing the Veil of National Security：Does China’s Banking IT Security Regulation Violate the TBT Agreement?”, *Asian Journal of WTO & International Health Law and Policy*, No. 2, 2016, SSCI.

21.《世界贸易组织法视角下的互联网自由与人权问题》，载《人权领域的国际合作与中国视角》，中国政法大学出版社，2017。

22.《从 WTO 到 eWTO：多边贸易规则的数据治理》，载《网络信息法学研究》2017 年第 1 期，中国社会科学出版社，2017。

23.《论经济主权在网络空间的形态与实现》，《中国信息安全》2017 年第 5 期。

24.《国家安全例外在互联网贸易中的适用及展开》，《河北法学》2017 年第 5 期。

25.《TBT 协定下的贸易自由与国家安全关切——基于中国网络安全和

信息化措施的应用》，《北方法学》2017 年第 5 期。

26.《论互联网自由的人权属性及其适用》，《法律科学》2017 年第 3 期，本文被人大复印报刊资料《国际法学》2017 年第 10 期全文转载。

27.《论网络经济主权的形成及其合作模式》，载《网络信息法学研究》2018 年第 2 期，中国社会科学出版社，2018。

28.《探索中国自由贸易试验区仲裁制度》，《人民法治》2018 年第 3 期。

29.《唤醒装睡的美国：基于美国对华单边贸易救济措施的分析》，《国际经济法学刊》2018 年第 3 期。

30.《互联网国际贸易的法治化与中国方案》，载《中国网络法治发展报告（2018）》，社会科学文献出版社，2018。

31.《论欧盟及其成员国在投资争端解决中的责任分配》，《欧洲研究》2018 年第 1 期，本文被人大复印报刊资料《国际法学》2018 年第 8 期全文转载。

32.《裁量余地原则在国际争端解决中的适用及其拓展》，《国际法研究》2018 年第 4 期。

33.《论作为消费者的数据主体及其数据保护机制》，《政治与法律》2018 年第 7 期，本文被人大复印报刊资料《经济法学、劳动法学》2018 年第 11 期全文转载。

34. “Strong Voice of the Times Defending the Multilateral Trade System-Book Review of Experiencing the WTO Appellate Body Personally”, *Journal of WTO and China*, Vol. 8, No. 1, 2018.

35.《美国经贸单边主义：形式、动因与法律应对》，《环球法律评论》2019 年第 1 期。

36.《〈美墨加协定〉对非市场经济国的约束及其合法性研判》，《拉丁美洲研究》2019 年第 1 期。

（三）主持项目

1. 2016 年司法部国家法治与法学理论研究部级科研青年项目：中国应对 WTO 网络安全争端法律问题研究。

2. 2016 年中国法学会后期资助项目：互联网规制的国际贸易法律问题研究。

3. 2016年中国法学会WTO法学研究会青年项目：多边贸易体制下的数据跨境流动规则研究。

4. 2018年中国法学会WTO法学研究会一般项目：WTO争端解决机制改革及其中国方案研究。

5. 2018年中国社会科学院青年社会调研项目：网络空间法治化治理机制实证研究。

6. 2018年国家社会科学基金青年项目：国际裁决的合宪性问题研究。

7. 2019年中国社会科学院国际调研与交流项目：国际电信联盟。

8. 2019年中国社会科学院与澳大利亚社会科学院合作研究项目：中澳服务贸易的法律框架及其升级路径研究——以教育和电信领域为研究对象。

（四）获奖情况

1. 2015年11月，获中国国际经济贸易法学研究会2015年年会优秀论文一等奖。

2. 2016年11月，获中国法学会中国法学青年论坛一等奖。

3. 2016年11月，获中国国际经济法学会2016年年会青年优秀论文二等奖。

4. 2016年12月，获安子介国际贸易研究奖学术鼓励奖。

5. 2017年12月，获中国法学会网络与信息法学研究会2017年年会优秀论文三等奖。

（五）媒体访谈

1.《向国际社会充分表达中国互联网人权自由》，中国人权网2016年10月24日。

2.《入世15年：深刻改变中国的经济法律制度》，法制网2016年12月9日。

3.《电子商务立法将网络空间法治化进程推向深处》，法制网2016年12月22日。

4.《奥迪滥用相对优势地位的价格歧视需立法禁止》，法制网2017年3月17日。

5.《市场经济不禁止差别待遇，但禁止不合理歧视》，《法制日报》2017年3月22日。

6.《打造网络空间法治化治理的中国方案》，《中国社会科学报》2017年9月15日。

7.《我国应做互联网贸易法治化推动者》，《经济参考报》2017年11月14日。

8.《自贸港探路全面开放新格局》（第二作者），《人民日报》2017年12月5日。

9.《佛首之谜等待揭开，先Get其中牵涉的法律问题》，法制网2018年9月14日。

任宏达

一　基本情况

自2017年起，就职于中国社会科学院国际法研究所国际经济法研究室，为助理研究员。此前，曾就读于北京航空航天大学和德国耶拿大学，先后取得德语学士学位、法学学士学位、法学硕士学位以及法学博士学位。其学术研究侧重于国际投资法、跨国并购和对外援助法。参与了一些前瞻性研究项目，在中外学术载体上发表过相关学术文章，部分对策建议得到积极反馈。同时，他还兼任最高人民法院“一带一路”司法研究基地研究人员、中国法学会部级会员联络员、中国特色社会主义理论体系研究中心研究人员、国际法研究所国际竞争法研究中心研究人员。

二 学术经历

（一）非典型学术经历

任宏达祖籍陕西宝鸡，其学术经历较为多元，具有丰富的跨学科背景。北京航空航天大学在高等教育阶段提供了德语文学的系统性训练。任宏达的本科毕业设计综合了语言学研究方法，利用计算机语料库技术自建数据库，对19世纪德国女权主义作家海德维西·得姆的中篇小说《成为你自己》（德语：Werder，die du bist）进行了文学分析。这篇著名小说以日记的形式展示了一位疑似有精神问题的妇女的意识流。可想而知，如果以传统的方式分析，几乎不知所云。而且作者在小说名字中玩了一个文字游戏，阴性定冠词die的指向并不明确，形成了一个开放式的命题，即应直译为“成为……（样）的你”。通过语料库的方法，全面梳理了文中阴性定冠词die的指向，从客观角度摆数据讲事实。分析得出，die一词不仅指女性，即一般意义上的女性应当成为女性自己，还指向了文中的灵魂（Seele）和精神（Psyche）等含义。换言之，女性应具有独立的思想和意识，以此改变当时不合理的社会秩序。通过分析，该文首次将这本小说名译为《成为你自己》。鉴于研究方法的创新性和结论的突破性，该文获得当年本科毕业论文最高分，是学术研究的第一次有益尝试。

在德语文学专业的学习之外，任宏达还完成了法学第二学位的学习。其间，参加曼弗雷德·拉克斯（Manfred-Lachs）国际空间法模拟法庭竞赛，对国际法产生了强烈兴趣。其法学本科论文《从皮诺切特案看国家豁免制度》获得了北京航空航天大学法学院的高度认可。

任宏达的硕士、博士阶段研究均在德国耶拿大学完成。耶拿大学全名弗里德里希·席勒大学（Friedrich-Schiller-Universität Jena），它有着500年的历史，许多为人熟知的大家，例如费希特、黑格尔、马克思等，都出自这所大学。其法学院常年占据CHE年度排名顶尖位置。硕士期间，其研究兴趣聚焦在公司治理方向。基于德国公司传统二元管理结构，其硕士论文

《论独立监事的独立性》在德国法和欧盟法框架内系统辨析与阐释了监事的独立性。德国的监事会充分体现多元性，其组成包括股东代表、上级公司派员、职工代表、金融专家（股份有限公司）、审计委员（规模以上公司）和独立监事（上市公司）等。但其多元性恰恰排除了一些任职的独立性，如股东代表、上级公司派员和职工代表。横向上，对金融专家、审计委员和独立监事的独立性要求散见于不同的法律序列当中，因此在概念上存在重合和交叉。纵向上，欧盟法、德国法、德国“软法”和司法实践也都对独立性有不同的要求与理解。监事的独立性瑕疵、独立性丧失的法律后果又较有争议。该文拨云见日，梳理了以上不同的概念和法律后果，强调尊重各公司监事会的自我认定。该文共计 52 页，引用文献 120 余个，脚注 550 多个，严格按照德国法学研究规范撰写。最终，该文获得优秀（gut）成绩。

博士阶段，任宏达继续跟随 Walter Bayer 教授从事研究。他的博士论文《并购中的特殊目的公司》主要研究外国企业收购中国非上市公司过程中使用特殊目的公司搭建复杂控股结构的法律原因与障碍，具体包含下列分议题：中国外商投资相关法律制度的法理学比较分析；市场准入以及对于外资并购的规制；规制（行政干预）的法技术角度比较分析；涉外并购中的民事关系法律适用问题；外资战略收购中国企业的并购结构演进；中国企业间接海外融资结构演进；等等。由于非上市公司收购信息的闭锁性，既往收购相关的文献主要关注于上市公司。该文使用经济学数据库对并购模型进行分析，从方法论上填补了空白。由于该研究的创新性，该文最终获得优秀论文成绩（拉丁语 magna cum laude）。全文共约 10 万字，2017 年 3 月由著名法学基金会“Johanna und Fritz Buch Gedaechtnis-Stiftung”资助出版。

（二）非典型工作经历

怀揣心中的学术理想，任宏达毕业后直接回国，来到中国社会科学院工作。在学术研究的同时，还在国际法研究所科研外事处进行实践锻炼，参与筹备若干重要国际、国内学术会议，参编学术文集，深入掌握科研管理、外事管理相关制度。

（三）项目研究

任宏达参与多项省部级研究项目，较为有代表性的如下。

1. 2017—2020 年，“一带一路”中的国际经济法问题，中国社会科学院创新工程研究所研究项目。

2. 2018 年，中国社会科学院特大项目“改革开放四十年百县（市、区）调查”——云南省瑞丽市，国家社科基金项目。

3. 2019—2023 年，“一带一路”法律风险防范与法律机制构建大型调研项目，中国社会科学院交办委托项目。

三　学术活动

国际法研究所为科研人员提供了良好的学术交流平台。在这一平台上，近年来任宏达参加了 30 余场国际、国内学术会议，与实务部门、国内外知名研究机构、国际组织、驻外使馆的专家学者进行了广泛深入的交流。

任宏达还组织筹办了多场国际性学术研讨会，其中具有代表性的是国际法论坛系列研讨会。国际法论坛此前已经连续举办十五届，在国内和海外国际法学界产生了较好的影响，享有很高的声誉。经过前十五届论坛的磨合，研讨会在主题选择、参会代表遴选以及会议安排等会议组织方面均积累了丰富的经验。以此为基础，相信在未来对参与筹办“一带一路”国际高峰论坛、二十国集团领导人峰会等国际性论坛可提供人才储备。

（一）参加的重要学术活动

1. 2017 年 5 月 19 日，“纪念日内瓦四公约 1977 年《附加议定书》通过 40 周年”国际研讨会，国际法研究所主办。

2. 2017 年 10 月 28 日，“WTO 法研究的中国视角”研讨会暨张月姣大法官新书发布会会议，国际法研究所主办。

3. 2017 年 11 月 5 日，“互联网金融创新与规范发展：国际经验与中国路径”研讨会，中国社会科学院国际法研究所、中国国际经济贸易法学研究会国际金融法专业委员会联合主办。

4. 2017 年 11 月 26 日，“重塑国际投资争端解决机制”青年国际法学者圆桌讨论会，国际法研究所主办。

5. 2018 年 3 月 26 日，PPP 合同性质及争议解决机制研讨会暨第二届社科仲裁圆桌会议，国际法研究所和北京仲裁委员会 PPP 研究中心共同举办。

6. 2018 年 4 月 8 日，中美经贸争端法律问题及其应对，国际法研究所主办。

7. 2018 年 4 月 20 日，中国法学会部级会员联络员工作座谈会，中国法学会主办。

8. 2018 年 5 月 24 日，最高人民法院“一带一路”司法研究中心研究基地年度座谈会，最高人民法院主办。

9. 2018 年 9 月 21 日，首届海事法治圆桌会议暨中国海事法治论坛，法学研究所、国际法研究所联合主办。

10. 2018 年 12 月 4 日，“深入学习贯彻实施宪法、坚定不移推进改革开放”座谈会，人民大会堂，全国人大常委会、中宣部和司法部联合主办，全国人大栗战书委员长发表重要讲话。

11. 2019 年 1 月 20 日，“当前国际法热点问题”研讨会，国际法研究所主办。

12. 2019 年 4 月 10 日，“当前国际法热点问题”研讨会，国际法研究所主办。

13. 2019 年 4 月 19 日，第二届海商法圆桌会议，国际法研究所主办。

（二）筹办的重要学术活动

1. 2017 年 12 月 2—3 日，中国社科论坛暨第十四届国际法论坛“新时期的国际法：变革、创新与发展”，中国社会科学院主办。

2. 2018 年 10 月 27—28 日，中国社科论坛暨第十五届国际法论坛“新时代改革开放与国际法”，中国社会科学院主办。

四 主要学术成果

（一）公开发表成果

1.《中国对外投资与东道国政策》（伦纳·库尔姆斯著，任宏达译，《国际法研究》2019 年第 1 期）

中国的海外投资在国际投资市场占据着越来越重要的位置，而一些国家的投资监管部门在对待国有企业或与政治关系密切的私营企业时，仍然戴着有色眼镜。该文以一些著名案例为基础，在借鉴经合组织和世界贸易组织国际惯例的基础上，为此类企业寻找更妥帖的国际标准和可行的原则。

2.《涉外股权收购合同关系的法律适用》（《国际法研究》2018 年第 1 期）

我国早期涉外投资立法对于外商投资设立了严格的审批制度，在面对日益复杂的全球化股权转让纠纷时，国内司法实践容易习惯性顺应公法思维，造成私法角度分析的缺位。在国际私法层面，股权转让涉及诸多民事关系。无论具有何种涉外因素，股权收购合同关系法律适用的出发点都应是合同准据法，其推导原则上依据《涉外民事关系法律适用法》第 41 条的普通规则，且《关于外国投资者并购境内企业的规定》第 22 条的特殊规则不能优先适用。涉及上市公司股票转让的合同关系在普通规则基础上应排除特征性履行说的适用。

3.《并购中的特殊目的公司》（Special Purpose Vehicles bei Mergers & Acquisitions，耶拿学术出版社，2017 年，ISBN：978 - 3 - 938057 - 57 - 5）

前文已介绍。

4.《在德国做法学教授，您准备好了么》，（《中国社会科学报》（法学版）2017 年 3 月 22 日，第 5 版）

该文以任宏达在德国法学院的经历为基础，介绍了德国法学学者成长的路径，相比于其他国家具有一定特点。由于德国法学学者成长的道路艰难，学者才更加珍惜自己的羽毛，更加尊重社会科学的研究。

（二）对策建议

作为法学学者，尤其是中国社会科学院研究人员，对于党和国家的重要法治战略和立法活动应作出学术回应并承担理论研究的责任。目前，任宏达的政策建议主要集中在国际投资、国际贸易以及对外援助三个方面，多篇政策建议受到党中央和国务院的高度关注。

“一带一路”法治化体系构建研究

刘敬东*

2013年，习近平主席提出共建丝绸之路经济带和21世纪海上丝绸之路的倡议，得到国际社会的广泛关注和积极响应。4年来，“一带一路”建设在全球范围取得重大进展。[①] 无论是从发展规模和覆盖范围，还是从国际影响力来评价，“一带一路”已成为当前全球经济发展的主要推动力。作为中国首倡的全球经贸发展新路径，“一带一路”的制度建设和发展模式对于21世纪全球经济治理最终能否成功将产生巨大影响。[②]

构建“一带一路”合作体系无非有两种路径可以选择：一条路径就是采取由中国主导、沿线国家以友好同盟关系为基础而形成的、封闭式经济同盟关系；另一条路径就是由中国与沿线各国共同协商建立以规则为导向、开放包容、民主透明的法治化体系。前者已被实践证明是一条不归路，历史经验和教训告诉人们，“小圈子式”的经济同盟模式尽管可能一时热闹，但最终却只能“昙花一现”、不可持续，在这方面，中国积累的教训是极为深刻的。[③] 以规则为导向、开放包容、民主透明的法治化路径，

---

* 刘敬东，中国社科院国际法所国际经济法室主任、研究员，最高人民法院民四庭原副庭长，中国法学会WTO法研究会副会长。

① 截至2017年，已经有100多个国家和国际组织参与“一带一路”建设，进度和成果超出预期。参见习近平2017年5月14日在“一带一路”国际合作高峰论坛开幕式上的演讲。http://news.xinhuanet.com/politics/2017-05/14/c_1120969677.htm，最后访问日期：2017年7月1日。

② 参见苏格《全球视野之“一带一路”》，《国际问题研究》2016年第2期。

③ 对中华人民共和国成立以来中国外交在国际法方面的经验与教训总结和研究，参见何志鹏、孙璐《新中国国际关系与国际法的起步》，载刘志云主编《国际关系与国际法学刊》第6卷，厦门大学出版社，2016，第156—161页。

不仅是建立新型国际关系的现实需求，更是国际关系保持稳定和可持续发展的必要保证。[①] 只有构建一套法治化体系，选择一条法治化的发展路径，实现国内法治与国际法治的良性互动，“一带一路”才能确保长期、稳定、健康发展。[②]

法治是人类共同的文明成果，通过国际合作制定国际规范，建立可预期的国际制度，进而逐步塑造公正、有效、法治化的全球治理模式是人类社会发展、进步的必然选择。在不断推进法治中国建设的同时，中国也需要在全球治理的法治化进程中阐述中国的立场，实现国际法治的中国表达。[③] 在当前国内法治建设进入新阶段以及国际经贸关系格局已发生重大历史性变化的今天，构建“一带一路”法治化体系应当成为法治中国建设以及改革全球治理体制的重要使命。

一 构建“一带一路”法治化体系的指导原则

坚持各国共商、共建、共享，遵循平等、追求互利，不仅造福中国人民，更造福沿线各国人民，这是“一带一路”建设确立的根本宗旨和最终目标，“一带一路”法治化体系必须围绕这一宗旨和目标。“一带一路”既植根于现有的国际经贸关系，又是对国际经贸关系的发展、创新，因此，“一带一路”法治化体系不仅要吸收借鉴全球经济治理的成功经验，更应因应国际关系的变化以及时代特点创新发展模式，推动全球治理体制的改革。

现有的全球经济治理体制是第二次世界大战后形成的、以发达国家为主导建立的治理体制。[④] 不可否认，这一治理体制及其法律制度为世界经济的增长与国际经贸关系的重建作出了历史性贡献，有其合理和积极的一

---

① “20世纪世界治理模式的进步就是不断迈向法制理想与目标的制度发展与制度建设进步，推动或促进国际经济贸易治理的法治化。”刘志云主编《国际关系与国际法学刊》第6卷，厦门大学出版社，2016，第89—90页。

② 参见赵骏《全球治理视野下的国际法治与国内法治》，《中国社会科学》2014年第10期。

③ 参见何志鹏《国际法治的中国表达》，《中国社会科学》2015年第10期。

④ 关税及贸易总协定、国际货币基金协定与世界银行被公认为战后世界经济发展的三大经济支柱，参见姚梅镇主编《国际经济法概论》，武汉大学出版社，1999，第622页。以上述三大法律制度为基础发展起来的国际货物贸易、国际服务贸易、国际人员流动、国际资本流动及国际支付结算等方面的法律规则覆盖了国际经济关系的方方面面，成为国际经济法的主要内容和渊源。

面，中国也是这一体系的长期参与者和受益者。但必须正视的是，这一治理体制主要反映了西方发达国家的立场，最终有利于西方发达国家，广大发展中国家只能服从它们的“治理”。基欧汉教授形容这种模式是一种“多国合作的俱乐部模式”，造成了国际民主的缺失。[①]

随着广大发展中国家经济实力的不断提升，这种“多国俱乐部”模式的不公正、不合理越发凸显。[②] 改革呼声愈发强烈，但美国等西方传统强国试图采取各种方法和手段来维系这一不合时宜的治理模式。中国等发展中国家经济实力大增导致美国丧失了在世界贸易组织（WTO）多边贸易体制中的绝对主导权，美国已不能像乌拉圭回合那样自行其是，故对新一轮多哈回合谈判采取长期拖延，甚至不惜放弃的立场。奥巴马执政期间，美国就开始从“多边”向“区域”性经贸谈判转向，其主导签署的《跨太平洋伙伴关系协定》（TPP）中“美国色彩”极其浓厚，尽管特朗普政府决定退出该协定，宣称将以双边谈判方式缔结所谓能实现美国利益最大化的经贸协定，但无论是区域性还是双边性谈判，美国维持其全球经济体系中霸权地位的意图仍十分明显。以提升中国等发展中国家投票权为核心的国际货币基金组织（IMF）改革，虽未影响到美国拥有的重大决策“否决权”，但对这一改革方案美国国会长时间不予批准，导致国际货币金融体系改革严重滞后，迫于国际压力美国最终同意了 IMF 投票权改革，但至今仍耿耿于怀。对于中国倡导建立的“亚洲基础设施投资银行”，美国起初非但不予支持，反而采取各种手段阻挠其西方盟友加入该行，唱衰意味十分强烈。上述做法无疑是逆国际形势发展的潮流而动，是霸权思想和“冷

---

① 他指出：“从 1944 年布雷顿森林会议开始，有关治理的关键机制就以‘俱乐部’的方式来运行。最初，少数富国的内阁部长及同一问题领域的部长级官员聚在一起制定规则。贸易部长们主导了 GATT；财政部长们则推动了 IMF 的工作；国防部长和外交部长会聚北约总部；央行行长则聚首国际清算银行。他们先秘密磋商，然后将相关协议提交国家立法机关并公布于众。直到最近，这种模式仍是不可挑战的。”〔美〕罗伯特·基欧汉：《局部全球化世界中的自由主义、权力与治理》，门洪华译，北京大学出版社，2004，第 249 页。又见刘志云《当代国际法的发展：一种从国际关系理论视角的分析》，法律出版社，2010，第 174 页。

② “三个国际组织都面临着重大的合法性与问责性危机，因为它们内部的投票与决策结构没有反映全球新的权力关系现实……要让国际经济组织在 21 世纪全球充满活力的经济中重要、负责、有效，就有必要进行重大的制度改革。政府领导人应当将这作为一项优先事务。”〔加拿大〕黛布拉·斯蒂格主编《世界贸易组织的制度再设计》，汤蓓译，上海人民出版社，2011，第 5 页。

战”思维的固守和延续。[①]

面对错综复杂的国际形势以及保护主义的甚嚣尘上，中国提出了具有包容、开放精神的“一带一路”倡议，向国际社会发出了支持贸易与投资自由化的强烈信号。[②] 在其推进过程中，理应顺应时代发展潮流，回应改革现有全球经济治理体制的呼声，以鲜明的时代特点创新治理模式，其核心是改变倚强凌弱、以大欺小的不公正、不合理的治理体系，推动全球经济治理向公正、合理的方向发展。[③]

结合“一带一路”的宗旨和目的以及改革全球经济治理的时代使命，在当前形势下，构建“一带一路”法治化体系应遵循以下三项原则。

第一，平等、互利原则。这一原则是构建“一带一路”法治化体系的首要指导原则。

中国倡导“一带一路”伊始就提出了共商、共建、共享的发展理念，遵循平等、追求互利的基本原则。这绝非一时冲动或权宜之计，而是中国总结历史经验、推动全球治理体系变革的长期战略。

中国从一个经济发展落后、经济实力弱小的国家发展成为当今世界第二大经济体，其经历的过程是艰苦和不平凡的。曾几何时，美国等西方发达国家动辄以各种借口对中国实施经济制裁，在中国加入 WTO 谈判中，这些国家罔顾中国的发展中国家地位，肆意抬高要价，以“非市场经济”、“特殊保障措施”等超 WTO 义务对中国企业和产品实行歧视性贸易政策，在其国内，针对中国投资长期施以“高标准”安全审查，使中国付出极高

---

① 美国上述对华政策转变本身反映了中美实力对比变化，美国已意识到其掌控全球事务能力在下降，也认识到中国崛起引发权势转移对现行国际体系的影响。赵华：《透视新“美国衰落”争论》，载刘志云主编《国际关系与国际法学刊》第 6 卷，厦门大学出版社，2016，第 201 页。

② “与 TPP 相比，‘一带一路’的合作机制突出表现为它的多元化和开放性。”李向阳：《跨太平洋伙伴关系协定与“一带一路”之比较》，《世界经济与政治》2016 年第 9 期。“‘一带一路’倡议下的国际贸易、国际金融和国际投资等国际经贸规则正在经历着不同意义上的重构。”张乃根：《“一带一路”倡议下的国际经贸规则之重构》，《法学》2016 年第 5 期。

③ “倡议充分体现了‘携手构建合作共赢新伙伴，同心打造人类命运共同体’这一全球治理新理念，有利于化解区域间经贸安排可能带来的矛盾与冲突，有助于展开各种形式的国际经贸合作，对于形成更加公平、合理的国际经贸新规则而言意义重大而深远。”参见张乃根《“一带一路”倡议下的国际经贸规则之重构》，《法学》2016 年第 5 期。

的经济代价。[①]“己所不欲，勿施于人”，中国绝不会将自己经历的痛苦强加于别国。

无论是全球治理模式改革要求，还是中国发展的历史经验均表明，“一带一路”体系建构必须遵循平等、互利原则，实现国际经济民主。我们应本着真诚的态度与沿线国家平等协商，通过实际行动取信于沿线国家，绝不以“老大”自居。应深刻认识到沿线国家充分参与“一带一路”合作体系创设的必要性，通过与沿线国家之间多边或双边磋商“一带一路”法律框架，不论是在投票权设置还是在规则制定方面，都要尊重并倾听各方意见和建议，真正将“一带一路”做成国际集体事业。在这一过程中，深入探寻和理解“一带一路”沿线国家各自真正需要什么，而不能主要由我们自己界定它们需要什么。平等和互利不可分割，“一带一路”建设必须强调公平的利益分配，甚至应偏惠于一些弱国贫国，追求实质平等，通过与沿线国家的真诚合作实现互利共赢的目标。[②]

第二，规则导向原则。这是“一带一路”法治化的核心，是营造稳定、可预见性发展环境的必然选择。

所谓规则导向，就是要求“一带一路”建设中的合作与开发活动遵循现有国际法原则和规则，尊重普遍适用的国际商业规则和惯例，进行全面的制度构建。同时，规则导向原则还要求参与“一带一路”建设的商事主体尊重东道国制定的法律，要求各国政府及司法机构在解决“一带一路”商事纠纷时尊重国际商事主体选择适用的法律以及相关国际公约和国际惯例。[③]

改革传统的全球治理模式，绝不意味着抛弃那些已被实践证明行之有效的国际法原则和规则，这些原则和规则是建立在科学基础之上的人类文明遗产，“一带一路”法治化体系构建应充分发掘和利用这些国际贸易投

---

① 市场经济地位之争不是一个单纯的法律和经济问题，而是美国赖以制衡中国的政治手段。参见孙昭《寸土必争的世贸争端》，知识产权出版社，2015，第11—14页。

② 时殷弘：《“一带一路”：祈愿审慎》，《世界经济与政治》2015年第7期。

③ 何志鹏认为，针对从实力本位向规则本位转型发展的当代国际制度，中国可以另辟蹊径，开启公平本位的导向。笔者认为，这是对规则本位的一种更高的要求，其实，公平是规则导向的应有之义。参见何志鹏《“一带一路”与国际制度的中国贡献》，《学习与探索》2016年第9期。

资法律制度中的宝贵资源。[①] 在此基础之上，建立一整套由条约、协定、合同、章程等法律文件构成的"一带一路"规则体系。[②]《联合国货物买卖合同公约》、《承认与执行外国仲裁裁决的公约》（即《纽约公约》）等国际商事条约为"一带一路"商事活动提供了规则范本。沿线各国属于不同的法系和法律文明，但平等保护原则、诚信原则、正当程序原则等均为其所尊崇，这些公认的基本法律原则亦应成为"一带一路"法治化体系中必不可少的普遍性法律原则。[③]

不断完善和创新现代国际法规则，同样是"一带一路"规则导向原则的重要要求。当前，新一轮 WTO 多边回合谈判举步维艰，环境保护、气候变化、互联网经济等新生事物亟待新的国际法规则予以规制。[④]"一带一路"应通过不断的规则创新，推动相关国际法规则进步。

规则导向原则还要求"一带一路"建立适合于自身特点的争端解决体系，及时、公正地解决沿线国家之间、东道国与投资者之间、商事主体之间可能产生的各种争端和纠纷。

第三，可持续发展原则。这是"一带一路"长期健康发展的根基，也是提升"一带一路"品质和国际形象的关键。

自 1992 年联合国环境与发展大会通过的《21 世纪议程》提出"进一步发展国际可持续发展法"的要求以来，国际可持续发展法有了令人瞩目的发展。[⑤] 现如今，可持续发展不仅是人类社会发展的总体目标，更是各国肩负的重要法律责任。作为国际合作的新形式，"一带一路"建设应坚

---

① 中国是现行国际秩序的受益者，改革传统治理模式并不意味着全部推倒重来。参见李鸣《国际法与"一带一路"研究》，《法学杂志》2016 年第 1 期。

② "一带一路战略的推进必须坚持规则导向，以实现国际区域法治的方式进行。我国要从贸易大国走向贸易强国，构建新型的国际合作发展空间和秩序，必须以规则和区域国际法治引领区域的合作和共同发展繁荣。"张晓君：《"一带一路"战略下自由贸易区网络构建的挑战与对策》，《法学杂志》2016 年第 1 期。

③ 有学者主张，应从更大的国际法角度研究"一带一路"体系构建，参见李鸣《国际法与"一带一路"研究》，《法学杂志》2016 年第 1 期。

④ 参见张乃根《"一带一路"倡议下的国际经贸规则之重构》，《法学》2016 年第 5 期。

⑤ 环境保护与经济发展相协调原则、行使主权权利不得损害境外环境原则、自然环境和环境的可持续利用原则、国际合作共谋可持续发展原则已成为可持续发展法的核心原则，参见赵建文《"一带一路"与"可持续发展法"》，《人民法治》2015 年第 11 期。

持可持续发展原则，并将这一原则落实为实际行动。①

在“一带一路”建设中，基础设施和能源领域始终是中国与沿线国家合作的优先领域，基础设施建设和能源开发又是生态环境风险的高发领域，面临着可持续发展的严峻考验。从地域上看，陆上丝绸之路经过欧亚大陆腹地，是全球生态问题突出地区之一，而海上丝绸之路沿岸国家大多是发展中国家，同中国一样正面临发展带来的环境污染困扰，“一带一路”沿线国家整体上分散在环境脆弱地区。② 以上因素决定了可持续发展对“一带一路”具有特殊意义。

过去一段时期，“中国环境威胁论”、“中国生态倾销论”等在国际上颇有市场。这些论调固然反映了西方国家的偏见，但一些中国投资者不顾当地环境乱采乱挖的现象也确有发生，这不但严重破坏中国的国际形象，也给中国企业造成严重的经济损失。能否将可持续发展原则落实到贸易、投资、基础设施建设等具体项目中，不仅关乎“一带一路”品质和形象，更关乎“一带一路”建设能否长期健康发展。

近年来，国际经济法律制度已将可持续发展作为重要的转型要素。③在国际投资仲裁实践中，可持续发展相关问题越来越引起仲裁庭的关注。④“一带一路”对于上述发展态势不能忽视，应将环境保护、气候变化、劳工保护、反腐败等具有可持续发展内涵的国际法规则纳入法治化体系之中。

构建“一带一路”法治化体系，平等、互利是根本指导原则，这是其

---

① 国家发展改革委、外交部和商务部2015年3月发布的《推动共建丝绸之路经济带和21世纪海上丝绸之路的愿景与行动》提出，在“投资贸易中突出生态文明理念，加强生态环境、生物多样性和应对气候变化合作，共建绿色丝绸之路”，“共建‘一带一路’……实现沿线各国多元、自主、平衡、可持续发展”。

② 宁红玲、漆彤：《“一带一路”倡议与可持续发展原则》，《武大国际法评论》2016年第1期。

③ 以国际投资法为例，最近缔结的国际投资协定中（2008—2013年）超过四分之三包含“可持续发展”的语言，2012年和2013年缔结的所有的投资协定都包含此类规定。2014年签署的18个国际投资协定大部分也都含有确保可持续发展目标的规制权条款。Gordon k. J. Pohl and M. Bouchard（2014），Investment Treaty Law，Sustainable Development and Responsible Business Conduct：A Fact Finding Survey，OECD Working Papers on International Investment，2014/01，OECD Publishing，p. 5. UNCTAD，World Investment Report 2015，p. 112. 转引自宁红玲、漆彤《“一带一路”倡议与可持续发展原则》，《武大国际法评论》2016年第1期。

④ 参见红玲、漆彤《“一带一路”倡议与可持续发展原则》，《武大国际法评论》2016年第1期。

宗旨所决定的，也是改革全球经济治理体系的要求；规则导向原则是法治化体系的核心，是稳定、可预见法律环境的必然选择；可持续发展原则是长期健康发展的根基，否则，"一带一路"将丧失正当性基础，最终"不可持续"。

指导原则确立后，制度内涵建设就成为关键。"一带一路"倡议的核心是推动中国与沿线国家之间开展经济贸易、投资、金融以及基础设施建设等领域的合作，国际贸易、投资、商事、海事规则等国际法律规则应成为"一带一路"法治化体系的制度内涵；"一带一路"建设涉及大量中国与沿线国家市场主体之间的民商事交往，中国与沿线各国的对外经贸法律制度建设以及涉外民商事法律制度亦不可或缺。因此，"一带一路"体系的制度内涵应当包括国际法、国内法两大领域，通过国际法、国内法规则的良性互动，实现法治化的发展目标。

二 "一带一路"法治化体系的国际法内涵

"一带一路"法治化体系的国际法内涵不仅应包括中国与相关国家和地区签署的既有双边、区域性及多边贸易与投资条约、协定，还应当吸纳国际经贸规则发展的最新成果，以贸易便利化为核心构建国际贸易法规则，以推进沿线国家的基础设施建设为工作重心创新国际投资规则，构建亚洲基础设施投资银行及丝路基金等开发性金融机构的国际金融法律规则，将构建一个代表21世纪国际经济法发展成果的国际条约体系作为其法治化的重要目标。①

在国际贸易、投资法领域，中国应与"一带一路"沿线国家一道，共同梳理现有双边、多边贸易和投资协定，以贸易、投资便利化为核心，推动与沿线国家和地区签订不同层级、不同水平的贸易投资协定。② 在这一

① 参见张乃根《"一带一路"倡议下的国际经贸规则之重构》，《法学》2016年第5期。

② 现有"一带一路"沿线国家签署的自由贸易协定仍体现出碎片化、自由化程度低、覆盖面窄等问题，参见张晓君《"一带一路"战略下自由贸易区网络构建的挑战与对策》，《法学杂志》2016年第1期。

进程中，以下法律条款应重点加以考虑。①

1. 环境条款

可持续发展原则要求参与“一带一路”建设的各国政府及其海外投资者必须肩负起保护海外投资环境的法律义务。中国与“一带一路”沿线国家应借鉴公认的国际环境公约、气候变化公约等国际环境法规则，结合各国经济发展水平和特点，共同谈判设计和制定“一带一路”中的环境条款。“一带一路”沿线国家大多属于发展中国家，面临经济发展与环境保护之间的协调困境，这无疑是一项艰巨的任务。②

2. 劳工条款

近些年来，劳工标准被国际贸易投资协定接纳的趋势越发明显，在“一带一路”贸易投资协定中确定基本劳工标准，不但符合国际经贸规则的发展趋势，对于沿线各国劳动者权益维护也是必要的。但在制定过程中，不能忽视这些国家大都属于发展中国家的现实，不能超过各国经济社会发展水平而设置过高标准，且应根据各国不同情况区别对待，为此，中国与沿线国家应开展充分协商，决不能强加于人。

3. 人权条款

当前，人权保护已逐渐渗透到国际贸易、投资法领域。③ 尽管可能存在争议，但无论是缔结新的贸易投资协定，还是建立亚投行等新的国际金融组织，人权都是绕不开的一个问题。“一带一路”建设以促进各国经济发展为目标，本身就是对国际人权事业的重大贡献，因此，“一带一路”不仅不应回避人权话题，而且应理直气壮地阐释对人权原则的理解。中国

---

① 我国应根据 WTO 的 RTA 规则，参考 TPP 的相关规定，在推进“一带一路”沿线国家或地区的 RTA 网络建设中逐步顺应国际经济法规则的新变化，根据不同国家或地区的特点，达成不同水平的 RTA，尤其要充分考虑将投资、环境、劳工规则纳入 RTA 中，参见张乃根《“一带一路”倡议下的国际经贸规则之重构》，《法学》2016 年第 5 期。

② 现阶段我国签订的投资协定在环境保护方面的规定仍处于较低水平，目前从中国已签订的 BITs 来看，仅在与新加坡和东盟签订的 BITs 中提到了环境保护的条款，但仍较为笼统，并且缺乏监督机制，中国现有 129 项 BITs 中仅有极个别 BITs 在序言中涉及健康问题。这是“一带一路”法治化进程中必须特别关注的议题。参见竺彩华、李诺《全球投资政策发展趋势与构建一带一路投资合作条约网络》，《国际贸易》2016 年第 9 期。

③ “国际贸易事务以及它影响我们赖以生存的社会的方式，特别是在过去几十年中已引发公众和政治家们的关注。” James Harrison, *The Human Rights Impact of the World Trade Organization*, Oxford and Portland, Oregon, Hart Publishing, p. 4.

应与沿线国家一道共同设计贸易投资领域中的人权条款，在贸易投资自由化与人权保护之间建立起法律上的平衡。①

4. 知识产权保护条款

高标准的知识产权保护成为新一代贸易投资协定的一个重要特征，包括延长著作权的保护时间、加强互联网知识产权保护、对临时性侵权行为的惩罚、降低侵犯知识产权行为的刑事门槛等。② 作为引领国际合作潮流的"一带一路"应借鉴、吸纳新一代贸易投资协定中知识产权保护条款的相关内容。当然，考虑到"一带一路"沿线国家多为发展中国家的实际情况，中国应与沿线国家根据不同情况，确立多元化知识产权保护标准。

5. 贸易便利化条款

贸易便利化对于"一带一路"建设显得尤为重要，"一带一路"的一项重要目标就是实现区域内商品和服务的互通有无，核心就是便利化。③ "一带一路"应特别关注货物通关、商品检验检疫、质量标准、电子商务规则等法律问题。通过程序和手续的简化、适用法律和规定的协调、基础设施的标准化和改善，创造一个协调的、透明的、可预见的营商环境。

除上述条款外，反腐败问题、国有企业问题、竞争法规则等也是新一代贸易投资协定中的重点规制领域，应引起中国与沿线国家高度重视，在这些领域设计具有自身特色的相应规则。④

在国际金融法领域，中国与参与各方就亚投行建立的宗旨和目的、份额、投票权分配、决策机制、投资导向及标准、成员方资格等充分协商，借鉴世界银行、亚洲开发银行等成功做法，汲取他们的教训，努力推动国

① Thomas Cottier, Joost Pauwelyn, and Elisabeth Burch, "Linking trade regulation and human rights in international law: an overview", in Thomas Cottier, Joost Pauwelyn and Elisabeth Burgi Bonanomi (eds.), *Human rights and international trade*, Oxford University Press, 2005. p. 21.

② TPP在知识产权规则方面的条款规定不仅超出了TRIPs规定的义务，而且与先前的《反假冒贸易规定（ACTA）相比，不仅覆盖面更广，而且涵盖了实体与程序两方面的规则。参见张乃根《"一带一路"倡议下的国际经贸规则之重构》，《法学》2016年第5期。

③ 促进投资便利化已成为全球投资政策发展的重要趋势，参见竺彩华、李诺《全球投资政策发展趋势与构建一带一路投资合作条约网络》，《国际贸易》2016年第9期。

④ 对于环境、劳工、人权保护、知识产权、反腐败等规则，应根据沿线各国的具体情况、逐步推进的做法缔结相关贸易投资协定。参见张晓君《"一带一路"战略下自由贸易区网络构建的挑战与对策》，《法学杂志》2016年第1期；又参见张莉《"一带一路"战略应关注的问题及实施路径》，《中国经贸导刊》2014年9月刊（下）。

际金融制度创新。①

亚投行决策机制设计应既考虑各国出资的份额大小，又考虑全体成员方的话语权，设计不同事项、不同类别的决策权分配方案，在投票权问题上真正做到实质平等。② 公平、透明、廉洁、高效应成为亚投行奉行的基本原则。公平，是亚投行建立的基础，亚投行对所有成员无论大小均公平对待；透明，是亚投行决策和运行的特色，亚投行全部决策及其过程均应公开、透明；廉洁，是亚投行成功的保障，亚投行自身建设以及投融资项目必须保持廉洁；高效，这一原则要求亚投行及时回应成员方诉求，减少繁文缛节，高效地为成员方提供服务。

亚投行成立以来成功运行，为"一带一路"建设作出了突出贡献，其制度设计应日臻完善，成为当今国际金融治理的典范。

三 "一带一路"法治化体系中的国内法内涵

在国际治理中，国内法治和国际法治始终相互贯通、相互渗透、相互影响，共同为国际治理的推进提供坚实的法律制度保障。③"一带一路"法治化要通过国内法治与国际法治的互动来实现，中国与沿线国家在充实"一带一路"国际法内涵的同时，应为"一带一路"营造良好的国内法律环境，平等保护各国商事主体利益。为此，各国应在投资者保护、涉外民商事审判、国际仲裁裁决承认与执行以及司法协助等领域加强合作，在条件成熟时，推动形成国际法规则。

根据"一带一路"建设的特点，其国内法内涵应包括两方面内容：一是与"一带一路"密切相关的涉外经贸法律制度建设；一是中国与沿线国家的涉外民商事法律制度及司法运用。

---

① 亚投行的成立与运行以及其制定的法律规则对于国际货币金融规则以及治理体系重构是具有突破意义的实质进展。参见张乃根《"一带一路"倡议下的国际经贸规则之重构》，《法学》2016 年第 5 期。

② IMF 的决策机制采用的是加权表决制，其缺陷是美国一家独大，有权否决 IMF 所有重要决策。WTO 采用的是"协商一致"原则，好处在于，不论国家大小，一律平等，均有权否决 WTO 的重要决策，但其弊端也十分明显——无法就国际贸易领域中的重要问题尽快作出决定，导致体制僵化。

③ 参见贺荣《论中国司法参与国际经济规则的制定》，《国际法研究》2016 年第 1 期。

在对外经贸法律制度建设方面，中国与沿线各国应特别注重贸易、投资领域的开放以及涉及公平市场环境的国内法问题。在这方面，中国已经作出巨大努力。自2013年上海自贸试验区设立以来，通过在自贸区内各项深化改革或扩大开放的制度实验，中国已初步建立了包括准入前国民待遇和负面清单制度在内的贸易投资法律创新体系。[①] 2016年8月，中国政府决定在辽宁省、浙江省、河南省、湖北省、重庆市、四川省、陕西省新设立7个自贸试验区，在更广领域、更大范围内形成各具特色、各有侧重的试点格局，推动全面深化改革扩大开放。[②]

中国不仅应将自贸试验区的成功经验适时转化为相关领域的国内立法，还应及时推广至中国与沿线国家签订的双边或区域性自贸协定之中，与此同时，将"一带一路"形成的国际法规则及时反映到国内自贸试验区制度之中，实现国内自贸试验区与"一带一路"持续互动。[③]

"一带一路"法治化体系的国内法内涵中另一个重要内容就是中国与沿线国家涉外民商事法律制度及其司法运用，这对于降低"一带一路"法律风险、增强投资者信心至关重要。近年来，中国在涉外民商事法律制度建设领域取得了重大进步，服务与保障"一带一路"的司法举措不断出台，展示了中国司法开放、包容的态度。

在涉外民商事领域，中国的司法机构一方面创新现有涉外民商事法律制度，通过审理涉"一带一路"建设相关案件，维护各类市场主体的合法权益，平等保护中外当事人的利益；另一方面，大力开展"一带一路"沿线国家之间的司法合作，推动各国间的司法协助，解决司法管辖冲突、国际平行诉讼问题和司法判决、仲裁裁决的承认与执行问题。通过上述举措，形成了有利于"一带一路"建设的良好国内司法环境。

2015年7月，最高人民法院颁布实施《最高人民法院关于人民法院为

---

① 已在上海、天津、福建和广东设置的自贸试验区形成可复制推广的制度经验，主要包括：以负面清单管理为核心的外商投资管理制度、以贸易便利化为重点的贸易监管制度、以资本项目可兑换和金融服务业开放为目标的金融创新制度、以政府职能转变为核心的事中事后监管制度。参见张乃根《"一带一路"倡议下的国际经贸规则之重构》，《法学》2016年第5期。

② 参见《国务院关于做好自由贸易试验区新一批改革试点经验复制推广工作的通知》，国发〔2016〕63号。http://www.gov.cn/zhengce/content/2016-11/10/content_5130918.htm，最后访问日期：2016年11月24日。

③ 参见张乃根《"一带一路"倡议下的国际经贸规则之重构》，《法学》2016年第5期。

“一带一路”建设提供司法服务和保障的若干意见》（以下简称《意见》）。[①] 该意见紧密结合“一带一路”建设的特点和我国涉外商事海事审判工作实践，借鉴国际先进司法理念，在管辖权、司法互惠、适用国际条约和惯例、外国法查明、涉外仲裁裁决的司法审查等多方面作出了创新性规定。[②]

1. 管辖权制度

《意见》在管辖权方面的规定总结借鉴了其他国家相关立法和司法判例，科学合理地确定涉“一带一路”案件的连结因素，为积极行使我国法院的司法管辖权迈出重要一步。同时，强调根据“意思自治”原则，充分尊重中外市场主体协议选择司法管辖的权利；通过与沿线国家的司法机构友好协商，减少涉外司法管辖的国际冲突，逐步与沿线国家建立司法合作渠道和机制，从而妥善解决国际间平行诉讼问题。[③]

2. 司法互惠

跨境送达、取证是国际民事诉讼必不可少的法律程序，承认与执行外国法院判决的重要性不必多言，如果得不到他国法院的承认与执行，当事人付出再高代价赢得的判决也只不过是一张废纸。《意见》提出在一定条件下中国法院将先行给予他国司法优惠，这对于沿线国家当事人而言不啻为一个重大利好。[④]

2017 年 6 月 8 日，第二届中国—东盟大法官论坛通过了《南宁声明》，第七项规定反向推定互惠关系的共识，这标志着互惠原则在司法实践中取得更大突破。[⑤] 尽管这仅是中国与东盟国家法院之间的重要共识，但中国

① 参见法发〔2015〕9 号文件，《最高人民法院关于人民法院为“一带一路”建设提供司法服务和保障的若干意见》，《人民法院报》2015 年 7 月 8 日。

② 法学专家解读《最高人民法院关于人民法院为“一带一路”建设提供司法服务和保障的若干意见》，《人民法院报》2015 年 7 月 8 日。

③ 参见法发〔2015〕9 号文件，《最高人民法院关于人民法院为“一带一路”建设提供司法服务和保障的若干意见》，《人民法院报》2015 年 7 月 8 日。

④ 石静霞《司法助力“一带一路”战略的有效实施》，《人民法院报》2015 年 7 月 8 日。

⑤ 《南宁声明》第七项规定：“区域内的跨境交易和投资需要以各国适当的判决的相互承认和执行机制作为其司法保障。在本国国内法允许的范围内，与会各国法院将善意解释国内法，减少不必要的平行诉讼，考虑适当促进各国民商事判决的相互承认和执行。尚未缔结有关外国民商事判决承认和执行国际条约的国家，在承认与执行对方国家民商事判决的司法程序中，如对方国家的法院不存在以互惠为理由拒绝承认和执行本国民商事判决的先例，在本国国内法允许的范围内，即可推定与对方国家之间存在互惠关系。”参见张勇健《“一带一路”背景下互惠原则实践发展的新动向》，《人民法院报》2017 年 6 月 20 日。

推动"一带一路"沿线国家司法互惠的意愿进一步彰显。

3. 适用国际条约和外国法

《意见》提出，人民法院应严格依照《维也纳条约法公约》第31条和32条规定的解释通则，根据条约用语通常所具有的含义按其上下文并参照条约的目的及宗旨对国际条约进行善意解释。[①]

这是我国第一次在国内重要司法文件中直接写入国际公认的条约解释通则，对于准确适用国际公约、提升国内民商事判决的国际公信力具有十分重要的意义。在国际商业交易中，已形成了大量各国普遍接受的国际惯例，准确适用这些国际惯例，对于案件裁判国际认可度提升无疑是非常积极的。[②]

根据《意见》规定，当相关案件涉及外国法律适用时，法院将依照我国《涉外民事关系法律适用法》等冲突规范的规定，全面综合考虑法律关系的主体、客体、内容、法律事实等涉外因素，充分尊重当事人选择准据法的权利，积极查明和准确适用外国法，消除沿线各国中外当事人国际商贸往来中的法律疑虑。[③]《意见》为"一带一路"建设参与者自由选择合同所适用的法律创造了良好条件，促使他们更愿意选择中国法院来解决民商事纠纷。

4. 司法支持国际仲裁

作为国际通行的跨国民商事领域纠纷解决方式，国际仲裁最终能否有效解决纠纷很大程度上依赖于主权国家对待仲裁的态度和司法立场。《意见》首次将支持仲裁作为一项法律原则纳入最权威司法文件。

在开展涉"一带一路"案件国际商事仲裁裁决司法审查工作时，人民法院将严格依照《纽约公约》对于依法应当承认和执行的仲裁裁决，依法及时予以承认和执行。对于那些尚未参加《纽约公约》的沿线国家仲裁机构作出的仲裁裁决，将本着互惠的原则对依法应当承认和执行的仲裁裁决，及时予以承认和执行。通过审理"一带一路"建设相关仲裁司法审查案件，中国法院将不断强化仲裁司法审查报告制度，推广仲裁司法审查案件统一归口涉外审判庭审查的工作机制，确保仲裁司法审查规范统一、公

---

① 参见法发〔2015〕9号文件，《最高人民法院关于人民法院为"一带一路"建设提供司法服务和保障的若干意见》，《人民法院报》2015年7月8日。

② 张晓君：《司法护航"一带一路"建设》，《人民法院报》2015年7月8日。

③ 参见法发〔2015〕9号文件，《最高人民法院关于人民法院为"一带一路"建设提供司法服务和保障的若干意见》，《人民法院报》2015年7月8日。

正高效。[①]

除以上创新外，《意见》特别提出，要研究“一带一路”建设中的国际经贸争端解决机制，探索司法支持贸易、投资等国际争端解决机制充分发挥作用的方法与途径，保障沿线各国双边投资保护协定、自由贸易区协定等协定义务的履行。[②] 这表明，中国司法机关将积极支持国际争端解决机制在“一带一路”建设中发挥作用，进一步保障中外投资者的合法权益。[③]

《意见》在涉外民商事法律领域作出的诸多创新彰显了中国将以包容、开放的态度推进“一带一路”法治化的决心和信心。为进一步落实这些举措，最高人民法院还应当深入研究国家主权豁免、“法庭之友”、法律援助、透明度等重要涉外民商事法律问题，及时推出相关司法政策。

除自身努力外，中国应通过各种渠道向“一带一路”沿线国家宣传中国涉外民商事法律及司法制度所取得的进步，还应与“一带一路”沿线国家充分利用现有司法合作平台，适时建立“一带一路”司法论坛，就涉“一带一路”民商事案件面临的法律问题以及司法协助问题进行协商，共同丰富“一带一路”法治化体系中的国内法内涵。[④]

四 “一带一路”法治化体系中的争端解决机制

争端解决机制是法治化进程中必不可少的环节，缺少公正、高效的争端解决机制，“一带一路”将无法保持长期、稳定发展。构建“一带一路”争端解决机制需要从国际、国内两个层面深思谋虑，需要国际争端解决机制与国内司法机制之间的有机结合。结合“一带一路”的特点，“一带一路”争端解决机制应遵循以下指导原则。[⑤]

---

① 参见法发〔2015〕9号文件，《最高人民法院关于人民法院为“一带一路”建设提供司法服务和保障的若干意见》，《人民法院报》2015年7月8日。

② 参见法发〔2015〕9号文件，《最高人民法院关于人民法院为“一带一路”建设提供司法服务和保障的若干意见》，《人民法院报》2015年7月8日。

③ 韩秀丽：《积极探索司法支持投资争端解决机制》，《人民法院报》2015年7月8日。

④ 现有“上海合作组织”最高法院院长会议、亚太首席大法官会议、中国—东盟大法官会议、金砖国家大法官会议等机制。参见贺荣《论中国司法参与国际经济规则的制定》，《国际法研究》2016年第1期。

⑤ 参见蒋圣力《论“一带一路”战略背景下的国际经贸争端解决机制的建立》，《云南大学学报》（法学版）2016年第1期。

1. 通过平等协商、谈判的方式解决争端

坚持各国共商、共建、共享的宗旨要求"一带一路"建设中一旦发生争端，当事各方应尽最大努力通过协商、谈判的方式加以解决，这应成为"一带一路"争端解决机制构建的首要原则。[①] 在这方面，WTO 争端解决机制可资借鉴。磋商是 WTO 案件进入实质审理之前的法定前置程序，使得成员方之间的大量贸易争端在磋商阶段就已妥善解决，并未进入实质审理。[②] 此外，无论案件在专家组阶段、上诉审阶段还是执行阶段，WTO 均鼓励争端各方通过协商、谈判的方式解决，确保许多争端不致进入最终的强制执行程序中。

中国与各沿线国家、政府应鼓励并促使国家间、投资者与东道国间、商事主体之间友好协商解决争端，应充分利用中国与沿线各国已搭建的平台，如中国东盟 10 +1 领导人会议机制、中国 - 中东欧国家合作机制、中国 - 阿拉伯国家合作论坛、中非论坛等多边合作机制协商解决相关经贸争端，创造团结友善、富有亲和力的合作氛围。

2. 尊重现代国际法规则及公认的国际商事规则

"一带一路"争端解决机制应充分尊重并运用现代国际法规则，各类商事主体之间争端解决也必须遵循国际商事交易规则，寻求可依据的共同法律基础。

这一原则还要求"一带一路"争端解决机制采取国际公认的仲裁、调解、斡旋等多元化纠纷解决方式，不仅应尊重 WTO 等国际机构作出的裁决以及国际投资仲裁裁决，还应当在其国内司法机构审理涉"一带一路"民商事案件中尊重并运用现代国际法规则和国际商事规则。[③]

---

① 参见蒋圣力《论"一带一路"战略背景下的国际经贸争端解决机制的建立》，《云南大学学报》（法学版）2016 年第 1 期。

② 参见 WTO《关于争端解决规则和程序的谅解》第 4 条规定。

③ 有的学者认为，"一带一路"争端解决机制不易照搬或直接诉诸既有的国际贸易争端解决机制，但笔者认为，这一观点有些偏颇，因为"一带一路"沿线许多国家都是 WTO 的成员以及《华盛顿公约》缔约国，相关贸易或投资争端诉诸 WTO 争端解决机制或《华盛顿公约》项下的投资仲裁机制是这些国家必须履行的国际条约义务。正确的做法是，应当将现有国际经贸争端解决机制与"一带一路"争端解决机制相结合，形成有机统一，共同为"一带一路"服务。参见蒋圣力《论"一带一路"战略背景下的国际经贸争端解决机制的建立》，《云南大学学报》（法学版）2016 年第 1 期。

3. 推动“一带一路”司法合作与协助

成功的争端解决机制离不开高效、便利的司法合作与协助机制。“一带一路”沿线国家文化传统不同，法律制度各异，横跨大陆法系、普通法系、伊斯兰法系等世界几大法系，这就需要在“一带一路”沿线国家间开展并推动司法合作与协助，以确保争端解决的最终成果落到实处。高效、便捷的司法合作与协助机制对于营造“一带一路”法治化营商环境的意义非同小可，中国与“一带一路”沿线国家应为此相向而行。

构建“一带一路”争端解决机制是一项复杂而艰巨的系统工程，不仅要依靠现有国际争端解决机制，还要依靠国内司法机制，只有将国际、国内两方面的机制有机结合，形成合力，才能真正实现公正、高效解决争端的最终目标。

中国与“一带一路”沿线许多国家都是 WTO 成员，也与许多沿线国家同属《华盛顿公约》缔约国，WTO 争端解决机制、《华盛顿公约》项下的国际投资争端解决中心等为“一带一路”争端解决提供了有效的法律途径。此外，中国与“一带一路”沿线国家还签署了区域性自由贸易协定和双边投资保护协定，这些协定中含有诸多争端解决条款和解决机制，应充分运用。①

在各方面条件成熟时，特别是符合“一带一路”沿线国家共同意愿的情形下，可结合“一带一路”的特点，共同构建“一带一路”创新性争端解决机制。目前，中国应与沿线国家一道探讨推动在亚投行、丝路基金等合作框架下建立新的争端解决机制的可能性。②

国内司法机制对于“一带一路”民商事主体之间的争端以及国际商事仲裁及投资仲裁裁决的承认与执行而言至关重要，理应成为“一带一路”争端解决机制的重要组成部分，沿线国家应为此开展广泛而深入的司法协助与合作。在这方面，中国的涉外民商事司法审判勇于开拓，已作出表率，还应进一步探讨建立国际商事法庭、国际商事调解委员会、国际仲裁机构“三位一体”的创新性涉外民商事司法机制。可见，理想中的“一带

---

① 我国与“一带一路”沿线国家签署的自由贸易协定情况，参见张晓君《“一带一路”战略下自由贸易区网络构建的挑战与对策》，《法学杂志》2016 年第 1 期。

② 参见蒋圣力《论“一带一路”战略背景下的国际经贸争端解决机制的建立》，《云南大学学报》（法学版）2016 年第 1 期。

一路"争端解决机制应当是一套多层次、立体化、国际机制与国内机制相互配合、良性互动的争端解决机制。

结 论

"一带一路"是中国在新的历史时期根据国际国内形势的新发展、新变化提出的重大倡议，得到了世界上许多国家和国际组织的响应，现已成为全球经济发展的重要推动力。只有构建科学的法治化体系，营造稳定的、可预见性的法治环境，才能确保"一带一路"建设的长期、稳定、健康发展。

平等互利原则、规则化导向原则、可持续发展原则是构建"一带一路"法治化体系应遵循的指导原则。这一体系应包括国际法和国内法两大内涵。在国际法方面，依靠中国与相关国家和地区签署的既有双边、多边贸易与投资合作机制，融入国际金融法、投资法和贸易法发展的最新成果，创新国际经贸规则，构建一个代表21世纪国际经济法发展成果的国际条约体系。在国内法方面，在对外经贸法律制度建设方面，中国与沿线各国应特别注重贸易、投资领域的开放以及涉及公平市场环境的国内法问题，改革、完善现有涉外民商事法律制度及司法运用，降低"一带一路"建设中的法律风险，平等保护中外当事人的利益，为此，应推动沿线国家之间的司法合作，解决司法管辖冲突、国际平行诉讼和司法判决、仲裁裁决的承认与执行等问题。中国已在这方面迈出坚实的一步，充分展示了开放、包容的态度。

"一带一路"法治化体系离不开公平、高效的争端解决机制，应坚持通过平等协商、谈判的方式解决争端、运用现代国际法规则及公认的国际商事规则解决争端、推动司法合作与协助的原则构建"一带一路"争端解决机制。中国与沿线国家应立足于现有国际争端解决机制，协商建立创新性争端解决机制，充分运用国内司法机制，形成一套多层次、立体化、国际机制与国内机制相互配合、良性互动的争端解决格局。

（本文原载于《政法论坛》2017年第5期）

国际货币体制的困境与出路

廖　凡*

由1944年布雷顿森林会议奠基的、以国际货币基金组织（International Monetary Fund，IMF）为核心的国际货币体制迄今为止已经走过了三分之二个世纪。近些年来，以“金砖四国”为代表的新兴经济体的崛起使得国际货币金融格局中的力量对比发生显著变化，建立在传统格局基础之上的IMF体制受到前所未有的挑战。不期而至的全球金融危机，更是集中凸显出这一体制所面临的困境：危机肇端于身为最发达经济体并在IMF唯一享有事实否决权的美国，并席卷全球主要发达国家，表明该体制存在整体性和根本性的问题。尽管改革IMF在当前已经成为共识，但关于改革的重心、途径和方向却尚无定论，对相关法律规则的阐释和探讨尤为欠缺。为此，本文拟从法律角度剖析IMF亟待改革的若干方面，以此揭示国际货币体制面临的主要困境，并尝试提出改革建议。

一　基本立场与切入角度

追本溯源，IMF体制本质上是美英两国政治妥协的结果。这种妥协导致IMF先天不足，在法定职能的广度、深度和有效性方面存在深刻缺陷。尽管《国际货币基金协定》（以下简称《基金协定》）在20世纪60年代和

* 廖凡，中国社会科学院国际法研究所科研处处长、研究员。

70 年代先后经历了两次重大修订,[①] 但上述缺陷并未得到实质性弥补。相反，第二次修订形成的“牙买加协定”，一方面正式终结了作为布雷顿森林体系基石的平价制度，确认了浮动汇率的合法性，另一方面却又没有规定任何稳定汇率和货币体系的硬性规则或制裁措施，使得 IMF 的初始功能被进一步削弱，固有缺陷更为突出。

20 世纪 90 年代以来的一系列金融危机（主要包括墨西哥金融危机、俄罗斯金融危机和亚洲金融危机，以及 21 世纪初的阿根廷金融危机）和 IMF 在其中不尽如人意的表现，促使人们反思既有国际货币体制的局限。事实上，在每次危机之后，国际货币体制的缺陷及其改革都会成为各国政府和学者讨论的主题。总体而言，作为现行国际货币体制的主导者，以美国为首的发达国家较为关注 IMF 运作的实效性，即其能否有效维护国际货币金融稳定和安全，成功推行符合其利益的原则和政策。因此，它们着重强调 IMF 危机处理能力的不足，建议从增强危机管理职能、提高危机预防能力、尽量缩短贷款期限、积极引导私人部门介入危机的预防和处理，以及加强同成员国及其他国际组织的合作等方面对 IMF 进行改革。[②] 与之相对，在国际货币体制中长期处于被动接受地位的发展中国家则更为关注 IMF 的代表性和公平性，即其是否是一个公正、民主、透明的国际组织，能否一视同仁地代表和体现不同成员国的利益和诉求。从这个角度出发，它们着重强调 IMF 在指导思想、价值取向、治理结构和决策机制上的缺陷，呼吁增加发展中国家在 IMF 中的份额和投票权，改变 IMF 监督的不对称性，改善 IMF 内部治理结构，增强 IMF 资金实力和贷款灵活性等。[③]

中国政府和学者在这一问题上的关注点同上述发展中国家基本立场较为接近，侧重于 IMF 作为一个多边国际组织，在代表性、公平性和民主性

---

① 第一次修订是在 1968 年 5 月 31 日（1969 年 7 月 28 日生效），核心内容是创设特别提款权这一新的国际储备形式；第二次修订是在 1976 年 4 月 30 日（1978 年 4 月 1 日生效），核心内容是浮动汇率合法化、黄金非货币化和储备资产多样化。1990 年 6 月 28 日还进行了第三次修订（1992 年 11 月 11 日生效），主要内容是增加基金份额和调整部分程序性规则，在重要性上不及前两次。

② 关于这方面的总结和分析，详见布雷顿森林机构改革研究课题组《国际货币基金组织改革》,《经济研究参考》2006 年第 49 期。

③ 关于这方面的总结和分析，详见布雷顿森林机构改革研究课题组《国际货币基金组织改革》,《经济研究参考》2006 年第 49 期；又见 Yilmaz Akyüz, “Reforming the IMF: Back to the Drawing Board”, *G－24 Discussion Paper Series* No. 38, November 2005。

方面的不足，主张以治理结构和决策机制为突破口对其加以改革，[①] 并在此基础上调整 IMF 的相关职能，具体建议包括修改份额计算方法和表决制度、调整贷款条件、实现资金来源与行政和决策过程分离、增强决策透明度、进一步明确和强化职能、确立更好的国际标准等。[②] 而在全球金融危机加速蔓延后，中国更是颇具创造性地率先提出在 IMF 特别提款权的基础上建立超主权储备货币的构想，[③] 并得到主要发展中国家的支持。

上述观点和建议从不同角度揭示了现行国际货币体制存在的种种缺陷，各有侧重，难言孰是孰非。笔者认为，对于我国而言，切入这一问题的关键在于把握中国在国际货币体制及 IMF 中的特殊地位。一方面，中国是发展中国家一员，在国际货币体制中长期处于发言权不足的非主导地位，因此改善 IMF 的治理结构和决策机制，使其真正多边化和民主化，是中国的自然诉求。另一方面，中国作为世界第三经济大国和第一出口大国，又具有不同于传统意义上发展中国家的某些特殊性，特别是，中国拥有超过 2.4 万亿美元的巨量外汇储备，高居世界第一，[④] 这使得中国在相关改革的探讨和论争中具有了不可或缺的重要地位。从这一现实出发，对国际货币体制缺陷及其改革的讨论应当兼顾实效性和公平性，以此为坐标反观现行体制所面临的困境，将构建更加协调和平衡的新体制作为改革目标。有鉴于此，本文将以 IMF 为核心的现行国际货币体制所面临的困境概括为四个主要方面，并结合近期改革实践和动态，探讨这一体制的未来发展方向。

---

① 例如，参见胡锦涛《通力合作共度时艰——在金融市场和世界经济峰会上的讲话》，《人民日报》2008 年 11 月 16 日；黄梅波《国际货币基金组织的内部决策机制及其改革》，《国际论坛》2006 年第 1 期；余锋《国际货币基金组织投票权分配制度及其改革：发展中国家的视角》，《环球法律评论》2009 年第 4 期。

② 参见王德迅、张金杰编著《国际货币基金组织》，社会科学文献出版社，2004，第 194 页。

③ 参见周小川《关于改革国际货币体系的思考》，中国人民银行网站：http://www.pbc.gov.cn/detail.asp? col = 4200&ID = 279，2010 年 7 月 3 日访问。以下网络资料的最后访问日期均为 2010 年 7 月 3 日。

④ 截至 2010 年 3 月底，中国的外汇储备总额为 2.447 万亿美元（参见国家外汇管理局网站 http://www.safe.gov.cn/model_safe/tjsj/tjsj_detail.jsp? ID = 110400000000000000, 21&id = 5），而居第二位的日本仅为 1.043 万亿美元（参见日本财务省网站 http://www.mof.go.jp/english/e1c006.htm），不到中国的一半。

二 现行国际货币体制的主要困境

（一）机构职能误入歧途

IMF初创之时的主要目标是维持国际收支平衡，防止国际贸易和支付体系崩溃的历史重演。为此，IMF力图确保一个建立在经由多边协商形成的可调整稳定汇率基础之上的有序支付体系，并对国际资本流动加以严格限制。其任务之一是向暂时处于国际收支逆差的国家提供周转资金，以免其实施紧缩性调整或者贸易和汇兑限制。成员国在IMF的提款权被严格限定在经常项目领域，不得用于弥补资本项目缺口，且IMF有权要求成员国实施资本控制，作为获取资金的条件。

主要工业国家之间政策的不一致和国际金融市场资本流动的迅速增长，促成了布雷顿森林体系解体和浮动汇率合法化。尽管在浮动汇率制下成员国仍然负有与外汇安排有关的一般义务（《基金协定》第4条第1款），但这些义务流于泛泛，缺乏约束力，对于IMF而言意义甚微。在此背景下，IMF的工作重心发生了转移。在20世纪80年代的拉美国家债务危机中，IMF联合其他多边机构向发展中国家提供大量贷款并进行广泛的债务重组安排，是这种转移的开始。而随着20世纪90年代以来金融危机在新兴市场经济体反复出现，危机贷款发展成为IMF的主要金融活动。据统计，在2003至2004财政年度内，对阿根廷、巴西和土耳其的危机贷款占到IMF提款和贷款总额的85%。[①] 换言之，IMF的主要职能已经从起初的通过多边汇率安排、资本流动控制和经常项目融资促进全球增长和稳定，转变为管理和解决新兴市场中因资本流动和汇率过度失稳而导致的资本项目危机。

如果说上述转变尚可解释为IMF形势之下的合理转型，那么IMF目前在发展领域的频繁介入，则更多的是误入歧途。创建IMF主要是为了确保工业大国对外支付和汇率的稳定，而不是维持发展中国家的国际收支平衡。在早期，欧洲工业国事实上也的确是IMF资金的主要使用国，因为提

① 参见IMF，*IMF Annual Report*（*2004*），Washington，D. C.，Table II. 6。

款权与成员国在IMF持有的份额成比例，而前者所占份额远高于后者。随着欧洲经济的恢复，尤其是欧洲货币体系的建立，欧洲国家对IMF的依赖逐渐减少，后者的活动因而开始更多地转向发展中国家。起初这些活动集中于同IMF传统职能相一致的短期经常项目融资，以后则越来越多地进入发展领域。这方面的标志性事件是1974年IMF推出“中期贷款”，用以解决持续存在的结构性国际收支问题。① 随即IMF又先后推出“结构调整贷款”和“扩充结构调整贷款”，以优惠利率向低收入国家提供资金，用于进行经济结构调整。1999年，IMF进一步推出“减贫与增长贷款”，取代扩充结构调整贷款，向低收入国家提供优惠利率融资，从而更加明确地以减少贫困、促进增长等发展事项为己任。

IMF促进货币和金融稳定的职责同减贫和发展固然有所关联，但仅此在逻辑上并不足以支持IMF涉足后者，因为贸易、劳工、卫生、环境、安全等诸多其他政策领域同样与减贫和发展有所关联。② 实际上，减贫和发展领域已有专司其职的多边金融机构，即世界银行和区域开发银行。它们通过向中低收入国家提供优惠贷款、政策建议、技术支持和知识共享来减少贫困，促进发展。在此情况下，IMF在这一领域的介入会产生若干问题。首先，结构性调整涉及农业、工业、贸易、投资、技术、金融、劳工市场和公共部门等政策领域内的广泛行动，需要来自研究和实践的专门知识以及关于制度和政策环境的大量信息，而IMF的现有机构能力并不具备作为多边开发银行特质的此种条件。③ 其次，尽管IMF声称其致力于同世界银行紧密协调以减少职能交叉和重复，但实际情况是它目前在发展领域的大

① 参见 Kenneth W. Dam, *The Rules of the Game: Reform and Evolution in the International Monetary System* (University of Chicago Press, 1982), p. 284。

② 关于这一点，有论者指出，IMF之所以转向发展中国家，在很大程度上是因为工业国不再依赖它作为流动性来源，它因而对这些国家的汇率和宏观经济政策失去了影响力。而如果在发展中国家只履行其原初职责——通过提供流动性弥补暂时性资本项目逆差，便利国际收支调整——又使其没有太多业务可以开展，因为后者的国际收支困难是结构性和持续性的，而不是周期性和暂时性的。这一背景，连同非洲在IMF中成员国席位的增多，是IMF推出长期贷款和优惠利率贷款的主要原因。参见 Yilmaz Akyüz, "Reforming the IMF: Back to the Drawing Board", *G-24 Discussion Paper Series* No. 38, November 2005, p. 6。

③ 参见 Dani Rodrik, *Why is There Multilateral Lending?*, NBER Working Paper No. 5160, National Bureau of Economic Research (Cambridge, Massachusetts, 1995); Christopher Gilbert, Andrew Powell & David Vines (1999), "Positioning the World Bank", *Economic Journal* 109 (1999), pp. 598-633。

部分工作都完全可以移交给世界银行来进行。这种职能重复不仅招致对机构存在价值的质疑，[①] 还会增加受援国在交叉领域协调二者不同措施的压力。最后，也是本文最为关注的，IMF 在发展领域的过多介入会占用和转移其有限的资源，从而影响其通过政策监督和危机管理来促进全球货币、金融和经济稳定的核心职能。正是在这种意义上，诺贝尔经济学奖得主约瑟夫·斯蒂格利茨指出："在 IMF 之外已经形成广泛共识，即 IMF 应当将自己限制在其核心领域，即管理危机，而不应再（在危机之外）涉足发展问题或转型经济。"[②]

（二）政策监督厚此薄彼

第二次修订之后的《基金协定》在第 4 条第 3 款规定，IMF 应当监督国际货币体系以保证其有效运行，并监督成员国遵守其根据该条第 1 款所应承担的一般义务；为此目的，IMF 应当严密监督成员国的汇率政策，并制定具体原则，在汇率政策上对所有成员国进行指导。这是一种妥协，既是对 IMF 失去货币平价守护职能的弥补，也可以视为各国为获得汇率浮动自由所付出的对价。

IMF 的监督包括两种形式，即双边监督和多边监督。双边监督是通过持续监测成员国的经济状况并在必要时同成员国进行磋商，[③] 对每个成员国的相关政策进行评估并提出建议，重点关注是否存在影响国内和外部稳定的风险，从而需要对经济或金融政策进行调整。多边监督则是对全球和地区经济趋势进行监测和评估，主要手段是定期发布《世界经济展望》、《全球金融稳定报告》和地区经济展望报告。比较而言，更具实质意义的是以国别为基础的双边监督。

然而，IMF 的双边监督存在明显的不对称性：对于国际收支逆差国的

---

① 例如，曾任美国财政部长和国务卿的美国经济学家乔治·普拉特·舒尔茨（George Pratt Shultz）就主张合并 IMF 和世界银行，因为二者的工作日趋重复。参见 George P. Shultz, *Merge the IMF and World Bank*, The International Economy, January/February, pp. 14 - 16 (1998)。类似主张还可见 Lindley H. Clark Jr.，"Let's Merge the World Bank and the IMF", *Wall Street Journal* Jan. 4, 1990; James B. Burnham, "The IMF and World Bank: Time to Merge", *The Washington Quarterly* 22 (1999)。

② Joseph E. Stiglitz, *Globalization and its Discontents* (W. W. Norton & Company, 2002), p. 232.

③ 根据《基金协定》第 4 条第 3 款第 2 项，成员国应当提供监督所需信息，并在 IMF 提出要求时就其汇率政策问题同前者进行磋商。

监督较为有力，而对顺差国的监督则相形见绌。造成这一局面的重要原因是《基金协定》关于监督的规定属于软法性规则，本身并无强制拘束力，监督实效取决于其他约束机制，而后者的运行是不对称的。这些约束机制主要包括 IMF 贷款的“条件性”和《基金协定》的“短缺货币”条款，下面分别加以讨论。

条件性是 IMF 贷款的标志性特征，它是指 IMF 的资金援助不是无条件或自动给予的，成员国在向 IMF 借款时必须按照 IMF 的要求对其经济政策进行调整，以解决那些导致其寻求资金援助的问题。条件性的法律渊源是《基金协定》第 5 条第 3 款第 3 项。该项规定，IMF 应当审查成员国的贷款申请是否符合《基金协定》条款以及根据这些条款所制订的政策。条件性不仅是成员国偿还贷款的保证，更使得 IMF 对成员国相关政策的监督、评估和建议以贷款条件的方式得到遵守和落实。考虑到条件性不只表现为事先的贷款申请标准（即所谓事先条件性），还包括对贷款条件落实情况的监督（即所谓“事后条件性”），[①] 其对于 IMF 发挥政策影响力的意义就更为明显。问题在于，条件性发挥作用的对象仅限于那些深陷国际收支逆差从而申请 IMF 贷款项目的成员国，对于项目外成员国则无能为力。如果说 IMF 初创时的主要贷款对象是欧洲国家，那么随着这些国家经济恢复从而不再符合贷款标准，IMF 贷款已经变得主要面向发展中国家，贷款条件也趋于严格。[②] 换言之，借助条件性来实施的监督只能约束有赖于 IMF 资金的国际收支逆差国，主要是贫困国家和发展中国家，而不能约束无求于 IMF 资金的国际收支顺差国，尤其是主要工业国家。这一点，在 20 世纪 80 年代的拉美债务危机和 90 年代的新兴市场金融危机中已经有所体现，而在美国次贷危机及其所引发的全球金融海啸中更是展现得淋漓尽致。

另一个可能的约束机制是《基金协定》第 7 条第 2 款、3 款，即所谓

---

① 参见 IMF, *Factsheet: IMF Conditionality*, http://www.imf.org/external/np/exr/facts/conditio.htm。

② 事实上，IMF 条件性的发展深受其主要成员国政治经济条件和利益变化情况的影响。起初美国坚持规定某种形式的条件性是为了防止对美元信贷的过度依赖，后来则利用条件性来追求其国家利益。相反，英国等欧洲国家起初因为需要 IMF 资金援助，对条件性持反对态度，但当其不再依赖 IMF 资金后，条件性对其也就不再成为问题。这使得条件性在 IMF 体制内得到巩固和强化。参见 Yilmaz Akyüz & Heiner Flassbeck, “Exchange Rate Regimes and the Scope for Regional Cooperation”, in Yilmaz Akyüz, ed., *Reforming the Global Financial Architecture—Issues and Proposals* (Zed Books, 2002), p. 98。

“短缺货币”条款。该条款规定，当某种货币发生普遍短缺，以致对该货币的需求明显严重威胁到 IMF 的供给能力时，IMF 可以正式宣布其为短缺货币，报告短缺原因并提出解决建议，同时授权其他成员国临时限制短缺货币的自由兑换。这是针对国际收支顺差国的约束机制，因为只有顺差国的本币才会因其他国家的进口用汇需求而发生短缺。根据该条款，IMF 可以要求短缺货币国对其国内货币和经济政策进行调整，以增加货币供应，并授权其他成员国暂停履行《基金协定》第 8 条下的经常项目自由兑换义务。

“短缺货币”条款的设计初衷是针对美国，因为美国几乎是当时唯一的债权国（顺差国），英国等欧洲国家需要美元供给以恢复经济。随着美国由顺差国变为逆差国，“美元荒”让位于“美元灾”，这一条款失去了其初始意义。同时，由于“普遍短缺”不同于一国或数国因为同多个其他国家之间的持续收支逆差而导致的外汇短缺，也不同于国际收支波动所带来的周期性临时外汇短缺，而是因各国普遍需要额外外汇资源来对某个特定国家进行支付而造成的短缺，所以这种短缺只可能是针对真正的对外贸易和投资大国，因为只有这样的国家才能同时对诸多其他国家形成高额国际收支顺差，从而对后者的外汇资源和外汇政策产生重大影响。[①] 因此在现实中，“短缺货币”条款发挥作用的空间颇为有限。

（三）治理结构力量失衡

IMF 在政策监督方面的厚此薄彼、用力不均，很大程度上源自其治理结构中的力量失衡。IMF 不实行一国一票制，而是以成员国所持有的基金份额为基础，实行类似于股份公司的“资本多数决”制度。份额如同公司股份一样，成为成员国在 IMF 中地位和权利的基本依据，一国在 IMF 中发言权的大小取决于其份额的多少。其中，IMF 创始成员国的份额于 1944 年参加布雷顿森林会议时商定，其他成员国的份额则由理事会决定。份额分配是国际政治经济力量对比的结果。初始分配方法由美国在布雷顿森林会议上提出：在计算一个成员国可认缴的份额时，该国国民收入总值、经济发展程度、战前国际贸易幅度等许多方面均予以考虑。这种方法显然对传

---

① 参见 E. M. Bernstein，“Scarce Currencies and the International Monetary Fund”，*The Journal of Political Economy* 53（1945），p. 1。

统发达国家最为有利。再者，份额公式是静态的，而各国经济发展却是动态的，如果前者不随后者作出相应调整，成员国在IMF中的份额就无法反映各国相对经济地位的变化。为此IMF于1963年和1983年分别对原份额公式进行了修改，但未能从根本上改变其结构或运作。① 其后虽一直存在关于修改份额计算公式的呼吁，但多年来提出过的各种方案均未能获得法定85%投票权的支持。②

IMF实行加权表决制。《基金协定》第12条第5款规定，每个成员国享有250票的基本投票权，此后按照所持有的份额每10万特别提款权折合1票。基本投票权是国家主权平等原则的体现，也是对资本多数决的一种制衡，对于份额不足的发展中国家具有一定意义。然而，两方面的情况发展使得基本投票权可能的制衡作用难以发挥。首先，随着IMF的多次普遍增资（增加份额），基本投票权在总投票权中的比重被日益稀释，从IMF成立之初的11.3%下降到现在的2.1%，③ 从在总投票权中勉强有一席之地变得几乎无足轻重。其次，美英等国借对《基金协定》进行修订之机，增多需要特别多数票方能通过的事项。④ 据统计，IMF成立之初，规定需经特别多数通过方能作出决策的条款有9项，1968年《基金协定》第一次修订后增加到18项，1976年第二次修订后更是增加到39项。⑤ 这变相降低了基本投票权的作用，使得发展中国家的实际发言权相对下降。

目前，美国在IMF中所持份额为371.493亿特别提款权，占总份额的

---

① 参见葛华勇主编《国际货币基金组织导读》，中国金融出版社，2002，第40页。

② 《基金协定》第3条第2款规定，份额可以在IMF理事会定期审议时（至少每五年一次）调整或视情况需要随时调整，但份额的任何变更（无论是针对全体成员国的变更还是针对个别成员国的调整）均须经理事会85%的特别多数票通过，非经此程序任何成员国的份额不得增加或减少。

③ 参见Edwin M. Truman, "Overview on IMF Reform", in Edwin M. Truman ed., *Reforming the IMF for the 21st Century* (Peterson Institute, 2006), p. 74。

④ 根据《基金协定》的相关条款，IMF的表决方式包括简单多数通过、特别多数通过和一致通过三种方式，特别多数又包括70%特别多数和85%特别多数两种。

⑤ 参见Ebere Osieke, "Majority Voting Systems in the International Labor Organization and the International Monetary Fund", *International and Comparative Law Quarterly* 33 (1984), p. 397。有论者指出，第一次增加是为了让欧洲经济共同体在关于设立特别提款权的某些事情上拥有否决权，而第二次增加则是为了让美国在欧佩克国家相对份额翻倍后继续拥有否决权。参见〔美〕斯蒂芬·D. 克莱斯勒《结构冲突：第三世界对抗全球自由主义》，李小华译，浙江人民出版社，2001，第135页。

17.09%；加权过后的总票数为371743票，占总投票权的16.74%。[①] 这意味着在诸如调整份额、出售IMF黄金储备、提供国际收支失衡援助及分配特别提款权等需要85%特别多数通过的重大事项上，美国拥有事实上的否决权。同样地，如果作为一个整体看待，那么欧盟国家总共拥有30%左右的投票权，远远超过该地区在世界经济中所占比例。这使得欧美国家在IMF内部占据绝对优势。相比之下，广大发展中国家，尤其是低收入国家，在IMF中的代表性严重不足。这种代表性不足主要表现在两个方面：一方面，随着全球经济的发展，新兴经济体在世界经济中所占比重日益增大，过度偏向欧美国家的份额计算方法已经严重滞后于现实；另一方面，以非洲为代表的低收入国家限于经济实力，投票权严重不足，在决策过程中日益边缘化。此外，传统上形成的IMF总裁由欧洲人担任、世界银行行长由美国人担任的惯例，进一步削弱了IMF治理结构和决策机制中的民主性。

这种治理结构中的力量失衡使得IMF易于被少数成员国所掌控，过度体现后者的政策立场和倾向。自20世纪80年代以来，IMF不遗余力地在全球范围内推行其与世界银行和美国财政部达成的所谓“华盛顿共识”，鼓吹金融自由化，就是一个突出例证。华盛顿共识是以财政节俭、私有化和市场自由化为支柱的一系列政策的通称，主要内容包括缩小政府规模、削减财政支出、放松监管、实施自由化和私有化等。尽管这些政策在应对拉美债务危机中起过一定积极作用，但有其适用的特定条件和局限，绝非放之四海而皆准的普遍真理。华盛顿共识的理论基础是单方面强调市场作用的“新自由主义”。作为新自由主义大本营的美国，早在20世纪80年代末就已经在国内逐步放弃新自由主义，转而强化政府职能。与此同时，美国却在国际社会继续大力鼓吹华盛顿共识，推行金融自由化和市场开放，其目的很大程度上在于维持和强化美国的竞争优势，为美国产业利益和金融利益的全球布局扫除障碍。从历史上看，建立IMF的本意是通过各国政府的经济合作和集体行动，矫正各行其是的各国经济政策所带来的灾难性后果，强调的是市场可能的失灵和政府应当扮演的积极角色。然而，近年来IMF却演变成为新自由主义最坚定的支持者和不遗余力的鼓吹者，

① 参见IMF, *IMF Members' Quotas and Voting Power, and IMF Board of Governors*, http://www.imf.org/external/np/sec/memdir/members.htm。

以致被批评为受“市场原教旨主义”（market fundamentalism）支配，① 其间变化耐人寻味。

（四）争端解决有心无力

近年来，汇率问题已经成为国际经贸争端中的重要争议点之一。全球金融危机过后的经济萧条导致贸易保护主义抬头，贸易摩擦加剧，各国在汇率问题上的分歧和争端更加凸显。迄今为止，这些争端都是通过政治和外交途径解决的，原因是按照世界贸易组织（以下简称 WTO）和 IMF 的分工，汇率问题属于后者管辖，② 而 IMF 却又缺乏相应的判断标准、操作规则和裁处机制。

如前所述，在固定汇率体系解体后，各国不再有义务将本国货币同他国货币的汇率维持在特定水平，IMF 也无权要求其这样做。根据《基金协定》第 4 条第 2 款第 2 项，成员国可以自由决定其外汇安排，包括：第一，以特别提款权或除黄金以外的其他指标为基准，确定本国货币的价值；第二，通过合作安排，使本国货币同其他一国或多国的货币保持比价关系；第三，成员国选择的其他外汇安排。换言之，对于成员国而言不再有必须接受的统一的汇率形成方式。

当然，如前所述，成员国仍需承担关于外汇安排的一般义务。根据《基金协定》第 4 条第 1 款，成员国承诺同 IMF 和其他成员国合作，以确保有秩序的外汇安排，促进汇率体系稳定。为此目的，成员国负有如下四项义务：第一，努力以自己的经济和金融政策来达到促进有秩序的经济增长这一目标，既有合理的价格稳定，又适当照顾自身的境况；第二，努力通过创造有秩序的基本的经济和金融条件和不会产生反常混乱的货币制度去促进稳定；第三，避免操纵汇率或国际货币制度来妨碍国际收支有效的调整或取得对其他成员国不公平的竞争优势；第四，奉行同本款所规定的保证不相矛盾的外汇政策。其中，具有实质意义的是第 3 项义务，即不得操纵汇率来妨碍国际收支有效调整或获取不公平竞争优势。这项义务也正

---

① 参见 Joseph E. Stiglitz, *Globalization and its Discontents* (W. W. Norton & Company, 2002), p. 202。

② 关于 WTO 和 IMF 在这方面的现有分工与合作，以及在笔者看来的可能安排，下文第三（四）部分将有进一步讨论。

是汇率争端所围绕的焦点。

问题在于，对于何为“操纵汇率”，《基金协定》并无进一步说明。尽管 IMF 在 1977 年通过《汇率政策监督决定》，将汇率操纵界定为“在外汇市场进行持续、大规模的单向干预”，但是对如何认定“持续”、“单向”和“大规模”，仍然缺乏具有可操作性的标准和方法。[①] 同样，对于何谓“妨碍国际收支有效的调整”或“不公平的竞争优势”，IMF 也没有给出答案和方法指引。

对于汇率争端，IMF 不仅缺乏明晰的判断标准，也没有正式的处理机制和相应的执行保证。IMF 处理汇率问题的主要手段是同成员国进行磋商。根据《基金协定》第 4 条第 3 款，IMF 应当监督成员国履行第 4 条第 1 款下的义务，并在必要时同后者进行磋商。通过磋商，IMF 向成员国表达自己对相关问题的意见并提出建议。由于磋商及其结果不具有强制性，IMF 所提建议也不构成成员国必须遵守的法定义务，因此对于成员国并无约束力。如果 IMF 希望对成员国进一步施加压力，根据《基金协定》第 12 条第 8 款，它可以将相关意见和建议非正式地传达给各成员国，并在获得 70% 以上投票权支持的情况下公布其磋商报告。但同样，这种做法只是诉诸成员国之间的舆论监督和政治压力，不具法律约束力。此外，尽管根据《基金协定》第 26 条第 2 款，IMF 对于违反汇率义务的成员国可以强制剥夺利益，包括宣布其丧失使用 IMF 普通资金的资格、中止其投票权乃至强制要求其退出，[②] 但一来如上所述，对于是否违反汇率义务本来就缺乏明晰的判断标准，二来 IMF 对于成员国不履行义务的行为一向倚重补救而不是制裁，[③] 罕有使用这些强制性措施。因此，总体而言，IMF 对于汇率争端的解决可以说是有心无力。

---

① 这一点可以从 IMF 成立以来从未认定过成员国操纵汇率并给予制裁这一事实得到印证。参见 Xinchen Sofia Lou, *Challenging China's Fixed Exchange Rate Regime: An Analysis of U. S. Options*, Hastings Int'l & Comp. L. Rev. 28（2005）, pp. 455, 477。

② 根据《IMF 协定》第 26 条第 2 款第 1—3 项的规定，对于未能履行《基金协定》义务的成员国，IMF 可以宣布其丧失使用 IMF 普通资金的资格；如该成员国在其后的合理期间内未能改正，IMF 经 70 % 以上投票权通过，可以中止该成员国的投票权；如该成员国在中止投票权后的合理期间内仍未能改正，则 IMF 经 85 % 以上投票权通过，可以要求该成员国退出。

③ 参见 Joseph Gold, *The Rule Of Law in the International Monetary Fund*, The International Monetary Fund Ser. No. 32（1980）, p. 21。

三　晚近改革与未来方向

针对上述困境，IMF 已经进行或启动了一些改革。其中，在双边监督和治理结构方面已经获得实质进展，但尚需进一步推进；而在职能定位和争端解决方面则仍徘徊不前，亟待突破。下面分别加以讨论。

（一）重塑核心职能

要保持自己在国际货币体制中的核心地位，真正实现促进全球金融稳定和贸易平衡的宗旨，IMF 必须回归和重塑其核心职能。首先，IMF 应当减少乃至放弃在中长期信贷、结构性调整和减贫项目等发展领域的介入，将这部分职能移交世界银行及区域发展银行，而专注于危机管理，即通过提供短期融资帮助陷入国际支付危机的成员国摆脱危机，缩短国际收支不平衡的时间并减轻其程度。其次，IMF 必须重塑其在维护货币和汇率稳定方面的传统职能，在浮动汇率制的约束性框架内，通过更积极的合作安排维持成员国间有秩序的外汇安排，从而不但管理危机，而且预防和减少危机。从目前情况看，第二点显得尤为必要。

如前所述，在固定汇率体系解体后，各国不再有义务采取统一的外汇安排，IMF 对固定汇率的“维系”被代之以对成员国汇率政策的“监督”，后者在不违反《基金协定》第 4 条义务的前提下有设定和调整其汇率的自由。尽管在此情况下美元不再具有唯一储备货币的法定特权，但由于美国在世界经济中的特殊地位，很多国家仍然在法律上或事实上采取了钉住美元的汇率浮动方式，从而形成所谓“美元本位”。在此背景下，有经济学家提出“布雷顿森林体系Ⅱ”的理论，即以美国为核心、中国等亚洲新兴市场国家为外围的事实上的固定汇率体系。在这一体系中，外围国家将其货币以低估的汇率与美元挂钩，以寻求出口驱动型经济增长；作为回报，它们将其所得重新投资于美国，让美国发挥稳定及最终消费者的作用。论者认为这一体系是对称、稳定和可持续的，因为其中外围国家有贸易顺差，美国有贸易逆差；外围国家输出商品，美国输出美元；外围国家积累债权，美国积累债务，双方各得其所。①

尽管“布雷顿森林体系Ⅱ”在一定程度上确实存在并在一定时期内维持了国际经济关系的稳定，但以美元特权为支撑的美国举债消费模式的不可持续性，决定了这一体系的不可持续性。美国总统奥巴马在二十国集团（以下简称 G20）第三次峰会（匹兹堡，2009 年 9 月）上呼吁中国增加消费、美国增加储蓄，就是一个有力的证明。因此，尽管提出这一理论的三位经济学家认为该模式在危机后仍然具有生命力，② 但寄望于这样一种模式来维持有秩序的外汇安排、维护货币和汇率稳定，无疑并不明智。讨论较多的改革路径有三条，即实现国际储备货币多元化、创设超主权储备货币和推进区域货币一体化。

储备货币多元化方案致力于改变美元在国际储备体系中“一币独大”的局面，以其他主要货币来分担储备货币职能，以减少国际货币体制对美元的依赖，对冲汇率波动风险。其中，欧元、日元和人民币是热门备选货币。然而现实是，日本低迷的经济不足以支撑起同美元分庭抗礼的强势日元；欧元背后是若干经济状况各异的独立主权国家，在货币政策方面难免掣肘；而人民币目前尚未完全实现资本项目下的自由兑换，还不是真正意义上的国际货币，遑论成为主要储备货币。因此，储备货币多元化在短期内较难实现。

超主权储备货币的设想是中国人民银行行长周小川在第二次 G20 峰会（伦敦，2009 年 4 月）前夕提出的，核心内容是在现有 IMF 特别提款权的基础上创设超主权的国际储备货币，作为美元的替代。应当说，作为终极目标，独立于任何主权国家之外的超主权储备货币无疑是值得追求的。实际上，在美元成为国际储备货币之前，无论是银本位制下的白银还是金本位制下的黄金，都是超主权的。问题在于，从现实来看，这一方案的实施

---

① 参见 Michael P. Dooley, David Folkerts-Landau & Peter Garber, “An Essay on the Rivived Bretton Woods System”, *NBER Working Paper 9971*, National Bureau of Economic Research, Cambridge, Massachusetts, 2003。需要指出的是，这里所说的“布雷顿森林体系Ⅱ”是对国际货币体系现况进行描述和解释的理论模式，与英国和法国在第一次 G20 峰会（华盛顿，2008 年 11 月）上所强调建立的“布雷顿森林体系Ⅱ”的含义有所不同；后者是对构想中的国际货币新体制的笼统称谓，其具体内容目前尚不明确。

② 参见 Dooley, Folkerts-Landau & Garber, “Bretton Woods Ⅱ Still Defines the International Monetary System”, *NBER Working Paper 14731*, National Bureau of Economic Research, Cambridge, Massachusetts, 2009。

面临难以逾越的法律障碍，即各国的货币主权。发行超主权储备货币意味着要有一个全球中央银行（不管采取何种形式，也不管是由 IMF 还是现有或新设的其他机构担任），意味着成员国必须让渡一部分货币主权给这个全球央行，还意味着各国必须在货币政策方面进行远比现在更为紧密的整合和协调。欧洲一体化程度之高，推出欧元尚且历尽艰辛，遑论创设这样一种世界性货币。从这一设想提出的时机看，它的真实意图或许只是在于表达中国对既有国际货币体制的批判态度，以及试探其他国家的立场和底线。

比较而言，推进区域货币一体化是更为现实可行的选择。通过区域内的货币协调与合作，减少区域内货币动荡，并增强抵御外部风险的能力，维护区域货币稳定，进而促进国际货币体系的稳定。而相关国家在地理上的接近以及相似的社会、历史和文化传统，也使得区域一体化的基础相对牢固。在这方面，欧洲货币一体化已经提供了很好的例证。目前，以东盟和中、日、韩“10 + 3”机制为核心的东亚区域货币合作也正在积极开展。[①] 在此背景下，IMF 应当对区域货币合作给予更多的关注和重视，并提供必要的政策、信息和技术支持，推进各国尤其是发展中国家和新兴市场的区域货币一体化进程，在此基础上强化对国际货币体制的机构影响力，重塑其维护货币和汇率稳定的核心职能。

（二）加强双边监督

2007 年 6 月，IMF 通过了《对成员国政策的双边监督决定》（以下简称《2007 年决定》），取代了施行 30 年之久的 1977 年《汇率政策监督决

---

① 亚洲金融危机之后，东盟十国和中、日、韩三国于 2000 年 5 月共同发起了旨在建立区域性货币互换框架的“清迈倡议”（Chiang Mai Initiative），随后在此框架内签订了大量双边货币互换协议。2006 年 5 月，第 9 届“10 + 3”财长会议对清迈倡议的主要原则进行了修订，明确各国在启动双边货币互换过程中执行集体决策机制，从而将清迈倡议从双边机制向多边机制转型的问题提上了日程。2009 年 5 月，第 12 届“10 + 3”财长会议就区域外汇储备库的全部关键要素达成一致，清迈倡议多边化取得重大进展。2010 年 3 月 24 日，清迈倡议多边化协议正式生效，建立起总规模为 1200 亿美元的区域外汇储备库，其核心目标是解决区域内国际收支和短期流动性困难，并对现有国际融资安排加以补充。2010 年 5 月，第 13 届“10 + 3”财长会议决定于次年设立“东盟中日韩宏观经济研究办公室”，作为独立区域监测机构，负责监测和分析地区经济，帮助多边机制尽早察知风险、迅速实施救助和有效作出决策。

定》(以下简称《1977 年决定》)。这是 IMF 在双边监督方面的重大变革。一方面,《1977 年决定》是在布雷顿森林体系解体后不久起草的,当时对于新体系如何运作存在相当大的不确定性,导致该决定存在固有缺陷;另一方面,在其后的 30 年间国际货币金融体系及其监督实践不断演进,而《1977 年决定》却几乎没有变化,从而与实践脱节。《2007 年决定》正是在此背景下出台的。

《2007 年决定》依据《基金协定》第 4 条制定,是对 IMF 双边监督政策的全面阐述。它的内容较为丰富,重点有如下四个方面:第一,引入了"外部稳定"这一概念,作为双边监督的统领原则;第二,明确了"汇率操纵"的概念,特别是将其同"根本性汇率失调"这一概念联系起来;第三,增加了应由 IMF 彻底考察并可能需要同成员国进行讨论的情形;第四,规定了双边监督的形式,强调监督的合作性、对话与劝说的重要性,以及保持坦诚和公平的必要性。

作为《2007 年决定》的核心概念,外部稳定是指不会或不太可能导致破坏性汇率变动的国际收支状况。外部稳定既涉及经常账户,也涉及资本账户;既包括一国国际收支的稳定,也包括该国国际收支状况对其他国家国际收支稳定的影响,亦即外溢效果。当一国国际收支状况不会或不太可能导致破坏性的汇率变动时,就实现了外部稳定。《2007 年决定》认为,最有效实现系统性稳定的途径是每个成员国实施能够促进本国外部稳定的政策,即与《基金协定》第 4 条第 1 款规定的成员国义务,特别是第 4 条第 1 款第 1—4 项规定的具体义务相一致的政策。① 外部稳定概念的意义在于它设定了 IMF 双边监督的范围:在双边监督中,IMF 的监督重点是成员国采取的那些对目前或未来的外部稳定可能产生显著影响的政策。据此,汇率、货币、财政和金融政策始终受到监督,而对于其他政策,只有当其显著影响目前或未来的外部稳定时,才予以考察。IMF 将评估上述政策是否有利于外部稳定,并就实现此目标所需的政策调整向成员国提出建议。②

《2007 年决定》对于汇率操纵问题作出了明确规定。它首先重申,只有当 IMF 认定一个成员国在操纵其汇率或国际货币体系,并且这种操纵是

---

① 《2007 年决定》第 4 条。
② 《2007 年决定》第 5 条。

为了阻止有效的国际收支调整或取得对其他成员国不公平的竞争优势时，该成员国才能被认为违反了《基金协定》第 4 条第 1 款第 3 项下的义务。该决定进而对操纵汇率和不公平竞争优势进行了解释。“操纵汇率”是指实施目的在于影响汇率水平并且实际影响了汇率水平的政策，这种影响既包括造成汇率变动，也包括阻止其变动。而“不公平的竞争优势”则要求，只有当 IMF 认定一个成员国是为了造成以汇率低估形式出现的根本性汇率失调而实施这些政策，并且造成这种失调的目的在于扩大净出口时，该成员国才能被认为为取得对其他成员国不公平的竞争优势而操纵汇率。此外，IMF 有责任根据所有可获得的证据，包括通过与有关成员国进行磋商，客观地评价成员国是否在履行第 4 条第 1 款规定的义务。其对于成员国就政策目的所作的任何陈述，在存在合理怀疑的情况下不得作出不利于成员国的判定。

在需要考察并在必要时同成员国进行讨论的具体情势方面，《2007 年决定》在《1977 年决定》的基础上进行了补充和修改，其中较为突出的一点是增加了“私人资本流动导致的对外部门显著脆弱性，包括流动性风险”这一项。① 这是对现实的承认。实际上，资本流动，尤其是私人资本流动，早已取代经常项目收支成为货币金融稳定的最大隐患。亚洲金融危机同国际游资或所谓“热钱”的冲击密不可分，而次贷危机之所以迅速蔓延成金融海啸，金融衍生产品在全球范围内无节制地泛滥是一个重要原因。在此背景下，加强对资本流动的监督，可以说是正当其时。不仅如此，IMF 还应对成员国，尤其是金融体系尚不发达、相关法律制度尚不健全的发展中成员国所采取的资本控制措施抱持更为开放的态度，不要轻言金融自由化和去管制化。②

上述规定为 IMF 双边监督提供了更具体、更清晰和更具操作性的依据，有助于增强双边监督的针对性和有效性。同时，《2007 年决定》强调“对成员国一视同仁，对情况相似的成员国采取相似的处理方法”的监督

① 《2007 年决定》第 15 条第 7 项。

② 《基金协定》并不要求成员国开放资本项目；换言之，为保障金融安全、防范金融风险而实施资本项目控制是成员国的权利。尽管如此，IMF 近年来一直致力于推行金融自由化和去管制化。

公平性,[①] 也有助于解决既有监督中厚此薄彼、用力不均的问题。这些都是值得肯定的发展。但应当看到,《2007 年决定》所构建的仍然是一种柔性监督,“对话和劝说是有效监督的关键支柱”。[②] 除关于操纵汇率和货币体系的内容外,该决定的相关规则仅为建议,而非成员国的义务。IMF 作出的某成员国没有遵守其中某项建议的认定也并不能导致推定该成员国违反了其所承担的《基金协定》第 4 条第 1 款下的义务。换言之,IMF 双边监督缺乏约束性和执行力的问题仍未得到根本解决。目前来看有可能作出的进一步努力,一是将 IMF 的双边监督同成员国之间的相互监督相联系,借助成员国的相互制约强化 IMF 监督的实效;[③] 二是完善 IMF 治理结构,推动 IMF 内部治理民主化,强化 IMF 的合法性和代表性,从而增强 IMF 监督的权威性和说服力。

(三) 完善治理结构

完善 IMF 治理结构的核心是改革现有的份额和投票权制度,改变发展中国家和新兴市场国家代表性不足、发达国家代表性过度的局面。在这方面,IMF 已经有所行动。2006 年 IMF 新加坡年会通过了一项决议,决定启动为期两年的改革计划。改革的第一步是个别增加中国、韩国、墨西哥和土耳其这四个相比经济实力而言代表性最为不足的成员的份额。作为改革的第二步,决议要求在 2008 年以前对于份额和投票权问题制定进一步的规则。在此基础上,IMF 于 2008 年 4 月通过一项意义深远的改革决议,采纳了新的份额计算公式并以此为依据增加 54 个国家(主要是新兴市场国家)的份额。决议还含有一项旨在增加低收入国家在 IMF 中发言权的《基金协定》修正案,内容包括:第一,将基本投票权增至目前的 3 倍,即 750 票,这是自 IMF 成立以来基本投票权的首次增加;第二,规定今后无论 IMF 如何发展,基本投票权数占总投票权数的比重均保持不变;第三,允许在执

---

① 《2007 年决定》第 8 条。

② 《2007 年决定》。

③ 例如,第三次 G20 峰会决定就有关国内政策建立“相互评估”(mutual assessment)机制,并建议由 IMF 来帮助进行此种相互评估。在 IMF 2009 年年会上,IMF 的政策指导机构国际货币金融委员会(IMFC)批准了这一建议,认为这对于 IMF 而言代表着一种新的双边监督种类。参见 IMF,“*Istanbul Decisions*” *to Guide IMF as Countries Shape Post-Crisis World*, http://www.imf.org/external/pubs/ft/survey/so/2009/NEW100609A.htm。

行董事会中代表非洲选区的两名董事各指定一名额外的候补董事。① 但由于《基金协定》规定，其任何修改在经理事会通过后，还需另行经五分之三以上并持有85%以上投票权的成员国接受方可生效，② 而截至目前接受这一修正案的成员国数目尚未达到要求，③ 因此这一决议尽管意义重大影响深远，但其真正付诸实践尚需时日。

即使上述改革方案获得不折不扣的实施，治理结构问题也远未解决。IMF内部权力失衡现状的矫正，不仅涉及份额和投票权的增加，还涉及既有的不合理份额比例的调整。2009年9月，第三次G20峰会决定，将5%的IMF份额从代表性过度的发达国家转移给代表性不足的有活力新兴市场国家和发展中国家，在2011年1月前完成此项工作。该决定应当说是一个好的开始，但还远远不够。首先，这一决定的落实有待前述份额和投票权修正案生效，并且份额如何从发达国家转移，转移后又如何在发展中国家之间分配等，还有很多问题需要解决。其次，上述改革方案和这一决定均不影响美国继续拥有15%以上的投票权，从而在IMF重大事项上继续享有事实上的否决权。④

在笔者看来，要解决治理结构中的权力失衡问题，还需要从以下两个方面努力。第一，变固定的份额计算公式为动态的投票权自动调整机制，按照事先设定的标准，如成员国在世界贸易中所占份额，定期自动调整投票权，从而充分反映各国经济地位和实力的变化。第二，全面审查《基金协定》，在合理的限度内削减那些需要经特别多数尤其是85%特别多数才

---

① 参见IMF, *IMF Quota and Voice Publications* (*June 2006 - April 2008*), http://www.imf.org/external/np/fin/quotas/pubs/index.htm。

② 《基金协定》第28条第1款规定："任何修改本协定的提议，不论其为成员国、理事或执行董事会所提出，应先通过理事会主席，然后由其提交理事会。如所提议的修改案经理事会通过，基金应用信函或电报征询各成员国是否接受该修正案。如有五分之三以上并持有85%以上投票权的成员国接受该修正案，基金即应将这一事实通知各成员国。"

③ IMF现有成员国186个，按照五分之三的比例计算，所需成员国数目为112个。截至2010年7月1日，已经接受修正案的成员国数目为84个。参见IMF, *Consents to the Proposed Amendments of the Articles of Agreement*, http://www.imf.org/external/np/sec/misc/consents.htm#a1。

④ 2010年4月25日世界银行通过的投票权改革方案提供了一个旁证。根据应第三次G20峰会要求作出的这一改革，世界银行的发达成员国向发展中成员国转移了3.13%的投票权，使后者的总投票权从44.06%提高到47.19%；其中中国的增幅最大，从2.77%提高到4.42%，成为仅次于美国和日本的世界银行第三大股东国。然而，改革后美国15.85%的投票权比例维持不变，仍然拥有在重大事项上的事实否决权。

能决定的事项，从而减少美国、欧盟等对 IMF 的过度控制。此外，如前所述，建立在美欧共治基础上的 IMF 总裁由欧洲人担任的惯例也与民主原则相背离。[①] 因此，改革 IMF 总裁遴选制度，使其以更为民主和公开的方式施行，并加强对管理层的有效监督，也是完善 IMF 治理结构不可或缺的环节。[②]

（四）促进争端解决

按照二战后国际经济体系设计者们的构想，货币和金融问题由 IMF 负责，贸易问题则由计划于其后成立的“国际贸易组织”负责。尽管后者由于种种原因以夭折告终，但作为其临时替代品的“关税与贸易总协定”却一直存续下来，并演变成为现在的 WTO。

虽然 WTO 拥有管辖国际贸易的广泛权力和强制性的争端解决机制，并且国际贸易同汇率政策和外汇安排日益密不可分，但 WTO 遵循了传统分工，将汇率和外汇措施排除在自己的管辖范围之外。1994 年《关税及贸易总协定》（以下简称 GATT 1994）第 15 条是 WTO 处理这一问题的法定依据。第 15 条第 2 款规定，当缔约方全体被提请审议或处理有关货币储备、国际收支或外汇安排问题的争端时，应与 IMF 充分磋商，接受 IMF 关于外汇、货币储备或国际收支的所有统计数据或其他事实的调查结果，并接受 IMF 关于某一缔约方在外汇问题上采取的行动是否符合《基金协定》的决定。第 15 条第 4 款和第 5 款则将 WTO 和 IMF 联系起来，勾勒出了二者合作的大致框架。第 4 款规定，缔约方不得通过外汇措施而使该协定各项条款的意图无效，也不得通过贸易行动而使《基金协定》各项条款的意图无效。第 5 款进一步规定，当缔约方全体在任何时候认为某一缔约方正在实施的有关进口支付和转移方面的外汇限制与 GATT 1994 对数量限制所规定的例外不一致时，应就此向 IMF 报告。IMF 和 WTO 于 1996 年达成的

---

① 事实上，《基金协定》第 12 条第 4 款第 1 项仅规定总裁由执行董事会选举，且理事和执行董事均不得担任总裁，并未附加任何地域条件。

② 这一点在第四次 G20 峰会（多伦多，2010 年 6 月）上得到了确认。成员国在联合发布的峰会宣言中承诺增强国际金融机构的合法性、可信性和有效性，建立公开、透明和择优的负责人及高管层遴选程序，并将在第五次 G20 峰会（首尔，2010 年 11 月）举行之前以更加广泛的改革为背景加强遴选工作。参见 G20，*The G－20 Toronto Summit Declaration*，http://g20.gc.ca/toronto-summit/summit-documents/the-g-20-toronto-summit-declaration。

协议对于二者之间的合作作了更明确的说明。根据这项协议，IMF 对于其批准针对经常性国际贸易支付或转移的限制措施的决定，批准歧视性货币安排或多重货币实践的决定，以及要求其成员国采取控制措施以防止大规模或持续资本外流的决定，均应通知 WTO。同时，IMF 同意参加由 WTO 国际收支平衡限制委员会针对某一 WTO 成员方为确保收支平衡而采取的措施所启动的磋商。[①]

概而言之，汇率和外汇措施属于 IMF 的专属管辖范围，当 WTO 在贸易争端中涉及这类问题时，必须移交 IMF，并接受后者的意见和结论。同时，IMF 有义务同 WTO 合作，就相关问题进行磋商。换言之，汇率争端不能在 WTO 争端解决框架内处理，而只能由 IMF 来作出决定。

然而，如前所述，IMF 传统上缺乏处理汇率争端的明晰标准和裁处机制。尽管《2007 年决定》对于"操纵汇率以获取不公平的竞争优势"有了明确界定，从而提供了更具可操作性的标准，但由于仍然缺乏类似于 WTO 专家组制度那样的独立、高效的争端解决机制，而是依赖成员国代表投票表决或达成一致，因此难以得出结论。即便有了结论，也仍然面临缺乏执行力和约束力的问题。

有鉴于此，笔者认为不妨在现有分工合作框架基础上大胆突破，将与贸易问题有关的汇率和外汇安排纳入 WTO 争端解决机制的管辖范围。这一构想看似激进，但"与贸易有关的知识产权"、"与贸易有关的投资措施"等概念，以传统眼光看来何尝不是如此？汇率和外汇安排同贸易问题的距离，未必比知识产权和投资措施更为遥远。况且，《2007 年决定》在界定获取不公平竞争优势时提出的"目的在于扩大净出口"这一要件，本身就同贸易密不可分。至于哪些具体措施构成"与贸易有关的汇率和外汇安排"，可以在接受这一原则的前提下，进一步探讨和辨析。一旦将特定汇率和外汇安排纳入 WTO 争端解决机制的管辖范围，IMF 在这些事项上可以类似于专家证人或"法庭之友"的身份提供专业意见，作为专家组或上诉机构最主要和最具说服力的裁判依据。从这个角度看，《2007 年决定》对于操纵汇率判断标准的明晰化，恰恰为此种进一步合作提供了可能。

---

① 参见 Agreement between the International Monetary Fund and the World Trade Organization（November 25，1996），para. 4 – 5。

四 结论

作为特定历史时期的产物，IMF 有其先天局限，不仅体现在技术操作和规则运行层面，更体现在权力结构和意识形态层面。由于担心 IMF 政策受到西方控制，苏联虽然在 1944 年签署了《基金协定》，但最终拒绝批准，这也成为触发美国冷战思维的原因之一。其后，随着紧张局势发展为冷战，已经加入 IMF 的波兰、捷克斯洛伐克、古巴等国相继退出，在苏联或中国影响范围内的其他大多数国家也完全置身于外，这使得 IMF 在很大程度上成为一个帮助稳定市场经济的资本主义俱乐部。[①] 冷战结束后，IMF 的成员覆盖范围虽然大为扩展，但其深受以美国为代表的发达国家控制和影响的现实却并未得到实质改变。这一点，从 IMF 近乎意识形态化地坚持所谓“华盛顿共识”，对遭遇金融危机的亚洲新兴市场国家及其他发展中国家执行片面有利于跨国金融集团的苛刻政策中可见一斑。[②] 唯其如此，斯蒂格利茨才尖锐地指出，IMF 在许多方面是不民主的，这种不民主的本质正是它未能倾听发展中国家声音的原因之一。[③]

可以说，在经过三分之二个世纪的发展之后，IMF 及其代表的国际货币体制已经走到了十字路口，改革完善还是推倒重来，是各国面临的共同抉择。从目前情况看，维持 IMF 在国际货币体制中的核心地位，在此基础上对其进行全面而深入的实质性改革，是更为可取的现实选择。[④] 综上所

---

① 参见国际货币基金组织《聚焦基金组织》（《基金组织概览》增刊第 35 期，2006 年 9 月），http://www.imf.org/external/pubs/ft/survey/chn/2006/090106c.pdf。

② 例如，关于 IMF 在亚洲金融危机中对泰国和韩国提供贷款时所附加的苛刻政策条件，可参见朱梦楠《国际金融学》，厦门大学出版社，1999，第 471 页；Hal S. Stott & Philip A. Wellons, *International Finance: Transactions, Policy and Regulation*, 8th ed. (Foundation Press, 2001), p. 1295。

③ 参见〔美〕约瑟夫·斯蒂格利茨《全球化及其不满》，夏业良译，机械工业出版社，2004，作者中文版序。

④ 可资佐证的是，尽管现行国际货币体制在此次金融危机中饱受指责，但各主要国家并未打算废弃 IMF 或限制其职能，而是选择对其进行改革和强化。例如，在第二次 G20 峰会上，各国决定大幅增加 IMF 的资金来源，从而使 IMF 成为这次峰会的最大赢家；在第三次 G20 峰会上，各国同意对 IMF 治理结构进行深入改革。可以说，在金融危机之后，IMF 的地位非但没有削弱，反而有所增强。

述，改革的基本目标和方向，一是梳理和重塑IMF相关职能，增强其对外运作的有效性；二是调整和平衡IMF权力结构，促进其内部治理的民主化。

需要指出的是，无论改革如何进行，最终都需要通过IMF法律体系中相关规范的修订和变动来实现。IMF法律体系不仅包括作为主体的《基金协定》，还包括理事会制定的章程和执行董事会制定的规则与条例，它们都对IMF及其成员国具有法律约束力。此外，理事会和执行董事会通过的决定也是具有约束力的法律文件。[①] 由于《基金协定》的修订极为困难，因此在不违反《基金协定》条款的前提下以规则与条例、决定等下位规范的形式先期落实某些改革举措，无疑是值得考虑的策略。此外，利用《基金协定》第29条赋予理事会和执行董事会的解释权，[②] 对《基金协定》相关条款作出更具开放性的解释，也是可能的途径。进而言之，IMF部分成员国之间签订的区域货币一体化协定或其他相关协定，在一定意义上也可以视为这一进程的一部分，其价值正如区域自由贸易协定之于WTO多边协定的发展。

相较于其他一些国际经济法律体制，如国际贸易法和国际投资法，争端解决机制和案例法的缺乏无疑是制约国际货币法律体制实效性的一个重要因素。货币主权的敏感性和个别成员国的绝对优势地位，使得在IMF体制内构建独立争端解决机制的设想短期内难以实现。在此背景下，可以考虑利用已被证实富有成效的WTO争端解决机制，将与贸易有关的货币领域争端渐进纳入其管辖范围，通过案例的累积逐步确立和强化相关争议事项的可诉性，从而为国际货币体制带来新的动力和活力。

在2009年伊斯坦布尔年会上，IMF总裁多米尼克·施特劳斯－卡恩在致辞中说道："现在，我们正处在一个关键时刻。历史告诉我们，当世界各国团结起来共同应对挑战时，我们就能够走上和平和繁荣的良性循环，

---

① 对于理事会的决定对成员国是否具有约束力，《基金协定》未作明确限制，这使得理事会可以通过对IMF及其成员国具有法律约束力的决定。此外，由于《基金协定》第12条明确规定，除该协定直接赋予理事会的权力外，理事会可以将其权力委托给执行董事会行使，因此执行董事会也可以通过具有法律约束力的决定。参见余元洲《国际货币基金组织法律制度改革研究》，武汉大学出版社，2001，第9页。

② 根据《基金协定》第29条，《基金协定》条款由执行董事会负责解释；若任何成员国不认同执行董事会的解释，可在3个月内提请理事会作出最终裁决。

避免冲突和停滞的恶性循环。"① 的确，长久以来由美欧发达国家所主宰的国际货币体制，在全球金融危机中前所未有地凸显出发展中国家，特别是以中国为代表的新兴市场国家的重要性。对于中国而言，IMF及其所代表的国际货币体制的改革既是挑战，更是机遇。只要正视现实，厘清定位，找准方向，中国完全可以在IMF改革以及未来的国际货币新体制中发挥更加积极的作用。

（本文原载于《法学研究》2010年第4期）

① 参见IMF，"*Istanbul Decisions*" *to Guide IMF as Countries Shape Post-Crisis World*，http://www.imf.org/external/pubs/ft/survey/so/2009/NEW100609A.htm。

欧盟与美国在合并控制领域的双边执法合作

黄　晋*

一　前言

随着经济全球化的进一步深入，合并控制领域的双边执法合作已经成为当前国家和超国家竞争主管机构执法常态化的必然选择。近年来，随着颁布实施合并控制制度的国家日益增加，多个竞争主管机构根据不同程序和实体标准进行同一合并审查的可能性大幅提高。鉴于同一交易会适用不同国家的竞争法律制度，各国反垄断执法机构完全有理由避免合并分析和救济行为的冲突。

尽管很多国家在合并控制的实体评估、程序和政策目标上存在一些差异，然而各国竞争主管机构还是采取了一些举措来促进协调和减少冲突。当前，最为重要的双边合作仍然是欧盟与美国两大反垄断司法辖区达成的旨在促进各自竞争执法的双边合作框架机制，这种合作框架机制有助于促进欧盟与美国在合并控制领域相互妥协、减少分歧和加强协调，其作用已经得到欧盟与美国竞争法学界的广泛认可。①

有鉴于此，本文将从欧盟与美国在合并控制领域双边合作的法律机制入手，着重分析欧盟与美国在合并调查中的通知、交流与信息交换、协

---

* 黄晋，中国社会科学院国际法研究所国际经济法研究室副主任、副研究员。

① 黄勇：《竞争法国际合作的现状与前景》，《山西大学学报》（哲学社会科学版）2004 年第 4 期，第 73 页。

调、礼让原则以及合并救济等多个方面的问题，以期为我国反垄断执法机构在合并控制领域开展双边合作提供一定的参考。

二 欧盟与美国在合并控制领域开展合作的法律机制

从 20 世纪 60 年代开始，欧盟委员会[①]与美国联邦贸易委员会和司法部反托拉斯局展开了非正式合作。这种合作以每年召开会议的方式逐步正式化。欧盟委员会和美国联邦执法机构还根据经济合作与发展组织（以下简称经合组织）1986 年发布、1995 年修改的《成员国间就影响国际贸易的限制性商业行为进行合作的推荐意见》（以下简称《推荐意见》）展开合作。[②]《推荐意见》涉及成员方在牵涉其他成员方重要利益的反竞争行为调查中相互通知、磋商和信息交换的有关内容。

《推荐意见》指出，成员方应当：在影响其他成员方重要利益的调查或者执法行动过程中及时通知后者；分享信息从而允许利益受影响的成员方向执行调查的成员方提出意见、进行磋商；在适当时协调平行调查；在彼此管辖范围内相互协助查明和取得信息；以及各方请求行为发生地国家的竞争主管机构采取行动，考虑处理影响其重要利益但发生在该国管辖地域外的反竞争行为。[③]

20 世纪 80 年代以来的一系列发展促使欧盟和美国竞争主管机构开始以更为正式和有组织的方式展开合作。第一，美国和欧盟的跨境贸易迅速增长，重复执法和双边执法冲突的风险加剧。第二，在 1998 年木材纸浆案（Wood Pulp）判决中，欧盟法院明确指出，由于加拿大与欧盟纸浆生产商之间的协议在欧盟内实施，因此欧盟委员会有权调查加拿大与欧盟纸浆生

---

① 《里斯本条约》生效后，“欧洲联盟（欧盟）”取代先前一直使用的“欧洲经济共同体（欧共体）”，原欧共体委员会变更为欧盟委员会。为写作方便，本文统一使用了欧盟委员会这一名称。

② Revised Recommendation of the OECD Council concerning Cooperation between Member Countries on Anti-competitive Practices Affecting International Trade, July 27 and 28, 1995, C (95) 130/FINAL.

③ Revised Recommendation of the OECD Council concerning Cooperation between Member Countries on Anti-competitive Practices Affecting International Trade.

厂商之间的卡特尔行为。[①] 欧盟法院的这一判决，伴随着《第139/2004号合并条例》的实施，很大程度上增加了欧盟与美国竞争主管机构管辖权冲突的可能性。[②] 第三，大量使用激励和宽泛性语言的经合组织推行《推荐意见》不足以解决竞争执法合作中的问题。第四，如果竞争主管机构希望避免对同一合并作出不同的审查决定，那么欧盟《第139/2004号合并条例》的实施使得这种合作至关重要。

当前，随着欧盟与美国在合并控制领域国际合作的进一步深入，这种合作已经变得日益制度化和规则化。以UTC/Goodrich为例。[③] 在该合并中，欧盟委员会、美国司法部和加拿大竞争局在合并审查中通过紧密合作确保了实体分析和时间方面的密切配合，最终使三家执法机构在同一天签发了各自的最终决定。

1. 1991年协定

1991年9月，欧盟与美国签署《欧共体委员会与美国政府关于适用各自竞争法问题的协定》（以下简称《1991年协定》）。[④] 由于法国等成员国质疑协定的有效性，欧盟法院在1994年判决中要求《1991年协定》应当由欧盟理事会和委员会以共同决定方式重新确认。[⑤] 1995年4月，欧盟理事会和委员会通过共同决定认可了该协定，协定生效日追溯至欧盟委员会

---

① Ahlstrm and Others v. Commission（"Wood Pulp"），Joined Cases 89，104，114，116，117，125－129/85，1988 E. C. R. 5193.

② Council Regulation（EC） No 139/2004 of January 2004 on the control of concentrations between undertakings（the EC Merger Regulation）（Text with EEA relevance），http://eur-lex. europa. eu/legal-content/en/ALL/？uri = CELEX：32004R0139，Last visited January 20 2018. 该条例是对原《第4064/89号合并条例》的修正，主要涉及共同体规模的集中控制应当向欧盟委员会进行事先申报并接受审查等内容。

③ European Commission，COMP/M. 6410 － UTC/Goodrich，Commission Decision dated 26 July 2012；US DOJ，26 July 2012；Canada Competition Bureau（statement），26 July 2012.

④ Agreement between the Government of the United States of America and the Commission of the European Communities regarding the application of their competition laws（1995 O. J. L95/47）. 《1991年协定》在欧盟的适用范围包括《欧盟运行条约》第101条和102条（原《欧共体条约》第81条和82条）《合并控制条例》以及欧盟内的其他实施条例；协定在美国的适用范围包括《谢尔曼法》、《克莱顿法》、《威尔逊关税法》和《联邦贸易委员会法》，但不包括法律中涉及消费者保护的条款。

⑤ France v. Commission，Case C－327/91，1994 E. C. R. I－3641. 在该案中，法国等成员国认为，根据条约规定，欧盟委员会没有签订类似协定的权利。最终，法院支持了成员国的观点，并要求理事会对协定进行重新确认。

签署协定之时。[①]《1991 年协定》为欧盟委员会和美国反托拉斯执法机构之间的国际合作提供了基本的框架。协定涉及签字各方的 5 项主要义务，分别是：通知对方执法活动有可能影响对方活动、交换信息、提供协助、在竞争执法中提供合作以及注意对方的重要利益。[②]

《1991 年协定》的条款都是非强制性的，条款的实施取决于欧盟与美国各竞争主管机构合作的意愿。[③] 协定没有制裁或者处罚不合作竞争主管机构的条款。虽然这有可能被认为《1991 年协定》的不足和缺陷，然而这样的规定恰恰反映了欧盟与美国竞争主管机构在签署协定时的愿望——限制双方主管机构在技术交流合作上的义务，将合作与交流纳入各国国内法和政策目标的调整范围。[④]

根据《1991 年协定》，欧盟与美国竞争主管机构可以分享各自法律没有禁止分享的信息，并且各方在取得对方提供的信息后应当保守秘密。鉴于欧盟和美国在竞争法律方面存在限制，初次申报以及经请求后提交的文件材料等保密信息均不得进行交换。[⑤] 未经信息来源方的同意，双方竞争主管机构也不可以向对方披露保密信息。[⑥] 实践中，欧盟与美国竞争主管机构均会要求交易申报方签署允许信息交换的权利豁免文件。

2. 1999 年行政安排

1999 年，欧盟与美国签署了《1999 年关于出席听证与会议的行政安排》（1999 Administrative Arrangement on Attendance）（以下简称《1999 年

---

① Decision of the Council and the Commission of 10 April 1995 concerning the Conclusion of the Agreement between the European Communities and the Government of the United States of America regarding the Application of their Competition Laws (95/45/EC, ECSC), published in 1995 O. J. (L95/47).

② 参见 Agreement between the Government of the United States of America and the Commission of the European Communities regarding the Application of their Competition Laws。

③ Art V (4), Agreement between the Government of the United States of America and the Commission of the European Communities regarding the Application of their Competition Laws.

④ Art. Ⅸ, Agreement between the Government of the United States of America and the Commission of the European Communities regarding the Application of their Competition Laws. 该条规定，协定适用的方式与欧盟与美国各自既有法律相一致，与各自州法或者成员国既有法律相一致。

⑤ Art. Ⅷ (1), Agreement between the Government of the United States of America and the Commission of the European Communities regarding the Application of their Competition Laws.

⑥ Art. Ⅷ (2), Agreement between the Government of the United States of America and the Commission of the European Communities regarding the Application of their Competition Laws.

行政安排》)，以竞争主管机构间备忘录的形式对协定各方在执法活动和交流方面的合作与协调作了进一步阐述。[①]

《1999年行政安排》详细解释了欧盟委员会和美国联邦反托拉斯执法机构与合并当事各方共同组织联合听证与会议的可行性。双方竞争主管机构一致同意允许对方接触自己的决策程序。欧盟委员会同意美国反托拉斯调查人员在涉及双方同时审查的跨境合并中列席委员会的听证。1999年双方的往来函件明确规定了这种安排。作为交换，美国反托拉斯执法机构同意开放其“定调会”（pitch meeting）——合并申报企业最后一次说服美国高层反托拉斯官员不要采取行动——这些问题同样也是欧盟委员会审查关注的事项。

需要注意的是，《1999年行政安排》设置了条件限制，出席听证和会议最终需要由欧盟与美国各自的竞争主管机构决定。这些限制包括：调查方必须同意对方代表的出席、双方必须确保保守秘密以及各方竞争主管机构在特定案件中可以拒绝对方机构的出席。

3. 欧盟与美国国际合作最佳实践

经历了2001年通用与霍尼韦尔合并案失败的合作机制以后，[②] 欧盟

---

① Bulletin EU 3 – 1999, Competition (18/43); 1999 Report from Commission to the Council and the European Parliament, at 5, COM (2000) 618 final (Oct. 10, 2000); Bulletin EU 3 – 1999, Competition (18/43); 1999 Report, at, COM (2000) 618 final.

② Case COMP/M. 2220, Commission decision of July 3, 2001 (2004 O. J. L 48/1). 在本案中，欧盟委员会和美国司法部在5个主要问题上得出了完全相反的结论：通用电气在大型商用飞机引擎市场合同订单中占有45%的份额是否构成市场支配地位；合并后的企业预计是否会捆绑销售航电和非航电设备，如果答案为是，那么它的排他策略是否能够成功；通用电气对飞机租赁业务的纵向整合是否会产生封锁效应；通用电气的财务能力是否能够通过要求霍尼韦尔在研发领域增加投资并为其客户提供更低价格的方式损害竞争；以及降价是否可以通过迫使竞争对手离开市场而损害竞争。通用电气和霍尼韦尔合并案以后，美国联邦反托拉斯执法机构和欧盟委员会努力避免双方的分歧，展开了“以平静和类似商业合作为特点”的执法合作。正如欧盟委员会副主席尼莉·克罗斯所说，“国际合作对于现代竞争主管机构至关重要……竞争主管机构间的积极双边合作具有不容置疑的价值”。需要注意的是，未来通用电气与霍尼韦尔合并案中所碰到的分歧预计会很少出现。这很大程度上反映了欧盟与美国竞争主管机构避免这种分歧的决心。美国反托拉斯执法机构认为，这种明显分歧非常令人担忧，主要原因有三。第一，在涉及全球市场的合并案件中，阻止合并的司法辖区会存在很强的外部效应，它的行为事实上否定了合并给全球消费者所带来的利益。第二，欧盟与美国之间不同的实体标准基本上肯定会增加与合并审查程序相关的交易成本，其结果是吓阻有利于竞争且提高效率的合并。第三，这种明显分歧会损害赞成反托拉斯执法的政治共识，这也是任何一方所不愿意看到的。

与美国合并工作组[①]开始着手准备《合并调查期间开展合作的最佳实践》(以下简称《国际合作最佳实践》)。[②] 2002 年 10 月，欧盟委员会与美国联邦反托拉斯执法机构正式发布了《国际合作最佳实践》。[③]《国际合作最佳实践》旨在“促进双方的执法机构充分了解彼此决策，减少双方得出不同结果的风险，促进在合并救济上的协调和一致性，提高欧盟与美国各自的调查效率，减少合并当事各方和第三方的负担，增加合并审查程序的整体透明度”。[④]《国际合作最佳实践》反映了欧盟与美国监管机构的共同观点，即定期交流对于避免审查决定的不一致是极为重要的。[⑤]

《国际合作最佳实践》是对过去欧盟与美国竞争主管机构在合并控制领域非正式合作实践的概括与总结。《国际合作最佳实践》强调了合并当事各方放弃保密权的重要性，虽然指南表明当事各方拒绝放弃保密权不构成妨碍竞争评估，但是指南仍强烈建议合并当事各方放弃该权利。[⑥] 指南还重复强调了联合会议的重要性，包括有欧盟竞争专员或者其代表以及美国联邦反托拉斯执法机构高级官员出席的会议等。[⑦] 更为重要的是，《国际合作最佳实践》讨论了协调合并程序中的时间问题，并建议或者通知联合会议应在调查程序的某些阶段召开。[⑧]

2011 年 10 月，在《国际合作最佳实践》发布 10 周年之际，欧盟委员会、美国司法部和联邦贸易委员会 3 家执法机构再次肯定了相互间有益的合作关系，并发布了修订后的《合并调查期间开展合作的最佳实践》（以

---

① 1999 年 10 月，欧盟委员会和美国联邦反托拉斯执法机构成立工作组以审查共同议题，从合并的个案中提取经验。工作组最初侧重于合并救济，工作组所作出的努力在欧盟委员会《关于救济的通告》中得以体现。

② “International Cooperation Best Practices on Cooperation in Merger Investigations”, October 30, 2002, available at http://europa. eu. int/comm/competition/mergers/others/eu_us. pdf.

③ International Cooperation Best Practices Guidelines in Merger Investigations.

④ International Cooperation Best Practices Guidelines in Merger Investigations, para. 2.

⑤ 参见 Charles A. James, “International Antitrust in the 21st Century: Cooperation and Convergence, before the OECD Global Forum on Competition”, Paris, France, October 17, 2001, http://www. oecd. org/daf/competition/prosecutionandlawenforcement/2438935. pdf. , last visited January 20, 2018。

⑥ Art. Ⅲ, International Cooperation Best Practices Guidelines in Merger Investigations.

⑦ Art. Ⅻ, International Cooperation Best Practices Guidelines in Merger Investigations.

⑧ Arts. Ⅳ, Ⅴ, International Cooperation Best Practices Guidelines in Merger Investigations.

下简称《最佳实践》）。[①]

三　合并调查中的通知、交流与信息交换

（一）合并调查中的通知、交流

欧盟与美国竞争主管机构在合并调查中负有对涉及对方重要利益的事项相互通知的义务。双方竞争主管机构在意识到各自的执法活动有可能影响对方的重要利益时有义务通知对方。[②] 在这里，需要通知的情况包括：请求对方提供位于对方司法辖区内的非公开信息；调查依据对方法律设立、组织或者从事经营的有关企业；调查对方司法辖区内发生的或者对方政府鼓励或者批准的行为；考虑对对方司法辖区内需要实施或者禁止的行为实施救济等。[③] 一般而言，重要利益容易受到来自对方执法活动、对方地域内的反竞争行为、根据对方法律实施合并行为或者在对方地域内对反竞争行为实施救济等因素的影响。[④]

《1991 年协定》对通知的时间作了安排。由于欧盟和美国在合并审查程序法律方面存在差异，因此协定对通知时间作了细化性规定。在欧盟，根据《第 139/2004 号合并条例》进行申报的交易，在交易通告公布在欧盟《官方通讯》上或者欧盟委员会决定启动第二阶段调查时，委员会应当

---

① BEST PRACTICES ON COOPERATION IN MERGER INVESTIGATIONS，http://ec. europa. eu/competition/mergers/legislation/best_practices_2011_en. pdf. Seehttp://ec. europa. eu/competition/mergers/legislation/best_practices_2011_en. pdf. 参见 http://ec. europa. eu/competition/mergers/legislation/best_practices_2011_en. pdf。又见 http://www. ftc. gov/sites/default/files/attachments/international-antitrust-and-consumer-protection-cooperation-agreements/111014eumerger. pdf，last visited January 20，2018。

② Art. Ⅱ（1），Agreement between the Government of the United States of America and the Commission of the European Communities regarding the application of their competition laws.

③ OECD，"Recommendation concerning International Co-operation on Competition Investigations and Proceedings 2014"，http://www. ftc. gov/system/files/documents/cooperation_agreements/140916cooperationagreeoecd. pdf.

④ Art. Ⅱ（2），Agreement between the Government of the United States of America and the Commission of the European Communities regarding the Application of their Competition Laws.

通知对方机构;[①] 在美国，美国联邦反托拉斯执法机构对拟议交易提出进一步信息请求或者材料（也称为“第二次请求”）或者决定反对既定交易时，联邦反托拉斯执法机构有义务通知对方竞争主管机构。[②] 至于其他事项，各方竞争主管机构应在申报时尽快通知对方，在任何情况下，通知应在通知方对交易提出正式反对或者作出决定前进行。[③]

在合并调查中，欧盟与美国竞争主管机构会就案件的情况进行相互交流。双方竞争主管机构的交流性质和次数取决于审查案件的特点。[④] 例如，在调查开始阶段，欧盟委员会和美国司法部或者联邦贸易委员会会在考虑合并性质和时间后就机构间协商的暂定时间达成一致。实践中，双方竞争主管机构间保持持续通气非常有益，特别是机构间磋商在调查的关键阶段尤为重要。[⑤]《最佳实践指南》指出，高级官员间的磋商在任何时候都是合适的；各竞争主管机构的高级官员应熟悉整个调查的关键问题；经济专家在合并调查的适当阶段也可以进行磋商。[⑥] 在拜耳与安内特合并案中，欧盟与美国竞争主管机构在调查中进行了持续交流。[⑦] 该案中，欧盟与美国竞争主管机构考虑了种子处理产品和杀虫剂、除草剂和杀菌剂市场如何在农业部门中占主要地位。[⑧] 经合并当事各方同意放弃保密权并推动欧盟与美国竞争主管机构间的深度合作，欧盟与美国竞争主管机构最终在对合并附加了无数剥离救济和其他条件后批准了该交易。[⑨]

鉴于双方竞争主管机构在调查开始阶段的合作颇为有益，《最佳实践

---

① Art. Ⅱ（3）（b），Agreement between the Government of the United States of America and the Commission of the European Communities regarding the Application of their Competition Laws.

② Art. Ⅱ（3）（a），Agreement between the Government of the United States of America and the Commission of the European Communities regarding the Application of their Competition Laws.

③ Art. Ⅱ（4），Agreement between the Government of the United States of America and the Commission of the European Communities regarding the Application of their Competition Laws.

④ Art. Ⅱ，Best Practices On Cooperation In Merger Investigations.

⑤ Art. Ⅲ，Best Practices On Cooperation In Merger Investigations.

⑥ Art. Ⅱ，Best Practices On Cooperation In Merger Investigations.

⑦ Bayer/Aventis Crop Science，Case No. COMP/M. 2547，available at http://ec. europa. eu/competition/mergers/cases/decisions/m2547_en. pdf. ，last visited in January 20，2018.

⑧ 参见 Commission Deepens Probe into Bayer's Acquisition of Aventis Crop Science，European Commission（Dec. 4，2001），available at http://europa. eu. int/rapid/pressReleasesAction. do? reference = IP/01/1736. ，last visited in January 20，2018。

⑨ 参见 Commission Deepens Probe into Bayer's Acquisition of Aventis Crop Science，European Commission（Dec. 4，2001）。

指南》建议，双方竞争主管机构应指定联系人员负责建立各机构相关调查人员的交流日程，与合并当事各方讨论协调各自调查时间的可能性，协调信息和证据的搜集以及要求合并当事各方和第三方当事人放弃保密权等事宜。①

（二）合并调查中的信息交换

《1991 年协定》对特定交易或者业务的基本信息交换进行了规定。②这意味着欧盟委员会与美国联邦反托拉斯执法机构在合并调查期间同意交换合并当事各方所提供的信息。然而，由于美国和欧盟对信息交换的法律规定存在不同，因此这种分歧必然对双方的合作措施产生一定的影响。③

例如，在欧盟，《理事会第 17/62 号条例》第 20 条或者其他竞争条例中有关条款所涉及的信息在任何情况下完全有可能不提供给美国联邦反托拉斯执法机构。④《第 1/2003 号条例》⑤和《第 139/2004 号合并条例》⑥同样禁止在调查程序期间披露从当事各方取得的信息。当然，在合并当事各方同意放弃其保密权从而促进欧盟双边合作时，信息交换是有可能实现的。有些人认为，跨国合并的当事方在交换保密信息有可能导致民事或者刑事责任的情况下是不太愿意放弃保密权的。⑦实践中，这种担心在涉及卡特尔和其他反竞争协议而非合并的案件中得到证实。在合并中，由于合并当事各方最不愿意见到的场景就是竞争主管机构禁止拟议交易，因此当事各方对信息交换持赞成态度，并且放弃保密权的程序成为一种习惯做法。

---

① 参见 Best Practices On Cooperation In Merger Investigations。

② Agreement between the Government of the United States of America and the European Communities regarding the application of their competition laws〔1995 OJ（L 131\38）〕, Art. Ⅲ.

③ Scoe B. Starek, Ⅲ, Former Commissioner, International Cooperation in Antitrust Enforcement, available at http://www.ftc.gov/public-statements/1997/09/international-cooperation-antitrust-enforcement#N_16_, September 29, 1997, last visited January 20, 2018.

④ Council Regulation 62/17, First Regulation Implementing Articles 85 and 86 of the Treaty, 1959—1962 O. J. Spec. Ed. 87. 这里的条约是指《罗马条约》。

⑤ Council Regulation（EC）No. 1/2003, of 16 December 2002, art. 20, 2003 O. J.（L L1/1）1.

⑥ ECMR, Art. 17.

⑦ 参见 Cornelis Canenbley, Michael Rosenthal, "Cooperation Between Antitrust Authorities In and Outside the EU: What Does it Mean for Multinational Corporations?", *European Competition Law Review* 26 (2006), pp. 185 - 218。

美国和欧盟关于信息交换的不同法律规定影响了双方竞争主管机构信息交换的范围。在美国，即使没有合并当事各方的同意，保密信息也可以传递给合作方的竞争主管机构。按照美国《1994 年国际反托拉斯执法协助法》，信息交流应遵循互惠原则。[①] 因此，只要一方竞争主管机构还能够提供保密信息，那么另一方就可以分享信息。然而，如上所述，欧盟委员会不可能将保密信息透露给美国联邦反托拉斯执法机构。因此，在合并当事各方决定双方竞争主管机构是否应披露保密信息时，这种情况不可避免地会对双方的合作程序提出挑战。结果就是，欧盟和美国的竞争主管机构在拥有不同信息时完全有可能会得出不同的结论。事实上，双方竞争主管机构不仅在评估反竞争影响方面有所不同，而且在市场份额及其他数据的计算上也是不同的。

合并当事各方放弃对有关信息的保密权可以促进欧盟与美国竞争主管机构的合作和信息交换。随着欧盟与美国反垄断司法辖区在合并审查实体法律方面的趋同，合并当事各方逐渐意识到在合并审查程序期间向所有竞争主管机构披露信息符合它们的最佳利益。在欧盟与美国竞争主管机构对合并交易进行反垄断审查过程中，特别是合并审查的第二阶段，双方竞争主管机构会要求合并当事各方提供信息以评估市场结构。这些信息基本是类似的，涉及合并当事各方的市场份额、相关产品或者服务的特征。因此，合并当事各方允许交换保密信息将极大促进双方竞争主管机构的合作，并使调查程序省时高效。

实践中，人们对《1991 年协定》的通知和披露条款存在误解，认为这为操纵合并审查打开了方便之门，理由是涉及某些战略性披露的企业如向合作中的欧盟与美国竞争主管机构提供不同数量的信息会影响两方竞争主管机构各自的决定。[②] 合并当事各方有时候确实会乐见欧盟与美国竞争主

---

① 参见 Charles S. Stark，“Chief of Foreign Commerce Section，Antitrust Division，US Department of Justice，International Aspects of Antitrust Enforcement：A US Perspective”（Feb. 13 – 14，1995），available at http://www. justice. gov/atr/public/speeches/0156. htm，last visited January 20，2018。

② Marianne Brun-Rovet，Joshua Chaffin，Caroline Daniel and James Harding，“US：Boeing's Skillful Lobbying Efforts，Financial Times”，Dec. 8，2003，available at http://www. corpwatch. org/article. php? id = 7856，last visited January 20，2018.

管机构之间的摩擦，正如波音与麦道合并案所出现的情况。[①] 在波音和麦道合并案中，美国联邦反托拉斯执法机构和美国政府对欧盟委员会作了大量游说工作以推动委员会赞成该合并。[②] 然而，这种案件在实践中非常少见，且在合并当事各方没有披露信息时，竞争主管机构间的合作程序只会放慢速度，当事各方将不得不分别应对各家竞争主管部门的审查。这明显会延长审查程序，更为重要的是，合并时间安排会大受影响。由于欧盟和美国在合并控制制度程序法律方面的差异，因此这是有可能出现的。

为避免这种破坏性影响，竞争主管机构通常会要求合并当事各方授权一揽子非披露豁免。[③] 这样欧盟与美国竞争主管机构就可以审查相同文件和信息，从而推动所有竞争主管机构在特定案件中作出类似决定。此外，按照《1999 年行政安排》和《最佳实践》，竞争主管机构和合并当事各方有机会见面、交换和讨论当事各方为合并评估所提供的信息。[④] 当前，为了方便当事各方提供必要信息，欧盟与美国竞争主管机构共同建立了问卷调查表为合并当事各方提供指导。[⑤] 问卷调查表为双方竞争主管机构共同关心事项所进行的决策提供了信息基础，它并不是竞争主管机构要求合并当事各方提供信息的官方正式文件或者表格。这样的安排进一步显示了欧盟与美国合作机制的灵活性和技术性特点。

---

① 参见 Marianne Brun-Rovet, Joshua Chaffin, Caroline Daniel and James Harding, "US: Boeing's Skillful Lobbying Efforts", *Financial Times* Dec. 8, 2003。

② Barry Schweid, "US Wants Europe Backing on Merger, AllPolitics", July 22, 1997, available at http://legalminds. lp. findlaw. com/list/antitrust/msg00527. html, last visited January 20, 2018.

③ Common use of this practice is reflected in Art. 1. 2. 1 of the Report from the Commission to the Council and the European Parliament on the application of the agreements between the European Communities and the Government of the United States of America and the Government of Canada regarding the application of their competition laws 1 January 2002 to 31 December 2002, available at http://ec. europa. eu/comm/competition/international/bilateral/canada/2002_report_en. pdf, last visited January 20, 2018.

④ US-EU Merger Working Group, Best Practices on Cooperation in Merger Investigations, http://ec. europa. eu/competition/mergers/legislation/best_practices_2011_en. pdf, last visited January 20, 2018.

⑤ William J. Kolasky, "Global Competition Convergence and Cooperation: Looking Back and Looking Ahead", American Bar Association Fall Forum, Washington DC, November 7, 2002, available at http://www. usdoj. gov/atr/public/speeches/200442. htm, last visited January 20, 2018.

四 合并调查中的协调

除了相互通知各自行动以及进行信息交换外，欧盟与美国竞争主管机构还相互协调各自的执法活动。[①] 在考虑协调执法活动是否存在必要性时，双方竞争主管机构会考虑资源的有效利用、信息收集的方便程度、执法目标的协调效果以及执法活动成本等问题。由于协调会对各竞争主管机构造成成本压力，因此双方竞争主管机构不得不在个案中衡量这种协调的成本与利益或者协调的程度和类型。[②] 当前，欧盟与美国竞争主管机构对涉及世界市场或者合并救济影响整个交易的案件进行了更为广泛的协调。

由于欧盟与美国竞争主管机构间的协调旨在避免相互冲突的审查方法和审查决定，减少重复的执法成本和充分利用各自的执法资源，因此，只有竞争主管机构调查时间表允许双方在合并调查过程中进行有效沟通，协调才是最为有效的。[③]

为便于协调，双方竞争主管机构采取了许多有效的做法，包括：在各自合并调查期间相互通知重要进展；尽力协调各自调查阶段，包括与合并当事各方和其他执法机构一起联合呼吁或者举行会议来讨论、协调各自的调查时间；提供作出审查决定所适用的时间表；在适当情形下要求所调查的当事各方和第三方当事人向合作中的对方竞争主管机构主动放弃保密权；在符合各自保密义务情况下分享公开信息；协调和讨论各自对案件的有关分析，包括市场界定、评估竞争效果和效率、竞争损害理论、经济理论以及检验这些理论的经验证据；协调合并救济的设计和实施；以及探索新的合作机制等。[④]

---

① 参见 Agreement between the Government of the United States of America and the Commission of the European Communities regarding the Application of their Competition Laws。

② Art. Ⅳ（2），Agreement between the Government of the United States of America and the Commission of the European Communities regarding the Application of their Competition Laws.

③ US-EU Merger Working Group，Best Practices on Cooperation in Merger Investigations.

④ OECD，"Recommendation concerning International Co-operation on Competition Investigations and Proceedings 2014"，http://www.ftc.gov/system/files/documents/cooperation_agreements/140916cooperationagreeoecd.pdf（last visited January 20，2018）. 又见 Art. Ⅱ（6），Best Practices On Cooperation In Merger Investigations。

合并当事各方的参与和配合对欧盟与美国竞争主管机构协调调查有着重要影响。如果合并当事各方在向欧盟与美国竞争主管机构申报合并后就与各竞争主管机构讨论协调的问题，那么交易通过审查的时间将明显缩短。因此，为促进双方竞争主管机构的讨论，合并当事各方在申报阶段就应向各竞争主管机构提供有关合并的基本信息，包括：合并当事各方的名称及活动、从事商业的地理范围、相关部门、交易在其他国家的申报、交易在各司法辖区申报的时间以及与合并时间有关的问题。①

跨境合并促进竞争主管机构协调的一个重要选择就是合并当事各方在欧盟和美国两大反垄断司法辖区展开平行申报。如果合并申报在欧盟和美国不是同时进行的，那么只有申报时间允许双方竞争主管机构在关键阶段进行协调才可以使合作具有意义。在考虑合并申报时间时，交易当事各方应考虑竞争主管机构的程序，特别是初始阶段；申报时间还应允许各竞争主管机构在调查关键决策阶段进行有意义的交流和合作。②

合并当事各方推动机构间协调的时间窗口有：欧盟委员会开始申报前磋商或者第一阶段调查以及美国联邦反托拉斯执法机构开始调查时，合并当事各方预计欧盟委员会以附带承诺方式在第一阶段批准合并以及美国联邦反托拉斯执法机构将签发第二次信息请求或者诉诸合并救济时，欧盟委员会启动第二阶段调查以及美国联邦反托拉斯执法机构签发第二次信息请求时。③

需要注意的是，欧盟与美国竞争主管机构在合并调查中的协调不影响各机构基于各自调查程序独立作出审查决定的权力。

五　合并调查中的礼让

在合并控制领域，法学界对国际礼让原则的解释存在高度分歧。④ 为

① Art. Ⅲ (9), Best Practices On Cooperation In Merger Investigations.

② Art. Ⅲ (10), Best Practices On Cooperation In Merger Investigations.

③ Art. Ⅲ (11), Best Practices On Cooperation In Merger Investigations.

④ Alexandr Svetlicinii, "Cooperation Between Merger Control Authorities of the EU and the U. S. A Viable Solution for Transatlantic Mergers?", *U. C. Davis Bus. L. J.* 7 (2006), http://blj.ucdavis.edu/archives/vol-7-no-1/cooperation-between-merger-control-authorities-of-the-eu-and-the-u.s..html, last visited January 20, 2018.

此，《1991 年协定》引入了传统礼让程序。根据该程序，各竞争主管机构方在执法的所有阶段均应考虑对方的重要利益，特别是在作出审查决定和使用合并救济的阶段。[①] 在波音与麦道合并案中，欧盟委员会在审查决定中“注意到了《欧盟与美国政府关于适用各自竞争法的协定》内容，特别是协定第 2 条和第 6 条的规定”[②]。

《1991 年协定》还引入了积极礼让程序。根据协定，一方竞争主管机构可以请求对方竞争主管机构在其司法辖区内启动适当执法活动，并在被请求方同意的情况下请求对影响请求方重要利益的反竞争行为实施救济；[③] 被请求活动属于违反被请求方竞争法律的反竞争行为；[④] 被请求方有义务决定是否启动执法活动，以及是否通知请求方作出决定的结果。[⑤] 《1991 年协定》积极礼让条款所规定的合作水平远远超过了美国双边条约、欧盟与中东欧国家间协定所包含的内容。[⑥]

积极礼让程序在《1998 年欧盟与美国积极礼让协定》（以下简称《1998 年协定》）中得到进一步解释。[⑦] 在某些情况下，一方竞争主管机构可以推迟或者中止其执法活动以支持对方竞争主管机构带头行动阻击存在问题的反竞争行为。[⑧] 然而，需要注意的是，由于欧盟和美国的合并程序规则均不允许延长或者中止合并调查，因此《1998 年协定》并不适用于合

---

① Art. Ⅵ (1), Agreement between the Government of the United States of America and the Commission of the European Communities regarding the application of their competition laws.

② Council Regulation (EEC) No. 4064/89, of 30 July 1997, Case No. IV/M. 877, available at http://ec. europa. eu/competition/mergers/cases/decisions/m877_19970730_600_en. pdf.

③ Art. Ⅴ (1) -Ⅴ (2), Agreement between the Government of the United States of America and the Commission of the European Communities regarding the application of their competition laws.

④ Art. Ⅴ (1), Agreement between the Government of the United States of America and the Commission of the European Communities regarding the application of their competition laws.

⑤ Art. Ⅴ (3), Agreement between the Government of the United States of America and the Commission of the European Communities regarding the application of their competition laws.

⑥ JOEL I. KLEIN, Acting Assistant Attorney General of U. S. Department of Justice, “The Internationalization of Antitrust: Bilateral and Multilateral Responses”, June 13, 1997, http://www. justice. gov/atr/public/speeches/1580. htm, last visited January 20, 2018.

⑦ 1998 O. J. (L 173) 28 Agreement between the European Communities and the Government of the United States of America on the application of positive comity principles in the enforcement of their competition laws173 28 -31 (1998). 1998 年 6 月，欧盟和美国修改了《1991 年协定》内的积极礼让条款。

⑧ Art. Ⅳ, 1991 Agreement.

并控制。虽然如此，欧盟与美国竞争主管机构对《1998 年协定》的评价还是很高的。正如前欧盟委员会竞争专员蒙帝所说，“这种颇具创新性的合作安排为双边合作带来了崭新的途径，为竞争主管机构间合理分摊执法负担提供了可能”①。

实践中，积极礼让原则在合并案件中并不常用。② 由于主张对合并交易具有管辖权的国家均设置了合并申报门槛，如欧盟对合并申报设置了共同体规模的门槛以及美国对合并申报设置了销售额门槛，因此合并当事各方不得不疲于应付来自各家竞争主管机构的审查。鉴于管辖权问题使得合并交易不可能移送给最适合对交易进行调查的单个竞争主管机构，当前各国竞争主管机构在合并调查方面的合作完全依赖于联合通知、讨论和协调。③

六 合并救济方面的合作

合并救济，又称为附条件批准集中，通常是指为了减少合并对竞争产生的不利影响，竞争主管机构对不予禁止的合并附加限制性条件的一种制度，是合并控制法律制度的重要组成部分。④ 鉴于合并救济在合并控制法律制度中的重要性，欧盟与美国竞争主管机构间的双边合作包括了双方在对合并当事各方施加救济和制裁措施方面的合作。

合作对双方竞争主管机构以及需要考虑救济的合并当事各方是非常有价值的。⑤ 跨国合并经常涉及多个司法辖区的管辖，这些司法辖区内的竞

---

① 参见 Cornelis Canenbley，Michael Rosenthal，“Cooperation Between Antitrust Authorities in and Outside the EU：What Does it Mean for Multinational Corporations?”，*European Competition Law Review* 26（2006）。

② Alexandr Svetlicinii，“Cooperation Between Merger Control Authorities of the EU and the U. S. A Viable Solution for Transatlantic Mergers?”，U. C. Davis Bus. L. J. 7（2006）. http://blj. ucdavis. edu/archives/vol-7-no-1/cooperation-between-merger-control-authorities-of-the-eu-and-the-u. s. html，last visited January 20，2018.

③ Alexandr Svetlicinii，“Cooperation Between Merger Control Authorities of the EU and the U. S. A Viable Solution for Transatlantic Mergers?”，U. C. Davis Bus. L. J. 7（2006）.

④ 金美蓉：《欧美反垄断制度中合并救济的一般原则》，《国家行政学院学报》2012 年第 3 期，第 64 页。

⑤ Art. Ⅰ，Best Practices On Cooperation In Merger Investigations.

争主管机构完全有可能根据各自国内法对合并交易适用国内救济和制裁。例如，在合并控制执法中，一方竞争主管机构所要求的承诺可能会超过了另一合作方所要求的内容。另外，当某个合并案件涉及全球市场或者至少影响欧盟和美国时，合并当事各方提供给各竞争主管机构使用的承诺就可能是相似或者相同的。此外，竞争主管机构通过合作也可以确保各竞争主管机构所接受的救济不会给合并当事各方带来相互冲突的义务。有鉴于此，合作无论对竞争主管机构还是对合并当事各方都是有意义且是必要的。

实践中，各竞争主管机构在对违规的竞争者施加救济措施时不会考虑相称性原则的适用问题。[①] 例如，在波音与麦道合并案中，为了保护共同体市场内的竞争，欧盟委员会在美国联邦反托拉斯执法机构没有提起诉讼情况下单方要求合并后的企业遵守有关承诺。[②] 因此，欧盟与美国竞争主管机构均认为在设计合并救济措施时机构间的合作与沟通有助于减少摩擦。

一般来说，欧盟与美国竞争主管机构在设计合并救济措施时会考虑合并当事各方的利益，协调合并救济措施建议的时间和内容，从而减少相互冲突的审查决定或者救济实施存在的困难。在不违反保密和披露义务情况下，双方竞争主管机构会在合并救济方面进行合作，与合并当事各方就有关救济进行讨论。

需要强调的是，一事不再理原则在欧盟等司法管辖区被严格解释。[③] 虽然欧洲初审法院在 Lysine 案中认为一事不再理使被告不再受到欧盟委员会发起的第二次制裁程序的影响，但是法院进一步指出，如果欧盟委员会施加的制裁是为了不同目的，那么重复制裁就是合法有效的。[④] 具体而言，虽然合并交易受到了美国联邦反托拉斯执法机构的制裁，然而美国联邦反

① Barry Schweid, "US Wants Europe Backing on Merger", *AllPolitics* July 22, 1997, available at http://legalminds. lp. findlaw. com/list/antitrust/msg00527. html, last visited January 20, 2018.

② Council Regulation (EEC) No. 4064/89, of 30 July 1997, Case No. IV/M. 877, available at http://ec. europa. eu/competition/mergers/cases/decisions/m877_19970730_600_en. pdf.

③ Alexandr Svetlicinii, "Cooperation Between Merger Control Authorities of the EU and the U. S. A Viable Solution for Transatlantic Mergers?", *U. C. Davis Bus. L. J.* 7 (2006). http://blj. ucdavis. edu/archives/vol-7-no-1/cooperation-between-merger-control-authorities-of-the-eu-and-the-u. s. html, last visited January 20, 2018.

④ Archer Daniels Midland v. Comm'n of the European Communities, Case C – 213/28, 2003 E. C. R. II – 2597.

托拉斯执法机构是为了保护美国市场公平竞争，因此，为了保护共同体市场内的有效竞争，欧盟委员会所发起程序以及施加的制裁就不应再适用一事不再理原则。

鉴于跨国公司在合并交易中不得不遵守不同国家竞争主管机构所施加的要求和制裁，欧盟竞争主管机构对该问题的态度引起了跨国公司的严重关切。考虑到《第139/2004号合并条例》规定的罚金是以相关企业的全球营业额为基础而非企业在共同体市场的实际营业额，欧盟委员会没有依据相称性原则制裁那些严重阻碍共同体市场有效竞争的跨大西洋合并的当事各方，实际处罚力度远远超过了欧盟委员会处罚欧盟内部的合并，这无形增加了欧盟与美国竞争主管机构对跨大西洋合并给予双重制裁的风险。①

以通用电气和霍尼韦尔合并案为例。② 该案恰恰反映了欧盟与美国竞争主管机构在不考虑对方司法辖区利益，且对混合合并有不同分析方法时所产生的有关救济的问题。该案中，美国联邦反托拉斯执法机构实际上放弃了对混合合并的反竞争评估，③ 并指出，混合合并的评估不再为美国反托拉斯执法机构视为对有效竞争的威胁。④ 与之相反，欧盟委员会的竞争分析依赖于组合效应理论和其他包括消除潜在竞争者在内的潜在长期效应理论，并认为应该对该合并交易实施剥离救济。美国联邦反托拉斯执法机构对此持批评态度，认为这些理论已经过时。然而从欧盟委员会的观点来

---

① Council Regulation （EC） No 139/2004 of 20 January 2004 on the control of concentrations between undertakings （the EC Merger Regulation）（Text with EEA relevance）, http://eur-lex.europa.eu/legal-content/EN/ALL/; ELX_SESSIONID = Hy0KJxFb2pvC22Nn1D6G7g XlV-vTpqprpxGPSn8vG2VGrzCfysTwl! 1769187027? uri = CELEX: 32004R0139, last visited January 20, 2018. 又见 Alexandr Svetlicinii, "Cooperation Between Merger Control Authorities of the EU and the U.S. A Viable Solution for Transatlantic Mergers?", *U. C. Davis Bus. L. J.* 7 （2006）. http://blj.ucdavis.edu/archives/vol-7-no-1/cooperation-between-merger-control-authorities-of-the-eu-and-the-u.s.html, last visited January 20, 2018。

② Case COMP/M.2220, Commission decision of July 3, 2001 （2004 O.J. L 48/1）.

③ "1968 Merger Guidelines included Section II Vertical Mergers", available at http://www.usdoj.gov/atr/hmerger/11247.htm, last visited January 20, 2018. "1984 Non-Horizontal Merger Guidelines （Section Ⅳ）", available at http://www.justice.gov/atr/public/guidelines/2614.htm, last visited July. 10, 2014, and 1992. "Horizontal Merger Guidelines", available at http://www.usdoj.gov/atr/hmerger/11250.htm, last visited January 20, 2018.

④ 参见 Albert A. Foer, "The Goals of Antitrust: Thoughts on Consumer Welfare", *Working Paper* 05－09, American Antitrust Institute, available at http://papers.ssrn.com/sol3/papers.cfm?abstract_id = 1103510。

看，这些分析方法符合欧盟竞争法及其政策目标。[①]

欧洲初审法院虽然肯定了欧盟委员会在通用电气和霍尼韦尔合并案中的决定，但是认为欧盟委员会存在许多错误，未能提供足够的事实证据佐证其调查。[②] 这最终促使欧盟委员会发布了《非横向合并指南》，并且将以后的审查决定建立在充分证据和严格的经济分析基础之上。[③]

通用电气和霍尼韦尔合并案以后，美国联邦反托拉斯执法机构和欧盟委员会努力避免双方的分歧，展开了“以平静和类似商业合作为特点”的执法合作。[④] 正如欧盟委员会副主席尼莉·克罗斯所说：“国际合作对于现代竞争主管机构至关重要……竞争主管机构间的积极双边合作具有不容置疑的价值。”[⑤] 在 Halliburton/Dresser 合并案件中，欧盟委员会依赖美国司法部的保证解决了对相关市场的担忧，从而减轻了委员会使用有限调查资源应付这一问题的压力。[⑥] 同样，在 WorldCom/MCI 合并案中，当合并救济为欧盟与美国双方竞争主管机构接受时，欧盟委员会也敦促美国联邦反托拉斯执法机构监督合并企业在美国国内遵守剥离救济。[⑦]

---

① Richard Burnley, “Who's Afriad of Conglomerate Mergers? A Comparison of the US and EC Approaches”, *World Competition* 28 (2005).

② Case COMP/M. 2220, Commission decision of July 3, 2001 (2004 O. J. L 48/1).

③ 参见 Nathalie Jalabert-Daury, Laurent et al. Competition Policies, IBLJ 87 - 105 (2006)。又见“Guidelines on the assessment of non-horizontal mergers under the Council Regulation on the control of concentrations between undertakings”, http://eur-lex. europa. eu/legal-content/EN/ALL/; ELX _ SESSIONID = S36NJv2VZ2fKL2t8vkzrSyB81QdWvFPYtgF8Sy928hQw2h5JMV6q!133325 4154? uri = CELEX: 52008XC1018 (03), last visited January 20, 2018。

④ Mario Monti, “Convergence in EU-US Antitrust Policy Regarding Mergers and Acquisitions: An EU Perspective”, UCLA Law First Annual Institute on US and EU Antitrust Aspects of Mergers and Acquisitions, Los Angeles, February 28, 2004 (Commission Press Release SPEECH/04/107).

⑤ Neelie Kroes, “Competition Commissioner, Regulating for competition and growth”, OECD Global Forum on Competition, Paris, February 17, 2005 (Commission Press Release SPEECH/05/98).

⑥ Case N° IV/M. 1140 - Halliburton/Dresser, http://ec. europa. eu/competition/mergers/cases/decisions/m1140_en. pdf.

⑦ “Report From the Commission to the Council and the European Parliament on the application of the agreements between the European Communities and the Government of the United States of America and the Government of Canada regarding the application of their competition laws”, http://ec. europa. eu/transparency/regdoc/rep/1/2002/EN/1 - 2002 - 45 - EN - F1 - 1. Pdf.

需要指出的是，欧盟与美国竞争主管机构在合并救济方面的分歧仍然存在。《1991 年协定》第 6 条虽然明确规定了避免执法活动中的冲突，但是由于协定缺乏实施程序，因此这种冲突仍然会反映在双方竞争主管机构对同一交易各自作出的审查决定中。一方竞争主管机构依据其竞争法域外适用的规定对合并交易施加救济和限制有可能违反对方的法律。以微软案为例，虽然该案并不涉及合并交易，但它展示了欧盟与美国竞争主管机构的分歧。[①] 在该案中，欧盟委员会和美国司法部先后开始调查微软，然而最终欧盟委员会和美国司法部基于各自的竞争法律对微软施加的救济完全不同。[②] 美国国会对该案的反应是非常恼火，而欧盟委员会则认为，整个程序完全符合《1991 年协定》第 6 条的规定。[③]

事实上，当前欧盟与美国各方已经接受了这样一种观点，即在合并控制领域，合作的目的不是使合作各方作出完全相同的审查决定。正如《最佳实践指南》第 1 条所指出的，合并调查期间的合作目的是使竞争主管机构作出的审查决定在可能情况下保持一致或者至少不存在冲突。[④] 从这方面而言，欧盟与美国竞争主管机构对通用电气与霍尼韦尔合并案各自不同的审查决定不是因为合作机制存在问题，而是由于双方在实体法律制度中存在差异。在该案中，美国司法部指出，通过在合并当事各方竞争的领域使用剥离救济，通用电气和霍尼韦尔合并交易不会影响市场竞争。欧盟委员会则基于两个主要异议禁止了合并：首先，欧盟委员会担心通用电气实行“混合捆绑”的政策，销售航电设备零件、非航电设备零件和飞机引擎，从而给没有全套产品线且在飞机引擎或者航电设备上没有市场支配地位的竞争者造成损害；其次，欧盟委员会担心作为全球最大的飞机购买者

---

① 参见 Markus Muller, “The European Commission's Decision against Microsoft: A Violation of the Antitrust Agreements between the United States and the European Union?”, *Eur. Compet. Law Rev* 26 (2005), pp. 309 - 315。

② 参见 Markus Muller, “The European Commission's Decision against Microsoft: A Violation of the Antitrust Agreements between the United States and the European Union?”, *Eur. Compet. Law Rev* 26 (2005), pp. 309 - 315。

③ 参见 Markus Muller, “The European Commission's Decision against Microsoft: A Violation of the Antitrust Agreements between the United States and the European Union?”, *Eur. Compet. Law Rev* 26 (2005), pp. 309 - 315。

④ Article. I, Best Practices On Cooperation In Merger Investigations.

通用飞机租赁公司（GECAS）会影响飞机制造商的决定从而将霍尼韦尔完全排除在产品采购之外。[①]

七　结语

随着同时适用不同竞争规则的机会增加以及世界经济一体化日益向纵深发展，合并控制执法上的双边合作已经变得越来越紧迫。[②] 欧盟与美国竞争主管机构间的双边合作框架为其他国家建立类似合作机制起到了参考作用。今后，各国竞争主管机构通过开展双边合作能够从一致行动、避免冲突的审查结果、支离破碎的救济措施以及取得更高效决定中获益。[③]

欧盟与美国在合并控制领域的双边合作体现了求同存异、协调发展的方针。欧盟与美国在合并控制的实体评估、程序和政策目标上存在一些差异，然而双方竞争主管机构还是采取了双边合作机制来促进合作和减少冲突。在遵守各自竞争法律的基础上，欧盟与美国竞争主管机构在合并调查的通知、交流和信息交换上加强合作；在不影响各竞争主管机构独立作出决定的情况下，欧盟与美国竞争主管机构以个案为基础，鼓励合并当事各方参与和配合审查，加强机构间的有效沟通，开展执法协调；在礼让方面，欧盟与美国竞争主管机构方在包括作出审查决定和使用合并救济等执法阶段会考虑对方的重要利益；在选择合并救济措施上，欧盟与美国竞争主管机构一方面既强调管辖权，另一方面又努力避免双方的分歧，在可能的情况下使各自作出的审查决定保持一致或者至少不存在冲突。

鉴于欧盟与美国竞争主管机构在双边层面竞争执法合作上的引领作用，我国有必要对此加以借鉴。《反垄断法》实施以来，我国反垄断执法

---

① William Kolasky, "U. S. and EU Competition Policy: Cartels, Mergers, and Beyond, Council for the United States and Italy, Bi-Annual Conference", New York, January 25, 2002. 又见 Donna Patterson and Carl Shapiro, "Trans-Atlantic Divergence in GE/Honeywell: Causes and Lessons", 17 Antitrust, Fall 2002, p. 18。

② Eleanor M. Fox, "Can We Control Merger Control? An Experiment, International Bar Association Competition Seminar, European University Institute", Florence, October 2, 1998.

③ 1997 Commission Report to the Council and the Parliament on the Application of the Agreement between the European Communities and the Government of the United States of America regarding the Application of their Competition Laws, COM (99) 439 of September 13, 1999, p. 12.

机构查处了许多在全球范围内有一定影响的案件。然而，在合并控制领域双边合作方面，我国反垄断执法机构与欧盟等反垄断司法辖区缺乏信息共享等合作机制，这影响了我国反垄断执法机构开展对外合作的能力，也不利于我国在审查具有全球影响的经营者集中案件中获取情报和发挥重要作用。当前随着我国已成为世界主要的反垄断司法辖区，我国应该抓住这一历史机遇，借鉴欧盟与美国在合并控制领域的合作机制，加强与其他国家商签竞争执法协定，更好地维护我国国内公平的市场竞争秩序。

（本文原载于《国际法研究》2014 年第 4 期）

“一带一路”背景下的国际海事司法中心建设

张文广*

“一带一路”是“丝绸之路经济带”和“21世纪海上丝绸之路”的简称。2013年9月7日，中国国家主席习近平在哈萨克斯坦纳扎尔巴耶夫大学发表题为“弘扬人民友谊共创美好未来”的重要演讲，倡议用创新的合作模式，共同建设“丝绸之路经济带”，以点带面，从线到片，逐步形成区域大合作。同年10月3日，习近平主席在印度尼西亚国会发表演讲时提出，东南亚地区自古以来就是“海上丝绸之路”的重要枢纽，中国愿同东盟国家加强海上合作，使用好中国政府设立的中国－东盟海上合作基金，发展好海洋合作伙伴关系，共同建设21世纪“海上丝绸之路”。

2015年3月28日，国家发展和改革委员会（以下简称“国家发改委”）、外交部、商务部三部委经国务院授权，联合发布了《推动共建丝绸之路经济带和21世纪海上丝绸之路的愿景与行动》（以下简称《愿景与行动》）。2017年6月20日，国家发改委和国家海洋局联合对外发布《“一带一路”建设海上合作设想》。这是自发布《愿景与行动》以来，中国政府首次就“一带一路”海上合作提出中国方案，北极航道被明确为“一带一路”海上合作的三大通道之一。

至此，“一带一路”的线路更加清晰。“一带”的走向是从中国出发，一是经中亚、俄罗斯至欧洲（波罗的海）；二是经中亚、西亚至波斯湾、地中海；三是至东南亚、南亚、印度洋。“一路”重点建设三条蓝色经济

* 张文广，中国社会科学院国际法研究所国际经济法研究室副研究员。

通道：一是以中国沿海经济带为支撑，连接中国—中南半岛经济走廊，经南海向西进入印度洋，衔接中巴、孟中印缅经济走廊，共同建设中国—印度洋—非洲—地中海蓝色经济通道；二是经南海向南进入太平洋，共建中国—大洋洲—南太平洋蓝色经济通道；三是积极推动共建经北冰洋连接欧洲的蓝色经济通道。

“一带一路”建设旨在打造包容开放的国际合作平台，是中国为世界提供的重要公共产品。2016 年第 71 届联合国大会第 A/71/9 号决议首次写入“一带一路”倡议。截至 2017 年 8 月 17 日，与我国签署共建“一带一路”合作协议的国家和国际组织已达 69 个。①

2017 年 5 月 14—15 日，“一带一路”国际合作高峰论坛在北京召开。这是“一带一路”框架下最高规格的国际活动，也是 1949 年以来由中国首倡，中国主办的层级最高、规模最大的多边外交活动，中国正成为全球治理变革进程的参与者、推动者、引领者。论坛通过《“一带一路”国际合作高峰论坛圆桌峰会联合公报》，承诺将秉持和平合作、开放包容、互学互鉴、互利共赢、平等透明、相互尊重的精神，在共商、共建、共享的基础上，本着法治、机会均等原则加强合作，尊重《联合国宪章》宗旨原则和国际法。

“一带一路”涉及多种运输方式，以及运输方式之间的联运。鉴于我国经济已经是高度依赖海洋的开放型经济，② 海运以及“海运 +”将在“一带一路”建设中发挥重要作用。

在“一带一路”建设中，法治是重要保障，司法作用不可或缺。③ 作为我国司法的国际窗口，涉外商事海事审判工作直接影响着我国司法的国际公信力，直接关系着国家海洋权益和国家利益的维护，直接决定着开放型经济新体制的司法环境。为做好“一带一路”的司法保障工作，2015 年 6 月，最高人民法院发布了《关于人民法院为“一带一路”

① 《69 个国家和国际组织与中国签署共建“一带一路”合作协议》，新华网 http://news.xinhuanet.com/fortune/2017－08/17/c_1121500544.htm，最后访问日期：2017 年 8 月 17 日。

② 国家海洋局：《科学规划统筹安排推动海洋经济迈上新台阶》，《中国海洋报》2013 年 1 月 21 日，第 3 版。

③ 车丕照：《“一带一路”建设与中国法院的国际担当》，《中国审判》2015 年第 15 期，第 16 页。

建设提供司法服务和保障的若干意见》（以下简称《意见》），统一法律适用，明晰裁判规则，为"一带一路"建设营造公平公正的司法环境，夯实"一带一路"建设的法治基础。[①]《意见》实施后，最高人民法院又陆续发布了《关于海事法院受理案件范围的规定》、[②]《关于海事诉讼管辖问题的规定》、[③]《关于审理发生在我国管辖海域相关案件若干问题的规定（一）》、[④]《关于审理发生在我国管辖海域相关案件若干问题的规定（二）》[⑤] 等多项司法解释以及《关于为自由贸易试验区建设提供司法保障的意见》。[⑥]

一 建设国际海事司法中心的提出历程

"海事司法中心"不是一个新提法。早在 1995 年底，时任最高人民法院院长任建新在第十七次全国法院工作会议上提出"在 2010 年之前，使我国成为亚太地区海事司法中心之一"。[⑦]"之一"表明亚太地区可以并存两个或两个以上的海事司法中心。事实上这个提法并没有引起媒体和学术界的太多关注。根据笔者在中国知网上的检索，关于"亚太海事司法中心"的文献不多。较有代表性的文章有二。第一篇刊登在 1997 年 12 月 1 日《瞭望新闻周刊》，题目为《我国正向亚太海事司法中心的目标迈进》。该文解释"亚太地区海事司法中心"的理由有：第一，海事审判工作已有法可

① 刘敬东：《"一带一路"建设的法治化与人民法院的职责》，《人民法治》2015 年第 11 期，第 17 页。

② 法释〔2016〕4 号，2015 年 12 月 28 日由最高人民法院审判委员会第 1674 次会议通过，自 2016 年 3 月 1 日起施行。

③ 法释〔2016〕2 号，2015 年 12 月 28 日由最高人民法院审判委员会第 1674 次会议通过，自 2016 年 3 月 1 日起施行。

④ 法释〔2016〕16 号，2015 年 12 月 28 日由最高人民法院审判委员会第 1674 次会议通过，自 2016 年 8 月 2 日起施行。

⑤ 法释〔2016〕17 号，2016 年 5 月 9 日由最高人民法院审判委员会第 1682 次会议通过，自 2016 年 8 月 2 日起施行。

⑥ 法发〔2016〕34 号。

⑦ 李国光：《提高海事审判公信力推进亚太海事司法中心建设》，《人民法院报》2014 年 9 月 3 日，第 2 版。经过多重验证，第十七次全国法院工作会议确实提出了在 2010 年之前将我国建设成为亚太地区海事司法中心的目标，但第十七次全国法院工作会议的召开时间不是文中所说的 1997 年，而是 1995 年。

依；第二，海事审判有完善的组织保证和人员保证；第三，海事审判工作成效显著。[①] 第二篇刊登在《法律适用》2004 年第 3 期，题目为《把我国建设成为亚太地区海事司法中心之一——全国海事法院派出法庭工作座谈会在深圳召开》。该文是新闻稿，“亚太地区海事司法中心”只是点到为止，并无太多论述。此后近十年，“亚太地区海事司法中心”很少被提及。

2013 年 11 月，在第二十二届全国海事审判研讨会上，时任最高人民法院副院长贺荣首次提出“大力推进国际海事司法中心建设，努力打造具有广泛国际影响力的海事司法品牌”[②]。

2014 年 9 月，在海事法院成立三十周年之际，最高人民法院发布了《中国海事审判白皮书（1984—2014）》，宣布中国海事审判初步确立亚太地区海事司法中心地位。其理由是“目前，我国是世界上设立海事审判专门机构最多最齐全的国家，也是受理海事案件最多的国家，具备较为完善的海事法院制度和海事司法服务保障体系”[③]。在中国海事审判三十周年座谈会上，全国人大常委会副委员长万鄂湘指出：“重点要在海事法治的质量及其国际影响力上下功夫，牢固确立我国在亚太地区海事司法中心的地位。”[④] 最高人民法院原副院长李国光认为，将我国建成亚太地区海事司法中心是由我国海洋大国和海运大国的地位决定的。“与其他国家相比，我国海事法院每年受理的海事海商案件数量及纠纷种类，无论是在亚太地区还是在全球海事司法领域都是最多的。我国当之无愧已经成为亚太海事司法中心。”[⑤] 从上述表述可见，此时所讲的“海事司法中心”，主要是从案件数量角度考虑。

在中国宣布成为亚太地区海事司法中心之后，学者将目光投向国际海事司法中心。2015 年 3 月发布的《中国海事司法透明度指数报告（2014）》中出现了“国际海事司法中心”的提法。该文的重点已由强调海事案件的

① 参见刘会生《我国正向亚太海事司法中心的目标迈进》，《瞭望新闻周刊》1997 年第 48 期，第 22—23 页。

② 张先明：《为海洋生态文明建设提供有效司法保障》，《人民法院报》2013 年 11 月 29 日，第 1 版。

③ 罗书臻：《中国海事审判初步确立亚太海事司法中心地位》，《人民法院报》2014 年 9 月 3 日，第 1 版。

④ 袁定波：《牢固确立亚太海事司法中心地位》，《法制日报》2014 年 9 月 3 日，第 1 版。

⑤ 李国光：《提高海事审判公信力推进亚太海事司法中心建设》，《人民法院报》2014 年 9 月 3 日，第 2 版。

数量转向强调海事审判的国际公信力和影响力。[①]

2015 年 7 月，《最高人民法院关于全面推进涉外商事海事审判精品战略为构建开放型经济新体制和建设海洋强国提供有力司法保障的意见》[②]第 14 条提出“善用法治思维主动研判大局。寻找构建创新型经济新体制、建设海洋强国与涉外商事海事审判的连接点，围绕‘走出去’企业法律风险防范、我国海洋权益保护、国际海事司法中心建设、海洋生态文明司法保障、自贸区法治保障、‘一带一路’法治保障……新问题、新情况开展前瞻性、预判性调研，及时形成调研成果……主动服务国家改革开放战略和建设海洋强国战略”。这是最高人民法院文件中首次出现“国际海事司法中心”的提法。2015 年 12 月，最高人民法院举行海事审判工作改革和发展专题会议，提出“把我国建设成为具有较高国际影响力的国际海事司法中心”的目标，[③] 并于 12 月在青岛成立了国际海事司法研究基地。

2016 年 1 月 23 日，在全国高级法院院长会议上，最高人民法院院长周强提出，要着眼于促进开放发展，围绕实施“一带一路”、海洋强国以及自由贸易区战略，加强商事、海事海商和涉外商事审判，推动完善法治化、国际化、便利化的营商环境，维护我国海洋主权和海洋权益。[④]

2016 年 2 月 17 日，新华社《经济参考报》刊发了笔者题为“海运大国应成为国际海事司法中心”的文章。[⑤]“国际海事司法中心”的提法进一步为海事界、司法界所熟悉。

然而，真正令“国际海事司法中心”成为国内外媒体报道重点的原因发生在 2016 年全国“两会”期间。2016 年 3 月 13 日，最高人民法院院长周强在向全国人民代表大会报告工作时提出，“人民法院将服务和保障‘一带一路’、海洋强国等战略实施，坚决维护国家主权、海洋权益和其他

---

① 参见中国社会科学院法学研究所法治指数创新项目组《中国海事司法透明度指数报告（2014）》，载《中国法治发展报告（2015）》（《法治蓝皮书》），社会科学文献出版社，2015，第 221 页。

② 法〔2015〕205 号。

③ 宁杰：《深入推进海事审判工作改革努力建设具有影响力的国际海事司法中心》，《人民法院报》2015 年 12 月 5 日，第 1 版。

④ 周强：《适应新常态司法要有新作为》，《人民日报》2016 年 1 月 28 日，第 5 版。

⑤ 张文广：《海运大国应成为国际海事司法中心》，《经济参考报》2016 年 2 月 17 日，第 6 版。

核心利益。加强海事审判工作，建设国际海事司法中心"①。国内外媒体迅速对"建设国际海事司法中心"这一提法进行了密集的报道。"中国已成为海事审判机构最多、海事案件数量最多的国家"，大多被境外媒体忽略，其关注的侧重点多是将"建设国际海事司法中心"与所谓"南海仲裁案"联系起来，认为中国试图另起炉灶。②

2016 年 3 月 14 日，外交部发言人在例行记者会上表示，"自 1984 年设立海事法院以来，中国海事审判工作取得了令人瞩目的成就，形成了专门化的海事审判体系，建立健全了海事审判制度。据了解，目前中国已是世界上海事审判机构最多、海事案件数量最多的国家，为加强海事审判工作，今年中国将建设国际海事司法中心。具体情况请你向有关部门了解"。③ 这一表态并没有消除境外媒体的困惑。

2016 年 3 月 18 日，最高人民法院召开全国法院学习贯彻十二届人大四次会议精神电视电话会议，周强院长在会上强调，"要加强商事、海事海商审判，积极推进国际海事司法中心建设，营造法治化、国际化、便利化的营商环境"④。同日，中国社会科学院发布《中国海事司法透明度指数报告（2015）》，阐释了国际海事司法中心的提出历程及重大意义。⑤ 2016 年 3 月 24 日，新华社《经济参考报》刊发了笔者的文章《建设国际海事司法中心需要顶层设计》。⑥ 上述两篇文章受到了境外媒体的关注和引用。2016 年 4 月 5 日，《外交学者》（*The Diplomat*）刊发了题为《中国海事法院——司法主权卫士》的文章，指出"将中国建设成为国际海事司法中

---

① 《两会授权发布：最高人民法院工作报告》，新华网，http://news.xinhuanet.com/politics/2016-03/20/c_1118384470.htm，最后访问日期：2017 年 8 月 12 日。

② 《中国想建国际海事司法中心，外媒有些躁动》，财新网，http://international.caixin.com/2016-03-14/100920077.html，最后访问日期：2017 年 8 月 12 日。

③ 《外交部发言人就今年中国将建设国际海事司法中心等答问》，中国政府网，http://www.gov.cn/xinwen/2016-03/14/content_5053356.htm，最后访问日期：2017 年 8 月 12 日。

④ 罗书臻：《切实回应人民群众期待坚持司法为民公正司法为"十三五"经济社会发展营造良好法治环境》，《人民法院报》2016 年 3 月 19 日，第 1 版。

⑤ 张文广：《加大中国海事司法公开力度，助力国际海事司法中心建设——在〈中国法治发展报告（2016）〉发布会上的发言》，中国法学网，http://www.iolaw.org.cn/showArticle.aspx?id=4708，最后访问日期：2017 年 8 月 11 日。

⑥ 张文广：《建设国际海事司法中心需要顶层设计》，《经济参考报》2016 年 3 月 24 日，第 8 版。

心，其目的在于提升中国法院的国际影响力和权威性，而不是设立新机构”①。至此，境外关于“建设国际海事司法中心”的质疑逐渐平息。

境外的质疑逐渐平息，国内的热度却越来越高。2016 年 11 月 15 日，中国审判理论研讨会海事海商审判理论专业委员会 2016 年年会在上海召开，与会代表围绕“推进国际海事司法中心建设的路径与行动”开展深入研讨。多家法院结合本院的实际情况和比较优势，探索国际海事司法中心建设方案。例如，浙江省高级人民法院出台《关于建设国际海事司法中心几点建议的报告》；宁波海事法院制定《关于积极参与国际海事司法中心建设的实施规划》；上海海事法院发布《上海海事法院五年发展规划纲要（2017—2021）》，明确提出“建设具有全球影响力的国际海事司法中心是我们的目标”；广州海事法院出台《学习周强院长讲话精神争当国际海事司法中心建设排头兵》，成立广州国际航运司法研究中心。②

回顾此次事件，“建设国际海事司法中心”成为境外媒体关注焦点的原因有二。其一，语言的差异。“建设”一词被媒体翻译成“setup”、“create”或“form”，并据此认为中国要成立新的机构——国际海事司法中心。其二，西方的焦虑。随着中国的快速发展，中国参与全球治理的能力和意愿不断增强，西方媒体对因中国实力上升而可能导致格局变化的焦虑与日俱增。不管中国情愿与否，中国的一举一动无不受到国际社会的广泛关注，中国政府在国际舞台上的“韬光养晦，绝不当头”时代已经基本结束。③

2017 年 3 月 12 日，最高人民法院院长周强在向全国人民代表大会报告工作时，对上一年度报告中提出的“加强海事审判工作，建设国际海事中心”工作部署作出了回应。从报告内容看，“建设国际海事司法中心”是为了服务保障“一带一路”建设和海洋强国战略，2016 年具体工作是“围绕把我国建设成为国际司法中心，指导各海事法院提升司法水平，加

---

① Susan Finder, “China's Maritime Courts: Defenders of ‘Judicial Sovereignty’”, The Diplomat, http://thediplomat.com/2016/04/chinas-maritime-courts-defenders-of-judicial-sovereignty/, last visited on 12 August, 2017.

② 张可心：《迈向国际海事司法中心》，《人民法治》2017 年第 5 期，第 10 页。

③ 张文显：《推进全球治理变革，构建世界新秩序——习近平治国理政的全球思维》，《环球法律评论》2017 年第 4 期，第 14 页。

强国际海事司法研究基地建设”。[①] 建设国际海事司法中心的路径更加清晰。

二 “建设国际海事司法中心”的主要原因

建设国际海事司法中心，目的是营造良好的法治环境，吸引中外当事人在中国解决海事纠纷，提升海事软实力和司法公信力，扩大中国海事审判的国际影响力，核心是把中国打造成“国际海事诉讼目的地”。只有大量的国际海事纠纷选择在中国诉讼，中国才能成为公认的国际海事司法中心。

（一）服务和保障国家战略实施

《2016年中国海洋经济统计公报》显示，2016年全国海洋生产总值70507亿元，占国内生产总值的9.5%。[②] 我国经济已经发展成为高度依赖海洋的外向型经济，对海洋资源、空间、海上通道安全的依赖程度大幅提高，在管辖海域外的海洋权益方面也需要不断加以维护和拓展。

党的十八大提出建设海洋强国战略，党的十八届五中全会进一步提出“拓展蓝色经济空间。坚持陆海统筹，壮大海洋经济，科学开发海洋资源，保护海洋生态环境，维护我国海洋权益，建设海洋强国”。海洋强国战略下，中国海事司法的职能定位包括：保障海洋经济活动健康有序，服务航运中心建设；保障涉海法律体系的特殊性，推动涉海法律体系的发展；保护公民、法人合法权益，维护国家海洋主权。[③] 当前，我国维护海洋权益的形势严峻。管辖地域、管辖案件的特殊性，使海事法院在维护国家司法主权等方面具有特别重要意义。扩大乃至积极行使海事司法管辖权，通过司法积累主权证据是维护国家海洋权益的重要途径。海事法院应根据《联

① 《最高人民法院工作报告》，最高人民法院网站，http://www.court.gov.cn/fabu-xiangqing-37852.html，最后访问日期：2017年8月12日。

② 《海洋局发布〈2016年中国海洋经济统计公报〉》，中国政府网，http://www.gov.cn/shuju/2017-03/17/content_5177987.htm，最后访问日期：2017年8月12日。

③ 司玉琢、曹兴国：《海洋强国战略下中国海事司法的职能》，《中国海商法研究》2014年第3期，第10—12页。

合国海洋法公约》和我国国内法的规定，积极行使沿海国、港口国、船旗国司法管辖权，公正审理海洋开发利用、海上事故纠纷，依法保护海洋权益，维护“蓝色国土”安全。①

党的十八届三中全会提出“构建开放型经济新体制”，要求“推进丝绸之路经济带、海上丝绸之路建设，形成全方位开放新格局”。市场经济是法治经济，开放型经济新体制是国际化、法治化的市场经济体制。② 作为法治的重要组成部分，司法越来越成为各国培育国际竞争优势的新领域。司法作为重要的法律手段，已经成为维护国家安全的重要方式。作为经济大国，中国需要借助国际民事诉讼制度在全球范围内保护利益；作为法治大国，中国需要提升司法服务水平，增强本国司法制度在全球争议解决市场的吸引力。③

党的十七大把自由贸易区建设上升为国家战略，党的十八大提出要加快实施自由贸易区战略。多个自贸试验区的《总体方案》均提出了“提升国际航运服务能级”、“增强国际航运服务功能”的建设目标，允许中资公司拥有或控股拥有的非五星红旗船，试点开展外贸集装箱在国内沿海港口和自贸试验区内港口之间的沿海捎带业务。有关沿海捎带业务的规定已经突破了《海商法》第4条关于只能由“五星红旗”经营沿海运输的规定。“中资外籍船舶沿海捎带”的实质性启动，其航线性质如何界定，将直接影响到法律适用的选择。④

此外，到2020年，上海将基本建成具有全球资源配置能力的国际航运中心，中国要实现建成具有国际竞争力的现代化海运体系阶段性目标，并以此为基础向建设海运强国迈进。⑤ 上述战略的实施，离不开海事司法的服务和保障。

---

① 海口海事法院：《海事司法在南海主权争议中的潜在价值和意义》，《法制日报》2014年12月24日，第9版。

② 汪洋：《加强涉外法律工作》，《人民日报》2014年11月6日，第6版。

③ 何其生：《大国司法理念与中国国际民事诉讼制度的发展》，《中国社会科学》2017年第5期，第123页。

④ 张勇健、刘敬东、奚向阳、杨兴业：《〈关于为自由贸易试验区建设提供司法保障的意见〉的理解与适用》，《人民法院报》2017年1月18日，第5版。

⑤ 《国务院关于促进海运业健康发展的若干意见》，国发〔2014〕32号。

（二）营造法治化、国际化营商环境

在国际竞争日益激烈的当下，营商环境已成为世界主要国家关注的重心，成为提升国际竞争力的重要手段。尽管取得了长足的进步，但我国的营商环境排名并不理想。在世界银行发布的《2017 年全球营商环境报告》中，中国的营商环境仅排第 78 位。[①]

在中央财经领导小组第十六次会议上，习近平总书记强调指出，“要改善投资和市场环境，加快对外开放步伐，降低市场运行成本，营造稳定公平透明、可预期的营商环境，加快建设开放型经济新体制，推动我国经济持续健康发展”[②]。

《最高人民法院关于为改善营商环境提供司法保障的若干意见》第 6 条规定：“依法审理各类涉外商事海事案件，服务和保障‘一带一路’等国家重大战略的实施。充分发挥审判职能作用，依法行使司法管辖权，公正高效审理各类涉外商事海事案件，平等保护中外当事人程序权利和实体权益。按照《最高人民法院关于人民法院为“一带一路”建设提供司法服务和保障的若干意见》，加强与‘一带一路’沿线国家的国际司法协助，完善相关工作机制，及时化解争议纠纷，为‘一带一路’建设营造良好法治环境。”[③]

国家统计局深圳调查队的统计结果显示，在影响营商环境的因素中，法治化排在第一位，超过七成企业在选择投资地时最看重的是公平公正的法治环境。[④] 法治环境已成为营商环境的核心要素。作为法治竞争力的核心组成部分，司法对于建立产权清晰、公平竞争、诚实守信的营商环境至关重要。[⑤]

---

① 郭言：《打造国际化法治化营商环境》，《经济日报》2017 年 8 月 4 日，第 9 版。

② 《习近平主持召开中央财经领导小组第十六次会议》，中国政府网，http://www.gov.cn/xinwen/2017-07/17/content_5211349.htm，最后访问日期：2017 年 8 月 12 日。

③ 《关于为改善营商环境提供司法保障的若干意见》，最高人民法院网站，http://www.court.gov.cn/fabu-xiangqing-56132.html，最后访问日期：2017 年 8 月 16 日。

④ 《广东：法治化营商环境成核心竞争力》，新华网 http://news.xinhuanet.com/fortune/2015-12/17/c_1117498481.htm，最后访问日期：2017 年 8 月 15 日。

⑤ 张勇健：《“一带一路”司法保障问题研究》，《中国应用法学》2017 年第 1 期，第 162 页。

（三）参与国际规则制定

国际规则的制定是国际博弈的结果，是各国政治、经济、外交综合实力的反映。改革开放以来，我国的综合国力不断提高，但是我国作为现行国际经贸规则适应者、遵循者的角色没有根本改变。这与我国的大国地位不相匹配。建设国际海事司法中心的目的之一就是谋求更大的规则话语权。

《中共中央关于全面推进依法治国若干重大问题的决定》要求积极参与国际规则制定，推动依法处理涉外经济、社会事务，增强我国在国际法律事务中的话语权和影响力，运用法律手段维护我国主权、安全、发展利益。

在中共中央政治局第19次集体学习时，习近平总书记强调，加快实施自由贸易区战略，是我国积极参与国际经贸规则制定，争取全球经济治理制度性权力的重要平台，我们不能当旁观者、跟随者，而是要做参与者、引领者，善于通过自由贸易区建设增强我国国际竞争力，在国际规则制定中发出更多中国声音，注入更多中国元素，维护和拓展我国发展利益。①

现行的国际航运、海事规则主要是由西方发达国家主导制定的，我国的利益和诉求并没有得到充分的体现和尊重。在规则已经成型或生效的情形下，推倒重来并非易事，也未必符合中国的利益。好的法律实践者能够利用法律的不确定性和未完成性去最大限度地维护本国的利益。即使现有的规则已经明确，也仍然可以就该规则的含义、该规则的限度、该规则的例外提出一系列的解释措施和解释思路，这种方式就有助于中国在现行的国际法体制框架之内寻求自己利益主张维护的可能。②

近年来，国际社会将国际争端司法化的趋势越来越明显。国内司法不仅可以通过案件审理对国际条约的解释和适用产生重要影响，而且还可以推动国际习惯以及国际法基本原则的形成和发展，甚至填补国际法领域的

---

① 《习近平主持中共中央政治局第十九次集体学习并发表重要讲话》，人民网，http://cpc.people.com.cn/n/2014/1207/c64094-26161930.html，最后访问日期：2017年8月12日。

② 何志鹏：《国际法治的中国方案——"一带一路"的全球治理视角》，《太平洋学报》2017年5月，第4页。

法律空白。[①]

我国司法机构具有参与国际规则制定的丰富实践经验，自身又是国际规则的适用者和解释者，理应在推动“一带一路”相关国际规则的制定和改革方面更有作为，积极地贡献司法智慧，提出中国法案，体现中国利益。[②] 丰富的司法实践经验和案例资源是中国的优势。在《中华人民共和国海商法》（修改建议稿）审核研究第一次工作会议上，最高人民法院民事审判第四庭副庭长王淑梅在开幕式致辞中透露，自1984年海事法院成立以来，中国海事法院审理的海事案件已经超过30万个。[③] 这些法律实践可为中国参与国际规则的制定提供重要支撑。

三 “建设国际海事司法中心”面临的主要困难与机遇

国际海事司法中心并无统一的标准。上海海事法院院长赵红在接受《人民法治》的专访时提出，成为国际海事司法中心，首先应具备四个核心要件：一是发达完备的海事法律体系；二是大量优质的海事案件；三是素质精良的海事法官队伍；四是高效完善的海事审判机制。评估是否成为国际海事司法中心的衡量因素包括以下四方面。一是国际关注度高。二是自身吸引力强。吸引更多的外籍当事人，基于海事裁判的国际公信力，主动选择到一国进行诉讼。三是国际影响力大。四是功能辐射力广。[④]

黄进教授认为，把中国建成国际仲裁中心的核心是要把中国打造成“国际商事仲裁目的地”，要有“四个一流”的意识：一是要有一流的法治环境；二是要有一流的仲裁法律制度；三是要有一流的仲裁管理服务；四是要有一流的仲裁品牌机构。[⑤] 这虽是针对“国际仲裁中心”而言，但对国际海事司法中心的界定也有一定的借鉴意义。

---

① 贺荣：《论中国司法参与国际经济规则的制定》，《国际法研究》2016年第1期，第9页。

② 张勇健：《“一带一路”司法保障问题研究》，《中国应用法学》2017年第1期，第165页。

③ 《〈中华人民共和国海商法〉（修改建议稿）审核研究第一次工作会议在我校举行》，大连海事大学网站，http://news.dlmu.edu.cn/a/yaowem/2017/0710/2699.html，最后访问日期：2017年8月12日。新闻报道中并无提及具体数字，但会议简报里有。

④ 参见何晶晶、李强《上海推进国际海事司法中心建设迈出坚实步伐——访上海海事法院党组书记、院长赵红》，《人民法治》2017年第5期，第12—13页。

⑤ 黄进：《建立中国现代仲裁制度的三点构想》，《中国法律评论》2017年第3期，第185页。

笔者认为，国际海事司法中心反映的是海事审判的地位、司法公信力和国际影响力，其核心是要把中国打造成"国际海事诉讼目的地"，衡量标准包括：第一，完善的海事法律制度；第二，涉外海事案件的数量和标的；第三，国际影响力，包括处理大案、新型案件的比例，裁决被普遍接受的程度，以及经典案例被学界接受和认可程度；第四，引领国际规则的创新。

（一）建设国际海事司法中心面临的主要困难

中国要成为国际海事司法中心，势必对原有的格局产生冲击。目前，伦敦、纽约、新加坡在国际海事纠纷解决中心建设中具有明显的优势。其共同的特点是：普通法系、工作语言是英语、航运要素聚集、司法公信力较高。

海事纠纷的解决途径主要有两种：诉讼和仲裁。国际海事纠纷解决传统上一直是"小诉讼、大仲裁"。① 当事人选择国际海事仲裁方式处理争议的原因主要是基于仲裁的执行力。截至 2017 年 8 月 1 日，世界上已有 157 个国家和地区加入《承认及执行外国仲裁裁决公约》（简称《纽约公约》），② 仲裁裁决在绝大多数国家能得到承认和执行。

就海事诉讼而言，自 2012 年以来，全国受理一审海事案件年均 2 万多件，远超英美等西方传统航运大国，我国已经成为世界上受理海事案件数量最多的国家。③ 但是，这些案件大多数都是与中国有关的案件，当事人都是外国人并选择在中国解决海事纠纷的案件数量不多。此外，我国法院审理的具有国际影响力并能引领国际规则发展的海事案件数量不多，这与我国的大国地位不相匹配。

尽管在港口吞吐量方面并无优势，英国仍然是世界公认的国际海事纠纷解决中心。英国法院的判决受到国际贸易界、海事界、司法界和学术界的广泛关注，并在一些国家得到援引或遵循。在海事仲裁领域，伦敦更是

---

① 汪闽燕：《中国成为国际仲裁中心还有多远》，《法制日报》2013 年 5 月 21 日，第 10 版。

② 关于《纽约公约》缔约国的具体信息，参见 http://www.uncitral.org/uncitral/en/uncitral_texts/arbitration/NYConvention_status.html，最后访问日期：2017 年 8 月 2 日。

③ 周强：《发挥海事司法职能服务保障国家海洋战略》，《中国审判》2014 年第 9 期，第 18 页。

一家独大。世界上75%的海事仲裁在伦敦进行，90%以上的造船合同选择英国法律作为适用法律，80%以上的造船合同选择在伦敦仲裁。①

英国能够成为国际海事纠纷解决中心的原因如下。第一，法律的稳定性和裁判的可预见性强。英国是判例法国家，海事文化悠久，经历了多年的发展，英国法和重要的海运公约的含义都比较明确，法官的整体水平较高，司法公信力较强。当事人愿意选择适用英国法解决纠纷。第二，大量的国际航运组织扎堆伦敦，由其制定并推荐使用的标准合同通常约定“适用英国法”、“伦敦仲裁”。第三，英国航运金融领域实力很强，银行是出资人，保险公司和互保协会通常是海事纠纷的最终买单人，其在合同条款的拟定方面具有很强的话语权，选择熟悉的法律并在“主场”解决纠纷是其理性的选择。第四，伦敦人才汇聚，产业链完整，能够发挥协同效应，以迅速且经济的方式解决纠纷。第五，路径依赖短期内难以改变。为了澄清英国法和国际海运公约的具体含义，海事界、贸易界已经支付了巨额的律师费用。对于商人而言，成本固然重要，但风险可控更加关键。除非其他选择具有明显的优势或是源于法律的强制性规定，商人通常不愿意改变原有做法。②

新加坡正在努力建设国际海事纠纷解决中心，并在一些重要领域赢得先机。优越的地理位置、便利的商业环境和高效管理，让新加坡第三次登上全球海事之都排行榜首。③ 全球七成的海事贸易使用波罗的海国际航运理事会（BIMCO）制定的标准合同。2012年11月，BIMCO在哥本哈根举行会议，正式批准并通过了一项决议，将新加坡列为继伦敦、纽约之后第三个国际海事仲裁地。④ 2016年11月，新加坡交易所（SGX）按计划完成收购波罗的海交易所，新加坡国际航运中心的地位更加巩固。

（二）中国建设国际海事司法中心的有利条件

尽管在国际海事规则制定领域，中国面临着严重的话语缺失和“话语

① 王纯：《中国建设国际海事司法中心》，《人民周刊》2017年第11期，第17页。

② 参见张文广《迈向海事司法强国》，《人民法治》2017年第5期，第54—55页。

③ 《报告：全球海事之都榜我国居首》，新加坡联合早报网，http://www.zaobao.com/finance/singapore/story20170427-753610，最后访问日期：2017年8月12日。

④ 吴明华：《擦肩而过的亚洲海事仲裁地之痒》，《航海》2013年第2期，第12页。

逆差"问题，但中国的硬实力仍在快速增长，这会给软实力的增长提供支撑。

1. 中国坚持对外开放的基本国策不会改变

2012年12月31日，十八届中共中央政治局就坚定不移推行改革开放进行第二次集体学习。习近平在主持学习时强调，坚持对外开放的基本国策，改革开放只有进行时没有完成时。[①]

2017年3月5日，李克强总理在政府工作报告里提出：积极主动扩大对外开放。面对国际环境新变化和国内发展新要求，要进一步完善对外开放战略布局，加快构建开放型经济新体制，推动更深层次更高水平的对外开放。[②] 根据检索，2017年度政府报告四次提及"海洋"，分别是"海洋权益"两次，"海洋强国"一次，"海洋经济示范区"一次。

目前，中国是全球第二大经济体，贸易大国、港口大国、航运大国、造船大国和海员大国。虽然中国尚不具备制定国际海事规则的主导权，但中国已经具备了国际海事规则能否生效或效力如何的否决权。中国在世界经济版图上的分量越重，中国成为国际海事司法中心的可能性就越大。

2. 航运要素聚集，航运中心东移

联合国贸易与发展组织（UNCTAD）《海运述评（2016）》显示，中国是世界第三大船东国，海运连接性指数全球第一。[③] 全球贸易超过50%的货运量由亚洲船东承运，亚洲船队运输力已占世界船舶总吨位的50%以上，全球90%的新造船也由亚洲完成。[④] 亚洲航运中心崛起趋势愈加明显。

国际海事司法中心与国际航运中心建设相互促进。2017年7月19日，《新华·波罗的海国际航运中心发展指数（2017）》和《上海国际航运中心建设蓝皮书2017》正式发布。全球排名前10航运中心中，5个位于亚洲，4个位于欧洲，1个位于美洲。全球综合实力排名前三位的国际航运中心

---

① 《习近平主持政治局集体学习：以更大的政治勇气和智慧深化改革》，人民网，http://cpc.people.com.cn/n/2013/0102/c64094-20070702.html，最后访问日期：2017年8月9日。

② 《李克强说，积极主动扩大对外开放》，新华网，http://news.xinhuanet.com/politics/2017-03/05/c_1120570695.htm，最后访问日期：2017年8月9日。

③ "Review of Maritime Transport 2016", http://unctad.org/en/pages/PublicationWebflyer.aspx?publicationid=1650, last visited on August 13, 2017.

④ 《全球贸易逾半由亚洲船东承运》，人民网，http://sh.people.com.cn/n2/2016/0519/c134768-28366854.html，最后访问日期：2017年8月9日。

分别为新加坡、伦敦、香港。上海排名第五。中国广州、青岛、宁波—舟山、天津、深圳、厦门、大连等港口也跻身国际航运中心行列。① 航运法治环境建设已成为推进国际航运中心软环境建设的重要方面。中国要由“吞吐量”的航运中心变为“定规则”的航运中心，重点在于提升制度性的话语权，具体包括制定国际公约、标准规则等方面，提升海运软实力，为国际海运问题解决提供更多的中国方案。②

3. 海事审判机构最多、海事案件数量最多

目前，全国10个海事法院在沿海沿江重要港口城市设立了39个派出法庭，并积极组织开展巡回审判，有效覆盖了我国管辖的全部港口和水域。我国海事法院每年受理的海事海商案件数量和纠纷种类，无论是在亚太地区还是在全球海事司法领域都是最多的。③ 随着“一带一路”建设的实施，海上经济活动更加兴旺，传统海事纠纷和新类型案件或将不断增多。中外当事人对我国司法环境的信任度不断提高，当事人协议选择中国法院诉讼解决纠纷的比例逐年上升。④

与此同时，中国海事司法的国际影响力不断上升。2016年度，上海海事法院审理的两起案例被法国航运界权威法律期刊《法国海商法杂志》登载，⑤ 英文版《中国海事商事法律报告》（Chinese Maritimeand Commercial Law Reports）也在行业领域负有盛名的英国英富曼（informa）的I-law平台上发布。

4. 中国开始走向世界海事立法舞台

丰富的案例，既给中国的海商法研究提供了素材，也提升了中国在国际海事界的地位和影响力。在《联合国全程或部分海上国际货物运输合同公约》（简称《鹿特丹规则》）制定过程中，中国代表团提出的书面提案

---

① 《2017年十大国际航运中心揭晓》，新华社，http://news.xinhuanet.com/mrdx/2017-07/21/c_136461351.htm，最后访问日期：2017年8月12日。

② 沈尚：《我国海运软实力透视》，《中国水运报》2016年10月1日，第8版。

③ 李国光：《提高海事审判公信力推进亚太海事司法中心建设》，《人民法院报》2014年9月3日，第2版。

④ 刘贵祥：《充分发挥司法职能服务保障“一带一路”建设》，中国审判网，http://www.chinatrial.net.cn/magazineinfo746.html，最后访问日期：2017年8月16日。

⑤ 《上海海事法院两起案例被法国权威海商法期刊登载并获好评》，上海海事法院网站，http://shhsfy.gov.cn/hsfyytwx/hsfyytwx/xwzx1340/hfzx1441/2016/12/28/d_306046.html，最后访问日期：2017年8月13日。

的数量在所有国家中位居第三，并在专家组会议中作出了巨大贡献。[①] 2012 年 10 月，国际海事委员会（CMI）第 40 届大会上提出的《承认外国船舶司法出售国际公约建议案草案》，是第一次由中国人主导并积极参与的国际公约的立法过程。2014 年 6 月 17 日，CMI 第 41 届会议正式通过了《关于外国船舶司法出售及其承认的国际公约草案》（简称《北京草案》）。如果公约未来能够生效，将被命名为《北京规则》。这在 CMI 一百多年的历史中还是第一次使用中国大陆的城市名字命名其国际文书。[②] 这将成为一个里程碑，预示中国真正开始走向世界海事立法舞台。[③]

四 "建设国际海事司法中心"的具体措施

建设国际海事司法中心是一项系统工程，需要顶层设计，统筹推进。

（一）完善涉海法律制度

"法治先行"是习近平总书记对全面深化改革提出的要求。2014 年 2 月 28 日，习近平同志在中央全面深化改革小组第二次会议上强调："凡属重大改革都要于法有据。在整个改革过程中，都要高度重视运用法治思维和法治方式，发挥法治的引领和推动作用，加强对相关立法工作的协调，确保在法治轨道上推进改革。"[④] 党的十八届四中全会进而明确提出，法律是治国之重器，良法是善治之前提。实践证明行之有效的，要及时上升为法律。实践条件还不成熟、需要先行先试的，要按照法定程序作出授权。对不适应改革要求的法律法规，要及时修改和废止。要加强法律解释工作，及时明确法律规定含义和适用法律依据。[⑤]

---

① 参见凯特·兰纳《〈鹿特丹规则〉的构建》，《中国海商法年刊》2009 年第 4 期，第 4—5 页。

② 参见李海《国际海事委员会的最新成果：〈北京草案〉》，《中国海商法研究》2014 年第 3 期，第 24 页。

③ 参见姚亚平《倾听中国好声音——国际海事委员会第 40 届大会侧记》，《中国海商法研究》2010 年第 2 期，第 2 页。

④ 《习近平主持召开中央全面深化改革领导小组第二次会议》，中国政府网，http://www.gov.cn/ldhd/2014 - 02/28/content_2625924.htm，最后访问日期：2017 年 8 月 11 日。

⑤ 《习近平：运用法治思维和法治方式推进改革》，人民网，http://cpc.people.com.cn/n/2014/1028/c64094 - 25919445.html，最后访问日期：2017 年 8 月 11 日。

我国的涉海法律体系远未形成。首先，我国宪法对海洋及相关问题没有作任何明确的规定。其次，我国“海法体系”缺乏系统性与协调性。再次，我国涉海法律尚未形成体系，缺陷严重，一些重要的法律尚未制定或者层次较低，比如我国至今没有制定海洋基本法、航运法、船舶法等等。最后，海洋程序立法滞后，目前我国法律中专门的海上程序法仅有《海事诉讼特别程序法》。[①]

海运领域现有三个生效公约同时并存，即1924年《关于统一提单若干法律规定的国际公约》（简称《海牙规则》）、1968年《修改关于统一提单若干法律规定的国际公约的协定书》（简称《维斯比规则》）和1978年《联合国海上货物运输公约》（简称《汉堡规则》）。然而，现有的三大国际海运公约只调整单一海运这一运输模式，而不能调整“海运+”，因此也就无法应对“一带一路”倡议下的“海铁联运”模式。2008年《鹿特丹规则》的创新点之一就在于统一“海运+”模式的多式联运规则。“一带一路”建设中，“海铁联运”将发挥重要作用。虽然《鹿特丹规则》是否能够生效尚不得知，但在国内修法或与其他国家签订双边协定时借鉴《鹿特丹规则》中先进的理念和规定却不失为一个可行的选择。

在我国《海商法》颁布并实施以来的二十余年里，国际贸易运输从形式到规模都有了很大的发展和变化。目前，《海商法》的修改工作已经启动。《海商法》修改的必要性主要体现在以下五个方面。第一，《海商法》不符合施行以来航运实践、航运经济和航运政策与发展战略的发展变化及其对海商立法的要求。第二，《海商法》不适应该法制定所遵循的具体原则的内容所发生的重大变化。第三，《海商法》缺失船舶污染损害赔偿制度。第四，《海商法》与一般民事法律存在不协调。第五，《海商法》部分内容存在不足与缺陷。[②]

本次修法与制定《海商法》时的情况大不相同：社会主义法律体系已经基本形成，最高人民法院出台了多部司法解释和3个指导性案例，各级法院审判经验、案例资源丰富，海商法的研究水平也有了很大的提高。

---

① 司玉琢：《“海上丝绸之路”的法律保障问题研究》，《中国审判》2015年第15期，第14页。

② 参见胡正良、孙思琪《我国〈海商法〉修改的基本问题与要点建议》，《国际法研究》2017年第4期，第53—58页。

《海商法》的修改应重视吸收中国司法经验，体现中国司法智慧，形成能被国际海事界普遍接受的“中国经验”、“中国规则”。

（二）改革海事司法机制

自1984年起，我国先后设立了10个海事法院，形成了“三级法院二审终审制”（海事法院——上诉审高级人民法院——最高人民法院）的专门法院体系。作为跨行政区域设立的专门法院，海事法院基本符合《中共中央关于全面深化改革若干重大问题的决定》提出的“司法机关的人、财、物由省一级统一管理及建立与行政区划适当分离的司法管辖制度”。但是，我国海事审判制度还存在以下的问题与不足。首先，海事法院的法律地位不明确；其次，海事法院的管理体制不顺；再次，海事专门审判体制没有贯彻到底，存在“一审专门、二审不专门”的问题，导致最高人民法院再审案件压力过大；最后，海事法院受理案件数量偏少，海事诉讼管辖有待完善。①

2014年9月，在中国海事审判三十年座谈会讲话中，最高人民法院院长周强指出：“要按照人民法院‘四五’改革纲要的要求，进一步完善海事法院管辖制度，围绕国家海洋开发战略，积极探索将相关海事行政、海事执行案件和其他涉海民事、刑事案件统一纳入海事法院专门管辖的新模式。”②

2015年2月，最高人民法院正式发布《最高人民法院关于全面深化人民法院改革的意见》，③ 并将之作为修订后的《人民法院第四个五年改革纲要（2014—2018）》贯彻实施。第5条规定：“改革海事案件管辖制度。进一步理顺海事审判体制。科学确定海事法院管辖范围，确立更加符合海事案件审判规律的工作机制。”

1. 设立海事高级法院

早在1999年，《人民法院五年改革纲要（1999—2003）》第43条就明

---

① 张文广：《改革和完善我国海事审判制度的几点建议》，《中国海洋大学学报》（社会科学版）2017年第2期，第11页。

② 周强：《发挥海事司法职能服务保障国家海洋战略》，《中国审判》2014年第9期，第19页。

③ 法发〔2015〕3号。

确提出“对设立海事高级法院进行研究”。[①] 设立海事高级法院，建立完整的海事专门法院体系，对进一步强化海事司法的专业性，更好地整合海事司法资源、统一海事司法的裁判尺度具有重要意义。

2. 试点涉海案件“三审合一”

自成立以来，海事法院受案范围不断拓展。2016 年 2 月 24 日，最高人民法院发布了《关于海事诉讼管辖问题的规定》和《关于海事法院受理案件范围的规定》。自 2016 年 3 月 1 日起，海事法院对海事行政案件行使管辖权，海事法院受理案件类型拓展至 108 项。然而，海事刑事案件至今尚未正式纳入海事法院的管辖范围，海事刑事案件零星分散于各地方法院审理。随着建设海洋强国、“一带一路”等国家战略和倡议的深入推进，海事司法作用更加凸显。加大海事司法改革力度，充分发挥海事司法职能作用，推行海事案件“三审合一”的呼声越来越高。[②]

2016 年 8 月 1 日，最高人民法院发布《关于审理发生在我国管辖海域相关案件若干问题的规定（一）》和《关于审理发生在我国管辖海域相关案件若干问题的规定（二）》（以下简称“涉海司法解释”），进一步明确人民法院作为沿海国法院对中国管辖海域的司法管辖权，为中国涉海行政管理部门对中国管辖海域实行综合管理，依法维护中国海上秩序、海洋安全和海洋权益提供了明确的法律依据。涉海司法解释内容涵盖刑事、民事和行政诉讼三个领域，具有较强的综合性。涉海司法解释的颁布，为人民法院充分发挥司法职能作用提供制度支撑，也给各级法院受理海事刑事案件提供了依据。

2017 年 7 月 6 日，宁波海事法院一审公开开庭审理了被告人艾伦·门多萨·塔布雷（Allan Mendoza Tablate）交通肇事一案。该案是我国海事法院自 1984 年成立以来首次受理海事刑事案件，[③] 标志着海事案件“三审合一”试点正式启动。

---

① 法发〔1999〕28 号。

② 参见司玉琢《保障海洋发展战略改革完善中国特色的海事司法管辖制度》，《中国海商法研究》2015 年第 2 期，第 28—29、32 页。

③ 罗书臻：《中国海事法院首次受理海事刑事案件》，《人民法院报》2017 年 6 月 6 日，第 3 版。

（三）提升中国海事司法公信力

建设国际海事司法中心的关键在于提高海事司法公信力和国际影响力。

1. 实施精品战略

涉外商事海事纠纷案件存在一个大致的“二八现象”。在所有的案件中，80%以上是常规性或常见案件，争议涉及的绝大多数问题均已由相关司法解释和指导意见解决。涉外民商事案件的上诉率为13%，海事案件的上诉率则仅有7%。①

2010年，第三次全国涉外商事海事审判工作会议提出了实施精品战略的总体要求。2015年，最高人民法院发布《关于全面推进涉外商事海事审判精品战略为构建开放型经济新体制和建设海洋强国提供有力司法保障的意见》，明确提出“实施涉外商事海事审判精品战略是实现涉外商事海事审判科学发展的总体要求，强调以精取胜，注重品牌效应，实现案件办理精品化、人员素质精英化、法官视野国际化、体制机制创新化，着力提高我国涉外商事海事司法的公信力”。

在精品战略的推进方面，应完善海事精品案件的发现、审理和提炼工作机制，加强对国际影响大、具有规则确立和宣示意义的海事案件的审理，如“中威”执行案、“加百利”轮海难救助合同纠纷案、美国康菲公司渤海溢油事故案、韩国韩进海运株式会社域外申请破产重组相关案件，逐步实现由学习、认知、适用国际规则到影响、引领、发展国际规则的重大转变。

2. 探索海事案例指导制度

伦敦、新加坡、纽约是全球公认的国际航运中心和国际海事纠纷解决中心，其共同的特点是法律制度完善，裁判尺度统一，裁判结果可预见性强。中国要成为具有较高影响力的国际海事司法中心，必须做到裁判程序透明，裁判结果公正，裁判尺度统一。

为进一步统一裁判尺度，《最高人民法院司法责任制实施意见（试行）》新创设了类案与关联案件检索机制，明确承办法官在审理案件时，应当对最高人民法院已经审结或正在审理的类案与关联案件进行全面检索，制作检索

① 罗东川：《开启涉外商事海事审判工作的新征程》，《中国审判》2014年第12期，第60页。

报告，并分情形作出处理。①

截至2017年8月17日，最高人民法院共发布了16批合计87个指导性案例，但是直接涉及海事的案例仅有3个。最高人民法院先后发布了两批共计18个涉“一带一路”典型案例（涉及海事的案例有6个）和2016年十大典型海事案例。为充分发挥司法的确认、示范、引领作用，中国应加大典型海事案例的发布力度，探索海事案例指导制度。在法律、司法解释、指导性案例没有改变，上诉审法院没有不同判决或其他充分理由的情形下，遵守由其发布的或上一级法院发布的典型海事案例，从而达到增加判决的可预见性、统一裁判尺度、提高海事司法公信力的目的。

3. 提升海事司法透明度

中国是“一带一路”建设的倡议者和推动者，各国必然更加关注中国司法体制的运行情况。以公开促公正，以公正树公信成为中国海事司法的必然选择。

在法院信息化建设方面，近几年我国的力度很大，进步很快。即使从全球范围内看，我国法院的信息化建设水平也不落后，在一些领域如庭审直播、大数据分析等甚至世界领先。截至2017年2月底，中国裁判文书网访问量突破62亿人次，覆盖210多个国家和地区，成为全球最有影响的裁判文书网。②

实践证明，加大海事司法公开力度，有利于提升海事司法公信力，有利于提升中国海事“软实力”，扩大海事审判的国际影响，提高海事司法的国际地位。中国海事司法透明度越高，海事司法公信力越强，当事人选择来中国法院进行诉讼的数量越多，建设国际海事司法中心的目标就能越早实现。

（四）扩大国际司法协助范围

管辖权是一国主权的主要组成部分，是国家主权在诉讼程序领域的集中表现。涉外管辖权有三重价值目标：维护国家主权、保护当事人利益、

---

① 李万祥：《最高法创新类案检索机制统一裁判尺度》，中国经济网，http://www.ce.cn/xwzx/gnsz/gdxw/201707/31/t20170731_24659759.shtml，最后访问日期：2017年8月12日。

② 《周强：中国裁判文书网成为全球最有影响的裁判文书网》，人民网，http://legal.people.com.cn/n1/2017/0312/c42510-29139896.html，最后访问日期：2017年8月12日。

促进和保障国际交往。[①] 一国根据国家利益自愿决定是否限制行使主权，并不是对主权的弱化，而正是行使主权的方式。[②] 国际司法协助是人民法院参与国际治理的重要环节，直接服务和保障“一带一路”建设。

依据我国《民事诉讼法》第282条的规定，条约和互惠是人民法院承认和执行外国民商事判决的法律依据。我国尚未加入海牙国际私法协会《选择法院协议公约》，而我国与“一带一路”沿线国签订包含民商事判决承认和执行内容的双边民商事司法协助条约数量偏少，国际条约发挥的作用较为有限。因此，如何理解和适用互惠原则，对于“一带一路”沿线国民商事判决在我国境内的承认和执行尤为重要。[③]

最高人民法院《关于人民法院为“一带一路”建设提供司法服务和保障的若干意见》，明确提出：要加强与“一带一路”沿线各国的国际司法协助，切实保障中外当事人合法权益，促进沿线各国司法判决的相互承认与执行；要在沿线一些国家尚未与我国缔结司法协助协定的情况下，积极促成互惠关系，积极倡导并逐步扩大国际司法协助范围。

2017年6月8日，第二届中国—东盟大法官论坛通过《南宁声明》。《南宁声明》第七项规定：“区域内的跨境交易和投资需要以各国适当的判决的相互承认和执行机制为其司法保障。在本国国内法允许的范围内，与会各国法院将善意解释国内法，减少不必要的平行诉讼，考虑适当促进各国民商事判决的相互承认和执行。尚未缔结有关外国民商事判决承认和执行国际条约的国家，在承认与执行对方国家民商事判决的司法程序中，如对方国家的法院不存在以互惠为理由拒绝承认和执行本国民商事判决的先例，在本国国内法允许的范围内，即可推定与对方国家之间存在互惠关系。”我国长期司法实践中一直强调实存互惠、事实互惠，《南宁声明》首次提出推定互惠关系共识，是对既有理解的重大突破。

（五）加强国际海事司法研究基地建设

习近平同志强调：“建设法治国家、法治政府、法治社会，实现科学

① 张勇健：《“一带一路”司法保障问题研究》，《中国应用法学》2017年第1期，第159页。

② 江伟主编《民事诉讼法专论》，中国人民大学出版社，2005，第448页。

③ 张勇健：《“一带一路”背景下互惠原则实践发展的新动向》，《人民法院报》2017年6月20日，第2版。

立法、严格执法、公正司法、全民守法，都离不开一支高素质的法治工作队伍。法治人才培养上不去，法治领域不能人才辈出，全面依法治国就不可能做好。”

海事法官的素质决定了海事司法的水平。中国要成为国际海事司法中心，需要有一支熟悉法律、航海、贸易知识，能够站在国际海事司法理论和实践最前沿、充分参与国际交流的高素质法官队伍。加大培训和国际交流力度，是提升海事法官素质的有效途径。

2015 年 12 月，最高人民法院国际海事司法研究基地和国家法官学院青岛海事分院同时成立。2017 年 3 月 10 日，最高人民法院民事审判第四庭庭长张勇健在法制网举办的“两会”系列访谈中表示，2017 年要继续加强最高人民法院国际海事司法研究基地的建设，支持上海、广东、浙江等地方建立国际海事基地。[①] “等”字表明，国际海事司法基地可能并不限于这三地。

国际海事司法基地既可以对中国法官进行培训，也可以对“一带一路”沿线国家法官进行培训。通过交流知识、交换经验，相互学习各自的法律制度和法律文化，将中国法“输出”到目标国家，又通过他们将沿线国家的法律信息带入我国。

（六）大力发展海事仲裁

国际海事仲裁作为航运法律服务的高端产业，历来是欧美海运业竞争与追捧的重点。[②] 中国企业在境外海事仲裁败诉率高达 95%。败诉的主要原因包括：中国企业在经营上可能不规范，不熟悉境外法律和仲裁程序，语言上不占优势，缺乏境外仲裁经验，存在法律文化差异，等等。[③]

中国海事仲裁委员会（简称“海仲委”）是中国海事仲裁的核心力量。2017 年 5 月 3 日，海仲委与中国国际经济贸易仲裁委员会正式“分家”。

---

① 《最高法：推进建立“一带一路争端解决中心”》，法制网，http://www.legaldaily.com.cn/index_article/content/2017-03/10/content_7047748.htm?node=5955，最后访问日期：2017 年 8 月 12 日。

② 王承杰：《发展海事仲裁事业助力“一带一路”建设》，《中国远洋航务》2016 年第 11 期，第 95 页。

③ 陶海青：《把中国建设成为国际仲裁中心》，《中国贸易报》2016 年 3 月 10 日，第 1 版。

独立运营后的海仲委明确了其发展定位：成为亚太海事仲裁中心及国际海事仲裁机构。海仲委秘书长顾超在接受记者采访时表示：“我们希望到2020年将海仲委打造成为国内外有一定影响的海事仲裁机构，2025年成为一流的国际海事仲裁机构，助力我国发展成为亚太及国际海事仲裁中心以及海事司法中心建设。”①

海事诉讼和海事仲裁是解决海事纠纷的主要途径。2016年，中国各级法院审结海事案件1.6万件，海仲委受案量总计69件，审结案件68件。近三年间，海仲委没有一起裁决被法院裁定撤销和不予执行。② 完善海事诉讼与海事仲裁的衔接机制，促进海事司法与海事仲裁的良性互动，有利于营造法治化、国际化的营商环境，助力国际海事司法中心建设。

2011年，上海市高级人民法院与中国海事仲裁委员会共同签署了《关于建立海事纠纷委托调解工作机制协作纪要》，标志着中国首个海事纠纷委托调解工作机制正式启动。上海海事法院依据《上海海事法院关于委托海事仲裁机构调解工作规定》，将两起因船上火灾引发的货损案件委托中国海事仲裁委员会上海分会进行调解。③ 2017年8月4日，中国海事仲裁委员会与广州海事法院签署了《关于建立海事纠纷委托调解工作机制合作备忘录》（简称《备忘录》）。与《备忘录》配套的《中国海事仲裁委员会华南分会接受人民法院委托调解规则》明确规定，海上、通海水域货物运输合同纠纷等八类海事纠纷被纳入委托调解范围。④

建设国际海事司法中心与发展海事仲裁相互配合，相互促进。一方面，人民法院依法对仲裁进行支持和监督，是维护仲裁公正和裁决执行力

---

① 万学忠：《服务海上丝绸之路法律界培育“并蒂莲花”》，《法制日报》2017年6月24日，第6版。

② 张维：《海仲委与贸仲委“分家”》，法制网，http://www.legaldaily.com.cn/index/content/2017-05/03/content_7132893.htm?node=20908，最后访问日期：2017年8月12日。

③ 《上海海事法院委托海仲调解两起案件取得良好效果》，上海海事法院网站，http://shhsfy.gov.cn/hsfyytwx/hsfyytwx/spdy1358/spdt1420/2017/07/21/2c9380995d37fd23015d65e8168a37d0.html，最后访问日期：2017年8月12日。

④ 《海仲委与广州海事法院建立海事纠纷委托调解工作机制》，中国海事仲裁委员会网站，http://www.cmac.org.cn/index.php?m=Article&a=show&id=3140，最后访问日期：2017年8月12日。

强有效的方式，更是提高仲裁公信力、促进仲裁事业健康发展的有力保障。[①] 另一方面，作为解决海事纠纷的有效途径之一，海事仲裁的繁荣与发展将减轻海事司法的重负，并利用其优势促进国际海事司法中心的建设。[②]

结语

目前，中国是全球第二大经济体。自 2013 年以来，中国成为世界第一货物贸易大国，90% 以上的外贸货物通过海运完成。中国还是第三大船东国，造船大国和海员大国。全球十大港口和十大集装箱港口中，中国均占据了七席。中国在海运领域的实力全球领先。然而，从《2017 新华 · 波罗的海国际航运中心发展指数报告》看，中国却无太大的优势。香港排名第三，上海排名第五，全球第一大港宁波—舟山仅排名第十八。[③] 可见，影响国际航运中心排名的关键因素是资源配置能力和软实力。中国应当由"吞吐量"的航运中心变为"定规则"的航运中心。

随着"一带一路"建设的推进，中国海事司法争取较高国际地位和国际影响力，积极参与国际规则的制定并引领国际规则的发展，已是紧迫的现实需求和大国的应有担当。中国应树立大国司法理念，加快推进国际海事司法中心建设。但是也不应忽视，自 1995 年提出至 2014 年宣布建成，中国成为亚太地区海事司法中心用了十九年时间。建设国际海事司法中心，确立中国海事审判在国际海事司法中的应有地位，也将是一个长期的过程。

（本文原载于《国际法研究》2017 年第 5 期）

① 沈红雨：《继续完善仲裁司法审查制度促进仲裁公信力提升》，《人民法院报》2015 年 9 月 26 日，第 1 版。

② 何晶晶、张慧超：《发展海事仲裁助力国际海事司法中心建设——专访中国海事仲裁委员会副秘书长兼仲裁院副院长陈波》，《人民法治》2017 年第 5 期，第 18 页。

③ 《2017 年十大国际航运中心揭晓》，新华网，http://news.xinhuanet.com/mrdx/2017－07/21/c_136461351.htm，最后访问日期：2017 年 8 月 2 日。

从《京都议定书》到《巴黎协定》：开启新的气候变化治理时代

何晶晶[*]

一 引言

2015 年 12 月的联合国巴黎气候变化大会在一片赞誉声中落下帷幕，达成的《巴黎协定》成为全球协同应对气候变化努力进程中的另一个里程碑。从《京都议定书》到《巴黎协定》，世界应对气候变化的治理机制发生了根本转变。从《京都议定书》主要依赖自上而下（top-down）的治理机制到《巴黎协定》的以自下而上（bottom-up）的治理机制为主，同时兼有自上而下治理成分的混合型治理机制（hybrid climate governance structure）[①]，《巴黎协定》无疑开启了新的气候变化治理时代。《巴黎协定》由于成功覆盖了全球 96% 的温室气体排放量，吸引 196 个《联合国气候变化框架公约》（UNFCCC）成员国中的 186 个成员国提交了国家自主贡献目标（Intended Nationally Determined Contributions，INDCs）而被广为肯定，被认为全球气候变化谈判在经历了哥本哈根气候变化大会以来的低潮与挫折之后的一次伟大胜利。

为了最大限度地赢得国家参与和支持，《巴黎协定》事实上放弃了《京都议定书》所遵循的“发达国家”和“发展中国家”两分法的格局，

---

* 何晶晶，中国社会科学院国际法研究所国际经济法研究室副研究员。

① Daniel Bodansky，Seth Hoedl，Gilbert Metcalf and Robert Stavins，“Facilitating Linkage of Climate Policies through the Paris Outcome”，*Climate Policy* 7（2015），p. 2.

虽然仍然秉承“共同但有区别责任”原则，但是重心已然不像《京都议定书》般强调发达国家的强制减排义务，而更多的是强调世界各国按照各自能力和自愿原则进行国家自主贡献减排模式。尽管“共同但有区别责任”原则仍然出现在《巴黎协定》的文本中，但是后半部分的“依据各自能力”已然成为更为重要的参照原则。在《巴黎协定》下，发达国家与发展中国家的“有区别的责任”主要体现在发达国家对发展中国家的资金和技术援助方面，在减排目标上已经不再区分。无论从治理机制、法律形式、法律基本原则、法律履约机制还是市场机制等方面，《巴黎协定》都与《京都议定书》有了本质的区别。需要指出的是，虽然当前《巴黎协定》获得一片盛赞，但是《巴黎协定》还存在许多亟待解决的关键问题，它只是一个好的起点，如果国际社会不在接下来的几年内积极赋予协定更为实质性的内容，不拿出真正的诚意来执行该协定，《巴黎协定》也许会沦为政治上作秀的尴尬协定。所以在“后《巴黎协定》时代”，国际社会面临的挑战还有很多。如何从国际法的角度去丰富《巴黎协定》内容和建立真正有效的履约机制，是国际社会在欢呼之后亟须认真思考的问题。

一 “形”、“神”各异的两个气候变化治理时代

（一）《巴黎协定》取代《京都议定书》的必然性

1.《京都议定书》的目标和特点

1997 年在日本京都召开的《联合国气候变化框架公约》缔约国第三次会议通过了《京都议定书》。《京都议定书》作为国际社会达成的第一个具有法律约束力的应对气候变化国际协定，无疑具有重要的历史进步意义。《京都议定书》要求发达国家在 2008 年到 2012 年实现其承诺的减排目标，并且建立了条约遵循机制（compliance mechanism）和专门的条约遵循委员会（compliance committee）来确保附件 B 所列国家达到其减排目标。[①]《京

① 《马拉喀什协定》建立了《京都议定书》的专门条约遵循委员会，来确保附件 B 所列国家实现《京都议定书》规定的减排目标。条约遵循委员会的职责包括：敦促缔约国达到其减排承诺、为缔约国提供帮助和建议、决定附件 B 所列国家是否遵循了《京都议定书》的减排要求和对于未实现减排承诺的国家实施惩罚措施。

都议定书》的第一阶段目标是附件 B 所列缔约国参照 1990 年的基准平均降低 5% 的温室气体排放量。2005 年《京都议定书》正式生效，在加拿大蒙特利尔召开的《联合国气候变化框架公约》第十一次大会也成为《京都议定书》缔约国的第一次大会，这次大会标志着国际社会开始通过对话达成战略性的国际合作行动来应对气候变化问题。当前，国际社会已进入《京都议定书》的第二个承诺期，该阶段的目标是附件 B 所列缔约国参照 1990 年的基准自 2013 年至 2020 年至少降低 18% 的温室气体排放量。《京都议定书》将在 2020 年被《巴黎协定》正式取代。

除了规定《京都议定书》附件 B 所列国家的强制温室气体减排目标外，《京都议定书》的一个重要特点同时也是一个伟大创新就是开启了碳市场化，把二氧化碳减排量变成能在碳交易市场上交易的商品，并且建立三种以市场为基础的灵活机制，即排放权交易机制（emissions trading），共同执行机制（joint implementation）和清洁发展机制（clean development mechanism）。《京都议定书》三大机制的主要目的就是帮助《京都议定书》缔约国低成本地实现其规定的减排目标，促使发展中国家走上低碳化的可持续发展道路，并且吸引资金开展碳减排项目。

2. 《京都议定书》的优点与局限性

（1）《京都议定书》的优点

《京都议定书》的先进性首先在于为了降低全球的温室减排成本而创造性地建立了三个以市场为基础的灵活机制，即针对附件 B 所列国家减排的排放权交易机制和共同执行机制，以及帮助发展中国家减排的清洁发展机制。其次，《京都议定书》赋予附件 B 所列国家在减排方式上的灵活性，即充分尊重国家主权，允许附件 B 所列国家自己决定本国的减排方式和制定符合本国国情的减排方针。最后，《京都议定书》体现了公平的原则，规定减排义务主要针对发达国家和那些对全球气候变化现状负有主要历史责任的国家，也就是《联合国气候变化框架公约》提出的共同但有区别责任原则。

（2）《京都议定书》的局限性

《京都议定书》虽然在气候变化国际立法发展历史中具有里程碑的意义，但是它也存在明显的不足和局限性。有鉴于此，《巴黎协定》取代《京都议定书》具有历史的必然性和进步性。正如 2014 年的政府间气候变化专门委员会（IPCC）报告所指出的“虽然具有法律约束力的《京都议定书》在实现UNFCCC所确立的目标和原则的道路上迈出了第一步，但是它并没有取得应该实现的目标……没有达到应该达到的环境成效标准（environmental effectiveness）。”①

首先，《京都议定书》的局限性体现在世界上最主要的温室气体排放国并没有被纳入强制减排中。美国作为世界上最大的碳排放国并没有批准《京都议定书》；同时世界上经济快速发展的几大发展中国家包括中国、印度、巴西和南非，它们的温室气体排放量已经超过许多发达国家，也没有被包括在条约中被要求实现强制减排目标。② 一些学者担心，没有这些碳排放大国的参与，《京都议定书》在很大程度上就是欧盟等国在履行减排承诺。而欧盟本身就已经制定了非常严格的减排目标，《京都议定书》的减排目标和欧盟本身制定的减排目标在很大程度上是相互重叠的，这使得《京都议定书》很难实现把全球气候变化控制在2度以内的目标。③

其次，由于《京都议定书》只有有限的附件B所列国家需要履行强制减排承诺，这就可能增加这些国家生产高碳排放商品（服务）的生产成本。从国际贸易角度来说，这些高碳排放产业就有可能转移到一些不用强制减排的国家来降低其生产成本，从而导致“碳泄漏”（carbon leakage）现象。

再次，另一个对《京都议定书》的担忧是，它的短期性可能会影响私营部门对低碳减排技术的投资。《京都议定书》的第一个承诺期只有5年（虽然已经平稳过渡到第二个承诺期），它的相对短期和未来前景的不确定

---

① 参见IPCC AR5 Working Group III报告中的第13章。Climate Change 2014：Mitigation of Climate Change IPCC Working Group III Contribution to AR5final report，chapter 13。网址：http://mitigation2014.org/英文原文：“The Kyoto Protocol was the first binding step toward implementing the principles and goals provided by the UNFCCC，but it has not been as successful as intended（medium evidence，low agreement）…the Protocol's environmental effectiveness has been less than it could have been.”

② Geoffrey Blanford，Richard Richels and Thomas Rutherford，“Revised Emissions Growth Projections for China：Why Post-Kyoto Climate Policy Must Look East”，Harvard Project on International Climate Agreements Discussion Paper 08－06，（2008），p. 8.

③ David Victor，*The collapse of the Kyoto Protocol and the Struggle to Slow Global Warming*（Princeton：Princeton University Press，2001），p. 26.

性，对私有企业的低碳减排投资有消极影响。而要有效刺激私有部门对低碳经营模式的投资，国际气候变化条约需要给市场一个长期的价格信号。①

最后，一些学者认为《京都议定书》的履约机制没有给附件 B 所列国家足够的刺激和约束力来敦促这些国家实现其减排承诺。②

事实上，《京都议定书》第一阶段的履约情况并不好。根据英国卫报（*The Guardian*）报道，附件 B 所列国家中，共有 12 个国家没有实现其承诺的减排目标，相当于大约三分之一的附件 B 所列缔约方没有实现承诺③。从全球范围来看，从 1990 年到 2011 年，全球的温室气体排放量增长了 11.3%，《京都议定书》并没有能遏制温室气体排放量增长的势头。除了减排目标方面的履约情况不令人满意，发达国家也没有积极履行对发展中国家提供资金和技术援助的承诺，《京都议定书》在推动发展中国家可持续发展方面也成效不佳。而《京都议定书》第二阶段的情况更不令人乐观，第二阶段的条约附件 B 所列国家即强制减排的国家只有部分欧洲国家和新西兰，即便完全实现其预设的减排目标也只能覆盖全球 14% 的全球温室气体排放量④。从这个角度来说，《京都议定书》第二阶段无论执行得多好，也已经失败了，无法有效推动全球温室减排。

相较而言，《巴黎协定》从一开始就赢得 186 个《联合国气候变化框架公约》缔约国的支持，相当于覆盖了全球 96% 的温室气体排放量，从条约的参与度来看，《京都议定书》被《巴黎协定》取代具有必然性。然而，只是基于覆盖国家的数量，就盲目乐观于《巴黎协定》的成果显然也是不科学的，因为这些令人振奋的数据背后有一个大大的前提，就是所有这些国家都能按照本国承诺的国家自主贡献目标（INDCs）进行减排。这个根本的前提就涉及《巴黎协定》的履约机制问题，如何使得这些缔约国在无

---

① Richard Newell, "International Climate Technology Strategies", The Harvard Project on International Climate Agreements Discussion Paper 08 - 12, (2008), p. 12.

② Scott Barrett, "A Portfolio System of Climate Treaties", The Harvard Project on International Climate Agreements Discussion Paper 08 - 13 (2008), p. 12.

③ "Has the Kyoto Protocol Made any Difference to Carbon Emissions?", The Guardian, http://www.theguardian.com/environment/blog/2012/nov/26/kyoto-protocol-carbon-emissions，最后访问时间：2016 年 4 月 2 日。

④ "Thanks to Paris, We Have a Foundation for Meaningful Climate Progress", The Conversation, http://theconversation.com/thanks-to-paris-we-have-a-foundation-for-meaningful-climate-progress-52525，最后访问日期：2016 年 4 月 2 日。

强制减排压力的情况下自觉自愿地实现自己的减排目标无疑是“后《巴黎协定》时代”面临的首要难题。

（二）《京都议定书》与《巴黎协定》的比较

《京都议定书》与《巴黎协定》在形式与实质上都存在根本不同，体现在治理机制、法律形式、法律基本原则、法律履约机制和市场机制等各方面。可以说，这两个条约分别代表了“形”、“神”各异的两个气候变化治理时代。

1. 治理机制

正如前文所述，《京都议定书》的治理机制是自上而下，它通过一种自上而下的方式为附件 B 所列国家制定了有法律约束力的强制减排目标，包括定量的国家减排标准（quantitative national performance standards）和为帮助其实现减排目标而制定的市场机制。这种方式旨在通过减排目标来鞭策各国采取符合本国国情的减排措施，从而达到全球减排的共同目标。自上而下的治理机制有着很好的出发点，希望通过总量控制来指导世界各国的减排行动。其他国际条约中也不乏自上而下治理机制的成功范本，比如 1987 年签署的《蒙特利尔破坏臭氧层物质管制议定书》（以下简称《蒙特利尔议定书》）也遵循了自上而下的机制，实施效果则非常显著。2003 年，时任联合国秘书长的科菲［安南（Annan）］称赞其为“迄今为止可能最为成功的国际条约”。① 然而，试图向《蒙特利尔议定书》学习的《京都议定书》虽然也推行自上而下的治理机制，虽然也是解决全球环境问题，但诸多因素导致实施效果不佳。在哥本哈根联合国气候变化大会谈判受挫以后，全球关于新的国际气候变化条约的谈判就基本放弃了自上而下的模式，开始探讨如何通过自下而上的管理方式，来重新构建全球应对气候变化的治理格局。从国际条约呈现的多样化的治理模式和各有成功及失败的结果可以看到，治理机制本身并不能决定一个国际条约的成败与否，一个国际条约采用何种治理机制取决于当时的国际政治、经济形势和大国博弈，两种机制本身各有优劣，最后国际条约采取何种治理方式则是多种因

① Bryan Green, “Lessons from the Montreal Protocol: Lessons for the next International Climate Change Agreement”, *Environmental Law* 39 (2009), p. 256.

素共同作用的结果。

《巴黎协定》最终采用的是自下而上为主、兼有自上而下成分的混合型治理机制。其中协定的自下而上治理机制主要体现在《巴黎协定》依靠缔约国提交的国家自主贡献目标来开展全球温室气体减排，每个缔约国减多少、采取什么样的形式减排是由各缔约国根据自身能力和特点来决定的。根据《巴黎协定》，各缔约方最晚于提交各自《巴黎协定》批准、加入或核准书之时通报它们的第一次国家自主贡献。纵观《巴黎协定》可以看到，国家自主贡献已经成为条约最为核心的内容。而协定保留的部分自上而下的治理机制成分则是体现在《巴黎协定》的检测、报告和核查（Monitoring，Reporting and Verification，MRV）机制上。比如，《巴黎协定》的第4条要求："……各缔约方应编制、通报它打算实现的下一次国家自主贡献……在通报国家自主贡献时，所有缔约方应根据第1/CP.21号决定和作为《巴黎协定》缔约方会议的《公约》缔约方会议的任何有关决定，为清晰、透明和了解而提供必要的信息……并参照第14条所述的全球总结的结果，每五年通报一次国家自主贡献……缔约方可根据作为《巴黎协定》缔约方会议的《公约》缔约方会议通过的指导，随时调整其现有的国家自主贡献，以加强其力度水平……约方通报的国家自主贡献应记录在秘书处持有的一个公共登记册上……缔约方应核算它们的国家自主贡献……并确保根据作为《巴黎协定》缔约方会议的《公约》缔约方会议通过的指导避免双重核算。"

从以上内容可以看到，《巴黎协定》给予了缔约国极大的自由度和自主性来决定国家自主贡献的减排目标和减排形式，从这个意义上来说是典型的自下而上的管理方式；同时，要求缔约国在提交自主贡献的相关信息上，要达到及时、透明和清晰的标准，在核算的方式和标准等问题上，又需要参照《巴黎协定》缔约方会议的指导进行，而且规定缔约国会议定期对全球国家自主贡献实现情况回顾总结，以确保国家自主贡献是在《巴黎协定》缔约国会议的宏观指导和监管下进行的，从而体现了从上而下的管理成分。

事实上，是否能真正基于全球统一的透明标准来实现缔约国的国家自主贡献目标，是关系《巴黎协定》是否有显著减排成效的重要因素。《巴黎协定》的透明标准是发达国家和发展中国家协商妥协的产物，意味着发展中国家需要在自主减排中同样遵循和发达国家一样严格透明的检测、报告和核算标准，这对于发展中国家相对不高的应对气候变化能力不仅是一个很大的挑战，也是对其能力提升的一个倒逼。可以预见的是，随着《巴黎协定》缔约国会议对《巴黎协定》的进一步丰富和完善，这种宏观指导的成分可能在国家自主贡献管理模式中的比重会加大，如此，《巴黎协定》的执行无疑将更加有效，也能充分发挥两种管理机制的互补优势。有鉴于此，本文采用了斯蒂文思（Stavins）等学者所提出的混合型治理机制来概括《巴黎协定》的治理模式，以突显自上而下的指导及监管对自下而上管理机制的重要补充作用。[①]

2. *法律形式*

对于《巴黎协定》的法律形式，虽然国际社会在2011年的德班会议[②]上就达成共识以“条约”（treaty）的法律形式呈现，但是条约中具体哪些方面的条款具有（或不具有）强制法律约束力则是巴黎会议前争论的一个热点问题。《维也纳条约法公约》第2条规定：“称‘条约’者，谓国家间所缔结而以国际法为准之国际书面协定，不论其载于一项单独文书或两项以上相互有关之文书内，亦不论其特定名称如何。”最终签署的《巴黎协定》依据德班会议的设计，采用了国际条约形式，也符合《维也纳条约法公约》关于“条约”的规定，对缔约国具有法律上的约束力。《巴黎协定》具有法律约束力，有利于获得国际社会的广泛认可和政治支持，也便于缔约国在国内法体系中通过纳入或转化方式加以适用以推动国内的应对气候变化行动。但是《巴黎协定》整体上的法律约束力不代表它的具体条文，特别是关系到温室气体减排的核心条款具有强制法律约束力，这也是《巴黎协定》和《京都议定书》在法律形式上最为显著的区别。

需要指出的是，条约的法律约束力是需要和其他几个相关但不同的概念区分的，包括法律文件的国内司法体系的适用（justiciable）、履约（enforcement）和条款的精确度（rule precision）。有学者认为，尽管在国内法

① Daniel Bodansky, Seth Hoedl, Gilbert Metcalf and Robert Stavins, “Facilitating linkage of climate policies through the Paris outcome”, *Climate Policy* 7 (2015), p. 2.

② 2011年德班平台（Durban Platform for Enhanced Action, ADP）关于新的国际条约的法律形式作了如下表述，称形成一个新的能够适用于所有公约缔约国的具有法律约束力的条约，这个条约应该不晚于2015年形成，并在2020年正式实施。参见UNFCCC网站：http://unfccc.int/bodies/body/6645.php，最后访问日期：2016年4月2日。

中这几个方面很可能是交织在一起的，但在国际法上这些方面往往并非重叠（Raustiala[①]，2005）。

根据《维也纳条约法公约》的第26条规定的“条约必须被遵守”原则，“凡有效之条约对其各当事国有拘束力，必须由各该国善意履行”，所以从条约遵守的角度来看，《巴黎协定》对于所有的缔约国都有法律约束力。在这点上，《巴黎协定》与《京都议定书》一样都是具有法律约束力的条约。

但是《巴黎协定》与《京都议定书》在履约和核心条款的精准度上有显著不同，集中体现在《巴黎协定》最为核心的国家自主贡献的减排条款不具有强制法律约束力，其采用的法律语言是“倡议性的”而非“强制要求性的”，并且在涉及国家自主贡献目标等条款规定上是不精确的，甚至是刻意模糊的。比如《巴黎协定》的第4条第2款“各缔约方应编制、通报并持有它打算实现的下一次国家自主贡献。缔约方应采取国内减缓措施，以实现这种贡献目标”。根据这样的规定，缔约方应采取相应的减排措施，但这样的执行并非强制性的，而更多的是基于自愿和自身能力进行。而且，对于减排的具体结果是否实现其订立的自主贡献目标，以及如果不能实现目标是否有惩罚措施方面，《巴黎协定》没有进一步的规定。换言之，《巴黎协定》在国家自主贡献等核心条款上的法律约束力更多是程序（procedure）上的而非实质（substance）性的。《巴黎协定》虽然规定了缔约国行为上的义务，即缔约国承诺就减排、适应、融资和能力建设等方面采取措施并报告相关信息，但是并没有结果上的义务，即缔约国并没有实现国家自主贡献承诺目标的强制结果义务。

3. *法律履约机制*

正如前文所述，法律履约机制的强制约束力是与条约本身的法律约束力不同的概念，两者也不互为条件。条约的履约机制主要涉及对于不履约行为是否有相应的惩罚措施，是否存在履约机制并非是一个法律文件是否具有约束力的必要条件。换句话说，具有法律约束力的条约可以不具有专门的履约机制来惩罚不履约行为，同样的，不具有法律约束力的法律文件

---

① Kal Raustiala, “Form and Substance in International Agreements”, *American Journal of International Law* 99 (2005), p. 593.

也可以具有惩罚机制来促进该法律文件的执行。从这样的标准划分，《京都议定书》是既有法律约束力又有履约机制的条约，而《巴黎协定》虽是具有法律约束力的协定，但是并没有真正有效的、惩罚非履约行为的履约机制，《巴黎协定》第 15 条规定“兹建立一个机制，以促进执行和遵守本协定的规定……机制应由一个委员会组成，应以专家为主，并且是促进性的，行使职能时采取透明、非对抗的、非惩罚性的方式……”《巴黎协定》这样一种非对抗的、非惩罚性的方式，被一些美国的学者（e. g. Kemp①，2015）所称道。他们认为《巴黎协定》应该保持这样的非强制履约的机制，只有如此《巴黎协定》才可能被美国国会批准，迎来更大程度的支持，避免出现《京都议定书》被美国拒绝批准的情况。但是从长远来看，如何敦促缔约国实现其国家自主贡献目标，仍然是“后《巴黎协定》时代”国际社会需要重点解决的问题。

令人欣慰的是，虽然《巴黎协定》没有强制履约机制，但是协定为促进条约的有效执行设立了透明度标准和定期回顾机制，关于透明度的安排包括“国家信息通报、两年期报告和两年期更新报告、国际评估和审评以及国际协商和分析”，以及对于协定的执行情况进行定期的全球总结和分析，并在 2023 年进行第一次全球总结②。这些制度设计大大提升了《巴黎协定》的执行力度，一定程度上弥补了协定缺乏惩罚性履约机制的不足。正如劳斯蒂亚拉（Raustiala）在分析国际条约是否具有有效的执行机制时指出，执行不力的国际条约往往既不具有对于非履约的惩罚性措施，也没有对于条约的执行情况进行定期分析和总结的机制。③ 所幸，《巴黎协定》虽没有对于非履约的惩罚性措施，但是设立了条约执行情况的回顾、总结和完善机制，只有能够真正基于缔约国提交的减排信息，总结并且不断完善其所设定的应对气候变化措施，《巴黎协定》才会成为具有显著环境成

① Luke Kemp, “Bypassing the ‘Ratification Straitjacket’: Reviewing US Legal Participation in a Climate Agreement”, *Climate Policy* 7 (2015), p. 4.

② 《巴黎协定》第 14 条关于协定执行情况的总结和分析有如下规定，“作为本协定缔约方会议的《公约》缔约方会议应定期总结本协定的执行情况，以评估实现本协定宗旨和长期目标的集体进展情况（称为全球总结）……作为《巴黎协定》缔约方会议的《公约》缔约方会议应在 2033 年进行第一次全球总结，此后每五年进行一次……”。

③ Kal Raustiala, “Form and Substance in International Agreements”, *American Journal of International Law* 99 (2005), p. 591.

效的真正国际法意义上的条约而非华而不实的政治宣言。这样的一种制度设计，也赋予了《巴黎协定》稳定性之外所需的灵活性。

4. 法律基本原则

《京都议定书》体现了国际环境法的诸多原则，特别是“共同但有区别责任原则”。基于这一原则，《京都议定书》在发展中国家和发达国家的减排目标问题上实行区别对待，考虑到发展中国家和发达国家在全球气候变化问题上的历史责任不同，它只要求附件 B 所列国家（主要是发达国家）遵循强制减排目标而发展中国家则可以自愿决定自己的减排目标。这一原则体现了对历史事实的尊重，对保护发展中国家的正当利益发挥了重要作用。然而《京都议定书》的这种区别对待影响了《京都议定书》的减排效果，缺少发展中国家参与强制减排的《京都议定书》不能有效达到减少全球温室气体排放的目标，甚至也影响了基于这一原则的清洁发展机制（CDM）的有效性。《巴黎协定》谈判过程中，对于是否保留“共同但有区别责任原则”以及如何在新的气候变化条约中体现该原则，发展中国家和发达国家两大阵营一直有着激烈的争论。美国等为首的发达国家虽然不敢公然提出废除“共同但有区别责任原则”，但是一直强调像《京都议定书》般把“共同但有区别责任原则”直接体现在发达国家和发展中国家不同的减排要求上，是对于“共同但有区别责任原则”的狭隘理解，也是导致《京都议定书》失败的一个重要原因。发展中国家则从发达国家温室气体排放的历史责任和发达国家自身较好的减排能力等方面出发，要求坚持保留“共同但有区别责任原则”。最终的《巴黎协定》保留了“共同但有区别责任的原则”，但是在“共同但有区别责任原则”后面又加上了“各自能力”，即“本协定的执行将按照不同的国情反映平等以及共同但有区别的责任和各自能力的原则”[①]，体现了发展中国家和发达国家的博弈和妥协。

《巴黎协定》在减排这一核心问题上不再区分发达国家和发展中国家，要求所有的缔约国都要依据各自能力提交国家自主贡献，从这个意义上来说，《巴黎协定》的“共同但有区别责任”已非《京都议定书》中的“共同但有区别责任”，而更多的重点是在新加上的“各自能力”

---

① 参见《巴黎协定》第 9 条。

原则上。当然，《巴黎协定》在发达国家对发展中国家的资金援助等问题上还保留了“共同但有区别责任原则”，但是发达国家在多大程度上能真正实践其承诺的资金、技术和能力建设援助则是“共同但有区别责任原则”是否能避免沦为只有“纸面效力”原则的关键所在。鉴于《京都议定书》时期发达国家资金落实不力的教训，在“后《巴黎协定》时代”，国际社会是否能够有效敦促发达国家根据《巴黎协定》第9条[①]的要求履行对发展中国家的资金援助无疑是比“共同但有区别责任原则”更为核心的问题。

5. 市场机制的存与废

《京都议定书》为了降低附件B所列国家的减排成本而设计的三种市场机制，能够有效帮助实现全球的低成本减排，并且赋予主权国家减排方式上的灵活性[②]。这三大灵活机制中的清洁发展机制还构成了发达国家把资金和技术转移到发展中国家以促进其减排的有效渠道，从而有利于鼓励发展中国家积极参与到全球的温室气体减排行动中。虽然《京都议定书》的三大灵活机制都还存在不足，需要在运作规则等方面进一步完善，然而这种尊重市场作用，充分利用市场刺激手段来进行减排的机制，无疑是充满创造性和先进性的，应该在新的联合国气候变化协定中保存和加强。然而《巴黎协定》并没有关于这三大市场机制的明确规定，但所幸的是《巴黎协定》的第6条为未来全球市场机制的构建留下了伏笔，“缔约方如果在自愿的基础上采取合作方法，并使用国际转让的减缓成果来实现国家自主贡献……兹在作为本协定缔约方会议的《公约》缔约方会议的授权和指导下，建立一个机制，供缔约方自愿使用，以促进温室气体排放的减缓，支持可持续发展……”而且《巴黎协定》的第7条第7款规定：“作为《巴黎协定》缔约方会议的《公约》缔约方会议应在第一届会议上通过本

① 《巴黎协定》第9条虽然没有明确发达国家对发展中国家资金援助的具体数额，但是关于《巴黎协定》决定的解释第54条提到，“发达国家有意在有意义的减缓行动和执行工作的透明度框架内，继续它们现有的到2025年的集体筹资目标；在2025年前，作为《巴黎协定》缔约方会议的《公约》缔约方会议将在考虑到发展中国家的需要和优先事项的情况下，设定一个新的集体定量目标，每年最低1000亿美元”。

② David Wirth, “The International and Domestic Law of Climate Change: A Binding International Agreement without the Senate or Congress?”, *Harvard Environmental Law Review 39* (2015), p. 526.

条第4款所述机制的规则、模式和程序。”可以预见的是，在接下来的缔约方会议上，国际社会将积极探讨如何建立一种基于自愿的全球自主贡献合作机制来促进缔约方之间在减排和可持续发展上的相互合作。但是，机制最终会以何种形式呈现，按照何种规则运作，与《京都议定书》时期的三大市场机制有何异同和关联，都是需要认真思考的重要问题。从上面的分析可以看到，在机制的“自愿性”和“目的”上（为了促进减排和可持续发展的双重目的），《京都议定书》与《巴黎协定》是有共同点的。

二 “后《巴黎协定》时代”的沉思与展望

基于上述讨论，笔者认为“后《巴黎协定》时代”国际社会还需要花很多力气来完善《巴黎协定》，把协定的关键条款和原则落在实处。其中，如何提高《巴黎协定》缔约国的履约积极性无疑是最为关键的问题。为了督促缔约国真正落实其承诺的国家自主贡献，构建有效的履约机制，国际社会需要从构建履约透明度框架与构建国家自主贡献的全球合作机制两个方面着重努力。需要指出的是，这两个方面本身存在逻辑上的关联且互为条件，一方面构建有效的缔约国履约透明度框架，需要建立能够对接各缔约国应对气候变化的全球合作机制；另一方面建立全球合作机制的一个重要前提，就是能够有相对统一的标准来实现国家自主贡献在不同国家和地区间的对接和转让，而且这样的转让需要有真实、可对比的信息作为前提。

（一）构建履约透明度框架，实现条约灵活性和有效性的双重目标

灵活性标准（flexibility）是衡量国际条约在面对重要的新信息和在变化的政治经济情况下，能否及时、灵活地调整相关法规来适应新形势发展的能力，这一标准也是衡量条约制度可行性的重要基准之一。[①] 同时灵活性标准还用于检验条约是否给予缔约国足够的灵活度和自主权，来决定本国的碳减排和气候适应措施的国家方针，从而更好地实现国家层面的应对

① Steffen Brunner, Christian Flachsland and Robert Marschinski, “Credible Commitment in Carbon Policy”, Climate Policy 12 (2012), p. 261.

温室气体减排策略和国际气候条约强制减排目标的有机融合，这对实现条约长期应对气候变化目标有积极作用。《巴黎协定》无疑符合国际条约的灵活性标准，它采取的国家自主贡献管理模式使得缔约国能够根据自身的情况来自主地决定该国的气候变化减排、适应目标以及目标的实现方式，这样的制度设计有利于吸引国家的广泛参与。然而《巴黎协定》的灵活性设计也会带来“搭便车”的问题，一些国家可能会基于“搭便车”的心理，在国家自主贡献中只是根据本国需要设定减排目标，而非根据协定要求设定真正投入巨大减排努力的目标，从而导致条约不能真正有效敦促缔约国积极努力地应对气候变化。换言之，《巴黎协定》虽然符合灵活性标准，但是如何同时实现条约的有效性标准则是一个棘手挑战。

正如前文所述，执行不力的国际条约往往既不具有对于非履约的惩罚性措施，也没有对于条约的执行情况进行定期分析和总结的机制。鉴于《巴黎协定》不具有强制履约措施的现状，提高条约的履约透明度和落实国家自主贡献的检测、报告和核查机制就成为敦促缔约国积极履约以实现《巴黎协定》灵活性和有效性双重目标的关键路径。当前提交的国家自主贡献无论在减排涉及的部门范围上、实现承诺的时间跨度上、环境成效衡量的标准上、计算减排成效的方法上，承诺的减排目标等方面都呈现出不同的形式①。这样的多样化形式无疑会增加《巴黎协定》构建相对统一透明的便于国家间横向对比的检测、报告和核查机制的难度。从功能性角度出发，一个旨在敦促缔约国积极履约的有效的检测、报告和核查机制需要至少符合以下几方面要求：第一，能够真实、及时、全面检测各缔约国完成国家自主贡献目标的情况，客观反映各缔约国真实的履约情况；第二，能够确立相对统一的标准来衡量比较不同国家的减排成效和减排努力，以便于国家之间相互监督各自的履约情况，降低“搭便车”的风险；第三，能够依据各缔约国的国家自主贡献成效全面、真实和及时地总结全球应对气候变化成效，以指导未来的缔约国国家自主贡献设计；第四，便利不同缔约国间的合作包括连接不同国家的碳市场和碳税体系；第五，该机制本身能够根据变化的国际形势和全球应对气候变化需求的改变来不断完善和

---

① Christina Hood, Liwayway Adkins and Ellina Levina, “Overview of INDCs Submitted by 31 August 2015”, *OECD Climate Change Expert Group Paper* No. 2015 (4), p. 6.

及时调整。

《巴黎协定》还可以借鉴其他国际条约在构建履约透明度框架方面的成功经验，比如《不扩散核武器条约》;[①] 在依靠国家自下而上自主汇报国家自主贡献信息的基础上，还可以采取其他辅助措施来提高收集的信息的可信度和精准度，比如由专家组进行无预警、定期实地抽查，独立的第三方核查审计（independent verification audit）或高科技远程卫星遥感，来监测大气中的温室气体排放情况。鉴于发展中国家可能缺乏足够的资金、资源、技术和能力来及时准确地监测和汇报本国国家自主贡献的实施情况，建议《巴黎协定》缔约方会议建立专项资金来援助有困难的发展中国家，并敦促发达国家在资金、技术和能力建设方面对发展中国家进行援助。此外，《巴黎协定》缔约方会议还需要对提供虚假履约信息的缔约国设立相应的惩罚措施，以惩戒试图在全球应对气候变化问题上“搭便车”的缔约国，提高缔约国整体的履约信心和积极性。

（二）构建国家自主贡献的全球合作机制，利用市场机制降低履约成本

如果说第一方面主要是从提高信息公开和透明来督促缔约国履行承诺，这一方面探讨的则是通过市场机制来刺激缔约国自觉、自愿地实现国家自主贡献，通过合作来减少缔约国的履约成本，充分调动私营部门的减排积极性。在《巴黎协定》下，全球国家自主贡献合作机制意味着一个国家或地区的减排成效也被另外一个国家或地区的减排体系认可，并且可以以某种形式比如碳排放信用额度（emission credit）的形式，在这个国家或地区的减排体系里进行交易、抵充和使用以达到低成本履约的目的。正如前文所讨论的，《巴黎协定》已经明确提出将构建基于自愿的国家自主贡献成效的国际转让机制，以促进缔约方之间在减排和可持续发展上的相互合作，以合作谋求实现低成本履约的双赢或是多赢目标。但是机制最终会以何种形式呈现、按照何种规则运作，则是需要国际社会深入讨论的问题。

---

① Jesse Ausubel and David Victor, “Verification of International Environmental Agreements”, *Annual Review of Energy and Environmental* 17 (1992), p. 21.

本文认为，鉴于当前提交的《巴黎协定》自主贡献目标和实现形式的多样化，基于自愿基础上的国际合作机制也可以以直接或非直接，双边或多边等多样化形式呈现。直接的国际合作机制指的是，不同国家或地区间达成共识，允许一个国家的碳排放信用额度（allowances or credits）等额或按照一定的兑换比例（at a trading ratio/exchange rate）在另外一个国家的减排体系（比如碳排放权交易机制）中使用，允许碳排放信用额度在合作国家的减排体系间转移、流通，这样的合作机制既可以是双边的也可以是多边的。间接的合作机制指的是，虽然两个国家的减排体系（比如碳排放权交易机制）并不直接认可双方的碳排放信用额度，但是它们都接受共同第三国的信用额度。在这样的机制下，它们通过共同的第三方实现了间接的碳市场连接并且因此影响彼此的碳市场交易价格。虽然碳排放权交易机制可能是最容易构成国际合作的市场减排机制，但是鉴于一些国家还没有推行碳排放权交易机制，建议在合作内容上，《巴黎协定》的全球国家自主贡献合作机制既可以连接不同国家（和地区）的碳排放权交易市场，也可以连接不同国家（和地区）间的碳税体系，或是把一个国家（和地区）的碳税体系与另一个国家（和地区）的碳排放权交易机制相连接。[①] 比如，在碳税的语境下，一国建立碳排放税收额度（Emission Tax Payment Credits，ETPCs），在不同国家的碳税体系间以及在碳税体系和碳排放权交易机制间买卖、转移。对于一些碳市场机制还没有建立起来的国家，还可以考虑把一些专项的气候减缓财政补偿（emission reduction subsidies）和其他基于政策的碳排放额度与碳税额度、碳排放权信用额度这些市场机制下的碳产品进行对接和交换，使得《巴黎协定》的国际合作机制能够最大限度地在不同国家间建立减排和可持续发展方面的合作。

构建国家自主贡献全球机制的最显著的好处是，缔约国通过寻求在所有该国合作的减排机制中最低成本的减排方法，来降低它实现国家自主贡献的成本，从而最终降低全球的减排成本和履约成本。国家自主贡献全球机制还有利于促进不同碳市场之间的碳排放额度的流通，从而增加碳市场的流动性，也可以降低由于不同国家碳政策严格程度不同而导致的“碳泄

---

① Matthew Ranson and Robert Stevens, “Post-Durban Climate Policy Architecture Based on Linkage of Cap-and-Trade Systems”, *The Chicago Journal of International Law* 13 (2013), p. 423.

漏”风险。[①] 国家自主贡献全球机制还有利于缔约国之间在相互合作的同时也加强相互间的监督，提高缔约国的履约积极性。同时，这样的全球连接机制也给予了参与机制的缔约国某种政治上和外交上的优势，有利于这些国家在国际舞台上获得碳话语权优势。而对于没有积极履约、没有参与全球合作机制或是怀有“搭便车”心理的国家会造成一种政治上的压力，这种现象可以被称为“气候俱乐部”现象[②]，也即同一气候俱乐部的国家在碳产品交易上的利益分享也仅限于该俱乐部成员，从而对没有参与俱乐部的国家造成促使其参加合作机制的正向压力和吸引力。需要指出的是，构建国家自主贡献全球机制最大的挑战是如何确保参与合作机制的缔约国全面及时地监测、报告和核查相关的减排信息，以确保在不同国家机制间交易的碳排放权额度和碳排放税收额度的真实性，避免碳排放额度在不同国家减排机制中的重复计算。这也再次凸显了自上而下的监管机制对于自下而上的国家自主贡献管理模式的不可或缺的引导和敦促作用，而且《巴黎协定》构建缔约国履约信息透明度框架是全球合作机制顺利运行的前提条件。

三 结语

联合国气候变化巴黎大会成功落幕，正式宣告一个气候变化治理时代被另一个时代所代替，鉴于《京都议定书》的明显不足，《巴黎协定》取代《京都议定书》也因此具有必然性和历史的进步性。但是这只是一个令人重燃希望的起点，“后《巴黎协定》时代”国际社会要面临的挑战还很多。《巴黎协定》的灵活性制度设计在最大程度上吸引了全球的广泛参与和支持，淡化了发展中国家与发达国家间的对立，却又由于强制履约机制的缺失而使得国际条约履约充满风险和不确定性。如何通过构建有效的履约透明度框架以实现条约的灵活性和有效性的双重目标，如何通过降低履约成本来提升履约积极性，都是国际社会在未来的缔约国会议上亟须解决

① Daniel Bodansky, Seth Hoedl, Gilbert Metcalf and Robert Stavins, “Facilitating Linkage of Climate Policies through the Paris Outcome”, *Climate Policy* 7 (2015), p. 2.

② William Nordhaus, “Climate Clubs: Overcoming Free-Riding in International Climate Policy”, *American Economic Review* 4 (2015), p. 1345.

的难题。带着这样的问题，本文从《京都议定书》和《巴黎协定》的“形”、“神”比较中来深入剖析《巴黎协定》在法律形式、法律原则和履约机制等方面的特点，并基于这样的分析来构建有效的履约透明度框架，包括条约执行情况的定期回顾机制和建立国家自主贡献全球机制这两方面，并对于如何提高缔约国的履约积极性、避免“搭便车”的风险提出建议。

（本文原载于《国际法研究》2016 年第 3 期）

法理学“指导”型知识生产机制及其困难

——从法理学教材出发

田　夫[*]

改革开放以来，中国法理学取得了巨大进步。其中，一个重要表现就是法理学教材的进步。从 20 世纪 50 年代继承苏联的“国家和法权理论”，到 20 世纪 80 年代的“法学基础理论”，再到 20 世纪 90 年代以后的“法理学”，单从名称来看，法理学教材的发展就烙下了深刻的时代印痕。不惟名称，法理学教材内容的发展也往往蕴含着丰富的时代气息。但是，较之于个性化色彩更强的法理学研究，由于特殊的教学功能以及由此决定的相关因素，法理学教材的发展仍显缓慢，甚至在很多问题上还残留着苏式法理学的痕迹。当然，苏式法理学也并非一无是处。对此，正确的态度应该是，全面、仔细地对苏式法理学对中国法理学教材的影响进行分析，然后去伪存真。这种影响集中表现在对如下问题的看法上：法理学与部门法学的研究对象是什么以及它们之间究竟是怎样一种关系？这个问题之所以是重要的，是因为对它的回答，必然涉及如何看待法理学作为一门学科得以独立存在的根据。就此问题而言，苏式法理学，基于法理学与部门法学具有不同的研究对象这一判断，认为法理学是部门法学的指导性学科，并在这种认识的支配之下，生产出了在逻辑上可以指导部门法学的法理学知识，因此，本文将法理学知识称为“指导”型知识。

然而最近，这种关于法理学知识之有效性的看法，却受到了来自各个方面不同程度的质疑，以致最终导致法学界对法理学教材的持续批评。但

---

* 田夫，中国社会科学院国际法研究所副研究员。

是，相对于各种场合口头上的批评，真正对法理学知识有效性乃至法理学教材展开有效批评的专门研究并不多。从既有研究来看，有学者指出，法理学与部门法学是指导与被指导的关系是法理学者自己给自己设置的障碍，也对法理学的法律关系等理论提出了质疑；[①] 有学者详尽梳理了法理学法律行为理论的流变，展示了法理学法律行为理论与民法学法律行为理论的分歧；[②] 有学者进一步考察了法理学法律行为理论对民法学法律行为概念的误读，并指出导致上述误读的根本原因可能在于语言翻译问题；[③] 有学者则对法理学法律体系理论提出了质疑。[④] 但是，由于研究视角等原因，既有研究均未从知识生产机制的角度考察法理学法律关系理论、法律行为理论等“指导”型知识产生的根源，也未将上述根源与对法律体系理论的批评结合起来。本文试图从“指导”型知识生产机制的角度对法理学知识及其有效性进行反思，进而重新审视法理学、部门法学的研究对象及其相互关系问题。

“指导”型知识生产机制的一般结构由基本原理和运行机制两个部分构成。其基本原理是，法理学的研究对象是整体性的、共同性的，部门法学的研究对象是部分性的、非共同性的，所以法理学是部门法学的指导性学科，享有生产“指导”型知识的特权。从法理学对部门法学的指导这一立场出发，“指导”型知识生产机制的运行机制分为正面向度和反面向度，正面向度是指法理学针对部门法学生产“指导”型知识的机制；当然，从部门法学有助于法理学丰富和发展的角度，部门法学也可能有助于“指导”型知识的生产，本文将部门法学帮助法理学生产“指导”型知识的机制称为“指导”型知识生产机制的反面向度。因此，本文对“指导”型知识生产机制正面向度与反面向度的提法，仅仅是在法理学与部门法学的关系向度的意义上而言的；从逻辑上讲，在展开对相关“指导”型知识的有效性的评价之前，无论是“正面向度”还是“反面向度”的提法，其本身都不意味着对“指导”型知识生产机制的价值判断。

① 参见刘作翔《法理学的定位——关于法理学学科性质、特点、功能、名称等的思考》，《环球法律评论》2008 年第 4 期。

② 参见黄金荣《法理学中的“法律行为”》，载郑永流主编《法哲学与法社会学论丛》2006 年第 2 期，北京大学出版社，2007，第 18—30 页。

③ 参见朱庆育《法律行为概念疏证》，《中外法学》2008 年第 3 期。

④ 参见冀祥德主编《法治的理念、制度与现实》，中国人民公安大学出版社，2013，第 6 页。

一 “指导”型知识生产机制：苏式法理学教材的一般看法

“指导”型知识生产机制深刻蕴含于法理学教材之中，而从历史的角度来看，法理学教材构成了1949年以后中国法理学学术传统形成与发展的核心。因此，在梳理苏式法理学教材关于“指导”型知识生产机制的一般看法之前，有必要先行介绍法理学教材的沿革史。

中国法理学教材从苏联法理学教材沿袭发展而来，自不待言。但准确地讲，苏联教材对中国教材的影响，其实是苏联教材中译本对中国教材的影响。在那个全面学习老大哥但同时又百废待兴的时代，直接使用苏联教材的学者毕竟是少数，大部分学者还是要仰仗苏联教材中译本。这一点决定了本文对苏联教材的考察其实是对苏联教材中译本的考察，也决定了这种考察还可能涉及对俄语中译的评价。顺便说明的是，由于本文涉及大量法理学教材，为简便计，正文中一律以“主编或作者（出版年份，译著为中文版出版年份）”简称。其中，对译著标明中文版出版年份而非原版出版年份的做法，正是出于从知识传播与生产的角度展开的考虑。通过对苏联教材中译本与中国教材出版年份的明确标示，更能直观、准确地考察苏联法理学影响中国的历史。

1949年以后，中国法理学教材经历了由最初的翻译苏联教材到后来的自编教材的过程。在20世纪50年代翻译的苏联教材中，“研究所（1954）”一书最具代表性，[①] 这表现在以下几个方面。第一，该书由苏联科学院法学研究所科学研究员集体编著，作者的身份与集体性决定了该书的权威性。第二，该书由中国人民大学马克思列宁主义关于国家与法权理论教研室翻译，并于1952年由中国人民大学初版、1954年再版，是中国人民大学这所“新中国普通高等法学教育基地”组织翻译的第一部苏联法理学教材。[②]

---

① 参见苏联科学院法学研究所科学研究员集体编著《马克思列宁主义关于国家与法权理论教程》，中国人民大学马克思列宁主义关于国家与法权理论教研室译，中国人民大学出版社，1954。

② 关于中国人民大学在中华人民共和国全面学习苏联法理论过程中的作用和地位，参见刘颖《法概念的跨语际实践：苏联法在中国（1948—1958）》，法律出版社，2011，第111—114页；关于“研究所（1954）”在1950年后法理学汉语类教学用书中客观上的时间排序，参见付子堂主编《法理学高阶》，高等教育出版社，2008，第564页。

据译者言："在苏联法学界编写的新的更完善的《国家与法权理论》教科书尚未出版以前，本书仍不失为一本较好的教科书。"[①] 事实上，后来出版的"卡列娃（1956）"的四位作者也来自苏联科学院法学研究所，[②] 其间的知识关联自不待言。而这两本教材也被认为是20世纪50年代的中国"使用比较广泛的教材"。[③] 第三，最重要的是，在该书中，能够找到"指导"型知识生产机制最原始，但同时也是最清晰的一般结构，对该结构的分析是反思这一机制的逻辑起点。

（一）"指导"型知识生产机制的一般结构

早在"研究所（1954）"第一章"国家与法权理论的对象与方法"中，就蕴含了"指导"型知识生产机制的一般结构。该章第一节"马克思列宁主义国家与法权理论的对象"这样论述国家与法权理论这一学科与其他法学学科的关系，也即"指导"型知识生产机制的基本原理："研究国家与法权的不仅是国家与法权理论这一学科，此外尚有许多其他法权学科：国家法、行政法、刑法、民法、集体农场法、家庭法、国际法、刑事诉讼法、民事诉讼法、法院组织法、土地法、财政法等。这些学科称之为'部门'或'专门'学科。它们的名称的本身即指出了每一门学科都是研究法权的个别部门，法权材料的个别部分，法权关系的个别规范而不是全部法权体系（法权体系是各个法权部门的一定的总和与统一，在第十五章'苏维埃社会主义法权体系'中将专门详细地论述）。"[④]

这段话表明，较之于国家与法权理论，其他法权学科因为研究对象是部门法所以是"部门"学科，而国家与法权理论"的对象是整个国家与法权。因此对各部门学科来说，它是一门共同性的学科。它所研究的问题，

---

① 苏联科学院法学研究所科学研究员集体编著《马克思列宁主义关于国家与法权理论教程》，中国人民大学马克思列宁主义关于国家与法权理论教研室译，中国人民大学出版社，1954，"译者的话"。

② 参见〔苏〕卡列娃等《国家和法的理论》（上册），李嘉恩等译，中国人民大学出版社，1956，"译者的话"。

③ 郭忠：《中国法理学教材发展的阶段和趋势——基于1950年到2010年教材出版情况和内容的分析》，《甘肃政法学院学报》2012年第4期。

④ 苏联科学院法学研究所科学研究员集体编著《马克思列宁主义关于国家与法权理论教程》，中国人民大学马克思列宁主义关于国家与法权理论教研室译，中国人民大学出版社，1954，第5页。

对其他有关国家与法权的科学有着共同的意义。这些问题就是该国家与法权的各个不同部门中所具有的共同性的问题”。[①]

如何体现这种共同性呢？教材继续指出：“没有一般的理论概念，如国家、法权、国家机构、国家职能、法权规范、法权关系等，便不能正确地来区分不同时代、不同国家间国家与法权的不同，不能发掘出苏维埃社会主义国家与法权同剥削者的国家与法权的本质区别，没有这些一般概念，就不可能进行研究法权的任何一个部门。马克思列宁主义国家与法权理论所研究的一般概念和理论原理对法权科学体系中之任何一门学科讲来，都是其基本原理和概念。”[②] 在这段话中，“指导”型知识生产机制开始了由基本原理到运行机制的理论推演——国家与法权理论要生产出适用于部门法学的一般理论概念和理论原理，“国家与法权理论这一学科所包含的理论原理，对一切其他各‘部门’学科都是共同的、必要的。”[③]

这种共同性与必要性到底能达到什么程度呢？教材指出：“把马克思列宁主义国家与法权理论视为其他各门学科的一个补充、辅助学科，把它视为只是那些不同的法学学科所包含的一般问题的‘概括’，它只是解答这些一般性的问题，它只是在学习上、在方法上来补充那些学科，免得在各部门学科中再来赘述这种一般问题，以上这些想法都是非常错误的。”[④] 这段话表明，“指导”型知识生产机制的指导性也即上述共同性与必要性已经达到了非常高的程度，它既不是补充性与辅助性的，也不是概括性的，而是高度适用性的。这个结论并非危言耸听——“国家与法权理论为一切‘部门’法权学科提供了基本原理。‘部门’法权学科在研究和论述

---

① 苏联科学院法学研究所科学研究员集体编著《马克思列宁主义关于国家与法权理论教程》，中国人民大学马克思列宁主义关于国家与法权理论教研室译，中国人民大学出版社，1954，第 5 页。

② 苏联科学院法学研究所科学研究员集体编著《马克思列宁主义关于国家与法权理论教程》，中国人民大学马克思列宁主义关于国家与法权理论教研室译，中国人民大学出版社，1954，第 7 页。

③ 苏联科学院法学研究所科学研究员集体编著《马克思列宁主义关于国家与法权理论教程》，中国人民大学马克思列宁主义关于国家与法权理论教研室译，中国人民大学出版社，1954，第 7 页。

④ 苏联科学院法学研究所科学研究员集体编著《马克思列宁主义关于国家与法权理论教程》，中国人民大学马克思列宁主义关于国家与法权理论教研室译，中国人民大学出版社，1954，第 7—8 页。

本门学科的基本问题时是以国家与法权理论所确定的这些原理、制度与概念为出发点的。”① 至此，“指导”型知识生产机制的指导性所具有的高度适用性已表现得淋漓尽致和无以复加。

相对于没有明确表述国家与法权理论要“指导”“部门”法权学科的苏联教科书，20 世纪 50 年代的中国教科书更进一步。“人大（1957）”在重申“研究所（1954）”有关国家和法权理论与部门法学研究对象不同这一观点之后，紧接着指出：“国家和法权理论所阐明的有关国家和法权的基本问题，对各专门法律学科有着指导意义；各专门法律学科的成就则有助于国家和法权理论内容的丰富和发展。”② 自此以后，尽管表述各异，但实质上，中国法理学教科书都保持了与“研究所（1954）”和“人大（1957）”相同的逻辑——法理学的研究对象是整体性的、共同性的，部门法学的研究对象是部分性的、非共同性的，所以法理学享有生产“指导”型知识的特权，进而对部门法学发挥指导作用。

（二）“指导”型知识生产机制的学制保障

如果说“研究所（1954）”第一章第一节是在学理层面事实上论证了“指导”型知识生产机制的话，那么第五节“国家与法权理论课程的内容与体系”的下面这段话则在学制层面保证了这一机制的高度适用性：“在高等法律学校中，应当最先讲授这门学科。把它作为研究一切部门法学学科的引言，作为一切法学学科的一般理论基础。这门学科应当使读者对国家与法权科学的基本具体问题有个一般概念，对读者在研究其他部门学科时将遇到的各种不同的现象有一原则的观点。”③

在“指导”型知识生产机制的一般结构与学制保障之间，存在双向的互动关系。一方面，一般结构决定了学制保障。既然“指导”型知识的功

---

① 苏联科学院法学研究所科学研究员集体编著《马克思列宁主义关于国家与法权理论教程》，中国人民大学马克思列宁主义关于国家与法权理论教研室译，中国人民大学出版社，1954，第 8 页。

② 中国人民大学法律系国家和法权理论教研室集体编写《国家和法权理论讲义》（上册），中国人民大学出版社，1957，第 3 页。

③ 苏联科学院法学研究所科学研究员集体编著《马克思列宁主义关于国家与法权理论教程》，中国人民大学马克思列宁主义关于国家与法权理论教研室译，中国人民大学出版社，1954，第 30 页。

能在于实现法理学对部门法学的指导，那么，就必须将法理学的讲授置于部门法学的讲授之前；否则，法理学对部门法学的指导就是没有意义的。另一方面，学制保障又巩固了一般结构。法理学既然要成为部门法学的指导性学科，就必须保证其提供的知识能够有效地指导部门法学。从学制的角度看，上述保证要经得起在法理学之后讲授的部门法学知识的检验，至少不要产生明显的矛盾。这就要求法理学研究者更加认真地研究“指导”型知识，这也就无形中强化了一般结构。

在此后的教材中，从字面表述上讲，“指导”型知识生产机制都没有像在“研究所（1954）”中那样表现得直接而全面，在有的教材中甚至难觅字面表述的踪迹。但需要强调指出的是，比字面表述重要得多的是教材内在的思维方式与逻辑结构。而一旦认真反思后者，就会发现，我们依旧深处“指导”型知识生产机制的历史脉络之中。下文将从“指导”型知识生产机制的运行机制开始分析，经由该机制的基本原理，最后分析该机制的理论基础。

二 “指导”型知识生产机制运行机制的正面向度：法律关系理论

从法理学教材的内在逻辑而言，所有的法理学知识对部门法学都是具有指导意义的，因而所有的法理学知识都是“指导”型知识。然而，除了反复的强调但同时又是含混的申明以外，教材并未明确告诉我们法理学是怎样具体地指导部门法学的，这就使得我们不得不去具体地考察教材的每个章节，去考察在这些章节之上法理学与部门法学的关系，进而思考何为“指导”这一问题。然而，一旦付诸具体章节，就可以发现“指导”呈现出三种基本的含义。第一种是意识形态意义上的，由于苏式法理学重在研究国家和法律的基本理论，而后者以阶级性著称，因此，这种意义上的“指导”保证了部门法学基本的政治正确方向。如果说这种意义上的“指导”随着法理学意识形态功能的淡化而渐告隐退的话，后两种意义上的“指导”则随着法学自主性的增强而逐渐凸显。第二种意义上的“指导”是在学科之间的参考与借鉴意义上而言的，与这种意义有关的章节一般不构成部门法学的内容，因而需要参考与借鉴法理学，但这恐怕不是“指导”的核心意义所在；因为如果是在参考与借鉴的意义上讲“指导”，法理学也需要参考与借鉴部门法学，那是不是意味着法理学也要接受部门法学的指导呢？很明显，法理学教材没有这个意思。第三种意义则符合了“指导”型知识的高度适用性，它是指法理学知识要高度适用于部门法学之中，而不是也不可能是相反的情况。在这种含义维度上，最典型的法理学知识莫过于法律关系理论和法律行为理论。因为法理学教材正是强调了法律关系和法律行为的一般理论框架可以适用于对部门法学的法律关系和法律行为的分析之中，与此同时，在法学研究与法学教育中，法理学指导部门法学的有效性所招致的绝大部分质疑也正是基于法律关系理论和法律行为理论。因此，本文将法律关系理论和法律行为理论作为“指导”型知识的典型。而如果考虑到“指导”型知识生产机制运行机制的正面向度与反面向度之分，法律关系理论正好对应着正面向度，法律行为理论正好对应着反面向度。

（一）法理学教材法律关系理论发展概述

法律关系是法律的基本概念。对法律的基本概念的研究是19世纪晚期至20世纪早期德语和英语国家法学的一个共同趋势，在前者，代表者是一般法理论，在后者，代表者是奥斯丁等人。[①] 尽管目前中文世界尚无研究考证彼时俄国法学界自身的发展状况以及对外国法学理论的借鉴状况，但可以确定的是，俄国法学界也展开了对法律的基本概念的研究，在法律关系领域也是如此。俄国当代学者马尔琴科在《国家与法的理论》的“法律关系”一章中，就不时引用俄国19世纪末20世纪初学者特鲁别茨柯伊、舍尔舍涅维奇、科尔库诺夫等人的法律关系理论。[②] 譬如舍尔舍涅维奇认为：“由法律规范规定的人们之间的日常生活关系的那一方面，就是法律关系。”[③]

苏联法理学在坚持马克思主义的基础上吸纳了沙俄时期法律关系理论

---

① 参见舒国滢《走出概念的泥淖——“法理学”与“法哲学”之辨》，《学术界》2001年第1期。

② 参见〔俄〕M.H. 马尔琴科《国家与法的理论》，徐晓晴译，中国政法大学出版社，2010，第427—439页。

③ 〔俄〕舍尔舍涅维奇：《法的一般理论》，莫斯科，1912，第568页；转引自〔苏〕斯塔利格维奇《社会主义法律关系理论的几个问题》，辛洁译，《政法译丛》1957年第5期。

的部分因素，将法律关系理论发展成为法理学教科书的重要一章。而中国法理学又紧随其后发展至今。“研究所（1954）”“社会主义社会的法权关系”一章在第一节“关于法权关系的概念”中开宗明义地指出：“法权规范调整着人们彼此之间的相互关系，他们相互的权利及义务，并因此而赋予它所调整之人们关系以一种特殊的性质——法权关系的性质：人们做为权利及义务的承担者而出现。法权关系就是人们做为法权规范所规定与保障之权利及义务的承担者而参与的人们相互间的关系。”① 可见，它一开始就将权利与义务作为法律关系的基本要素。进一步地，它将权利与义务运用到了对各部门法法律关系的分析上去。

“研究所（1954）”法权关系这一章分为概念、要素、法的事实的内容安排，基本上延续到20世纪80年代中期的中国法理学教材之中。值得注意的是，在“陈守一、张宏生（1981）”一书中，出现了在实质意义上改造法律关系概念的尝试。该书“社会主义法律关系”一章由沈宗灵所撰，该章第一次尝试突破既有的法律关系理论。尽管该章依然将法律关系界定为“人们根据法律规定而结成的各种权利和义务的关系”，② 但该章第二节“权利、职权和义务的概念”明显试图将职权作为法律关系的一项要素。

不但如此，该节第一次从中西比较的角度论述了权利、职权与权力的关系。该节指出：“法律上的权利这一用语最早来源于以《查士丁尼民法大全》为代表的罗马法……但罗马法中讲的权利是指以财产权为中心的一般民事权利。以后到十七、十八世纪资产阶级反封建斗争时，新兴资产阶级的政治、法律思想家将权利这一概念不仅适用于资产阶级的财产权，而且也扩大到所谓公民权，即政治权利。十九世纪的资产阶级法学家不仅确认法律关系的主体有自然人与法人之分，而且法人中又分为公法人和私法人，公法人即指国家或国家机关。因而权利和义务的概念同样适用于国家机关、其他团体和个人。”③ 所以，“权利和职权、权限或权力这些概念是等同的”。④

---

① 苏联科学院法学研究所科学研究员集体编著《马克思列宁主义关于国家与法权理论教程》，中国人民大学马克思列宁主义关于国家与法权理论教研室译，中国人民大学出版社，1954，第479页。

② 陈守一、张宏生主编《法学基础理论》，北京大学出版社，1981，第348页。

③ 陈守一、张宏生主编《法学基础理论》，北京大学出版社，1981，第353—354页。

④ 陈守一、张宏生主编《法学基础理论》，北京大学出版社，1981，第353页。

但是，“在我国，国家机关作为法律关系主体时，不能笼统地讲享有权利。在有的场合下，可用‘权利’一词，但在绝大多数场合下，似用‘职权’一词为宜。”[①] 沈宗灵意识到了国家机关作为主体参加民事法律关系与宪法法律关系的区别，他进一步明确区分了职权和权利，概括而言：第一，职权的主体是国家机关，权利的主体是公民；第二，权利一般与个人利益相联系，而职权只代表集体或国家利益；第三，与权利不同，职权与义务、职权与职责事实上是合二为一的；第四，职权意味着权力，与国家的强制力密切联系，而公民在其权利遭到侵犯时，一般只能要求国家机关的保护，而不是由公民来强制实施。[②]

此后，沈宗灵还陆续发表了《对霍菲尔德法律概念学说的比较研究》、《权利、义务、权力》等文，深化了对法律关系理论的探讨。[③] 在前一篇论文中，沈宗灵重点比较了霍菲尔德的学说与中国法律中相应概念的异同。在后一篇论文中，沈宗灵重点论述了权利、义务、权力等概念。这两篇论文与“陈守一、张宏生（1981）”都体现了沈宗灵发展法律关系理论的两大资源：一是中国的现行部门法规范，二是霍菲尔德等人的法律关系理论。这客观上表明了沈宗灵思考法律关系要素问题的努力。沈宗灵的核心贡献可以归纳为，他注意到了权利与权力的关系在中国和西方（包括苏联）的根本差异——在中国，权利与权力在主体、法益以及各自与义务和国家强制力的关系等方面均有根本差异；而在西方，则不存在上述差异。

但也必须承认，沈宗灵并未发展出一套有机整合苏式法理学法律关系理论、两大法系法律关系理论的法律关系理论。而此后的大部分教科书更是未在法律关系一章像沈宗灵那样明确区分权力（职权）与权利，依旧坚持着权利义务二要素理论。这样做的结果正如刘作翔所指出的：“中国现有法理学对法律关系的理论，只能部分地解释民事法律关系，而不能充分地说明刑事法律关系、行政法律关系、宪法法律关系，因此，中国现有法理学关于法律关系的理论，常常在法学实践中和法律实践中不具有充分的

---

① 陈守一、张宏生主编《法学基础理论》，北京大学出版社，1981，第 354 页。

② 参见陈守一、张宏生主编《法学基础理论》，北京大学出版社，1981，第 354—355 页。

③ 参见沈宗灵《对霍菲尔德法律概念学说的比较研究》，《中国社会科学》1990 年第 1 期；沈宗灵《权利、义务、权力》，《法学研究》1998 年第 3 期。

说服力和解释力。”[①]

（二）法律关系理论在部门法中的应用：以刑事法律关系为例

在法律关系理论尚未成熟之时，就着急着要去“指导”部门法学，其间的仓促，是可想而知的。然而，基于“指导”型知识的功能，这样的“指导”确实发生了，这主要表现在所谓刑事法律关系的问题上。

有趣的是，中国法学界关于刑事法律关系的研究，是从法理学者舒国滢的《刑事法律关系初探》一文开始的。[②] 舒国滢在该文中从苏联法学界对刑事法律关系的研究出发，认为：“刑事法律关系的主体是国家和犯罪人，其内容表现为一方享有刑罚权，另一方履行刑罚义务，同时也享有不受‘法外用刑’的权利：其客体是刑事权利和义务所指向的目标，即实现刑罚本身。”[③] 他还进一步指出：“只有使人们在认识上接受‘刑事处罚是一种权利（而不是权力）关系’这一观念，才能提高个人的法律意识，从而使人们能自觉地避免或制止适用法律过程中可能出现不依法办事、拘情枉法、‘司法专横’等非法现象的发生。”[④]

舒国滢将刑事法律关系的内容界定为权利与义务的做法，对此后关于刑事法律关系的研究产生了一定影响，[⑤] 但也遭到了质疑。张小虎明确指出：“这或许是受法理学法律关系界说的影响。其实，法理学法律关系界说的本身就有着一定的局限性，是‘苏联＋民事法律关系’的模式。应当说，由于刑事法律关系的特殊性，其内容并不表现为‘权利与义务’，而是‘权力与责任’。”[⑥]

事实上，从30年前舒国滢发表上述论文一直到现在，对刑事法律关系的研究一直未成为中国刑法学研究的主流。这其中，除了刑法学自身发展的因素使然外，法理学自身薄弱的法律关系理论未能为刑事法律关系提供合适的理论基础未尝不算是一个原因，这也为下文深入反思法律关系理论

---

① 刘作翔：《法理学的定位——关于法理学学科性质、特点、功能、名称等的思考》，《环球法律评论》2008年第4期。

② 参见舒国滢《刑事法律关系初探》，《法学评论》1985年第6期。

③ 舒国滢：《刑事法律关系初探》，《法学评论》1985年第6期。

④ 舒国滢：《刑事法律关系初探》，《法学评论》1985年第6期。

⑤ 参见刘生荣《论刑事法律关系》，《中外法学》1993年第2期。

⑥ 张小虎：《论刑事法律关系的内容》，《中国刑事法杂志》2000年第2期。

的知识生产机制提供了契机。

（三）法律关系理论的知识生产机制

通过上文的梳理可以看出，自苏联将法律关系要素界定为权利义务之后，这一直被苏中法理学通说和绝大部分教材所遵循，并被当然地认为可以适用到对部门法的分析中去，直至遭到各种形式的质疑。为了反思法律关系理论的知识生产机制，还需与欧陆和英美的相关理论展开比较。

前文已述，对法律的基本概念的研究是 19 世纪晚期至 20 世纪早期德语和英语国家法学的一个共同趋势。尽管限于语言、资料的原因，笔者不能直接考察德国的一般法理论，但可以通过相关资料考察其对法律关系的思考。考夫曼在介绍一般法理论时整理出了法律关系的体系。他指出，权利是法律关系的核心。所谓权利，即："由法律取得可以独自贯彻法律所保护利益（法益）的意志力。"[①] "法律关系有公法的、私法的及社会法的三种。"[②] 相应地，权利也有公法上的权利、私法上的权利和社会权三种。公法上的权利包括国家对于个人的权利和个人对于国家的权利，进一步地，考夫曼引用耶利内克的观点，将个人对于国家的权利细分为基本的与自由的权利、参与的权利、正面的请求权。私法上的权利依其内容分为绝对权、相对权、形成权。

相比于一般法理论，在法律关系理论上对后世产生更大影响的是美国法学家霍菲尔德。后者在其名篇《司法推理中应用的若干基本法律概念》、《司法推理中应用的基本法律概念》中所言"基本法律概念"就是专指法律关系。他指出，那种认为"一切法律关系皆可化约为'权利'与'义务'"的认识是一种臆断，是"清晰理解、透彻表述以及正确解决法律问题的最大障碍之一"。[③] 为此，他提出了权利——无权利、特权——义务、权力——无权力、豁免——责任四组相反关系和权利——义务、特权——无权利、权力——责任、豁免——无权力四组相关关系。他认为，各种法律关系皆能纳入上述相反关系和相关关系之中，进而被加以准确、科学的分析，直至正确解决法律问题。

---

① 〔德〕考夫曼：《法律哲学》，刘幸义等译，法律出版社，2004，第 158 页。
② 〔德〕考夫曼：《法律哲学》，刘幸义等译，法律出版社，2004，第 159 页。
③ 〔美〕霍菲尔德：《基本法律概念》，张书友译，中国法制出版社，2009，第 26 页。

本文并不旨在研究一般法理论和霍菲尔德的法律关系理论，而是通过对其的初步概述展现19世纪晚期至20世纪早期欧陆、英美法学对法律关系问题的基本思考。尽管这两种理论在理论传统、研究旨趣等问题上差异不小，但它们都反映出了一个共同特征，即它们都没有将权利义务作为不可细化的因素运用到对法律关系的分析中去，而是均在各自法制传统的基础上在不同情形中对法律关系作了不同的细化分析，以真正适应相应情形的需要。

反观苏联法理学，并没有对权利义务作任何进一步的细化，而是想当然地认为权利义务可以适用到对任何部门法法律关系的分析之中。如果说，这种认识的弊端在不严格区分权力与权利的苏联还不明显的话，那么，它在严格区分权力与权利的中国则暴露无遗，直至导致诸如上文已述的刑法学者对法理学法律关系理论的质疑等各种批评。究其根本，这种弊端是在不结合部门法的实际情况的前提下，机械适用权利义务二要素的法律关系理论的结果。

三 “指导”型知识生产机制运作机制的反面向度：法律行为理论

上文通过梳理法律关系理论，展现了“指导”型知识生产机制运行机制的正面向度。实践证明，因循这一向度产生的“指导”型知识是无效的。那么，从部门法学有助于法理学的向度即反面向度出发生产“指导”型知识的效果又如何呢？法理学教材中的法律行为理论正好是考察这一向度的最佳范例。

与法律关系理论不同，法律行为理论是在20世纪90年代才成为“指导”型知识的。但在教科书中，法律行为理论早已存在，这是怎样一回事呢？在20世纪90年代以前，法律行为理论并未独立成章，法律行为只是法律事实的下位概念，而法律事实理论是作为法律关系理论的一部分而存在的。从上述关系似乎可以认为，作为法律关系理论的一部分而存在的法律行为理论也是“指导”型知识。实则不然，因为，在20世纪90年代以前，法理学界关于法律行为这一概念本身并未形成统一的用法，而且存在很大的不同。这种差异不仅仅是表述形式上的差异，而且直接关涉到了法律行为这一概念的存在与否。如果连法律行为概念都不存在，法律行为理论怎么可能成为“指导”型知识呢？而从知识论的角度来看，正是20世纪90年代以前法理学界关于法律行为概念用法的实质差异，构成了理解20世纪90年代以后法律行为理论的必要背景。因此，对前者的梳理，也就成为理解后者的前提。

（一）法律行为存在吗？——20世纪90年代以前的法律事实理论

如果考虑到“法律事实”一节最初是作为法律关系一章的内容而出现的这一事实，从逻辑上便可以就该节内容作出与本文第二部分一致的沙俄时代考察。事实也印证了这一点，特鲁别茨科伊将法律事实定义为：“应该把法律事实理解为所有能够使法得到确立和终止的现实状况和事件。”① 马尔琴科对此评论道：“所谓‘法得到确立和终止’指的是‘法律关系得到确立和终止’。”② 而在法律事实的分类上，马尔琴科则指出：“在十月革命前的俄罗斯法学界，曾尝试过把事件比照行为，按照法律规范对它们的评价特点把事件划分为合法事件和违法事件。H. M. 科尔库诺夫甚至因此而分出了法律事实的四个范畴：合法行为、合法事件、违法行为、违法事件。”③

苏联法理学继承了沙俄法理学的法律事实理论，据黄金荣考证，在苏联教科书中，在法律事实的分类这一问题上，主要存在两脉不同的表述。一脉将法律事实的分类表述为法律行为和法律事件，一脉将法律事实的分类表述为行为和事件。④

法律事件/法律行为一脉以“杰尼索夫（1948）”为代表，据称，这本早在1948年就翻译过来的苏联法理学教材已经包含了法律事实一节。“法律将成立新的权利关系、变更或消灭旧的权利关系与之联系起来的事实，名曰法律事实。”⑤ 法律事实又分为法律事件和法律行为——“有的事实并

---

① 〔俄〕M. H. 马尔琴科：《国家与法的理论》，徐晓晴译，中国政法大学出版社，2010，第437页。

② 〔俄〕M. H. 马尔琴科：《国家与法的理论》，徐晓晴译，中国政法大学出版社，2010，第437页。

③ 〔俄〕M. H. 马尔琴科：《国家与法的理论》，徐晓晴译，中国政法大学出版社，2010，第438—439页。

④ 参见黄金荣《法理学中的“法律行为”》，载郑永流主编《法哲学与法社会学论丛》2006年第2期，北京大学出版社，2007，第18—20页。

⑤ 〔苏〕杰尼索夫：《国家与法律的理论》，方德厚译，中华书局，1948，第448页。

不依赖国家、国家机关、公务员或公民之意志而发生，称为法律事件”；[①]“凡国家、国家机关、公务员、法人、有行为能力的公民意志之结果的法律事实，名曰法律行为”。[②] 法律行为又分为合法的与违法的两个类型。可见，“这本书关于法律事实、法律行为的概念与我们现在的观念已经没有多大的差异”。[③]

行为/事件一脉以“罗马什金等（1963）”为代表。后者的法律事实理论在内容上与“杰尼索夫（1948）”保持一致的情况下，将法律事实的两大类别分别由法律事件和法律行为改为了事件和行为，行为则进一步划分为合法行为与违法行为。[④]

“杰尼索夫（1948）”中存在法律行为概念，而“罗马什金等（1963）”中根本不存在法律行为概念。这里面究竟是怎样一回事呢？是苏联法理学家本身就存在这种差异，还是另有原因？“杰尼索夫（1948）”的确使用了法律行为概念，但该书在法律事实的分类图中，又将法律事实分为了事件与行为。[⑤] 这不免令人怀疑，在杰尼索夫的本意中，行为与法律行为真的存在本质性的差异吗？会不会只是语言使用的问题？遗憾的是，由于该书未附相应俄语，制约了对该书的进一步考察。但对此后法理学教材的继续研究，将逐步揭开事情的真相。

“人大（1957）”涉及相关的俄语问题。[⑥] 尽管该书是中国教材，但“社会主义法权关系”一章由熟悉俄语的孙国华所撰。孙国华既未采纳法律行为概念，也未采纳行为概念，而是选择了法的行为这一概念。相应地，法律事实也变成了法的事实。法的事实包括法的事件和法的行为，法的行为又分为合法行为和违法行为。“合法行为中又可分为有取得一定权利承担一定义务的意思表示的行为，我们把它叫做法律作为，和没有这种

---

① 〔苏〕杰尼索夫：《国家与法律的理论》，方德厚译，中华书局，1948，第448页。

② 〔苏〕杰尼索夫：《国家与法律的理论》，方德厚译，中华书局，1948，第448页。

③ 黄金荣：《法理学中的“法律行为”》，载郑永流主编《法哲学与法社会学论丛》2006年第2期，北京大学出版社，2007，第19页。

④ 参见〔苏〕罗马什金、彼得罗果维奇、图曼诺夫主编《国家和法的理论》，中国社会科学院法学研究所译，法律出版社，1963，第480—483页。

⑤ 参见〔苏〕杰尼索夫《国家与法律的理论》，方德厚译，中华书局，1948，第449页。该图最上方应为“法律事实”，而非“法律事件”。

⑥ 参见中国人民大学法律系国家和法权理论教研室集体编写《国家和法权理论讲义》（下册），中国人民大学出版社，1957，第329页，注①。

意思表示，但行为的结果，依法自然产生一定权利义务的行为，我们把它叫做法律行动。”[①] 孙国华将合法行为分为法律作为和法律行动的做法，对于不熟悉俄语的中国人而言，如果不仔细辨析它们的含义，很容易产生将它们与法的行为相混淆的可能。孙国华意识到了这种可能，为此，他专门加注指出：“民法学中的法律作为，有个专门术语，俄文为 сделка，所以 сделка 译为民事法律作为较妥，而有些书籍中 сделка 被译为法律行为，这就往往易于使人把它和法的行为（юридическиядействия）相混，其实它只是法的行为中的合法行为之一。”[②] 也就是说，在孙国华的理解中，法的行为（юридическиядействия）与法律作为（сделка）是严格有别的。

如果按照孙国华的上述观点，法律行为这一术语本可以不存在。然而，事实并非如此。一方面，将 сделка 译为法律作为的做法远远不能被民法学界所接受。将 сделка 译为法律行为一直是民法学界的通例。[③] 另一方面，孙国华的法的行为的概念也未被此后的中国法理学所接受，沿用“杰尼索夫（1948）”一脉的法律行为概念的做法所在多有。于是，这在逻辑上就造成了在俄语中有严格区别的 сделка 与 юридическиядействия 在汉语中存在同一译法进而相互混淆的可能。后来的学术史表明，这种可能不但成为现实，而且激发了远胜于译法争议的概念之争。在 20 世纪 90 年代激化的这场争论，直接确立了法律行为理论“指导”型知识的地位。

（二）20 世纪 90 年代以后作为“指导”型知识的法律行为理论

根据黄金荣的考察，20 世纪 80 年代的中国法理学教科书中，采纳法律行为/法律事件一脉和行为/事件一脉的同时存在。[④] 而在 20 世纪 90 年代以后，法律行为/法律事件一脉逐渐取得上风——在一些法理学教材中，“‘法律行为’不仅只是一个在‘节’中才提到的概念，而且它还被升格为一‘章’的标题。从这些教材关于法律行为的论述看，法律行为概念在

---

① 中国人民大学法律系国家和法权理论教研室集体编写《国家和法权理论讲义》（下册），中国人民大学出版社，1957，第 329 页。

② 中国人民大学法律系国家和法权理论教研室集体编写《国家和法权理论讲义》（下册），中国人民大学出版社，1957，第 329 页，注①。

③ 参见鄢一美《俄罗斯当代民法研究》，中国政法大学出版社，2006，第 215 页。

④ 参见黄金荣《法理学中的“法律行为”》，载郑永流主编《法哲学与法社会学论丛》2006 年第 2 期，北京大学出版社，2007，第 21—22 页。

法理学中之所以能够平步青云，在很大程度上要归功于1993年张文显教授所著之《法学基本范畴研究》的出版。”[①] 该书将法律行为列为法学的基本范畴，原因如下：第一，“法律的调整对象是行为”；[②] 第二，“法律行为体系是动态的法律现实……因此，只有理解了构成法律事实的法律行为，才能对法律现象有一个全面而深刻的理解”；[③] 第三，“法律的效力和实效存在于法律行为之中，行为是检验法律规范效力和实效的主要标准，行为使法律中的各个要素（主体、客体、权利、义务、责任等）相互联系和转化”；[④] 第四，法学本身的性质要求人们必须研究行为，“法学实际上是一门行为科学”。[⑤] 不难看出，张文显在这里赋予了法律行为远超过引起法律关系的发生、变更和消灭的法律行为的意义，因而也就不难理解他将法律行为列为法学的基本范畴的原因。

与既往做法不一样的是，张文显对法律行为的考察逐渐摆脱苏式教科书的影响，他鲜明地将法律行为的词源追溯至了德语Rechtsgeschäft，他通过对该词的语义分析认为：“法律行为的原初语义是合法的表意行为。”[⑥] 但他继续指出：“在苏联的法学理论体系中，‘法律行为’是一个涵括一切有法律意义和属性的行为的广义概念和统语，而不限于狭义的合法的表意行为。”[⑦] 毫无疑问，张文显接受了法律行为/法律事件一脉对法律行为的定义，但他又认为这一脉与德语Rechtsgeschäft是有学术关联的，只是前者扩大了后者的含义而已。

但是，张文显将Rechtsgeschäft与苏联法理学的法律行为勾连起来的做法，显然不能得到民法学者的认可。德国民法中的Rechtsgeschäft，在俄语中的对应词是сделка，而非юридическиядействия，而сделка的含义从未改变，即“主体以意思表示为要素，为了达到一定法律后果的有目的、有意识的行为”。[⑧] 对于张文显的做法，不仅是民法学者不认可，就连法理学

① 黄金荣：《法理学中的“法律行为”》，载郑永流主编《法哲学与法社会学论丛》2006年第2期，北京大学出版社，2007，第23页。
② 张文显：《法学基本范畴研究》，中国政法大学出版社，1993，第124页。
③ 张文显：《法学基本范畴研究》，中国政法大学出版社，1993，第125页。
④ 张文显：《法学基本范畴研究》，中国政法大学出版社，1993，第126页。
⑤ 张文显：《法学基本范畴研究》，中国政法大学出版社，1993，第126页。
⑥ 张文显：《法学基本范畴研究》，中国政法大学出版社，1993，第129页。
⑦ 张文显：《法学基本范畴研究》，中国政法大学出版社，1993，第130页。
⑧ 鄢一美：《俄罗斯当代民法研究》，中国政法大学出版社，2006，第215页。

者也不认可。于是，我们在“张文显（1999）”中，看到了舒国滢（该书法律行为一章作者）退一步的论证策略：“一般意义上的‘法律行为’应是各法律部门中的行为现象的高度抽象，是各部门法律行为（宪法行为、民事法律行为、行政法律行为、诉讼法律行为）与各类别法律行为（如合法行为、违法行为、犯罪行为等）的最上位法学概念（或法学范畴）。这个最上位概念的德文名词是 Rechtsakt（英文 juristic act 或 legal act），它所描述的，是包括 Rechtsgeschäft 在内的一切具有法律意义的行为现象。”[①] 舒国滢的上述观点，奠定了法理学教材迄今为止法律行为理论的基本格局，[②] 同时也进一步宣告了法律行为理论的“指导”型知识性质——法律行为是一个法理学的一般概念。

（三）法律行为理论的知识生产机制

从概念本身存在的不确定，到成为一般概念，法律行为理论的发展史表明，面对法律行为概念（民法学）的悠久传统，法律行为理论（法理学）在不断调适自己，直至确立自身“指导”型知识的地位。前文在论述“指导”型知识生产机制时也曾指出，部门法学也可能有助于法理学“指导”型知识的生产。然而，法律行为理论（法理学）面对法律行为概念（民法学）的这种调适，可以解释为一种部门法学对法理学的助益吗？

对 20 世纪 90 年代以前的法律事实理论的梳理表明，юридическиядействия 原本存在多种汉译，法律行为并不是唯一的译法。吊诡的是，在 сделка 上承 Rechtsgeschäft 一直被汉译为法律行为的民法学传统面前，юридическиядействия 的译法却最终也确定为法律行为。于是，便产生了法理学与民法学间法律行为概念的冲突。

解决这个问题的办法原本很简单，其实就是在 юридическиядействия 与 сделка 间选择其一更改译法。麻烦在于，法理学与民法学谁也不愿意进行更改。在这种情况下，针对这么一个翻译问题，公允的办法应该是，考察法律行为概念在中文世界的使用史，进而看看能否得出合适的结论。而一旦诉诸历史，民法学显然占了上风。正如朱庆育所言：“我国在清末民

① 张文显主编《法理学》，高等教育出版社、北京大学出版社，1999，第 101 页。
② 参见张文显主编《法理学》，高等教育出版社、北京大学出版社，2011，第 102 页。

初法律继受之始，即以法律行为对译 Rechtsgeschäft，并从此深植于法学著述立法之中，是否有必要改变传统，为了迎合受苏联译著影响的法理学将 juristischeHandlung 称为‘法律行为’之要求，而强行改变既定译名？”①

在面临“行为”与“法律行为”两种选择的20世纪80年代，法理学教材本来具备弃“法律行为”选“行为”的时机。然而，事实恰恰与此相反。难道这仅仅是由于不熟悉语言而导致的选择错误吗？不然。对此问题的检讨，从根本上涉及作为“指导”型知识的法律行为理论的知识生产机制。

作为一种试图为部门法学提供指导的机制，“指导”型知识生产机制一经形成，就具有一切机制皆具有的稳定性，这种稳定性进而会成为维持机制本身存在的重要力量。法律行为理论在20世纪90年代成为“指导”型知识的事实，正是“指导”型知识生产机制稳定性的重要证明。前文已指出，张文显之所以大力提高法律行为理论的地位，一个重要原因就是“为各部门法学研究具体法律领域的行为提供一般原理”。② 为此，他甘愿冒着招致民法学者批评其修改 Rechtsgeschäft 意义的风险，也要将法律行为概念从民法学上升到法理学之中。在意识到这一点颇难实现之后，舒国滢采取了退一步的论证策略——他将法律行为（法理学）的德文名词从 Rechtsgeschäft 变为了 Rechtsakt，并继续强调法律行为概念的法理学性质。要注意的是，变化的不仅仅是名词。张文显是要将法律行为（法理学）建立在 Rechtsgeschäft 这一学术传统之上，而舒国滢似乎多多少少有了仅仅在语词对应的意义上诉诸 Rechtsakt 的意思。即使后者后来在 Rechtsakt 之前又给法律行为（法理学）增加了一个德文词——Rechtshandlung，情况似乎也是如此。③

但事实上，舒国滢将法律行为（法理学）的德文名词从 Rechtsgeschäft 变为 Rechtsakt 的做法，已经表明法理学认可了 Rechtsgeschäft 属于民法学

---

① 朱庆育：《法律行为概念疏证》，《中外法学》2008年第3期。另：朱庆育在该文中已经敏锐地指出，导致法理学界与民法学界法律行为概念之争的根源，应该是相关俄语的翻译问题，只是未明确进行俄语考证而已。而这里的德语 juristische Handlung，正是对应着俄语 юридическия действия。

② 张文显：《法学基本范畴研究》，中国政法大学出版社，1993，第127页。

③ 参见张文显主编《法理学》，高等教育出版社、北京大学出版社，2011，第102页。

这一主张。[①] 进一步地，从逻辑上可以推导出，为了保证概念的同一性，法律行为（法理学）必须更名，除非 Rechtsgeschäft 不能译为法律行为。换句话说，身处汉语世界里的法律行为（法理学）的正当性不是建立在 Rechtsakt 或 Rechtshandlung 能译为法律行为这一点之上，而是建立在 Rechtsgeschäft 不能译为法律行为这一点之上。遗憾的是，包括法理学者在内的绝大部分学者，都认可 Rechtsgeschäft 应该翻译为法律行为这一点。[②]

进一步地，如果 Rechtsgeschäft 的法律行为这一译法不能被否定，法律行为（法理学）就必须更名。然而，事实却并非如此。这只能说明，法理学教材在“指导”型知识生产机制固有力量的支配之下，在理应让步的情况下拒绝作出任何让步。除此之外，找不到其他原因。进一步地，可以看出，法理学对“指导”型知识的生产不是以部门法学帮助法理学的方式实现的，而是以法理学理由不足地向部门法学争夺概念的方式实现的。这也与“指导”型知识生产机制的初衷相背离，因为“研究所（1954）”在阐明部门法学在研究和论述本学科的基本问题中要以法理学所确定的原理、原则与概念为出发点这一点时所紧接着强调的一句话：“国家与法权理论不能仅以个别法权学科所研究的和为它所总括起来的材料为基础。”[③] 但事实上，法理学中“指导”型知识的生产，恰恰事与愿违。

四 “指导”型知识生产机制的理论基础及其批判

上文通过检讨法律关系理论和法律行为理论，分别考察了“指导”型知识生产机制运行机制的正面向度和反面向度。考察的结论是，作为一种

---

① 参见张文显主编《法理学》，高等教育出版社、北京大学出版社，1999，第 100 页。

② 米健和田士永是两个罕见的例外，但他们关于 Rechtsgeschäft 翻译的争论是民法内部的争论，且至少到现在为止，未取代通说的地位。相关争论，参见米健《法律交易论》，《中国法学》2004 年第 2 期；田士永《物权行为理论研究——以中国法和德国法中所有权变动的比较为中心》，中国政法大学出版社，2002，第 20 页；朱庆育《法律行为概念疏证》，《中外法学》2008 年第 3 期。

③ 苏联科学院法学研究所科学研究员集体编著《马克思列宁主义关于国家与法权理论教程》，中国人民大学马克思列宁主义关于国家与法权理论教研室译，中国人民大学出版社，1954，第 8 页。

旨在向部门法学提供指导的知识，“指导”型知识并不能有效地指导部门法学；法理学要么生产不能妥当地适用到部门法学之中的“指导”型知识（正面向度），要么通过向部门法学争夺概念的方式生产不正确的“指导”型知识（反面向度）。

然而，上文只是从运行机制层面论证了“指导”型知识生产机制的无效性，但这并不意味着该生产机制在基本原理层面就必然是无效的。从逻辑上讲，如果基本原理是正确的，那么，只要解决运行机制中的问题，“指导”型知识生产机制依然是可以成立的。而从研究对象问题入手，正是要从基本原理层面研究该机制。

“指导”型知识生产机制的基本原理可以归结为法理学与部门法学具有不同的研究对象这一点。那么，法理学与部门法学具有不同的研究对象这一判断是否成立呢？对此问题的分析，将引发出隐藏在基本原理之后的“指导”型知识生产机制的理论基础——法律体系理论。

“研究所（1954）”正是通过明确的引用（指向），表明了旨在划分部门法的法律体系理论是部门法学以相应的部门法为研究对象这一观点的理论基础，① 而这一观点不过是法理学与部门法学具有不同的研究对象的另一种表述。因此，对“指导”型知识生产机制基本原理正确性的考察，归结到了对法律体系理论正确性的考察之上。

（一）“指导”型知识生产机制的理论基础——法律体系理论

以调整对象和调整方法为划分标准的法律体系理论是苏式法理学批评公私法之分的产物，这源于列宁的著名论断：“我们不承认任何‘私法’，在我们看来，经济领域中的一切都属于公法范围，而不属于私法范围。”② 苏联法学家据此认为公法与私法只是资产阶级对法的分类，③ 不能作为国家与法权理论中法律体系理论的基础。既然如此，法律体系理论又将建立

---

① 参见苏联科学院法学研究所科学研究员集体编著《马克思列宁主义关于国家与法权理论教程》，中国人民大学马克思列宁主义关于国家与法权理论教研室译，中国人民大学出版社，1954，第5页。

② 《列宁全集》第36卷，人民出版社，1959，第587页。

③ 参见苏联科学院法学研究所科学研究员集体编著《马克思列宁主义关于国家与法权理论教程》，中国人民大学马克思列宁主义关于国家与法权理论教研室译，中国人民大学出版社，1954，第530—532页。

在什么样的理论基础之上呢？

苏联法学界先后就此展开了广泛的讨论，在1938—1940年的第一次讨论后，主流意见认为："法分为部门的基础是实体标准——受法调整的关系的特殊性或法律调整对象"。[①]"研究所（1954）"全面体现了主流意见。

该书指出："如果想按照法权规范的性质，按照规范本身的属性来分类，那末我们所得的是分成不同种类的规范，但不是法权体系，因为规范的分类若是由规范本身出发，可以按各种不同的根据来进行。"[②] 于是，他们引用了马克思的《〈政治经济学批判〉序言》——"法权关系……无论是从它自己本身，或是从所谓人类精神底共同发展上都不能得到了解的，相反，法权关系是根源于物质生活关系。"[③] 因此，"为了使法权规范的分类有科学和客观的根据起见，应当由法权所调整的和确认的社会关系出发。因此法权体系的建立，必须根据法权所调整的社会关系。必须根据一定种类的社会关系的联系和差别，把法权规范分成各类，并确定各类法权规范的界限"。[④] 很明显，这里建立法权体系的标准是法权所调整的社会关系。苏联法学家遂根据社会关系将法律体系划分为以下法律部门：国家法、行政法、财政法、民法、劳动法、土地法、集体农庄法、家庭法、刑法、审判法。[⑤]

尽管此后法律体系理论还经历了从唯一标准（调整对象）说向主辅标

① 〔俄〕B. B. 拉扎列夫主编《法与国家的一般理论》，王哲等译，法律出版社，1999，第161页。

② 苏联科学院法学研究所科学研究员集体编著《马克思列宁主义关于国家与法权理论教程》，中国人民大学马克思列宁主义关于国家与法权理论教研室译，中国人民大学出版社，1954，第532页。

③ 转引自苏联科学院法学研究所科学研究员集体编著《马克思列宁主义关于国家与法权理论教程》，中国人民大学马克思列宁主义关于国家与法权理论教研室译，中国人民大学出版社，1954，第532页；原文为，"法的关系正像国家的形式一样，既不能从它们本身来理解，也不能从所谓人类精神的一般发展来理解，相反，它们根源于物质的生活关系"。《马克思恩格斯选集》第2卷，人民出版社，2012，第2页。

④ 苏联科学院法学研究所科学研究员集体编著《马克思列宁主义关于国家与法权理论教程》，中国人民大学马克思列宁主义关于国家与法权理论教研室译，中国人民大学出版社，1954，第532页。

⑤ 参见苏联科学院法学研究所科学研究员集体编著《马克思列宁主义关于国家与法权理论教程》，中国人民大学马克思列宁主义关于国家与法权理论教研室译，中国人民大学出版社，1954，第534页。

准（以调整对象为主、调整方法为辅）说的演变和中国的发展，但“研究所（1954）”中的法律体系理论还是构成了迄今为止法理学教科书中法律关系理论的主体，而调整对象标准也构成了苏式法理学法律体系理论的质的标准。

（二）法律体系理论批判

然而，法律体系理论事实上是存在根本缺陷的。对这种缺陷的批评，可以从逻辑和历史两个维度展开。

从逻辑维度上讲，法律体系理论存在循环论证的根本错误。不妨再回到“研究所（1954）”，该书在指出建立法律体系的标准是法律所调整的社会关系后紧接着指出：“社会关系（经济的和其他的关系）既是法权调整的对象，就表现在法权关系中。社会关系和与它相适应的法权关系（也就是特种的社会关系），是各种各样的。因此，调整社会关系的法权，虽然根本上是统一的，但也按照与一定数量的法权规范及相应的法权关系有关的某类社会关系的特点而加以区别并分成各种部门。”[①] 注意，尽管法律关系也是社会关系，但是“特种的”社会关系，区别于作为其事实原型的社会关系（下文所言“社会关系”就指作为事实原型的社会关系）。然而，一旦社会关系与法律关系这一区分成立，新的问题又来了——既然已经明确建立法律体系的标准是社会关系，而这里又指出法律要“按照与一定数量的法权规范及相应的法权关系有关的某类社会关系的特点而加以区别并分成各种部门”；也就是说，社会关系这一建立法律体系的标准本身也是有一定标准的，后一种标准就是“与一定数量的法权规范及相应的法权关系有关”。于是，循环论证出现了：建立法律体系的标准本来是社会关系，而社会关系本身有赖于参考法律规范及相应的法律关系来鉴别，但法律关系又是由法律规范调整社会关系而形成。这一循环论证可以图示如下：

法律体系→社会关系→法律规范相应的法律关系→法律规范社会关系

① 苏联科学院法学研究所科学研究员集体编著《马克思列宁主义关于国家与法权理论教程》，中国人民大学马克思列宁主义关于国家与法权理论教研室译，中国人民大学出版社，1954，第533页。

在上图中，建立法律体系的标准到底是社会关系还是法律关系这一问题是无解的——循环论证正是法律体系理论的逻辑谬误。因此，尽管教科书区分了社会关系与法律关系，但这种区分对认识建立法律体系的标准而言并无助益。之所以犯下这一逻辑谬误，从根本上而言，是法律体系理论在划分标准的问题上一方面保持马克思主义的社会学基调（法律关系根源于物质生活关系），一方面又接受大陆法系法律关系理论的结果。若将两者相比较，前者体现了法的社会性，后者体现了法的自主性。作为一种外在面向的马克思主义社会理论，本不必进入法律体系这一内在面向的法律理论领域；但苏式法理学却坚持以法的社会性消解法的自主性，进而从根本上导致了法律体系理论循环论证的逻辑谬误。

同时，这种区分本来是要突出作为法律调整对象的社会关系，但法理学的这种努力其实并未受到部门法学的认可，后者还是将调整对象理解为法律关系。譬如民法调整对象，按照法理学的界定，这一定是社会关系，但民法学所言的作为民法调整对象的平等主体的财产关系和人身关系必然是法律关系。

从历史维度上讲，正如李林所言："以苏联为代表的社会主义国家法律体系部门划分的实际意义，或许其政治价值大于其学术和实践价值，它存在的主要目的是解决法律体系姓'资'姓'社'的问题，其次才是按照法律科学和法学传统来建构一个国家的法律体系。因为只有用这种划分理论和方法，才能取代公法和私法这种以承认私有制为经济基础合法前提的划分标准，才能彰显出这种新型法律体系的公有制性质，及其比资本主义社会更先进的社会主义本质。由于不采用上述部门法的划分方法仍然可以建构一个国家的法律体系，而且千百年来世界上绝大多数国家都不采用这种方法，但并不影响其法律体系的形成、存在和发展。"① 换句话说，以调整对象为主要划分标准的法律体系理论对法律体系的划分实质上是无用的、不必要的。

既然法律体系理论在理论维度上是错误的，在历史维度上是无用和不必要的，也就否定了法律体系理论。既然法律体系理论已被否定，那么，

① 冀祥德主编《法治的理念、制度与现实》，中国人民公安大学出版社，2013，第6页。

部门法学以相应的部门法为研究对象这一观点也就没有了立足之地。若如此，法理学与部门法学具有不同的研究对象这一“指导”型知识生产机制的基本原理就难以成立了。而对“指导”型知识生产机制的从运作机制到基本原理乃至理论基础的批判，也逐步完成。

五 余论

在结束对“指导”型知识生产机制的批判之后，对本文而言，依然遗留下了一个至关重要的开放性问题：法理学与部门法学的关系应当何为？之所以说这个问题是开放性的，既是因为对它的回答已经超出本文的主题，又是因为对它的回答不必囿于传统意义上的社会主义法系。在与苏联、中国在法制传统上有着密切联系的德国，就存在处理法学学科间关系的不同方案。譬如，考夫曼指出：“在科学理论中，人们将实义客体理解成科学所研究的具体对象之整体。相反，形式客体则指研究这个整体的特殊视角（因此，形式客体有时被称为‘研究客体’）。对每一种科学来说，形式客体是其独特之处，而实义客体则为多种科学共有。譬如，‘法’，是全部法学学科共同的实义客体，民法，国家法，行政法，刑法是在各自的形式客体上相异的。最近还可以看到，实义客体一直在不停地分裂成许多形式客体。”① 考夫曼这段话正是论述了全部法学学科间的关系。它认为法学学科之间以研究客体相区别，这看似与苏式法理学部门法学以相应的部门法为研究对象这一观点相一致，实则不然。考夫曼所谓的研究客体，是指形式客体，而非实义客体。法学学科之间以研究客体相区别，却共享实义客体。换句话说，实义客体对法学学科的区分而言并无意义。而在苏式法理学中，研究对象的意义恰是等同于考夫曼笔下的实义客体，而非研究客体。有意思的是，考夫曼区分研究客体而非实义客体的立场，客观上被相对而言未受苏式法理学法律体系理论实质影响的国际法（这里的国际法，是与国内法相区分而言的，包含国际公法、国际私法和国际经济法，

① 〔德〕考夫曼、哈斯默尔主编《当代法哲学和法律理论导论》，郑永流译，法律出版社，2002，第5页。

即“三国”）所佐证。[①] 不妨以国际经济法为例介绍相应观点，国际经济法学者认为，国际经济法与国际公法存在相当的交叉关系，与国际私法则存在有限的交叉关系。[②] 有学者甚至进一步认为，针对相同的国际法问题，“三国”学者均能予以研究，“但侧重面可能相同，也可能不同。”[③] 显然，上述观点只是区分了“三国”的研究客体，而非实义客体。当然，考夫曼的观点是否完全适合于中国，还可以继续探讨，但至少它为我们提供了研究法学学科间关系的另一条思路，存在值得借鉴的可能与空间。

总而言之，在“指导”型知识生产机制无效性的背后，是重新界定法理学与部门法学关系的问题。可喜的是，法理学界已经注意到了此问题。[④] 当下需要继续做的，无疑是深化对该问题的研究。

（本文原载于《北方法学》2014 年第 6 期）

---

① 苏式法理学一向认为，法律体系是由一国现行法组成的体系，所以国际法不是一个独立的法律部门。但有意思的是，国际法学者大多主张，国际法是独立的法律部门（由于不同的国际法学者对“三国”相互关系的看法不同，大家对于“三国”能否分别成为一个独立的法律部门各持己见，但这并不影响他们认为国际法是独立的法律部门）。导致法理学与国际法这种分歧的原因主要有以下几点。第一，从国际法发展的历史维度来看，国际法学者起初所理解的法律部门，并不是苏式法理学意义上的法律部门。以国际经济法为例，其先驱施瓦增伯格就主张，国际经济法应当成为一个国际公法的 special branch of law，但正如学者指出的，“special branch of law 是指在传授国际公法原则和知识时更专业的知识领域。在此语境下，branch of law 与我国学者将国际经济法描述为‘法律部门’的含义不同。同理，西方学者将国际经济法视为 branch of international law 时，他们实际上是将国际法视为一个学科或知识体系（discipline），而不是真正的独立存在的法律规范体系”（莫世健主编《国际经济法》，中国政法大学出版社，2008，第 9 页）。第二，基于国际法与国内法都具有一定的调整对象这种相似性等原因，再加上部分国际法学者没有注意到施瓦增伯格式的 branch of law 与苏式法理学法律部门概念的区别，以至于他们客观上无视苏式法理学有关法律体系不包含国际法的理论预设，得出了国际法也是一个苏式法理学意义上的法律部门的结论。然而，从正文中讨论的研究客体与实义客体这一语境来看，国际法实质上又没有受到部门法学以相应的部门法为研究对象这一苏式法理学基本观点的实质影响。所以，正文作出如此判断。

② 参见黄东黎主编《国际经济法》，社会科学文献出版社，2006，第 31—33 页。

③ 莫世健主编《国际经济法》，中国政法大学出版社，2008，第 16 页。

④ 一个代表性的研究，参见陈景辉《法理论为什么是重要的——法学的知识框架及法理学在其中的位置》，《法学》2014 年第 3 期。

对外财政援助决定权的宪法制约

——德国联邦宪法法院对欧元区援助法案的违宪审查

毛晓飞*

2009年爆发的欧债危机不仅困扰着深陷主权债务的国家，同时也影响了整个欧元区的金融稳定。作为欧洲经济的“火车头”，联邦德国成为解决危机的“关键人物”，承担了约27%的援助份额，为欧元区各成员国之最。有不少德国民众对此表示担忧，认为这将给本国的财政带来难以估量的负担，德国因此承担了过度的违约责任风险，且援助只会是杯水车薪，无法根本解决负债国家因长期经济结构性问题所产生的庞大财政开支。部分反对者转向了联邦宪法法院，以期通过宪法诉讼阻止欧元区金融援助法案的生效。作为德国宪法守护者与诠释者的联邦宪法法院在政治法律化的帷幕下被推到了台前，它必须对联邦议会的相关法案作出违宪审查。通过一系列的判决，联邦宪法法院重申了联邦议会作为“人民最直接的代表”所拥有的国家财政决定权，这是一项连议会自身都无权随意转让的宪法权力。因此，可能影响国家财政的对外援助决定也必须由联邦议会作出，而且还要遵循基本法所设置的法律界限，以保证决定权不被架空。本文将通过对司法判决的分析展示联邦宪法法院为德国参与欧元区财政援助行动所确立的基本法律框架。

一　对欧元区援助法案的违宪审查

从最初2010年5月德国援助希腊法案到2012年9月对金融稳定机制

---

* 毛晓飞，中国社会科学院国际法研究所国际经济法研究室助理研究员。

法案合宪性审查的尘埃落定，联邦宪法法院在两年里受理了上万份宪法诉讼申请。这些诉讼中有以公民个人或团体名义提起的宪法申诉（Verfassungsbeschwerde）[①] 和由联邦议员和党团提起的机构争议（Organstreit）[②]。诉讼针对的法案、被指控的政府行为以及相关的请求权不尽相同，这是因为随着欧元区主权债务危机的不断持续和蔓延，相应的救助措施也在发生动态变化，从最初单一的援助希腊，到设立暂时性欧洲金融稳定基金（Europäische Finanzstabilisierungsfazilität，EFSF）以帮助其他陷入债务危机的欧元区成员国，再进一步建立长期性的欧洲金融稳定机制（Europäischen Stabilitätsmechanismus，ESM），从而产生不同类型的多轮宪法诉讼。为了能够清晰地梳理相关诉讼请求和司法判决，有必要在此简单地回顾一下欧债危机的演化以及德国政府所参与的金融援助方案。

（一）集体性援助方案

欧洲主权债务危机始于希腊。希腊于 2001 年加入欧洲经济货币联盟。[③] 该联盟通过 1992 年 2 月 7 日签署的马斯特里赫条约[④]建立，其目的是让成员国能够使用单一货币并由统一的中央银行体系来负责货币政策，以促进欧洲共同市场的发展。2002 年欧元作为统一货币被使用。为确保统一货币政策下的财政纪律，加入欧元区的成员国同时通过了稳定与增长公约，[⑤] 要求成员国的财政赤字水平最多不超过国民生产总值的 3%，公共债

---

① “宪法申诉”是指，联邦宪法法院依据基本法第 93 条 1 款 4a 项可以对任何人提出的对其基本权利或其依第 20 条第 4 项、第 33 条、38 条、101 条、103 条、104 条所享之权利造成损害的公权力行为作出宪法裁决。见 Grundgesetz für die Bundesrepublik Deutschland vom 23 Mai 1949（BGBl. S. 1），zuletzt geändert durch das Gesetz vom 11. Juli 2012（BGGl. l S. 1478）。

② “机构争议”是指，联邦宪法法院依据基本法第 93 条 1 款 1 项可以对最高宪法机构及其成员之间就权利义务范围的争议作出宪法裁决。最高宪法机构通常包括联邦总统、联邦议会、联邦参议员、议会委员会、联邦政府、党派以及联邦议员和联邦政府部长。例如，联邦会议对联邦总统签署未经其批准的法案而提起机构争议。

③ Entscheidung des Rates 2000/427/EG vom 19. Juni 2000 gemäβ Artikel 122 Absatz 2 des Vertrages über die Einführung der Einheitswährung durch Griechenland am 1. Januar 2001，ABl Nr. L 167/19.

④ Verträge über die Europäische Union，ABl Nr. C 191/1，29. 07. 1992；BGBl II S. 1253.

⑤ Entschlieβung des Europäischen Rates über den Stabilitäts-und Wachstumspakt Amsterdam，17. 06. 1997，ABl Nr. C 236/1.

务水平不超过国民生产总值的60%。[①] 然而，希腊政府因担心自己无法达标，便从一开始就与美国的投资银行合作，采用诸如货币掉期交易等所谓的“金融创新工具”使负债率在账面上可以符合联盟的要求。[②] 2004年经欧盟统计局重新计算发现，希腊政府的赤字水平实际上高达3.7%。2009年，希腊政府的财政赤字水平为国民生产总值的12.7%，而公共债务水平则超过国民生产总值的113%，接近规定水平的两倍。[③] 鉴于希腊恶劣的财政状况，全球三大信用评级机构惠誉、标准普尔和穆迪相继调低了希腊的主权信用评级，由此拉开了欧盟国家主权债务危机的帷幕。随后，葡萄牙、爱尔兰、西班牙、意大利等国也暴露出类似问题，从而引发了整个欧元区的货币信用危机和银行业系统性风险。2010年4月23日，希腊正式向欧盟和国际货币基金组织提出财政援助的申请，掀开了欧元区国家集体救助行动的序幕。[④] 欧元集团成员于2010年5月2日发表声明同意在国际货币基金组织的三年援助计划中以双边借款形式向希腊提供总数为800亿至1100亿欧元的援助，第一年为300亿欧元。每个参与国提供的份额依据其在欧洲中央银行缴纳的份额计算。德国在15个欧元区成员国（不包括希腊）中承担27.92%的份额，[⑤] 援助金额为224亿欧元，第一年为84亿欧元。[⑥] 德国联邦议会于2010年5月7日批准了《保障货币联盟金融稳定

① Verordnung (EG) Nr. 1467/97 vom 7. Juli 1997 über die Beschleunigung und Klärung des Verfahrens bei einem übermäβigen Defizit, ABl Nr. L 209/6，后经 Verodnung (EG) Nr. 1056/2005 des Rates vom 27. Juni 2005 zur Änderung der Verordnung (EG) Nr. 1467/97 über die Beschleunigung und Klärung des Verfahrens bei einem übermäβigen Defizit 修订，ABl Nr. L 174/5，但是3%的标准没有变动。Artikel 1 des Protokolls (Nr. 12) über das Verfahren bei einem übermäβigen Defizit des Vertrags über die Arbeitsweise der Europäischen Union, ABl C 83/1, 30.03.2010.

② “Wie Goldman Sachs den Griechen zur Seite sprang”, Handelsblatt, http://www.handelsblatt.com/unternehmen/banken/derivategeschaefte-wie-goldman-sachs-den-griechen-zur-seite-sprang/3376400.html，最后访问日期：2013年12月3日。

③ “Pressemitteilung des Rates für Wirtschaft und Finanzen <ECOFIN-Rat>”, 16.02.2010, http://www.consilium.europa.eu/Newsroom，最后访问日期：2012年11月22日。

④ “Statement on the support to Greece by Euro-area Members States”, 11.04.2010, http://europa.eu/rapid/press-release_MEMO-10-123_en.htm; “Joint statement by European Commission, European Central Bank and Presidency of the Eurogroup on Greece”, IP/10/446, 23.04.2010, http://europa.eu/rapid/press-release_IP-10-446_en.htm，最后访问日期：2012年11月22日。

⑤ Gesetzentwurf der Fraktionen der CDU/CSU und FDP, BTDrucks 17/1544, S.4.

⑥ Gesetzentwurf der Fraktionen der CDU/CSU und FDP, BTDrucks 17/1544, S.1.

的承担希腊共和国支付能力法》（简称“货币联盟与金融稳定法”）以确保对希腊的援助。①

2010年5月9日，欧盟财长理事会决定设立欧洲金融稳定机制，由两个部分构成：一是基于欧盟条例的欧洲金融稳定机制；二是基于欧元区成员国以国家间协议成立的一个以借款和贷款为目的的公司，即欧洲金融稳定基金，其目的是帮助陷入国债危机的成员国获得财政支持。欧洲稳定基金于2010年6月7日依照卢森堡法律成立，其组织形式是股份公司，职责是帮助陷入危机的欧元区国家发行债券、发放贷款和给予授信额度。基金的股份参照成员国向欧洲中央银行缴纳的份额，限期运行3年。② 整个救助计划资金高达7500亿欧元，其中欧洲金融稳定机制部分为600亿欧元，欧洲金融稳定基金4400亿欧元，还有来自国际基金组织的2500亿欧元。③ 2010年5月22日德国联邦议会通过了《承担欧洲稳定机制保障义务法》（简称“稳定机制法”），其中规定援助金额的上限为2110亿欧元。④

然而，欧洲金融稳定基金仅是一种临时性措施。考虑到成员国的财政结构性转变并非朝夕之事以及稳定欧洲金融体系之必要，欧元区政府首脑早在2010年底就已开始酝酿一种长期的金融稳定机制。在2010年12月16日和17日的欧盟理事会上，成员国政府首脑原则上同意修改欧盟运行条约的第136条，⑤ 并增加第3款，为集体性援助行动提供法律依据。⑥ 鉴于金融市场的持续动荡，欧元区国家成员于2011年7月21日同意签署《欧洲稳定机制条约》。该条约形成一个由成员国构成的“国际金融组织”（第1条）。当出现需要保护欧元区及其成员国金融稳定的必要情形时，欧洲稳

---

① Gesetz zur übernahme von Gewährleistungen zum Erhalt der für die Finanzstabilität in der Währungsunion erforderlichen Zahlungsfähigkeit der Hellenischen Republik（Währungsunion-Finanzstabilitätsgesetz-WFStG），BGBl I S. 537.

② 从2010年6月到2013年6月。

③ BverfG，2 BvR 987/10 vom 7. 9. 2011，http://www.bverfg.de/entscheidungen/rs20110907_2bvr098710.html，Rn. 18，最后访问日期：2012年11月22日。

④ Gesetz zur übernahme von Gewährleistungen im Rahmen eines europäischen Stabilisierungsmechanismus（Stabilisierungsmechanismusgesetz-StabMechG），BGBI I S. 627，§1.

⑤ Beschluss des Europäischen Rates 2011/199/EU vom 25. März 2011 zur Änderung des Artikels 136 des Vertrags über die Arbeitsweise der Europäischen Union hinsichtlich eines Stablitätsmechanismus für die Mitgliedstaaten，deren Wärung der Euro ist，ABl. L91/1.

⑥ 第3款规定，使用欧元的成员国可以建立一个稳定机制并在必要情形下而启动它，以保障欧元货币区的稳定。为保障提供的必要金融援助必须遵循严格的条件。

定机制应当对其成员国在严格的、与金融援助工具相匹配的条件下予以救助（第 12 条）。援助方式包括以贷款形式发放的短期或者中期稳定救助（第 14 条），在初级市场上的援助基金（第 15 条）。[①] 2012 年 1 月 23 日召开的欧盟国家财长会议正式通过该条约，并于 2012 年 2 月 2 日由成员国驻布鲁塞尔的大使签字。[②] 2012 年 3 月 2 日欧元区成员国又签订了《经济与货币联盟的稳定、合作和运行条约》。[③] 为了兑现国际承诺，德国议会于 2012 年 6 月通过了一系列同意建立欧洲稳定机制的法案，以实现条约的国内法转换。在欧洲稳定机制高达 7000 亿欧元的总资本中，800 亿需要成员国以现金方式支付，6200 亿则作为通知即付资本。德国承担了其中的 27.15%（217 亿欧元现金和 1683 亿欧元的资金承诺）。也就是说，在极端情况下德国财政必须负担 1900 亿欧元的援助资金。[④]

（二）从精英到大众的宪法诉讼

作为欧元区的经济强国，德国一方面深知自己在解决欧债危机中的作用以及切身利益所在，但是另外一方面也对这种援助方式的有效性表示怀疑。尤其是在负债国家经济表现依然低迷的情况下，似乎让人在近期难以看到危机解决的曙光。德国联邦银行行长燕斯 · 魏德曼（Jens Weidmann）在一份公开意见中表示，集体救助措施会使债务国依赖共同体的赔偿责任，会减低债务国来自资本市场的压力，反而不利于国家财政控制。[⑤] 德

---

① Vertrag zur Einrichtung des Europäischen Stabilitätsmechanismus zwischen dem Königreich Belgien, Der Bundesrepublik Deutschland, der Republik Estland, Irland, der Hellenischen Republik, dem Königreich Spanien, der Französischen Republik, der Italienischen Republik, der Republik Zypern, dem Grossherzogtum Luxemburg, Malta, dem Königreich der Niederlande, der Republik Österreich, der Portugiesischen Republik, der Republik Slowenien, der Slowakischen Republik, der Republik Finnland, T/ESM/Anhang III/de 1, 21. 07. 2011.

② "Unterzeichnung des EMS-Vertrags", http://www.bundesfinanzministerium.de/Content/DE/Standardartikel/Themen/Europa/Stabilisierung_des_Euro/Finanzhilfemechanismen/2012-01-27-esm.html，最后访问日期：2012 年 11 月 22 日。

③ Vertrag über Stabilität, Koordinierung und Steuerung in der Wirtschafts-und Währungsunion (SKSV), BTDrucks 17/9046, S. 6 ff.

④ Gesetz zur finanziellen Beteiligung am Europäischen Stabilitätsmechanismus (ESM-Finanzierungsgesetz-ESMFinG), BGBl. I S. 1918, § 1.

⑤ Stellungnahme von Dr. Jens Weidmann, Präsident der Deutschen Bundesbank, 19. 09. 2011，联邦银行官方网站 http://www.bundesbank.de/Redaktion/DE/Pressemitteilungen/BBK/2011/2011_09_19_stellungnahme_weidmann_haushaltsausschuss.html，最后访问日期：2012 年 11 月 22 日。

国经济研究所所长汉斯－维尔纳·森（Hans-Werner Sinn）警告说欧元区的“救助伞”对德国来说是“无法预估的冒险”和“踩上了经济增长的刹车”，因为德国实际上是在为其他欧元区国家的债务埋单，会增加德国自身的再融资成本。① 在联邦议会中也不乏反对之声。自由民主党（FDP）议员弗兰克·谢夫勒（Frank Schäffler）批评欧盟理事会是对欧盟条约中规定的“不援助条款”的“集体性违反”，而且导致了“经济政策的中央化和欧盟的超国家经济决策权”。②

在一片质疑声中，联邦宪法法院收到了要求对联邦议会批准的欧元区金融援助法案进行违宪审查的诉讼申请。提起诉讼的不仅有议会议员、前政府官员，还包括来自学界的教授和一些民间团体的代表。依照时间顺序及所针对的救助法案可概括为这样三轮具有重大影响意义的宪法诉讼。

第一，从2010年5月开始，针对德国议会通过的同意对希腊实施金融援助和建立欧洲金融稳定基金的法案，以法学教授卡尔·阿尔布莱希特·沙赫特施耐德（Karl Albrecht Schachtschneider）和基督教社会联盟党（CSU）议员彼德·高伟乐（Peter Gauweiler）为首的反对者向法院递交了诉状，认为相关法案违反了基本法，要求法院颁布“紧急禁令”（einstweilige Anordnung）以防止法案的生效。联邦宪法法院于2010年5月7日和6月9日对紧急禁令申请作出了驳回判决，称未查明政府在对希腊实施紧急援助和设立金融稳定基金时就德国财政和经济所承担风险的评估中有重大错误，而且，法院对此只能实施有限的司法审查。③ 对于诉状涉及违宪指控的实质性审查，法院决定于2011年9月7日作出判决。最终判决结果是：联邦议会的财政自主权并未因援助法案而丧失，基本法所保护的德国公民的选举权和根本的民主制度也未受到侵害，因而并不构成违宪，但同时强调法案需要保证联邦议会对援助措施的有效监督。④

---

① Fehlentscheidung: “Ifo-Institut verdammt Euro-Rettungsschirm”, 20.05.2010, Handelsblatt, http://www.handelsblatt.com/politik/konjunktur/nachrichten/fehlentscheidung-ifo-institut-verdammt-euro-rettungsschirm/3440846.html，最后访问日期：2012年11月22日。

② 见其个人网页 www.frank-schaeffler.de，最后访问日期：2012年11月22日。

③ BVerfG, 2 BvR 987/10 vom 7.5.2010, http://www.bverfg.de/entscheidungen/rs20100507_2bvr098710.html; BVerfG, 2 BvR 1099/10 vom 9.6.2010, http://www.bverfg.de/entscheidungen/rs20100609_2bvr109910.html，最后访问日期：2012年11月22日。

④ BverfG, 2 BvR 987/10 vom 7.9.2011.

第二，鉴于金融市场上的危机未见缓解，欧元区成员国政府首脑决定赋予金融稳定基金更加灵活的工具，以保证对陷入危机国家的紧急援助。2011 年 6 月 21 日在欧盟理事会上决定向欧洲金融稳定基金缴足最初设定的最高资本限额 4400 亿欧元，允许欧洲金融稳定基金在初级和二级市场上购买国家债券。为履行此项承诺，联邦议会于 2011 年 10 月 9 日修改了稳定机制法，规定在特别紧急和保密情况下德国联邦议会对稳定机制的监督权可以通过一个由议会预算委员会成员组成的特别委员会来实施。① 针对这一规定，议员彼德·高伟乐提起了机构争议，要求宪法法院裁决作为联邦议会议员（但未成为特别委员会的成员）所享有的基本法第 38 条 1 款 2 句保障的权利受到了侵害。2011 年 10 月 27 日，联邦宪法法院发出了紧急禁令，要求联邦议会在联邦宪法法院对违宪问题作出实质性审查前不得将有关援助的决定权授予特别委员会。② 联邦宪法法院在 2012 年 2 月 28 日的最终判决中认定相关规定违宪。③ 这一判决可以说是涉欧元区救助宪法诉讼的第一个成功案例。接下来，联邦议会的联盟 90 和绿党党团又再次提起了机构争议，控告以总理默克尔夫人为首的联邦政府在与欧元区其他成员国准备建立欧洲稳定机制和制订欧元加计划时违反了德国基本法第 23 条 2 款 2 句保护的议会知情权，未将 2011 年 2 月 21 日欧盟委员会有关建立欧洲稳定机制的文本、2011 年 4 月 6 日的条约草案、2011 年 2 月 4 日有关提升欧洲竞争力计划和欧盟委员会与欧盟理事会 2011 年 2 月 25 日的“提高欧元区经济政策合作 - 主要内容与方案”提交给联邦议会。联邦宪法法院于 2012 年 6 月 19 日作出判决支持了申请人的主张。④ 这样在机构争议中，联邦议员和党团再次获得胜利。

第三，更大规模的宪法诉讼出现在 2012 年 6 月联邦议会表决通过一系列关于批准建立长期性欧洲金融稳定机制的法案，主要包括《2011 年 3 月

① Entwurf eines Gesetzes zur Änderung des Gesetzes zur Übernahme von Gewährleistungen im Rahmen eines europäischen Stablisierungsmechanismus, BT Drucks 17/6916.

② BVerfG, 2 BvE 8/11 vom 27. 10. 2011, http://www. bverfg. de/entscheidungen/es20111027_2bve000811. html，最后访问日期：2012 年 12 月 3 日。

③ BVerfG, 2 BvE 8/11 vom 28. 2. 2012, http://www. bverfg. de/entscheidungen/es20120228_2bve000811. html，最后访问日期：2012 年 12 月 3 日。

④ BVerfG, 2 BvE 4/11 vom 19. 6. 2012, http://www. bverfg. de/entscheidungen/es20120619_2bve000411. html，最后访问日期：2012 年 12 月 3 日。

25日欧盟理事会修改欧盟运行条约第136条有关欧元区成员国稳定机制决议法》（简称“修改欧盟条约第136条法”）[①]、《关于2012年2月2日欧洲稳定机制条约法》（简称“欧洲稳定机制法”）[②]、《财政参与欧洲稳定机制法》[③] 以及《关于2012年3月2日经济与货币联盟的稳定、合作和运行条约法》（简称“货币联盟稳定合作运行法”）[④]。这次有数量众多的反对者转向了联邦宪法法院，他们要求法院尽快颁布“紧急禁令”以阻止相关法案的签署和生效，并请求对法案内容进行违宪审查。与前两轮的“精英诉讼”（提起诉讼者多为联邦议员、学者和前政府官员）不同的是，本轮诉讼中有了更多普通民众自愿组成团体的参与，也更具“大众”色彩。一个名为“更多民主”的团体对外发布了准备提起宪法诉讼的消息并公开征集加入者的授权签名。[⑤] 根据法院判决书的显示，有11718名当事人参加了这一团体诉讼。[⑥] 本轮诉讼的类型既包括以公民身份提出的宪法申诉，也包括联邦议会左翼党团提出的机构争议。联邦宪法法院将这些诉讼作为共同诉讼进行合并审理，并于2012年9月12日作出了单一判决：驳回紧急禁令请求，但对议会通过相关法案提出了限制性条件，即（1）欧洲稳定机制条约第8条5款1句所规定的德国的最高支付义务不得超过条约第Ⅱ附件中所规定的总额，且没有任何一个条约的条款会被解释为要求德国在没有德国代表人同意的情况下履行更高的支付义务；（2）欧洲稳定机制条约第32条5款、第34条和第35条1款不得有碍联邦议会和联邦参议院的

---

① Gesetz zu dem Beschluss des Europäischen Rates vom 25. März 2011 zur Änderung des Artikels 136 des Vertrages über die Arbeitsweise der Europäischen Union hinsichtlich eines Stabilitätsmechanismus für die Mitgliedstaaten, deren Währung der Euro ist, BTDrucks 17/9047.

② Gesetz zu dem Vertrag vom 2. Februar 2012 zur Einrichtung des Europäischen Stabilitätsmechanismus, BTDrucks 17/9045; 17/10126; 17/10172.

③ Gesetz zur finanziellen Beteiligung am Europäischen Stabilitätsmechanismus (ESM-Finanzierungsgesetz-ESMFinG), BTDrucks 17/9048.

④ Gesetz zu dem Vertrag vom 2. März 2012 über Stabilität, Koordinierung und Steuerung in der Wirtschafts-und Währungsunion, BTDrucks 17/9046, 17/10125.

⑤ 相关媒体报道见 ESM und EU-Fiskalpakt, Däubler-Gmelin kündigt Verfassungsklage an, http://www.faz.net/aktuell/wirtschaft/esm-und-eu-fiskalpakt-daeubler-gmelin-kuendigt-verfassungsklage-an-11715391.html，最后访问日期：2012年11月22日。

⑥ BVerfG, 2 BvR 1390/12 vom 12.9.2012, http://www.bverfg.de/entscheidungen/rs20120912_2bvr139012.html，最后访问日期：2012年11月22日。

广泛知情权。[1]

尽管以上总结尚不能包括欧元区金融救助宪法诉讼的全部细节，另有少数与程序问题有关的诉讼，诸如对联邦宪法法院法官中立性的指控等，但已可以大致描绘截至目前宪法诉讼的轮廓。从一开始只有少数联邦议员和知识精英发起，逐步发展到有越来越多普通德国公民参与的大众诉讼。这显示了一方面民众因为德国为解决其他成员国主权债务危机所承担财政负担和违约责任不断加码而感到不满。另一方面也展示了法律不仅是熟练掌握法律工具的精英表达不同意见的方法，也是法治国家为每个公民维护自身权利提供的可能。

联邦宪法法院违宪审查的范围涉及法案中所有可能与基本法相冲突的条款，这些条款是联邦议会批准政府履行其在欧元集团层面所作出的国际承诺的国内法转换。鉴于欧盟运行条约第 123 条和第 125 条原则上排除成员国或欧洲中央银行向其他欧元区成员国以贷款或担保方式进行援助的欧盟法义务，因此除了少数援助资金（约 600 亿欧元）来自欧盟财政以外，绝大部分的紧急援助款项都通过欧元区成员国之间订立新的国际条约而产生。[2] 因此，违宪审查主要涉及基本法与国际法的关系。尽管欧元区集体性援助行动本身也引起了有关欧盟法方面的争议，但这并非联邦宪法法院相关审查的重点。

宪法诉讼的类型既有关乎宪法机构在相关事务中职权范围的机构争议，也有援引宪法基本权利的个人宪法申诉。从判决来看，联邦宪法法院尽管承认了个人诉讼中作为公民原告的适格性（主要基于第 38 条 1 款的选举权），但却基本否认了欧元区集体性救助法案可能对德国公民的基本权利构成损害，因而个人宪法申诉的请求均被法院驳回。在机构争议中，联邦宪法法院则表现出积极的态度，更多地支持了作为申请人的联邦议会议员和党团提出的诉讼请求，甚至是依申请发出了需重大利益权衡才可作出的紧急禁令，而类似请求在个人申诉中却被驳回。从这两种不同倾向的判决中可以看出，联邦宪法法院在努力强化联邦议员和联邦议会的权力，相

---

① BVerfG，2 BvR 1390/12 vom 12. 9. 2012，http://www. bverfg. de/entscheidungen/rs20120912_2bvr139012. html，最后访问日期：2012 年 11 月 22 日。

② Hanno Kube/Ekkehart Reimer，“Grenzen des Europaesichen Stabilisierungsmechanismus”，*NJW 2010*，1911（1911）.

对限制政府、欧盟机构以及公民的权利，以此来保障宪法规定的民主原则不会在解决欧元区危机时被架空。

二　国家财政的决定者：联邦议会

判断欧元区集体性救助法案是否合宪的关键问题在于：谁有权决定以何种方式使用公民纳税形成的国家财政资金用来帮助那些陷入国债危机的欧元区成员国。这本质上关涉国家财政决定权的归属问题。不论是最初针对希腊的财政援助，还是作为临时性援助的欧洲金融稳定基金及其后续的以长久保持欧洲金融稳定为目的的欧洲金融稳定机制，都要求那些尚有余力的成员国可以从国家财政中支出或预留一笔款项作为对陷入危机国家的贷款或者担保资金。这样的救助无疑会导致当下或未来救助国的额外财政负担，其最终负担者自是本国国民。那么，这种决定应当由人民自己还是可以通过相关的国家机关来代表人民作出呢？是议会，还是政府？这种权力是否可以转让给超国家组织的欧盟呢？联邦宪法法院给出的答案是：国家财政的决定权只属于联邦议会。

（一）不可转让的宪法权力

联邦宪法法院在判决中认定，必须由联邦议会而不是联邦政府或欧盟机构对国家的财政政策完全负责。[①] 国家财政决定权属于议会职权，而且这是一项不可随意转让的职权，否则便会损害基本法第 38 条 1 款所保护的公民选举权。[②] “……德国联邦议会的预算权不能通过财政政策方面的授权以不确定的方式交予其他机构。所承担的赔偿义务的金额越大，那么相应批准法中的德国联邦议会的控制权也就应当更加有效。尤其是，不论是整体方案还是单一措施，都不允许在没有事先实质同意的情况下导致国家财政方面不可预测的负担，不管是支出还是收入方面。禁止预算权的转让不是要限制立法者的财政权，而恰恰是为了予以保护。”[③] 法院认为，决定国

---

① BVerfG, 2 BvR 1390/12 vom 12. 9. 2012, Rn. 196.

② BVerfG, 2 BvR 1390/12 vom 12. 9. 2012, Rn. 210.

③ BVerfG, 2 BvR 1390/12 vom 12. 9. 2012, Rn. 212; BVerfG, 2 BvR 987/10 vom 7. 9. 2011, Rn. 124.

家财政收入与支出是宪治国家“民主自治能力”（demokratische Selbstgestaltungsfaehigkeit）的一个基本要素，是民意表达的核心内容之一。[①] 但由于人民无法对全部收支方案逐一进行表决，因此可以通过自由平等选举产生的联邦议会来掌握国家的财政权，代表人民作出负责任的决定。[②] 联邦议会对国家预算承担的责任和义务不能通过“不确定的财政授权”（unbestimmte haushaltspolitische Ermächtigungen）向其他主体转让，尤其是通过法律使得国家财政在无联邦议会明确同意的情况下面临无法预估的负担。[③]

在肯定联邦议会职权的同时又加以限制会产生这样一个逻辑疑问：如果认为联邦议会是代表人民决定公共开支的宪法机构，人民只能通过撤换议员来间接地影响国家财政政策，而不是通过诸如全民公决的直接方式，那么也就意味着，联邦议会在其合法存续时期是国家财政的最高决策者，享有财政自治权。对其全部或部分转让权力的限制无疑又是似乎在否定其自治权。对此，联邦宪法法院的解释是，国家财政权与基本法第 20 条 1 款和 2 款以及第 79 条 3 款所保护的“宪法核心特征”（Identitätskern der Verfassung）紧密相关，是德国保障政治自由空间的必要条件，国家可以不受欧盟机构或其他国家的外在影响而能够自行决定收入和支出，长期保持“自己决定的主人”（Herr seiner Entschlüsse）。[④] 在德国基本法中，属于宪法核心特征的规定包括民主、法治与社会国家、共和、联邦以及维护人的尊严，是连联邦议会也无权通过修宪加以改变的基本规范（第 79 条 3 款）。基本法第 20 条 1 款和 2 款确立的民主原则不能通过联邦议会的法律而被改变，即便是为了达到欧盟一体化和国际合作的目的。因此，即使在欧盟这样的国家间政府体系中，被选举的德国议员及其组成的联邦议会也应当作为人民的代表对国家财政的根本性决定拥有控制权。[⑤]

（二）代议制民主是议会财政决定权的基础

国家财政权之所以被赋予议会，而不是政府，是遵循了严格的代议制

① BVerfG, 2 BvR 1390/12 vom 12.9.2012, Rn. 210.
② BVerfG, 2 BvR 1390/12 vom 12.9.2012, Rn. 211.
③ BVerfG, 2 BvR 987/10 vom 7.9.2011, Rn. 125.
④ BVerfG, 2 BvR 1390/12 vom 12.9.2012, Rn. 213.
⑤ BVerfG, 2 BvR 1390/12 vom 12.9.2012, Rn. 213.

民主理论，对授权民主加以某种程度的限制。“德国联邦议会是人民最直接的代表，由选举产生的代表全体人民的议员所组成，他们构成了人民的代表。基本法第 38 条 1 款 2 句所保障的议员代表地位是议会具有代表性的基础，使之可以作为‘特别机构’实施来自人民的国家权力。”[①] 根据德国基本法第 38 条 1 款的规定，联邦议会议员通过普遍、直接、自由、平等及秘密的选举产生。议员为全体人民之代表，不受命令与训令之拘束，只服从其良心。该条款在联邦宪法法院看来是保障德国“公民自治”（Selbstbestimmung der Bürger）和“自由平等参与国家权力”（freie und gleiche Teilhabe an der Staatsgewalt）的一项公民基本权利。[②] 也正是以公民选举权为基点，联邦宪法法院对成员国国家的代议制民主和欧盟的民主性作出了决定性的区分。法院明确表示，后者在代议制民主方面不同于成员国。实际上早在 2009 年的里斯本条约判决中法院就已作出了清晰表达，并在欧元区集体性救助法案的判决中大量援引了该判决的要旨。里斯本条约判决起因于 2008 年 4 月 24 日德国联邦议会批准了 2007 年 12 月 13 日的里斯本条约和修改基本法第 23 条、45 条和 93 条的法案以及在欧盟事务中扩大和加强德国议会和联邦参议院权的法案。里斯本条约作为进一步加强欧洲联盟的协定，替代了 2004 年 10 月 29 日未获所有成员国通过的欧盟宪法。[③] 即便如此，不少德国人依然对欧洲一体化行动表示反对，尤其是联邦议会中的反对党团和议员通过机构争议和个人宪法申诉将里斯本条约的合宪性问题交由联邦宪法法院审查。尽管法院最终并未认定里斯本条约违反基本法所保护的公民自由平等选举权和代议制民主，[④] 但却鲜明地指出，目前欧盟所体现的民主原则与成员国通过平等选举权所实现的代议制民主之间虽有相似性，但从自由平等选举和构成有效决策的多数原则来看，欧盟的状况不同于现有的联邦国家。[⑤] 成员国实施民主选举的基本规则是“一人一票”（one man, one vote）的机会均等的选举权。[⑥] 而里斯本条约第 14 条 2 款 1 项 3 句却规定欧盟议会代表的比例原则，这处于“国际法上的国家平等原则与国家法

① BVerfG, 2 BvE 8/11 vom 28. 2. 2012, Rn. 101.

② BVerfG, 2 BvR 1390/12 vom 12. 9. 2012, Rn. 208.

③ AblEU Nr. C 310, S. 1.

④ BVerfG, 2 BvE 2/08 vom 30. 6. 2009, Rn. 277.

⑤ BVerfG, 2 BvE 2/08 vom 30. 6. 2009, Rn. 277.

⑥ BVerfG, 2 BvE 2/08 vom 30. 6. 2009, Rn. 279.

上的选举权平等原则之间”。[①] 法院进一步指出，欧盟议院共有最多750个议席（包括议会主席）；没有一个成员国可以单独拥有超过96个议席并且没有一个成员国要少于6个议席（里斯本条约第14条2款1项2—4句）。这导致人口少的成员国获得的加权比重要超过人口密集成员国的12倍。[②] 例如，来自德国或法国的一名议员将代表857000名本国公民，而一名来自马耳他的议员只代表67000名本国公民。[③] 由此可见，欧盟的民主有过多的邦联色彩，而非成员国的民主形态。[④] 此外，欧盟理事会、部长理事会、欧盟委员会以及欧盟法院原则上也都根据国家投票权来决定。因此，作为体现民主自治能力的国家财政决定权就必须由通过自由平等选举产生的成员国议会及其议员来最终掌握，而不能通过授权赋予不完全符合代议制民主原则的国家或超国家组织。

三 对外财政援助中的宪法制约机制

尽管议会的财政决定权被联邦宪法法院解释为一种不可转让的宪法权力，但不能就此理解为法院否定议会在不失去决定权的情况下不能部分或有条件地转让财权。否则，此前联邦议会所批准的建立和维持欧元货币联盟的条约及相关欧盟条例都应被视为违反基本法，因为这些条约和欧盟法律或多或少都会影响成员国的财政自治权。在违宪审查中，联邦宪法法院肯定了联邦议会部分转让其财政权的可能，但必须受到基本法的宪法性约束，具体可归纳为以下三个内容。

（一）有限的单项授权

根据联邦宪法法院的解释，联邦议会只能通过有限的单项授权（begrenzte Einzelermächtigung）向超国家组织部分地让渡自己的财政权，而绝不能进行空白授权，否则便是违宪。[⑤] “不允许出现这样一种对其他国家的

① BVerfG, 2 BvE 2/08 vom 30. 6. 2009, Rn. 284.

② BVerfG, 2 BvE 2/08 vom 30. 6. 2009, Rn. 284.

③ BVerfG, 2 BvE 2/08 vom 30. 6. 2009, Rn. 285.

④ BVerfG, 2 BvE 2/08 vom 30. 6. 2009, Rn. 288.

⑤ BVerfG, 2 BvR 1390/12 vom 12. 9. 2012, Rn. 209.

意志决定承担赔偿责任的国际法义务，尤其是当可能导致难以预料的后果的情况下。每个可能让联邦在国际或者欧盟范围内实施影响财政支出的救助措施必须经德国联邦议会单独批准。”① 法院担心笼统的授权会导致欧盟这样的超国家组织的职权膨胀和未经成员国同意的越权行为，因为在法院看来，超国家组织权力的合法性来源到目前为止仍是成员国人民的权利，“通过不断增加的职权和逐步跨越一致同意的门槛或是迄今为止不断增强的政府性，欧盟政权的这种不断自我发展就德国宪法而言都源自人民自治的行动自由”②。

在1993年有关《马斯特里赫条约》和2009年《里斯本条约》的违宪审查中，联邦宪法法院就已强调了有限的单项授权原则，反对国家机关将“职权的职权”（Kompetenz-Kompetenz）转让给欧盟或其相关机构。③ 所谓“职权的职权”就是指授予权力的权力，譬如立法者授予政府有权制定市场规则或者是维护公共秩序的职能，或是政府授权特别组织以负责动植物检疫或者公共卫生事务的职能，等等。获得这种职权的被授权者可再行设定相关权力或是可以自行决定将其权力转让，从而相较于明确事项的授权可获得更为广泛的职权扩张空间。为了防止这种情况在成员国向欧盟转让国家财政权时出现，联邦宪法法院要求，立法者在批准和执行欧盟义务的法案时必须配合有效的预防机制，以“保留自己作为立法机构对欧盟责任的履行”④。

（二）监督权的议会保留

为了保障联邦议会的财政决定权不会落空，联邦宪法法院认为无论如何应当保证议会对财政支出款项的监督权和知情权，即便支出部分已得到联邦议会的事先同意，也必须保留对使用过程和结果的监督。“只要是超国家的协定由于其数额会对本国预算权产生结构性的改变，如承担担保责任，该责任履行会影响到国家财政的自主性，或者是参加一种相应的金融

---

① BVerfG, 2 BvR 1390/12 vom 12.9.2012, Rn. 214.

② BVerfG, 2 BvE 2/08 vom 30.6.2009, Rn. 233.

③ BVerfG, 2 BvE 2/08 vom 30.6.2009, Rn. 233; BVerfG, 2 BvR 1390/12 vom 12.9.2012, Rn. 209.

④ BVerfG, 2 BvE 2/08 vom 30.6.2009, Rn. 239.

保障体系，不仅需要德国联邦议会单独的批准，而且还必须保障对支出资金有某种形式的足够的议会监督。”[①] 法院作出这种限制的目的在于，让联邦议会能够对德国对外承担赔偿责任及对预算的影响保持一种长期的监控。[②] 在审查联邦议会的稳定机制法时，联邦宪法法院特别指出，法案第32条第5款，第34条和第35条第1款的规定不能妨碍联邦议会和联邦参议员所享有的广泛知情权。第32条第5款规定了对欧洲金融稳定机制有关文件管理的不可侵犯；第34条要求欧洲金融稳定机制管理委员会和领导机构的成员履行保密义务，不得泄露职务秘密；第35条第1款赋予欧洲金融稳定机制管理委员会和领导机构成员及其他工作人员以从事与职务相关的行为以及官方文件和资料的司法豁免权。这些权利有可能使成员国议会或议员在向本国参与欧洲金融稳定机制的政府机构或者官员在索取信息时受到阻碍，后者以履行保密义务或享有豁免权为由而拒绝提供，从而损害议会的知情权和监督权。有关欧盟一体化进程中对联邦议会和联邦参议院参与权的保障问题，联邦宪法法院早在里斯本条约判决中就已强调，这种权力不能通过议会自己的法案而被剥夺，否则就是违反了基本法所设置的宪法要求。[③]

（三）正当程序

多个机构争议都涉及对外援助事务中联邦议会与联邦议员及党团之间的权利义务关系，联邦宪法法院因而在判决中就联邦议会行驶国家财政决定权的正当程序问题作出了宪法解释。同样以公民的平等选举权和代议制民主为出发点，法院认为，不论数量多寡，联邦议会中的各党派议员作为“人民代表”具有同等性，[④] 即他们在议会决策中享有完全平等的权利[⑤]，包括知情权、话语权、表决权和监督权等等。在决定国家对外财政援助时，联邦议员也享有同等的权利。最能体现这一原则的是通过全体大会讨论和表决来确定相关事项，然而，在国家实践中，为了提高议事效率，出于专业化的考虑，议会通常会设立负责财政和预算事务的专门委员会负责

---

① BVerfG, 2 BvR 1390/12 vom 12. 9. 2012, Rn. 214.

② Franz C. Mayer/Christian Heidfeld, Eurobonds, “Schuldentilgungsfonds und Projektbonds-Eine dunkle Bedrohung?”, *ZRP 2012*, 129 (130).

③ BVerfG, 2 BvE 2/08 vom 30. 6. 2009, Rn. 406.

④ BVerfG, 2 BvE 8/11 vom 28. 2. 2012, Rn. 102.

⑤ BVerfG, 2 BvE 8/11 vom 28. 2. 2012, Rn. 104.

审查政府提交的预算案，并就相关内容举行听证，收集更多的信息，以便作出专业性判断。德国的情况也同样如此。法院也承认，联邦议会的财政委员会在实践中发挥了重要作用并得到广泛的认可。这也就意味着，国家财政事务也并非一定要通过所有议员参加的全体大会来决定，也可以授权一个小型的专业委员会，这也符合基本法第40条1款2句规定的联邦议会的“事务自治”（Geschäftsordnungsautonomie）。[①]

但问题是，由于参加小型专业委员会的议员数量有限，可能会限制未参与议员的权利。正如在修订稳定机制法时，联邦议会将在紧急状态下将是否实施财政援助的决定权授予一个比预算委员会规模更小的9人特别委员会，从而使得更多的联邦议员被排除在决策之外。联邦宪法法院认为，尽管设立特别委员会本身并不违宪，但对此还是需要一定的限制以保障议员的权利：[②] 一是委员会人员构成要符合“镜式反映”（Spiegelbildlichkeit）[③]，也就是说，委员会中议员名额的分配要能够反映议会中党派政治力量的分布；二是要保证非委员会成员议员最低限度的知情权。[④] “……单个议员原则上还享有知情权和控制权，即有权获得可以对政府财政计划作出独立专业判断的相关信息以及修改申请，还有对财政决定的控制权。向非委员会成员的议员通报可以降低授权对议员权利的限制和不公平待遇的程度，并且使得议会大会原则上可以恢复自己的决定权。”[⑤]

另外，联邦宪法法院力图在不改变政府制定和提交财政预案由议会进行审查和批准的基本运行框架下，对政府规划预算（主要是在欧元集团层面讨论集体性救助方案时）的程序提出了要求，即政府须履行及时、全面的告知义务，以保障议会和议员的知情权。“这种告知必须能够为德国议会尽早和有效地对政府决策施加影响打开方便之门。只有在获得充分信息的前提下，联邦议会才能够参与和影响欧洲联合的进程，可以对一个事务的赞成与反对进行讨论和提供意见。告知不能只是将议会置于一个被动理解者的角色。”[⑥] 在政府向议会和议员通告有关欧洲联合事务（基本法第

① BVerfG, 2 BvE 8/11 vom 28.2.2012, Rn. 115.

② BVerfG, 2 BvE 8/11 vom 28.2.2012, Rn. 125.

③ BVerfG, 2 BvE 8/11 vom 28.2.2012, Rn. 126.

④ BVerfG, 2 BvE 8/11 vom 28.2.2012, Rn. 131.

⑤ BVerfG, 2 BvE 8/11 vom 28.2.2012, Rn. 131.

⑥ BVerfG, 2 BvE 4/11 vom 19.6.2012, Rn. 107.

23 条第 2 款第 2 句）时必须做到：内容全面、信息及时且言简意赅。[①]

四 判决影响的法律关系

通过一系列对欧元区金融救助法案的违宪审查，联邦宪法法院明确了在国家对外财政援助中不同法律主体之间尚不完全明晰的法律关系，尽管还不是全部。这主要涉及联邦议会与联邦政府、联邦议会与议员和党团、联邦议会与公民以及德国与欧盟之间的法律关系。下文将对此逐一分析。

（一）联邦议会与联邦政府

通过宪法判决更加清晰的是，联邦议会包括联邦参议院拥有决定是否以及在多大程度上提供对外财政援助的权力，而且这一宪法权力不可以被随意转让，甚至连联邦议会自身也无权自行决定完全让渡给其他国家或者超国家组织。尽管判决本身针对的是欧元集团的集体救助行动，但影响力可及德国参与的所有可能对国家财政产生影响的集体援助活动包括国际货币基金组织的援助行动。相对而言，联邦政府仅有代表德国参与国际财政援助的谈判权，可以拟定援助方案及承担国际责任的具体内容，但最终需得到联邦议会的同意。那些可能会过度限制联邦议会的财政决定权、知情权以及监督权的政府承诺很可能会被视为违宪。此外，通过对机构争议的宪法判决更为明确的是，联邦政府有义务将对外援助谈判的内容及时、全面和简明扼要地向联邦议会传递，否则也可能违反基本法。不过，对于在判决中法院所强调的对外援助承诺不能对国家财政产生“不可预测的负担”（nicht überschaubare haushaltsbedeutsame Belastungen）或让议会失去“对财政的全面负责”（haushaltspolitische Gesamtverantwortung），[②] 法院没有进一步澄清评判标准。至于有限的单项转让是否也会导致议会财政决定权的丧失以及如何避免的问题，法院没有作出相应的解释，因而可能成为未来宪法争议的焦点。

---

① BVerfG, 2 BvE 4/11 vom 19. 6. 2012, Rn. 116ff.

② BVerfG, 2 BvR 1390/12 vom 12. 9. 2012, Rn. 212; BVerfG, 2 BvR 987/10 vom 7. 9. 2011, Rn. 124.

（二）联邦议会与议员和党团

在多个涉及联邦议会与议员和党团法律关系的判决中，法院承认联邦议会作为一个由议员组成的宪法机构可以根据内部事务自治的原则对国家财政事务的审议和表决进行程序性安排，而且可以成立人数较少的特别委员会以提高议事效率，因此少数党派议员被排除在决策程序之外本身并不违宪。但是，为了保障基本法所保护的公民平等选举权，必须保证类似特别委员会的组成或审议表决程序能够真实反映联邦议会中党派政治力量的分布，以及联邦议员最低限度的知情权。对于依据平等选举权的宪法阐释无疑值得商榷，因为设立特别委员会或表决程序是依据相关事务的性质和效率因素而决定，而非从选举权的平等性中推演出来。令人担忧的是，这样可能会限制议会决策、决议和组建机构的自由空间。马丁·纳特斯海姆（Martin Nettesheim）教授认为："如果相关议会决策性机构没有人数众多的议员参加就成为损害平等原则的表面证据需要予以抗辩，那么联邦宪法法院所要求的'审查密度'就会挤压议会的自由决策权。这种表面的结果平等将剥夺议会自由组织其机构的权力，从而影响宪法保障的议会代表制中的议会决策能力。"[①] 由此可能导致的一个结果是，联邦议会就对外财政援助法案的表决也许需要更长的时间，而这与应对欧债危机时需要成员国政府快速反应的要求之间是存在差距的。

（三）联邦议会与公民

联邦宪法法院在一系列判决中的基本立足点可以归纳为对代议制民主理论的重述，是建立在公民行使自由平等选举权所产生的能够代表人民意志的议会民主基础之上的。联邦议员通过选民的直接选举而产生。联邦宪法法院认为，由全体议员组成的联邦议会就是"人民最直接的代表"。[②] 而联邦政府的组成，尽管是由联邦议会中占多数的党派或党团组建而成，也具有民主合法性，但显然不同于议会的直接民主性。这样，关于公民"民主自治能力"的财政事务也就应当由最能体现人民意志的宪法机构来决

① Martin Nettesheim, "Verfassungsrecht und Politik in der Staatsschuldenkrise", *NJW 2012*, 1409 (1411).

② BVerfG, 2 BvE 8/11 vom 28. 2. 2012, Rn. 101.

定。国家财政权属于联邦议会保留的权力，不能够随意被架空。对议会代表制的重申也同时意味着联邦宪法法院倾向于否定直接地参与民主，如通过全民公决方式来决定国家重要的财政政策。在联邦宪法法院看来，人民依然是需要被代表的，但必须是那些被直接选举的代表。

（四）德国与欧盟

同样基于直接选举产生的议会为中心的代议制民主，联邦宪法法院认为，欧盟作为超国家组织的民主性不能与成员国比肩，因为欧盟的议事和决策机构包括欧盟议会的组成与成员国国家机构的民主产生并不完全一致。欧盟依然维系着国际法意义上的主权国家平等原则，从而相对挤压了基于公民个体的平等原则。欧盟法意义上的"欧盟公民"并不具有完全独立的法律主体资格，必须依附于其作为成员国公民的主体资格。联邦宪法法院的这一观点也符合有关欧盟公民法律主体资格的通说。[①] 欧盟依然是一个"由主权民主国家构成的具有法人资格的联盟"。[②] 里斯本条约并不是欧盟宪法，它没有使得欧盟议会成为能够代表欧盟公民意志的核心机构，而且从中也无法解读出成员国建立欧盟国家的意愿。[③] 欧盟与成员国之间的法律关系依然被认定为国际法上的关系，是主权国家之间通过国际条约形成的联盟关系，而非近似国内法上的联邦与州政府之间的关系。这表明，在形成欧元区集体性救助方案时，欧盟机构的权力是有限的，它必须来自联邦议会有限的单项授权，否则就会违背基本法的精神。

总体而言，联邦宪法法院在国家对外财政援助中构建了一个以联邦议会为权力本源的核心框架，局部加强了联邦议员和党团在议会中的权利，且在某种程度上限制了联邦政府以及欧盟机构的职权。其目的在于维护代议制民主下的人民自治权。如以效率与民主、团结与民主的范畴而言，法院无疑将天平更多地倒向了民主。

---

① Albert Bleckmann, "Der Vertrag über die Europäische Union", *DVBl 1992*, *335* (*336*).

② BVerfG, 2 BvE 2/08 vom 30. 6. 2009, Rn. 278.

③ BVerfG, 2 BvE 2/08 vom 30. 6. 2009, Rn. 277.

五 结语

联邦宪法法院为德国政府参与集体性欧债危机解决机制最终亮起了“绿灯”，但也设置了减速缓行的“黄灯”，即德国政府必须在获得联邦议会依照基本法规定充分履行其财政决定权的情况下，才可作出有效的对外财政援助承诺。而且，联邦议会在实施这一宪法权力时自身也必须遵循基本法所设置的宪法约束机制，尤其是要符合有限的单项授权、监督权的议会保留以及正当程序的基本原则。即便是为了维护欧盟的团结与欧元的稳定，也不能脱离这一基本宪法框架，只有这样才能够使德国的对外财政援助行动保持在以民主为依托的法治轨道上。总之，在“救他”和“自救”之间、在“欧洲团结”和“国家主权”之间、在“克服历史”与“引领欧洲”之间，联邦宪法法院紧紧抓住了民主和程序正义的标杆，以求在后民族国家结构的历史背景下达到利益与团结之间的平衡。

（本文原载于《欧洲研究》2013 年第 2 期）

从限权到赋权：面向未来的互联网贸易规则

孙南翔*

正如经济合作与发展组织（OECD）所言，几乎所有的经济和社会活动都能在网络空间中进行。① 互联网贸易甚至成为当前贸易的主要形式。本质上，人类通过互联网技术创造出一个与实体空间相平行的网络世界，并促进跨境贸易更加自由化和便利化。正如罗斯坦·纽沃斯（Rostam Neuwirth）所言，历史上的贸易与法律的发展交织在一起，而且二者与科学技术的革新也紧密相连。② 由于世界各国都共存于相互依赖的网络空间中，③ 互联网贸易具有内在的全球性与国际性，互联网贸易也需按国际性贸易规则的方式进行调整。

互联网贸易需要新规则吗？该问题成为新时期多边或双边贸易协定无可回避且尚存争议的问题。与传统的实物贸易不同，互联网贸易的差异性表现在两个层面：其一，互联网承担传输功能，其创造出一个普遍的、具有目的性的网络，进而能够支持任何类型的服务；④ 其二，在互联网贸易

---

* 孙南翔，中国社会科学院国际法研究所国际经济法研究室助理研究员。

① OECD，“Guide to Measuring the Information Society 2011”，Paris：OECD Publishing，2011，p. 14.

② 参见 Rostam J. Neuwirth，“Global Market Integration and the Creative Economy：The Paradox of Industry Convergence and Regulatory Divergence”，*Journal of International Economic Law* 18（2015）；Bernard Hoekman and Beata Smarzynska Javorcik ed.，“Global Integration and Technology Transfer”，Washington DC：The World Bank，2006；J. C. Somers，“Impact of Technology on International Trade”，*American Journal of Economics and Sociology* 21（1962）。

③ 参见〔美〕罗伯特·基欧汉、约瑟夫·奈《权力与相互依赖》（第四版），门洪华译，北京大学出版社，2012，第 237—295 页。

④ 参见 Timothy Wu，“Application-Centered Internet Analysis”，*Virginia Law Review* 85（1999），pp. 1189 - 1193。

中，如美国贸易代表迈克尔·弗罗曼（Micheal Froman）所言，信息流动与货物移动同样重要。[①] 根据欧洲国际政治经济中心报告，限制信息将降低大约8%的全球生产总值。[②] 遗憾的是，贸易政策制定者在当前仍未就信息自由事项达成一致意见。

由于互联网贸易与实物贸易的差异性，互联网贸易需要新的贸易规则。以《跨太平洋伙伴关系协定》（TPP）、《美韩自由贸易协定》、《欧盟与加拿大全面经济和贸易协定》等为例，本文对国际性贸易协定规则进行类型化区分，将现有的互联网贸易规则分为确权性规则、限权性规则与赋权性规则。上述三种类型的规则共同促进互联网贸易的自由发展。由此，本文试图回答以下三个核心问题：互联网贸易是否需要以贸易协定的方式进行规制，互联网贸易是否需要新的贸易规则以及互联网贸易需要什么样的贸易规则。在回答上述问题后，本文对现有的互联网贸易规则进行实证分析，以此预判规则升级的趋势，并为我国实践提供一定的启示。

一　互联网贸易及其与国际性贸易规则的关联性

诚如哈米德·马姆杜（Hamid Mamdouh）所言，大多数的贸易自由化都是自发的。[③] 技术的变革、市场的需求变动共同推动贸易自由化的纵深发展。在互联网贸易领域，由于市场与技术的深层次作用，其需要新的贸易规则进行调整。

（一）互联网贸易概念及其规制方式

1. 互联网贸易的概念

传统上，贸易自由化与便利化都是以贸易协定的方式进行推动。然

---

① 参见 WTO Public Forum, "USTR Warns Poor countries Would Be the Biggest Losers if Bali Fails", https://www.wto.org/english/news_e/news13_e/pfor_01oct13_e.htm, last visited on 25 March 2016。

② 参见 Matthias Bauer, Hosuk Lee-Makiyama, Erik van der Marel, Bert Verschelde, "The Costs of Data Localisation: A Friendly Fire on Economic Recovery", ECIPE Occasional Paper No. 03/2014。

③ Hamid Mamdouh, "Services Liberalization, Negotiations and Regulation: Some Lessons from the GATS Experience", in Aik Hoe Lim, Bart De Meester eds., *WTO Domestic Regulation and Services Trade: Putting Principles into Practice* (Cambridge: Cambridge University Press, 2014), p. 325.

而，互联网贸易结合了互联网与贸易的双重属性。在定义上，随着互联网技术发展，互联网贸易涵盖所有与互联网有关的贸易活动，包括通过互联网进行的货物贸易、服务贸易，以及将互联网作为分销媒介的服务等形式。本质上，互联网贸易与电子商务并不完全相同。根据世界贸易组织（WTO）的定义，"电子商务"被理解为"通过电子方式对货物和服务的生产、分销、营销、销售或交付的活动"。[①] 然而该定义并不等同于当前的互联网贸易。"电子商务"概念范围远小于互联网贸易，例如，萨沙·文森特（Sascha Vincent）将信息技术产品与服务、网络基础设施服务、电子贸易服务和数字产品等与互联网贸易相关的活动都概括为互联网贸易。[②] 狭义的电子商务仅包括电子贸易服务。

更进一步的，美国政府认为电子商务区别于传统商业贸易的主要方面在于其承担着"销售货物或服务的电子职责（electronic obligations）"。这意味着以电子形式达成的任何商业合同都被视为电子交易，即使其在网络之外履行相关的义务。例如，根据美国政府认为由网络书店销售的书籍也构成电子交易，尽管该货物是以传统的信件形式投递。[③] 换言之，互联网贸易不仅限于以电子方式提供交易的服务，还包括提供电子服务的产品贸易。理论上，互联网贸易还涉及电信等其他领域。毫无疑问，互联网贸易概念是开放的、发展的、面向未来的。换言之，互联网贸易概念随互联网技术的发展而发生变化，例如，当前的云计算、物联网等服务也被纳入互联网贸易的框架之中。

2. 国际性贸易协定对互联网贸易的规制

虽然互联网贸易的概念存在一定的模糊性，然而，互联网贸易需要并且已经为国际性贸易协定所调整。具体如下。

第一，互联网需要以国际性机制进行治理。一方面，由于网络空间的虚拟性、无边界性和电子化，单一国家无法对所有网络活动和行为进行排

---

① World Trade Organization，"Work Programme on Electronic Commerce"，http://www.wto.org/english/tratop_e/ecom_e/wkprog_e.htm，last visited on 26 March 2016.

② 参见 Sascha Wunsch-Vincent，*WTO*，*E-commerce and Information Technologies*，*From the Uruguay Round through the Doha Development Agenda*（Geneva：UN ICT Task Force，2005）。

③ United States Census Bureau，"Quarterly Retail E-Commerce Sales 1st Quarter 2006"，http://www.census.gov/mrts/www/data/html/06Q1.htm，last visited on 26 March 2016.

他性的管辖。[①] 互联网的建立与发展依赖国际层面的协同与合作。本质上，在网络空间进行的贸易活动具有全球性与国际性。由此，互联网贸易法具备全球公共产品的属性，其表现为互联网领域的法律全球化和法律国际化；另一方面，任何国内的互联网规制措施均具有一定域外性，甚至产生全球范围内的溢出效应。[②] 因此，互联网贸易需要国际性的机制进行协调。

第二，互联网技术促使产品贸易网络化。随着互联网技术的推广，更多的产品以服务方式而体现，该现象被称为产品服务化趋势。[③] 例如，在现实中，唱片、书籍等已逐渐转化为服务的方式进行销售。产品服务化的重要推动力在于产品贸易的网络化。当前，互联网已不仅为一项具体的服务，其更成为产品交易的重要平台。网络平台包括搜索引擎、社交媒体、电子商务平台、应用商店、价格比较网站等，它们在社会和经济生活中的作用愈发凸显，使得消费者能够发现互联网信息和商机，进而最大化地利用电子商务。[④] 由此，互联网贸易与贸易活动密切相关，甚至成为众多贸易活动的主要形式。

第三，实际上，互联网贸易已经为国际性贸易协定所调整。在条约文本上，以多边贸易协定为例，《服务贸易总协定》（GATS）第 14 条规定，在满足一定条件下，成员方可以采取保护个人隐私和安全的措施。同时，《电信附件》第 5 条规定，在满足合理的和非歧视的适用方式或不构成服务贸易的变相限制的前提下，成员方可采取保护信息安全和保密性所必要的措施。在 WTO 争端解决实践中，“美国博彩案” 和 “中国视听产品案” 阐明多边贸易协定对互联网贸易的可适用性。在 “美国博彩案” 中，该案上诉机构认为美国的禁令限制了互联网赌博活动。[⑤] “中

---

① 参见 Yochai Benkler, “Internet Regulation: A Case Study in the Problem of Unilateralism”, *European Journal of International Law* 11 (2000)。

② Steven R. Salbu, “Regulation of Borderless High-Technology Economies: Managing Spillover Effects”, *Chicago Journal of International Law* 3 (2002).

③ 参见 Hosuk Lee-Makiyama, “Future-Proofing World Trade in Technology: Turning the WTO IT Agreement (ITA) into the International Digital Economy Agreement (IDEA)”, *ECIPE Working Paper* No. 04 (2011)。

④ 上述的网络平台存在规制不足，例如其透明度不高，导致相比于用户而言，网络平台具有强大的议价能力等。参见 European Commission, “A Digital Single Market Strategy for Europe”, COM (2015) 192, 2015, p. 11。

⑤ United States-Measures Affecting the Cross-Border Supply of Gambling and Betting Services, Report of the Appellate Body, WT/DS285/AB/R, 7 April 2005, pp. 166 – 167.

国试听产品案”上诉机构认为中国对试听产品分销的承诺拓展至以互联网作为分销媒介的形式。[①] 由此，互联网贸易已经成为国际性贸易协定的管辖事项之一。

有学者认为互联网贸易可在国际电信联盟、信息社会世界高峰会议、互联网管制论坛（Internet Governance Forum）、联合国人权事务委员会、OECD 及其他场合进行调整。[②] 然而，必须明确的是，不同国际性机制的核心宗旨与目的并不完全相同。例如，国际电信联盟所解决的是信息通信技术的融合和发展；联合国人权事务委员会解决的是保障个人的权利。更重要的是，国际性贸易协定常具备完善的贸易救济措施与强有力的争端解决机制，其具有其他机制无法媲美的比较优势。虽然人权义务等可能与信息流动相关，但是上述协定与机制并不具有全球性的拘束力，并且缺乏可执行性。[③] 正是基于如上原因，贸易协定被认为规制跨境信息流动的最佳手段。

（二）互联网贸易的特征及其贸易规则需求

如前文所述，互联网贸易需要以贸易协定的方式进行调整，那么随后问题转为互联网贸易是否需要新的贸易规则？笔者认为答案是肯定的。其根本原因在于互联网贸易与传统的实物贸易存在显著差异。

1. *互联网技术是传统贸易协定的外生变量*

虽然贸易是自古以来就有的社会行为，然而每次技术革命都将贸易活动的范围拓展至更远之处。以工业技术、航海技术为代表的近代技术革命推进了国际贸易的发展；20 世纪末期的信息技术革命则为互联网贸易的开展提供了科技基础与现实条件。

有学者指出，互联网发展本身并不产生新的问题。[④] 然而，网络空间

---

① China-Measures Affecting Trading Rights and Distribution Services for Certain Publications and Audiovisual Entertainment Products, Report of the Appellate Body Report, WT/DS363/AB/R, 21 December 2009, para. 396.

② 参见 Michael L. Rustad, *Global Internet Law in a Nutshell* (2nd Edition), (New York: West Academic Publishing, 2013), pp. 118 – 121。

③ Mira Burri, “Should There Be New Multilateral Rules for Digital Trade?”, International Centre for Trade, and Sustainable Development and World Economic Forum Paper, 2014, p. 1.

④ 参见 Joel P. Trachtman, *The Future of International law: Global Government* (Cambridge: Cambridge University Press, 2013), p. 85。

的产生不仅加剧解决古老难题的紧迫性，更产生了一系列新问题，其需要实质性的制度创新。① 虽然作为科学技术，互联网的影响早已超过电力、燃油机、蒸汽机等其他发明创造的成果，② 然而，在缔结 WTO 协定时，成员方并未意识到互联网将给嗣后的经济社会带来的显著变化，其并没有实质性地将技术改革纳入条约中。实物贸易与互联网贸易差异的决定性因素之一在于科学技术，其为传统贸易协定的外生变量。

归纳而言，互联网具有四种与先前技术相区别的特征：其一，互联网使实时的全球信息（包括图像的和视听的材料）传输成为可能；其二，互联网使个人和组织与其他人的交流成为可能，其提供点对点、点对多和多对多的通信渠道；其三，互联网的参与方能够匿名地进行通讯；其四，通过数据库、搜索引擎和机器人，互联网成为前所未有的信息接收工具。③ 基于上述新特征，诸多现存的贸易规则无法解决与电子技术相关的贸易问题，④ 更无法在贸易自由与个人权利保障之间达成平衡。例如，电子技术产生了货物与服务归类问题上的模糊性，同时，互联网使消费者权利更加脆弱。上述客观情势变化都挑战着传统贸易协定的合法性。

2. 互联网贸易的信息对价

传统上，所有的产品购买、销售与现金流紧密相关。虽然一些互联网贸易产生金钱上的给付行为，但是众多的互联网服务提供商充当信息流动和数据传输的平台，其难以满足传统的金钱对价理念。关于信息流动问题，有学者认为信息构成全球公共产品，因为其对经济发展、生产力提高和创新等具有重要的作用。⑤ 然而，免费的“公共产品”难以准确衡量贸易商的趋利动机，更难以将贸易商的行为纳入政府的规制范围中。

在互联网贸易中，服务对价并非总是金钱，还包括信息。互联网贸易

① 参见 Joel P. Trachtman，*The Future of International law：Global Government*（Cambridge：Cambridge University Press，2013），p. 89。

② 参见 OECD，“Broadband and the Economy：Ministerial Background Report”，OECD Doc. DSTI/ICCP/IE（2007）3/FINAL，2007，p. 8。

③ Rolf H. Weber，*Regulatory Models for the Online Word*（Netherlands：Kluwer Law International，2002），p. 41.

④ 参见 Mira Burri，“Should There Be New Multilateral Rules for Digital Trade？”，International Centre for Trade，and Sustainable Development and World Economic Forum Paper，2014，p. 1。

⑤ 参见 Adeno Addis，“The Thin State in Thick Globalism：Sovereignty in the Information Age”，*Vanderbilt Journal of Transnational Law* 37（2004）。

存在众多的双头市场或多头市场，[①] 其更多提供的是零价格的服务。由此，约翰·纽曼（John Newman）创新性地主张互联网企业提供的服务并不以索取服务费用为目的，而是以信息关注与获取用户隐私为对价。[②] 换言之，不存在金钱性对价并不能表明互联网产品不产生贸易价值。以搜索引擎为代表的网络服务提供商是以获取信息关注和隐私的方式，销售其互联网服务，其中，消费者实际上以隐私为代价，支付其服务费用。

毫无疑问，在互联网时代，信息不仅是互联网贸易赖以存在的根基，更充当着通货的作用。由此，贸易协定也应规制此类看似“免费”，但实际为贸易的活动。例如，TPP 服务章节明文规定，服务提供者并不需要与其消费者产生金钱上的来往。换言之，服务提供者包括提供免费电子商务的服务商。[③] 由此，与传统的金钱性给付方式并不相似，互联网贸易需要新的规则文本。

3. 传统的多边贸易协定的局限性

传统的多边贸易协定并未能处理互联网贸易产生的新问题。回溯历史，1998 年，WTO 成员方同意延长对电子传输不施加关税的国家实践，其被称为《电子传输的免税备忘录》。同时，成员方启动全方位审查与电子商务相关的贸易议题的工作计划。2001 年，WTO 成员方启动多哈发展回合谈判，其包括为适应电子商务和信息技术需求的规则谈判。[④] 尽管成员方达成一致意见，尚不对电子传输施加关税，然而现有的多边贸易协定仍存在不可调和的矛盾。

第一，传统的贸易规则无法自动拓展至新的产品形式。虽然乌拉圭回合谈判取得举世瞩目成果，然而当年谈判未能预见到货物和服务在信息时

---

① 参见 Rachel Block，“Market Access and National Treatment in China-Electronic Payment Services：An Illustration of the Structural and Interpretive Problems in GATS”，*Chicago Journal of International Law* 14（2014），pp. 677–679。

② 参见 John M. Newman，“Antitrust in Zero-Price Markets：Foundations”，*University of Pennsylvania Law Review* 164（2015），pp. 149–203；John M. Newman，“Antitrust in Zero-price Markets：Applications”，The University of Memphis Research Paper No. 150，2015。

③ 进一步的，跨境服务的行为被定义为从一缔约成员方境内转移到其他成员方境内的服务；从一成员方境内生产，并被传送至其他成员方的国民的服务；或者从一成员方的国民转移到另一成员方境内的服务。参见 TPP 第 10.1 条。

④ 参见 Sascha Wunsch-Vincent，*WTO*，*E-commerce and Information Technologies*，*From the Uruguay Round through the Doha Development Agenda*（Geneva：UN ICT Task Force，2005），p. 1。

代更新换代的周期加快，而且新型的、综合性的和多功能的产品与日俱增。现有的 WTO 协定文本仍具有模糊和不确定之处。以数字产品归类为例，成员方尚无法确定电子产品到底归属货物还是服务，抑或是受到多重规则的重叠适用。该类规则的模糊或空白不仅削弱了成员方的合理预期，更引发了由规则不确定性而产生的贸易争端，增加了贸易商的经济成本，更减损了多边贸易规则的正当性。

第二，前互联网时代的多边贸易规则无法保障互联网的贸易平台功能。在 GATS 签署时，电信服务仍处于“前互联网”时代。承诺减让表仅识别出 14 种不同类型的电信服务。前 7 种被认为基础性的；而后 7 种被视为具有附加价值的。在实践中，升级版的网络充当着贸易平台的功能。互联网并非创造出一种新的服务，而是创造出一种新的平台，其他服务可以该平台为基础进行。这意味着《电信附件》对基本服务自由化的承诺与当前的互联网服务的规制措施不具有强相关性。例如，《电信附件》并未对互联网的传输功能、信息交换功能进行确认。更进一步的，前互联网时代，谈判缔约方将互联网服务分为以传输为目的的电信服务与以内容为目的的试听服务。然而，新产生的服务类型具备传输性与内容目的性的双重属性，例如，即时媒体视频服务、网络电话等。①

第三，通过文本模糊性，成员方具有实施贸易限制政策的灰色空间。由于多边贸易协定并未意识到互联网的信息传输功能，其未能明确地保护互联网的媒介功能。成员方可通过特定的互联网规制措施，实施“非黑非白”的贸易限制政策。例如，在航空运输中，增加服务信息可获得性和附加服务的成本将降低该航空公司在特定市场的竞争能力。在旅游服务中，若不能通过当地旅游机构采用的电脑预定系统，服务提供者可能无法完成相应的服务，也不能及时处理服务，从而导致服务时间延迟，② 这可能对服务造成贸易障碍，然而，上述障碍是否违反 WTO 协定的问题仍存争议。

更为重要的是，跛行的 WTO 体制难以满足互联网贸易的规则需求。贸易谈判曾为 WTO 的三大核心机制之一，然而多边贸易规则正经历行动

---

① 参见 Shin-yi Peng，“GATS and the Over-the-Top Services：A Legal Outlook”，*Journal of World Trade* 50（2016），pp. 22 - 23。

② Bernard Hoekman，Carlos A. Primo Braga，“Protection and Trade in Services：A Survey”，*Open Economies Review* 8（1997），p. 292.

困境。自2001年多哈发展回合启动以来，至今新一轮的谈判成果寥寥无几。[①] 由此，现有的多边贸易协定仍无法满足互联网贸易的需求。

二 互联网贸易规则的类型化划分与规则创新路径

自20世纪80年代起，随着计算机、软件和卫星等技术的出现，以美国和日本为首的国家主张将信息自由纳入贸易协定的管辖范围中，然而，由于其他国家认为此举将对国家主权构成威胁，会削弱国家对跨境信息流动的控制能力，[②] 国际社会最终并未缔结有拘束力的贸易规则。随着互联网贸易、手机电话和云技术的发展，跨境信息流动再次成为贸易协定谈判中的热点议题。如西方学者所言，互联网加速了新的法律规则的发展。[③] 在贸易领域，互联网规则的发展也呈现出新的特征。

（一）国际性贸易规则的类型化划分

多边贸易协定的根本宗旨在于促进贸易的自由化与便利化。[④] 一般而言，多边贸易协定存在两种实现自由贸易的方式——积极一体化与消极一体化。管理去中心化（policed decentralization）禁止多边贸易协定成员方采纳歧视性的政策，其一般被称为消极一体化；相互承认和协调则要求成员方积极创造条件便利国际贸易，其被称为积极一体化。[⑤] 虽然二者目标具有同一性，然而，消极一体化与积极一体化的实际效果并不完全相同。消极一体化要求缔约方不造成国内产品与外国产品间的歧视待遇；积极一体化则要求缔约方采取统一的、协调的贸易政策。总体而言，积极一体化

---

① 多哈发展回合的成果仅包括《贸易便利化协议》、《公共健康宣言》。与谈判相关的人力、物力、资金和时间相比，规则升级成本远高于其收益。

② Susan Aaronson, “Why Trade Agreements are not Setting Information Free: The Lost History and Reinvigorated Debate over Cross-Border Data Flows, Human Rights, and National Security”, *World Trade Review* 14 (2015), p. 672.

③ JR. Henry H. Perriht, “The Internet is Changing the Public International Legal System”, *Kentucky Law Journal* 88 (2000), p. 895.

④ 例如，《建立世界贸易组织的马拉喀什协定》序言提及WTO协定的根本宗旨是贸易自由化和便利化。

⑤ Federico Ortino, *Basic Legal Instruments for the Liberalization of Trade: A Comparative Analysis of EC and WTO Law* (Oxford: Hart Publishing, 2004) p. 12.

路径的开放程度远大于消极一体化。

正如乔尔·特拉赫特曼（Joel Trachtman）所言，在贸易自由化上，第一层次为确定对待贸易产品与服务的国民待遇和最惠国待遇；第二层次是促使各国贸易措施符合比例性要求，并且以科学为基础确定贸易政策；第三层次则反映出各国贸易政策的积极协调过程。[①] 未来的贸易条款的更新体现为从第二层次向第三层次迈进的过程。现有的互联网贸易规则也体现出上述特征。在互联网贸易中，最为典型的新规则包括阻止电子贸易壁垒的规则与赋予贸易商电子权利的规则。

以美欧的互联网贸易规则为例。在美国经济中，由于信息技术具有至关重要的作用，其将电子贸易作为谈判协定中的优先事项。特别是，美国希望建立起限制信息流动的明确规则，其主要的关注点反映在审查与过滤机制、数据中心及其服务器本地化要求、隐私权保护等事项。[②] 然而，其他国家却担心美国对信息控制能力的加强将损害本国利益。例如，出于消费者保护的关切，欧盟对互联网贸易自由的推动进程相对较缓慢。欧盟自由贸易协定多采用在服务贸易章节处理信息技术产品合作与电子商务融合的事项。[③] 除规定阻止电子贸易壁垒外，欧盟对外签署的自由贸易协定（FTAs）一般不对信息流动作出承诺。美欧分歧也体现在对《安全港协议》的不同态度上。[④]

归纳而言，美国与欧盟之间的分歧无外乎两个层面。其一，如何有效地甄别并避免电子贸易保护措施，该规则的目标在于确保互联网贸易的正常和有序开展；其二，如何定义“电子权利”（digital rights），其目标在于确保互联网贸易的进一步发展，并实现国家间的协同政策。由此，笔者将

---

① 参见 Joel P. Trachtman, *The Future of International law: Global Government* (Cambridge: Cambridge University Press, 2013), p. 201。

② 参见 Susan Ariel Aaronson, "What does TPP mean for the Open Internet?", www.gwu.edu/~iiep/assets/docs/papers/TPP%20Policy%20Brief%20EDIT.pdf, last visited on 20 Feb., 2016。

③ 参见 Sacha Wunsch-Vincent, Arno Hold, "Towards Coherent Rules for Digital Trade: Building on Efforts in Multilateral Versus Preferential Trade Negotiations", in Thomas Cottier eds., *Trade Governance in the Digital Age* (Cambridge: Cambridge University Press, 2012), pp. 192–193。

④ 近期欧盟法院将促进自由贸易的安全港原则裁定为无效，因为其违反了欧盟条约对基本权利的保护。参见 Maximillian Schrems v. Data Protection Commissioner, Judgment of the Court (Grand Chamber), Case C–362/144, 6 October 2015。

互联网贸易相关的新规则区分为两类：一为限制政府权力的规则，主要体现为消极一体化的方式实现贸易自由；二为赋予贸易商权利的规则，其反映以积极一体化的路径实现贸易自由。当然，韩国、加拿大等其他国家与地区的分歧也集中反映在如何实施互联网贸易规制措施以及如何保障个人的合法权利上。

具体而言，自由贸易协定也有相似的反映。例如，韩国与美国签署的FTA规定了电子商务的信息自由流动规则；而韩国与欧盟签署的FTA并不存在信息自由的规定。[①] 国际社会其他国家也不存在统一观点，欧盟和加拿大的FTA并不包含信息自由的条款；加拿大与哥伦比亚FTA则包括明确的信息自由和隐私权的规则。[②]

（二）传统的限权性路径：对政府权力的有力约束

信息与权力相关，权力要么维护信息自由流动，要么阻碍信息的流动。[③] 政府权力的不当使用将产生贸易壁垒。近期，电子保护主义概念愈发得到国际社会的重视。美国和欧盟等都单边地批评其他国家的规制措施构成互联网贸易障碍。由此，电子保护主义成为互联网自由贸易的显著挑战之一。

电子贸易壁垒被视为电子保护主义的表现形式。互联网贸易与实物贸易的显著差别在于贸易对象的无形性、服务过程的虚拟性与服务效果的即时性。若信息跨境流动并不需要相应的有形物的跨境转移，那么相应的贸易无须履行海关程序。本质上，互联网贸易必须采取某种形式的联系，要么通过直接的实体联系，要么通过通信网络。成员方政府对贸易的阻碍也体现在阻止贸易商与消费者进行联系上。美国国际贸易委员会报告将“电

① 参见 European Commission, “European Union-South Korea Free Trade Agreement”, http://ec.europa.eu/trade/policy/countries-and-regions/countries/south-korea/, last visited on 15 May 2016。

② 参见 European Commission, “Consolidated Canada-European Union Comprehensive Economic Agreement Text”, http://trade.ec.europa.eu/doclib/docs/2014/september/tradoc_152806.pdf, last visited on 20 September 2015; Government of Canada, “Chapter 15 Electronic Commerce of Canada-Colombia Free Trade Agreement”, http://www.international.gc.ca/trade-agreements-accords-commerciaux/agr-acc/colombiacolombie/chapter15-chapitre15.aspx? view = d, last visited on 9 March 2016。

③ D. E. Denning, “Power over Information Flow”, in Ramesh Subramanian and Eddan Katz eds., *The Global Flow of Information: Legal, Social and Cultural Perspectives* (New York: New York University Press, 2011), p. 271.

子保护主义”视为对电子贸易的障碍或阻碍，其包括当地成分要求、分化的数据隐私和保护规则、不充分的知识产权保护与不明确的法律框架、持续增长的网络审查制以及传统的不必要的关税程序等。[①]

对抗电子保护主义的有力措施在于限制国内规制权力。新服务的发展受到碎片化的规制和监管的挑战，并且尚不存在受认可的国际标准。[②] 由此，限制政府权力的互联网贸易规则体现在确保国家的规制要求与合法目标相关，并且不超过其必要限度的负担。此方法为传统的消极一体化的贸易自由路径。

（三）新型的赋权性路径：给予贸易商的电子权利

李·牧山浩石（Hosuk Lee-Makiyama）曾发布研究报告主张通过创设《国际数字经济协定》（International Digital Economy Agreement）实现互联网贸易自由化。具体而言，牧山浩石认为在新事情上，WTO 还有很多与互联网相关的工作需要完成，包括电信服务领域。同时，WTO 应建立起对数字经济贸易的承诺，将原先承诺拓宽至互联网服务。[③] 由此，互联网贸易自由仍需要拓展原先 WTO 协定的承诺范围。

传统上，有效促进服务贸易自由化的手段主要关注两类重要的生产要素——商业存在（资本）和劳动力移动（人员）。[④] 然而，对互联网贸易而言，放松资本和劳动力移动限制能在一定程度上实现贸易自由的功能，

---

① 参见 United States International Trade Commission, Digital Trade in the US and Global Economies, Part I, Investigation No. 332 – 532 Publication 4415, July 2013, paras. 5. 1 – 5. 36。有学者认为国家对互联网的干预体现为：将知识产权转移作为外国企业获得市场准入的条件、要求外国企业以与本国公司合资的方式进入本国市场、将抵消或本地成分作为赋予外国公司的合同的条件。参见 Iva Mihaylova, “Could the Recently Enacted Data Localization Requirements in Russia Backfire?”, *Journal of World Trade* 50 (2016), p. 314。

② 参见 Aik Hoe Lim, Bart De Meester, “Addressing the Domestic Regulation and Services Trade Interface: Reflections on the Way Ahead”, in Aik Hoe Lim, Bart De Meester eds. , *WTO Domestic Regulation and Services Trade: Putting Principles into Practice* (Cambridge: Cambridge University Press, 2014), p. 333。

③ 参见 Hosuk Lee-Makiyama, “Future-Proofing World Trade in Technology: Turning the WTO IT Agreement (ITA) into the International Digital Economy Agreement (IDEA)”, ECIPE Working Paper No. 04/2011. , p. 23。

④ Panagiotis Delimatsis, *International Trade in Services and Domestic Regulations: Necessity, Transparency, and Regulatory Diversity* (Oxford: Oxford University Press, 2007) p. 63.

然而，对其更重要的是，对跨境数据流动和计算机网络的限制将直接破坏贸易的持续进展。[①] 换言之，贸易商的电子权利主要体现在信息权及相关的隐私权保障上，甚至还包括互联网的接入权。

在信息权上，贸易谈判者需要更新多边贸易协定的电子商务条款，进而避免挑选条约，并且确保全球互联网维持一个自由贸易区。[②] 赋予贸易商信息权旨在创造互联网的全球可贸易环境。2008 年 6 月，在韩国首尔举办的 OECD 部长级会议以“互联网经济的未来”为主题，最终形成《首尔宣言》。该宣言指出，各国将致力于在加强网络可信性与安全性的前提下，建立起公正平等的规制环境，并维持开放的信息自由流动的环境，保障互联网经济成为全球共享之物。[③]

在确保贸易商应有的信息权基础上，在互联网上，几乎所有的贸易产品都能以数据或信息的方式储存、运输、分销和营销，互联网贸易规则涉及消费者的信息保护等权利。在多边层面上，OECD 起草了《关于平衡隐私权、安全和数据自由流动的自愿性原则》。[④] 该原则承认政府保障隐私权和安全的正当性需求，但通过数据质量、目的明确、限制利用、安全保护、公开和个人参与等原则，强调以明文方式保障经济性信息在全球的自由流动。[⑤] 然而，该原则未具备强制性的拘束力。

除信息权外，互联网接入权也是电子权利的内在要素之一。然而，美国和欧盟对其具有不同认识。主要表现在以下三方面。第一，在法律背景上，欧盟国家具有人权保护的完整体系；而美国则倾向于信息自由。第

---

① Panagiotis Delimatsis, *International Trade in Services and Domestic Regulations: Necessity, Transparency, and Regulatory Diversity* (Oxford: Oxford University Press, 2007) p. 78.

② 参见 Mira Burri, “Should There Be New Multilateral Rules for Digital Trade?”, *International Centre for Trade, and Sustainable Development and World Economic Forum Paper*, 2014。

③ OECD, “The Seoul Declaration for the Future of the Internet Economy”, http://www.oecd-ilibrary.org/science-and-technology/the-internet-economy-on-the-rise/declaration-for-the-future-of-the-internet-economy-the-seoul-declaration_9789264201545-4-en, last visited on 6 May 2016.

④ 其全称为《OECD 隐私权和个人数据跨境流动保护指南》。除隐私权外，在互联网经济框架下，OECD 还关注电子识别和认证、儿童权益保护、密码体系、互联网治理等领域。参见 OECD, “Internet Economy”, http://www.oecd.org/sti/ieconomy/, last visited on 23 March 2016。

⑤ OECD, “OECD Guidelines on the Protection of Trans-border Flows of Personal Data”, http://www.oecd.org/internet/ieconomy/oecdguidelinesontheprotectionofprivacyandtransborderflowsofpersonaldata.htm, last visited on 23 March 2016.

二，在权利属性上，在以法国为代表的部分欧盟国家中，互联网接入权是基本的人权；而美国将接入权视为发展议题，而非人权议题。第三，在规制手段上，欧盟和美国对国家与企业在保护隐私中的作用与功能配置有不同主张。① 毋庸置疑，至少在贸易层面上，互联网接入权构成国家发展的权利，甚至是增加中小企业贸易机会的重要方式。例如，TPP 第 24 章“中小企业”规定应通过提供网络信息和链接的方式，增加中小企业的贸易机会。

需要注明的是，WTO 协定本身具有相对特定的适用范围，不可能解决互联网规制的所有问题，其可拓展的互联网规制的领域建立在与贸易的相关性之上。② 然而现有的双边贸易协定甚至将承诺义务拓展至贸易领域之外，包括人权事项等。

三 新型贸易协定的互联网规则文本

2011 年，谷歌公司发布的研究报告中，提出两项 21 世纪互联网贸易议程，分别为：其一，政府应该减小现有 WTO 框架内的缝隙（gaps），进而确保 GATS 能适用于所有的互联网贸易；其二，政府应谈判能够符合当前信息经济的新规则，并将它们包括在双边和多边贸易协定中。③ 按照前述思路，新型的互联网贸易规则也可分为确权性规则、限权性规则和赋权性规则。由于互联网贸易在 21 世纪初逐渐兴起，其产生与发展的过程较短，下文对互联网贸易规则分析主要以晚近签署或公开的 TPP、美国—韩国 FTA、欧盟—加拿大《全面经济和贸易协定》等为主。

① 关于欧盟和美国对跨境信息流动的不同策略和行为，参见 Susan Aaronson，“Why Trade Agreements are not Setting Information Free：The Lost History and Reinvigorated Debate over Cross-Border Data Flows，Human Rights，and National Security”，*World Trade Review* 14（2015），pp. 687 - 691。

② Fredrik Erixon，Hosuk Lee-Makiyama，“Digital Authoritarianism：Human Rights，Geopolitics and Commerce”，*ECIPE Occasional Paper* No. 5/2011，p. 17.

③ Google Corporation，“Enabling Trade in the Era of Information Technologies：Breaking Down Barriers to the Free Flow of Information”，2011，p. 12，www. transnational-dispute-management. com/article. asp？key = 1658，last visited on 4 November 2015.

（一）确权性规则：对WTO协定可适用性的确认

关于缔结于20世纪90年代的WTO协定是否可调整互联网贸易的问题，理论和实践均存有一定争议。[①] 在理论上，文森特主张WTO协定可适用于电子商务，以及以电子方式提供的服务（electronically supplied services）等新兴贸易领域。[②] 在争端解决实践中，美国和中国曾分别在“美国博彩案”和“中国试听产品案”中主张其在缔约时无法预见互联网技术的兴起，因而WTO协定不应适用于新的产品形式。[③] 然而，上述案件的专家组和上诉机构均认为，对WTO协定的可适用性分析应依赖条约解释的惯常方式，最终确定了WTO协定对争议产品的可适用性。然而，专家组和上诉机构反复强调WTO协定的适用应在考虑特定案件的实施情形和法律语境下，以逐案分析的方式进行确定。[④] 换言之，现有的争端解决机制并未能提供WTO协定对互联网贸易的可适用性的明确保障。在协定文本缺乏可预见性的前提下，个案分析的裁决思路难以解决所有与贸易相关的互联网规制问题。

为实现互联网贸易规则的稳定性和可预见性，在双边贸易协定中，各缔约方直接明文规定WTO协定能够适用于互联网贸易规则。例如，在加拿大—哥伦比亚FTA中，其第1502条“一般条款”规定，“缔约方认识到由电子商务能提供经济增长与机会，以及WTO规则可适用于电子商务领域”。

该类型的规则为确权性规则，其在双边贸易安排中，缔约方重新确认WTO协定对互联网贸易的可适用性，进而以协定的方式确定缔约方的权利和义务。确权性规则连接WTO协定与双边贸易协定，一方面，在WTO协

① 参见Sacha Wunsch-Vincent，“The Internet，Cross-Border Trade in Services，and the GATS：Lessons from U. S. -Gambling”，*World Trade Review* 5（2006），pp. 323－324。

② 参见Sacha Wunsch-Vincent，“The Internet，Cross-Border Trade in Services，and the GATS：Lessons from U. S. -Gambling”，*World Trade Review* 5（2006），pp. 323－324。

③ 参见United States-Measures Affecting the Cross-Border Supply of Gambling and Betting Services，Panel Report，WT/DS285/R，10 November 2004，para. 6. 285；China-Measures Affecting Trading Rights and Distribution Services for Certain Publications and Audiovisual Entertainment Products，Report of the Appellate Body，WT/DS363/AB/R，21 December 2009，para. 408。

④ United States-Import Prohibition of Certain Shrimp and Shrimp Products，Report of the Appellate Body，12 October 1998，WT/ DS58/AB/R，para. 159.

定适用中，由于双边贸易协定可能构成解释时的“相关国际法文件”，甚至为嗣后协定，[①] 因此，该确权性规则避免了专家组和上诉机构的保守性裁决。另一方面，由于在 WTO 协定的条约解释上，目前对 WTO 协定与互联网贸易之间的相关性仍未明确。换言之，在大前提尚未明确的情况下，双边贸易协定的确权性规则的适用效果尚存疑惑。由此该确权性规则似乎构成双边贸易协定的“无效率的自白”。

（二）限权性规则：对抗不必要的电子贸易壁垒

由于电子保护主义的存在，在 WTO 协定外，缔约方建立符合互联网贸易需求的新规则具有迫切性和必要性。除确认性规则外，消极一体化的传统贸易规则制定路径也反映在互联网贸易规则中，其集中体现于缔约方明文限制不必要的电子贸易壁垒。

美国—韩国 FTA 首次规定了电子商务中的信息自由流动规定，第 15.8 条规定：“认识到信息自由流动对贸易便利化，以及保护个人信息的重要性，成员方应该致力于避免对跨境电子信息流动施加或维持不必要的障碍（unnecessary barriers）。”[②] 相似的，在加拿大—哥伦比亚 FTA 中，第 1502.4 条“一般条款”也规定，缔约方认识到避免以电子方式实施不必要的贸易障碍的重要性。[③]

关键问题在于如何理解“不必要的电子贸易障碍”概念。根据加拿大—哥伦比亚 FTA，缔约方的义务包括两个层面：其一，缔约方不应以不适当的电子方式阻碍贸易；其二，与其他方式采取的贸易相比，缔约方不应对电子方式提供的贸易施加更具限制性的措施。

本质上，对抗电子保护主义的核心在于实现互联网贸易的非歧视性。第一，其要求确保缔约方不能因为产品或服务以电子方式表现，就否认该产品或服务的法律效果、有效性或可执行性。换言之，这就将非歧视待遇

① 参见孙南翔《论发展的条约解释及其在世贸组织争端解决中的适用》，《环球法律评论》2015 年第 5 期，第 161—178 页。

② 该自贸区协定已于 2012 年生效适用。

③ 美国与日本签署的信息与通信技术服务贸易原则第 2 条、美国与欧盟信息、通信技术服务贸易原则第 2 条等都有相似的规则。参见 Shin-yi Peng，“GATS and the Over-the-Top Services：A Legal Outlook”，*Journal of World Trade* 50（2016）。

拓展至互联网交易中。[①] 第二，限权性条款确认了“技术中性”（technological neutrality）的原则，禁止因为技术使用方式对货物或服务制定不合理的差别待遇。

当然，互联网贸易的限权性规则还应区分“必要的贸易限制措施”与“不必要的贸易限制措施”。根据《维也纳条约法公约》第31条和第32条确定的条约解释的文本方法，一方面，“必要的”被理解为“不可或缺的”；另一方面，也可被理解为“对目标作出贡献”。WTO协定发展出一系列关于“必要性”的案例，甚至影响其他国际性裁决机构的推理方式与裁决思路。在WTO争端解决实践中，其认为WTO协定的“必要的”含义更倾向于“不可或缺的”，而非仅仅是“有贡献”。[②] 条约积极性义务的“必要的”解释与例外条款的“必要性”解释相似，一般应考察争议中的利益或价值的重要性、措施实现目标的贡献程度、措施的贸易限制性，以及其他潜在的可替代性措施。[③] 换言之，必要的贸易限制措施应对合法目标具有贡献，并且具有相对较低的贸易限制性。

实践中，针对限权性规则而言，美国与欧盟国家间并不存在显著分歧。例如，欧盟与韩国、欧盟与加勒比地区国家的自由贸易协定也要求缔约方尽量避免对电子商务施加不必要的规制障碍。[④] 2015年，欧洲议会委员会、欧洲经济与社会委员会等共同发布的《欧洲单一电子市场策略》文件也致力于消除欧洲市场的电子贸易壁垒。然而，也有学者指明现有互联网贸易的限权性规则的缺陷。具体而言，现有的规则适用于所有的影响信息流动的措施，并且适用于所有的电子产品，不管其构成货物还是服务，然而，该条款“致力于”以术语定义缔约方的义务，实际上并不具有拘束力。进一步的，谷歌公司认为应明确“致力于消除障碍”的含义，并且将

① Rolf H. Weber, “Digital Trade and E-commerce: Challenges and Opportunities of the Asia-pacific Regionalism”, *Asian Journal of WTO and International Health Law and Policy* 10 (2015).

② Korea-Measures Affecting Imports of Fresh, Chilled and Frozen Beef, Report of the Appellate Body, WT/DS161/AB/R, 11 December 2000, para. 161.

③ Brazil-Measures Affecting Imports of Retreaded Tyres, Report of the Appellate Body, WT/DS332/AB/R, 3 December 2007, para. 178.

④ European Commission, “International Affairs: Free Trade Agreements”, http://ec.europa.eu/enterprise/policies/international/facilitating-trade/free-trade/index_en.htm#h2-2, last visited on 9 March 2016.

该条款的义务适用于所有的电子信息流动，而不仅仅是“跨境的”信息。[①] 由此，TPP 协定第 14.11 条指出，实现合法公共政策目标的措施应满足两个条件：①不得以构成任意或不合理歧视的方式适用，或对贸易构成变相限制；②不对信息传输施加超出实现目标所需要的限制。毫无疑问，该条款使得限权性规则更具有可明确性，并增加对贸易规制措施的适用方式的约束。

（三）赋权性规则：信息自由及其例外

尽管避免电子贸易主义的规则能够减少阻碍互联网贸易发展的壁垒，然而，消极一体化本身难以从根本上实现全球的自由贸易。在互联网领域尤为如此。与传统实物贸易相比，互联网贸易的兴起与发展更需要赋予贸易商电子权利作为保障，以此实现全球互联网规制的统一化。

信息是互联网贸易发展的基础。与互联网贸易相关的赋权性规则的构建以信息自由为前提。其主要包括赋予贸易商以信息自由权、互联网接入权，以及禁止当地成分要求等。

在信息自由权上，以 TPP 为例，在“电子商务”章节中，其要求成员方确保全球信息和数据的自由流动，并承诺不施加对当地数据处理中心的限制，同时其要求软件源代码不应该被要求转让或进行评估。TPP 还直接规定缔约方不应对电子传输征收税收，且不可通过歧视性措施或彻底屏蔽来支持国内生产者或服务者。除避免新的电子贸易障碍外，美国与智利、新加坡、秘鲁、哥伦比亚等贸易协定规定任何缔约方都不能进行当地成本要求。本质上，禁止对数据中心进行当地成本要求，推动了信息的自由流动。相似的，加拿大和哥伦比亚 FTA 也包括确保信息自由流动、透明度和隐私权保护的规则。

除正面规定信息自由的权利外，现有的互联网贸易规则也通过鼓励设置协调的标准实现信息的自由化。正如苏姗·艾伦森（Susan Aaronson）所言，在隐私权上，美国和欧盟存在难以调和的矛盾。根据美国法，网络隐私权为消费者权利，然而在欧盟、澳大利亚和加拿大等，隐私权被视为须

---

① 参见 Google Corporation，“Enabling Trade in the Era of Information Technologies: Breaking Down Barriers to the Free Flow of Information”，2011，p. 14。

经政府保护的人权权利。[①] OECD《隐私权和个人数据跨境流动保护指南》序言指出，尽管各国隐私权保护立法使得贸易规则具有可预见性，然而，不同国家立法的差异构成个人数据跨境自由流动的障碍。由此，协调网络隐私权分歧的方式只能通过协同性的标准。例如，欧盟与加勒比地区国家要求在数据保护领域进行合作，并且要求缔约方实现与欧盟标准相协同的数据保护标准。

需要注明的是，信息自由并非是绝对的，也受到例外条款的限制。现有自由贸易协定并未否认国家的互联网规制权。例如，TPP 第 14.11 条规定对电子方式跨境传输的自由化要求不得阻止缔约方为实现合法公共政策目标而采取或维持的限制性措施。[②] 正如美国国际贸易委员会报告所反复强调的，对数据流动的必要限制应当符合现有的贸易规则。[③] 现有的贸易规则通常以一般例外与安全例外的方式实现贸易自由与政府合法性规制间的平衡。

在互联网贸易语境下，例外规则也有细微的变化。以欧盟与加拿大起草的《全面经济和贸易协定》为例。其中，安全例外规则的“维持和维护国际和平与安全的国际义务”并未与《联合国宪章》相联系，[④] 而是笼统地规定“本协定不阻止为实现国际和平和安全目的国际义务，缔约方采取其认为对保护必要安全利益必要的行为”。换言之，与 GATT1994 相比，该双边贸易协定拓展了对“国际和平和安全”的理解，进而使其更可适用于网络和平与安全的语境。

四 展望与启示

本质上，WTO 协定建立在消极一体化的基础上，其核心目标在于确保

① Susan Aaronson, “Why Trade Agreements are not Setting Information Free: The Lost History and Reinvigorated Debate over Cross-Border Data Flows, Human Rights, and National Security”, *World Trade Review* 14 (2015), p. 682.

② TPP 第 14.11 条规定实现合法公共政策目标的措施应满足两个条件：（a）不得以构成任意或不合理歧视的方式适用，或对贸易构成变相限制；（b）不对信息传输施加超出实现目标所需要的限制。

③ 该报告指出，现有的贸易规则要求限制措施应是非歧视的、比例性的和公开透明的，并且应是最小贸易限制性的措施。

④ GATT1994 第 21（c）规定：本协定的任何规定不得解释为阻止任何缔约方为履行其在《联合国宪章》项下的维护国际和平与安全的义务而采取的任何行动。

成员方单边施加的政策与措施不构成不必要的或歧视性的贸易障碍。[①] 以消极一体化为导向的WTO协定未能满足美国为主的网络大国的利益需求。从《国际服务贸易协定》（TiSA）的谈判可见一斑。[②] 除涉及传统的服务贸易规则外，TiSA还涉及包括跨境数据流动、禁止本地化措施等敏感事项。[③] 由此，众多专家学者建议TiSA谈判认真对待新的贸易形式，关注乌拉圭回合后的电子贸易革命，并且将贸易便利化、网络中性等规定到文本中，进而实现网络空间的跨境交易自由。[④] 值得说明的是，除上述分析的规则外，互联网贸易的规则还涉及知识产权保护、中小企业能力建设等。[⑤]

如赫特曼乔尔所言，事实上，国际法的成长与国内法相似，先是确定基本的财产权与安全规则，随后转向创造公共产品和规制目的的政策。[⑥] 互联网贸易规则的发展亦应循此路径。双边贸易规则以确权性规则为主，目前美欧之间在限权性规则上已达成一致，然而在赋权性规则上，美欧仍

---

① Petros C. Mavroidis, "Driftin Too Far from Shore-Why the Test for Compliance with the TBT. Agreement Developed by the WTO Appellate Body is Wrong, and What Should the AB Have Done Instead", *World Trade Review* 12 (2013).

② 2012年2月，以美国、澳大利亚、欧盟为主的WTO成员方组成"服务真正好友"成员集团启动对服务贸易的全面协定的谈判，该协定被称为TiSA。截至2015年10月，TiSA共进行了13轮谈判，并计划在2016年6月前继续进行四轮新谈判。参见 Australian Government, "Department of Foreign Affairs and Trade, Trade in Services Agreement", http://www.dfat.gov.au/trade/agreements/trade-in-services-agreement/Pages/trade-in-services-agreement.aspx, last visited on 3 March 2016。

③ TiSA泄露的关于电子商务附件草案包括"开放的互联网、互联网接入与使用"条款，其规定：在遵守所适用的法律下，任何缔约方应该确保其领土内的消费者能够：（a）基于他们的选择，可接入和使用在互联网上的服务和应用程序；（b）若相关设备不对网络造成损害，可使用他们选择的设备连接互联网；（c）在互联网接入服务提供者的网络管理操作（network management practices）下，可获得信息。参见 Our World is not For Sale, "Briefing on Leaked US TISA Proposal on E-Commerce, Technology Transfer, Cross-Border Data Flows and Net Neutrality", http://www.ourworldisnotforsale.org/en/report/briefing-us-tisa-proposal-e-commerce-technoloy-transfer-cross-border-data-flows-and-net-neutr, last visited on 20 May 2016。

④ Pierre Sauve, "A Plurilateral Agenda for Services? Accessing the Case for a Trade in Services Agreement (TISA)", NCCR Working Paper No. 2013/29, May 2013, pp. 14－15.

⑤ 参见 Brian Bieron, Usman Ahmed, "Regulating E-commerce through International Policy: Understanding the International Trade Law Issues of E-commerce", *Journal of World Trade* 46 (2012): 545－570。

⑥ 参见 Joel P. Trachtman, *The Future of International law: Global Government* (Cambridge: Cambridge University Press, 2013), p. 1。

存在尚未调和的矛盾。毫无疑问，赋权性规则将是下一代的互联网贸易规则的核心。值得说明的是，虽然 TTIP 尚未最终达成文本，2015 年 6 月欧盟委员会发布的欧盟文本建议中，第 5—2（2a）条规定了比例性测试，而非必要性测试。① 换言之，除美国推动自由贸易外，欧盟也在尽力削弱政府权力滥用的可能性。

对中国而言，网民数量已占据全球第一，我国已成为互联网贸易大国。近期，我国大力推行“互联网+”战略，其本身需要公平、透明、自由和开放的互联网贸易环境。总体而言，结合国际性贸易规则的未来趋势，在未来签署的自由贸易协定中，我国可以把握以下三个方面。

第一，我国应避免实施电子保护主义的贸易政策。近期，我国启动《服务贸易创新发展试点方案》，强调将依托大数据、物联网、移动互联网、云计算等新技术推动服务贸易模式创新，打造服务贸易新型网络平台。② 新型服务贸易网络平台的建设与发展需要自由的贸易环境，核心在于消除一切形式的不必要的电子贸易障碍。

第二，作为网络大国和信息大国，我国应合理区分贸易性的信息权和非贸易性的信息权。在贸易领域，除非符合现有的一般例外或安全例外规则，否则应避免限制与贸易相关的信息流动。在政治等其他领域，应主张信息的非贸易性，特别是基于我国国情现状，以合理的方式对网络信息进行治理。例如，在网络出版服务上，由于网络出版物并非简单的提供贸易信息，而是以内容为其核心价值，因而互联网并非是简单的信息媒介功能，其体现非贸易性的信息内容。基于此，我国可合理地对其出版内容服务及其服务提供者进行限制。③

第三，我国应发挥例外条款作用，实施合法的互联网规制措施。国际性贸易协定并不否认缔约方按照国家利益、公共利益与私人利益对互联网贸易进行限制。虽然有学者可能对例外情形是否成为一般规定持批评态度，但是例外规则对缔约方是必要的，因为缔约方本身对更紧密的合作有

① 参见 European Commission，“European Union's Proposal for TTIP Services，Investment and E-commerce Text”，http://trade.ec.europa.eu/doclib/docs/2015/july/ tradoc_153669.pdf，last visited on 20 February 2016。

② 国务院：《国务院关于同意开展服务贸易创新发展试点的批复》（国函〔2016〕40 号），成文日期：2016 年 2 月 22 日。

③ 参见 2016 年 3 月 10 日施行的《网络出版服务管理规定》第 8 条第 3 款。

需求，而其对保留规制空间具有合法的和政治性的理由。[①] 我国应通过例外条款，构建符合国际性贸易协定的互联网规制措施。

当然，与其说对赋予贸易商的电子权利产生分歧，不如说各国对互联网贸易相关的信息的定义存在极大分歧。正如艾伦森所反复追问的，现有的贸易协定到底是规制所有的信息流动，还是那些与商业交易相关的信息?[②] 该问题将考验谈判各方的智慧。然而，正如文森特和亚诺所期待的，多边和优惠贸易谈判最终将形成对电子贸易规制的一致性措施。[③] 2016 年，OECD 将在墨西哥坎昆召开以电子经济为主题的部长级会议，其将关注互联网开放性、电子互信、全球互联性等领域。[④] 对互联网贸易自由而言，这似乎又燃起一缕崭新的希望。

（本文原载于《当代法学》2016 年第 5 期）

---

① Armand de Mestral, "When Does the Exception Become the Rule? Conserving Regulatory Space under CETA", *Journal of International Economic Law* 18 (2015).

② 参见 Susan Aaronson, "Why Trade Agreements are not Setting Information Free: The Lost History and Reinvigorated Debate over Cross-Border Data Flows, Human Rights, and National Security", *World Trade Review* 14 (2015), p. 678。

③ 参见 Sacha Wunsch-Vincent, Arno Hold, "Towards Coherent Rules for Digital Trade: Building on Efforts in Multilateral Versus Preferential Trade Negotiations", in Thomas Cottier eds., *Trade Governance in the Digital Age* (Cambridge: Cambridge University Press, 2012), pp. 192 – 193。

④ 此外，OECD 分别于 1998 年、2008 年召开关于电子商务、互联网经济未来的部长级会议。参见 OECD, "Meeting the Policy Challenges of Tomorrow's Digital Economy", http://www.oecd.org/internet/ministerial/, last visited on 23 March 2016。

涉外股权收购合同关系的法律适用

任宏达*

一 问题的引入

近年来随着中外经济交往的快速发展，涉外并购交易数量猛增，国内相关民事纠纷数量自2010年以来呈几何倍数增长。① 人民法院在对案情进行实质分析之前首先需解决法律适用问题，而既往案例存在“合而治之”的情况。以2010年“金华（中国）有限公司、天津汇英实业有限公司、赵英机诉汇英（加拿大）有限公司股权转让纠纷案”为例，② 该案中目标公司“天津汇英公司”（下称“天津公司”）是外商合资企业且依法未成

---

* 任宏达，中国社会科学院国际法研究所国际经济法研究室助理研究员。

① 在中国裁判文书网中使用“涉外”、“股权”、“转让”、“民事案由”等关键词的组合，可以看大致的趋势，2010年仅有四起案例而2016年有166起案例与之相关。具体而言，裁判年份2010年共有11个搜寻结果，其中4个案件涉及股权转让纠纷，参见：http://wenshu.court.gov.cn/list/list/? sorttype = 1&number = BK54VD38&guid = 9509922f-a974-e4743fce-d7ef96e79f88&conditions = searchWord + QWJS + + + 全文检索：涉外%20 股权%20 转让 &conditions = searchWord + 2010 + + + 裁判年份：2010&conditions = searchWord + 民事案由 + + + 一级案由：民事案由；裁判年份2016年共有201个搜寻结果，其中166起案件涉及股权转让纠纷，参见 http://wenshu.court.gov.cn/list/list/? sorttype = 1&number = LVBRKGB2&guid = f2684697-766c-eabe9c4b-5619f030099e&conditions = searchWord + QWJS + + + 全文检索：涉外%20 股权%20 转让 &conditions = searchWord + 民事案由 + + + 一级案由：民事案由 &conditions = searchWord + 2016 + + + 裁判年份：2016&conditions = searchWord + 股权转让 + + + 关键词：股权转让；查询及整理时间为2017年12月12日。

② 参见天津市高级人民法院判决书，2010年9月27日，〔2010〕津高民四终字第3号，资料来源：http://wenshu.court.gov.cn/content/content? DocID = f02feac9-b647-11e3-84e9-5cf3fc0c2c18，最后访问日期：2017年12月12日。

立股东会，董事会代为行使职能，其董事主要为赵某、董某夫妻二人。其间该公司大部分股份以低价转让给了由赵氏家族控制的香港公司，随后赵董二人离婚并产生财产纠纷。董某以原持股公司（成立于加拿大）之名向人民法院起诉，请求确认《股权转让协议》及天津公司《董事会决议》无效、返还股权并赔偿损失。两审法院均将该案件定性为涉外股权转让合同纠纷，随后都依据合同准据法确定了“整个案件”应当适用我国法律：其中一审援引了《关于审理涉外民事或商事合同纠纷案件法律适用若干问题的规定》（以下简称《涉外民商事纠纷规定》）[①] 第4条第2款；二审则适用了《合同法》第126条第1款的最密切联系原则。该案体现了涉外股权转让纠纷的常见特征，即当事人诉求往往包含了多种不同的民事关系。具体而言，此案中包含《股权转让协议》的效力、《董事会决议》的效力、股权的返还、侵权责任赔偿这四类民事关系，而仅以合同准据法为依据判断整个案件的法律适用显属不当。类似的处理方式还存在于2014年的海南东林公司案中。[②]

2012年最高人民法院出台了《最高人民法院关于适用〈中华人民共和国涉外民事关系法律适用法〉若干问题的解释（一）》[③]（以下简称《法律适用法释一》），其第13条规定案件涉及两个或者两个以上的涉外民事关系时，人民法院应当分别确定应当适用的法律。该条款以司法解释的形式既阐明了法律适用对象问题，又对人民法院的审判提出了更高的要求。但是这种“分而治之”的思路在实践中存在两个层面的挑战：宏观层面，合而治之的思路高效便捷，不论依据正确与否，最终适用法院地法一般不会出错，相反分而治之的思路虽合乎法理但低效烦琐；微观层面，长久以来我国立法习惯将涉外并购相关协议强制适用我国法律，这一公法的刻板印象蒙蔽了强制适用的初衷，从而干扰司法审判真正从私法角度出发，援引

① 法释〔2007〕14号（已失效），发布于2007年7月23日，自2007年8月8日至2013年4月8日有效；失效依据为《最高人民法院关于废止1997年7月1日至2011年12月31日期间发布的部分司法解释和司法解释性质文件（第十批）的决定》，法释〔2013〕7号，第76项。其第4条第2款规定：“当事人未选择合同争议应适用的法律，但均援引同一国家或者地区的法律且未提出法律适用异议的，应当视为当事人已经就合同争议应适用的法律作出选择”。

② 参见海南省高级人民法院判决书，2014年12月22日，〔2014〕琼民三终字第2号，资料来源：http://wenshu.court.gov.cn/content/content?DocID=763e0211-77e1-4359-827f-42d821870872，最后访问日期：2017年12月12日。

③ 法释〔2012〕24号，发布于2012年12月28日，自2013年1月7日起生效。

恰当的条款以及进行充分的说理。

针对宏观层面的问题需要从国际私法的角度系统研究涉外并购中各类民事关系的法律适用，以学术研究推动司法效率的提升，而本文则先行聚焦实践中最常见的合同关系。微观层面，在阐明合同关系的范围及法律基础之后，本文重点讨论外资并购中的收购合同是否应当强制适用我国法律。其中，以实证研究的方式表明强制适用的现行法依据在实践中的尴尬地位及消极影响，进而从股权转让限制技术发展的新视角否定了强制适用的现实意义，本文的主要论点亦基于此种新视角，最终提出合同关系法律适用的出发点应正本清源地回归到合同准据法上来。

二 涉外股权收购合同、合同纠纷与合同关系

实践中公司收购合同（Sale and Purchase Agreement，SPA）[①] 依据其标的的不同又可以分为两类：资产收购合同与股权收购合同。资产收购合同的标的可以丰富多样，既可能包括债权、动产、不动产、知识产权等传统标的，也可能包括客户资源、市场份额、生产流程等非传统标的。[②] 股权收购合同的标的则主要是目标公司的股权，甚至可能是多个目标公司（包括外国公司）的股权。从出让方角度来看，资产收购合同的主体是目标公司本身，而股权收购合同的主体是目标公司的股东。就受让方而言，其可以是任何自然人、法人等主体，但就公司并购的专业性来看不应将其视为普通消费者。在无法律及政府规制的约束下，[③] 股权收购合同的具体内容有较大的自治空间，一般都会包含一些“法律适用条款”。[④] 目前我国立法

① 即使在德国的并购实践中，涉外并购合同的行文一般也使用英语，vgl. Oliver Duys/ Kerstin Henrich：Der Unternehmenskaufvertrag nach anglo-amerikanischem Muster in：Hölters （Hrsg. ） HandbuchUnternehmenskauf，7. Aufl. 2010，Teil XVI，Rn. 1ff。

② Vgl. Göthel，StephanR. ：in：Reithmann/Martiny （Hrsg. ） InternationalesVertragsrecht，8. Aufl. 2015，Kapitel 10 Rn. 6. 2479.

③ 对于股权转让合同内容的基本要求，参见《关于外国投资者并购境内企业的规定》，商务部令 2009 年第 6 号，第 22 条，其针对外资并购；《外商投资企业投资者股权变更的若干规定》，〔1997〕外经贸法发第 267 号，第 10 条，针对外商投资企业股权变更。

④ 针对法律适用条款的法律适用，详见沈涓《法律选择协议效力的法律适用辨析》，《法学研究》2015 年第 6 期；德国法框架下详见 Thomas Rauscher：Internationales Privatrecht，4. Aufl. 2012，§10 Rn. 1151f。

未对股权收购合同的性质作出明确规定，《最高人民法院关于审理买卖合同纠纷案件适用法律问题的解释》第45条第1款认为其可以参照适用民法中关于买卖合同的规定，[①] 在此基础上本文认为股权收购合同一般可以视为债法意义上的普通民事买卖合同。

具有涉外因素的合同产生的民事关系是一种涉外民事关系。这些涉外因素可能涉及主体是外国人，标的物在中国境外，产生、变更或者消灭民事关系的法律事实发生在中国境外等情形。[②] 具体案情中这些涉外因素可以无限复杂地叠加，但需明确的是“外商投资企业”[③] 这一因素并非是判断某股权收购合同是否涉外的绝对标准，也就是说并非所有涉及外商投资企业的股权收购都具有涉外因素，[④] 下文中最高人民法院的一则判决就持此种观点。[⑤]

如果收购各方围绕涉外股权收购合同产生纠纷并诉至人民法院，人民法院应首先处理法律适用问题。最高人民法院2005年12月26日印发的法发〔2005〕26号《第二次全国涉外商事海事审判工作会议纪要》第46条规定：“合同争议包括合同是否成立、成立的时间、效力、内容的解释、履行、违约责任，以及合同的解除、变更、中止、转让、终止等争议。”然而在公司并购这一专业领域，合同的履行可能意味着报批程序、股权的转让、目标公司的许可、股东名册的登记、工商登记及外汇转换等一系列程序。从私法角度来看上述大部分程序不涉及合同关系本身，从公法角度来看其很有可能受到政府规制，因此本文将“合同的履行”排除于合同关

① 参见《最高人民法院关于审理买卖合同纠纷案件适用法律问题的解释》，法释〔2012〕8号，第45条第1款：“法律或者行政法规对债权转让、股权转让等权利转让合同有规定的，依照其规定；没有规定的，人民法院可以根据合同法第124条和第174条的规定，参照适用买卖合同的有关规定。”

② 参见《最高人民法院关于适用〈中华人民共和国涉外民事关系法律适用法〉若干问题的解释（一）》，法释〔2012〕24号，第1条。

③ 其指广义上的外商投资企业，包括中外合资经营企业、中外合作经营企业、外资企业、外商投资股份有限公司等我国法律及行政法规规定的企业形式。

④ 参见蔡毅《论审理涉外股权纠纷案件之法律适用》，《法律适用》2006年第7期；另有观点，崔志伟、贺晓翊《关于审理涉外股权转让纠纷的法律思考》，《人民司法》2010年第7期。

⑤ 参见下文第四部分（一）小节博泰隆公司股权转让案，最高人民法院，（2013）民四终字第1号，资料来源：http://wenshu.court.gov.cn/content/content? DocID = 0a553fe1-91b b - 4c83 - 9aa4 - 839aa0abb960，最后访问日期：2017年12月12日。

系或合同争议之外。文本所讨论的股权收购合同关系涵盖合同的效力、合同的订立、变更、转让、终止和撤销以及违约责任（合同之债）等内容。

三　涉外股权收购合同法律适用的立法依据

（一）合同关系法律适用的普通规则

从1987年实施的《民法通则》（2009年修正）第145条确立以来，直到1999年《合同法》第126条，2011年实施的《涉外民事关系法律适用法》（以下简称《法律适用法》）第41—43条，我国立法与司法实践的历史发展都坚持以“合同准据法”这一准据法表述公式来判断合同关系应当适用的法律。[①] 就如何推导普通民事合同的合同准据法（lexcontractus）这一问题，横向对比可以发现目前我国[②]与欧盟[③]的处理方式较为相似：首先承认当事人意思自治；在缺乏一致意思自治情况下，适用特征性履行说；当前两种方式无法确定准据法或者当合同明显与其他国家有更密切联系时，适用“最密切联系原则”。[④] 因此不论是从纵向的历史发展还是横向的法律对比角度来看，处理普通合同关系存在成熟的立法依据。

（二）含有普通涉外因素的股权收购合同的普通规则

前文认定股权收购合同是债法意义上的普通民事买卖合同，其应区别于劳动合同及消费者合同，[⑤] 因而其合同准据法的推导不应适用《法律适用法》第42条和第43条的特殊规定（特殊连接点）。如股权收购合同仅具有一般涉外因素，例如合同签署地在境外或标的为外国公司股权，其合同准据法应由《法律适用法》第41条进行推导。如若合同准据法指引到

---

① 参见陈卫佐《涉外民事关系法律适用法的中国特色》，《法律适用》2011年第11期，第49页。

② 参见《法律适用法》第41条。

③ 参见，Regulation（EC）No593/2008 of the European Parliament and of the Council of 17 June 2008 on the law applicable to contractual obligations（RomeI），Official Journal of the European Union 4. 7. 2008，p. L117/6；以下简称《罗马I规则》；参见其第3条及以下。

④ 参见欧盟《罗马I规则》第4条第3款、4款。

⑤ 关于消费者合同的判断，参见于颖《〈涉外民事关系法律适用法〉第42条评析》，《法学评论》2011年第2期。

外国法律，最终虽不能规避法定的股权转让限制，但能否规避公司章程设置的限制仍需在后文第六部分（一）小节讨论。

（三）具有特殊涉外因素的股权收购合同法律适用规则

现行外商投资法律制度对于两大类并购交易进行普遍地规制：其一，指外商投资企业股权的变更；其二，指外国投资者收购境内内资企业股权（以下简称外资收购）。[①] 立法对于这两类交易设定了严格的行政审批制度，并规定相关协议强制适用我国法律。鉴于相关规定错综复杂，需要首先排除不适用于股权收购合同法律适用的规定。

1. 易混淆应排除的特殊规则

从1979年《中外合资经营企业法》的颁布至今，外商投资企业法都明确规定外商投资企业的设立必须经审批机关批准，其公司章程需要报批且自批准后才能生效。[②] 此外中外合资经营企业及中外合作经营企业的合资（作）合同同样需要报批且批准后生效。[③] 此类合同是指合营（作）各方为设立合营（作）企业就相互权利、义务关系达成一致意见而订立的文件，[④] 其本质是股东之间达成的仅具有债务约束力的合同（joint venture contract）。我国法律以明确的方式对于此类合同的法律适用进行了干预，例如《合同法》第126条第2款规定："在中华人民共和国境内履行的中外合资经营企业合同、中外合作经营企业合同、中外合作勘探开发自然资源合同，适用中华人民共和国法律。"同时《中外合作经营企业法实施细则》（2014年修正）第55条又进一步明确："合作企业合同的订立、效力、解释、履行及其争议的解决，适用中国法律。"由此观之，以绿地投资为模板的外商投资企业法要求企业设立及变更过程中的合营合同强制适用中国法律，但其从各方面都有别于股权收购合同，因此上述法律规定不

---

① 并非指外资企业作为目标公司或主体进行的收购。

② 参见《中外合资经营企业法》（2016年修正）第3条第1句；《中外合资经营企业法实施条例》（2014年修订）第14条；《中外合作经营企业法》（2016年第二次修正）第5条第1句；《中外合作经营企业法实施细则》（2014年修正）第11条；《外资企业法实施细则》（2014年修正）第10条第1款第3项，第16条。

③ 如存在外商合资企业（仍被视为狭义外资企业）的情况，外资企业合同仅需备案，参见《外资企业法实施细则》（2014年修正）第10条第3款。

④ 参见《中外合资经营企业法实施条例》（2014年修正）第10条第1款；《中外合作经营企业法实施细则》（2014年修正）第10条第3款。

应适用于涉外股权收购合同。此外依据《外资企业法实施细则》(2014年修正)第79条的规定:“外资企业与其他公司、企业或者经济组织以及个人签订合同,适用《中华人民共和国合同法》。”如前文所述,股权收购合同的主体并非企业本身,因而该针对狭义外资企业的规定同样不适用于相关涉外股权收购合同。

2. 外商投资企业股权变更及外资收购的特殊规则

现行三部外商投资企业法及其行政法规虽明确干预了外商投资企业股权转让,但并未就股权收购合同的法律适用进行明确规定。仅在部门规章层面的〔1997〕外经贸法发第267号《外商投资企业投资者股权变更的若干规定》第3条规定,企业投资者股权变更应遵守中国有关法律、法规,并按照本规定经审批机关批准和登记机关变更登记。同时依其第20条第1句:“股权转让协议和修改企业原合同、章程协议自核发变更外商投资企业批准证书之日起生效。”换言之,立法并未明确要求标的为外商投资企业股权的收购合同强制适用我国法律。此外,在外国投资者收购境内内资企业股权这一前提下(外资收购),部门规章《关于外国投资者并购境内企业的规定》(商务部令2009年第6号,以下简称《外资并购规定》)第22条规定:“股权购买协议、境内公司增资协议应适用中国法律……”这是现行法中对于此类股权收购合同法律适用作出的明确规定。已失效的《涉外民商事纠纷规定》第8条中也明确规定,三资企业股权转让合同(第8条第4项)以及外商收购内资企业股权合同(第8条第6项),其在中国履行的,适用中国法律。由此观之最高人民法院曾明确支持以上两大类并购交易中,收购合同强制适用我国法律。[①] 这些条款最终如何运用到司法实践中,需要引入以下实证研究。

四 外资收购中的收购合同法律适用实证研究

本文选取了最高人民法院两则具有对比性的民事案例进行研究。两案中均含有外资收购合同关系,但判决中的法律适用依据并不相同。

① 参见陈纪忠《〈关于审理涉外民事或商事合同纠纷案件法律适用若干问题的规定〉的理解与适用》,《人民司法》2007年第17期。

（一）外资收购中的当事人意思自治

2013年最高人民法院就博泰隆公司股权转让案进行了审判。[①] 该案中目标公司“博泰隆有限责任公司”（下称“海南公司”）原为海南省注册的内资企业，原股东分别为北京安能信达公司（占股份的40%）及自然人李某（占股份的60%）。李某欲将其股权转让，收购方原为香港注册的中惠（中国）公司（下称“中惠香港公司”），该公司的两家中国子公司分别是中惠南京公司（中外合资企业）及中惠海南公司（外资企业）。2007年李某与中惠香港公司签订《股权转让合同一》，该合同约定股权首先由中惠南京公司直接收购，继而转让给中惠香港公司。随后李某与中惠南京公司签订《股权转让合同二》并完成了股权转让。然而2009年中惠南京公司却与中惠海南公司签订《股权转让合同三》，将其在目标公司的股权悉数转让给了中惠海南公司。此后原股东北京安能信达公司与中惠集团就公司经营管理等问题产生纠纷，北京安能信达公司与李某上诉至最高人民法院请求解除“股权转让合同一、二、三”、返还股权并赔偿利息损失。

如前文所述特殊规则，案涉《股权转让合同一》签订时目标公司的性质为内资企业，合同主体（收购方中惠香港公司）具有涉外因素且被视为外国投资者[②]，因而撤销《股权转让合同一》这一问题的法律适用属于《外资并购规定》第22条的适用范围，应适用中国法。同时该合同确系得到了履行，[③] 换言之正是依据该合同李某才与中惠南京公司签订了《股权转让合同二》并最终完成转让，因而该问题也可适用当时有效的《涉外民商事纠纷规定》第8条第6项规定。然而判决书中二审最高人民法院将案件首先定性为股权转让合同纠纷：涉及三份合同，一是与中惠香港公司之间的《股权转让合同一》，系涉外合同关系，合同中明确约定适用中国法，

---

① 参见最高人民法院判决书，2013年12月11日，(2013)民四终字第1号，资料来源：http://wenshu.court.gov.cn/content/content? DocID = 0a553fe1 - 91bb - 4c83 - 9aa4 - 839aa0abb960，最后访问于2017年12月12日。

② 参见《外资并购规定》第57条。

③ 一审法院认为：“李某同中惠南京公司签订的股权转让协议，中惠南京公司同中惠海南公司签订的股权转让协议，均系为履行安能信达公司、李某同中惠中国公司签订的《博泰隆公司股权转让协议》，达到最终由中惠中国公司受让和持有涉案股权而签订的协议。”

依《民法通则》第 145 条第 1 款规定适用中国法；《股权转让合同二、三》没有涉外因素（即前文所述外商投资企业并非绝对是涉外因素），是纯国内民事法律关系，当然适用中国法。显然该案中区分了各民事关系的法律适用问题，但以普通规则判断了外资收购中的《股权转让合同一》的法律适用。该案的案情及判决说明了两方面内容。第一，股权收购合同本身、合同的履行与股权的转让是三个不同维度的概念：股权收购合同的生效并不一定意味着履行，案涉《股权转让合同一》的履行也未导致股权的转让以及目标公司类型的转变。因此以履行地作为收购合同法律适用规则前提条件的，例如《涉外民商事纠纷规定》第 8 条或《中华人民共和国外国投资法（草案征求意见稿）》第 164 条[①]，这样的立法技术本身存在缺陷。第二，最高人民法院判决中的说理具有重要的价值导向，以合同准据法为依据判断《股权转让合同一》的法律适用，至少说明当事人意思自治在外资收购中得到过支持。然而该案判决后一年的相似案例中，最高人民法院又给出了不同的说理依据。

（二）外资收购中强制适用我国法律

在 2014 年的白沙洲公司案中，[②] 目标公司“白沙洲公司”原为湖北省注册的内资企业，收购方中国高速集团公司（下称中国高速），成立于百慕大后又在香港登记。2007 年中国高速与股东签订了股权转让协议（以下称阴合同）且最终执行，协议主要约定：以市场价格收购股东股权、部分价款以可换股票据支付（实质为股权置换）、适用香港法律解决争议。此种交易类型属于外资收购，依据《外资并购规定》具有股权置换的交易需要更为严格的审批程序。为规避商务部门更严格的审批程序以及外汇管理制度，收购各方同时签订了专门用于报批的阳合同且最

① 《中华人民共和国外国投资法（草案征求意见稿）》（自 2015 年 1 月 19 日由商务部公布）第 164 条：“外国投资者签订的在中国境内履行的投资合同，适用中国法律。”

② 参见最高人民法院判决书，2014 年 12 月 31 日，（2014）民四终字第 33 号，资料来源：http://wenshu.court.gov.cn/content/content? DocID = 3699635c - 4edf - 4051 - a5b8 - f948efb96b07；该案一审湖北省高级人民法院判决书，2014 年 5 月 30 日，（2011）鄂民四初字第 00001 号，资料来源：http://www.court.gov.cn/zgcpwsw/content/content? DocID = 1a1a8de0 - 1b53 - 4da8 - a4c9 - bab2e697639f，最后访问日期：2017 年 12 月 12 日。

终获批，合同约定：以较低金额收购股权、现金股权交易、合同适用中国法律。后各方产生纠纷上诉至最高人民法院并主要讨论阳合同是否无效。最高人民法院在该案中认为此种规避破坏了国家对外商投资、对外投资的监管秩序和外汇管理秩序，属于双方恶意串通，损害国家利益，也属于以合法形式掩盖非法目的，依《合同法》第52条第2项、3项规定，认定该合同无效。此处因本案股权转让属于境外投资者并购境内企业而认为有关协议“依法”（未直接援引法条）应当适用中国法，并再次明确阳合同中的法律适用条款（即使约定适用中国法）无效，不影响中国法律的强制适用。

（三）强制适用依据的尴尬处境及消极影响

以上最高人民法院两则案例均未直接引用部门规章及相关司法解释，反映了外资并购中收购合同强制适用依据在立法层级上的尴尬处境。虽然具体援引的条款及说理各不相同，但最高人民法院通过这些案例以及曾发布的司法解释清晰地传达了一种信号：坚定支持外资并购审批制度，并从结果上将相关协议的法律适用指引到我国法律。而当这种信号传达下层法院时，其消极影响越来越大。2013年上海市黄浦区法院在外资收购个案中认为：案涉《股权转让协议》标的为中国公司法人的股权，根据《法律适用法》第4条之规定，本案应直接适用中国法律的相关规定。① 换言之，朴素观点认为只要目标公司是“中国公司”，以其股权为标的的收购合同就应适用中国法律。这种“安全”的操作方式更加忽视强制适用的合理依据。其背后暗含着司法实践对于适用外国法律的担忧，尤其担心当事人选择外国法律以此规避我国涉外并购的相关审批制度。② 然而近年来学界关于股权转让限制技术手段的研究已取得重大进展，因而可以从法技术角度重新审视这一担忧。

---

① 参见上海市黄浦区人民法院判决书，2014年10月29日，（2013）黄浦民二（商）初字第1088号），资料来源：http://wenshu. court. gov. cn/content/content? DocID = d39a7c07 - 9048 - 4a2f - af63 - 87d82ee43703，最后访问日期：2017年12月12日。

② 参见陈纪忠《〈关于审理涉外民事或商事合同纠纷案件法律适用若干问题的规定〉的理解与适用》，《人民司法》2007年第17期。

五 股权转让限制技术手段综述

有限责任公司股权的转让需首先签订股权收购合同，现行法并未对其生效的形式要件（如公证）[①] 作出特殊规定，因此在无其他前提条件下（如附条件、附期限、需审批等）合同自签订时生效。在合同生效的基础上，主流观点认为股权的转让依据《公司法》（2013 年修正）第 73 条第 1 句规定，自收购方登记在股东名册上时生效，此处的登记是公示行为（事实行为）。[②] 而工商登记依据《公司法》第 32 条第 3 款第 2 句仅具有对抗第三人的效力。[③] 这种观点可以总结为形式主义的股权变动模式，即合同生效加公示行为才能导致股权转让。此外还有诸如“（债权）意思主义”的观点大致认为股权自收购合同生效即完成转让。[④] 新近观点采“意思主义”这一措辞，并以德国法模式为背景承认股权转让过程中的处分行为，且该处分行为适用债权让与的路径。[⑤] 实质上该观点是承认股权收购合同（负担行为）之外还存在关于股权转让的合意[⑥]（处分行为）。虽然以上观点在现阶段仍有较大分歧，但学界就两点问题已取得一致看法：其一，承

---

① 地方性法规及规章可能会有要求；参见刘俊海《论有限责任公司股权转让合同的效力》，《暨南学报》（哲学社会科学版）2012 年第 12 期。

② 参见叶金强《有限责任公司股权转让初探——兼论〈公司法〉第 35 条之修正》，《河北法学》2005 年第 6 期，第 32 页；刘俊海《论有限责任公司股权转让合同的效力》，《暨南学报》（哲学社会科学版）2012 年第 12 期；实践中并非所有有限责任公司都设置了股东名册，参见杨瑞峰《股权转让合同的生效与股权变动》，《法律适用》2007 年第 10 期；周友苏《试析股东资格认定中的若干法律问题》，《法学》2006 年第 12 期。

③ 参见杨瑞峰《股权转让合同的生效与股权变动》，《法律适用》2007 年第 10 期；刘俊海《论有限责任公司股权转让合同的效力》，《暨南学报》（哲学社会科学版）2012 年第 12 期；曹兴权《股东优先购买权对股权转让合同效力的影响》，《国家检察官学院学报》2012 年第 10 期。

④ 参见综述性文章，李建伟《有限责任公司股权变动模式研究——以公司受通知与认可的程序构建为中心》，《暨南学报》（哲学社会科学版）2012 年第 12 期；范健、王建文：《公司法》，2011，第 352 页及以下；王欣新《公司法》，2012，第 198 页及以下。

⑤ 完全是德国法律及一致学术观点对于德国有限责任公司股权转让的法技术角度分析；详见张双根《股权善意取得之质疑》，《法学家》2016 年第 1 期。

⑥ 德语文献中会直接使用处分行为一词，此处的合意即指合同，为行文以示区别才使用合意一词，德语文献中不存在这种措辞上的区别。

认（收购）合同与合同的履行之间的区分；[①] 其二，基于法律行为的股权变动建立在（收购）合同生效的基础之上。[②]

不论基于以上何种角度的分析，一般情况下股权的转让受到三个维度的限制：第一，公司内部层面限制，例如章程规定股权转让需经其他股东或公司机构批准；第二，法律及行政法规层面限制，例如《公司法》第 71 条第 2 款以及三部外商投资企业法中涉及股权转让的政府审批等规定；[③] 第三，政府各机构通过规章文件进行的规制层面限制，主要指商务部的《外资并购规定》。在缺乏上述观点纷争之前，限制股权转让会被自然而然地理解为限制股权收购合同的生效。例如《公司法》第 71 条第 2 款第 1 句规定："股东向股东以外的人转让股权，应当经其他股东过半数同意。"有观点会认为此处其他股东的许可是收购合同生效的前提，[④] 实践中也有个案认为未经其他股东许可则股权收购合同未生效。[⑤] 再例如外商投资企业的股权转让以及外资并购都需经相关部门批准，且股权收购合同是报批材料中的一项，但实践和文献会自然而然地将批准理解为收购合同的生效要件，未经批准的合同未生效。[⑥] 随后实践中产生了大量的涉及报批的法

---

① 参见宋国良、臧峻月《股权变动登记程序存在瑕疵的不影响股权转让合同的效力》，《人民司法》2009 年第 20 期；曹兴权《股东优先购买权对股权转让合同效力的影响》，《国家检察官学院学报》2012 年第 10 期；叶金强《有限责任公司股权转让初探——兼论〈公司法〉第 35 条之修正》，《河北法学》2005 年第 6 期；蔡立东《行政审批与权利转让合同的效力》，《中国法学》2013 年第 1 期。

② 参见张双根《股权善意取得之质疑》，《法学家》2016 年第 1 期。

③ 参见《中外合资经营企业法实施条例》(2014 年) 第 20 条第 1 款；《中外合作经营企业法实施细则》(2014 年修正) 第 23 条第 1 款；《外资企业法实施细则》(2014 年修正) 第 22 条。

④ 参见雷新勇《有限公司股权转让疑难问题探析》，《法律适用》2013 年第 5 期；刘俊海《论有限责任公司股权转让合同的效力》，《暨南学报》(哲学社会科学版) 2012 年第 12 期；杨瑞峰《股权转让合同的生效与股权变动》，《法律适用》2007 年第 10 期。

⑤ 参见广州市中级人民法院判决，2014 年 6 月 5 日，〔2014〕穗中法民二终字第 574 号，资料来源：http://www.court.gov.cn/zgcpwsw/content/content? DocID = cb4ea44c - a25b - 4687 - 8a73 - 33a18ea27f38；另有观点认为收购合同可撤销，参见河北省承德市中级人民法院，2014 年 2 月 12 日，〔2014〕承民初字第 00028 号，资料来源：http://wenshu.court.gov.cn/Content/Content? DocID = acfaf4c8 - 314c - 4bf3 - af3d - 4b8dd1c06968，最后访问日期：2017 年 12 月 12 日。

⑥ 参见《合同法》第 44 条第 2 款：法律、行政法规规定应当办理批准、登记等手续生效的，依照其规定；《最高人民法院关于适用〈中华人民共和国合同法〉若干问题的解释（一）》(法释〔1999〕19 号) 第 9 条；《最高人民法院关于审理外商投资企业纠纷案件若干问题的规定（一）》(法释〔2010〕9 号) 第 1 条第 1 款第 1 句：当事人在外商投资企业设立、变更等过程中订立的合同，依法律、行政法规的规定应当经外商投资企业审批机关批准后才生效的，自批准之日起生效；未经批准的，人民法院应当认定该合同未生效。

律纠纷，即收购合同签订后出让方不履行报批且无须承担违约责任（合同未生效），面对这些问题最高人民法院只能以司法解释的形式暂时设定所谓的报批义务。[①] 而以上股权模式纷争提供了新的干预思路，即各维度的转让限制不应狭义地理解为限制股权收购合同的生效，还可以理解为对于合同的履行的干预。[②] 这些观点并非寄希望于应然法，而是基于现行法律解释得出，优势在于实质上限制了股权转让的同时不轻易否认转让各方之间债权合同的效力。

六 涉外股权收购合同法律适用的重新梳理

本节从法技术角度依次分析合同准据法与股权转让过程中各维度限制的关系，系统梳理各类涉外情况下合同关系的法律适用问题。

（一）普通涉外股权收购合同的法律适用与章程限制的规避

《公司法》第 71 条第 2 款以法定的形式规定有限责任公司股权向外部人员转让需经其他股东同意（法定限制），紧接着其第 71 条第 4 款以但书的形式赋予了公司章程就此类问题的自治空间，即章程可以约定股权转让是否需要经其他股东或公司机构许可（章程限制）。因此该条所谓的法定限制不宜被视为《法律适用法》第 4 条意义上的强制性规定。然而不论合同关系适用哪国法律，其仍不能规避章程限制，因为合同履行中的各民事关系，尤其是有限责任公司股权的转让（个案中被称为股权转让的前提条件）是由法人属人法来调节的。[③] 假设目标公司注册地及主营业地均在中

---

① 参见《最高人民法院关于审理外商投资企业纠纷案件若干问题的规定（一）》（法释〔2010〕9 号）第 6—9 条。

② 参见曹兴权《股东优先购买权对股权转让合同效力的影响》，《国家检察官学院学报》2012 年第 10 期；王东光《论股权转让的双重限制及其效力》，《公司法律评论》2010 卷，上海人民出版社，2010；叶金强《有限责任公司股权转让初探——兼论〈公司法〉第 35 条之修正》，《河北法学》2005 年第 6 期；蔡立东《行政审批与权利转让合同的效力》，《中国法学》2013 年第 1 期；刘贵祥《论行政审批与合同效力》，《中国法学》2011 年第 2 期。

③ 德国法参见 Bayer，Walter，in：Lutter/Hommelhoff GmbHG，2012，Anh II zu § 4aRn. 29，§15 Rn. 33；Reichert，Jochem/Weller，Marc-Philippe：in：MünchenKomm GmbHG，2015，§15 Rn. 170，172；中国司法判决参见福建省高级人民法院判决书，2014 年 11 月 17 日，〔2014〕闽民终字第 119 号，该案认为“因 SMART 公司（目标公司）在美国 （转下页注）

国，经法人属人法指引得出股权转让的前提条件适用中国法，同时章程约定股权的转让需经公司机构或其他股东批准，此时以某外国法处理转让双方之间合同纠纷（如合同之债、合同的效力）并不意味着股权的转让同样适用该国法律。这种情况下收购合同即使生效也无法导致股权的变动。假如法人属人法将股权转让的前提条件指引到 A 国法律，按照相同的推理逻辑也可以得出合同关系适用 B 国法律也无法规避 A 国公司法框架下的章程限制。因此前文中所提具有普通涉外因素的股权收购合同，其合同准据法确信应由《法律适用法》第 41 条推导。

（二）外商投资企业股权变更中的收购合同法律适用与审批制度的规避

公司法双轨制下的三部外商投资企业法虽然理论上是组织法，但至今都扮演着保护和引导外商投资的历史角色，其具有公法强制性属性。因而涉及股权转让行政审批以及合营（作）他方许可的条款应被视作《法律适用法》第 4 条中的强制性规定。换言之《中外合资经营企业法实施条例》第 20 条、《中外合作经营企业法实施细则》第 23 条以及《外资企业法实施细则》第 22 条依据《法律适用法》第 4 条及最高人民法院《法律适用法释一》第 10 条不经冲突规则指引而直接适用，当事人就此问题的法律选择不发生选择的效果。首先，前文已说明以上条款并未要求收购合同强制适用我国法律，此时合同关系适用外国法律不影响行政程序中政府对于“股权的转让”的审批。其次，如按照前述新观点将合营他方的许可解释为限制“股权的转让”，则当事人意思自治与此种限制互不干扰，最大限度地维护了股权转让双方以及合营各方之间的利益。因而此处收购合同的法律适用应依据法人属人法判断。

（三）外资收购中强制适用条款正当性讨论

作为外资并购实践中的重要依据，《外资并购规定》明确干预两类外

（接上页注③）内华达州登记注册，故对于本案涉及的 SMART 公司组织机构及该公司股权转让手续是否办理完毕问题，则应依据《法律适用法》第 14 条的规定，适用美国内华达州法律。”资料来源：http://wenshu.court.gov.cn/content/content? DocID = 5fdf4dcc - 767d - 4b9b - b559 - 2931fc414489，最后访问日期：2017 年 12 月 12 日。

商收购交易：外国投资者（直接），[①] 或者通过其在中国设立的投资性公司（间接，但不绝对具有涉外因素），[②] 收购中国境内内资企业的股权（股份）或增资。在这两类交易中《外资并购规定》第22条明确规定股权购买协议应适用中国法律。商务部的这种要求一定是技术手段而不是目的本身，其最可能担心外国法的适用可以规避外资并购审批程序。虽然整个程序仅以部门规章这种尴尬的形式确立下来，但这种担心是不必要的。外资并购审批制度的整体设计理念是，外商收购后导致内资企业转制成为外商投资企业，并将其审查重新纳入了外商投资企业法框架内。[③] 因而审批制度最终都由外商投资企业法明确规定，司法程序中合同关系适用外国法律不影响行政程序中政府对于特定交易的审查，而且根据上述并购规制新思路此处的审查应着重干预合同的履行而非合同的生效。

在司法程序内仍需讨论《外资并购规定》第22条能否直接在判决中援引。首先，其作为部门规章的条文不能被视为《法律适用法》第4条中的强制性规定，因而不能不经冲突规范指引而直接适用。在开启冲突规则的论证之后，前文分析得出普通涉外股权收购合同的合同准据法主要由《法律适用法》第41条推导。由此产生了上位法的普通冲突规范与下位法的特殊冲突规范之间的冲突，亦即条款适用顺序问题。如果法庭优先适用下位法，判决中则应说明其有足够的正当性。[④] 在以上规避审批事由之外，强制适用我国法律还可能涉及合同关系的三个规制目标：交易的价格、[⑤] 支付的期限、[⑥] 付款的方式[⑦]。因此其正当性还需以目的论为导向就此三方面分别讨论。

就并购交易的价格而言，《外资并购规定》第14条第1款第3句规定："禁止以明显低于评估结果的价格转让股权或出售资产，变相向境外

① 参见《外资并购规定》第2条。

② 参见《外资并购规定》第52条第1款；投资性公司是特殊的外商投资企业，其设立有特别的审批要求。

③ 参见普吉《解析〈外国投资者并购境内企业暂行规定〉》，《中国外资》2003年第7期。

④ 参考张霞《判决书中的法律论证》，《政法论丛》2005年第5期。

⑤ 参见《外资并购规定》第14条第1款。

⑥ 参见《外资并购规定》第17条（特殊条款）第27条及以下。

⑦ 参见《外资并购规定》第16条第1款。

转移资本。”[①] 该条款限制折价并购主要为配合资本项目的外汇监管，防止利用并购形式恶意向境外转移资本。[②] 目前对于资本项目的外汇管理手段仍以数量控制和行政审批为主，[③] 自《法律适用法》生效以来外汇管理相关法律法规已经可以依据《法律适用法》第 4 条不经冲突规范指引而直接适用。[④] 而就合同关系强制适用我国法律即非外汇管理的技术手段，[⑤] 也并非资本管制的政策趋势，[⑥] 从立法论角度来看，更无须以低位阶的《外资并购规定》维护高位阶的外汇管理立法目标。

就交易的支付期限而言，依《外资并购规定》第 16 条第 1 款，[⑦] 外国投资者应在期限内（经审批最多一年）向转让方支付全部对价。该规定最初可以追溯到《〈中外合资经营企业合营各方出资的若干规定〉的补充规定》[⑧] 第 1 条，[⑨] 其出台的背景应是 1992 年至 1994 年间的“中策事件”。[⑩] 20 世纪 90 年代中策事件中，外国投资者拒绝或者延期支付对价，而中国的龙头国有企业因为缺乏并购经验或者因为行政干预[⑪]缺少有效的救济方式。这一问题的实质是并购中交易各方的风险控制问题，而在今天适用于买卖双方的风险控制手段丰富多样：开设第三方管存账户（escrowaccount），

---

① 其可追溯到《外国投资者并购境内企业暂行规定》（对外贸易经济合作部、国家税务总局、国家工商行政管理总局、国家外汇管理局令 2003 年第 3 号）第 8 条第 3 款。

② 参见普吉《解析〈外国投资者并购境内企业暂行规定〉》，《中国外资》2003 年第 7 期。

③ 参见张大龙《我国资本项目外汇管理的现状及对策探讨》，《吉林金融研究》2015 年第 8 期。

④ 参见《法律适用法》第 4 条，最高人民法院《法律适用法释一》第 10 条第 4 项。

⑤ 参见罗纲《外资 PE 并购境内企业引起的跨境资本流动及其外汇管理》，《时代金融》2013 年第 1 期。

⑥ 参见付伟《资本管制变迁及中国资本管制改革研究》，《西南金融》2017 年第 5 期；宋娴《中国（福建）自由贸易试验区外汇管理创新探索》，《福建金融》2015 年第 4 期；马骏《人民币离岸市场与资本项目开放》，《金融发展评论》2012 年第 4 期。

⑦ 同于《外国投资者并购境内企业暂行规定》（对外贸易经济合作部、国家税务总局、国家工商行政管理总局、国家外汇管理局令 2003 年第 3 号），第 9 条第 1 款。

⑧ 对外经合部、国家工商行政管理局令 2 号，已失效，有效期自 1997 年 9 月 29 日至 2014 年 3 月 1 日。

⑨ 参见梅新育《解析外资并购新规》，《新理财》2006 年第 11 期。

⑩ 参见梅新育《解析外资并购新规》，《新理财》2006 年第 11 期；对于“中策事件”，详见胡峰《跨国公司在华并购问题研究》，博士学位论文，华东师范大学，2003，第 44 页。

⑪ 参见杨镭《跨国并购与政府规制——兼论中国对外资并购的规制》，博士学位论文，中国社会科学院研究生院，2003，第 107 页。

第三方（或银行）担保，[1] 风险对冲条款，[2] 以及新近出现的并购保险[3]等等。换言之，无须以收购合同强制适用我国法律的形式维护不复存在的规制目标。

就交易对价而言，收购方可以以任何形式（包括人民币资产）[4] 支付转让价款，但以外国投资者的股权作为支付对价（股权置换）则受到严格的规制。[5] 这一制度的历史出发点是限制及引导境内企业以红筹模式海外上市，因此仅有一种形式的股权置换被允许：境外上市公司股票置换境内内资企业股权。[6] 这里涉及上市公司股票收购交易中收购合同法律适用问题，该问题也是对于本文通篇以非上市公司股权转让为例的一个补充。随着计算机及网络技术的飞速发展，世界上多数股票交易所都会使用中央结算系统以实现超短时间内巨量交易的成交。而随着沪港通、深港通抑或其他全球化交易途径的出现，股票收购方、出让方、交易所所在地、中央结算系统服务器所在地都有可能不在同一法域之中。在此情况下欧盟《罗马I规则》对于合同准据法的推导有了较为成熟的规定。简言之《罗马I规则》第4条第1款第h项规定，在多边（结算）系统下缔结的合同，如未达成一致的法律选择，其应直接适用证券市场地法。[7] 我国现行法虽未有此类详细规定但其思路值得借鉴：收购上市公司股票的合同，其合同准据法的推导应首先尊重当事人意思自治，缺乏一致法律选择时按最密切联系原则适用证券市场地法，从而排除了特征性履行说的使用。由此观之，此

---

① 参见宋政平《外国投资者并购境内企业中的担保问题初探》，《山东审判》2012年第6期。

② 参见姜军、赵慧芳《交易结构化：中联重科海外并购案例的再分析》，《财务与会计》2013年第1期；风险对冲的条款：例如锁定期，优先受让权，跟卖权，卖出期权，特别卖出期权等等。

③ 详见张广宝、刘淑莲、施继坤《并购保证及补偿保险：机理、释义及展望》，《保险研究》2011年第7期。

④ 参见《外资并购规定》第17条。

⑤ 参见《外资并购规定》第27—50条。

⑥ 参见《外资并购规定》第27—29条。

⑦ 第4条第1款第h项直译："买卖《欧共体第2004/39号指令》第4条第1款第17项所界定的有价证券的合同，如其在一个多边系统中缔结，该多边系统遵循非自由裁量规则以及受单一法律管辖并促成大量第三方权益的汇集，则合同适用该法律。"条文中并未明确使用"证券市场地法"这一措辞，仅说对于该多边系统具有决定性作用的法律，具体需就何种证券交易所进行分类讨论；详见 Dieter Martiny，in：MünchenerKommentarzumBGB（6. Auflage 2015），RomI-VO，Art. 4，Rn. 162；FrancoFerrari，in：Ferrari/Kieninger/Mankowskiu. a.，InternationalesVertragsrecht（2. Auflage2011），VO（EG）593/2008Art. 4，Rn. 57。

类涉及外国上市公司股票转让的收购合同，强制适用中国法律显然不妥。

《外资并购规定》自2003年生效以来就是涉外并购实践中最为重要的法律依据之一，然而随着涉外并购相关法律法规的逐步出台，诸多规制目标已逐步被这些法律部门所取代。从目的论角度来看，强制适用中国法既非唯一选择，也非最佳选择。因而本文不认为司法审判中《外资并购规定》第22条具有足够的正当性优先于《法律适用法》第41条适用。换言之，外资并购中的收购合同（合同关系）的法律适用仍主要应由合同准据法判断。

七 结论性观点

涉外股权收购合同是债法意义上的普通民事买卖合同，国际私法中合同关系涵盖合同的效力、合同的订立、变更、转让、终止和撤销以及违约责任（合同之债）等具体问题，但不应涉及合同的履行。收购合同的法律适用，不论其具有何种涉外因素，应主要由合同准据法判断，合同准据法则主要依照《法律适用法》第41条推导。如合同准据法指引到某外国法，不影响其他民事关系的法律适用，不妨碍公司章程对于股权转让的限制，更无法影响行政程序中政府依据我国法律对于特定交易的审查。在重新审视强制适用的初衷之后，《外资并购规定》第22条不应优先于《法律适用法》第41条。对于转让上市公司股票的合同，其合同准据法的推导在普通规则基础上应排除特征性履行说的适用。

（本文原载于《国际法研究》2018年第1期）

走向繁荣的国际法学

（全六卷）

TOWARDS THE PROSPERITY OF
INTERNATIONAL LAW STUDIES (SIX VOLUMES)

2009
~
2019

中国社会科学院国际法研究所十周年所庆纪念文集

【国际人权法卷】

莫纪宏　总主编
孙世彦　主　编

社会科学文献出版社
SOCIAL SCIENCES ACADEMIC PRESS (CHINA)

国际人权法研究室合影

2019 年 1 月 20 日，首届国际法热点问题研讨会

2019 年 2 月 8 日至 11 日，莫纪宏所长出席亚太法律协会第一届人权会议

2018 年 10 月 27 日至 28 日，莫纪宏研究员出席中国社会科学论坛暨第十五届国际法论坛

2012年6月13日，柳华文研究员做客人民网“强国论坛”，解读《国家人权行动计划（2012-2015年）》

2009年6月西班牙马德里，戴瑞君（左二）、柳华文（右三）参加第二十次中欧人权研讨会

2019 年 6 月 18 日，柳华文研究员参加中国人权研究会代表团与爱尔兰众议院议长肖恩·奥法乔尔会谈

2018 年 12 月 4 日，柳华文研究员主持第八届中美司法与人权研讨会

2017 年 12 月 2 日至 3 日，陈泽宪出席中国社科论坛暨第十四届国际法论坛

2010 年 6 月西班牙马德里，陈泽宪（左二）、刘海年（左四）参加中国 - 欧盟人权研讨会

2019 年 6 月维也纳，孙世彦、曲相霏、戴瑞君参加 2019 中欧人权研讨会

2017年12月澳大利亚悉尼，国际人权法研究室研究人员陈泽宪（右二）、柳华文（右一）、孙世彦（左一）、戴瑞君（左二）访问澳大利亚人权委员会

2014年10月日内瓦联合国总部，朱晓青（左一）和戴瑞君（左五）观摩联合国消除对妇女歧视委员会审议中国履约报告后，与消歧委员会委员邹晓巧（右四）合影

2017 年 5 月瑞士日内瓦，戴瑞君（左二）与越南、印度尼西亚学者及其他中国学者访问联合国总部

2017 年 5 月瑞士日内瓦，戴瑞君（右一）等访问联合国人权事务高级专员办事处

2018 年 6 月韩国首尔，戴瑞君参加第十届世界宪法大会

序

推动中国国际法学不断走向繁荣

1949 年 10 月 1 日，中华人民共和国中央人民政府宣告成立，结束了旧中国近百年半殖民地半封建受压迫受奴役的历史。中国人民从此站起来了！

在中国共产党和中国政府的坚强领导下，70 年来，中华人民共和国不断总结经验，克服困难，实现突破和发展，取得社会主义建设事业的伟大成就。特别是改革开放 40 年来，中国实现了经济腾飞和社会进步，中国的国际地位和影响力前所未有。2012 年党的十八大召开以来，中国特色社会主义进入新时代，中国人民实现了从站起来、富起来到强起来的发展过程，中国日益走近世界舞台的中央，中华民族比以往任何时候都更加接近实现中华民族伟大复兴的中国梦！

中华人民共和国的成立和 70 年来的发展历程，为中国国际法学的发展创造了良好的政治、经济、社会和历史条件。以周鲠生、陈体强、李浩培、王铁崖、韩德培等老一辈中国国际法学者为代表的中国国际法人为中国国际法理论研究和实践工作的起步和发展作出了卓越的贡献，为中国国际法学研究和教学做了大量奠基和铺路的工作。

1978 年 12 月 13 日，邓小平同志在党的十一届三中全会前召开的中央经济工作会议上发表了《解放思想，实事求是，团结一致向前看》的讲话，明确提出“要大力加强国际法的研究”。如春风，如号角，中国国际法研究获得极大的鼓舞。中国国际法学迎来了发展的春天。1980 年 2 月，中国国际法学会成立，中国社会科学院副院长宦乡担任首任会长。

中国社会科学院是中国国际法学的研究重镇。1959 年，也就是中国科

学院哲学社会科学部建立法学研究所之后的第二年，法学研究所成立了国际法组。1977 年 5 月，经党中央批准，中国社会科学院在中国科学院哲学社会科学部基础上正式组建。1978 年 9 月，中国社会科学院法学研究所国际法组改建为国际法研究室。

2002 年又是中国发展历程中一个不平凡的年份。这一年，中国改革开放渐入佳境，中国正式加入世界贸易组织；这一年，中国批准了作为“国际人权宪章”重要内容的联合国《经济、社会和文化权利国际公约》。也是这一年，在时任中国社会科学院院长李铁映的推动下，经中央机构编制委员会办公室批准，在国际法研究室基础上成立了国际法研究中心，使其成为与法学研究所平行的院属所局级机构。

国际法研究中心成立后，中国社会科学院国际法学研究获得进一步加强和推进。2009 年 9 月，经中央机构编制委员会办公室批准，国际法研究中心正式更名为国际法研究所。到今天，国际法研究所刚好成立 10 年了！

陈泽宪研究员任国际法研究所首任所长。2017 年 9 月至 2018 年 11 月，现任法学研究所所长、中国社会科学院学部委员陈甦研究员代行国际法研究所所长职责。2018 年 11 月，莫纪宏研究员开始担任国际法研究所所长。国际法研究所正是在国家经济发展和社会进步取得历史性突破，中国在国际社会地位极大提升、国际影响力不断扩大的背景下诞生的。它的成立和发展承载了党和国家繁荣和发展中国国际法学的使命。

10 年来，国际法研究所与外交部、商务部等相关政府部门密切联系，与中国国际法学会等全国性国际法研究学会、学术机构一道，积极进取，努力推动中国国际法学走向繁荣。依托学科和人才优势，国际法研究所设有国际公法、国际经济法、国际私法和国际人权法 4 个研究室，还设有海洋法治研究、竞争法研究和国际刑法研究领域的 3 个非实体中心以及最高人民法院“一带一路”司法研究基地。依托国际法研究所国际法专业的博士点和硕士点，博士、硕士研究生和博士后研究人员的指导工作也得到了加强。

2014 年创刊的《国际法研究》是中国第一本获得正式刊号的国际法专业原创中文期刊，国际法研究所是其主要主办单位和主编单位。该刊在国际法研究领域学术期刊的发文转载率方面处于全国领先地位，已经成为国际法学界重要的学术展示和交流平台。一年一度的国际法论坛已成功举办

15 届，成为中国社会科学院院级国际研讨会的学术品牌，吸引了国内外权威和知名专家的积极参与。在刘楠来、王可菊、陶正华、林欣等前辈国际法学家的关心和鼓舞下，国际法研究所一大批中青年国际法学者正在成为国际法学界的学术骨干。

值此国际法研究所 10 周年所庆之际，我们出版文集，选粹研究人员的研究成果，包括《国际法研究》发表过的有影响力的论文，回顾走过的历程，展示当下的风貌，既是国际法研究所成长道路上的一个小结，更是展现坚定的再创辉煌的决心。

中国倡导的"一带一路"建设正在世界范围内获得越来越多、越来越大的发展成就，推动构建人类命运共同体的中国主张日益获得国际社会的广泛支持和积极响应。

前路不乏机遇和挑战，中国社会科学院国际法研究所全体同仁必将以只争朝夕的精神，不忘初心、牢记使命，与全国国际法学同仁一道，推进中国国际法学不断走向繁荣！

莫纪宏

2019 年 8 月 20 日

目录

Contents

国际人权法研究室简介

一 概况

中国社会科学院法学研究所早在1994年就成立了中国社会科学院人权研究中心，这是中国最早的人权研究机构。2002年中国社会科学院国际法研究中心成立以后，也把国际人权法作为其重要的研究领域之一，研究人员当时主要隶属国际公法研究室。2009年，国际法研究中心更名为国际法研究所，同时设立国际人权法研究室。

国际人权法研究室成立时有研究人员3人，即赵建文、柳华文和戴瑞君，赵建文任研究室主任。为明晰研究室归属之目的，国际法研究所原所长陈泽宪也列入国际人权法研究室。2011年，曲相霏加入国际人权法研究室；2012年，柳华文改任《国际法研究》编辑部主任；2016年，赵建文退休，孙世彦、钟瑞华分别从国际公法研究室、国际经济法研究室调入，孙世彦任国际人权法研究室负责人（2016—2018年）、主任（2018年至今）。

国际人权法研究室现有专职研究人员4人：孙世彦研究员、曲相霏研究员、戴瑞君副研究员和钟瑞华助理研究员。国际法研究所所长莫纪宏研究员、中国社会科学院图书馆法学分馆副馆长刘小妹研究员，也列入国际人权法研究室。国际人权法研究室人员均有在国外长期访学、工作的经历。国际人权法研究室除了从事国际人权法领域的研究和教学，还广泛参与我国的对外人权活动，包括以各种方式参与中国提交联合国人权机构的报告的撰写和联合国人权机构对这些报告的审议。

二　主要研究成果

国际人权法研究室以国际人权法为主要研究对象。国际人权法学科是一个广泛的交叉学科，除了以国际人权法为对象的研究，还包括对其他国际法领域中可能与人权有关的现象和问题以国际人权法为视角进行的研究；在中国的语境中还包括，以国际人权法为视角和参照，对中国的有关人权政策、法律和实践的研究。

在国际法研究所，除了国际人权法研究室的研究人员以人权及相关法律问题为主要研究领域之外，其他部门的研究人员也有许多人权领域的研究成果。限于篇幅，本卷只收入曾经或目前隶属国际人权法研究室的在职研究人员，以及供职于《国际法研究》编辑部的李西霞的优秀论文。本部分所述研究成果涵盖国际法研究所而非仅仅国际人权法研究室在国际人权法学科的主要研究成果。这些成果，按类型可以分为书籍（包括专著、译著和论文集）、论文、报刊文章、资料汇编等公开出版物以及大量的内部报告；按内容则可以分为对人权基本理论问题的研究，对中国人权理论、法律和实践的研究，对国际人权公约的研究，对具体人权和特别群体人权的研究，对人权与国际法领域中其他现象和问题的关系的研究，对域外人权问题的研究，等等。本卷收入的大部分是在学术刊物上发表的论文，但基本上涵盖了上述所有内容类型。

（一）人权基本理论

人权基本理论是包括国际人权法在内的整个人权法制度的理论基础。国际人权法学科重视对人权基本理论的研究。这方面的代表性成果是曲相霏的专著《人权离我们有多远：人权的概念及其在近代中国的发展演变》（清华大学出版社，2015）和收入本卷的莫纪宏的论文《论人权的非道德性》。此外，国际人权法学科还广泛研究了人权的主体问题[①]、人的尊严与

---

① 曲相霏：《人·公民·世界公民：人权主体的流变与人权的制度保障》，《政法论坛》2008年第4期。

人权的关系问题[①]以及人权理论在中国的演变历史[②]。

（二）中国人权理论、法律和实践

国际人权法学科重视对中国人权理论、法律和实践的总结和宣传。这方面的代表性成果是收入本卷的柳华文的论文《改革开放四十年与中国人权发展道路》、刘小妹的论文《以新时代人权发展事业推动构建人类命运共同体》，张卫华的论文《构建人类命运共同体的人权之维》（《人权》2017 年第 5 期），廖凡的论文《人类命运共同体的人权与主权内涵》（《吉林大学社会科学学报》2018 年第 6 期）以及柳华文的专著《中国的人权发展道路》（中国社会科学出版社，2018）。此外，国际人权法学科还广泛研究了人权在中国的主流化与本土化[③]、中国特色社会主义人权观[④]、人权与中国梦[⑤]、中国对人权的立法和司法保障[⑥]等问题。

（三）国际人权公约

国际人权公约是国际人权标准的核心载体，因而是国际人权法学科的研究重点，在以国际人权公约为核心的国际人权法律制度的总体情况、各项国际人权公约、这些公约的某些内容以及这些公约与中国的关系等方面都有大量的研究成果。

在国际人权法学科中，一个重要问题是联合国人权制度的总体情况，这方面的代表性成果是柳华文的论文《联合国与人权的国际保护》（《世界经济与政治》2015 年第 4 期）和专著《联合国核心人权公约与机制》（湖南大学出版社，2016）。国际人权法学科同时关注国际人权法对国内法的影响，这方面的代表性成果是收入本卷的戴瑞君的论文《论基本权利制度变迁之国际人权法动因》。

---

① 柳华文：《以尊严论解读人权》，《人权》2011 年第 1 期；曲相霏：《人的尊严与人权保障》，《人权》2013 年第 2 期。

② 曲相霏：《十九世纪末二十世纪初人权语词在中国的使用》，《法学家》2008 年第 4 期。

③ 柳华文：《论人权在中国的主流化与本土化》，《学习与探索》2011 年第 4 期。

④ 柳华文：《中国特色社会主义人权观——结合习近平致“2015 北京人权论坛”贺信的解读》，《国际法研究》2016 年第 5 期。

⑤ 柳华文：《切实尊重和保障人权与实现中国梦》，《人权》2013 年第 2 期。

⑥ 刘小妹：《人权保障立法中的重大理论与现实问题研究》，《学术动态》2008 年第 25 期；《中国人权司法保障制度的特点与举措》，《法律适用》2014 年第 11 期。

对于《经济、社会和文化权利国际公约》，代表性成果是柳华文的专著《论国家在〈经济、社会和文化权利国际公约〉下义务的不对称性》（北京大学出版社，2005；社会科学文献出版社，2019）和柳华文主编的《经济、社会和文化权利可诉性研究》（中国社会科学出版社，2008）。[①] 对于《公民权利和政治权利国际公约》，代表性成果是朱晓青与柳华文合著的《〈公民权利和政治权利国际公约〉及其实施机制》（中国社会科学出版社，2003）。另外，赵建文和孙世彦还广泛而深入地研究了《公民权利和政治权利国际公约》规定的义务、克减、保留，与国内法律制度的关系等问题。[②] 孙世彦对《公民权利和政治权利国际公约》（同时涉及《经济、社会和文化权利国际公约》）中文本问题的研究，具有一定的国际影响力。[③]

国际人权公约研究中一个很重要的方面是其实施机制。这方面的代表性成果是朱晓青的论文《〈公民权利和政治权利国际公约〉的实施机制》（《法学研究》2000 年第 2 期）[④]、戴瑞君的论文《联合国人权条约机构体系的加强进程——联合国人权保护机制的最新发展》（《环球法律评论》2013 年第 6 期）[⑤]。在国际人权公约的国内实施方面，代表性成果是戴瑞君的专著《国际

① 另见孙世彦《〈经济、社会、文化权利国际公约〉研究述评——从〈《经济、社会、文化权利国际公约》：评论、案例和资料〉谈起》，《国际法研究》2014 年第 5 期。

② 如赵建文《论人权公约的克减条款》，《法学家》1996 年第 5 期；《〈公民权利和政治权利国际公约〉的保留和解释性声明》，《法学研究》2004 年第 5 期；《论国际法与宪法的效力关系——〈公民权利和政治权利国际公约〉的视角》，《时代法学》2004 年第 6 期；《国际人权条约当事国义务的范围》，载《中国国际法年刊（2009）》，世界知识出版社，2010。孙世彦：《从〈公民权利和政治权利国际公约〉看人权的普遍性与相对性》，《人权》2009 年第 4 期；《〈公民及政治权利国际公约〉与国内法律制度——一些基本认识》，《法治研究》2011 年第 6 期；《〈公民及政治权利国际公约〉的域外适用——人权事务委员会对“在其领土内和受其管辖的一切个人”的解释》，载《中国国际法年刊（2010）》，世界知识出版社，2011；《〈公民及政治权利国际公约〉缔约国的义务》，社会科学文献出版社，2012。

③ 孙世彦：《有关 International Covenant on Civil and Political Rights 中文本的若干问题》，载徐显明主编《人权研究》第 4 卷，山东人民出版社，2004；“International Covenant on Civil and Political Rights: One Covenant, Two Chinese Texts?”, *Nordic Journal of International Law* 75（2006）；《〈公民及政治权利国际公约〉的两份中文本：问题、比较与出路》，《环球法律评论》2007 年第 6 期；“The Problems of the Chinese Texts of the International Human Rights Covenants: A Revisit”, *Chinese Journal of International Law* 15（2016）；《国际人权公约中文本问题之再探讨：兼与司马晋、黄旭东商榷》，《台湾人权学刊》2016 年第 3 卷第 4 期。

④ 另见朱晓青《论联合国人权国际保护的执行措施》，《法学研究》1994 年第 4 期；《关于联合国妇女人权保护机制的健全与完善》，《妇女学苑》1997 年第 2 期。

⑤ 另见戴瑞君《论联合国人权条约监督机制的改革》，《法学杂志》2009 年第 3 期。

人权条约的国内适用研究：全球视野》（社会科学文献出版社，2013）。

国际人权法学科的一个研究重点是中国与国际人权公约及其各项制度的关系。这方面的代表性成果是莫纪宏的专著《国际人权公约与中国》（世界知识出版社，2005）[①] 以及陈泽宪主编的《〈公民权利与政治权利国际公约〉的批准与实施》（中国社会科学出版社，2008）。就批准《公民权利和政治权利国际公约》，莫纪宏提出制定一部整合国际人权公约中的普遍人权与中国宪法以及其他法律、法规所保护的个人权利的中华人民共和国人权保障法。[②] 孙世彦则在中国批准该公约的背景中分析了其理解和解释问题；[③] 赵建文提出了创新性的提议，即中国应该接受联合国人权条约规定的个人申诉机制。[④]

（四）具体人权和特别群体人权

国际人权法学科重视对具体人权的研究，特别是结合国际人权法的研究。在公民权利和政治权利方面，代表性成果是莫纪宏的《表达自由的法律界限》（中国人民公安大学出版社，1998）等。在经济、社会和文化权利方面，代表性的成果是曲相霏研究受教育权的论文《受教育权初探》（《政法论坛》2002 年第 3 期）[⑤]、研究健康权的论文《国际法事例中的健康权保障》（《学习与探索》2008 年第 2 期）[⑥]。在第三代人权方面，代表性成果是赵建文有关自决权与和平权的论文[⑦]以及柳华文有关发展权的论文[⑧]。

---

① 另见莫纪宏、宋雅芳《论国际人权公约与国内宪法的关系》，《中国法学》1999 年第 3 期；莫纪宏《两个国际人权公约下缔约国的义务与中国》，《世界经济与政治》2002 年第 8 期。

② 莫纪宏：《批准〈公民权利和政治权利国际公约〉的两种思考进路——关于法治与人权价值次序的选择标准》，《首都师范大学学报》2007 年第 6 期；莫纪宏主编《人权保障法与中国》，法律出版社，2008。

③ Shiyan Sun, "The Understanding and Interpretation of ICCPR in the Context of China's Ratification", *Chinese Journal of International Law* 6 (2007).

④ 赵建文：《应接受国际条约中的个人申诉机制》，《环球法律评论》2013 年第 2 期。

⑤ 另见曲相霏《析受教育权平等》，《山东大学学报》（哲学社会科学版）2003 年第 5 期；《部属高校的“人为地方化”与受教育权平等》，《法学》2009 年第 11 期。

⑥ 另见曲相霏《外国宪法事例中的健康权保障》，《求是学刊》2009 年第 4 期；《公民有自助透析的自由》，《太平洋学报》2009 年第 8 期；《气候变化背景下的健康权保障》，《人权》2016 年第 6 期。

⑦ 赵建文：《人民自决权的主体范围》，《法学研究》2008 年第 2 期；《人民自决权与国家领土完整的关系》，《法学研究》2009 年第 6 期；《和平权的缘起与演进》，《人权》2015 年第 6 期。

⑧ 柳华文：《人权：环境保护与发展权》，《人权》2013 年第 1 期。

国际人权法学科特别重视对特别群体人权的研究，尤其是对妇女权利（以及与之关联的性别问题和家庭暴力问题）、儿童权利和残疾人权利的研究。在妇女权利和性别平等方面，代表性成果是柳华文的论文《性别平等：联合国人权条约机构的实践及其启示》（《法学杂志》2009 年第 8 期）、收入本卷的李西霞的论文《论国际人权法对妇女健康权的保护》。[①] 在儿童权利方面，代表性成果是柳华文主编的《儿童权利与法律保护》（上海人民出版社，2009）。[②] 曲相霏对残疾人权利有广泛而深入的研究，其代表性成果包括《〈残疾人权利公约〉与残疾人权利保障》（《法学》2013 年第 8 期）；[③] 特别是对“合理便利”的研究，这方面的代表性成果是收入本卷的《残疾人权利公约中的合理便利——考量基准与保障手段》。[④] 柳华文也曾研究中国残疾人权利保障事业的基本特点。[⑤] 对特别群体人权的研究还包括对老年人权利和外国人权利的研究。[⑥] 收入本卷的钟瑞华的论文《论消费者权利的性质》就包括从人权角度对消费者权利的性质的分析。

（五）人权与国际法领域中其他现象和问题的关系

人权并不局限于国际人权法领域，还与国际法其他领域中的现象和问题发生联系、相互作用。国际人权法学科关注这些交叉领域内的问题，并在人

---

① 另见李西霞主编《妇女社会权利的保护：国际法与国内法视角》（上下册），社会科学文献出版社，2013；朱晓青《妇女人权法律保护的发展与变化——基于国际人权公约和国内法视角的考察》，《人权》2015 年第 6 期；李西霞《中国反女性就业歧视法律制度研究——基于国际人权法的视角》，《人权》2017 年第 1 期。

② 另见柳华文《中国儿童权利保护新趋势——评〈中国儿童发展纲要（2011—2020 年）〉》，《中国妇运》2012 年第 3 期；《设立弃婴岛与儿童权利保护》，《人权》2014 年第 1 期；《儿童权利保护不可顾此失彼》，《群言》2017 年第 4 期。

③ 另见曲相霏《保障精神和智力障碍人的生命与尊严》，《河南省政法管理干部学院学报》2010 年第 2 期。

④ 另见曲相霏《“合理便利”概念的起源和发展》，《人权》2015 年第 6 期；《〈残疾人权利公约〉的“合理便利”理念在我国教育领域的运用》，《人权》2017 年第 3 期；《“合理便利”的特点及其在我国就业领域的适用》，《人权》2018 年第 2 期。

⑤ 柳华文：《中国残疾人权利保障事业的基本特点》，《残疾人研究》2017 年第 2 期。

⑥ 例如见柳华文《发展与人权：关于老龄化问题的思考》，《人权》2009 年第 2 期；《关于制定联合国〈老年人权利公约〉的初步研究》，载《中国国际法年刊（2012）》，法律出版社，2013；戴瑞君《外国人权利的法律保护——从国际法到中国法的考察》，《人权》2014 年第 5 期。

权与贸易、人权与引渡、人权与人口流动、人权与气候变化、人权与腐败等问题上进行了有特色的研究。在人权与贸易的关系方面，代表性成果是刘敬东的论文《国际贸易中的人权》(《法学研究》2009 年第 4 期)、《人权保护还是贸易保护？——以劳动权为视角的理论思考》(《国际经济法学刊》2010 年第 2 期)。[①] 在人权与引渡方面，代表性的成果是柳华文的论文《美洲人权法院引渡第一案的意义及其启示》〔《东南大学学报》（哲学社会科学版）2016 年第 6 期〕、郝鲁怡的论文《引渡中的人权问题探究》（《国际法研究》2015 年第 6 期）。在人权与人口流动方面，代表性成果是柳华文的专著《〈联合国禁止贩运人口议定书〉研究：以人权法为视角》（社会科学文献出版社，2010）。[②] 在人权与气候变化方面，代表性成果是何晶晶的论文《气候变化的人权法维度》（《人权》2015 年第 5 期）以及《〈巴黎协定〉的人权维度》（《人权》2017 年第 6 期）。在人权与腐败的关系方面，代表性成果是孙世彦的论文《腐败如何损害人权》（《法制与社会发展》2013 年第 6 期）。[③]

（六）域外人权问题

国际人权法学科也关注区域性人权制度以及国际人权法与其他国家的关系等域外人权问题。对区域性人权制度，代表性研究成果是中国最早研究欧洲人权制度的学者之一朱晓青的专著《欧洲人权法律保护机制研究》（法律出版社，2003）以及论文《欧洲一体化进程中人权法律地位的演变》（《法学研究》2002 年第 5 期）。[④] 在国际人权法与其他国家的关系方面，代表性成果是李庆明的论文《国际人权条约与美国法院的双重标准》(《人权》2013 年第 5 期)。[⑤] 李庆明还曾专门研究美国的《外国人侵权行为

---

① 另见李西霞《在自由贸易区制度中积极构建我国主张的劳工标准》，《人权》2014 年第 6 期；《自由贸易协定中劳工标准的发展态势》，《环球法律评论》2015 年第 1 期。

② 另见柳华文《论禁止人口贩运的基础》，《江海学刊》2016 年第 2 期。

③ 另见柳华文《〈联合国反腐败公约〉履约审议机制刍议》，《当代法学》2014 年第 1 期。

④ 另见孙世彦《人权研究的新进展——评〈欧洲人权法院判例评述〉》，《武汉大学学报》（社会科学版）2002 年第 1 期；《欧洲人权制度中的“自由判断余地原则”述评》，《环球法律评论》2005 年第 3 期；李庆明《国家豁免与诉诸法院之权利——以欧洲人权法院的实践为中心》，《环球法律评论》2012 年第 6 期；郝鲁怡《欧盟妇女劳动权利保护的法律制度研究》，中国社会科学出版社，2013；蒋小红《贸易与人权的联结——试论欧盟对外贸易政策中的人权目标》，《欧洲研究》2016 年第 5 期。

⑤ 另见戴瑞君《批准人权公约与切实保障人权不能等同——以美国法院对一项国际人权公约的适用为例证》，《法学》2009 年第 2 期。

法》，其中包括该法与人权的关系。[①]

（七）译著

除了上文介绍的主要论文和专著以外，国际人权法学科对中国人权研究的另一重大贡献是国外人权著作的译介。这方面的代表性成果包括：孙世彦、毕小青翻译的曼弗雷德·诺瓦克的《〈公民权利和政治权利国际公约〉评注》（修订第二版，三联书店，2008）；[②] 柳华文翻译的曼弗雷德·诺瓦克的《国际人权制度导论》（北京大学出版社，2010）；孙世彦翻译的本·索尔、戴维·金利和杰奎琳·莫布雷的《〈经济社会文化权利国际公约〉：评注、案例与资料》（法律出版社，2019）等。这些译著中有许多属于中国人权研究领域，特别是国际人权法研究领域，引用最频繁的参考书籍。国际人权法研究室将从2019年起陆续翻译出版“核心国际人权公约评注”，将世界范围内研究人权公约的优秀著述译介给中国人权学界。

三 总结和展望

国际人权法学科的研究范围非常广泛，基本覆盖了国际人权法所涉及的所有领域。国际人权法学科的研究问题非常现实，除了关注国际人权法领域本身的实践和发展，更为重要的是，关注国际人权法对中国法治建设的作用和意义。国际人权法无论是作为一个法律部门还是一个法学学科，在中国为人所知的历史都不长。因此，国际人权法学科的一个重要任务是架起一座“桥梁”，帮助国内人权界和法学界了解国际人权法领域的最新实践发展、国际人权法研究领域的最新学术成果。

在新时代，国际人权法学科将继续起到“世界与中国之间的人权之桥”的作用。国际人权法学科将继续研究国际人权法领域本身的实践和发展，使国内人权界和法学界能经由国际人权法学科的工作和成果了解这一

---

① 李庆明：《美国〈外国人侵权请求法〉研究》，武汉大学出版社，2010。

② 其英文第一版的中文版为〔奥〕曼弗雷德·诺瓦克：《民权公约评注》，毕小青、孙世彦主译，三联书店，2003。

领域在世界层面的最新发展情况。国际人权法学科将继续研究国际人权法对中国法治建设的作用和意义，将国际人权法中可用于中国法治建设的资源提炼出来，为中国尊重和保障人权的事业作出进一步的贡献。最重要的是，国际人权法学科将更多地从“人权之桥”的中国一端走向世界一头，即努力做到两点：一是更多地发挥向外部世界展现中国人权领域实践情况和研究成果的作用，二是更多地参与国际层面的人权讨论和话语建设并为这种讨论和建设作出中国应有的贡献。

研究室成员简介

莫纪宏

一　基本情况

1965 年生，汉族，江苏靖江市人，法学博士。现为中国社会科学院国际法研究所所长、研究员，中国社会科学院研究生院教授、博士生和硕士生导师，中国社会科学院大学特聘教授。专业方向为宪法学、立法学、行政法学和国际人权法学。重点研究领域是宪法哲学、依宪治国理论、宪法监督制度与合宪性审查理论、基本人权理论、国际人权法实施机制、紧急状态制度、国家安全与公共安全理论等。

莫纪宏研究员目前担任的主要社会职务和兼职有：国际宪法学协会名誉主席（终身）、中国法学会常务理事、中国法学会学术委员会委员、中国宪法学研究会常务副会长、北京市法学会立法学研究会会长、中国法学会立法学研究会副会长、中国法学会律师法学研究会副会长等。

莫纪宏研究员1986年毕业于北京大学法律学系，1989年在中国社会科学院研究生院获得法学硕士学位，1994年在中国社会科学院研究生院获得法学博士学位。1989—1990年在中国社会科学院政治学研究所工作，1991—2018年在中国社会科学院法学研究所工作，2018年至今在中国社会科学院国际法研究所工作。1993年被破格晋升为副研究员，2001年晋升研究员，2004年被聘为国际人权法方向博士生指导老师，2004年获得中国法学会“全国十大杰出青年法学家”称号。2013年入选人力资源和社会保障部“国家百千万人才工程”并被授予“有突出贡献中青年专家”荣誉称号。2015年获得国务院政府特殊津贴。2017年入选中宣部文化名家暨“四个一批”人才、第3批国家“万人计划”哲学社会科学领军人物。他还担任最高人民检察院专家咨询委员，全国“五五”、“七五”普法中央讲师团成员，中国法学会“百名法学家报告团”成员，北京市人大常委会法制顾问，北京市人民政府法律咨询专家，北京市依法治市宣传顾问，广东省委法律顾问，等等。2017年4月至2018年3月，任中共甘肃省张掖市委副书记（挂职）。

莫纪宏研究员曾长期在国外著名大学和研究机构担任客座教授和访问学者。1995年在日本东京大学法学部做客座研究员，1998年在挪威人权研究所做访问学者，2001年在瑞典隆德大学做访问学者，2002年在瑞士佛里堡大学做访问学者。

莫纪宏研究员指导的国际人权法方向的博士生已毕业9名，在读的有3名。指导宪法、行政法方向的博士后近20名，法学和法律硕士达60名，进修生10名，本科生2名。

二 科研活动与贡献

在30年的科研工作中，莫纪宏研究员主持和参加了所内外和院内外组织的许多重大课题的论证和研究工作，积极参与国家立法活动，先后参与了百余部法律、法规、规章和党内法规的起草、论证和咨询工作，许多重要学术研究成果获得省部级以上奖励，撰写的近百篇内部研究报告许多得到党和国家领导人的批示肯定，先后获得三等奖以上中国社会科学院优秀对策信息奖60余项，中国知网收录的论文350余篇，《新华文摘》转摘近10篇，人大复印报刊资料全文转摘20余篇。主要科研成绩包括以下几个方面。

（一）积极参与或者组织国家重点课题和中国社会科学院重点项目的研究工作，并取得了一批比较有分量的学术成果

1. 主持2007年国家社科基金重大课题“党的领导、人民当家做主与依法治国有机统一”，顺利完成结项。

2. 主持2017年国家社科基金重点项目“民间规范与地方立法”，正在顺利推进。

3. 主持和参加党的十八届四中全会决定的专家建议稿论证和起草工作，该稿是决定起草小组的重要参考资料。

4. 参加中国社会科学院组织的“全面深化改革书系”，撰写出版《法治中国的宪法基础》。

5. 参加中国社会科学院组织的“习近平新时代中国特色社会主义思想学习丛书”，撰写出版《全面依法治国建设法治中国》。

6. 主持2015年中国社会科学院国情调研项目“宁夏回族自治区宗教事务依法管理的状况研究”，2017年中国社会科学院国情调研项目“地方法治研究”，2018年中国社会科学院国情调研项目“生态文明建设与生态法治意识”。

7. 主持中国社会科学院2019—2022大型调研项目“‘一带一路’法律风险防范与法律机制构建”。等等。

（二）积极参加国家立法活动，许多重要的立法建议被采纳，结合立法活动所编著和出版的一些著作成为立法活动的重要参考资料

1. 参加了防震减灾立法工作和我国防震减灾法律体系的构建工作，先后担任《破坏性地震应急条例》立法起草小组副组长，《中华人民共和国防震减灾法》立法起草小组成员，《发布地震预报的规定》、《抗震设防要求管理条例》和《地震重点监视防御区条例》立法起草小组顾问。为配合防震减灾立法工作，编著了《外国紧急状态法律制度》（法律出版社，1994)，该著作成为防震减灾立法确立地震应急制度的重要法律依据。

2. 参与了《戒严法》、《国防法》、《立法法》、《监察法》、《公务员法》、《人民检察院组织法》、《人民法院组织法》、《慈善法》等法律的立法论证及咨询工作，撰写了《戒严法律制度概要》(法律出版社，1996)一书，该著作成为《戒严法》、《国防法》规定戒严制度的重要参考资料。

3. 参加了《突发事件应对法》起草小组，是《国家安全法》立法起草小组的重要成员。

4. 参与了2004年现行宪法第四次修改的咨询和宣传工作、2018年现行宪法第五次修改的立法咨询和宣传工作，提出的许多很好的修宪建议被修宪小组采纳。

5. 对参与国家和地方立法活动的经历和经验作出了系统总结，撰写出版《为立法辩护》(武汉大学出版社，2007)。

(三) 积极响应中国社会科学院党组和院领导提出的“精品工程”、“创新工程”的号召，在理论结合实践的基础上，尤其是结合参加国家立法活动的实践经验，及时地就我国法制建设中的重大问题撰写内部报告，其中多篇报告引起党和国家领导人的关注，60多篇报告获得中国社会科学院颁发的优秀信息和优秀对策成果奖以及其他类型的省部级奖励，产生了广泛的社会影响

1. 1999年，针对我国驻南使馆遭北约飞机轰炸以及“法轮功”等紧急危机事件，结合对紧急状态法律制度进行的长期研究所取得的成果，撰写了《建立国家紧急事务预警反映机制》的内部报告。该报告受到党和国家领导人的高度重视。

2. 获得党和国家领导人批示，并获得中国社会科学院优秀对策信息一等奖以上的主要对策信息包括:《代表法》修改应注意的几个问题，2011年9月，特等奖；加强《选举法》修改宣传工作的建议，2011年9月，一等奖；关于宣布形成有中国特色社会主义法律体系应当认真对待的几个理论问题，2011年9月，一等奖；需做好衡阳贿选事件的法律善后工作，2015年6月，一等奖；全国人大不宜修改全国人大常委会制定的法律，2015年6月，一等奖；制定国家荣誉法要体现“科学立法”精神，2016年6月，一等奖；不宜用立法手段干预宗教习俗的存留，2016年6月，一等奖。

（四）加强对宪法基础理论的研究，出版个人专著12部

其中，《宪法审判制度概要》（中国人民公安大学出版社，1998）是国内宪法学界系统研究宪法审判制度的第一本学术著作。《表达自由的法律界限》（中国人民公安大学出版社，1998）通过全面介绍挪威最高法院对“羞示”案件所作出的判决，系统地分析了现代宪法审判制度在保障基本人权方面的功能，在研究宪法审判案例方面作了有益的尝试。《政府与公民宪法必读》（中国人民公安大学出版社，1999）详细介绍了1999年宪法修正案的产生背景、内容、意义、理论和实践上的价值等，是全面理解现行宪法及其修正案的最全面的参考书。《现代宪法的逻辑基础》（法律出版社，2001）第一次以逻辑学的方法阐述了现代宪法的基本原理，将宪法定位为价值法，并详细地探讨了宪法的正当性、确定性、有效性等价值特性，指出了宪法制度的设计必须以宪法价值为基础。《“非典”时期的非常法治》（法律出版社，2003）比较系统地介绍了我国灾害法和紧急状态法的立法状况以及有关非典防治的法律对策。《国际人权公约与中国》（世界知识出版社，2005）比较全面和系统地介绍了《公民权利和政治权利国际公约》及《经济、社会和文化权利国际公约》所确立的基本人权体系及实施机制。《实践中的宪法学原理》（中国人民大学出版社，2007）汇集了作者对实践中的宪法问题进行系统性理论思考的宪法学观点和理念。《为立法辩护》（武汉大学出版社，2007）全面系统地收集了作者参与国家和地方立法的立法资料以及作者自己根据立法需求和立法技术就某些方面的社会问题起草的专家立法建议稿。《宪法学原理》（中国社会科学出版社，2008）运用比较宪法学和规范宪法学的方法，对世界各国成文宪法文本中的宪法制度进行归纳和总结，构建了崭新的宪法学原理体系。《法治中国的宪法基础》（社会科学文献出版社，2014）列入“全面深化改革书系”，对法治中国建设过程中的各种宪法问题进行了全面系统的归纳、总结和分析，提出了依宪治国的理论框架和主要学术观点。《法治中国与制度建设》（方志出版社，2016）收录了作者对法治中国制度建设中的一些重大理论和实践问题的学术思考、方案和建议。

三 主要学术观点

莫纪宏研究员在以下几个方面为我国宪法学和人权法理论研究的完善

作出了自己独特的贡献。

1. 依法治国的实质就是依宪治国

在法学界最早明确提出了“依法治国的实质就是依宪治国”的观点。认为，贯彻“依法治国”的精神不仅要求在一个法治社会中的所有社会关系都必须接受法律规则的评价，做到“有法可依”，更重要的是，应当保障“依法治国”的前提是法律自身的问题必须用法治的手段加以解决。要解决法律自身存在的矛盾必须通过实施宪法加以实现。因此，如果不突出宪法在依法治国中的核心地位，依法治国在实践中就有可能演变成人治的规范化或者人治的新形式。

2. 法律与道德的二元化是“人治”的产物

最早提出道德与法律的二元化是“人治”的产物的观点。认为，在“人治”情况下，由于统治者与被统治者分离，统治者按照自己的意志行事，制定法律约束被统治者。对于统治者而言，法律和道德是合一的；但对被统治者来说，法律和道德就是分离的，因为法律体现的是统治者的意志，这种意志可能不符合被统治者的要求。由于被统治者的意志不能成为法律，这样就产生了被统治者对统治者的一种主观要求，这种要求来源于被统治者，约束的对象是统治者。因此，道德的理念是约束统治者的，不是约束被统治者的。故在“人治”形式下，社会中就存在两种统治理念，一种是统治者的“法治”理念，另一种就是被统治者的“德治”理念。

3. 宪法权利在国内法上的法律效力高于国际人权公约中的普遍人权

认为对于一个国际人权公约的参加国而言，承担有关国际人权公约下的义务的前提是《维也纳条约法公约》的有关规定。也就是说，国际人权公约中的普遍人权不能直接对公约参加国产生法律上的拘束力，必须通过国际人权公约本身所具有的国际法性质对公约参加国产生国际法上的效力。由于公约参加国大多数以议会通过的有关法律予以批准，所以，国际人权公约在国内法上的法律效力只能相当于议会制定的法律。从法律效力上来看，经过议会批准的国际人权公约中的普遍人权在其重要性上只能确定为一般法律权利，这种权利在国内法中所受到的保护不得超过宪法权利所受到的保护。议会只有经过特定程序，通过修改宪法才能将已经批准的国际人权公约中的普遍人权上升到宪法权利的水平予以保护。

4. 人权是权利制度辩证发展的产物

最早提出了“人权是权利制度辩证发展的产物”的观点。认为人权与权利是两个具有独立价值的哲学范畴。权利旨在设定一种实现利益的资格，权利制度存在的目的就是最大限度地实现利益。人权强调人的尊严和人自身的价值，它是在权利制度发展过程中产生的概念，目的是限制滥用权利制度将人自身也作为一种利益进行交换和分配。因此，人权制度是权利制度辩证否定的产物，是为了纠正权利制度在实现利益方面的弊病，使权利制度更好地为人类服务。

5. 人权具有区别于道德的独立价值

从法律的公共道德性出发，指出人权的道德性必须通过法律制度体现出来，离开法律判断，人权的道德性不具有公共性。而在法律制度下，人权价值的取舍不完全受制于公共道德的要求，还要受到社会现实的客观性、国家利益、公共利益、自由目标等本体论、认识论等因素的制约，所以，人权的正当性不完全来自道德评价，人权也具有非道德性。人权的非道德性主要强调人权的正当性应当从历史唯物主义和辩证法的视角来考察。人权本身具有一定的客观性，受到社会经济文化条件因素的制约，人权是在现实的社会关系中实现的。人权离不开道德评价，但是，人权价值背后的利益冲突导致人权的价值取舍不完全受制于道德要求，人权本身是历史的产物，也是在社会发展过程中不断向前发展的。所以，考察人权的正当性基础应当关注人权的道德性与非道德性之间的辩证统一关系。人权的道德基础不能简单地停留在人权的规范要求上，在社会关系的框架中来考察人权的特性，需要重视人权所追求的人格利益在现实中可以得到制度保障的实际状况和程度。人权性质过于主观化不利于人权事业的发展。

6. 加强对法律、行政法规、自治条例和单行条例、规章的合宪性审查

与合宪性审查相关的一系列学术论文对在中国现行法律体制下如何进行科学和有效的合宪性审查提出了系统的学术建议。《论法律的合宪性审查机制》一文从现行宪法第 5 条所规定的法制统一性原则出发，指出法律与行政法规、地方性法规一样都属于合宪性的审查对象，但与对行政法规、地方性法规合宪性审查制度设计不同的是，对行政法规、地方性法规的合宪性审查目前在立法法上有明确的程序和机制，但对法律的合宪性审查却缺少相应的程序与机制。作者从我国现行宪法所确立的人民代表大会制度的基本特征和要求出发，指出在我国目前全国人大及其常委会享有国家立法权同时又能够修改宪法、解释宪法的立法体制下，法律的制定主体

与法律合宪性审查主体之间具有同一性，因此，采用西方国家“对立”或“对抗”式的法律合宪性审查方式与我国党领导立法的政治体制不相吻合，在制度上唯一可行的办法就是充分发挥全国人大及其常委会内部监督机制的作用，特别是发挥全国人大宪法和法律委员会在保证法律合宪性方面的作用。在对法律的合宪性审查上只采取“相一致”或“不相一致”的审查结论，对于“不相一致”情形可以采取修改宪法或受审查的法律，或者是以解释宪法或受审查的法律的方式进行相应处理，从而保证法律与宪法之间的高度一致性，维护宪法权威和法律正当性。在《论行政法规的合宪性审查机制》一文中，从我国现行宪法、立法法以及相关法律法规的规定出发，全面和系统地梳理了现行法律制度框架内行政法规合宪性审查的制度设计、运行机制及特征、审查效果及效力等与行政法规合宪性审查机制相关的基本法律制度的内涵，对于相同和相似的制度设计作了归纳，概括了我国行政法规合宪性审查机制的特征，并基于对行政法规合宪性审查机制现状的分析，结合我国当下的政治体制和法律制度实际，提出了建立健全行政法规合宪性审查机制应当关注的几个重要的理论与实践问题。指出，要真正地在实践中推动行政法规的合宪性审查机制的建设，需要从中国的实际出发，重点抓好行政法规制定过程中行政法规草案与宪法之间的一致性，从而提升行政法规的立法质量。对于来自外部的行政法规的合宪审查，则要根据立法法的相关规定，结合党领导立法的原则，根据行政法规所具有的中央法规的特性，妥善地作出制度安排，从而维护行政法规作为中央法规的权威，保证宪法的有效实施。《自治条例和单行条例合宪性审查的法理和分层》一文，从《中华人民共和国立法法》规定的自治条例和单行条例属于应当受全国人大常委会合宪审查对象的相关制度设计出发，通过分析现行宪法、立法法、民族区域自治法等法律对自治条例和单行条例立法机制确认的特点，指出对自治条例和单行条例的合宪性审查应当区分两个层面：一是对自治区的自治条例和单行条例的合宪性审查；二是对自治州、自治县的自治条例和单行条例的合宪性审查。其中，前一项审查只能是生效前的合宪性审查，后一项审查则应当是生效后的违宪审查。认为，我国宪法和立法法上所规定的自治条例和单行条例批准生效程序上的特殊性，导致对自治条例和单行条例的立法监督很难简单地套用“下位法服从上位法”的原则，必须严格地按照自治条例和单行条例的法律效力等级加以区分，建立分层次的合宪性审查机制。由于立法法规定了全国人大常委会对包含由其批准的自治区的自治条例和单行条例进行合宪性审查的制度，在合宪性审查实践中可能就会产生全国人大常委会自己审查自己批准的自治条例和单行条例生效行为的合宪性问题，这就形成了全国人大常委会的自我监督。因此，要在合宪性审查的实践中着力推进对自治条例和单行条例的合宪性审查工作，就必须区分不同情形，只有这样才能对症下药、有所成就。《论规章的合宪性审查机制》一文，从我国现行宪法、立法法和相关法律法规的文本出发，全面系统地归纳和总结了我国现行法律制度框架内规章的合宪性审查的制度和机制特征，明确地提出了规章的合宪性审查是一项已经存在、尚待完善的立法监督制度。从分析规章的三种类型出发，提出了可以通过宪法修改或宪法解释的方式，在现行宪法与国务院部门规章、地方政府规章和军事规章之间建立形式上的法律联系，从而为规章的合宪性审查提供形式合宪的法理基础。并指出，目前关键的制度设计就是要把规章纳入立法法所规定的由全国人大常委会进行违宪审查的对象的范围，以保证规章的合宪性审查工作的权威性。

四 代表作简介

1.《现代宪法的逻辑基础》

莫纪宏研究员在该书中运用宪法逻辑学的分析方法，对目前我国宪法学界所探讨的一系列最前沿的基础性理论问题发表了自己独特的见解。具体来说，该书具有以下三个方面的重要特征。（1）在方法论上具有创新意义。作者提出，宪法属于价值现象，因此，分析宪法现象的基本方法必须体现价值的基本特性，即应当将宪法放在手段与目的的因果关系逻辑链中，通过探讨宪法的正当性（合法性）、合理性、确定性和有效性等基本价值属性来认识宪法现象的基本特征。作者将上述分析方法贯穿于全书的始终，旨在通过宪法逻辑学的方法论来发现那些长期隐藏在宪法现象背后由于没有恰当的方法论而未被发现的价值规律。在作者看来，宪法学是历史学与逻辑学的统一，宪法逻辑学是人类理性的最高体现，因为它的方法论是采用最有效的方法来解决最复杂的社会问题。宪法逻辑学的建立对于推进道义逻辑学的逻辑形式和逻辑规律的发展具有非常重要的意义。（2）对一些重要的宪法理论问题作了全新的法理解释。如，结合《立法法草案》

作者着重分析了制宪权与立法权的本质界限，指出忽视制宪权在构建宪法制度中的基础性作用，就无法克服由于缺少制宪权而产生的各种价值矛盾。作者提出，制宪权、主权、全民公决权以及社会权利等都属于价值概念，它们的存在是为了解决宪法的正当性问题，是不应随意抛弃的重要的宪法范畴。此外，作者还提出了宪法学理论研究应当加以重视的新的宪法学范畴，如国际民主原则、国际法治原则、宪法责任、宪法程序等，这些新的宪法学范畴的建立有利于从整体上推进宪法学理论研究的深度、广度发展，具有开拓性的作用。

2.《审视应然性——一种宪法逻辑学的视野》

莫纪宏研究员在该论文中第一次从认识论的角度就法学理论界长期争论的法的“应然性”问题提出了自己独特的见解。该论文运用宪法逻辑学的方法，从本体论、认识论和价值论三个角度探讨了“应然性”的内涵，指出在价值论意义上的“应该”的逻辑形式表现为确定性和不确定性两个价值区域。传统法学理论中的“应该”受到了价值判断主体的主体性的过度影响，因此，在逻辑形态上表现为不确定的“应该”，以此为基础很难形成具有普遍价值的“应然性”命题。作为确定性的“应该”表现为以认识论为基础而产生的“不得不”。“不得不”作为一种能力判断是被传统的法哲学所遗忘的范畴，它可以避免“假设”理论给应然性造成的过度不确定性，因此，应当将“不得不”作为考察具有最低程度确定性的“应该”的逻辑准则。作者在该文中指出，传统法学理论在分析“事实问题”与“价值问题”上的根本缺陷就是将“事实问题”与“价值问题”混淆或者没有发现两者之间的差异。为了解决“事实问题”与“价值问题”之间的逻辑过渡，应当以认识论为基础，在“事实判断”与“价值判断”之间引入“能力判断”的分析方法，实现本体论、认识论和价值论三种分析方法上的统一。作者基于对应然性的逻辑分析，指出宪法的价值属性分为应然的宪法和宪法的应然性两个方面，两者属于不同的价值范畴，民主、人权等价值都属于应然的宪法，是宪法正当性的来源，而不应当将这些价值完全视为“合宪性”的产物，还由此区分了“前宪法现象”与“宪法现象”在构建宪法价值体系中的不同功能，强调现代宪法的价值核心是一种“法治法”。

3.《论宪法原则》

在该论文中，莫纪宏研究员对确定宪法原则的标准作了新的探索。作者认为，宪法原则的功能在于“反对特权现象”，宪法制度必须以“反对特权”为目的来设计相应的手段性措施，这是宪法制度构造的逻辑起点，由此可以产生“目的性的宪法原则”与“手段性的宪法原则”两类互为因果的宪法原则体系。作为“目的性的宪法原则”，它要求所有的宪法制度设计必须服务于“反对特殊的权力原则”、“反对特殊的权利原则”和“反对特殊的权势原则”，不符合这三个“目的性的宪法原则”要求的宪法制度都不具有正当性。作为“手段性的宪法原则”，它要求在设计国家权力体系、公民权利体系以及国家权力与公民权利之间的关系体系时至少从逻辑上应该解决各种特权现象产生的制度可能性问题。可以分两个层次来设计“手段性的宪法原则”，即首要性宪法原则和辅助性宪法原则。首要性宪法原则是以突出宪法权威为核心的，包括人民主权原则、宪法至上原则、剩余权力原则和剩余权利原则。辅助性宪法原则以突出立法机关制定的法律的权威为核心，包括法律优先原则、法律保留原则、依宪授权原则、依法行政原则和人权的司法最终性救济原则。

五　重要学术作品目录

（一）著作

1.《宪法审判制度概要》，中国人民公安大学出版社，1998。

2.《表达自由的法律界限》（译著），中国人民公安大学出版社，1998。

3.《政府与公民宪法必读——中华人民共和国宪法修正案全景透析》（编著），中国人民公安大学出版社，1999。

4.《现代宪法的逻辑基础》，法律出版社，2001。

5.《“非典”时期的非常法治》，法律出版社，2003。

6.《国际人权公约与中国》，世界知识出版社，2005。

7.《实践中的宪法学原理》，中国人民大学出版社，2007。

8.《为立法辩护》，武汉大学出版社，2007。

9.《宪法学原理》，中国社会科学出版社，2008。

10.《法治中国的宪法基础》，社会科学文献出版社，2014。

11.《法治中国与制度建设》，方志出版社，2016。

（二）论文

1.《法律行为的几重透析》，《中国社会科学院研究生院学报》1988 年第 3 期。

2.《法律评价的过程及其标准》，《中国社会科学院研究生院学报》1989 年第 6 期。

3.《合法行为的含义及其意义》，《中国社会科学院研究生院学报》1991 年第 6 期。

4.《选民选举意向结构甄析》，《中国法学》1992 年第 3 期。

5.《加大执法监督力度，提高执法监督水平》，《求是》1996 年第 7 期。

6.《依宪治国是依法治国的重要保证》，载王家福等主编《依法治国，建设社会主义法制国家》，中国法制出版社，1996。

7.《依宪治国是依法治国的核心》，《法学杂志》1998 年第 3 期。

8.《论国际人权公约与国内宪法的关系》，《中国法学》1999 年第 3 期。

9.《论国际法与国内法关系的新动向》，《世界经济与政治》2000 年第 9 期。

10.《论人权的司法最终救济性》，《法学家》2001 年第 3 期。

11.《论宪法原则》，《中国法学》2001 年第 4 期。

12.《审视应然性——一种宪法逻辑学的视野》，《中国社会科学》2001 年第 6 期。

13.《论公民的宪法意识》，《求是》2002 年第 6 期。

14.《诉权是现代法治社会第一制度性人权》，《法学杂志》2002 年第 4 期。

15.《两个国际人权公约下的义务与中国》，《世界经济与政治》2002 年第 8 期。

16.《受教育权宪法保护的内涵》，《法学家》2003 年第 3 期。

17.《中国紧急状态立法的状况及特征》，《法学论坛》2003 年第 4 期。

18.《论宪法关系》，《法学研究》2003 年第 1 期。

19.《宪法程序的类型以及功能》，《政法论坛》2003 年第 2 期。

20.《紧急状态入宪的意义》，《法学家》2004 年第 4 期。

21.《人权制度的概念分析》，《法学杂志》2005 年第 1 期。

22.《违宪主体论》，《法学杂志》2006 年第 1 期。

23.《宪法在司法审判中的适用性研究》，《北方法学》2007 年第 3 期。

24.《论宪法与其他法律形式的关系》，《上海政法学院学报》2007 年第 6 期。

25.《批准〈公民权利和政治权利国际公约〉两种思考进路》，《首都师范大学学报》（社会科学版）2007 年第 6 期。

26.《宪法学与公法学的关系》，《江汉大学学报》（社会科学版）2008 年第 1 期。

27.《论对社会权的宪法保护》，《河南省政法干部管理学院学报》2008 年第 3 期。

28.《应当高度关注“基本权利”的保障义务》，《法学》2009 年第 4 期。

29.《论立法的技术路线》，《广东社会科学》2009 年第 4 期。

30.《从宪法第 100 条看宪法适用理论的缺失》，《社会科学战线》2009 年第 9 期。

31.《论宪法与基本法律的效力关系》，《河南社会科学》2010 年第 5 期。

32.《对我国立法监督制度缺陷的探讨》，《江苏行政学院学报》2010 年第 4 期。

33.《“公民”概念在中国宪法文本中的发展》，《人权》2010 年第 4 期。

34.《论人权的非道德性》，《广东社会科学》2011 年第 2 期。

35.《论执政党在我国宪法文本中的地位演变》，《法学论坛》2011 年第 4 期。

36.《辛亥革命前夕各国立宪文本的特征比较》，《法学研究》2011 年第 5 期。

37.《论文化权利的宪法保护》，《法学论坛》2012 年第 1 期。

38.《宪法实施的评价方法及其影响》，《中国法学》2012 年第 4 期。

39.《我们应当怎样修改宪法》，《清华法学》2012 年第 6 期。

40.《宪法原则在宪法学理论研究体系中的地位及发展》，《法学论坛》2012 年第 6 期。

41.《法治与小康社会》，《中国法学》2013 年第 1 期。

42.《直面“三个挑战”：衡阳贿选事件的法理透析》，《法学评论》

2014 年第 2 期。

43.《坚持党的领导与依法治国》,《法学研究》2014 年第 6 期。

44.《依宪治国重在制度建设》,《理论视野》2015 年第 3 期。

45.《习近平依宪治理思想的形成及特征》,《法学杂志》2016 年第 5 期。

46.《党内法规体系建设重在实效》,《东方法学》2017 年第 4 期。

47.《国家监察体制改革要注重对监察权性质的研究》,《中州学刊》2017 年第 10 期。

48.《论加强合宪性审查的机制制度建设》,《广东社会科学》2018 年第 2 期。

49.《论行政法规的合宪性审查机制》,《江苏行政学院学报》2018 年第 3 期。

50.《论规章的合宪性审查机制》,《江汉大学学报》(社会科学版) 2018 年第 3 期。

51.《合宪性审查机制建设的 40 年》,《北京联合大学学报》(人文社会科学版) 2018 年第 3 期。

52.《以宪法修改为契机全面推进依宪治国》,《西北大学学报》(哲学社会科学版) 2018 年第 4 期。

53.《论宪法保留原则在合宪性审查中的应用》,《法治现代化研究》2018 年第 5 期。

54.《论法律的合宪性审查机制》,《法学评论》2018 年第 6 期。

55.《习近平依宪治国与依宪执政重要论述的理论价值与实践意义》,《治理现代化研究》2019 年第 2 期。

56.《自治条例和单行条例合宪性审查的法理及分层》,《甘肃社会科学》2019 年第 2 期。

孙世彦

一　基本情况

1969 年生,中国社会科学院国际法研究所研究员、国际人权法研究室主任，中国社会科学院研究生院法学系教授。

孙世彦研究员于 1991 年、1994 年在吉林大学法学院取得法学学士、法学硕士学位，1999 年于中国社会科学院研究生院取得法学博士学位。1994—2003 年任吉林大学法学院助教、讲师、副教授，吉林大学理论法学研究中心研究人员。2003—2004 年为瑞典隆德大学罗尔·瓦伦堡人权和人道法研究所访问教授（Visiting Professor）。2004 年 4 月受聘担任中国社会科学院国际法研究中心副研究员；2005 年 12 月正式调入中国社会科学院国际法研究中心，任副研究员、国际公法研究室主任；2012 年 12 月晋升研究员，继续担任国际法研究所国际公法研究室主任；2016 年 5 月调任国际人权法研究室负责人，2018 年 7 月至今任国际人权法研究室主任。

孙世彦研究员曾经在乌得勒支大学荷兰人权研究所、美国哥伦比亚大学法学院、奥斯陆大学挪威人权研究所、加拿大多伦多大学法学院、英国皇家国际事务研究所等学术机构长期访学。

孙世彦研究员目前是中国国际法学会理事、中国人权研究会理事，《国际法研究》副主编，《中国国际法年刊》、《中国国际法学刊》、《红十字国际评论》编委会成员。

孙世彦研究员的主要研究领域为国际人权法，发表中文论文 30 多篇、英文论文 5 篇，出版专著 1 部、主编 8 部、译著 5 部。

二　主要研究成果

1. 国际人权法施予国家的义务

《论国际人权法下国家的义务》（《法学评论》2002 年第 2 期）是中国最早系统研究国家根据国际人权法所承担之义务的学术成果，提出国际人权法施予国家承认、尊重、保障和促进以及保护人权四个方面的义务。《〈公民及政治权利国际公约〉的域外适用——人权事务委员会对“在其领土内和受其管辖的一切个人”的解释》（《中国国际法年刊（2010）》，世界知识出版社，2011）根据人权事务委员会的实践全面分析了《公民及政治权利国际公约》缔约国的域外义务。《国际人权条约的持续效力》（载朱晓青主编《变化中的国际法：热点与前沿》，中国社会科学出版社，2012）深入研究了在国际人权条约的退出和继承的问题以及适用于中国香港和澳门的特别问题。《〈公民及政治权利国际公约〉缔约国的义务》（社会科学文献出版社，2010）全面探讨了《公约》缔约国义务的形式、性质、范围和国内履行。

2.《公民权利和政治权利国际公约》

除了研究该公约缔约国的义务外，这方面的成果还有："The Understanding and Interpretation of ICCPR in the Context of China's Ratification" (*Chinese Journal of International Law*, Vol. 6, No. 1, 2007)、《从〈公民权利和政治权利国际公约〉看人权的普遍性与相对性》（《人权》2009 年第 4 期）、《〈公民权利和政治权利国际公约〉与国内法律制度——一些基本认识性》（《法治研究》2011 年第 6 期）、《从〈公民及政治权利国际公约〉第 14 条第 5 款看最高人民法院对刑事案件的一审管辖权》（《当代法学》2014 年第 1 期）。在这一方面最重要的成果是对该公约中文本问题的研究：《〈公民及政治权利国际公约〉的两份中文本：问题、比较和出路》（《环球法律评论》2007 年第 6 期）；"International Covenant on Civil and Political Rights: One Covenant, Two Chinese Texts?" (*Nordic Journal of International Law*, Vol. 75, Issue 2, 2006)；针对境外学者就这一问题的恶意揣测，则以 "The Problems of the Chinese Texts of the International Human Rights Covenants: A Revisit" (*Chinese Journal of International Law*, Vol. 15, No. 4, 2016)、《国际人权公约中文本问题之再探讨：兼与司马晋、黄旭东商榷》（《台湾人权学刊》2016 年第 3 卷第 4 期）予以回应。

3. 人权教育问题

在国内较早从事有关人权教育特别是大学人权法教学的研究。发表论文《大学法律教育中人权法教学的现状与思考》（《人权》2005 年第 6 期）、"Human Rights Education and Research in China: The Contribution of The Raoul Wallenberg Institute" (Jonas Grimheden and Rolf Ring, eds., *Human Rights Law: From Dissemination to Application-Essays in Honour of Göran Melander*, Martinus Nijhoff, 2006)，与李步云教授共同主编《人权案例选编》（高等教育出版社，2008），主编《中国大学的人权法教学——现状与展望》（科学出版社，2009）。

4. 人权著作翻译

与多位学者合作翻译了《民权公约评注》（三联书店，2003），并与毕小青合作翻译了该书的修订版《〈公民权利和政治权利国际公约〉评注》（三联书店，2008），这两本书是中国人权学界经常引用的资料之一。还曾翻译出版《全球化走向文明：人权和全球经济》（中国政法大学出版社，2013）以及《〈经济社会文化权利国际公约〉：评注、案例和资料》（法律出版社，2019）。

曲相霏

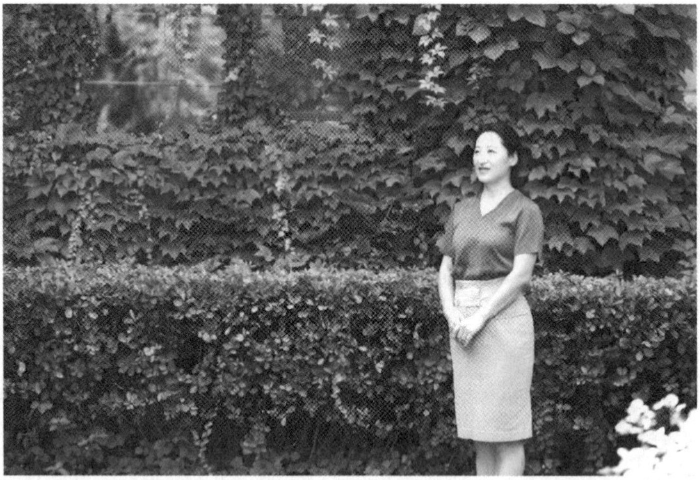

一 基本情况

中国社会科学院国际法研究所研究员，中国社会科学院研究生院法学系教授。

曲相霏研究员在山东大学获得法学学士、法学硕士和法学博士学位，在中国人民大学法学院从事宪法与行政法学博士后研究，曾任山东大学法学院讲师、副教授，加拿大维多利亚大学中加学者交换项目（CCSEP）访问学者，瑞典隆德大学罗尔·瓦伦堡人权与人道法研究所访问学者，曾赴国外高校和相关机构短期访学多次。

曲相霏研究员目前担任《国际法研究》编辑、全国妇联权益部副部长、中国法学会法理学研究会常务理事、北京市法学会教育法学研究会理事等职。

曲相霏研究员的主要研究领域为人权哲学、人权史、人权法，尤为关注人权主体理论和受教育权平等、健康权、残障者权利、城镇化发展与农村土地权利保障以及女性权利保障。曲相霏研究员主张学以致用，在人权研究中以问题为导向，超越单一学科的界限，采用多学科多角度的研究方法，综合运用国际法与国内法的理论和规范，在人权研究中重视底层视角，关注特定群体和特定人权的制度保障。

曲相霏研究员出版个人专著1部，合著4部，独立发表人权领域专业学术论文40余篇，其中在《中国法学》、《法学》、《政法论坛》等权威期刊发表学术论文十几篇，《人权主体界说》、《人权的正当性与良心理论》、《人·公民·世界公民：人权主体的流变与人权的制度性保障》、《残疾人权利公约中的合理便利——考量基准与保障手段》等论文在学界产生了一定的影响。

二　主要学术观点

曲相霏研究员在专著《人权离我们有多远：人权的概念及其在近代中国的发展演变》中综合人权研究的不同领域和视角，分析探讨了一系列人权基本理论问题，在法理和法史两个方面丰富了当前的人权研究，获得了学界的赞誉。曲相霏研究员主张，人权理论需要建立在对人权主体的预设之上，人权主体的转换也意味着人权理论的重建。曲相霏研究员从历史维度考察了自由主义人权主体理论的产生，指出了自由主义人权主体理论以及自由主义人权理论的局限性，考察了自由主义的人权文本中人权主体的真实范围，认为自由主义人权理论应该在社群主义和后现代主义的批评中反思和发展，尤其应当重视人的多样性，把人权理论建立在真实的具体的人之上。

曲相霏研究员主张，普遍性是人权的内在逻辑，也是人权的正当性所在。人权的普遍性首先是人权主体的普遍性。由于人权的内容决定于人权的主体，因而人权的普遍性不仅要求人权主体形式上的普遍性，更要求人权理论揭示存在殊异的人权主体各自的独特性，承认并尊重存在差异的人权主体对人权的特殊和特定要求。能与普遍的、多样的和具体的人相契合的人权才能真实保障每一个人的尊严，才称得上是普遍人权。

曲相霏研究员以人权主体与人权内容之间的相关性理论为前提，支持了20世纪以来人权内容的扩展，试图建构以人的尊严为核心的人权体系。她还对人权的来源问题和人权文化进行了思考，认为人权的正当性作为一个价值判断没有真假之分，人权反映了价值判断的情感属性，是以人们的心理反应和感情体验为元基础建立起来的道德观念的产物。曲相霏承认人权与文化之间有着密切的关系，认为文化相对主义是普遍人权理念面临的一大挑战，但尊重文化的特殊性并不意味着承认人权的文化相对性，在人权问题上有着价值上无法中立之处。她提倡“自省的人权普遍主义”，即在人权普遍主义的基础上充分考虑不同文化、不同传统、不同价值观。

曲相霏研究员还考察分析了近代中国人权概念的产生和演变。“人权”语词自19世纪末20世纪初传入中国后，就有着不同于西方人权概念的显著特征。在100多年的时间里，中国曾发生过多次人权运动，人权语词也几经沉浮。随着人权理论的发展和社会的变迁，中国的人权概念在人权主体、内容、价值等方面都历经演变，至今仍在发展之中。曲相霏研究员考察了“人权”汉字语词的形成，分析了人权语词如何传入中国，研究了中国“人权”概念的最初含义和主要内容，并分阶段考察了各个时期“人权”概念的发展，包括新文化运动时期的“人权”概念、20世纪30年代“人权运动”中的“人权”概念、抗战时期“人权运动”中的“人权”概念、民权保障同盟和民盟的“人权”概念、中华人民共和国成立前中国共产党的“人权”概念等，论述了在这些不同的时间段中国“人权”概念的内涵变异，以及中国人权概念与人权保障实践的关联。

三 主要研究成果

曲相霏研究员在具体人权领域的研究还取得了下面一些主要成果。

1. 受教育权平等研究

曲相霏研究员发表了《受教育权初探》（《政法论坛》2002年第3期）、《析受教育权平等》[《山东大学学报》（哲学社会科学版）2003年第5期] 等文章，从法理角度系统分析了受教育权的权利形态、内容和受教育权平等的内涵、要求。发表《部属高校的“人为地方化”与受教育权平等》（《法学》2009年第11期）、《中央需强化公民受教育权的平等保护》（《南方都市报》2013年5月10日）等文章，参编《大学招生与宪法平等》（译林出版社，2010），对中国普通高等学校招生考试中的机会平等进行了系统细致的分析，提出了保障受教育权平等的具体对策建议。

2. 健康权研究

《国际法事例中的健康权保障》（《学习与探索》2008 年第 2 期）和《外国宪法事例中的健康权保障》（《求是学刊》2009 年第 4 期，人大复印报刊资料《宪法学、行政法学》2009 年第 11 期全文转载）是中国较早以健康权为研究对象的学术文章。健康权研究的成果还包括《公民有自助透析的自由》（《太平洋学报》2009 年第 8 期）、《气候变化背景下的健康权保障》（《人权》2016 年第 6 期）等。

3. 残障权利研究

这方面的研究成果有《保障精神和智力障碍人的生命与尊严》（《河南省政法管理干部学院学报》2010 年第 2 期）、《〈残疾人权利公约〉与残疾人权利保障》（《法学》2013 年第 8 期）、《〈残疾人权利公约〉与我国残疾模式的转换》（《学习与探索》2013 年第 11 期，人大复印报刊资料《国际法学》2014 年第 4 期全文转载）等。

4. 合理便利研究

合理便利是国际人权法中的一个新概念，是反歧视的一个新手段。《残疾人权利公约中的合理便利——考量基准与保障手段》（《政法论坛》2016 年第 2 期）一文对合理便利的要素、特征、考量基准、保障手段、正当性等问题作了综合分析，是国内较早系统研究合理便利的学术文章之一。关于合理便利的文章还包括《“合理便利”概念的起源和发展》（《人权》2015 年第 6 期）、《〈残疾人权利公约〉的“合理便利”理念在我国教育领域的运用》（《人权》2017 年第 3 期）、《“合理便利”的特点及其在我国就业领域的适用》（《人权》2018 年第 2 期）等，对合理便利从理论到实践进行了考察分析。

5. 城镇化建设与农村土地权利保障

农村土地问题是中国一个重大的理论与现实问题，曲相霏研究员对此问题作了持续的思考，发表了《完善农村集体土地征收程序的思考》（《学习与探索》2012 年第 6 期）、《消除农民土地开发权宪法障碍的路径选择》（《法学》2012 年第 6 期，人大复印报刊资料《宪法学、行政法学》2012 年第 10 期全文转载）等论文，合著《城市化进程中农民权利保障》（中国民主法制出版社，2012，撰稿6万字），发表《一刀切的村居改造运动和城市化建设必须停止》（《中国经济时报》2011年2月28日）、《被“城镇化”的民主困局》（《长城月报》2011年6月刊）等评论文章。

刘小妹

一 基本情况

1977年生，湖北省洪湖市人，法学博士。1995年9月至1999年7月就读于中南财经政法大学经济法系，获法学学士学位；1999年8月至2001年8月任职于中山大学附属中学，先后获评初级教师、二级教师；2001年9月至2007年7月，就读于中国政法大学法学院，获法学硕士、博士学位；2007年8月至2009年12月进入中国社会科学院法学研究所博士后流动站；2009年12月至今任职于中国社会科学院国际法研究所。

现为中国社会科学院国际法研究所研究员，中国社会科学院研究生院教授、硕士生导师，中国社会科学院大学长聘教授，中国社会科学院图书馆法学分馆副馆长。兼任中国宪法学研究会副秘书长、北京市法学会立法学研究会副秘书长、宁夏社会科学院特聘研究员、全国妇联专家库专家、北京市“七五”普法讲师团成员、山西省“七五”普法讲师团成员等社会职务。专业方向为宪法学、立法学和行政法学，重点研究领域为人民代表大会制度、立法制度、首都制度、基层治理、人权理论。在教学方面主要讲授宪法学，于 2014 年、2015 年、2018 年 3 次荣获法学系“十佳教师”称号；指导硕士研究生 7 名，4 名已毕业。

二 主要科研活动和科研成果

入职国际法研究所近 10 年来，既致力于宪法学和法治建设的理论基础和中国特质研究，积极跟进监察体制改革、国家机构改革、立法体制机制建设、首都法治建设、基层法治建设等重点领域，出版专著 4 部，发表学术论文 20 余篇；又关注中国法治建设的现实问题，积极组织、参与国家级、省部级课题和各单位委托项目的研究工作，深入法治实践领域开展调研，撰写研究报告和内部报告 30 余篇。

（一）主持和参与大量课题研究

1. 主持国家社科基金课题 2 项：“社区公民参与机制及其法治保障研究”（2010 年）和“改革开放四十年百县调研通州项目”（2018 年），其中 2018 年课题被评定为优秀，研究报告《高水平建设城市副中心》收入《改革开放与中国县域发展（上）》（社会科学文献出版社，2018）。

2. 主持其他课题 10 项：深圳市行政审判中心智慧法院建设研究，深圳市盐田法院委托课题，2019 年；北京市信访法治化指数研究，北京市信访办委托课题，2018 年；《公共机构节能条例》立法后评估项目，司法部、国管局共同委托，2018 年；首都功能定位和功能实现的立法保障研究，中国社会科学院国家治理智库课题，2018 年；保障首都功能实现的立法研究，北京市法学会课题，2017 年；换届选举中的法律问题研究，四川省什邡市委托课题，2016 年；京津冀协同发展背景下首都立法问题研究，北京市法学会课题，2016 年；基层民主自治中的法治保障，北京市法学会课题，2015 年；首都核心功能实现的法治保障研究，北京市政府法制办委托课题，2014 年；城市社区公民参与的法治保障研究，中国社会科学院青年科研启动基金项目，2010 年。

3. 参与课题研究 20 余项。其中，担任国家社科基金重大（点）课题子课题负责人 2 项：“党的领导、人民当家做主与依法治国有机统一”（2007 年）和“民间规范与地方立法”（2017 年）。担任中国社会科学院国情调研和重点课题子项目负责人 3 项：“地方法治研究”（2017 年）、“依法治国与国家治理现代化”（2017 年）和“法治国家、法治政府、法治社会三个一体建设研究”（2018 年）。

（二）积极关注法治建设的现实问题和热点问题，及时开展应用对策研究

撰写内部报告近 20 篇，荣获中国社会科学院优秀对策一等奖 1 篇（2016 年），三等奖 3 篇（2016 年和 2017 年）；在《人民日报》发表理论文章 2 篇，其中《法治强国的中国道路》一文获中宣部优秀理论文章奖；撰写研究报告 10 余篇，其中《增强民政指标体系科学性推进国家治理能力现代化》（2015 年）获民政部全国民政政策理论研究三等奖。

（三）注重基础理论研究

出版专著 4 部，合著 2 部，发表论文 20 余篇，研究报告 10 余篇。代表作有《京津冀协同发展背景下首都立法问题研究》、《基层自治的法治之维》、《省级地方立法研究报告——地方立法双重功能的实现》、《人大制度下的国家监督体制与监察机制》、《以新时代人权发展事业推动构建人类命运共同体》等。

三 主要研究领域和学术观点

1. 持续关注立法制度和立法实践，分别从国家立法体制机制、省级立法实践、专项立法和基层法治建设的立法保障等宏观、中观、微观层面开展理论和实证研究。《立法改革与法律体系构建》一文和每年在《法治蓝皮书》发布的年度立法报告总结了改革开放 40 年来，特别是近年来的立法成就、经验和不足。专著《省级地方立法研究报告》基于对 5637 件省级地方性法规的大数据分析，呈现省级地方立法的总体规律和特点，阐述并分析在“统一、分层次”的立法制度中，省级地方立法所具有的实施国家法律和创制地方法规的双重功能及其实现机制。专著《基层自治的法治之维》对基层民主、基层自治领域的法律制度进行了梳理和研究，认为现行宪法、地方组织法、村居委员会组织法构建的城乡二元选举格局，使得基层选举对国家民主政治建设的“溢出效益”非常有限，而基层参与、基层自治则有更大的作用空间，因此加强这方面的国家法和民间法研究和建设尤为重要。首都法是新兴的研究领域，从 2014 年接受北京市政府法制办委托至今，主持了4个与首都法相关的课题，出版了智库报告《京津冀协同发展背景下首都立法问题研究》，并在《北京市法学会的年度课题研究报告丛书》（2017年）、《博士后论丛》（2017年）、《改革开放与中国县域发展（上）》（2018年）和《北外法学》（2019年第1期）上发表了2篇研究报告和2篇论文，这些研究提出了关于首都和首都功能的内涵界定，提出了与之相应的权责关系和法律制度构建。此外，还对党内法规立法、地方环境立法、核心价值观入法等专题进行了研究，撰写了多篇内部报告，有的被采用和批示。

2. 人大制度和代表理论研究。为给研究生讲授“人大制度与选举制度”专题课，对代表理论和人大制度史资料进行了细致研读，形成了一些阶段性成果。结合监察体制改革，撰写了《人大制度下的国家监督体制与监察机制》一文，从人大制度和代表理论的视角，对监督国家机关和监督国家机关工作人员的“二元”监督体制进行了阐释和剖析，提出人大对监察委员会的监督不宜采用报告工作的方式，而应由监察委员会向同级人大常委会作专项工作报告，同时采取多种监督机制充实和革新人大对监察委员会的监督方式。

四　代表作简介

1.《基层自治的法治之维》

民主不仅仅是一种价值观念，更重要的还是一种政治实践。只有通过民主政治的实践，才能了解中国社会可能发展出什么样的民主政治，以及如何进一步改进已有的民主政治实践。该书回顾历史，观照现实，分析理论，提出了四个方面的创见。（1）在民主政治建设的“上”“下”双重路径、基层自治的“上”“下”双向推动、选举民主和参与民主的共同发展、村民自治与居民自治的二元格局下，分析城乡基层自治对民主的“溢出效应”及其作用方式和范围。（2）将社区参与视为参与民主实验的、训练的场域，实证考察和分析了社区参与的政治效能感。（3）超越单纯的“法治保障”的局限，解析了基层自治制度的多重法治维度，即基层自治既需要国家法治建设的有力保障，又直接参与和促进着国家的法治建设；既是法治社会建设最重要的场域，又为法治国家、法治政府建设提供坚实基础和发展要素；既受国家法律制度的硬规制，又有村规民约等民间社会规范的软约束。（4）详细梳理了基层自治的现行法律和政策依据，提出了健全和完善基层自治的法律体系的设想和具体建议。本书扩展并丰富了关于基层民主和社会治理创新的研究视域和研究成果。

2.《人大制度下的国家监督体制与监察机制》

该文认为，在人民代表大会制度及民主集中制的国家机构组织活动原则下，监督权承载了“以权力制约权力”的重要现代治理功能。监察体制改革通过整合监察权重构国家监督体制和宪法权力结构，形成了人民代表大会制度下的监督国家机关和监督国家机关工作人员的“二元”监督体制。“二元”监督体制中监督机关与监督人员既相互衔接配合，又彼此交叠牵制。“二元”监督体制和兼职代表制下，人大对监察委员会的监督不宜采用报告工作的方式，而应由监察委员会向同级人大常委会作专项工作报告，同时采取多种监督机制充实和革新人大对监察委员会的监督方式。本文从代表理论和民主集中制原则的视角对“二元”监督体制的构建、对人大及其常委会监督监察委员会的合理方式进行了有创见的分析，这些观点和分析方法对于健全和完善国家监察制度和人民代表大会制度具有重要的理论意义和参考价值。

3.《以新时代人权发展事业推动构建人类命运共同体》

2017年以来，“构建人类命运共同体”的理念、思想相继写入中国共产党的十九大报告、党章和中国宪法序言，以及联合国大会、安理会和人权理事会决议，既确立了中国的大国外交战略，又彰显了中国对全球治理的巨大贡献。“构建人类命运共同体”的概念、内涵和思想是党的十八大以来逐步提出并形成的，但是构建超越民族国家的共同价值观和世界性秩序的思想资源和国际合作实践却源远流长。该文的创见在于：一方面，溯源中国古代儒家“大同社会”、古希腊城邦共同体思想、欧洲的空想社会主义理论、康德的“世界主义”理论、马克思恩格斯《共产党宣言》中的自由人联合体思想及其他古今中外从人类角度出发构建共同体的思想资源，回顾了二战后建立的联合国及区域性人权机构、人权保护体系在保护基本人权和维护世界和平、构建战后世界秩序中的有效实践及其局限性；另一方面，提出“构建人类命运共同体”也是以共同创造人类的美好未来为根本目标，以保障人权的充分实现为价值基础和具体路径的。具体是指，以生存权、发展权和追求幸福权为首要人权，通过在人权领域促进合作共赢，推进新时代人权发展事业，推动构建一个更加可实现的、更加公平正义的世界新秩序。

五　主要学术成果目录

（一）著作

1.《信访学概论》（参著），中国民主法制出版社，2012。

2.《领导干部法治读本》（参著），党建读物出版社，2016。

3.《省级地方立法研究报告——地方立法双重功能的实现》（独著），中国社会科学出版社，2016。

4.《“总体法治宣传教育观”的理论与实践》（参著），中国社会科学出版社，2016。

5.《京津冀协同发展背景下首都立法问题研究》（独著），中国社会科学出版社，2017。

6.《基层自治的法治之维》（独著），中国社会科学出版社，2018。

（二）论文、文章类

1.《公民参与行政立法的理论思考》，《行政法学研究》2007 年第 2 期。

2.《法律、法规与宪法的冲突研究》（第二作者），载《案例宪法研究》（第 1 辑），群众出版社，2008。

3.《人权保障立法中的重大理论与现实问题研究》，《学术动态》2008 年第 25 期。

4.《儒家视野下的群己关系》，《博士后交流》2009 年第 1 期。

5.《“基本法律”制度背后宪法价值的困境》（第二作者），载《中国宪法年刊》（2008），法律出版社，2009。

6.《新闻自由的权利属性》，载《宪法研究》（第 10 卷），四川大学出版社，2009。

7.《社区公民参与立法的途径和程序》，载《立法过程中的公共参与》，中国社会科学出版社，2009。

8.《宪法的修辞：变迁着的公民身份及其表述方式》，《吉首大学学报》（社会科学版）2009 年第 5 期。

9.《浅析城市社区公民参与立法的途径》，《法学杂志》2009 年第 10 期。

10.《城市社区公民参与的法治化路径》，载《宪法研究》（第11卷），黑龙江大学出版社，2010。

11.《论“以人为本”与突发事件应对》（第二作者），《法制与经济》2010年第2期。

12.《中英代议机关的立法权比较——从民主与法治的视角考察》，载《法治新视界：比较法的分析》，社会科学文献出版社，2011。

13.《中国近代权利观的形成和演变》，载《中国民主评论》（第2卷），中国社会科学出版社，2013。

14.《浅析城市社区治理中的“群众参与”理论》，载《依法治国与推进国家治理现代化》（第五届博士后论丛），中国社会科学出版社，2014。

15.《城市社区参与机制之省思》，《黑龙江省政法管理干部学院学报》2014年第5期。

16.《外国专家学者眼中的四中全会》，《光明日报》2014年11月10日。

17.《中国人权司法保障制度的特点与举措》，《法律适用》2014年第11期。

18.《维护国家安全应充分尊重和保障人权》，《光明日报》2015年7月18日。

19.《法治强国的中国道路》（第二作者），《人民日报》2015年10月26日。

20.《〈国家安全法〉充分体现人权保障原则》，《人民法治》2016年第8期。

21.《习近平法治道路思想探析》，《法学杂志》2016年第5期。

22.《我国“互联网+党建”新模式成绩斐然》（第二作者），《人民论坛》2017年第1期。

23.《更加自觉自信地走中国道路》，《人民日报》2017年8月27日。

24.《体现科学立法、民主立法、依法立法要求》，《中国纪检监察报》2018年3月17日。

25.《中国共产党领导是中国特色社会主义最本质的特征》，《中国纪检监察报》2018年3月21日。

26.《为中华民族伟大复兴提供有力宪法保障》，《中国纪检监察报》

2018 年 3 月 28 日。

27.《简述国外首都与首都圈立法》，载《开创法治中国建设新局面》（第六届博士后论丛），中国社会科学出版社，2018。

28.《立法改革与法律体系构建》，载《中国法治（1978—2018）》，社会科学文献出版社，2018。

29.《寻求网络民情与司法审判的良性互动》（第二作者），《人民论坛》2018 年第 7 期。

30.《以新时代人权发展事业推动构建人类命运共同体》，《国际法研究》2018 年第 3 期。

31.《人大制度下的国家监督体制与监察机制》，《政法论坛》2018 年第 3 期。

32.《北京城市副中心的功能定位及其立法保障研究》，《北外法学》2019 年第 1 期。

33.《机构改革与组织法律体系的革新》，《西北大学学报》（哲学社会科学版）2019 年第 3 期。

（三）研究报告

1.《广东省人大代表制度创新》，载《广东经验：法治促进改革开放》，社会科学文献出版社，2012。

2.《政府立法与规范性文件监管》，载《广东经验：法治政府建设》，社会科学文献出版社，2014。

3.《2013 年的中国立法》，载《中国法治发展报告（2013）》，社会科学文献出版社，2014。

4.《十六大党章丰富纪律检查工作的内涵》，载《党章中的纪律》，中国方正出版社，2015。

5.《加强和改进人大立法、提高立法质量》，载《法治中国的地方经验：广东样本》，社会科学文献出版社，2015。

6.《2014 年的中国立法》，载《中国法治发展报告（2014）》，社会科学文献出版社，2015。

7.《2016 年的中国立法》，载《中国法治发展报告（2016）》，社会科学文献出版社，2017。

8.《2017 年的中国立法》，载《中国法治发展报告（2017）》，社会科学文献出版社，2018。

9.《高水平建设城市副中心》，载《改革开放与中国县域发展（上）》，社会科学文献出版社，2018。

10.《2018 年的中国立法》，载《中国法治发展报告（2018）》，社会科学文献出版社，2019。

戴瑞君

一　基本情况

1980 年生，内蒙古五原县人，现为中国社会科学院国际法研究所副研究员，中国社会科学院研究生院副教授、硕士研究生导师。

戴瑞君副研究员 2003 年毕业于北京交通大学法律系，获法学学士学位；研究生就读于中国社会科学院研究生院法学系国际法专业，先后于 2006 年、2009 年获法学硕士、法学博士学位。曾在美国哥伦比亚大学法学院、芬兰赫尔辛基大学法学院和英国牛津大学法律系长期访学。戴瑞君副研究员于 2006 年进入中国社会科学院国际法研究中心国际公法研究室工作，2009 年调入国际人权法研究室，历任研究实习员、助理研究员、副研究员。2015 年受聘为中国社会科学院研究生院硕士生指导老师，招收国际公法、国际人权法方向硕士研究生。

戴瑞君副研究员目前担任香港基本法澳门基本法研究会理事、中国社会科学院法学研究所性别与法律研究中心秘书长，入选北京市法学会北京市“百名法学英才”，受聘北京市“十三五”时期妇女儿童发展研究专家。

戴瑞君副研究员的主要研究领域为国际公法和国际人权法，重点研究的问题有国际法与国内法的关系、条约法、国际人权法基本理论与实施机制、性别平等与妇女人权、特别行政区对外事务权等。主持国家社科基金项目“国际条约在中国法律体系中的地位分析与制度设计研究”、中国社会科学院重点项目“国际人权条约的国内适用研究”、全国人大常委会港澳基本法项目“特别行政区对外事务权研究”等。出版学术专著1部（《国际人权条约的国内适用研究：全球视野》），合著著作1部（《人权法学的新发展》），参著著作、教材多部，在《法学研究》、《法学》、《环球法律评论》、《国际法研究》、《法学杂志》、《人权》等杂志发表学术论文、文章近30篇，译著、译文若干。

戴瑞君副研究员曾赴多国进行学术交流，先后向第七、第九、第十届世界宪法大会，第六届亚洲国际法学会双年会等国际学术会议提交论文。多次就国内立法、中国履行联合国人权条约的国家报告等事项发表咨询意见和建议；发表内部研究报告10余篇，曾获中国社会科学院优秀对策研究奖二等奖一项、三等奖两项。

二　主要学术成果

1. 国际人权法的实施机制

《论联合国人权条约监督机制的改革》（《法学杂志》2009年第3期）、《主权、人权与中国——以联合国人权保护机制及其改革为视角》（《国际法研究》第7卷，社会科学文献出版社，2012）、《联合国人权条约机构体系的加强进程——联合国人权保护机制的最新发展》（《环球法律评论》2013年第6期）、《联合国人权审议机制的后续跟踪程序研究》（《国际法学论丛》第9卷，中国方正出版社，2014）等系列论文跟踪研究了联合国保护人权的宪章机制和条约机制的改革进程及成效，指出国际人权机构不断增强效力的动机与其资源短缺、工作积压之间的矛盾，提出国际人权实施机制走出困境的根本有赖于各国完善国内人权保障制度，在国内做好人权保障与救济工作。

2. 国际法与国内法的关系

《认真对待国际法——基于对亚洲各国宪法文本的考察》（《国际法研究》2016 年第 4 期）呈现了亚洲各国宪法处理国际法与国内法关系的共性和趋势：大多数国家明确承诺遵守国际法，同时赋予国际法尤其是国际人权法以优先效力，国际法日益得到重视和善待。《国际人权条约的国内适用研究：全球视野》（社会科学文献出版社，2013）以国际人权条约的国内适用为切入点，证成接受国际人权标准与国家对人权的宪法、立法、司法和行政保障之间的互动关系。《论基本权利制度变迁之国际人权法动因》（《广东社会科学》2015 年第 3 期）则聚焦宪法基本权利制度的变迁，通过实例证明国际人权法在这一变迁过程中的实际影响力。

3. 特别行政区对外事务权

特别行政区对外事务权的核心是缔结和适用国际条约。《国际条约在特别行政区的缔结和适用问题研究》（《香港基本法澳门基本法论丛》2013 年第 2 辑，中国民主法制出版社，2013）围绕近十个理论和实践问题，从缔约程序、权责关系、适用范围、适用方式、法律地位等角度进行研讨，提出对策建议。针对实践中其他国家对特区对外事务权的误解，《中国缔结的双边条约在特别行政区的适用问题——兼评“世能诉老挝案”上诉判决》（《环球法律评论》2017 年第 5 期）一文进行了澄清，同时也提出中国有必要尽快解决国际条约适用于特区的制度安排对第三方的效力问题。

4. 性别平等与妇女人权

这方面的研究成果有“Promoting Domestic Implementation of CEDAW in China”（载莫纪宏主编《世界宪法研究》第 1 辑，中国环球文化出版社，2007）；《妇女社会权利的国际监督机制》（载李西霞主编《妇女社会权利的保护：国际法与国内法视角》，社会科学文献出版社，2013）；《谁为妇女的家务劳动买单——国际人权法的视角》（载李林等主编《人权保障与法治建设：中国与芬兰的比较》，社会科学文献出版社，2014）。此外，译著《联合国〈消除对妇女一切形式歧视公约〉评注》即将由社会科学文献出版社出版。

钟瑞华

一　基本情况

1975年生，江苏沛县人，中国社会科学院国际法研究所国际人权法研究室助理研究员，主要研究领域为法宗教学、宗教自由和消费者法。1997年、2000年获中国政法大学法学学士、法学硕士学位，2005年于中国社会科学院研究生院获法学博士学位。曾在美国埃默里大学法学院、加州大学圣芭芭拉分校长期访学。

二　主要科研成果

（一）论著（文）

1.《中国“三包”制度总检讨》，载《清华法学》第6辑，清华大学出版社，2005（《中国社会科学文摘》2005年第4期摘发）。

2.《美国消费者集体诉讼初探》，载《环球法律评论》2005年第3期（人大复印报刊资料《诉讼法学、司法制度》2005年第10期全文转载）。

3.《从绝对权利到风险管理——美国的德莱尼条款之争及其启示》，《中外法学》2009年第4期。

4.《哈罗德·J. 伯尔曼：美国当代法律宗教学之父》，《比较法研究》

2017 年第 5 期。

5.《消费者权益及其保护新论》，中国社会科学出版社，2018。

（二）译著（文）

1.《消费者权利是人权吗?》（Sinai Deutch 著），载《公法研究》第 3 卷，商务印书馆，2006。

2.《规制是如何失灵的?》（Cass R. Sunstein 著），载《规制研究》第 1 辑，格致出版社、上海人民出版社，2008。

3.《权利革命之后：重塑规制国》（Cass R. Sunstein 著），中国人民大学出版社，2008。

4.《宪法的起源与演变》（与他人合译自德文版，Dieter Grimm 著），载《现代宪法的诞生、运作和前景》，法律出版社，2010。

5.《西方法律和宗教传统中的非婚生子女》（John Witte 著），人民出版社，2011。

6.《法律与新教：路德改革的法律教导》（John Witte 著），中国法制出版社，2013。

7.《从圣礼到契约：西方传统中的婚姻、宗教与法律》（John Witte 著），中国法制出版社，2014。

8.《西方传统中法宗教学的兴起》（John Witte 著），《华东政法大学学报》2015 年第 1 期。

三　代表作简介

1.《从绝对权利到风险管理——美国的德莱尼条款之争及其启示》

美国《食品、药品和化妆品法》中的德莱尼条款，绝对禁止任何致癌的添加剂而不论其实际风险大小，这种严苛的立场不仅没有取得预期的效果，反而产生诸多弊端，最终导致其被部分废除。该文在绝对权利和风险管理的理论框架内梳理了围绕德莱尼条款的种种争议，指出德莱尼条款之争的启示在于：食品安全的绝对权利观既不可取亦不可行，在当下的风险社会中，应当从风险管理的视角进行食品安全规制，有限度地容忍食品供应中存在的可忽略风险。论文发表后被广泛引用，对引导政府及民众以科学理性的态度对待食品安全问题发挥了一定作用。

2.《哈罗德·J. 伯尔曼：美国当代法律宗教学之父》

美国著名法学家哈罗德·J. 伯尔曼因在法律与宗教跨学科研究领域的开拓性贡献而被誉为“法律宗教学之父”，其代表作《法律与宗教》、《法律与革命》等均属该领域的奠基性作品，对于世俗化法学研究范式的返魅、法律宗教学学术标准的设定、法律宗教学学科地位的最终确立发挥了关键性作用。伯尔曼及其著述，是研究美国乃至西方当代法律宗教学的起点。该文发表后引起了部分学界同行的关注，获得较好的评价，推动了对美国当代法律宗教学这一新兴学术领域的研究。

3.《消费者权益及其保护新论》

该书以消费者权益的概念性分析为基点，对消费者权益保护的法律路径进行了体系化研究。首先，探讨了有关消费者法保护对象的各种问题，重点梳理了消费者权利概念的产生和发展，分析了消费者权利的性质、特征和类型，并厘清了消费者利益的范围和特征。其次，论述了消费者权益的私法保护和公法保护模式，指出消费者权益的保护必须“双轨”，其中私法保护部分重点探讨了消费者接近正义制度，公法保护部分聚焦于消费者保护规制的相关问题。最后，选取中国消费者权益保护实践中的若干具体制度事例，对书中提出的一些基本观点予以印证和运用。

论人权的非道德性

莫纪宏[*]

最近二十几年，我国学界对人权的基本理论进行了深入和系统的研究，其中，对于人权的正当性和价值基础的研究，可以说是比较有特色的。大多数论著在区分人权与法律权利的同时，指出了人权的道德性，也就是说，人权是一种道德意义上的权利，人权具有道德性。但在研究人权的道德性时，对于人权的道德基础的“可靠性”和“确定性”的表述，却很少有深入论述和探讨。因此，对于人权正当性和价值基础的研究，目前仍然处于比较粗浅的状态。本文从人权的非道德性的角度入手，试图打破以往学界论述人权性质的常规视角，通过论证人权所具有的非道德性，来为人权的价值基础提供一种新的解释方法。

一 关于人权的道德性的几种观念及评析

所谓人权的道德性，是指人权具有道德意义。在某种角度上，可以将人权的道德性简化为“道德意义上的人权”或者是“道德人权”。刘升平、郭道晖教授在合著的《人权的几个基本理论问题》中，对人权作为道德意义上的权利的含义表述得非常清晰。他们认为，“人权首先是一种道德意义上的权利，它所依据的，从根本上讲，是‘把人当人看待’的道德原则，而不是国家的法律。在现代社会，任何法律都要规定国民的权利和义务，但不是任何法律都尊重人权。在当今世界，国家的法律只有尊重人

---

* 莫纪宏，中国社会科学院国际法研究所研究员。

权、体现人权、维护人权，才能在道德上被认为是合法的，并因此享有权利和尊严。违反这样的法律，既要受到法律的制裁，也要受到道德的谴责。如果一个国家的法律敢于践踏人权，那么就会出现这样的情形：法律上合法的行为在道德上非法，法律上非法的行为在道德上合法，这样便会导致社会秩序的混乱。长期以来，有不少人看不到人权作为一种道德权利所具有的起始性、权威性，仿佛人权是可以由国家法律任意表现、可以由法定权利完全取代的，例如，将人权等同于公民权，或将公民权等同于人权。这种认识，在理论和实践上都造成了一定的危害”。[①] 很显然，上述观点中存在着三个基本价值判断：一是人权是一种道德意义上的权利；二是道德意义上的人权与法律规定的权利不能完全等同起来；三是人权与法定权利之间存在价值冲突，人权不一定合法，合法的权利也不一定符合人权的要求。就上述三个基本价值判断来看，将人权与法定权利的价值属性分开，这在逻辑上比较清晰，在制度上也能够找到实例。但是，断言人权是道德意义上的权利这样的命题必须经过符合学术规范要求的证明，而人权不一定合法，合法的权利不一定符合人权的要求，则在逻辑上会导致人权与法律价值目标之间的冲突。逻辑上可能存在的问题是：为什么合法的权利不一定符合人权的要求？为什么不能将符合人权的要求直接写入法律？为什么立法者要故意设计人权与法律之间价值冲突的制度机制？很明显，这样的问题对于上述观点所提出的学术挑战都是致命的。至少可以发现上述三个关于人权的基本价值判断带有作者自身强烈的“主观性”和“任意性”。

关于人权道德性的另外一种表述思路最有代表性的是李步云教授提出的人权的三种形态论。李步云教授认为：人性的第二个基本要素是德性，其主要内容有平等、博爱、正义。人是一种有伦理道德及其无限追求的高级动物，这是人区别于一般动物的一个根本点。人生性就有“仁爱心”、“同情心”、“怜悯心”、“恻隐心”，并在人与人之间相互依存、相互影响的关系和交往中逐渐养成平等、博爱、正义等为核心的一套伦理道德观念。当我们说人权的本来含义是一种“应有权利”时，它就已经包含有道德的意蕴。当我们依人道主义原则救助弱势群体、依现代民主理念既要服

① 参见刘升平、夏勇主编《人权与世界》，人民法院出版社，1996，第2页。

从多数又要保护少数时，人权的伦理性也是显而易见的。他还对人权的三种形态的内涵作了非常精辟的论述：“学界有许多种对于人权的分类方法，例如将人权分为国际人权与国内人权、个人人权与集体人权、基本人权与非基本人权等等。我们认为无论哪种分类方式都不可能脱离人权的三种形态，即应有人权、法定人权和实有人权。应有人权，是指人之为人依据其社会属性和自然属性所应当享有的权利。应有人权是对人之为人的一种肯定，它向人们昭示人之为人的根本内涵。法定人权，是指通过宪法和法律的规定将应有人权确定化、具体化，将抽象的权利变为相对具体的权利。法定人权一方面向人们昭示着人权的具体内容，一方面又为受侵害的人权提供保障的途径。但不同的国家甚至某一国家在不同的历史时期，对法定人权的规定都不一样，所以法定人权的范围很难确定。在民主法治社会里，法定权利是最为可靠的人权，是最能得到实现的人权。实有人权，是指在应有人权的范围之内，公民所实际能够享有的各种权利，它不仅仅限于法律的规定，因为法律规定的权利在有些时候公民并不能真正地享有，而法律没有规定的权利，公民并不一定不能享有，因为我们这个社会并不仅仅只有法律这样一种调整社会关系的准则，社会进步组织的章程、风俗习惯、乡规民约以及道德乃至宗教，同样可以使人享有某些权利。”① 李步云教授的上述论述，首先肯定了人权作为一种道德权利的特性，并且以“应有人权”来表述人权的“道德性”或者是道德意义上的人权。其次，李步云教授上述观点明显不同于刘升平、郭道晖的地方是，李步云教授并没有将作为道德意义上的人权与法定权利的价值关系对立起来，而是通过将道德权利、法定权利和实有权利统一为人权存在的三种形态，将法定权利视为人权的一部分，并且在道德权利与法定权利之间作了两者相互一致的价值关系表述，即“应有人权”必须通过“法定人权”加以制度化和具体化，法定人权是道德意义上的人权的制度表现形式，两者之间不存在价值冲突。不仅如此，李步云教授还认为，道德人权既可以表现为“法定人权”，也可以通过其他途径来实现，因此，“应有人权”并不完全需要“法定人权”来加以实现，由此，法定人权在实现应有人权方面只是起到了主

① 李步云：《人权与宪法精神》，中国人权网，http://www.humanrights.cn/html/2014/3_0606/156.html，最后访问日期：2019 年 4 月 18 日。

要的作用，而不是履行了保障道德人权全部实现的功能。就李步云教授的人权的三种形态理论来说，它在逻辑上也有不可克服的内在矛盾。主要有以下两个问题需要进一步加以论证：一是为什么“应有人权”不能完全“法定人权”化，人权进入法律通过法律途径来加以保障需要什么条件；二是为什么“应有人权”不可能完全地“实际享有”，不能实际享有的人权为什么说是“应有人权”，其中的“应有”是依据什么价值标准来判断的？很显然，要回答上述两个问题也是很困难的。综观李步云教授提出的人权的三种形态观，其对人权存在的表现形式的表述具有很强的“形式逻辑”上的直观性，无法有效地来分析现实生活中存在的各种人权问题。

当代西方学者关于人权的特性的观点更是众说纷纭、莫衷一是。但有一个特点是很明显的，即绝大多数观点都将人权与道德紧密地联系在一起，承认人权的道德因素或者是认可人权作为一种道德权利，主张人权应当接受道德的评价。著名法理学家沈宗灵先生在总结西方人权学说的基础上，对西方人权学者有关人权概念的解释，特别是有关人权的定义作了近十项归类，主要有以下几种代表性观点：（1）人权是那些属于每个男女的道德权利，它们之所以为每个男女所有，仅仅因为他们是人（英国的麦克法兰）；（2）基于人仅因作为人这一事实而被认为当然具有的权利就是人权（日本的宫泽俊义）；（3）人权是平等地属于所有人的那种普遍的道德权利（美国的温斯顿）；（4）只有作为最低限度道德标准的人权概念才是经得起辩驳的（英国的米尔恩）；等等。①

由此可见，人权是一个与道德问题纠缠在一起的概念。但是，人权到底是在何种意义上与道德联系在一起的，是整个人权价值都属于道德价值体系的一部分，还是人权价值与道德价值密切相关，彼此发生一定的联系？这些问题并没有在人权教科书或论著中得到明确的说明，可以说，是目前人权理论中最为混乱的。人权与道德关系的模糊混乱状况，也直接地影响到人权的实践活动。在人权的国内法实践中，存在着人权的“阶级性”和“人民性”的争议；在人权的国际法实践中，也存在着“人权”与“主权”关系的对立。所以说，正确地认识人权的道德性以及人权与道

① 沈宗灵：《二战后西方人权学说的演变》，载刘升平、夏勇主编《人权与世界》，人民法院出版社，1996，第111—113页。

德的关系，是人权理论得以向前深入发展的逻辑前提，否则，很难断言我们今天的人权理论与以往相比究竟进步了多少。仅以清末立宪时期学界和政界对人权的理解而言，其中关于权利与义务关系的论述，至今也无法在逻辑和制度上加以超越。以笔者阅读的出版于1906年的中国社会科学院图书馆法学分馆藏书《立宪纲要》[①] 的论述为例，其对权利与义务关系的理解以及因此而对人权观念的看法，迄今仍有很好的借鉴意义：

> 立宪国之臣民与未立宪国之臣民何所以异乎？一言以断之，曰立宪国之臣民对于国家享有种种之权利，亦即负有种种之义务而已。不若未立宪之臣民，仅负义务未能享有权利者也。因是二者之分，则立宪政体与专制政体不同之大要，已可略识而。立宪国之臣民与未立宪国之臣民对于国家之关系，亦于是乎大异。夫权利与义务，乃同时并生，一面享权利，即一面负义务。一面负义务即一面享权利。故天下无无权利之义务，亦无无义务之权利。彼立宪国之臣民，其爱国也，既深且挚，而其受国家之保护也，亦极周洽者。岂有异术者？

不难看出，上述关于权利与义务关系的论述，以个人与国家之间的关系为基础，强调了“没有无权利的义务，也没有无义务的权利”这样的权利思想，对于人权的实践和法律保护来说，是非常具有实效的价值主张。恐怕难以用简单的论述来超越。

二 从历史唯物主义看人权的非道德性

既然人权问题深陷道德问题的陷阱，那么，能否跳出人权与道德之间关系的窠臼呢？也就是说，在理论上论证人权与道德无关，或者是人权在本质上不属于道德的范畴，只是可以运用道德来加以评析？笔者曾就“人权与道德权利的同一性”问题当面请教过哈贝马斯先生，[②] 哈贝马斯的回

---

① 《立宪纲要》，光绪丙午（1906年）季秋北洋官报局印。

② 该问题是笔者在2001年4月17日哈贝马斯在中国社会科学院学术报告厅举行的“人权的文化间性”主题演讲会上提出的。

答是："人权在法律和道德之外，是一个具有独立性的价值。"哈贝马斯先生这一答复意味着人权作为道德权利以及法律权利在相关性上欠缺逻辑上的证明。而在此之前，笔者在阅读国内人权学者的著作时，看到的多是人权是一种道德权利的论点。其实，从相关性角度来看，这样的观点是很成问题的。因为人权如果以道德作为自身的逻辑基础，就意味着被称为人权的东西必须接受道德的评价，那么，"好的、善的"人权与"坏的、恶的"人权在逻辑上就是成立的。如果将人权的属性沦落到道德评价的陷阱中，毫无疑问，人权将失去普遍主义的意义。这一点，与"作为人应当享有的"在逻辑上是自相矛盾的。所以，应当排斥人权与道德权利的相关性，至少人权应当独立于道德权利。①

笔者认为，要真正解决人权的性质问题，必须从马克思主义的历史唯物主义出发，将人权放在历史发展的过程中，放在社会关系的结构中来考察，才能解开人权问题上诸多理论困惑。马克思主义认为，权利无论是作为一种要求、一种政治主张，还是作为法定权利，它的产生、实现和发展，都必须以一定社会的经济条件为基础，"权利永远不能超出社会的经济结构以及由经济结构所制约的社会的文化发展"。② 这就是说，人权不是纯粹道德意义上的主观遐想或者一厢情愿，必须具有现实性，而这种现实性，来自社会发展的程度，受制于社会经济基础与上层建筑之间关系的变化。特别是，人权具有历史性，会随着历史的发展而呈现出不同的要求。马克思和恩格斯在《论波兰问题》中雄辩地指出："1791 年的波兰宪法到底宣布了什么呢？充其量也不过是君主立宪罢了，例如宣布立法权归人民代表掌握，宣布出版自由、信仰自由、公开审判、废除农奴制等等。所有这些当时竟被称为彻头彻尾的雅各宾原则！因之，先生们，你们看到了吧，历史已经前进了。当年的雅各宾原则，在现在看来，即使说它是自由主义的话，也变得非常温和的了。"③ 而且人权的实现离不开特定的国家载体，即在现实中的人权，总是依托一定的主权国家来实现，没有空洞的人权承诺的存在。正如马克思在《哥达纲领批判》中指出的那样："既然德国工人党明确地声明，它是在'现代民族国家'内，是在自己的国家即普

① 莫纪宏：《现代宪法的逻辑基础》，法律出版社，2001，第 74 页。

② 《马克思恩格斯选集》第 3 卷，人民出版社，1972，第 12 页。

③ 《马克思恩格斯选集》第 1 卷，人民出版社，1972，第 291 页。

鲁士德意志帝国内进行活动，——否则，它的大部分要求就没有意义了，因为人们只要求他们所没有的东西——那么，它就不应该忘记主要的一点，这就是这一切美丽的东西都建立在承认所谓人民主权的基础上，所以它们只有在民主共和国内才是适宜的。”① 与此同时，人权作为历史的范畴，也是不断发展的。马克思主义认为，应当用发展的观点来看待权利。人权，从作为一种理想和理论提出到发展成为资产阶级革命的旗帜；从作为一种政治口号到发展成为政治实践的结果，即权利的法定化。权利的领域从国内法对权利的肯定发展到国际法和国际社会的共同关心和共同维护；权利的主体从个人人权发展到集体人权；权利的内容从最基本的平等、自由和安全的生存权，扩展到政治、经济、文化、社会、发展、和平等更广泛的范围。人们对权利概念的理解和认识也随之发展和不断深化。另外，权利的实现是一个渐进的过程，它受到政治、经济、文化、社会、传统等各种条件的制约，超越于现实提供的可能条件而提出过高的要求，或者滞后于社会发展的现实要求而拒不发展权利，都不符合马克思主义的权利发展观。因此，“代替那存在着阶级和阶级对立的资产阶级旧社会的，将是这样一个联合体，在那里，每个人的自由发展是一切人的自由发展的条件”。②

从马克思主义的历史唯物主义史观来看待人权与道德的关系，不论一个特定时期、特定社会、特定国家，人们如何去理解人权的性质和内涵，人权作为人与人交往的社会关系的产物和必要条件，本身具有很强的“客观性”，它并不是以谁的主观爱好为转移的。人权是以人的存在和发展的充分必要条件作为自身正当性的基础，不应被主观爱好或者是兴趣选择所左右。在阶级社会中，人权只能存在于国家的法律之中，而无法游离于法律之外。因为在法律之外，不存在公共道德的价值基础。法律之外的道德要求不具有公共性，只能以团体或个体道德的形式存在。所以，从制度意义上看，将道德权利与法律权利明确加以区分是缺少逻辑依据和制度背景的。法律作为最低限度的公共道德，是人权自身客观性的存在方式。如果法律都不肯定某种权利的正当性，那么，在实践中，以人权为理由来提出

① 《马克思恩格斯选集》第3卷，人民出版社，1972，第21页。
② 《马克思恩格斯选集》第1卷，人民出版社，1972，第273页。

某种人格利益的要求并不能为公共道德所认同。因此，“法外无权”基本上可以解决道德权利与法律权利之间价值冲突的问题。也就是说，“应有”的人权必须是“法定”的，“法定”的人权也必须是“实有”的。“应有”的人权不能“法定”，那么，其“应有”的正当性只能依靠个人或者是团体爱好或者是兴趣的支持，不能成为公共道德的价值选择；“法定”的人权如果不能“实有”，则“法定”的人权就是虚假的。当然，“法定”人权的“实有”性与通过“法定”人权获得的实际人格利益是两个不同概念。“实有人权”指获得人权的“可能性”，而基于这种“可能性”能否实现具体的人格利益，则需要其他条件的辅助，与“法定”的条件无关。

由此可见，人权的道德性是从属于法律的道德性。作为公共道德的集中体现，凡是得到法律肯定的人权，都具有公共道德的正当性基础；凡是法律没有规定的，任何关于实现人格利益的要求，都只能是人权主张者个人的爱好和要求，缺少现实的社会关系的基础。人权只能在法律中实现其正当性。故人权具有当然的“合法性”，在逻辑和制度上不存在所谓“人权不一定合法”这样的命题和推论。当然，法外的人权也不具有公共道德的意义。因此，离开了法律来抽象地谈论人权的道德性，在理论上是很难找到落脚点的，人权的道德性服从法定性，故人权的非道德性是人权的重要特征，人权不能任意使用道德上的“好人权”、“坏人权”来简单地加以评析。

三 人权的道德性与非道德性的价值关系

强调人权的非道德性，并不意味着在逻辑上就完全排除了人权与道德之间的关系。人权与道德之间的关系是通过法律来加以确立的。因为阶级社会的法律本身就具有很强的道德性，法律本质上是公共道德的体现，法律如果表现私人道德，这样的法律就是不公正的，不是现代法治意义上的法律，而是人治意义上的法律。故法律外的人权的非道德性与法律之中的人权的道德性之间是辩证统一的。在法律之外，人权不可能有统一的标准；在法律之中，人权必须依据法律作出判断，尽管这种法律判断带有过多的价值倾向或者是道德选择。

法律之中的人权，其道德性必须服从法律自身的判断。因此，法律规范的规范要求和价值选择在很大程度上决定了人权的道德走向。特别是涉及不同人权之间发生价值冲突时，基于法律判断所作出的人权选择才是有现实意义的。而在法律之外，由于人权的非道德性，人权无法解决不同人权观之间的价值取舍，法律外对人权的道德评价基本上是失效的。仅以两则著名的人权案件为例，就可以比较好地说明，在法律判断之外，是无法确定人权的道德基础的。

一是“罗伊诉韦德案”①，这是美国联邦最高法院处理过的比较著名的涉及人权价值冲突和取舍的案件。

1969 年，一位化名杰内 · 罗伊的妇女和其他人一起向得克萨斯州限制堕胎的法令提出挑战。该法令规定，除非因为维护孕妇的生命，州内一律禁止妇女实施堕胎手术。罗伊主张：得克萨斯州限制堕胎的法令剥夺了她在妊娠中的选择权，因为她既无钱到可以合法堕胎的州进行手术，又不能终止妊娠，所以，分娩之后不得不将孩子交给不知身份的人收养。得克萨斯州限制堕胎的法令使她无法自主地决定在什么时间、以什么方式、为何种理由而终止妊娠。被告得克萨斯州政府在诉讼中辩称：生命始于受孕而存续于整个妊娠期间，所以，怀孕妇女在整个妊娠过程中都存在着保护胎儿生命这一国家利益。宪法中所称的“人”包括胎儿在内，非经正当法律程序而剥夺胎儿生命是联邦宪法修正案第 14 条所禁止的行为。

该案最终上诉到美国联邦最高法院。1973 年，联邦最高法院以 6∶3 的多数意见裁定，得克萨斯州限制堕胎的法令过于宽泛地限制了孕妇在妊娠过程中的选择权，侵犯了联邦宪法修正案第 14 条所保护的个人自由，构成违宪。

美国联邦最高法院以布莱克门大法官为代表的多数意见支持了罗伊的诉讼请求。

布莱克门大法官在判决中认为，虽然联邦宪法没有明文规定公民享有隐私权，但是无论是权利法案提供的特定保障，还是联邦宪法修正案第 9 条所确认的“剩余权利原则”，或者是联邦宪法第 14 条修正案确认的未经正当程序不可剥夺的“自由”，都为公民隐私权的保护提供了广阔的宪法空间，而“隐私权的广泛性足以涵盖妇女自行决定是否终止妊娠的权利”。

---

① Cf. Roe v. Wade, 410 U. S. 113, 1973.

只有个人权利才是宪法所保护的基本权利和法定自由。司法对基本权利的保护应当遵循下列规则：限制基本权利的法律违反宪法，除非限制是为了维护某种“不可抗拒的国家利益”，而限制措施又没有超出实现立法目的所必需的限度。在罗伊一案中，首先应当承认妇女堕胎权是宪法所保护的个人隐私权。但是，也应当看到，决定堕胎与否的个人隐私并不是绝对自由的。在妊娠期间，存在两种“重要和正当”的国家利益：一是保护孕妇健康；二是保护潜在生命。政府得在同时考虑上述两种国家利益的基础上制定限制堕胎的法律。这两种利益在妊娠期间同时存在，各自在某一个时间点内成为不可抗拒的国家利益。在罗伊案件中，得克萨斯州法律对堕胎作了过于宽泛的限制，即没有区分妊娠早期和晚期的堕胎，只是将抢救母亲生命作为允许堕胎的唯一理由，而排除了堕胎所涉及的其他利益，因此，得克萨斯州法律违反了宪法修正案第 14 条正当程序条款。

布莱克门大法官认为，在考虑保护孕妇健康与保护胎儿生命两种不同的国家利益时，存活的可能性是划分潜在生命的国家利益和妇女选择权的一条基本界限。所谓存活的可能性就是指胎儿能够脱离母体、借助人工辅助而成为生命。为了在这两种利益之间划分一个明确的界限，布莱克门等多数法官将妊娠期分为三个阶段：第一阶段在妊娠头 3 个月，堕胎危险性小于正常分娩，政府没有必要为保护孕妇健康而限制堕胎，孕妇可以与医生商量之后，自行决定是否堕胎，不受法令限制；第二阶段是在妊娠头 3 个月之后，胎儿具有在母体外存活的可能性之前，堕胎危险性增加，政府得以保护孕妇健康为目的限制堕胎，但是，限制手段只能以孕妇健康为必要；第三阶段是在胎儿具有脱离母体存活的可能性（一般第 24 周至第 28 周）之后，政府可以为了保护潜在生命或者孕妇健康而采取包括禁止堕胎在内的措施，除非堕胎是为了挽救孕妇的生命。

伦奎斯特法官在此案中代表少数意见认为，罗伊案例由于与婚姻无关，因此，它不涉及隐私权问题。从 36 个州有关堕胎的立法史来看，妇女的堕胎权利一直受到不同程度的限制，不可能是一项“基本权利”，因此，不应当受到任何特殊保护。

从上述案件可以看出，在怀孕妇女的健康权与胎儿的生命权之间存在价值冲突，而解决这种冲突的制度手段只能依据法律判断。一方面，法律判断引进了国家利益的概念，从某种意义上可以说，遵从国家利益也是一种道德要求，是公共道德的体现；但另一方面，在这两种人权之间可以依据制度上的设计，来使得彼此都得到不同程度的实现，这种制度设计完全是以“正义”为特征的，体现了“自由”价值的特性。因此，人权在法律判断的尺度内，首先要服从“自由”价值，而自由价值不能简单地归入道德的范畴，自由本身具有客观性和必然性，属于本体论和认识论的范围，是道德伦理和价值论的前提，而不是相反。

二是联邦德国宪法法院处理的“艺术自由的宪法限制案”①。该案涉及两种人权需要在宪法范围内同时获得保护的时候，根据公共利益的要求，可以在两种受保护的人权之间设立优先保护秩序。

1933 年，作家克劳斯·曼从德国流亡，于 1936 年在阿姆斯特丹出版了名为《魔鬼》的小说。二战后，根据柏林出版商的要求，他计划再版该书。小说的主人公黑福根是一名演员，由于想在艺术上获得辉煌而结交纳粹分子从而改变了自己的政治信念。该小说涉及心理精神等社会条件方面的内容。该小说是作者以他的前妹夫格林更斯的生活经历创作的，格林更斯曾经与作者的妹妹生活了近 20 年时间，后来又离婚。小说主人公的所有特征与作者前妹夫完全吻合。

1963 年 8 月，名为尼芬鲍肯的女性出版商向社会预告要出版该小说。对此，格林更斯（1963 年 10 月死亡）的养子向汉堡地方法院提起诉讼，主张该小说侵犯了格林更斯的人格权，要求法院禁止该小说的出版。原告在诉状中辩称，任何熟悉三四十年代德国戏剧史的读者，都必然会将小说主人公黑福根与格林更斯联系起来。在该小说中，作者将许多可以辨认的事实综合起来，加上一些故意虚构的情节，对格林更斯的人格肆意进行贬损，已经不属于一般意义上的“艺术作品”了，不过是对他人名誉和人格进行贬损的“实话小说”，为此，原告养子请求禁止出版商出版该小说。

一审汉堡地方法院依据基本法第 5 条第 3 款驳回了原告的诉讼请求。出版商于 1965 年在附加“本小说人物纯属虚构”的注意事项之后出版了该小说。对此，原告于 1965 年 11 月 23 日向汉堡高等法院提起上诉。汉堡高等法院支持了原告的请求，并且说明了下列理由：该小说伤害了格林更斯的名誉和名声。该小说既不是他的传记，也不是二三十年代的德国戏剧

① Cf. BverfGE 30，173，Beschluβ v. 24. 2. 1971.

史，对于了解德国戏剧史的读者来说，主人公与格林更斯是比较容易区分的，但是，对于不了解格林更斯行为习惯的人来说，像该小说对主人公行为这样的描写，读者就很难区分哪些是创作的，哪些是真实的。而小说作者加上的“本小说人物纯属虚构”的注意事项并不能消除此种影响。小说关于主人公个人生活的描写，有煽动读者情绪的愿望。因此，小说作者以及出版商不能引用基本法第 5 条第 3 款。该小说只不过是诽谤文书。基本法第 5 条第 3 款不能超越对其他基本权利的保护。在与基本法第 1 条、第 2 条所规定的人的尊严以及人格的自由发展相抵触的时候，权衡利益是必要的。就本案来说，已经侵犯了格林更斯的受基本法第 1 条保护的人格尊严。在这一点上，作为被诉人的出版商的利益应当后退。

出版商继续上诉到联邦最高法院，但是败诉。联邦最高法院认为，作为原告的被上诉人养子的人格权保障应当受到一定限制，但是基于民法第 823 条第 1 款的规定，应当承认原告适格，另外上诉人所主张的艺术自由也应当受到制约。

对此，出版商向联邦宪法法院提起了诉讼。出版商认为，联邦最高法院的判决违背了基本法第 1 条、第 2 条第 1 款、第 5 条第 1 款和第 3 款，比例原则以及法的安定性。

联邦宪法法院驳回了起诉，但有 2 名宪法法官持有不同意见。

联邦宪法法院提出了下列判决理由。

（1）基本法第 5 条第 3 款第 1 句，是涉及艺术与国家关系的重要的基本规范。该规范同时也保障个人的自由。

（2）艺术自由，从艺术创作活动的角度来看，包括艺术作品的上演和传播。

（3）出版商可以援引艺术自由的权利。

（4）艺术自由不受基本法第 5 条第 2 款以及第 2 条第 1 款后半段的限制。

（5）对艺术自由的保障与宪法上所保障的人格自由发生冲突的时候，应当考虑宪法的价值序列。在这种场合下，基本法第 1 条第 1 款所保障的人的尊严必须受到特别关注。首先，艺术自由不得侵犯他人的权利或触犯宪法秩序和道德准则。根据联邦宪法法院所确定的判例，基本法第 2 条第 1 款的规定是一项概括性的可加以补充的规定。艺术自由不得随意地侵犯受基本法保护的其他领域。其次，作为自由权，并不是没有限制地加以保障。基本法第5条第3款所保障的艺术自由，如同其他基本权利一样，应当在社会共同体的作用中来谋求自身的自由发展，人权从来就是伴随着自身的责任。艺术的自由受保障的界限，在没有一般法律规定或者规定事项不清晰的情况下，应当根据宪法自身的价值规定和价值序列来加以推导。在宪法价值的顶端，是基本法第1条所规定的人的尊严，这是必须特别加以留意的。最后，所有艺术作品，在有真实的生活模型存在的情况下，实际上是现实世界和美学世界的一体化。艺术在展开自身的活动领域时，也应当在其他社会活动中来展开自身的活动。在本案的情况下，正如原审法院正确地指出的那样，根据格林更斯养子依基本法第1条第1款的请求，应当对艺术自由的一部分出版书籍的自由作出限制。

毫无疑义，人格权和艺术自由都属于现代意义上的“人权”，都具有自身的道德基础，但是，如果需要在这两种道德权利之间作出取舍或者排序的话，就无法再依据道德原则来评价了，必须依靠法律判断所赖以进行的司法正义原则和公共利益原则。与“罗伊诉韦德案”一样，“艺术自由的宪法限制案”也充分展现了在法律判断之外，是无法对所谓人权的道德性作出准确的评估的，缺少公共道德作为道德基础的人权，在现实中不具有实现的可能性。为此，人权的价值基础不仅来自道德要求和道德选择，也与客观的社会需求和社会的发展密切相关。人权的正当性必须立足于道德与自由两种正当性的考虑，必须通过法律判断的方式来获得自身的现实性。而在法律判断的区间内，个人权利往往与国家利益密切相关，带有很强的客观性。这一点，在一百年前日本学者工藤重义著《日本法制要旨》[①]中有很好的表述。在该书中，工藤重义专门论述了“权利与道德”的关系，特别是对人权背后个人对国家的责任以及权利不得滥用等人权的本质问题发表了独特的很有学术见地的看法，对于认识人权的非道德性都有较好的启发作用。他认为：

权利之义，如前所述。由国法之保护而得主张者是也。而国法

① 〔日〕工藤重义：《日本法制要旨》，陆辅译述，上海商务印书馆，光绪三十三年六月初版（1907年版），第32—33页。

者，实为国民共同生活之要件。以此主张为国家所认之权利，固皆为正当之行为，无悖于道德者矣。然非惟无所相悖，必相依相扶，足以保国家之安全秩序者也。例如今有行窃盗者，若被害者而主张自己之权利，不请求国家之刑罚，则何以能保国家之安全乎？于个人之损害，虽为可忍，然其宽纵毒害国家者之责，也不能免矣。天下之人，有多为如斯之措置者，则盗贼将繁殖跋扈于国内。因此而为国家衰颓之基，亦未可料也。是故凡主张自己正当之权利者，不但为自己个人计而已，抑亦吾人对于国家之一大责任。此吾人所确信者也。然世人往往有以为主张权利而仰国法之制裁，如一大罪恶，目为非道之行为者。呜呼，其误亦甚矣。虽然吾人于此，亦非为极端之反对。如彼损一厘，失一毫，亦不之恕。妄好健讼，不使他人穷蹙不止者，固亦非吾等所赞成。如斯者，虽摈斥之为滥用权利，妄使国法保护者，亦无不可也。要之不失于宽，不流于酷，宽严得其所，择中庸至正之途而主张之，是为国家所要求于吾人，而道德亦不外乎此矣。况吾人生于明治之盛代，国法之完美，灿如日星。故关于权利行使之责任，亦益加重大，可不勉哉。

由此可见，人权的正当性不完全来自道德上的要求和评价，必须将人权放到整个社会关系的框架中，放到历史发展的空间内，特别是结合人权的实现途径——法律制度来认识，才能准确地加以界定。因此，所谓“人权高于主权”、“人权的绝对性”等命题都是不可靠的，应当将其置于辩证法的视野中加以评析，才能准确把握人权的性质，避免人权保护事业受到过多的道德因素的干涉。

四 小结

综观目前人权的诸理论和各种学说，对人权的性质作道德解剖的居多，而跳开道德理论的束缚，认真关注人权的非道德性的观念寥寥无几，因此，常常会出现人权的道德要求与人权的实现严重脱离的问题。就其理论渊源来说，将人权过度地予以道德化，必然就会以道德的要求来构建人权的正当性基础和人权的内涵，由此也就会滋生人权问题上的价值冲突。

而在人权实现的过程中，支撑人权的道德要求所要追求的目标带有很强的主观性，没有考量人权实现的各种主客观条件，特别是将人权置于法律判断之外，其结果必然是人权的主观道德要求与人权要求所要获得的人格利益实现之间的巨大差异。将人权严格置于法律判断之中，给人权赋予道德正当性之外的本体论和认识论的依据，可以使人权的实现具有更好的客观性。所以，人权的客观性在法理上完全可以支持人权的非道德性。考察人权必须从道德与非道德两个尺度来进行。而在对人权加以法律保护时，也要考虑到人权规范与人权利益实现的结合，也就是说，人权所追求的人格利益的结果获得事实上的法律认可的程度决定了人权要求的现实性。作为权利救济机制的司法判断，在现代法治社会中，以保障宪法所保障的基本权利为目标的宪法法院，在弘扬人权正当性的过程中，起着非常重要的决断作用。

（本文原载于《广东社会科学》2011 年第 2 期，收入本卷时略作修改）

改革开放四十年与中国人权发展道路*

柳华文**

一　引言

2016年8月22日，联合国开发计划署和国务院发展研究中心历时两年完成的《中国人类发展报告2016》（以下简称《报告》）在北京发布。《报告》指出，根据人类发展指数测算，中国已成为高水平人类发展国家，是30多年中人类发展领域进步最快的国家之一。①

1980年，中国处于改革开放之初。根据联合国开发计划署的测算，当时中国还属于低人类发展水平国家。伴随着改革开放，中国在1995年成为中等人类发展水平国家，2011年成为高人类发展水平国家。在2010年后，中国的人类发展指数开始超过世界平均水平。在1990年尚属于低人类发展水平组别的47个国家中，中国是唯一跻身高人类发展水平组的国家。

《报告》指出，中国的人类发展体现在收入与减贫、健康、教育和政治社会参与等各方面，其中经济的快速增长起到了关键作用。20世纪70年代末的经济体制改革打破了计划经济的束缚，极大地释放了增长潜力，

* 本文是作者参与的国家社科基金重大项目“人权问题若干重大基础理论研究”（项目编号：2016MZD009）的阶段性成果。

** 柳华文，中国社会科学院国际法研究所副所长、研究员，中国社会科学院人权研究中心执行主任。

① 联合国开发计划署驻华代表处、国务院发展研究中心：《中国人类发展报告2016》，中译出版社，2016，第17—30页。

带来了持续30多年的年均近10%的高速经济增长，这对促进中国的人类发展至关重要。从1980年到2010年的30年间，中国收入指数的增幅排名全球第一。对中国人类发展指数的增长因素的分析表明，30年间经济（收入）增长对人类发展指数增长的贡献达到了56.26%，其中在1980年到1990年间的贡献率更是高达65.53%。收入的快速增长让大量人口摆脱了贫困，不仅提高了物质生活水平，也大大扩展了机会和选择。义务教育在全国普及，人人有学上的目标基本实现。尽管城乡教育的质量差距仍然较大，农民工子女入学困难，城市“择校”现象严重，少数民族人口较多的地区高中毛入学率均低于全国平均水平，但是义务教育的平等性还是显著增强。20世纪80年代以来，健康指标逐步改善，人均预期寿命从1981年的67.9岁提高到2010年的74.8岁，高于70岁的世界平均水平。特别是在2000到2010年的十年间，预期寿命提高了3.4岁，进步显著加快。

中国是世界上最大的发展中国家，并且取得了高速发展。同时，中国的发展是人类的发展，是人权保障的进步，用“巨变”来形容也并不为过。

科学的评价可以准确衡量发展的幅度，同时还可以看到，在发展道路与模式上，中国突破了人权有无、好坏的简单评判，将人权放在了经济发展与社会进步的大背景下加以考虑和推进。改革开放以来，中国将法治、发展和人权结合起来，形成了三位一体的国家治理和发展模式，体现了中国文化的整体性思维特征。[①]

加拿大的约翰·汉弗莱（John Humphrey）是联合国人权司的首任司长，他在20世纪80年代末出版的专著中指出，国际法曾经是水平式的，因为它仅仅规定了国家间的横向关系，但现在它是垂直式的，纵向延伸到了国家中的每个公民。汉弗莱因此预言：“从现在起100年后，当历史学家就20世纪的国际法著书立说的时候，他们就会说，在这个体系的历史上这些发展是最重要的和最彻底的。”[②] 的确，人权保护的国际化深刻影响了国际法，一国的国际交流与合作及其对国际人权治理的态度和做法也是该国人权事务的重要内容。

① 参见柳华文《法治、发展和人权：中国道路的三个基本维度》，《人权》2014年第6期。

② 约翰·汉弗莱：《国际人权法》，庞森等译，世界知识出版社，1992，第209页。

本文拟回顾和考察改革开放40年来中国的人权发展道路及其特点，包括在中国共产党和中国政府领导下以发展促人权的理念和模式，全面推进法治与人权事业，特别是用宪法、法律和政策保障来改善人权的成就与特点，以及中国参与国际人权治理的新发展和新趋势。

二　中国梦也是人权梦

2018年3月11日，中华人民共和国第十三届全国人民代表大会第一次会议通过了新的宪法修正案。修正案充实和加强了有关中国共产党的全面领导的内容，在宪法第一章“总纲”第1条第2款“社会主义制度是中华人民共和国的根本制度”后增加了“中国共产党领导是中国特色社会主义最本质的特征”。①

中国共产党是执政党，是国家的最高政治领导力量，这是以国家的根本大法为依据。中国的经济发展和社会进步是在中国共产党和中国政府的领导下实现的。中国共产党和中国政府对国家和社会的正确和坚强领导，是中国社会主义现代化建设的有力保障。

在中国共产党第十九次全国代表大会上完成了最新修改，于2017年10月24日正式通过的《中国共产党章程》（以下简称《章程》）规定：“中国共产党是中国工人阶级的先锋队，同时是中国人民和中华民族的先锋队，是中国特色社会主义事业的领导核心，代表中国先进生产力的发展要求，代表中国先进文化的前进方向，代表中国最广大人民的根本利益。”这是中国共产党的政治定位和责任担当。与人权密切相关，《章程》在“总纲”中明确申明“尊重和保障人权”。《章程》还提到，要“逐步消灭贫穷，达到共同富裕，在生产发展和社会财富增长的基础上不断满足人民日益增长的美好生活需要，促进人的全面发展”，“必须坚持以人民为中心的发展思想”，“做到发展为了人民、发展依靠人民、发展成果由人民共享”。②

改革开放40年来，中国社会主义市场经济建设取得了令人瞩目的成

① 引自中国普法网，http://www.legalinfo.gov.cn/index/content/2018－03/22/content_7509863_3.htm，最后访问日期：2018年8月15日。

② 《中国共产党章程》，人民出版社，2017，第1、8页。

就，在总量上已成为世界第二大经济体。不同时期、不同国情之中，中国对于发展的内涵、外延和任务有着不同的认识和理解，这是一个与时俱进、不断探索的过程。对于解决亿万人口的温饱问题来说，经济建设的重要性非常直接和明了。因此，从改革开放起，以经济建设为中心长期以来是中国发展政策的要义。2002 年，中国共产党第十六次全国代表大会提出社会主义经济建设、政治建设、文化建设“三位一体”的新任务。2007 年，中国共产党第十七次全国代表大会进一步发展为经济、政治、文化、社会“四位一体”的总体布局，体现了对社会建设前所未有的重视。2012 年，中国共产党第十八次全国代表大会正式归纳出“五位一体”的发展格局，即兼顾经济建设、政治建设、文化建设、社会建设和生态文明建设，提出了全面和科学发展的新概念。2017 年，中国共产党第十九次全国代表大会强调要坚持新发展理念。习近平在报告中指出，发展是解决我国一切问题的基础和关键，发展必须是科学发展，必须坚定不移贯彻创新、协调、绿色、开放、共享的发展理念。

2004 年，中国共产党第十六届中央委员会第四次全体会议通过了《关于加强党的执政能力建设的决定》，首次从提高党的执政能力的角度专门提出要“尊重和保障人权”。实际上，在中国共产党和中国政府的领导下，中国的发展格局和理念一直将以人为本作为突出特征。

2013 年 3 月，第十二届全国人民代表大会选举产生了以习近平同志为核心的新一届国家领导人。以习近平同志为核心的新的领导集体响亮地提出了努力实现“中国梦”的施政目标。2013 年 3 月 17 日，在第十二届全国人民代表大会第一次会议的闭幕会上，习近平发表了关于“中国梦”的重要讲话。他郑重指出：“中国梦归根到底是人民的梦，必须紧紧依靠人民来实现，必须不断为人民造福。”习近平还特别阐述了“中国梦”与整个中华民族和每个公民的关系——“中国梦是民族的梦，也是每个中国人的梦”。[①] 同一天，李克强在与中外记者见面时表示：“我们要尽力使改革的红利惠及全体人民，使老年人安度晚年、年轻人充满希望，使我们的国家生机勃勃。”[②]

---

① 《习近平谈治国理政》，外文出版社，2014，第 40 页。

② 《李克强总理等会见采访两会的中外记者并回答提问》，http://news.xinhuanet.com/2013lh/2013-03/17/c_124469054_10.htm，最后访问日期：2018 年 3 月 1 日。

此后，习近平多次在不同场合阐述“中国梦”的深刻内涵。2015 年 9 月 25 日，习近平在访问美国时指出：“中国人民实现中华民族伟大复兴中国梦的过程，本质上就是实现社会公平正义和不断推动人权事业发展的进程。”① 这直接指明了中国梦与中国人权事业的关系。在 2017 年 10 月召开的中国共产党第十九次全国代表大会上，习近平在大会报告中明确提出，新时代“我国社会主要矛盾已经转化为人民日益增长的美好生活需要和不平衡不充分的发展之间的矛盾”，“必须坚持以人民为中心的发展思想，不断促进人的全面发展、全体人民共同富裕”。

归根结底，对于中国这样一个世界上最大的发展中国家而言，中国梦也是发展梦、人权梦。以发展促人权是中国将发展与人权密切结合的重要方式，与联合国为倡导落实“千年发展目标”推出的《2030 年可持续发展议程》中的思路完全一致。中国的减贫工作就是其中的典型实例。就过程而言，它反映了中国由党和政府主导，动员社会参与，同时实现发展和人权目标的制度优势。改革开放 40 年来，中国成立了专门的扶贫工作机构，确定了重点扶持地区和群体，安排专项资金，在全国开展了有计划有组织的大规模开发式扶贫。先后实施了《国家八七扶贫攻坚计划（1994—2000 年）》、《中国农村扶贫开发纲要（2001—2010 年）》和《中国农村扶贫开发纲要（2011—2020 年）》等中长期扶贫规划。2012 年中国共产党第十八次代表大会以来，中国开始实施精准扶贫、精准脱贫的基本方略，提出在 2020 年实现贫困人口全部脱贫、贫困县全部摘帽的历史性目标。改革开放以来，中国有 7 亿多贫困人口摆脱贫困，中国对全球减贫的贡献率超过 70%。中国成为世界上减贫人口最多的国家，也是世界上率先完成联合国千年发展目标的国家。中国减贫行动的巨大成果是中国人权进步的最显著标志。

总之，以“中国梦”的提出为标志，中国将“发展梦”和“人权梦”推向了新的时代。可以说，中国人权事业是中国共产党和中国政府在道路自信、理论自信、制度自信和文化自信的基础上，在中国特色社会主义人权观指导下的伟大实践。“中国梦”是对这一伟大实践的生动概括。

---

① 杜尚泽、陈丽丹：《习近平同美国总统奥巴马共同会见记者》，《人民日报》2015 年 9 月 26 日。

三　新的人权原点

1949年10月1日，中华人民共和国成立，中国人民从此走上了独立自主的新征程。之后，中国面对诸多挑战，克服重重困难，发展历经曲折。从20世纪70年代末开始，中国走出了一条改革开放的成功之路。2018年是中国改革开放40周年。从1978年开始的40年来改革开放的进程，是中国不断走向繁荣、富强、文明与和谐的过程，是中国与世界互动更加频繁、与各国人民联系更加密切的过程，是中国人权事业不断加快发展、获得突破、取得丰硕成就、形成有益经验的过程。

1978年12月18日召开的中国共产党第十一届中央委员会第三次全体会议拉开了改革开放的序幕，它是中华人民共和国成立以来中国历史上具有深远意义的伟大转折。全会公报除了提出以经济建设为中心的新的发展道路之外，还专门指出“宪法规定的公民权利，必须坚决保障，任何人不得侵犯”这一历史性的重大转折来之不易。

现代人权概念是世界文化交融的产物。它起源于西方启蒙运动，英国的约翰·洛克（John Locke）和法国的让-雅克·卢梭（Jean-Jacques Rousseau）等启蒙思想家对于近代意义上人权概念的形成起到了非常重要的作用。在18世纪末的美国独立战争和法国大革命中，又产生了大量的人权文献，特别是1776年美国的《独立宣言》、1789年法国的《人权和公民权宣言》以及1789年美国的《宪法修正案》，它们推动了人权概念和思想的形成。

中国的优秀历史文化中存在珍贵的人权文化资源，充满了民本、民权思想以及关爱儿童、妇女、老人的价值观。中国在春秋战国时期就产生了“天下为公”的概念和天下体系的思想，之后经过不断演进和发展，逐渐具有平均、平等、公平、正义等内涵。[①] 中国传统哲学思想对国家与社会的治理、对于构建更加公平与正义的国际秩序都具有启发意义。

20世纪初，在延续了两千年的封建专制统治的尽头，中国出现了倡导

---

① 参见柳华文《天下为公，文明和谐》，载周溯源主编《社会主义核心价值观概述语征文选集》，中国社会科学出版社，2012，第323—329页。

包括人权在内的新文化的启蒙运动。当时，陈独秀就认为：“自人权平等之说兴，奴隶之名，非血气所忍受。世称近世欧洲历史为‘解放历史’——破坏君权，求政治之解放也；否认教权，求宗教之解放也；均产说兴，求经济之解放也；女子参政运动，求男权之解放也。”而且，科学与人权“若舟车之有两轮焉……国人欲脱蒙昧时代，羞为浅化之民也，则急起直追，当以科学与人权为重”。[①]

同西方国家一样，人权思想也在近现代的中国萌芽和发展。而且，中国也为国际人权文书的制定和起草作出过杰出贡献。第二次世界大战后，人权原则被进一步提升到国际层面，逐渐成为世界各国的普遍追求。相比于18世纪法国的《人权宣言》，1948年12月10日联合国大会通过的《世界人权宣言》不但大大拓展了人权观，而且丰富了人权的内容，吸收和融合了世界各大宗教与文明的价值观。《世界人权宣言》的第1条就规定：“人人生而自由，在尊严和权利上一律平等。他们赋有理性和良心，并应以兄弟关系的精神相对待。”其中使用“良心”一词便是当时的中国代表、南开大学的创办人之一张彭春的建议，体现了儒家文化的价值观。[②]

中华人民共和国成立后，获得彻底民族独立的中国人民翻开了人权保障新的一页。中华人民共和国的第一部宪法诞生于1954年9月20日。在第一届全国人民代表大会第一次会议上，这部宪法以全票赞成获得通过。它确立了国家的根本政治制度，首次规定“中华人民共和国的一切权力属于人民”。宪法的第三章则是公民的基本权利与义务。在当时的历史条件下，中国的普通公民对国家与社会、国家与个人之间的相互关系还缺乏充分理解，但在制宪过程中，制宪者已经注意到个人的宪法地位问题。在之后的宪法修改中，也基本沿用了这一框架。

1966年5月至1976年10月的“文化大革命”使党、国家和人民的事业遭受严重挫折和损失。十年间，中国的经济、社会和法治建设受到了严重影响。在此背景下，中国共产党在1978年作出了正确决策，开始了改革开放、发展经济、完善法治、保障人权的新征程。

---

① 引自陈独秀《独秀文存（一）》，亚东图书馆，1939，第3、9页。

② 参见孙平华《张彭春：世界人权体系的重要设计师》，社会科学文献出版社，2017；Sun Pinghua, *Historic Achievement of a Common Standard: Pengchun Chang and the Universal Declaration of Human Rights*, Singapore: Springer Nature Singapore, 2018。

从 1979 年起，中国连续多年派代表以观察员身份列席联合国人权委员会会议。1981 年，中国在联合国经济和社会理事会上当选人权委员会成员。1980 年 7 月 17 日，中国政府签署《消除对妇女一切形式歧视公约》，同年 11 月 4 日向联合国交存批准书，此举开启了中国批准联合国核心人权公约的进程。

改革开放以来，中国已先后加入 20 多项国际人权公约和议定书，除上述《消除对妇女一切形式歧视公约》外，还包括《经济、社会和文化权利国际公约》、《消除一切形式种族歧视国际公约》、《禁止酷刑和其他残忍、不人道或有辱人格的待遇或处罚公约》、《儿童权利公约》、《残疾人权利公约》等。没有签署或者批准的有 1990 年联大通过的《保护所有移徙工人及其家庭成员权利国际公约》和 2006 年联大通过的《保护所有人免遭强迫失踪国际公约》。此外，中国已经批准但是尚未加入《公民权利和政治权利国际公约》。不过，根据 2016 年 9 月国务院授权国务院新闻办公室发布的《国家人权行动计划（2016—2020 年）》，中国政府正在“继续推进相关法律准备工作”，为批准《公民权利和政治权利国际公约》创造条件。①

1978 年既是改革开放的起点，也是中国人权事业发展的新原点，更是中国与世界发生更加紧密的联系的开始。

四 人权的宪法保障

1982 年，中国的现行宪法出台，其对公民的权利和义务作出了新的规定。这是一部具有中国特色、符合社会主义现代化建设需要的宪法。它将“公民的基本权利和义务”放置在总纲之后，使其成为第二章，突出了宪法保护公民基本权利的作用。改革开放以来，中国正是在 1982 年《宪法》的基础上不断探索适合国情的人权发展道路。

人权研究在中国也经历了思想不断解放的过程。20 世纪 80 年代末 90 年代初，东欧剧变、苏联解体，以美国为首的西方国家在人权领域对中国进行歪曲和攻击。在此背景下，1991 年 1 月，中共中央宣传部理论局专门

① 国务院新闻办公室：《国家人权行动计划（2016—2020 年）》，人民出版社，2016，第 43 页。

组织会议，提出了8个研究课题，要求立即着手收集资料，编写一套人权研究资料丛书。这套丛书后来于1993年由四川人民出版社出版。这次会后，中国社会科学院、中共中央党校、北京大学、中国人民大学、中国法学杂志社等单位纷纷召开人权座谈会。人权的讨论和研究范围迅速延伸扩大，对人权的理论与实际问题的探讨也全面展开。法学家们先后前往南亚和北美考察人权状况，据此给中央写了60多份报告。①

1991年11月2日，国务院新闻办公室发表《中国的人权状况》白皮书。这是中国政府向世界公布的第一份人权官方文件。在中国政府的首份人权白皮书中，人权被称为“伟大的名词”，强调实现充分人权是“中国人民和政府的一项长期的历史任务”，并提出“生存权是中国人民的首要人权”。邓小平高度肯定了该白皮书，他表示：“这是一篇大文章，是一篇好文章。”②

1995年10月，江泽民在接受外媒采访时谈到了人权的普遍性原则，这是中国领导人首次公开承认人权的普遍性。③ 1996年2月8日，江泽民在中共中央举办的法制讲座上发表讲话，正式提出了“依法治国”的概念。④ 此后的1997年，“尊重和保障人权”首次被写入中国共产党第十五次全国代表大会报告。1999年，“依法治国”被写入宪法。

2004年3月14日，在第十届全国人民代表大会第二次会议上，新的宪法修正案以2863张赞成票获得通过，“国家尊重和保障人权”被写入宪法。对此，全国人大常委会委员信春鹰认为，人权入宪是中国社会主义民主和法制建设达到一个新水平的标志，必将对推进中国的人权事业，实现社会全面进步，产生重大而深远的影响；“国家尊重和保障人权入宪，体现了我国宪法的基本精神”。⑤

张文显等则指出：“中国1982宪法、2004宪法修正案折射了官方意识形态关于个体、社会和国家之间关系的重新考量和阐释，表现出在保持对

---

① 参见刘海年《新中国人权法治60年》，载李林主编《中国法治建设60年》，中国社会科学出版社，2010，第320—324页。

② 刘海年：《新中国人权法治60年》，载李林主编《中国法治建设60年》，中国社会科学出版社，2010，第325页。

③ 吴兢：《未来30年中国人权保障将更广泛》，《人民日报》2008年12月3日。

④ 《江泽民文选》第1卷，人民出版社，2006，第511—512页。

⑤ 信春鹰：《国家尊重和保障人权——关于人权入宪的历史意义》，《求是》2004年第9期。

社会平等、集体认同、共同福利的尊奉的同时，释放和归还曾被不正当压抑和否定的生命个体的个性、尊严、自由和利益，表征对于主权在民社会治理模式的反思和探索，对于中国人权事业和政治文明的推进意义重大。”①

现在，保护人权已经被写进了指导中国国民经济和社会发展的“十一五”、“十二五”和“十三五”规划，也写进了执政党中国共产党的《章程》和党的第十五次至第十九次全国代表大会的报告中。2004 年中国修订《宪法》，实现“人权入宪”，为中国人权事业的进一步发展奠定了坚实的根本法基础。

中国宪法的改革与发展既是中国政治体制改革的法律成果，又是进一步扎实推进这一改革的法律基础。2018 年 3 月，第十三届全国人民代表大会第一次会议通过的宪法修正案就体现了这一作用。

1982 年《宪法》公布施行后，根据改革开放和社会主义现代化建设的实践经验和发展需要，全国人大于 1988 年、1993 年、1999 年、2004 年先后 4 次加以修正，共通过了 31 条宪法修正案，使宪法紧跟时代步伐，不断与时俱进。最新的宪法修正案是对宪法的第 5 次修正，其对现行宪法作出了 21 条修改，其中 11 条与设立国家监察委员会相关，这是中国政治体制的历史性突破和重大发展。这有助于反腐和廉洁政府、廉洁社会的建设，对于人权保障同样意义重大。

宪法是国家的根本大法，宪法实施是推行法治、建设法治国家的首要任务。② 2018 年 3 月，第十三届全国人民代表大会第一次会议根据宪法修正案决定设立宪法和法律委员会，这是加强和推动宪法实施和监督的一项突破。

总之，中国现行宪法与人权密切相关。2012 年 12 月 4 日，在首都各界纪念现行宪法公布施行 30 周年大会上，习近平表示我国宪法“有力促进了人权事业发展”。习近平指出：“公民的基本权利和义务是宪法的核心内容，宪法是每个公民享有权利、履行义务的根本保证。”他强调：“我们要依法保障全体公民享有广泛的权利，保障公民的人身权、财产权、基本政治权利等各项权利不受侵犯，保证公民的经济、文化、社会等各方面权

---

① 张文显、刘红臻：《人权的宪法载列与保障》，载中国人权研究会编《“人权入宪”与人权法制保障》，团结出版社，2006，第 112 页。

② 李林、翟国强：《健全宪法实施监督机制研究报告》，中国社会科学出版社，2015，第 1 页。

利得到落实，努力维护最广大人民根本利益，保障人民群众对美好生活的向往和追求。”①

中国宪法对于尊重和保障人权原则的明确规定与强调，符合国际社会加强人权保障的潮流。现行宪法为中国人权事业的发展奠定了坚实的根本法基础。

五 人权的法律保障

以宪法为基础，中国人权保障的法律体系已经取得了长足的进步。到2010年底，中国已制定现行有效法律236件、行政法规690多件、地方性法规8600多件，并完成了对现行法律和行政法规、地方性法规的集中清理。因此，2011年1月24日，时任全国人大常委会委员长的吴邦国在北京宣布，以宪法为统帅，以宪法相关法、民法商法等多个法律部门的法律为主干，由法律、行政法规、地方性法规等多个层次的法律规范构成的中国特色社会主义法律体系已经形成。

形成中国特色社会主义法律体系的基本经验是坚持以人为本、立法为民，坚持走群众路线，深入推进科学立法、民主立法。这也包括积极借鉴外国经验，吸收和转化以联合国国际人权公约为代表的国际人权标准。

例如，《物权法》是中国迈向第一部民法典的起点，是中国法治建设的里程碑。因为它直接涉及公民的基本财产权利，调整的对象是物权，保障的却是人权。2005年7月10日，全国人大常委会办公厅正式公布《物权法》草案，向社会公开征求意见。2007年3月16日，历经8次审议后，《物权法》在第十届全国人民代表大会第五次会议上高票通过。作为权利启蒙的物权是现代社会人权的物化表达，因此《物权法》的基本精神是对基本人权中的财产权的一种平等保护。如何防止公权力对公民基本财产权的侵犯是《物权法》实施中需要着重解决的问题，《物权法》的颁布对于保障和完善中国的基本人权体系具有里程碑式的意义。②

民法被誉为“社会生活的百科全书”，与人权保障关系密切。中国立

① 《习近平谈治国理政》，外文出版社，2014，第136、140、141页。

② 袁兵喜：《论〈物权法〉的人权底蕴》，《广州大学学报》（社会科学版）2009年第1期。

法机关计划在2020年完成中华人民共和国成立以来首部民法典的制定。全国人大常委会委员徐显明曾在审议《民法总则（草案）》时表示，“民法应该具有现代精神，而现代精神的核心是应该体现尊重和保障人权”。由于法院裁判时不能援引宪法，他建议把宪法中列举的权利尽可能地民事化。①

2017年3月15日，第十二届全国人民代表大会第五次会议表决通过了《中华人民共和国民法总则》（以下简称《民法总则》），中国朝着制定民法典的方向迈出了坚实一步。《民法总则》通过全面确认和保障公民的民事权利，在相当程度上起到了有效规范公权力的作用，为中国国家治理的现代化奠定了制度基础。梁慧星认为，民法是私法的基本法，它以对人的保护为核心，以权利为本位，系统全面地规定了自然人、法人、非法人组织在民事活动中享有的各种人身、财产权益。在具体内容方面，《民法总则》增加了对胎儿利益、个人信息、一般人格权、特定人格权的保护，这些都强化了对个人权利的保护。《民法总则》在民法通则的基础上修改、完善了民事权利体系，强化了保护民事权利的观念，在世界上开创了于《民法总则》中系统规定民事权利的立法模式。中国人权保护的法治建设也由此进入一个新时期。②

与民事法律的完善相应，中国的刑事法律同样体现了在人权保障方面的立法进步。一方面，中国是联合国《禁止酷刑公约》的缔约国；另一方面，虽然中国尚不是《公民权利和政治权利国际公约》的缔约国，但是中国的国内立法和司法也充分考虑和吸收了其宗旨、原则和规则。此外，《刑事诉讼法》也兼顾着打击犯罪和保障人权，有人称之为人权“小宪法”。1979年，在改革开放之初拨乱反正的关键时刻，中国的第一部刑事诉讼法获得通过。在它的基本原则中，主持立法工作的彭真亲笔加上了一句话：“保障无罪的人不受刑事追究。”1996年，《刑事诉讼法》迎来首次大幅修改。收容审查制度被取消，“对抗式”诉讼被吸收。在最后一次研讨会上，全国人大常委会分管立法的副委员长王汉斌明确支持规定“疑罪从无”的原则。

许多人将诉讼中的非法证据称为“毒树之果”，刑事司法中的刑讯逼

① 徐显明：《民法典应充分体现“尊重和保障人权”》，《中国人大》2016年第14期。

② 梁慧星：《民法总则的时代意义》，《人民日报》2017年4月13日。

供是古今中外冤假错案的重要来源。2010 年 5 月 9 日，“杀害”同村村民、在监狱已经服刑多年的河南商丘农民赵作海，因“被害人”赵振晌的突然回家，被宣告无罪释放。而此时，赵家已经为此家破人亡。经查，赵作海当初之所以违心认罪，完全是被刑讯逼供、屈打成招。[①] 刑事错案的发生在任何社会、任何国家都不可避免，关键在于要构建针对刑事错案的预防和救济机制，通过立法和司法预防冤假错案这种严重侵犯人权的现象的发生。2012 年 3 月，第十一届全国人民代表大会第五次会议审议通过新的刑事诉讼法修正案，完善了非法证据排除制度，首次规定不得强迫任何人证实自己有罪。该修正案还进一步规定了律师在侦查阶段的法律地位。特别是此次修订明确将“尊重和保障人权”写入《刑事诉讼法》第 2 条，这明显体现了促进人权的立法取向。

刑事诉讼法的发展脉络反映了中国刑事法律从单纯注重打击犯罪向人权保障方向发展的过程。改革开放以来，中国的《刑法》不断修订，大量减少可适用死刑的罪名，这标志着中国刑法从“国权”刑法向“民权”刑法的转变，这也是受国际人权保护运动影响、侧重人权保障的表现。[②]

传统中国有重男轻女的陋习，保障男女平等在中华人民共和国成立以后被确立为基本国策。男女同工同酬和婚姻自由是中国妇女解放的重要举措。改革开放以来，性别平等在中国更加深入人心。除了制定、修订和实施《妇女权益保障法》等相关法律之外，借鉴外国经验和国际人权条公约的标准，中国在反对家庭暴力和针对妇女的歧视方面也不断取得进展。2015 年 12 月 27 日，全国人大常委会通过了《反家庭暴力法》，实现了立法突破。该法规定了公安告诫、人身安全保护令和强制报告等制度。在 2016 年 3 月 1 日《反家庭暴力法》正式施行的当天，湖南省长沙市妇联代家庭暴力受害人周某向岳麓区人民法院递交了人身安全保护令申请书，并得到了法院支持。这是湖南省首份单独立案的人身安全保护令，也是中国第一份由妇联代为申请的人身安全保护令。

法治不仅是静态的法律文本，还意味着对社会生活和社会实践的动态影响。在中国特色社会主义法律体系基本形成、总体上解决了有法可依的

---

① 李奋飞等：《正义的救赎——影响中国法治进程的十大刑案》，人民出版社，2016，第 31—34 页。

② 刘仁文：《从国权刑法迈向民权刑法》，《法制日报》2011 年 2 月 16 日。

问题之后，实现有法必依、执法必严、违法必究就显得更为突出、更加紧迫。

2013年2月23日，习近平在主持第十八届中央政治局第四次集体学习时指出，全面建成小康社会对依法治国提出了更高要求。他强调，“全面推进科学立法、严格执法、公正司法、全民守法，坚持依法治国、依法执政、依法行政共同推进，坚持法治国家、法治政府、法治社会一体建设，不断开创依法治国新局面”。①

2014年10月20日至23日，中国共产党第十八届中央委员会第四次全体会议在北京召开。这是改革开放以来，中国共产党首次召开以依法治国为主题的中央全会。会议通过了《中共中央关于全面推进依法治国若干重大问题的决定》（以下简称《决定》）。此次会议承前启后，是中国法治发展历程中的一个重要节点。社会主义的法治中国建设不同于其他国家的法治建设，它是中国共产党的领导、人民当家作主和依法治国的有机统一。在十八届四中全会上，习近平在对《决定》的起草工作的说明中指出：“党和法治的关系是法治建设的核心问题。”他强调：“对这一点，要理直气壮讲、大张旗鼓讲。要向干部群众讲清楚我国社会主义法治的本质特征，做到正本清源、以正视听。”②《决定》规定的是中国法治事业的蓝图，也是通过法治保障人权的纲领。

在全面推进依法治国的背景下，中国的司法体制改革取得显著成效。立案审查制变为立案登记制，这使得公民在行使诉权时获得了更多的便利和保障；最高人民法院在深圳、沈阳、杭州、重庆等地设立了巡回法庭，这有利于克服地方保护主义，促进司法公正；司法系统还成功加强了审判流程、庭审活动、裁判文书、执行信息这四大公开平台的建设，有力促进了“阳光司法”，增强了司法的透明度，对于通过司法渠道保障人权具有重要意义。

2013年12月28日，全国人大常委会通过废止劳动教养制度的决定，对正在被依法执行劳动教养的人员，解除劳动教养，剩余期限不再执行。如此一来，缺少坚实的法律基础，不能满足依法由司法机关在保障公民获

---

① 《习近平谈治国理政》，外文出版社，2014，第144页。

② 《关于〈中共中央关于全面推进依法治国若干重大问题的决定〉的说明》，《人民日报》2014年10月29日。

得充分、公正审判权的前提下剥夺公民人身自由的劳动教养制度终于废止。这是中国法制史上的标志性事件，是中国日益重视公民权利、人权保障法治化的重要体现。

2015 年 8 月 29 日，习近平签署国家主席特赦令，根据第十二届全国人大常委会第十六次会议关于特赦部分服刑罪犯的决定，对参加过抗日战争、解放战争等四类服刑罪犯实行特赦。截至 2015 年年底，依法特赦服刑罪犯 31527 人。特赦作为一项宪法制度，在中国 1954 年宪法、1978 年宪法和 1982 年宪法中都有规定，但是在 1975 年后的 40 年中从未适用过这项制度。这次在举国纪念抗日战争和世界反法西斯战争胜利 70 周年的历史时刻，特赦部分罪犯体现了中国共产党和中国政府在法治和人权领域的制度自信，体现了保障人权、德治与法治兼顾的制度特征。这也是中国以法治保障人权的新实践。

六　人权的政策保障

所有国家制定的法律都要付诸实施，这既包括刑法、民法等操作性强、传统上可以直接诉诸司法救济的法律，也包括指导性强但操作性相对较弱、除司法救济外还有更多社会保障需求的法律，后者如《妇女权益保障法》和《未成年人保护法》。实现法治需要落实所有法律，这不能仅靠司法机关，更要依靠全社会的共同参与。法律在打击违法犯罪时可能立竿见影，但是要真正应对社会问题，往往需要辅以科学、有效、系统的社会治理。在这一方面，政府的决策和政策性措施具有重要意义。

政府保障人权的阶段性政策文件虽然不具有像法律条文一样的法律约束力，但是它们是落实尊重和保障人权的宪法原则以及相关法律法规的关键措施，是结合政府职责分配和任务制定的国家规划，是宪法和法律在政府工作中的具体化。这些政策措施要求中央和地方各级政府部门予以切实执行，它们既具有指导性，又具有较强的可操作性，对促进和保障人权有重要意义。其中的典型案例就是中国制定和发布的《国家人权行动计划》。

1993 年维也纳世界人权大会通过了《维也纳宣言和行动纲领》，建议每个成员考虑制定和实施国家行动计划，明确本国为促进和保护人权所应采取的步骤。但是，此后只有约 30 个国家着手制定国家人权行动计划，其中仅 8 个国家制定了三次以上的国家人权行动计划。中国是联合国安全理事会的常任理事国，更是联合国人权理事会的理事国，已经批准了 20 多个国际人权条约。制定《国家人权行动计划》表明中国政府对于实施联合国人权条约规定的国际义务的真诚态度，更展现了切实推进人权事业的坚定立场、主动性和积极性。

2008 年对于中国来说是一个非同寻常的年份，这一年中国首次举办了奥运会，标志着中国走向世界的新阶段。也是在这一年，笔者参与了中国首个国家人权行动计划的起草工作。2009 年 4 月 13 日，经国务院授权，国务院新闻办公室发布《国家人权行动计划（2009—2010 年）》。这是中国第一次制定以人权为主题的国家规划，是一个历史性突破，堪称中国人权事业发展的里程碑。事实上，所有政府部门的工作都与人权相关，但是仅仅相关还不够，还应当主动地从人权的视角来规划和行动，最大化地保障人权。首次发布的《国家人权行动计划》是政府开始从人权视角来规划自身工作的标志。

根据第一个行动计划的规定，由国务院新闻办公室和外交部牵头，国家立法和司法机关、国务院相关职能部门以及人民团体、社会组织等组成国家人权行动计划联席会议机制，负责统筹协调计划的执行、监督和评估。2011 年 7 月 14 日，国务院新闻办公布《〈国家人权行动计划（2009—2010 年）〉评估报告》，对首期行动计划的执行情况作了全面评估。报告指出：计划规定的各项措施得到有效实施，预定的各项目标如期实现，各项指标均已达标，其中约 35% 的约束性指标、50% 以上的涉民生指标提前或超额达标。

2012 年 6 月 11 日，国务院新闻办发布第二个国家人权行动计划，即《国家人权行动计划（2012—2015 年）》。2016 年 6 月 14 日，《〈国家人权行动计划（2012—2015 年）〉实施评估报告》发布。报告表示，经过各方共同努力，行动计划规定的目标任务如期完成。

在总结第一、二期国家人权行动计划的执行情况和实施经验的基础上，依据国家尊重和保障人权的宪法原则，遵循《世界人权宣言》和有关国际人权公约的精神，结合《中华人民共和国国民经济和社会发展第十三个五年规划纲要》的部署，2016 年 9 月 29 日中国政府制定发布了《国家人权行动计划（2016—2020 年）》，确定从 2016 年到 2020 年中国尊重、保护和促进人权的目标和任务。

长期以来，中国的社会治理呈现出“大政府—小社会”的特征，还不能充分适应现代社会的治理需求。在继续发挥党和政府主导作用的同时，中国社会参与治理的能力和水平仍然需要提升。为此，中国共产党和中国政府提出了社会建设的任务，要努力发挥人民群众的积极性、主动性和创造性，扩大公民的政治和公共参与，发挥群团组织的建设性作用。2015 年 7 月，中共中央在北京召开党的群团工作会议，这在中国共产党的历史上还是第一次。一年后，中共中央办公厅、国务院办公厅印发《关于改革社会组织管理制度促进社会组织健康有序发展的意见》，其中强调发挥社会组织的积极作用，包括支持社会组织在创新社会治理、化解社会矛盾、维护社会秩序、促进社会和谐等方面发挥作用，使之成为社会建设的重要主体。

《国家人权行动计划（2016—2020 年)》的导言中规定，“合力推进”是制定和实施该行动计划的基本原则之一，即“政府、企事业单位、社会组织共同促进人权事业的发展”。计划具体规定：支持新闻和网络媒体设立人权专题频道或栏目，普及人权知识，传播人权理念；支持和鼓励企事业单位加强人权教育、培训，培育人权文化，包括在境内外投资中将尊重和保障人权作为决策的重要考虑因素；支持高校开展人权通识教育，提升高校、科研院所开展人权重大理论与实践问题研究的能力；建设中国特色新型高端人权智库。特别是在实施与监督的章节中规定：“尊重人民主体地位，创新社会治理机制，发挥社会组织在实施《行动计划》过程中的建设性作用……鼓励新闻媒体广泛宣传《行动计划》的内容，并在《行动计划》的实施中发挥监督作用。”

“软法”的概念源于国际法，是指那些由不同国际组织或者机构制定、未经国家正式认可、不具有法律约束力，但是在实践中发挥了指导性并具有操作性的规则。“软法”在国内法研究中方兴未艾。专业性、行业性社会组织和基层群众自治组织在国家机器之外进行的规范化治理产生了“软法之治”，在公共治理中发挥着不可替代的作用。重视和发挥好社会力量及其规范化治理的建设性作用，有利于国家治理的现代化，当然也适用于在全社会普及和促进人权保障。与人权相关的国家政策文件是法律与社会治理之间的一座桥梁，它们肯定并强调了社会组织和社会工作者在人权工作中的积极作用。①

① 参见柳华文《软法与人权和社会建设》，《人权》2012 年第 2 期。

需要指出的是，中国关于人权保障的国家政策不仅促进了法律在社会生活中的落实，同时也密切结合了国际法和国内法，体现了国际人权法的宗旨、目标和精神。这些政策包括2007年发布的《中国反对拐卖妇女儿童行动计划（2008—2012年）》、2013年发布的《中国反对拐卖人口行动计划（2013—2020年）》以及2011年发布的《中国妇女发展纲要（2011—2020年）》与《中国儿童发展纲要（2011—2020年）》。

以《中国反对拐卖人口行动计划（2013—2020年）》为例。它开篇就规定："为有效预防、依法打击拐卖人口犯罪，积极救助、妥善安置被拐卖受害人，切实维护公民合法权益，依据有关国际公约和我国法律，制定《中国反对拐卖人口行动计划（2013—2020年）》。"考察国家人权行动计划也会发现，其篇章布局、术语使用、具体举措、人权工作任务与指标的设置，也都兼顾了国内法和国际法标准。

改革开放以来，中国人权事业在法治化、制度化轨道上不断前行，已经进入有计划、有步骤、迅速发展的时期。

七　促进国际人权治理

国内现代化建设和人权事业的持续发展为中国的对外开放和国际交流奠定了坚实基础。20世纪70年代末、80年代初，中国改革开放的总设计师邓小平提出了"韬光养晦"的外交政策，这符合当时和之后很长一段时期里的中国国情，有效扩大了对外交往与合作。

美国等部分西方国家在国际人权领域的双重标准曾经严重影响联合国的人权工作。自1990年起，联合国人权委员会中一度出现了西方国家以"中国的人权状况"为名提出的反华提案。中方根据程序规则，以不采取行动的动议还击，即要求委员会对西方的提案不采取任何行动，不讨论也不表决。在人权委员会上中国连续11次挫败反华提案，这说明政治性、选择性地指责具体国家的动议不得人心。[①] 中国主张在平等和互相尊重的基础上开展对话和交流。中国与美国、英国、澳大利亚等许多西方国家就人

---

① 参见李林蔚、陶甜《难忘16年前的那个春天——访联合国人权小组会专家陈士球》，《人民日报》（海外版）2006年3月17日。

权问题进行了多轮对话，邀请联合国和其他国家的众多人权官员和专家访华，并派出代表团赴一些国家就国际人权领域的问题交换意见和看法。

40 年来，中国在国际人权交流领域日益活跃。1995 年 9 月，中国在北京举办了联合国第四次世界妇女大会和非政府组织妇女论坛，此次大会也是妇女权利保障史上一个里程碑。2003 年 12 月，第五十九届联合国大会向中国残疾人联合会主席邓朴方颁发了联合国人权奖。自 1989 年起中国开始派出军事观察员参加联合国维持和平行动，1992 年就派出总人数 800 人的工程大队赴柬埔寨。截至 2018 年 1 月 24 日，中国累计派出维和人员近 4 万人次。2015 年，习近平出席联合国成立 70 周年系列峰会，在会上他宣布建立中国 - 联合国和平与发展基金，该基金在斡旋调解、维和及反恐能力建设、2030 年可持续发展议程、难移民等领域开展了 30 个具体项目。①

中国积极参加人权领域国际规则的起草和制定。中国积极参与了联合国《儿童权利公约》、《残疾人权利公约》等公约的起草工作，在以《联合国气候变化框架公约》为主渠道的气候变化国际谈判中发挥了建设性作用，推动了气候变化《巴黎协定》的达成和生效。除公约之外，中国还参加了《发展权利宣言》、《保护民族、种族、语言、宗教上属于少数人的权利宣言》、《维也纳宣言与行动纲领》、《和平权利宣言》等人权文件的起草。

中国重视国际人权文书对促进和保护人权的重要作用，对于已经批准或者加入的人权公约，认真履行条约义务，及时向条约机构提交履约报告。中国积极参与联合国人权机制，包括认真参与联合国人权理事会和联合国人权条约机构的工作，并充分考虑人权审议过程中有关国家和机构提出的建议与意见，结合中国国情对合理可行的建议加以采纳和落实。

随着中国综合实力的提高和国际形势的变化，中国对外政策的调整逐渐提上日程。作为对世界经济增速贡献最大、经济总体规模和实力不断增长、国际事务参与程度越来越深、国际治理能力不断增强的中国来说，大国外交既是中国外交的选择，也是国际社会的期望。

例如，2006 年联合国改革人权机制，撤销人权委员会，建立人权理事会，此后在所有按规则可以参选的理事会选举中，中国均成功当选。而

① 《2018 年 1 月 24 日外交部发言人华春莹主持例行记者会》，http://www.fmprc.gov.cn/web/wjdt_674879/fyrbt_674889/t1528436.shtml，最后访问日期：2018 年 3 月 9 日。

且，2016年10月28日，中国第四次高票当选联合国人权理事会成员时，得票数高达180票，足以显示国际社会对中国人权事业所取得的成就的认可，也可以看到各国对中国在国际人权领域中发挥作用的深切期望。新的形势意味着，基于改革开放不断取得的成就，中国外交在世界上应有更多的作为、担当和贡献，也意味着要承担和面临更多的压力和挑战。

2017年10月，中国共产党第十九次全国代表大会正式确立了习近平新时代中国特色社会主义思想。十九大报告中写入了中国特色大国外交的概念，并提出构建新型国际关系、构建人类命运共同体的对外关系新主张。报告指出："中国秉持共商共建共享的全球治理观，倡导国际关系民主化，坚持国家不分大小、强弱、贫富一律平等，支持联合国发挥积极作用，支持扩大发展中国家在国际事务中的代表性和发言权。中国将继续发挥负责任大国作用，积极参与全球治理体系改革和建设，不断贡献中国智慧和力量。"

2018年3月11日，第十三届全国人民代表大会第一次会议通过了新的宪法修正案，在宪法序言第12自然段中"中国坚持独立自主的对外政策，坚持互相尊重主权和领土完整、互不侵犯、互不干涉内政、平等互利、和平共处的五项原则"后增加"坚持和平发展道路，坚持互利共赢开放战略"的表述，并将"发展同各国的外交关系和经济、文化的交流"修改为"发展同各国的外交关系和经济、文化交流，推动构建人类命运共同体"。构建人类命运共同体是对中国自20世纪50年代以来始终主张的和平共处五项原则的坚持和发展，是宪法性原则、目标和理念。

人权领域的国际交流与合作是中国特色大国外交的重要内容，国际人权治理也是中国倡导的新型国际治理的组成部分。国际人权治理的目标和模式决定了各国及其人民能否平等、公平、公正地参与国际人权交流与合作。各国应当通过国内努力与国际合作的合力，共同促进国际人权事业的健康发展。

2013年3月，习近平在莫斯科国际关系学院发表重要演讲。他指出："人类生活在同一个地球村里，生活在历史和现实交汇的同一个时空里，越来越成为你中有我、我中有你的命运共同体。"① 数年来，习近平多次在

① 《习近平谈治国理政》，外文出版社，2014，第272页。

国际国内的重要场合谈及人类命运共同体。

和平与发展是时代的主题。人类命运共同体的理念在人权领域突出表现为中国特色社会主义人权观，强调了和平权与发展权。习近平在致2015北京人权论坛的贺信中提到了两个“坚定不移”，即中国坚定不移走和平发展道路，坚定不移推进中国人权事业和世界人权事业。2016年12月4日，习近平在致“纪念《发展权利宣言》通过三十周年”国际研讨会的贺信中强调，发展是人类社会永恒的主题，联合国《发展权利宣言》确认发展权利是一项不可剥夺的人权，中国将为人类发展进步作出更大贡献，国际社会要以联合国2030年可持续发展议程为新起点，努力走出一条公平、开放、全面、创新的发展之路，实现各国共同发展。他强调，中国积极参与全球治理，着力推进包容性发展，努力为各国特别是发展中国家共享发展成果创造条件和机会。①

2015年9月，习近平在联合国成立70周年系列峰会上全面阐述了打造人类命运共同体的重要内涵。2017年1月，习近平在日内瓦万国宫出席“共商共筑人类命运共同体”高级别会议上发表了题为《共同构建人类命运共同体》的主旨演讲。在演讲中，习近平主张共同推进构建人类命运共同体伟大进程，坚持对话协商、共建共享、合作共赢、交流互鉴、绿色低碳，建设一个持久和平、普遍安全、共同繁荣、开放包容、清洁美丽的世界。② 2017年2月27日，中国外交部部长王毅于人权理事会第34次会议开幕当天，在《人民日报》发表题为《促进和保护人权，携手构建人类命运共同体》的文章。文章指出：“人类命运共同体理念植根于源远流长的中华文明，契合国际社会求和平、谋发展、促合作的共同愿望，为应对当前突出全球性挑战指明了根本出路，对完善国际人权治理也具有重要启示。”③

中国的主张在联合国引发了强烈反响。2017年2月13日，联合国社会发展委员会第55届会议一致通过“非洲发展新伙伴关系的社会层面”决议，呼吁国际社会本着合作共赢和构建人类命运共同体的精神，加强对

---

① 习近平：《致“纪念〈发展权利宣言〉通过三十周年国际研讨会”的贺信》，《人民日报》2016年12月5日。

② 习近平：《共同构建人类命运共同体——在联合国日内瓦总部的演讲》，《人民日报》2017年1月20日。

③ 王毅：《共同促进和保护人权，携手构建人类命运共同体》，《人民日报》2017年2月27日。

非洲经济社会发展的支持。这是联合国决议中首次写入构建人类命运共同体。2017年3月17日，联合国安理会以15票赞成一致通过关于阿富汗问题的第2344号决议。决议强调，应本着合作共赢精神推进地区合作，以有效促进阿富汗及地区安全、稳定和发展，构建人类命运共同体。2017年3月23日，联合国人权理事会第34次会议通过关于“经济、社会、文化权利”和“粮食权”的两个决议，明确表示要“构建人类命运共同体”，这是人类命运共同体概念首次被写入人权理事会决议。

2018年3月23日，联合国人权理事会第三十七届会议通过了中国提出的“在人权领域促进合作共赢”的决议。该决议体现了联合国最重要的人权机构对全球人权治理的新认识、新主张，决议首次将构建新型国际关系、构建人类命运共同体同时写入联合国文件。它强调各国要坚持多边主义，加强人权领域对话与合作，实现合作共赢。其途径就是构建相互尊重、公平正义、合作共赢的新型国际关系，构建人类命运共同体。这标志着中国的主张逐渐成为世界的主张。

建设人类命运共同体思想是新时期中国外交的重要指导，蕴含着深刻的国际法内涵。[①] 未来，人类命运共同体思想还将深刻影响国内法和国际法的互动以及国内与国际法治的发展。在此意义上，构建人类命运共同体作为构建公正、合理的国际人权治理体系的重要主张，是中国对国际人权发展的重要贡献。

当然，值得注意的是，尽管中国提出的概念和主张在联合国获得了肯定和认可，但是不能急于求成或者在短期内寄予过高期望。在国际法意义上，联合国人权理事会等机构的决议本身往往不具有法律约束力，只是生成国际法的辅助渊源，在形成国际条约和国际习惯等正式国际法的过程中具有积极意义，但还不是正式的国际法。国际法是一个成熟度更高、稳定性更强的话语、规则和专业人才体系。一国对于国际社会特别是国际法方面的积极贡献，往往需要一个长期努力的过程。

中国的人权理念、思想和主张反映到国际社会、呈现在多边舞台上这一事实具有重要的意义。这不是中国单方面表达和传输话语的过程，而是一个与国际社会互动，相互沟通、学习和理解的过程，是一个“你中有

---

① 李赞：《建设人类命运共同体的国际法原理与路径》，《国际法研究》2016年第6期。

我”、“我中有你”的主动发声、积极融合的过程。

中国在国际人权治理中如何对待既有国际人权框架和体系？这也是一个需要回答的问题。荷兰学者汤姆·茨瓦特（Tom Zwart）发现，中国的人权观无意挑战既有的人权机制，而只是挑战西方对这一人权机制的某些解释。中国愿意在现有人权机制内行动，而不是在人权机制外加以质疑。① 2018 年 2 月 28 日，中国常驻联合国日内瓦办事处和瑞士其他国际组织代表俞建华大使在联合国人权理事会第 37 次会议上阐述了中国的立场和主张，他表示在构建新型国际关系、构建人类命运共同体的目标下，中国主张以发展促人权、以安全促人权、以合作促人权、以公平促人权，“中国始终是国际人权治理的参与者、建设者和贡献者，始终积极推动国际人权事业健康发展”。②

总之，在中国特色社会主义人权观的指引下，中国不仅在国内有效推动人权事业的发展，也在积极参与国际人权治理，为国际人权事业的健康发展贡献智慧。

八 结语

改革开放40 年来，在中国共产党和中国政府的领导下，中国不仅经济快速发展，而且在政治、文化、社会和生态文明建设等诸多领域也取得令人瞩目的成就，这使得中国的人权事业不断进步和发展。在道路自信、理论自信、制度自信和文化自信的基础上，中国形成了新的人权自信。

正如习近平在 2015 年 9 月 1 日致 2015 北京人权论坛的贺信中所说：“长期以来，中国坚持把人权的普遍性原则同中国实际相结合，不断推动经济社会发展，增进人民福祉，促进社会公平正义，加强人权法治保障，努力促进经济、社会、文化权利和公民、政治权利全面协调发展，显著提高了人民生存权、发展权的保障水平，走出了一条适合中国国情的人权发

① 汤姆·茨瓦特：《在遵行中挑战：为中国的人权立场赢得更多支持》，曲相霏译，《国际法研究》2017 年第 1 期。

② 俞建华：《坚持合作共赢共促人权发展——在人权理事会第 37 次会议高级别会议一般性辩论中的发言》，http://www.mfa.gov.cn/ce/cegv/chn/hyyfy/t1538414.htm，最后访问日期：2018 年 3 月 9 日。

展道路。”①

如何正确看待一国的人权发展呢？2012 年 2 月 14 日，时任国家副主席的习近平在美国国务院出席时任美国副总统约瑟夫·拜登（Joseph Biden）和时任国务卿希拉里·克林顿（Hilary Clinton）共同举办的欢迎午宴并致辞，在致辞中就人权等问题开诚布公地交换了意见。他表示，中国人口多，区域差异大，发展不平衡，在进一步改善民生和人权状况方面，还面临不少的挑战，中国政府将继续从本国国情出发，坚持以人为本，始终把人民愿望和要求放在心上，采取切实有效的政策措施，大力促进社会公平、正义与和谐，推动中国人权事业不断取得新的进展。他特别强调，改革开放 30 多年来，中国人权事业取得了有目共睹的巨大成就，但在人权问题上没有最好，只有更好。②

2017 年 11 月 20 日，习近平在中央全面深化改革领导小组第一次会议上强调要“始终牢记改革只有进行时、没有完成时”。③ 人权保障和法治建设不会一蹴而就、一劳永逸，而是需要长期不懈的努力。

改革开放使中国经济快速发展，社会发生巨大进步；改革开放使中国民主与法治建设不断突破，稳步推进；改革开放使中国人权事业在适应本国国情的基础上依法推进、全面推进、渐进推进，并逐步走向世界，积极参与国际交流与合作，为国际人权治理贡献智慧和力量。在包括“发展梦”和“人权梦”在内的中国梦的鼓舞下，中国特色社会主义人权观既植根于中国文化和中国国情，又越来越紧密地与世界相连，越来越深刻地与人类命运共同体的理念和精神相通。在改革开放 40 年后，中国全面推进改革开放的步伐将更加坚定，也将迎来人权事业全面快速发展的崭新阶段。

（本文原载于《世界经济与政治》2018 年第 9 期）

---

① 习近平：《致“二〇一五·北京人权论坛”的贺信》，《人民日报》2015 年 9 月 17 日。

② 焦莹、沈静：《习近平：人权问题没有最好只有更好》，http://www.chinadaily.com.cn/hqgj/jryw/2012-02-16/content_5163467.html，最后访问日期：2018 年 8 月 17 日。

③ 霍小光等：《风生水起逐浪高——党的十九大以来以习近平同志为核心的党中央坚定不移推进全面深化改革述评》，《人民日报》2018 年 8 月 6 日。

以新时代人权发展事业推动构建人类命运共同体*

刘小妹**

2017年以来，构建人类命运共同体的理念、思想相继写入中国共产党的十九大报告、党章和中国宪法序言以及联合国决议、联合国安理会决议、联合国人权理事会决议，彰显了中国对全球治理的巨大贡献。构建人类命运共同体的倡议是从全人类的角度，来考虑如何建立新型的、合理的国际关系和国际秩序，如何“共同创造人类的美好未来”。[①] 虽然其概念、内涵和思想是党的十八大以来逐步提出并形成的，但是构建超越民族国家的共同价值观和世界性秩序的思想资源和国际合作实践却源远流长。在这些思想理论和国际实践中，人权保障都是建立理想世界的终极目标和根本动力。构建以“为中国人民造福”，“为世界各国人民造福”为目标的人类命运共同体同样体现着深厚的人民情怀，[②] 因此，完善以生存权、发展权和追求幸福权为内涵的新时代人权保障事业，是推进“构建人类命运共同体”历史进程的具体路径和主要抓手。

---

* 本文系教育部“人权教育与培训基地项目”课题“人权与中国政治发展研究”（15JJD820026）的阶段性成果。

** 刘小妹，中国社会科学院国际法研究所研究员。

① 《坚持和平发展道路，推动构建人类命运共同体》，《光明日报》2017年10月19日，第4版。

② 习近平：《携手建设更加美好的世界——在中国共产党与世界政党高层对话会上的主旨讲话》，《人民日报》2017年12月2日，第2版。

一 人类命运共同体思想的由来及基本内涵

进入21世纪以来，国际形势发生了深刻复杂的变化。世界多极化、经济全球化、社会信息化、文化多样化深入发展，新兴市场国家和广大发展中国家快速崛起，日益改变国际力量对比，也日益重塑国际关系理论和实践。与此同时，发展鸿沟日益突出、地区冲突频繁发生、国际恐怖主义肆虐、世界经济复苏乏力等众多难题困扰着人们，“西方中心论”① 价值观下的国际关系理念和国际格局已难以为继，整个世界都在孜孜寻求新的治理之道。

（一）人类命运共同体思想的由来

在改革开放以来我国经济社会发展的基础上，面对国际新形势，以习近平同志为核心的党中央站在人类历史发展进程的高度，深入思考“建设一个什么样的世界、如何建设这个世界”等关乎人类前途命运的重大课题，提出了国际社会日益成为一个“你中有我、我中有你”的“人类命运共同体”的重大判断。②

2011年9月，国务院新闻办公室发表《中国的和平发展》白皮书指出，“不同制度、不同类型、不同发展阶段的国家相互依存、利益交融，形成‘你中有我、我中有你’的命运共同体”。这是“命运共同体”概念的首次被提出。③ 2012年10月，党的十八大报告向世界郑重宣告：“合作共赢，就是要倡导人类命运共同体意识，在追求本国利益时兼顾他国合理关切，在谋求本国发展中促进各国共同发展，建立更加平等均衡的新型全球发展伙伴关系，同舟共济，权责共担，增进人类共同利益。”这是中国共产党正式提出“人类命运共同体意识”。

---

① 柯文：《在中国发现历史——中国中心观在美国的兴起》，林同奇译，中华书局，2002，第7—8页。西方中心观有三种模式：“冲击—回应”模式（impact-response model）、“传统—近代”模式（tradition-modernity model）和帝国主义模式（imperialism model）。三种模式都认为19、20世纪中国所可能经历的一切有历史意义的变化只能是西方式的变化，而且只有在西方冲击下才能引起这些变化。

② 赵可金：《人类命运共同体思想的丰富内涵与理论价值》，《前线》2017年第5期。

③ 《“人类命运共同体”大事记》，《人民日报》（海外版）2017年7月9日，第5版。

“你中有我、我中有你”的“互嵌式”人类命运共同体思想有着深厚的中国传统文化渊源。中国文化关于人的本质的定义，是“关系本位”[①]的，即“人者仁也”[②]。“仁”一作“人二”，通常理解为，仁是由“人”和“二”组合而成，就是“二”个人之间，是相互内在性、相互关联的人和人之间的统一体；[③] 二作“身心”，“从身从心”，是指将他人放在心上，也就是“心中思人”，与“仁者，爱人”同义，[④] 表现为“己欲立而立人，己欲达而达人”[⑤] 的行为准则。由此，“仁”在人与人的相互内在、相互关联中，达成了人我融合、人我一体，乃至“万物一体”之仁，也就是“你中有我、我中有你”的人类命运共同体。这也是“仁”的思想资源，在继张彭春将“良心”观念引入《世界人权宣言》后，[⑥] 再次为国际人权理念注入中国智慧。

十八大以后，中国开始在国际舞台上，逐渐阐释构建人类命运共同体的新型国际关系的理念和内涵，并得到国际社会的广泛认同和赞誉。2013年3月23日，习近平在莫斯科国际关系学院发表演讲，第一次向世界传递对人类文明走向的中国判断：“这个世界，各国相互联系、相互依存的程度空前加深，人类生活在同一个地球村里，生活在历史和现实交汇的同一个时空里，越来越成为你中有我、我中有你的命运共同体。”[⑦] 2015年9月28日，习近平在第70届联合国大会一般性辩论时明确提出“携手构建合作共赢新伙伴，同心打造人类命运共同体”的政治主张。[⑧] 2016年9月3日，在B20峰会开幕式主旨演讲中，习近平再次呼吁树立人类命运共同体意识，以全球伙伴关系来应对挑战。2017年1月18日，习近平主席在日内瓦万国宫出席“共商共筑人类命运共同体”高级别会议，并发表题为《共同构建人类命运共同体》的重要演讲，全面深入系统阐述人类命运共

① 参见《梁漱溟全集》第3卷，山东人民出版社，1990，第79—95页。

② 《礼记·中庸》。

③ 李景明：《“仁”辨释》，曲阜师范大学孔子研究会、曲阜师范大学孔子研究会所编《孔子儒学与当代社会文集》，齐鲁书社，1991，第391页。

④ 白奚：《“仁”字古文考辨》，《中国哲学史》2000年第3期。

⑤ 《论语·雍也》。

⑥ 亓同惠：《〈世界人权宣言〉里的中国元素——张彭春其人、其事、其功》，《读书》2018年第1期。

⑦ 《习近平谈治国理政》，外文出版社，2014，第272页。

⑧ 《习近平谈治国理政》第二卷，外文出版社，2017，第526页。

同体理念，在国际上引起热烈反响和高度评价。此后不久，2017 年 2 月 10 日，联合国社会发展委员会第 55 届会议协商一致通过“非洲发展新伙伴关系的社会层面”决议，“构建人类命运共同体”理念首次被写入联合国决议。① 2017 年 3 月 17 日，联合国安理会一致通过关于阿富汗问题第 2344 号决议，强调要本着合作共赢精神，维护地区安全、稳定与发展，构建人类命运共同体。② 2017 年 3 月 23 日，联合国人权理事会第 34 次会议通过关于“经济、社会、文化权利”和“粮食权”的两个决议，明确表示要“构建人类命运共同体”，这是人类命运共同体理念首次载入联合国人权理事会决议，③ 标志着这一理念成为国际人权话语体系的重要组成部分。2017 年 11 月 2 日，第 72 届联合国大会裁军与国际安全委员会（联大一委）会议闭幕，“构建人类命运共同体”的理念写入“防止外空军备竞赛进一步切实措施”和“不首先在外空放置武器”两份安全决议，这是这一理念首次纳入联合国安全决议。④ 2018 年 3 月 23 日，联合国人权理事会第 37 次会议通过中国提出的“在人权领域促进合作共赢”决议，决议呼吁各国共同努力，构建相互尊重、公平正义、合作共赢的新型国际关系，构建人类命运共同体，强调各国要坚持多边主义，加强人权领域对话与合作，实现合作共赢。⑤ 这是人类命运共同体理念再次载入人权理事会决议。

基于国际国内理论、实践和舆论的积淀，2017 年 10 月，党的十九大报告把坚持推动构建人类命运共同体作为新时代坚持和发展中国特色社会主义的基本方略之一，并写入新修改的《中国共产党章程》。⑥ 12 月 1 日，习近平在人民大会堂出席中国共产党与世界政党高层对话会开幕式，并发表题为《携手建设更加美好的世界》的主旨讲话，对如何推动构建人类命

---

① 《“构建人类命运共同体”首次写入联合国决议》，《人民日报》（海外版）2017 年 2 月 13 日，第 1 版。

② 《安理会决议呼吁各国构建人类命运共同体》，新华网，http://www.xin-huanet.com/2017-03/18/c_1120651440.htm，最后访问日期：2018 年 4 月 10 日。

③ 《人类命运共同体理念首次载入联合国人权理事会决议》，《人民日报》2017 年 3 月 25 日，第 2 版。

④ 《“构建人类命运共同体”中国理念再次写入联合国决议》，《人民日报》2017 年 11 月 3 日，第 21 版。

⑤ 《联合国人权理事会通过决议呼吁“两个构建”》，《光明日报》2018 年 3 月 25 日，第 8 版。

⑥ 《中国共产党第十九次全国代表大会文件汇编》，人民出版社，2017。十九大报告下引文同出处。

运共同体的一系列重大理论和实践问题进行了深入阐述。

2018 年 3 月 11 日，十三届全国人大一次会议审议通过《中华人民共和国宪法修正案》，将“推动构建人类命运共同体”作为国家外交战略写入宪法序言，上升为国家意志，成为我国外交政策理念在国家法治价值上的最高宣示。这也是 1982 年宪法公布施行后，首次对宪法中关于外交政策方面的内容进行充实完善。这次宪法修正案包含的外交理念和内涵，弘扬了《联合国宪章》的宗旨和原则，同时也是中国倡导的“和平共处五项原则”在新时代的延续和创造性发展，反映了中国在世界大变局中的国际治理观和国际秩序观，为国际法的发展提出新的价值追求，也将为国际法的发展带来新的动力，促进国际法向更加公正合理的方向发展。①

综上所述，构建人类命运共同体思想，既反映了当代国际关系现实，又将人类共同价值和中华优秀文化在新高度上发扬光大。2017 年以来，联合国决议、联合国安理会决议、联合国人权理事会决议相继写入“构建人类命运共同体”，体现了这一理念不仅得到广大会员国的广泛认同，而且在国际人权领域也引起普遍反响，彰显了中国对全球治理的巨大贡献。

（二）人类命运共同体思想的基本内涵

构建人类命运共同体思想的内涵极其丰富、深刻。从党的十八大报告将“构建人类命运共同体”在合作共赢的新型国际关系范畴内提出，到 2015 年习近平在第 70 届联合国大会一般性辩论时对构建人类命运共同体面向全世界作出阐释，再到党的十九大报告指出构建人类命运共同体就是要推动建设相互尊重、公平正义、合作共赢的新型国际关系，建设持久和平、普遍安全、共同繁荣、开放包容、清洁美丽的世界，人类命运共同体思想的内涵不断丰富和发展。

学界对构建人类命运共同体的内涵作了多层次多角度的阐释，涉及传统文化、国际主义、生态有机体、法治文明、共生论以及人类共同价值等。② 这些论述从不同的视角，分析了人类命运共同体的中国特性、内在结构、实践内涵、共生性质和国际意义。基于学界的研究，综合而论，笔

① 王毅：《坚定不移走和平发展道路　推动构建人类命运共同体》，《人民日报》2018 年 3 月 14 日，第 15 版。

② 张继龙：《国内学界关于人类命运共同体思想研究述评》，《社会主义研究》2016 年第 6 期。

者认为人类命运共同体思想的基本内涵包含以下几个方面。

第一，构建人类命运共同体的基础是要坚持中国一贯主张的和平共处五项原则，即在世界大发展、大变革、大调整时期，和平与发展仍然是时代主题，强调倡导国与国之间的和平相处。

第二，构建人类命运共同体的核心理念是和平、发展、合作、共赢，即要和平不要战争，要发展不要贫穷，要合作不要对抗，要共赢不要单赢，在尊重各国主权意志的基础上，构建相互尊重、公平正义、合作共赢的新型国际关系。

第三，人类命运共同体的构建方式是平等互信的新型权力观、义利相兼的新型义利观、包容互鉴的新型文明观和“结伴不结盟”的新型交往观。[①]

第四，构建人类命运共同体的着力点涵盖政治、安全、经济、文化、生态等五个方面，[②] 即建立平等相待、互商互谅的伙伴关系，营造公道正义、共建共享的安全格局，谋求开放创新、包容互惠的发展前景，促进和而不同、兼收并蓄的文明交流，构筑尊崇自然、绿色发展的生态体系。[③]

第五，构建人类命运共同体的实现机制是共同安全、共同发展、共担责任，[④] 即坚定奉行双赢、多赢、共赢理念，在谋求自身安全时兼顾他国安全，努力走出一条互利共赢的安全之路；秉持共商共建共享的全球治理观，奉行互利共赢的开放战略，在追求本国利益时兼顾他国合理关切，在谋求本国发展中促进各国共同发展；呼吁各国积极参与全球治理体系改革和建设，践行国际责任，支持联合国发挥积极作用。

第六，构建人类命运共同体的价值目标和宗旨是以保障人权在世界范围内的充分实现为宗旨，增进世界人民的共同利益、整体利益和长远利益。

二　人类命运共同体思想的历史渊源

从人类角度出发，构建超越民族国家的全球价值观和世界性秩序，古

① 李爱敏：《“人类命运共同体”：理论本质、基本内涵与中国特色》，《中共福建省委党校学报》2016 年第 2 期。

② 杨洁篪：《推动构建人类命运共同体》，《人民日报》2017 年 11 月 19 日，第 6 版。

③ 王毅：《携手打造人类命运共同体》，《人民日报》2016 年 5 月 31 日，第 7 版。

④ 刘传春：《人类命运共同体内涵的质疑、争鸣与科学认识》，《毛泽东邓小平理论研究》2015 年第 11 期。

今中外的思想家不乏这方面的论述，如，中国古代儒家提出的“大同世界”、古希腊城邦共同体思想中的“理想国”、18 世纪空想社会主义者提倡和实践的“乌托邦社会主义”、德国古典主义思想家康德提出的“世界政府”、马克思恩格斯共产主义社会中的“自由人联合体”等。这些思想虽然路径不同，但深切关怀人类共同利益与命运，追求理想社会共同体的目标是一致的，都反映了从人类整体利益出发，构建最有利于人类社会生存的组织形式的思想探索和理论努力。

（一）中国古代儒家的“大同社会”

儒家大同思想是中国古代思想家对于人类美好社会的理想追求。“天下为公”、“大同社会”的理想首先在《礼记·礼运》篇提出：“大道之行也，天下为公。选贤与能，讲信修睦，故人不独亲其亲，不独子其子，使老有所终，壮有所用，幼有所长，矜寡孤独废疾者，皆有所养。……是谓大同。”可见，“公”、“信”、“仁”、“和”是大同社会的四个基本价值理念，其中“仁”又是实现大同社会的基本条件。如前所述，当将“仁”定义为个体将他人切身之事完全视为己所关心之事，且以一种为整体的善服务的方式行事时，我们便进入了“公”的世界——一个“仁人”与“仁性社群”共存共生的“天下为公”的大同世界。这里的“公”脱离了政府、朝廷的范畴，是关怀普遍、全体的价值观，也是平等对待事物的心态，更暗含着天下为天下人所有的观念。[①]

儒家“博施于民而能济众”[②] 的至善“大同社会”理想，在中国的近现代转型和建设中，不断被赋予新的内涵，如康有为《大同书》对大同社会的思考，孙中山“真正的民生主义，就是孔子所希望的大同世界”[③] 的天下为公理念和兴国计划，熊十力对传统儒家大同思想的现代阐释，费孝通“各美其美，美人之美，美美与共，天下大同”的十六字箴言，等等。当下中国，儒家的大同思想与人类命运共同体之间更是有着“天下为公”的价值共识，贯穿着“公平正义”的治理理念，蕴涵着“和而不同”的文

① 陈弱水：《公共意识与中国文化》，新星出版社，2006，第 77—83 页。

② 《论语·雍也》。

③ 《孙中山文集》，团结出版社，1997，第 269 页。

化理念。[①] 可见，中国传统文化强调和合理念，主张天下为公，推崇不同国家、不同文化“美美与共、天下大同”，蕴含着丰厚的人类命运共同体基因。[②]

（二）古希腊的城邦共同体思想

追求普遍必然性的古希腊知识论传统，奠定了西方文明的理性基础。这一理性主义哲学发端于惊异（wonder）“我”的存在，强调人的理性，要求认识自身。由此，“人”从“自然”中分离出来，并基于理性构建新的政治统一体——城邦（polis）。城邦是一个基于共同的“正义感”的道德共同体，这种共同的“正义”或称之为“善”，是以共同的社会观念和社会伦理为基础的，因此维系公民间联系的不是亲情、地域或血浓于水这类人性自然温情，而是对共同目标的选择和承诺。[③] 由此，城邦存在的目的便是促进并实现这种共同的“善”。共同的“善”在一定意义上也是共同利益，它奠定了公共生活的基础。在公共生活中，在个人与城邦的关系中，个人被叠加了城邦成员的身份资格以及相应的公共责任，转换成了城邦的公民。

柏拉图的“理想国”是古希腊城邦共同体思想的集中体现。在《理想国》中，柏拉图从正义是关于整体的德性出发，以追求所有人的至善生活为根本价值目标，描绘出一个完美优越的城邦：具有智慧、勇敢、节制和正义的品质，且“国家的正义在于三种人在国家里各做各的事”。[④] 在这里，正义是关于整体的幸福，是“为了全体公民的最大幸福”而“铸造一个整体的幸福国家”。[⑤] 虽然，柏拉图的“理想国”不是世界主义的，而是针对“公民”的一个特殊城邦，但它构建了城邦共同体与公民的逻辑、范式、理念和思想，理想国实现了从个人理性到城邦理性、从个人正义到城邦正义的跨越和融合，后世只需再次扩展“理性”的空间范围，[⑥] 便可以

① 孙聚友：《儒家大同思想与人类命运共同体建设》，《东岳论丛》2016 年第 11 期。

② 杨洁篪：《推动构建人类命运共同体》，《人民日报》2017 年 11 月 19 日，第 6 版。

③ 徐贲：《阿伦特公民观述评》，爱思想网，http://www.aisixiang.com/data/14941.html，最后访问日期：2018 年 4 月 10 日。

④ 〔古希腊〕柏拉图：《理想国》，郭斌和、张竹明译，商务印书馆，1986，第 169 页。

⑤ 〔古希腊〕柏拉图：《理想国》，郭斌和、张竹明译，商务印书馆，1986，第 420 页。

⑥ 参见李峻登《政治哲学的形而上学：西方超验型公共理性传统及其变迁研究——主要基于哲学王 VS 弥撒亚的高度》，博士学位论文，苏州大学，2009，第 106 页。

超越城邦共同体思想中的利己主义和民族主义，构建针对“人类”的共同体。罗马时期的斯多亚学派以“宇宙理性”构建“宇宙公民”的思想，[①]正是“理性”空间延展的开端。

（三）欧洲的空想社会主义理论

空想社会主义（utopian socialism）即乌托邦社会主义，主张建立一个没有阶级压迫和剥削以及没有资本主义弊端的理想社会。空想社会主义流行于19世纪初期的西欧，是现代社会主义思想的来源之一，其代表人物是莫尔、欧文、圣西门和傅立叶。托马斯·莫尔在1516年以对话体文学游记的形式撰写的《乌托邦》中构建了“国家层面：经济公有，政治民主；社会层面：秩序公正，和谐共富；个人层面：行善修德，幸福为本”的三维空想社会主义价值观，[②]描绘了令人向往的理想国度。《乌托邦》被恩格斯称作“共产主义思想的微光”，为后来的社会主义理论奠定了思想基础。值得一提的是，1825年约翰·格雷为捍卫“欧文计划”而专门写作的《人类幸福论》，作为一种天赋人权的幸福权和斯密、李嘉图的价值学说作为批判的武器，深刻批判了英国产业革命以来所实行制度的严重缺陷，并提出了以人的幸福为愿景的社会主义制度设想。[③]

然而，乌托邦思想在现代社会失去了自信、认同和活力。1968年被称为最后的乌托邦时代。此后尽管有布洛赫、霍克海默、阿多诺、本雅明、马尔库塞等反偶像崇拜的乌托邦思想家在力推乌托邦愿景和乌托邦思想，但乌托邦思想总体上遭受了严重的挑战与危机，在多重围困下不断走向衰落。[④]“我们世纪的伟大著作都是反乌托邦的或苦托邦（kakotopia）的，即对世界的这样一种展望，在这样的世界中，作者认同的所有价值都已经被无情粉碎了。”[⑤]这或许正是西方价值观及其指导下的国际秩序无力回应当前各种世界难题的原因之一。

---

① 高秉江：《古希腊超越论传统与普世主义的形成》，《广东社会科学》2012年第4期。

② 段光鹏：《莫尔的空想社会主义价值观凝练及其当代启示》，《大连干部学刊》2017年第1期。

③ 〔英〕约翰·格雷：《人类幸福论》，张草纫译，商务印书馆，1963，第3页。

④ 王爱松：《乌托邦与历史的多种可能性》，《文艺理论与批评》2018年第1期。

⑤ 〔波兰〕莱泽克·科拉科夫斯基：《经受无穷拷问的现代性》，李志江译，黑龙江大学出版社，2013，第148页。

（四）康德的“世界主义”理论

受同时代启蒙思想家的影响，在市民社会的建立上，康德秉持契约论观点。早在1784年，康德在《世界公民观点下的普遍历史观念》中就提出了自然状态经由社会契约直接达成共和制的思想，“大自然使人类的全部禀赋得以发展所采用的手段就是人类在社会中的对抗性”，“大自然迫使人类去加以解决的最大问题，就是建立起一个普遍法治的公民社会”。[①]

永久和平才是人类的终极目标。因此，个体经历社会契约而结成市民社会后，继而要再经由共和国家的契约而达成永久和平、进入世界公民状态。由此，在《永久和平论》中，康德建立了一个三级结构：“根据一个民族的人们的国家公民权利的体制”、“根据国家之间相互关系的国际权利的体制”和“根据世界公民权利的体制”。[②] 其中，“公民”是核心概念，而“国家公民”则是“世界公民”的基础和前提。永久和平还需要一个保障，当主权国家不愿将主权转移给世界主权而建立“世界共和国”时，各国建立契约形成和平联盟就是一个可行的替代方案。康德指出，由于和平联盟并非世界国家，因此要以世界公民权利为补充以实现永久和平。

康德以普遍理性和共同人性的道德哲学，论证了世界主义的正当性，为当代世界主义者提供了阐释世界主义的理论依据；同时，其和平联盟的思想为哈贝马斯的“世界联盟国家”[③]、赫尔德“定位在联邦制和邦联制之间”[④] 的世界主义共同体思想等各种形式的“国家联合体”理论与实践奠定了思想基石。

（五）《共产党宣言》中的共产主义社会

19世纪中叶，马克思、恩格斯在《共产党宣言》中通过分析和揭示资本主义社会形态的弊端和历史局限性，认为国家终将消亡，并提出了“自由人联合体”思想：“代替那存在着阶级和阶级对立的资产阶级旧社会的，

---

① 〔德〕康德：《历史理性批判文集》，何兆武译，商务印书馆，1996，第6—8页。

② 〔德〕康德：《历史理性批判文集》，何兆武译，商务印书馆，1996，第105页。

③ 彭霄：《全球化、民族国家与世界公民社会——哈贝马斯国际政治思想述评》，《欧洲研究》2004年第1期。

④ 〔英〕戴维·赫尔德：《民主与全球秩序：从现代国家到世界主义治理》，胡伟等译，上海人民出版社，2003，第244页。

将是这样一个联合体，在那里，每个人的自由发展是一切人的自由发展的条件。”① 之后，马克思、恩格斯在不同的著作中以不同方式多次阐释了他们的这一思想，并以“自由人联合体”指称人类理想的未来社会——共产主义，强调“真正的共同体，即自由人的联合体与共产主义社会是等同的，它是人类理想的生活形态”。②

马克思终其一生探求无产阶级夺取政权及其争取人类解放的社会理想和价值关怀。建立“自由人联合体”，提出社会主义和共产主义的人类未来社会模型，是对在未来社会中人的存在方式的展望，更是无产阶级追求自身解放、实现人的自主而全面发展的思想指导。③ 首先，生产力和交往的高度发展是促进联合的前提条件，只有这样，个人在物质生产和精神生产中才能融入世界历史进程并且获得自由与全面发展，成为具有社会关系的现实的自由人。其次，马克思强调了国际合作在人类解放道路上的重要性，即“联合的行动，至少是各文明国家的联合的行动，是无产阶级获得解放的首要条件之一”。④ 再次，“自由人联合体”涉及个人与联合体两个核心要素的辩证关系：一方面“只有在共同体中，个人才能获得全面发展其才能的手段，也就是说，只有在共同体中才可能有个人自由”⑤；另一方面，在联合体中“每个人的自由发展是一切人的自由发展的条件”⑥。最后，“自由人联合体”以实现人的自由全面发展为价值旨归。人类命运共同体正是“自由人联合体”的继承发展和现实方案，是以追求共同利益、共同解放和所有人的自由全面发展为目的的理想社会形态。

综上，人类社会永恒的主题是发展，人类发展的最高境界是彼此共同发展。在人类文明史上，为构建一个理想的共同体，思想家们不懈探索，提出了各种方案。这些思想、理论和方案，为构建人类命运共同体储备了丰富的思想资源。与此同时，构建人类命运共同体也必将在应对国际新形势、解决世界新难题的实践中，创造性地丰富和发展人类文明关于共同体的思想。

---

① 《马克思恩格斯选集》第1卷，人民出版社，2012，第422页。

② 陈东英：《马克思的共同体思想的主要来源和发展阶段》，《哲学动态》2010年第5期。

③ 参见唐成涛《〈共产党宣言〉中的人类命运共同体思想探究》，《江西广播电视大学学报》2017年第1期。

④ 《马克思恩格斯选集》第1卷，人民出版社，2012，第419页。

⑤ 《马克思恩格斯选集》第1卷，人民出版社，2012，第199页。

⑥ 《马克思恩格斯选集》第1卷，人民出版社，2012，第422页。

三 人权保障理念在构建人类命运共同体中的作用

人类命运共同体与作为“类”的人密切相关，故人类命运共同体要建立在相对稳定的社会关系秩序基础之上，必须以保障基本人权为前提。从历史发展的角度观察，人权观念的产生以及对保障人权义务和责任的制度构建，成为推动国际社会加强相互合作并逐渐形成比较稳定的国际关系秩序的重要价值基础。与此同时，构建人类命运共同体的重大理念也体现了人权发展的时代精神，它要求建设一个持久和平、公平安全、共同繁荣、开放包容、清洁美丽的世界，正是当今世界人权事业发展在生存权、发展权、健康权、和平权、安全权、环境权等方面的具体表现，反映了世界人权事业朝着更加全面、协调、平衡、包容、可持续的方向发展。[①] 二战后在人权保障领域开展的国际合作实践，是形成人类命运共同体思想的重要基础。

（一）罗斯福的“四大自由”理念与战后和平秩序的构建

面对第二次世界大战给全世界人民造成的深重灾难，特别是战争对人的生命和基本权利造成的严重践踏，1941 年 1 月 6 日时任美国总统富兰克林·罗斯福在《致国会的年度咨文》中提出了建立以“四大自由”为核心的战后世界新秩序，[②] 即在全世界任何地方，人人都有发表言论和表达意见的自由、以自己的方式崇拜上帝的自由、免于匮乏的自由和免除恐惧的自由。[③]“四大自由”彰显了对人类社会整体文明存在状况和未来发展命运的高度关切，使得超越于具体国家和民族观念的限制、在“类”的意义上的“人”得到了国际社会的普遍关注，人类的共同命运成为二战后构建国际关系秩序的重要议题。

“四大自由”的价值目标是要追求对人的基本权利最低限度的承认和保障，并将尊重人权作为构建国际关系、重建世界秩序的价值基础。虽然

---

① 刘明：《“构建人类命运共同体与全球人权治理”理论研讨会综述》，《人权》2017 年第 4 期。

② 高珮莙：《罗斯福的“四大自由”怎样改变世界?》，人民网，http://history.people.com.cn/n/2015/0717/c372327-27318706-2.html，最后访问日期：2018 年 4 月 10 日。

③ 〔美〕罗斯福：《罗斯福选集》，关在汉编译，商务印书馆，1982，第 279 页。

在 1945 年旧金山会议上挪威和新西兰曾特意提出将“四大自由”作为联合国所有成员应遵循的原则，但此提议未被通过。《联合国宪章》的宗旨和原则也因此采用了更为笼统的表达。[①]“四大自由”思想对二战后形成联合国这一维护国际社会安全、保障人权价值的国际性组织起到了奠基性作用，是《联合国宪章》和《世界人权宣言》的重要思想来源，为人权的国际保护实践提供了思想基础。

（二）《联合国宪章》中的人权保障理念及特征

1945 年 4 月 25 日，联合国国际组织会议在美国旧金山开幕，6 月 25 日与会代表一致通过了《联合国宪章》（以下简称《宪章》），10 月 24 日《宪章》生效，联合国随之正式宣告成立，这是国际社会规划二战后和平体制的一项重大成就。《宪章》在序言中明确地表达了对“基本人权”的关切，“重申基本人权，人格尊严与价值，以及男女与大小各国平等权利之信念”；并将“促成国际合作”作为联合国存在的宗旨。此外《宪章》第 13 条、第 55 条、第 56 条、第 62 条和第 68 条分别明确了联合国和各会员国在促进和保障基本人权方面的具体责任。[②]《宪章》关于人权问题的规定，是全人类对两次世界大战惨痛经历的总结和反思，表达了对世界和平与安宁的渴望，对现代国际人权的发展具有现实指导意义。《宪章》作为二战后最重要的国际法文件，把对人权的保障与国际社会的基本秩序以及人类社会的整体命运紧密地结合在一起，在维护国际社会安全秩序、保障基本人权方面发挥了重要作用，并为探索人类命运的共同内涵奠定了坚实的法律基础。

（三）《世界人权宣言》中的人权秩序

1948 年 12 月 10 日，联合国大会通过第 217A（Ⅲ）号决议并颁布《世界人权宣言》（以下简称《宣言》）。[③] 作为第一个专门的人权问题国际

---

① Brice Dickson, “The United Nations and Freedom of Religion”, *International and Comparative Law Quarterly* 44 (1995), p. 332.

② 《〈联合国宪章〉关于人权有哪些原则性规定》，《人民日报》2005 年 2 月 25 日，第 9 版。

③ UN General Assembly Resolution 217 (Ⅲ), “International Bill of Human Rights”, 10 December, 1948, G. A. Res. A/RES/217 (Ⅲ), pp. 71 – 77. Available at: http://www.un.org/en/ga/search/view_doc.asp? symbol = A/RES/217 (Ⅲ)，最后访问日期：2018 年 3 月 17 日；胡志强主编《中国国际人权公约集》，中国对外翻译出版公司，2004，第 249 页。

文件，《宣言》奠定了现代国际人权法的基石，对后来世界人民争取、维护、改善和发展自己的人权产生了深远影响。《宣言》对于二战后国际人权保护秩序的建立起到了定海神针的作用，特别是为国际社会的人权保护提供了一个可以共同遵循的“共同标准”（common standard）[①]。更为关键的是，《宣言》所主张的“共同标准”关系到人权所具有的“普遍性”，涉及人类的共同利益，关乎人类的共同命运。所以，从人类命运共同体思想渊源来看，《宣言》所主张的“作为所有公民和所有国家努力实现的共同标准”的人权，已经构成了人类命运共同体的“价值基础”。正因为人类社会有共同的人权价值标准，国际社会才比以往任何时候更加关注所有公民和所有国家的整体利益、关切人类的共同命运。

（四）联合国人权保护体系与联合国在战后世界秩序重建中的作用

由于《联合国宪章》没有给“人权”一词下定义，经社理事会早在1946年的第一届会议上就决定成立一个核心的人权委员会，并建议这个委员会起草一个“国际权利法案”（International Bill of Rights），以诠释宪章中的人权概念。1947年人权委员会在第二次会议上决定，“国际权利法案”（草案）应该包括三个部分：一是一份宣言草案，宣示一般原则；二是一份公约草案，规定可以产生法律义务的具体权利；三是关于执行措施的草案。[②]

1948年《世界人权宣言》在形成完整的人权思想方面功不可没。《宣言》将公民权利和政治权利、经济与社会权利以及平等和非歧视原则整合在一起，强调了所有权利的相互依存和不可分割性。这一点在多年后被维也纳世界人权大会再次肯定，并进一步强调和扩展了权利平等和平等权利。1966年，联合国通过《公民权利和政治权利国际公约》和《经济、社会和文化权利国际公约》，将《宣言》所确立的各项原则具体化，并设立相应的保障人权实现的机制，形成了以《宣言》和“两公约”为基础的“国际人权宪章”。此外，为了保证公约的内容得到更好实现，联合国还通过了两公约的受理申诉任择议定书和公民权利公约废除死刑任择议定书。

---

① 《世界人权宣言》序言。

② UN Doc. E/600. cf. *Yearbook of the United Nations* (*1947 - 1948*), p. 572.

除了由宣言、公约和任择议定书组成的“国际人权宪章”之外，联合国还通过了构成联合国人权保护法律体系的核心公约，即普遍性的核心人权条约，包括《消除一切形式种族歧视国际公约》、《消除对妇女一切形式歧视公约》、《禁止酷刑和其他残忍、不人道或有辱人格的待遇或处罚公约》、《儿童权利公约》、《保护所有移徙工人及其家庭成员权利国际公约》、《残疾人权利公约》、《保护所有人免遭强迫失踪国际公约》以及与上述公约相配套的多个任择议定书，它们共同构成了联合国人权保护体系。

联合国人权保护体系在联合国维护国际社会安全秩序方面起到了非常重要的推动和保障作用。以联合国产生的各种人权保护文件为依托，在“宪章机构”和“条约机构”的推动下，通过保障人权，已经在国际社会达成了基本共识，即普遍人权与人的尊严和人类社会的整体命运密不可分。二战后之所以在联合国的作用下维护了长久的世界和平，相当程度上与保障人权的国际法和国内法机制之间的共同发力，以及普遍人权观念的广泛传播并逐渐成为世界各国普遍认可的共同价值有着内在的逻辑联系。把关心个人的人权与关注人类社会的整体命运有机结合起来，并采取积极有效的措施努力实现《联合国宪章》、《世界人权宣言》等重要的国际法文件所强调的建立国际社会秩序、维护国际社会长久和平和安全等目标，为形成科学和系统的人类命运共同体思想提供了丰富的理论基础和实践经验。

（五）区域性人权保护体系在维护世界和平中的作用

二战后，除了联合国层面的人权保护体系有力地推动了人类命运共同体思想的产生，区域性人权保护体系也与联合国人权保护体系密切配合，共同维护了战后的世界和平秩序。欧洲继 1950 年通过《欧洲保护人权和基本自由公约》之后，又通过了《欧洲社会宪章》以及禁止酷刑和保护少数民族权利的公约。后来，欧盟通过了《欧盟基本权利宪章》并制定了一系列的相关指令，在区域人权法的发展中起到了重要作用。1951 年生效的《美洲国家组织宪章》包含保护人权的条款，随后通过的《美洲人的权利和义务宣言》被视为对宪章中人权条款的进一步诠释，它与 1978 年生效的《美洲人权公约》成为美洲人权法的核心。此外，美洲地区还通过了保障经济、社会、文化权利，禁止酷刑，保护所有人免遭强迫失踪，保障妇女权利及残疾人权利的多项条约。1986 年生效的《非洲人权和民族权宪章》奠定了非洲人权法的基石。另外，非洲地区还制定了保护儿童、妇女和难民权利的专项人权条约。

区域性国际组织一直重视人权在成员国或缔约国境内的有效实施。1950 年通过的《欧洲人权公约》即包含设立监督公约执行情况的机构和程序的条款。根据该公约的规定，欧洲先后于 1955 年和 1959 年成立了欧洲人权委员会①和欧洲人权法院，负责监督缔约国对该公约的履行。欧洲的模式给美洲和非洲提供了借鉴。如今，三个区域组织均出现了以人权委员会或人权法院为中心的人权实施机制。虽然这些机制在具体职能和监督效力方面有所不同，但都已成为对国家人权状况进行经常性监督的制度化机制。

综上所述，围绕保护基本人权这一共同标准而形成的战后国际秩序，以承认和尊重人的尊严为前提，通过保护个人基本自由和权利，把对个人权利的保护与对国家、民族乃至人类整体命运视域下的集体人权保护有机地结合在一起，富有实效地建立了有利于人类社会文明不断健康发展、和平安全的国际秩序长久有效持续的国际关系崭新格局，为人类命运共同体从思想理念到制度实践再到国际社会普遍认同提供了丰富的国际合作和共同发展的经验，为人类命运共同体作为国际社会共同奋斗的理想奠定了可靠的制度基础。

四 以发展新时代人权保障事业为契机，逐步推进人类命运共同体构建的历史进程

（一）保障生存权、发展权和追求幸福权是新时代中国特色社会主义人权事业的重要使命

人权是社会的、历史的、具体的，也是发展变化的。每个国家都有自己的国情和发展阶段，不同国家或同一国家的不同时期人权的具体内涵是不同的。西方国家长期以来试图通过推进政治权利的改进方式，进而构建

① 1994 年 11 月 1 日通过的《保护人权和基本自由欧洲公约》第 11 号议定书生效后，欧洲人权委员会被取消。

国际秩序的方案，存在巨大的不合理性。[①] 构建人类命运共同体，从人权的角度看，是一种以保障人权为核心价值的关于人类未来发展的设想，是站在发展中国家的立场上提出的一种主张。

重视生存权与发展权，是中国推进人类命运共同体建设的基本经验和行动方案。生存是人类最基本的需求，是首要的人权，是享受其他权利的前提和基础。1991 年 11 月 1 日，国务院新闻办公室发布首个《中国的人权状况》白皮书，提出并阐明“生存权是中国人民长期争取的首要人权”的基本立场和具体实践。人权的内容是分层次的，生存权也是不断发展的权利。有学者认为，生存权包括生命本位的第一代生存权、尊严本位的第二代生存权和安全本位的第三代生存权，包括本源性权域、派生性权域和关联性权域。[②] 其实，权利的分代是一种学理分析，历史地看，生存权的内容的确在不断地深化、拓展和丰富，但是一般来说并不存在截然分开的代际区别。而从根本上说，生存权保障水平提高和保护范围扩展的根本途径就是“发展”。

正是在“稳定解决了十几亿人的温饱问题，总体上实现小康”的经济社会发展成就基础上，党的十九大报告对新时代我国社会主要矛盾的认识发生了深刻变化，指出我国社会主要矛盾已经转化为人民日益增长的美好生活需要和不平衡不充分的发展之间的矛盾。同时表明中国共产党人的初心和使命，就是为中国人民谋幸福，为中华民族谋复兴。从人权保障的角度来看，这里的“美好生活需要”和“为中国人民谋幸福”，实现了从仅仅满足“物质文化需求”的低度生存权，到实现“美好生活需要”、“获得幸福感”的高层次生存权的跨越，丰富和发展了“生存权”的内涵：一方面，提高了生存权的保障水平，并由此对发展和发展权有了新的要求；另一方面，满足“美好生活需要”和“获得幸福感”的权利需求，扩展了生存权的保障范围，即人民群众对幸福的追求权，也就是现代宪法学上的“追求幸福权”。由此，笔者认为，发展权和追求幸福权成为全面建成小康社会进程中必须关注的两个最重要的人权，也体现了新时代人权内涵的不断丰富和发展。

---

① 杨建军：《国家治理、生存权发展权改进与人类命运共同体的构建》，《法学论坛》2018 年第 1 期。

② 汪进元：《论生存权的保护领域和实现途径》，《法学评论》2010 年第 5 期。

发展是解决“不平衡不充分的发展”与“美好生活需要”之间矛盾的根本途径，与此相应，“发展权”保障也必然成为人权法治保障制度建设的重心。第一，与“美好生活需要”相对应，“发展”的内涵和要求有了新的变化，发展不仅追求速度和数量，更要保证结构和质量，要在民主、法治、公平、正义、安全、环境的价值要求下，实现平衡、充分的发展，即必须坚持以人民为中心的发展思想，不断促进人的全面发展、全体人民共同富裕；第二，充分保障人民的“平等发展权利”，成为实现社会主义现代化的内在要求，是新时代中国特色社会主义人权保障事业的重要使命；第三，“唯有发展，才能消除全球性挑战的根源；唯有发展，才能保障人民的基本权利；唯有发展，才能推动人类社会进步”①，发展权是“构建人类命运共同体”的关键手段。

“追求幸福权”起源于美国《独立宣言》中的自然权利，② 1946 年日本宪法第 13 条明确规定了个人的“幸福追求权”，③ 并在学理上把“幸福追求权”放置在“生存权”的权利体系中加以考察。④ 笔者认为，追求幸福权符合以人类福利为国际法效力基础的新理念。传统的国际法效力基础源于国家之间的合意，这是一种程序法则，是一种形式合法性。这些法律原则和规则是在国家交往过程中形成的，更多体现了有话语权的国家的意志和利益，而不一定是对人类共同体的审慎考量，也不一定是出于理性、良知的判断。

综上所述，生存权、发展权、追求幸福权是一种交叠关系，发展权、追求幸福权都是生存权的重要内涵，是不同层次的生存权，三者之间前一种权利是后一种权利的基础，后一种权利是在前一种权利基础上发展起来

---

① 中国国务院新闻办公室：《发展权：中国的理念、实践与贡献》，新华网，http://www.xinhuanet.com/politics/2016-12/01/c_1120029207.htm，最后访问日期：2018 年 4 月 10 日。

② 1776 年 7 月 4 日生效的美国《独立宣言》宣称：“We hold these truths to be self-evident, that all men are created equal, that they are endowed by their Creator with certain unalienable Rights, that among these are Life, Liberty, and the pursuit of Happiness。”（“我们认为这些真理是不言而喻的：人人生而平等，造物者赋予他们若干不可剥夺的权利，其中包括生命权、自由权和追求幸福的权利。”）

③ 1946 年《日本国宪法》第 13 条规定：全体国民都作为个人而受到尊重。对于谋求生存、自由以及幸福的国民权利，只要不违反公共福利，在立法及其他国政上都必须受到最大的尊重。

④ 〔日〕大须贺明：《生存权论》，林浩译，法律出版社，2001。

的。保障生存权、发展权和追求幸福权是新时代中国特色社会主义人权发展事业的重要使命，也是推动构建人类命运共同体的重要手段。中华人民共和国成立60多年来，中国共产党和中国政府不断推动经济社会发展，增进人民福祉，促进社会公平正义，显著提高了人民生存权、发展权的保障水平，走出了一条适合中国国情的人权发展道路。[①] 解决新时代社会主要矛盾，构建新型国际关系，必须继续依靠法治和人权的手段，也就是在法律制度上有效、充分地保障生存权、发展权和追求幸福权的实现，这就要求国家有效地履行在保障基本人权方面应当承担的重要责任。

（二）加强政府保障人权的责任是推动构建人类命运共同体的政治基础

一方面，正如李步云教授所言，由于保障人权是构建人类命运共同体的根本任务，构建人类命运共同体，充分实现全人类的人权，就成为全人类的共同价值追求，是国际社会所有组织和世界各国政府的共同职责所在；[②] 另一方面，构建人类命运共同体，必须加强政府保障人权的国内责任和国际责任。

首先，因应新时代社会主要矛盾的结构性变革，政府保障人权的国家责任也要相应提升。为解决“人民日益增长的物质文化需要同落后的社会生产之间的矛盾”，政府保障人权的首要责任是立足于保障人民的“生存权”；而应对“人民日益增长的美好生活需要和不平衡不充分的发展之间的矛盾”，政府除将“生存权”作为人权保障的重要责任之外，“发展权”以及“追求幸福权”应当成为新时代政府在保障人权方面最重要的保护对象，保障人权的具体制度措施也要相应地转型升级，“提质增效”。

其次，中国始终是世界和平的建设者、全球发展的贡献者、国际秩序的维护者，[③] 因此，在构建人类命运共同体的历史进程中，中国政府还要

---

① 柳华文：《人权进步的中国被世界寄予厚望》，《人民日报》（海外版）2016年11月1日，第2版。

② 刘明：《“构建人类命运共同体与全球人权治理”理论研讨会综述》，《人权》2017年第4期。

③ 习近平：《在庆祝中国共产党成立95周年大会上的讲话》，新华网，http://www.xinhuanet.com/politics/2016－07/01/c_1119150660.htm，最后访问日期：2018年4月10日。

大力承担保障人权的国际责任，既积极提供“一带一路”建设、亚洲基础设施投资银行、金砖国家发展银行、南南合作援助基金和中国—联合国和平与发展基金等构建人类命运共同体的公共产品，[①] 为世界创造更多合作机会，努力推动世界各国共同繁荣；又认真关注国际法在国内法中的效力，真正拿出勇气来建立符合构建人类命运共同体要求的国际法新秩序，自觉地践行由我们主导的新的国际法秩序。

综上，为推动构建人类命运共同体提供可靠的国内法保障机制，进而为推动构建人类命运共同体的国际合作奠定坚实的制度保障平台，这是中国作为一个负责任的大国应当担负的历史使命，与国家的命运、人民的命运乃至全人类的命运都有着千丝万缕的联系。

（三）推动共同安全是保障人权、建设人类命运共同体的应有之义

人类历史上战乱频仍，生灵涂炭，教训惨痛而深刻。要和平、不要战争是各国人民朴素而真实的愿望，也是古今中外人类命运共同体思想的基本出发点，更是国际法理论发轫并兴起的直接推动力。建设一个持久和平的世界，根本要义在于国家之间要构建平等相待、互商互谅的伙伴关系。[②] 主权平等，是数百年来国与国规范彼此关系最重要的准则，也是联合国及所有机构、组织共同遵循的首要原则。主权平等，真谛在于国家不分大小、强弱、贫富，主权和尊严必须得到尊重，内政不容干涉，都有权自主选择社会制度和发展道路。[③]

建设一个持久和平的世界，维护共同安全是基本前提。恐怖主义、网络攻击、重大传染性疾病、气候变化等非传统安全面临的各种威胁和危险在当今世界持续蔓延，人类社会面临着越来越多的共同挑战。今天，世界上任何一个国家都不可能独善其身，人类越来越利益交融、安危与共。在这种新形势下，习近平提出的“总体国家安全观”，强调重视传统安全的同时，也要把“自身安全与共同安全”有机地结合起来。关注“共同安

---

① 杨建军：《国家治理、生存权发展权改进与人类命运共同体的构建》，《法学论坛》2018年第1期。

② 杨洁篪：《推动构建人类命运共同体》，《人民日报》2017年11月19日，第6版。

③ 习近平：《共同构建人类命运共同体——在联合国日内瓦总部的演讲》，人民网，http://politics.people.com.cn/n1/2017/0119/c1001-29033860.html，2017年1月20日发布，最后访问日期：2018年4月10日。

全”实质上是人类共同命运的内在要求。一方面，只有各国树立共同、综合、合作、可持续的安全观，并以对话协商、互利合作的方式解决安全难题，人类命运共同体才有生存的环境；另一方面，要建立维护“共同安全”的国际合作机制，也必须推动构建人类命运共同体，并在共同体内确立和分配维护人类“共同命运”的国际责任，从而推进全球安全治理，建立和维护和平安全的国际关系新秩序。将推动共同安全纳入构建人类命运共同体，这一理念与联合国的共同安全的和平理念高度契合，给充满不确定的世界指明了方向。①

安全权本身也是一项自然权利和人权。通过对自然法理论的溯源，尤其是霍布斯的主权和公民理论，可以清楚地看出安全权与人权之间的深刻勾连。安全权是行使其他人权不可或缺的一项人权，每个人都有权享有能够达到的、有益于体面生活的最低限度标准的安全权。② 1776 年《弗吉尼亚权利法案》（Virginia Declaration of Rights）第 1 条开宗明义地宣扬了天赋人权的思想：“所有人都是生来同样自由与独立的，并享有某些天赋权利，当他们组成一个社会时，他们不能凭任何契约剥夺其后裔的这些权利；也就是说，享受生活与自由的权利，包括获取与拥有财产、追求和享有幸福与安全的手段。”其中，安全权就是“享受生活与自由”的天赋人权的重要内容，也是享有其他人权的基础。基于此，推动共同安全、保障安全权也是发展新时代人权保障事业的必要内容，是充分实现其他人权的前提条件，是构建人类命运共同体的题中应有之义。

五　结语：构建人类命运共同体必须以保障人权的充分实现为根本目标

从人类角度出发，构建人类命运共同体思想的历史渊源中，儒家大同世界、柏拉图理想国、空想社会主义、康德的世界公民、马克思恩格斯的自由人联合体，都是建立在对“人”的人性、本质、存在方式或幸福感的

① 《综述：联合国热评“构建人类命运共同体”理念再次写入联合国决议》，新华网，http://www.xinhuanet.com/2017－11/02/c_1121896404.htm，最后访问日期：2018 年 4 月 10 日。

② 张洪波：《作为人权的安全权：比较、内涵及规律》，《南京社会科学》2013 年第 5 期。

终极追求上。二战后建立的联合国及区域性人权机构、人权保护体系，更是以保护基本人权和维护世界和平为主要使命，构建战后世界秩序的有效实践。

进入21世纪，面对国际新形势，构建新型国际关系和人类命运共同体也必将以保障人权的充分实现为根本目标和具体路径。其一，中国《国家人权行动计划（2016—2020年）》明确提出，坚持以人民为中心的发展思想，“把保障人民的生存权和发展权放在首位，将增进人民福祉、促进人的全面发展作为人权事业发展的出发点和落脚点”，这正体现了张伟教授所主张的“人类命运共同体的构建应当以尊重和保障人权为核心价值观”的理念；其二，中国是一个社会主义国家，写入《中国共产党章程》和宪法修正案的“构建人类命运共同体”思想和战略，与《共产党宣言》中“自由人联合体”的理想社会形态一脉相承，都是以为人类谋福祉、为世界求大同和实现每个人的全面自由发展为根本目标，可见，“人类命运共同体本身就是一个以人权为最高价值追求的人权共同体”①。正是在这个意义上，作为习近平新时代中国特色社会主义思想重要组成部分的“构建人类命运共同体”思想是根植于马克思“自由人联合体”思想，并将其丰富发展的伟大中国实践。

（本文原载于《国际法研究》2018年第3期）

---

① 刘明：《“构建人类命运共同体与全球人权治理”理论研讨会综述》，《人权》2017年第4期。

论基本权利制度变迁之国际人权法动因

戴瑞君*

20世纪70年代中期，荷兰学者对142个国家的成文宪法与《世界人权宣言》（以下简称《宣言》）进行了详细的比较研究，得出的结论认为，一部宪法中的规定与《宣言》的规定相仿，可能不是受国际的而是受国内的政治法律思想的启发，还可能是受已有宪法的启发，甚至《宣言》的诞生也是导源于1948年之前制定的宪法。① 此项研究采样截止时（1976年3月31日），《公民权利和政治权利国际公约》刚刚生效一周，②《经济、社会和文化权利国际公约》生效不足三个月；③ 其他今天人们所熟悉的核心国际人权条约绝大部分仍处于起草阶段或尚未生效。

上述研究之后的近40年里，国际人权法体系和各国宪法的基本权利制度均取得了长足发展。一方面，第二次世界大战之后，国际人权法日新月异，法律体系日臻完善，成为国际法中发展最快的法律部门。另一方面，各国纷纷调整宪法基本权利制度，尤其是20世纪90年代以降，各国宪法中基本权利的主体、权利类型、权利保障机构乃至权利救济制度等内容均发生了显著的变化。宪法基本权利制度最近40年间的发展变迁与国际人权法的发展之间是否存在某种对照、呼应关系，国际人权法是否在一定程度

---

* 戴瑞君，中国社会科学院国际法研究所副研究员，法学博士。

① 荷兰学者该项研究选取的对象是1976年3月31日前刊登在A.P.布劳斯坦和G.H.弗朗茨编辑的《世界各国宪法汇编》中的142个国家的成文宪法。详细内容参见〔荷〕亨利·范·马尔赛文、格尔·范·德·唐《成文宪法的比较研究》，陈云生译，华夏出版社，1987。

② 《公民权利和政治权利国际公约》于1976年3月23日生效。

③ 《经济、社会和文化权利国际公约》于1976年1月3日生效。

上促成了宪法基本权利制度的变迁，很值得再作考察。因此，本文主要选取“国际人权宪章”[①] 生效之后制定或修订的宪法作为研究对象，以宪法基本权利主体、基本权利类型、基本权利保障机构、基本权利救济途径等方面的发展变化为线索，探讨这些发展变化同国际人权法之间的内在关联，进而考证国际人权法在宪法基本权利制度变迁进程中的作用与贡献。

一 “基本权利制度”与“国际人权法”

本文在以下范畴内讨论国际人权法与基本权利制度变迁之间的关系。

（一）国际人权法

国际人权法是国际法的一个法律部门，它以国际人权条约和习惯国际人权法为主要法律渊源，是人权国际保护的法律基础，也是国际社会监督国家履行人权保障义务的主要法律依据。国际人权法规定个人或团体享有的人权、国家保障人权的法律义务、国际社会监督国家履行人权保障义务的机构及程序等内容。

国际人权法主要由联合国层面的人权法律体系和区域层面的人权法律体系组成。联合国层面目前已经形成了包括 9 项核心人权条约和其他普遍人权文件在内的内容较为完备的人权法律体系。这 9 项核心人权条约分别是《消除一切形式种族歧视国际公约》、《经济、社会和文化权利国际公约》、《公民权利和政治权利国际公约》、《消除对妇女一切形式歧视公约》（以下简称《妇女公约》）、《禁止酷刑和其他残忍、不人道或有辱人格的待遇或处罚公约》（以下简称《禁止酷刑公约》）、《儿童权利公约》、《保护所有移徙工人及其家庭成员权利国际公约》、《残疾人权利公约》以及《保护所有人免遭强迫失踪国际公约》。在区域层面，欧洲、美洲、非洲也分别形成了以《欧洲保护人权和基本自由公约》（以下简称《欧洲人权公约》）、《美洲人权公约》和《非洲人权和民族权宪章》为核心的区域人权法律体系。本文将着重考察上述核心人权条约对宪法基本权利制度变迁的影响效力。

---

① “国际人权宪章”是对《世界人权宣言》、《公民权利和政治权利国际公约》、《经济、社会和文化权利国际公约》的总称。

（二）基本权利与基本权利制度

基本权利概指一国宪法确认的个人或个人组成的群体所享有的权利。现代宪法作为人民权利的保障书，几乎都包含一份基本权利清单。由于宪法在一国法律体系中的至上性和根本法地位，基本权利对个人而言具有根本重要性，从而区别于一般的法律权利。

概括而言，基本权利可以看作国际人权法所言之“人权”在国内法，特别是在一国宪法中的反映。然而，二者在内涵和外延上并不完全对应。国际人权法所确认和保护的“人权”具有享有主体的普遍性和权利内容的普遍性，即人权是每个人，不分种族、肤色、性别、语言、宗教、政治或其他见解、国籍或社会出身、财产、出生或者其他身份等任何区别而均应享有的权利，是每个人在公民、政治、经济、社会、文化等各个领域均应享有的权利。因此，国际人权法所确认的人权通常被称为普遍人权。相比之下，宪法的基本权利清单长期以来主要罗列的是“公民”的基本权利，即基本权利的享有以取得公民资格为前提；此外在内容上，各国宪法虽能或多或少地反映国际人权法确认的普遍人权，但往往并不能全面覆盖普遍人权的内容。

宪法基本权利制度是以宪法基本权利清单为核心，以保障基本权利的实现为宗旨的法律制度。它主要由基本权利的主体、基本权利的内容、基本权利的保障机构以及基本权利的救济制度等内容组成。一般而言，各国的立法机关、行政机关和司法机关履行宪法职责的过程也是保障基本权利的过程；同时，多数国家的宪法赋予了最高司法机关或者专门的宪法审判机关以救济基本权利的职能。

二　基本权利制度变迁之国际人权法对照

近年来，特别是20世纪90年代以后，许多国家颁布了新宪法或对宪法基本权利制度加以完善，基本权利的主体有所扩展，基本权利的内容不断丰富，基本权利的传统保障机制和救济途径得到了扩展和延伸。基本权利制度各个方面的发展变迁展现出对国际人权法的明确呼应。

（一）基本权利主体的扩展与国际人权法

人权是每个人的权利。人权主体的普遍性为国际人权法反复申明。为此，国际人权法一方面确认了人权为各国境内受其管辖的所有人，无分种族、肤色、性别、语言、宗教、民族本源、社会阶层、财产、出生或其他身份，一律平等享有的原则；另一方面逐条规定了各项人权的主体是“人人”、“所有人”、“任何人”、“每个人”，而只在政治权利等屈指可数的极个别条款中出现了“公民”是权利主体的规定。

过去很长一段时间，宪法中的基本权利往往只是“公民”的“特权”。如今，在一国领土内生活的人不再只是公民，还有越来越多的外国人、无国籍人，居住国宪法中“公民的基本权利”已难以满足这些人的基本权利需求。伴随国际人权法被各国广泛接受，国际人权法所蕴含的普遍人权观念正在宪法基本权利制度中体现出来，基本权利的主体已经开始突破“公民”的藩篱，逐步扩展到更大范围的“人”。

一些国家的宪法以总括性的条款规定，除特别说明外，基本权利为本国境内的所有人享有，或者规定宪法中的公民权利也适用于本国境内的外国人。例如，乍得 1996 年宪法第 15 条规定，合法进入乍得共和国的外国人，除政治权利外，与乍得公民享有同样的权利和自由。捷克 1992 年《基本权利和基本自由宪章》第 42 条第 2 款规定，外国人享有宪章保障的人权和基本自由，除非法律明确规定某些权利或自由仅适用于公民。有些国家在宪法的具体条文中将权利主体逐条规定为每个人。

有些宪法将基本权利的章节名称从过去的“公民权利”修改为“个人权利”、“人的权利”或“人和公民的权利”。例如，秘鲁 1993 年宪法第一章规定的就是“人的基本权利”；俄罗斯 1993 年宪法第二章规定了“人和公民的权利与自由”。还有一些国家免去了对基本权利主体的限定，直接规定“基本权利”。例如，芬兰 2000 年宪法取代了 1919 年颁布的《芬兰宪法法案》，新宪法第二章的题目由原来“芬兰公民的一般权利和法律保护”改为“基本权利和自由”，基本权利的主体不再局限于芬兰公民。①

---

① The Parliament of Finland, the Ministry for Foreign Affairs, and the Ministry of Justice, *The Constitution of Finland*, Helsinki: VammalanKirjapaino Oy, 2001.

上述宪法已不再囿于对基本权利的传统理解，而将权利的主体逐步扩大到“所有人”。这是受到普遍人权观念影响的一个明证。鉴于这些宪法大多修订或制定于“国际人权宪章”生效之后，可以乐观地假设国际人权法在一定程度上推动了宪法关于基本权利主体规定的积极变化。

（二）基本权利内容的丰富与国际人权法

对于哪个领域的权利是人权，或者某一领域内哪些权利属于人权，各国的认识并不一致。这种认识分歧直接反映在宪法对基本权利的规定中。过去，各国宪法强调公民权利和政治权利，轻视经济、社会、文化领域的权利，妇女、儿童、少数群体的权利也很少直接体现在宪法中。相比之下，国际人权法强调“一切人权均为普遍、不可分割、相互依存、相互联系”,[①] 它以列举不同领域、不同群体人权的形式诠释了人权在内容上的普遍性。伴随越来越多的国家批准多项人权条约，宪法基本权利的内容也日渐丰富起来。

1. 宪法确认了经济、社会、文化权利的基本权利地位

经济、社会和文化权利一度被认为不应算作人权，而只是国家的社会政策。正如本文开篇提到的 20 世纪 70 年代中期荷兰学者的研究所展示的，被调查的 142 个国家的宪法中只有 10 部宪法用到了“经济权利”这个词或是类似的词；只有 5 部宪法用了“文化权利”这个词或类似的词。[②] 然而时至今日，《经济、社会和文化权利国际公约》已经拥有 163 个缔约国，即全世界 80% 以上的国家已经接受了经济、社会和文化权利属于基本人权的观念。这一变化在宪法中的体现就是越来越多的宪法确立了经济、社会、文化权利的基本权利地位。例如苏里南 1987 年宪法、哥伦比亚 1991 年宪法、捷克 1992 年《基本权利和基本自由宪章》、波兰 1997 年宪法、阿尔巴尼亚 1998 年宪法、莫桑比克 2005 年宪法等都将经济、社会与文化权利作为基本权利清单的一个独立部分加以规定。

有的国家通过宪法改革不断增强对经济、社会、文化权利的保障。例如，巴西 1988 年宪法第 6 条明确规定了社会权利，指出“教育、健康、工

---

① *Vienna Declaration and Program for Action*, A/CONF. 157/24 (1993), Part I, Ⅲ para. 5.

② 〔荷〕亨利·范·马尔赛文、格尔·范·德·唐：《成文宪法的比较研究》，陈云生译，华夏出版社，1987，第 135—136 页。

作、休闲、安全、社会保障、保护母亲和儿童、援助贫困者是本宪法规定的社会权利”；2000年，该国第26号宪法修正案增加了“居住权”作为社会权利的内容之一；2010年，第64号宪法修正案又增加了“食品权”作为社会权利的一项内容。[①] 葡萄牙1976年宪法通过后，截至2005年共进行了7次修订，工人的权利、健康权、住房权等内容在修订过程中不断得到强化。[②]

确立“经济、社会、文化权利”的基本权利地位，表明了各国对人权内容普遍性认知的提升，对各类人权彼此联系、相互依存、不可分割的性质的肯定。这一进展，同《经济、社会和文化权利国际公约》以及其他国际人权条约中的相关内容被各国广为接受密切关联。

2. 宪法比照国际人权法强化了对特定群体权利的保护

各国宪法近年来的发展呼应了国际人权法对妇女、儿童、残疾人、少数人权利的专门保护。此处仅以宪法对妇女权利、儿童权利的专门保护为例详加说明。

联合国通过的《妇女公约》是保障妇女人权的国际纲领。目前，该公约已有188个缔约国，这为公约对各国基本权利制度产生影响创造了机遇。该公约通过后，许多国家比照公约丰富和增强了宪法对妇女权利的保障。例如，比利时2002年2月26日修正宪法时，为原来关于“平等”的第10条增加第3款“保障男女平等”。德国1994年第42号基本法修正案修改了基本法第3条第2款，在原来“男女享有平等权利”的基础上增加了一句“国家应促进男女平等的实际贯彻，并致力于消除现存的歧视”。[③] 埃塞俄比亚1994年宪法第35条关于“妇女权利”的规定更是全面转述了《妇女公约》的核心内容。宪法直接援用人权条约的语言来诠释基本权利，是人

---

① CONSTITUIÇÃO DA REPúBLICA FEDERATIVA DO BRASIL DE 1988。该文本包含了2010年7月13日之前的66次修正。可访问 http://www.planalto.gov.br/ccivil_03/constituicao/constituicao.htm，最后访问日期：2015年1月22日。

② 比较葡萄牙1976年宪法和经7次修订后的2005年宪法可以看到，宪法增加了个人权利，减少了个人义务，强化了国家的人权保障义务。可访问 http://app.parlamento.pt/site_antigo/ingles/cons_leg/Constitution_VII_revisao_definitive.pdf，最后访问日期：2010年7月31日。

③ 1994年10月27日第42号基本法修正案是《德国基本法》通过以来几个主要的修正之一。修正后的第3条第2款确认了国家为实现男女平等可以采取特别措施。参见 Susanne Baer, “The Basic Law at 60 – Equality and Difference: A Proposal for the Guest List to the Birthday Party”, *German Law Journal* [special issue: the Basic Law] 11 (2010), p. 60。

权条约推进宪法基本权利最直接的体现。

关于儿童权利，1990 年生效的《儿童权利公约》得到了除美国和索马里之外的联合国所有会员国的接受。该公约获广泛接受极大地推动了近年来宪法对儿童权利的保护。在各国的宪法规定中，有的直接以《儿童权利公约》来确定宪法保护的儿童权利的范围，有的在具体条款中体现该公约的内容和原则。例如，根据哥伦比亚 1991 年宪法第 44 条的规定，儿童“应该享有宪法、法律、哥伦比亚批准的国际条约所承认的权利”。柬埔寨 1993 年宪法第 48 条第 1 款规定，国家保护《儿童权利公约》中规定的儿童权利，特别是生命权、受教育权、战争中的保护以及免受经济和性剥削。

区域人权条约和联合国核心人权条约在内容上具有较高的一致性，二者相互巩固、相互补充，共同促进宪法基本权利制度的完善。而某些区域人权条约包含的独到内容对缔约国宪法所产生的独特影响则显而易见。例如，1981 年生效的《非洲人权和民族权宪章》（以下简称《宪章》）以其内容涵盖三代人权，并强调权利与义务的统一性而著称，它不仅规定了内容广泛的经济、社会和文化权利，而且规定了自决权、发展权与环境权等集体人权。《宪章》通过后的 10 年间，非洲各国纷纷制定了包含权利法案的新宪法。这些新宪法明显呼应了《宪章》中关于人权的主张。许多国家在宪法的序言中引用《宪章》作为国家所保障的人权的根本依据。截至 2003 年的一项统计显示，就经济、社会和文化权利的规定而言，非洲 53 个国家的宪法中，43 个国家规定了贸易自由权，49 个国家规定了财产权，40 个国家规定了受教育权，40 个国家规定了劳动者权或与劳动相关的权利，32 个国家规定了社会保障权，34 个国家规定了健康权。此外，非洲大部分国家的宪法还规定了集体人权，其中 30 个国家规定了自决权，25 个国家规定了发展权，28 个国家规定了环境权。[①] 由此可见，区域人权条约对宪法基本权利的影响有时更加直接和明显。

（三）基本权利保障机构的扩展与国际人权法

由政府公权力保障基本权利是人权保障的传统模式。国际人权法要求

---

① 参见 Christ of Heyns（ed.），*Human Rights Law in Africa*（Vol. 2），Leiden：Martinus Nijhoff Publishers，2004。

国家采取一切适当措施保障人权的实现，这些措施包括但不限于立法机关制定法律、行政机关执行法律以及司法机关的公正审判。然而，公权力本身易于膨胀和被滥用的倾向促成了新的人权保障机制的发展，即政府公权力之外的专门的人权保护机构。

1978 年，联合国呼吁各国建立促进和保护人权的国家机构。[①] 1991 年“关于国家人权机构地位的巴黎原则”获得通过。[②] 1993 年联合国大会鼓励国家根据“巴黎原则”建立和加强国家人权机构（National Human Rights Institutions，NHRIs）。[③] 虽然国际人权法本身没有明确要求国家成立国家人权机构，但是鉴于国家人权机构在保护和促进人权方面可以发挥的重要作用，各人权条约机构纷纷通过一般性评论表达了支持的观点。例如，经济、社会和文化权利委员会在其第 10 号一般性评论中肯定了“国家人权机构在保护经济、社会和文化权利方面的作用”，并认为建立“促进和保护人权的国家机构”是缔约国履行公约义务的一项重要措施。[④] 消除种族歧视委员会建议“设立国家机构推动落实《公约》”。[⑤] 儿童权利委员会肯定“独立的国家人权机构是促进和确保执行《儿童权利公约》的重要机制”。[⑥]

在联合国人权机构的倡导和推动下，各国纷纷创建了适合本国国情的国家人权机构，并通过宪法明确其地位和职能。例如，菲律宾 1987 年宪法、马拉维 1994 年宪法、阿尔巴尼亚 1998 年宪法、匈牙利 2003 年宪法均通过专章或专门条款来规定相应的国家人权机构的设立及职能。截至 2013 年 2 月，世界范围内成立的 100 余个国家人权机构中，已有 69 个被国家人

---

① *National Institutions for the Promotion and Protection of Human Rights*, A/RES/33/46 (1978)。该文件认可了关于保护和促进人权的国家和地方机构的运行准则。

② 联合国于 1991 年在法国巴黎召开了关于国家人权机构的国际研讨会，会上通过了“关于国家人权机构地位的原则”，简称“巴黎原则”。参见 E/CN. 4/1992/43 (1991), p. 46。

③ *National Institutions for the Promotion and Protection of Human Rights*, A/RES/48/134 (1994), paras. 11&12.

④ UN Committee on Economic, Social and Cultural Rights, *General Comment No. 10, the Role of National Human Rights Institutions in the Protection of Economic, Social and Cultural Rights*, E/1999/22 (1998), p. 122, Annex V.

⑤ *General Recommendation XVII (42) on the Establishment of National Institutions to Facilitate the Implementation of the Convention*, A/48/18 (1993), p. 117.

⑥ UN Committee on Rights of the Child, *The Role of Independent National Human Rights Institutions in the Promotion and Protection of the Rights of the Child*, CRC/GC/2002/2 (2002).

权机构国际协调委员会确认为完全符合“巴黎原则”的标准。[①] 国家人权机构在传统的公权力之外，通过整合社会力量，形成了保护和促进基本权利的社会机制，在监督和协助政府执行国际人权法，保障普遍人权方面已经和正在发挥着重要作用。

（四）基本权利救济路径的延伸与国际人权法

1. 国际人权法充当基本权利之诉的审判依据

如上文所述，宪法基本权利在内容上正呈现出不断向国际人权法靠拢的趋势。与此同时，国际人权法也被频繁地用来解释宪法的基本权利，有些国家的宪法法院在审理基本权利案件时甚至直接援用国际人权条约作为审理案件的依据。国际人权法所蕴含的精神不仅被宪法基本权利所吸收，而且被宪法法院生动地诠释在具体的案例中，直接作用于对个人基本权利的救济。例如，西班牙宪法法院曾于 1991 年明确援引《儿童权利公约》第 40 条第 2（b）款，据以判定少年法庭以往采取的程序违宪。[②] 又如，哥伦比亚宪法法院于 1992 年根据《妇女公约》第 11 条的规定，确立了家务劳动应有报酬的判例。[③] 再如，法国最高上诉法院在 2005 年 5 月 18 日的决定中第一次以十分明确的方式适用了《儿童权利公约》“最高民事厅……在向涉案各方说明之后，决定自动依据《儿童权利公约》第 3 条第 1 款和第 12 条第 2 款提出论点”，从而肯定了该条约超越法国本国法律的地位。[④]

2. 基本权利救济途径向国际层面延伸

国际人权法规定的个人申诉程序为个人或团体提供了用尽国内救济后进一步获得救济的机会，以补充国内法对基本权利救济的不足。近年来，一方面越来越多的国际人权条约增设了个人申诉程序，另一方面越来越多的国家通过宪法确认了个人在用尽国内救济后向国际人权机构申请救济的权利。这使得对基本权利的救济途径从国内延伸到了国际。例如，俄罗斯

---

① 数据来源于联合国人权高专办公室网站 http://www.ohchr.org/EN/Countries/NHRI/Pages/NHRIMain.aspx，最后访问日期：2015 年 1 月 22 日。

② Report of the Committee on the Rights of the Child，A/51/41（1996），para. 270.

③ Report of the Committee on Elimination of Discrimination against Women，A/50/38（1995），para. 606.

④ 案例转引自 *The Universal Implementation of International Human Rights Treaties*，A/HRC/Sub. 1/58/5（2006），para. 51。

1993年宪法第46条第3款规定，根据俄罗斯联邦缔结的国际条约，在用尽国内救济后，人人有权向政府间机构提出保护人权和自由的申诉。秘鲁1993年宪法第205条规定，在用尽国内救济后，当事一方如果认为自己由宪法赋予的权利仍然受到损害，可以向根据秘鲁批准的条约或协定建立的国际法庭或机构申诉。

（五）国际人权法促成基本权利制度变迁的总体特征

越来越多的国家构建起了较为完备的宪法基本权利保障制度：基本权利的主体正在从具有一国国籍的公民扩展到每一个人；基本权利的内容正在从公民权利、政治权利扩展到经济、社会和文化权利；基本权利的保障正在从传统的立法、司法、行政机关的保障扩展到由国家人权机构参与的专门人权机构的保障；基本权利的救济途径正在从常规的司法机关的救济扩展到更高级别的宪法救济，从国内救济扩展到国际机构的救济。在宪法基本权利制度逐步走向完善的过程中，国际人权法的启发和影响作用显而易见。

首先，国际人权法是新近起草的宪法中基本权利制度的标杆，指引着宪法基本权利制度改革的方向。如果说人权条约同20世纪50年代前后制定的宪法间关系尚不明确，那么对于“国际人权宪章”生效后颁布的宪法，特别是20世纪90年代之后制定的宪法来说，人权条约发挥着重要的示范作用。在这些新宪法中随处可以找到国际人权条约的用语。

其次，与全球性人权条约相比，区域人权条约对缔约国宪法的影响也许更加直接和显著。这不仅是因为相互毗邻的地理位置、比较接近的文化传统以及存在组织结构较为紧密的区域组织使得区域性的文件更易被属于该区域的国家接受和贯彻；还因为一些区域性人权条约规定了比全球性条约更加严格的执行措施。

最后，国际人权法对宪法基本权利制度不同组成部分的影响程度有所不同。其中，宪法基本权利清单对国际人权法的呼应最为有力。相比之下，基本权利的保障机构虽然在国际人权法的影响下朝着多元的方向发展，而且世界范围内一半以上的国家成立了专门的人权机构，但是真正独立发挥有效作用的机构仍然有限。对基本权利的救济而言，虽然有相当数量的国家表示接受国际机构提供的救济途径，但是将这项承诺在宪法中予以确认的并不多见。

三　国际人权法促成基本权利制度变迁何以可能

国际人权法是宪法基本权利制度变迁的一个重要动因。来自国际和国内两方面的原因为国际人权法在基本权利制度演进过程中发挥积极影响创造了条件。

（一）人权的国际监督机制为国际人权法在国内发挥效力提供制度保障

国际人权法不仅规定普遍人权和国家保障人权的义务，而且创设了促进权利义务得以实现的国际监督机制。人权国际监督机制的关注点和落脚点是国际人权法在国内的落实情况，而完善的宪法基本权利制度是实现国际人权法的首要一步，也是人权国际监督机制努力促成的目标之一。

为促进各国切实贯彻国际人权法，在全球层面，联合国建立了监督人权保障的宪章机制和条约机制。宪章机制以联合国人权理事会为核心机构，以普遍定期审查制度、特别程序和申诉程序为制度依托，对联合国所有会员国的人权状况，尤其是履行国际人权法的状况进行定期的和经常性的监督。人权理事会是由政府代表组成的政治性机构，其对国家人权状况的审查结论，在影响力和执行力方面往往较专家组成的条约机制更为有力。

条约机制由依国际人权条约成立的条约机构，通过审议国家履约报告、受理国家间指控和个人申诉、赴缔约国实地调查访问等途径实现对缔约国履行人权条约状况的监督。每项监督活动之后，条约机构均会发表指导国家履行人权条约的意见或建议。由独立专家组成的条约机构，其意见或建议对缔约国来说虽然并不具有正式的法律拘束力，但实际上已逐步得到了各缔约国的重视和不同程度的采纳。

近年来，为促使国家遵守和执行人权国际监督机制的审议结论，宪章机制和条约机制逐步形成了各自的后续跟踪程序（Follow-up Procedure），不断跟进和督促国家执行审议结论，有力地加强了人权国际监督机制在各国国内的实际影响力。此外，两套机制还通过一系列改革措施，不断向有强制力的机制发展。

区域层面的人权监督机制较联合国机制更为有力，其典型代表是欧洲人权机制。1998 年改革之后的欧洲人权法院[①]具备了对《欧洲人权公约》体系的发展具有决定性影响的极大权限。这是因为该公约第 32 条授权人权法院对“所有与公约的解释和适用相关的问题”享有排他的最终决定权，也就是说人权法院实际上有权决定自己的管辖权范围。又据该公约第 46 条，缔约国“保证在其作为当事方的任何案件中遵守法院的终审判决”，判决的执行还有部长委员会的监督作保障。这种制度上的安排，促使缔约国在国内认真贯彻《欧洲人权公约》和欧洲人权法院的判决，并在必要情况下对宪法基本权利制度作出调整。

（二）国家广泛接受国际人权法为其影响基本权利制度创造现实条件

一般而言，国际条约只对缔约国产生法律拘束力。以国际人权条约为主体的国际人权法在世界范围内被广泛接受，使得国际人权法能够对几乎所有国家产生拘束力。其中，联合国人权条约得到了成员国的普遍批准。截至 2014 年 10 月 1 日，批准《经济、社会和文化权利国际公约》、《公民权利和政治权利国际公约》、《消除一切形式种族歧视国际公约》、《妇女公约》、《禁止酷刑公约》、《儿童权利公约》这 6 项核心人权条约中的一项或几项的国家已占联合国 193 个会员国的 90% 以上。对个人申诉程序而言，目前所有联合国核心人权条约的条约机构均具备了受理个人申诉的职能。其中，同意本国公民向人权事务委员会[②]提交申诉的国家已达 115 个，占批准该公约国家总数的 68%；另有 105 个国家同意个人向消除对妇女歧视委员会[③]提交申诉，占批准国总数的 56%。这些数字仍在不断攀升。[④]

从国家对区域人权条约的接受程度看，截至 2014 年 10 月 1 日，欧洲理事会 47 个成员国均批准了《欧洲人权公约》；美洲国家组织 35 个成员

① 1994 年欧洲理事会通过了《欧洲人权公约第十一议定书》，议定书决定以单一、常设、全职的欧洲人权法院取代过去由欧洲人权委员会和欧洲人权法院并立的双重人权保障机制。1998 年，新的欧洲人权法院成立。新法院不仅具备受理个人申诉、国家间申诉以及发表咨询意见的权力，而且有权管辖在申诉或咨询案中提出的与公约和议定书的解释和适用有关的所有事项。

② 人权事务委员会（human rights committee）是监督《公民权利和政治权利国际公约》实施情况的条约机构。

③ 消除对妇女歧视委员会是根据《妇女公约》设立并监督该公约执行情况的条约机构。

④ 以上数据统计自联合国条约集，可访问 http://treaties. un. org，最后访问日期：2015 年 1 月 22 日。

国均是《美洲国家组织宪章》的缔约国，其中25国批准了《美洲人权公约》；非洲联盟53个成员国全部加入了《非洲人权和民族权宪章》。此外，区域人权条约下的个人申诉程序更具优势。以欧洲为例，接受欧洲人权法院的管辖对缔约国来说是强制性的。欧洲人权法院发挥影响力的机会从其每年数以万计的受案数量即可略见一斑。20世纪60年代，欧洲人权委员会受理的案件是49件，70年代是163件，80年代是455件。1998年新的欧洲人权法院成立后案件激增到18200件，2006年一年的受案数量更是高达50500件之多。[①] 如此充足的案源，为该条约体系对各国的基本权利制度产生影响开辟了广阔的空间。

（三）宪法中凸显国际人权法的地位为其在国内得到实施提供坚实基础

过去，各国宪法一般只概括性地规定国际条约与国内法的关系，较少专门规定某类条约的地位。近年来，伴随国际人权条约影响力不断增强、普遍人权观念逐渐深入人心，越来越多的国家在宪法中对人权条约在国内法律体系中的地位，及如何在国内适用人权条约作了专门规定。有的国家甚至赋予人权条约以等同宪法的地位。例如，阿根廷1994年宪法第75条明确规定《美洲人的权利和义务宣言》、《世界人权宣言》、《美洲人权公约》、《经济、社会和文化权利国际公约》、《公民权利和政治权利国际公约》等10余项国际人权文件具有宪法的效力等级。更多的国家明确规定经批准的人权条约具有优于普通法律的地位。还有许多国家将国际人权条约作为解释宪法基本权利的依据，这为国家根据国际人权条约来丰富宪法基本权利的内涵创造了机会。在宪法中明确国际人权条约在一国法律体系中的地位，是国际人权条约能够在国内得到正确适用，并充分发挥影响力的坚实基础。

四 国际人权法对中国基本权利制度的影响

中国接受国际人权法始于20世纪80年代初。1980年11月4日，中国

---

① Helen Keller, Alec Stone Sweet (eds.), *A Europe of Rights: The Impact of the ECHR on Domestic Legal Systems*, Oxford: Oxford University Press, 2008, p. 20.

批准了《消除对妇女一切形式歧视公约》，这是对中国产生法律拘束力的首个国际人权条约。次年，中国批准了《消除一切形式种族歧视国际公约》。随后，中国又相继批准了《禁止酷刑公约》（1988 年）[①]、《儿童权利公约》（1992 年）、《经济、社会和文化权利国际公约》（2001 年）以及《残疾人权利公约》（2008 年）等 6 项联合国核心人权条约。尽管中国尚未批准《公民权利和政治权利国际公约》，但并不意味着中国没有义务保障个人的公民权利和政治权利。这是因为，一方面中国已经签署了《公民权利和政治权利国际公约》，签署条约的法律效力意含签署国已初步同意受该条约的拘束，在批准条约之前，签署国不得采取破坏该条约目的和宗旨的行动。[②] 另一方面，中国已经批准的其他人权条约反复确认了所有人平等享有所有人权的原则。所以，根据已经接受的国际人权法，中国承担了尊重、保护和实现在其管辖范围内所有人的普遍人权的国际法律义务。

接受国际人权法是否在一定程度上影响着中国宪法基本权利制度的走向？

中国现行宪法于 1982 年颁布之时将基本权利制度集中规定于第二章，定位在“公民”的基本权利，内容包括公民的人身自由和信仰自由，公民参与政治生活的权利，经济、社会、文化权利以及特定群体的权利等方面的共 27 项基本权利。这样的制度设计应该说更多的是承接了中国历部宪法的传统并借鉴了相关国家的有益经验，[③] 尚难发现受国际人权法影响的直接证据。之后，现行宪法经历了几次修正，历次修正均将基本权利制度向前推进一步。其中 2004 年的第四次修正从多个方面加强了对宪法基本权利的保障。此次修正的最大亮点是在“公民的基本权利与义务”一章增加了“国家尊重和保障人权”的宪法原则，“人权”这一术语第一次出现在中国的根本法中。“人权”入宪引起了各界的广泛关注，学者们普遍认为，人权入宪意义深远，它修正了中国的人权主体观，从前的公民人权观被现在的一切人的人权观所取代；修正了宪法的基本权利体系，将过去封闭的列举式权利体系变为开放的体系，为保障宪法中没有列举的人权提供了依

① 括号中标明的是中国批准相应公约的年份。

② 《维也纳条约法公约》第 18 条第 1 款规定：“一国负有义务不得采取任何足以妨碍条约目的及宗旨之行动：（甲）如该国已签署条约或已交换构成条约文书而须经批准、接受或赞同，但尚未明白表示不欲成为条约当事国之意思；……”

③ 关于中国现行宪法基本权利制度确立历程的论述，可参见韩大元《基本权利概念在中国的起源与演变》，《中国法学》2009 年第 6 期。

据；它还修正了中国的人权标准观，将人权标准从国家现行法律规定的标准扩展为国际人权条约下接受的人权标准。[①]

不难看出，学者们多以国际人权法中的普遍人权观来解读“人权”入宪的意义。尽管“国家尊重和保障人权”被放在了“公民”基本权利的章节，从条文结构上难以突破权利主体的局限，但是学者们略带理想主义的解读并非空穴来风，“人权”入宪也并非一蹴而就。自 1991 年中国政府发布首份《中国的人权状况》白皮书，首度公开表达中国对人权保护的立场以来，中国就在不断对国际人权法的发展作出回应，并在这个过程中不断发展自己的人权观。1991 年，中国政府强调人权的特殊性，指出“人权状况的发展受到各国历史、社会、经济、文化等条件的制约，是一个历史的发展过程”。[②] 1995 年，中国政府在谈到人权实现的条件时指出“和平与发展是当今世界的两大主题，也是实现普遍人权和基本自由的必不可少的前提”；国际合作的目标是建设一个“和平稳定、经济发展和普遍享有人权的世界”。[③] 由此，中国政府开始承认人权普遍性的一面，即所有人“普遍享有人权”。对于人权的国际监督，2000 年，中国政府认为递交履行人权条约的国家报告是为了“增进有关公约机构和国际社会对中国人权状况的了解”。[④] 2003 年，中国政府开始主张“应充分考虑和利用联合国现有的法律、人权文书和监督机制”，[⑤] 但是对于如何利用联合国的人权法律并未详述。2004 年，中国政府表示要“重视国际人权文书在促进和保护人权方面发挥的重要作用，……采取一系列措施履行公约义务，并根据公约规定及时提交履行公约情况的报告，接受联合国条约机构的审议”。[⑥] 中国政

---

① 关于人权入宪的深远意义的讨论，可参见莫纪宏等《人权法的新发展》，中国社会科学出版社，2008，第 179 页；韩大元《基本权利概念在中国的起源与演变》，《中国法学》2009 年第 6 期；徐显明《宪法修正条款修正了什么》，载中国人权研究会编《“人权入宪”与人权法制保障》，团结出版社，2006，第 44—49 页。

② 中华人民共和国国务院新闻办公室：《中国的人权状况》，1991 年 11 月。

③ 中华人民共和国国务院新闻办公室：《中国人权事业的进展》，1995 年 11 月。

④ 中华人民共和国国务院新闻办公室：《2000 年中国人权事业的进展》，2001 年 4 月，第七部分第二段。

⑤ 中华人民共和国国务院新闻办公室：《2003 年中国人权事业的进展》，2004 年 3 月，第八部分第二段。

⑥ 中华人民共和国国务院新闻办公室：《2004 年中国人权事业的进展》，2005 年 4 月，第七部分第二段。

府认为履行国际人权条约和接受国际机构监督均是法律义务。2008年，中国政府再次确认要“充分发挥国际人权公约在促进和保护本国人权方面的积极作用”。[①] 从2009年开始，中国先后制定了《国家人权行动计划（2009—2010年）》和《国家人权行动计划（2012—2015年）》。两份行动计划从结构到措辞与国际人权法的规定保持了一致，行动计划中所规定的权利在很多方面超越了现行宪法对基本权利的保障，反映了中国政府对人权的最新理解，这些理解更加全面，也是符合国际人权标准的理解。

综上所述，国际人权法对中国人权观念以及基本权利制度的影响是潜移默化的，“人权”入宪是这一影响过程的标志性事件，它为此后中国采取更加积极的措施完善基本权利制度、保障普遍人权奠定了基石。

五　结论

联合国成立的前40年，保护人权的国际规范体系迅速生成，但大量规范被束之高阁。而20世纪90年代以降，情况发生了明显转变。联合国层面的人权条约被写入各国宪法，人权条约被当作标准应用到审判实践中。区域层面，如欧洲人权法院，其浩如烟海的判例为各国法院广泛引用。种种迹象表明，国际人权法已经从最初的“宣示型”规范发展为“实施型”规范，甚至显露出“强制型”规范的端倪。受其影响，宪法基本权利制度呈现出不断向国际人权法靠拢的趋势。

不可否认，宪法基本权利制度的发展变化是多种因素共同作用的结果。在诸多因素中，国际人权法已经和正在产生的深刻影响不容忽视。宪法基本权利制度的发展变化是在国际人权法已被各国广泛接受的大环境下发生的；这些变化所体现出来的人权主体的普遍性、人权内容的普遍性等特征是对国际人权法所蕴含的普遍人权观念的有力印证。

（本文原载于《广东社会科学》2015年第3期）

① 中华人民共和国国务院新闻办公室：《中国的法治建设》，2008年2月，第三部分。

《公民及政治权利国际公约》的两份中文本：问题、比较与出路

孙世彦*

“International Covenant on Civil and Political Rights”（ICCPR）① 是“国际人权宪章”的重要组成部分，也是公民权利和政治权利领域中最为广泛、最为权威的国际法律文件。ICCPR 于 1966 年 12 月 16 日由联合国大会第 2200 A（XXI）号决议通过，1976 年 3 月 23 日生效，截至 2007 年 3 月 13 日，已经有 160 个缔约国和 6 个签署国。中国于 1998 年 10 月 5 日签署了 ICCPR，并且一直在积极考虑并致力于尽快批准该文书。

自中国签署 ICCPR 之后，中国学者一直非常关注其批准和实施问题，并进行了大量的研究、出版了不少的成果。然而，在考虑批准和研究 ICCPR 的过程中，几乎从来没有任何机构或学者关注所使用的 ICCPR 的中文本的版本出处、内容正误和法律效力等问题。尽管一些学者在其相关研究中已经察觉就该文书的中文标题而言就存在“公约”与“盟约”的混乱，以及目前在联合国和中国广为使用的 ICCPR 的中文本，与其作准英文本相比，在许多措辞和用语上有程度不同的差异，② 但是，似乎从没有人深究这些问题的原因和可能造成的后果。笔者经调查发现，实际上 ICCPR 有两个中文本：目前在联合国和中国广为使用的 ICCPR 的中文本不是作准文

* 孙世彦，中国社会科学院国际法研究中心研究员。

① 这是该法律文书的英文全称和缩略语。由于本文涉及该法律文书具有不同中文标题的问题，因此下文一般以 ICCPR 或《公约》指代该法律文书，但并不必然指其英文本或中文本。

② 如参见陈光中主编《〈公民权利和政治权利国际公约〉批准与实施问题研究》，中国法制出版社，2002，第 101、226、318 页；杨宇冠《人权法——〈公民权利和政治权利国际公约〉研究》，中国人民公安大学出版社，2003，第 260 页。

本，而且充满了错误；而 ICCPR 的作准中文本则鲜为人知、几被遗忘。因此，本文将揭示这两个文本的存在，举例分析两个文本的不同措辞和用语可能造成的对于 ICCPR 的不同理解，论证两个文本的不同法律地位和效力，表明这一问题对中国批准和实施 ICCPR 所可能产生的重大影响，并探讨应该如何认识与解决这一独特、重要、紧迫的问题。

一　问题的发现与提出

根据 ICCPR 第 49 条和第 53 条的规定、《维也纳条约法公约》中可适用的规定以及相关的国际实践，对于 ICCPR 的文本可以确知的是：该文书有 5 个同一作准文本，即中文、英文、法文、俄文及西班牙文文本，该 5 种文本具有同等的法律效力；ICCPR 的 5 种作准文本，是由参加 ICCPR 草拟的国家同意、联合国大会通过、获得 35 件批准书或加入书而生效的文本；这些作准文本被交存联合国档库，其正式副本则由联合国秘书长发布并分送 ICCPR 的所有缔约国和签署国。[①] 根据联合国的实践，在交存联合国档库后，ICCPR 的所有作准文本均刊载在《联合国条约集》（United Nations Treaty Series，简称 U. N. T. S.）上。这样所形成的包括中文本在内的 5 种作准文本，正如“作准”所指，是国际法意义上唯一合法有效的 ICCPR 文本。除非此后根据法定程序被修正，并导致其所有 5 种作准文本或仅只某一文本的修正，否则，这 5 种文本仍是 ICCPR 的法定作准文本。

然而，就 ICCPR 的中文本而言，则有一个完全不同的、奇怪的现象，即刊载在《联合国条约集》上的作准中文本，[②] 与联合国目前广为使用的中文本并非同一文本。比较这两份文本，会发现两者无论在具体用语还是行文方式上都有重大差别，甚至连标题都不尽相同，作准本的标题为《公民及政治权利国际盟约》，而联合国目前广为使用且更为人熟知的中文本

① 联合国于 1967 年 3 月 29 日确立了 ICCPR 正式副本并于 1994 年 5 月 17 日发布了这些副本。Depository Notification C. N. 61. 1967. TREATIES - 1 （18 May 1967）；Procès-verbal of Ratification of the Original of the Covenant，Depository Notification C. N. 8. 2002. TREATIES - 1 （3 January 2002）.

② U. N. T. S. Vol. 999，p. 202 （1976）.

的标题则是《公民权利和政治权利国际公约》（有时也作《盟约》）。根据笔者掌握的资料，前一文本最早出现在 1966 年联合国大会通过 ICCPR 的第 2200 A（XXI）决议中文本的附件中，① 后来又刊载在《联合国条约集》上（以下简称“先前本”）。而后一文本出现的最早日期，至少可以追溯至联合国于 1973 年编辑的《人权——联合国国际文件汇编》②，并在此后被联合国用于几乎所有人权文件汇编等出版物③（以下简称“后来本”）。后来本在中国也使用得极为广泛，刊载在众多学术网站上和人权文件汇编中，④ 并且是许多学者研究 ICCPR 时的文本依据。⑤ 有一定证据表明，中国有关国家机关在考虑对 ICCPR 的签署与批准时，依据的也是该文本。⑥ 相比而

---

① ICCPR 通过时的中文本，见 http://daccessdds. un. org/doc/RESOLUTION/GEN/NR0/783/02/IMG/NR078302. pdf? OpenElement。但是，该文本与载于《联合国条约集》上的作准中文本相比，有几处微小差别，看起来主要是印刷技术方面的错漏。

② ST/HR/1，1974.

③ 如参见联合国《人权：国际文件汇编》，ST/HR/1/Rev. 3，1988；《人权国际文件汇编》，ST/HR/1/Rev. 6（Vol. I/Part 1），2002；联合国人权事务高级专员办事处《核心国际人权条约》，ST/HR/3，2006；联合国人权中心“人权概况介绍”第 2 号《国际人权宪章》中文本，附件，1988。

④ 网站如中国人权研究会：http://www. humanrights. cn/china/rqfg/R120011127112054. htm；中国法律法规网：http://www. falvfagui. com/falv/Article/xianzhengzhuanti/200607/1015063. html。汇编如董云虎、刘武萍编著《世界人权约法总览》，四川人民出版社，1991，第 972 页；中国社会科学院法学研究所《国际人权文件和国际人权机构》，社会科学文献出版社，1993，第 22 页；冯林主《中国公民人权读本》，经济日报出版社，1998，第 365 页；北京大学法学院人权研究中心《国际人权文件选编》，北京大学出版社，2002，第 16 页（但其使用的名称是《公民权利和政治权利国际盟约》）；胡志强《中国国际人权公约集》，中国对外翻译出版公司，2004，第 27 页。

⑤ 以“后来本”为基础的对 ICCPR 的研究成果如彭锡：《〈公民权利和政治权利国际公约〉国际监督机制研究》，吉林人民出版社，2001；陈光中主编《〈公民权利和政治权利国际公约〉批准与实施问题研究》，中国法制出版社，2002；杨宇冠《人权法——〈公民权利和政治权利国际公约〉研究》；朱晓青、柳华文《〈公民权利和政治权利国际公约〉及其实施机制》，中国社会科学出版社，2003；陈光中主编《〈公民权利和政治权利国际公约〉与我国刑事诉讼》，商务印书馆，2005；莫纪宏《国际人权公约与中国》，世界知识出版社，2005，第 263—336 页；刘连泰《〈国际人权宪章〉与我国宪法的比较研究——以文本为中心》，法律出版社，2006，第 85—133、144—228 页。

⑥ 中国外交部的网站没有公布任何一个版本的全文，而只是指出中国已经签署了《公民权利和政治权利国际公约》（后来本的标题），见 http://www. mfa. gov. cn/chn/wjb/zzjg/tyfls/wjzdtyflgz/zgygjrqf/t94508. htm。不过，外交部条约法律司编的《中华人民共和国多边条约集》上刊载的是后来本（第八集），法律出版社，2006，第 30—47 页。

言，载有先前本的学术资料或使用该文本的研究著述则极少。[①]

就同一项ICCPR存在两份中文本这一现象导致了三方面的国际法律问题。其一，先前本与后来本究竟有何区别？两者仅仅在语言形式上有所不同，还是另有实质内容的差异？如果两者的某些内容有实质差异，究竟哪一个文本更加符合ICCPR制定者的意图，与ICCPR的目的和宗旨更加一致？其二，从国际法的角度，究竟应该如何理解ICCPR存在两种不同的中文本的情况以及这两者之间的关系？其三，这一现象对中国考虑批准和将来实施ICCPR会产生怎样的作用和影响？这一现象可能导致哪些法律和其他问题？应如何应对？这三方面的问题将在下文依次加以讨论。

二　两个文本的若干明显差别

必须对比这两个中文本以揭示这两者的确是不同的文本。对比之前应该强调以下几点。第一，这一部分只是挑选了若干明显的例证以说明两个中文本的差别，并没有穷尽这两个文本的所有不同，也不涉及某些在其他作准文本中也可能引起不同理解和争议之处。第二，对比的主要方法是依循《维也纳条约法公约》规定的有关条约解释的规则，同时参考某些学者的见解。第三，在对比时，主要根据ICCPR的作准英文本[②]对两个中文本的差别进行判断与评价，这意味着对于两个中文本中有差别的条款，将主要根据这些条款与英文本中相对应条款的一致程度来衡量它们中究竟哪一个更加符合ICCPR的目的和宗旨。但必须指出的是，之所以采用英文本作为评判的标准完全是基于实用的考虑，而不是因为英文本在法律上具有比中文本或其他作准文本更高的效力。从逻辑上说，如果没有一个中立的第三者作为标准，评判有差异的两个事物是不可能的，而使用英文本作为这样的客观标准是合适的：在起草ICCPR时，大多数的讨论都是围绕英文本展开的，可以认为英文本准确体现了起草者的意图；而且，在ICCPR的5种

① 如见王铁崖、田如萱《国际法资料选编》，法律出版社，1986年第2版，第166页；王德禄、蒋世和《人权宣言》，求实出版社，1989，第35页；李龙、万鄂湘《人权理论与国际人权》，武汉大学出版社，1992，第307页；罗玉中、万其刚、刘松《人权与法制》，北京大学出版社，2001，第728页（但其所用的标题为《公民权利和政治权利国际公约》）。

② U. N. T. S. Vol. 999, 1976, p. 171.

文本中，英文本在世界范围内使用的程度最高，有关 ICCPR 以及公民权利和政治权利的概念、规则和语汇主要是以其英文本为基础发展起来的。

（一）名称与标题："公约"还是"盟约"？

一个经常令研究者感到困惑的问题是，与 ICCPR 中的"Covenant"对应的中文词似乎有"盟约"和"公约"两个。而且即使在联合国的中文文献中，也是忽而"盟约"、忽而"公约"，令人无所适从。这一问题的澄清不仅涉及两个中文本的差别，而且也涉及先前本名称的一个变化。先前本的名称——在 2002 年 1 月 3 日被更正前——为《公民及政治权利国际盟约》，而后来本的名称为《公民权利和政治权利国际公约》（有时也作《盟约》）。对比这两个名称，会发现除了两处形式上的不同外，最主要的差别是：与英文本中的"Covenant"对应的，在前者中是"盟约"，在后者中是"公约"。在中文中，"盟约"被解释为"缔结同盟时所订立的誓约或条约"，[①] 因此"盟约"更多地用于指称某些组织性、构成性文件，故而其适用范围要小于可泛指任何多边约束性文件的"公约"。[②] 因此"公约"可能更适于指称由联合国主持通过的、包括 ICCPR 在内的多边性人权条约。[③] 而在英文中，"Covenant"与"Convention"的差别则远比中文中"盟约"与"公约"的差别要小。《布莱克法律辞典》对"Convention"的一项释义是：An agreement or compact，esp. one among nations；a multilateral treaty，对"Covenant"的释义是：1. A formal agreement or promise，usu. in a contract；2. Treaty。[④] 可见这两者并没有实质的差别。也许正是以上原因导致了在 2001—2002 年 ICCPR 作准中文本的更正，即以"公约"替代作准中文本标题和文本中的"盟约"一词。对此，本文将在第三部分中进行更为详细的介绍。

---

① 《现代汉语词典》对"盟约"的释义，商务印书馆，1994，第 778 页。

② 《现代汉语词典》（第 386 页）对"公约"的释义是："条约的名称之一。一般指三个或三个以上的国家缔结的某些政治性的或关于某一专门问题的条约。"

③ 实际上，国际人权领域中除两个 Covenants 以外的其他重要条约的名称都是"Convention"/"公约"，如 Convention on the Rights of the Child /《儿童权利公约》。

④ 分别见 *Black's Law Dictionary*（West，7th ed.，1999），p. 332，p. 369，p. 370. 但该书在第 5 版中对"Covenant"的释义是"An agreement，convention，or promise of two or more parties"（*Black's Law Dictionary*，West，5th ed.，1979，p. 327）。

（二）第 2 条第 1 款："民族本源"还是"国籍"？

ICCPR 第 2 条第 1 款规定的是缔约国承担尊重和保证在其领土内和受其管辖的一切个人无差别地享有 ICCPR 所承认的权利的原则。对此，先前本的表述是："本盟约缔约国承允尊重并确保所有境内受其管辖之人，无分种族、肤色、性别、语言、宗教、政见或其他主张［、］民族本源或社会阶级、财产、出生或其他身分等等，一律享受本盟约所确认之权利。"后来本的表述是："本公约每一缔约国承担尊重和保证在其领土内和受其管辖的一切个人享有本公约所承认的权利，不分种族、肤色、性别、语言、宗教、政治或其他见解、国籍或社会出身、财产、出生或其他身份等任何区别。"

从中可以看出，在不得作为差别待遇的根据中，两个文本有一个显著的不同，即先前本中的"民族本源"和后来本中的"国籍"，在英文本中，相对应的短语都是"national…origin"。那么，"民族本源"和"国籍"中的哪一个与"national origin"的意思更为接近呢？

从法律角度来看，"民族本源"和"国籍"显然是两个不同的概念。"民族本源"即一个人的民族出身并不必然与"国籍"有关，即使同一个国家的国民也可能有不同的民族本源或出身；而"国籍"指某个人拥有的、作为某一国家国民或公民的资格，因此不同国籍的人完全可能具有同样的民族本源或出身，反之亦然。

从纯粹语言的角度讲，英文中与"国籍"对应的"nationality"一词[①]可以是"national origin"的义项之一，而且两者可能有重叠的涵盖范围——这仅仅是在事实而非法律的意义上。例如，在"美籍华人"这样一种称谓中，这两个概念的区别就清晰、典型地体现出来：一个"美籍华人"在一方面，与生活在任何地方的华人具有一样的"民族本源"，即生为华人；在另一方面，却又与所有美利坚合众国的国民——无论其"民族本源"为何——具有一样的"国籍"即身为美国公民。那么，差别如此之大、绝不能被混淆的"民族本源"和"国籍"中两个概念中，哪一个更能体现 IC-

① 《世界人权宣言》第 15 条规定的是享有国籍的权利，其对应的英文词即为"nationality"而非"national origin"。

CPR 中有关规定的本义，更贴近英文本中的“national origin”？首先，如同其他不得作为歧视的理由如种族、肤色、性别、语言、宗教等一样，“民族本源”是一个事实，对此事实法律无法加以改变；但是“国籍”则是一个不同于这些事实因素的法定概念，可以依法改变。其次，有极少数基于国籍的差别待遇是 ICCPR 所明文允许的，例如第 25 条所规定的政治权利只能为“公民”（英文本中为“citizen”）所享有。因此，很难想象该条一方面将政治权利仅赋予“公民”即拥有所关涉之缔约国国籍的人，另一方面——按照后来本第 2 条第 1 款的措辞——又称这种权利的享有不受国籍的限制。[①] 再次，监督 ICCPR 之实施与执行的人权事务委员会在“居耶诉法国案”中的说明极为清楚地否定了“national origin”具有“国籍”的含义。需要指出的是，该案涉及 ICCPR 第 26 条即法律的平等保护和非歧视的规定，但其中列举的禁止歧视的理由在用语上与第 2 款第 1 款的用语完全一致，因此对第 26 条中的“national origin”的解释完全适用于对第 2 条第 1 款的理解。在该来文中，易布拉依玛·居耶（Ibrahima Gueye）等提交人声称他们由于自己的国籍而受到了歧视。但人权事务委员会在对该案最后意见中指出，“国籍本身没有出现在第 26 条列举的被禁止的歧视理由之中，……国籍属于第 26 条第 2 句话中提到的‘其他身分’”。[②] 最后，ICCPR本身的其他条款也可以作为证明。第 24 第 1 款规定对儿童的保护措施不得有任何歧视，在英文本中，歧视的根据也包括“national origin”（其对应词在先前本和后来本中也分别是“民族本源”和“国籍”）。而第 24 条第 3 款的英文本规定儿童有权取得“nationality”（两个中文本中与之对应的词均为“国籍”）。这可以说明，在英文本中，“national origin”与“nationality”的含义是不一样的，否则它不会在同一条（即第 24 条）的不同两款（即第 1 款和第 3 款）中使用两个不同的术语。所有这些证据都清楚地表明，先前本中的“民族本源”更符合 ICCPR 的目的和宗旨以及对 ICCPR 的解释，与英文本中的“national origin”具有更为接近甚至相同的含义，而后来本中的“国籍”一词将导向完全不同的解释以及与 ICCPR 的

① 人权事务委员会也只是称“一般而言，本公约所订各项权利适用于每个人，不论国家间对等原则，亦不论该个人的国籍或无国籍身份”，而没有绝对地禁止在本国公民和外侨之间的区别对待。见人权事务委员会第 15 号一般性意见，第 1—2 段（1983）。

② *Gueye et al. v. France*, Communication No. 196/1985, para. 9. 4.

目的和宗旨不相容的法律后果。

（三）第14条第3款（d）项[①]：“辩护人”还是“法律援助”?

该项规定的是刑事案件中被告人的辩护权利。被告人可以自行辩护，也可以通过他人辩护。但对于“他人”究竟是谁，先前本和后来本的表述是不一样的：先前本为“到庭受审，及亲自答辩或由其选任辩护人答辩；未经选任辩护人者，应告以有此权利；法院认为审判有此必要时，应为其指定公设辩护人，如被告无资力酬偿，得免付之”；后来本则是“出席受审并亲自替自己辩护或经由他自己所选择的法律援助进行辩护；如果他没有法律援助，要通知他享有这种权利；在司法利益有此需要的案件中，为他指定法律援助，而在他没有足够能力偿付法律援助的案件中，不要他自己付费”。两个中文本的最显著不同是先前本作“辩护人”之处，后来本为“法律援助”（英文本相对应的用语是“legal assistance”）。

就英文本中的“legal assistance”而言，如果该用语出现在其他语境中，在中文中理解为“法律援助”也许并无不妥。然而，对该项中出现的这一表达决不能作此简单理解，而要考虑到该规定的目的和宗旨。按一位权威学者的分析，该项的规定可以被分为一系列个别的权利，包括：亲自为自己辩护；选择自己的辩护人；被告知获得辩护人的权利；获得免费的legal assistance。[②] 由此看来，先前本中以“辩护人”对应“legal assistance”是妥当的。后来本中的对应词“法律援助”的问题在于，在现代汉语法律语言中，“法律援助”已经取得了约定俗成的含义，即指某一案件的当事人由专业法律人帮助进行诉讼，但无力支付该服务，因此这种法律帮助为免费或由第三方付费的情况。但这种意义上的法律援助在英文中是“legal aid”，可以理解为“免费的法律帮助（free legal assistance）”，因此与更广义的“legal assistance”具有迥然不同的含义，不可混为一谈。[③] 后

① 在先前本中，此处为“（卯）项”；在后来本中，此处为“（丁）项”。为避免繁杂与混淆，此处采用英文本的标记方式。下文对第14条第3款（e）项采用同样的处理方式。

② Manfred Nowak, *UN Covenant on Civil and Political Rights-CCPR Commentary* (N. P. Engle, 2nd. ed., 2005), Article 14, para. 58. 这也得到了人权事务委员会的一系列案例法的确认。

③ 例如，《布莱克法律辞典》中将“legal aid”解释为“Free or inexpensive legal services provided to those who cannot afford to pay full price”（*Black's Law Dictionary*, 7th ed., 1999, p. 903）。该辞典中没有收入“legal assistance”一词。

来本使用的“法律援助”容易让人误以为在任何刑事案件中，无论被告的经济承担能力如何，国家都有义务为其提供免费的辩护人。这样的理解将极大地扩展缔约国的相应义务，完全与该项的意图不符。实际上，该项最后提到的在被告人自己无力支付“legal assistance”的情况下，为其指定的、无须他自己付费的“legal assistance”才是通常所说的“法律援助”。[①]

（四）第14条第3款（e）项：谁诘问/讯问证人？

ICCPR 第14条第3款（e）项规定了受刑事控告者讯问证人的权利。对此，先前本的行文是“得亲自或间接诘问他造证人，并得声请法院传唤其证人在与他造证人同等条件下出庭作证”；后来本是“讯问或业已讯问对他不利的证人，并使对他有利的证人在与对他不利的证人相同的条件下出庭和受讯问”；[②] 英文本则是“To examine, or have examined, the witnesses against him and to obtain the attendance and examination of witnesses on his behalf under the same conditions as witnesses against him”。

先前本该项前半句话中的“间接诘问证人”比较令人费解，而后来本中的相对应部分则更让人莫名其妙。从上下文来看，在第14条第3款的每一项之前，都可以加上“every one [accused] shall be entitled to”[③]（按后来本即“[被指控的人] 人人有资格”），这样该句可以扩展为“[被指控的人] 人人有资格讯问或业已讯问对他不利的证人”。什么叫“有资格……业已讯问证人”？完全无法理解。

为了正确地理解该规定的本义，我们首先需要看看英文表达的一种用法：Someone has something done。其含义是，某人的某件事情完成了，但该事并非该某人自己做的，而是由未加指明的他人做的。例如，He has his watch sold 的意思是他卖了自己的表，但不是亲自卖的，而是通过他人比如寄卖商店卖掉的。这句话的含义与 He has sold his watch（他自己把表卖

---

① 参见 *O. F. v. Norway*, Communication No. 158/1983, para. 5.6。

② 不过，在联合国人权事务高级专员办事处最新出版的《核心国际人权条约》（ST/HR/3, 2006年）中，该项前半句的行文是“直接或间接讯问对他不利的证人”，比较接近先前本的意思。

③ 例如，人权事务委员会第13号一般性意见英文本论及该项规定时，就称“Subparagraph 3（e）states that the *accused shall be entitled to* examine or have examined the witnesses against him...”（Human Rights Committee, General Comment No. 13, para. 12, 1984）。

了）是很不一样的，尽管这两句翻译成中文很可能都是“他卖了自己的表”。同样，He is entitled to have his watch sold 和 He is entitled to sell his watch 的含义也不一样，尽管译成中文都是“他有权把表卖掉”。这里，“to”后面的动词（sell 或 have）决定了他是亲自卖表还是经由他人卖表。回头看 ICCPR 中这一部分的英文表述：“To examine，or have examined，the witnesses against him”。从语法上看，显然“examine”前面的“to”也限定后面的“have examined”，只不过为了行文方便省略了。因此，这应该是 Someone has something done 的用法。那么为什么不表述为“to have the witness against him examined”而是“［to］have examined，the witnesses against him”呢？这是为了与前面的“to examine”共用一个宾语、行文简洁起见。因此，如果把英文本该半句话展开还原，则分别是：every one accused shall be entitled to examine the witness against him 和 every one accused shall be entitled to have the witness against him examined。前一句话很好理解，即任何被告都有权利自己诘问他造证人/讯问对他不利的证人。后一句则表明任何被告都有权利让他人，一个第三者（例如律师）诘问他造证人/讯问对他不利的证人。反观两个中文本，先前本用的“间接”一词，尽管不很理想，但仍体现了这层意思；而后来本中令人无法理解的表述恐怕只能归结为一个翻译错误，即很可能是将“have the witness against him examined”理解成了现在完成时，并且因为在中文中没有过去时和现在完成时的明显区别，翻译成了“业已讯问”。对先前本的正确和后来本的错误，人权事务委员会在其第 13 号一般性意见中对该项的解释也可以作为证明：“第 3 款（e）项规定，被告应可讯问或可要求由他人讯问对他不利的证人，并使对他有利的证人在与对他不利的证人相同的条件下出席和受讯问。”①

（五）第 18 条第 1 款：如何行使宗教和信仰自由？

ICCPR 第 18 条第 1 款保障的是个人的思想、良心和宗教自由。对于如何行使这一权利，先前本规定“此项权利包括保有或采奉自择之宗教或信仰之自由”；与之对应的后来本的表述则是“此项权利包括维持或改变他的宗教或信仰的自由”。可以发现，两者最大的差别是使用了不同的动词：

① 人权事务委员会第 13 号一般性意见（1984），第 12 段，着重号为笔者所加。

"保有或采奉"和"维持或改变"（英文本中与之对应的词组则是"to have or to adopt"）。在法律中，任何微小的差别都可能导致不同的法律后果，因此绝不能忽视。那么，这两种不同的中文表述中，究竟哪一个更符合该规定的目的和宗旨呢？

要正确地理解这一问题，我们可以首先从ICCPR的立法史着手，了解为什么英文本使用了特定的动词"have"与"adopt"而非其他词汇。如果我们对照《世界人权宣言》和ICCPR，就会发现这两份文书的许多条款极其相近甚至雷同，这是因为ICCPR本来就是对《宣言》宣布之权利的具体化和法律化，所以ICCPR在许多方面保持着与《宣言》的一致性。但是，规定同样权利的《宣言》第18条与ICCPR第18条在本段所涉及的用词上却有较大不同。《宣言》第18条中与ICCPR第18条第1款第二句话前半段对应的部分的英文是："this right includes freedom to *change* his religion or belief"。可以发现，该部分用的动词是"change/改变"。为什么在ICCPR第18条的英文本中没有使用"to change"，而换之以"to have or to adopt"呢？实际上，联合国人权委员会最初提出的该款草案的表述与《宣言》的相应部分是类似的，即"to maintain or to change his religion"。然而，这一表述遭到了某些伊斯兰国家的强烈反对，并因而改成了目前的表述。① 尽管可以认为"adopt a religion of [his] choice"也意味着一个人有权利退出一个宗教社团而加入另一个，但非常清楚的是，在ICCPR英文本中，没有使用"to maintain or to change"而代之以"to have or to adopt"是刻意的。② 因此，中文本也必须反映这一微妙而不可忽略的细节。相比而言，先前本中的"保有或采奉自择之宗教或信仰"的表述接近起草者的本意，也与英文本的表述相近。而后来本使用"改变"一词则完全没有体现起草者的微妙用意。

---

① 参见Marc J. Bossuyt, *Guide to the "Travaux Préparatoires" of the International Covenant on Civil and Political Rights* (Dordrecht, Martinus Nijhoff, 1987), pp. 357 - 358。

② 在有关第18条的第22号一般性意见英文本中，人权事务委员会也只是称，它认为"the freedom to 'have or to adopt' a religion or belief necessarily entails the freedom to choose a religion or belief, including the right to replace one's current religion or belief..."，而没有使用"change"一词（Human Rights Committee, General Comment 22, 1993, para. 5）。令人遗憾的是，在第22号一般性意见的相应中文本中，在与"replace"对应之处，依然使用了"改变"，尽管"replace"的最准确意思是"代替、替代、取代"。

三　问题的定性与解决

很明显，就 ICCPR 存在着两个中文本。以 ICCPR 的英文本为参照标准进行比较，先前本——至少就用来比较的部分而言——对该法律文书的目的和宗旨有更加准确的体现，而后来本中则存在着诸多严重的问题和错误，除了以上列举的以外，就 ICCPR 第 4 条第 3 款、第 5 条第 2 款、第 7 条、第 9 条第 3 款、第 14 条第 1 款、第 23 条第 4 款、第 25 条（c）项和第 27 条等，后来文中的谬误也比比皆是。

在现当代国际条约法律实践中，由于语言差异、法律传统和制度不同或起草过程中的技术问题等诸多原因，不同作准文本之间存在差异甚至某些规定上的实质不同，是屡见不鲜甚至不可避免的。从这一角度而言，如果目前在联合国和中国广泛使用的标题为《公民权利和政治权利国际公约》的 ICCPR 的中文本（后来本）是作准中文本，则它与其他 4 种作准本具有同等法律效力，该文本与其他文本如英文本存在差异因而也是正常的，这一问题可以按照《维也纳条约法公约》中有关条约解释的规定加以解决。

但是，从本文第一部分介绍的情况来看，至少 ICCPR 在通过时的作准文本是先前本。那么，是否有可能在 ICCPR 通过和生效以后，其作准中文本已经根据法定程序被修正——即后来本是对先前本的修正与取代？按照相关国际法规则，对条约的任何改变可能经由两种途径。首先，根据《维也纳条约法公约》第 39 条和第 40 条第 1 款的规定，某一条约若对其自身的修正有规定，则修正应按此规定进行。因此，对 ICCPR 的任何修正（英文中为“amendments”），应依据其第 51 条的规定而进行。这样的修正可以被称为实质性修正，但 ICCPR 从未根据该规定和程序加以修正。

其次，即使在准备原初文本的过程中极为小心，由于某些实际的原因，对某一条约的原初文本进行技术性更正（英文中为“corrections”）可能仍是必要的。这些可能构成对某一条约之原初文本进行更正的原因是：（1）在打字或印刷、拼写、标点、标数中存在形式性错误和类似错误；（2）条约的原初文本与通过条约的外交会议的正式记录缺乏一致性；（3）在构成条约之原初文本的不同作准文本之间缺乏和谐一致。[1]

然而，即使这样的更正也有严格的程序。联合国秘书长作为保存人，可以自己或者应某一或某些参与条约之起草和通过的国家的要求，将更正提议通知所有参加缔约会议的国家、所有签署国和缔约国。只有在一个设定的适当期限内提议的更正未遭到反对时，才可以认为这些更正得到了通过。然后，这些更正就将对原初文本实际生效并由一位经授权的官员签署，一份相应的订正记事录（*procès-verbal* of rectification）将由保存人以保存通知（depositary notification）的形式递送给所有签署国和缔约国，[2] 而且任何更正都将由联合国记录、建档、公布。

根据联合国多边条约的保存记录，到目前为止仅有两次依该程序对ICCPR的更正，一次有关西班牙文本，[3] 一次有关中文本。对中文本的修正经过是：中国政府向联合国秘书长提出ICCPR作准中文本标题和文本中使用“盟约”是一个错误并建议以“公约”替代。联合国秘书长于2001年10月5日向所有有关国家发出通知，提议进行更正并征求任何可能的反对意见。[4] 在设定的90天的异议期满而没有国家表示反对后，联合国主管法律事务的副秘书长汉斯·考雷尔（Hans Corell）于2002年1月3日签署记事录（*Procès-verbal*），正式以“公约”取代作准中文本标题和文本中出现的“盟约”一词。[5] 因此，从严格的法律角度而言，ICCPR的正式中文名称从1966年12月16日获得通过到2002年1月3日，一直是《公民及政治权利国际盟约》，只有在2002年1月3日以后，才改为《公民及政治权利国际公约》。然而，此次对ICCPR作准中文本的修正，没有提到或暗示任何存在两个不同中文本的情况或它们之间的差异。

除了这一记载在联合国多边条约的保存记录中的更正以外，在联合国的

---

① Treaty Section of the Office of Legal Affairs, United Nations, *Summary of Practice of The Secretary-General as Depositary of Multilateral Treaties*, ST/LEG/7/Rev. 1, para. 48 (1999). 参见 Depository Notification C. N. 782. 2001. TREATIES - 6 (5 October 2001)。

② Treaty Section of the Office of Legal Affairs, United Nations, *Summary of Practice of The Secretary-General as Depositary of Multilateral Treaties*, ST/LEG/7/Rev. 1, paras. 49 - 59 (1999).

③ 该修正有关西班牙文本中的一处印刷错误。见 U. N. T. S. Vol. 1057, p. 407 (1977); United Nations, *Multilateral Treaties Deposited with the Secretary-General: Status as at 31 December 2001*, Vol. 1, p. 181 (2002)。

④ Depository Notification C. N. 782. 2001. TREATIES - 6 (5 October 2001).

⑤ Depository Notification C. N. 8. 2002. TREATIES - 1 (3 January 2002).

正式条约记录中没有任何信息表明对《公约》的作准中文本还有任何其他的修正或更正。在不存在相反证据的情况下可以得出结论，即目前广泛使用的后来本并没有取代《公约》的作准中文本，因此也不具有任何法律效力。而刊载在《联合国条约集》上并由联合国于1994年确立其正式副本的中文本，即先前本，结合2002年生效的对该文本的订正，才一直是唯一作准的、权威的《公约》中文本，并且和其他4个作准文本具有同等的法律效力。尽管如此，联合国本身却在30多年里一直将后来本当作“正式”或“官方”中文本加以使用，而且主要基于这一原因，导致了在中国对《公约》的理解和研究主要——如果不是全部——以后来本为文本基础。毕竟，谁会怀疑联合国出版物（如《人权国际文件汇编》中使用的《公约》中文本）不是作准文本呢？然而，任何条约都是“国家间所缔结之国际协定”，都代表了缔约国之间的同意，这意味着也要求只有在获得所有有关国家——缔约国、签署国，甚至是仅只参与了条约的起草的国家——的同意时，才能对条约进行修正或更正。正如以“公约”替代“盟约”而更正ICCPR作准中文本的过程和程序所显示的，即使这样一个微小的、“技术性的”更正，即使是由联合国启动，也需要所有缔约国和签署国的同意（尽管是以不存在反对的形式）。除了所有有关国家的完全同意以外，除非某一条约另有规定，否则任何国际组织——包括联合国或作为许多多边条约保存机关的联合国秘书长——或任何国家都没有任何权利或权力擅自对条约的作准文本作出任何改变。尽管国际法不禁止任何国家、组织或个人在作准文本之外，创制使用某一作准文字的新文本（后来本就是这样的一个文本），但是没有所有有关国家的同意，这样的文本将没有任何法律上的效力与价值。

对于联合国目前广为使用的中文本即“后来本”的来源及其始作俑者，本研究迄今没有发现任何记录。然而，后来本究竟何时、由谁、如何炮制出来，从法律角度而言是无关紧要的，因为如果本研究的发现属实，则已经可以决然地确定“后来本”不是作准文本，也没有任何法律效力。即使30多年来联合国在其有关人权的中文出版物中几乎压倒性地使用后来本，也绝对没有改变其“冒牌货”的地位与性质，或赋予其任何法律效力。作准本与“后来本”的法律性质、地位与效力的差异，是“真”与“伪”的不同，是决不可混为一谈的“正统”与“僭越”的区别。

那么，这一奇特现象的法律意义和后果是什么？对中国正在研究的批准会有怎样的影响？可以肯定的是，无论中国在签署或将来批准《公约》时依据哪一个中文本，从国际法的角度看，对中国产生相关法律效力的，都是《公约》的作准文本（包括作准中文本）及其内容。然而，至少从目前中国学者研究《公约》的情况来看，我们考虑批准《公约》的主要依据是后来本。尽管已经证明后来本在法律上是无效的，但假如它与作准文本的差异仅仅只是某些语言形式的、词语使用的差异，假如这些差异不会实质性地影响对《公约》的理解和适用，那么仅仅从技术角度而言，依据后来本考虑批准也许并无不可。但是，本文第二部分的抽样对比研究已经清楚地表明，后来本中有相当多的表述或者歪曲了《公约》的规则和要求，或者完全不知所云。《公约》是一份法律文件，绝对容不得一点似是而非，因为任何微小的偏差都可能导致不同的法律效果。尽管中国尚未批准《公约》，但是目前就可以肯定的是，如果中国以后来本为基础理解、研究并批准《公约》，将会出现一些麻烦的、难堪的法律后果。例如，在审议缔约国报告时，由于依据的文本不同，人权事务委员会和中国政府可能就《公约》某些条款的释义出现分歧。

那么，为避免这些恶劣情况的出现，我们应该怎么办？第一，我们必须明确地认识到，中国政府和学者在考虑和研究《公约》的批准问题时，所依据的很可能是一个毫无法律效力且充满错误的赝品；并认识到，如果依据该文本批准和实施《公约》，可能造成严重的政治影响和无法预料的法律困境。第二，我们必须正确认识、严肃对待这一问题，祛除任何可能存在和产生的、认为这一问题仅仅是无关紧要的“翻译问题”而轻描淡写、等闲视之的态度，明确承认后来本在法律性质上的无效和具体内容中的谬误。第三，中国政府应该通知联合国就《公约》的中文本存在的问题，提请和敦促联合国有关部门寻求相应的解决方案。第四，从法理角度而言，我们现在应该抛弃后来本，而依据作准中文本来考虑批准与实施《公约》的事项。第五，我们应该将探察与研究《公约》存在两个中文本的问题的结果广而告之，避免中国的任何部门、机构或人员继续将错就错地按照后来本来认识、理解和研究《公约》。

不过，以上办法只是防止情况进一步恶化的暂时措施，并不能从根本上解决问题。根本上的解决办法似乎很明显：弃用后来本而在联合国和中国

“复活”作准中文本。但是，情况远非如此简单。在此，有两个实际情况必须加以考虑。首先，作准中文本的表述方式较为古旧，其中有许多用词用语已经不很符合现代通用汉语和法律表述的习惯，因此不利于《公约》在中国的宣传推广。其次也更为重要的是，由于联合国有关人权的部门在其文件中普遍使用后来本，因此该文本在中国也广为流传，被认为是《公约》的正式中文本，已经成为我们理解和研究《公约》的基本标准和主要依据。其结果是，目前中文中有关人权特别是公民权利和政治权利以及《公约》的用语和词语在相当大程度上是以后来本为基础确立和发展起来的。在这种情况下，如果突然间完全放弃后来本而彻底回到作准本，联合国与中国都将面临以作准中文本为基础转换中文中的人权概念与词语，乃至于重构整个人权话语方式的重负。从任何角度来看，这样的解决方案都将造成无数的困惑与混乱，例如已经熟悉了后来本中的用词用语甚至完全以这些词语来思考《公约》的中国人权学者，很有可能因为词语的差别与转换而陷入“失语”状态。因此，以牺牲后来本为代价而启用作准文本仅仅在理论上是正确的，在法律上是正当的，但是从实际可能性和可行性角度而言，是极为困难甚至根本不可能圆满完成的。解决存在两个中文本及其造成的一系列困难的问题，必须从现实出发，既尊重作准中文本作为唯一法定有效中文本的法律地位，又考虑后来本已经在联合国和中国广为流传和使用几十年的实际情况，提出法律规则上和现实操作中都可以接受同时又导致最小困难与麻烦的解决方案。

目前看来，以下解决方式也许从法律角度可以接受，从操作角度比较可行。该方法即是对作准文本进行“更正”——当然这样的更正绝不能被认为是因为该文本存在任何错误。在更正中，实质内容上必须坚持作准中文本的规定，但在用词、用语、风格和形式上，在符合《公约》的目的和宗旨的条件下，可以尽量结合与参考后来本。因为这样“更正”的中文本在任何意义上都不包含对《公约》条款的实质性修正，所以没有必要启动《公约》第 51 条规定的修正程序，而只需遵照已经适用过的将“盟约”改为“公约”的更正方法和程序即可。由此方法和程序产生的新的《公约》中文本将取代原先的作准文本而成为《公约》新的作准中文本，联合国也应该在其有关《公约》和人权的所有中文文件和出版物中使用这一新的作准中文本。以这样的方式产生的新的作准中文本，将在最大限度上平衡以上提到的各种考虑，并以最方便和最节省的方式解决问题。

更正作准中文本的技术性工作既可以由联合国有关部门进行，也可以由中国方面承担。考虑到联合国各部门中通晓中文的人权专业人员非常缺乏，而中国在近年来已经进行了大量有关《公约》的研究并积累了丰富的知识，因此这一任务由中国承担比较合适。同时，由中国政府将新的文本提交联合国秘书长进入后续程序，也能体现中国作为国际社会中负责任的一员对于国际人权事业的积极、严肃、认真的态度。不过，究竟以何种方式、在什么程度上更正作准中文本，则是另外一个需要有关各方都加以关注和认真研究的问题。

在这里可以进一步指出的是，这种文本的混乱并不仅限于《公民及政治权利国际公约》的中文本，也发生在若干其他国际人权文书中。实际上，除《公民及政治权利国际公约》外，"国际人权宪章"的另外两份核心文书即《经济社会文化权利国际公约》和《世界人权宣言》也都有两种中文本。就中国已经于2001年3月27日批准的《经济社会文化权利国际公约》而言，其问题与ICCPR完全一样，也是在1966年12月16日通过、1976年1月3日生效并刊载于《联合国条约集》上的中文本即作准中文本[①]之外，另有一份广为流传和使用的标题为《经济、社会、文化权利国际公约》的非作准文本。[②] 与其作准中文本和英文本相比，该非作准文本中也有相当多的错误与偏差。但是，从中国提交经济、社会、文化权利委员会的初次缔约国报告、[③]该委员会的会前工作组为审议中国的报告准备的"问题清单"[④] 以及委员会对中国的初次报告作出的结论性意见[⑤]来看，似乎联合国、经社文权利委员

① U. N. T. S. vol. 993，1976，p. 22. 该文书在通过与生效时的正式中文标题是《经济社会文化权利国际盟约》。于更正ICCPR中文本的同时，按照同样的程序，由《经济社会文化权利国际盟约》全体缔约国和签署国同意，其作准中文本标题和文本中的"盟约"也由"公约"取代，见 Depository Notification C. N. 781. 2001. TREATIES - 6（5 October 2001）；Depository Notification C. N. 7. 2002. TREATIES - 1（3 January 2002）。但同样，此次修正没有提到该文书存在两个不同中文本的情况或它们之间的差异。

② 全国人大的官方网站上公布的也是这一文本，见 http://www. npc. gov. cn/zgrdw/wxzl/wxzl_gbxx. jsp？dm = 010608&pdmc = 010608。

③ "缔约国根据《公约》第16条和第17条提交的初次报告：中华人民共和国"，E/1990/5/Add. 59，2004年3月9日。

④ 经济、社会、文化权利委员会会前工作组，"审议中华人民共和国就《经济、社会、文化权利国际公约》第1至第15条所述权利执行情况提交的初步报告（E/1990/5/Add. 59）时须处理的问题清单"，E/C. 12/Q/CHN/1，2004年6月7日。

⑤ 经济、社会和文化权利委员会的结论性意见："中华人民共和国（包括香港和澳门特别行政区）"，E/C. 12/1/Add. 107，2005年5月13日。

会和中国都没有意识到《经济社会文化权利国际公约》存在两个中文本的问题。这两份中文本之间的差异及其法律后果也从来没有得到关注和研究。但是，由于这也将造成与《公民及政治权利国际公约》类似的一系列的问题，因此也需要认真对待。就《世界人权宣言》这一最权威、最具影响力的国际人权文书而言，也存在着两种中文本：一种是联合国大会于1948年12月10日通过的中文本，另一种是目前广为流传的、来源同样不明的中文本。这两个文本竟然都刊载在联合国的官方网站上。[①] 当然，由于《世界人权宣言》在严格意义上不是有法律约束力的条约，该文书存在两个中文本的问题与两公约存在两个中文本的问题在法律性质上是不一样的，当有另外的认识与解决方式。

四 结语

《公约》存在两个中文本的问题在30余年间一直没有被认识到，但这种情况不能再继续下去了。一方面，国际社会不应该容忍《公约》这一严肃而重要的法律文件存在如此严重而荒唐的缺陷；另一方面，拥有13亿人口的中国正在尊重和保障人权的道路上快速前进，并且极为严肃地考虑着批准和实施《公约》的问题，但《公约》的中文本存在的问题将对处于中国领土内和受其管辖的个人——这些人占到了世界人口的五分之一——享有公民权利和政治权利的范围和程度产生无法预测的但很可能是消极的影响。因此，为了整个国际人权事业的健康发展，为了中国建设法治社会、尊重和保障人权的需要，为了中国能更好地参与国际人权活动、履行国际人权义务，有关各方——中国、联合国乃至整个国际社会——必须在中国批准《公约》之前，从现在就开始以共同的努力认真对待和妥善解决这一问题。

（本文原载于《环球法律评论》2007年第6期）

① 通过时的文本见“联合国文献：研究指南”：http://www.ods-dds-ny.un.org/doc/RESOLUTION/GEN/NR0/044/86/IMG/NR004486.pdf?OpenElement. 通行中文本见联合国人权事务高级专员办事处的网站：http://www.unhchr.ch/udhr/lang/chn.htm；以及联合国官方中文网站：http://www.un.org/chinese/work/rights/rights.htm。

论国际人权法对妇女健康权的保护

李西霞*

妇女健康权的保护是国际人权法的重要内容，也是相关国际人权条约缔约各国应承担的国际义务。长期以来，对妇女健康的忽视已经成为世界各国普遍存在的一个问题。妇女由于性别原因而经常在法律和事实上受到歧视，她们健康权的行使也因而受到严重影响。[①] 另外，全球范围内普遍存在的对人类健康的各种挑战也使得对妇女健康权的保护面临更多的困难。虽然各国政府对妇女健康权的保护已经给予了广泛的关注和高度的重视，但由于国际层面对健康权的规范内容存在不同的理解以及健康权作为社会权利的实现严重依赖本国经济和社会的发展水平，世界各国对妇女健康权的保护水平高低不一，并且存在诸多不尽如人意之处。为了更好地保护妇女健康权并促进其实现，研究国际人权法中关于妇女健康权保护的相关规定，探讨构成妇女健康权保护立法的最基本因素，对发展和完善国家层面保护妇女健康权法律制度具有重要意义。本文将着重分析国际人权法对妇女健康权保护的相关规定、缔约国保护妇女健康权的义务、非歧视原则以及监督机制。

一　对“健康”一词定义的理解

到目前为止，被普遍接受的关于“健康”的定义是 1948 年《世界卫

* 李西霞，中国社会科学院国际法研究所副研究员。

① 参见 R. Cook, *Women's Health and Human Rights: The Promotion and Protection of Women's Health through International Human Rights Law* (Geneva: World Health Organization, 1994), p. 6。

生组织宪章》导言给出的定义。它认为，“健康是指人的生理、心理和社会适应能力的完好状态，而不仅仅是指没有疾病或身体处于虚弱状态”。[①] 笔者认为，这一定义包含了以下三个方面的内容：第一，它强调健康政策的制定超出了常规的健康内容，涵盖了影响健康的社会因素；第二，它表明健康是一种完好状态，这种状态包括生理、心理和社会适应能力三个方面；第三，它具有相对性。研究国际人权法对妇女健康权保护的规定应当建立在对健康定义全面而正确的理解上。

二 对妇女健康权规范内容的理解

（一）对健康权规范内容的理解

健康权首先是由《世界卫生组织宪章》予以明确承认和规定的：“享有最高可能达到的健康标准是每个人的一项基本权利，而不得有种族、宗教、政治信仰、经济或社会状况的区分。”1966 年通过的《经济、社会和文化权利国际公约》对健康权作了全面规定。该公约第 12 条规定，缔约国承认人人有权享有能达到的最高的身体和心理健康的标准。同时，还列举了缔约国为实现这项权利应采取的若干步骤，包括：降低死胎率和婴儿死亡率，使儿童得到健康的发育；改善环境卫生和工业卫生的各个方面；预防、治疗和控制传染病、风土病、职业病以及其他的疾病；创造保证人人在患病时能得到医疗照顾的条件。对健康权作出规定的其他国际人权文件包括《世界人权宣言》、《消除对妇女一切形式歧视公约》、《消除一切形式种族歧视国际公约》、《儿童权利公约》、《残疾人权利公约》等。尽管上述国际人权文件对健康权作出了规定，但并没有对健康权的规范内容进行明确界定，也就是说没有界定健康权具体包括的权利内容。

对于这个问题，经济、社会和文化权利委员会（以下简称“经社文权利委员会”）在其第 14 号一般性意见中明确指出，健康权不仅指享有及时和适当的医疗保健的权利，而且指享有健康的基本决定因素的权利，包括安全的食物、营养、住房，洁净的饮用水，健康的工作场所和健康的环

① 《世界卫生组织宪章》于 1946 年 7 月 22 日在纽约通过，1948 年 4 月 7 日生效。

境，等等。[①] 也就是说，经社文权利委员会把健康权解释为一项全部包括在内的权利。

为了不使健康权在内容上过于庞杂而无从实施，学者和相关联合国机构在理论上提出了“健康权的核心内容”这一概念，[②] 主张健康权核心内容应符合世界卫生组织的“所有人的健康”和“初级卫生保健”战略。[③] 该战略规定：“有一个健康底线，在任何国家，均不得有人发现自己低于此标准。”[④] 这一标准应在发达国家和发展中国家普遍适用，而无论其可利用的资源如何。20 世纪 70 年代，该战略又规定了一系列的基本卫生服务，包括孕期、儿童健康保健和计划生育；主要传染病的免疫注射；对常见疾病和外伤的适当治疗；提供基本药物；关涉普遍健康的问题以及预防和控制这些问题的方法的教育；促进食物提供和适当的营养；充分提供安全用水和基本卫生。虽然这个标准已经提出许多年，但仍为许多学者视为健康权的核心内容。[⑤] 与此同时，其他学者则对核心健康权概念提出异议，认为这个概念容易产生误导，很可能导致健康权的其他方面内容被视为不重要并因而被忽视。[⑥]

实践中，各缔约国对《经济、社会和文化权利国际公约》第 12 条规定的健康权所作的报告内容各不相同。例如，英国的国家报告在对《公约》第 12 条规定的健康权进行报告时，主要报告了卫生服务、社会和社

① 经社文权利委员会第 14 号一般性意见，第 11 段。

② 经社文权利委员会第 3 号一般性意见，第 10 段。A. P. M. Coomans，“Clarifying the Core Elements of the Right to Education”，in A. P. M. Coomans and G. J. H. van Hoof（eds.），*The Right to Complain about Economic，Social and Cultural Rights*，1995，pp. 11 – 27，转引自〔挪〕艾德等《经济、社会和文化权利》，黄列等译，中国社会科学出版社，2003，第 198 页。

③ World Health Organization，“Primary Health Care：Report of the International Conference on Primary Health Care”，Alma-Ata，USSR，6 – 12 September 1978，Health For All Series No. 1，1978，Chapter 3，para. 50.

④ World Health Organization，“Global Strategy for Health for All by the Year 2000（Adopted in WHO resolution WHO. 34. 36）”，1981，Chapter 3，p. 31，para. 1，转引自〔挪〕艾德等《经济、社会和文化权利》，黄列等译，中国社会科学出版社，2003，第 199 页。

⑤ 〔挪〕艾德等：《经济、社会和文化权利》，黄列等译，中国社会科学出版社，2003，第 199 页。

⑥ 〔荷兰〕伯吉特·托贝斯：《健康权》，载国际人权法教程项目组编写《国际人权法教程》第 1 卷，中国政法大学出版社，2002，第 342 页。

区服务、卫生项目和政策三项内容，[①] 而把第 14 号一般性意见第 4 段提到的健康的决定因素，如食物，营养，住房，清洁的饮用水，卫生、健康的工作场地和健康的环境包括在《经济、社会和文化权利国际公约》第 11 条规定的“生活水平”部分。[②] 而法国在对《经济、社会和文化权利国际公约》第 12 条规定的健康权进行报告时，则报告了“自由和人类尊严的一般性原则”、“卫生体制”、“法国人口的健康和社会统计数据”以及“公共卫生项目”等四项内容。[③] 由此可见，无论从理论层面还是从实践层面，都应该对健康权的规范内容进行更系统深入的研究，以便为国际社会达成共识提供依据。鉴于此，笔者认为，妇女健康权的规范内容最起码应保有上文提及的健康权的核心内容。

（二）妇女健康权的规范内容

尽管在理论上对健康权保护的规范内容仍存在不同观点，实践中也有不同的做法，但第 14 号一般性意见第 13 段至 17 段具体阐述的健康权内容仍是妇女健康权保护的重要依据。

第 14 号一般性意见指出：“《经济、社会和文化权利国际公约》第 12 条第 2 款并不完全的举例，规定了各国采取行动的准则。它提出了一些具体措施的通用例子，这些措施都在第 12 条第 1 款对健康权的广泛定义范围内，从而说明了这项权利的内容。”[④]

第 12 条第 2 款（a）项规定了产妇、儿童和生育健康权：“‘降低死胎率、婴儿死亡率和使儿童得到健康的发育’可理解为需采取措施，改善儿童和母亲的健康、性和生育健康服务，包括实行计划生育、产前和产后保健、紧急产科服务和获得信息以及根据获得的信息采取行动所需的资源。”[⑤] 性与生育健康是妇女健康权的一个重要组成部分，它既包括对产妇的健康保护，也包括对女婴的健康保护。这项权利内容与妇女的健康保护有着特别密切的关系。

---

① E/C. 12/4/Add. 8, paras. 12. 02 - 12. 35.

② E/C. 12/4/Add. 8, paras. 11. 01 - 11. 147.

③ E/1990/6/Add. 27, paras. 550 - 594.

④ 经社文权利委员会第 14 号一般性意见，第 13 段。

⑤ 经社文权利委员会第 14 号一般性意见，第 14 段。

第 12 条第 2 款（b）项规定了享有健康的自然和工作环境的权利。改善环境卫生和工业卫生的各个方面主要包括：采取预防措施避免职业事故和疾病的发生；保证充分供应安全洁净的饮用水和基本卫生条件；防止和减少人们接触有害物质，如放射性物质和有害化学物质，或其他直接或间接影响人类健康的有害环境。第 12 条第 2 款（b）项还包括适当的住房、安全、卫生和工作条件，充分供应食物和适当的营养，劝阻酗酒、吸烟、吸毒和使用其他有害药物。① 这项健康权保护的一般性规定包含了对妇女健康权的保护。

第 12 条第 2 款（c）项规定了预防、治疗和控制疾病的权利。预防、治疗和控制传染病、地方病、职业病的权利，要求对与行为相关的健康问题建立预防和教育计划［如性传播疾病（特别是艾滋病/病毒）及有害于性卫生和生育卫生的行为］，改善健康的社会要素（如安全的环境、教育、经济发展和性别平等）。得到治疗的权利，包括在事故、流行病和类似的对健康有危害的情况下，建立一套应急的医疗保健制度，及在紧急情况下提供救灾和人道主义援助。控制疾病，指各国单独或共同努力（特别是提供相关技术、使用和改善分类流行病监督及数据收集工作），执行和加强免疫计划及传染病控制的其他战略。② 这项权利内容对妇女健康保护有着更为重要的意义，因为从一般意义上讲，性传播疾病、不良的性卫生和生育卫生的行为以及影响健康的其他因素（如不利于健康的传统习惯等）也在更大程度上损害着妇女的健康。

12 条第 2 款（d）项规定了享受卫生设施、货物或服务的权利。创造保证人人在患病时能得到医疗照顾的条件包括：平等和及时地提供基本预防、治疗、康复的卫生保健服务，以及卫生教育；定期检查计划；对流行病、一般疾病、外伤和残疾给予适当治疗，最好是在社区一级；提供必需药品；适当的精神健康医疗和护理。另一个重要的方面，是改善和进一步加强民众参与，提供预防和治疗保健服务。

根据经社文权利委员会第 14 号一般性意见，上述各项只是缔约国义务的一部分而非全部。这表明，妇女健康权的规范内容包括医疗保健的权利

① 经社文权利委员会第 14 号一般性意见，第 15 段。

② 经社文权利委员会第 14 号一般性意见，第 16 段。

和享有健康的基本条件的权利。

根据第14号一般性意见，健康权既包括自由也包括权利：自由指控制自己健康和身体的权利，包括性自由和生育自由、免于干涉的自由（如免于酷刑、强制医疗和实验的自由）；权利指享有健康制度保护的权利，即人们能够享有最高的健康水平的平等机会。

第14号一般性意见认为，健康权的各种形式和层次包括以下相互关联的基本要素，其具体实施将取决于特定缔约国的现实条件。（1）可用性是指缔约国必须提供足够数量的、行之有效的公共卫生和卫生保健设施、商品和服务以及卫生计划。（2）可获得性是指这些卫生设施、商品和服务必须是经济上和地理上容易使用的，并且所有人都不受歧视地容易使用这些设施、物品和服务。此外，可获得性还包括查找、接受和传播有关卫生问题的信息和意见的权利，前提是获得信息不应损害个人健康资料保密的权利。（3）可接受性是指所有的卫生设施、商品和服务必须遵守医学道德并符合文化习惯，即尊重个人、少数民族、各民族和社区的文化习惯，照顾性别和生命周期的要求，并且能尊重隐私和改善有关人员的健康状况。（4）质量是指卫生设施、商品和服务不仅应在文化上是可以接受的，而且必须在科学和医学上是适当的和高质量的。这要求医疗人员有较高的技能、药品和医院设备获得科学认证并且没有超过有效期、安全和洁净的饮用水、适当的卫生条件等。①

另外，值得注意的是，妇女享有健康权不应理解为保有身体健康的权利，而应该理解为一项享有实现能够达到最高健康标准所必需的各种设施、商品、服务和条件的权利。因为，第12条第1款的“能够达到最高的体质和心理健康标准”的概念，既考虑了个人的生理和社会经济先决条件，也考虑了国家掌握的资源。有一些方面不可能完全在国家与个人的关系范围内解决，具体而言，国家不能保证健康，它也不能保护人类健康免受各种可能疾病的影响。因此，遗传因素、个人是否易患疾病和追求不健康或危险的生活方式，都可能对个人的健康产生不利影响。②

① 经社文权利委员会第14号一般性意见，第12段。

② 经社文权利委员会第14号一般性意见，第8—9段。

三 国际人权法对保护妇女健康权的规定

健康权，即享有能达到的最高的身体和心理健康标准的权利，是一项基本的人权，在许多国际人权条约和宣言中得到承认和保障。但是，国际人权法并不存在一个专门的全面规定妇女健康及其基础要素的法律条款，相关的规定和解释分散在不同的法律文件中。从广义上讲，与妇女健康权有关的法律条款包括健康权的一般条款、对妇女健康进行保护的特别条款。

1. 规定健康权的一般条款

1948 年通过的《世界人权宣言》第 25 条规定，“人人有权享受为维持他本人和家属的健康和福利所需的生活水准，包括食物、衣着、住房、医疗和必要的社会服务”，“母亲有权享受特别照顾和协助”。该条规定使得健康的含义在《世界人权宣言》的宪章性条约上法律化了，为健康权的发展标准和机构层面的建设奠定了基础。

《经济、社会和文化权利国际公约》第 12 条对健康权作出了全面规定（如上所述），是对《世界人权宣言》第 25 条的详尽阐述。

1965 年通过的《消除一切形式种族歧视国际公约》第 5 条（e）款（4）项规定缔约国应保证人人有不分种族、肤色或民族或人种在法律上一律平等的权利，尤其享有公共卫生、医疗保健、社会保障和社会服务的权利。

1989 年通过的《儿童权利公约》第 24 条第 1 款规定：“缔约国确认儿童有权享有可达到的最高标准的健康，并享有医疗和康复设施。缔约国应努力确保没有任何儿童被剥夺获得这种保健服务的权利。”该条第 2 款还详细列举了缔约国为充分实现这种权利应特别采取的适当措施。这些措施包括：降低婴幼儿死亡率；确保向所有儿童提供必要的医疗援助和保健，侧重发展初级保健；消除疾病和营养不良现象，包括在初级保健范围内利用现有可得的技术和提供充足的营养食品和清洁饮用水，要考虑到环境污染的危险和风险；确保母亲得到适当的产前和产后保健；确保向社会各阶层，特别是向父母和儿童介绍有关儿童保健和营养、母乳育婴优点、个人卫生和环境卫生及防止意外事故的基本知识，使他们得到这方面的教育并帮助他们应用这种基本知识；开展预防保健、对父母进行指导，以及计划生育教育和服务。

2006年通过的《残疾人权利公约》第25条规定：残疾人有权享有可达到的最高健康标准，不受基于残疾的歧视。缔约国应当采取一切适当措施，确保残疾人获得考虑到性别因素的医疗卫生服务，包括与健康有关的康复服务。缔约国尤其应当：（1）向残疾人提供其他人享有的，在范围、质量和标准方面相同的免费或费用低廉的医疗保健服务和方案，包括在性健康和生殖健康及全民公共卫生方面；（2）向残疾人提供残疾特需医疗卫生服务，包括酌情提供早期诊断和干预，并提供旨在尽量减轻残疾和预防残疾恶化的服务，包括向儿童和老年人提供这些服务；（3）尽量就近在残疾人所在社区，包括在农村地区，提供这些医疗卫生服务；（4）要求医护人员，包括在征得残疾人自由表示的知情同意基础上，向残疾人提供在质量上与其他人相同的护理，特别是通过提供培训和颁布公共和私营医疗保健服务职业道德标准，提高对残疾人人权、尊严、自主和需要的认识；（5）在提供医疗保险和国家法律允许的人寿保险方面禁止歧视残疾人，这些保险应当以公平合理的方式提供；（6）防止基于残疾而歧视性地拒绝提供医疗保健或医疗卫生服务，或拒绝提供食物和液体。

2. 对妇女健康进行保护的特别条款

1979年通过的《消除对妇女一切形式歧视公约》第12条是对妇女健康进行保护的特别条款。该条款规定："缔约各国应采取一切适当措施，消除在保健方面对妇女的歧视，保证她们在男女平等的基础上取得包括有关计划生育的保健服务"；"缔约国应保证为妇女提供有关怀孕、分娩和产后期间的适当服务，必要时给予免费服务，并保证在怀孕和哺乳期间得到充分营养"。除该公约第12条规定外，《公约》第11条第1款（e）和（f）项以及14条第2款（b）和（h）项对妇女健康权的保护的规定都超出了医疗保健的范围，涉及了影响妇女健康的经济社会因素。该公约第11条第1款（e）和（f）项分别规定：妇女"享有社会保障的权利，特别是在退休、失业、疾病、残废和老年或在其他丧失工作能力的情况下，以及享有带薪假的权利"；"在工作条件方面享有健康和安全保障，包括保障生育机能的权利"。该公约14条第2款（b）项和（h）项分别规定缔约国应保证农村妇女"有权利用充分的保健设施，包括计划生育方面的知识、辅导和服务"和"有权享受适当的生活条件，特别是在住房、卫生、水电供应、交通和通讯方面”。

除上述国际人权条约外，对妇女健康权作出规定的其他相关文件还包括联合国人权条约机构通过的一般性意见和一般性建议。虽然人权条约机构关于健康权的一般性意见没有法律约束力，但它们是构成理解人权公约的重要文件。“一般性意见可影响对于条约条款含义的澄清，也有助于加强《经济、社会和文化权利国际公约》诸条款由法院直接适用的可能性。”① 经社文权利委员会在其2000年通过的第14号一般性意见中对健康权的内容进行了系统化，并力求明确缔约国的义务。它对健康权的理解作出了权威性的解释，包括健康权的定义、范围、国家义务、国际义务的违反、国家义务的履行等。消除对妇女歧视委员会于1999年通过的第24号关于妇女与健康的一般性建议在其第12段明确承认妇女的健康权利有别于男子的显著特点和因素，如生理因素（月经周期及其生育功能和更年期）、社会经济因素（这些因素对妇女总体或某些妇女群体而言是有差别的，如男女在家庭和工作场所中的不平等关系可能消极地影响妇女的营养和健康、接受教育的问题、基于性别的暴力）、心理因素（如抑郁，特别是产后抑郁）以及不严格保守病人隐私信息（会阻碍妇女不愿寻求咨询和治疗，从而给她们的健康和福祉带来不利影响。由于某些妇女健康问题如暴力、性和生育健康问题非常敏感并且在一般情况下比较忌讳，再加上妇女在社会中的地位一般较低，使得妇女隐私显得尤为重要）。② 儿童权利委员会通过的第3号关于艾滋病毒/艾滋病与儿童权利一般性意见阐述了青少年健康和发展的问题。这些一般性意见和一般性建议无疑是对妇女健康权的保护范围的具体化，发展了国际人权文件相关规定的一致性并增强了国际人权条约的法理基础。

2002年，人权委员会任命了一位健康权特别报告员。特别报告员的各种报告澄清了包括妇女健康权在内的健康权的各种规范和义务，包括健康权和其他因素如贫困、歧视、千年发展目标、性与生殖健康、暴力等关系的信息。另外值得注意的是，联合国大会通过的相关宣言（如《在民族或族裔、宗教和语言上属于少数群体的人的权利宣言》、《消除对妇女的暴力

① 〔挪〕艾德等：《经济、社会和文化权利》，黄列等译，中国社会科学出版社，2003，第44页。

② 消除对妇女歧视公约委员会第24号一般性建议，第12段。

行为宣言》)、联合国人口与发展大会（1994 年）和联合国第四次世界妇女大会（1995 年）通过的文件，以及世界卫生组织和国际劳工组织的相关规定都有助于澄清妇女健康权的内容和标准。

对健康权作出主要规定的《经济、社会和文化权利国际公约》和经社文权利委员会通过的第 14 号一般性意见、其他国际人权条约及其相应的条约监督机构对健康权的相关规定、联合国大会通过的相关宣言、世界卫生组织和国际劳工组织的相关规定构成了审视各国妇女健康权发展的基础。

四 缔约国保护妇女健康权的义务

妇女健康权的保护要求缔约各国履行一系列不同性质的义务。

1. 逐步实现和立即实现的义务

《经济、社会和文化权利国际公约》第 2 条第 1 款要求缔约国采取步骤，使用一切适当方法，尤其是包括立法方法，逐步实现包括妇女健康权在内的经济、社会和文化权利。逐步实现的含义是，缔约国有义务尽可能迅速和有效地实现健康权。尽管在实现妇女健康权方面的义务具有逐步的性质，但是该公约的缔约国还有一些立即实现的义务，如缔约国有保证非歧视和公平治疗的立即义务，有采取深思熟虑、具体的和有针对性的步骤完全实现妇女健康权的立即义务。

2. 尊重、保护和实现的义务

经社文权利委员会第 14 号一般性意见要求缔约国在妇女健康权方面承担三个层次的义务。

《经济、社会和文化权利国际公约》第 12 条第 1 款要求缔约国承认“人人有权享有能达到的最高的身体和心理健康的标准”，意味着缔约国应该保障妇女平等享有卫生服务的机会并免于各种对其健康造成的侵害。尊重妇女健康权的义务意味着缔约国不能剥夺或限制妇女享有预防和治疗等卫生服务的平等机会，也不得对妇女的健康状况和需要推行歧视性做法。缔约国不得阻止妇女参与健康方面的事务，也不得违法实施损害妇女健康的活动，如造成环境污染的活动。① 健康权的有关规定要求缔约国尊重妇

① 经社文权利委员会第 14 号一般性意见，第 33—34 段。

女的生育权，不应限制得到避孕和其他保持性健康和生育健康手段的途径，不应审查、扣押或故意提供错误的健康信息。[①] 违反尊重的义务包括“违反《经济、社会和文化权利国际公约》第12条所确定的标准的国家行为、政策或者法律，可能导致的身体伤害、不必要的疾病和可以预防的死亡”，比如由于法律上或事实上对妇女的歧视而致使她们无法享有医疗设施、商品和服务等。[②]

保护妇女健康权的义务要求缔约国通过法律或采取其他措施保障妇女有平等的机会得到第三方提供的卫生保健和卫生方面的服务，并保障妇女免于第三方对其施加的任何侵害。[③] 比如，缔约国应当确保卫生部门的私有化不会对保健设施、物品和医疗服务的可用性、可获得性、可接受性和质量构成威胁；缔约国应当确保执业医生和其他卫生专业人员满足适当的教育、技能标准和职业道德规范；缔约国还应该保证妇女不受有害传统习俗的伤害，如女性生殖器割礼。[④]《消除对妇女一切形式歧视公约》第12条第1款规定，缔约各国应采取一切适当措施，消除在保健方面对妇女的歧视，保证她们在男女平等的基础上取得包括有关计划生育的保健服务。该公约第12条第2款进一步规定，缔约各国应保证为妇女提供有关怀孕、分娩和产后期间的适当服务，于必要时给予免费服务，并保证在怀孕和哺乳期间得到充分营养。消除对妇女歧视委员会通过的第24号一般性建议在其第13段要求缔约国承担责任，以保障在男女平等的基础上妇女享有卫生保健服务以及卫生相关的信息和教育。

实现妇女健康权的义务要求缔约国为全面实现妇女健康权采取适当的法律、行政、预算、司法、促进和其他措施。具体讲，就是要求缔约国在国家的政治和法律制度中充分承认健康权，制定全国卫生政策和实现妇女健康权的详细计划。缔约国必须保证提供卫生保健（包括对主要传染病的免疫计划），保证妇女能平等地获得基本健康要素（如富于营养的安全食物和清洁饮用水、基本的卫生条件和适当的住房和生活条件）。公共卫生基础设施应提供性和生育卫生服务（包括母亲的安全知识），特别是在农

---

① 经社文权利委员会第14号一般性意见，第34段。

② 经社文权利委员会第14号一般性意见，第50段。

③ 经社文权利委员会第14号一般性意见，第33、35段。

④ 经社文权利委员会第14号一般性意见，第35段。

村地区。各国必须保证医生和其他医务人员经过适当培训，提供足够数量的医院、诊所和其他卫生设施，促进和支持建立提供咨询和精神卫生服务的机构，并充分注意到在全国的均衡分布。①

缔约国有责任保证其立法、行政和政策有益于以上三个层次义务的履行。另外，还应该建立有效的司法制度，否则将构成对《经济、社会和文化权利国际公约》第 12 条的违反。对于健康权实现的逐渐义务的不同理解和诠释不应违背上述三个层次的义务。

3. 核心义务

除上述义务外，实现妇女健康权还要求缔约国履行一项核心义务。②经社文权利委员会要求，缔约国应确保最低限度基本健康权水平的核心义务：确保不受歧视地使用卫生设施、物品和服务的机会，特别是边缘群体和弱势群体（如妇女）；确保获得适当和安全的食品、基本住所、住房、卫生条件、清洁的水源的机会；提供世界卫生组织确定的基本药品；确保平等地分配所有卫生设施、物品和服务；制定和实施确保每个人健康权的国家公共卫生战略和行动计划。③

除了国内层次的义务外，妇女健康权的实施还要求缔约国承担国际援助和合作方面的义务（《经济、社会和文化权利国际公约》第 2 条第 1 款）。比如，缔约国有义务尊重在其他管辖地区健康权的实现，确保国际协议不会对健康权产生不利的影响，确保它们在国际组织（如世界贸易组织、世界银行和国际货币基金组织）里的代表在讨论所有政策时都对健康权有足够的考虑。④

五　妇女健康权的保护与非歧视原则

基于性别的歧视常常针对妇女，是世界范围内导致妇女疾病和侵犯妇女健康权的原因之一。比如，对妇女的歧视往往造成妇女不能得到适当的信息、充分营养及保健和计划生育的平等权利，导致妇女营养不良并患上

---

① 经社文权利委员会第 14 号一般性意见，第 33、36 段。

② 经社文权利委员会第 3 号一般性意见，第 10 段。

③ 经社文权利委员会第 14 号一般性意见，第 43 段。

④ 经社文权利委员会第 14 号一般性意见，第 38—42 段。

慢性疾病。虽然性别歧视的原因和后果在各缔约国之间有所不同，但是妇女受到歧视是普遍现象，而且性别歧视的总体趋势不利于妇女和女童的健康状况。所以，缔约国按照国际人权公约的规定履行非歧视义务，对于有效保障妇女健康权非常重要。

第一，非歧视原则是妇女健康权平等保护的根本要素。《世界人权宣言》第 7 条规定："法律之前人人平等，并有权享受法律的平等保护，不受任何歧视。人人有权享受平等保护，以免受违反本宣言的任何歧视行为以及煽动这种歧视的任何行为之害。"

第二，《经济、社会和文化权利国际公约》第 2 条第 2 款对非歧视原则作出了规定，即缔约国有义务保证公约所宣布的权利应予普遍行使，而不得有例如种族、肤色、性别、语言、宗教、政治或其他见解、国籍或社会出身、财产、出生或其他身份等任何区分。该公约第 3 条要求缔约各国承担保证男子和妇女在该公约所载一切经济、社会及文化权利方面有平等的权利。该原则在适用于《经济、社会和文化权利国际公约》第 12 条规定的健康权时，意味着缔约国应该平等地、非歧视地实现包括妇女健康权在内的所有人的健康权，这是一项立即义务，而不是逐步实现的义务。

经社文权利委员会在第 14 号一般性意见中进一步明确承认了基于性别的歧视。第 14 号一般性意见强调，为了消除对妇女的歧视，缔约国必须既要在其健康相关的政策、规划、项目和研究中引入性别视角又要制定实施妇女健康权的全面的国家战略。它建议缔约各国："为了更好地促进男性和妇女的健康，应将性别视角引入与本国的健康相关的政策、规划、项目和研究中。基于性别的方法承认，生理和社会文化因素在影响男性和女性的健康方面发挥着重要作用。"① 这说明，首先，缔约国应建立和完善使妇女参与健康政策的决策程序的机制。消除对妇女歧视委员会建议缔约国应当"促进妇女参与与女性健康服务有关的项目与政策的计划、实施和管理过程"。② 其次，缔约国还应该考虑到社会经济文化因素对妇女健康的负面影响。这些因素包括但不限于：（a）妇女较低的社会经济地位所导致的质量较低或相对缺乏的医疗服务不能满足她们的需求；（b）不良的文化和宗

① 经社文权利委员会第 14 号一般性意见，第 20 段。
② 消除对妇女歧视委员会第 24 号一般性建议，第 31 段。

教因素，如女性生殖器割礼、重男轻女等，在一定程度上会阻碍妇女接受医疗服务；（c）环境因素，包括不安全的工作条件和就业歧视，会不同程度地影响妇女的健康；（d）不公平的受教育机会，也是影响妇女健康的一个重要因素；（e）基于性别的暴力通常是针对女性，也是一个导致妇女不健康的普遍原因；（f）法律和政策中存在的阻碍妇女获得健康服务的障碍。“为了消除针对妇女的歧视，必须制定和实施在妇女的整个生命周期内实现其健康权的综合性国家战略。这项战略应包括对女性疾病的预防和治疗的干预，以及提供全面的高质量的、文化上可接受的、经济上负担得起的卫生保健服务，包括性健康和生殖健康服务。国家战略的主要目标是降低妇女健康的风险，特别是降低产妇死亡率和保护妇女免受家庭暴力的伤害。消除一切干扰妇女获得卫生服务、教育和信息，包括性健康和生殖健康的障碍。采取预防、促进和补救行动，保护妇女免受那些使她们不能充分享有生育权的有害的传统文化习俗和规定的影响。”①

第三，《消除对妇女一切形式歧视公约》第 1 条把“对妇女的歧视”定义为：任何区别、排斥或限制，其影响或目的均足以妨碍或否认妇女不论其婚姻状况在男女平等的基础上认识、享有或行使在政治、经济、社会、文化、公民或任何其他方面的人权和基本自由。该公约要求缔约国不仅有义务禁止歧视性行为（第 2 条），而且有义务采取适当措施，保证妇女得到充分发展和进步，以确保她们在与男子平等的基础上行使和享有人权和基本自由（第 3 条）。另外，该公约第 4 条还规定，旨在加速实现男女事实上的平等而采取的暂行特别措施不能被认为是歧视。《消除对妇女一切形式歧视公约》第 12 条强调了妇女平等享有医疗保健服务、计划生育服务和产前及产后保健。消除对妇女歧视委员会通过的第 24 号一般性建议对《消除对妇女一切形式歧视公约》第 12 条关于妇女与保健作了系统化的阐述和解释。第 24 号一般性建议第 13 段规定：“各缔约国确保人人在男女平等的基础上获得保健服务的责任意味着必须尊重、保护和实现妇女的健康权利。缔约国有责任确保立法、行政行动和政策履行这三项义务。它们还必须建立有效司法行动的制度。”该建议指出，假设某一保健制度不提供预防、诊查和治疗妇女特有的疾病的服务，那么，此种消除对妇女

① 经社文权利委员会第 14 号一般性意见，第 21 段。

歧视的措施就被认为是不适当的。如缔约国拒绝在法律上许可为妇女提供某种生殖健康服务，那就是歧视。例如，保健部门如因良心理由拒绝提供此类服务，即应采取措施确保将妇女转至其他保健机构。[①]

第四，《消除一切形式种族歧视国际公约》第 5 条（e）项规定强调了健康权背景下的平等和非歧视原则。

第五，《儿童权利公约》在序言中承认了两性之间的平等，并在公约第 2 条第 1 款规定了禁止歧视："缔约国应遵守本公约所载列的权利，并确保其管辖范围内的每一儿童均受此种权利，不因儿童或其父母或法定监护人的种族、肤色、性别、语言、宗教、政治或其他见解、民族、族裔或社会出身、财产、伤残、出生或其他身份而有任何差别。"该条规定保障了女童在平等的基础上享受健康权。

第六，联合国《在民族或族裔、宗教和语言上属于少数群体的人的权利宣言》第 4 条规定，"各国应采取必要的措施确保属于少数群体的人可在不受任何歧视并在法律面前完全平等的情况下充分而切实地行使其所有人权和基本自由"，为少数民族妇女平等地享有健康权提供了保障。

第七，基于性别的暴力常常针对女性，既是一种严重的歧视形式，也是一个导致妇女健康状况不良和侵犯妇女健康权利的普遍原因。《经济、社会和文化权利国际公约》第 14 号一般性意见规定，缔约国对妇女的暴力行为（包括对那些施加家庭暴力的男性）不加以保护或起诉施暴的人意味着没有履行保护妇女健康权的义务。[②] 消除对妇女歧视委员会第 19 号一般性建议要求缔约各国采取一切必要的法律及其他措施，为妇女提供免于基于性别的暴力的有效保护，包括：有效的法律措施，包括保护妇女免受一切形式暴力的刑事制裁、民事救济和赔偿条款，特别是包括家庭暴力和虐待、职场性骚扰及性暴力；防范性措施，包括用来改变有关男女社会角色和地位的公众信息和教育项目；保护性措施，包括为那些暴力受害妇女或遭受暴力威胁的妇女提供庇护难所、咨询服务、康复以及支持服务。但由于条约机构所通过的一般性建议本身对缔约各国不具有法律约束力，世界范围内对妇女的暴力行为仍然普遍存在。缔约国政府需

① 消除对妇女歧视委员会第 24 号一般性建议，第 11 段。

② 经社文权利委员会第 14 号一般性意见，第 51 段。

要在其法律中对保护妇女作出明确规定，已经明确规定禁止暴力行为的，则需要有效地予以实施。

六 妇女健康权实施的监督机制

首先，联合国人权制度下保障包括妇女健康权在内的经济、社会和文化权利的主要文件是《经济、社会和文化权利国际公约》。该公约第16条所确立的报告程序是对该公约实施进行国际监督的一个重要措施。缔约国报告自1987年起由经社文权利委员会负责审议。经社文权利委员会成立于1985年，是联合国负责监督《经济、社会和文化权利国际公约》缔约国履行条约义务情况的机构。该委员会由人权专家组成，负责审议各缔约国定期向联合国提交的关于该国促进和保护经济、社会和文化权利所采取的步骤以及在保护人权方面所取得进展的报告，根据这些报告和联合国专门机构送来的其他报告，向经济和社会理事会提出一般性意见。它的目的是：帮助缔约国履行其报告义务；提请缔约国注意其提交的报告中的不足之处，建议改进报告程序的方法；促进缔约国、各国际组织和专门机构逐渐和有效地充分实现经济、社会和文化权利的活动。实践中，经社文权利委员会通过的一般性意见，尤其是关于健康权的一般性意见，对解释《公约》中的妇女健康权利以及相应的条约义务作出了巨大的贡献。

其次，《经济、社会和文化权利国际公约任择议定书》允许缔约国承认经社文权利委员会有权接受并审查符合条件的受害者来文，是监督妇女健康权实施的另一项重要措施。该任择议定书于2008年12月10日由联合国大会通过，并应于第10件批准书或加入书交存联合国秘书长之日起3个月发生效力。该任择议定书对个人申诉程序作了详细规定，妇女对侵犯其健康权的行为可以向经社文权利委员会投诉以寻求救济的措施。虽然该任择议定书目前尚未生效，但个人申诉程序在《公约》生效后将对妇女健康权的促进和实现有着重要的现实意义。

最后，对妇女健康权实施的监督还可以依赖《消除对妇女一切形式歧视公约》第17条所设立的消除对妇女歧视委员会。消除对妇女歧视委员会的主要职责包括：根据《公约》第18条规定审查缔约国报告；根据《消除对妇女一切形式歧视公约任择议定书》的规定接受和处理个人申诉、对缔约国内严重或系统侵犯《公约》所载权利的情况进行调查；发布一般性意见。这些措施可被用于监督有关妇女健康、计划生育服务、产前产后保健、艾滋病防治等的实施。可以说，《消除对妇女一切形式歧视公约》建立了比较完善的监督措施，可以依据这些规定在符合条件的情况下请求委员会保护妇女健康权。

一旦健康权受到侵害，受害者应当能够在国内或国际上通过有效的司法或其他渠道来进行申诉。[①] 尽管国际监督机制的作用非常重要，但它对妇女健康权的保护往往是辅助性的。国家层面的监督机制和司法救济是妇女健康权实现的更为重要的途径，妇女健康权保护的基础仍然是国际人权法的国内适用。所以，缔约国通过发展和完善其国内卫生法律制度来实施国际人权条约中的相关规定，才是有效保护妇女健康权的最重要的途径。

结　论

综上所述，国际人权法对妇女健康权的保护作了较为全面的规定，这些规定同时也意味着各缔约国必须履行的国际义务。但是，妇女健康权的实现在很大程度上仍有赖于各缔约国国内法律的发展和完善。笔者认为，审视国际法上关于妇女健康权的相关规定，决定构成立法的根本要素，是亟须研究的一个重要课题，因为它对建立和完善国内层面的妇女健康权保护法律制度有根本性的意义。也只有建立和完善国内层面的妇女健康权保护的法律制度，才能更好地保障妇女健康权的充分实现。

（本文原载于《少数人的权利》，社会科学文献出版社，2010）

① 经社文权利委员会第 14 号一般性意见，第 59—62 段。

残疾人权利公约中的合理便利

——考量基准与保障手段

曲相霏*

在联合国目前所有核心国际人权公约中，唯一一个明确规定了合理便利[①]概念的是《联合国残疾人权利公约》（United Nations Convention on the Rights of Persons with Disabilities，英文简称 CRPD，下文简称《残疾人权利公约》或《公约》）。[②]《公约》不仅将合理便利作为一个关键概念给予定义，[③]

---

* 曲相霏，中国社会科学院国际法研究所研究员，法学博士。

① 《公约》中文文本中的合理便利对应英文文本中的“reasonable accommodation”。但是严格而言，“便利”与“accommodation”从词义上并不是恰当的对应词，这两个语词也都不是《公约》理念的最佳表达。其实，中文中的“合理调适”与英文中的“reasonable adjustment”不仅相互对应，也非常明确地体现了《公约》的精神和理念，更为适当。但是《公约》已经通过和生效，现在所能做的就是对《公约》的措辞给予符合《公约》本意的清晰解释。值得注意的是，2012 年 10 月残疾人权利委员会对中国《首次履约报告》提出的《结论性意见》的中文作准文本使用了“合理照顾”来对应英文中的“reasonable accommodation”，这是不恰当的，应予纠正。本文除在直接引用原文时尊重原文的表达方式，在中文行文中统一使用《公约》中文作准文本采用的合理便利这一表达。

② 2006 年 12 月 13 日该公约及其任择议定书经第 61 届联合国大会通过，2007 年 3 月 30 日开放给各国签署，2008 年 5 月 3 日正式实施。截至 2015 年 10 月 23 日，该公约有 160 个签署国和 159 个缔约国，其任择议定书有 92 个签署国和 88 个缔约国，见 http://treaties. un. org/Pages/ViewDetails（最后访问日期：2015 年 10 月 23 日）。《公约》的英文版本使用的是“persons with disabilities”，只在引用《关于残疾人的世界行动纲领》（World Programme of Action Concerning Disabled Persons）时使用了“disabled person”。《公约》的中文版本使用的是“残疾人”。中国法律法规通用“残疾人”。本文引用《公约》及相关法律法规文献资料时，使用原文称呼。其他情况下，视行文方便同等使用“残疾人”、“残障人士”、“身心障碍人”、“障碍人”、“障碍者”等称呼。

③ Gerard Quinn and Charles O'Mahony, “Disability and Human Rights: A New Field in the United Nations”, in C. Krause and M. Scheinin (eds.), *International Protection of Human Rights: A Textbook* (Turku/Abo: Abo Academi University Institute for Human Rights, 2nd revised edn., 2012), p. 269.

并且规定“不提供合理便利构成歧视”从而将提供合理便利置于“平等和反歧视”的法律原则之中。缔约国“确保”提供合理便利的规定也被誉为《公约》中最重大和最有用的规定。[①]

中国是《残疾人权利公约》的缔约国。在中国所批准或加入的国际人权公约中，《残疾人权利公约》直到今天仍然具有独特性，因为中国不仅推动并在一定程度上领导了《公约》的起草和通过，[②] 位列《公约》的第一批签署国，[③] 更在批准《公约》时没有作出任何保留，[④] 这在中国批准或加入的人权公约中是唯一的。[⑤] 为了与《公约》保持一致，中国在批准《公约》之前还迅速修订了《中华人民共和国残疾人保障法》（下文简称《残疾人保障法》）。[⑥] 然而，也许是因为当时人们对《公约》中合理便利所涉及问题的广泛性和基本性没有足够重视，《残疾人保障法》在修订时只是在个别条文中规定了若干为残疾人提供“便利”的要求，[⑦] 既没有使

---

① Rosemary Kayess and Philip French, “Out of Darkness into Light: Introducing the Convention on the Rights of Persons with Disabilities”, *Human Rights Law Review* 8 (1) (2008), pp. 1 - 34.

② Quinn and O'Mahony, “Disability and Human Rights: A New Field in the United Nations”, p. 275.

③ 中国在《公约》开放签署日当天（2007 年 3 月 30 日）就签署了《公约》。2008 年 6 月 26 日全国人大常委会批准了《公约》。2008 年 8 月 31 日《公约》在中国正式实施。

④ 美国到目前仍未加入该《公约》，而加拿大、澳大利亚等西方发达国家在批准或加入《公约》时都作了保留。

⑤ 包括《残疾人权利公约》在内，目前联合国共有 9 大核心国际人权公约，中国已经批准或加入了其中 6 个，而在批准或加入时中国没有作出任何保留的目前还只有《残疾人权利公约》。《公约》不仅受到中国的欢迎，还赢得了世界性的赞誉。在《公约》的开放签署日，有 82 个国家签署了《公约》，创下了联合国的历史纪录，这使得《公约》成为联合国历史上在开放签署日获得最多签署国的公约。当日还有 44 个国家签署了《公约》的《任择议定书》，牙买加还直接批准了《公约》。除了在开放签署日获得最多签署国，《公约》还创下了其他若干个第一：它是人类进入 21 世纪后通过的第一个国际人权公约；是联合国第一个开放给区域一体化组织（如欧盟）签署和批准的人权公约；在联合国历史上第一次由受公约直接影响的人士积极有效地参与公约的制定过程，大量残疾人和残疾人组织在《公约》制定过程中发挥了重要作用；是联合国历史上磋商和制定速度最快的公约，从联合国大会决定设立“拟订全面的综合的保护和促进残疾人权利和尊严的国际公约特设委员会”（Ad Hoc Committee，下文简称“特设委员会”）来考虑制定公约的问题，到《公约》获得通过，仅用了 5 年时间。

⑥ 2008 年 4 月全国人大常委会对 1991 年《残疾人保障法》进行了修订，以符合《公约》的要求。

⑦ 例如第 25 条、第 50 条、第 56 条等。

用合理便利概念，也没有关于合理便利的概括性规定。[①] 在中国目前的规范性法律文件中，唯一明确规定了合理便利的是2015年4月21日教育部和残疾人联合会联合发布的《残疾人参加普通高等学校招生全国统一考试管理规定（暂行）》（下文简称《规定》）。[②] 但是该《规定》不仅法律效力级别低，也只涉及普通高等学校招生全国统一考试这一事项。而合理便利则不仅是残疾人权利保障的手段，还涉及财产权和经济自由等受宪法保障的公民基本权利，涉及教育、就业、医疗、交通、居住等生活的方方面面。合理便利的全面实施不仅会给普通社会生活带来影响，还会给司法活动带来新的挑战。在中国的法律体系中，只有基本法律才能承担得起规定合理便利的任务。

2010年8月30日中国根据《公约》第35条关于缔约国提交报告的规定，向联合国残疾人权利委员会提交了《首次履约报告》（Initial Report of China），[③] 2012年10月残疾人权利委员会对中国的《首次履约报告》提出了《结论性意见》（Concluding Observations）。在该《结论性意见》中，委员会在肯定中国为履行《公约》所作出的努力和所取得的成就的同时，也对中国提出了一系列建议，其中一条建议就是关于合理便利。委员会表示中国法律还没有关于合理便利的明确规定，在为残疾人提供合理便利方面存在着不足，建议中国“在法律中加入对合理便利的定义”，并且“该定义应反映《公约》中的定义，涉及在特定案例中在超越一般性无障碍问题之外应用必要和适当的修改与调整”。委员会还建议中国“应确保在法律中明确承认，拒绝提供合理便利构成基于残疾的歧视”。[④]

基于上述背景，本文试图从学理上考查分析《公约》中合理便利的内容、特征、判断标准和保障手段等基本问题，研究探索其对中国的挑战和可能产生的影响，为中国的履约和完善残疾人权利保障作准备。

---

① 尽管全国人民代表大会常务委员会法制工作委员会编写的《残疾人保障法释义》一书将合理便利纳入关于《残疾人保障法》第3条“基于残疾的歧视”的解释，但该书并不是中国的法律渊源。参见信春鹰主编《中华人民共和国残疾人保障法释义》，法律出版社，2008，第15页。

② 《残疾人参加普通高等学校招生全国统一考试管理规定（暂行）》，新华网，http://education.news.cn/2015-05/15/c_127804329.htm，最后访问日期：2015年9月3日。

③ CRPD/C/CHN/1.

④ CRPD/C/CHN/CO/1.

一　合理便利的要素：哪些便利？何为合理？

在起草《公约》时，“合理便利”这一概念在国际法上尚未得到充分定义，许多国家对其存在理解上的模糊甚至误解。起草《公约》的过程也是合理便利概念逐渐明晰的过程。①《公约》最终文本对合理便利定义如下：

“‘合理便利’是指根据具体需要，在不造成过度或不当负担的情况下，进行必要和适当的修改和调整，以确保残疾人在与其他人平等的基础上享有或行使一切人权和基本自由。”②

虽然合理便利的定义十分清晰，但是合理便利究竟包括哪些具体内容、哪些便利是合理的哪些便利是不合理的、判断合理便利的方法和工具是什么等问题，《公约》无法一一作出详尽规定。本文将结合各国关于合理便利的法律和实践、《公约》起草过程中的讨论以及联合国残疾人权利委员会在处理个人来文时所给出的意见，对“合理”和“便利”分别予以分析，以廓清合理便利可能涵盖的范围和内容。

（一）合理便利中的便利

在《公约》草案第1版给出了合理便利的定义之后，③起草《公约》的代表们对“便利”的内容即进行必要和适当的“改造和调整”，再没有产生实质性的分歧。这一方面是因为“便利”比较易于理解和表达，没有造成误解；另一方面是因为《公约》草案中的“便利”与已有的各国法律和实践所支持的“便利”在内容上并无二致。不过，由于《公约》将合理便利置于“平等和反歧视”的原则之中，并且对“便利”涉及的范围和领

---

① Ad Hoc Committee on a Comprehensive and Integral International Convention on the Protection and Promotion of the Rights and Dignity of Persons with Disabilities，参见 http://www.un.org/esa/socdev/enable/rights/adhoccom.htm，最后访问日期：2015年10月11日。

② 其英文表述如下：“Reasonable accommodation means necessary and appropriate modification and adjustments not imposing a disproportionate or undue burden, where needed in a particular case, to ensure to persons with disabilities the enjoyment or exercise on an equal basis with others of all human rights and fundamental freedoms.”

③ http://www.un.org/esa/socdev/enable/rights/ahcwgreporta7.htm，最后访问日期：2015年6月11日。

域没有作任何限制，《公约》中的“便利”和已有的各国法律和实践所支持的“便利”相比，更为广泛和全面。

1. 便利的广泛性和全面性

合理便利是在就业领域反歧视的过程中发展起来的，长久以来在某些国家以及欧盟，为残疾人提供合理便利的法律义务仍然主要局限于就业领域。在《公约》起草过程中，特设委员会成员普遍认为，需要使合理便利的概念“既宽泛又灵活”（both general and flexible），以确保它易于适应不同的领域。[①]《公约》所规定的“便利”从一开始就是开放性的，没有任何特定领域的限定，不仅渗透于残疾人的教育、就业、医疗等日常生活的方方面面，并且渗透于所有环节和所有程序步骤之中，这使得《公约》中的合理便利前所未有地全面和广泛。

除了没有特定领域和事项的限定，《公约》中“便利”的广泛性和全面性也能从下列几个方面体现出来。

第一，提供合理便利的场所。《公约》所要求的提供合理便利的场所，不仅包括公共场所、工作场所、公寓住宅、学校医院等常规场所，还包括监狱、拘留地等这些特殊场所。《公约》第 14 条第 2 款规定：“缔约国应当确保，在任何程序中被剥夺自由的残疾人，在与其他人平等的基础上，有权获得国际人权法规定的保障，并应当享有符合本公约宗旨和原则的待遇，包括提供合理便利的待遇。”2014 年 4 月残疾人权利委员会处理的来自阿根廷的来文，就涉及缔约国为接受刑事监禁的残疾人的医疗康复和日常生活提供合理便利的义务。委员会根据《公约》第 14 条第 2 款指出，缔约国有义务对拘留地点加以改造，采取相关措施作出充分、合理的调整，确保来文当事人能够与其他囚犯同等进入监狱的各个场所并使用监狱提供的各种服务，确保被剥夺自由的残疾人能够自主生活，并能够在拘留地点充分参与生活的方方面面。[②] 该事例反映了《公约》所包含的“便利”的全面性和广泛性。

第二，合理便利的权利主体即需要者。《公约》所保障的合理便利并不只限于残疾人本人，即不仅残疾人本人可以基于自己所面临的障碍而提

---

① http://www.un.org/esa/socdev/enable/rights/ahc3.htm，最后访问日期：2014 年 12 月 24 日。

② CRPD/C/11/D/8/2012. http://tbinternet.ohchr.org/_layouts/treatybodyexternal/TBSearch.aspx?Lang=en&TreatyID=4&DocTypeCategoryID=6，最后访问日期：2015 年 6 月 18 日。

出合理便利的要求，与残疾人有关联的其他人（通常为残疾人的家属）也可以基于残疾人的特殊需要而以其自己的社会身份和名义提出合理便利要求。这是因为“基于残疾的歧视”往往不仅涉及残疾人本人，还涉及与残疾人有关系的非残疾人，例如需要照顾残疾子女的职业女性。[①] 残疾人权利委员会在针对西班牙的结论性意见中就明确要求西班牙将残疾基础上的保护扩展到与残疾人有关联的人或事等领域。[②] 中国立法部门组织编写的《中华人民共和国残疾人保障法释义》一书也指出，“禁止基于残疾的歧视”所保护的对象“除了残疾人以外还包括与残疾人有联系的人或组织，如残疾人的配偶、残疾人的亲属、残疾人的照料者、残疾人的同事、残疾人的工作单位、残疾人的供养和托养机构、残疾人组织等”，对上述对象的歧视都属于“基于残疾的歧视”。[③]

第三，合理便利的义务主体即提供者。《公约》对提供合理便利的义务主体也没有作任何限定，这使得任何社会主体都可能成为提供合理便利的义务主体，这种不列负面清单的方式大大增加了提供合理便利的可能性。为行文方便，这一规定的合理性将在下文关于合理便利的保障部分再予以分析。

2. 便利的分类

尽管《公约》中的“便利”十分全面和广泛，但我们仍然能够通过分类的方式将“便利”的内容具体化。从目前各国的法律和司法实践来看，[④] 合理便利中的“便利”既包括各种物质性便利，又包括各种非物质性便利。在具体个案中，便利可能同时包括物质性便利和非物质性便利。

（1）物质性便利

物质性便利是指物质方面的“修改和调整”。例如，在就业领域，根据美国《残疾人法案》，雇主有义务对工作环境进行改进或调整，以使残

---

① *Coleman v. Attridge Law and Steve Law*, European Court of Justice, Case C－303/06, Opinion of the Advocate Gene Council Directive（EC）2000/78, Establishing a General Framework for Equal Treatment in Employment and Occupation 2000, 31 January 2008.

② 参见 Conclusion Observation of the Committee on the Rights of Persons with Disabilities: Spain, UN doc. CRPD/C/ESP/CO/1, 19 October 2011, para. 19。

③ 信春鹰主编《中华人民共和国残疾人保障法释义》，法律出版社，2008，第 15 页。

④ 美国是最早规定合理便利的国家，美国的实践也为其他国家提供了参照。目前各国对合理便利的规定呈现出相似性，其中菲律宾的法律规定更是与美国的基本相同。因此本文在分析合理便利的要素时将主要以美国为例来加以说明，辅之以其他国家的相关情况。

疾雇员可以完成关键的工作内容，或使残疾雇员可以和类似情形的非残疾雇员一样“平等享有雇用的利益和权利”。为达到这个目的，雇主应设法使现有的、供雇员使用的设施也能够方便残疾雇员进入和使用，必要时雇主应添加或改造设备装置。[①] 以色列《残疾人平等法》规定，在就业领域为残疾人提供的物质性调适不仅包括“工作场所内的设备调适”，还可以是“工作场所的调适”。[②] 这意味着可以为残疾雇员选择其他适合的“工作场所”，例如居家工作或单独安排一个安静的工作间。英国 1995 年的《残障歧视法案》第 6 段第 3 分段也规定，雇主为有身心障碍的雇员提供的物质性便利包括“对经营场所进行调整”和“分配其去不同的工作场所”。[③]

根据个案的具体情况，物质性便利包括的内容其实非常广泛，甚至五花八门。例如在美国的一个案件中，由于有残疾人住户对某些化学物质过敏，法院根据美国《公平住宅法案》判令住宅的负责人采取适当措施，例如撤走可能导致该住户过敏的地毯，或停止使用某些涂料或杀虫剂。[④] 在此案件中，对地毯、涂料、杀虫剂等进行的调整，就属于环境和场所方面的物质性便利。再如，根据当事人的特定需要，为视力障碍者提供纸质盲文材料或阅读器，为身体障碍者提供拐杖或轮椅，都属于物质性便利。

（2）非物质性便利

为残疾人提供的非物质性便利是指对通常的、一般性的程序、规则、政策、标准、要求、期限等非物质性要素作出调整，或为残疾人提供人员方面的特别协助。从目前各国的立法和法律实践来看，非物质性便利比物质性便利更为复杂多样，涉及的方面也更广泛。

例如在就业领域，美国《残疾人法案》要求雇主提供的非物质性便利包括：对申请工作的程序进行改进或调整，使适格的残疾求职者可以获得被雇主考虑的机会；为残疾雇员调整工作内容，提供兼职工作或修改工作日程，重新分配到空缺的岗位，适当调整或修改考试、培训材料或政策以

---

① Americans with Disabilities Act of 1990 (ADA), Sec. 12111. Definitions.

② *Israel's Equal Rights for People with Disabilities Law*, 5758 (1998).

③ *The United Kingdom's Disability Discrimination Act of 1995*.

④ *Roe v. Housing Authority of the City of Boulder*, 909 F. Supp. 814, 822 – 823 (D. Colo. 1995). http://www.accessiblehousing.org/rights/accommodations.asp，最后访问日期：2015 年 3 月 23 日；*Radecki v. Joura*, 114 F.3d 115 (8th Cir. 1997), http://www.accessiblehousing.org/rights/accommodations.asp，最后访问日期：2015 年 3 月 23 日。

及其他类似的便利。[①]

在住房领域，根据美国《公平住宅法案》，据不完全统计，已经在实践中得到肯定的非物质性便利包括：为需要导盲犬的视力障碍人或其他需要动物陪伴或辅助的残疾人改变“禁止宠物”规则；[②] 为具有行动障碍的残疾人预留最近距离的停车位而改变“先到先停”规则；在禁止非住户使用洗衣房的社区，允许无法自己去洗衣房洗衣的残疾人由其朋友、家人或助理帮助其使用洗衣房；为需要助理留宿以完成日常照顾的残疾人改变禁止非住户留宿的规定；在申请住房的程序中为听力障碍者提供免费的手语协助；因身心障碍而需要提前结束租期改换住房的残疾人不得被视为违约，并应优先获得需要的住房；因精神障碍而打扰了其他住户或违反住宿规则的精神障碍人，可以先行治疗，在此治疗期间不得被驱逐；[③] 等等。

英国1995年的《残障歧视法案》第6段第3分段也详细规定了雇主为有身心障碍的雇员提供便利时可能采取的一些步骤和措施，其中多项内容涉及非物质性便利，包括“将身心障碍人的一些工作职责分配给其他人；转移该身心障碍人去填补一个已有的空缺岗位；调整工时；允许身心障碍人旷工以进行康复、评估或治疗；给身心障碍人提供培训或安排其接受培训；修改指令或参考手册；修改测试或评估程序；提供监督指导”。[④] 以色列的《残疾人平等法》规定，在就业领域为残疾人提供的非物质性调适应包括“工作要求的调适，工作时间、招聘测试、引导培训和工作实践的调适”。[⑤]

综上所述，根据个案的具体情况，非物质性便利可以是简化的求职程序，提供给智力障碍人的简单易懂的工作指示，单独安排的轮班时间（例如灵活的、可选择的工作时间，非全日制工作时间），[⑥] 降低的工作指标，

---

① ADA. Sec. 12111. Definitions.

② 28 C. F. R. §36.104，http://www.accessiblehousing.org/rights/accommodations.asp，最后访问日期：2015年3月23日。

③ *Roe v. Housing Authority of the City of Boulder*，909 F. Supp. 814，822－823（D. Colo. 1995），http://www.accessiblehousing.org/rights/accommodations.asp，最后访问日期：2015年3月23日。

④ *The United Kingdom's Disability Discrimination Act of 1995.*

⑤ *Israel's Equal Rights for People with Disabilities Law.*

⑥ *London Underground Ltd. vs. Edwards*［1997］IRLR157.

改变了的工作方式和工作内容（例如简单重复性的工作），特别的人员辅助，等等，难以尽述。上文提到的2015年4月21日中国教育部和残疾人联合会联合发布的《规定》所列举的大部分便利都属于非物质性便利。[①]该文件还规定，招生考试机构应在保证考试安全和考场秩序的前提下，根据残疾考生的残疾情况和需要以及各地实际，为残疾考生提供"其他必要且能够提供的合理便利"，这使得为残疾人考生提供其所需要的电子试卷也成为可能。

联合国残疾人权利委员会处理的第一份来文就是关于《公约》中的合理便利的。2012年5月，残疾人权利委员会对这份来自瑞典的来文作出了处理意见。[②]来文当事人是一位患有慢性结缔组织异常症的残疾人，为了防止病情恶化，其唯一的康复手段是水疗，但其身体状况使其难以离开住所前往医院或其他康复机构。如果该当事人要继续在该社区生活，在其住所建造一个水疗池是对其最有利的选择，也几乎是唯一的有效选择。但按照政府的相关城市发展规划，其住所所在的区域不允许进行这样的扩建，法院也没有支持当事人的请求。残疾人权利委员会认为，水疗池对保障该来文当事人的健康权至关重要，建筑规划本身也为改动留下了空间，该改动也不会为缔约国带来"过度和不当负担"，因此缔约国应当为当事人提供该合理便利。[③]该事例中残疾人权利委员会认为缔约国应当为当事人提供的"便利"，就是一种非物质性便利。

---

① 例如，为考生提供现行盲文试卷；提供大字号试卷；免除外语听力考试；优先进入考点、考场；考点、考场配备专门的工作人员（如引导辅助人员、手语翻译人员等）予以协助；允许视力残疾考生携带答题所需的盲文笔、盲文手写板、盲文作图工具、橡胶垫、无存储功能的盲文打字机、台灯、光学放大镜、盲杖等辅助器具或设备；允许听力残疾考生携带助听器、人工耳蜗等助听辅听设备；允许行动不便的残疾考生使用轮椅、拐杖，有特殊需要的残疾考生可以自带特殊桌椅参加考试；适当延长考试时间；等等。该文件同时也规定了一些物质性便利，例如设立环境整洁安静、采光适宜、便于出入的单独标准化考场；考点、考场设置文字指示标识、交流板等；配设单独的外语听力播放设备；提供能够完成考试所需、数量充足的盲文纸和普通白纸。

② 截至2015年6月19日，联合国残疾人权利委员会已经接受了8项来文。其中2项来自瑞典，2项来自匈牙利，英国、德国、巴西和阿根廷各1项。匈牙利的两个案件，一个是关于视障者使用自动取款机，另一个涉及匈牙利智力障碍者关于选举权的来文则仅关注第12条及第29条。

③ CRPD/C/7/D/3/2011. http://tbinternet.ohchr.org/_layouts/treatybodyexternal/TBSearch.aspx?Lang=en&TreatyID=4&DocTypeCategoryID=6，最后访问日期：2015年6月18日。

（二）合理便利中的合理

《公约》并不要求义务主体为残疾人提供所有便利而只要求提供合理便利，“合理”是《公约》中合理便利的一个关键要素。无论什么便利，只有当它是“合理”的时候，义务主体才负有提供的义务。根据《公约》，“合理”包含四个标准：第一，有效（effective）；第二，必要（necessary）；第三，适当（appropriate）；第四，不造成过度或不当负担（not imposing a disproportionate or undue burden）。

1. 合理即有效

《公约》文本并没有直接提出“有效”标准，但是《公约》指出合理便利应当根据“具体需要”。“有效”的便利必定是针对当事人的“具体需要”从而能够产生预期效果的，也只有能够针对当事人的“具体需要”而产生预期效果的便利才算得上是“有效”的便利。可见，“有效”既是便利的特征，也是“合理”的标准。例如，一位视力障碍者参加考试，相关机构为其提供了盲文试卷，但该视力障碍者实际上并无使用盲文的能力，那么提供盲文试卷的做法就没有针对该视力障碍者的“具体需要”，不能产生使其实质性参加考试的效果，因此提供盲文试卷的做法就构不成“便利”，更遑论合理便利。

2. 合理即必要

《公约》在规定合理便利时，明确指出合理便利是根据具体需要“进行必要和适当的修改和调整”。可见，“必要”和“适当”是“合理”的标准。

在美国 1995 年的桑德案①中，法院认为，即使一项便利是有效的且不会产生很多费用，但如果提供该便利不是必要的，雇主即不必提供。该案原告请求雇主为其修改办公楼厨房的水池和台面，以便利其使用。但法院审理后认为，雇主没有义务为有身心障碍的雇员提供跟其他人绝对相同的工作环境，该案原告可以使用雇主承诺为其安装的厨房搁板，并使用浴室里的水池，因此法院认为雇主没有必要为原告修改办公楼厨房的水池和厨房台面。

笔者认为，桑德案判决值得肯定的一点是，其确认了雇主没有义务为有身心障碍的雇员提供跟其他人绝对相同的工作环境。按照合理便利的原

① *Vande Zande v. State of Wisconsin Dept. of Administration*, 44 F. 3d 538 (7th Cir. 1995).

理，提供合理便利在更多时候正是要求义务主体为当事人提供不同的条件和环境。不过，该案原告所要求的便利（即得到合适的厨房台面和水池）并不因为雇主已经承诺要为其提供厨房搁板和其可以使用浴室的水池就失去了必要性。在该案中，雇主只是为原告提供了一种关于合理便利的选择。而在《公约》起草过程中，特设委员会第三届会议工作组的意见明确指出，工作组原则上认为不应当强迫一个人接受任何特定的合理便利，尽管工作组广泛同意如果存在一系列合理便利并且每一个便利按规定又是合理的，那么个人无权根据个人喜好去选择其他便利。[①] 该案判决涉嫌强迫原告接受雇主所提供的特定的一种便利。不过，该案雇主是否应当按照原告的要求修改厨房水池和台面的高度，仍然需要按照判断合理便利的基本方法来进行综合考察。如果原告的要求是合理的，不会导致不合比例的负担，则雇主应当尊重原告的意愿，按照原告的要求来修改台面和水池。

3. 合理即适当

《公约》明确规定“适当”也是“合理”的标准之一。上文提到的1995年美国的桑德案也提供了关于什么是“适当”的一个例子。该案原告要求雇主允许其居家办公。但在雇主为原告提供办公场所的合理便利之后，原告即可以在办公室工作，因此居家办公首先不具有特别的必要性。另外，原告的主要工作为秘书工作，完成其大部分工作都需要团队合作，为保证工作质量还应当接受必要的监督，因此法院认为该案原告居家工作是不适当的，雇主没有义务为原告提供居家办公的便利。[②]

2007年英国的拉蒂夫案[③]提供了关于“适当”的另一个例子。拉蒂夫是一位接受过会计训练的盲人，她要求项目管理协会（Project Management Institute）允许她在一台配置了她的屏幕阅读软件（scree-reading software）的电脑上进行职业考试，但项目管理协会按照其针对盲人候选人的已有的标准程序，只同意为拉蒂夫提供阅读器，同时可以延长其考试时间。该案

① http://www.un.org/esa/socdev/enable/rights/ahc3.htm，最后访问日期：2014年12月24日。

② *Vande Zande v. State of Wisconsin Dept. of Administration*, 44 F. 3d 538 (7th Cir. 1995).

③ *Project Management Institute v. Latif* [2007], Industrial Relations Law Reports 579，转引自 Anna Lawson, “Reasonable Accommodation in the Convention on the Rights of Persons with Disabilities and Non-Discrimination of Employment: Rising to the Challenges?”, In C. O'Mahony & G. Quinn, (eds.), *The United Nations Convention on the Rights of Persons with Disabilities: Comparative, Regional and Thematic Perspectives* (Belgium: Intersentia, 2015)。

判决认为，项目管理协会在为拉蒂夫提供合理便利方面是失败的，因为其提供的便利对拉蒂夫而言并不适当（proper）。

现实生活十分复杂，不同的人所面临的障碍可能千差万别。即使所面对的障碍是相同或相似的，不同的人也可能有不同的习惯和偏好。对一个人有效且适当的便利，对另一个人就未必同样有效和适当。因此，在具体个案中，究竟哪种便利是必要的、适当的，应该经由合理便利的提供者与需要者双方通过对话来沟通和协商，合理便利的义务主体尤其要尽可能地尊重权利主体的偏好和习惯，综合考虑各种相关因素。

4. 合理即不造成过度或不当负担

提供合理便利是否应当以“不造成过度或不当负担（不合比例的负担）”（not imposing a disproportionate or undue burden）为限，在《公约》起草的过程中代表们产生了分歧。例如，欧洲残疾论坛（European Disability Forum，EDF）、世界盲人联盟（World Blind Union，WBU）、全球精神治疗使用者和幸存者网络（The World Network of Users and Survivors of Psychiatry，WNUSP）都认为，“不合比例的负担”是一个很困难的概念，它有可能被用来进行歧视，《公约》应该限制提供合理便利的例外。[①] 国家人权机构组织也建议删除“不合比例的负担”，认为这样义务主体就没有借口不履行其义务。[②]

从经济分析的视角来看，为身心障碍人提供某种便利在很多情况下确实要给提供者带来一定的经济负担。尽管许多便利设备或措施同时也能够为非身心障碍人带来方便，而且从长远来看，有了这些便利之后身心障碍人也能够创造更多经济价值，但是提供者为此要承担的经济成本毕竟是客观存在的。此外，为身心障碍人提供合理便利所付出的经济成本还涉及受宪法保护的财产权和契约自由，而如果提供合理便利将导致提供者承受巨大经济负担甚至影响企业的正常运转，那又将造成新的社会不公。因为从社会公平的角度来看，身心障碍人在社会中所遭受的许多障碍都是历史形

---

① UN Convention on the Rights of People with Disabilities，Third session of the Ad Hoc Committee-Daily summary of discussions related to Article 7，http://www.un.org/esa/socdev/enable/rights/ahc3sum7.htm，最后访问日期：2014 年 12 月 24 日。

② UN Convention on the Rights of People with Disabilities，Third session of the Ad Hoc Committee-Daily summary of discussions related to Article 7，http://www.un.org/esa/socdev/enable/rights/ahc3sum7.htm，最后访问日期：2014 年 12 月 24 日。

成的，移除这些障碍的义务也应当由整个社会来承担，不应当要求某一个义务主体（如雇主或学校）来独自承担。所以，提供合理便利应该作为一种临时补救措施，或者是特殊情况下的一种有益补充，这种临时补救措施或有益补充不能要求特定义务主体代替整个社会来承担责任，而应当以不给义务主体带来过度负担为限，过度负担可以成为义务主体免责的理由。

从《公约》起草过程中的背景材料来看，当时联合国考察的十多个国家以及欧盟在规定提供便利的义务时，也都对便利作了“合理”、“不造成过度或不当负担”这样的限定。在各国立法中，“过度或不当负担”的具体表达方式包括“过度负担（undue burden），过度的、不正当的、不合理的困难（undue，unjustifiable or unreasonable hardship），不合理的破坏（unreasonable disruption），不合理的要求（unreasonable requirement），不正当的、不合理的或重大的花费（unjustified，unreasonable or significant costs）”，等等。[①]《公约》最终采纳了限定条件，只有“不造成过度或不当负担”的便利才是《公约》支持的合理便利。笔者认为这是一个折中的考虑，也是一个公正的决定。

二　合理便利的判断方法

《公约》没有明确指出判断一项便利是不是合理便利的具体方法。比较各国的法律和实践、《公约》的背景材料和残疾人权利委员会的实践，可以得出如下一些结论。

（一）坚持“特定个案情况下的合理性”

各国在规定合理便利时，都坚持“特定个案情况下的合理性”，[②] 即判断一项便利是否合理，必须也只能结合该特定个案中的各项因素进行考察，除此之外别无他法。例如，美国联邦平等就业机会委员会 1999 年 3 月

---

① Department of Economic and Social Affairs, “The Concept of Reasonable Accommodation in Selected National Disability Legislation” (A/AC. 265/2006/CRP. 1), http://www. un. org/esa/socdev/enable/rights/ahc7bkgrndra. htm，最后访问日期：2014 年 12 月 24 日。

② Department of Economic and Social Affairs, “The Concept of Reasonable Accommodation in Selected National Disability Legislation”.

发布的旨在澄清提供合理便利义务的就业指南就特别强调，在判断一项便利是否构成“过度困难”时，不能一刀切地作决定，而应考虑与特定雇主提供特定便利的成本或困难相关联的资源和环境等各项要素，根据特定个案的具体情况作判断。

（二）运用比例原则进行衡量

各国在考察合理便利时，都用潜在的比例原则来衡量这些便利或调适可能影响到的所有相关主体的权利、利益和负担。①

1. 成本/收益的经济分析是基本的衡量工具，但一定的经济成本是义务主体不能拒绝的

成本/收益的经济分析方法是考察合理便利的一个基本的、重要的分析工具，在某些领域（例如住宅领域）的个案中甚至是一个决定性的工具。② 需要明确的是，提供者为提供合理便利而付出一定的经济成本是合理便利所内含的要求，合理便利所排斥的只是会造成过度负担的成本。爱尔兰关于合理便利的曲折的立法实践提供了一个例证。爱尔兰 1996 年的《就业平等法案》要求雇主为雇员或申请者提供合理便利，但是爱尔兰最高法院认为，尽管该法案的目的值得颂扬，但是不能要求雇主承担本来应该由社会整体承担的责任，该法案侵犯了雇主享有的宪法上的财产权和经济活动的自由。③ 该法案因此不得不进行修改，之后的爱尔兰 1998 年《就业平等法案》在第 16 条（3）（c）项作出新的规定：如果提供一项便利给雇主带来的成本支出超过“微不足道”（a nominal cost）的程度，这项便利就不能被视为“合理”。该法案第 34（3）项还进一步规定，如果不允许进行某种区别对待的结果是成本的显著增加，那么该区别对待就不构成歧视，不违反法律。④ 爱尔兰的这一做法受到欧盟的反对，《2004 年就业平等法案》最终用“不合比例的负担”取代了“微不足道”这一标准。

正如加拿大索品卡法官（Sopinka J.）在一起雇佣案件中明确指出的，

---

① Department of Economic and Social Affairs, “The Concept of Reasonable Accommodation in Selected National Disability Legislation”.

② *HUD v. Ocean Sands, Inc.*, HUDALJ 04－90－0231－1（September 3, 1993）, http://www.accessiblehousing.org/rights/accommodations.asp，最后访问日期：2015 年 3 月 23 日。

③ *Re Article 26 and the Employment Equality Bill*（1997）2 Irish Reports 321.

④ *Ireland's Employment Equality Act of 1998.*

"过度"（undue）一词的使用表明，一定的经济成本和困难是雇主在提供合理便利时应当接受的，只有当成本和困难达到过度的程度时，才可以成为雇主不提供便利的理由。[①] 美国1995年的一个判决也明确指出，"合理"意味着并不要求义务主体"尽最大可能的努力"，因此考虑成本是必要的，不管雇主多么强大、多么具有经济实力，雇主为提供便利所付出的成本都不应和提供便利所带来的好处极端不成比例。[②]

根据美国《残疾人法案》，判断一项便利的花费时，需要考虑的因素包括但不限于：所需便利的性质及要花费的成本；机构实体中可用于提供合理便利设施的所有财政资源；机构实体的所有资源的总量；等等。[③] 美国联邦平等就业机会委员会1999年3月发布的就业指南还特别指出，雇主应该确定从外部（例如国家康复机构）获得相关资金以帮助其支付合理便利的成本的可能性；雇主还应当考虑退税额或税收抵免的资格，并应确定员工是否愿意支付可能会造成不当负担的部分成本。澳大利亚人权和平等机会委员会认为，关于雇主的花费，应当考虑可识别的净成本或收益（net costs or benefits），或者对雇主可能产生的整体影响，而不是简单的直接成本或预付成本或总成本（direct or upfront or gross costs）。在考量成本时应当考虑下列一些因素：直接成本；因雇佣残疾人及进行相应调整所可以取得的任何税收抵消、补贴或其他经济收益；与提供或将要提供给情况相似但没有残疾的员工的设备或设施相比，为残疾员工提供的合理调适将增加多少额外的成本；等等。[④]

2. 综合考察个案中的各种相关因素，而不仅仅是经济考量

美国《残疾人法案》还规定，如果设定的标准是与工作相关的和必要的，并且是残疾人无法通过合理便利来达到的，那么该标准可以作为对抗歧视指控的辩护。[⑤] 该法案同时规定，在判断合理便利时，除了考虑经济成本，需要考虑的因素还包括：与雇佣人数有关的机构实体的商业规模；

---

① *Central Okanagan School District No. 23 v. Renaud* [1992] 2 S. C. R. 970.

② *Vande Zande v. State of Wisconsin Department of Administration* [42 44 F. 3d 538 (7th Cir. 1995)].

③ ADA. Sec. 12111. Definitions.

④ Department of Economic and Social Affairs, "The Concept of Reasonable Accommodation in Selected National Disability Legislation".

⑤ ADA. Sec. 12113.

便利设施的数量、类型与地点；机构实体的工作方式，包括它的组成、结构以及劳动力的功能；该机构实体的地理位置；便利设施与所涉机构实体的行政或财政关系；便利设施对环境的影响；等等。[①] 另外，如果一个机构实体能够证明，改变其政策、实践或程序包括高等教育（中学后教育）的学术要求等将从根本上改变其商品、服务、设施、特权、优势或涉及的场所等的性质，或将导致不恰当的过分负担，则可以不作改变。[②] 根据美国《残疾人法案》，提供合理便利也不应当给身心障碍人本人或其他人造成健康或安全方面的直接威胁。当然，判断是否会构成这种直接威胁，需要根据医学标准，考虑潜在风险和危害的性质、严重程度、发生的可能性和紧迫性等一系列要素。[③] 如果提供某种便利极有可能导致某些严重后果，则提供这种便利就不是合理的。

在加拿大，提供一项便利是否将导致“不当负担”也取决于很多因素，健康、安全和花费都应当纳入考虑。在决定雇佣关系中提供某种便利是否构成“不当负担”时，加拿大的法院曾考虑了如下一些因素：金融成本；对集体协议的破坏；对公众服务的中断；其他员工的风纪斗志；劳动力和设备的可替换性；雇主的行动规模（可能涉及雇主承担成本和改变劳动力的能力）；安全；对雇主的商业运行的干扰；总体经济环境。在决定教育系统提供某项便利是否构成“不当负担”时，法院则考察了下列一些因素：提供该项便利所需的金融资源；该便利对其他学生将产生的影响（包括程度和种类）；该便利对教育程序和教育规划的影响；该便利对教职员工和其他学生（包括其他有身心障碍的学生）可能产生的其他不寻常的风险。[④]

三　合理便利的特征

（一）合理便利的个人化

合理便利的基本特征是它的个人化，即它针对的是具体个人的具体需

① ADA. Sec. 12111. Definitions.

② ADA. section 12201 (f) and ADA. Sec. 12182.

③ ADA. Sec. 12113. Defenses (b).

④ Department of Economic and Social Affairs, “The Concept of Reasonable Accommodation in Selected National Disability Legislation”.

求，是为满足特定个人的特定需求而设计和提供的。从人权原理来看，合理便利反映了人权保障的更高层次。人权具有普遍性，但如果人权保障不能考虑到每一个特定的具体的人维护其尊严的特定需求，则人权的普遍性就得不到体现。因此，真正的普遍人权必定能落实到每一个具体的人，能满足每一个特定的人保障其尊严的特定需求。[①] 而提供合理便利比起其他人权保障手段来说，更着眼于人的多样性，更贴合每一个个体人的特定需要，更个人化，也因而更能体现人权的普遍性。从已有的法律规范和法律实践来看，合理便利的个人化表明：一个人就可以提出合理便利的要求。[②] 只要一个人有某种需要，就可以向义务主体提出提供合理便利的要求，合理便利也可以只为一个有需要的人提供。

（二）合理便利的协商性

合理便利的个人化决定了合理便利的协商性，即提供者应当为需要者提供什么样的合理便利，应当由双方经过协商来确定。合理便利的需要者应当向提供者提出清晰的要求，提供者应当充分尊重需要者对合理便利的意见，在不造成过度负担的前提下满足其需要。例如，美国的公共政策方针（the public policy guideline）明确规定，提供给个人的便利应当是建立在个案情况基础上的经过雇主和雇员互动的同意。[③]

（三）合理便利一般要求提供者尽积极义务

提供合理便利一般需要提供者采取具体的积极行动，作出上文所述各种物质性或非物质性的调整。要求提供者采取积极行动一般都直接规定在各国关于合理便利的定义之中，例如加拿大《公平就业法》（*Employment Equity Act*）就直接要求义务主体积极行动。《公约》在规定合理便利时也明确指出义务主体要“进行必要和适当的修改和调整”，这也表明提供合理便利一般而言是一项需要采取积极行动的义务。也正因为此，提供合理

---

① 参见曲相霏《人权离我们有多远——人权的概念及其在近代中国的发展演变》，清华大学出版社，2015。

② 黄裔：《合理便利概念的浅析》，载《反歧视评论》（第1辑），法律出版社，2014。

③ Department of Economic and Social Affairs, “The Concept of Reasonable Accommodation in Selected National Disability Legislation”.

便利才需要以不给义务主体造成“过度或不当负担”为条件。而传统的反歧视大多只要求义务主体尽不作为的消极义务，故传统的反歧视不需要考虑是否会造成“过度或不当负担”。

（四）合理便利要求提供者根据需要者的具体情况提供“区别对待”

合理便利的一个重要特征就是，它要求提供者根据需要者的具体情况提供区别对待。这一点也使合理便利与传统的反歧视手段有了显著区别。传统反歧视无论是消除直接歧视还是消除间接歧视，目的都是实现“同等对待”（identical treatment），即确保任何群体都不会因为群体的特殊性（如性别、种族、宗教信仰等）而受到区别对待。而提供合理便利的义务则恰恰相反，它要求义务主体充分考虑权利人的特殊需求，并针对这一特殊需求提供区别对待或优待（more favorable treatment）。[①] 忽略个体的需要，一味地坚持同等对待并不会带来真正的平等，反而会使不平等变得更加严重。因此个体的特殊需求应当被考虑，并且应当采取适当的措施满足这些需求，以避免个体因自身的需求无法得到满足而面临障碍。[②]

（五）合理便利应建立在提供一般性无障碍设施的基础之上或作为其临时补充

2012 年 10 月残疾人权利委员会对中国《首次履约报告》提出的《结论性意见》明确指出，合理便利的定义“涉及在特定案例中在超越一般性无障碍问题之外应有必要和适当的修改与调整”。[③] 委员会的这一意见表明，合理便利的提供应当建立在已经为身心障碍人提供了一般性无障碍设施的基础之上。一般性无障碍设施是通用设计，而合理便利涉及在特定案例中针对特定身心障碍人的超越了一般无障碍设施的需要，或者在无障碍设施不可得的情况下，提供必要的和适当的便利。这表明，并不是有了完

---

① Lisa Waddington, “Reasonable Accommodation: Time to Extend the Duty to Accommodate Beyond Disability?” *NTM | NJCM-Bulletin* 36（2011），pp. 186 - 198，Available at SSRN：http://ssrn.com/abstract = 1847623，最后访问日期：2015 年 6 月 19 日。

② Stephen L. Darwall, *Equal Freedom: Selected Tanner Lectures on Human Values*（Ann Arbour: University of Michigan Press, 1995）. 参见黄裔《合理便利概念的浅析》，载《反歧视评论》（第 1 辑），法律出版社，2014。

③ CRPD/C/CHN/CO/1.

善的无障碍设施之后，身心障碍人就不需要再提出合理便利的要求。因为无障碍设施是一般性的、面向所有人的，而每个身心障碍人所承受的损害不同，在受教育、工作和生活中所面对的问题也可能不同，其需求就可能有差别，合理便利就是在已经提供了无障碍设施的前提下，再为有需要的个人提供个性化的便利。当然，如果无障碍设施本身就是缺乏的，则身心障碍人就不得不提出更多的合理便利要求。

四　合理便利的保障

（一）缔约国保障合理便利的义务

合理便利最早出现在雇佣领域，并且很长一段时间内主要局限于雇佣领域。在美国、加拿大等国的法律和司法实践中，雇主最早被要求承担提供合理便利的义务。随着合理便利理念的逐渐发展，合理便利也逐渐扩展到教育、医疗、住宅、餐饮、娱乐、交通等领域，提供合理便利的义务主体也从雇主扩展到学校、医院、住宅所有人和管理人以及其他提供公共服务的部门，但比较而言雇佣就业领域仍然是各国要求提供合理便利的一个主要领域，雇主仍然是提供合理便利的主要义务主体。

各国国内法关于合理便利的立法和实践也表明，政府和私有主体在法律上都承担着直接提供合理便利的义务，尤其在公共医疗、公共教育等领域，政府更是合理便利的直接提供者。不过，对私有雇主来说，其公司或机构的性质和规模（包括雇员的人数），往往对提供合理便利构成一个限制条件。例如，加拿大《公平雇佣法》第 4 条规定，该法适用于联邦服务机构、皇家公司、与联邦政府的工作和业务有关联或其管辖下的有 100 人或更多员工的私营部门雇主。[①] 美国《残疾人法案》把雇员人数达到 15 人（某些特殊情况下达到 25 人）作为需要提供合理便利的门槛。[②] 美国《康复法案》则只约束联邦政府机构和受联邦援助或与联邦有合同关系（并达

① http://laws. justice. gc. ca/eng/acts/E - 5. 401/page - 3. html#docCont，最后访问日期：2015 年 5 月 1 日。

② ADA. Sec. 12111 (5).

到一定的金额）的雇主和机构。[①]

在《公约》通过之前，国家本身并没有促进合理便利的义务。特设委员会第四届会议明确提出国家对提供合理便利应负确保性责任，[②] 即《公约》虽然并不要求国家自己直接提供全部合理便利，但国家有责任积极行动，通过立法、行政、司法等一切可能的手段和措施，确保为身心障碍人提供合理便利。简而言之，根据《公约》，缔约国对合理便利承担着三种不同性质的义务。

一是直接提供合理便利的义务。例如《公约》第 27 条（工作和就业）明确规定缔约国应当"在公共部门雇佣残疾人"，从《公约》第 24 条（教育）、第 25 条（健康）等相关条文也可以推导出缔约国在向公众提供医疗、教育、交通等公共产品和公共服务时有义务为身心障碍人提供合理便利。

二是"确保"其他社会主体为身心障碍人提供合理便利的义务。《公约》第 4 条（一般义务）、第 5 条（平等和不歧视）、第 14 条（自由和人身安全）、第 24 条、第 27 条等一系列条文都明确规定缔约国"确保"向身心障碍人提供合理便利。前文提到，《公约》没有对提供合理便利的义务主体作任何限定，没有像上述有些国家的国内法那样设置提供合理便利的私有主体应达到的规模等门槛条件。笔者认为，这里可能有三方面的考虑：其一，《公约》作为国际人权法规范的是缔约国的义务和责任而不是其他私有社会主体的行为，因此没有必要直接针对这个问题作出规定；其二，从《公约》力图促进提供合理便利的精神来看，《公约》不对提供合理便利的义务主体列负面清单、作硬性限制的做法，可以大大提高提供合理便利的可能性；其三，也是最重要的，就是《公约》关于提供合理便利以"不造成过度或不当负担"为条件的规定，实际上完全能够吸收关于雇员人数、公司或机构的性质和规模等一系列考量因素，没有必要再作硬性的门槛规定。基于同样的理由，《公约》实际上没有对合理便利的义务主体作出任何其他限制。根据《公约》可以推导出如下结论：合理便利的义

---

① Section 504 of Rehabilitation Act.

② UN Convention on the Rights of People with Disabilities Fourth session of the Ad Hoc Committee-Daily Summary. http://www.un.org/esa/socdev/enable/rights/ahc4sumart03.htm，最后访问日期：2015 年 5 月 1 日。

务主体是非常广泛的，任何可能与身心障碍者产生联系的主体都有可能成为合理便利的义务主体。换句话说，《公约》实际上要求缔约国将合理便利的义务主体扩展到所有相关的人和组织，在某些特殊情况下也有可能包括个人。所有这些社会主体都由国家来确保其直接承担提供合理便利的义务。

三是促进合理便利的义务。提供合理便利的义务是一项“即刻的义务”，即要求提供者即刻行动来提供合理便利。这一点也使合理便利与无障碍有了区别，无障碍建设只能根据社会的发展水平按计划逐渐进行。合理便利的水平也要受到客观条件的限制，与社会的发展程度相关。《公约》第 4 条规定，“缔约国承诺确保并促进充分实现所有残疾人的一切人权和基本自由，使其不受任何基于残疾的歧视”，为了实现这个目的，缔约国承诺“应当采取一切适当措施”。《公约》第 5 条又规定，“为促进平等和消除歧视，缔约国应当采取一切适当步骤，确保提供合理便利”。例如，缔约国可以为合理便利提供财政补贴，培训专业人员或提供关于合理便利的专家支持，发展出更多样、更灵活的就业模式，等等，这些都可以大大提高合理便利的水平和效果。

（二）缔约国确保提供合理便利的具体措施

“确保提供合理便利”是缔约国对保障合理便利承担的三项重要义务中的一项，为了履行这一义务，缔约国至少应当采取下列两大措施。

1. 在法律中明确规定合理便利

前文提到，联合国残疾人权利委员会在审议中国的《首次履约报告》后提出的《结论性意见》中，建议中国“在法律中加入对合理便利的定义”。[①] 在法律中明文规定合理便利对于保障合理便利具有积极意义。虽然传统的消除歧视（尤其是消除间接歧视）的手段和方法在一定程度上也能达到提供合理便利的目的，但是，传统的消除歧视与提供合理便利之间还是有显著的区别。首先，按照传统的反歧视理论，义务主体只要做到不加深、不巩固或不强化已经存在的不平等就可以了，换言之，传统的反歧视法律一般只要求义务主体尽消极义务。其次，传统的消除歧视的手段和方法一般只被用来回应群体的平等权诉求，而提供合理便利则并不需要具有

① CRPD/C/CHN/CO/1.

相同或相似特征的所有人都具有这种便利需要。最后，二者之间的最大区别是，传统的反歧视手段和方法追求的目的仍然是实现“不同的人得到相同的对待”，而提供合理便利追求的目的则是“给不同的人以与其要求相适应的不同的对待”。尽管传统的反间接歧视的概念经过发展已不再强调形式上的相同，但其根源和本质仍是“实现不同群体之间的相同对待及群体之间的平衡”。也就是说，传统的消除间接歧视要求一个人所受到的待遇与他自身的特质或其所属群体的身份认同没有关系。[①] 而提供合理便利却要求一个人所受到的待遇（即提供合理便利）与他自身的特殊情况（可能与他所属的群体的情况一致，也可能与他所处的群体的情况不完全一致）密切相关。

不过，随着反歧视理论的发展，合理便利与传统的反歧视手段和方法的这些区别已经变得不这么清晰了。在今天，传统的反歧视理论已经能够包容某些合理便利的要求。例如，澳大利亚 1992 年的残疾歧视法案并没有明确规定“合理调适”（reasonable adjustment），只是在第 6 段规定了“间接歧视”（indirect discrimination），要求“消除对身心障碍人不利的不合理的要求”。而澳大利亚人权和平等机会委员会在解释该法案时明确指出，该法案“毫无疑问要求提供合理便利”。[②] 加拿大也是在平等和反歧视的框架中为身心障碍人提供合理便利，埃尔德里奇一案就是一个典型案例。该案判决认为，当政府提供一项普遍的利益时，必须采取积极措施消除障碍，让身心障碍人与他人同样享有该利益，以实现实质平等，在该案中消

① Anna Lawson, *Disability and Equality Law in Britain*: *The Role of Reasonable Adjustment* (Hart Publishing, 2008), p. 26; Sandra Fredman, “Equality: A New Generation?”, *Industrial Law Journal* 30 (2001), p. 145; Dagmar Schiek and others, *Cases, Materials and Text on National, Supranational and International Non-Discrimination Law* (Hart Publishing, 2007), p. 35; Marianne Gijzen, *Selected Issues in Equal Treatment Law*: *A Multi-Layered Comparison of European, English and Dutch Law* (Intersentia, 2006), p. 39; Sandra Fredman, “Disability Equality: A Challenge to the Existing Anti-Discrimination Paradigm?”, in Anna Lawson and Caroline (eds.), *Gooding Disability Rights in Europe from Theory to Practice* (Hart Publishing 2005); Lisa Waddington and Anna Lawson, *Disability and Non-Discrimination Law in European Union*: *An Analysis of Disability Discrimination Law within and beyond the Employment Field* (European Union, 2009). 参见黄裔《合理便利概念的浅析》，载《反歧视评论》（第 1 辑），法律出版社，2014。

② Department of Economic and Social Affairs, “The Concept of Reasonable Accommodation in Selected National Disability Legislation”.

除障碍就表现为要为听力障碍者提供手语服务。[①] 英国伦敦地铁公司一案（London Underground Ltd. v. Edwards）也在消除歧视的框架中为当事人提供了合理便利。[②] 可见，消除歧视发展到今天已经可以包含提供合理便利的要求。或者可以说，提供合理便利是传统反歧视手段与方法的新发展。[③] 合理便利只在传统反歧视的基础上更进一步，在一般化的提供无障碍设施的基础上更进一步，从而直接针对特定个人的多样化需要。

不过，虽然消除歧视的手段发展到今天，从理论上来讲已经可以包含提供合理便利的要求，在一些国家的实践中也起到了提供合理便利的作用，但是对大多数国家来讲，在法律中规定合理便利仍然具有必要性。因为法律的明确规定可以避免反歧视理论和实践的不确定性和不统一性，使提供合理便利具有明确的法律依据，尤其对于反歧视理论和实践都还处于起步阶段的国家而言，在法律中明确规定合理便利更具有理论和现实意义。

有观点认为，提供合理便利需要资源投入，需要积极作为，合理便利作为欧美立法传统之下的一个个体色彩浓重的概念，依赖于司法审判来推动义务主体的主动行为，与中国残疾人权利保障的发展路径不同，中国的残疾人权利保障立法更强调整体环境的改善，强调集体权利的实现。[④] 对合理便利的这种担忧不无道理，但同时也应当辩证分析。提供合理便利的确在大多数情况下是一项积极义务，客观上需要根据可利用的资源来逐渐实现。但是，我们也应当看到相反的一面。第一，《公约》要求提供的是“合理”便利而不是所有便利，“合理”意味着不能超出可利用的最大资源，超出可利用的最大资源的便利就不是合理便利。第二，在“提供合理便利是提供可利用的资源范围之内的便利”这一前提下，“提供合理便利”

---

① *Eldridge v. British Columbia*（*Attorney General*）［1997］，3 S. C. R. 624.

② 伦敦地铁公司案（*London Underground Ltd. v. Edwards*）（No. 2）一案的判决指出，根据常识，女性比男性更多地承担照顾未成年孩子的责任，地铁公司的新轮班方案将使单亲母亲难以在照顾未成年孩子的同时继续胜任其工作，因此构成对女性的间接歧视，地铁公司应当根据爱德华兹女士（Ms. Edwards）的特别需求而为其单独安排轮班时间，这相当于要求地铁公司为爱德华兹女士提供合理便利。*London Underground Ltd. v. Edwards*［1997］IRLR157.

③ Christine Jolls，“Accommodation Mandate”，*Stanford Law Review* 53（2000），pp. 223 - 306.

④ 参见李敬《〈残疾人权利公约〉中的不歧视原则》，载《反歧视评论》第1辑，法律出版社，2014。

也包括“行动的义务”和“结果的义务”两个方面。只要特定残疾人在特定情况下所需要的便利是合理的，相关义务人提供该合理便利的“行动的义务”就是即刻的，就应当是“立即生效的”（immediately effect）。这意味着提供者要马上在合理时间内采取行动，尽管特定残疾人获得该便利的结果可能需要一段时间才能达成。第三，如前所述，便利包括物质性的便利和非物质性的便利，提供合理便利实际上并不一定都需要较大的资源投入。而且，在有些特殊情况下，相关方只要不反对、不作为，残疾人就可以得到其所需要的便利。第四，合理便利作为一个与特定个人的特定正当需要相关联的概念，正是要补足一般性无障碍措施的不足，也只有在相关方拒绝提供合理便利的情况下，才可能需要司法审判机关的介入。除了司法审判机关的介入，也还有一些非司法机构或准司法机构能够提供同样的功能。因此，合理便利尽管是一个英美法传统中孕育出来的个人色彩较重的概念，在其他地域并非没有生根发芽的可能。在一定意义上，国际人权法的功能之一就是普及这些具有超地域性的概念和理念。

2. *在法律中明确规定拒绝提供合理便利构成歧视并应承担相应的法律责任*

将拒绝提供合理便利的行为认定为歧视，是目前国家保障合理便利的一个十分重要的法律手段。美国《残疾人法案》、英国《残障歧视法案》和欧盟《平等就业条例》都作了这样的规定，加拿大1999年的梅奥瑞一案也明确提出，若无合理的理由，拒绝提供合理便利便构成法律所禁止的歧视。[①]《公约》在国际人权法中第一个提出“拒绝提供合理便利构成歧视”，这一做法在《公约》起草过程中就产生了分歧。有一些成员认为《公约》应主要用来约束缔约国，因此不应强制缔约国在其相关国内立法中使用合理便利这一概念，也不宜把私人实体没有提供合理便利的行为定性为违反不歧视原则。[②]《公约》没有采纳这一观点。笔者认为，《公约》的做法是值得称许的。国际人权法确实是用来约束缔约国的，但这并不妨碍国际人权法规定缔约国反歧视的具体手段。

---

① *British Columbia*（*Public Service Employee Relations Commission*）*v. BCGSEU*［1999］Supreme Court Judgments 26274［1999］3 SCR 3.

② http://www.un.org/esa/socdev/enable/rights/ahc3.htm，最后访问日期：2014年12月24日。

（三）合理便利的证明责任

在关于合理便利的证明责任方面，各国立法、法律解释和司法判例都支持“谁主张谁举证”的基本原则，即把证明“过度或不当负担”的责任分配给了应当提供合理便利的一方，而权利主体即身心障碍人则有责任证明其所要求的便利或调适是合理的。[①] 例如，欧盟《平等就业条例》第10条规定，个人认为受到不平等待遇时，法庭或其他主管机构应“确保由被告证明其未违背平等待遇原则”。[②] 美国和加拿大的案例法还显示，尽管合理便利的概念适用于不同领域和基于不同原因的歧视，但适用的标准并不相同。在与身心障碍有关的案例中，提供合理便利的义务适用很严格的审查标准，只有在极少数情况下义务主体才可以以“过度的负担”为免责理由。[③]

五 总结与反思

（一）合理便利的正当性基础

前文提到，合理便利涉及财产权和契约自由等宪法性权利。尽管合理便利本身即附带自我限制条件，以不给提供者“造成过度或不当负担”为限度，但毫无疑问的是，提供合理便利在很多情况下需要提供者承担超出“微不足道”的负担，通常是一定的经济成本。合理便利的正当性基础是什么，合理便利如何通过合宪性审查，是合理便利理论需要解决的一个根本问题。

笔者认为，人权主体的转型、人权内容的扩张、人与人之间的连带关系的强化以及财产权的社会义务理论等，都为合理便利的正当性提供了支持。私有财产神圣不可侵犯和契约自由在古典人权理论中占据着至关重要

① Department of Economic and Social Affairs, “The Concept of Reasonable Accommodation in Selected National Disability Legislation”.

② Council Directive (EC) 2000/78, “Establishing a General Framework for Equal Treatment in Employment and Occupation 2000”.

③ Waddington, “Reasonable Accommodation: Time to Extend the Duty to Accommodate Beyond Disability?”, pp. 186 - 198.

的位置，19 世纪初制定的《法国民法典》体现的正是这种人权理论。20 世纪以后，自由主义人权理论的缺陷开始逐渐得到修正，人权主体开始从抽象的理性主体向现实的、具体的、多样化的人转化，儿童、老人、身心障碍人这些最初被自由主义人权理论忽视的人现在被承认为人权的主体。人权主体的转型带来了人权内容的扩充，社会权利开始登上人权的舞台，成为民事权利和政治权利的补充。[①] 而社会权利的保障往往需要社会财富的再分配，需要对财产权予以限制。与此同时，人与人之间的社会连带关系也越来越得到正视，其所内含的财富的社会连带关系带来了财产权理论的新发展。由于财富的获得不再完全是个人自我奋斗的产物而是在社会连带关系中产生的，尤其是一些人的生存和发展可能严重依赖其他人的财产，财产权开始被认为附带着社会义务，从而也不再是绝对的了。财产权的社会义务理论起源于德国，《魏玛宪法》第 153 条第 3 款是该理论的最好表达："所有权负有义务，财产权的行使要以公共福祉为目的。"这就要求财产权应当为了维护社会正义和公共利益而自我限缩，"在个人张扬其财产自由的同时，应使其财产亦有助于社会公共福祉的实现，也就是能够促进合乎人类尊严的人类整体生存的实现"。[②] 正是由于财产权负有社会义务，因此可以对财产权进行某些限制，并且可以不予补偿，因为这种限制是对一切相关财产的普遍限制，不同于征收、征用等特别限制，征收、征用等特别限制必须予以公正补偿。合理便利对提供者的财产权和契约自由的限制，可以被视为财产权的社会义务的一种体现，换言之，提供合理便利的义务是所有财产权的所有者都承担的不需要特别补偿的普遍社会义务。

20 世纪 70 年代联合国和平与人权司司长卡雷尔·瓦萨克提出连带权理论，他认为连带权是基于人类的博爱和必不可少的连带而产生的人权，这些权利只能通过社会所有参与角色的共同努力才能实现。[③] 在现代社会里，过群体生活是人们所需要的也是人们难以摆脱的，人们因此

---

① 关于人权主体转型与人权内容扩张的系统分析，参见曲相霏《人权离我们有多远——人权的概念及其在近代中国的发展演变》，清华大学出版社，2015，第 1 章、第 3 章。

② 张翔：《财产权的社会义务》，《中国社会科学》2012 年第 9 期。

③ 参见卡雷尔·瓦萨克《人权的不同类型》，张丽萍、程春明译，载《法哲学与法社会学论丛》第 4 辑，中国政法大学出版社，2001。

互相依赖、互相影响。每个社会主体都可能既是提供者，又是接受者。只有所有社会角色都承担起一定的社会责任，人的尊严才能得到更好的保障。这也是要求所有社会主体普遍承担提供合理便利义务的正当性所在。

尽管因为财产权承担着社会义务因而可以要求财产权在得不到特别补偿的前提下受到限制，对财产权的这种限制本身也必须受到严格限制，应当由法律来明确规定，并且不能过度，否则就是对财产权的侵犯。这就是为什么合理便利应当由基本法律来规定并且必须通得过比例原则的考量。

（二）合理便利对中国的挑战及其可以发挥的积极作用

中国是《残疾人权利公约》的缔约国，并在一定程度上推动了《公约》的制定和通过，有义务履行《公约》关于合理便利的规定。联合国残疾人权利委员会也已经明确建议中国“在法律中加入对合理便利的定义”，这就对中国立法提出了挑战。而如果中国在基本法律中明确规定合理便利，那又将给整个社会带来新的挑战，因为合理便利的实施几乎涉及所有社会主体，尤其是就业、教育和公共服务等领域的社会主体。另外，由于在个案中不提供合理便利即构成歧视，具有可诉性，这又将不可避免地给司法机关带来新的任务和新的挑战。

在美国、加拿大等国的实践中，合理便利已经被证明是一项比较有效的反歧视工具。它在给中国带来挑战的同时，也将对推动中国的残疾人权利保障发挥非常积极的作用。前述教育部和残疾人联合会联合发布的《残疾人参加普通高等学校招生全国统一考试管理规定（暂行）》已经使一些残疾人从中受益。[①] 中国多年来推行的按比例安排残疾人就业制度和残疾人就业保障金制度在实践中遭遇了一系列问题，已经引起了人们对这两项制度的反思。[②] 在此情况下，无障碍建设和提供合理便利给我们提供了新的思路和方法，例如，政府可以用这些年来节余的大量残疾人保障金为

① 《残疾高考生连出黑马 残疾考生应享合理便利》，人民网，http://xj.people.com.cn/n/2015/0629/c188521-25402787.html，最后访问日期：2015年8月23日。

② 相关综述参见曲相霏《〈残疾人权利公约〉与中国的残疾人权利保障》，《法学》2013年第8期。

合理便利提供财政补助，从而推动残疾人就业。实际上 2015 年 9 月 9 日印发的《残疾人就业保障金征收使用管理办法》也为这一做法提供了法律支持。[①] 总而言之，加快对合理便利的研究、立法和实施具有十分积极的意义。

（本文原载于《政法论坛》2016 年第 2 期）

① 《管理办法》第三章“使用管理”部分明确规定，残疾人就业保障金可用于“补贴用人单位安排残疾人就业所需设施设备购置、改造和支持性服务费用。补贴辅助性就业机构建设和运行费用”。《关于印发〈残疾人就业保障金征收使用管理办法〉的通知》，财政部官网，http://szs.mof.gov.cn/bgtZaiXianFuWu_1_1_11/mlqd/201509/t20150914_1458276.html，最后访问日期：2015 年 5 月 20 日。

论消费者权利的性质

钟瑞华*

自1962年3月15日美国总统肯尼迪在向国会提交的“消费者权利咨文”中明确提出消费者4大基本权利即安全权、知情权、选择权和意见被听取权以来，消费者权利的种类及范围不断扩充，消费者权利逐步发展成为一个内容丰富、独具特色的权利束。① 虽然消费者权利存在的时间才不

---

* 钟瑞华，中国社会科学院国际法研究所助理研究员。

① 1963年，国际消费者组织联盟（International Organisation of Consumer Unions，简称IOCU，现称Consumers International，中文译名为国际消联）以肯尼迪提出的4项权利为基础，再加上消费者受教育权、求偿权、基本需求权及良好环境权等4项内容，提出了消费者的8大权利及消费者的认知、行动、关心社会、保护环境和团结等5大义务。此外，不仅日本、加拿大、澳大利亚及欧洲各国等发达国家，而且印度、泰国、菲律宾、马来西亚等发展中国家也纷纷通过消费者保护立法乃至在宪法中承认并规定了消费者权利；1985年联合国大会通过《联合国保护消费者准则》，在国际层面上以国际法文件的形式提出要确保满足消费者的6项合理需求，并于1999年修改时增加了第7项需求，即“促进可持续消费形式”。

国际消联提出的8项消费者权利如下。（1）基本物质需求权（The Right to Satisfaction of Basic Needs）。获得基本、必需的商品和服务以及充分的食物、衣服、住房、健康治疗、教育和卫生条件的权利。（2）安全权（The Right to Safety）。消费者的生命和健康免受危险产品、生产过程以及服务等伤害的权利。（3）知情权（The Right to be Informed）。获得作出正确的消费决定所需要的信息，以及免受不实的或引人误解的广告或标识的诱导或欺骗的权利。（4）选择权（The Right to Choose）。以具有竞争力的价格和满意的质量获得多种产品和服务的权利，在垄断的情况下，国家应保证质量满意、价格合理。（5）意见被听取权（The Right to be Heard）。通过代表反映消费者利益，保证国家政策的形成和执行、产品和服务的开发符合消费者利益的权利。（6）获得救济权（The Right to Redress）。消费者的正当请求获得合理、迅速、便捷解决，以及损害获得赔偿的权利。（7）受教育权（The Right to Consumer Education）。为了能够作出正确的消费决定，明了其基本权利和责任而获得充分的知识和技巧的权利。（8）良好环境权〔The Right to a Healthy （转下页注）

过五六十年，但它对世界各国乃至国际经济、政治和法律秩序都形成了很大的冲击，美国总统肯尼迪甚至将消费者利益等同于国家利益。[①]世界上许多国家乃至欧盟、国际消联和联合国等国际组织纷纷通过法律文件甚至宪法正面确认消费者权利，并采取各种措施对其实施保护。相应地，消费者（保护）法也日益引起法律学者的重视并逐渐发展成为一个年轻的法律分支。但总体看来，消费者保护法基础理论的研究还非常有限，消费者权利仍然只不过是一个非常笼统的概念和指称而已，其法律性质、内部构成和类型划分等问题迄无定论。相比较于西方国家而言，我国消费者保护运动起步较晚，这方面的研究尤其欠缺。消费者权利是消费者保护法的核心制度之一，而在与消费者权利有关的诸多基本问题之中，消费者权利性质问题具有更加基础性的理论意义；对消费者权利性质的理解甚至决定着一国消费者保护法的整个制度构成和体系安排。有鉴于此，本文将主要围绕消费者权利这一经济、政治和法律现象，结合国内外学者的研究成果，展开对消费者权利性质的讨论。

（接上页注①）Environment〕。在适宜的环境中生活和工作的权利，并且要求所处的环境不会危及当代人及子孙后代的福利。

从世界各国的规定看，不同国家赋予消费者的权利虽然主要内容基本相同，但由于法律文化传统和具体社会经济条件的差异，在具体规定和文字表述方面存在一些差异。例如德国法中的消费者保护撤回权（Das Verbraucherschützende Widerrufsrecht）属于比较有特色的工具性消费者权利之一，并且构成德国 2002 年债法改革的核心内容，德国还强调并重视消费者的环境权；美国则非常关注消费者索赔权赖以实现的制度保障（the Access to Justice），并注重通过多样化的行政管制工具预先保护消费者免受伤害。

我国《消费者权益保护法》规定的消费者权利有安全权（第 7 条）、知情权（第 8 条）、选择权（第 9 条）、公平交易权（第 10 条）、索赔权（第 11 条）、结社权（第 12 条）、受教育权（第 13 条）、受尊重权（第 14 条）和监督权（第 15 条），共计 9 项。不仅权利种类丰富，而且在权利义务关系的设计上也独具特色，详见下文。此外尚须注意的是，消费者权利是一种新型权利，存在时间不过五六十年，目前尚处在不断的发展和扩张之中。随着经济发展和社会进步，消费者权利的内容必然更加丰富。

本文的讨论主要以国际消联的规定为蓝本，并适当涉及一些国家特别是我国《消费者权益保护法》的特殊规定。若非特别指出，本文所指的消费者权利或消费者基本权利主要包括国际消联列举的 8 项权利以及我国《消费者权益保护法》中规定的结社权和公平交易权等。

① K. Rajeshwar Rao and P. Krishnama Chary, "Basic Ingredients for Effective Consumer Protection", in D. Himachalam (ed.), *Consumer Protection And The Law* (Aph Publishing Corporation, 1998), p. 76.

本文首先总结归纳了我国理论界对消费者权利性质的两种不同认识——“特别民事权利论”和“人权论”,[①] 并在分析和评价这两个观点的基础上提出了自己的看法。本文认为，消费者权利具有复合性和层次性的特征。首先，各项具体的消费者权利其性质并不一致。消费者的所有基本权利均是人权，主要属于经济、社会和文化权利（社会权）；部分基本消费者权利不仅是人权，还同时是民事权利；部分基本消费者权利则仅是人权而不具有私权性。是为消费者权利的复合性。其次，作为人权的消费者权利与作为私权的消费者权利并非处于同一个层次。作为人权的消费者权利是整个消费者保护法的统率和灵魂，贯穿于所有消费者保护制度之中；作为私权的消费者权利则仅存在于消费者保护民事特别规范之中，属于民事权利中的债权并主要通过债法制度和民事责任制度得到保障。是为消费者权利的层次性。全面准确地把握消费者权利的复合性和层次性，不仅有助于深化对消费者权利制度的了解，更可以为梳理消费者保护法不同组成部分的相互关系及整合性质各异的消费者保护规范群提供理论上的指导；而且，从人权（社会权）的高度看待消费者的基本权利有助于提高对消费者的保护，特别是有助于实现对消费者身体健康和生命安全等基本生存要求的满足和实现。

一　特别民事权利论

特别民事权利论是我国民法理论界对消费者权利性质的主流观点，并且充分体现在我国《消费者权益保护法》对于9项消费者权利的定义之中。

---

① “特别民事权利论”基本上是我国民法学者的主流观点，主要代表学者及其著述为：李昌麒、许明月编著《消费者保护法》（法律出版社，1997）；张严方《消费者保护法研究》（法律出版社，2003）。另外，也经常在民法学者间听到“消费者权利为特别民事权利”的笼统说法。此外，我国现行《消费者权益保护法》第二章“消费者的权利”对消费者诸权利的定义非常鲜明地体现出“消费者权利是民事权利”的色彩。“人权论”则主要为我国一些经济法学者所主张。我国台湾地区和国外也有学者主张消费者权利是人权或应该承认消费者权利的人权身份。

（一）特别民事权利论的主要内容①

1. 消费者权利是民事权利

特别民事权利论认为，消费者权利是消费者在购买、使用商品或接受服务时依法享有的受法律保护的权利。②“事实上，消费者权利为民事权利即私权之一种：消费者权利的主体是消费者，其义务主体是经营者，两者皆为私法（民法）上的主体，即此种权利是发生在私法上主体间的权利，故其当然具有私法性质。”③ 可见，特别民事权利论研究消费者权利性质的出发点是：消费者权利是消费者和经营者之间的权利关系，存在于消费者和经营者之间因购买商品或接受服务的消费行为而产生的民事法律关系中。从法律上讲，消费者和经营者地位平等，适用的法律也是民事法律。因此，消费者权利是民事权利。但是，消费者权利不是纯粹的民事权利，具有自己的特殊性。

2. 消费者权利是“特别”民事权利或“现代”民事权利

在将消费者权利定性为民事权利的前提下，特别民事权利论进一步承认消费者权利具有特殊性，认为“对于消费者权利，我们不能只简单地理解为是一种民法上的民事权利”；④ 并且从理论上总结了消费者权利区别于传统民事权利的特征：⑤（1）消费者的权利是消费者所享有的权利，即消费者身份是享有消费者权利的前提；（2）消费者的权利通常是法定权利，即由法律的直接规定而产生；（3）消费者的权利是法律基于消费者的弱者地位而特别赋予的权利，体现了法律对消费者特殊保护的立场。

---

① 梁慧星是我国最早关注消费者权利性质的学者之一，早在1991年就著有《消费者运动与消费者权利》一文，对消费者权利的性质有精辟论述；1997年，李昌麒和许明月的《消费者保护法》一书，进一步深入论证了消费者权利的性质及特点；2003年，张严方的博士论文《消费者保护法研究》出版成书，主张消费者权利为现代民事权利。由于《消费者保护法》和《消费者保护法研究》的观点区别不大，本文此处一并加以分析；梁慧星的观点则另有详细介绍。

② 参见李昌麒、许明月编著《消费者保护法》，法律出版社，1997，第76页。

③ 张严方：《消费者保护法研究》，法律出版社，2003，第564页。

④ 李昌麒、许明月编著《消费者保护法》，法律出版社，1997，第76页。

⑤ 参见李昌麒、许明月编著《消费者保护法》，法律出版社，1997，第76、77页。

（二）我国《消费者权益保护法》的有关规定与特别民事权利论①

通过上述介绍可知，特别民事权利论的本质特征就是在坚持消费者权利是民事权利的前提下，用消费者相对于经营者的弱势地位论证消费者权利的正当性，并肯定其不同于普通民事权利的特殊之处。分析我国现行《消费者权益保护法》关于消费者权利的有关规定，可以发现，特别民事权利论在《消费者权益保护法》关于消费者权利的规定中得到了非常充分的体现。主要表现如下。

1. 作为“权利束”的消费者权利的概念

我国《消费者权益保护法》第 2 条规定：“消费者为生活消费需要购买、使用商品或者接受服务，其权益受本法保护；……”虽然本条并没有采取“消费者权利是……”，或者“……是消费者权利”的表述方式，但联系本条在《消费者权益保护法》中所处的重要位置（第 2 条），并结合我国学者在理论上对消费者权利所作的定义，可以看出，第 2 条包含了《消费者权益保护法》对消费者权利的“原则性”定义。例如，根据上文所引特别民事权利论的定义，消费者权利是“消费者在购买、使用商品或接受服务时依法享有的受法律保护的权利”；还有的定义是“所谓消费者的权利，就是国家法律规定或确认的公民为生活消费而购买、使用商品或者接受服务时享有的不可剥夺的权利”②；等等。总之，不论表达方式有何不同，这些定义都强调了《消费者权益保护法》第 2 条规定的“消费者”、“生活消费”、“购买、使用商品或者接受服务”和“权益”等几个要素。因此可以认为，我国研究消费者权利的学者正是从本条规定总结出了消费者权利的普遍性概念。那么，第 2 条规定的特征是什么呢？从其所使用的关键语词看，该条规定为消费者权利的存在划定了时空范围：消费者权利是消费者在消费过程之时（时间要素），在与经营者进行购买商品或接受服务的交往之中（空间要素）所享有的权利。从第 2 条在《消费者权益保

① 由于我国研究消费者权利性质的著作，包括明确主张特别民事权利论的作品，大部分发表于《消费者权益保护法》实施生效之后，而且它们对于各项消费者权利的具体论述也基本以《消费者权益保护法》为依据，本文认为，特别民事权利论在相当程度上是对现行《消费者权益保护法》进行推导和总结的产物。

② 王保树主编《经济法原理》，社会科学文献出版社，1999，第 263 页。

护法》中所处的位置及与其他条文的关系看，紧随其后，《消费者权益保护法》第 3 条又规定："经营者为消费者提供其生产、销售的商品或者提供服务，应当遵守本法；……"这样，《消费者权益保护法》第 3 条和第 2 条共同发挥作用，将消费者权利"锁定"在消费者和经营者之间的双方法律关系中，这完全与特别民事权利论所强调的前提相契合。

2. 各项"具体"的消费者权利的概念

如果说《消费者权益保护法》第 5 条和第 6 条又分别规定了"国家"和"全社会"在保护消费者权利方面的责任，从而对前述第 2 条和第 3 条形成制约和平衡，缓和了将消费者权利局限于消费者和经营者之间的色彩，那么，《消费者权益保护法》对于各项具体消费者权利所下的定义则更加确凿地凸显了特别民事权利论在其中的主导地位。

《消费者权益保护法》第二章"消费者的权利"共 9 条，分别规定了安全权、知情权等 9 项具体的消费者权利。本文认为，这 9 条对消费者诸权利的规定纯粹是"民事权利式"的。首先，从其采用的表达方式看，这 9 条规定所采用的主语主要是"消费者"，频繁使用的措辞是"消费者在（因）购买、使用商品和接受服务（时）"（第 7、10、11、14 条）、"消费者有权（……）要求经营者……"（第 7、8 条）和"消费者享有……的权利"（第 9、10、12、13、14、15 条）。且不说各条规定的具体内容，单是这些词语就奠定了消费者权利是特别民事权利的基调。其次，从内容看，这几条中对单项消费者权利所下的定义完全是民事权利的"翻版"。例如：《消费者权益保护法》第 9 条对消费者选择权的规定是："消费者享有自主选择商品或者服务的权利。消费者有权自主选择提供商品或者服务的经营者，自主选择商品品种或者服务方式，自主决定购买或者不购买任何一种商品、接受或者不接受任何一项服务。消费者在自主选择商品或者服务时，有权进行比较、鉴别和挑选。"这根本就是民法意思自治和合同自由的当然要求。此外，《消费者权益保护法》对于安全权（第 7 条）、知情权（第 8 条）、公平交易权（第 10 条）、索赔权（第 11 条）等的规定也与此类似，[①] 此处不一一引述。

---

① 《消费者权益保护法》第 12 条关于结社权及第 15 条关于监督权的规定比较特殊。关于这两项权利，下文还会有所涉及。

总而言之，对于消费者权利，我国民法学界的主流观点是在承认私法主体平等的基础上强调消费者的弱者地位，进而将消费者权利定性为特别民事权利；《消费者权益保护法》的有关规定更是完全符合特别民事权利论的基本精神。

（三）特别民事权利论的贡献和局限性

特别民事权利论强调经营者在尊重和维护消费者权利方面的义务和责任，注重通过民事救济方式为消费者权利提供保护，抓住了消费者权利的一个方面，从而在一定程度上解释了消费者权利的性质。尤其是，特别民事权利论从消费者的弱者地位出发深刻地洞察到了消费者权利与传统民事权利的不同之处，从而正确地强调了需要对消费者权利提供的特殊保护。但是，本文认为，强调消费者权利相对于传统民事权利的“特别性”或“现代性”并不足以充分而全面地说明消费者权利的性质，特别民事权利论在理论解释和实践指导上均具有很大的局限性。具体分析如下。

1. 完全无法解释某些消费者权利

消费者权利是一个集合概念，其中已经定型化的具体权利就多达八九项。消费者权利既包括安全权（生命健康权）、索赔权等比较容易理解和接受的传统概念，又包括随经济发展而新近形成的或正在形成之中的新型概念，如良好环境权和受教育权。此外，还有一些具体的消费者权利虽然保留或采用了传统称呼，却被赋予了崭新的含义。这些新型消费者权利或“扩张”了的权利的含义根本无法通过传统私权理论加以解释。

这一点在新近才形成的一些消费者权利上表现得非常明显。可以消费者受教育权为例加以证明。消费者教育虽然是最近才发展而成的一个概念，却被认为是消费者主义成功的一个前提条件。[①] 从长远的角度看，消费者受教育权属于消费者权利体系中比较基础而又意义重大的一项权利。大致而言，消费者教育是指，有意识地培养个人生活所需要的技巧、观念和理解力等各种能力，以保证消费者能够获得为其所在的价值观和文化框架所允许的最大满足以及资源的最大效用。

---

① Francis Cherunilam, “Consumer Protection-Rationale and Methods”, in D. Himachalam (ed.), *Consumer Protection And The Law* (Aph Publishing Corporation, 1998), p. 11.

至于消费者教育的目标，可总结为：(1) 帮助消费者更好地管理其金钱、时间和能源等资源，从而使有限的资源获得最大满足；(2) 帮助消费者更加聪明地购买商品或接受服务，在市场上获得最有价值的东西；(3) 帮助消费者更加聪明地使用商品并享用服务，从所拥有的东西中获得最大效用；(4) 帮助消费者成为一个更好的消费者公民，使其行为不仅有利于提高个人的经济地位，也构成对消费者群体福利的民主手段。此外，消费者教育还应该考虑环境保护问题，并意识到不同的消费模式所造成的环境污染和生态失衡等问题。①

消费者教育的方式包括正式和非正式两种，正式的消费者教育构成学校课程的组成部分；② 非正式的消费者教育主要针对那些非在校生进行。

通过上述对消费者教育的概念、目标及实现方式的介绍可以看出，消费者教育显然不是仅仅通过消费者或经营者的努力就可以实现的。例如，在现代消费者教育比较成功的日本，“消费者教育事业，起始于60年代初期，由消费者组织先行倡导，引起国家重视并在立法中给予肯定。消费者教育成为消费者行政机构的任务之一，学校也建立了消费者教育制度。随之消费者问题引起企业界的关注，于是也将消费者教育引入企业活动，作为其加强与消费者联系的纽带之一”。③ 可见，消费者受教育权的实现需要消费者组织、政府、企业、消费者个人的通力合作，尤其是需要政府的大力支持。消费者教育需要的不仅仅是政府的消极不干涉，更要求政府积极作为，促其实现。因此，消费者受教育权的性质绝非简单的一句“特别民事权利”可以概况的。

消费者良好环境权是这方面的另一个典型例子。大致而言，消费者的环境权是指消费者有权要求健康、安全的生活和工作环境的权利，并且要不危及当代人和子孙后代的福利。显而易见，消费者个人对环境的影响是微乎其微的，将环境权的实现寄希望于个人乃天方夜谭；将环境权仅仅理解成消费者在购物或接受服务时有权要求经营者提供良好购物环境的权利

---

① Anitha H. S. and M. Com, “Consumer Education”, in D. Himachalam (ed.), *Consumer Protection And The Law* (Aph Publishing Corporation, 1998), p. 131.

② 例如，《联合国保护消费者准则》第36条规定：“消费者教育应在适当情况下成为教育系统基本课程的组成部分，最好成为现有科目的一部分。”

③ 许思奇：《中日消费者保护制度比较研究》，辽宁大学出版社，1992，第635页。

更是荒谬。必须在个人和国家的关系中理解消费者的良好环境权，而这在特别民事权利论是不可能的。

2. 不能充分解释某些消费者权利

有些具体的消费者权利产生的时间相对较早，也比较适于用特别民事权利论进行解释。但是，由于消费者问题的复杂性，这些权利还有超越于私权之外的维度，例如知情权和公平交易权。如果依据特别民事权利论加以定义，则知情权是消费者依法享有了解与其购买、使用的商品和接受的服务有关的真实情况的权利。相应地，经营者应该客观、真实地向消费者提供关于商品的价格、产地、生产者、用途、性能、规格、费用等有关情况。这确实是消费者知情权的应有之义，甚至构成知情权基本的和核心的内容。但是，知情权的作用范围到此并没有停止，它还要求“国家及消费者保护组织应对此进行监督，通过检查、受理投诉等方式督促经营者披露有关信息，保证消费者的知悉权不受侵犯”。[①] 例如，《日本消费者保护基本法》第 12 条规定：“国家为使消费者能自主地营其健全的消费生活，应就商品及服务有关知识之普及、情报之提供、生活设计有关知识之普及，以及对于消费者之启发活动加以推进，并就合理消费行为教育之实施采取必要之措施。”《联合国保护消费者准则》也有类似规定。

能够证明国家在实现消费者知情权方面的责任的最佳例子是 20 世纪 90 年代在整个欧洲市场引起恐慌的“疯牛病”（BSE）丑闻：英国 1984 年爆发了严重污染牛肉的“BSE”病毒，并由英国扩展到其他国家。必要的应对措施不仅在国家层面甚至在欧盟层面都一再被拖延。欧盟 1994 年才禁止用“动物饲料”（造成污染的主要原因）喂牛；迟至 1996 年才宣布全面禁止进口英国牛肉制品——但为期仅为半年。其间，英国逾 80 人死于“克雅氏病”（“Creutzfeld-Jacob”，简称 CJD）的一种变体，而这种疾病正是“BSE”病原体所致。德国和其他一些欧盟国家也发生了此类病例。“BSE”给欧盟各国造成的损失极为惨重。[②]

轰动一时的“BSE”丑闻在许多方面对消费者保护都有启发意义，但本文此处关注的问题则是：“BSE”丑闻中，基于种种原因，欧盟各国都或多

---

① 李昌麒、许明月编《消费者保护法》，法律出版社，1997，第 83 页。

② Eike von Hippel, “Präventiver Verbraucherschutz: Vorbeugen ist besser als Heilen”, *Politik und Zeitgeschichte*, B24/2001, ss. 16 – 18.

或少存在隐瞒事实真相、侵害消费者知情权的做法。例如，在英国，危机最初爆发的时候，政府说牛肉是安全的；1990 年，当时的农业部长 John Gummer 和其爱女在食用牛肉汉堡时声明："味道美极了！我根本不怕吃牛肉汉堡。没有什么可担心的"；直至 1995 年有关部门的部长们还在异口同声地强辩说，"目前尚没有科学证据表明'BSE'可以被传染给人类，也没有证据证明吃牛肉能导致 CJD"。[①] 随着形势的恶化，英国政府 1996 年才不得不承认，人类受传染的轻度危险是存在的。但没过几天，农业部长 Douglas Hogg 又安慰消费者说："现在吃英国牛肉，危险极小——一般而言，英国牛肉是安全的。"[②]直到 2000 年 10 月 26 日英国政府才公布了长达 10 卷的疯牛病调查报告，记录了疯牛病被发现及扩散的情况，其中许多内容触目惊心。不仅英国如此，甚至在消费者保护特别是食品卫生和安全方面一向注重预防原则的德国政府最初也曾多次声明，德国没有"BSE"病毒，德国的牛肉是安全的；后来鉴于消费者罢工以及牛肉市场的崩溃，德国政府才不得不在荒乱之中采取措施，而在 2000 年 11 月欧盟决定普遍禁止使用动物饲料之前，德国对疑似病例一直都秘而不宣。

作为公认的知情权的义务主体，牛肉食品的经营者固然有义务告知消费者与"疯牛病"有关的事实真相，但是，考虑到"BSE"对消费者身体健康和公共安全造成的严重威胁，考虑到政府全面、充分掌握信息资源的绝对优势地位，当"BSE"肆虐欧洲，消费者茫然不知所措时，政府就没有责任告知消费者危险的存在及如何尽量避免这些危险吗？当然，对于政府的这一责任也可以从公共安全等其他角度理解，但是，从消费者保护的角度看，直接而简便的思路就是承认国家也是知情权的义务主体，肯认其在直接实现消费者知情权方面的法律责任，甚至承认消费者知情权对国家的直接请求效力，使消费者可以要求国家提供信息或损害赔偿。总之，虽然国家因此而承担的义务的可诉性等仍然是有必要深入研究的问题，但无论如何，"BSE"之类的事件确实能引发我们的思考：或许消费者的知情权并不如特别民事权利论所理解的如此简单，在有些情况下，它还要求国家必须提供有关信息，如公布疫情等。

---

① John Major 在 1995 年 12 月的讲话，见 1996 年 3 月 21 日《卫报》（*The Guardian*）。

② Terry Marsden, Andrew Flynn and Michelle Harrison, *Consuming Interests* （UCL Press, 1999）, p. 188.

消费者公平交易权是特别民事权利论不能充分解释的另一个典型例子。公平交易是私法自治和身份平等的当然要求，是民事活动应当遵循的基本原则之一，当然也适用于消费者和经营者之间的商品购买或提供服务的活动。而《消费者权益保护法》专门规定公平交易权，除强调经营者在出售商品或提供服务时要讲究公平之外，最重要、最基本的含义应该是要求国家通过各种措施创造、保证公平的交易环境，为公平交易的实现提供充分的前提条件，例如通过反不正当竞争法保证充分自由的竞争环境，通过价格法对价格进行调控监管，保证合理定价，等等。很难设想，没有国家对市场环境的有效监管，没有自由充分的竞争，个体消费者能够在消费交易中希求公平。毕竟，“竞争是消费者最好的朋友”。

3. 逻辑上难以自圆其说

用特别民事权利论解释消费者权利并指导消费者保护立法，也有难以自圆其说的地方。这一点可以我国《消费者权益保护法》为例加以说明。正如上文所指出的，从《消费者权益保护法》第 7 条及其以下各条可以看出，《消费者权益保护法》中规定的消费者权利确实是特别民事权利（不过，第 12 条和第 15 条是例外）。但是，如果把《消费者权益保护法》中的上述规定解释为特别民事权利，就容易令人产生疑问：《消费者权益保护法》规定的安全权、公平交易权、知情权、受尊重权等本来就是“民法中的人”理所当然享有的权利，何用《消费者权益保护法》重复规定？难道没有《消费者权益保护法》规定的公平交易权，经营者就可以进行不公平交易？没有《消费者权益保护法》规定的求偿权，消费者在身体或经济利益遭受损害时，就无权索赔？显然，《消费者权益保护法》的目的并非简单重复规定民法中本就存在的权利，而应该另有精义所在。

就此而言，体现最充分的是消费者索赔权制度。其实，即使没有消费者保护法的专门规定，消费者也有权要求经营者对其因购买商品或服务所遭受的财产和人身损害提供赔偿，此为民法侵权行为法的应有之义。鉴于消费争议发生频繁、消费争议标的额小、消费者在信息和经济上的弱势地位等因素，消费者保护法中的索赔权意在强调索赔权的可兑现性，也就是说，国家有义务采取立法、行政乃至司法程序等各种措施为消费者的索赔权提供便捷、廉价、公平的实施机制。这可以从有关的国际法文件中得到证明。例如，《联合国保护消费者准则》第32条规定："各国政府应制定或维持法律和（或）行政措施，使消费者或在适当情况下使有关组织能通过迅速、公平、耗资少和便于利用的正式或非正式程序取得赔偿。此类程序应特别照顾低收入消费者的需求。"第33条规定："各国政府应鼓励所有企业以公平、迅速和非正式的方式解决消费争端，并设立可以向消费者提供协助的自动机制，包括咨询服务和非正式投诉程序。"第34条规定："应向消费者提供关于可获取的赔偿和其他解决争端程序的资料。"由上述规定可以看出，消费者索赔权不在于宣布消费者"有"权索赔，而是首先强调各国"政府"的责任，要求政府积极主动提供切实可行的措施和方案，贯彻落实消费者的索赔权。理解了这一点，就很容易理解为什么虽然我国《消费者权益保护法》第39条规定了"和解、调解、投诉、仲裁和诉讼"等五种解决消费争议的途径，而消费者却抱怨"投诉无门"了。其理论上的重要原因是，我国《消费者权益保护法》对于消费者权利采取的是特别民事权利论，对消费者权利的保护也以私法保护为主，消费者权利据以实现的种种制度基本是普通私权保护制度的翻版，没有照顾到消费争议的特殊性，没有达到"迅速、公平、耗资少和便于利用"的要求，因此在现实可行性上就大打折扣。偏离《消费者权益保护法》专门强调消费者各项权利的真实意图而宣示"9大权利"或列举"5种解决途径"最终都只能使法律规定沦为一纸空文。

上述分析表明，用特别民事权利论定义消费者权利不能体现消费者权利自身的意义，忽视了消费者权利概念独立存在的价值，在理论上欠缺说服力。其实，境外学者、有关国际法文件及外国立法对消费者权利的界定几乎均是从国家义务或责任的角度出发，采取消费者"有权要求"或"有权要求当局"、"政府应"等表述方式，而并非在消费者和经营者之间的关系中定义消费者权利。①

4. 限制了对消费者权利的保护

实际上，人权和私权的主要区别是义务主体和实施机制的不同。人权

---

① 参见王泽鉴《消费者的基本权利与消费者的保护》，《民法学说与判例研究》第3卷，中国政法大学出版社，1998，第17页；林金吾《消费诉讼制度之研究》，中国台湾地区《司法研究年报》第17辑第10篇，1997；《联合国保护消费者准则》各条；日本《消费者保护基本法》第7—16条。

强调国家的义务，要求国家在立法、行政和司法等各个环节都必须尊重、保护并促进其实现；私权的义务主体是社会上的其他私人，且主要通过私法制度获得保障。因此，将消费者权利局限和束缚在私法中的特别民事权利论固然巩固了公民的私权，似乎符合公民利益，但因疏于强调国家的义务，所以并不利于对消费者权利的保护。

民法对民事权利的保护模式基本上是救济式的，遵循“民事权利（民事义务）——侵害权利（违反义务）——民事责任”的模式。只有当民事权利遭到实际侵害或面临非常真实的危险，且当事人诉请国家保护时，民事保护程序才启动。民法救济这种被动性和事后性的特征，与消费者权利要求预防性保护的思想相背离，显然不适于保护消费者权利。一方面，由于消费者在信息、经济乃至心理等各方面均处于弱者地位，很难预期个体消费者具有构成私权救济方式前提的权利意识和自卫能力；另一方面，消费争议的标的额一般都不大，成本和效益的分析也往往使消费者对启动民事救济程序望而却步。所以，私法不足以保护消费者权利。这一点也是许多学者在深入研究消费者保护法之后得出的一致结论。例如德国学者埃克·冯·希佩尔（Eike von Hippel）认为，“个体消费者在具体案件中常常难以实现其享有的权利，而当供方拟制了通常对其单方有利的习惯性一般交易条件时，情形更是如此。这再次证明了消费者的劣势地位。因此，毫不奇怪的是，对许多消费者的实证调查表明，事后措施无法令人满意”。[①] 英国消费者保护法研究者格瑞特·G. 豪厄尔（Geraint G. Howells）和斯蒂芬·韦瑟里尔（Stephen Weatherill）也曾说，“然而，消费者法律工作者日益承认私法的局限性。我们怀疑私法在保护消费者方面的有效性。这并不是说消费者无法受益于已经增多的私法权利，而是说其他的方法可能更有效，而且私法权利的扩张具有不平衡的趋势”。[②] 我国台湾地区专门研究消费者保护法的朱柏松教授也认为，“虽说消费生活行为与市民生活行为相同，系属人与人间具有相对性、私法性的行为，不过，一旦消费者在消费过程中受有损害，势将难予依现存私法体

---

① Eike von Hippel，“Präventiver Verbraucherschutz：Vorbeugen ist besser als Heilen”，s. 16.

② Geraint G. Howells，Stephen Weatherill，*Consumer Protection Law*（Dartmouth Publishing Co Ltd.，1995），p. 112.

系，特别是民事法律规范获得有效之救济”。[1] 从上述诸引论可以看出，私法无法充分保护消费者权利在理论上已经是不争的事实。固守消费者权利为民事权利的观点则必然将消费者权利的保护局限于私法领域，并最终限制对消费者权利的保护。

综上所述，特别民事权利论虽然强调了消费者权利的“特别性”或“现代性”，但在理论上仍然存在解释力不足和说服力不强的弊端，在实践中也限制了对消费者权利的保护。

二 人权论

与特别民事权利论不同，人权论为我们提供了观察消费者权利的另一个视角。

（一）人权论的主要内容

综合言之，人权论主要从如下两个方面理解消费者权利的性质。[2]

1. 消费者权利的依据在于“经济的公平与正义”

随着资本主义的高速发展，自由放任市场经济的弊端越发凸显，其表现之一是经济上的自由平等被打破，劳工、消费者等在社会、经济上处于绝对的弱势地位，基本生存甚至受到威胁。基于此，强调社会安全福利和经济公平正义的理念逐步形成，特别是二战以后，在社会主义思想和资本主义思想的相互激荡、共产主义价值与民主主义价值的相互抗争之下，经济的公平和正义更受重视并开始对各国的法律制度建设形成影响。到20世纪60年代，上述理念由“纲领性规范”的理想层面进步到“实在法化”的层面，消费者权利概念的产生和发展正是其表现之一。因此说，消费者权利是强调“经济公平与正义”的产物。

---

① 朱柏松：《消费者保护法之成立、构成及若干问题之提起》，载《消费者保护法论》，翰芦图书出版有限公司，1999。

② 参见梁慧星《消费者运动与消费者权利》，载《民法学说判例与立法研究》，中国政法大学出版社，1993，第265、266页；史际春主编《经济法教学参考书》，中国人民大学出版社，2002，第204、205页；李鸿禧《保护消费者权利之理论体系——经济的人权宪章之新谱系》，载“国立”台湾大学法学丛书编辑委员会编辑《宪法与人权》，元照出版公司，1999。

2. 消费者的各项权利都以“生存权的基本人权”为起点和目的[①]

作为经济、社会上的弱者的权利，消费者权利的核心目的是确保消费者的生命健康和安全，维护消费者的基本生存人权。各项具体的消费者权利都是围绕这一目的设计的。例如，知情权保障消费者获得有关商品的各种信息和情报，最终目的是确保消费者自身的安全和自卫；良好环境权关注消费者的生存和工作环境，直接关系到消费者的生存安全。另外，消费者的基本物质需求权、健康权等无不如此，甚至消费者的选择自由，也显著地向生存权倾斜。关于竞争政策的问题、公权力的介入问题，其结果也无非是在现实经济社会中确保消费者的生存权。

就认可并强调消费者相对于企业的弱势地位而言，人权论和特别民事权利论并没有区别。人权论与特别民事权利论的根本不同在于，人权论认为在市场经济高度发达、“大量生产，大量销售，大量消费”的特定社会背景中，消费者在信息、经济、组织等各方面均处于绝对的弱势，有予以特别保护之必要。而且，在消费者和经营者之间为满足个人消费目的的经济交往中，消费者的交易行为是消费行为，目的在于获得食物、衣服、住房、医疗等维持自身生存所必需的基本物质条件；经营者进行交易的目的则在于最大限度地获取经济利益，属于营利行为。相对于企业对经济利益的追求而言，消费者的生命安全和生存需要更应该得到保护。总之，对消费者进行特别保护的根本原因是：在科学技术、市场经济和人类文明高度发达的时代背景下，在人类消费行为这一特定活动领域中，个人难以控制的各种危险性因素逐渐产生并迅速增加，甚至威胁到人类自身的生存。为此，有必要特别关注人类的生存安全。消费者保护法和消费者权利的产生则恰好反映了人们在这一特定场景下维护自身生存的努力。

---

① 此外，有的学者还对此进行了补充，认为当人的生存需要得到满足后，高层次的需求也产生了，它体现为人的求知、审美的满足。消费者权利的实现即是对每个人的发展的肯定。因此，消费者权利也是人的发展权。并且，就所发挥的功能而言，消费者权利还是社会安定剂。参见史际春主编《经济法教学参考书》，中国人民大学出版社，2002，第205页。本文认为，虽然从发展权的层面和从社会功能的角度认识消费者权利有助于加深对其的理解和认识，但是，把握人权论的基本内涵仍应该仅仅扣牢如下一点：消费者权利存在的依据在于生存权。

（二）国内学术界对人权论的不同态度

我国学术界对人权论的态度并不一致，可分为否定和肯定两种观点。

1. 人权论基本上遭到了民法学者的否定

大部分民法学者认为消费者权利产生并存在于消费者和经营者的民事交易之中，因此主张消费者权利是特别民事权利。实际上，人权论基本上没有引起民法学者的重视，少数接触这个问题的学者也对其持否定态度。例如，我国最早关注消费者权利性质问题并对日本的人权论进行介绍的梁慧星老师并不支持人权论的核心观点。他虽然认为“消费者权利与传统民法上的权利在性质上是不同的”，但同时也表示，“对于所谓消费者权利以生存权为根据之点，应有特别斟酌之必要”。① 总之，梁慧星老师一方面洞察到了消费者权利具有不同于传统民事权利之处，另一方面也对人权论表示了异议，认为对其“应有特别斟酌之必要”。从目前民法理论界在消费者权利性质方面的研究成果看，基本上没有突破梁慧星老师的这两点基本认识。

但是，虽然特别民事权利论是民法理论界的主流观点，国家在消费者保护领域中却确实发挥着非同一般的积极作用，人权论对消费者权利的强大解释力也不容忽视。因此，基本上遭到民法学界否定的人权论在经济法理论上却获得了通说的地位。

2. 人权论是我国经济法学界的主流观点

在我国，研究消费者保护法的学术力量除了民法学者外，还有经济法学者。从目前国内民法学和经济法学的教材编写体例上看，民法理论界对消费者保护法的研究多为因人而异，就事论事，是支离破碎的，作为“部门法”的、“整体”的消费者保护法在民法学中尚无立足之地；经济法学的教材却几乎是无一例外地将其与反垄断法、反不正当竞争法等并列作为市场规制法进行编写。而且，鉴于消费者权利在我国现行《消费者权益保护法》中占据的核心地位，各种经济法教材都用了相对多的篇幅对其进行论述，其中大多数还专门论及消费者权利的性质。从总体上看，经济法学

① 梁慧星：《消费者运动与消费者权利》，载《民法学说判例与立法研究》，中国政法大学出版社，1993，第268页。

界对消费者权利的性质采取了人权论的观点。其中比较有代表性的说法是：

“消费者的权利是《消费者权益保护法》的核心，是保护消费者法律关系的主要内容，是人类在生活消费过程中应享有的基本权利，是生存权的重要组成部分。”①

“消费者权益保护法的理论基础，可以从多种不同的角度来加以说明。从哲学的角度说，是有关人权的各种理论。”② “消费者权利作为一种基本人权，是生存权的重要组成部分。由于消费者权利是人类在生活消费过程中应享有的权利，因此，法律必须予以保障，以使消费者的基本人权从应然的权利转化为法定的权利。”③

“消费者权利的基本性质是生存权、发展权和其他基本人权，是包含财产权、人身权等多种民事经济权利在内的综合权利。”④

其中也不乏较为深入的论述。例如，有学者不仅宣称消费者权利是“消费者为进行生活消费应该安全和公平地获得基本的食物、衣服、住宅、医疗和教育的权利等，实质即以生存权为主的基本人权”，而且认为“保护消费者权益专门立法是人权法律保障的重要方面，体现出国家对以生存权为主的基本人权的确认和伸张。……而本世纪以来，消费者权益保护法律制度在各国的陆续建立，进一步表明法是确认与保障人权实现的有力工具”，甚至还将消费者保护法抬高到了与美国1776年《独立宣言》、1791年《人权法案》，法国1789年《人权与公民权利宣言》等同的崇高历史地位，并且宣称，“在现代市场经济条件下，全社会人人都是消费者，国家如不通过专门立法对交易中处于弱者地位的消费者给予特别保护，人权保障就是徒具虚名”。⑤

此外，我国台湾地区及国外一些公法学者、经济法学者或民法学者也

---

① 潘静成、刘文华主编《中国经济法教程》，中国人民大学出版社，1999，第646页。

② 杨紫烜主编《经济法》，北京大学出版社、高等教育出版社，1999，第195页。

③ 见杨紫烜主编《经济法》，北京大学出版社、高等教育出版社，1999，第195页；杨紫烜、徐杰主编《经济法学》，北京大学出版社，2001，第176页；侯怀霞主编《经济法学》，北京大学出版社，2003，第265页。

④ 吴宏伟主编《经济法》，中国人民大学出版社，2003，第209页。

⑤ 漆多俊主编《经济法学》，武汉大学出版社，1998，第222、223页。

曾论及消费者权利的人权性。[①] 例如，赖源河先生认为，“现代之消费者可谓不论愿意与否均已被卷入交易社会，且在该社会里其生命及健康，或作为生活基础之财产等，总括言之，即作为人类而生存之权利，已陷于危机。……若果如斯，则宪法上所保障之生存权，在身为消费者的这一方面而言，可谓已正受侵犯。因此，在此背景之下，‘消费者之权利’乃屡被主张，而此权利之主张，无非是生存权之必然的结果”，而“所谓生存权，乃人民为维持其生存，得向国家要求予以扶助之权利”。[②]

（三）人权论的贡献与欠缺

经济法学者直接承认消费者权利的人权性质，认可国家在消费者权利保护方面的职责和作用，坚持强调消费者权利具有超越于私权之上的维度。这是经济法学在消费者保护法基本理论方面不容忽视的贡献。从对消费者保护实践的指导意义上看，人权论将消费者权利提升到人权的高度，强调国家在消费者权利保护中的义务和作用，有助于增强对消费者保护的力度。

从目前理论研究所取得的成果看，虽然经济法学理论洞察到了消费者权利的人权性质，但仍存在很多有待深入探讨之处；而且人权论对我国消费者保护立法和实践也基本上没有发挥任何实质性影响。虽然经济法学总论方面的知识有助于我们相对全面地理解消费者保护法，但实际上，对于作为经济法分论的消费者保护法，我国经济法学界的研究基本上还停留在对现行《消费者权益保护法》进行释义的层次上，失之于肤浅。这一点从各种经济法学教材的相关内容以及消费者保护法专著的稀少可见一斑。具体到对消费者权利性质的分析，经济法学理论界研究的上述局限性体现得非常明显。虽然上文所引各种经济法学教材均声称消费者权利是“生存权的组成部分”或“基本人权”，却并没有继续探讨如下基本问题：消费者权利为什么是人权？如果消费者权利确实是人权，则它是一种什么样的人

① 例如，以色列西奈·多伊奇及日本金泽良雄教授等人（参见梁慧星《消费者运动与消费者权利》，载《民法学说判例与立法研究》，中国政法大学出版社，1993，第266页）。此外，王泽鉴先生也曾间接说道“当局对于上述五项基本人权必须加以尊重，应该采取各种措施，促其实现”（参见王泽鉴《消费者的基本权利与消费者的保护》，载王泽鉴《民法学说与判例研究》第3卷，中国政法大学出版社，1998，第17页）。

② 赖源河：《公平交易法与消费者保护之研究》，《中兴法学》1986年总第14期。

权？主张消费者权利是人权有何意义？一言以蔽之，“消费者权利是人权”对消费者保护法理论研究及对消费者保护法制建设有何启示？事实上，没有详细论证甚至根本没有关注到这些问题正是人权论在我国法学界遭到忽视乃至否定的重要原因之一。

此外，由于“人权”本身就是一个备受争议的概念，泛泛地宣称消费者权利是人权而不深入具体论述有关问题，在理论和实践中的意义也确实不大。

三　作为人权的消费者权利

为对人权论进行必要的补充，下文着重论述消费者权利之为人权的原因、消费者权利在人权序列中的地位以及承认消费者权利人权性的理论和实践意义。

（一）消费者权利符合人权的实质性要求

国内消费者权利性质人权论的主张者虽然宣称消费者权利本质上是人权，但均没有深入论证消费者权利之为人权的原因，说服力较差。对于人权论的支持者而言，论证消费者权利是人权仍然是必须补的功课。

论证消费者权利是人权必须面对的一个前提问题是：何为人权？虽然这是一个众说纷纭的问题，并不存在关于人权的统一概念，但学者们还是总结出了人权的一些本质特征，并以此为基础形成了据以考察人权的一些指导性方针。大致言之，这些指导性方针包括：（1）人权应该与整个人类社会或者所有的人相关，是为人权的普遍性；（2）人权是人作为人的权利，人权的首要关怀是个人，强调个人的尊严、荣誉和发展，是为人权的至关重要性；（3）人权是个人据以对抗强大政府的权利。[①]

本文认为消费者权利完全符合人权的这些实质性特征。

第一，消费者权利完全符合人权的普遍性要求。虽然有人可能会反驳说，消费者权利只是“消费者”的权利，因此不是“人人”可以享有

---

① 参见〔以〕西奈·多伊奇《消费者权利是人权吗?》，钟瑞华译，载《公法研究》第3卷，商务印书馆，2006，第490页。

的权利，无法满足人权的普遍性要求。但是，正如有学者论述的，“如果说人权是‘人作为人就享有的权利’这句话可以成立的话，那么它也绝对不仅仅是指‘人在任何时候任何情况下都享有的权利’，还包含了‘人在一些特定时候或者特定情况下所享有的权利’，一些情况下还包含了‘一些特定的人在特定情况下享有的权利’。这主要包括两种情形：第一种情形是人在特定情况下所享有的权利。例如，人在受刑事指控或者被拘禁的情况下的权利，……对这些特定的情形下的人和特定的人进行特殊保护完全是由其所具有的至关重要性决定的，这也是人权公约为什么选择一些情形而不规定其他情形、选择某些特定的人而不是其他特定的人的原因所在。对于人在特定情形下的权利，至少在‘人人’在特定情形下可以享有这个意义上仍然是具有普遍性的；……”① 本文认为，与人在受刑事指控或被拘禁的情况下享有人权一样，消费者权利正属于“第一种情形”，是“人在一些特定情况下所享有的权利”。虽然人们习惯上将消费者权利称为“弱势群体”的权利，但在现实经济生活中，“人人皆可为消费者”，即工人、农民、知识分子、商人、公务员、腰缠万贯的富豪、食不果腹的乞丐、精通法律的法学家等均可以消费者的面目出现。因此，消费者并非独立的社会群体和阶层，消费者权利是个人而不是群体的权利。消费者权利是人在作为消费者从事消费活动时所享有的权利，是特定场景中的人权。

第二，消费者权利也完全符合人权的至关重要性标准。消费者权利不仅仅涉及消费者的经济利益，其核心的关注点乃消费者的身体健康和生命安全。从这一点上可以说，消费者权利完全符合人权的至关重要性标准。尤其是在现代社会中，人的衣食住行均通过消费行为获得，而由于消费者本人根本无法控制其中的许多危险，个人的生命安全完全依赖于外在于本人的许多因素，从而使个人遭遇危险的概率、不可预期性和无法控制性均大大增加。其实，这也正是为什么现代市场经济国家强调对消费者的特殊保护、消费者保护法迅速发展成为重要的法律分支的根本原因。21 世纪初，我国发生的导致数百名婴幼儿罹患严重营养不良症，十数名婴幼儿死

① 黄金荣：《经济和社会权利的可诉性问题研究》，博士学位论文，中国社会科学院研究生院，2004，第 17、18 页。

亡，时间跨度长达一年多，影响几乎遍及全国的“阜阳劣质奶粉案”[①] 就充分地表明：消费者权利不仅仅关乎缺斤少两、价高质低等“鸡毛蒜皮”的小事，而且关乎“人命”的大事；消费者生命权和健康权案件也并非都是“啤酒瓶爆炸”、“瓦斯炉爆炸”或“电视机着火”等偶尔发生的、伤害人员较少的疑难案件，而有可能是导致多人死亡的、跨时长、影响范围广的重大事故。“阜阳奶粉事件”证明，消费者权利与每一个人的基本生存和身体健康息息相关，是以生存权为依据的基本人权。与其说“阜阳劣质奶粉事件”是“消费者保护案件”，不如说它是一次重大的“人权事故”，与其将生命权、健康权、知情权等权利笼统地称为“消费者权利”，不如说“消费基本权”或“人的消费权”更能反映消费者权利的本质和重要性。更何况，有充分的理由相信，像“阜阳劣质奶粉”之类的事件在我国远远不止一起，例如令人谈虎色变而又无可奈何的“地沟油事件”，其危害程度就丝毫不比“阜阳劣质奶粉事件”小。

第三，虽然消费者权利并非直接针对来自国家和政府的侵害，但必须承认的是，现代社会中的大型商业组织不像在同等条件下进行讨价还价的个人，而更像控制个人消费者的政府，消费者和公司之间的关系类似于个人和政府的关系。有消费者保护工作者总结认为，现代公司巨型化发展造成了严重的恶果。首先，公司掌握着巨大的权力，而这些权力又是毫无制约的。消费者保护激进主义者甚至主张，大型公司就是政府：公司收入富可敌国，公司能够收税（通过其控制价格的能力），公司能够决定人的生死（通过忽视产品安全问题），公司对生活质量和环境也发挥着极大的影响。虽然公司的权力不啻政府的权力，但公司却不受公共控制并且不承担问责性。因此，公司变得越发肆无忌惮、一意孤行并腐败透顶。其次，公司制度使相关个人不必亲自为自己的行为承担责任。就公司的法律性质而言，公司可以保护其工作人员不必承担个人责任。公司的巨大规模和地理跨度及官僚机构在作出决定的公司成员和直接承担批评压力的人之间形成了巨大的防护屏。在不负责任的面纱后面，所有的个人责任感都蒸发得无影无踪，人性中最坏的部分则如脱缰的野马，公司领导和管理人员违法乱

① 关于“阜阳劣质奶粉事件”，《南方周末》、《新京报》及《中国青年报》在 2004 年 4 月下旬及 5 月份及其后均有较为详细的报道。

纪，欺骗消费者，随意高抬价格，并糟蹋环境——尽管他们在私人生活中可能是本社区的柱石。甚至有人创制了“公司政治”（corpocracy）一词，以形象地揭示现代公司高度发展所造成的后果。“公司政治”一方面意味着公司的统治，从而暗示出公司权力的无限膨胀性及其与政府权力的相似性；另一方面，“公司政治”还凸显出现代公司的运作与官僚政治一样，是冷淡而迟钝的。① 鉴于公司等大型商业组织在现代社会中对个人生活及整个社会所发挥的作用和影响，在一个消费者导向的社会中，个体消费者的保护是维护人的尊严——特别是对抗巨型商业组织、垄断、卡特尔和跨国公司——的一部分。②

虽然国际人权公约并没有将消费者权利列举为人权的一种，但从人权的实质性要件上看，消费者权利完全符合人权之为人权的各种标准。因此，可以认为消费者权利是一种新型人权。事实上，也确实有学者专门撰文，要求承认消费者权利的人权身份。③ 此外，现代人权理论认为人权的价值基础在于人之为人的尊严，这也为承认消费者权利是人权提供了坚实的理论根据。正如上文所分析的，在现代消费社会中，关注消费者的个人权利，保护消费者的身体健康和生命安全，保护个人消费者免受势力强大的企业的肆意侵害是维护人的尊严的必然要求；不赋予个人公平交易权、公正合同权和司法救济权乃忽视人的尊严。因此，可以认为消费者权利是建基于人的尊严之上的人权。

（二）消费者权利主要体现为人权中的经济、社会、文化权利

从消费者权利产生的原因和契机、消费者权利的特征以及有关国际公约的内容看，消费者权利可以归于人权中的经济、社会和文化权利及社会权的一种。

1. *消费者权利作为对市场经济弊病的应对之一*

消费者权利是资本主义市场经济发展到特定阶段的产物，其与劳动者

---

① Robert N. Mayer, *The Consumer Movement: Guardians of the Marketplace* (Twayne Publishers, 1989), pp. 70 - 73.

② 〔以〕西奈·多伊奇:《消费者权利是人权吗?》，钟瑞华译，载《公法研究》第3卷，商务印书馆，2006，第478页。

③ 〔以〕西奈·多伊奇:《消费者权利是人权吗?》，钟瑞华译，载《公法研究》第3卷，商务印书馆，2006，第493页。

权利、环境权、社会保障权等一样，是作为应对资本主义市场经济高度发展所造成的社会弊病的措施而产生的。

在自由资本主义阶段，虽然资本主义国家已经开始对消费者提供特殊保护，但由于资本主义发展所造成的社会弊病仍然只不过初露端倪，传统的法律框架依旧足以容纳并解决这些问题，国家不干预私人生活的自由权观念并没有受到根本性的冲击和挑战，“消费者权利”据以产生的社会条件还不充分，还没有必要从民事权利中专门剥离出“消费者权利”概念以应对消费者问题。19 世纪末 20 世纪初，资本主义由自由竞争阶段发展到垄断阶段。这一时期，自由竞争阶段所推崇的极端个人主义和经济放任自由极大地解放了生产力，西方社会在经济发展和科技进步方面均获得了长足进展，但资本主义高度发展的外部性也日益显露出来并导致了一系列社会弊病，而20 世纪正是资本主义矛盾在各个社会领域集中凸显的时期。这时候，如果仍然信奉传统的自由主义观念，严守国家不干预政策，那些因各种原因在竞争中处于下风的个体，很可能出现生存危机。因此，为维持资本主义社会体制的存在，维持个人自由赖以存在的制度框架，国家不得不积极干预经济活动，对那些由于自由竞争而被无情地抛到社会底层的弱势群体进行特殊保护。于是，要求国家积极干预社会生活，关注弱势群体生存利益的社会权观念由此而生。

在这样的时代背景中，为解决贫富分化、劳资对立和严重失业等问题产生了社会保障权和劳动者的权利，为解决资源过度开发和环境污染问题产生了环境权，为解决消费者问题产生了消费者权利。而从人权发展史的角度看，社会保障权、劳动者权利、环境权和消费者权利等其实都是人权在特定场景中的具体体现;[①] 消费者权利乃这种社会权“新型权利观念”在消费生活领域的体现，可以称之为“人的消费权”。

① 关于资本主义经济的发展、消费者权利、以生存权为基础的社会权之新型人权谱系这三者之间的关系，可参见李鸿禧《保护消费者权利之理论体系——经济的人权宪章之新谱系》，载李鸿禧《宪法与人权》，“国立”台湾大学法学丛书编辑委员会编辑，元照出版公司，1999，第 496—501 页。例如，其中曾论道：“于是法学界就有不少学者，从生存权的基本人权理念中，引申、演绎、阐述消费者权利乃是确保并实施消费者消费商品以求生活之生存权，而赋予基本人权之性格，将之列入战后新形成之人权谱系中。”见该书第 503 页。

2. 消费者权利与社会权的目的和特征相一致

社会权和自由权乃人权中的两大类型，其中社会权又称为经济、社会和文化权利。社会权的“特质在于为了实现社会经济生活中的实质自由、平等，可要求国家积极介入保障的权利”。[①] 其一方面赋予公民要求维持基本生存及生活的权利，另一方面要求国家必须架构各种保障制度，预防新的弱势群体的产生。本文认为，消费者权利强调国家对作为弱者的消费者提供积极的扶助和帮助，属于人权中的社会权。

作为两类不同的人权，自由权和社会权存在一些区别。自由权是资本主义成立阶段的产物，社会权则是资本主义垄断阶段的产物。自由权是一种与夜警国家和自由国家的国家观相对应的基本人权，社会权则是与福利国家或积极性国家的国家观相对应的基本人权。自由权是在国民自由的范围中要求国家的不作为的权利，社会权则主要是在社会上对经济上的弱者进行保护与帮助时要求国家进行作为的权利。[②] 总而言之，社会权强调自由经济体制“应与社会权互相调和，并予以适当限制，尤其是借资本再生过程而形成资本型财产时，若构成侵害他人生存权（如劳动者、消费者……），或对环境构成破坏、污染等，即须受较严格的合理限制，达到社会整体生活的安全、和谐与幸福”，[③] 并认为国民有权要求国家权力整体考量社会经济生活中的各种利害冲突关系且介入调整，以架构出一个“使任何个人能在社会独立存在”的最起码法秩序，达到谋求社会和谐并继续发展的目标。可见，社会权的目的在于消除伴随资本主义的高度化发展而产生的贫困和失业等社会弊病，为此要求国家积极地干预社会经济生活，保护和帮助弱者。

而消费者权利的内容是消费者在“生活消费”这一与人的生存息息相关的活动中所体现出的经济、身体乃至精神利益，消费者权利与其他私权的不同之处是要求国家的积极介入，强调国家在保护和帮助消费者方面的职责和义务。国家介入的方式和强度决定了消费者权利不再是民事权利，而成了完全符合社会权特征和要求的新型人权，消费者权利正是社会权在消费活动领域中的体现。

---

① 许庆雄：《宪法入门Ⅰ人权保障篇》，元照出版公司，1998，第139页。

② 〔日〕大须贺明：《生存权论》，林浩译，吴新平审校，法律出版社，2001，第12页。

③ 许庆雄：《宪法入门Ⅰ人权保障篇》，元照出版公司，1998，第138页。

（三）认识并承认消费者权利人权性的现实意义

认识并承认消费者权利的人权性不仅能够从理论上加深对消费者权利本质的理解，并整合消费者保护法的体系建构，而且在实践中还有助于指导消费者保护法制建设，并在立法、行政和司法等方面加强对消费者的基本权利的保护。认识并承认消费者权利人权性的现实意义如下。①

1. 平衡消费者权利与其他基本权利或经济政策的冲突

如果不承认基本的消费者权利是人权，当其与其他宪法性权利发生冲突的时候，由于法院倾向于优先保护宪法性权利，消费者权利将因此受到影响。然而，如果接受消费者权利是人权，则它们就可以和作为宪法性权利的财产权、择业自由权、自由经营权等并驾齐驱，从而能够在平等的基础上和其他人权进行竞争。

承认消费者权利的人权性，使消费者权利自身最终成为一项独立的人权，有助于增强消费者保护工作的独立地位，使其不再仅仅是经济政策的附属或推动经济发展的工具。这一点对我国的消费者保护实践工作尤为重要。其实，我国的消费者保护政策从来没有获得过独立地位，对经济政策和产业政策自始至终具有很强的依附性。例如，现行《消费者权益保护法》就明确规定不仅要“保护消费者的合法权益”，而且要“维护社会经济秩序，促进社会主义市场经济健康发展”。这意味着消费者利益从来就没有被作为独立存在的利益加以对待过，消费者福利只不过是其他政策的反射利益而已。很长时间以来，我们都是为了“刺激消费，拉动内需”而保护消费者利益的。既然可以为了“刺激消费，拉动内需”而保护消费者，当然也可以为了同样的目的或任何其他别的目的而牺牲消费者利益，消费者保护政策的从属性及其地位的不稳固性由此可见一斑。从观念上提高对消费者权利的认识，从消费基本权的高度看待消费者权利和消费者保护问题并赋予消费者政策独立地位，有助于从理论上指导我国目前消费者

① 有人曾提及承认消费者权利为人权具有如下“优点”：（1）在消费者立法不完备的地方制定专门的消费者保护法；（2）改善已有法律和规章的贯彻实施；（3）平衡消费者权利与合同自由或职业自由等其他人权之间的冲突；（4）促进政府和司法机关在既定法律规则和规范的框架内进行干预；（5）解释当前的法律规则以避免与其他人权相冲突。参见〔以〕西奈·多伊奇《消费者权利是人权吗?》，钟瑞华译，载《公法研究》第3卷，商务印书馆，2006，第480页注②。

保护工作停滞不前的消极被动状态。

2. 通过国家责任保护消费者利益

人权与私权的主要区别之一是义务主体的不同，作为人权的消费者权利要求国家在立法、行政等各个方面承担尊重、保护和实现的义务。当国家没有履行或没有有效履行保护消费者的义务和职责时，就必须承担责任，这是对消费者权利的更好保障。既然消费者权利属于经济、社会和文化权利的一种，则关于经济、社会和文化权利可诉性的争议①当然也适用于消费者权利，那么，如果国家没有履行或有效履行保护消费者权利的义务，消费者能否通过诉讼请求国家直接承担责任，即作为人权的消费者权利是否构成一种司法权利？

欧洲法院在一些案件判决中要求没有履行义务的成员国对因此遭受损害的消费者直接承担损害赔偿责任，从而在这方面作出了卓越的贡献。比较著名的案例是20世纪90年代初德国的“MP-Travel”案。② 该案基本案情如下。1993年8月，由于“MP-Travel und Marlo-Reisen”旅游公司的破产，数千名德国度假者被困在美国佛罗里达、土耳其和葡萄牙的度假胜地。宾馆和航空公司拒绝继续向游客提供预订的服务，因为它们知道作为旅游举办人的“MP-Travel und Marlo-Reisen”旅游公司已经没有支付能力。许多游客为了能够重返家园，不得不再次支付飞机票。据《明星》（*Stern*）杂志报道，当时的受害人高达两万。后来人们发现，联邦政府没有按照欧盟要求在1993年1月1日前适时地转化适用1990年欧洲共同体理事会《一揽子旅游指令》③ 是造成游客被困的原因。因为虽然《一揽子旅游

① 许多人认为，经济、社会和文化权利的内容抽象、欠缺法的明确性、司法救济程度很低，因此应主要通过立法裁量和行政措施得到实现和保护，并在立法怠惰或行政怠惰之时，根据三权分立原则，以选举或罢免手段实行控制［参见郑贤君《论宪法社会基本权的分类与构成》，载《中国法学会宪法学研究会2003年年会论文集》（上册），2003，第260页］。也有许多人主张经济、社会和文化权利的可诉性，部分国家也存在这样的实践（参见黄金荣《经济和社会权利的可诉性问题研究》，博士学位论文，中国社会科学院研究生院，2004）。

② Nobert Reich, “A European Concept of Consumer Rights: Some Reflections on Rethinking Community Consumer Law”, in Jacob S. Ziegel (ed.), *New Developments in International Commercial and Consumer Law* (Hart Publishing, 1998), p. 449.

③ Council Directive 90/314/EEC，中文全称为“欧洲共同体理事会1990年6月13日关于一揽子旅游的指令”。

指令》规定所有旅游举办人必须就破产危险进行投保，以确保在无力支付的情况下由保险公司办理合同约定的旅游服务，但由于德国根本没有转化适用该指令，也就是说这种保险在德国还没有成为法律义务，“MP-Travel und Marlo-Reisen”旅游公司也就没有就这种情况进行投保。这对消费者造成的后果是，他们必须再次支付费用才能重返家园。于是，受害的游客在1994年将德国联邦政府告上波恩地方法院，要求损害赔偿。德国法院将该案提交卢森堡的欧洲法院，欧洲法院1996年作出判决：由于拖延实施《一揽子旅游指令》，德国政府必须承担责任，赔偿消费者因旅游公司破产所遭受的全部损失。人们并不确切地知道，德国政府到底为此支付了多少金钱，司法部说是1400万马克，消费者协会估计付给游客的各种赔偿可能高达2000万马克。

此外，欧盟还在其他一些案件中追究了成员国的责任。当然，关于国家在何种情况下应向消费者承担何种责任的问题，欧洲法院目前仍然处于摸索阶段。是否国家违反任何欧盟一级立法或二级立法规定的消费者保护义务都必须直接向消费者承担责任，目前尚不明确。但有一点可以肯定，国家责任不仅在过去而且在将来都是落实消费者权利的重要武器。例如，自“MP-Travel”案后，德国开始通过法律科以德国境内的旅游举办人强制保险义务。如果不是害怕承担国家责任，德国政府就不可能作出这种规定。

我国尚未发生消费者要求国家承担责任的案件，消费者权利针对国家的可诉性在理论上也还没有引起人们的注意。其原因主要在于：首先，理论界关于消费者权利法律属性的见解并不一致，研究也不深入，尚没有从人权法义务的高度认识国家保护消费者权利的义务；其次，消费者权利在我国是通过一般法律而不是宪法得到承认，尚未取得宪法性权利的地位。这两个因素就决定了，在我国，无论是理论上还是实践中，国家保护消费者权利的义务的可诉性问题均处于极度的边缘化状态。本文认为，就目前的情况而言，关于消费者权利在我国是否构成司法权利的问题，可以分立法怠惰和行政怠惰两个层次加以分析。立法怠惰是指国家立法机关没有有效地履行通过立法保护消费者权利的义务。对于这种情况，如果法律尚没有制定，就不存在判断法律的可行性和有效性的问题，但可以（也只能）通过民主程序建议立法机关制定特定法律规范；如果法律已经制定并实施，却因质量低劣无法实现保护消费者的目的，由于我国司法机关不具有违宪审查权，因此也不能获得司法救济。例如，虽然我国《消费者权益保护法》规定的“五种”解决消费争议的途径无法保证消费者索赔权的实现，构成立法怠惰，但消费者并不能获得司法救济。行政怠惰是指行政机关没有履行法律所科以的保护消费者权利的义务。对于这种情形，如果行政机关的不作为侵犯了消费者的合法权益，并符合提起行政诉讼的法定要件，消费者可以通过行政诉讼程序获得救济。但总的来看，由于我国立法中对于有关机关保护消费者权益的职责规定得不很明确，实践中消费者权利获得行政诉讼保护的可能性也不大。

四 作为私权的消费者权利

在国际消费者组织联盟所列举的消费者基本物质需求权、安全权、选择权、知情权、意见被听取权、结社权、索赔权、受教育权、良好环境权等基本权利中，安全权、选择权、知情权、意见被听取权和索赔权等既是人权又是私权，本文所指的“作为私权的消费者权利”主要就是指这些权利的私权维度。当然，需要注意的是，由于消费者权利自身发展的动态性特征，目前无论是对“作为人权的消费者权利”，还是对“作为私权的消费者权利”的范围和具体类型的描述都只能是初步而简略的。从目前已经获得的成果看，对作为私权的消费者权利的理论研究已经比较成熟，而且多以产品责任、格式合同或特定交易方式等具体制度为对象。下文仅从与此处核心论题有关的角度对作为私权的消费者权利加以简要说明。

（一）消费者权利私权性的形成和变迁

虽然只有部分基本的消费者权利具有私权性，但私权性对全面理解消费者权利的法律属性并建构相应的权利保护体系却具有独特而显著的地位。

首先，从消费者保护法各部分的产生看，最早的一批消费者保护法基本上是民事规范，以民法特别规范的形式存在。例如，世界上最早的一批分期付款买卖法，同时也是世界上相对比较早的一批消费者保护法规范，分别于 1894 年、1896 年和 1900 年在德国、奥地利和法国制定，其目的在于限制厂商片面强加于消费者的苛刻契约条件。有学者曾总结这一时期消费者保护法的特征为："资本主义国家通过各种民事特别法，对旧的私法自治原则加以变通。这是直接调整消费者与生产经营者之间权利义务的法律，因而与消费者的关系最为密切，也是消费者保护法中最先得到发展的部分。"[①] 其实，这些对民事"私法自治原则"进行变通的民事特别法不仅当时，即便是现在仍然是消费者保护法中基本而重要的组成部分。

其次，从各项具体消费者权利的产生和发展历史看，消费者权利最初脱胎于民事权利，体现出显著的私权性；消费者权利的人权性是消费者权利发展到一定阶段才逐渐显明出来的。最早提出的消费者权利，如知情权、选择权和索赔权等，关注点在于消费者和经营者的关系，强调的是经营者的义务，基本上是私权；随着消费者运动的深入，消费者权利的类型和性质也发生了根本性变化。一方面，许多公权色彩浓重的新型权利，如消费者的结社权、基本物质需求权、良好环境权等开始被提出并得到重视；另一方面，对于那些较早产生的索赔权等权利，国家也日益强调其实际的贯彻落实。例如，为保障消费者索赔权的实现，促进对消费者保护的"接近正义"（access to justice），以美国为代表的西方国家进行了积极的探索，力求通过立法或者行政程序等为消费者提供更加便利、快捷的纠纷解决机制。这种做法强调国家在立法等方面的"制度框架提供义务"，从而使索赔权逐渐突破原先的民事色彩并因而获得了公权性。不过，索赔权等权利同时仍然保持了其原来的私权性。

因此，无论就消费者权利的产生历史，还是就消费者权利当前的性质特征而言，私权性都是消费者权利性质的一个方面，是分析消费者权利性质的起点和基础。而且，由于消费者保护民事特别规范仍然是当前世界各国消费者保护法的重要组成部分，厘清消费者权利的私权性及其与消费者权利人权性的关系对于研究这部分消费者保护法规范具有特别的理论指导意义。

（二）作为私权的消费者权利与消费者保护民事特别法

正如作为人权的消费者权利贯穿整个消费者保护法一样，作为私权的消费者权利或者说消费者权利的私权维度当然存在于民法之中并统率所有

---

① 谢次昌主编《消费者保护法通论》，中国法制出版社，1994，第52页。

的消费者保护民事特别规范。作为私权的消费者权利不仅是消费者保护民事特别法与其他部门法中消费者保护法规范的连结点，它也有助于我们梳理消费者保护民事特别法与其他民事规范的关系。

在诸种类型的民事权利中，作为私权的消费者权利属于债权，具体体现为消费者要求经营者提供的商品或服务具有必要的安全性，要求经营者提供关于商品或服务的必要信息，要求消费者能够自主选择提供商品的经营者和商品或服务，以及要求经营者就其因购买商品或接受服务所遭受的人身或财产损害进行赔偿的权利，等等。这些权利都是私法中的请求权。相应地，民法中确认并保障这些权利的制度基本上是债法上的制度，例如，意在解决产品不合理危险的产品责任制度在民法中以特别侵权行为法的形式得到表达，其与产品检验、产品标准等管制法一起构成关注消费者安全权的规范群。只不过前者采取的是事后救济的民法手段，后者采取的是预防性救济手段。为专门强调消费者和经营者之间消费交易的特殊之处，学者们用“消费者合同”特指这类协议，并专门设计了许多不同于普通合同的权利义务关系，如定式合同中的信息提供义务及其解释规则、消费者购物后的“考虑期”制度等，以平衡交易双方的利益关系。另外，消费者的索赔权乃利用民法中的民事责任特别是财产补偿制度对消费者和经营者之间遭到破坏的利益关系进行恢复。

总而言之，作为私权的消费者权利属于民事权利中的债权，并通过消费者合同制度、产品责任制度（特别侵权行为之一）和民事责任制度而得到表达和实现。这样，虽然各种消费者保护民事特别规范看似各不相关，但作为私权的消费者权利却成为贯穿、支配并整合这些制度的“脉络”。

结　论

特别民事权利论和人权论都在一定程度上触及消费者权利的本质，但这两种观点对消费者权利性质的把握或者不够全面，或者不够深入，都不足以构成对消费者权利性质的完备说明。主要存在于我国民法学界的特别民事权利论未能全面把握消费者权利的性质，其根本不足在于仅在消费者和经营者的关系之中理解消费者权利的本质，而忽视了国家所应承担的积极义务与职责，从而造成了理论上欠缺解释力、实践中限制对消费者权利的保护等消极后果；基本上在经济法理论界占主流地位的人权论虽然认识到消费者权利涉及国家、经营者和消费者之间的三方关系，从而正确地体认到消费者权利具有超越于私权之外的效力维度并强调国家的义务，却由于没有深入论证，也没有对有关问题进行必要的探讨而欠缺说服力。

特别民事权利论和人权论对消费者权利性质的认识都是不全面的，其主要原因在于民法学和经济法学在基本理念和研究方法等方面存在根本性差异。从法学理念上讲，民法强调政治国家和市民社会的二元划分，尊崇私法自治，固守权利本位，因此难以接受为“国家干预”张目的人权论。不仅如此，从直观上看，消费者权利最初又确实发端并体现于消费者和经营者之间的民事法律关系之中，许多具体消费者权利的私权维度也非常重要而显著。因此，民法学者在研究消费者保护法时，一般会更多地关注作为民事主体“具体人格”的消费者因其弱势地位所享有的各种特殊权利，并将其定性为特别民事权利。

与此相反，经济法本来就是“国家干预之法”，经济法学者必然会更多地关注国家在保护消费者方面所采取的政策及发挥的作用，因此他们在把握消费者权利的性质时，多会强调国家的责任。实际上，国内绝大多数经济法教材在“消费者保护法”一章中均会专辟章节讨论“国家对消费者权利的保护”或“国家的义务”问题。但由于缺少坚实的“权利本位”观念作指导，经济法学者对消费者权利的论述基本上仅限于对《消费者权益保护法》的释义，而没有在理论上进行细致深入的探讨，更少关注各项具体的消费者权利。

（一）消费者权利性质的复合性和层次性

正确把握消费者权利的性质必须以两点为前提：一是综合民法学和经济法学通过不同观察视角所得出的不同结论，在国家、经营者和消费者的三方关系中把握消费者权利的性质，力求获得对消费者权利性质比较全面的认识；二是抛弃“消费者权利”的笼统指称，深入分析各项具体的消费者权利，分别对其加以定性，从而将对消费者权利性质及其他相关问题的研究推向深入。因此，消费者权利具有复合性和层次性。

1. 消费者权利的复合性

消费者权利并非单项权利，而是一个包含若干具体权利的权利束。不仅各项具体权利的性质不一致，而且同一项消费者权利还可能具有两种性质，是为消费者权利的复合性。

首先，一些基本的消费者权利具有两种“身份”，不仅是人权，而且是私权，包括选择权、知情权、获得救济权（索赔权）和安全权等。作为人权的消费者权利存在于消费者和国家之间，其要求国家积极主动承担保护和扶助的义务，发挥的是积极作用。作为私权的消费者权利存在于消费者和经营者之间，其要求经营者对消费者承担私法上的不侵害义务或损害赔偿责任，发挥的是消极和防御作用。其次，一些基本的消费者权利只具有人权性而并非私权，包括基本物质需求权、意见被听取权、受教育权、良好环境权和结社权等。这类消费者权利只具有一种“身份”，存在于消费者和国家之间，要求国家积极提供帮助和保护的义务，发挥的是积极作用。

总而言之，根据其性质，可将基本的消费者权利分为“既是人权又是私权的消费者权利”和“纯粹人权的消费者权利”两类。消费者权利的复合性不仅表示消费者权利或为人权或为私权，而且还表示同一种消费者权利也可能既是人权又是私权。

2. 消费者权利的层次性

作为人权的消费者权利贯穿整个消费者保护法领域，作为私权的消费者权利则只存在于消费者保护民事特别法之中。

消费者权利的私权性和消费者权利的人权性并非各不相关，消费者权利的私权性派生于消费者权利的人权性，作为人权的消费者权利要求国家采取立法、行政和司法等多种措施进行保护的需要，是对作为人权的消费者权利的制度性保障，具有工具性意义。作为人权的消费者权利必然要求国家通过制定法律（宪法或一般性法律）、设立机构（行政机构）、设计救济程序（行政或司法）等多种方式提供保护。在国家为保护消费者权利而制定和提供的法律框架中，民事权利义务制度也构成对消费者权利的制度性保障之一。进一步说就是，制定消费者保护法是国家在履行保护消费者权利的义务，而当国家为履行其义务而立法时，如果对民事主体之间的权利义务关系进行干预，消费者权利就有可能在消费者和经营者之间发生，如果国家并没有就某项消费者权利设计民事权利义务关系，则该项具体权利就只是人权而不是私权。因此，从功能上说，作为私权的消费者权利其实是作为人权的消费者权利的实现手段，并不具有终极意义。

理解了消费者权利的复合性和层次性不仅能够调和特别民事权利论和人权论的冲突和对立，而且能够为探讨消费者保护法的性质，梳理、整合消费者保护法的体系提供一个可能的思路。

（二）从消费者权利性质的特点看消费者保护法的性质和体系

其实，正如理论研究中所表现出来的一样，消费者权利性质问题和消费者保护法的性质问题确实是不可分的。在二者的关系中，消费者保护法以承认和保护消费者的权利和利益为目标，而消费者权利的性质则决定着其需要何种法律规范的保护。因此，消费者权利的性质决定了消费者保护法的构成和性质，消费者保护法的性质则反映着消费者权利的性质。消费者权利的复合性和层次性在消费者保护法中必然有所体现。

1. 消费者保护法组成部分的复杂性及其规范的多样性

消费者权利的复合性决定了其必然需要各种法律手段的保护，并具体体现为消费者保护法组成部分的复杂性和消费者保护法律规范的多样性。

正如上文所述，一方面，消费者权利并非单一的权利，而是一个包含多项具体权利的权利束。其中既有消费者的生命安全权、公平交易权等人身和财产方面的实质性权利，又有注重程序保障的索赔权等技术性权利；既有可以从传统民法理论得到部分解释的安全权、知情权等私权性较强的权利，又有民法理论根本无法说明的环境权、受教育权、结社权等社会性权利，等等。另一方面，消费者权利的性质还体现出复合性，有的消费者权利既是人权又是私权，有的消费者权利只是人权而不是私权。消费者权利类型的多样性及性质的复合性决定了消费者保护法在组成部分和性质方面的复杂性。

消费者保护法内容丰富，成分复杂，性质各异，不可一概而论。其中既有定式合同、产品责任等典型的民法制度，更有食品监管、药品监管等行政法上的制度，甚至还包括追究严重侵害消费者权益的违法犯罪行为的刑法规范；既有对于消费者权利和经营者义务的实体性规定，又有为实现消费者实体权利而设置的小额诉讼、调解制度、消费者申诉等程序性规定；既有针对国家、经营者和消费者的行为规范，又有关于消费者组织、消费者保护行政机构的设置等法律主体的规定，等等。从消费者保护法的组成部分和内容上看，消费者保护法是包括刑法、民法和行政法，实体法和程序法的综合法律部门，消费者保护法的性质因而体现出很大的“多样性”。其实，传统上公私法划分的二元模式以及现有的部门法分类根本无法不露痕迹地完全“消化掉”消费者保护法，关于消费者保护法到底是民事特别法还是经济行政法或任何其他类似的争论也都是没有意义的，对其的研究必须超越传统的公私法划分以及现有的部门法体系。而这正是消费者权利性质复合性的必然要求和具体体现。

2. 消费者权利对消费者保护法的体系整合功能

消费者权利性质的复合性部分地解释了消费者保护法组成部分的复杂性，而消费者权利性质的层次性则有助于我们在种类繁多、性质各异的消费者保护法规范中梳理出一条比较清晰的思路，尤其有助于我们厘清其中不同性质的规范群之间的关系，明确其在消费者保护法中各自不同的“身份”。

首先，作为人权的消费者权利在所有消费者保护法规范群中处于统帅地位，无论是国家关于消费者问题的政策性规定，还是民法、行政法或刑法规范，还是为保护消费者权利而设置或成立的行政机构、司法机构或者民间组织等，均服务于作为人权的消费者权利。国家对上述种种制度的设计和执行只不过是履行其保护人权的义务和职责而已。

其次，消费者权利的私权性只是消费者权利在较低层次上的性质，主要体现在私法领域。国家为保护消费者权利而设计所有民事规范是作为人权的消费者权利的制度性保障。作为消费者权利保护手段之一的民法规范与商品检验、行政许可等行政管制以及追究经营者刑事责任的刑法规范处于平等的地位，只不过是消费者保护法的组成部分而已。

（本文原载于《法大评论》第4卷，中国政法大学出版社，2005，收入本卷时略有修改）

走向繁荣的国际法学

（全六卷）

TOWARDS THE PROSPERITY OF
INTERNATIONAL LAW STUDIES (SIX VOLUMES)

2009
~
2019

中国社会科学院国际法研究所十周年所庆纪念文集

【《国际法研究》卷】

莫纪宏　总主编
柳华文　李西霞　主　编

社会科学文献出版社
SOCIAL SCIENCES ACADEMIC PRESS (CHINA)

《国际法研究》莫纪宏主编、柳华文副主编

《国际法研究》编辑合影

2014 年 2 月 26 日，国际法研究所在京举办《国际法研究》期刊座谈会

2017 年 11 月 4 日，《国际法研究》编辑部举办“贯彻党的十九大精神，繁荣中国国际法学”研讨会

2018 年 8 月，时任主编陈泽宪（中）与编辑合影

2014 年 5 月 9 日，《国际法研究》编辑部举行集体审稿会

2018 年 4 月 27 日，《国际法研究》编辑部访问厦门大学法学院

2018 年 12 月 2 日，李庆明获得北京市国际法学会 2018 年年会青年论文奖一等奖，
刘楠来荣誉学部委员颁奖

2018年11月，《国际法研究》被中国社会科学评价研究院评定为“2018年度中国人文社会科学期刊AMI综合评价”新刊核心期刊

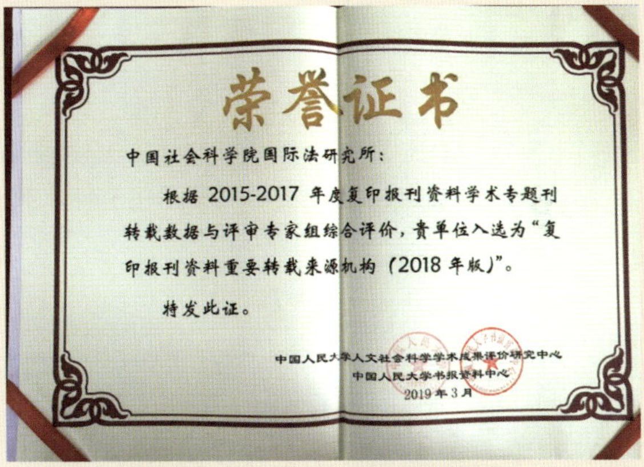

2019年3月，中国社会科学院国际法研究所入选“复印报刊资料重要转载来源机构（2018年版）”

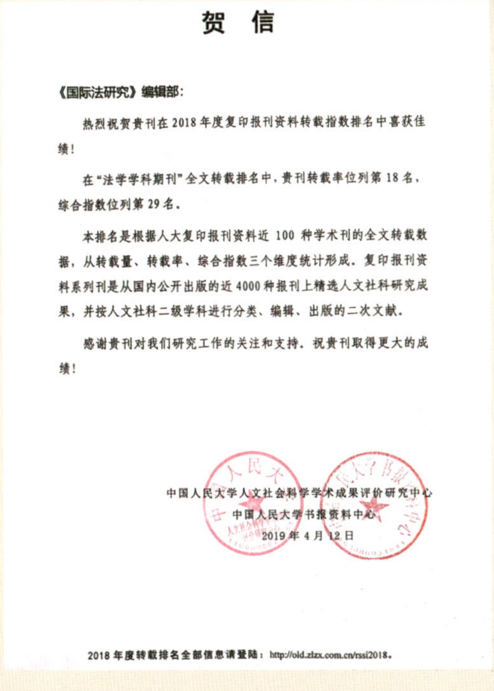

贺 信

《国际法研究》编辑部：

热烈祝贺贵刊在2018年度复印报刊资料转载指数排名中喜获佳绩！

在“法学学科期刊”全文转载排名中，贵刊转载率位列第18名，综合指数位列第29名。

本排名是根据人大复印报刊资料近100种学术刊的全文转载数据，从转载量、转载率、综合指数三个维度统计形成。复印报刊资料系列刊是从国内公开出版的近4000种报刊上精选人文社科研究成果，并按人文社科二级学科进行分类、编辑、出版的二次文献。

感谢贵刊对我们研究工作的关注和支持。祝贵刊取得更大的成绩！

中国人民大学人文社会科学学术成果评价研究中心
中国人民大学书报资料中心
2019年4月12日

2018年度转载排名全部信息请登陆：http://oid.zlzx.com.cn/rssi2018。

在2018年度复印报刊资料“法学学科期刊”转载指数排名中，《国际法研究》的全文转载率位列第18名

2016 年 10 月 22 日至 23 日，李西霞参加人权领域的国际合作与中国视角国际研讨会

2016 年 12 月 10 日至 11 日，李西霞在中国社会科学论坛暨第十三届国际法论坛“和平发展与国际法治”研讨会上发言

2017 年，李西霞在墨西哥国立自治大学访学

2016 年 6 月，罗欢欣在联合国总部参加第四十届国际海洋法年会

2015 年 5 月，罗欢欣在巴黎联合国教科文组织参加世界和平大会

2013 年 7 月，罗欢欣在北京参加第二届南海合作与发展论坛

2019 年 8 月 2 日，何田田在北京参加中国社会科学评价研究院和泰勒－弗朗西斯出版集团（Taylor & Francis Group）共同主办的“国际期刊审稿人培训”

序

推动中国国际法学不断走向繁荣

1949 年 10 月 1 日，中华人民共和国中央人民政府宣告成立，结束了旧中国近百年半殖民地半封建受压迫受奴役的历史。中国人民从此站起来了！

在中国共产党和中国政府的坚强领导下，70 年来，中华人民共和国不断总结经验，克服困难，实现突破和发展，取得社会主义建设事业的伟大成就。特别是改革开放 40 年来，中国实现了经济腾飞和社会进步，中国的国际地位和影响力前所未有。2012 年党的十八大召开以来，中国特色社会主义进入新时代，中国人民实现了从站起来、富起来到强起来的发展过程，中国日益走近世界舞台的中央，中华民族比以往任何时候都更加接近实现中华民族伟大复兴的中国梦！

中华人民共和国的成立和 70 年来的发展历程，为中国国际法学的发展创造了良好的政治、经济、社会和历史条件。以周鲠生、陈体强、李浩培、王铁崖、韩德培等老一辈中国国际法学者为代表的中国国际法人为中国国际法理论研究和实践工作的起步和发展作出了卓越的贡献，为中国国际法学研究和教学做了大量奠基和铺路的工作。

1978 年 12 月 13 日，邓小平同志在党的十一届三中全会前召开的中央经济工作会议上发表了《解放思想，实事求是，团结一致向前看》的讲话，明确提出“要大力加强国际法的研究”。如春风，如号角，中国国际法研究获得极大的鼓舞。中国国际法学迎来了发展的春天。1980 年 2 月，中国国际法学会成立，中国社会科学院副院长宦乡担任首任会长。

中国社会科学院是中国国际法学的研究重镇。1959 年，也就是中国科

学院哲学社会科学部建立法学研究所之后的第二年，法学研究所成立了国际法组。1977 年 5 月，经党中央批准，中国社会科学院在中国科学院哲学社会科学部基础上正式组建。1978 年 9 月，中国社会科学院法学研究所国际法组改建为国际法研究室。

2002 年又是中国发展历程中一个不平凡的年份。这一年，中国改革开放渐入佳境，中国正式加入世界贸易组织；这一年，中国批准了作为“国际人权宪章”重要内容的联合国《经济、社会和文化权利国际公约》。也是这一年，在时任中国社会科学院院长李铁映的推动下，经中央机构编制委员会办公室批准，在国际法研究室基础上成立了国际法研究中心，使其成为与法学研究所平行的院属所局级机构。

国际法研究中心成立后，中国社会科学院国际法学研究获得进一步加强和推进。2009 年 9 月，经中央机构编制委员会办公室批准，国际法研究中心正式更名为国际法研究所。到今天，国际法研究所刚好成立 10 年了！

陈泽宪研究员任国际法研究所首任所长。2017 年 9 月至 2018 年 11 月，现任法学研究所所长、中国社会科学院学部委员陈甦研究员代行国际法研究所所长职责。2018 年 11 月，莫纪宏研究员开始担任国际法研究所所长。国际法研究所正是在国家经济发展和社会进步取得历史性突破，中国在国际社会地位极大提升、国际影响力不断扩大的背景下诞生的。它的成立和发展承载了党和国家繁荣和发展中国国际法学的使命。

10 年来，国际法研究所与外交部、商务部等相关政府部门密切联系，与中国国际法学会等全国性国际法研究学会、学术机构一道，积极进取，努力推动中国国际法学走向繁荣。依托学科和人才优势，国际法研究所设有国际公法、国际经济法、国际私法和国际人权法 4 个研究室，还设有海洋法治研究、竞争法研究和国际刑法研究领域的 3 个非实体中心以及最高人民法院“一带一路”司法研究基地。依托国际法研究所国际法专业的博士点和硕士点，博士、硕士研究生和博士后研究人员的指导工作也得到了加强。

2014 年创刊的《国际法研究》是中国第一本获得正式刊号的国际法专业原创中文期刊，国际法研究所是其主要主办单位和主编单位。该刊在国际法研究领域学术期刊的发文转载率方面处于全国领先地位，已经成为国际法学界重要的学术展示和交流平台。一年一度的国际法论坛已成功举办

15届，成为中国社会科学院院级国际研讨会的学术品牌，吸引了国内外权威和知名专家的积极参与。在刘楠来、王可菊、陶正华、林欣等前辈国际法学家的关心和鼓舞下，国际法研究所一大批中青年国际法学者正在成为国际法学界的学术骨干。

值此国际法研究所10周年所庆之际，我们出版文集，选粹研究人员的研究成果，包括《国际法研究》发表过的有影响力的论文，回顾走过的历程，展示当下的风貌，既是国际法研究所成长道路上的一个小结，更是展现坚定的再创辉煌的决心。

中国倡导的“一带一路”建设正在世界范围内获得越来越多、越来越大的发展成就，推动构建人类命运共同体的中国主张日益获得国际社会的广泛支持和积极响应。

前路不乏机遇和挑战，中国社会科学院国际法研究所全体同仁必将以只争朝夕的精神，不忘初心、牢记使命，与全国国际法学同仁一道，推进中国国际法学不断走向繁荣！

莫纪宏

2019年8月20日

目录

Contents

《国际法研究》编辑部简介

一　机构概况

《国际法研究》编辑部是中国社会科学院国际法研究所的下属部门，于2012年6月正式成立。《国际法研究》期刊的现任主编是国际法研究所所长莫纪宏研究员，副主编是柳华文研究员和孙世彦研究员。柳华文研究员担任编辑部主任，李西霞副编审担任编辑部副主任。编辑部成员现有4名，分别是柳华文研究员、李西霞副编审、罗欢欣副研究员、何田田助理研究员，另有国际人权法研究室的曲相霏研究员、国际私法研究室的李庆明副研究员和国际公法研究室的郝鲁怡副研究员兼任责任编辑。①

编辑部的职责是围绕《国际法研究》的办刊宗旨，遵守国家相关政策和制度，在编辑、校对、审稿等办刊过程中，严把期刊质量关，树立期刊特色品牌和国际法研究所的学术品牌。《国际法研究》的办刊宗旨是深入、全面、准确地对国际法领域的法律制度和观念进行研究；反映国内外国际法理论和法律制度发展的最新动态及研究成果，打造国际法领域的高端学术平台。

二　《国际法研究》的创办沿革与编辑部成立

中国社会科学院国际法研究所是中国社会科学院专门从事国际法研究

---

① 莫纪宏、孙世彦、曲相霏研究员在《国际人权法卷》作了详细介绍，李庆明副研究员在《国际私法卷》作了详细介绍，郝鲁怡副研究员在《国际公法卷》作了详细介绍，本卷编辑部成员简介部分只收录4名专职成员的简介。

的科研机构，其前身是中国社会科学院国际法研究中心（2002 年 10 月至 2009 年 9 月）、中国社会科学院法学研究所国际法研究室（1978 年 9 月至 2002 年 9 月）和国际法组（1959 年至 1978 年 8 月）。《国际法研究》最早作为集刊由国际法研究中心创办，其发展及沿革凝聚着现期刊编辑部和原集刊编委会的共同努力。

国际法研究所/中心自 2002 年 10 月成为中国社会科学院下属的独立所级机构以来，一直力求创办一本国际法专业的标志性刊物并希望能申请到刊号，以填补我国作为发展中大国缺少国际法专业期刊的空白，并为建立马克思主义国际法学术阵地和国内外学术交流平台发挥重要作用。2006 年 8 月，国际法研究中心创立《国际法研究》（集刊）并正式出版第 1 卷，内容涵盖国际公法、国际经济法和国际私法等国际法诸领域。此后，直到 2013 年获得批准刊号，《国际法研究》在 8 年内共出版了 9 卷，历卷的执行主编有：沈涓主编了第 1 卷、第 5 卷和第 9 卷；孙世彦主编了第 2 卷、第 6 卷和第 7 卷；黄东黎主编了第 3 卷和第 8 卷；赵建文主编了第 4 卷。历任主编及编委所倾注的心血为《国际法研究》的发展积累了宝贵的经验。

2011 年，国际法研究所获准为中国社会科学院创新工程项目下的创新单位，作为集刊的《国际法研究》亦获得专项资助。2012 年 3 月 22 日，经法学研究所和国际法研究所联合党委会研究决定，向院里正式提出建立《国际法研究》编辑部的请示。2012 年 6 月，《国际法研究》编辑部正式成立。在院所两级领导的大力支持和编辑部成员的努力下，编辑部成立的第二年，2013 年 12 月，国家新闻出版广电总局正式批复同意创办《国际法研究》期刊，作为中文双月刊，每年出版 6 期，大 16 开，逢单月 15 日出版。

三 编辑部工作效果与成绩

办刊以来，编辑部在院所两级领导的指导下，坚持正确的政治方向和舆论导向，遵守《中华人民共和国著作权法》，严格遵守办刊纪律，顺利完成期刊出版工作。自 2014 年《国际法研究》（双月刊）创刊以来，每期按期出刊。编辑部在 2017 年和 2018 年的两所年度优秀评选中获得优秀。并且，《国际法研究》在国际法学界与实务界已经获得了良好的声誉，初步树立了严谨、专业、有深度的学术刊物品牌形象。

（一）精益求精，严把审稿和校稿关

《国际法研究》是国内第一本原创性国际法中文期刊，编辑部对审稿和校稿的要求是专业、严格和审慎。编辑部为了严格遵守办刊纪律，维护刊物形象，在审稿和编校方面，坚持匿名审稿制度、三审三校制度、责任编辑负责制度和集体审稿制度。在细化责任编辑专业分工的基础上，严格遵守学术性和规范性，对于一些涉及敏感问题的论文，坚持集体审稿制，在编辑部内集体审校和把关的同时，也邀请编辑部以外的权威专家参加审稿。责任编辑除了对文章内容把关，对文章格式、概念、用语以及标点符号均反复校对，务求引领国际法研究的规范化，在学术上坚持精益求精。

（二）所刊文章在国际法各专业领域具有代表性

作为国际法的专业期刊，编辑部在组稿时特别注意所刊文章的专业覆盖性与学术代表性。以 2017 年出版的 6 期为例，6 期共刊发国际法学领域论文 47 篇，其中国际公法论文 26 篇，国际经济法论文 11 篇，国际私法论文 10 篇，各自在发表论文总量中所占的比例为 55.3%、23.4%和 21.3%。国际公法全年论文中在国际法立场和热点问题上体现中国主张和中国学者观点的有 19 篇：涉及人权 6 篇、海洋法 5 篇、国际人道法 4 篇、国际刑法 4 篇。国际经济法全年论文中，随着中国“一带一路”倡议的提出，国际商事仲裁、涉外投资等方面的热点文章得到重点展示。国际私法的论文不限于纯理论探讨，还突出了对涉外（国际）民商事诉讼中实践问题的关注。截至 2017 年底，《国际法研究》全年刊发的论文约 123 万字。

（三）组建专栏，把握理论方向，反映最新动态

国际法问题既是理论问题，又是现实问题，编辑部为了突出国际法的专业特色，回应国际法的最新理论与现实问题，陆续开设了系列专栏。

譬如，从 2016 年第 2 期开始设立“专家学者评南海仲裁案”栏目。当时菲律宾政府单方提起的“南海仲裁案”正进入程序“审议”和“裁决”阶段，是国际国内关注的热点，也是国际法上的重要理论与现实问题。该栏目 2016 年第 2 期共刊发 3 篇论文，2016 年第 3 期共刊发 4 篇论

文。该专栏是国内最早就“南海仲裁案”相关“裁决”作出权威性和专业性解读的专栏，它的设置得到学术界和实务部门的支持。专栏的多篇文章得到外交部、国家海洋局等机构的高度重视，并作为中国国际法学者的声音予以推广。该专栏刊发的多篇论文收录进中国国际法学会《中国国际法年刊：南海仲裁案管辖权问题专刊》再次发表。该专栏为《国际法研究》带来了良好的学界声誉，影响很大。

与此类似，《国际法研究》还相继开设了“国际人权法专栏”（2017 年第 1 期）、“国际刑事法院被害人参与问题研究专栏”（2017 年第 2 至 4 期）、“纪念日内瓦公约 1977 年《附加议定书》通过 40 周年专栏”（2017 年第 4 期）、落实“‘一带一路’倡议与国际法专栏”（2017 年第 5 期）等。

此外，编辑部还刊发了将国际法与马克思主义理论结合起来开展研究的系列论文。这方面的论文有《论中国司法参与国际经济规则的制定》（2016 年第 1 期）、《中国特色社会主义人权观——结合习近平致“2015 · 北京人权论坛”贺信的解读》（2016 年第 5 期）、《建设人类命运共同体的国际法原理与路径》（2016 年第 6 期），以及《人类命运共同体对国际法的理论创新——与“对一切的义务”的比较分析》（2018 年第 2 期）等。

（四）专业转载度与认可度稳步提升

经过编辑部同仁的积极努力，《国际法研究》（双月刊）经过多项学术指标综合评定，入选 2017《中国学术期刊影响因子年报》统计源期刊，位列中国知网 CNKI《中国学术期刊影响因子年报（人文社会科学 · 2017 版）》发布的“影响因子人文社科排序：38/94”。2018 年 11 月 16 日，《国际法研究》入选“中国人文社会科学期刊 AMI 综合评价新刊核心期刊”。

《国际法研究》所刊载的文章在权威的专业转载刊物上获得了很高的转载度与认可度。截至 2018 年 3 月，人大复印报刊资料《国际法学》转载《国际法研究》46 篇论文，《中国社会科学文摘》转载 6 篇，《新华文摘》数字版转载 2 篇。在 2018 年 3 月发布的《2017 年度转载指数排名及分析报告》和《2017 年版复印报刊资料重要转载来源期刊研制报告》中，《国际法研究》在“法学学科期刊排名”中，全文转载量指标为第 21 名（转载数 11），全文转载率排名指标为第 15 名（22%），综合指数排名指标为第 18 名（综合指数 0.489706）。《国际法研究》继续入选“复印报刊资料重要转载来源期刊”。

（五）利用数据平台推介期刊和发挥影响力

为推介《国际法研究》，编辑部除通过参加学术会议、调研等方式进行推广外，还与时俱进，通过各种现代化数据与多媒体平台对期刊进行宣传和推广。

2014 年 1 月 21 日，“国际法研究杂志”官方认证微博登录新浪平台；此后，《国际法研究》每一期的稿件全文均在中国法学网进行推介，还陆续通过中国社会科学院图书馆按期上线中国知网；中国社会科学网、中外法学服务平台（WELLS）也数次转载《国际法研究》目录及部分论文；中国法学会中国法学创新网在“刊海纵览”栏目刊载《国际法研究》每期摘要。

2016 年 4 月，《国际法研究》主办单位中国社会科学院国际法研究所与国家哲学社会科学学术期刊数据库达成作品使用协议。同月，微信订阅号“国际法研究”开通。编辑部官方网站（采编系统）亦于 2017 年开始全面运行，使期刊基本实现网上投稿、派稿与审稿，实现在线化、透明化与便捷化办公。

四 编辑部组织开展学术活动

为了发现、交流和展示中国国际法学者的优秀研究成果，把握国际法发展的趋势和动态，保持必要的宣传引导和舆论导向，编辑部还精心组织和开展了一系列活动，比较有代表性的有以下几项。

（一）举办《国际法研究》期刊座谈会

2014 年 2 月 26 日，由中国社会科学院国际法研究所主办的《国际法研究》期刊座谈会在中国社会科学院法学研究所、国际法研究所新会议室举行。出席会议的有外交部条法司、边界与海洋事务司及国家海洋局海洋发展战略研究所等来自实务部门的领导，还有中国国际法学会、中国国际经济法学会、北京大学、中国人民大学、北京师范大学、对外经济贸易大学、外交学院、国际关系学院、厦门大学、海军军事学术研究所等高校和科研机构的代表以及《中国法学》、《法学研究》、《环球法律评论》等兄弟期刊和中国社会科学院法学研究所、国际法研究所的代表。

（二）举办“贯彻党的十九大精神，繁荣中国国际法学”研讨会

2017 年 11 月 4 日，《国际法研究》编辑部举办了“贯彻党的十九大精神，繁荣中国国际法学”研讨会。来自外交部、国防部、环境保护部、国际关系学院、厦门大学、北京大学、外交学院、中国政法大学、北京理工大学、大连海事大学、宁夏大学、武汉大学等单位的理论与实务专家，以及《中国国际法年刊》、《法学研究》、《比较法研究》、《政法论坛》、《边界与海洋研究》、《武大国际法评论》、《南海法学》、《太平洋学报》、《北大国际法与比较法评论》等编辑部和中国民主与法制出版社的多位主编、副主编、编审和编辑共计 40 余人参加了本次研讨会。

（三）与厦门大学法学院共同主办“国家的回归与国际法律秩序的重建”研讨会

2018 年 4 月 28 日至 29 日，《国际法研究》编辑部与厦门大学法学院在厦门共同主办“国家的回归与国际法律秩序的重构”研讨会。《国际法研究》编辑部、厦门大学法学院国际法创新团队和华东政法大学、西安交通大学、东南大学、苏州大学、福州大学、河北经济贸易大学等高校的学者，围绕该主题进行了深入的交流和探讨。

五　前景与展望

在看到成绩的同时，编辑部也需要总结经验、正视《国际法研究》面临的挑战与压力。未来，编辑部将继续不忘初心，砥砺前行，不辜负时代赋予我们的重要使命：继续加强政治理论、时事政策与专业学习与培训；坚持学者办刊，尤其强调要培养责任编辑的专业能力；继续完善责任编辑制，继续推行集体审稿制；进一步扩大作者专家库和外审专家库建设；多交流，“走出去”。未来，编辑部将加强与国际法专家学者、国内知名高校法学院，以及其他刊物编辑部的交流；继续密切结合国际法理论和实践，与时俱进，做好选题策划。根据当前国际法相关的局势发展预判，积极主

动地捕捉国际法学界热点和焦点问题，做好选题策划工作，尤其要争取让国内外知名学者、有潜力的青年学者，在《国际法研究》上刊发有影响的优秀稿件。

“创新无止境，发展路正长。”《国际法研究》编辑部全体同仁必定继续努力，按时按质完成出版工作，使《国际法研究》期刊的办刊水平和出刊质量再上新台阶。

编辑部成员简介

柳华文

一　基本情况

1972年生，山东省栖霞市人，法学博士。现为中国社会科学院国际法研究所副所长、研究员，中国社会科学院法学研究所国际法研究所联合党委委员，中国社会科学院研究生院教授、博士研究生导师和硕士研究生导师，中国社会科学院人权研究中心执行主任，中国社会科学院国际法研究所《国际法研究》副主编、编辑部主任。重点研究领域是国际法基本理论、国际人权法、国际条约法、国际组织法、国际争端的解决、禁止贩运人口、反腐败领域的国际合作等。

柳华文研究员目前担任的主要社会兼职有第三届外交部国际法咨询委员会委员，中国国际法学会《中国国际法年刊》主编，亚洲国际法学会执委，荷兰跨文化人权研究中心执委，北京国际法学会副会长，中国行为法学会软法研究会副会长，中国国际法学会常务理事，中国海洋法学会常务理事，中国人权研究会常务理事，中国经济社会理事会理事，中国社会科学院青年人文社会科学研究中心常务理事，国务院妇女儿童工作委员会办公室实施中国儿童发展纲要项目专家，中国政法大学人权研究院、西南政法大学人权研究院、中华女子学院等校兼职教授，云南省法治政府建设专家，等等。

柳华文研究员 1995 年毕业于西南政法大学法律系，获法学学士学位；1998 年毕业于北京大学法学院，获国际法专业法学硕士学位；2003 年毕业于北京大学法学院，获国际法专业博士学位。2000 年 9 月起入职中国社会科学院。2000—2002 年在法学研究所工作，任助理研究员。2002—2006 年在国际法研究中心工作，任副研究员、国际法研究中心科研处副处长。2006—2010 年，在法学研究所工作，任副研究员，科研处副处长、处长。2010 年 4 月至 2019 年 4 月担任国际法研究所所长助理。2019 年 4 月起担任国际法研究所副所长。2011 年晋升研究员。2016 年被聘为国际公法方向博士生导师。2016 年获国务院政府特殊津贴。曾获聘外交部第二届国际法咨询委员会委员、文化部进口网络游戏专家审查委员会委员、世界经济论坛全球峰会反腐败与透明度理事会理事、中国青少年研究会国际青年研究专家委员会委员、北京电视台科教节目中心特约法学专家等。

柳华文研究员曾在国外大学和研究机构担任访问学者，2002 年在瑞典隆德大学罗尔·瓦伦堡人权与人道法研究所和挪威奥斯陆大学挪威人权研究中心、2004 年在荷兰阿姆斯特丹大学国际法研究中心、2009 年在挪威科学与文学院担任访问学者。

柳华文研究员正在指导国际法方向的博士和硕士研究生。

二 科研活动与贡献

在近20年的科研工作中，柳华文研究员主持和参加了所内和院内外组织的许多重大课题的论证和研究工作，积极参与涉国际法领域的国家立法和政策文件起草工作，以专家身份参与我国在人权等领域的对外交往实践，包括参加政府层面组织或者非政府层面组织的人权对话与研讨，联合国人权机制下人权条约履约审议会议、国别审议会议，联合国《反腐败公约》履约审议准备工作等。许多重要学术成果获得省部级以上奖励，撰写的多篇内部报告得到党和国家领导人批示的肯定，先后获得中国社会科学院优秀对策信息奖，在国内外发表中文或者英文论文和文章百余篇，多篇论文获人大复印报刊资料《国际法学》、《中国政治》等的全文转载。1篇论文被收入澳门人文社会科学30年研究回顾文选。

（一）积极参与或者组织国家社会科学基金、中国法学会和中国社会科学院等重点项目的研究工作，主要有以下几项

1. 正在主持马克思主义理论研究和建设工程重大项目“中国人权问题若干重大基础理论研究”子课题“中国人权评估指标体系研究”。

2. 正在承担外交部国际法咨询委员会项目“关于人类命运共同体思想在国际法领域的应用研究”等。

3. 正在主持中国社会科学院创新工程项目“构建人类命运共同体、促进全球治理体系变革的国际法保障研究”。

4. 正在参与中国社会科学院2019—2022大型调研项目“‘一带一路’法律风险防范与法律机制构建”。

5. 主持中国残联重点课题“《残疾人权利公约》国际履约情况及对我国的启示”，已结项。

6. 主持中国法学会课题“联合国《巴勒莫议定书》与我国法律改革”研究，已结项。

7. 主持中国人权研究会课题“人权公共外交研究”，已结项。

8. 主持中国社会科学院中国廉政研究中心课题“黄海勇诉秘鲁案及其启示研究”，已结项。

9. 主持中国社会科学院和意大利研究委员会合作课题“《经济、社会和文化权利国际公约》和千年目标在中国和意大利的实施”，已结项。

10. 主持中国社会科学院法学研究所承担的联合国人权事务高级专员办公室与中国政府技术合作项目“经济、社会和文化权利的可诉性”，已结项。

（二）积极参加国家立法和政策文件活动，许多重要的建议获得立法或者决策机关采纳，积极发挥专家作用，参与智库外交、法律外交以及其他国际法实务工作，主要有以下几项

1. 2006 年担任全国妇联参与修订《未成年人保护法》项目专家。长期担任国务院妇女儿童工作委员会办公室实现《中国儿童发展纲要（2011—2020 年）》项目专家，参与儿童法律保护相关的专家工作，包括中期评估等工作。多次参加民政部、教育部等有关部门组织的有关儿童工作的政策或者行政立法工作座谈会。

2. 2008 年，多次为中国政府履行联合国人权公约国家履约报告提供意见和建议，为中国政府参与联合国人权理事会普遍性定期审议（国别审议）国家报告的撰写提供意见和建议。多次以专家身份参与国务院新闻办公室人权白皮书的撰写或者为其提供意见和建议。

3. 2011 年 4 月 13 日，经国务院授权，国务院新闻办公室发布了首个《国家人权行动计划（2009—2010 年）》。2008 年，柳华文作为专家参与了该计划的起草工作。在计划发布后向国内外机构和公众介绍和宣讲该计划。参与了计划的实施总结和评估工作，包括总结评估报告的撰写工作。也参加了《国家人权行动计划（2012—2015 年）》的起草和其他相关工作。

4. 2012 年 1 月，撰写为全国人大、政协“两会”直播提供手语翻译的内部报告获得批示，中央电视台当年 3 月开始为“两会”直播提供手语翻译。

5. 2012 年前后多次参加我国接受联合国《反腐败公约》履约审议相关会议，提供专家意见和建议。2014 年前后，多次以理事身份参加世界经济论坛全球峰会透明度与反腐败理事会会议。

6. 2014 年，经美洲人权法院批准，以专家证人身份参与美洲人权法院黄海勇诉秘鲁案，为该案成为有利于我国追逃追赃工作的国际人权法案例作出了贡献。

7. 多次参加最高人民法院、公安部等组织的反拐立法研讨会、个案分析会，应邀为法官培训班、全国妇联系统代表等就反对人口拐卖作专题授课。

8. 参加了2008年以来中国人权研究会、中国人权发展基金会主办的“北京人权论坛”历届会议，参与了多次论坛的筹备工作。

9. 多次牵头组织由中国社会科学院法学研究所和人权研究中心作为中方组织方承办的中国—欧盟非政府层面的人权司法研讨会，多次参加中欧、中美、中英、中澳、中德等人权对话和研讨会议。

10. 2016年，在应对菲律宾政府单方面提起“南海仲裁案”过程中，以专家身份参与国内外重要研讨会，包括在所谓仲裁裁决发布前夕赴荷兰海牙参加了“南海仲裁案”国际研讨会、赴中国香港参加了“南海仲裁案”国际研讨会，直接主持了《中国国际法年刊：南海仲裁案管辖权问题专刊》编辑出版工作。

三 主要学术观点

1. 国际法与国内法是两个不同的法律体系。两者有联系又有区别，国际法有自身的特点和运作规律。研究国际法应该懂得国内法，同时要研究中国外交史、国际关系史、外交与国际关系理论。国际法研究应该有本国立场和全球视野，以实证研究为主，必要时应将法律与历史及当代的政治、经济、文化、社会、军事等因素相结合开展研究。

2. 人的尊严是人权法的基础。安全、发展和人权是联合国改革和发展的三大支柱，国际社会出现“人权主流化”的趋势。在国内，法治、发展和人权是国家发展相互联系、相辅相成的三个基本维度。人人享有人权，同时所有人权是一个整体。不能孤立或者简单地看待人权，人权发展需要立足国情，与法治和经济发展水平相统一。在国际社会，中国以合作促发展、以发展促人权的主张与联合国对可持续发展议程的倡导一致。

3. 国际人权法首先是国际法，遵循国际法的发展和运作规律。国家间在平等和相互尊重的基础上开展人权交流与合作符合国际人权法的本质规律。人权条约存在实质性要求较高、较为丰富，而程序性义务单一、薄弱的问题。人权标准的实现主要依靠国内社会的努力，加强国际实施机制有合法性与正当性之问，需要区分应有法和现行实在法，积极而又稳妥地推进联合国人权机制的改革与发展。

4. 海洋法有了很大的发展，但是《联合国海洋法公约》远未满足国际社会海洋实践的现实需求，该公约未明确规定的问题还需要通过一般国际法的考察寻找国际法规范。即使如此，海洋法领域的法律不明现象仍然突出。从海洋法的发展史来看，是海洋法适应国家实践，不是国家实践适应海洋法。国际法是国家海洋实践的根据。同时国家是国际法制定和实施的主体，海洋法的解释与适用，应该慎重和严谨，不能为个别国家、机构或者学者的主张左右。

5. 国际法是以主权国家为主形成的国际社会的法律规范，其适用环境、发展和运作规律与国内法在国内社会中的适用有很大区别，不能用国内法思维简单套用、分析国际法问题。比如，软法的概念和作用，非政府组织的概念和作用等，在国内法和国际法上、在国内社会和国际社会范畴下，往往是不同领域的问题，有联系，更有区别，不能混同。源于国内法与国际法无边界的混同，相关领域存在许多对国际法问题的迷思和错误认识。国际法上也有不容忽视的软法现象和软法之治，需要给予重视和研究。

四　代表作简介

（一）著作

1.《论国家在〈经济、社会和文化权利国际公约〉下义务的不对称性》

《经济、社会和文化权利国际公约》是“国际人权宪章”中的“人权两公约”之一。中国政府已于 2001 年正式批准了该公约。本书概括了国家在公约下法律义务的性质和特点，阐明了国家实质性义务的多层次性和丰富性以及国家程序性义务的单一性和薄弱性，分析了两者存在不对称性的原因，国际社会为了改变这种不对称性而进行的努力，公约《任择议定书》制定与实施面临的机遇和挑战。本书借鉴欧洲一体化过程中强调的辅助性原则的理论和实践，对国家在该公约下义务的不对称性进行了创造性的解读，指出了其合理性与不合理性，并提出解决这种不对称性的建议。从本书对《经济、社会和文化权利国际公约》下国家义务不对称性的研究，可以探索关于国际人权机制与国家主权关系的一些规律性的认识。

2.《〈联合国禁止贩运人口议定书〉研究——以人权法为视角》

人口贩运是一种古老的犯罪，在今天又死灰复燃，呈现严峻态势。作者认为，《联合国禁止贩运人口议定书》既是打击跨国有组织犯罪的武器，更是促进人权保护的根据。近年来，联合国将人权视角纳入反拐工作。基于对人格尊严的强调，议定书重新制定了贩运人口的定义，扩大了贩运人口概念涵盖的罪名及其范畴。议定书在预防与打击犯罪并重的基础上，特别强调被害人保护，使国际立法呈现“三位一体”的模式。该议定书经中国立法机关批准，2010 年起对中国生效。实施议定书，需要立足国情，总结经验，进一步加强国内立法，进一步建立和完善反拐工作机制。作者强调，开展社会治理创新，实现法治包括软法之治，是实施国际标准、加强反拐工作的新趋势。

（二）论文

1.《从国际法角度评析 1887 年中葡〈和好通商条约〉》

1887 年中葡《和好通商条约》是中国近代史上唯一一个规定澳门法律地位的国际条约。本文以此约为主线，从国际法角度比较学术界论点，进行法理分析与评价：条约为澳门规定的是一种特殊的租借地的地位；澳门勘界之争本身不影响条约效力，葡方严重违约才使条约的效力发生动摇；1928 年中国国民政府废除此约在法律上是有效的；澳门问题在当代获得解决，体现了国际法在中国的一种实践。国际法是外交办案成功的必要条件，即没有国际法不行，仅依靠国际法不一定可行。外交抉择和行动不仅要有法律角度的考虑，还要受国际环境、国家意识形态、政治、经济及军事等因素的综合影响。

2.《改革开放 40 年与中国人权发展道路》

改革开放 40 年来，根据联合国开发计划署的评估，中国是在人类发展领域中进步最快的国家。中国坚持把人权的普遍性原则同中国实际相结合，走出了一条适合中国国情的人权发展道路。中国实现了经济发展和社会进步，并以“中国梦”的提出为标志，将发展梦和人权梦推向新的时代。1978 年既是中国改革开放的起点，也是中国人权保障新的原点，此后中国开始加强与世界的联系。中国不断深化对法治和人权的认识，加强人权的宪法保障，实现了“人权入宪”；中国人权保障的法律体系基本建成，立法不断取得突破，法律实施得到加强并不乏创新；中国响应联合国的号召，制定实施国家人权行动计划，中国人权事业进入有计划、有步骤迅速发展的时期；中国提出构建新型国际关系、构建人类命运共同体，人权领域的国际交流与合作逐渐深入和加强，并作出独特和建设性的贡献，成为国际人权治理的参与者、建设者和贡献者。

五 重要学术作品目录

（一）个人著作

1.《〈公民权利和政治权利国际公约〉及其实施机制》（与朱晓青合著），中国社会科学出版社，2003；社会科学文献出版社，2019。

2.《论国家在〈经济、社会和文化权利国际公约〉下义务的不对称性》，北京大学出版社，2005；社会科学文献出版社，2019。

3.《经济、社会和文化权利可诉性研究》（主编），中国社会科学出版社，2008。

4.《儿童权利与法律保护》（主编），上海人民出版社，2009。

5.《〈联合国禁止贩运人口议定书〉研究：以人权法为视角》，社会科学文献出版社，2011。

6.《人权知识联合国核心人权公约与机制》，湖南大学出版社，2016。

7.《人权领域的国际合作与中国视角》（副主编），中国政法大学出版社，2017。

8.《中国的人权发展道路》，中国社会科学出版社，2018。

（二）译著

〔奥〕曼弗雷德·诺瓦克：《国际人权制度导论》，柳华文译，北京大学出版社，2008。

（三）论文

1.《从国际法角度评析 1887 年中葡〈和好通商条约〉》，《中国边疆史地研究》1999 年第 2 期。

2.《发展与人权：关于老龄化问题的思考》，《人权》2009 年第 2 期。

3.《性别平等：联合国人权条约机构的实践及其启示》，《法学杂志》2009 年第 8 期。

4.《逻辑框架法对哲学社会科学课题管理的启示》，《社会科学管理与评论》2010 年第 3 期。

5.《正确认识人权是开展人权教育的前提》，《广州大学学报》（社会科学版）2010 年第 5 期。

6. “Can Rapid Economic Growth Benefit More? Review of the Medical Care Reform in Shenmu County in China”, *Journal of Asia Public Policy*, Vol. 3, No. 3, November 2010.

7. “Gender Equality and Human Rights: ICCPR and its Impacts in China”, in Pauline Stolz, etc. (eds.), *Gender Equality, Citizenship & Human Rights: Controversies and Challenges in China and the Nordic Countries*, Routledge, 2010.

8.《以尊严论解读人权》,《人权》2011 年第 1 期。

9.《论哲学社会科学研究的后期资助制度》,《社会科学管理与评论》2011 年第 2 期。

10.《论人权在中国的主流化与本土化》,《学习与探索》2011 年第 4 期。

11.《软法与人权和社会建设》,《人权》2012 年第 2 期。

12.《中国儿童权利保护新趋势——评〈中国儿童发展纲要（2011—2020 年)〉》,《中国妇运》2012 年第 3 期。

13. “Children’s Rights Protection Enters New Stage in China”, *Human Rights*, 2012, No. 1.

14. “Soft Law, Human Rights and Social Construction”, *Human Rights*, 2012, No. 3.

15.《人权：环境保护与发展权》,《人权》2013 年第 1 期。

16.《切实尊重和保障人权与实现中国梦》,《人权》2013 年第 2 期。

17.《论法律作为一个整体促进人权》,《人权》2013 年第 5 期。

18.《关于制定联合国〈老年人权利公约〉的初步研究》,《中国国际法年刊（2012)》，法律出版社，2013。

19.《设立弃婴岛与儿童权利保护》,《人权》2014 年第 1 期。

20.《〈联合国反腐败公约〉履约审议机制刍议》,《当代法学》2014 年第 1 期。

21.《联合国与人权的国际保护》,《世界经济与政治》2015 年第 4 期。

22.《和平共处五项原则：继往开来的国际法基本原则》,《中国国际法年刊（2014)》，法律出版社，2015。

23.《论禁止人口贩运的基础》,《江海学刊》2016 年第 2 期。

24.《中国特色社会主义人权观——结合习近平致“2015·北京人权论坛”贺信的解读》，《国际法研究》2016 年第 5 期。

25.《美洲人权法院引渡第一案的意义及其启示》，《东南大学学报》（哲学社会科学版）2016 年第 6 期。

26.《中国残疾人权利保障事业的基本特点》，《残疾人研究》2017 年第 2 期。

27.《改革开放 40 年与中国人权发展道路》，《世界经济与政治》2018 年第 9 期。

28. “Starting from system building: child rights protection and the non-discrimination principle in China”, in Marit Skivenes and Karl Harald Søvig (Editors), *Child Rights and International Discrimination Law: Implementing Article 2 of the United Nations Convention on the Rights of the Child*, *Routledge Research in International Law*, 1st Edition, Routledge, February, 2019.

（四）文章

1.《领土庇护违反国际法：与石之瑜先生商榷》，新加坡《联合早报》2012 年 5 月 19 日，言论版。

2.《全面推动，重在行动——与时俱进的新一期人权行动计划》，《光明日报》2012 年 6 月 13 日，第 3 版。

3.《推进法治中国也要以人为本》，《法制日报》2012 年 11 月 17 日，第 7 版。

4.《重视发挥软法的作用》，《人民日报》2013 年 9 月 16 日，第 8 版。

5.《人权审查须坚持原则》，《人民日报》2013 年 9 月 25 日，第 3 版。

6.《法治、发展和人权：中国道路的三个基本维度》，《光明日报》2014 年 12 月 31 日，第 3 版。

7.《中国残疾人权利保障道路的基本特点》，《光明日报》2016 年 12 月 5 日，第 4 版。

8.《改革开放四十年与中国人权发展道路》，《光明日报》2018 年 12 月 14 日，第 11 版。

李西霞

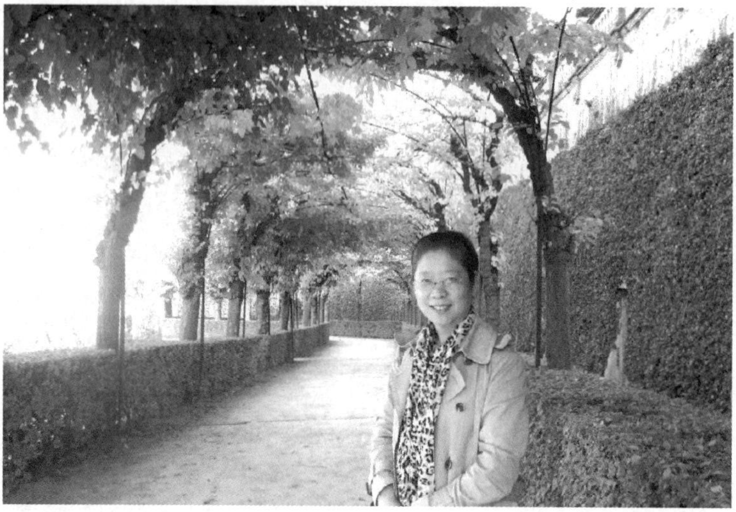

一　基本情况

中国社会科学院国际法研究所《国际法研究》编辑部副主任、副编审、副研究员。主要研究领域：国际劳工标准、人权法、妇女社会权利和社会保障法。

李西霞副研究员担任的主要社会职务有：农工党北京市委第十二届社会法律专门工作委员会副主任委员，农工党东城区区委委员，中国社会法研究会理事，中国国际法学会理事等。

1983—1987 年，就读于河南大学外语系英语语言文学专业，获英语学士学位；1987—1989 年，就读于西安交通大学外语系英语应用语言学专业硕士研究生班；2000—2003 年，就读于对外经济贸易大学法学院法律硕士专业获法律硕士学位；2008—2017 年，先后赴瑞士弗里堡大学、加拿大阿尔伯特大学、瑞典斯德哥尔摩大学、墨西哥国立自治大学做短期访问学者。

二　主要科研贡献

李西霞的研究成果曾获以下重要奖项：《建议在自贸区谈判中推行我

国主张的劳工标准》，获中国社会科学院2014年优秀对策信息对策研究类二等奖。《妇女社会权利的保护：国际法与国内法视角》（社会科学文献出版社，2013），获2016年“王金玲性别研究奖励基金”优秀成果三等奖。

三 主要学术观点

1. 建议在自由贸易协定中纳入我国可接受的劳工标准。自1995年1月1日世界贸易组织成立以来，自由贸易区在全球范围内呈快速发展态势。这一发展引发了区域性经贸规则的重构，其中一个重要方面就是自由贸易区劳工标准的建立。这一区域经贸规则突破了世界贸易组织拒绝纳入劳工议题的现行规则，实现了国际贸易与劳工标准不同程度的挂钩，对多边贸易体制形成挑战，并对国际贸易和劳动者保护产生重大影响。尤其是在过去的20多年里，欧盟、美国、加拿大这三个主要经济体在一系列自由贸易协定中纳入劳工标准的缔约实践，已经形成了不同模式的区域性劳工规则，并对贸易和投资产生了不同程度的影响，对此不可能完全回避。在此情势下，加快实施自由贸易区战略和推进“一带一路”建设，可在自由贸易协定中纳入我国主张的劳工标准，并进一步推动形成我国可接受的区域性劳工规则。

2. 妇女社会权利是妇女人权的重要组成部分，国际层面和国内层面均予以承认。由于妇女在身体结构和生理素质方面与男性有着先天不同，妇女担负着生育子女的社会使命，加上普遍存在的文化偏见以及传统性别歧视等观念，使得她们社会权利的保障和实现往往面临更多的困难和更大的挑战。因此，在对妇女提供平等保护的同时，应强调对妇女权利给予特殊保护，以实现实质平等。中国政府一直高度重视妇女发展和男女平等。对妇女社会权利的保护，已经形成了立法、行政和司法的保护体系。

3. 生育产假制度是保护生育妇女的重要制度之一。国外基于生育产假制度创建的新生儿父亲陪护假和父母育儿假制度，极大地推动了男女两性在有偿工作中的机会平等和无偿家务劳动中的责任分担，显著提高了生育保护水平。目前我国为应对人口老龄化问题，采取的措施之一是在全国统一实施“全面两孩”政策，以期鼓励生育。这在客观上要求建立新生儿父亲陪护假和父母育儿假等配套制度，促进对生育妇女的保护。

四 代表作简介

1.《自由贸易协定中的劳工标准》

本书从国际法层面，全面梳理了全球贸易自由化背景下国际贸易与劳工标准关系的不同理论，并对将国际贸易与劳工标准挂钩的相关实践进行了概述。本书主要探讨了欧洲联盟、美国和加拿大这三个主要经济体自由贸易区劳工标准实体性权利和劳动争端解决机制、建构依据和发展特征，并揭示其发展趋势；同时分析了中国自由贸易协定纳入的劳工条款，进而提出构建我国可接受的自由贸易协定中劳工标准的对策性建议。围绕这些中心议题，本书还探讨了世界贸易组织和国际劳工组织对国际贸易与劳工标准关系的态度、欧洲联盟内部的劳工标准、国际劳工组织核心劳工标准以及全球范围内自由贸易协定中劳工标准的发展态势。这项研究是关于自由贸易区劳工标准构建最新发展态势的研究成果，对我国自由贸易区劳工标准的构建具有重要的借鉴和参考价值。本书的出版，对于进一步加强自由贸易区劳工标准的理论、政策与制度研究，构建我国主张的自由贸易协定中的劳工标准，具有重要理论价值和实践意义。

2.《妇女社会权利的保护：国际法与国内法视角》

本书从国际法和国内法两个层面，全面梳理了妇女社会权利法律保护的不同理论观点，比较借鉴了国际人权法、区域人权法和国别人权法的有益经验，深入探讨了妇女作为社会弱势群体之社会权利法律保护的若干理论和实践问题。剖析了中国当前社会保障、妇女生育保护、劳动保护、就业权、健康权、反家暴立法等方面的最新情况，也对荷兰、英国、瑞士、德国、法国和澳大利亚等国家妇女社会权利保护状况进行了比较研究。这些研究既是人权与法治研究的重要组成部分，也是关于妇女人权保护法治问题研究的延续和深化。本书的出版，将有助于进一步加强妇女社会权利法律保护的理论与政策研究，为完善妇女社会权利保障的法治机制提供借鉴。

3.《生育产假制度发展的国外经验及其启示意义》

为应对人口老龄化问题，我国从 2016 年 1 月 1 日起在全国统一实施“全面两孩”政策，以期鼓励生育。然而，“全面两孩”政策的有效实施，在一定程度上有赖于建立完善的配套制度，如新生儿父亲陪护假和父母育儿假制度。因此，研究国外新生儿父亲陪护假和父母育儿假制度，将为我国提供借鉴意义。鉴于德国和瑞典分别首创产假和新生儿父亲陪护假制度，本文以德国、瑞典和中国为例，比较研究这三个国家的相关制度安排，为我国建立新生儿父亲陪护假和父母育儿假制度提供学理依据和制度借鉴。

五　重要学术作品目录

（一）著作

1.《社会保险改革与法制论文集》（副主编），社会科学文献出版社，2005。

2.《社会保障法》（译著），北京大学出版社，2006。

3.《少数人的权利》（合作主编），社会科学文献出版社，2010。

4.《法治新视界：比较法的分析》（副主编），社会科学文献出版社，2011。

5. *On Minority Rights*（合作主编），Paths International Ltd.（UK），2012。

6.《妇女社会权利的保护：国际法与国内法视角》（第一主编），社会科学文献出版社，2013。

7. *Protection of Women's Social Rights: from International and Domestic Law Perspectives*（English Version）（第一主编），Paths International Ltd.（UK），2016。

8.《自由贸易协定中的劳工标准》（专著），社会科学文献出版社，2017。

（二）论文

1.《医疗保险模式的比较与研究》，载邹海林主编、李西霞副主编《社会保险改革与法制论文集》，社会科学文献出版社，2005。

2.《中韩医疗保险制度比较研究》，载田禾主编《亚洲法论坛》（第一卷），中国人民公安大学出版社，2006。

3.《“拒签”事件：谁为“孕妇之死”担责?》，《中国医疗前沿》2008年第1期。

4.《论国际人权法对妇女健康权的保护》，载李林、李西霞、丽狄娅·F. 巴斯特主编《少数人的权利》，社会科学文献出版社，2010。

5.《〈经济、社会和文化权利国际公约〉缔约国报告撰写准则的历史沿革及其启示》，载李林主编、李西霞副主编《法治新视角：比较法的分析》，社会科学文献出版社，2011。

6.《生育假制度比较研究：德国、荷兰和中国》，载李西霞、弗莱纳·巴斯特主编《妇女社会权利的保护：国际法与国内法的视角》，社会科学文献出版社，2013。

7.《在自由贸易协定中积极构建我国主张的劳工标准》，《人权》2014年第6期。

8.《自由贸易协定中劳工标准的发展态势》，《环球法律评论》2015年第1期。

9.《全球贸易自由化进程中劳工标准体系的分化与发展》，《社会发展研究》2015年第1期。

10.《论〈跨太平洋伙伴关系协定〉谈判中美国劳工标准目标及对我国的启示意义》，《中国劳动》2015年第20期。

11.《生育产假制度发展的国外经验及其启示意义》，《北京联合大学学报》（人文社会科学版）2016年第1期。

12.《整合城乡居民基本医疗保险制度的若干思考——以北京市为例》，《中国劳动》2016年第20期。

13.《中国反女性就业歧视法律制度研究——基于国际人权法的视角》，《人权》2017年第1期。

14.《试论TPP劳工标准、其影响及中国的应对策略》，《法学杂志》2017年第1期。

15.《欧盟自由贸易协定中的劳工标准及其启示》，《法学》2017年第1期。

16.《加拿大自由贸易协定劳工标准及其启示》，《河北法学》2018年第4期。

（三）文章

1.《以法治方式推进社区首诊分级诊疗》，《中国社会科学报》（理论版）2016年5月4日。

2.《借助国际法推进一带一路建设》，《中国社会科学报》2018年5月2日。

3.《依法推进职工医保个人账户改革》，《中国社会科学报》2019年4月3日。

罗欢欣

一 基本情况

湖南新化人，法学博士，现为中国社会科学院国际法研究所副研究员，《国际法研究》（双月刊）责任编辑。专业方向为国际法学和法理学；重点研究领域是和平解决国际争端、国家主权与领土问题、海洋法问题、国际法基本理论与文化。

罗欢欣的主要社会兼职有：中国国际法学会会员、中国海洋法学会会员、辽宁省法学会海洋法学会常务理事（2015 年受聘）、中国太平洋学会海洋维权与执法研究分会理事（2017 年受聘）。

罗欢欣 2002 年毕业于湘潭大学法学院，获湘潭大学法学学士学位，同年通过国家首次司法考试，获法律职业资格证书；2003 年获得律师执业资格证书并先后在湖南湘渝律师事务所、北京市德恒律师事务所长沙分所从事律师工作；2006年进入北京大学法学院学习，2008年获得北京大学法律硕士学位并在北京大学法学院继续攻读国际法专业的博士学位；2011年获得北京大学现代日本研究中心结业证书并赴日本短期交流；2012年作为联合培养博士生赴英国剑桥大学劳特派特中心学习1年（其间又赴意大利威尼斯人权学院获得短期培训证书）；2013年取得北京大学法学博士学位并进入国际法研究所工作；2016年赴美国纽约哥伦比亚大学访学1年。

罗欢欣自2013年进入国际法研究所工作以来，参加国家社会科学基金重大课题2个，作为课题负责人主持国家部委重要横向课题3个并参与国家部委其他委托与横向课题多个，主持并完成本所重点课题1个。其主持或参与的课题涉及国家海洋重要立法问题、国家领土主权与权益维护问题以及突发事件与重要案例的应对问题等。其发表的中英文学术成果、单独或参与撰写的研究报告等亦涉及对国家重要领土与海洋权益争端的分析和处理。其研究秉持大胆创新与小心求证精神，敢于攻破疑点和难点，受到相关部门与学界的好评，她因此获得国家相关部委横向课题资助，并在2016年下半年被借调到外交部数月以参与国家紧要课题研究。此外，罗欢欣的著作还获得中国社会科学出版社的英文翻译与出版资助，其多篇论文在相关专业领域亦获得奖项并被人大复印报刊资料转载，许多评论文章亦为新华网、人民网、凤凰网等各界媒体广为转载，其本人亦受邀担任过电视台及相关媒体的评论人。

二　代表作简介

（一）著作

《论国际法上的琉球地位与钓鱼岛主权

此著作由罗欢欣在北京大学攻读博士学位期间的成果修改而成。钓鱼岛问题在2012年日本“国有化”事件发生后一度成为热点，但在罗欢欣写作其博士论文时，钓鱼岛并未受到大的关注。并且，当时在国际法上将琉球的领土地位作为一个问题来探讨甚为鲜有，此前历史学界对此有所提及时被冠以高度敏感的标签，似乎质疑琉球的地位就要遭受危害中日关系的政治“讨伐”。所以，罗欢欣立意将琉球领土的法律地位与钓鱼岛主权结合起来研究，体现了她善于发现问题、敢于攻克难题，并有较好的对重大课题的学术操控能力。该书的创新性主要体现在三个方面：一是对琉球的法律地位这个被视作“悬案”的难点问题进行法律的定性分析；二是弥补国内学界在钓鱼岛主权研究上国际法专论之欠缺；三是综合历史与实在法的方法进行分析论证。该书中的部分历史文件和地图由罗欢欣亲自查证收集，较重要的一些国际文件的英文原文，她都尽量放入引注或将图片附于文后，以供查证；该书同时较严格地遵从条约国际法与习惯国际法规则，注意对规范性文件的实在国际法效力进行区分、识别和探讨。

（二）论文

1.《国际法上的领土权利来源：理论内涵与基本类型》

本文写作基于在钓鱼岛争端与南海争端众说纷纭的大背景下，我国国内对领土主权问题的探讨，仍然大多停留在对传统的“领土取得模式”的关注，这一定程度上造成我们对争端中的事实解释不足，对外界的深度回应不够。本文指出，在领土争端的司法实务中，作为争端方的国家需要证明其在特定领土上建立主权的行为、事实依据、来源、证据或证明，这就是国际法上的领土权利来源问题。“先占”等五种领土取得模式尽管绝大部分已经过时，但它们仍然属于传统的领土权利来源范畴。新发展的一些可以独立构成领土权利来源的主要有：条约、新国家的建立、有权机构或国际组织的处置和一国放弃/默认的国家单方行为等。值得注意的是，“有效控制”虽然备受关注，但它并不能单独达到建立领土主权的效果，只有当它和“领土放弃/默认”等国家单方行为结合在一起时，才可以发挥关键作用，并导致领土主权的变化。

2.《国家在国际造法进程中的角色与功能——以国际海洋法的形成与运作为例》

本文写作基于罗欢欣承担的课题：在建设海洋强国的国家战略目标下，中国如何把握自身在国际海洋秩序中的角色定位。本文指出，现代国际秩序是建立在以《联合国宪章》为核心的国际法的基础上的，国际海洋秩序亦是受现代海洋法原则与规则所调整的一种法律秩序。在新时代背景下，国家尤其需要正视自身在国际造法进程中的角色与功能。根据《国际法院规约》第 38 条所反映的国际法渊源，新的国际法规则由国家制定，它们主要通过条约或发展习惯国际法来造法。因此国家既是国际法规则的缔造者也是其约束的对象；国际造法是一项综合、立体的过程，除了国际法的技术性内容外，其背后体现了国际关系与政治的复杂博弈。以国际海洋法的形成与运作为例，发展中国家在理论准备、现实介入、政治决策与规则取舍上均与发达国家存在较大差距，这里面有西方发达国家的法律文化具备先天优势的原因，也有发展中国家对自身在国际造法中的角色认识不足、影响力发挥不够的原因。深度参与国际造法，对中国的海洋强国建设意义重大。

三　重要学术作品目录

（一）著作

《论国际法上的琉球地位与钓鱼岛主权》，中国社会科学出版社，2015。

（二）论文

1.《国际法院在解决领土争端中的局限性》，《上海政法学院学报》2010 年第 1 期，同年被全文收录于人大复印报刊资料《国际法学》。

2.《中俄边界争端中的国际法争议》，《东方法学》2010 年第 2 期。

3.《论 9·7 钓鱼岛事件中的国家责任问题》，《政法学刊》2010 年第 6 期。

4.《论 1972 年前美国“统治”冲绳的法律依据》，载《未名日本论丛》第 6 辑，社会科学文献出版社，2011。

5.《海内外钓鱼岛研究四十年：比较与评述》，载《日本研究报告（2013）》，社会科学文献出版社，2013。

6.《论琉球在国际法上的地位》，《国际法研究》2014 年第 1 期。

7.《琉球问题所涉“剩余主权”论的历史与法律考察》，《日本学刊》2014 年第 4 期。

8.《认清我国海洋维权的国内国际两个大局》，《祖国》2014 年 12 月 27 日，海洋问题专刊。

9.《国际法上的领土权利来源：理论内涵与基本类型》，《环球法律评论》2015 年第 4 期。

10.《〈美国国际法杂志〉南海专刊文章述评》,《北方法学》2016 年第 4 期。

11.《日本 1972 年后“管理”琉球的非法性》,载《筹海文集》(第二卷),海洋出版社,2016。

12.《论南海仲裁案实体裁决对陆地权源的非法处理——以仲裁庭对岛礁地位的认定为考察对象》,《国际法研究》2016 年第 5 期。

13.“Language Challenges in the China Sea Dispute”,美国威廉 & 玛丽学院 Comparativejurist,2016 年 12 月 26 日英文专栏文章。

14.《人类命运共同体思想对国际法的理念创新——与“对一切的义务”的比较分析》,《国际法研究》2018 年第 2 期,同年被全文收录于人大复印报刊资料《国际法学》。

15. 中国国际法学会编《南海仲裁案裁决之批判》(The South China Sea Arbitration Awards: A Critical Study),中英文同时出版,外文出版社,2018。

16.《国家在国际造法进程中的角色与功能——以国际海洋法的形成与运作为例》,《法学研究》2018 年第 4 期。

(三)文章

1.《钓鱼岛问题:警惕日本的冒进与深沉》,《法制日报》2012 年 8 月 7 日,环球法治七日谭版。全文被人民网、环球网、凤凰网、中国新闻网以及解放军军事网等转载。

2.《港人保钓:主权宣示与国际法自信》,《法制日报》2012 年 8 月 21 日,环球法治港澳台版。

3.《钓鱼岛系中国固有领土:有史为凭、法理确凿》,《法制日报》2012 年 9 月 25 日,环球法治七日谭版。全文被人民网、环球网、凤凰网、中国新闻网等转载,并收录于人民网(理论版)。

4.《撒切尔:拯救英国的女人》,《法制日报》2013 年 4 月 16 日,环球法治七日谭版。

5.《人类命运共同体对国际法的理念创新》,《中国社会科学报》2018 年 2 月 7 日,第 1390 期。

何田田

一 基本情况

中国人民大学国际法学博士，现为中国社会科学院国际法研究所助理研究员，《国际法研究》（双月刊）编辑。主要研究国际争端研究、国际刑法、国际人道法和海洋法。获北京市法学会“百名法学英才”称号。

二 主要研究成果

（一）专著

《征募儿童的战争罪——以“国际刑事法院第一案”为视角》，社会科学文献出版社，2018。

（二）中文论文

1.《菲律宾提交“南海问题国际仲裁”的国际法分析》，《太平洋学报》2013 年第 12 期，人大复印报刊资料《国际法学》2015 年第 6 期全文转载。

2.《菲律宾南海仲裁案管辖权与可受理性裁决书评析——以事实认定和证据使用为角度》,《国际法研究》2016 年第 2 期，该文同时载入《中国国际法年刊：南海仲裁案管辖权问题专刊》。

3.《徘徊在法律与科学之间——国际法院的专家指定》,《当代法学》2018 年第 1 期，人大复印报刊资料《国际法学》2018 年第 5 期全文转载。

4.《论国际法院与专家证据——以 1994 年国际法院“陆地和海洋边界案”为视角》,《国际法研究》2019 年第 2 期。

（三）英文论文和文章

1. “Manila's arbitration has evidence problem”, *China Daily*, May 6th, 2016。

2. “Commentary on Award on Jurisdiction and Admissibility of the Philippines-instituted Arbitration under Annex VII to the UNCLOS：A Discussion on Fact-Finding and Evidence”, (2016) 2 *Chinese Journal of Global Governance.*

3. “Book Review：Philosophy of International Law”, (2017) 16 *Chinese Journal of International Law* (SSCI 期刊)。

4. “Book Review：James Gerard Devaney, Fact-Finding before the International Court of Justice”, (2018) 17 *Chinese Journal of International Law* (SSCI 期刊)。

三 学术观点

关于“南海仲裁案”以及国际争端解决中的程序与证据问题，代表性观点如下。第一，“南海仲裁案”的仲裁庭对菲律宾单方启动的仲裁案所涉诉求没有管辖权。根据裁决书，仲裁庭不当地采纳、采信和联系了菲律宾单方提供的证据，得出了与事实并不一致的结论。第二，国际性法庭或仲裁庭的程序与证据问题，与国内实践既有众多相似之处，又有自己的特点。其中，证据问题的国际法实践灵活具体，有很强的类型与个案特点。

国际法的发展动态及值得关注的前沿问题

黄惠康*

当今世界正经历第二次世界大战以来未有之大变局，乱象纷呈，国际法作为国际关系和国际秩序“稳定器”的作用更趋重要。“治国者，以奉法为重”，大国外交必重国际法。习近平指出：“我们应该创造一个奉行法治、公平正义的未来。要提高国际法在全球治理中的地位和作用，确保国际规则有效遵守和实施，坚持民主、平等、正义，建设国际法治。”①

党的十八大以来，在习近平外交思想指引下，中国特色大国外交在实践中尊重国际法、坚持运用和发展国际法的特征更加鲜明。基于不断增长的综合国力和影响力，中国正逐渐从国际法的“接受者”、“跟跑者”向“参与者”、“建设者”转变，在气候变化、自由贸易、互联互通等领域更是成为“引领者”。中国要实现综合国力和国际影响力领先的强国目标，需要在更广范围、更深层次、更高水平运用国际法，积极参与引领全球治理体系改革。

---

* 黄惠康，联合国国际法委员会委员、中国外交部国际法咨询委员会主任委员、外交部条约法律司前司长、浙江大学光华法学院客座教授、武汉大学国际法研究所博士生导师。本文系作者在2018年浙江省国际法研究会年会和湖北省国际法学会年会上的两次主旨发言基础上撰写而成的。文中的见解仅为作者的个人观点，不代表作者服务的任何机构或组织的立场。

① 《习近平在气候变化巴黎大会开幕式上的讲话（全文）》，新华网，http://www.xinhuanet.com//world/2015-12/01/c_1117309642.htm，最后访问日期：2018年12月14日。

一 当前国际法的总体发展态势

（一）全球治理体系和国际秩序变革加速推进，制度性权力和未来秩序主导权之争成为大国博弈的主战场

以英国“脱欧”和美国“退群”为代表，“黑天鹅”与“灰犀牛”同行，传统安全与非传统安全交织，恐怖主义、难民危机、网络安全等非传统安全问题更趋突出，发达国家内部逆全球化民粹主义思潮暗流涌动，单边保护主义政策抬头，撬动了新一轮国际战略格局的调整。“冷战”结束以来，以相对稳定的中美俄欧双边和三边关系为机轴的大国关系、以世界贸易组织规则为核心的国际贸易体系、以美俄核裁军条约为基础的国际军控体系、以《联合国气候变化框架公约》及其《巴黎协定》为指引的应对气候变化机制、以联合国安全理事会为核心的集体安全体制等重大国际关系和国际机制，受到了不同程度的冲击，全球治理面临严重“赤字”和重大挑战。以我国为代表的新兴大国主动引导全球治理体系变革取得新的进展，我国在全球治理中的影响力、引导力得到制度化的巩固和拓展，同时面临大国博弈的新挑战。未来，国际秩序主导权之争仍将在国际关系的各个领域深入发展。在此背景下，作为国际法学者和法律外交实践者，我们要坚持以公平正义为理念，积极参与全球治理体系改革和建设，倡导国际关系民主化和法治化。既要从战略层面提出用好国际法服务中国特色大国外交的思路、建议，也要从微观层面就国际法的前沿问题提出中国方案，将我国提出的全球治理、国际法治理念转化为国际法领域的具体立场、主张。

（二）国际竞争从传统陆地疆域向包括海洋、极地、外空、网络在内的新疆域拓展的态势愈发明显，海洋领域规则制定和实施持续走深走实

国家管辖范围以外区域生物多样性养护和可持续利用问题，公海保护区、深海基因、大陆架和专属经济区划分、国际海底资源开发、极地治理、海平面上升等前沿问题以及争端解决机制问题受到各国高度重视。涉

及海域管辖、岛礁归属、大陆架划界等海上热点问题多发频发，且呈常态化、多边化、司法化之势，国际海底资源勘探开发竞争激烈，极地形势更趋复杂。我国在涉海方面面临的挑战有所增加。21 世纪是海洋世纪，中国确定了海洋强国战略。新的形势要求我国国际法学界紧密跟踪海洋法的最新理论与实践发展，不断提高运用海洋法服务建设海洋强国目标的能力，丰富和强化我国海洋权益主张的法理依据，在人类命运共同体思想的指引下，努力推动构建更加公平合理的国际海洋法律秩序。

（三）网络空间战略地位不断上升，在国际议程中的位置加速前移，制网权之争已悄然拉开帷幕①

各方围绕网络技术、网空治理、网络安全和规则制定展开激烈较量。一方面，信息技术、智能技术和网络技术发展方兴未艾，新一轮社会化互联网技术革命正在酝酿；另一方面，网络国际治理严重滞后。大国在网络空间的军力角逐不断升级，网络战风险增加；网络安全、信息安全危机四伏，网络攻击事件愈演愈烈，网络犯罪尤其是网络金融诈骗多发高发；网络领域渗透与反渗透、垄断与反垄断国际斗争日趋复杂；网络领域发展不平衡、规则不健全、秩序不合理等问题亟待解决。② 网络空间安全事关各方重大利益，已成为集政治、外交、安全、法律、经济和文化等多重因素于一体的重大战略问题。③ 西方与中俄等新兴国家阵营对垒的态势日渐清晰。双方围绕网络自由与网络主权、网络空间军事化与网络和平利用、民间与政府、技术垄断与公平参与这几对矛盾展开博弈。核心的一点是抢抓网络技术和网络空间秩序的主导权。2018 年上半年美国制裁中兴公司所暴露出来的问题表明，在网络领域，我们面临的挑战十分严峻。各国应在相

① 17、18 世纪各大国争夺制海权，19、20 世纪争夺制空权。有学者认为，21 世纪，谁能主导网络空间，谁就能主导整个世界。托夫勒曾预言：“谁控制了信息，谁控制了网络，谁就控制了世界。”参见〔美〕阿尔温·托夫勒、海蒂·托夫勒《创造一个新的文明——第三次浪潮的政治》，陈峰译，上海三联书店，1996，第 31 页。

② 我国受境外网络攻击、黑客攻击的数量和规模前所未有，受网络窃取、网络监听形势严峻，特别是斯诺登揭露的美国全球监听计划——“棱镜”计划，不仅威胁个人的隐私与数据安全，更是对国家主权的大范围和深层次的侵犯。

③ 习近平指出：“没有网络安全就没有国家安全，没有信息化就没有现代化。”参见《中央网络安全和信息化领导小组第一次会议召开 习近平发表重要讲话》，中央网信办，http://www.cac.gov.cn/2014-02/27/c_133148354.htm，最后访问日期：2018 年 12 月 14 日。

互尊重、相互信任的基础上，加强对话合作，推动互联网全球治理体系变革，共同构建和平、安全、开放、合作的网络空间，建立多边、民主、透明的全球互联网治理体系。[①]

（四）气候变化谈判进入转折期，各方加紧谋划未来全球环境治理体制

经各方共同努力，2015 年巴黎气候大会达成历史性的《巴黎协定》，并快速生效，“巴厘路线图”谈判进程终结硕果。[②] 然而，美国特朗普新政府推行“逆全球化”的“美国优先”政策，宣布将退出《巴黎协定》，对全球气候治理带来一定冲击，但《巴黎协定》将继续有效，国际合作应对气候变化的势头依然强劲。当前重点是继续合作落实《巴黎协定》，制定相关细化规则，推动协定有效运行。后续细则谈判由 20 多项议题组成。经过各国的共同努力和艰苦谈判，2018 年 12 月 16 日在波兰卡托维兹闭幕的联合国气候变化大会成功通过《巴黎协定》实施细则，细则谈判如期收官。卡托维兹会议是全球气候治理进程的重要节点，开启了全球合作应对气候变化的新时代，对维护气候治理多边机制和合作势头具有重要意义。同时，《巴黎协定》的落实工作仍然任重道远，在减缓、适应、资金等方面面临不少挑战。“独行快，众行远。”面对气候变化全球挑战，各国应认真贯彻公平、“共同但有区别的责任”和“各自能力”等基本原则，不断凝聚政治共识，携手合作，促进全球绿色、低碳和可持续发展。

2017 年以来，在法国总统马克龙的推动下，法国积极倡议制定《世界环境公约》。经过多轮磋商，第 72 届联合国大会于 2018 年 5 月 10 日通过了题为“迈向《世界环境公约》”的程序性决议，[③] 就是否制定《世界环

---

① 在 2015 年第二届国际互联网大会上，习近平提出了全球互联网治理的“四项原则”：尊重网络主权、维护和平安全、促进开放合作、构建良好秩序。为了共同构建网络空间命运共同体，习近平还提出了“五点主张”：第一，加快全球网络基础设施建设，促进互联互通；第二，打造网上文化交流共享平台，促进交流互鉴；第三，推动网络经济创新发展，促进共同繁荣；第四，保障网络安全，促进有序发展；第五，构建互联网治理体系，促进公平正义。参见《习近平出席第二届世界互联网大会开幕式并发表主旨演讲》，中央网信办，http://www.cac.gov.cn/2015-12/16/c_1117480642.htm，最后访问日期：2018 年 12 月 14 日。

② 2016 年 11 月 4 日，《巴黎协定》正式生效，现有缔约方 184 个（含欧盟）。

③ 联合国大会决议：《迈向〈世界环境公约〉》，ARES72277（2018），第 2—3 页。

境公约》作出分步走的程序性授权和安排：请联合国秘书长就国际环境法治存在的问题和不足向第73届联合国大会提交技术报告；在联合国大会设立特设工作组，审议上述报告并视情讨论一项国际文书的范围、指标和可行性，并于2019年上半年向联合国大会提出建议，包括召开政府间会议通过国际文书等等。① 这项决议的通过，标志着国际环境法领域的“造法”努力取得了阶段性进展。未来发展值得继续关注。

（五）国际法成为对外斗争和扩大国际影响的重要抓手

近年来，围绕西亚北非局势、伊朗核问题、朝鲜半岛局势、安理会改革、南海争议、中美贸易战等热点和难点问题，相关各方均十分注重以法律为抓手谋划应对之策、抢占道义高地，国际博弈中的法律战更趋激烈。即使特朗普政府大肆推行单边主义贸易保护措施，表面上也打着维护世界贸易组织“公平”贸易体制的旗号，并在世界贸易组织内娴熟地玩弄“法律牌”。法理之争成为塑造国际秩序、赢得制度性权力的重要方面，特别是中小国家越来越重视利用国际司法和仲裁程序谋利或造势。国际立法、国际司法对国际关系的影响不断上升，外交与法理愈加密不可分。

一个值得关注的新动向是，中小国家在国际舞台上联合发声、发挥影响，甚至联手向大国提出挑战的趋势在发展。前者如，51个小岛国向联合国大会第六委员会联合提议，请国际法委员会审议海平面上升对小岛国的影响问题；非洲联盟成员集体要求请国际法委员会审议“普遍管辖权”问题。后者如，在众多中小国家的强力推动下，联合国大会通过了《禁止核武器条约》，引来安理会五个常任理事国发表联合声明，集体反对，这在联合国历史上十分罕见；在联合国大会关于提请国际法院就涉及查戈斯群岛的两个问题出具咨询意见的决议表决中，安理会五个常任理事国中无一赞成票，不是反对，就是弃权，这也十分罕见；在2017年11月举行的国际法院法官选举中，竞选连任的英国籍法官格林伍德（Christopher Greenwood）意外地在6选5的竞选中败给了来自索马里、巴西、黎巴嫩、印度等国的候选人，成为唯一一个出局者。1946年国际法院成立以来，英国首

---

① 包括中国在内的143国投了赞成票，美国、俄罗斯、菲律宾、叙利亚、土耳其5国投了反对票，白俄罗斯、伊朗、马来西亚、尼加拉瓜、尼日利亚、沙特阿拉伯、塔吉克斯坦7国弃权。

次在该法院丧失法官席位。此前，在 2016 年 11 月举行的联合国国际法委员会换届选举中，法国提名的候选人竞选连任失败，英国和俄罗斯候选人以本区域最低得票当选，险遭淘汰。

我国是联合国安理会常任理事国和最大的发展中国家，正在日益走近世界舞台的中央，在当今国际社会居于十分重要而特殊的地位。要树立正确的历史观、大局观、角色观，深入分析世界转型过渡期国际形势和国际法发展演变的规律和动态，准确把握历史交汇期我国外部环境的基本特征，善用法律手段应对和化解发展过程中面临的各种风险挑战。要坚持维持世界和平、促进共同发展的外交宗旨，坚持独立自主的和平外交政策，始终不渝走和平发展道路，始终不渝奉行互利共赢的开放战略，以深化“四位一体”外交布局为依托，积极推动建设相互尊重、公平正义、合作共赢的新型国际关系，构建人类命运共同体。要大力弘扬正确的义利观，在同发展中国家交往中坚持义利并举、义重于利，增进与发展中国家的团结合作。这是中国特色大国外交得道多助的重要基础，在新时代应不断发扬光大。要积极参与全球治理体系改革和建设，倡导国际关系民主化和法治化，推动国际秩序朝更加公正合理的方向发展。

二　当前国际法前沿值得关注的九大问题

当前，在国际法和条约法律外交领域，一些重大的前沿法律问题值得学界给予特别关注和深入研究。

（一）人类命运共同体与国际法

人类命运共同体思想是习近平新时代中国特色社会主义思想的重要组成部分，是党的十八大以来中国外交的重大理论创新成果。2018 年 3 月，与“坚持和平发展道路”、“坚持互利共赢开放战略”一起，“推动构建人类命运共同体”的思想被载入国家根本大法。这是我国外交政策理念在国家法治上的最高宣示，也是中国外交进入推动构建人类命运共同体新时代的法律标志。准确把握人类命运共同体思想的国际法内涵，积极探索在国际治理的各具体领域融入命运共同体思想，既是推进新时代中国特色大国外交的必然要求，也是中国国际法学界的共同使命。

推动构建人类命运共同体，不是“另起炉灶”，也不是推倒重构，而是要在以《联合国宪章》为核心的现有国际法律秩序的基础上，致力于建设一个持久和平、普遍安全、共同繁荣、开放包容、美丽清洁的世界。

外交的灵魂在于王道，法律的生命在于行动。人类命运共同体思想作为中国外交的王道，需要国际法的固化和支撑。人类命运共同体理念已写入了联合国相关决议，《中华人民共和国和俄罗斯联邦联合声明》、《上海合作组织成员国元首理事会青岛宣言》、《中非合作论坛北京峰会宣言》等多边或双边文件。下阶段，应积极推动通过具体国际规则体现和落实上述理念，使其真正落地生根，并焕发持久生命力。希望学界共同做好人类命运共同体理念的国际法阐释和宣介工作，积极探索在各具体领域外交实践中体现和落实人类命运共同体理念的具体路径，使我国推进人类命运共同体理念的实践成为我国不断培育和扩大国际影响力和制度性权力的过程。

（二）“一带一路”法治保障

共建“一带一路”是我国今后相当长时期对外开放和对外合作的管总规划，也是人类命运共同体理念的重要实践平台，法治保障是其中的重要一环。下列法律问题值得研究。

1. 条约网络的构建。当前“一带一路”条约网络构建工作已经起步并已初具雏形，但还存在不少短板。一是覆盖的国家和领域还不全面，需要拓展；二是现有经贸条约还不太适应新形势，需要升级换代；三是如何用好已有多边条约和机制，深入参与制定新公约新机制，需要加强研究。

2. 风险防范机制。与“一带一路”建设相关的法律问题相当复杂，风险不小。有效应对法律风险，一个重要环节就是要立足各国现实情况，将相关政策问题法律化。利用法律的正式性、稳定性、可预测性等特质克服政治和商业决策中的不确定性，从而使“一带一路”合作与交往走上法治化轨道，在相对稳定的法律框架下实现共同发展和互利共赢。这个法律框架应遵循“共商共建共享”和平等互利的原则，尊重当事人选择可适用法律的自由，发生法律冲突时选择相应规则来解决。

三是争端解决机制。“一带一路”国际合作，分歧争端难免，迫切需要建立高效、公正、便捷的争端解决机制。有两种基本思路：一是用好用足现有机制；二是在充分调研的基础上考虑设立新机制。考虑到“一带一路”聚焦经济领域的合作，国家、公民、法人等不同主体间争端都可能存在，需要区分情况分类施策。

（三）《禁止核武器条约》与全面核裁军进程

核武器是悬在人类头上的“达摩克利斯之剑”，从长远看，应该全面禁止并最终彻底销毁，实现无核世界。迄今，国际社会已先后缔结《禁止在大气层、外层空间和水下进行核武器试验条约》（1963）、《不扩散核武器条约》（1968）、《全面禁止核试验条约》（1996）等国际公约，多边核不扩散法律体制总体稳定牢固，但近年来在国际核裁军领域，有核国家与多数无核国家间在如何进一步推进核裁军的问题上矛盾十分突出。2016 年 10 月，奥地利、墨西哥等国推动第 70 届联合国大会通过决议，要求就禁止核武器谈判，制定一项具有法律约束力的文书。[①] 2017 年 3 月该谈判进程正式启动，有 130 多个国家参加，其中绝大多数是亚非拉国家。主要有核国及多数北约成员国均未参加。[②] 2017 年 7 月 7 日，联合国大会以 122 票赞成通过了《禁止核武器条约》，要求全世界各国立刻停止几乎所有与核武器相关的活动，比如研发、制造、生产乃至持有。在此次表决中，包括中国在内的安理会五个常任理事国拒绝参与投票。此公约涉及复杂的法律问题，主要包括核武器在现行国际法中是否合法，《不扩散核武器条约》规定的核裁军谈判义务的范围，《禁止核武器条约》对非缔约国的效力，对核不扩散机制的冲击，以及对核有关行业的实体和个人的影响等。联系

---

① 美国、俄罗斯、英国、法国 4 个有核国家投了反对票，中国、印度、巴基斯坦投了弃权票。

② 外交部新闻发言人指出，中方充分理解相关国家希望早日实现无核武器世界的愿望，但应坚持在现有多边裁军机制下处理，另起炉灶、破坏协商一致原则可能只会适得其反。所以，中方决定不参加谈判。中国外交部重申，“尽管不参与谈判，中方坚定支持最终全面禁止和彻底销毁核武器的立场没有改变”。参见《2016 年 10 月 28 日外交部发言人陆慷主持例行记者会》，外交部，https://www.fmprc.gov.cn/web/fyrbt_673021/t1411135.shtml，最后访问日期：2018 年 12 月 14 日；《2017 年 3 月 20 日外交部发言人华春莹主持例行记者会》，外交部，https://www.fmprc.gov.cn/web/fyrbt_673021/t1447096.shtml，最后访问日期：2018 年 12 月 14 日。

到2014年马绍尔群岛在国际法院起诉拥核国家案,[①] 表明核裁军中的法律因素日益突出。2018年10月29日，中俄美法英五国发表声明，共同反对《禁止核武器条约》。声明强调，五国一直在按照1968年《不扩散核武器条约》对核武器进行削减。该条约在防止核武器的威胁扩散到全球方面发挥了重要作用，极大控制了核战争的风险，还给民用核技术提供了重要的框架，造福了人类。五国一致强调，实现一个“无核武器”的世界是各国共同的目标，只要这不会损害世界的安全。声明表示，“恰是在这样的前提下，我们反对《禁止核武器条约》”。理由是，“我们坚信只有考虑国际安全形势，一步步来，才是实现一个无核武器世界的最佳办法”。声明进一步阐述了《禁止核武器条约》的几个硬伤，例如忽视了国际安全形势和地区的挑战，也没有增加各国间的互信与透明，甚至还会给《不扩散核武器条约》的执行带来阻碍和困难。因此，五国表示：“我们不会支持、签署或批准《禁止核武器条约》。该条约不会对我们的国家产生任何法律强制效力……我们也希望考虑支持该条约的国家可以认真考虑这会给世界和平与安全带来的影响。”[②]

（四）国际司法机构与国际法的解释与适用

国际司法机构，特别是联合国国际法院，一直被许多国家视为公平正义的化身，在国际法的解释与适用中发挥重要作用，不仅决定有关争端个案的解决，也在很大程度上影响国际法的发展方向，一直是大国博弈和争夺的重要阵地。近年来，国际性司法裁判机制趋于加强。越来越多的条约规定了以司法手段解决争端的义务和程序，主权国家接受国际司法机构管辖的压力增大，在人权、环境、海洋法领域尤其明显。国际海洋法法庭和其他第三方争端解决机构或机制在受理、审理国家间涉海争端时出现了严

---

① 例如，可参见 Obligations concerning Negotiations relating to Cessation of the Nuclear Arms Race and to Nuclear Disarmament（Marshall Islands v United Kingdom），International Court of Justice，https://www.icj-cij.org/en/case160，最后访问日期：2018年12月14日。

② “Joint Statement by China，France，Russian Federation，United Kingdom and United States”，The Ministry of Foreign Affairs of the Russian Federation，http://www.mid.ru/en_GB/maps/cn/-/asset_publisher/WhKWb5DVBqKA/content/id/3384609#flag-popup，最后访问日期：2018年12月14日。

重的“扩权和滥权”问题。[①] 普遍司法管辖权趋于扩大，对侵犯人权的追诉趋于国际化。最新趋势是将所谓侵犯人权的罪行列入所谓的“普遍管辖权”，并限制司法豁免的适用范围，对一国现任或前任领导人进行刑事追诉的案例增加。“国家主权与全球治理”、“不干涉内政与保护的责任”、“国内管辖与国际管辖”三组矛盾激烈折冲对撞。国际管辖的范围在扩展，“国内和国际混合管辖区域”在增多，深刻影响着国家决策空间和行为模式。[②] 而国际法院、国际刑事法院、国际海洋法法庭、欧洲人权法院、美洲人权法院等国际或区域司法机构，愈来愈多地直接或间接地介入了一些国际热点问题或敏感问题。争权、扩权、滥权倾向日趋明显。[③] 甚至联合国大会都有了建立具有独立刑事侦查权的辅助机关的冲动。[④] 因此，有必要结合国际形势与我国发展现状，提高我国在国际司法活动中的影响力。作为政府和学界共同努力的方向之一，从人才培养、制度建设、机制创新多角度入手，寻求突破。还要高度重视国际法学的研究方法，无论是理论研究还是法律实务，都要十分重视对国际法院案例的研究。

（五）条约履约机构和缔约国大会扩权动向

与此同时，除国际司法机构外，条约履约机构等具有一定准司法或监督职能的机构，也不同程度地出现了扩权倾向。主权的人本化趋势进一步加强，消除所谓“有罪不罚”的呼声日高，道义天平明显向个人倾斜。这是法律与政治相互作用、相互影响的必然结果，也是各国抢占国际新秩序制高点的博弈在法律上的必然反映。[⑤] 自 2009 年联合国人权高级专员办事处启动有关改革进程以来，人权条约机构监督职责不断强化，工作的选择

---

① 钟声：《仲裁庭扩权滥权严重损害国际法治》，《人民日报》2016 年 5 月 11 日，第 3 版。

② 参见黄惠康《当代国际法的若干发展趋势》，《西安政治学院学报》2013 年第 4 期。

③ 总体而言，在相当长时间内，美欧国家将继续保持国际司法领域的优势主导地位。我国对国际司法机构的影响力，碍于诸多原因同主要大国相比还有较大差距，这与我国的国际地位和国际影响力也不相称。

④ 参见朱利江、杨承甫《论联大设立叙利亚“国际公正独立机制”的不法性》，《武大国际法评论》2017 年第 5 期。

⑤ 人权保护的政治化倾向进一步发展，“政治问题法律化”、“法律问题政治化”、“国内问题国际化”、“国际问题国内化”，对主权平等、不干涉内政等国际法基本原则造成冲击。对他国内政的干涉手段，已从政治施压、经济制裁、武力干涉，发展到通过国际司法机制追究行为人的刑事责任。

性和政治化倾向日益严重。我国是联合国六项主要人权条约的缔约国，涉及经济社会文化权利，反对种族主义，禁止酷刑，妇女、儿童和残疾人权利等重要领域，人权机构改革进程中的扩权动向，对我们应对履约工作有重要影响。① 环境类条约缔约国会议也有类似趋势。《联合国防止荒漠化公约》缔约国会议决定，在公约框架下就全球土地退化问题建立工作组，这可能会超出公约规定的防治荒漠化目标的适用范围。《濒危野生动植物种国际贸易公约》的管辖范围应该是进出口贸易，但是公约缔约方会议以保护濒危野生动植物为由，对缔约国国内贸易措施也提出要求。这些条约履约机制或者缔约国大会的扩权趋势，既是各领域国际治理日益加强的结果，也对有关国际规则和制度的确定性产生一定冲击，长远来看对国际法治会产生影响。

（六）国际法院“查戈斯群岛咨询意见案”

2017 年 6 月 22 日，第 71 届联合国大会以 94 票赞成、15 票反对、65 票弃权的表决结果，通过了由毛里求斯推动非洲组国家提出的第 71292 号决议，② 提请国际法院就涉及查戈斯群岛的两个问题出具咨询意见：（1）在查戈斯群岛与毛里求斯分裂的情况下，毛里求斯 1968 年独立时非殖民化进程是否已经完成；（2）英国继续管理查戈斯群岛有何法律后果。这是一个政治上很敏感的问题，既牵涉非殖民化进程中的历史纠葛，又有双边领土主权争端特征，还涉及国际法院的咨询管辖权。③ 国际法院已启动咨询程序，并邀请各国提交书面意见和出席听证程序。目前看，各国在法院应否发表

---

① 我国是下列人权公约的缔约国：《经济、社会和文化权利国际公约》、《消除一切形式种族歧视国际公约》、《禁止酷刑和其他残忍、不人道或有辱人格的待遇或处罚公约》、《消除对妇女一切形式歧视公约》、《儿童权利公约》、《残疾人权利公约》、《儿童权利公约关于买卖儿童、儿童卖淫和儿童色情制品问题的任择议定书》和《儿童权利公约关于儿童卷入武装冲突问题的任择议定书》。

② “Request for an Advisory Opinion of the International Court of Justice on the Legal Consequences of the Separation of the Chagos Archipelago from Mauritius in 1965”, Resolution Adopted by the General Assembly on 22 June 2017, ARES71292.

③ 从联大决议投票情况看，安理会五大常任理事国中除英、美投反对票外，其余全部投了弃权票，即五大常任理事国中无一赞成票，这种情况比较少见。反对和弃权的国家加起来，和赞成的国家数量比，基本上一半对一半。

咨询意见的问题上分歧严重。毛里求斯及其支持方认为非殖民化是联合国大会的职权，国际法院有权应联合国大会的请求发表咨询意见。英、美等国则认为查戈斯群岛问题本质上属于毛英间的双边争端，根据“当事国同意原则”，未经当事另一方（英方）的同意，不能诉诸国际法院。毛里求斯在道义上获得了众多发展中国家的同情，声势不容小觑。另一方面，查戈斯群岛问题涉及英美重大利益，两国势必运用国际政治和法律领域的软硬实力，全力阻止国际法院发表对其实质不利的意见。如何处理，确实是对法院智慧的考验。后续进展情况需要密切跟踪研究。

鉴于此案涉及重要的国际法问题，中国政府高度关注，决定向国际法院提交书面意见。2017 年联合国大会表决通过有关决议时，中国投了弃权票并作解释性发言。2018 年 9 月 3 日至 6 日，国际法院在海牙举行了口头程序，听取双方当庭陈述，两军对垒，阵营分明，观点对立，交锋激烈。[①]从各方提交的书面意见和口头陈述看，中国在联合国大会的解释性发言和向法院提交的书面意见的主要观点得到各方的肯定和认同。[②]

（七）美英法对叙利亚动武的合法性问题

2018 年 4 月 7 日，叙利亚首都大马士革东郊杜马镇发生疑似化学武器袭击事件。西方认定此系叙利亚政府所为，但叙利亚政府坚决否认。4 月 14 日，美国联合英国和法国，对叙利亚发动空袭，并称空袭是为了“惩罚或报复叙利亚政府使用化学武器的行为”，以震慑叙利亚政府，防止其再次使用化学武器。英国政府还公布了其司法大臣的法律意见，声称空袭叙利亚属于必要的“人道主义干预”，是为了缓解叙利亚日益严重的人

① 毛里求斯、英国、南非、德国、阿根廷、澳大利亚、巴西、美国、印度、以色列、肯尼亚、尼日利亚、塞尔维亚、泰国等 22 个国家和非洲联盟出庭陈述。鉴于中国已在书面意见中全面阐述了核心主张和关切，中国决定不参加口头程序。和中国有类似关注和持类似立场的俄罗斯、法国、韩国等国也未参加口头程序。参见“Legal Consequences of the Separation of the Chagos Archipelago from Mauritius in 1965 (Request for Advisory Opinion)”, International Court of Justice, https://www.icj-cij.org/en/case169，最后访问日期：2018 年 12 月 14 日。

② 毛里求斯积极评价中国“承认国际法院在履行联合国非殖民化职能方面发挥重要作用”，并表示同意中国主张的“法院的咨询意见不应触及纯属双边领土主权争端”立场。英国、德国认为中国在维护“当事国同意原则”方面“表达了重要关切”。

道危机。①

单边“人道主义干预”背离联合国集体安全机制，② 对禁止使用武力原则造成冲击，值得密切关注。首先是如何更有效发挥安理会作用的问题。安理会是联合国集体安全机制的核心，但常常会因为大国博弈而无法有效运作，这往往给一些国家采取单边措施提供借口。如何维护安理会权威，需要研究和探索。其次是如何应对“人道主义干预”卷土重来。此次英国重弹“人道主义干预”老调，虽在实证法上站不住脚，但仍不乏支持者。③ 西方谋求“人道主义干预”合法化的企图和行动从来就没有停止过，值得研究并依法予以驳斥。

（八）全球海洋治理及“南海仲裁案”后续法律问题④

当前，全球海洋治理问题受到国际社会高度重视。随着人类对海洋资源的大规模开发利用，污染排放、过度捕捞、滥采资源等一系列不合理不可持续的行为频发，给海洋生态带来了巨大的压力。海上安全风险也呈上升态势，特别是非传统安全威胁日益突出。台风、海啸等严重自然灾害多发；溢油、危险化学品泄漏等海上突发事故增多；海盗、非法捕鱼等事件屡见不鲜。在这些危机面前，任何一个国家和地区都不能独善其身，需要各国携手合作、守望相助，共同确保海洋和人类社会的可持续发展。

制定一份具有法律约束力的关于国家管辖范围以外区域生物多样性（Biodiversity Beyond National Jurisdiction，BBNJ）养护和可持续利用问题国际协定是当前全球海洋治理中的当务之急。该协定被视为《联合国海洋法

---

① 从现行国际法的原则和规则来判定，美、英、法此次单边动武明显违反国际法。既无联合国安理会授权，三国也未受到叙利亚的“武力攻击”，不存在任何意义上的“自卫”问题；“惩罚或报复”也没有国际法依据；“人道主义干预”理由难以服众。

② 2005 年联合国大会通过的世界首脑会议成果文件，明确国际社会在履行保护的责任时，应以外交等和平手段为主，在例外情况下通过武力履行该责任须获得安理会的明确授权。

③ 一些西方学者认为应将叙利亚危机当作发展、完善“人道主义干预”规则的良机。例如有学者认为，应该为“人道主义干预”规则的适用设立清楚、可操作的门槛，即从“大规模的人道危机”转变为“性质严重的人道危机，如使用生物化学武器等”，也就是从“量”的标准过渡到“质”的标准。

④ 详见黄惠康《关于国际海洋法前沿值得关注的十大问题》，《边界与海洋研究》2019 年第 1 期。

公约》框架下的第三份执行协定。[①] 目前，谈判正在进行之中，主要涉及下列五大问题：海洋遗传资源、海洋保护区的划区管理工具、环境影响评价、能力建设和技术转让以及跨领域问题。

此外，关于公海保护区问题、在他国专属经济区内的军事活动问题、岩礁和低潮高地的法律地位问题、大陆架和专属经济区划界的新动向、第三方争端解决机制问题、国际海底资源开发规章、南极和北极的国际治理以及“南海仲裁案”的后续法律问题，都值得进行深入研究。

我国应对“南海仲裁案”的政治、外交与法律斗争已告一段落，但不会一劳永逸地终结。中国与东盟国家就“南海行为准则”的磋商还在进行之中，仲裁案裁决的法律影响及后续走向问题仍不可小觑，需要密切关注，相关的法律问题也值得继续深入研究。西方和个别南海声索国仍会伺机发难或捣乱，国际法学界也会不时就相关法律问题发表评论或意见。个人以为，我们不宜再主动发起南海仲裁案法律问题之公开论战，但对于个别南海声索国重燃南海问题司法化的可能图谋应保持警惕，并始终保持政治和外交上的高压态势。对于学界的学术探讨则可保持平常心，只要不是有意在政治上与我为敌，可以不与其论争，我国学者也可以自由参与学术研讨，增信释疑。

（九）推进理论和实践创新，构建中国特色国际法学体系

随着综合国力和国际地位提升，中国越来越多地承担国际规则的引领者和塑造者的角色。国际社会高度关注中国的国际法治观，我们参与国际规则的博弈也需要以中国的国际法治观为引领。为此，我们要配合中国特色大国外交理论和实践的发展需要，打造和完善中国特色国际法治观，从理论和实务的角度深入研究人类命运共同体等重大外交思想，推动国际法理论创新符合中国国际法治观的对外宣示，此外还要做好机制体制创新。

---

① 《联合国海洋法公约》框架下的第一份执行协定是1994年《关于执行1982年12月10日〈联合国海洋法公约〉第十一部分的协定》，第二份执行协定是1995年《执行1982年12月10日〈联合国海洋法公约〉有关养护和管理跨界鱼类种群和高度洄游鱼类种群的规定的协定》。目前，1994年协定有缔约国150个，1995年协定有缔约国89个。

三　结语

新时代中国特色大国外交正日益走向世界舞台中央。我们要推进建设相互尊重、公平正义、合作共赢的新型国际关系，构建人类命运共同体，建设持久和平、普遍安全、共同繁荣、开放包容、清洁美丽的世界。这都要求我们更加重视国际法，坚定推进国际法治。国际法是国际关系理论与实践发展的结晶。“政治上有利，道义上有理，法律上有据”，这是外交的最佳状态，而让法治的精神在国际关系中王道浩荡，则是现代外交的一大目标。每一个国际法学人都要怀着对法律的敬重，以自己的专长为国家外交和世界和平事业作贡献，努力开创国际法学研究的新局面。

（责任编辑：何田田）

（本文原载于《国际法研究》2019 年第 1 期）

人类命运共同体与国际法

徐　宏*

推动构建人类命运共同体，是习近平新时代中国特色社会主义思想的重要组成部分。2018 年 3 月 11 日第十三届全国人民代表大会第一次会议通过《中华人民共和国宪法修正案》，将“推动构建人类命运共同体”写入宪法，① 意味着我国以国家根本大法的形式对此向全世界作出庄严法律承诺，为国际法的发展开辟了新境界，指明了新方向，催生了新动力。

“法者，治之端也。”② 在国际层面将构建人类命运共同体思想真正落地生根，必须深入挖掘这一思想的国际法内涵，认识其对于当代国际法发展的引领作用，并在工作中树立国际法意识，强化国际法思维，妥善运用国际法这一“国际通用的语言”，推动其从国家意志向国际共识、从思想理念向具体制度的转化。

一　构建人类命运共同体思想契合当代国际法发展大势

构建人类命运共同体思想回答了“建设一个什么样的世界，如何建设这个世界”这一“时代之问”，属于国际关系和外交政策的理念范畴。而国际法则是对国家相互关系上行为的规范，③ 是对国家之间的关系加以规

---

* 徐宏，外交部条法司司长。本文仅代表作者的个人观点。

① 参见《中华人民共和国宪法》序言第 12 段。

② 参见《荀子·君道》。习近平 2017 年 1 月 18 日在联合国日内瓦总部所作《共同构建人类命运共同体》的演讲中援引此句强调推行国际法治的重要性。

③ 周鲠生：《国际法》，武汉大学出版社，2007，第 1 页。

范的原则、规则和制度的总体。[①] 二者处理的都是国际关系问题，都属于上层建筑，相互之间有着密不可分的联系。理念引领方向，规则决定成效；规则服务于理念，而理念的落实也离不开规则。所以，构建人类命运共同体思想的时代先进性，需要放到国际法发展的历史长河中加以考察。

首先，从马克思主义唯物史观揭示的法律本质及人类社会发展规律看，构建人类命运共同体思想的提出顺应了时代要求。马克思指出："法的关系正像国家的形式一样，既不能从它们本身来理解，也不能从所谓人类精神的一般发展来理解，相反，它们根源于物质的生活关系，这种物质的生活关系的总和，……人们在自己生活的社会生产中发生一定的、必然的、不以他们的意志为转移的关系，即同他们的物质生产力的一定发展阶段相适合的生产关系，这些生产关系的总和构成社会的经济结构，即有法律的和政治的上层建筑竖立其上并有一定的社会意识形式与之相适应的现实基础。"[②] 国际法伴随国家的产生而产生，伴随国际关系的发展而发展，其演变轨迹，归根到底是由其所处时代国际社会的经济基础决定的。我国著名国际法学者周鲠生先生就曾指出，国际法是随着国家的产生，在国际交往过程中形成的。每一个时代凡属有许多国家并立，互相交往，自然就有适应这个时代社会经济制度的国际交往规则或习惯产生。[③] 马克思主义揭示了社会主义必然取代资本主义的历史规律。1848 年《共产党宣言》中描绘的奋斗目标是："代替那存在着阶级和阶级对立的资产阶级旧社会的，将是这样一个联合体，在那里，每个人的自由发展是一切人的自由发展的条件。"[④] 这是一个渐进的、需要长期奋斗的进程。历史发展到今天，"自由人联合体"所需的"物质存在条件"尚未成熟，国际社会仍由主权国家组成，资产阶级仍占优势地位，社会主义与资本主义两种社会制度呈现出长期并存竞争的态势。这决定了国际法作为主权国家之间的行为规范仍然需要存在。但是，随着经济全球化的发展以及世界多极化、社会信息化、文化多样化的深入，各国日益相互依存，利益交融，命运与共，比以往任

① 王铁崖：《国际法引论》，北京大学出版社，1998，第 2 页。

② 《〈政治经济学批判〉序言》，载《马列著作选编（修订本）》，中共中央党校出版社，2011，第 98 页。

③ 周鲠生：《国际法》（上卷），商务印书馆，1981，第 40—41 页。

④ 《共产党宣言》，载《马列著作选编（修订本）》，中共中央党校出版社，2011，第 226 页。

何时候都需要各国同舟共济，共同维护和促进世界和平与发展，这要求国际法制度与时俱进。构建人类命运共同体思想的提出，正是契合了世界历史发展的要求，指明了新时代国际法的方向与目标。

其次，从中华优秀传统文化的传承看，构建人类命运共同体思想有着深厚的历史文化根基。中华传统文化以整体和谐为最大特征，强调“以和邦国”、“天下为公”，追求“天下大同”的理想。在国家间交往中，中华文明还历来崇尚“兼相爱，交相利”，坚信“义利并举、以义为先”，“己所不欲、勿施于人”的原则，重视各国之间建立和而不同、和睦相处、平等互利的友好关系。在法治方面，也在很早就形成了一系列约束国家行为的规则和惯例。在这些规则及其背后规则意识基础上，中国古代历经“止有‘际’而非‘国’”的春秋战国和“止有‘国’而非‘际’”的王朝更迭,① 又在近代受到西方国际法的冲击和百年战争洗礼，逐渐形成了中国看待世界、看待自身的独特视角,② 这些都成为人类命运共同体思想的重要文化源泉。

再次，从中国共产党的使命看，构建人类命运共同体思想的提出体现了新时代中国共产党推进全球治理和国际法治的责任担当。中国共产党将马克思主义的国际主义思想发扬光大，逐步形成了中国特色的国际观包括国际法治观。党的十九大报告指出：“中国共产党是为中国人民谋幸福的政党，也是为人类进步事业而奋斗的政党。中国共产党始终把为人类作出新的更大的贡献作为自己的使命。”③ 党的最高理想和最终目标是实现共产主义。在中国共产党领导中国人民进行社会主义革命和建设事业的征程中，一直坚定奉行独立自主的和平外交政策，提出并积极践行和平共处五项原则。60 多年来，“历经国际风云变幻的考验，和平共处五项原则作为一个开放包容的国际法原则，集中体现了主权、正义、民主、法治的价值观”。④ 中国在重大国际和地区问题上秉持正义，坚定捍卫以《联合国宪章》

---

① 陈顾远：《中国国际法溯源》，商务印书馆，1931，第 10 页。

② 李适时：《夯实人类命运共同体的国际法治基础》，载《中国国际法年刊（2017）》，法律出版社，2018，第 16—17 页。

③ 习近平：《决胜全面建成小康社会 夺取新时代中国特色社会主义伟大胜利——在中国共产党第十九次全国代表大会上的报告》，人民出版社，2017，第 57—58 页。

④ 习近平：《弘扬和平共处五项原则建设合作共赢美好世界——在和平共处五项原则发表 60 周年纪念大会上的讲话》，《人民日报》2014 年 6 月 29 日，第 2 版。

为核心的国际法基本原则和国际关系基本准则，坚持和平解决国际争端和历史遗留问题。中国以建设性姿态参与国际规则制定，已参加了几乎所有普遍性政府间国际组织，缔结了500多项国际公约和2万多项双边条约，[①] 成为全球治理的重要力量、国际法治的坚定维护者和建设者。习近平在出席气候变化巴黎大会开幕式上的讲话中指出："我们应该创造一个奉行法治、公平正义的未来。要提高国际法在全球治理中的地位和作用，确保国际规则有效遵守和实施，坚持民主、平等、正义，建设国际法治。"[②] 构建人类命运共同体思想正是为当今世界如何治理、如何建设国际法治，建设什么样的国际法治指明了方向，贡献了中国智慧、中国方案，充分体现了中国特色社会主义的道路自信、理论自信、制度自信、文化自信。

最后，从国际法自身发展的轨迹和逻辑看，构建人类命运共同体思想的提出为国际法的未来发展指明了新的价值目标。美国国际法学者路易斯·亨金（Henkin）说："就国家间关系而言，文明的进步可以被视为从武力到外交，再从外交到法律的历史演进。"[③] 国际法在每个历史时期所反映的价值目标，体现的都是当时国际社会的价值追求，代表的是占优势地位的国家及其统治者的利益，这又归根到底决定于经济基础和国际分工的发展程度。在17、18世纪资产阶级革命时期，资产阶级提出和倡导了一系列指导国际关系的准则，包括国家主权原则、不干涉内政原则、国家平等原则等。[④]《威斯特伐利亚和约》标志着近代国际法的诞生，这一时期国际法的核心价值是主权独立和平等。但这种独立和平等只适用于所谓资产阶级"文明国家"之间，掩盖不了资本贪欲的野蛮扩张。在"国际法"旗号掩盖下，西方国家通过烧杀抢掠、推行海外殖民、签署不平等条约、划分势力范围、建立租界和领事裁判权制度等，侵夺广大发展中国家的正当权益，充分暴露了他们所谓"主权独立和平等"的虚伪性。两次世界大战对国际法造成了极大的破坏，同时也唤醒了世界各国人民，和平成为国际社会最为关切的焦点问题。不使用武力、民族自决、和平解决国际争端等国

① 参见中华人民共和国外交部条约法律司编《中国国际法实践案例选编》，世界知识出版社，2018，第9页。

② 《习近平谈治国理政》（第二卷），外文出版社，2017，第529页。

③ Louis Henkin, *How Nations Behave: Law and Foreign Policy* (New York: Columbia University Press, 1979), p. 1.

④ 王铁崖：《国际法》，法律出版社，1981，第64页。

际法原则和集体安全体制得以确立，《联合国宪章》及其他有关国际文件确定的国际关系基本准则和国际法基本原则得到普遍接受。随着社会主义国家的兴起以及民族独立解放运动的蓬勃发展，发展中国家的力量不断壮大，对国际法产生的影响也越来越大。特别是中国提出和倡导的和平共处五项原则，被公认为国际法基本原则，① 发展权被承认为基本人权。冷战结束后，特别是进入21世纪以后，国际社会的相互联系、相互依存、相互影响日益增多，国际法逐渐从“共处法”走向“合作法”，把关注点更多投入国家间的合作。上至太空，下达海底，大到全球气候，小至衣食住行，都成为国际法调整的范围，新的国际法规范不断涌现。正如习近平指出：“数百年来列强通过战争、殖民、划分势力范围等方式争夺利益和霸权逐步向各国以制度规则协调关系和利益的方式演进。现在，世界上的事情越来越需要各国共同商量着办，建立国际机制、遵守国际规则、追求国际正义成为多数国家的共识。”② 当前，世界正处于大发展大变革大调整时期，国际格局面临数百年未有之变局。世界日益成为地球村，和平与发展是国际社会的共同追求，应对全球性挑战也越来越需要各国加强合作。在此背景下，习近平勇立时代潮头，以卓越的全球视野和世界胸怀提出构建人类命运共同体思想。这一思想超越了旧的文明和利益局限，为国际法指出了以人类为中心、以人类社会整体利益和共同的前途命运为依归的根本价值追求，反映了全人类的普遍愿望，使新时代中国国际法观赢得了道义制高点。

二　构建人类命运共同体思想具有丰富的国际法内涵

人类命运共同体思想包括“持久和平、普遍安全、共同繁荣、开放包容、清洁美丽”五大支柱，都具有丰富的国际法内涵。

持久和平是构建人类命运共同体的基本前提，也是国际法的永恒主

① 联合国副秘书长兼法律顾问苏亚雷斯在出席“和平共处五项原则与国际法的发展”国际研讨会时表示：和平共处五项原则对国际法和国际关系的影响十分重大，他作为联合国法律顾问，每天都能感受到五项原则的影响。苏亚雷斯：《和平共处五项原则影响无时不在》，《人民日报》2014年6月10日，第23版。

② 《习近平在中共中央政治局第二十七次集体学习时强调：推动全球治理体制更加公正更加合理 为我国发展和世界和平创造有利条件》（2015年10月12日），《人民日报》2015年10月14日，第1版。

题。和平一向是国际社会的崇高追求，是国际法的首要目标。1899 年第一次海牙和平会议和 1907 年第二次海牙和平会议确立了和平解决国家间争端的基本原则，1928 年《巴黎非战公约》明确表达了世界各国力求避免战争的共同追求，这些思想和原则在 1945 年《联合国宪章》中得到了充分体现。二战结束后的 70 多年里，虽然世界规模的大型战争得以避免，但区域战争、小型战争从未间断。一些国家以所谓“普世价值”为名，行一己之私，通过对国际法上“不使用武力”原则例外情形的扩大解释，鼓吹“人道主义干预”，滥用“保护的责任”，以武力干涉其他国家内政，破坏国际和平稳定，冲击国际法的宗旨和原则。针对这一情况，中国提出构建人类命运共同体，并将“持久和平”列为人类命运共同体五大支柱之首，意义十分重大。中国主张，建设一个持久和平的世界，根本要义在于国家之间要构建平等相待、互商互谅的伙伴关系。“要相互尊重、平等协商，坚决摒弃冷战思维和强权政治，走对话而不对抗、结伴而不结盟的国与国交往新路。”[①] 这就要求在国际法的解释和适用上，必须秉持善意，以有利于实现持久和平为出发点，准确理解和切实贯彻主权平等、不干涉内政、不使用武力、和平解决国际争端等国际法原则。正如习近平指出的，主权平等是数百年来国与国规范彼此关系最重要的准则；主权平等，真谛在于国家不分大小、强弱、贫富，主权和尊严必须得到尊重，内政不容干涉。[②]

普遍安全是构建人类命运共同体的根本保障，也是国际法的首要任务。一个人也好，一个国家也好，一旦自身安全得不到保障，一切都无从谈起，因此各国都将安全问题置于关乎自身生死存亡的高度。这方面的国际法规则和制度也不断发展。《联合国宪章》将“维护国际和平与安全”作为联合国的首要宗旨，[③] 规定了一系列原则，确立了以“大国一致”为基础的集体安全体制。一些区域国际组织也建立了地区安全机制。随着恐怖主义、环境、能源、难民、传染性疾病、粮食安全等非传统领域安全问题日益突出，国际社会制定了一系列新的国际条约，并依托相关国际组织

---

① 杨洁篪：《推动构建人类命运共同体》，载《党的十九大报告辅导读本》，人民出版社，2017，第 91 页。

② 习近平《习近平谈治国理政》（第二卷），外文出版社，2017，第 539 页。

③ 《联合国宪章》第 1 条规定，联合国的首要宗旨是：“维持国际和平及安全；并为此目的：采取有效集体办法，以防止且消除对于和平之威胁，制止侵略行为或其他和平之破坏；并以和平方法且依正义及国际法之原则，调整或解决足以破坏和平之国际争端或情势。”

开展合作。然而，安全问题并没有得到有效解决。当前国际安全形势动荡复杂，传统安全威胁和非传统安全威胁相互交织。而一些国家仍然固守冷战思维、军事同盟，把自身绝对安全置于他国安全和国际社会普遍安全之上，其结果只能是使这个世界更不安全。习近平指出："我们要摒弃一切形式的冷战思维，树立共同、综合、合作、可持续安全的新观念。"① 这就要求在国际法上，切实落实《联合国宪章》的规定，充分发挥联合国及其安理会在止战维和方面的核心作用，遵守并发展安全领域的国际规则，反对动辄诉诸武力或以武力相威胁，反对简单地"以暴制暴"、"以战止战"，而要以和平、法治、对话和建设性的方式，不断推进安全领域的合作。

共同繁荣是构建人类命运共同体的物质基础，也是国际法的根本目标。当今国际格局正加速演变，新兴市场国家和发展中国家崛起已经成为不可阻挡的历史潮流，经济全球化、社会信息化极大解决和发展了社会生产力，给全世界创造了前所未有的发展机遇。但南北差距依然存在，发展鸿沟依然巨大。一方面，在联合国主导下，国际社会制定和实施了千年发展目标和 2030 年可持续发展议程。另一方面，在一些国家出现了单边主义、实用主义、贸易保护主义和"逆全球化思潮"，他们仍然推行赢者通吃、零和博弈、强买强卖、唯我独尊的处事方式，给国际经济发展前景蒙上阴影。习近平指出，开放带来进步，封闭导致落后。重回以邻为壑的老路，不仅无法摆脱自身危机和衰退，而且会收窄世界经济共同空间，导致"双输"的局面。② 中国提出构建人类命运共同体，就是主张各国"要同舟共济，促进贸易和投资自由化便利化，推动经济全球化朝着更加开放、包容、普惠、平衡、共赢的方向发展"。③ 这就要求在国际法上，要创造和维护良好的制度环境，推动变革全球治理体系中不公正不合理的安排，通过国际法治，实现权利平等、机会平等、规则平等；要维护世界贸易组织规则，支持开放、透明、包容、非歧视的多边贸易体制，推动建设开放型世界经济；切实落实千年发展目标和 2030 年可持续发展议程，使发展成果惠

---

① 《习近平谈治国理政》（第二卷），外文出版社，2017，第 523 页。

② 习近平：《中国发展新起点 全球增长新蓝图——在二十国集团工商峰会开幕式上的主旨演讲》，《人民日报》2016 年 9 月 4 日，第 3 版。

③ 习近平：《决胜全面建成小康社会 夺取新时代中国特色社会主义伟大胜利——在中国共产党第十九次全国代表大会上的报告》，人民出版社，2017，第 59 页。

及世界各国人民。

开放包容是构建人类命运共同体的文明纽带，也是国际法的思想根基。在相当长的历史发展阶段，国际关系和国际法呈现相当严重的“西方中心主义”，非西方国家的文明受到歧视、排斥。《联合国宪章》确立了尊重各国不分政治制度、宗教或意识形态，均享有平等权利的原则，联合国教科文组织通过的《保护和促进文化表现形式多样性公约》进一步确认了文化多样性的重要意义。但实践中，“文明冲突论”仍然大行其道，意识形态领域的斗争愈趋激烈。一些国家以社会制度和意识形态划线，将不满足其所谓“文明标准”的国家单方面认定为“失败的国家”、“独裁的国家”，排除在所谓“自由主义”秩序之外，通过歪曲解释国际法或炮制新的国际法理论，粗暴干涉有关国家内政。事实上，在对待不同文明的态度上做不到开放包容，而是采取居高临下、唯我正统的态度，就不可能真正做到相互尊重、平等合作，并且会妨碍国家间正常关系的发展，甚至会加剧国际和地区冲突。习近平指出：“文明没有高下、优劣之分，只有特色、地域之别。文明差异不应该成为世界冲突的根源，而应该成为人类文明进步的动力。……不同文明要取长补短、共同进步，让文明交流互鉴成为推动人类社会进步的动力、维护世界和平的纽带。”① 各国只有在真正平等、相互尊重、取长补短、求同存异的基础上形成协商民主的氛围，才能真正做到共同推进国际法治，共同构建人类命运共同体。

清洁美丽是构建人类命运共同体的生态追求，也是国际法的前沿领域。地球是人类赖以生存的共同家园。环境问题是全球性挑战，需要各国携手合作，共同应对。建设生态文明和清洁美丽的世界、维护完善的地球生态系统是人类社会的共同福祉。实现可持续发展、共建地球美丽家园是国际环境治理的重要课题，特别是要通过国际环境法规则体系，在利用、保护和改善环境问题方面加强规范和协调，推动人与自然和谐发展。国际上，从 1987 年可持续发展概念提出，到里约环境与发展宣言、联合国千年发展目标，再到 2030 年可持续发展议程，全球生态文明建设理念持续发展演进，不断深入人心。2030 年可持续发展目标为构建清洁美丽的世界提出了全球纲领。气候变化、生物多样性、防治荒漠化、化学品管理等环境领

---

① 《习近平谈治国理政》（第二卷），外文出版社，2017，第 544 页。

域的国际条约，为建设清洁美丽的世界提供了可操作的国际规范。中国自古就有“天人合一”、和谐共生的观念。中国生态文明理念具有深厚的文化底蕴和悠久的历史传承，并在中国特色社会主义理论和实践中衍生出新内涵，迸发出新活力。中国立足可持续发展内在需求，采取切实政策行动，大力推进国内生态文明建设。同时，中国展现积极负责任国家形象，建设性参与国际合作和多边进程，对气候变化《巴黎协定》的达成和生效作出历史性贡献，就国际环境治理规则体系提出中国方案，“成为全球生态文明建设的重要参与者、贡献者、引领者”。[①] 习近平指出：“建设生态文明关乎人类未来。国际社会应该携手同行，共谋全球生态文明建设之路，牢固树立尊重自然、顺应自然、保护自然的意识，坚持走绿色、低碳、循环、可持续发展之路。”[②] 将清洁美丽作为人类命运共同体的核心要素之一，呼应了各国人民共建美丽家园的迫切愿望，契合了国际法发展的前沿和最新趋势。当今，有关环境和可持续发展等领域的国际规则制定方兴未艾，日益成为大国博弈新焦点和“造法”新阵地。中国主张应坚持“国家主权原则”、“共同但有区别的责任原则”、“国际合作原则”等国际法原则，坚持《巴黎协定》等国际环境条约达成的共识，不断丰富新的国际法规则，推动国际环境治理和生态文明建设取得新进展。

三 构建人类命运共同体思想是对当代国际法的弘扬和发展

推动构建人类命运共同体，不是要“另起炉灶”再造一个新的国际法体系，而是在继承中创新，在创新中发展，推动国际法规则与时俱进，适应人类社会发展的需要。

（一）构建人类命运共同体思想是对和平共处五项原则等国际法基本原则的继承和弘扬

60 多年前，中国与印度、缅甸共同倡导提出互相尊重主权和领土完

① 《党的十九大报告辅导读本》，人民出版社，2017，第 6 页。
② 《习近平谈治国理政》（第二卷），外文出版社，2017，第 525 页。

整、互不侵犯、互不干涉内政、平等互利、和平共处五项原则，因应了广大发展中国家反帝、反殖、反霸的时代要求，反映了发展中国家追求独立、自主、自强、发展的普遍诉求，开启了不同意识形态和社会制度国家之间交往的合作旅程。60多年来，和平共处五项原则已成为中国独立自主和平外交政策的基石，同时也被国际社会广泛认同和遵循，成为指导国与国关系的基本准则和国际法基本原则。习近平指出："新形势下，和平共处五项原则的精神不是过时了，而是历久弥新；和平共处五项原则的意义不是淡化了，而是历久弥深；和平共处五项原则的作用不是削弱了，而是历久弥坚。"[①] 推动构建人类命运共同体，必须以和平共处五项原则作为基本遵循，并赋予其新的时代意义。如果说60多年前提出和平共处五项原则时，强调的侧重点在于几个"互"字，重点是不同国家相互之间"共存"、"共处"，反映的主要还是新生社会主义国家和弱小发展中国家对于正常存续的起码要求的话，那么构建人类命运共同体思想则是重点强调一个"共"字，即要求在共存的基础上，追求共同利益，承担共同责任，加强合作，实现共进。从这个意义上说，人类命运共同体语境下的和平共处五项原则，是60多年前提出的该原则的升级版，是站在新的时代前沿，提出了更高层次的追求。正如中国外交部前副部长刘振民指出："五项原则作为一个开放包容的国际法原则体系，60年来不断被赋予新的内涵，从'和平共处'到'和平发展'，到'和谐世界'，再到'合作共赢'的'命运共同体'，既有传承，更有发展，必将以其强大的生命力和广泛的适用性，继续为世界的和平与发展作出重要贡献。"[②]

公认的国际法基本原则还体现在《联合国宪章》、1970年《关于各国依联合国宪章建立友好关系及合作之国际法原则之宣言》、1974年《各国经济权利和义务宪章》等文件中。特别是《联合国宪章》建立了以联合国为核心的多边主义国际秩序，确立了以安理会为核心的集体安全机制，确立了尊重国家主权和领土完整、主权平等、不干涉内政、和平解决争端等

① 习近平：《弘扬和平共处五项原则　建设合作共赢美好世界——在和平共处五项原则发表60周年纪念大会上的讲话》（2014年6月28日），新华网，http://www.xinhuanet.com/politics/2014-06/28/c_1111364206.htm，最后访问日期：2018年9月13日。

② 刘振民：《遵循五项原则携手构建命运共同体》，载中华人民共和国外交部条约法律司编《中国国际法实践案例选编》，世界知识出版社，2018，第135页。

重要原则，形成了战后国际关系的基本行为规范。当前，《联合国宪章》所确立的国际秩序框架、安全机制、行为规范和价值理念依然有效，依然是现代国际法和国际关系的基石。习近平指出，“当今世界发生的各种对抗和不公，不是因为联合国宪章宗旨和原则过时了，而恰恰是由于这些宗旨和原则未能得到有效履行”。[①] 近年来发生在伊拉克、利比亚、叙利亚等国的事件充分表明，强权政治仍大行其道，国际法基本原则并未得到很好的遵守。在国际社会仍由主权国家组成、国家间仍存在各种差异和利益分歧的现实下，国家主权原则和不干涉内政原则仍然是国际法最重要的原则。倡导构建人类命运共同体，不是要贬损这些原则，不是要建立“世界政府”，更不是为西方鼓吹“人道主义干预”、滥用“保护的责任”背书，而是正本清源，拨乱反正，在坚持主权平等基础上，尊重文明多样性，尊重各国自主选择的发展道路，倡导国际法基本原则的统一普遍适用。同时，该坚持的坚持，该改写的改写，该纠偏的纠偏，该创新的创新，突出对人类社会整体性的关注，扩大利益交汇点，不断充实新内涵，以建设性方式促进各国开展合作，共建更加美好的世界。

（二）构建人类命运共同体思想是对国际法上共同体理论及实践的借鉴和升华

一般而言，共同体是指人们在共同条件下结成的集体。在人类生活的不同层面、不同领域、不同范围，都会形成各种各样的共同体。[②] 国际法上，共同体思想久已有之。康德（Kant）早在1795年发表的《永久和平论》中就提出：“国际法应以自由国家的联盟为基础。”[③] 他理想中的“联盟”实际上就是后来欧洲经济共同体、欧共体、欧盟的实践。[④] 1944年联合国成立前夕，国际法学家凯尔森（Kelsen）提出，为了解决持久和平问题，需要在国际法框架中，通过一个具有一定程度的集中化，但不超越

---

① 《习近平在中共中央政治局第二十七次集体学习时强调：推动全球治理体制更加公正更加合理　为我国发展和世界和平创造有利条件》（2015年10月12日），《人民日报》2015年10月14日，第1版。

② 刘建飞：《人类命运共同体的现实与未来》，《学习时报》2018年6月11日，第1版。

③ 〔德〕伊曼努尔·康德：《永久和平论》，何兆武译，上海人民出版社，2005，第19页。

④ 曾令良：《欧洲联盟法总论：以〈欧洲宪法条约〉为新视角》，武汉大学出版社，2007，第28页。

“国际共同体”的通常模式之组织。[①] 联合国就是这个“国际共同体”的载体。这种共同体理论和实践在冷战和单一霸权时代被严重扭曲，成为西方国家推行其价值观、干涉别国内政的借口和工具。

随着人类社会的进步，国际共同体的含义也随之丰富和发展。联合国前秘书长安南（Annan）在1999年一次非政府组织会议上发表题为“国际共同体的含义”的演讲，从人类的共同机遇、共同挑战以及国际法作用等角度进行了阐述。[②] 2012年党的十八大报告首次提出“要倡导人类命运共同体意识”。5年多来，习近平在多个重要国际场合阐述构建人类命运共同体的理念，使之日益深入人心。党的十九大报告又将“推动构建人类命运共同体”作为新时代坚持和发展中国特色社会主义的基本方略之一，全面阐述了其内涵。可以看出，构建人类命运共同体思想，汲取了传统“国际共同体”理念的进步因素，是对“国际共同体”理念的重大创新，也必然带来相关国际法的巨大飞跃。由于构建人类命运共同体思想的先进性和感召力，在其提出后的短短几年里，已得到国际社会广泛认同和响应，并已多次被写入联合国决议。[③]

（三）从国际法角度看，构建人类命运共同体思想具有鲜明的时代性、系统性和实践性

构建人类命运共同体思想的时代性，集中体现在它对“人类命运”的关切和聚焦。当今世界，没有哪个国家能够独自应对人类面临的各种挑

---

① Hans Kelsen, *Peace Through Law* (Chapel Hill: The University of North Carolina Press, 1944), pp. 12 – 13.

② 安南在演讲中说：“是什么使我们连结成为一个国际共同体？宽泛而言，是因为我们有一个为所有人寻求更美好世界的共识，正如《联合国宪章》中所载明的；是因为我们面对气候变化和大规模杀伤性武器的共同的脆弱感；是因为国际法框架；是因为感受到共同的机遇，这使我们建立共同市场以及联合国等机构。联合起来，我们更强大。”参见Secretary-General, Examines “Meaning of International Community” in Address to DPI/NGO Conference, http://www.un.org/press/en/1999/19990915.sgsm7133.doc.html，最后访问日期：2018年8月20日。

③ 包括2017年2月联合国社会发展委员会一致通过的“非洲发展新伙伴关系的社会层面”决议（后由经社理事会通过）；2017年3月联合国安理会一致通过的关于阿富汗问题第2344号决议；2017年3月联合国人权理事会通过的关于“经济、社会、文化权利”和“粮食权”两个决议；2017年11月第72届联大一委通过的“防止外空军备竞赛进一步切实措施”和“不首先在外空放置武器”两份决议；2018年3月联合国人权理事会通过的“在人权领域促进合作共赢”决议等。

战，也没有哪个国家能够退回到自我封闭的孤岛。那种以邻为壑、零和博弈的旧思维，越来越显现出其落后性、反动性。特别是随着国际力量对比发生深刻变化，新兴市场国家和一大批发展中国家快速发展，在追求本国利益时兼顾他国合理关切，在谋求本国发展中促进各国共同发展，建立国际政治经济新秩序，已成为当代国际社会的主旋律。构建人类命运共同体思想顺应了时代呼唤，直指人类社会面临的问题，着眼于揭示规律，破解难题。第一次在“共同体”之前冠以“人类命运”的定性，准确界定了新形势下建设“国际共同体”的出发点和落脚点，符合马克思主义科学原理。“马克思主义博大精深，归根到底就是一句话，为人类求解放。……马克思主义之所以具有跨越国度、跨越时代的影响力，就是因为它植根人民之中，指明了依靠人民推动历史前进的人间正道。”① 晚近国际法的发展已经呈现出以人类为中心的趋势，比如人权保障制度的发展、人类共同继承财产等国际法律制度的确立、全球环境保护国际法律制度的日益丰富等。通过国际法对国家行为进行规范，归根到底是为了使人类免于匮乏，免于恐惧，有尊严地生活。这里讲的“人类”，既是指向每一个人，更是将人类社会作为一个整体。“命运”则是指共同的前途（shared future）。将全人类的共同前途作为国际共同体建设的总目标和总依归，这就超越了文明冲突、冷战思维、零和博弈等旧观念，站在了时代发展和人类进步的制高点上，体现了当代国际法的先进价值。同时，从文化底蕴看，它熔铸“世界大同”、“天人合一”等中华优秀传统文化思想，与西方人文主义精神等进步思想相融通，找到了东西方思想共振区、共鸣点、公约数，易于为国际社会理解认同。

构建人类命运共同体思想的系统性，体现为它作为一个科学完备的体系，对国际法带来的全方位、全局性影响。首先，人类命运共同体的建构要从“价值共同体、利益共同体、责任共同体”三个维度入手。② 而不论是价值、利益还是责任，都体现为国际法所界定的国家间权利义务的划分和对人类共同利益的保障。其次，构建人类命运共同体思想中的“持久和

---

① 参见习近平《在纪念马克思诞辰200周年大会上的讲话》，《人民日报》2018年5月5日，第2版。

② 参见李适时《夯实人类命运共同体的国际法治基础》，载《中国国际法年刊（2017）》，法律出版社，2018，第18页。

平、普遍安全、共同繁荣、开放包容、清洁美丽”五大要素，涉及政治、安全、经济、文化、生态等各个领域，涵盖了人类生活的方方面面。将这五个方面作为一个整体并列，又揭示出其彼此之间相互渗透、相互影响、相互联系、互为因果的紧密联系和务必整体推进、协调并进的实现路径。从国际法角度看，当代国际法已形成了较为完备的体系，但需要应对的新问题仍层出不穷。解决任何一个领域的问题都不可能采取孤立的、割裂的规则体系，而要彼此兼顾，综合统筹，协调并进。再次，实现上述目标还有赖于民主立法、善意遵法和公正司法的有机统一。习近平指出：“世界命运应该由各国共同掌握，国际规则应该由各国共同书写，全球事务应该由各国共同治理，发展成果应该由各国共同分享”；[①] 法律的生命在于付诸实施，“在国际社会中，法律应该是共同的准绳”，“适用法律不能有双重标准”，“各国都应该依法行使权利，反对歪曲国际法，反对以‘法治之名’行侵害他国正当权益、破坏和平稳定之实”；[②] “各国和国际司法机构应该确保国际法平等统一适用，不能搞双重标准，不能‘合则用、不合则弃’，真正做到‘无偏无党，王道荡荡’。[③] 最后，构建人类命运共同体思想的主体是国际社会全体成员。这一思想由中国提出，但无法由中国独力推动，更不能强加于人，而是需要世界各国不分大小、贫富、强弱，遵循“共商共建共享”原则，携起手来，平等参与。同时，大国往往是决定战争与和平的关键因素，也对地区和世界和平与发展负有更大责任，因此在构建人类命运共同体过程中，大国应该作出更大的贡献，而不能搞唯我独尊、恃强凌弱的霸道。[④]

构建人类命运共同体思想的实践性，表明这一思想不是停留在理论和概念上的空洞口号，而是与实践紧密结合的。毛泽东指出：“理论的基础是实践，又转过来为实践服务。判定认识或理论之是否真理，不是依主观

---

① 《习近平谈治国理政》（第二卷），外文出版社，2017，第540页。

② 习近平：《弘扬和平共处五项原则　建设合作共赢美好世界——在和平共处五项原则发表60周年纪念大会上的讲话》（2014年6月28日），新华网 http://www.xinhuanet.com/politics/2014-06/28/c_1111364206.htm，最后访问日期：2018年9月13日。

③ 《习近平谈治国理政》（第二卷），外文出版社，2017，第540页。

④ 杨洁篪：《推动构建人类命运共同体》，载《党的十九大报告辅导读本》，人民出版社，2017，第91—92页。

上觉得如何而定，而是依客观上社会实践的结果如何而定。”[①] 党的十八大以来，中国围绕推动构建人类命运共同体，率先垂范，采取了许多有力举措，体现了负责任的大国担当。中国提出一系列外交新理念，包括深入阐述中国梦的世界意义、建设全球伙伴关系、构建以合作共赢为核心的新型国际关系以及新发展观、新安全观、正确义利观、全球治理观、国际法治观等，引领了时代潮流；中国与30多个国家和区域确认共建命运共同体，与100多个国家和地区建立不同形式的伙伴关系，已形成遍布全球的“朋友圈”；中国倡导成立亚洲基础设施投资银行和金砖国家新开发银行，在应对气候变化等国际谈判中发挥积极建设性作用，深度参与全球治理体系变革，推动人类命运共同体理念向规则和制度转化，均取得重要阶段性成果；中国发起成立的上海合作组织成立17年来，坚持践行互信、互利、平等、协商、尊重多样文明、谋求共同发展的“上海精神”，已在多个领域取得重大成果，发展成为当今世界幅员最广、人口最多、潜力巨大的综合性国际组织，为构建人类命运共同体发挥了重要的先导作用；[②] 中国提出的“一带一路”倡议作为当今世界规模最大的国际合作平台和各方普遍欢迎的全球公共产品，成为人类命运共同体建设的重要实践平台。“一带一路”建设已经在许多国家取得实实在在的成果，100多个国家和国际组织积极支持参与，一大批有影响力的标志性项目成功落地，为中国同世界各国共同发展注入了新动力，[③] 给各国人民带来了看得见摸得着的好处，也增进了各国对构建人类命运共同体思想的认知和认同，显示了这一思想的强大感召力和实践指导意义。

四 高度重视运筹国际法，助力推动构建人类命运共同体

推动构建人类命运共同体，是新时代中国外交工作的总目标、总纲

① 《毛泽东著作选编》，中央党校出版社，2002，第73页。

② 2018年6月10日举行的上海合作组织青岛峰会通过的《上海合作组织成员国元首理事会青岛宣言》载明，“确立构建人类命运共同体的共同理念”，使之成为上海合作组织成员国最重要的政治共识和努力目标。参见《人民日报》2018年6月11日，第3版。

③ 参见王毅《坚定不移走和平发展道路推动构建人类命运共同体》，《人民日报》2018年3月14日，第15版。

领、总战略。它具有时代先进性，蕴含强大真理力量，发展前景光明。将这一思想理念转化为国际共识，贯彻到具体实践，需要找准切入点和抓手，多策并举，善做善成。“天下从事者，不可以无法仪，无法仪而其事能成者无有也。”① 除从政治、经济、理论、宣传等方面着力外，妥善运筹好国际法方面的工作，是必不可少的一环。

（一）高举国际法旗帜，进一步夯实推动构建人类命运共同体的国际法基础

必须看到，尽管历史车轮滚滚向前，但世界的转型过渡不会一帆风顺。国际秩序大变革大调整大发展，不仅将使世界面临的不确定性、不稳定性日益突出，也将加剧新兴大国与守成大国围绕规则和制度性权力的较量。当前，逆全球化、民粹主义、贸易保护主义、国家中心主义等思潮盛行，地缘热点和全球性挑战此起彼伏，这都是世界进入转型过渡期的集中表现。我国推动构建人类命运共同体面临严峻复杂形势。一些国家动辄拿所谓“基于规则的秩序”说事，将它们单方面的国际法主张强行贴上“普世”标签，指责中国“不守规矩”，展开“舆论战”，并借炮制“南海仲裁案”等挑起“法律战”，侵害中国利益，抹黑中国形象。越是面对这种形势，我们越要坚定信心，越要把国际法的旗帜举得更高。在推动构建人类命运共同体实践中，坚定维护以《联合国宪章》宗旨和原则为基础的国际秩序，坚持和平共处五项原则等国际法基本原则和国际关系基本准则，旗帜鲜明地反对选择性适用或曲解、滥用规则，树立中国是国际法真正的、坚定的维护者和建设者的正义形象。

（二）以构建人类命运共同体思想为统领，大力推动理论创新，逐步建立起中国特色的国际法理论体系

进一步深入挖掘构建人类命运共同体思想在国际法上的科学内涵和指导意义，与中国特色的发展观、安全观、合作观、文明观、全球治理观相结合，总结归纳出科学完整的理论体系和规则体系。主动将国际法、国际秩序以及相应的制度性权力、国家形象、软实力作为统筹考虑国内国际两

① 参见《墨子·法仪》。

个大局的重要方面，在更加广阔的层面考虑自身利益，区分当前利益和长远利益、局部利益和核心利益，落实正确义利观，在切实维护国家核心利益的前提下推进国际社会整体利益。在坚持主权平等和不干涉内政原则的前提下，加强对建设性介入等重大国际法问题的研究，为我国更好地参与解决国际和地区热点问题提供有力的法律支撑。研究解决将国际法纳入国内法律体系的问题，巩固中国重诺守信的良好形象。以我为主、兼收并蓄、突出特色，努力以中国智慧、中国实践为世界法治文明建设作出贡献；在中国特色国际法理论体系的构建过程中，对世界上的优秀法治文明成果，既要积极吸收借鉴，也要加以甄别，有选择地吸收和转化，不能囫囵吞枣、照搬照抄。①

（三）全方位深度参与国际规则制定，在全球治理体系变革中进一步发挥引领作用

全球治理关系国内改革发展，关系我国实现民族复兴的外部环境，也是推动构建人类命运共同体的重要方面。在更广领域更高水平参与全球治理，继续发挥大国作用，积极参与全球治理体系改革和建设，推动国际秩序向更加公正合理的方向发展。始终坚持和维护以联合国、世界贸易组织等多边机制为核心的全球治理体系，积极推动全球经济治理体系变革，增强发展中国家的代表性和发言权。更好运筹上海合作组织等区域合作组织的作用，并根据需要和条件不断创新国际合作机制和平台，使其在推进具体领域合作方面发挥更大作用。继续发挥在全球气候治理领域的引领作用，加大参与深海、极地、外空、网络等新兴领域全球治理和规则制定，将“共商共建共享”的全球治理观落到实处。大力推进“一带一路”规则体系建设和法治保障工作，推动与有关国家的双边、多边合作条约法律体系的完善，预防、解决“一带一路”建设过程中涉及投资、贸易、劳工标准等可能出现的争端，确保“一带一路”建设在法治基础上行稳致远，进而为人类命运共同体的构建树立成功典范。

---

① 参见《习近平在中国政法大学考察时强调：立德树人德法兼修抓好法治人才培养 励志勤学刻苦磨炼促进青年成长进步》，《人民日报》2017 年 5 月 4 日，第 1 版。

（四）统筹国内国际两类规则，用好国际法手段，维护和拓展国家利益

构建人类命运共同体的五大方面内容与国内经济建设、政治建设、文化建设、社会建设和生态文明建设“五位一体”总体布局高度契合，是国内发展战略的国际版。应当牢固树立国际法工作为国内改革发展稳定服务的意识，努力实现为“五位一体”提供服务的全覆盖。坚决维护国家主权、安全和发展利益，打赢我国发展进程中可能遇到的各类“法律战”，做到政治上有利、道义上有理、法律上有据。

（五）加强国际交流和传播，使基于人类命运共同体思想的中国国际法观更加深入人心

人类命运共同体需要世界各国共同构建，与之相关的国际法也不能搞孤芳自赏、自说自话。应当妥善处理好“中国特色”与“世界公认”的关系，在对外阐释与人类命运共同体有关的国际法理论时，运用世界通用的国际法话语，言之有物，扎实有据。同时，通过政府和学术界等多层面的国际交流与研讨，争取形成最广泛的共识和共同国际法立场。人类命运共同体总体上是一个新概念，其国际法内涵还需进一步阐述厘清，由中国倡议转变为国际共识不可能一蹴而就。对此，我们既要有战略信心，也要有战略耐心，不强加于人，不急于求成，采取开放包容、灵活务实的态度，尽可能通过沟通交流，逐步增信释疑，凝聚共识，争取最大公约数。①

（责任编辑：郝鲁怡）

（本文原载于《国际法研究》2018 年第 5 期）

① 例如 2018 年 6 月通过的联合国外空会议 50 周年纪念大会成果文件《规划未来外空全球治理发展方向》指出：“在和平探索和利用外层空间领域实现命运的共同愿景（shared vision for the future），为全人类谋福利与利益。”虽然未直接采用“人类命运共同体”的表述，但实质意思一样。

本体、对象与范围[*]

——国际组织法学科基本问题之探讨

饶戈平[**]

一 引言

国际组织是国家间多边合作的产物，推动和加速了全球化时代的到来。所谓全球化时代，在很大程度上也可以说是一个国际组织的时代。国际组织，特别是政府间国际组织，是国际社会组织化、全球化的载体，是国际社会法律秩序和国际体制的组织形态。当前世界上各类国际组织或机构的数目已接近7万个，国际组织活跃的领域覆盖了国际社会的方方面面，可以说是无所不至，无处不在。世界上重大问题的解决几乎都离不开相关国际组织的作用。

一方面，国际组织对主权国家的渗透程度和影响力度日益加深，国际组织的活动不仅对一国政府的对外政策和国际法实践，而且对国家内部的社会生活，诸如贸易、环境、个人权利保护等问题也都有深刻的影响。另一方面，国际组织是一个国家必须善加利用的活生生的国际资源。参与国际组织是国家对外关系、外交政策的重要组成部分，国际组织所代表的国际社会公共利益，也包含了各国的国家利益。一个大国、强国的作用，很大程度上体现在其动员、影响、利用国际机制的能力。实践表明，有效借助国际组织是西方大国建构其全球影响力和话语权的必由之路。不妨说，对国际组织的认识、参与和利

---

* 本文缘起得益于与陈一峰博士的多次深度讨论，谨此表示真诚的谢意。

** 饶戈平，北京大学法学院教授。

用程度，是衡量一个国家对外关系是否成熟、是否明智和有力度的重要标志。

国际法学界对于国际组织的关注，始于19世纪后期在欧洲出现的“国际行政联盟”，此后又有对国际联盟和国际劳工组织等国际组织进行的专门研究。但是直到第二次世界大战以后，国际组织才呈现出雨后春笋般的发展态势，学界从20世纪五六十年代开始才跳出对个别国际组织的关注，尝试对国际组织整体开展一般化的研究，从理论上对国际组织的组织特性加以重视，并使得国际组织法成长为现代国际法学科的一个重要分支。鲍维特（Bowett）于1963年初版的《国际组织法》（*The Law of International Institutions*）和谢默思（Schermers）1972年初版的《国际机构法》（*International Institutional Law*）①，可视作国际组织法学科确立的重要标志。在全球化不断深化的今天，国际组织法研究也进一步拓展和丰富，不仅鲍氏和谢氏的教科书在保持再版和更新，新的国际组织法教科书也不断在欧洲和美国问世，为国际组织法的研究增添了活力。② 以国际组织法作为专门研究领域的《国际组织法评论》杂志也于2004年问世，成为汇聚和推动国际组织法研究的重要平台。

30多年来，我国学界、实务界对国际组织的认识程度有了很大提升。国际组织法研究从无到有，从了无生息到崭露头角，逐渐发展起来。一些高校设置了国际组织法的相关课程，一些部委设置了专责国际组织的机

① 参见 Derek W. Bowett, *The Law of International Institutions*（Stevens & Sons Limited, 1963）; Henry G. Schermers, *International Institutional Law*（Leiden: A. W. Sijthoff）, the first two volumes（Structure, Functioning and Legal Order）published in 1972 and a third volume（Teaching and Materials）in 1974。在此之前，英国国际法学者、国际劳工局局长詹克斯（Jenks）于1962年也出版了其专著《国际组织法》（*The Proper Law of International Organizations*），侧重对国际组织内部行政管理（从公法的角度）、组织外部交往（从私法的角度）作了研究，但是从国际公法本身对国际组织的分析只有很少的篇幅。这种研究视角并未成为后续国际组织法研究的主流方法。参见 C. Wilfred Jenks, *The Proper Law of International Organizations*（London: Stevens & Sons Limited, 1962）。

② C. F. Amerasinghe, *Principles of the Institutional Law of International Organizations*（Cambridge: Cambridge University Press, 2nd Revised Edition, 2005, 初版于1996年）; Jan Klabebrs, *An Introduction to International Organizations Law*（Cambridge: Cambridge University Press, 3rd edn., 2015, 初版于2003年）。美国学界对国际组织法教材也有所发展，柯吉斯教授的国际组织法最早出版于1977年，近来美国学界又开始了对国际组织法新的研究兴趣。Frederic Kirgis, *International Organizations in Their Legal Setting*（West Publishing Co. 2nd edn., 1993, 初版于1977年）; Michael P. Scharf and Paul R. Williams, *The Law of International Organizations: Problems and Materials*（Carolina Academic Press, 3rd edn., 2013, 初版于2001年）。

构，开始有了一批关注国际组织法的学者和专家。可以说，国际组织作为国际法不可或缺的组成部分，在教学与实践中都有了较为充分的展示，学界比以往任何时候都更加关注国际组织法这门学科，诚堪嘉许。

但是整体来看，我国学界对国际组织的研究和教学还是比较薄弱、比较落后的。不论是就整体研究、对基本理论和基本问题的研究而言，还是就类别组织、个别组织的深入研究而言，大多数工作似乎还停留在对知识的介绍、章程的诠释以及对个别、局部问题的分析上，其成果数量和质量都难如人愿。最明显的是，在国际组织法学科的研究对象、研究范围、研究方法、核心内容等问题上，国内学界的认识还是比较模糊、薄弱的，讨论得也不充分。倘若对这些问题缺乏清晰的认识，很难设想能够把握住这门学科的精髓，而对这些问题的回答，不仅需要密切跟踪国际组织的发展现实，需要对国际组织法这一学科的基本框架和方法作深层次的思考，而且为适应我国认识和参与国际组织的实际需要，也应该在国际学术讨论中表达中国学界的思考和声音。

二　国际组织法的研究对象：对国际组织的再定义

我们通常可以把国际组织法理解为用以规范和调整国际组织的建立和运作的所有法律原则、规则、章程和制度的总称，虽然学界对此存在不同的认识。对国际组织的定义问题，不单纯是一个概念上的争论，更重要的是表明了对国际组织法这一学科的研究对象和范围的判断和界定。对于什么是国际组织，哪些是构成国际组织必不可少的要素，尚没有一个被普遍接受的定义。①。总结西方学界的主流意见，一般认为，一个国际组织需要

① 作为国际法委员会“国际组织责任”特别报告员，意大利国际法教授加亚（Gaja）在其第一次报告中指出，之所以“就国际组织无法达成一个令人满意的定义，主要困难是当下被认为是‘国际性’的组织具有极大的多样性”。参见 First Report of the Special Rapporteur, Giorgio Gaja，A/CN. 4/532（March 26，2003）。最终国际法委员会在其“国际组织责任条款草案”第 2 条采纳了如下工作定义：“为本条款的目的，‘国际组织’是指根据条约或受国际法制约的其他文书建立的具有独立国际法律人格的组织。国际组织的成员除国家以外，还可包括其他实体。”这个定义强调了国际组织须具有国际法律人格，主要是考虑到不具有国际法律人格的国际组织难以在国际法上承受国际责任，此类国际组织的责任问题不必适用该条款草案。条款草案文本，参见联大决议 A/Res/66/100（2011 年 12 月 9 日）。

具备以下要素：主要成员是主权国家，以国际条约为基础，具备自己的独立意志，并设有常设机构。[①] 此种定义下的国际组织，确切地说，仅仅能够涵盖现今的协定性政府间组织。传统上，国际组织法的研究对象主要是国家通过条约成立的政府间国际组织，因此，协定性政府间组织也就习惯性地构成整个国际组织法研究的基础模型。

从历史上看，国际组织法的研究的确始于对协定性政府间组织的关注。国际联盟、国际劳工组织和联合国等典型的协定性国际组织，为国际组织法的发展和成熟积累了大量的研究素材和实践经验。协定性政府间组织的组织特点非常鲜明，具有国际法律人格，构成自成一类的国际法主体，受国际法规范；有利于学界借鉴国际法学的知识和话语体系，从国际法主体、国际法渊源、特权与豁免、条约法等问题对此类国际组织加以研究。不可否认的是，协定性政府间国际组织始终是国际多边合作中最为重要、最值得关注的一种形态。

同时值得注意的是，二战后，特别是冷战结束后，国际组织整体呈现出井喷式的发展态势，然而协定性国际组织数目的增长速度却在放慢甚至相对萎缩。从数量上看，协定性政府间组织曾在 20 世纪 80 年代中期发展到其最高峰，1985 年为 387 个。此后协定性政府间组织的发展就开始进入缓慢下降的趋势，到 2002 年降为 232 个，到 2011 年回升为 251 个，数量较其最高峰而言减少了约三分之一。[②] 相反，其他形态的政府间组织却风生水起，蓬勃发展。例如在人权领域，各类条约机构已经成为推动和监督国家履约、对人权条约进行解释和适用的重要机制，其数目成倍地增长。再如环境领域，1972 年以后，缔约方大会制度也逐渐成为国际环境条约所普遍采纳的制度。

总结来说，在过去三四十年的国际实践中，产生并活跃着大量非传统

---

① 西方学界对于国际组织的定义和构成国际组织的要素意见并不完全一致。有代表性的讨论可以参见 Philippe Sands & Pierre Klein, *Bowett's Law of International Institutions* (London: Sweet & Maxwell, 6th edn., 2009), pp. 15 - 16; Felice Morgenstern, *Legal Problems of International Organizations* (Cambridge: Grotius Publications, 1986), pp. 19 - 26; Henry G. Schermers & Niels M. Blokker, *International Institutional Law* (Leiden: Martinus Nijhoff Publisher, 5th Revised Edition, 2011), pp. 30 - 47。

② Union of International Associations (ed.), *Yearbook of International Organizations* (Brill, 48th edn., 2011/2012), pp. 33 - 35.

的政府间国际组织形态。这些国际组织形态，可以大致归纳为如下四种情况。[①] 一是国家间集团型组织（即 G 型组织），典型的如八国集团（G8）、二十国集团（G20）等。在某种程度上，亚太经济合作组织（APEC）也属于此类组织形态。此类组织由国家参与，其行为方式也受到国际法约束，虽然机制化程度较低，但是在组织化和机构化的层面上明显高于定期会议制度。正是这种组织化的特征，才有在克里米亚事件之后，美国等西方国家中止了俄罗斯在八国集团中的成员资格。二是条约机构，这是最大量也是最活跃的一类新生的政府间组织形态。国家为了应对国际社会的特定问题，制定了一些多边条约，同时附带性地成立了以执行、监督和落实条约为目的的机构。条约机构多见于贸易、环境、人权、电讯等领域，其数目数以千计。三是协定性组织中具有对外职能的内部机构。这主要是指具有普遍性管理职能的国际组织中的有一定对外职能的内部机构，例如作为联合国主要机构之一的国际法院，作为联合国大会附属机构的联合国开发计划署、联合国环境规划署、联合国人权事务高级专员办公室等以及欧盟下属的欧盟委员会等等。这些内部机构几乎是以独立活动的身份出现在国际舞台，尽管它们只是特定国际组织的一个内部机构。权威的《国际组织年刊》（*Yearbook of International Organizations*）往往把它们作为一个独立实体统计进国际组织的数目之中。四是国际组织间的联合机构或项目，例如联合国艾滋病防治署等。近年来，国际组织之间尝试着通过建立联合机构或者项目来处理国际社会的问题。一个问题的解决往往涉及国际社会的方方面面，不光是单个国际组织，还连带其他政府间和非政府间组织，甚至还有特定国家。通过这种多样化的多边合作形式，往往可以形成国际社会的合力，避免多头管辖和不必要竞争，从而更好更有效地处理问题。当然，上述四种非传统形态的国际组织之外，肯定还存在其他有待发掘的形态，需要我们继续探索。

这些非传统的政府间组织形态在实际上适应和满足了国际多边合作的社会需求，极大地丰富并扩展了国际组织的职能，也构成了国际社会非常重要的活动舞台。然而，按照传统的国际组织定义，条约机构、集团型组

---

① 对非传统形态国际组织的详细考察和分类，参见饶戈平、胡茜《全球化时代国家间多边合作的组织型态》，载饶戈平主编《全球化进程中的国际组织》，北京大学出版社，2005，第 36—90 页。

织等都很难算作正式的国际组织。谢默思和布洛克在其《国际机构法》里以集团型组织的机构化程度相对较低而将其排除在国际组织之外，① 而条约机构因其不具有自己独立的意志而同样被排除在外。② 这些新形态的国际组织由于不具备先入为主的协定性国际组织的典型特征，在法理上无法进入国际组织法的研究范畴。

然而无法否认的是，上述国际合作的新形态，同样是国家间多边合作的产物和载体，也具有不同程度的机构化形态，并且都是依据国际法在积极参与和影响国际事务，没有理由被排斥在国际组织法的研究范围之外。传统的国际组织法学对国际组织采取了一个比较僵硬、刚性的定义，实有削足适履之嫌，不敷所用。实践的发展需要我们突破传统的认识，需要对国际组织的现有界定进行再思考、再探索，形成符合实际的新认识，以便使国际组织法的研究对象能够囊括所有这些国际多边合作的新形态、新本体，更好地回应国际社会常青不谢的实践。

有鉴于此，笔者尝试着对政府间国际组织提出一种新的界定，简要表述如下：所谓政府间国际组织，就是适用于国家间多边合作的、依据国际法运作的制度性安排。这个定义包含以下三个要素。一是要满足国家间多边合作的需求。政府间国际组织本身就是多边主义的产物，是为了满足这种需求才产生的，这是本质特征。二是要有一定的制度化或者机构化形态。前述五种组织形态，都是常设性、有制度、有载体的组织形式，而并非临时的、松散的、无所依托的组合。这是机制特征，也是国际组织区别于国际会议、国家间条约关系的根本方面。三是依据国际法运作。这些组织都依据国际法行事，多数可以在国际法上承受权利和义务，具有法律特征。对国际组织的这一尝试性新定义，一方面力图抓住国际组织的核心特征，同时也力图最大限度地包容现有的各类形态的政府间多边合作形式，以一种开放的、与时俱进的理论包容来回应国际社会的实践。从这一界定出发，凡是符合上述标准的各类政府间多边合作形式都可被称为国际组织，都构成国际组织法的研究对象。

---

① 参见 Henry G. Schermers & Niels M. Blokker, *International Institutional Law* (Leiden: Martinus Nijhoff Publisher, 5th Revised Edition, 2011), pp. 32 – 33。

② 参见 Henry G. Schermers & Niels M. Blokker, *International Institutional Law* (Leiden: Martinus Nijhoff Publisher, 5th Revised Edition, 2011), pp. 44 – 46。

需要指出的是，对国际组织采取新的定义，并不仅仅进一步扩大了国际组织法的研究范围，同时也对现有国际组织法的知识结构提出了新的问题和挑战。这些新形态组织的法律地位、成员构成、职能范围、组织机制、程序规则，以及和其他国际法主体间的关系等问题，各有其特性，和传统的协定性政府间组织有明显区别，但是又都有其共性，汇合成为国际组织的整体。凡此种种，都需要分别加以考察和分析，进而补充、修改和丰富现有的国际组织法体系。同时要强调的是，国际组织法还似有必要在一定程度上将国际非政府间组织纳入自己的研究范围。众所周知，国际法学传统上是不包括对非政府组织的研究的，然而国际现实逼迫我们不得不重新考虑是否要继续坚持这一立场。非政府间国际组织的数量已逾6万个，占全部国际组织数目的八成以上，已经成为全球化时代国际社会不可或缺的“完全参与者”（联合国赋予的称呼）。非政府组织是国际关系中的非国家行为体，代表了国际合作的民间组织形态，可以说是风起云涌的国际市民社会的一种载体。非政府间国际组织也以各种形式参与了全球性、区域性国际制度的构建，与政府间国际组织发生大量的交往，其作用委实不容小觑。但是如天文数字般庞大的非政府组织却因为不具有国际法的主体资格，整体上也不能直接承受国际法上的权利与义务，向来未被正式列入国际法的研究视野。现代国际法亦缺乏专门规范非政府组织的原则、规则以及制度，只有在联合国系统，在咨询非政府组织的过程中才形成了一些内部管理规则，然而这些规则不具有普遍性，也并非正式意义上的法律，无法起到规范一般非政府组织的作用。不妨说，除受制于驻在国国内法的约束外，非政府组织在国际社会尚处在无法可依、无法可管的状态。这种现状对国际秩序和国际法提出了重大挑战：要不要规范、用什么规范以及如何规范数以万计的国际非政府组织？如何把非政府组织作为一个特殊对象列入国际法、国际组织法的研究范畴，对这一问题的解决对当代国际组织法而言，似乎已成为一项刻不容缓的任务了。

三　国际组织法的研究范围

就确定国际组织法学科的研究范围而言，界定国际组织仅仅是第一步，接下来还有必要处理好研究过程中始终面临的三对关系。

一是关于国际组织内部法律秩序和外部法律秩序的关系问题。如同国家一样，每个国际组织都有各自的法律秩序。作为国际法的主体以及国际社会的独立成员，国际组织法律秩序包括内部和外部两个方面。内部法律秩序通常也称为国际组织的内部法，或者说是组织机构法，涉及国际组织内部运作中适用的一般性法律原则、规则、章程和制度。就组织机构法而言，至少可包括组织的基本文件，法律地位，成员资格，组织机构，机构职能，组织机构的议事、决策和投票程序，组织内部的管理制度等多个方面。外部法律秩序则是指调整国际组织与包括成员国在内的其他国际法主体交往过程中所发生的法律关系，其中涉及的问题包括对外缔约、承认和求偿、特权与豁免、组织的监督实施机制、制裁机制、争端解决机制以及国际组织的责任等问题。外部法关注的是组织运作过程中所适用的国际法原则、规则和制度，既包括国际组织章程、国际组织参加的条约，也包括其他可适用于国际组织的国际法一般规则。[①] 比较而言，国际组织的内部法更像一个国家的国内法，而外部法涉及的基本上是国际法，更像一个国家的对外关系法。内部法和外部法相互作用、相辅相成、缺一不可，共同构成一个组织的法律秩序。

从传统上看，组织机构法向来是国际组织法学科研究的主要方面，谢默思和布洛克的《国际机构法》和阿蒙雷辛格（Amerasinghe）的《国际组织机构法原理》即为代表。从国际社会的实践来看，国际组织的外部行为具有对外交往的特性，往往具有重大的社会影响，其中涉及的大量法律问题无法仅仅从组织机构法的角度予以解决。不过，国际组织的内部法和外部法，在实践中往往很难严格地加以区分。随着全球化的深入，国际组织承担越来越多的全球治理职能，行使广泛的国际权力，国际组织的外部法律秩序越来越受到关注和重视。[②] 因此，今后国际组织法的研究，在继续关

① 国际法院在1980年“世界卫生组织与埃及于1951年3月25日所定之协议的解释”的咨询意见中指出：“国际组织是国际法主体，因此受国际法一般规则、组织章程及其所参加条约所施加之任何义务的约束。”参见 International Court of Justice，*Interpretation of the Agreement of 25 March 1951 between the WHO and Egypt*，*Advisory Opinion*，I. C. J. Reports 1980，pp. 89 – 90。

② 对于国际组织管理行为的外部性问题，包括人权保护、环境义务等问题，正在引发学界越来越多的关注。例如 Jan Wouters，et al.，*Accountability for Human Rights Violations by International Organizations*（Antwerp：Intersentia，2010）。

注组织机构法的同时，应当更多地将组织外部法律秩序纳入自己的研究视域，注重内部法律秩序和外部法律秩序的互动关系。

二是作为机构法和程序法的国际组织法，与实体国际法问题/领域之间的关系。不少学者主张区分国际组织的机构法（institutional law）和实体法（substantive law），而将国际组织法的教材写作限定于前者。[①] 从国际组织法教科书的写作来看，这样的主张无可厚非，毕竟国际组织的实体法所涉领域已经渗透到国际法的几乎每一个领域，如果要把国际组织涉及的每个实体法领域都包容进来，不啻写作一本国际法百科全书。国际组织法学科研究，一方面固然要在全局上对国际组织从事比较性质的、一般性的研究，需要开展理论和学说方面的探索和归纳，另一方面尤其有必要强化对特定、个别国际组织的专门研究。国际组织的实践都是在具体的国际法领域内开展的，涉及具体的国际法问题，表现为多样性特色；国际组织法一般问题的研究，不能替代对单个国际组织的具体、深入、跟踪性的研究。若要充分认识和善加利用国际组织，我们更迫切需要的似乎是对特定国际组织的有深度研究、能解决实际问题的专家而非一般泛泛而论的杂家。因此需要强化对特定的国际组织、对特定类型的国际组织（如经济类、安全类、环境类的国际组织）开展深入研究。在这方面，国内学者以往的研究较多偏重于联合国、世界贸易组织、欧盟、世界银行、国际货币基金组织，以及联合国系统的一些专门机构，针对其他国际组织的专门性、有深度的研究还太少。对于这些具体的、个别的国际组织的研究，必须紧密结合具体国际法领域或者实体国际法问题。正是在此过程中，国际组织的机构法和程序法才能充分展现鲜活的生命力和实际效用。

沙赫特（Schachter）和乔伊尔（Joyner）在1995年主编的《联合国法律秩序》一书中，归纳了与联合国体系有关的18个实体法领域，包括武力与军备控制、人权、自决权、难民和移民、妇女、劳工、经济关系与发展问题、教育科学文化和信息、环境、海洋法、海运、通讯与邮政、民

---

① 参见 Jan Klabbers, *An Introduction to International Organizations Law*（Cambridge: Cambridge University Press, 3rd edn., 2015）, p. 2; Henry G. Schermers & Niels M. Blokker, *International Institutional Law*（Leiden: Martinus Nijhoff Publisher, 5th Revised Edition, 2011）, pp. 27－28。

航、外层空间、卫生、粮食与农业、国际犯罪、国际私法的统一。[1] 现在二十年过去了，联合国体系所涉及的实体法领域，已经远远超出了上述18个领域的范围。在国际组织法教科书的写作上，固然可以侧重国际组织的一般性问题，但是在日常的学术研究中应当大力提倡对国际组织的个别研究，提升对国际组织法和国际法研究的深度，两者不可偏废。

三是国际组织法和一般国际法研究之间的关系。每个国际组织都有其内外部法律秩序，甚至在一定意义上，每个国际组织都是自成体系的自给自足的法律和政治系统。但是，不可忽视的是，国际组织身处国际法律秩序之中，是在整个国际法的大环境中依据国际法开展活动的，国际组织和国际法密切相关。国际组织法是国际法学科的一个重要分支，国际组织成立和运作的方方面面都受到国际法制约，国际组织同时也在影响和改变着国际法系统本身。国际组织大大拓展和丰富了国际法理论和学说的范畴，充实和发展了当代国际法的内容。这表现在很多方面：国际组织的出现，带来了国际法上主体概念的扩大；作为一个独立的国际法律人格者，国际组织使得国际法律体系趋向于多元化和多样性。国际组织的出现，在某些领域使得原本是水平的国际法律秩序出现了垂直化的现象，并且在一定程度上使得国际法和国内法的疆界变得模糊。[2] 此外，国际组织对于国际社会的造法过程产生了结构性影响，促进了国际法渊源形式的扩展，也赋予国际造法概念以新的内涵。[3] 尽管《国际法院规约》第38条已有相关规定，但在实践中，国际组织的重要决议及国际组织本身的章程对国际法渊源的扩大都有影响。二战以来，国际组织日渐成为现代国际法发展的一个主要动力和渊源。

同样值得关注的是，国际组织也推动国际法的实施机制产生革命性变化。[4] 国际法自身有着传统的实施机制，主要是通过国家自我遵守或自助的方式来实施。但自从国际组织出现以来，特别是二战后国际组织得到了

---

① Oscar Schachter & Christopher Joyner, *United Nations Legal Order* (two volumes, New York: Cambridge University Press, 1995).

② 参见 Henry G. Schermers & Niels M. Blokker, *International Institutional Law* (Leiden: Martinus Nijhoff Publisher, 5th Revised Edition, 2011), pp. 5 - 7。

③ 对此问题的专门探讨，参见 Jose Alvarez, *International Organizations as Law-Makers* (New York: Oxford University Press, 2005)。

④ 详见饶戈平《国际组织与国际法实施机制的发展》，载饶戈平主编《国际组织与国际法实施机制的发展》，北京大学出版社，2013，第3—30页。

长足发展，国际组织事实上也参与了国际法的实施过程。尽管在大部分情况下，这只是作为一项辅助手段，是国家实施机制的补充。国际组织实际参与国际法实施的例子很多，像联合国这样的政治性组织，以及如北约、非洲联盟、美洲国家组织这样的区域性组织，都直接参与了区域性、全球性和平与安全方面的实际运作，在很大程度上能够使国际法实施机制具有强有力的执行效果。在这方面，人权、贸易、裁军等领域表现得尤为明显。

因此国际组织法学科研究，在注重国际组织自身及其运作之外，还有必要关注国际组织对于国际法发展的影响以及两者的互动关系。这些问题从性质上来说更多的属于国际法领域，但是国际组织法学者谙熟国际组织的运作和实践，往往能够提供自己独到的经验和认识，拓展和深化国际法本身的学科知识。

四 国际组织法学科中的“法”

在探讨了国际组织法研究的对象和范围以后，还有一个本体性质的问题没有回答，那就是作为一个学科，什么是国际组织“法”？国际组织法所研究的究竟是作为国际组织这一国际现象整体的法，还是单个国际组织的法？如果存在法，那么是一个什么性质和形态的法？作为法律，其渊源又是什么？这些问题解决好了，国际组织法的研究才是有根基、有方向的。

有意思的是，虽然国际组织法作为一个学科和研究领域获得了很大发展，但是对何谓国际组织“法”这个本体问题，学界始终语焉不详。欧洲早期的两本最主要的国际组织法教科书，鲍维特1963年的《国际组织法》和谢默思1972年的《国际机构法》，完全回避了这个问题，虽然这并不妨碍两位学者将其研究对象和领域定性为法律，而不是法理学、组织、机构或者政治。谢默思和布洛克在其2011年第五版的《国际机构法》一书中反复用了国际机构法（international institutional law）或者国际组织的机构法（institutional law of international organizations）的措辞，并且明确主张国际组织法应列为国际法下面的一个次级学科。① 但令人不解的是，这部将

① 参见 Henry G. Schermers & Niels M. Blokker, *International Institutional Law* (Leiden: Martinus Nijhoff Publisher, 5th Revised Edition, 2011), p. 27。

近1300页的教科书从头到尾没有给何谓国际机构法下一个明确的定义。桑兹（Sands）和克莱恩（Klein）修订的第六版《鲍维特国际组织法》，仅仅用了不到一页的篇幅对国际组织法作了一个欲语还休的说明，仅仅提到说“并不排除存在一个国际组织共通法的可能性”，让人感觉更多的是在刻意回避而不是意在具体讨论。[①] 芬兰赫尔辛基大学国际法教授克莱伯斯（Klabbers）是当前国际法和国际组织法研究的领军人物，但是其在2015年出版的第三版《国际组织法导论》一书中，同样回避了这个问题，只是一般地援引说“有社会，即有法”。[②] 也曾有个别学者对国际组织法的这个本体问题作了讨论，但显然并没有获得学界的一般性接受。[③]

这些国际组织法专家对于国际组织法这个概念本身采取了回避的态度，显然并非出于疏忽，而是有深层原因的。最根本的原因，恐怕在于到底什么是国际组织法，在他们看来仍然是一个不明确的、见仁见智的、实践中也仍然在不断发展的问题。然而，既然要主张把国际组织法作为一个独立学科来认识和研究，就不能长期回避这个本体性问题。可以说，对这个问题的认识和回答，从根本上影响到国际组织法是否构成一个独立的学科，影响到国际组织法作为一个学科的定位以及具体的研究方法等理论和学术问题，同时也在规范的层面上不可避免地影响我们对各种具体的国际组织法问题的正确认识和解决。

其实，困扰国际组织法概念的最根本的问题在于，是否存在一个专门调整国际组织的、具有一般性、对各类国际组织都可以统一适用的国际法规范体系，抑或说国际组织法研究是否仅仅是对国际组织存在的若干共同法律问题加以比较研究的领域。诚然，林林总总的国际组织各不相同，每

---

① 参见 Philippe Sands & Pierre Klein, *Bowett's Law of International Institutions* （London: Sweet & Maxwell, 6th edn., 2009）, pp. 16 – 17。

② Jan Klabbers, *An Introduction to International Organizations Law*. 尽管担任过赫尔辛基大学国际组织法教授，但是克莱伯斯教授对于国际组织法是否构成一个独立的学科提出了质疑，但是他认为这并不减损在大学里教授国际组织法的必要性。参见 Jan Klabbers, “The Paradox of International Institutional Law”, 5 *International Organizations Law Review* 151 （2008）: 151 – 173。

③ 参见 C. F. Amerasinghe, *Principles of the Institutional Law of International Organizations* （Cambridge: Cambridge University Press, 2nd Revised Edition, 2005, 初版于1996年）, pp. 13 – 21; Finn Seyersted, *Common Law of International Organizations* （Leiden: Martinus Nijhoff Publisher, 2008）, pp. 1 – 29。

个国际组织都自成体系，都有其不同的法律秩序，都有其独特的原则、规则和具体实践。但是所谓国际组织法究竟是旨在揭示和构建一个具有普遍适用效力的规范性体系，抑或说仅仅是一个对各个国际组织的法律和实践加以比较研究或个别研究的学术领域，这似乎是一个我们无法推诿、有必要加以明确的重大问题。

学界对此问题的专门讨论虽然有限，但将他们歧见纷呈的论述汇总一下，还是可以归纳出以下四种基本立场的。第一种意见一枝独放，以塞耶斯泰德（Seyersted）为典型代表。他在其著作《国际组织的共通法》（*Common Law of International Organizations*）中认为，国际实践中存在一套完整的、可以一般适用于所有国际组织的法律。他强调自己所研究的，是政府间国际组织的共通法（common law）。“尽管各类政府间国际组织存在种种差别，但是存在一套事实上对包括超国家组织在内的所有政府间国际组织都适用的重要的习惯法。”[①] 按照塞耶斯泰德的观点，这套国际组织的共通法并非来源于国际组织的章程性文件，而是在国际组织的实践中发展出来的习惯法。从内容上来看，包括处理组织内部关系的内部法、处理组织对外与国家关系相关的国际公法，以及处理组织对外与私人关系的冲突法规则。[②] 显然，塞耶斯泰德在这里把国际组织法定位为具有一般性的习惯法、共通法。第二种意见则是针锋相对，以法国学者勒泰（Reuter）为代表。他认为，不存在一个统一的、适用于所有国际组织的国际组织法，而是每个国际组织都有其自身的组织法，因此所谓国际组织法只能是一个复数的法（laws of international organizations），[③] 是每个单个的国际组织法律和实践的总和。在他看来，国际组织法似乎是汇集众多国际组织的单个法律体系的一个大拼盘。第三种意见独辟蹊径，以谢默思和布洛克为代表。他们认为，国际组织尽管千差万别，但是在日常运作过程中遭遇的大量问题却很有类似之处，而且这些问题都有其法律方面的共性，因此国际组织法是以

① Finn Seyersted, *Common Law of International Organizations* (Leiden: Martinus Nijhoff Publisher, 2008), p. 1.

② Finn Seyersted, *Common Law of International Organizations* (Leiden: Martinus Nijhoff Publisher, 2008), pp. 21 - 23.

③ 转引自 C. F. Amerasinghe, *Principles of the Institutional Law of International Organizations* (Cambridge: Cambridge University Press, 2nd Revised Edition, 2005, 初版于 1996 年), pp. 16 - 17。

国际组织的章程性文件为基础，对各个国际组织所可能遇到的共同问题进行的一种比较研究。[①] 一个国际组织的法律和实践并不能当然地适用于另一个国际组织，但是可以彼此借鉴，有参考意义而非规范性效力。给人的印象是，他们似乎在有意无意地用对国际组织的研究方法去取代对国际组织法的定性。第四种意见接近于折中派，以阿蒙雷辛格为代表。他一方面承认每个国际组织都有其特殊性，每个国际组织都有其独特的原则和规则体系，同时又主张国际社会已经在国际组织的某些问题上发展出了一些可以广泛适用的法律原则。因此，国际组织法既包括各个国际组织的章程等基本文件，也包括某些可以一般适用的法律原则、某些实践中发展出来的习惯法，以及某些协定性国际法规则，等等。[②]

上述意见表明了不同学者对于国际组织法性质和范围的不同认知，各有其真知灼见和合理性，很难简单地加以肯否或取舍，也凸显了从学术上解决这一问题的难度，很难期待短时间内能够达成一种共识。值得注意的是，这些不同认识还在很大程度上影响了学者个人对国际组织法的研究方法、研究重点和研究内容等核心问题的看法。例如，塞耶斯泰德力图发现和建构“国际组织的共通法”，注重研究中的归纳和演绎方法，重点在于阐明国际组织法的一般规则，在体系上注重围绕国际组织运行建构一个体系完整的国际组织法。而谢默思和布洛克则彻底贯彻了比较研究的方法，注重对国际组织实践的总结和类型化，注重对国际组织共同机构问题的发掘，而对国际组织法的体系性和系统性关注程度不够，在一定意义上对国际组织法的理论发掘是相对贫乏的。

笔者认为，国际组织法具有许多不同于国际法其他分支学科的特点，在现实生活中更多的是表现为一个个国际组织的具体的、特定的法律规范，我们不能以国际法其他学科的惯常的标准或模式来要求、衡量国际组织法。纵使国际社会不存在一个统一的成文的国际组织法典，也没有一个可以普遍适用于所有政府间国际组织的法律体系，但这些丝毫不能否认实

---

① 参见 Henry G. Schermers & Niels M. Blokker, *International Institutional Law* (Leiden: Martinus Nijhoff Publisher, 5th Revised Edition, 2011), pp. 21 - 28。

② 参见 C. F. Amerasinghe, *Principles of the Institutional Law of International Organizations* (Cambridge: Cambridge University Press, 2nd Revised Edition, 2005, 初版于 1996 年), pp. 13 - 21。

践中的确存在规范国际组织的法律，也难以忽略国际组织法学科确立的正当性，而是需要用新的更加开放的思维来看待国际法行列中的这一特殊成员。对国际组织法的认识既可以基于规范意义的层面，也可以基于学科意义的层面，既要注意两者的区分，也要注意两者的关联。就规范意义上来说，国际组织法是用以规范、调整政府间国际组织的建立和运作的所有原则、规则、章程和制度的总称。从学科内容上来看，国际组织法不仅包括每个国际组织的个别法，也包括适用于国际组织的一般原则和习惯法规则；不仅包括国际组织法的基本文件、组织决议、运作实践等组织内部法，也包括组织参加或者缔结的条约法规则，还包括调整国际组织对外关系方面的国际法律人格、权力、缔约、承认、特权与豁免、使节派驻、组织责任等一般国际法原则和规则。从国际实践发展来看，这些一般性质的国际法原则和规则，正在日益成为国际法学界的研究重点，国际组织法研究也日益从比较研究转向规范性研究。

作为一个独立学科的国际组织法，其中的“法”除了在实践中体现为对国际组织的具体规范外，更多强调的是法律研究方法，指的是国际法学者运用规范的视角和法律的思维去研究国际组织运作中存在的各种法律问题，推动国际组织运作的法治化、规范化。面对国际组织这一活生生的社会现象，向来有不同学科、不同视角的研究方法，包括政治学的、经济学的、历史学的、社会学的等方法。国际组织法学科强调的是从法律的角度对国际组织这一充满多样性的现象加以研究和规范，从规范性的角度切入，实然法和应然法并重。换言之，国际组织法作为一个学科，强调的是国际法学者在研究国际组织方面特有的视角、方法、维度和价值取向。正是这种独特性，使得国际法学者得以在对何谓国际组织“法”存在争议的情况下，能够推动形成一个独立的国际组织法学科。也正因此，国际组织法的学科内容具有相当的开放性，尤其是在教材写作方面。不同学者对于哪些问题应该纳入国际组织法、基于何种体系和原则来梳理和阐述国际组织法，往往带有鲜明的个人见解。

当然，规范意义上的国际组织法和学科意义上的国际组织法是密切关联的。规范意义上的国际组织法，构成了国际组织法学科研究的基础和主要方面；同时，对国际组织法在规范层面上的不同理解，也往往导致在国际组织法研究上的不同发展方向。

在研究国际组织的法现象和法要素过程中，还有以下两个方面的问题值得注意。第一是硬法和软法的问题。国际组织法的研究对象既包括所谓硬法，即严格符合国际法形式渊源的原则和规则，也包括大量的所谓软法，最典型的就是国际组织的决议。国际组织决议的法律基础、形式和效力各有不同，有建议和决定之分，有对内决议和对外决议之分，但它们都是国际组织有效影响国际社会生活的重要方式，均应当纳入国际组织法的研究范围。第二是内部法和外部法的问题。调整组织内部各种关系的内部法跟以调整国家间关系为对象、以条约和习惯为主要形式的传统国际法显然不同，前者在性质上究竟是属于国际法的范畴，还是自成一类的国际组织法范畴，仍然有待于在理论上进一步探讨。至于国际组织的外部法，从国际组织法研究的角度来看，随着国际组织在全球治理背景下对外行使国际权利的情况日益增多，加强对国际组织外部法的研究已经刻不容缓了。

五　结语

综上所述，本文试图仅就国际组织法学科研究中的三个基础性问题进行探讨。首先，强调厘清学科研究对象的必要性。国际组织法不能仅仅把目光聚焦于协定性政府间组织，还必须同时关注大量存在的其他多边合作的组织形态。在此基础上笔者提出了对国际组织重新界定的思考，将所谓国际组织定义为：适用于国家间多边合作的、依据国际法运作的制度性安排。其次，强调国际组织法的研究范围，提出其中应重点关注的三对关系，即内部法与外部法的关系、国际组织机构法与实体国际法的关系、国际组织法与国际法发展的关系。指出国际组织法研究应从传统的机构法、程序法视角跳出来，把自己置身于整个国际法的大环境下来发展，关注二者的互动关系。最后，试图对国际组织法的“法”的定位和定性进行探索。一方面指出国际社会尚不存在一部普遍适用于所有国际组织的统一的国际组织法法典，国际组织法大量地表现为各个国际组织的多样化的法律秩序；另一方面又强调各国际组织中存在着共同的法律问题，需要就其一般性法律原则、规则和制度进行基础性研究，推动形成适用于各国际组织的普遍性法律规范和法理基础。当然，以上这些观点不过是笔者个人不很成熟的观察与见解，纯属探索之言、一家之说，目的主要在于引发、促进学界的争鸣。

其实，国际组织法学科的基本问题远不限于上述三点，还有一些重大问题，诸如本学科的核心内容、基本理论、研究方法、学术流派，以及中国学界的当务之急等等，都是大有必要探讨、厘清的。限于篇幅的原因，本文尚未能涉及，期待此后可以继续讨论。

一个学科的成熟往往是在丰富实践的积累过程和持续充分的学术探讨过程中逐步取得的。当前，虽然很少有人再质疑国际组织法作为国际法一个分支学科存在的必要性，但并非意味着这一学科已经足够成熟，已经具备足够的学术根基了。国际组织法学科产生的时间按理说已经不算短了，但严格说来，整个学界对其似乎仍然缺乏深度的基础性研究，还有一些基础性的理论问题存在争议，还缺乏重大的理论性突破，在学科体系上还存在一些明显的虚点和盲点，亟待加强研究、完善成熟，亟待学界的重视和投入。不过，这一状况也恰恰从另一方面说明了国际组织法学科的发展潜力和发掘空间，学界在这方面可以拓荒耕耘、大有作为。殷切期待国内学界有识之士能够携手砥砺，为这一学科的发展贡献自己的学术智慧和才华。

（责任编辑：李西霞）

（本文原载于《国际法研究》2016 年第 1 期）

中国（上海）自由贸易试验区的“名”与“实”[*]

——相关概念的国际经济法学解读

车丕照[**]

自2013年8月30日《全国人民代表大会常务委员会关于授权国务院在中国（上海）自由贸易试验区暂时调整有关法律规定的行政审批的决定》通过以来，国务院已于同年9月18日批准并印发了《中国（上海）自由贸易试验区总体方案》，上海市人民政府也随后公布了《中国（上海）自由贸易试验区管理办法》。中国（上海）自由贸易试验区（以下简称“上海自贸区”）已在万众瞩目下启程。然而，由于种种原因，有关上海自贸区的一些表述并不能准确传达出其真实的含义，因此，有必要加以解读。①

一　名为“自由贸易区”，实为“自由投资贸易区”

上海自贸区的名称为“自由贸易区”，但如果仅将其理解为实行“自由贸易的区域”那就是一种误解了。事实上，从全国人大常委会、国务院和上海市政府的一系列规定来看，上海自贸区不仅是一个自由贸易区，更

---

* 本文为作者主持的国家社会科学基金重点项目“国际经济秩序的中国立场研究”（项目批准号：13AFX029）的阶段性研究成果之一。

** 车丕照，清华大学法学院教授。

① 已有学者开始作这种“解读”工作，如龚柏华《厘清上海自贸区法治理念是其建设的根本》，载龚柏华主编《上海自贸区法研究与动态》（内部学习交流资料）2013年12月总第2期。

是一个“自由投资区”。

首先，从全国人大常委会对国务院的相关授权决定来看，该项授权的唯一内容就是授权国务院在上海自贸区内，“对国家规定实施准入特别管理措施之外的外商投资，暂时调整《中华人民共和国外资企业法》、《中华人民共和国中外合资经营企业法》和《中华人民共和国中外合作经营企业法》规定的有关行政审批”。对于那些不属于禁止或限制类的外商投资，由原先实行的审批制改为备案制。也就是说，设立上海自贸区首先需要变动的法律是投资方面的法律，而不是贸易方面的法律。就此推断，上海自贸区首先是要在引进外资方面实行特殊法律制度的区域。

其次，从国务院批准并印发的《中国（上海）自由贸易试验区总体方案》的内容来看，促进国际投资是其中的重要内容。该方案概括出自贸区有5大任务，分别是：加快政府职能转变、扩大投资领域的开放、推进贸易发展方式转变、深化金融领域的开放创新和完善法制领域的制度保障。可见，在投资、贸易和金融三大领域当中，投资被列为首位；而无论是“贸易发展方式转变”还是“金融领域的开放创新”，无一不与投资相关；而“政府职能转变”和“法制完善”也必将涉及投资管理体制的转变和投资法制的完善。

最后，上海自贸区设立之后所出台的与现行制度最为不同的一项规定是上海市人民政府于2013年9月29日颁布的《中国（上海）自由贸易试验区外商投资准入特别管理措施（负面清单）（2013年）》。该项规定开启了上海自贸区外资法改革的试验。按照该项规定，对负面清单所列之外的领域，将外商投资项目由核准制改为备案制（国务院规定对国内投资项目保留核准的除外），同时，将外商投资企业合同章程审批也改为备案管理。负面清单列明了上海自贸区限制外资进入的产业领域，同时也列明了禁止外资进入的产业领域。上述特别管理措施既适用于绿地（新建）投资，也适用于并购投资。

“自由贸易区”以国际投资作为其主要内容是一种常见的国际实践。自由贸易区的原型是13世纪末一些欧洲国家出现的自由港（free port）。那时的自由港对于打破封建割据、疏通贸易渠道和促进商品流转发挥了积极的作用。后来，在借鉴自由港经验的基础上，许多国家设立了自由贸易区。自由贸易区实质上是划在一国关境以外的、与自由港具有同等地位的区域。所不同的是自由港必须是港口或港口的一部分，而自由贸易区则可设在远离港口的地方。进入自由贸易区的商品（除另有限定外）不交关税，也不办理海关手续。商品进区后，可以拆散、储存、分级、分类、修理、加工、重新包装、重新标签、重新出口，海关不予控制。但自由贸易区内的商品要运进自由贸易区所在国的其他地区，则要办理报关手续，缴纳进口税。

如果说自由港及自由贸易区的主要作用在于吸引外国船只、商品的进入，从而增加各项费用收入，发展转口贸易的话，那么，20 世纪 60 年代之后出现的加工出口区（manufacture and export zone）则以吸收外资和国外先进技术、发展国内产业和扩大商品出口为主要目的。各国的加工出口区都设立一些吸引外资的优良条件，外国投资者既可以在加工出口区内独资兴办企业，也可以与所在国的官方资本或私人资本合办企业或进行其他形式的合作。区内企业所用原材料、零配件和加工设备的进口及产品出口通常可享有关税减免待遇，区内企业还可依较低税率缴纳企业所得税，外国投资者所分得的利润或其他收益可自由汇往国外，不受外汇管制的限制。加工出口区的当地政府还在水电供应、通信、交通等方面为外国投资者提供良好的基础设施和廉价的公共服务。由于加工出口区具备上述优越条件，因而对于吸引外国投资发挥了很大的作用。

自 1979 年以来，我国陆续创办的经济特区、经济技术开发区与其他国家所创办的加工出口区具有相同的性质。这些特别经济区域与其他区域不同的地方在于通过实行一些特殊的经济法律制度（如税收减免、简化行政审批）并提供优良的基础设施和公共服务，吸引外来投资，发展当地产业并扩大出口。上海自贸区与我国现存的经济特区及各种类型的开发区在性质上是一致的。虽然冠以“自由贸易区”的名称，但并不以扩大进出口（包括转口）贸易作为其主要功能，而以实体经济的发展作为其主要内容。没有实体经济支撑的国际贸易是不能持久的。同样，没有自主知识产权支撑的实体经济也是没有国际竞争力的。从这个意义上讲，上海自贸区不仅要以吸引和促进投资为主要任务，更要明确如何促进具有自主知识产权和国际竞争力的产业的形成和发展。

二　名为“准入前国民待遇”，实为“准入的国民待遇”

在全国人大常委会对国务院的授权决定中没有“投资准入前国民待

遇”的表述。在国务院批准和印发的《中国（上海）自由贸易试验区总体方案》中，明确要求上海市人民政府“探索建立投资准入前国民待遇和负面清单管理模式”，“对外商投资试行准入前国民待遇”。上海市人民政府颁布的《中国（上海）自由贸易试验区管理办法》也明确规定：“自贸试验区实行外商投资准入前国民待遇，实施外商投资准入特别管理措施（负面清单）管理模式”。然而，外资“准入前国民待遇”不是一个表述准确的概念。

国民待遇（national treatment）是指一国政府给予其他国家的自然人、法人及其他实体或来自其他国家的货物、服务和投资等不低于其给予本国自然人、法人及其他实体或本国货物、服务和投资等的待遇。国民待遇原则的实质是非歧视，即平等地对待本国人与外国人、本国货物和外国货物、本国投资和外国投资等。

虽然国民待遇原则反映了“平等”、“公平竞争”等与市场经济相一致的理念，但是从国际法角度来看，除非一个国家对其他国家作出允诺，否则该国没有义务给予其他国家的人、物和投资等以国民待遇。但事实上，绝大多数国家都通过双边协定和多边公约彼此承担了给予对方的人、物和投资等国民待遇的国际法义务。例如，在国际货物贸易领域，世界贸易组织（WTO）的160个成员方均基于《关贸总协定》（GATT）的规定而彼此给予来自其他成员方的货物以国民待遇。

然而，一国在对其他国家承担给予国民待遇义务的时候，通常包含一个前提，即只有在对方的国民或公司、货物、投资等进入本国之后，才能给予其国民待遇。例如，GATT关于国民待遇的规定是：“任何缔约方领土的产品进口至任何其他缔约方领土时，不得对其直接或间接征收超过对同类国产品直接或间接征收的任何种类的国内税或其他国内费用”（第3条第2款）；“任何缔约方领土的产品进口至任何其他缔约方领土时，在有关影响其国内销售、标价出售、购买、运输、分销或使用的所有法律、法规和规定方面，所享受的待遇不得低于同类国产品所享受的待遇”（第3条第4款）。在《中国加入工作组报告书》中，中国所承诺的也是对“已进口产品”（imported products）即市场准入后的产品给予国民待遇。①

① 见《中国加入工作组报告书》第二部分（经济政策）第一项。

关于投资的国民待遇问题，一般的实践也是在外资进入东道国之后才给予国民待遇。例如，我国政府与日本政府于 1988 年 8 月 27 日签订的《中华人民共和国和日本国关于鼓励和相互保护投资协定》第 3 条第 2 款规定："缔约任何一方在其境内给予缔约另一方国民和公司就投资财产、收益及与投资有关的业务活动的待遇，不应低于给予该缔约一方国民和公司的待遇。"这里规定的国民待遇显然是来自对方的投资进入本国市场之后才能享有的。2005 年 11 月 14 日签署的《中华人民共和国和西班牙王国关于促进和相互保护投资的协定》第 3 条第 2 款规定："缔约一方应给予缔约另一方投资者在其境内的投资及与投资有关活动不低于其给予本国投资者的投资及与投资有关活动的待遇。"这里的国民待遇也只能在市场准入之后才能享有。

然而，美国等国家一直致力于将投资的国民待遇从市场准入之后提前到市场准入阶段。《美国双边投资协定范本（2012 年）》将国民待遇分为"投资者"的国民待遇和"投资"的国民待遇。其表述分别为："缔约方给予另一缔约方投资者的待遇应不低于其在国内类似情形下在设立、获取、扩大、管理、实施、运行、出售或其他形式的投资处置给予国内投资者的待遇"；"各缔约方给予的投资待遇不应当低于在类似情形下给予在其领土内本国投资者在设立、获取、扩大、管理、实施、运行、出售或其他形式的投资处置方面的待遇"。[①] 这里的关键词是"设立"（establishment）、"获取"（acquisition）和"扩大"（expansion）。"设立"就是新建投资（绿地投资），"获取"等同于通过并购所进行的投资，而"扩大"则是增加投资。要求缔约国在对方投资者"设立"、"获取"和"扩大"时就给予国民待遇即意味着在投资者和投资进入对方国家的市场时（市场准入时）即给予国民待遇。因为《美国双边投资协定范本（2012 年）》所要求的国民

① 相应的英文表述为："Each Party shall accord to investors of the other Party treatment no less favorable than that it accords, in like circumstances, to its own investors with respect to the establishment, acquisition, expansion, management, conduct, operation, and sale or other disposition of investments in its territory"; "Each Party shall accord to covered investments treatment no less favorable than that it accords, in like circumstances, to investments in its territory of its own investors with respect to the establishment, acquisition, expansion, management, conduct, operation, and sale or other disposition of investments。"见《美国双边投资协定范本（2012 年）》第 3 条。

待遇从市场准入后前移至市场准入前，因此，被许多人称作“准入前的国民待遇”。

事实上，这种国民待遇应称作“市场准入的国民待遇”，而不是“市场准入前的国民待遇”。“待遇”总是与特定事项相联系的。当国家之间约定，或一国向其他国家允诺给予对方的投资者或投资以“国民待遇”，一定要明确在何种事项上给予这种待遇。传统上所说的，东道国给予进入本国市场之后的外资以“国民待遇”，是指外资进入东道国之后，在管理、实施、运行以及出售或其他形式的投资处置方面（也即《美国双边投资协定范本（2012 年）》所列的“management”、“conduct”、“operation”、“sale”或“other disposition of investments”）享有不低于东道国给予其本国国民的待遇。所谓“市场准入前的国民待遇”也必须明确在何种事项上给予外国投资者和外国投资以国民待遇，而这些事项按照《美国双边投资协定范本（2012 年）》的表述即“设立”、“获取”和“扩大”。如果不与特定的事项相联结，而只是从时间角度的“之前”或“之后”来表述，是难以确定相关国家在“国民待遇”问题上的权利义务关系的。

将外资的国民待遇前移到市场准入阶段，并不意味着外国投资者和外国投资在市场准入阶段即可享受与东道国的投资者和投资完全相同的待遇。从当今的国际实践来看，还没有哪一个国家向其他国家允诺过，可以就市场准入给予外国投资者和外国投资以完全的国民待遇。因此，“市场准入阶段的国民待遇”必须与“负面清单”相结合，即对那些不能在市场准入阶段给予外国投资者和外国投资国民待遇的产业列出一个清单。《中国（上海）自由贸易试验区外商投资准入特别管理措施（负面清单）（2013 年）》就是这样一份清单。

一个国家就外国资本可以进入的产业领域是列“负面清单”还是“正面清单”[①] 似乎区别不大：“正面清单”未列入的产业就应该属于“负面清单”的内容，而“负面清单”未列入的产业即应属于“正面清单”的内容。如果有 100 个产业的话，是列出允许外资进入的 80 个产业，还是列出不准外资进入的 20 个产业，效果应该是一样的。既然如此，为什么在制

---

① 有人将我国现行的《外商投资产业指导目录》称作“正面清单”，其实是不准确的。因为我国的《外商投资产业指导目录》从市场准入角度将产业分为“鼓励”、“允许”、“限制”和“禁止”四类，既包括“正面清单”，也包括“负面清单”。

度设计上会有“正面清单”与“负面清单”之争呢？原因主要有两点。第一，产业类型并非固定不变。因此，当出现一个新的产业时，在实行“正面清单”的情况下，它不在清单之内，东道国可自主决定是否允许外资进入这一产业；而如果实行的是“负面清单”制度，那么，未列入“负面清单”的产业即应为外资可以进入的产业领域。所以，实行“正面清单”制度对东道国来说显然是更为主动和稳妥的一种方式。第二，“正面清单”通常是一个国家自行设立和维持的，而“负面清单”则是两个或更多的国家之间谈判的结果。因此，一个国家可自行变更其单方面制定的“正面清单”，却无法变更以条约形式确定下来的“负面清单”（除非条约有相应约定）。如果是单方面制定“正面清单”，则制定者可自行就清单作出解释，而如果是以条约形式确定的“负面清单”，则需要缔约方一致的解释或者由争端解决机构加以解释。[①] 可见，“负面清单”使得一个国家在外资准入的产业领域事项上，将原本可以自行决定的问题转换为必须与缔约对方协商确定的事项。《中国（上海）自由贸易试验区外商投资准入特别管理措施（负面清单）（2013 年）》规定：“根据外商投资法律法规和自贸试验区发展需要，负面清单将适时进行调整。”将来我国与其他国家签署双边投资协定时，是否彼此允许保有此种“调整权”是需要认真研究的问题。

还需要指出的是，关于投资的国民待遇问题，我国学界长期存在一种误解，以为 WTO 的《与贸易相关的投资措施协议》（《TRIMs 协议》）已经给各缔约方施加了投资领域中实行国民待遇的义务。例如，有人认为，“《TRIMs 协议》旨在要求一国对于来自他国的直接投资在其资本运作的各个方面及环节给予国民待遇”，[②] 这种说法是对《TRIMs 协议》的误读。《TRIMs 协议》的确涉及国民待遇问题，但《TRIMs 协议》所要求的国民待遇并不是外资的国民待遇，而是相关货物的国民待遇。《TRIMs 协议》所禁止的违背国民待遇原则的投资管理措施是指违背《关贸总协定》第 3 条的投资管理措施；《TRIMs 协议》之所以要禁止“当地成分措施”（local

---

① 如在美国诉我国“出版物案”（DS363）中，我方曾试图将我国在《服务贸易具体承诺减让表》第 2D 部分（视听服务）对“录音制品分销服务”的承诺，解释为只适用于以物理形式存在的录音制品的分销，而并不包括录音制品的电子化分销。但中方的这一解释并未获得 WTO 专家组和上诉机构的支持。有关该案的述评，参见李成钢主编《世贸组织规则博弈：中国参与 WTO 争端解决的十年法律实践》，商务印书馆，2011，第 343—368 页。

② 邹立刚：《TRIMS 协定与我国对外资的待遇标准》，《法商研究》1999 年第 1 期。

content TRIMs）和“贸易平衡措施”（trade-balancing TRIMs），是因为这两类措施使得进口商品处于比本国商品更为不利的地位，而不是因为这些措施使得外资比内资处于更为不利的地位，尽管这些措施可能真的会使外资（而不仅是外国货物）受到歧视待遇。

还有学者认为，WTO 要求各成员方在市场准入方面给予外资和外国投资者以国民待遇，认为：“我国目前所给予外资的国民待遇是不全面的，与国际通行的做法及与 WTO 有关协定的要求还有很大距离，突出地表现在外资企业既享受许多内资企业享受不到的‘超国民待遇’，如各种税收优惠等；又受到较多限制，如对外资投向服务业的限制。”[①] 对外资投向服务业的限制是一种市场准入的限制。即使我国已按照入世时的承诺扩大了服务业的开放领域，在市场准入方面，我们仍然没有使外国投资者与本国投资者处于平等地位。如前所述，《TRIMs 协议》规定的国民待遇并不是外资或外国投资者的国民待遇，而是 GATT 第 3 条所要求的外国货物的国民待遇。因此，在《TRIMs 协议》项下，各成员方并没有义务在市场准入方面给予外资以国民待遇。那么，《服务贸易总协定》（GATS）是否就市场准入方面的国民待遇问题作出了一般的要求呢？回答也是否定的。虽然 GATS 第 17 条规定，成员方在实施影响服务提供的各种措施时，对满足减让表所列条件和要求的其他成员的服务或服务提供者，应给予其不低于本国服务或服务提供者的待遇。但 GATS 对国民待遇原则的规定，只适用于成员方已作出承诺的服务部门。任一成员方都可以通过与其他成员方的谈判来确定其市场开放的领域和国民待遇的赋予。也就是说，如果没有具体的承诺，无论是在市场准入环节，还是在市场准入之后，每个成员方就外国投资者和外国投资的国民待遇问题均不承担一般的义务。

三 名为“与国际接轨”，实为“自主选择”

《国务院关于印发〈中国（上海）自由贸易试验区总体方案〉的通知》要求将上海自贸区建设成“具有国际水准的投资贸易便利、监管高效便捷、法制环境规范的自由贸易试验区”。《中国（上海）自由贸易试验区

---

① 王立东：《完善我国外资国民待遇的法律问题》，《当代法学》2002 年第 1 期。

总体方案》三次谈到“国际化和法治化”，并多次提到“与国际高标准相适应”、“与国际接轨”等。《中国（上海）自由贸易试验区管理办法》也规定，要“探索建立与国际投资和贸易规则体系相适应的行政管理体系”。“与国际接轨”似乎已成为上海自贸区的基本特征之一。

其实，“与国际接轨”是一个容易被误解的概念，需要加以说明。

首先，一个国家并不负有“与国际接轨”的义务。是否“与国际接轨”，完全可以自行决定。由于相关文件里所谈到的“与国际接轨”都是在与法律制度有关的语境之下，因此，“与国际接轨”应该是与“国际法律规则接轨”。国际法律规则基本上可分为两类：一类是国际条约规则，另一类是国际习惯规则。从本文研究的角度来看，国际条约也可分为两类，一类是我国为缔约方的国际条约，另一类是我国不是缔约方的国际条约。就前者而言，我国既然选择了缔结或加入该条约，就必须遵守条约规则，与这些条约规则“接轨”，是不言而喻的事情。就后者而言，由于我国不是条约的缔约方，条约规则对我国没有约束力，我国是否参照这类条约的规定来确立自己的外资、外贸管理规范，是我国可以自行决定的事情。换言之，我们并不负有与这类国际规则“接轨”的义务。国际习惯是指“作为通例之证明而经接受为法律者”。[①] 国际习惯规则的确立需要两个构成要件，即各国的反复的类似的行为和被各国认为具有法的约束力。国际习惯在历史上曾是国际法的主要渊源，但由于其具有内容不易确定及形成时间缓慢等缺陷，所以，其地位目前已被国际条约所取代。国际习惯曾被认为是具有普遍约束力的国际法规则，但当今的国际实践则普遍赞同：一项国际习惯规则不能约束一贯地明确地反对这一规则的国家。[②] 因此，如果在外资、外贸管理方面存在国际习惯规则，我们的立场也不应该是简单地与其“接轨”，而是根据自己的判断进行自主选择。

其次，某些规则或做法是否构成“国际规则”尚需甄别。就外资的

---

① 联合国《国际法院规约》第 38 条。

② 见联合国国际法院就“英挪渔业案”（Anglo-Norwegian Fisheries Case）和哥伦比亚诉秘鲁的“庇护案”（Colombia-Peru Asylum Case）所作的判决，分别参见联合国国际法院主页上公布的判决书：http://www. icj-cij. org/docket/index. php? p1 = 3&p2 = 3&k = a6&case = 5&code = ukn&p3 = 4，最后访问日期：2014 年 3 月 13 日；http://www. icj-cij. org/docket/index. php? p1 = 3&p2 = 3&k = f8&case = 7&code = cp&p3 = 4，最后访问日期：2014 年 3 月 13 日。

“市场准入阶段国民待遇”加“负面清单”的做法而言，目前还很难说它已经是一种“国际规则”。从多数国家的实践来看，“国民待遇”是外资和外国投资者进入东道国之后才能享有的待遇。同大多数国家一样，我国以往与其他国家签订的双边投资协定中，各缔约方所承诺的国民待遇只限于市场准入之后，而且，还将赋予对方投资者及投资国民待遇的义务限定在“在不损害缔约一方可适用的法律法规的前提下”。例如，在我国政府与贝宁政府于2004年2月18日签订的《关于促进和保护投资的协定》中，关于国民待遇的规定是：“在不损害其法律法规的前提下，缔约一方应给予缔约另一方投资者在其境内的投资及与投资有关活动不低于其给予本国投资者的投资及与投资有关活动的待遇。”[①] 协定中对“投资”的定义为：“缔约一方投资者依照缔约另一方的法律和法规在缔约另一方领土内所投入的各种财产。”[②] 将国民待遇原则的适用前移到市场准入阶段是美国全力推动的。即便如此，在美国已签署的40多个投资协定中，也只有卢旺达、乌拉圭、加拿大和韩国等为数不多的国家接受了“负面清单”的做法。[③] 因此，我国关于外资和外国投资者国民待遇原则适用的立场转变，只能说是与美国的做法“接轨”，[④] 而不能说是与“国际接轨”。

最后，“接轨”或“不接轨”自身不说明什么问题，“接轨”问题的本质是一国对“国际规则”所持的立场，不应一概地强调或反对“与国际接轨”。国际规则是国际秩序的基础，也影响甚至决定了各国间的利益分配格局。由于国际社会不存在超国家的政府，国际规则的确立方式主要是

---

① 其英文表述为：“Without prejudice to its laws and regulations, each Contracting Party shall accord to investments and activities associated with such investments by the investors of the other Contracting Party treatment not less favorable than that accorded to the investments and associated activities by its own investors”。

② 其英文表述为：“The term ‘investment’ means every kind of assets invested by investors of one Contracting Party in accordance with the laws and regulations of the other Contracting Party in the territory of the later”。

③ 温先涛：《〈中国投资保护协定范本〉（草案）论稿（一）》，《国际经济法学刊》第18卷第4期，北京大学出版社，2012，第188页。

④ 2014年1月15日，为期两天的第11轮中美投资协定（BIT）谈判在上海落幕，中美双方在此轮会谈上正式开始文本谈判。中美BIT谈判启动于2008年。2013年7月11日，在第五轮中美战略与经济对话过程中，中方宣布以“准入前国民待遇和负面清单”为基础与美方进行投资协定的实质性谈判。有专家预计，在本轮文本谈判中，有可能涉及“负面清单”本身内容的谈判商定。

国家间的约定，因此，国际规则与国际秩序必然会更多地反映强国的意志。中国作为一个国际贸易和国际投资的大国，在国际经济规则的创设过程中，将有更多的机会表达自己的意愿。同时，我国政府根据自身情况的变化而调整自己就某些国际规则和制度的立场也属正常情况，没有必要将这种立场调整贴上“与国际接轨”的标签。就“市场准入阶段国民待遇”问题而言，10 年前的中国主要是一个吸收外资的大国，那时候讨论“市场准入的国民待遇”并不适宜，因为这意味着我国将主要作为义务主体，而很少享受利益。今天的情况则完全不同，我国在保有资本输入大国地位的同时，也成为资本输出大国。如何保障我国企业顺利进入外国市场成为一个十分现实的问题。同时，30 多年的经济发展也使我国国内产业抗冲击的能力大为提高，因此，我国政府与他国政府探讨彼此给予“市场准入阶段的国民待遇”就摆上议事日程。第二次世界大战以来，美国一直是国际贸易和国际投资的大国，对国际经济规则的制定起决定性作用，这就决定了中美两国的投资协定谈判肩负着塑造未来的国际投资规则的使命。因此，当今的“国际规则”是什么已经不重要，是否与其“接轨”也不重要，重要的是中美投资协定谈判以及正在同时进行的《跨太平洋伙伴关系协议》(TPP)① 和《跨大西洋贸易与投资伙伴关系协定》（TTIP)② 谈判会对我国的利益产生何等影响，以及如何保证未来国际经济秩序的公平性。从这个意义上说，当我们谈到上海自贸区的时候，还是不要忽略其全称中的“试验”二字。

（责任编辑：曲相霏）

（本文原载于《国际法研究》2014 年第 1 期）

---

① 《跨太平洋伙伴关系协议》(Trans-Pacific Partnership Agreement，简称 TPP)，其前身是《跨太平洋战略经济伙伴关系协定》(Trans-Pacific Strategic Economic Partnership Agreement)，由新西兰、新加坡、智利和文莱四国发起。2008 年 9 月，美国总统奥巴马宣布参与 TPP 谈判。2009 年 11 月，美国正式提出扩大跨太平洋伙伴关系计划。从此，美国开始全方位主导 TPP 谈判。

② 《跨大西洋贸易与投资伙伴关系协定》(Transatlantic Trade and Investment Partnership，简称 TTIP)，其谈判方为欧盟与美国，因此又称为“欧美自由贸易协定”。2013 年 7 月 8 日，欧美启动了 TTIP 的首轮谈判。

关于菲律宾南海断续线仲裁请求的管辖权问题

——《联合国海洋法公约》第298.1（a）（i）项下的排除和海洋权利之争

张新军*

一 前言

2015年10月29日，应菲律宾共和国请求依据1982年《联合国海洋法公约》（以下简称《公约》）附件七建立的仲裁庭，在荷兰海牙对菲律宾所称依据《公约》就中国和菲律宾有关南海"海洋管辖权"的争端单方面提起的强制仲裁（以下简称"南海仲裁案"）的管辖权和受理可能性问题作出了裁决。[①] 被菲律宾作为核心诉求而分别列入其第一和第二项仲裁请求[②]的有

---

* 张新军，清华大学法学院副教授。

① *Award on Jurisdiction and Admissibility*, 29 October 2015, http://www. pcacases. com/web/sendAttach/1506，最后访问日期：2016年2月23日。

② （1）China's maritime entitlements in the South China Sea, like those of the Philippines, may not extend beyond those permitted by the United Nations Convention on the Law of the Sea（"UNCLOS" or the "Convention"）；（2）China's claims to sovereign rights and jurisdiction, and to "historic rights", with respect to the maritime areas of the South China Sea encompassed by the so called "nine-dash line" are contrary to the Convention and without lawful effect to the extent that they exceed the geographic and substantive limits of China's maritime entitlements under UNCLOS. *Award on Jurisdiction and Admissibility*, para. 101, p. 34.

关南海断续线的诉求，被仲裁庭视为有关海洋权利来源的争端，[①] 归结为一个“《公约》框架下的有关历史性权利的争端”。[②] 仲裁庭以中国历史性权利主张的性质和有效性事关实体问题判断为由，认定由此产生的可能的管辖抗辩不具有完全的先决性质，因而在判决中宣告将第一和第二项下的南海断续线仲裁请求的管辖权判断延后至实体问题审理阶段。

从仲裁庭就菲律宾第一和第二项请求的管辖权问题所作的结论来看，由于仲裁庭将菲律宾有关南海断续线的请求排他地归结为“《公约》框架下的有关历史性权利的争端”，而不考虑判断南海断续线可能依据的其他海洋权利来源，因此仲裁庭关于此问题的下一步审理很可能会仅仅考虑中国基于《公约》第 298 条所作的声明是否排除了“历史性权利”这一个问题。这是本文将要讨论的关于《公约》第 298.1（a）（i）项[③]的解释的一个问题。[④]

另外，将菲律宾有关南海断续线的仲裁请求限于历史性权利问题，不仅偏离了菲律宾第一、第二项仲裁请求的文本结构，也与南海断续线在中菲争端水域的基本地理事实不符。如果菲律宾有关南海断续线的诉求根据争端水域的基本事实和仲裁庭的初步判断涉及对其他海洋权利来源的判断，则仲裁庭在实体问题审理阶段可能仍然不得不重新考虑这些和其他的海洋权利来源相关的争端特别是中国主张主权的岛礁在《公约》第 121 条解释或适用上的争端，是否作为与划界相关的一揽子争端已经被中国基于《公约》第 298 条所作的声明所排除的问题。这是本文将要讨论的有关《公约》第 298.1（a）（i）项的解释的另一个问题。

---

① *Award on Jurisdiction and Admissibility*, para. 164, p. 64.

② *Award on Jurisdiction and Admissibility*, para. 168, p. 66 [“a dispute about historic rights in the framework of the Convention”].

③ 《公约》298.1（a）（i）项的英文文本如下：Article 298 Optional exceptions to applicability of section 2 1. When signing, ratifying or acceding to this Convention or at any time thereafter, a State may, without prejudice to the obligations arising under section 1, declare in writing that it does not accept any one or more of the procedures provided for in section 2 with respect to one or more of the following categories of disputes：（a）（i）disputes concerning the interpretation or application of articles 15, 74 and 83 relating to sea boundary delimitations, or those involving historic bays or titles, provided that a State having made such a declaration shall, …

④ 笔者有关这一解释问题的初步讨论，见 Xinjun Zhang, “‘Setting Aside Disputes and Pursuing Joint Development’ at Crossroads in South China Sea”, in Jing Huang and Andrew Billo (eds.), *Territorial Disputes in the South China Sea：Navigating Rough Waters*（London：Palgrave Macmillan, 2014), p. 46。

二　菲律宾关于南海断续线的仲裁请求涉及的海洋权利

如上所述，仲裁庭将菲律宾有关南海断续线的第一、第二项仲裁请求作为有关海洋权利来源的一个争端处理。参照国际法院判例对类似请求的处理，其第一项请求是“以定义、原则或规则为形式的一系列假设，以此支撑所提之争点但并不构成其主张的精确和直接的表述”。[①] 这样来看，仲裁庭将两项请求作为一个争端，并非没有道理。然而，菲律宾第二项仲裁请求的对象是中国南海断续线内的（1）中国所主张的“主权权利和管辖权”和（2）中国所主张的“历史性权利”。可见，菲律宾有关南海断续线的仲裁请求所涉及的海洋权利来源，在文本结构上是两个并列的海洋权利来源，而不仅是一个历史性权利。仲裁庭在对菲律宾有关南海断续线的仲裁请求这一争端的定性上，一方面认为其是有关海洋权利来源之争，一方面又认定其只限于海洋权利来源之争中有关历史性权利的争端。这样的定性解释，明显背离了菲律宾仲裁请求的文本。

同时，这样的定性解释也不合乎菲律宾有关南海断续线仲裁请求的目的，而请求目的恰恰是仲裁庭自己在本案中给出的有关争端定性的两个基准之一。[②] 在第二项请求中，菲律宾明确要求仲裁庭宣布中国南海断续线内的主张超出了《公约》下中国能具有的海洋权利的地理和实体限度。很明显，这一请求的目的是要求仲裁庭判断中国的南海断续线是否符合《公约》，挑战的是中国所主张的南海海洋权利的存在和范围。[③] 为实现菲律宾的这一请求目的，仲裁庭将不得不面对争议水域中的多个海洋权利，包括菲律宾仲裁请求第二项文本所明示的中国所主张的“主权权利和管辖权”。

正是由于上述请求目的的存在，在判断南海断续线是否符合《公约》时，不考虑中国所主张的“主权权利和管辖权”将无法最终达到解决南海

---

① 参见 *Fisheries* (*United Kingdom v. Norway*), I. C. J. Reports 1951, p. 126. 对提交文件的类似处理，参见 *The Minquiers and Ecrehos case*, Judgment, I. C. J. Reports 1953, pp. 50 - 52.

② *Award on Jurisdiction and Admissibility*, para. 153, p. 59.

③ *Award on Jurisdiction and Admissibility*, para. 157, p. 61.

断续线争端的目的。由于中国对争议水域中岛礁的主权主张，中国对南海断续线内水域的主张仍然可以被视为代表了中国主权在《公约》上能够产生的合法的海洋权利的范围。特别是在菲律宾的巴拉望岛和南沙诸岛之间，南海断续线（两段）并未超出南沙诸岛的若干大岛（太平岛等）的200海里或350海里。对于这些南沙诸岛的大岛，仲裁庭自身也认为“有必要考虑中国所主张的任何南海的海洋地物产生的海洋（权利）区域，无论是否为中国现时占领”。[①] 如果在下一步的实体问题审理阶段，仲裁庭对南沙诸岛中的若干大岛的判断和国际法学界的主流观点一致，[②] 即认定其为可以拥有专属经济区和大陆架的岛屿而非《公约》第121（3）条下的礁石的话，那么即使仲裁庭认为自身对历史性权利有管辖权并且否定相关历史性权利的法律效力，也不能就此判断这一水域中的南海断续线在《公约》上的合法性问题。[③]

三 《公约》第298.1（a）（i）项下的排除和其他海洋权利来源之争

南海断续线内中国所主张的“主权权利和管辖权”，与争议水域内能够主张专属经济区和大陆架的海洋地物的法律性质相关。仲裁庭一方面认

---

① *Award on Jurisdiction and Admissibility*, para. 154, p. 60.

② Robert C. Beckman and Clive H. Schofield, “Defining EEZ Claims from Islands: A Potential South China Sea Change”, *International Journal of Marine and Coastal Law* 29 (2014): 210; Alex G. Oude Elferink, “The Islands in the South China Sea: How Does Their Presence Limit the Extent of the High Seas and the Area and the Maritime Zones of the Mainland Coasts?”, *Ocean Development & International Law* 32 (2001): 178. One commentator, however, was of the view that none of the Spratly features could at present to be capable of sustaining human habitation or economic life of their own. 参见 Marius Gjetnes, “The Spratlys: Are They Rocks or Islands?”, *Ocean Development & International Law* 32 (2001): 201。

③ 当然，如果在管辖阶段，仲裁庭根据先决问题审理时相应的证据标准和仲裁庭应当周知之事实（judicial notice），对南沙诸岛中类似太平岛这样的大岛就得出了上述结论的话，仲裁庭将支持中方立场文件中所提出的基于陆地决定海洋原则定性争端的管辖异议，只能得出其不具有管辖权的结论（至少是对巴拉望岛和南沙诸岛之间的南海断续线）。遗憾的是，仲裁庭并没有尝试这么做。中方的这一管辖异议见 Position Paper of the Government of the People's Republic of China on the Matter of Jurisdiction in the South China Sea Arbitration Initiated by the Republic of the Philippines (2014/12/07), http://www.fmprc.gov.cn/mfa_eng/zxxx_662805/t1217147.shtml., paras. 11 – 13，最后访问日期：2016年2月23日。

为“有必要考虑中国所主张的任何南海的海洋地物产生的海洋（权利）区域，无论是否为中国现时占领”，一方面又将争议水域内高潮时露出水面的所有海洋地物在《公约》第121（3）条的解释或适用上就其是否能够拥有自己的专属经济区和大陆架的问题，作为悬案问题放在实体问题审理阶段处理。仲裁庭将和《公约》第121（3）条解释或适用相关的争端，归结为和海洋权利来源相关的争端。[①] 这一海洋权利来源之争，是菲律宾有关南海断续线的仲裁请求中针对中国所主张的“主权权利和管辖权”的关键所在。

仲裁庭在《公约》第121（3）条关于岛礁性质的争端问题的解释或适用上，认为岛礁性质的争端既不是岛礁主权争端，也不是和海洋划界有关的争端，因而明确认定自身对此具有管辖权。[②] 这一判断否定了中方在管辖权立场文件中有关本案争端定性的两个一般性管辖异议。[③] 本文仅就作为海洋权利来源之争的有关《公约》第121（3）条的解释和适用问题是否落入《公约》第298.1（a）（i）项的排除范围展开讨论。[④]

菲律宾自己也承认，《公约》第298.1（a）（i）项所排除的并不直接是海洋划界，而是“关于划定海洋边界的第15条、第74条、第83条在解释或适用上的争端”。[⑤] 上述解释或适用上的争端，通过“关于（relating to）”这一措辞，与划定海洋边界相关联。从爱琴海大陆架一案（*Aegean Sea Continental Shelf*）中国际法院确认大陆架划界是“关于”领土主权问题这一判断[⑥]来看，本案将要考虑的海洋权利来源问题必然也是“关于”划定海洋边界的。因此考虑海洋权利来源争端是否为《公约》第298.1（a）（i）项所排除这一问题的核心是，海洋权利来源特别是《公约》第121（3）条的解释或适用上关于岛礁性质的争端，是否落入“第15条、第74

---

① *Award on Jurisdiction and Admissibility*, para. 169, p. 66.

② *Award on Jurisdiction and Admissibility*, para. 400, pp. 141 – 142; para. 404, pp. 143 – 144.

③ *Award on Jurisdiction and Admissibility*, para. 158, p. 61.

④ 先行研究中有初步的支持性结论。参见 Natalie Klein, *Dispute settlement in the UN Convention on the Law of the Sea* (Cambridge: Cambridge University Press, 2005), p. 276。另参见 Barbara Kwiatkowska and Alfred H. A. Soons, “Entitlement to Maritime Areas of Rocks Which Cannot Sustain Human habitation or Economic Life of Their Own”, *Netherlands Yearbook of International Law* 21 (1999): 181。

⑤ *Award on Jurisdiction and Admissibility*, para. 374, p. 132.

⑥ *Aegean Sea Continental Shelf*, Judgment, I. C. J. Reports 1978, paras. 84, 86, pp. 35 – 36.

条、第83条在解释或适用上的争端”之内。

《公约》第74条和第83条，通过共通的4个分款，设置了和划界相关的一系列的法律条件和权利义务关系。其解释和适用问题涉及最多的第1款，也并非严格意义上的划界——该款并不强求划出一条海上边界。因为如果对划界作这样的解释的话，“不现实并且过于正式”。[①] 第1款所要求的，是“在国际法院规约第38条所指国际法的基础上以协议划定，以便得到公平解决”。这一条款规定的是当事国在划界过程中以含糊的所谓“国际法院规约第38条所指国际法的基础”为定义的权利义务。这样“简单和不精准的定义方式”，在解释上将“允许广泛地考虑那些和划界相关的条约和习惯法规则”。[②]

在《公约》生效前的有关大陆架划界案件中，在解释或适用习惯法规则时，与海洋权利或海洋权利来源相关的问题构成划界争端的“基本要素”[③] 或“关联问题”。[④] 韦尔（Prosper Weil）也将（涉及大陆架的）权利视为划界的核心。[⑤] 在《公约》生效后，海洋权利和权利来源也是有关《公约》第74条、第83条的解释或适用的争端的核心。在巴巴多斯诉特立尼达和多巴哥一案（*Barbados v. Trinidad and Tobago*）中，仲裁庭认为“当事方在可适用的规则的问题上都无法达成一致，更不用说双方一定会对适用其认可的规则后所可能形成的任何分界线无法达成一致”。[⑥] 在该案件中，适用规则的不一致主要是指《公约》上有关大陆架权利制度的相关条款，特别是第76条、第56条和第77条。同样的推理如果运用在南海仲裁案的话，作为海洋权利来源之争的《公约》第121（3）条的解释或适

---

① *Arbitration between Barbados and the Republic of Trinidad and Tobago*，http://www.pca-cpa.org/showfile.asp? fil_id = 178，para. 198（“unrealistic and formalistic”），最后访问日期：2016年2月23日。

② *Arbitration between Barbados and the Republic of Trinidad and Tobago*，para. 222.

③ *Aegean Sea Continental Shelf*，Judgment，para. 83，p. 35.

④ *Continental Shelf*（*Libyan Arab Jamahiriya/Malta*），Judgment，I. C. J. Reports 1985，para. 27，p. 30.

⑤ Prosper Weil，*The law of Maritime Delimitation*：*Reflections*，trans. from the French by Maureen MacGlashan（Cambridge：Grotius Publication，1989），p. 49.

⑥ *Arbitration between Barbados and the Republic of Trinidad and Tobago*，para. 198.（“the Parties could not even agree upon the applicable legal rules shows that a fortiori they could not agree on any particular line which might follow from the application of appropriate rules.”）

用的争端，必然有效地构成有关《公约》第74条、第83条解释或适用的争端。这也是中方在管辖权立场文件中对此问题的基本立场。①

但是仲裁庭并没有在《公约》第298.1（a）（i）项的文本基础上，回应中方在管辖权立场文件中提出的管辖异议，即包括岛礁性质在内的一系列海洋权利之争均作为和划界相关的整体和系统的一揽子争端为中国基于《公约》第298条所作的声明所排除。仲裁庭在本案中对基于《公约》第298条声明所作排除的解释脱离了《公约》第298.1（a）（i）项的文本结构，把焦点放在了是否排除“划界”这一问题上。菲律宾更是主张《公约》第298.1（a）（i）项所排除的是“实际划界”，并进而主张这一“实际划界”仅在沿岸国海洋权利重叠的前提下产生。② 仲裁庭支持了菲律宾的这一解释立场，认为“海洋边界可以在……有着重叠海洋权利的国家间划分”。③ 这样，仲裁庭和菲律宾一样将《公约》第298.1（a）（i）项下的排除限定于存在海洋权利重叠水域的“划界”争端。

假定仲裁庭对《公约》第298.1（a）（i）项下的排除所作的解释是正确的，那么中国和菲律宾在争议水域是否存在海洋权利重叠的问题，也涉及《公约》第121条的解释或适用，即对特定岛礁性质的判断。以黄岩岛为例，在其周边200海里以内，除了与其相距118海里的菲律宾的吕宋岛，没有其他高潮时高于水面的岛礁的存在。但正是由于这样的地理事实，中菲之间的争端水域潜在地存在中方基于黄岩岛主权与菲律宾吕宋岛方向的海洋权利重叠，因而必然具有划界之情形。是否存在海洋权利的重叠以至于被《公约》第298.1（a）（i）项排除，这一问题本身取决于黄岩岛是岛还是礁这一悬案问题；而仲裁庭对这一悬案问题的管辖权，又必须通过回答其是否为《公约》第298.1（a）（i）项所排除这一问题来解决。很显然，这里的管辖权问题存在着蛋和鸡的循环推理的陷阱。

在国际法院审理的国际民航组织理事会一案（*ICAO Council*）中，曾出现过类似的陷阱。该案中，原告印度根据《芝加哥公约》第84条和

① *Position Paper of the Government of the People's Republic of China on the Matter of Jurisdiction in the South China Sea Arbitration Initiated by the Republic of the Philippines*, para. 67.

② *Award on Jurisdiction and Admissibility*, para. 374, p. 132.

③ *Award on Jurisdiction and Admissibility*, paras. 155 - 156, pp. 60 - 61.

《过境协定》第2条第2款有关理事会决定的上诉的规定，将国际民航组织理事会原审案件有关管辖权的决定提交至国际法院。被告巴基斯坦对这一上诉的主要管辖异议是，原告所依据的上诉条款，仅允许国际法院对国际民航组织理事会作出的实体问题的决定具有上诉管辖，而不包括国际民航组织理事会自身的管辖问题的决定。[①] 按照这一解释，国际法院对国际民航组织理事会决定的上诉管辖，取决于理事会是否具有对原案的管辖权这一悬案问题；而这一悬案问题的管辖权，又正是《芝加哥公约》第84条和《过境协定》第2条第2款上诉管辖的规定所面临并需要解决的问题。国际法院从两个条约中的上诉管辖规定入手，作出了以下的判断：

> 法庭认为理事会有关其自身是否可以管辖案件的决定……本质上是严重影响本案两造地位的实体性问题，尽管它并不能决定最终的实体问题。因此，法院认为，从规定（上诉）管辖的相关条约条款的目的上看，理事会有关其自身管辖权的最终决定无法和其有关实体问题的最终决定区分。[②]

国际法院在此问题上进一步阐释：

> 尽管有关（理事会）管辖权的决定不能决定本案“最终的实体问题”，这仍然是一个实体性质的决定，因为如果这一决定推翻了有关管辖的假设，这将使得整个案件就此结束。具有这样效果的决定很难说其重要性比实体问题的决定要小，它要么完全排除（案件审理），要么通过对管辖权基础——这是任何实体问题决定的不可缺失的基础——存在的肯定，允许（进一步的案件审理）。因此一个管辖权的决定毫无疑问是作为整体看待的案件的组成部分，并应当在原则上视同为任何可以上诉的实体问题的决定。[③]

---

① *Appeal Relating to the Jurisdiction of the ICA0 Council*, Judgment, I. C. J. Reports 1972, para. 14, p. 52.

② *Appeal Relating to the Jurisdiction of the ICA0 Council*, para. 18, p. 56.

③ *Appeal Relating to the Jurisdiction of the ICA0 Council*, para. 18, p. 56.

回到南海仲裁案中，仲裁庭同意中方有关划界是一个整体和系统过程的看法，并认为海洋权利问题仅仅是这一过程的起点。[①] 这样的话，即使仲裁庭将《公约》第298.1（a）（i）项的解释仅限于排除“划界”，则依照国际法院在国际民航组织理事会一案的推理，岛礁的法律性质这一海洋权利来源之争也将为《公约》第298.1（a）（i）项所排除。仍然以黄岩岛为例，如果判断黄岩岛为礁石的话，将无从划界，而具有这样效果的决定很难说其重要性要比“划界”的决定小；而如果判断黄岩岛为岛的话，则此决定将成为“划界”争端为《公约》第298.1（a）（i）项所排除。无论如何，对黄岩岛是岛还是礁的判断，尽管不能决定最终的“划界”，但毫无疑问应该被视同为必须排除的“划界”问题〔如果《公约》第298.1（a）（i）项解释为排除“划界”的话〕。

由于仲裁庭将与巴拉望岛相对的南沙诸岛中高潮时露出水面的所有岛礁都作为《公约》第121条解释或适用的悬案问题，上述推理也适用于关于这些岛礁性质争端的管辖权问题上，因此关于这一问题的结论应和仲裁庭的结论相反，即应该决定这一问题为《公约》第298.1（a）（i）项所排除。由于围绕中国主张的黄岩岛和南沙诸岛的法律性质这一海洋权利来源之争，是菲律宾有关南海断续线的仲裁请求中针对中国所主张的“主权权利和管辖权”的关键所在，即使不考虑《公约》第298.1（a）（i）项下是否排除了历史性权利这一仲裁庭自设的可能的管辖权问题，仲裁庭也将不具有对菲律宾关于南海断续线的仲裁请求的管辖权。

四　历史性权利和《公约》第298.1（a）（i）项下的排除

对于仲裁庭自设的管辖权问题即历史性权利（historic rights）是否能为中国基于《公约》第298条所作的声明所排除，菲律宾当然主张是不能。其理由是：第一，《公约》第298.1（a）（i）项所能排除的“历史性

① *Award on Jurisdiction and Admissibility*, para. 155, p. 60.

海湾或所有权”（historic bays or titles）限定于主权性质的海洋权利；第二，中国在南海主张的历史性权利并非主权性质的海洋权利。①

就第二点而言，中国政府坚持南海断续线内包括南沙诸岛和黄岩岛等的主权，却并没有澄清南海断续线在海洋权利主张上的意义。尽管如此，中国政府在南海断续线内的西沙群岛划定了直线基线；不仅如此，中国政府反复声明包括在南海断续线内的南海水域的航行自由不受阻碍。② 仲裁庭或许认定上述国家实践在现代海洋法上表明了南海断续线内水域并非全部为主权性的，③ 从而支持菲律宾的主张。

问题在于《公约》第 298. 1（a）（i）项中的“历史性海湾或所有权”（historic bays or titles）的解释能否仅仅限定为主权性质的海洋权利。在南海仲裁案庭审中原告律师花了大量的篇幅，讨论《公约》第 298. 1（a）（i）项的不同语言版本中的“历史性海湾或所有权”（historic bays or titles），试图论证这一点。④ 但这也恰恰说明，关于“历史性海湾或所有权”（historic bays or titles）在解释上客观存在着问题。

《公约》第 298. 1（a）（i）项对“历史性海湾或所有权”（historic bays or titles）没有定义。《公约》涉及“historic bay（s）or title（s）”的条款只有《公约》第 10. 6 条和第 15 条。因此，有很有力的学说支持与《公约》第 298. 1（a）（i）项中的“历史性海湾或所有权”（historic bays or titles）

---

① “Final Transcript Day 2 - Jurisdiction Hearing” - 08 - 07 - 2015（English）, http://www.pcacases.com/web/sendAttach/1400, p. 58, p. 62，最后访问日期：2016 年 3 月 3 日；“Final Transcript Day 1 - Merits Hearing” - 24 - 11 - 2015（English）, http://www.pcacases.com/web/sendAttach/1547, p. 15, p. 47，最后访问日期：2016 年 3 月 3 日。

② *Foreign Ministry Spokesperson Hong Lei's Regular Press Conference on February* 29, 2012, http://www.fmprc.gov.cn/eng/xwfw/s2510/2511/t910855.htm，最后访问日期：2013 年 11 月 12 日。

③ 在丰塞卡湾这一多国共享的历史性海湾中，作为现代海洋法的变则（“an anomaly in terms of the modern law of the sea”），存在着沿岸国合意设置的 3 海里排他的管辖和主权水域，以及和现行的对构成内水的湾的法律地位的理解不一致（“at odds with the present general understanding of the legal status of the waters of a bay as constituting ‘internal waters’”）的无害通航。*Land, Island and Maritime Frontier Dispute*（*El Salvador/Honduras: Nicaragua*（*intervening*））, I. C. J. Reports 1992, paras. 392 - 393, pp. 593 - 594.

④ “Final Transcript Day 2 - Jurisdiction Hearing” - 08 - 07 - 2015（English）, http://www.pcacases.com/web/sendAttach/1400, pp. 70 - 72.，最后访问日期：2016 年 3 月 3 日。被告律师自身也注意到俄文版本并不支持其说法。

相关的争端仅指上述两个条款的解释或适用的争端，[①] 而这两个条款中的 historic bay（s）or title（s）明确所指的是主权性水域。但从《公约》第 298.1（a）（i）项的文本结构来看，上述这样的解释存在问题。因为该条款的前半段已经排除了《公约》第 15 条的解释或适用，而历史性所有权（historic title）却又明文规定在《公约》第 15 条中。这样，《公约》第 298.1（a）（i）项前半段对《公约》第 15 条的解释或适用的排除，即已排除了该条款文本中明文规定的历史性所有权（historic title）的解释或适用。《公约》第 298.1（a）（i）项后半段的 "historic titles" 即使和第 15 条的单数形式历史性所有权（historic title）不构成两者性质差别的决定因素，在解释结论上两者的性质也一定是不同的。因为如果不是这样的话，《公约》第 298.1（a）（i）项后半段的 "historic titles" 的排除就是多余的。

由于《公约》第 15 条规定的是领海划界之规则，其中的历史性所有权（historic title）一定是指向主权性质的水域。《公约》第 298.1（a）（i）项后半段的 "historic titles" 性质与此不同，必然包括非主权性质的历史性水域。对于 historic title（s）这样的定性，在联合国 1957 年和 1962 年有关历史性水域和历史性海湾的两个文件中都有所体现。[②]

和《公约》第 298.1（a）（i）项前半段排除与划界相关的第 15 条、第 74 条、第 83 条的解释适用不同，《公约》第 298.1（a）（i）项后半段 "historic bays or titles" 甚至不和划界直接关联。这样，围绕 "historic bays or titles" 的《公约》合规性的争端，即使其合规性问题涉及的是有关海洋

---

① Treves argued, "…according to article 286, compulsory jurisdiction applies only to deputes concerning the interpretation or application of the Convention. It would seem to follow that compulsory jurisdiction can concern historic bays and titles only to the extent that the dispute concerns the interpretation or application of article 10, para. 6, and article 15". T. Treves, "The Jurisdiction of the International Tribunal for the Law of the Sea", in P. Chandrasekhara Rao and Rahmatullah Khan (Eds.), *The International Tribunal for the Law of the Sea: Law and Practice* (Hague: Kluwer Law International, 2001), p. 121.

② *Juridical Regime of Historic Waters, Including Historic Bays* (1962), para. 183, p. 25. ["there seems to be no doubt that, in principle, a historic title may exist also to other waters than bays, such as straits or archipelagos, or in general to all those waters which can form part of the maritime domain of a State."] *Historic Bays: Memorandum by the Secretariat of the United Nations* (1957), para. 199, p. 37. ["The application of the theory is not limited to bays. It tends to be applied also to straits, to the waters within archipelago and, generally, to the various areas capable of being comprised in the maritime domain of the State."]

权利来源（sources of maritime entitlement）的其他条款引起的解释和适用问题，也将被排除。同样的排除构造也反映在《公约》第298.1（b）项有关军事活动的排除和《公约》第298.1（c）项安理会所采取行动的排除上。和上述排除需要证明相关的活动是不是军事活动或安理会所采取行动这样的事实问题一样，历史性权利（historic rights）的存在也将作为事实问题确认。在这一点上，仲裁庭却又令人困惑地将历史性权利（historic rights）的有效性（validity）作为实体问题留作下一步审理时决定。然而，仲裁庭如果不是单纯进行事实确认而是进入有关历史性权利的有效性问题的判断的话，其本身对这一问题是否拥有管辖权就成为问题。①

五 结论

菲律宾有关中国南海断续线的仲裁请求，挑战的是中国的海洋权利主张。这一挑战，明显和划界“相关”。无论菲律宾挑战的是南海断续线内中国主张的“主权权利和管辖权”还是“历史性权利”，都有可能落入《公约》第298.1（a）（i）项下，为中方基于《公约》第298条的声明所排除。

仲裁庭在考虑菲律宾有关中国南海断续线的仲裁请求时，完全忽略了“历史性权利”之外的其他海洋权利来源之争，尤其关键的是有关岛礁性质的《公约》第121（3）条的解释或适用之争能否落入《公约》第298.1（a）（i）项下这一问题。但仲裁庭在处理菲律宾直接提出的有关岛礁性质的《公约》第121（3）条的解释或适用的仲裁请求时，未能展开对《公约》第298.1（a）（i）项的解释，导致最后认定自身具有管辖权。

在实体问题审理中依职权重新考虑在先决问题审理中已予考虑的管辖权问题，这样的做法，在国际法院的审判实践中，特别是在被告缺席时，

---

① Philip Saunders（加拿大达尔豪斯Dalhousie大学法学院教授）在中国南海研究院2016年1月24日举办的“Symposium on the Historic Rights and the South China Sea Arbitration”会议上所作的题为“Compulsory Adjudication of Disputes over Historic Rights and Title: Implications for the China-Philippines Arbitration”的发言中，提及这一观点。

并非无例可循。[1] 只有在穷尽并扫清了所有海洋权利来源上的管辖障碍后，仲裁庭才能确定对菲律宾有关南海断续线的仲裁请求具有管辖权。同时，如果仲裁庭在实体问题审理中判断关于《公约》第298条的声明排除了“历史性权利”这一自设的管辖异议成立的话，仲裁庭也将无权审理菲律宾有关南海断续线的请求。这样，即使仲裁庭对其他海洋权利来源上中方已提出的管辖异议存在疏忽，也将不影响这一结论。

（责任编辑：曲相霏）

（本文原载于《国际法研究》2016年第2期）

① *Fisheries Jurisdiction* (*United Kingdom v. Iceland*), Merits, Judgment, I. C. J. Reports 1974, paras. 42 – 48, pp. 20 – 23. *Military and Paramilitary Activities in and against Nicaragua* (*Nicaragua v. United States of America*), Merits, Judgment, I. C. J. Reports 1986, paras. 32 – 35, pp. 26 – 28.

中国外交抗议在南海仲裁程序中的法律意义

叶　强*

引　言

2014年12月7日，中国外交部受权发表《中华人民共和国政府关于菲律宾共和国所提南海仲裁案管辖权问题的立场文件》（以下简称《立场文件》）。[①]《立场文件》从《联合国海洋法公约》（以下简称《公约》）及相关国际法的角度，向国际社会表明中国认为菲律宾所提南海仲裁案仲裁庭没有管辖权的立场，阐明中国不接受、不参与仲裁的国际法依据，指出菲律宾单方面将南海争议提交国际仲裁的违法之处。[②] 值得注意的是，12月15日是仲裁庭确定的中国提交辩诉状（Counter-Memorial）的截止时间。对此，仲裁庭的回应是："仲裁庭注意到，截至2014年12月16日，中国并未提交其辩诉状，且中国政府重申它不接受、不参与菲律宾单方面提起的仲裁。仲裁庭进一步注意到，其成员收到了中国于2014年12月7日发布的《立场文件》，并且中国政府向书记官处表明'转交上述立场文件不

---

* 叶强，中国南海研究院、中国南海研究协同创新中心助理研究员。

① 《中华人民共和国政府关于菲律宾共和国所提南海仲裁案管辖权问题的立场文件》，外交部网站，http://www.fmprc.gov.cn/mfa_chn/zyxw_602251/t1217143.shtml，最后访问日期：2014年12月20日。

② 《外交部受权发表中国政府关于菲律宾所提南海仲裁案管辖权问题的立场文件》，外交部网站，http://www.fmprc.gov.cn/mfa_chn/zyxw_602251/t1217144.shtml，最后访问日期：2014年12月20日。

得被解释为中国接受或参与仲裁'。"[1] 同时，仲裁庭要求菲律宾对中国政府的公开声明（即《立场文件》，笔者注）作出适当的回应。[2]

自菲律宾就南海争议向中国发出仲裁通知，单方面提起仲裁程序以来，中国政府一直否定仲裁庭对案件的管辖权。此次《立场文件》的发表是迄今为止中国方面级别最高、论述最全面的一次管辖权抗辩，并且已通过外交渠道将该《立场文件》送达常设仲裁法院书记官处。中国政府同时强调转交上述《立场文件》不代表中国接受或参与仲裁。

一般而言，在国际司法和仲裁程序中，若当事国反对法院或法庭对案件行使管辖权，往往要通过“先决性抗辩”程序（Preliminary Objections，或称“初步反对”程序）加以实现。这种抗辩的提出属于庭审“附随程序”（Incidental Proceedings）的组成部分。当事方须参与司法或仲裁程序，并按照法定程序提交书状，才能使法院或法庭审理这一抗辩。因此，中国“不参与”仲裁的立场，似乎削弱了向仲裁庭主张管辖权抗辩的有效性。然而，在国际实践中，国际司法和仲裁机构除了依据当事国提交的“先决性抗辩”中止对案件实体问题的审理之外，还可能依据其他事由先行审理对案件的管辖权。因此，在“南海仲裁案”中，中国政府的一系列外交抗议，包括发表的《立场文件》的法律效力，应结合国际司法实践认真加以评估。

一 《立场文件》发表的背景与性质

《立场文件》的核心内容是否定仲裁庭对菲律宾所提仲裁请求的管辖权。《立场文件》从三个方面指出“仲裁庭对于菲律宾提起的仲裁明显没有管辖权”：首先，菲律宾提请仲裁事项的实质是南海部分岛礁的领土主权问题，超出《公约》的调整范围，仲裁庭无权审理；其次，以谈判方式解决在南海的争端是中菲两国通过双边文件和《南海各方行为宣言》所达成的协议，菲律宾单方面将有关争端提交强制仲裁违反国际法；最后，菲

① 《新闻稿：菲律宾诉中国仲裁案（第3号）》，常设仲裁法院网站，http://www.pca.cpa/org/showfile.asp? fil_id = 2848，最后访问日期：2014年12月20日。

② 《新闻稿：菲律宾诉中国仲裁案（第3号）》，常设仲裁法院网站，http://www.pca.cpa.org/showfile.asp? fil_id = 2848，最后访问日期：2014年12月20日。

律宾提出的仲裁事项构成中菲两国海域划界不可分割的组成部分，而中国已根据《公约》的规定于2006年作出声明，将涉及海域划界等事项的争端排除适用仲裁等强制争端解决程序。[①]

上述观点是自2013年1月22日，菲律宾根据1982年《公约》第287条和附件七就中菲有关南海争议提起强制仲裁程序以来，中国一直坚持的立场。2013年2月19日，中国政府退回菲律宾的照会及所附《仲裁通知》，表示中国不接受菲律宾单方面提起的仲裁，最重要的原因是："由直接有关的主权国家谈判解决有关争议，是东盟国家同中国达成的共识"；[②] 菲律宾的诉求是"对双方均主张的岛礁的主权归属进行判定"，"是两国在南海部分海域的海洋划界问题"；"中国政府于2006年已经根据《公约》第298条的规定提交了声明，将涉及海洋划界等争端排除在包括仲裁在内的强制争端解决程序之外"，仲裁庭没有管辖权。[③]

根据《公约》附件七第3条，即使当事一方不参加仲裁员的指派和仲裁庭的组建，另一方仍可通过国际海洋法法庭相关机制完成上述工作。2013年6月，由5人组成的仲裁庭组建完毕，仲裁程序正式转入仲裁庭主导的程序。[④] 第一次仲裁庭会议于2013年7月在海牙召开。8月27日，仲裁庭发布《第1号程序令》，制定了仲裁《程序规则》，并确定2014年3月30日为菲律宾提交诉状（Memorial）的时间。[⑤] 对此，中国向常设仲裁

① 《外交部受权发表中国政府关于菲律宾所提南海仲裁案管辖权问题的立场文件》，外交部网站，http://www.fmprc.gov.cn/mfa_chn/zyxw_602251/t1217144.shtml，最后访问日期：2014年12月20日。

② 《2013年2月19日外交部发言人洪磊主持例行记者会》，外交部网站，http://www.fmprc.gov.cn/mfa_chn/wjdt_611265/fyrbt_611275/t1014798.shtml，最后访问日期：2014年12月20日。

③ 《外交部发言人华春莹就菲律宾推进设立涉中菲南海争议仲裁庭事答记者问》，外交部网站，http://www.fmprc.gov.cn/mfa_chn/wjdt_611265/fyrbt_611275/t1035477.shtml，最后访问日期：2014年12月20日。

④ 《外交部发言人华春莹就菲律宾推进设立涉中菲南海争议仲裁庭事答记者问》，外交部网站，http://www.fmprc.gov.cn/mfa_chn/wjdt_611265/fyrbt_611275/t1035477.shtml，最后访问日期：2014年12月20日。

⑤ PCA Press Release：Arbitration between the Republic of the Philippines and the People's Republic of China：Arbitral Tribunal Establishes Rules of Procedure and Initial Timetable，http://www.pca-cpa.org/showfile.asp? fil_id=2311，最后访问日期：2014年12月20日。

法院递交照会，重申中方不接受仲裁的一贯立场，表明将不参与仲裁程序。[①]

2014 年 3 月 30 日，菲律宾向仲裁庭提交诉状，阐述了仲裁庭管辖权、菲律宾诉求的可受理性以及争议的实体问题。在诉状中，菲律宾叙述了对案件适用法律与相关证据的分析，以证明仲裁庭对菲律宾所提出的所有主张具有管辖权，每项主张都应该得到裁判，最后对每项主张提出了它所寻求的具体救济。对此，中国再次回应称，“不接受菲方就中菲南海争端提起的国际仲裁”，原因还是在于，“不论菲方对其诉状如何包装……问题的实质是双方围绕岛礁主权和海域划界的争端。2006 年，中国依据《公约》作出声明，已将上述争端排除出仲裁程序”，“这是中国与东盟国家共同签署的《南海各方行为宣言》的明确规定，也是中菲双方在一系列双边文件中达成的共识。菲方有义务履行自己的承诺”。[②]

2014 年 5 月，仲裁庭发布《第 2 号程序令》，确定 12 月 15 日为中国提交回应菲律宾诉状的辩诉状的截止日期。常设仲裁法院于 5 月 21 日再次收到来自中国的照会。在照会中，中国重申其“不接受菲律宾提起的仲裁”的立场以及该照会“不应被视为中国接受或参与了仲裁程序”。[③]

可见，中国在“南海仲裁案”仲裁程序的推进过程中，不仅一直通过外交途径向菲律宾持续表明反对其单方面发起并推进仲裁的立场，而且向仲裁庭（包括其常设机构——常设仲裁法院书记官处）多次表明“不接受、不参与”仲裁的立场及其法律依据——仲裁庭对本案没有管辖权。

在国际司法和仲裁实践中，如果当事一方（主要是“被告”方）认为另一方（主要是“原告”方）提请法庭裁决的诉求属于法庭没有管辖权的或不可裁决的（Non-justiciable）事项，国际司法和仲裁机制中往往通过授予当事方“先决性抗辩”的权利来实现诉辩权利平衡。在“南海仲裁案”中，仲裁庭制定的仲裁《程序规则》第 20 条明确规定了有关“先决性抗

---

① PCA Press Release：Arbitration between the Republic of the Philippines and the People's Republic of China：Arbitral Tribunal Establishes Rules of Procedure and Initial Timetable，http://www.pca.cpa.org/showfile.asp?fil_id=2311，最后访问日期：2014 年 12 月 20 日。

② 《外交部发言人洪磊就菲律宾向中菲南海争端仲裁庭提交诉状答记者问》，外交部网站，http://www.fmprc.gov.cn/mfa_chn/fyrbt_602243/dhdw_602249/t1142318.shtml，最后访问日期：2014 年 12 月 20 日。

③ PCA Press Release：Arbitration between the Republic of the Philippines and the People's Republic of China，http://www.pca.cpa.org/showfile.asp?fil_id=2638，最后访问日期：2014 年 12 月 20 日。

辩”的提出及审理程序。其中，第2款规定：“对仲裁庭无管辖权的抗辩，至迟应在辩诉状中提出”；第3款规定：“对于此类抗辩，仲裁庭应作为先决问题作出裁定”。① 在国际实践中，当事国既可能在辩诉状中阐述对管辖权的抗辩，也可能在提交辩诉状前的任何阶段单独提交对管辖权的抗辩。② 一旦法庭裁定此种抗辩具有“完全的先决性”，则会中止对案件实体问题的审理，同时设立独立阶段专门审理管辖权问题。值得注意的是，这一条款中并未提及在仲裁程序之外的任何其他管辖权抗辩行为的方式和效力。

从仲裁参与的程序来说，仲裁案《程序规则》规定，“当事方的书面陈述应按下述方式传送：提交方应通过电子邮件将其书面陈述的电子副本传送给另一当事方、仲裁庭及书记官处，同时应附证据及法律依据”。③ 然而，中国的《立场文件》并非按此程序提出。该《立场文件》在前言中明确指出：“本立场文件不意味着中国在任何方面认可菲律宾的观点和主张。本立场文件也不意味着中国接受或参与菲律宾提起的仲裁”。因此，《立场文件》并不是中国关于仲裁案的辩诉状，也不是程序意义上的“先决性抗辩”，它在性质上仍然延续了“外交抗议”这一政治方式。

那么，以具有政治属性的《立场文件》为形式的对仲裁庭管辖权的外交抗议，是否能够具备法律效果以及具备何种程度的法律效果，就需要通过国际司法实践进行分析，而非通过法律文本（如仲裁《程序规则》）分析。

二 《立场文件》的法律效果

（一）不以“先决性抗辩”为依据的管辖权审理程序：国际司法实践

与仲裁《程序规则》相类似，《国际法院规则》通过第79条规定了

---

① Rules of Procedure, http://www.pca.cpa.org/showfile.asp? fil_id = 2504，最后访问日期：2014年12月20日。

② 这种提交以专门的“Preliminary Objections”文书为形式。例如，常设仲裁法院受理的“毛里求斯诉英国仲裁案”（*The Republic of Mauritius v. The United Kingdom of Great Britain and Northern Ireland*）中，英国向仲裁庭提交了先决性抗辩（Preliminary Objections of the United Kingdom）。参见常设仲裁法院网站，http://www.pca.cpa.org/showpage.asp? pag_id = 1429，最后访问日期：2014年12月20日。

③ Rules of Procedure, http://www.pca.cpa.org/showfile.asp? fil_id = 2504，最后访问日期：2014年12月20日。

“先决性抗辩”的具体程序，以此授权案件当事国对国际法院管辖权提出异议。[①] 然而，不依据该程序提出的管辖权异议抗辩在国际司法实践中一直存在，并且近年有逐渐增多之势。

在“诺特鲍姆案”中，列支敦士登向法院递交请求书以后，被告国危地马拉的外交部长致信法院院长，主张法院对本案没有管辖权。在该信函（Communication）中，危地马拉认为其“接受法院任择性强制管辖权条款的声明已经于1952年1月26日起中止效力”。[②] 随后，法院将该立场视为“先决性抗辩”，并采取了相应的审理程序。[③]

在此之后，“渔业管辖权案”、“核试验案”、“爱琴海大陆架案”、“德黑兰外交人质案”、“边境武装冲突案”以及“尼加拉瓜军事和准军事行动案”等案件中，被告国一方都没有提出正式的“先决性抗辩”，没有遵守《国际法院规则》第79条所规定的“先决性抗辩”程序，而是以信函、通告等外交文件形式来主张国际法院没有管辖权。除了“德黑兰外交人质案”以外，国际法院对其他案件都决定暂时中止对实体问题的审理，先行处理案件的管辖权和可受理性问题，并且都作出了关于管辖权问题的独立判决，在事实上（*de facto*）采取了与“先决性抗辩”相同的处理程序。[④]

在“爱琴海大陆架案”中，被告国土耳其在递交给国际法院的立场通知中，告知法院应援引希腊对《和平解决国际争端总议定书》所附的第二项保留来裁定自身不具备对本案的管辖权。对此，希腊认为，因为土耳其没有依照《国际法院规则》提出“先决性抗辩”，因此上述通知不能被视为对保留的援引。[⑤] 但是国际法院并不认同希腊的主张，指出：“为了查明法院是否对本案具有管辖权，法院应考虑包括缺席被告国提出的‘诉讼程序

---

① Rules of Court (1978), http://www.icj.cij.org/documents/index.php? p1 = 4&p2 = 3&p3 = 0，最后访问日期：2014年12月20日。

② *Nottebohm case* (*Liechtenstein v. Guatemala*) (Preliminary Objection), Judgment of November 18th, 1953, I. C. J. Reports 1953, p. 118.

③ *Nottebohm case* (*Liechtenstein v. Guatemala*) (Preliminary Objection), Judgment of November 18th, 1953, I. C. J. Reports 1953, p. 118.

④ 〔日〕杉原高嶺：《国际司法裁判制度》，王志安、易平译，中国政法大学出版社，2007，第216页。

⑤ *Aegean Sea Continental Shelf Case* (*Greece v. Turkey*), Judgment of 19 December 1978, I. C. J. Reports 1978, para. 41.

外的通知’（extra-procedural communications）在内的所有要素”。[①] 最终，国际法院不仅考虑了土耳其的非正式通知，而且作出了拒绝对希腊所提交的案件行使管辖权的判决。

在“边境武装冲突案”中，被告国洪都拉斯的外交部长致信法院，认为法院对尼加拉瓜提交的案件不具备管辖权，希望法院首先对本案的管辖权和可受理性问题进行审理。对此，经双方当事国协商达成合意，国际法院设定了独立的管辖权审理程序。[②]

在“尼加拉瓜案”中，国际法院认为，“现阶段对管辖权问题的审查，是依据 1984 年 5 月 10 日的命令，由法院自身决定开始的程序，而不是依据美国提出的‘先决性抗辩’而开始的程序”。同时，法院认为，“对美国所提出的法院缺乏管辖权的主张，依据该抗辩程序进行审理是适当的。按照《国际法院规则》第 79 条第 7 款，美国所提出的多边条约保留的抗辩并非仅仅只具有先决性”。[③] 这样，在一方当事国以某种形式对管辖权提出异议时，尤其是被告国在提出异议的同时又缺席的情况下，国际法院自行设定了管辖权问题的审理程序。尽管这是《国际法院规则》中没有规定的程序，但国际法院是自身管辖权的决定者。因此，即使在当事国缺席时，法院也有义务判断自身的管辖权，这是源于《国际法院规约》第 53 条第 2 款的义务。[④]

在“德黑兰外交人质案”中，国际法院指出：“根据法院规约第 53 条的一般法理，法院必须首先自行审查案件中是否存在任何‘先决性问题’（preliminary question），即法院对案件是否具有管辖权以及原告诉求是否具备可受理性。这种‘先决性问题’的存在与否应从案件的全部信息中去寻

---

① *Aegean Sea Continental Shelf Case* （*Greece v. Turkey*），Judgment of 19 December 1978，I. C. J. Reports 1978，para. 42.

② *Case Concerning Border and Transborder Armed Actions* （*Nicaragua v. Honduras*），Order of 22 October 1986，I. C. J. Reports 1986，pp. 551 – 552.

③ *Case Concerning Military and Paramilitary Activities in and against Nicaragua* （*Nicaragua v. United States of America*），Jurisdiction of the Court and Admissibility of the Application，Judgment of 26 November 1984，I. C. J. Reports 1984，para. 76.

④ Statute of the Court，http://www. icj. cij. org/documents/index. php? p1 = 4&p2 = 2&p3 = 0，最后访问日期：2014 年 12 月 20 日。

找。如果此种问题存在，法院应中止对实体问题的审理程序。”① 在本案中，法院面临伊朗通过信件（letters）表达反对法院管辖权的情况，因此，法院认为应“首先考虑伊朗分别于 1979 年 12 月 9 日和 1980 年 3 月 16 日递交的两封信件中所宣称的法院不应受理本案”的抗辩。② 但是，在该案中，法院没有先行审理管辖权问题，而是在实体问题审理阶段对管辖权异议进行了探讨，并且在对实体问题的判决中阐明了结论。③ 这种做法的原因在于，法院认为管辖权的存在是十分明显的。法院在本案“临时措施”命令中就已经认定“管辖权是明显存在的”，“伊朗在其信件中所声称的理由不能成为法院行使管辖权的障碍”。④

需要指出的是，能够满足法院规定“临时措施”最低条件的“初步管辖权”（*prima facie* jurisdiction）的存在，通常并不能使法院免除先行审理管辖权的义务。例如，在“核试验案”中，国际法院在“临时措施”命令以及设定管辖权审理程序的命令中均指出，原告国所提出的法律论证仅仅为管辖权的存在提供了初步的（*prima facie*）基础，⑤ 法院仍然需要先行审理管辖权，才能将那些需要慎重探讨的法律问题或异议阐释清楚。因此，在法院将当事国以递交外交文件的方式提出管辖权异议的行为视为“先决性抗辩”的情况下，除非法院能够判断出对案件的管辖权明显存在，否则都应当设定单独的管辖权审判程序。

2014 年 11 月 26 日，根据《公约》附件七设立的“北极日出号案”（the Arctic Sunrise Arbitration）仲裁庭对该案管辖权问题的裁决，不仅延续了国际司法实践的一般法理，更为今后的国际司法和仲裁实践提供了重要指引。

---

① *Case Concerning United States Diplomatic and Consular Staff in Tehran* (*United States of America v. Iran*), Judgment of 24 May 1980, I. C. J. Reports 1980, p. 18, para. 33.

② *Case Concerning United States Diplomatic and Consular Staff in Tehran* (*United States of America v. Iran*), Judgment of 24 May 1980, I. C. J. Reports 1980, p. 18, para. 33.

③ *Case Concerning United States Diplomatic and Consular Staff in Tehran* (*United States of America v. Iran*), Judgment of 24 May 1980, I. C. J. Reports 1980, pp. 18 – 20, paras. 33 – 38.

④ *Case Concerning United States Diplomatic and Consular Staff in Tehran* (*United States of America v. Iran*), Request for the Indication of Provisional Measures, Order of 15 December 1979: I. C. J. Reports 1979, p. 14, para. 31. *Case Concerning United States Diplomatic and Consular Staff in Tehran* (*United States of America v. Iran*), Judgment of 24 May 1980, I. C. J. Reports 1980, p. 20, para. 38.

⑤ *Nuclear Tests Case* (*New Zealand v. France*), Request for the Indication of Interim Measures of Protection, Order of 22 June 1973, I. C. J. Reports 1973, p. 138.

在本案中，荷兰在仲裁程序中多次要求仲裁庭先审理案件的管辖权问题。2014年2月27日，荷兰在评论仲裁《程序规则草案》时指出，俄罗斯于2013年10月22日发表的外交照会应被视为对仲裁庭管辖权的抗辩。① 在该照会中，俄罗斯指出："对'北极日出号'的调查行为属于俄罗斯作为沿海国的权利。俄罗斯于1997年2月26日批准《公约》时已经发表声明，对有关行使主权权利和管辖权的执法行为不接受《公约》第15部分第二节的强制管辖。因此俄罗斯不接受仲裁，不参与口头程序。"② 2014年3月3日，俄罗斯再次递交了上述照会并重申不参与仲裁。③ 荷兰在2014年9月1日递交的诉状第59段再次提出，俄罗斯的上述照会应被视为对仲裁庭管辖权的抗辩，应根据仲裁《程序规则》第20条第3款的规定将其作为"先决问题"，④ 从而请求仲裁庭将庭审程序分成两个阶段，即先裁定仲裁庭对本案的管辖权，再审理案件可受理性和实体问题。2014年11月14日，仲裁庭向当事双方发送了《第4号程序令》草案，拟针对俄罗斯的外交照会先行审理管辖权问题。对此，荷兰表示支持；俄罗斯未作评论。11月21日，仲裁庭通过了《第4号程序令》，确认将仲裁程序分为两个阶段，先对管辖权问题进行裁决。⑤ 在5天后，仲裁庭作出了"管辖权裁决"。但是，仲裁庭在裁决中并未指出其设定先予裁决管辖权程序的详尽法理依据，而仅从仲裁程序的角度谈及荷兰的多次请求。

值得注意的是，仲裁庭在裁决中首先强调，"本裁决仅针对俄罗斯的管辖权抗辩进行审议，不涉及除该抗辩之外的任何其他管辖权问题、可受

① PCA Case No. 2014 - 02, Award on Jurisdiction, para. 18, http://www.pca.cpa.org/showfile.asp? fil_id =2845，最后访问日期：2014年12月20日。

② PCA Case No. 2014 - 02, Award on Jurisdiction, para. 9, http://www.pca.cpa.org/showfile.asp? fil_id =2845，最后访问日期：2014年12月20日；Note Verbale from the Russian Federation to the PCA dated 27 February 2014, http://www.pca.cpa.org/showfile.asp? fil_id =2532，最后访问日期：2014年12月20日。

③ PCA Case No. 2014 - 02, Award on Jurisdiction, para. 19, http://www.pca.cpa.org/showfile.asp? fil_id =2845，最后访问日期：2014年12月20日。

④ PCA Case No. 2014 - 02, Award on Jurisdiction, para. 41, http://www.pca.cpa.org/showfile.asp? fil_id =2845，最后访问日期：2014年12月20日。

⑤ PCA Case No. 2014 - 02, Award on Jurisdiction, paras. 44 - 47, http://www.pca.cpa.org/showfile.asp? fil_id =2845，最后访问日期：2014年12月20日。

理性问题或实体问题”。[①] 这显然不同于以往根据《公约》附件七成立的仲裁庭在实体问题的裁决中首先依职权对管辖权和可受理性问题进行“一揽子”审查的固定模式。仲裁庭不仅将管辖权审理程序前置并独立出来，而且进一步增强了对当事国非正式抗辩的重视程度。虽然该裁决最终否定了俄罗斯依据批准《公约》时的保留声明排除仲裁庭强制管辖权的效力，但这一管辖权裁决程序在国际司法实践上却具有重要意义。

根据以上对国际司法和仲裁实践的分析，可以得出以下结论。

首先，国际实践已经认可了除正式“先决性抗辩”之外，当事国以非正式形式提出的管辖权异议的效力：法庭有义务中止对实体问题的审理程序，同时对自身管辖权问题进行仔细考量。

其次，除非法庭可以明显判断出对案件具有管辖权，否则对管辖权的审理程序应独立进行且先予裁决。

《公约》附件七下的仲裁庭继承了国际法院在处理当事方非正式管辖权抗辩方面的法理，但并未对其进行过多的论述和解释。而国际法院经过数十年的实践，更倾向于将自身这种依职权审理管辖权的义务归结为《国际法院规约》第53条第2款下的义务。鉴于《公约》附件七第9条，[②] 以及“南海仲裁案”《程序规则》第25条第1款均规定了与《国际法院规约》第53条第2款措辞相同的内容，[③] 那么，仲裁庭在审理菲律宾所提交的案件的过程中，也有理由将国际法院已经明确的法理在本案中阐释清楚。

（二）《立场文件》对仲裁庭先行作出管辖权裁决的效力

2014年12月17日，仲裁庭要求菲律宾对中国政府的《立场文件》作出回应。截至本文完稿时，尚不清楚菲律宾对此作何回应。菲律宾外交部发言人曾在中国《立场文件》发表后表示“菲律宾政府注意到了该立场文件”，“中国的主张并无新意，我们对此早已清楚，并且在诉状中已经进行

---

① PCA Case No. 2014 - 02, Award on Jurisdiction, para. 59, http://www.pca.cpa.org/showfile.asp? fil_id = 2845，最后访问日期：2014年12月20日。

② Annex VII Article 9 Default of Appearance, http://www.un.org/Depts/los/convention_agreements/texts/unclos/closindx.htm，最后访问日期：2014年12月20日。

③ Rules of Procedure, Article 25, http://www.pca.cpa.org/showfile.asp? fil_id = 2504，最后访问日期：2014年12月20日。

了回应”。[①] 由此可以看出，中菲两国在关于仲裁庭管辖权问题上存在明显的分歧和意见对立。因此，如果参照前文分析的国际司法实践，仲裁庭有义务将中国在本案中持续对仲裁庭行使管辖权的反对和抗辩，特别是《立场文件》的提出，视为仲裁程序中的“先决性抗辩”，据此在审理实体问题以前单独设立管辖权审理程序，并对本案管辖权和可受理性问题作出独立的裁决。

在“北极日出号案”中，荷兰在仲裁程序中多次要求仲裁庭先审理案件的管辖权问题。由于该案仲裁庭在对管辖权的裁决中并未论及设定管辖权裁决程序的特殊法理，很容易使人理解为荷兰的请求是仲裁庭先行审理管辖权的先决条件，从而认为，如果在“南海仲裁案”中菲律宾并未将中国《立场文件》视为具有“先决性抗辩”的效力、不建议仲裁庭先予审理管辖权问题，或者要求仲裁庭在实体问题的裁决中一并审理管辖权问题，那么《立场文件》似乎无法对仲裁程序产生法律效果。然而，严格说来，菲律宾是否提出此种主张对仲裁庭的影响应当是微乎其微的。即使在菲律宾反对先行审判管辖权问题，而中国政府又不作表态的情况下，仲裁庭仍要依照职权对本案的管辖权问题先行审理并作出独立裁决。理由有三。

首先，“北极日出号案”的先例效果在于，仲裁庭应当事国请求设立独立的管辖权裁决程序，不意味着在当事国不请求或反对设立这一独立程序的情况下，仲裁庭就不能依职权设立。

其次，仲裁庭是否负有依职权设立该程序的义务，取决于既有的国际实践所形成的一般义务（这在前文中已经分析过了）。

再次，“南海仲裁案”以及“北极日出号案”的仲裁《程序规则》第20条——先决性抗辩——均未要求对管辖权的审理程序以当事国同意为条件。这一条款中虽然指出仲裁庭在作出决定前应征求当事方的意见，但这种意见仅限于表达该抗辩是否具有“完全初步的性质”。也就是说，当事方的意见仅能够制约正式向仲裁庭提交的“先决性抗辩”，而对于非正式抗辩，仲裁庭只能依职权作出决定。

---

① “Challenges Mount to Beijing’s South China Sea Claims”, *VOA News*, 15th December 2014, http://www.vietnamtribune.com/index.php/sid/228539561，最后访问日期：2014年12月20日。

最后，需要指出的是，在对管辖权的判断上，“北极日出号案”明显简单于“南海仲裁案”。这仅仅从俄罗斯提交给仲裁庭的照会内容与中国《立场文件》内容的比较上就能得出如此明显的结论。[①] 从而，就问题的复杂程度而言，既然“北极日出号案”仲裁庭对案件管辖权问题都进行了单独审理，“南海仲裁案”的管辖权问题显然更应该通过先行审理决定。

因此，中国政府针对“南海仲裁案”发表的《立场文件》在仲裁程序上具有——至少在理论上应当具有——十分重要的作用。如果仲裁庭尊重和遵循一以贯之的法理和实践，则有理由相信仲裁庭会将《立场文件》视为中国对本案仲裁庭管辖权的抗辩，依职权设立独立的先行审理管辖权的程序（中止对实体问题的审理），并对中国《立场文件》中所质疑的全部管辖权和可受理性问题进行审理和裁决。

三　结论和展望

由于中国政府在签署和批准《公约》时就概括性地默示接受了国际仲裁的强制管辖，使得中国成为“被告”的风险随时存在。尽管依据《公约》附件七设立的仲裁庭无权解决领土争端，同时中国政府在2006年根据《公约》对涉及海洋划界、军事活动等的争端作出保留，不接受《公约》规定的强制性争端解决程序管辖，但鉴于中国周边海洋争端形势日趋复杂，很难避免部分国家基于政治目的的“滥诉”。可以预见，今后一段时期，周边国家免不了想要和中国“法庭相见”。而中国基于政策考量可能仍然不会参与国际司法和国际仲裁来解决类似的主权争议。在这种情况下，进行“庭外法律斗争”具有重要意义。

在国际法上，无论是根据条约还是特别协议来提起国家间诉讼或仲裁，裁判的根本基础都在于当事国的同意。[②] 为了防止“滥诉”，国际司法实践中形成了专门的管辖权抗辩制度，为的就是再给国家同意原则加上一道“安全阀”。而“庭外法律立场”对国际司法和仲裁机构的程序进展具

---

① *Note Verbale* from the Russian Federation to the PCA dated 27 February 2014, http://www.pca.cpa.org/showfile.asp? fil_id=2532，最后访问日期：2014年12月20日。

② 〔日〕杉原高岭：《国际司法裁判制度》，王志安、易平译，中国政法大学出版社，2007，第203页。

有重要的制约作用，对中止实体问题审理程序、先行审理管辖权具有直接效力。有鉴于此，《立场文件》等庭外表态方法，不失为综合运用法律技术和外交途径确保国家利益与战略稳定的有效方式。

（责任编辑：罗欢欣）

（本文原载于《国际法研究》2015 年第 2 期）

对美国国务院报告质疑中国南海断续线的评析与辩驳*

黄　瑶　黄靖文**

2014年12月5日，美国国务院网站发表题为《海洋界限——中国在南中国海的海洋主张》（Limits in the Seas, China: Maritime Claims in the South China Sea）报告（以下简称美国报告或报告），该报告由美国海洋、国际环境和科学事务局撰写并发布，基于对中国在南海的海洋主张的分析，美国较详细地说明了它对中国南海问题的立场，特别质疑了中国地图上的南海“断续线”（dashed-line）。美国报告的分析围绕南海断续线地图的特征、主张相关性及其合法性等问题加以展开。可以说，报告意见对我国地图所示的断续线的国际法效力几乎完全持否定态度。①

中国地图上南海诸岛海域外围的那些断续线，简称“南海断续线”或“断续线”，又称南海“U”形线（U-shaped Line）或“九段线”（Nine-dash Line）。经过中国的长期实践，这条南海诸岛外围海域的界线发展为一条历史性权利线。不过，迄今为止，中国官方对断续线的性质及法律地位尚未作出明确的表态。在此种背景下，美国国务院所发报告对断续线的性质提出了

---

* 本文的研究与写作获得国家社科基金重大项目“南海断续线的法理与历史依据研究”（14ZDB165）的资助，特此致谢。

** 黄瑶，中山大学法学院教授、中国南海研究协同创新中心研究员；黄靖文，中山大学法学院硕士研究生。

① 美国报告在首页特别声明其内含的研究成果在一些具体问题上代表美国政府的观点，但不必然意味着美国接受中国有关的海洋主张。Bureau of Oceans and International Environmental and Scientifie Affairs, U. S. Department of State, “Limits in the Seas, China: Maritime Claims in the South China Sea”, Dec. 5, 2014, p. 1, http://www. state. gov/documents/organization/234936. pdf，最后访问日期：2015年1月2日。

三种可能的解释，分别是："断续线作为对岛屿的主张"（Dashed-Line as a Claim to Islands）、"断续线作为国界线"（Dashed-Line as a National Boundary）和"断续线作为历史性主张"（Dashed-Line as a Historic Claim）。这也对应了当前理论界的几种主流观点，即把断续线的性质解释为"岛屿归属线"、"国界线"和"历史性主张线"。[①] 报告援引1982年《联合国海洋法公约》（以下简称《海洋法公约》或《公约》）的有关制度作为研究的主要国际法基础，并据此分析每种解读是否符合国际海洋法。报告结论否定了断续线作为边界之划分的国界线的合法性，也否定了断续线包含中国的"历史性水域"或"历史性权利"主张，只认可中国可能将断续线作为"岛屿归属线"，即认为断续线只是反映了中国对线内岛屿的主权主张。[②]

美国试图通过质疑南海断续线以削弱断续线在维护中国海洋权益中的重要地位，并与菲律宾在2014年3月向国际仲裁庭提交的诉状内容相呼应，似有制造国际舆论压制中国的意图。为此，本文在梳理美国报告的论点和论据基础上，选取对报告基本结论起决定作用的四个关键问题作为切入点，在分析每一个关键问题时首先评析报告的主要观点，再指出问题并作出可能的回应，以期为理解和辨析美国的立场、维护中国断续线地图的重要地位提供参考。此四个关键问题是：中国是否只对断续线内的岛屿提出主权主张？断续线使用国界线图例的真实意图为何？中国是否对断续线内水域提出历史性主张？中国在南海的历史性主张是否具有合法性？

一　中国是否只对断续线内的岛屿提出主权主张

（一）美国报告的观点：断续线只可能是"岛屿归属线"

"岛屿归属线"是美国报告分析的第一种关于断续线的解释。报告在分析断续线地图的性质与目的时，指出"在地图的海洋上划线作为一种实

---

① 为便于表述，本文对报告关于断续线性质的三种解释"断续线作为对岛屿的主张"、"断续线作为国界线"、"断续线作为历史性主张"及其具体含义作出归纳，称之为"岛屿归属线"、"国界线"和"历史性主张线"，不再援用原表述。

② Bureau of Oceans and International Environmental and Scientific Affairs, US Department of State, "Limits in the Seas, China: Maritime Claims in the South China Sea", pp. 23 – 24.

用有效的办法识别一群岛屿，这种做法并不罕见”①，肯定了中国意图通过断续线对线内的岛屿主张陆地主权的效力，但并不认同断续线具有主张岛屿主权之外的任何其他目的，也就是说，断续线只能是单纯的“岛屿归属线”。报告列举了中国的法律和声明以及断续线地图本身作为依据。

美国报告提到其注意到了中国长期以来主张对断续线内南海诸岛及其附近海域（adjacent waters）拥有主权的一贯立场，② 但同时通过对个别中国国内法和声明作出解读，报告否定中国还根据断续线主张任何《海洋法公约》规定之外的海洋权利。为此，报告提出两项关键事实支持这一观点。

其一，关于2009年和2011年中国呈交联合国的照会。报告对两份照会提及的“附近水域”、“相关水域”、“主权权利和管辖权”进行解释，指出：“这些岛屿‘附近’海域的‘主权’可能指12海里领海，根据国际法，那里确实是‘主权’地带。同理，‘主权权利和管辖权’可以理解为是指《海洋法公约》规定的专属经济区和大陆架的权利，因为《公约》用同样的术语描述沿海国家在这些区域的权利。‘相关海域’和‘海床和底土’则可以理解为是指专属经济区和大陆架。”

其二，关于1958年《中华人民共和国政府关于领海的声明》（以下简称1958年领海声明）。报告认为，该声明的第一段承认中国大陆与包括西沙、南沙群岛在内的沿海岛屿隔有公海，而公海是不受任何国家管辖的海域，显示中国在1958年没有对其断续线内的全部海域提出主张。③

---

① Bureau of Oceans and International Environmental and Scientific Affairs, US Department of State, “Limits in the Seas, China: Maritime Claims in the South China Sea”, p. 11.

② 2009年，越南与马来西亚向联合国大陆架界限委员会提交了南海地区的200海里外大陆架划界案申请，中国向联合国提交照会表示抗议，并重申对南海的各项权利主张。美国报告引述了中国2009年提交联合国的照会上的声明，认为该照会内容支持了断续线只是“岛屿归属线”的解释。在2009年的照会中，中国声明：“中国对南海诸岛（islands in the South China Sea）及其附近海域（adjacent waters）拥有无可争辩的主权，并对相关海域（relevant waters）及海床和底土享有主权权利和管辖权（见附图）。”中国在2011年再次向联合国提交照会，并重申：“中国对南海诸岛及其附近海域拥有无可争辩的主权，并对相关海域及海床和底土享有主权权利和管辖权。中国在南海的主权及相关权利和管辖权有着充分的历史和法律根据。”中国2009年5月7日照会，联合国，http://www.un.org/depts/los/clesnew/submissions_files/mysvnm33_09/chn_2009re mys vnm.pdf；中国2011年4月14日照会，联合国，http://www.un.org/depts/los/clesnew/submissions_files/mysvnm33_09/chn_2011_re_phl.pdf，最后访问日期：2015年1月3日。

③ Bureau of Oceans and International Environmental and Scientific Affairs, US Department of State, “Limits in the Seas, China: Maritime Claims in the South China Sea”, pp. 11 - 12.

基于上述认识，报告对断续线作为“岛屿归属线”作出评价，认为中国必须另行根据国际海洋法主张海洋权利。虽然报告在表面上肯定了“岛屿归属线”具有一定程度的可能性和合理性，但断续线的法律效力却深受报告所质疑。报告认为岛屿的外延仅包括高潮时露出水面的地形，不包括低潮高地和类似曾母暗沙的水下地形（submerged features），岛屿的海域权利需要根据《公约》第121条“岛屿制度”的规定予以明确，并支持菲律宾通过仲裁程序解决南海哪些海洋地形属于岛屿的问题。① 此外，报告认为由于南海岛屿的主权归属仍存在争议，相应地，中国的海洋主张也存在争议。②

应当指出，报告列举的种种依据也只能构成对断续线有关主张的初步推论，不仅是因为中国尚未明确断续线内的海洋权利主张，从而为美国提供了任意解读的机会，更重要的是，报告只将其论述局限在《海洋法公约》，却不充分考虑中国自古以来在南海的行为和主张。同时，报告对中国国内法、声明存在相当程度的曲解。事实上，中国不仅对断续线内的海域提出了主张，中国还对线内所有的南海诸岛及其他地理构造主张主权，报告认为断续线只可能是“岛屿归属线”的观点难以成立。③

① Bureau of Oceans and International Environmental and Scientifie Affairs, U. S. Department of State, “Limits in the Seas, China: Maritime Claims in the South China Sea”, pp. 12 – 13；目前，从一些学者的研究结论中可以保守估计，南海断续线内能依据《海洋法公约》第121条主张专属经济区和大陆架的海洋地形数量十分有限，只有永兴岛、太平岛南威岛、中业岛等几个面积较大的岛屿符合相关的标准。参见 Alex G. Oude Elferink, “The Islands in the South China Sea: How Dose Their Presence Limits the Extent of the High Seas and the Area and the Maritime Zones of the Mainland Coasts?”, (1993) 32 *Ocean Development and International Law* 169, p. 178; Michael Richardson, Energy and Geopolitics in the South China Sea: Implication for ASEAN and Its Dialogue Partners (Singapore: Institute of Southeast Asian Studies, 2009), p. 15; Robert W. Smith, “Maritime Delimitation in the South China Sea: Potentiality and Challenges”, (2010) 41 *Ocean Development and International Law* 214, p. 221; Yann-huei Song, “The Applications of Article 121 (3) of the Law of the Sea Convention to the Five Selected Disputed Islands in the South China Sea”, http://nghiencuubiendonvn/en/conferences-and-seminars –/505 – the-application-of-article – 1213 – of-the-law-of-the-sea-convention-to-the-five-selected-disputed-islands-in-the-south-china-sea，最后访问日期：2015年1月2日。

② Bureau of Oceans and International Environmental and Scientific Affairs, US Department of State, “Limits in the Seas, China: Maritime Claims in the South China Sea”, pp. 13 – 14.

③ Bureau of Oceans and International Environmental and Scientific Affairs, US Department of State, “Limits in the Seas, China: Maritime Claims in the South China Sea”, p. 24.

（二）对美国报告的反驳：中国对断续线内的权利主张不限于岛屿的领土主权

1. 应正确理解中国照会指称的“相关海域”的合理内涵

首先，报告将中国照会中的“附近海域”解释为领海有其法理基础，但同样作为非《海洋法公约》术语的“相关海域”则不宜解释为专属经济区和大陆架，因为“相关”（relevant）一词意味着海域的范围需要根据参照对象来确定。一方面，2009 年照会提及“相关海域”（relevant waters）的同一句话末尾括号内表示“见附图”，可以表明“相关海域”指代断续线内除“附近海域”之外的其他范围。其次，中国照会指称的“主权权利和管辖权”虽然是《公约》的术语，但中国多次将这些权利和历史依据紧密联系在一起。例如，2011 年照会声明：“中国在南海的主权及相关权利和管辖权有着充分的历史和法律根据。”又如，中国人民解放军副总参谋长王冠中在 2014 年的香格里拉对话会上指出：“中国在南海的主权、主权权利、管辖权主张是在长期的历史发展过程中形成的。”① 我国外交部发言人在回应美国助理国务卿拉塞尔（Daniel R. Russel）在国会听证会上对断续线的质疑时，也指出：“中国在南海的海洋权益是历史形成的。”② 可见，中国官方这些表态都说明中国对“主权权利和管辖权”的理解并不局限于《公约》，这些概念与大陆架和专属经济区之间缺乏绝对的联系，其主张范围包括中国依据习惯国际法对断续线内海域所享有的历史性权利。

2. 应合理解读中国 1958 年领海声明

关于中国 1958 年领海声明，依照美国的解释，中国承认断续线内海域存在公海，所以该声明似乎成为中国维护断续线主张的一根软肋。然而，从该声明的公布背景来看，中国 1958 年领海声明的目的在于宣告中国的领土主权范围，反击美国对中国台湾地区的军事威胁，而非宣告完整的各种

---

① 《解放军副总长就九段线问题答问：中国在南海主权有 2000 多年历史》，《人民日报》（海外版）2014 年 6 月 3 日，第 1 版。

② 《外交部发言人洪磊就美国务院官员涉南海言论答记者问》，中华人民共和国外交部，http://www.fmprc.gov.cn/mfa_chn/wjdt_611265/fyrbt_611275/t1126662shtml，最后访问日期：2015 年 1 月 4 日。

类型的海域权利主张。①

此外，对公海概念的认识应结合领海声明发布之时的国际法发展背景。1958 年 4 月，第一次联合国海洋法会议讨论并通过了《公海公约》，规定："称'公海'者谓不属领海或一国内水域之海洋所有各部分。"同时，该公约第 2 条通过列举"公海自由"的内容，明确了公海内各国的权利义务，这些由各缔约国平等享有的权利包括航行自由、捕鱼自由、铺设海底电缆和管道自由以及公海上空飞行自由。② 可见，中国通过该声明表明尊重南海部分水域内其他国家所享有的种种公海自由，而不是对整片南海主张主权，但这并不排斥中国主张在断续线内海域继续享有与前述公海自由不相互冲突的其他传统海洋权利，如历史性权利。值得注意的是，第一次海洋法会议只在有限的范围内讨论了历史性海湾，历史性海湾的具体制度和其他类型的历史性权利都成了会议的遗留问题，留待国家实践和判例的发展。③ 并且，公海的概念并不排斥历史性权利。

3. 中国对南海诸岛及其他地理构造提出主权主张

在 2009 年和 2011 年的照会中，中国声明对"南海诸岛"拥有主权。中国在外交文件中常用到的"南海诸岛"（islands in the South China Sea）一词，结合中国 1958 年领海声明和 1992 年《中华人民共和国领海与毗连区法》，其地理范围具体指东沙群岛、西沙群岛、中沙群岛和南沙群岛，这四组群岛均位于断续线以内。

学者高之国和贾兵兵认为："九段线代表着线内所有的南海诸岛的所有权。换言之，在九段线内，中国是对南海诸岛及其他地理构造享有主权的。"④

① 中国 1958 年《中华人民共和国政府关于领海的声明》指出："台湾和澎湖地区现在仍然被美国武力侵占，这是侵犯中华人民共和国领土完整和主权的非法行为。台湾和澎湖等地尚待收复，中华人民共和国政府有权采取一切适当的方法在适当的时候，收复这些地区，这是中国的内政，不容外国干涉。"参见周鲠生《我政府关于领海的声明的重大意义》，《世界知识》1958 年第 18 期。

② 1958 年《公海公约》第 1 条、第 2 条。

③ 参见李任远《国际法中的历史性权利研究》，博士学位论文，厦门大学，2014，第 21—27 页。

④ Zhiguo Gao and Bingbing Jia, "The Nine Dash Line in the South China Sea: History, Status, and Implications", (2015) 107 *American Journal of International Law* 98, pp. 123 – 124.

鉴于岛屿（islands）在《海洋法公约》第121条中有特定的内涵①，在《海洋法公约》的语境下，“南海诸岛”的表述不能完整涵盖南海四组群岛的所有地理构造。因此，尽管对“南海诸岛”这一习惯用语的理解不应受到《海洋法公约》的掣肘，但为了避免歧义，使用“南海诸岛及其他地理构造”比“南海诸岛”更加可取，两者具有相同含义。通过上述对“南海诸岛”和“南海诸岛及其他地理构造”含义的梳理，可以发现，中国在断续线内的主权主张并不限于《海洋法公约》第121条所指的岛屿，而是对断续线内四组群岛的岛、礁、滩、沙作为整体提出主权主张。换言之，作为南海四组群岛各组成部分的暗沙、浅滩和暗礁（诸如曾母暗沙）等水下地形亦属于中国拥有。

在断续线内，中国的主权主张并非只针对某一个或某几个岛屿的主权主张，而是概括性地对整个断续线水域内的所有岛、礁、滩、沙等提出的主权主张，这是中国南海权利主张的特殊之处。其依据主要有两个方面。一是中国历史上将南海诸岛作为一体的历史事实。中国历史上在相当长一段时间内都将南海诸岛、礁、沙洲等作为一个整体处理，只是未明确采用“整体性”这一概念。譬如，中国历史上将整个南海地区都统称为“涨海”，将西沙群岛称为“九乳螺洲”、“七洲”等，同时，将南沙群岛称为“万里石塘”、“万里长沙”等。从命名来看，在很长的历史时期里，对南海岛屿的称谓采用的多是群岛名，未涉及对每一个岛屿的具体命名，这也从一个侧面反映了南海诸岛的整体性。二是《海洋法公约》中有关整体性的规定，即《公约》中关于群岛的定义对南海的海洋地形地貌是否构成群岛的判断也产生影响。群岛的整体性观念在《公约》第46条对群岛的界定中得到了具体体现。该条指出，构成群岛的“岛屿、水域和其他自然地形在本质上构成一个地理、经济和政治的实体，或者在历史上一直被视为此种实体”。目前，已经有一些海洋地质和地球物理实测的研究表明南海断续线总体上也是南海与其东部、南部和西部陆区以及岛区的巨型地质边

① 《海洋法公约》第121条第1款对岛屿作出定义：“岛屿是四面环水并在高潮时高于水面的自然形成的陆地区域。”

界线，南沙岛礁原属中国华南大陆南缘，后因南海的形成裂离至现今的位置。[①] 换言之，这些科学研究的结论证明了南海的海洋地形满足了第46条中“地理实体”的要求。那么，南海的海洋地形是否构成第46条指称的“经济和政治实体”？可以说，南海诸岛礁在行政区划上总体经历了从西沙群岛、南沙群岛、中沙群岛办事处（1959年）到三沙市（2012年）的变化，诸多事实依据支撑此项整体性要求的验证。因此，中国可以通过整体性概念对南海诸岛及其他地理构造概括性地主张，这种整体性主张并不缺乏历史和法理的依据。

二 断续线使用国界线图例的真实意图

（一）美国报告的观点：否认断续线是“国界线”

美国报告在分析断续线作为“国界线”的可能性时认为，1947年断续线地图用国界线的图例标注断续线的事实，暗示了断续线的意图是中国与邻国的海上边界。然而，报告并不认可这种解释，理由包括：断续线不是划界协议的产物；断续线缺乏坐标和连续性；在划界时给予岛屿过多的地位，不符合国家实践和国际法理。此外，报告指出，即便断续线是中国单方面的海洋边界主张，也无法解决中国在线内主张何种权利或管辖权的问题，因为断续线距离岛屿超过领海12海里的宽度，一些线段不仅接近其他国家的海岸，而且部分或全部处在中国主张的任何岛屿陆地200海里之外。[②]

针对报告提出的质疑，可以肯定的是，断续线并非中国与有关邻国划界协议的产物，因为没有证据显示断续线地图公开前中国和这些邻国有过海上划界谈判，但是，单方提出的边界并非没有法律意义。断续线使用国界线图例表达了我国单方的海洋边界主张，其真实意图也必须在此背景下进行探究。

---

① 参见夏戡原、夏综万、赵明辉、孙珍《我国南海历史性水域线的地质特征》，《海洋学报》2014年第5期；谢文彦、王涛、张一伟《南沙群岛海域断裂体系构造特征及其形成机制》，《热带海洋学报》2007年第6期。

② Bureau of Oceans and International Environmental and Scientific Affairs, U. S. Department of State, “Limits in the Seas, China: Maritime Claims in the South China Sea”, pp. 14 – 15.

（二）对美国报告的反驳：断续线具有作为单边主张界线的意义与目的

在国际判例中，单方提出的边界并非没有法律意义。在1977年“比格尔海峡仲裁案”中，仲裁庭认同阿根廷的观点，即该案中争端双方提交的地图均不是1881年阿根廷和智利双边条约的一部分，但认为那些非经合意达成的而是由单方面制作、遵照和采纳的地图并非完全没有价值，即便这些地图本身不具有终局效力，它们所具有的价值可能包括解释当事国的意图（在条约缔结前）、表达当事国对条约的理解（在条约缔结后），或者传达政府当时的立场。① 地图的绘制和公布是国家行为的表现形式之一，官方绘制的断续线地图反映了当时中国政府的立场。在领土争端中，单方面通过地图的方式提出主张范围的做法十分寻常，经过当事国之间一番相互妥协后，单方的主张范围往往超出最终争端解决方案所确立的范围。② 所以，中国单方面通过断续线地图表明本国的领土和海洋主张符合国际惯例，是正常的国家行为。

正确理解中国运用国界线图例所传递的制图目的和相关主张，必须结合绘图当时的历史背景。1933年法国侵占南沙“九小岛事件”引发中国官方和民间的强烈抗议。以此为背景，中华民国政府水陆审查委员会在1934年着手审定南海各岛礁的名称，1935年出版的《中国南海各岛屿图》确定中国领土的最南端至少应在北纬4度的曾母滩（今曾母暗沙）。1946年中国接收曾在二战期间被日本占领的南海岛屿，1947年内政部会同有关部门讨论了《西南沙范围及主权之确定与公布案》，肯定抗战前南海的领土范围，并根据海军巡弋南海后所得资料，重新审定了各岛屿名称并绘制《南海诸岛位置图》，至此断续线正式出现在官方地图之中。③ 这些事实表明，在断续线地图出现前，中国南海立场的重心是捍卫岛礁主权，以对抗帝国

---

① Beagle Channel Arbitration（Argentina vs Chile），Report of International Arbitral Awards，1977，para. 141.

② Sourabh Gupta，“Testing Chinas and the State Departments nine dash line claim”，Pac Net，No88，Pacific Forum CSIS，Dec 15，2014，http://csis org/files/publication/141215_Pac1488 pdf，最后访问日期：2015年2月5日。

③ 参见贾宇《南海问题的国际法理》，《中国法学》2012年第2期；郑志华《南海地图的法理解读与包容性海洋秩序的建构》，博士学位论文，上海交通大学，2013，第57—68页；Zhiguo Gao and Bingbing Jia，“The Nine-Dash Line in the South China Sea：History，Status，and Implications”，（2015）107 *American Journal of International Law* 98，pp. 100 - 102.

主义的入侵。在此背景下，断续线使用国界线图例的基本和首要目的不是对线内海域主张主权，而是宣示线内岛礁主权。[①] 有鉴于此，报告根据现代海域划界规则和实践所总结的要素（如确定的坐标、连续的线、岛屿在划界中不具有完全的效力等）来评价 60 多年前公布的断续线地图是没有道理的。

尽管断续线的基本和首要目的是宣示线内岛、礁、滩、沙的主权，但断续线的完整含义并不限于此，它还反映了中国在南海所享有的某种历史性权利，这也解答了报告关于“中国在线内主张何种权利或管辖权”的问题。据当时参与绘图的内政部方域司第三科科长王锡光和绘图员鞠继武等的回忆，该线是按照中国所属的南海各岛礁与周边国家岸线、岛礁的中间线画出[②]，这种画法与当时已经逐步形成的海域等距离中间线划界方法并非简单的“不谋而合”。报告虽未对这一说法予以直接回应，但报告在介绍断续线地图描述的地理情况时，认为断续线部分线段的位置更接近邻国的陆地海岸，这与断续线大致位于中间线的说法存在矛盾。[③]

然而，如果考虑到断续线地图的沿革，断续线地图最初的画线方法确实契合了中间线划界方法。以 1947 年地图为例，该地图使用国界线图例在菲律宾的巴拉望省和马来西亚的婆罗洲之间海域划了一段明显的中间线，说明断续线很可能是单方面提出的海域外部界限。有充分的历史证据证明中国在断续线所包围的海域内已经形成了某种历史性权利，从这个意义上说，断续线不仅是南海岛礁主权的范围线，还是南海历史性权利的外部界限。只是，当年水陆审查委员会在制作断续线地图时，没有具体说明有关海洋权利的性质及其与断续线之间的联系。不少中国学者相信，断续线还

---

① 林金枝教授认为断续线是南海诸岛的外围范围线，是承袭私人出版的地图的画法，只不过范围线包围的岛群有变化，因此，范围线也不断扩大。李金明教授认为断续线基本是沿着南海诸岛的外围岛礁画就，把整个南海诸岛环绕起来，断续线这种画法使用的是一种地理速记的简单方法，这种方法在 19 世纪末和 20 世纪初曾在国际间广泛使用。不过，这两位学者并未就断续线内海域是否存在历史性权利展开讨论或给出结论。

② 转引自郑志华《南海地图的法理解读与包容性海洋秩序的建构》，博士学位论文，上海交通大学，2013，第 68 页。

③ Bureau of Oceans and International Environmental and Scientific Affairs, US Department of State, “Limits in the Seas, China: Maritime Claims in the South China Sea”, pp. 4 – 6.

可能具有潜在的海洋边界剩余功能。①

基于以上分析，断续线使用国界线图例进行绘制并非没有意义和价值。作为单方主张的界线，其基本目的首先是宣示对线内岛、礁、滩、沙的主权，其剩余功能是作为潜在的海洋权利界线，划分中国的历史性权利与其他邻国海洋权利的边界。

三　中国是否对断续线内水域提出了历史性主张

（一）美国报告的观点：否认中国历史性主张的存在

除了评说“岛屿归属线”和“国界线”的观点外，美国报告还将讨论的重点放在第三种关于断续线的可能解释上，指出断续线地图的目的是表明一种所谓历史性主张（historic claim），可能是对海洋区域的主权主张（“历史性水域”或“历史性所有权”），或者是其中一些权利的集合（“历史性权利”）②。报告认为，评价断续线是否为“历史性权利线”的前提是中国是否提出了相关的历史性主张。

尽管报告承认可以通过解读中国政府的某些声明和行为，为断续线作为“历史性主张线”的解释提供基础③，但报告质疑这些事实是否足以证

① 参见 Zhiguo Gao and Bingbing Jia，“The Nine-Dash Line in the South China Sea：History，Status，and Implications”，（2015） 107 *American Journal of International Law* 98，p. 108；李金明《南海断续线的法律地位：历史性水域、疆域线、抑或岛屿归属线?》，《南洋问题研究》2010 年第 4 期。

② Bureau of Oceans and International Environmental and Scientific Affairs，US Department of State，“Limits in the Seas，China：Maritime Claims in the South China Sea”，p. 15.

③ 美国报告提及的相关依据包括：（1） 1998 年《中华人民共和国专属经济区和大陆架法》第 14 条规定：“本法的规定不影响中华人民共和国享有的历史性权利”；（2） 2011 年照会声明：“中国在南海的主权及相关权利和管辖权有着充分的历史和法理依据”；（3） 尽管不能归结到中国政府，但中国一些机构和评论员认为，断续线地图描述了中国在南海的历史性权利；（4） 中国外交部发言人称对仁爱礁、曾母暗沙，或对“南海及其岛屿”享有主权，因而中国可能根据历史性水域对南海主张主权；（5） 2012 年，中国海洋石油总公司在越南中部海岸对面海域为一批石油勘探区块招标，其中两个区块在中国主张的岛屿的 200 海里专属经济区之外；（6） 其他国内法暗示中国可能基于《海洋法公约》之外的依据主张海洋权利，如 1999 年颁布的《中华人民共和国海洋环境保护法》规定中国管辖的海域除了内水、领海、毗连区、专属经济区和大陆架外，还包括“其他海域”。Bureau of Oceans and International Environmental and Scientific Affairs，US Department of State，“Limits in the Seas，China：Maritime Claims in the South China Sea”，pp. 15 – 17.

明中国提出了历史性主张。根据爱尔兰学者西蒙斯（Clive. R. Symmons）在《海洋法中的历史性水域》一书中的观点，报告认为提出历史性主张的国家必须使主张为国际社会所周知，正式通知似乎是提出历史性主张的必要步骤，只有这样，其他国家才有机会通过抗议等方式进行否认，或者对这一主张予以默认。①

据此，美国报告中指责中国并未实际提出明确的“历史性水域”或“历史性权利”主张，认为中国的国内立法和断续线地图不符合一项“正式”、“官方”的历史性主张所应满足的标准。报告认为，在法律上，1998年《中华人民共和国专属经济区和大陆架法》第14条是“保留条款”，本身没有提出主张，也没有提到断续线地图；1999年《中华人民共和国海洋环境保护法》第2条所提及的“其他海域”在性质、依据和地理范围上不明确，也没有提出任何历史性主张。中国2011年呈交联合国的照会虽然提到中国的“主权和相关权利与管辖权”有着“历史和法理依据”，但是，就像1998年立法一样，这封照会本身不构成一项主张的声明，且“历史依据”可能仅指中国对南海岛屿的依据，不是中国对断续线内海域的权利依据。至于1958年的领海声明，该声明宣布南海存在公海，并且对渤海的历史性水域地位提出主张，若中国将断续线内海域视为历史性水域，那么在与渤海相关的主张中也应有所提及。②

那么断续线地图本身是否构成海洋主张的正式通知呢？报告也对此持否定观点。报告指出1947年的《南海诸岛位置图》没有提及海洋权利主张，该地图用中文在国内出版也不构成广而告之、提醒国际社会出现海洋权利主张的行为，且中国出版的各种断续线地图也因缺乏准确性、明确性和一致性而无法表达海洋权利主张的性质与范围。

（二）对美国报告的反驳：未全面理解中国的对外表态

判断中国是否对断续线内海域提出了历史性主张，必须首先明确中国可能提出哪种历史性主张，以避免将从未提出的主张强加于中国而造成错误。

---

① Bureau of Oceans and International Environmental and Scientific Affairs, US Department of State, “Limits in the Seas, China: Maritime Claims in the South China Sea”, p. 17.

② Bureau of Oceans and International Environmental and Scientific Affairs, US Department of State, “Limits in the Seas, China: Maritime Claims in the South China Sea”, pp. 18 – 19.

与历史性主张相关的概念包括历史性所有权（historic title）、历史性水域（historic waters）和历史性权利（historic rights），这些概念之间存在一定的联系与区别。意大利学者吉欧雅（Andrea Gioia）在阐释历史性所有权时，认为历史性所有权是国家经过历史性强化的过程，是取得陆地或海洋领土的渊源和证据。[①] 理论界普遍认可历史性水域是历史性所有权在海洋取得上的体现，国家在其历史性水域中享有主权，历史性海湾是典型的历史性水域。[②] 历史性权利是指国家对某些海域在历史上一直享有的权利，这些权利已经被习惯国际法规则所确认，得到国际条约的承认和尊重。[③] 历史性权利在不同的场景下有不同的内涵，有时与历史性所有权是同一概念，有时仅指国家在一定范围海域内长期、稳定从事的资源开发活动等实践所产生的权利，后者是一种尚未达到领土主权高度的权利，包括历史性捕鱼权和历史性航行权等。[④] 结合美国报告的上下文，报告反复提及的历史性主张是指历史性水域主张或非主权性质的历史性权利主张。尽管报告注意到了历史性水域和历史性权利在概念上的区别，但报告在论述时常常将两者混为一谈，其基本逻辑是：中国并未有效地提出历史性水域主张，因此中国没有提出历史性主张。由此可见，报告的论述实际上存在概念混淆与逻辑混乱。

报告指出，中国外交部发言人称对仁爱礁（Second Thomas Shoal）、曾母暗沙（James Shoal），或对"南海及其岛屿"（the South China Sea and the islands）享有主权，因而中国可能根据历史性水域对南海主张主权，唯一依据是中国外交部发言人的表态。然而，笔者查阅相关记录后发现，中国

---

① Andrea Gioia, "Historic Titles", Max Plank Encyclopeida of Public International Law (online edition), http://opil. ouplaw. com/view/101093/lawepil/9780199231690/law - 9780199231690 - e705rskey = 7gh5sm&result = 1&prd = EPIL，最后访问日期：2015 年 1 月 15 日。

② 参见 Clive R Symmons, *Historic Waters in the Law of the Sea: A Modern Re-Appraisal* (The Hague: Martinus Nijhoff Publishers, 2008), Chapter 2.

③ 王军敏：《国际法中的历史性权利》，中共中央党校出版社，2009，"内容提要"第 1 页。

④ 联合国秘书处在 1958 年准备的《历史性海湾备忘录》（Historic Bays Memorandum）在说明对历史性海湾或历史性水域的权利时使用了不同用语，既使用了"历史性权利"（historic rights），也使用了"历史性所有权"（historic title）。联合国第一次海洋法会议在讨论直线基线问题时提出了历史性通过权（historic rights of innocent passage），联合国第二次海洋法会议在讨论扩大领海宽度、专属渔区问题时提出了历史性捕鱼权问题（historic rights of fishing）。王军敏：《国际法中的历史性权利》，中共中央党校出版社，2009，第 40—41 页。

外交部从未声称对整个南海拥有主权，美国报告对外交部表态的解读存在错误和偏差。报告引用印度《经济时报》（Economic Times）的一篇报道，指出中国外交部一位发言人在2011年9月15日的记者会上称："我在此重申，中国对南海及其岛屿拥有无可争议的主权。"① 事实上，发言人姜瑜在这场记者会上的原话是："我愿重申，中国对南沙群岛及其附近海域拥有无可争辩的主权，中国在南海的主张有充分的历史和法理依据。"姜瑜的表述与2009年和2011年的两封中国照会一致，她还指出："中国在南海的主权、权利和相关主张是在长期的历史过程中形成的，并且一直由中国政府所坚持。我们对南海诸岛的主权是建立在发现、先占和长期、持续、有效管理的基础之上。《联合国海洋法公约》未赋予任何国家把本国专属经济区和大陆架主张扩展到其他国家领土上的权利，也并未限制或否定一国在历史上形成并持续主张的权利。"② 另外，中国确实一直对仁爱礁、曾母暗沙等没于水下的海洋地形主张主权，主要原因正如前文所述，中国将这些水下地形（submerged features）视为南沙群岛的一部分而予以概括性地主张主权。与菲律宾和美国的有关观点不同，中国拒绝将这些水下地形视为南海邻国大陆架主张的一部分。由此可见，报告未免有断章取义解读中国外交部表态的嫌疑。

（三）对美国报告的反驳：中国的历史性权利主张以长期实践为基础

如前所述，报告所列举的上述事实无法证明中国的历史性主张可能是一项"历史性水域"或"历史性所有权"主张。根据联合国秘书处1962年的研究报告，历史性水域可能构成领海或内水，③ 国家对历史性水域拥有主权，而中国在南海的历史性主张很难说是一种历史性水域主张。自1947年断续线地图公布以来，中国政府并未限制外国船只的自由航行和外

---

① "China warns on South China Sea Oil", Economic Times, Sep. 15, 2011, cited in Bureau of Oceans and International Environmental and Scientific Affairs, US Department of State, "Limits in the Seas, China: Maritime Claims in the South China Sea", p. 16.

② 《2011年9月15日外交部发言人姜瑜举行例行记者会》，中华人民共和国外交部，http://www.mfa.gov.cn/mfa_chn/fyrbt_602243/jzhsl_602247/t859330shtml，最后访问日期：2015年1月5日。

③ 参见"Juridical Regime of Historic Waters, Including Historic Bays", Doc A/CN4/143, in Yearbook of International Law Commission (1962), Vol II, p. 23, paras. 160 - 167。

国航空器在该海域上空飞越。近年来，中国政府声明南海的航行自由不受影响，没有任何国家包括中国对整个南海提出主权声索。[①] 报告揣测中国提出“历史性水域”和“历史性所有权”主张缺乏客观现实根据。

面对报告的种种质疑，中国外交部作出了回应。2014 年 12 月 9 日，在中国外交部例行记者会上，发言人洪磊如此评价该报告：“中国在南海的主权和相关权利主张是在长期的历史过程中逐步形成的，并为历代中国政府长期坚持。”[②] 这与前述中国人民解放军副总参谋长王冠中的说法一致，表明中国并未依赖 1947 年的断续线地图提出新的海洋权利主张，更不是通过后续的各项海洋立法、照会和声明才明确中国的历史性主张。反观报告，所有否认历史性主张存在的依据都是 1947 年后的现代资料，报告并未回归到更久远的历史当中去还原事实。

那么，结合历史，中国的历史性主张的内涵到底有哪些？中国通过何种形式提出了历史性主张？如前所述，在排除了中国在南海断续线内的历史性主张是一种历史性水域主张之后，中国对线内海域的权利主张除了《海洋法公约》所赋予的那些权利之外，是具有其他内容的历史性权利主张。通过对国家实践的考察可发现，提出历史性权利主张的形式没有严格的标准，不要求沿海国在提出历史性权利主张时必须以立法或地图等方式说明权利的性质、依据和地理范围，也不要求沿海国指明是何种具体的“历史性权利”。

国际仲裁庭在 1998 年“厄立特里亚和也门案”的裁决中认定两国在红海南部许多世纪以来的捕鱼、航行活动创设了某种历史性权利。[③] 也就

---

① 2012 年 2 月 29 日中国外交部新闻发言人洪磊在例行记者会上指出：“南海争议的核心是部分南沙岛礁领土主权争议和南海部分海域的划界争议。需要指出的是，没有任何国家包括中国对整个南海提出主权声索……事实证明，南海的航行自由和安全从来不是问题，没有因为南海争议受到任何影响。”《2012 年 2 月 29 日外交部发言人洪磊举行例行记者会》，中华人民共和国外交部，http://www.fmprc.gov.cn/mfa_chn/wjdt_611265/fyrbt_611275/t909551shtml，最后访问日期：2015 年 1 月 5 日。

② 《2014 年 12 月 9 日外交部发言人洪磊主持例行记者会》，中华人民共和国外交部，http://www.mfa.gov.cn/mfa_chn/fyrbt_602243/t1217733shtml，最后访问日期：2015 年 1 月 5 日。

③ 仲裁庭指出：“许多世纪以来盛行于红海南部的捕鱼的传统自由、穿梭于两岸之间的无障碍航行通道的作用以及两岸民众对有关岛屿的共同使用，均构成创设某种‘历史性权利’的重要因素，这些因素的积累通过历史性巩固构成一种尚未达到领土主权高度的且对双方都有利的‘国际地役权’。” Phase I: Territorial Sovereignty and Scope of Dispute (Eritrea/Yemen), Award of the Arbitral Tribunal, PCA, 1996, para. 126.

是说，仲裁庭在该案中认为历史性权利主张体现在沿海国对海域长期的实际利用行为，厄立特里亚和也门两国均未说明海域历史性主张的具体类型、性质和依据，但这并不妨碍仲裁庭认定历史性权利的存在。在1982年"突尼斯－利比亚大陆架划界案"中，突尼斯所主张的历史性权利源于长期以来突尼斯在近岸的地中海水域和海床的捕鱼活动和利益，突尼斯认为这种开发行为的古老性、行使渔业资源所有权和管辖控制权的持续性以及第三国的容忍和承认，导致突尼斯取得了对这片海床的历史性权利。[①] 突尼斯主张并取得历史性权利的行为不是基于公开宣告和正式通知，而是历史上不断累积的资源开发和管理行为。因此，历史性权利是一项远古的权利，源于沿海国在历史演进过程中对海域的开发与利用，包括沿海国的航行、捕鱼和其他资源开采行为。这些行为长期、稳定存在的事实本身便反映了沿海国的历史性主张，更无须所谓的"正式通知"，历史性主张的内容由沿海国在相关海域的具体实践所决定。

回顾中国自古以来在南海海域的开发、利用和管理实践，丰富的史料表明中国在南海的活动包括：巡航、捕鱼、通航、打击海盗、海难救助，以及科学测量与调查等。[②] 历史上，中国在南海的管理活动还得到了南海周边国家的支持和协助。[③] 自1947年断续线地图公布以来，中国在南海的历史性主张通过实践得到延续和强化，在断续线内积极开展资源开发、执法维权、测量调查、科学考察、定期巡航等活动。中国所主张的历史性权利是通过各个历史阶段累积而成的。沿海国开发、利用海洋的能力是从原始走向现代的过程，在不同阶段，中国在南海的历史性权利内容也随着对南海更广阔、更深层的开发而发生变化，从传统的渔业权发展到包括勘探、开发矿藏资源在内的各类海洋活动的权利。

中国在1998年《专属经济区和大陆架法》的第14条中对"历史性权利"作出规定，并在2011年提交给联合国的照会中声明"南海的主权及相关权利和管辖权有着充分的历史和法律根据"，以此重申和强调历史性

① Case Concerning the Continental Shelf (Tunisia/Lybia Arab Jamahiriya), Judgment, ICJ Reports 1982, para. 98.

② 参见袁古洁、李任远《历史性权利对海洋权利的影响——兼及中国南海权利主张》，《中山大学法律评论》第11卷第3辑，广西师范大学出版社，2014。

③ 参见傅崐成《南（中国）海法律地位之研究》，台湾123资讯有限公司，1996，第62—85页。

主张。可以说，与其他主张历史性权利的国家相似，中国在南海的历史性主张和有关权利是在漫长的历史过程中逐步形成的，并一直存在，更不是如报告所称的，是在最近几年才提出的新主张，此应为国际社会尤其是南海周边国家所知晓。概言之，长期的历史实践表明中国对断续线内海域提出了历史性主张，这种历史性主张并非报告所强调的历史性水域主张，而是区别于历史性水域的历史性权利主张。结合中国的各项实践，中国在南海断续线内所主张并享有的历史性权利具体内容包括典型的历史性捕鱼权、历史性航行权，以及对矿藏等资源勘探、开发的权利和对相关海域的管辖权。①

四　中国历史性主张的合法性问题

（一）美国报告的观点：否认中国历史性主张的合法性

美国报告从《海洋法公约》和一般国际法两方面否认中国在南海断续线内历史性主张的合法性。

一方面，报告认为，即便中国的历史性主张存在，该主张也不会得到《海洋法公约》的承认。因为《公约》的文本和起草历史清楚表明，除了涉及近岸的历史性海湾和领海划界的历史性所有权，现代国际海洋法不承认以历史为基础拥有海域管辖权，《公约》也未规定历史性主张可以作为例外来减损沿海国对专属经济区、大陆架海域享有的主权权利和管辖权。也就是说，美国认为《公约》已完整地规定了历史性权利在国际海洋法中的性质和地位，《公约》未提及的历史性权利是违法且无效的。报告指出，《公约》全面地规定了所有海洋法律制度，航行、油气资源开发和渔业活动都由《公约》加以调整，因此一个国家不可以基于“一般国际法”来主

① 中国学者高之国和贾兵兵认为：“‘九段线’在经历60余年演变后，已经成为对历来属于中国的南海诸岛主权的宣示，并包括对在这些岛屿及其周围海域中从事渔业、航行，以及包括矿藏等资源勘探开发等其他海洋活动的历史性权利。”中国学者贾宇、金永明也持相近的观点。Zhiguo Gao and Bingbing Jia, “The Nine-Dash Line in the South China Sea: History, Status, and Implications”, (2015) 107 *American Journal of International Law* 98, p. 108；参见贾宇《南海问题的国际法理》，《中国法学》2012年第2期，第33页；金永明《中国南海断续线的性质及线内水域的法律地位》，《中国法学》2012年第6期。

张《海洋法公约》规定之外的历史性水域或历史性权利。①

另一方面，报告也分析了在中国提出历史性水域主张的情况下，中国的历史性水域主张并不满足一般国际法所要求的三项要素。首先，美国认为中国并未对南海实施公开的、众所周知的、有效的管辖，因为中国有关断续线的主张并不明确，缺乏地理上的前后一致性和精确性；其次，中国的管辖行为不具有连续性，可以从其他南海争端当事国长期、广泛利用南海的事实中发现，中国并未在南海行使主权或排他性的管辖权；最后，没有外国国家对中国在南海行使权利的行为表示默认，因为中国在2009年向联合国呈交照会和断续线地图后，多个争端当事国迅速表示抗议，美国也要求中国尽快澄清其主张。②

（二）对美国报告的反驳：中国的历史性主张并不违反《海洋法公约》

严格地讲，美国关于国际海洋法的认知是片面的，该报告在理解《海洋法公约》和解读历史性权利上都存在偏颇，其否定中国历史性权利主张的合法性之大前提无法成立。

首先，《海洋法公约》并未解决所有海洋法问题，正如《公约》前言所述，“本公约未予规定的事项，应继续以一般国际法的规则和原则为准据”。

其次，《海洋法公约》第10条、第15条、第51条、第298条等规定体现了《公约》对历史性权利的吸收和转化，然而这种吸收和转化并不完全，《公约》并未取代历史性权利的法律制度。

美国塞缪尔国际咨询公司研究员吉普塔（Sourabh Gupta）在评论该美国报告时认为，中国能在非排他和非专属的基础上（on a non exclusive and non exclusionary basis）在断续线内海域主张传统捕鱼权，因为《海洋法公约》第123条关于半闭海渔业合作规定和第62条关于沿海国主张专属经济区时尊重他国传统捕鱼活动的规定均认可这一类历史性权利。③ 只是，该

① Bureau of Oceans and International Environmental and Scientific Affairs, U S Department of State, “Limits in the Seas, China: Maritime Claims in the South China Sea”, pp. 19 – 21.

② Bureau of Oceans and International Environmental and Scientific Affairs, U S Department of State, “Limits in the Seas, China: Maritime Claims in the South China Sea”, pp. 21 – 22.

③ Sourabh Gupta, “Testing China's and the State Department's nine dash line claim”, Pac Net, No 88, Pacific Forum CSIS, Dec 15, 2014, http://csis.org/files/publication/141215_Pac1488.pdf, 最后访问日期：2015年2月5日。

学者的观点仍然过于保守，因为绝大部分历史性权利，特别是《海洋法公约》未加以详细规定的非主权性质的历史性权利，虽然存在条约法上的空白，却不缺乏习惯国际法上的根据。1982 年国际法院在“突尼斯 - 利比亚大陆架划界案”中谈及突尼斯主张的历史性捕鱼权时指出：“一般国际法没有为历史性水域或历史性海湾规定单独的制度，只是为每一个具体的、公认的历史性水域或历史性海湾的情形作了特殊规定。实际情况显然是，历史性权利或历史性水域概念与大陆架概念是由习惯国际法中的不同法律制度所支配。”[①] 虽然该判决是在《海洋法公约》正式通过前作出的，但国际法院充分考虑到了海洋法的最新发展，因此，国际法院就历史性权利在国际法中的地位发表的意见与解释和适用《公约》相关条款直接相关。[②] 这表明，历史性权利的有关概念继续受到《海洋法公约》以外的一般国际法规则的支配。

事实上，南海争端相关国也从未将解决南海划界问题的国际法规则限定在《海洋法公约》这一部公约里。譬如，2002 年《南海各方行为宣言》指出要根据包括《海洋法公约》在内的公认的国际法原则，解决领土和管辖权争议。[③] 2008 年 10 月《中越联合声明》也指出，中越两国将按照包括 1982 年《海洋法公约》在内的国际法所确认的法律制度和原则，寻求双方均能接受的基本和长久的解决办法。[④] 可见，南海国家在处理南海问题时，均认为应尊重和适用包括《海洋法公约》在内的有关海洋法规则。美国作为非南海国家，不应当擅自排除一般国际法特别是历史性权利有关制度在南海争端中的适用。

---

① Case Concerning the Continental Shelf (Tunisia/Lybian Arab Jamahiliya), Judgment, I C J Reports 1982, para. 100.

② 王军敏：《国际法中的历史性权利》，中共中央党校出版社，2009，第 32 页。

③ 2002 年《南海各方行为宣言》第 4 条：“有关各方承诺根据公认的国际法原则，包括 1982 年《海洋法公约》，由直接有关的主权国家通过友好磋商和谈判，以和平方式解决它们的领土和管辖权争议，而不诉诸武力或以武力相威胁。”

④ 2008 年 10 月《中越联合声明》是中越两国最新的双边重要文件，第 6 项声明：“双方就维护南海和平稳定坦诚友好地交换了意见，重申恪守两国高层共识及《南海各方行为宣言》精神，保持海上问题谈判机制，按照包括 1982 年《联合国海洋法公约》在内的国际法所确认的法律制度和原则，寻求双方均能接受的基本和长久的解决办法，同时积极研究和商谈共同开发问题，以便找到适合的模式和区域。”《中越双边重要文件》，中华人民共和国外交部：http://www. mfa. gov. cn/chn//pds/ziliao/tytj/zcwj/t821559htm，最后访问日期：2015 年 1 月 5 日。

（三）对美国报告的反驳：中国的历史性主张并不违反一般国际法

报告依据一般国际法对所谓中国的历史性水域主张之合法性提出挑战，其论据的基本前提存在错误，因为诸多事实表明中国从未对整个南海提出主权主张。中国所提断续线内相关水域的历史性主张的内涵不是历史性水域，而是非主权性质的历史性权利。相应地，该报告所援引的有关历史性水域三项构成要素也不能直接适用于中国的历史性权利主张，因为这三项要素主要参照 1962 年联合国秘书处《包括历史性海湾在内的历史性水域法律制度》的报告内容，是通过总结历史性海湾、历史性水域的国家实践和国际法原则而得出的研究结论。[①]

即便如此，作为广义的历史性权利的一种，历史性水域的构成要素对检验中国在南海的历史性权利的存在有一定程度的参照价值。下面逐一分析这三项要素。首先，尽管中国并未对整个南海行使主权，但中国在南海断续线内海域公开实施权利的行为是不容置疑的，这在前文关于中国历史性主张存在与否的讨论中已经论及。其次，报告称南海许多岛屿由马来西亚、菲律宾、越南占领，又称多个南海国家的海域权利主张伸入南海并进行资源开发活动，但这些事实不能撼动中国历史性权利的合法性。因为，历史证据证明中国在南海的历史性权利产生和确立的时间早于外国的占领和开发行为，外国的行为因此构成非法的侵占活动。最后，关于外国是否对中国在南海实施权利的行为表示默认的问题，美国提到的外国抗议发生在 2009 年之后。事实表明，越南、菲律宾等南海国家在 1948 年至 2009 年间均未对中国公布和实施的断续线提出任何抗议，长期的沉默证明这些国家对中国南海历史性权利予以默认。

五 总体评价

综上所述，报告在回答前述四个关键问题时存在不少事实和法律依据上的问题，报告企图否认中国政府对断续线内的权利主张的结论无法成

① 参见“Juridical Regime of Historic Waters, Including Historic Bays”, Doc A/CN 4/143, in Yearbook of International Law Commission, (1962), Vol II, pp. 13 - 19, paras. 80 - 133.

立。报告基于有限的依据，错误地将断续线性质认定为“只可能反映了对岛屿的主张”①，限制了断续线内中国的主权、主权权利和管辖权主张，这种“岛屿归属线”说不能完整地反映断续线地图的本意。而“国界线”说更是对地图的一种机械解读，虽然断续线地图以宣示线内岛礁主权为基本目的，但不排除中国在线内海域主张并实际享有某种历史性权利。

相比较之下，“岛礁归属线”和“历史性主张线”的叠加解释更具合理性与合法性。中国政府对断续线内的权利主张，既包括对线内岛、礁、滩、沙的主权主张，也包含对线内相关海域的各项历史性权利的主张。断续线还具有作为未来与南海邻国海洋划界界线的剩余功能。实际上，中国在南海所主张的各项权益的合法性主要源于丰富的法理和历史依据，而非断续线地图本身。断续线地图只是中国南海各项主张的重要标志和载体，其内涵亦随着中国实践的发展而不断丰富。

在中国尚未澄清南海断续线性质的背景下，美国采取先发制人的策略，通过推测性论述，对断续线性质提出三种选择性解读，主要体现了美国对自身利益的考量。美国报告将断续线的意图单纯地解释为中国对线内岛屿的主权主张，并主张仅根据《海洋法公约》确定中国的海洋权利。美国这一举措的动机，着眼于维持美国在南海的军事活动现状，避免干扰美国航行自由和战略安全利益的实现。对此，有学者在评价美国和菲律宾等南海国家近期对中国的抨击时，指责各方欠缺长远眼光、智慧与均衡，戴着民族主义眼罩给予中国不公正的待遇。② 整体而言，结合美国政府近期的南海政策，这份研究报告的政治意义远大于法律意义。

（责任编辑：罗欢欣）

（本文原载于《国际法研究》2015 年第 3 期）

---

① Bureau of Oceans and International Environmental and Scientific Affairs, U S Department of State, "Limits in the Seas, China: Maritime Claims in the South China Sea", p. 24.

② Mark Valencia, "Provoking China on South China Sea Issues is a Dangerous Tactic", South China Morning Post, Feb. 2, 2015, http://en. nanhai. org. cn/index. php/Index/Research/paper_c/id/40 html，最后访问日期：2015 年 2 月 4 日。

尊重并保证尊重国际人道法

——1949 年《日内瓦四公约》共同第 1 条的解构分析

李　强*

一　共同第 1 条的由来

很少有人在意共同第 1 条为什么会成为《日内瓦四公约》① 的第一个条款。考虑到《日内瓦四公约》是当今世界上接受程度最高的公约，厘清这个问题对于准确理解共同第 1 条的法律地位十分有帮助。②

---

* 李强，中国政法大学法学院副教授，法学博士。

① 《日内瓦四公约》是对 1949 年 8 月 12 日在日内瓦外交会议上通过的四部公约的总称，它们分别是《改善战地武装部队伤者病者境遇之日内瓦公约》（以下简称《日内瓦第一公约》）、《改善海上武装部队伤者病者及遇船难者境遇之日内瓦公约》（以下简称《日内瓦第二公约》）、《关于战俘待遇之日内瓦公约》（以下简称《日内瓦第三公约》）、《关于战时保护平民之日内瓦公约》（以下简称《日内瓦第四公约》），上述四部公约均于 1950 年 10 月 21 日正式生效。此外，为了弥补《日内瓦四公约》的某些不足，国际社会又于 1977 年 6 月 8 日分别通过了《1949 年 8 月 12 日日内瓦第四公约关于保护国际性武装冲突受难者的附加议定书》（以下简称《第一附加议定书》）和《1949 年 8 月 12 日日内瓦四公约关于保护非国际性武装冲突受难者的附加议定书》（以下简称《第二附加议定书》），两个《附加议定书》均于 1978 年 12 月 7 日正式生效。《日内瓦四公约》及其 1977 年两个《附加议定书》构成现代国际人道法的首要渊源。

② 截至目前，1949 年《日内瓦四公约》有 196 个缔约国，ICRC，"Treaties，States Parties and Commentaries"，https://ihl-databases.icrc.org/applic/ihl/ihl.nsf/INTRO/470，最后访问日期：2017 年 6 月 1 日。这意味着全世界所有主权国家均已批准或加入上述公约。从某种意义上说，这些公约全球适用。参见 ICRC，*Commentary on the First Geneva Convention: Convention (I) for the Amelioration of the Condition of the Wounded and Sick in Armed Forces in the Field* [hereafter "ICRC updated Commentary on the First Geneva Convention"]（Cambridge: Cambridge University Press，2017），p. 119，para. 342。

从条约法的角度看，《日内瓦四公约》将使用共同第1条这样措辞的约文置于条约之首是极不寻常的。该条明显包含对“约定必须遵守”原则的昭示，“约定必须遵守”原则对于所有条约来说，简直是不证自明的公理。纯粹法学派的汉斯·凯尔森（Hans Kelsen）甚至将其视为构成所有法律体系之基本规范的首要规则，处于金字塔的顶端。[①] 因此在一般情况下，条约约文不会明确重复此项原则，因为按照1969年《维也纳条约法公约》对这项原则的阐释，一旦国家同意接受某项条约的约束，在该条约对其生效后就有善意履行的当然义务。最为常见的策略是，在条约序言中载明“兹议定条款如下”或“以昭信守”等字样。而条约的第一个条文所载内容，主要有三种模式：第一种，表明条约的目的和宗旨，如1945年《联合国宪章》；第二种，对条约中使用的重要术语进行定义，如1984年《禁止酷刑和其他残忍、不人道或有辱人格的待遇或处罚公约》；第三种，澄清条约的适用范围，譬如前面提到的1969年《维也纳条约法公约》；还有其他一些特例，在此不逐一赘述。由此可见，就《日内瓦四公约》而言，涉及适用范围的共同第2条成为第1条才更合乎常理，那么共同第1条又是如何产生的呢？

自1864年第一部《日内瓦公约》诞生起，直至1899年和1907年两次海牙和平会议期间产生的大量涉及战争规则的条约，没有一部包含类似共同第1条的表述。它的雏形最早出现于1929年关于伤病员和战俘的两个《日内瓦公约》中，分别为第25条第1款和第82条第1款，措辞完全一致且置于“公约的适用与执行”这一部分之下：“缔约各国应在任何情况下尊重本公约的各项规定。”但对该款的理解却不能与现在的共同第1条等同，因为这两个条文都还有第2款，即“战时遇有一交战国并未参加本公约，则本公约的规定仍应在参加本公约的交战国之间具有拘束力”，可见它与“普遍参加条款”（si omnes clause）的废除是密切相关的。因此，它们出现在条约正文当中是由于涉及具体的条约义务，而非仅仅是对“约定必须遵守”原则的宣示。不过，最初的草案中这两个条款本是连在一起的，但在后来的起草过程中被分成两个独立的段落，以致新版的评注认为

① 〔奥〕汉斯·凯尔森：《法与国家的一般理论》，沈宗灵译，中国大百科全书出版社，1996，第404页。

第1款由此具备了独立的含义。[①] 即便这种理解有其一定的道理，但这种独立性与后来的共同第1条相比仍是相当有限的。

1948年5月，为了能在同年八月份于斯德哥尔摩召开的第17届国际红十字大会上提出一系列新的保护战争受难者的国际公约草案以供大会讨论，红十字国际委员会（International Committee of the Red Cross，ICRC）率先起草完成了相关约文，其中共同第1条就几乎是现在的样子，只不过在“各缔约国”之后多了一句“以其人民的名义”。[②] 与此同时，这个底版源自1929年《日内瓦公约》的条文还被移至草案第1条这一显著的位置。这一变化是相当突兀的，虽然ICRC没有明确给出这样做的理由，但从它对这一条文内涵的阐释中却可见端倪：“ICRC认为有必要强调，若要该公约的保护制度有效，各缔约国不能仅限于自身实施公约。它们必须在其权力范围内采取一切措施，保证构成公约之基础的人道原则得以普遍适用。”[③] 因此，将该条置于公约之首这种看似画蛇添足的做法，实质上是要各缔约国作出正式和庄严宣告，以强化这一条文的重要性。ICRC甚至添了一句“以其人民的名义”，就是想将各缔约国人民自身也与尊重和保证尊重公约之原则联系起来，从而加强公约的有效性。如果考虑到两次世界大战期间，大多数当时既存的战争法条约都遭到破坏，这种做法就不难理解了。

ICRC草拟的共同第1条在红十字与红新月国际大会期间经过微调之后，[④] 就在第二年提交缔约方外交大会审议，由缔约方外交大会设置的一个联合委员会负责。然而令人意外的是，地位如此重要的条文，在缔约方外交大会期间只有意大利、挪威、美国和法国四个国家的代表发表了一些看法并由ICRC作了一些解释，除此以外再没有过什么实质讨论。[⑤] 就这

---

① 参见ICRC updated Commentary on the First Geneva Convention, p. 38, para. 123。

② ICRC, *Draft Revised or New Conventions for the Protection of War Victims*, Geneva, May 1948, article 1, p. 4, http://www.loc.gov/rr/frd/Military_Law/pdf/RC_Draft-revised.pdf，最后访问日期：2017年6月1日。

③ 参见ICRC, *Draft Revised or New Conventions for the Protection of War Victims*, Geneva, May 1948, Remarks on Article 1, p. 5。

④ 删除了“以其人民的名义”这个短语。

⑤ *Final Record of the Diplomatic Conference of Geneva of 1949*, Vol. II, Section B, p. 53, https://www.loc.gov/rr/frd/Military Law/pdf/Dipl-Conf-1949-Final_Vol-2-B.pdf，最后访问日期：2017年6月1日。

样，共同第1条没有经过任何修改就戏剧性地诞生了。

从上述有限的一些评论中看，对《日内瓦四公约》共同第1条的理解并非没有争议。对于参加1949年缔约方外交大会的各国代表为什么对讨论该条兴致索然，我们无从得知真相，但最有可能的原因之一就是该条的措辞未与具体的义务相联系，从而没有吸引各国的关注。也正是因为如此，共同第1条为有关各方的解读留下了余地，也为应对当代武装冲突带给国际人道法的挑战提供了规则上的转圜空间。不过这样的条款和规定方式近乎成为绝响，除了少量条约重述了该项义务以外，这种措辞再不见于其他国际人道法条约。①

二 “各缔约国承诺”

众所周知，共同第1条的新颖之处在于，它不仅为缔约国设定了善意履行《日内瓦四公约》的基本义务（“尊重本公约”），还增添了保证其得到善意履行的衍生义务（“保证本公约之被尊重”）。从条约法的视角单独来看，共同第1条使用“各缔约国承诺……”这样的措辞再正常不过，但若对《日内瓦四公约》进行整体考察，则会发现它与公约其他部分似乎并非完全自洽。问题的根源在于《日内瓦公约》在“缔约国”（High Contracting Parties）这一标准用语之外，还引入了“冲突各方”（Parties to the conflict）的概念。② 有意思的是，“冲突各方”这种表达在《日内瓦四公约》中出现的频次之高，不但不亚于“缔约国”，甚至犹有过之，但这两类用语所指向的对象又不完全一致。在共同第2条所指的国际性武装冲突（包括占领）中，冲突各方可能包含非缔约国；而在共同第3条所指的非国际性武装冲突中，冲突各方中则必然有非国家武装团体（non-State armed groups）。这样的冲突方显然不能为“缔约国”这一概念所涵盖，但公约又没有对这

① 重申共同第1条所包含之义务的条约包括：1977年《第一附加议定书》第1条第1款，1989年《儿童权利公约》第38条第1款，2005年《1949年8月12日日内瓦公约关于采纳一个新增特殊标志的附加议定书》第1条第1款和2013年《武器贸易条约》的序言、“原则”第5段。其中，只有1977年和2005年这两个《附加议定书》仍将这样的规定置于条约首位，特别应注意1977年《第一附加议定书》的特殊地位。

② 其措辞的变体还包括诸如“冲突之各方”（each Party to the conflict）和“冲突之一方”（the Party to the conflict）。

两类用语之间的关系作进一步阐释。那么应当如何理解“各缔约国承诺”的义务范围呢？它对非缔约国和非国家武装团体会产生怎样的影响呢？

（一）缔约国

毫无疑问，缔约国才是共同第 1 条中“尊重”（respect）和“保证尊重”（ensure respect）两项义务的主体，而不是冲突各方。就“尊重”的义务而言，它意在体现各缔约国本身对《日内瓦四公约》的适用。换言之，所有可归因于某一缔约国的机关、团体或个人的行为都可纳入该范畴。譬如，从各公约的具体规定来看，可能包括缔约国的武装部队、军事当局和立法机关等。[①] 就“保证尊重”的义务而言，它则是一种全新的创造，意在鼓励各缔约国在其权限范围内采取一切措施来保证《日内瓦四公约》中的基本人道原则得到普遍适用。然而，各缔约国究竟有义务保证“谁”来尊重，各公约均未提供明确答案。一种较易接受的理解是，“保证尊重”之义务对内及于行为不可归因于该缔约国的个人或团体（从某种意义上说就是全体人民），对外则可针对其他所有缔约国，无论其是冲突之一方还是保护国或者中立国。

此外，还有一个不容忽视的方面是，共同第 1 条之所以选择使用“各缔约国”一词而非“冲突各方”，也考虑到《日内瓦四公约》中还有大量平时即可实施的条款。使用更具一般意义的“缔约国”能最大限度地保证这些公约的充分适用。

（二）非缔约国

根据条约对第三国既无损也无益的一般原则，非缔约国显然没有尊重《日内瓦四公约》的法律义务。[②] 从逻辑上讲，只有在非缔约国接受并援用公约之规定时，缔约国才要保证非缔约国尊重这些公约。[③] 不过，共同第 1

---

① 《国家对国际不法行为的责任条款草案》第 4 条，载《国际法委员会报告第五十三届会议》，A/56/10，第 61 页，http://legal. un. org/docs/? path = . /ilc/documentation/english/reports/a_56_10. pdf&lang = EXP，最后访问日期：2017 年 6 月 1 日。

② 这里暂不考虑习惯国际法的问题。

③ 即共同第 2 条第 3 款规定的事实适用：“冲突之一方虽非缔约国，其他曾签订本公约之国家于其相互关系上，仍应受本公约之拘束。设若上述非缔约国接受并援用本公约之规定时，则缔约各国对该国之关系，亦应受本公约之拘束。”

条设定的这两项义务其实是相互独立的，“保证尊重”的义务并不一定以相对方“承诺尊重”为前提。事实上，缔约国仍可以在自身权力范围内采取可行措施来履行上述义务。譬如在消极义务方面，缔约国可以做到不鼓励、不支持非缔约国破坏公约的行为；在积极义务方面，缔约国可以采取不违背国际法基本原则的措施来预防破坏公约的行为或防止这类行为进一步扩大，如外交对话、武器禁运以及运用普遍管辖权惩治出现在境内的犯罪人等。

需要指出的是，在《日内瓦四公约》已获得全球批准的背景下，上述探讨可能理论意义大于实际意义。但包含相同条款的《第一附加议定书》迄今为止仍未获得全球批准。[①] 这也从侧面说明，对这个问题的讨论仍有其必要性。

（三）非国家武装团体

从历史的角度看，共同第1条中缔约国所负的“保证尊重”义务，原本就是针对非国际性武装冲突中非国家武装团体的。在《日内瓦四公约》草案酝酿之初，摆在ICRC面前的一个难题就是，如何让冲突之一方的非国家武装团体尊重这些公约？这旨在对西班牙内战的经验教训作出回应，但彼时尚未有成熟的理论来解释为何国家之间签订的条约可以为非国家武装团体创设国际义务，因为后者从未参与条约的制定过程，也不可能成为缔约之一方。后来该问题在ICRC法律部主任克洛德·皮尤（Claude Pilloud）的潜在影响下，形成了这样一种解决方案，在共同第1条中为缔约国增加一项“保证本公约之被尊重”的义务（还包括后来被删掉的“以其人民的名义”这样的用语），意在让一国通过代表全体人民作出承诺，使其领土内之人民的所有部分都事实上受到公约的约束。[②] 在1949年外交会

---

① 截至目前，《第一附加议定书》共有174个缔约国。ICRC，“Treaties, States Parties and Commentaries”，https://ihl-databases.icrc.org/applic/ihl/ihl.nsf/INTRO/470，最后访问日期：2017年6月1日。

② 参见Frits Kalshoven，“Chapter 31：The Undertaking to Respect and Ensure Respect in all Circumstances：From Tiny Seed to Ripening Fruit”，in Frits Kalshoven，*Reflections on the Law of War：Collected Essays*（Leiden & Boston：Martinus Nijhoff Publishers，2007），p.675。

议期间，挪威和美国就支持进行这样的解读。[①] 因此，非国家武装团体在非国际性武装冲突期间所负的义务可以说是缔约国“保证尊重”义务的衍生品，是公约之效力及于缔约国全境及其全体人民的结果。迄今为止，已经产生许多理论来解释《日内瓦四公约》，特别是共同第3条为什么可以直接为非国家武装团体创设国际义务，[②] 在这里不过多赘述，但可以援引塞拉利昂特别法庭在2004年一项裁决中的论断作为例子：“目前已达成一致意见的是，即使只有国家才能成为国际条约的缔约方，但武装冲突中的所有当事方，不论国家还是非国家行为体，都应受到国际人道法的约束。”[③]

与之相关的另一个问题是，非冲突之一方的其他缔约国是否也应承担保证非国家武装团体尊重公约的义务？至少在消极义务方面，答案是肯定的，国际法院关于“在尼加拉瓜和针对尼加拉瓜的军事和准军事活动案”（尼加拉瓜诉美国）的判决中就印证了这一点。[④] 国际法院在关于“在被占领巴勒斯坦领土修建隔离墙的法律后果”的咨询意见中也事实上认可了该义务的存在。[⑤] 值得一提的是，新版评注认为，除了缔约国以外，政府间的国际组织和非国家武装团体也都负有保证其成员尊重《日内瓦四公约》的义务。[⑥] 这种观点中所蕴含的价值导向值得肯定，但其是否已构成实在法义务仍值得商榷。

三 “在一切情况下”

“在一切情况下”这一限定语不仅存在于《日内瓦四公约》的共同第1条中，在其他条款中也多有提及。若要把握这个限定语的确切含义，就

---

① 挪威代表认为该条的目的是“保证全体人民尊重这些公约”，美国代表附议挪威代表的观点。参见 *Final Record of the Diplomatic Conference of Geneva of 1949*, Vol. II, Section B, p. 53。

② 参见 Andrew Clapham, *Human Rights Obligations of Non-State Actors* (Oxford & New York: Oxford University Press, 2006), p. 280。

③ Special Court for Sierra Leone, *Prosecutor v. Sam Hinga Norman* (CDF case), Case No. SCSL - 2004 - 14 - AR72 (E) - 131, The Appeals Chamber, Decision on Preliminary Motion based on Lack of Jurisdiction (Child Recruitment), 31 May 2004, para. 22.

④ *Military and Paramilitary Activities in and against Nicaragua* (*Nicaragua v. United States of America*), Judgment of 27 June 1986 (Merits), I. C. J. Reports 1986, p. 114, para. 220.

⑤ *Legal Consequences of the Construction of a Wall in the Occupied Palestinian Territory*, Advisory Opinion of 9 July 2004, I. C. J. Reports 2004, pp. 199 - 200, paras. 158 - 159.

⑥ *ICRC updated Commentary on the First Geneva Convention*, pp. 40 - 43, paras. 131 - 142.

必须从源头谈起。

在1929年形成伤病员和战俘两个《日内瓦公约》的外交会议上，各国普遍赞同要采取办法克服此前各战争法公约中一直存在的“普遍参加条款”所带来的不良影响。此时，英国代表团的一个提案受到欢迎，其措辞是：“各缔约国有义务在一切情况下尊重本公约的各项规定，除非遇有一交战国并未参加本公约：在这种情况下，本公约各项规定在该国与其他交战国之间不适用，但参加本公约的交战国之间仍应尊重本公约的规定。”[①] 可以看出，这个短语最早出现时，在很大程度上只是一个没有太多实际意义的副产品，它的存在只是为了烘托和强调该草案的后半句，它本质上并非绝对性的。“在一切情况下”这个短语后来被赋予全新的理解，得益于两次重大改变：第一次是1929年外交会议，起草委员会将英国的提案润色后分成两个独立的段落，使该限定语初步获得了独立的意义；第二次是1949年外交会议，该限定语随之被挪至公约之首，完全脱离了原来例外规定的影响。结合历史与当代，“在一切情况下”至少应作如下理解。

（一）它意味着“普遍参加条款”的废除

“在一切情况下”这一短语的使用原本就与“普遍参加条款”的废除密切相关。在1929年以前，无论海牙法还是日内瓦法，[②] 大多数战争法公约都存在这样的条款，规定公约仅适用于所有交战国都已参加公约的情形，一旦有非缔约国参与冲突，则会导致公约对冲突所有当事国丧失拘束力。[③]

---

① “Actes de la Conférence diplomatique de Genève de 1929”, quoted from Frits Kalshoven, *Reflections on the Law of War: Collected Essays*, p. 670.

② 自成文的现代国际人道法规则出现以来，一直有两股法律潮流在沿着相对独立的道路发展演进。一支被称为日内瓦法，它主要涉及对武装冲突受难者的保护，即那些丧失战斗力的作战人员和没有参加敌对行动的平民，自1864年第一部《日内瓦公约》起，历经1906年、1929年、1949年的不断完善和补充；另一支被称为海牙法，以1899年和1907年两次海牙和平会议通过的十几部国际公约为代表并因此而得名，主要涉及限制或禁止战争的某些具体手段和方法。直至1977年两个《附加议定书》通过，分别将“保护”和“限制”纳入其中，这两股法律潮流才发生融合，使日内瓦法和海牙法的区分彻底成为历史，真正意义上统一的国际人道法体系才得以形成。

③ 例如，1907年《关于改善战地武装部队伤者和病者境遇的公约》第24条规定：“本公约的规定，仅在缔约国内的两国或数国间发生战争时，对这些国家有约束力。如果交战国之一不是本公约的签署国，则本公约的规定不具有约束力。”再如1907年《陆战法规和惯例公约》第2条规定：“第一条所指章程及本公约各条款，应在缔约国之间，并且只有在交战各方都是缔约国时方能适用。”

显然，“普遍参加条款”意在维护条约的相互性，但造成的客观结果是，那些本应在武装冲突期间适用的公约，却从武装冲突一开始被排斥在外了。它的负面影响在第一次世界大战期间还不十分明显，但在第二次世界大战期间却让国际社会饱尝恶果，甚至流毒至今，因为很多包含“普遍参加条款”的公约目前仍有法律效力。①

在 1929 年的初次尝试之后，国际社会在 1949 年外交会议上进一步加强了在这方面的努力。“在一切情况下”这个短语不仅被提至共同第 1 条统领全篇，其废除“普遍参加条款”的意图还被共同第 2 条第 3 款第 1 句加以明确：“冲突之一方虽非缔约国，其他曾签订本公约之国家于其相互关系上，仍应受本公约之约束。”换言之，缔约国之间适用公约，不受非缔约国是否参战的影响。此外，“在一切情况下”还意味着，缔约国也别想通过退约机制随意规避公约义务。《日内瓦四公约》均规定：“如缔约国于作退约通知时已卷入冲突，则其退约须待至和议成立后，并在有关本公约所保护之人员之释放及遣返之工作完毕后，始能生效。”②

不过，“普遍参加条款”的废除没有触及一个模糊地带，那就是在缔约国与非缔约国发生双方冲突时，缔约国自身是否还受公约义务的约束？如果不考虑共同第 2 条第 3 款第 2 句规定的事实适用（de facto application），仅从条约法的角度来说，公约无法适用于这种冲突，但其中的实质义务仍然拘束缔约国，并且缔约国应予以“尊重”并“保证尊重”，这不

① 譬如 1907 年第二次海牙和平会议订立的各公约，尤其是《陆战法规和惯例公约》（1907 年海牙第四公约）及其附件《陆战法规和惯例章程》，目前仍具有法律拘束力。不过，这些公约对于中国是否仍有拘束力尚存疑问。当时的清政府代表中国批准了几乎所有海牙宣言和海牙公约，后来的中华民国政府予以继承。中华人民共和国成立之初，《共同纲领》第 55 条规定：“对于国民党政府与外国政府所订立的各项条约和协定，中华人民共和国中央人民政府应加以审查，按其内容，分别予以承认，或废除，或修改，或重订。”这意味着，中华人民共和国政府对于条约的继承并不是当然的。但当时这一规定主要是针对各项不平等条约，实质上没有触及国际人道法领域的条约。但根据外交部网站“中国参加国际公约情况一览表（1875—2003）”，所列仅包含两次海牙和会上订立的《和平解决国际争端公约》，这是否证明中国已不承认其他海牙公约的法律效力？但仍然要强调，《海牙章程》中的大部分规则不仅为后续国际人道法条约所继承，其中许多也构成习惯法。参见“中国参加国际公约情况一览表（1875—2003）”，外交部，http://www.mfa.gov.cn/chn//pds/ziliao/tytj/tyfg/t4985.htm，最后访问日期：2017 年 6 月 1 日。

② 日内瓦第一至第四公约，分别为第 63 条第 3 款、第 62 条第 3 款、第 142 条第 3 款和第 158 条第 3 款。

仅反映了习惯法，而且在某种程度上已构成一种“对世义务”（obligation erga omnes）。就这一点而言，从《日内瓦四公约》的退约机制中也能找到部分证据：“退约仅对该退约国有效，但并不减轻冲突各方依国际法原则仍应履行之义务，此等原则系产自文明人民间树立之惯例，人道法则与公众良心之要求。”[①]

（二）它意味着一种“对世义务”

由于《日内瓦四公约》已获全球批准，探讨如下问题可能更有意义：缔约国尊重并保证尊重公约的义务，是否以其他缔约国同样履行义务为前提？“在一切情况下”这一限定语给出了否定的答案。正如ICRC所说，“公约的可适用性可基于相互性原则，但在尊重公约方面没有相互性”。[②]这一点也得到了1969年《维也纳条约法公约》的认可，明确规定“条约因违约而终止或停止施行”不适用于“各人道性质之条约内所载关于保护人身之各项规定”。[③] 除了公约以外，各国的实践以及国际和国内法庭的判例均支持这种解读，即作为一项法律的一般原则，具有人道性质的法律义务不以相互性为前提。[④] 换言之，共同第1条所指缔约国尊重并保证尊重《日内瓦四公约》是一项对世义务。

（三）它意味着“诉诸战争权”与“战时法”的严格分离

这层含义意在昭示：无论一场战争是“正义的”还是“非正义的”，无论是侵略战争还是抵抗侵略的战争，各缔约国尊重并保证尊重公约的义务均不受影响。这种解读在1929年和1949年外交会议上均未被提及，却是“在一切情况下”的应有之意。它最初是为了回应冷战期间的苏联阵营所持立场——因为《联合国宪章》禁止侵略，所以排除了侵略者主张受国

---

① 日内瓦第一至第四公约，分别为第63条第4款、第62条第4款、第142条第4款和第158条第4款。

② 马尔科·萨索利、安托万·布维耶主编《战争中的法律保护》（第二版），第一卷，红十字国际委员会，2006，第120页；〔比〕让-马里·亨克茨、〔英〕路易丝·多斯瓦尔德-贝克主编《习惯国际人道法——规则》，法律出版社，2007，第470页，规则140。（简称ICRC《习惯国际人道法研究》）

③ 1969年《维也纳条约法公约》第60条第5款。

④ 关于国家实践和法庭判例的介绍，参见ICRC《习惯国际人道法研究》，第470—471页，关于规则140的评注。

际人道法保护的权利。[①] 这显然与国际人道法的目的和宗旨相悖。可以说，在国际法目前的发展状况下，“诉诸战争权”与“战时法”的严格分离是保证国际人道法得到有效遵守的基本前提，任何缔约国都不能在冲突的合法性方面找到不尊重公约的合理借口。

（四）它意味着可平时适用

这层含义则意在强调共同第 1 条作为“一般义务”的性质。在 1929 年外交会议上，这个问题最早是由中国代表团提出来的。中国代表团很不理解为何要将公约的拘束力限定于战时，毕竟还是有不少规定，例如使用红十字和红新月标志的规则、涉及武装部队教育的立法和其他措施以及惩治违法行为等，都是要在平时实施的。这一关切很快得到提出草案的英国代表团的响应，并最终由各国达成这样的共识，即“在一切情况下”尊重公约之各项规定的义务可被解读为包括平时。[②] 而对于 1949 年《日内瓦四公约》而言，这种理解已在共同第 2 条第 1 款中得到回应（“于平时应予实施之各项规定之外……”）。

最后，必须强调的是，尽管 1929 年外交会议时各国尚无此意图，但 1949 年《日内瓦四公约》共同第 1 条中的“在一切情况下”也涵盖非国际性武装冲突。在这种冲突中，各缔约国必须尊重并保证尊重共同第 3 条所列之最低限度的人道法义务。

四 “尊重本公约”

共同第 1 条使用“尊重”（respect）一词，而不是更为常用的“遵守”（comply with）等类似词语，实质上为各缔约国履行公约义务提出了更高的标准。与遵守相比，“尊重”一词更强调内心认同和主观意愿，而不依赖于外在力量的强迫。事实上，正如路易斯·亨金（Louis Henkin）所说，外

---

① 参见 Frits Kalshoven, *Reflections on the Law of War: Collected Essays* (Leiden & Boston: Martinus Nijhoff Publishers, 2007), pp. 698 – 699。

② 参见 Frits Kalshoven, *Reflections on the Law of War: Collected Essays* (Leiden & Boston: Martinus Nijhoff Publishers, 2007), pp. 671 – 672。

部强制“并不是确保法律得到遵守的唯一方法，甚至不是主要的方法”。[1] 任何外部约束机制都不如唤起内心主动守法的意识，这一点对《日内瓦四公约》乃至整个国际人道法来说尤为重要。

长期以来，由于强制执行及制裁机制的不足，国际人道法的有效性一直受到质疑，现实主义者认为它有严重理想化的倾向，更严厉的批评者甚至认为，国际人道法从头到尾都是伪善的。[2] 然而大量事实已表明，守法之人通常并非出于对制裁的畏惧，而制裁也不足以震慑真正的犯罪者。那么，各缔约国应如何来实现对《日内瓦四公约》的尊重呢？

（一）约文普及

知晓法律是尊重法律的前提。重要的是，各缔约国应让全体国民意识到，《日内瓦四公约》所体现的是法律规则而非道德宣言。正如 ICRC 出版的《战争中的法律保护》一书中所言：“在多数情况下，只要人们认识到国际人道法是由各国和国际社会接受的适用于武装冲突中的法律，而不仅是职业空想家某些善良的愿望，他们就会愿意遵守这一法律。”[3] 因此，恰当的普及和传播国际人道法知识至关重要。考虑到这一点，各公约的执行部分均包含一个共同条款，规定了普及约文的义务：

> 各缔约国在平时及战时应在各该国尽量广泛传播本公约之约文，尤应在其军事，并如可能时在公民教育计划中，包括本公约之学习，俾本公约之原则为全体人民，尤其武装战斗部队、医务人员及随军牧师所周知。[4]

就这项义务而言，首先，约文传播之首要对象是武装部队，公约能否得到有效遵守和实行与之紧密相关。各缔约国应将公约的内容纳入军事教育计

---

① 参见 Louis Henkin, *How Nations Behave: Law and Foreign Policy* (New York: Columbia University Press, 2nd edition, 1979), p. 92。

② 〔美〕约翰·法比安·维特：《林肯守则：美国战争法史》，胡晓进、李丹译，中国政法大学出版社，2015，序言部分。

③ 马尔科·萨索利、安托万·布维耶主编《战争中的法律保护》（第二版），第一卷，红十字国际委员会，2006，第 357 页。

④ 日内瓦第一至第四公约，分别为第 47 条、第 48 条、第 127 条和第 144 条。

划，以便武装部队全体人员周知。除此以外，公约还为相当等级的指挥官施加了额外的义务，规定“冲突各方应通过其总司令保证以上条款之详细执行”。1977年《第一附加议定书》第87条对此又进一步加以补充和细化，还通过第82条特别要求“于必要时有法律顾问，对各公约和本议定书的适用以及就此问题发给武装部队的适当指示，向相当等级的军事司令官提供意见”。

其次，应向平民居民传播约文，鼓励平民进行相关学习。这一点之所以重要，除了平民应当知晓武装冲突期间国际人道法赋予的各项保护和限制外，还因为他们可能是武装部队或其他非国家武装团体成员的潜在来源。必须强调的是，尽管有“如可能时”这一限定语，但这并不意味着将公约之学习纳入公民教育计划是一个可选项，而是考虑到某些联邦国家的中央政府可能在教育事项上没有这种权力。实践中，这项义务的履行可以更为多样化。例如，截至2015年9月，世界上已有包括中国在内的107个国家建立了国际人道法国家委员会，其职责中很重要的一项就包括普及和传播国际人道法；再如，ICRC建立了探索人道法国际项目，旨在向13至18岁的青少年介绍国际人道法的基本规则，并在超过60个国家中成功推行。①

最后，传播约文的义务涵盖平时与战时。此外，各缔约国还应相互通知本公约的正式译文，同时包括该国实施公约的法律和规则。这项义务亦由传播义务衍生而来。

（二）规范内化

规范内化是尊重法律的核心。实践已表明，知晓法律并不必然导致守法的结果。战场上的士兵受环境、心理、情感等多种因素的影响，原始的暴力冲动很容易压制理性判断，从而带来严重后果。在2005年举世震惊的“哈迪塞屠杀”事件中，遭遇路边炸弹袭击的美国海军陆战队员由于过激反应和报复心态，随后枪杀了24名伊拉克平民，其中还包括2岁左右的儿童。② 因此，重要的是将国际人道法训练成为士兵的本能反应，使其成为第二天性，而不是给士兵口袋里装上写满《日内瓦四公约》规定的小卡

① 关于国际人道法国家委员会以及探索人道法项目的详细介绍，可访问红十字国际委员会官方网站：http://www.icrc.org，最后访问日期：2017年5月31日。

② 参见 Paul von Zielbauer，“Marines' Trials in Iraq Killings Are Withering”，*New York Times*，30 August 2007，at A1。

片，这就是规范的内化。

然而，在《孤独的幸存者》一书中，在谈到以国际人道法为核心的交战规则时，一名前海豹突击队员却描绘了战场上士兵的真实心态："这些规则非常明确：除非我们受到攻击，或者已经明确地辨认出敌人及其敌对意图，否则不得开火。这非常光明磊落。但是这究竟将美国士兵置于何地呢？他们可能已经连续执勤数天，不断遭到射击，一直在躲避火箭弹和简易炸弹的攻击，蒙受了伤亡，已经筋疲力尽，而且可能还有点惊慌……"①

正是战场上士兵的这种处境，让人们很容易接受降低守法标准是正当的。这反映出一种普遍的自我矛盾心态：人们对于和平时期的非法杀戮行为零容忍，却对武装冲突期间的相同行为报以更大的宽容，将其作为战争的副产品而理所当然地接受。其严重后果在越战期间臭名昭著的"美莱村大屠杀"中得到了充分反映，参与屠杀的许多美军士兵都将其归咎于受害者的命运不济。事后的调查表明，这正是因为国际人道法从未通过训练内化到他们的行为之中。②

规范的内化有助于为国际人道法创造良好的遵守环境，能够塑造武装部队整体的行为模式，从而对个体的行为产生积极影响，特别是在两难的境地中作出恰当的选择。③

（三）违法制裁

违法制裁是尊重法律的保障。但因为现实的制约，这种保障是有限度的，是促进遵守国际人道法的辅助方法。由于证据不易获得和保存，大量违反国际人道法的行为无法通过法律机制得到有效制裁，这也是批评者们质疑国际人道法有效性的根据之一。在"哈迪塞屠杀"事件中，犯罪的士

---

① 〔美〕马库斯·鲁特埃勒、〔美〕帕崔克·罗宾逊：《孤独的幸存者》，赵宏涛译，湖北长江出版集团、长江文艺出版社，2015，第13—14页。

② 参见 Elizabeth Stubbins Bates, "Towards Effective Military Training in International Humanitarian Law", (2014) 96 (895/896) *International Review of the Red Cross* 795, p. 803。

③ 2005年在阿富汗开展的"红翼行动"中，含《孤独的幸存者》的作者在内的4名海豹突击队员在执行先期侦察任务时被3名当地牧羊人发现。在杀与不杀之间犹豫时，4名士兵最终投票决定，由于1人弃权，该书作者投下了关键的一票，主张将3人放走。结果3个牧羊人很快就将4名海豹队员的行踪报告给了塔利班。在随后的突围战斗中，除作者外，其余3人全部阵亡。坦率地讲，这样的结果确实会极大地影响国际人道法的说服力，这也是当代不对称冲突带给国际人道法的挑战之一。

兵就险些逃脱法律的惩罚，因为最初的报告显示，15 名平民在路边炸弹爆炸中死亡，另有 9 名叛乱分子在交火中被击毙。[①] 这种机制上的“缺陷”虽并非国际人道法所独有，却因为武装冲突的存在而被严重放大。事实上，与惩罚和威慑相比，国际人道法中的制裁机制更重要的作用是营造守法的氛围，表明结束有罪无罚现象的决心，并重申行为的准则。因此，就像路易斯·亨金所期望的，真正“有效的法律系统并不是一个尽可能多地惩罚违法者的系统，而是一个只有少量违法行为需要受到惩罚的系统”，[②] 应依靠制裁以外的其他方式来阻止潜在的违法者。

我们不能单纯依赖制裁机制来促进守法，但也不能认为这种机制可有可无。盲目的失望或者过高的期待都会形成偏见，因此必须正确认识到这种机制所能发挥的作用。《日内瓦四公约》要求各缔约国制定必要立法将所列之严重破坏公约的行为犯罪化，建立普遍管辖权对行为人加以刑事制裁，甚至为这类行为承担相应的国家责任。[③]

总而言之，实现共同第 1 条所说的“尊重”，是内外因素合力的结果，而且以内因为主导，外因为辅助。要更好地遵守《日内瓦四公约》，必须唤起人们内心的认同和信任。与传播国际人道法和制裁违法行为相比，规范的内化是更为艰难的工作。正如 ICRC 所提及的，“与不懂规则的人相比，那些了解规则但已经认为规则无用的人或许更加危险，因为克服无知比克服悲观容易”。[④]

五 “保证本公约之被尊重”

1949 年外交会议期间，意大利代表团在评价“保证尊重”这个用语时曾表示，它“要么是多余的，要么就是引入了一个国际法的新概念”。[⑤] 很

---

① 参见 Tim Mcgirk, “Collateral Damage or Civilian Massacre in Haditha?”, Time, 19 March 2006。

② 参见 Louis Henkin, *How Nations Behave: Law and Foreign Policy* (New York: Columbia University Press, 2nd edition, 1979), p. 93。

③ 日内瓦第一至第四公约，分别为第 49—51 条、第 50—52 条、第 129—131 条和第 146—148 条。

④ 马尔科·萨索利、安托万·布维耶主编《战争中的法律保护》（第二版），第一卷，红十字国际委员会，2006，第 420 页。

⑤ 参见 *Final Record of the Diplomatic Conference of Geneva of 1949*, Vol. II, Section B, p. 53。

显然，后一种说法才是中肯的。“保证尊重”是《日内瓦四公约》赋予各缔约国的一项全新义务，首次出现于共同第1条。但遗憾的是，其确切含义并没有得到进一步阐释。作为共同第1条的起草者和提出者，ICRC对于“保证尊重”义务的理解始终坚定，强调各缔约国“应在其权力范围内采取一切措施，保证各公约中的基本人道原则得以普遍适用”。[①] 换言之，“保证尊重”义务旨在加强各缔约国的责任，不能“独善其身”，而要“兼济天下”。不过，《日内瓦四公约》本身并未给出如何履行这项义务的明确指南，但基于国际法原理、国家实践和国际判例，我们可以勾勒出如下基本标准。

（一）合法性

共同第1条旨在强化《日内瓦四公约》义务的神圣性，并没有打破现有国际法体系的任何意图。因此，各缔约国履行“保证尊重”这项衍生义务，不得背离现有可适用的国际法规则，特别是《联合国宪章》所载之各项基本原则。譬如，一国不得以结束另一国严重违反公约为由，单方面对该国擅自使用武力或以武力威胁或者以其他方式侵犯该国的主权。但反过来说，现有的国际法规则和原则也决不为一国严重违反公约提供保护伞。考虑到公约义务的对世性，某一缔约国严重违反公约的行为不得被视为其内部事务，哪怕这种行为发生在该国境内的非国际性武装冲突的背景下。因此，必须谨慎衡量行为的界限，尤其对于采取单方措施的缔约国来说。

在大多数情况下，更为稳妥的做法是诉诸集体措施，尤其是在联合国的框架内。《第一附加议定书》第89条特别强调了履行“保证尊重”义务的这种可能性：“在严重违反本公约或本议定书的情形下，缔约各方承诺在与联合国合作下按照联合国宪章采取共同或单方行动。”譬如，在波斯尼亚和黑塞哥维那、卢旺达、刚果、塞拉利昂、利比里亚等地发生武装冲突期间，联合国均依据安理会决议向这些国家派遣了维和特派团，履行保证冲突各方尊重国际人道法的职责。[②]

---

① 参见 *Final Record of the Diplomatic Conference of Geneva of 1949*, Vol. II, Section B, p. 53。

② 例如，联合国安理会1993年第872号决议（卢旺达），S/RES/872（1993）；1995年第1031号决议（波斯尼亚－黑塞哥维那），S/RES/1031（1995）；1999年第1234号决议（刚果民主共和国），S/RES/1234（1999）；1999年第1270号决议（塞拉利昂），S/RES/1270（1999）；2003年第1509号决议（利比里亚），S/RES/1509（2003）；等等。

（二）有效性

考虑到武装冲突的复杂性，可以合理地认为“保证尊重”是一项手段义务，而非结果义务。在一切情况下公约都得到尊重是一个理想的目标，只有采取务实的态度才能促使各缔约国真正承担起保证尊重的义务。这项义务由消极义务和积极义务两个部分组成：前者意味着各缔约国不得鼓励实施违反公约的行为；后者则意味着各缔约国应主动采取措施，促使违反公约的冲突当事方回到尊重公约的轨道上来。2007 年第 30 届红十字与红新月国家大会题为“重申和实施国际人道法”的第 3 号决议明确认可了这种解读。[①] 综合上述义务，它们意味着要做到以下几个方面。

1. 不鼓励

不鼓励意味着各缔约国不得鼓动、帮助或协助冲突一方违反公约或为其违法行为提供便利，不论是在舆论上还是在资金和物资支持等实质方面，亦不得承认严重违反国际人道法所制造之局势的合法性。将这项消极义务立法化的典型例子是 2013 年的《武器贸易条约》，它为缔约国转让公约所列之常规武器的行为设定了严格的评估标准，其中一项就是“是否会用于犯下或有助于犯下严重违反国际人道法的行为”，即“严重违反 1949 年《日内瓦四公约》的行为，实施针对受保护民用物品或平民的袭击或其作为缔约国的国际文书所规定的其他战争罪”。[②] 事实上，早在 1986 年，国际法院就已经在“在尼加拉瓜和针对尼加拉瓜的军事和准军事活动案”的判决中认可了这种消极义务的存在。[③]

2. 不纵容

不纵容意味着各缔约国应采取一切可行措施预防并终止违反公约的行为，这是一项积极义务。实践中，这项义务的履行取决于多种因素，包括公约文本的传播规模、立法状况、缔约国当局与行为发生地的地理距离以

---

① 2007 年第 30 届红十字与红新月国际大会第 3 号决议第 1 部分（尊重和确保尊重）第 2 条：“强调所有国家都有义务不鼓励武装冲突的任何一方违反国际人道法，并运用其影响力，单独或者通过多边机制防止和制止违反国际法的行为。”

② 《武器贸易条约》，2013 年 4 月 2 日通过，2014 年 12 月 24 日生效，第 6 条第 3 款。

③ *Military and Paramilitary Activities in and against Nicaragua*, Judgment of 27 June 1986, para. 220.

及与行为人之间的政治联系或其他联系的强度等。[①] 而且，各缔约国所负的义务性质虽然相同，程度却有差异。很明显，对冲突当事方有着更大影响力的缔约国就应承担更高的义务。譬如，如果一国负责教育、培训另一国的武装部队并且为该国提供武器装备和资金支持，基于这种影响力，前者就比其他国家承担更多的保证后者尊重国际人道法的义务，因为其采取措施会更加便利和有效。

3. 不姑息

不姑息意味着各缔约国应采取一切可行措施，在国内和国际层面支持将严重违反国际人道法的行为人绳之以法。其中，在国内层面，《日内瓦四公约》规定了调查程序，《第一附加议定书》补充了另一项机制，即国际人道实况调查委员会。[②] 同时，各缔约国还可以基于普遍管辖权启动国内的刑事诉讼。在国际层面，则是支持国际刑事司法机制，各缔约国履行“保证尊重”的义务在这一点上体现得尤为明显。譬如，在安理会通过决议建立前南斯拉夫问题国际刑事法庭时，中国其实并不赞同这样的法律安排，但仍然对决议投了赞成票（之后还向刑庭派遣法官），正是为了将犯有违反国际人道法罪行的人绳之以法。[③]

总之，缔约国履行“保证义务”的措施是多样化的，但由于该义务的内容并没有被明确界定，因此具体采取何种措施很大程度上交由各缔约国自由裁量。

（三）相称性

各缔约国采取措施履行“保证尊重”义务时，还必须满足相称性标准，这就意味着这些措施不仅是合法的，也是合理的。这项标准很容易被忽视，却十分重要。如前所述，缔约国可采取的措施有多种类型，所产生的效果也各不相同。因此，在关注这些措施的有效性时，还必须考虑到其所带来的附带影响。现在很多制裁措施更多地直接针对当权者，以避免对

---

① *Case concerning Application of the Convention on the Prevention and Punishment of the Crime of Genocide* (*Bosnia and Herzegovina v. Serbia and Montenegro*), Judgment of 26 February 2007, ICJ Reports 2007, p. 154, para. 430.

② 1977 年《第一附加议定书》，第 90 条。

③ 联合国安理会第 3217 次会议临时逐字记录，1993 年 5 月 25 日，UN Doc. S/PV. 3217。

弱势群体带来不利影响。例如在2011年利比亚冲突期间，由于存在严重违反国际人道法的现象，联合国安理会就针对利比亚领导人及其亲属发布了旅行禁令并冻结其资产。[①] 此外，相称性还意味着各缔约国不能以克减公约的保障措施为代价来履行“保证尊重”的义务，对于冲突当事方而言尤其如此。对于各公约所保护的对象，均禁止各缔约国施以报复。

最后，需要补充强调的一点是，缔约国履行“保证尊重”的义务并不以自身卷入国际性或非国际性武装冲突为前提。特别是在国际性武装冲突中，中立法没有为中立国克减这项义务提供依据，这就意味着，在不歧视的基础上对待所有冲突当事方的要求并不会免除中立国“保证尊重”的义务。

六 结语

《日内瓦四公约》共同第1条的诞生极富戏剧性。它的雏形本打算解决公约的平时适用以及“普遍参加条款”的废除问题，却最终由共同第2条加以解决；它引入“保证尊重”这一全新的概念，旨在解决公约在非国际性武装冲突中的适用问题，却最终由共同第3条加以解决。共同第1条未给缔约国创设任何具体义务，因此，其重要性也就长期以来受到忽视。但事实上，共同第1条超越了“约定必须遵守”原则的传统意涵，为缔约国施加了更大的责任。由于共同第1条义务的内容不具体，也有人质疑该条的有效性。[②] 然而，共同第1条中所使用的“承诺”（undertake）一词表明，它绝不是一个道义上的宣誓，而是一项实在的法律义务。国际法院在“在尼加拉瓜和针对尼加拉瓜的军事和准军事活动案”中明确指出，共同第1条规定的义务不只是源于公约自身，还源于人道法的一般原则，公约只是对这些原则进行了具体表达。[③] 在后续的《防止及惩治灭绝种族罪公约》的适用案中，国际法院更是进一步确认，“承诺”一词的通常含义“是

① 联合国安理会第1970号决议，《针对阿拉伯利比亚民众国的局势规定并实施武器禁运、旅行禁令以及资产冻结》，S/RES/1970（2011），2011年2月26日，执行部分第15段至第21段。

② 新版评注中列举了一些有代表性的看法。See *ICRC updated Commentary on the First Geneva Convention*, p. 54, footnote 93.

③ *Military and Paramilitary Activities in and against Nicaragua* (*Nicaragua v. United States of America*), I. C. J Report1986, Judgement, para. 220.

正式的允诺，是约束自身，是保证或承诺，是同意，是接受一项义务……而非仅仅是一种劝告或决心”。[①] 确实，共同第1条的履行在很大程度上要由各缔约国自行决定，但这并不意味着这项义务就是随意的。根据1969年《维也纳条约法公约》所确立的条约解释原则，共同第1条必须放在《日内瓦四公约》甚至国际人道法的整体框架下进行解读，并可以通过后续的国家实践予以补充和完善。

（责任编辑：何田田）

（本文原载于《国际法研究》2017年第4期）

① *Case Concerning Application of the Convention on the Prevention and Punishment of the Crime of Genocide* (*Bosnia and Herzegovina v. Serbia and Montenegro*), p. 61, para. 162.

国际法院与共同利益的保护：实践、发展与影响*

宋　杰**

共同利益（common interest）的保护问题是当代国际法上的一个重要理论与实践问题。从理论角度来看，什么叫共同利益，其法理基础何在？此种利益相对于其他利益有何不同？其对于国际社会意味着什么？从实践角度来看，国际社会在共同利益的保护上建立了哪些机制？为了保护共同利益，国家是否有权采取单独或集体行动？一旦国家有权采取行动，是否应遵循一定限制？国家基于此所采取的行动，同传统国际法上的干涉有何区别？所有这些问题，都将在实践中存在，同样也需要依赖于实践提供答案。国际法院在近年来的司法实践中已经作出了一定回应。此种回应与相应国家的实践，必将对共同利益的保护产生重要影响，会给干涉问题在国际法上的发展提供一定的理论依据与实践指引，也会深刻地影响到国家未来的行为模式。因此，共同利益的保护问题及国际法院的相关司法实践，无疑值得深入研究。

本文将从国际法院司法实践的角度来讨论国际法上共同利益的保护问题。文章分四部分。第一部分对共同利益概念的提出及其发展进行讨论。第二部分对国际法院的相关司法实践进行梳理，来讨论此概念的实践性后果。第三部分则从此概念对国际法和国家实践影响的角度进行分析和评论。最后是总结部分。

---

* 本文系国家社科基金项目“国际法上的司法干涉问题研究”（项目号：13BFX145）的阶段性成果。

** 宋杰，法学博士，浙江工商大学法学院教授。

一 共同利益概念的提出及其发展与升华

从国际法院的司法实践来看，共同利益的保护经历了三个阶段：概念的提出阶段，随后发展阶段，以及完美“升华”阶段。在第一个阶段，国际法院仅仅提出了共同利益的概念，抽象地指出了其基本特征。但对于此概念的“法律性”，尤其是“规范性含义”，国际法院则没有触及。这见之于“灭绝种族罪公约保留咨询意见案”（Reservations to the Convention on Genocide）。随后，在“巴塞罗那电力、电车和电灯公司案”（Barcelona Traction, Light and Power Company）中，以此概念为基础，国际法院提出了对一切义务这个新概念。相较于共同利益概念，这是一个规范意义上的法律概念。并且，通过《防止及惩治灭绝种族罪公约》，共同利益的概念与对一切义务的概念发生了“偶遇”。而在“比利时诉塞内加尔有关或引渡或起诉义务问题案”（Belgium v. Senegal）（以下简称“或引渡或起诉义务问题案”）中，国际法院则将共同利益与对一切义务这两个概念“完美”地结合并赋予了其实践性后果。

（一）共同利益概念的提出及其特征

共同利益的概念最早是国际法院在“灭绝种族罪公约保留咨询意见案”中提出来的。

该案中，在论及《防止及惩治灭绝种族罪公约》是否允许保留，如果允许保留，可以提出何种保留等问题时，国际法院认为，要回答这些问题，就有必要考虑公约的目的等。国际法院指出，公约纯粹是为了人道和文明的目的而拟定的，一方面是为了保障某些人群的存在，另一方面是为了确认和赞同最基本的道德原则。“在这样的公约中，缔约国是没有自己的任何利益的，它们有且仅有一个共同利益（common interest），即实现这些崇高的目的，而这些目的正是公约存在的理由。因此，在这样的公约中，既不能论及其给国家自身所带来的利弊问题，也不能说在权利和义务之间维持完全的契约上的平衡。”①

① Reservations to the Convention on Genocide, Advisory Opinion, I. C. J. Reports 1951, p. 23.

在这段论述中，可以看出，国际法院提出了共同利益的概念，认为《防止及惩治灭绝种族罪公约》体现了共同利益。同时，共同利益至少有两个重要特征。(1) 共同利益贵在共同二字，个别利益或自身利益是被排除的事项。正因如此，国家不能在共同利益所涉事项上追逐、计较自身利弊得失。(2) 确立共同利益的条约不同于一般的契约性条约。后者追求的是彼此间权利与义务关系上的均衡。而前者追求的可能是国家承担完全的义务，而无丝毫自身权利；或者，即使国家享有相关权利，此种权利与国家自身利益也没有任何直接联系。换言之，国家基于此类公约所享有的权利与义务之间既不具有均衡性，也不具有均等性。

共同利益的上述重要特征也经当时的联合国秘书长针对该公约草案第17条[①]所作评论证实。秘书长指出，"（就保留问题而言）公约没有就保留的一般范围问题进行规定，是因为这样的公约并不处理国家自身的利益问题，而是关涉维护国际秩序的一个问题"。[②] 由此可见，共同利益完全不同于国家的个别利益，其与国际秩序息息相关。

国际法院针对公约提出了共同利益这个概念，也指出了其重要特征，但对于这么一个重要的概念，仅仅抽象地概括其特征显然远远不够。此概念是不是一个法律上的概念？如果是，其规范性含义是什么？其在实践中会产生何种法律后果？所有这些问题，国际法院都未涉及。国际法院需要在实践中进一步回应这些问题。

（二）共同利益概念的发展：对一切义务概念

与回应上述这些问题有关，国际法院在"巴塞罗那电力、电车和电灯公司案"中进一步提出了对一切义务（obligation erga omnes）概念。国际法院指出："有必要在国家对国际共同体整体所负的义务和在外交领域对另一国所负的义务之间划一条基本界限。在本质上，前者涉及所有国家的利害关系。鉴于与此等义务有关的权利的重要性，可以认为所有国家都对保护这些权利具有法律上的利益，这些权利同时也是（国家）对一切所负的义务。"

---

① 本条涉及公约的保留问题，但具体规定则是空白，没有草拟任何内容。

② Secretariat Draft E/447, in Hirad Abtahi and Philippa Webb, eds., *The Genocide Convention: The Travaux Préparatoires* (Leiden and Boston: Martinus Nijhoff Publishers, 2008), p. 255.

“就当代国际法而言，这些义务既源于诸如对侵略行为、灭绝种族行为的非法性的宣告，也源于有关保护基本人权的国际法原则与规则，包括免受奴役和禁止种族歧视的规则。这些所保护的权利有的已成为一般国际法的一部分，其他的则由普遍性或准普遍性的国际文件所赋予。”[①] 从上述阐述可看出，国际法院将国家所承担的义务“一分为二”：对个别国家承担的对等、互惠的义务和对作为整体的国际共同体所承担的对一切义务。后者涉及所有国家的利害关系，所有国家在监督对一切义务的履行上都“享有法律上的利益”。国际法院举例称，对一切义务至少包括四类，即针对侵略行为的义务、针对灭绝种族行为的义务、针对奴役的义务和针对种族歧视的义务。前两者属于对整体性严重非法行为的宣告，而后两者，则属于对基本人权的保护范畴。无论是表达还是范围，对一切义务概念的法律性和规范性都超过了共同利益。

由于预防和惩治灭绝种族行为义务被包含在对一切义务之中，而国际法院此前在“灭绝种族罪公约保留咨询意见案”中又声称，国家对预防和惩治灭绝种族行为享有共同利益，因此，至少在预防和惩治灭绝种族行为义务事项上，对一切义务和共同利益发生了“偶遇”，二者产生了联系。尽管如此，一方面，相较于共同利益，对一切义务是“升华”，还是更为规范性的表达，国际法院并没有澄清。另一方面，对一切义务在实践中会产生何种实践性后果，国际法院同样没有明确。只有在“或引渡或起诉义务问题案”中，国际法院才既直接回应了二者间的关系，又澄清了其实践性后果。

（三）共同利益与对一切义务的实践性结合

国际法院在 2012 年 7 月 20 日的“或引渡或起诉义务问题案”判决中，讨论了国家基于《禁止酷刑和其他残忍、不人道或有辱人格的待遇或处罚公约》（以下简称《禁止酷刑公约》）所承担义务的性质及比利时是否有权援引塞内加尔的国家责任问题。国际法院首先指出，由于《禁止酷刑公约》序言强调了公约的目的与宗旨，即“在全世界更有效地开展反对酷刑……

① Barcelona Traction, Light and Power Company, Limited, Judgment, I. C. J. Reports 1970, p. 32.

的斗争”，基于此规定，在确保预防酷刑及一旦酷刑发生、行为实施者不应出现“有罪不罚”现象事项上，所有公约当事国均享有共同利益。一旦酷刑实施者出现在一国（以下简称所在国）领土内，无论其发生在何地，也不论实施者或受害者国籍为何，所在国均有义务启动对其所犯罪行的调查，并将相关案件提交本国主管机关以便起诉。在监督所在国履行上述义务事项上，所有其他公约当事国均享有共同利益。这一共同利益也意味着，国家所承担的义务是对所有其他公约当事国所承担的义务。根据“巴塞罗那电力、电车和电灯公司案”判决中有关对一切义务的阐述，其他国家在保护此类权利上都“享有法律利益”。这一义务可称为“对所有公约当事国承担的对一切义务”（obligations ergo omnes partes）。所有公约当事国在监督此义务的履行上均享有利益。在此意义上，国际法院特别强调，国家基于《禁止酷刑公约》相关条款所享有的此种共同利益，类似于国家基于《防止及惩治灭绝种族罪公约》相关条款享有的共同利益。[①] 国际法院还指出，国家在执行《禁止酷刑公约》相关义务上享有共同利益意味着，每个公约当事国均有权要求违约国终止违约行为，都有权去援引其应承担的国家责任。[②]

通过上述阐述可看出，国际法院首先肯定了国家在监督他国履行公约义务上享有共同利益，然后以此为基础，强调了国家基于公约所承担义务的性质，即对所有其他公约当事国承担的义务。尽管国际法院使用了“对所有公约当事国承担的对一切义务”这一措辞，但此措辞与对一切义务概念并没有实质性区别，只是后者的适当修正而已。

值得注意的是，在本案中，国际法院第一次直接在实践中将共同利益和对一切义务结合在一起。为了凸显这两个概念的内在联系和逻辑关系，国际法院在论述的时候，既援引了在“灭绝种族罪公约保留咨询意见案”中的前述相关论述，也援引了其在“巴塞罗那电力、电车和电灯公司案”中的前述相关论述。国际法院认为，一旦国家承担了对一切义务，在监督该义务的履行上，所有其他国家都将享有共同利益。同样地，一旦国家基于某一事项享

① Questions Relating to the Obligation to Prosecute or Extradite (Belgium v. Senegal), Judgment, I. C. J. Reports 2012, p. 449.

② Questions Relating to the Obligation to Prosecute or Extradite (Belgium v. Senegal), Judgment, I. C. J. Reports 2012, p. 450.

有共同利益，相对国在该事项上所承担的义务即为对一切义务。共同利益与对一切义务实际上是一个硬币的两面，二者具有密不可分的内在联系。

根据国际法院在本案中的相关论述，一旦国际法院认定国家在对一切义务上享有共同利益，国家即有权要求违约国终止其违约行为，有权援引其所应承担的国家责任。根据国际法委员会对“援引”（invocation）这个规范性概念的界定，实际上意味着：国家有权通过国际法庭等很正式的形式来向不法行为国主张权利，要求其承担相应的国家责任。[①] 也就是，为了保护共同利益，国家应该有权通过国际法庭（如国际法院）来援引不法行为国的国家责任。由于国家在所诉事项上不享有自身的利益，追求保护的是作为整体的国际共同体的利益，此类诉讼，在国际法中被称为“actio popularis”，即公益诉讼。[②] 对于此类公益诉讼，国际法院持何种立场？下部分将对此进行讨论。

二 基于共同利益的诉讼：国际法院的相关司法实践

在自身具体物质性利益没有遭受到损害的情形下，国家能否单纯地基于共同利益而通过国际法院来援引不法行为国的国家责任，这既具有理论性，也具有实践性。就理论角度而言，涉及国家在国际法庭的出庭权问题；而从实践角度来看，一个国家在自身利益没有遭受到直接损害的情形下对另一国的介入，实际上构成了对另一国的干涉，在一定程度上还会使其成为一国打压另一国的法律工具，因而具有高度的政治性，涉及复杂的国际关系、国际政治和国家的行为模式。因此，对于国家的此类行为，国际法院的司法实践极为谨慎，经历了一个从徘徊到回避，然后到积极回应的发展过程。

本部分将首先讨论出庭权的概念，然后在此基础上讨论国际法院的相关司法实践。

---

① International Law Commission, Draft Articles on Responsibility of States for Internationally Wrongful Acts, with Commentaries, 2001, Commentaries to Article 42, p. 117. para. 2, http://legal. un. org/docs/? path = . /ilc/texts/instruments/english/commentaries/9_6_2001. pdf&lang = EF，最后访问日期：2017 年 6 月 5 日。

② 国内学者有将其翻译为“群众行动”的。《国际公法百科全书 · 国际法院、国际法庭和国际仲裁的案例》（第二专辑），陈致中、李斐南译，中山大学出版社，1989，第 489 页。

（一）出庭权的含义与特征

出庭权有不同的英文表述，如 locus standi，standing，legal standing，jus standi，title to sue 等，但正如《国际公法百科全书》所指出的，它并没有一个统一的定义。① 在国内法中，其一般是指拥有权利的个体或群体通过向司法机构提起诉讼，期待获得司法机构支持的一种权能或资格。② 在国际法中，则是指一项条件，通过此条件限定了寻求援引不法行为国国家责任的国家与确定谁应承担违反责任的法律规则这二者之间的关系。③ 那些寻求援引不法行为国国家责任的国家只有能够证明自身在监督相应规则的履行上享有法律利益，才会享有出庭权。

一般而言，出庭权有如下三个特征。（1）出庭权是当事国诉诸法庭并获取法庭保护的前提和基础。没有出庭权，当事国将无法指望获得司法保护。（2）出庭权与利益、损害等密切相关。国家只有在某一事项上享有利益，并且其利益因某一不法行为而遭受损害，才享有出庭权。④（3）当事国一旦享有出庭权，就有权期待法庭积极回应自身诉求。

其中，最重要的特征是第二个。只有在存有利益、损害的情形下，当事国才享有出庭权。但无论对利益还是损害的界定都存在重大争议。就利益而言，由于"每个国家都是自身利益的法官"，⑤ 如何界定利益——例如，利益应仅限于有形的物质性利益，还是也可以包括无形的非物质性利益——便是出庭权理论和实践中非常重要的问题。而就损害而言，此种损害到底是实质性的还是非实质性的，答案同样重要。就共同利益的保护而言，由于其既涉及利益含义也涉及损害范围的确定，其是否能"径自"赋予国家以出庭权，无疑尤为敏感而复杂。

---

① Franz Matscher, "Standing before International Courts and Tribunals", in Bernhardt, eds., *Encyclopedia of Public International Law* (Oxford: Oxford University Press, 2012), p. 594.

② Leslie A. Stein (eds.), *Locus Standi* (Sydney: The Law Book Company Limited, 1979), p. 3.

③ Christian J. Tams, *Enforcing Obligations Erga Omnes in International Law* (Cambridge: Cambridge University Press, 2005), p. 26.

④ Christian J. Tams, *Enforcing Obligations Erga Omnes in International Law* (Cambridge: Cambridge University Press, 2005), p. 28.

⑤ Dissenting Opinion of Judge Morelli, South West Africa Cases (Ethiopia v. South Africa; Liberia v. South Africa), Preliminary Objections, Judgment, I. C. J. Reports 1962, p. 570.

(二) 国际法院与基于共同利益出庭权相关的司法实践

国际法院有关此问题的立场与实践可分为三个不同阶段。

1. 徘徊与回避阶段：从“西南非洲案”到“东帝汶案”

国际法院审理的第一个有关案件是埃塞俄比亚和利比里亚诉南非的“西南非洲案”(South West Africa Cases)。在该案中，当两原告国于1960年11月4日以“国联前会员国”的身份提起针对南非的诉讼时，原告国自身具体性物质利益并未遭受到损害，正因如此，南非提出了4项先决反对，认为原告国没有出庭权。在1962年驳回南非先决反对的判决中，国际法院指出，委任制度的首要宗旨是“促进委任统治地人民的福祉及其发展”，为实现此目的，在监督委任统治国遵守相对于委任地人民、国联和国联会员国的义务方面，国联会员国被认为享有法律权利或利益，享有出庭权，因而有权根据委任统治书第7条援引南非的国家责任。[①] 尽管如此，由于国际法院法官于1963年经过定期改选，法官构成发生了变化，在1966年第二阶段判决中，国际法院却又判称自己对此案无管辖权，[②] 理由是：委任统治书条款分为两类，即行为条款和特别利益条款，当前争端涉及的是行为条款。而就行为条款而言，要解决原告国是否享有法律权利或利益的问题，就必须判断执行委任统治书的权利是专属于国联还是同时也包括国联会员国。通过对《国际联盟盟约》第22条的解释，国际法院否定了国联会员国享有此权利。因此，国际法院认为，原告国尽管满足了出庭权的属人性条件，但没有满足出庭权的属物性条件。[③] 在论证过程中，对于原告国基于“必要性”而强调自身出庭权重要性的论点，国际法院认为，这实

---

① South West Africa Cases (Ethiopia v. South Africa; Liberia v. South Africa), Preliminary Objections, Judgment, I. C. J. Reports 1962, pp. 342 – 345.

② 有关因法官构成变化而导致法院判决“走向”发生改变的分析，参见 Andronico O. Adede, “Judicial Settlement in Perspective”, in A. S. Muller, D. Rai and J. M. Thuránszky, eds, *The International Court of Justice—Its Future Role after Fifty Years* (Dordrecht: Martinus Nijhoff Publishers, 1997), pp. 52 – 53, especially foot note 9; Detlev F. Vagts, “The International Legal Profession: A Need for More Governance?”, *America Journal of International Law* 250 (1996) 90 (2): 256。

③ South West Africa Cases, Second Phase, Judgment, I. C. J. Reports 1966, pp. 17 – 39. 关于此案的更多介绍和评论，参见宋杰《国际法中普遍性法律利益的保护问题研究——基于国际法庭和国家相关实践的研究》，中国人民大学出版社，2012，第38—53页。

质上是要求法院允许公益诉讼；尽管某些国家的国内法承认此权利，但当前国际法是不承认的。[①] 由于此判决实质上相当于推翻了先决反对判决，不仅造成原告国不满意，就是部分法官，也认为此判决背离了常设国际法院的类似法理。[②]

在澳大利亚和新西兰诉法国的“核试验案”（Nuclear Tests）中，两原告国均从对一切义务角度阐述了自身所享有的出庭权。

澳大利亚在论及其出庭权时认为，法国在空中核试验上所承担的义务（即不进行空中核试验）为对一切性质的义务，就此义务而言，“用国际法院在‘巴塞罗那电力、电车和电灯公司案’中所用的话来说就是，‘由于此义务所涉权利的重要性，所有国家在此权利的保护上都享有法律利益’”，[③] 因此，在确保法国遵守其所承担的不从事空中核试验义务事项上，澳大利亚享有法律利益；在向国际法院寻求获得一份宣告性判决的事项上，自己享有出庭权。[④]

与澳大利亚不同，新西兰在诉状中首先对自己的权利要求进行了分类。其指出，在5项权利要求中，a项、b项[⑤]权利要求同c项、d项、e项权利要求不一样。前者反映的是在保护所有人的安全、生命、健康及保护全球环境上的共同利益，法国在此方面所承担的义务是对一切义务。[⑥] 在此意义上，新西兰指出，尽管在不同个案中，法律利益的含义各不相同，但从趋势看，其含义是随国际法的发展而扩大的。随着国际社会间的相互依赖性增强，国

① South West Africa Cases, Second Phase, Judgment, I. C. J. Reports 1966, pp. 45 – 48.

② 杰塞普（Jessup）法官认为，无论是在少数者保护还是在劳工保护方面，国际法均承认国家即使自身或其国民没有遭受直接损害，也有权保护的普遍性法律。常设国际法院在“梅梅尔地区规章解释案”中即支持了国家的此类实践，认可了国家的出庭权。参见 Dissenting Opinion of Judge Jessup, South West Africa Cases (Ethiopia v. South Africa; Liberia v. South Africa), Preliminary Objections, Judgment, I. C. J. Reports 1962, pp. 373 – 378。

③ Australian Memorial, para. 448, http://www.icj-cij.org/files/case-related/58/9443.pdf，最后访问日期：2017年5月10日。

④ Australian Memorial, para. 449.

⑤ 此两项权利要求为：（a）国际共同体的所有成员，包括新西兰，免遭核试验所产生的放射性尘降污染和危害的权利；（b）国际共同体的所有成员，包括新西兰，免遭人为产生的对陆地、海洋和空中环境所带来的放射污染的权利。

⑥ Memorial on Jurisdiction and Admissibility Submitted by the Government of New Zealand, para. 191, http://www.icj-cij.org/docket/files/59/9451.pdf，最后访问日期：2017年5月30日。

际法正越来越从强调保护单个国家的权利转向强调保护国际共同体所享有的公共利益和公共福祉。而随着此种发展，国际法也承认，单个国家在通过司法执行的方式来执行上述规则上享有法律利益。新西兰强调，如果后者不发展（即通过国家诉讼等方式来执行有关保护公共利益的规则），缺乏通过司法执行的方式来保护的相应实体性规则将会越来越多。[①] 新西兰认为，就 a 项和 b 项权利要求而言，自己寻求保护的是国际共同体的利益；新西兰强调，正是基于国际法院在"巴塞罗那电力、电车和电灯公司案"所阐明的法理，自己才启动当前诉讼，期待诉求所涉及的权利能得到保护。[②]

由于法国发表了不再进行空中核试验声明，国际法院认为，法国的这一单方面声明是对整个国际社会所作的承诺，具有约束力，[③] 从而认为两原告国的诉求目的已经消失，因而决定不再作出相应裁决。[④] 而对于两原告国提出的出庭权问题，国际法院在判决中并未触及，因而失去了一次发展此问题相关法理的机会。

在 1995 年葡萄牙诉澳大利亚的"东帝汶案"（East Timor）中，葡萄牙为了证明自己享有出庭权，特别强调了其作为经联合国授权的"管理当局"，是为国际社会公共利益服务的。澳大利亚反驳了此论点。澳大利亚认为，一国要通过国际法院来提起诉讼，就必须证明其在诉讼事项上享有法律利益。一般在国际法中不存在支持葡萄牙所提出的为国际公共利益服务的原则。除非葡萄牙能够证明，澳大利亚所承担的义务具有对一切性质，否则其无权提起诉讼。无论是基于国际公共利益服务，还是基于其他目的，一国均无权以公益诉讼的方式提起诉讼。澳大利亚还认为，对于国际法院在"巴塞罗那电力、电车和电灯公司案"中有关对一切义务的阐述不应从反面去理解。尽管国际法院在该案中也指出，"这些所保护的权利有的已经成为一般国际法的一部分，其他的则由普遍性或准普遍性的国际文件所赋

① Memorial on Jurisdiction and Admissibility Submitted by the Government of New Zealand, paras. 194 – 196.

② Memorial on Jurisdiction and Admissibility Submitted by the Government of New Zealand, para. 211.

③ Nuclear Tests (Australia v. France, New Zealand v. France), I. C. J. Reports 1974, para. 50.

④ 尽管如此，国际法院也可能意识到自身这种有些武断性质的认知可能不太妥当，于是，在判决的第 60 段授权新西兰在判决基础受到影响时可再次向法院请求对情势进行审查。关于此点，参见邵沙平主编《国际法院新近案例研究》，商务印书馆，2006，第 258—291 页。

予”，但国际法院却并未说，每一项对一切义务都具有公益诉讼的性质，因而可以据此采取诉讼行动。[①] 令人遗憾的是，对于当事国有关出庭权问题的争议，国际法院同样选择了回避。国际法院指出，由于葡萄牙的诉求涉及作为第三方的印度尼西亚，根据“从罗马移出黄金货币案”（Monetary Gold Removed from Rome in 1943）中所确立的“第三方同意”规则，自己对本案无管辖权。[②]

通过上述案例可看出，国际法院在此阶段内先后提出了共同利益的概念和对一切义务的概念。但是，鉴于其敏感性和对国际关系的重大影响，对于基于共同利益的出庭权问题，在不同个案中，国际法院的立场与实践有所不同，甚至在同一案件的不同阶段，其前后实践也迥然有别。但总体而言，除个别情形外，对于国家的此类诉讼及相关主张，国际法院的立场是谨慎和保守的，刻意避免正面和直接回应。由于国家的此种行为高度类似于国内法中的公益诉讼，在国际法其他领域，如国家责任法等发展没有出现重大突破的情形下，考虑到国际社会的可能反应及相关实践的可能影响，国际法院采取保守立场是可以理解的。

2. 积极回应阶段：从“灭绝种族罪公约适用案”到“或引渡或起诉义务问题案”

冷战终结后，对于国家基于共同利益的出庭权问题，国际法院的实践开始进入积极回应的新阶段。这一阶段肇始于波黑诉塞尔维亚的“灭绝种族罪公约适用案”（Bosnia and Herzegovina v. Serbia and Montenegro）。

在 2007 年 2 月 26 日有关该案的实体判决中，国际法院在解释《防止及惩治灭绝种族罪公约》第 1 条中所规定的预防义务的含义时指出，所有国家都承担预防义务。公约要求国家采取一切合理的措施进行预防。当国家在其权力范围内没有采取一切有效的措施去预防灭绝种族行为发生时，就应承担相应责任。[③] 通过这一阐述，国际法院实际上提出了“作为一种义务存在的干涉”概念。当灭绝种族行为发生时，不论灭绝种族行为发生

---

① Counter Memorial of the Government of Australia, paras. 258 - 263, http://www.icj-cij.org/files/case-related/84/6837.pdf，最后访问日期：2017 年 6 月 8 日。

② East Timor（Portugal v. Australia），Judgment，I. C. J. Reports 1995，p. 101，paras. 25 - 26.

③ Application of the Convention on the Prevention and Punishment of the Crime of Genocide（Bosnia and Herzegovina v. Serbia and Montenegro），Judgment，I. C. J. Reports 2007，pp. 220 - 225.

于何地，国家均有义务采取行动进行干涉。一旦国家没有适当履行预防义务，其他国家有权通过适当方式来援引其国家责任。[①] 尽管国际法院没有阐述国家能通过哪些具体方式援引另一国的国家责任，但由于明确肯定了国家有权采取行动，因此，在基于共同利益出庭权问题上，相对于此前在此问题上的刻意回避立场而言，上述阐述明显推进了一大步。

而在“或引渡或起诉义务问题案”中，国际法院则更进一步明确肯定了比利时基于共同利益所享有的出庭权。

该案中，比利时在论及自身的出庭权时，首先援引了国际法院在“巴塞罗那电力、电车和电灯公司案”中有关对一切义务的阐述，认为，基于“或引渡或起诉义务”的习惯国际法地位，考虑到其目的与宗旨，即终结有罪不罚，每一个国家都必须履行此义务，并且，此义务是对作为整体的国际社会承担的，每一当事国均有权在不考虑受害者国籍的情形下援引不法行为国的国家责任。在此基础上，比利时进一步援引了《国家对国际不法行为的责任条款草案》（以下简称《国家责任条款草案》）第 48 条及其评注，[②] 认为自己有权基于“受害国以外的国家”这一身份而享有出庭权。[③] 比利时的上述论点并未遭到塞内加尔的实质性反对。[④]

国际法院认为，比利时是否享有出庭权，有必要首先考虑公约当事国这一身份是否足以使其有权援引不法行为国的国家责任。国际法院通过对《禁止酷刑公约》序言的解读，通过将其与“灭绝种族罪公约保留问题咨询意见案”及“巴塞罗那电力、电车和电灯公司案”中的相关阐述相结合，认为《禁止酷刑公约》每个公约当事国在监督他国履行相关义务上都享有共同利益。由于国家在监督他国履行公约义务上享有共同利益，国家有权要求另一国停止违约行为；一旦该另一国不履行公约义务，国家有权援引其国家责任。因此，作为公约当事国，比利时在监督塞内加尔履行基

---

① 宋杰：《“保护的责任”：国际法院相关司法实践研究》，《法律科学》2009 年第 5 期。

② Yearbook of the International Law Commission, 2001, vol. 2, Part 2, p. 126.

③ I. C. J. Judgment of 20 July 2012, Case Concerning Questions relating to the Obligation to Prosecute or Extradite (Belgium v. Senegal), Memorial, paras. 5. 15 - 5. 16, http://www.icj-cij. org/files/case-related/144/16933. pdf, 最后访问日期：2017 年 5 月 10 日；CR 2012/6, http://www.icj-cij. org/files/case-related/144/144 - 20120319 - ORA - 01 - 01 - BI. pdf, 最后访问日期：2017 年 5 月 10 日。

④ 有关塞内加尔的反应，参见 CR 2012/7, pp. 17 - 19, http://www.icj-cij. org/files/case-related/144/144 - 20120319 - ORA - 01 - 01 - BI. pdf, 最后访问日期：2017 年 5 月 12 日。

于公约第6（2）条、第7（1）条所承担义务事项上享有出庭权。[①]

必须注意的是，国际法院此阶段对基于共同利益出庭权问题给予正面、积极的回应，是与三个重要背景息息相关的。

（1）冷战终结的背景。冷战的终结标志着国家之间单纯地基于意识形态的对立和对抗得到了有效的缓解，不同国家在关涉国际社会重大利益的事项上更容易达成共识。保护国际社会的整体性利益、共同应对严重的全球性危机也就具备了可能。[②] 作为一种重要保护工具，基于共同利益的公益诉讼的出现，当然也就顺理成章。

（2）国家责任法的发展。2001年，联合国国际法委员会二读通过了《国家责任条款草案》。在该草案中，第42条有关“受害国援引不法行为国的国家责任”的规定、第48条有关“受害国以外的国家援引不法行为国的国家责任”的规定和第54条有关“受害国以外的国家采取合法措施”的规定，都承认和赋予了国家在一定情形下基于共同利益而对不法行为国采取一定行动的权利；在这些权利之中，通过国际法庭来采取行动当然是有效途径之一。既然《国家责任条款草案》已经提供了规范基础，国际法院通过实践来回应这些规范，当然不存在任何问题。

（3）人权法与国际刑法发展所带来的影响同样不应忽视。人权法与国际刑法都是冷战终结之后国际法发展最快的部门之一。多个临时性、混合型国际刑事法庭的设立，以及常设性的国际刑事法院的设立，便是这两个领域快速发展的结果。通过刑法保护基本人权既强化了国际法的执行机制，也反映了国际社会在维护公共秩序、公共道德等上所达成的共识。对于国际法院而言，此种被强化的执行机制和所形成的共识无疑具有启示意义。国家是否同样可以通过国际法院来强化实施国际法，即使相关事项并没有直接损害本国物质性利益？例如，单纯地基于保护公共利益的目的？一旦国家将这些问题诉诸实践，来到国际法院提起公益诉讼，国际法院是

① Case Concerning Questions Relating to the Obligation to Prosecute of Extradite，Belgium v. Senegal），I. C. J. Judgment of 20 July 2012，paras. 66 - 70，http://www.icj-cij.org/files/case-related/144/144 - 20120720 - JUD - 01 - 00 - EN. pdf，最后访问日期：2017年5月11日。

② Christian J. Tams，*Enforcing Obligations Erga Omnes in International Law*（Cambridge：Cambridge University Press，2005）；Maurizio Ragazzi，*The Concept of International Obligations Erga Omnes*（Oxford/ New York：Oxford University Press，2000）.

否应该像其他法庭一样，基于保护公共秩序、公共道德或基本人权的目的而予以积极回应？在此背景下，其他法庭的实践当然会对国际法院的相关司法实践产生示范性影响。

3. 扩大适用阶段："南极捕鲸案"和"停止核军备竞赛和实行核裁军的谈判义务案"

"或引渡或起诉义务问题案"在基于共同利益的出庭权上无疑具有特别重要的意义：其实际上是一个象征，标志着国际法院已经改变了自身此前有关这个问题的"徘徊和犹豫"的态度，转而采取正式的支持立场。这一新的法理确立后，很快就对随后的个案产生了明显的积极影响。这主要体现在"南极捕鲸案"（Whaling in the Antarctic）和"停止核军备竞赛和实行核裁军的谈判义务案"（Obligations concerning Negotiations relating to Cessation of the Nuclear Arms Race and to Nuclear Disarmament）中。

2010 年 5 月 31 日，针对日本每年在南极捕鲸的行为，澳大利亚在国际法院提起了针对日本的诉讼，即"南极捕鲸案"。2014 年 3 月 31 日，国际法院判决日本败诉。

在该案中，尽管日本并没有在任何程度上质疑澳大利亚的出庭权，但毫无疑问，澳大利亚的出庭权正是建立在共同利益之上。澳大利亚并不追求自身的任何利益，其致力于维护的是鲸这种物种在南极海域的可持续发展。

澳大利亚是根据《国际捕鲸管制公约》提起相关诉讼的。纵观公约具体规定，却没有任何一项实体性条款授予了国家在监督公约的执行上以具体的权利，相反，相应的权利应主要由根据公约所设立的国际捕鲸委员会负责行使。公约中同国家监督相关的规定，仅仅是公约序言中的两段，分别是"（各国）认为，为了保护鲸类及其后代丰富的天然资源，是全世界各国的利益"，和"认为，在不致引起广泛的经济上或营养上的不良影响下，尽速实现鲸类资源达到最适当的水平，是共同的利益"。[①]

值得注意的是，无论是在申请书中还是在诉状中，澳大利亚对自身的出庭权只字不提。澳大利亚对出庭权问题的回避，可能正是因为其意识到

---

① 《国际捕鲸管制公约》序言。来源：http://www.china.com.cn/environment/txt/2003-01/24/content_5267588.htm，最后访问日期：2017 年 6 月 10 日。

了公约具体条文并没有授予个别当事国以监督的权利，单纯地依赖于公约序言中上述两段的规定来论证自身的出庭权，在法理上容易遭到日本的质疑。就此意义而言，回避提及此问题也是一种策略。而从日本的反应来看，其明显地忽视了此问题：在其辩诉状中，日本对澳大利亚的出庭权同样不置一词。

在原被告双方均对出庭权问题及与此相关的可受理性问题沉默的背景下，国际法院在最终判决中同样对此问题视而不见，径直对实体争议作出了裁决。但有了这样一个有效先例，国家基于公约所享有的监督权就被确立了下来。任何公约当事国，都有权监督其他公约当事国履行公约的行为。一旦其认为另一公约当事国的某一行为违背了基于公约所承担的义务，即使相关行为并没有直接损害本国具体利益，其也有权通过国际法院来援引该不法行为国的国家责任。

马绍尔群岛共和国（以下简称“马绍尔”）于 2014 年提起的针对英国、巴基斯坦、印度等三个国家的“停止核军备竞赛和实行核裁军的谈判义务案”，同样涉及基于共同利益的出庭权问题。由于其申请书完全相同，下面仅以其诉英国案为例展开讨论。

本案涉及的主要是对《不扩散核武器条约》第 6 条的解释与适用问题。[①] 为了论证自身有权起诉英国，马绍尔指出，英国基于《不扩散核武器条约》第 6 条所承担的义务是对整个国际社会承担的，是对一切性质的义务；每个国家在监督该义务的履行上都享有法律利益。[②] 很显然，马绍尔是将自身基于条约规定所享有的出庭权建立在该义务的对一切性质之上的，认为基于此而享有共同利益，因而有权监督英国履行相应义务。至于英国的相应行为是否直接侵犯了马绍尔的利益，则并非问题的关键。

遗憾的是，在 2016 年 10 月 5 日针对英国先决反对所作出的判决中，国际法院支持了英国所提出的第一个先决性反对主张——即马绍尔在递交请求书时，未能成功地证明其与英国之间存在可裁决的争端（a justiciable

① 《不扩散核武器条约》第 6 条规定：“每个缔约国承诺就及早停止核军备竞赛和核裁军方面的有效措施，以及就一项在严格和有效国际监督下的全面彻底裁军条约，真诚地进行谈判。”

② Application Instituting Proceedings Against the United Kingdom, submitted on 24 April 2014 by the Republic of the Marshall Islands, para. 85, http://www.icj-cij.org/files/case-related/160/18296.pdf，最后访问日期：2017 年 5 月 12 日。

dispute)，因此，国际法院对马绍尔的请求没有管辖权，或者，其请求不具有可受理性。国际法院认为，由于英国没有意识到，或不可能未意识到（could not have been unware），马绍尔当时是在宣称英国违背了自身承担的国际义务，因此，不能认为彼此之间存在着争端，[①] 国际法院对本案没有管辖权。由于国际法院并没有在任何程度上回应马绍尔基于“对一切”权利而享有的出庭权问题，从而丧失了自“或引渡或起诉义务问题案”后一个很好的进一步发展自身有关此问题的法理的机会。

通过上述两个案例可以看出，在基于共同利益的出庭权获得国际法院的认可之后，其明显地对其他国家和国际法院的后续实践产生了影响：首先，受“或引渡或起诉义务问题案”这样一个成功先例的影响，其他国家也纷纷在国际法院主张自身基于共同利益所享有的出庭权；其次，所涉事项范围已经从保护基本人权的公约如《禁止酷刑公约》等，扩展到了保护物种的《国际捕鲸管制公约》及保护环境的《不扩散核武器条约》。然而，此种影响目前仅体现在国家行为层面。从国际法院角度来看，国际法院的反应还是比较谨慎的，其并没有在“或引渡或起诉义务问题案”的基础上“更进一步”。国际法院的相关法理，迄今仍停留在“或引渡或起诉义务问题案”的层面。

三　国际法院相关司法实践的影响

国际法院对国家基于共同利益的出庭权的认可，既会对国际法的发展产生深远影响，又会对国家的行为模式和国际法院自身产生重要影响。

（一）对国际法发展的影响

国际法院相关司法实践与《国家责任法条款草案》相关规定形成了互动，丰富了国家责任的援引形式，促进了国家责任法的“实践性”发展；同时，其会影响国际法领域内与干涉相关的规范，会为其发展提供一定的

① Obligations Concerning Negotiations Relating to Cessation of the Nuclear Arms Race and to Nuclear Disarmamant（Mashall Islands v. United Kingdom），Preliminary Objections，Judgment of 5 October 2016，para. 57，available at：http://www.icj-cij.org/files/case-related/160/160 – 20161005 – JUD – 01 – 00 – EN. pdf，最后访问日期：2017 年 5 月 12 日。

理论与实践依据。

1. 为《国家责任条款草案》第48条提供了“支持性”案例，并与其未来发展构成“良性互动”

《国家责任条款草案》自2001年二读通过以来，由于围绕其中的一些重要条款，如第42条、第48条和第54条等存在争议，没能达成共识，目前依然维持着“草案”的形态。从各国“就今后对条款采取的任何行动提出书面意见”的建议来看，[①] 短时间内国际社会也没有将其制定成国际条约的意愿。[②] 尽管如此，从国家实践的角度来看，国际法院有关“或引渡或起诉义务问题案”、“南极捕鲸案”的判决，都可以构成对第48条提供支持的积极性案例，并会被编入联合国秘书长提交给联合国大会的相关报告之中。[③] 而就“停止核军备竞赛和实行核裁军的谈判义务案”而言，尽管国际法院并没有就基于“共同利益”出庭权的问题进行任何回应，没有进一步发展自身在此问题上的相关法理，却并不意味着在国家行为层面，国家就不可以在此问题上进一步通过国际法院来进行“试探”。如果马绍尔群岛共和国再次起诉，并将自身的出庭权完全建立在基于“对一切”权利所享有的共同利益上，国际法院是否会继续认为“争端”不存在？答案并非当然如此。

《国家责任条款草案》第48条是有关“受害国以外的国家援引不法行为国的国家责任”的规定。由于此条赋予了受害国以外的国家在监督和执行对一切义务上的权利，认可了其在此事项上所享有的公共利益，在很大程度上是有利于有相应意愿的国家通过利用此条来合法地对他国进行干涉的。正因如此，发达国家和发展中国家对于此条有着截然不同的立场。发达国家认为其有利于自身对他国进行干涉，因此大力支持；发展中国家则

① 对于业已编纂完成的草案，《国际法委员会章程》第23条规定：“1. 委员会可向大会建议：(a) 报告既已发布，不必采取行动；(b) 以决议方式表示注意，或通过这项报告；(c) 向会员国推荐这项草案，以求缔结一项公约；(d) 召集会议以缔结一项公约。2. 大会认为合适时，得将草案送回委员会重新审议或重新起草。”

② 部分国家有关草案未来处理结果的意见，参见联合国文件：A/62/63，A/65/96，A/68/69。

③ 自2004年始，根据大会第59/35号决议，联合国秘书长即开始编制国际性法院、法庭和其他机构援引国家责任条款的裁判汇编，迄今已经提交了多份相关报告。参见联合国文件：A/62/62，A/62/62/Add. 1，A/62/63，A/62/63/Add1，A/65/76，A/68/100等。

坚决反对。[1] 在两类国家存在明显分歧的背景下，如果贸然决定召开外交会议，将草案制定为相关国际公约，相当程度上会因不同国家间分歧太大而导致会议“流产”。这样，国际法委员会努力的成果就会“付诸东流”。

在此背景下，与其冒以上风险还不如继续维持目前的草案形态。这样做的好处在于，草案形态既不妨碍相关国家援引其中的任何规定，也不妨碍国际法院等司法机构在实践中对其任何条款的援引，从而提供“国家和国际社会实践”的证据。相关实践“证据”一旦累积，不仅会吸引更多国家和国际法庭采取同样的实践，更主要的是，从国际法发展的阶段角度来看，[2] 还有利于相应规范的国际化而更早地被国际社会主流所接受，最后形成相应的国际习惯，或被载入普遍性的国际条约之中。

正是在上述意义上，国际法院对国家基于共同利益出庭权的认可，既给《国家责任条款草案》第48条提供了直接的支持性案例，又有利于他国类似实践的更好、更快发展。在《国家责任条款草案》的规定和国际法院的实践之间，二者明显地形成了“互相影响、互相促进”的互动关系。

2. 丰富了国家责任的援引形式

在传统国际法中，国家责任的主要援引形式是受害国援引不法行为国的国家责任。受害国以外的国家，一般无权援引不法行为国的责任。此种机制设计与传统国际法中的国家权利义务关系的对等、互惠特点是相匹配的。而在现代国际法中，国家间的权利义务除了对等、互惠以外，还有大量“对一切”权利义务的存在。由于对一切权利义务涉及作为整体的国际共同体的利益，每一个国家在监督该类义务的履行上都享有法律上的共同利益。因此，在机制设计上，就必然要求有新的、另外的机制与之匹配。《国家责任条款草案》第48条的制定逻辑和基点正在于此。通过此条的规定，受害国以外的国家就获得了在一定情形下对他国不法行为进行介入的

① 例如，中国代表在第62届联大六委就“国家对国际不法行为的责任”议题发言时，就建议“删除”第48条和第54条的相关规定。参见《中国代表马新民在第62届联大六委关于“国家对国际不法行为的责任”议题的发言》（2007年10月23日），http://www.fmprc.gov.cn/ce/ceun/chn/ldhy/ld62/t375207.htm，最后访问日期：2017年6月10日。

② 一般都认为，国际法的发展要经历三个阶段，分别是：个别国家的实践，更多国家的跟进，最后国际化，即形成相应的国际习惯或被制定为国际条约。关于此点的研究，参见Andrea Birdsall, *The International Politics of Judicial Intervention* (London and New York: Routledge, 2009), p. 2。

权利。此条的规定实质上完善了国家责任的援引机制。

国际法院对国家基于共同利益出庭权的确认，实质上就相当于为《国家责任条款草案》的上述新规定“背书”。这一实践一旦确立，就为受害国以外的国家通过国际法院来援引不法行为国的国家责任开辟了一个新途径。

与此同时，国际法院的司法实践还丰富和超越了国家责任的援引机制。在传统国际法中，两种责任援引机制都是独立使用的。国家要么以受害国的身份援引，要么以受害国以外的国家身份援引，没有出现一个国家在一个案例中同时主张两种身份的情形。而在“或引渡或起诉义务问题案”中，第一次出现了两种责任援引机制同时并存和叠加的情形：比利时尝试同时以“受害国”和“受害国以外的国家”这两种不同身份来援引塞内加尔的国家责任。

在论及其“受害国”身份时，比利时指出，自己依据《禁止酷刑公约》有关“或引渡或起诉”的规定而向塞内加尔提出了引渡请求，享有“特别利益”，有权以“受害国”的身份提起诉讼。[①] 此外，考虑到“或引渡或起诉义务”的终极目的在于打击“有罪不罚”，此义务不仅约束所有《禁止酷刑公约》当事国，也同时约束所有其他国家。国家基于此所承担的义务不仅针对公约当事国，基于一般国际法，也同时针对所有其他国家。《禁止酷刑公约》的每一当事国均有权在不考虑受害者国籍的情形下援引不法行为国的国家责任。[②]

而在论及其“受害国以外的国家”身份时，比利时指出，基于“或引渡或起诉义务”的习惯国际法地位，国家所承担的此义务是对作为整体的国际社会承担的。同时比利时认为，国际法委员会在评论《国家责任条款草案》第48条时明确强调，“一国如果违背了旨在保护国家集团或整个国际社会的特定义务，受害国以外的国家也有权援引该不法行为国的国家责

① I. C. J. Judgment of 20 July 2012, Case Concerning Questions Relating to the Obligation to Prosecute or Extradite (Belgium v. Senegal), Memorial, paras. 5.17 – 5.18, http://www.icj-cij.org/docket/files/144/16933.pdf，最后访问日期：2017年5月10日。

② CR 2012/6, paras. 54 – 61, http://www.icj-cij.org/docket/files/144/16963.pdf，最后访问日期：2017年5月10日。

任”，[①] 因此，其有权基于“受害国以外的国家”这一身份而享有出庭权。[②]

对于比利时同时主张两种援引身份的行为，国际法院并没有提出质疑。因此，在国家责任的援引形式上，此案具有创新性和启示性意义，那就是，两种援引形式可以同时并存，可以叠加。国家责任的援引形式因此而得以更丰富。

3. 为国际法中干涉规范的进一步发展提供了理论和实践“依据”

传统国际法是拒绝干涉的。即使一国是基于人道原因的干涉，在传统国际法中也会遭受到强烈质疑和反对。干涉遭受到质疑与传统国际法规范主要是“共存”规范的特质相吻合的。因为在“共存”国际法中，各国重视的是彼此之间管辖权的独立性和排他性，强调的是彼此间的不干涉。主权独立和平等原则具有优先于其他国际法原则的重要性。

但在冷战终结之后，“合作”国际法的重要性日益凸显。很多问题的处理，如环境问题、恐怖犯罪问题等，都具有跨国性。对于这些问题，仅凭一国之力是无法应对和解决的。国际合作是解决诸如此类问题的唯一途径。人类命运共同体的观念日益受到国际社会的重视。在此背景下，国际法的发展也出现了新变化、新趋势。其中最明显的，莫过于与干涉相关的概念、理论的提出及相关实践的出现。这其中，既包括“保护的责任”概念的提出，也包括含有赋予国家在一定条件下合法干涉他国条款的《国家责任条款草案》的二读通过，还包括作为国际法热点关注的人道干涉理论的提出及相关实践的出现等。

而从国际法院对国家基于共同利益出庭权的认可及对比利时相关行动的支持性判决来看，至少在《禁止酷刑公约》的语境内，相关干涉行为就合法化了。再结合“南极捕鲸案”和“停止核军备竞赛和实行核裁军的谈判义务案”，干涉的合法化在多个不同的公约语境内明显呈现出扩张的趋势。因此，从理论与实践互动的角度来看，国际法院的相关司法实践都将会为干涉行为在一定范围内的合法化提供重要的理论和实践支撑。而这对

① Yearbook of the Internatioanl Law Commission, 2001, vol. 2, Part 2, p. 126.

② I. C. J. Judgment of 20 July 2012, Case Concerning Questions Relating to the Obligation to Prosecute or Extradite (Belgium v. Senegal), Memorial, paras. 5.15 – 5.16, http://www.icj-cij.org/files/case-related/144/144 – 20120720 – JUD – 01 – 00 – EN.pdf, 最后访问日期：2017 年 5 月 10 日。

于干涉问题在国际法体系内的进一步发展，无疑将产生极为重要的影响。

（二）对国家行为模式和国际法院自身的影响

从对国家行为模式影响的角度来看，国际法院的相关论述和实践会鼓励、推动国家现有的干涉实践以及更多国家来国际法院进行公益诉讼。

国际法院对比利时基于共同利益出庭权的认可及判决比利时胜诉，会被那些有干涉意愿的国家——比利时也包含在这些国家之中——所重视和积极利用。这些国家将此视为使干涉合法化的一种重要途径，同时考虑利用这个平台对不法行为国进行干涉，去援引不法行为国的国家责任。

正因如此，可以看到，自“或引渡或起诉义务问题案”之后，共同利益出庭权被确认所起的“示范”效应已经开始显现：“南极捕鲸案”及“停止核军备竞赛和实行核裁军的谈判义务案”即为例证。考虑到上述三类案件所涉及的义务范围：从保护基本人权的条约到保护物种和环境的条约，接下来，其他国家是否也会同样主张自身基于共同利益而享有出庭权，将基于某一条约的解释与适用的争端提交至国际法院？那么，公益诉讼会不会如“潮水一般”地涌向国际法院？一旦真的如此，考虑到国际法院的现有资源和处理案件的能力——在现有模式下，国际法院每年需处理的案件已让其在“满负荷”地运转——这么多的案件，是否会让国际法院“瘫痪”？国际法院是否有能力保证公平、有效地作出回应，及时、高效地处理相关案件？特别是，一旦争端涉及人权条约的解释与适用，考虑到此类争端的高度敏感性，国际法院该如何处理急剧增多的同类争端？也许正是基于对这些问题的担忧，在“停止核军备竞赛和实行核裁军的谈判义务案”中，尽管马绍尔群岛共和国同时主张了自身基于对一切权利而享有共同利益的出庭权，国际法院在先决性反对判决中依旧“视而不见”，不作任何回应。国际法院在此案中的谨慎和保守，在一定程度上可以缓解上述问题出现的可能性，避免相关法理“激进式”发展。

四　结语

通过对国际法院前述实践的研究可以看出，在共同利益的保护上，国际法院的相关法理经历了一个缓慢发展和转变的过程。其中，“灭绝种族罪公约保留咨询意见案”和“巴塞罗那电力、电车和电灯公司案”是基础性案例。通过这两个案例，国际法院明确地肯定了国家基于对一切义务所享有的共同利益，此类利益完全不同于国家基于对等义务所享有的互惠利益；但对于此种利益的实践性后果，尤其是国家是否有权据此在国际法院采取诉讼行动，国际法院在长期司法实践中却一直避免给予肯定性回应。

随着国际刑法、国际人权法和国家责任法的新发展，一些新概念、新理论的提出以及一些相关实践的出现，国际法院开始改变此前的立场，对共同利益的保护开始采取积极态度。“灭绝种族罪公约适用案”是一个开端，“或引渡或起诉义务问题案”则是一个标志，标志着国际法院在共同利益的保护问题上形成了新的法理。而国际法院在“南极捕鲸案”中的实践则构成了一个超越。因为国际法院虽然没有直接提及基于共同利益的出庭权问题，却在实体判决中予以“内在性”解决，以相当于直接肯定的方式认可了澳大利亚基于共同利益的出庭权。然而，在“停止核军备竞赛和实行核裁军的谈判义务案”中，国际法院却采取了一定的谨慎立场，并没有将相关法理进一步推进。国际法院的此种克制与保守，部分原因可能在于担心更多类似案件在短时间内“涌入”国际法院，从而既让自身无力承担，也不利于当前国际关系的稳定和国际法秩序的维护，就此意义而言，国际法院在此案中的相对保守实践是可以理解的。

从历史视角来看，国际法院的相关司法实践在很大程度上属于对常设国际法院相关司法实践的“回归”和超越。说是“回归”，是因为常设国际法院在两个案件中，即“温布尔登案”（Case of S. S. “Wimbledon”）[①] 和“梅梅尔地区规章解释案”（Case of Interpretation of the Statute of the Memel Territory）[②]，同样认可了原告国基于“共同利益”所享有的出庭权。说其超越，是因为国际法院对程序的处理、概念的提出及其论证角度都比常设国际法院更详尽、更精细、更完美。国际法院不仅提出了共同利益的概念，提出了对一切义务的概念，还将二者结合起来，并在此基础上肯定了基于共同利益的出庭权。

国际法院有关基于共同利益的司法实践将会对国际法的发展带来重要

---

① P. C. I. J, Series A, No. 1.

② P. C. I. J, Series A/B, No. 49.

影响。一方面，其给《国家责任法条款草案》第48条提供了实践性案例，另一方面，其给国际法上的干涉问题提供了新视角。由于基于共同利益的出庭权实际上会为国家通过国际法院来对他国进行司法干涉提供重要实践工具，这既会使干涉问题在国际法院这个平台“合法化”，也可能会使公益诉讼在国际法院出现“扎堆”的现象。尽管国际法院已经开始有意识地在此方面加以控制，但是，此类实践也会给干涉问题在国际法上的进一步发展提供重要的理论依据与实践“证据”。考虑到干涉问题的敏感性及不同国家对此问题的不同立场，国际法院有关共同利益的司法实践既给国际法的发展带来了重要机遇，同时也带来了挑战。因此，对于国际法院此种实践的总结，既应基于国际法院这个平台，也应超越这个平台，有必要将其放在国际法的未来发展趋势的框架体系内进行研究。

（责任编辑：郝鲁怡）

（本文原载于《国际法研究》2017年第5期）

被害人参加国际刑事法院诉讼的方式*

凌　岩**

《罗马规约》允许在国际刑事法院（以下简称“法院”）管辖下的犯罪的被害人参加法院诉讼程序。被害人除个别出庭表达自己的意见和关注外，一般来说，只要被害人愿意，他们不必亲自到法院去参与诉讼。在大多数情况下，被害人都通过法律代理人参与诉讼，向法院提出他们的意见和关注。

一　被害人的法律代理人

（一）法律代理人的条件

被害人可以自由选择他们的法律代理人。在国际刑事法院，法律代理人的条件与辩护律师的条件一样，必须是一个在国际法或刑法和刑事诉讼法方面具有至少十年经验的律师、法官或检察官，能流利运用法院的工作语言（英语或法语）。[①] 律师不是国际刑事法院的职员，法院书记官处将合格的律师列在名册上，通过向被害人提供律师名单，帮助被害人找到一个法律代理人。当有较多被害人时，分庭也可以要求被害人选择一个法律代理人，以保证诉讼的有效性。如果被害人选择遇到困难，分庭可请书记官

---

* 本文是国家社科基金项目“国际刑事法院的理论与实践”的中期成果，项目号11BFX136。

** 凌岩，中国政法大学教授。

① 国际刑事法院《程序和证据规则》第22条。

处替他们选择。如果被害人付不起代理人费用，书记官处可以援助和决定法院支付的法律援助范围，[①] 但不保证能代被害人支付法律代理人的全部费用。

此外，书记官处成立了被害人公共律师办公室，在被害人参与诉讼以及要求赔偿方面向被害人及其法律代理人提供支持和援助。该办公室的成员也可以被指定为被害人的法定代理人。

国际刑事法院是第一个允许被害人由律师代表参与诉讼的国际性刑事法庭，没有先前的经验可以参照。法院内各个分庭在实践中采取了一些适合所处理案件的做法。尤其在参与诉讼的被害人人数太多时，一个法律代理人不容易与每个被害人都取得联络，听取他们的意见，故由一名代理人代表所有的被害人显然不可行，在这种情况下，分庭会为被害人分组和任命代理人，例如，在“检察官诉本巴案”（The Prosecutor v. Jean-Pierre Bemba Gombo，以下简称“本巴案”）中，大量的被害人是以犯罪发生地分组的，分庭任命了两名共同代理人代表两个组的被害人。[②]

此外，按照国际刑事法院《程序和证据规则》（以下简称《规则》）第 90 条第 4 款的规定，被害人的法律代理人要照顾被害人的利益。如果被害人之间有利益冲突，必须要为不同利益的被害人团组任命不同的共同法律代理人。不过，观点不同不一定会产生利益冲突。例如受同一攻击的被害人可能对攻击的手段有不同看法，而他们的利益并无不一致。但是如果对攻击了甲村还是乙村有不同看法，则存在利益冲突。民族不同有时也会引起利益冲突，政治倾向不同也是利益冲突。在犯了罪的被害人和未犯罪的被害人之间也可能有利益冲突。[③] 例如在“检察官诉恩塔甘达案”（Prosecutor v. Ntaganda，以下简称“恩塔甘达案”）中，被害人被分为两个利益不同的组，一组为 140 个儿童兵（既是被害人又曾参与犯罪），另一组为

---

① 国际刑事法院《程序和证据规则》第 90 条；国际刑事法院《书记官处条例》第 112 条和第 113 条。

② ICC，Prosecutor v. Bemba，“Decision on common legal representation of victims for the purpose of trial”，ICC－01/05 －01/08－1005，10 November 2010，para. 21.

③ ASF Report，“Modes of Participation and Legal Representation”，pp. 22－23，http://www.asf.be/wp-content/uploads/2013/11/ASF_IJ_Modes-of-participation-and-legal-representation. pdf，最后访问日期：2017 年 6 月 12 日。

受武装攻击的980名被害人，由两名律师分别作为两组被害人的共同法律代理人。[①] 在“检察官诉卡汤加等人案”（Prosecutor v. Germain Katanga and Mathieu Ngudjolo Chui，以下简称“卡汤加案”）中的被害人也是这样分组和被代表的。[②] 但是在“检察官诉阿布·加尔达·班达和耶尔波·侯赛因案”（Prosecutor v. Abu Garda Banda and Jerbo Hussein，以下简称“班达等人案”）中，维和部队的驻地受到了武装攻击，有两名平民在维和驻地的院落中工作，由于维和驻地受到攻击，他们的生命受到威胁，看到维和士兵的伤亡，他们受到了心理伤害，预审分庭承认他们是被害人，他们与其他受攻击的维和部队的被害人不同。[③] 但是预审分庭给所有的被害人任命了一个共同代理人，并没有认为这两名被害人与其他被害人的利益有冲突。[④]

开始，在预审阶段，代理人尼斯（Nice）和狄克逊（Dixon）代表这两名苏丹籍被害人参与诉讼。这两名代理人是苏丹工会联盟和苏丹国际辩护团为被害人安排的。苏丹工会联盟和苏丹国际辩护团这两个组织都是同情苏丹政府的，曾以法庭之友干预过“检察官诉对奥马尔·哈桑·艾哈迈德·巴希尔案”（The Prosecutor v. Omar Hassan Ahmad Al Bashir，以下简称“巴希尔案”），反对法院对巴希尔的管辖权。在该案确认指控听讯前两天，检察官提出紧急请求反对两名被害人由尼斯和狄克逊代表参与诉讼。检察官认为这两个组织在巴希尔案上失败了，现在变换为被害人代理人参与此案的诉讼。[⑤] 辩方也要求更换该两位法律代理人，认为苏丹的这两个组织意在借此平台推进苏丹政府的议事日程和达到苏丹政府的目的。这两个组织被认为更关心的是苏丹政府的利益，而非两名达尔富尔被害人的利益。

---

① ICC, Prosecutor v. Ntaganda, ICC－01/04－02/06－449, “Decision on victims' participation in trial proceedings, 6 February 2015”, para. 1; ICC, Prosecutor v. Lubanga, “Decision on victim's participation”, 18 January 2008, para. 97.

② See also Prosecutor v. Germain Katanga and Mathieu Ngudjolo Chui, “Order on the organisation of common legal representation of victims”, ICC－01/04－01/07－1328, 22 July 2009, para. 7.

③ ICC, Prosecutor v. Banda and Jerbo, “Decision on Victims' Participation at the Hearing on the Confirmation of the Charges”, ICC－02/05－03/09－89, 29 October 2010, paras. 28－29.

④ ICC, Prosecutor v. Banda and Jerbo, “Order inviting the Registrar to appoint a common legal representative”, ICC－02/05－03/09－209, 6 September 2011.

⑤ Emily Haslam and Rod Edmunds, “Victim Participation, Politics and the Construction of Victims at the International Criminal Court: Reflections on Proceedings in Banda and Jerbo”, *Melbourne Journal of International Law* 14 (2013): 740.

如两名被害人法律代理人得到这两个组织的支持和资助参与诉讼，他们的行为不可能不受这两个组织的影响。[①] 诉讼两方都希望更换两名被害人的这两名代理人，以保障诉讼的正直和两被害人的利益。但是，预审分庭并没有同意更换，理由是未能证明被害人与这两个苏丹组织之间有利益冲突。[②] 后来，在审判阶段，书记官处为该案的89名被害人安排了共同代理人，取代了这两名代理人。[③]

（二）指派法律代理人的标准

除了法院规定的被害人法律代理人的条件外，书记官处根据被害人的意见或其自己的分析，会确定一些法律代理人的标准，分庭也会根据其对案件或情势的理解提出自己的标准。例如在本巴案中，第三审判分庭优先考虑任命该国的律师和被害人国籍国的律师。分庭说：鉴于本案的具体情况，分庭特别强调需要尊重《法院条例》（以下简称《条例》）第79条第2款规定的当地习俗，共同法律代理人最好说被害人的语言，与被害人享有共同的文化和知晓他们的现实情况，以便更有意义地代理被害人，与被害人沟通和向分庭传递被害人的意见和关注。[④] 但有人指出，被害人未必都喜欢由本国的律师代理。在有些案子中，被害人可能喜欢本国籍的律师，因为他们更理解冲突的根源和他们所受的损害。而在另一些情况下，被害人也许更喜欢外国律师，因为怕当地律师受贿。最重要的是在指派律师时要征求被害人的意见。[⑤]

在“检察官诉威廉·鲁托等人案”（Prosecutor v. Ruto et al.）中，预

---

① ICC, Prosecutor v. Banda and Jerbo, “Defence Application to restrain legal representatives for the victims a/1646/10 & a/1647/10 from acting in proceedings and for an order excluding the involvement of specified intermediaries”, ICC-02/05-03/09-113, 7 December 2010.

② Emily Haslam and Rod Edmunds, “Victim Participation, Politics and the Construction of Victims at the International Criminal Court: Reflections on Proceedings in Banda and Jerbo”, *Melbourne Journal of International Law* 14 (2013): 741.

③ ICC, Prosecutor v. Banda and Jerbo, “Notification of appointment of common legal representatives of victims”, ICC-02/05-03/09-215, 14 September 2011.

④ ICC, Prosecutor v. Bemba, “Decision on common legal representation of victims for the purpose of trial”, ICC-01/05-01/08-1005, 10 November 2010, para. 11.

⑤ ASF Report, “Modes of Participation and Legal Representation”, p. 29.

审分庭和审判分庭在为被害人指派律师时都要求考虑以下有关因素：[①] 已建立了被害人的信任，或能够建立这样的关系；能够和愿意在工作中以被害人为中心；在被害人被允许参与的诉讼中，熟悉被指控犯罪发生的国家；先前的刑事审判经验表明具有相关专业和经验；有代表大量被害人群体的经验，和在有关科研领域进行过专门研究；准备好花费大量的时间与大量被害人联络，跟踪法院诉讼的进展，在诉讼中采取适当步骤，保持与法院的充分联系；掌握基本的信息技术知识。

在该案中，审判分庭要求代理人驻在当地，认为法律代理人驻在肯尼亚就能更好地为被害人的利益服务。法律代理人与被害人越近就越容易与被害人沟通，以保证有意义地代表被害人。但也有人认为，驻在当地并不意味着与被害人接近和征求被害人的意见，而且如果由法律代理人的助手在当地与被害人联络和沟通，代理人驻在当地就不那么重要了。任命能驻在当地的代理人更应该考虑的可能是代理人的安全以及保证其独立的需要。[②]

（三）指派法律代理人的方式

国际刑事法院不同的分庭对被害人的法律代理人采取了不同的指派方式。在"检察官诉卢班加案"（The Prosecutor v. Thomas Lubanga Dyilo，以下简称"卢班加案"）的审判中，法庭指派了两个代理人团队分别代表两组被害人，被害人公共律师办公室的律师代表有双重地位的个人被害人。[③] 在卡汤加案和本巴案的审判阶段，在征求了被害人的意见后为两组不同的被害人分别指派了共同的法律代理人，并请他们再任命一位律师助理，以协助他们工作。[④] 在"检察官诉巴博案"（Prosecutor v. Gbagbo，以下简称巴博案）中，法庭则采用了被害人公共律师办公室的律师和法院外律师的

---

① ICC, Prosecutor v. Ruto et al., "Decision on Victims' Participation at the Confirmation of Charges Hearing and in the Related Proceedings", ICC - 01/09 - 01/11 - 249, 5 August 2011, paras. 69 - 74; ICC, The Prosecutor v. William Samoei Ruto and Oshua Arap Sang, ICC - 01/09 - 01/11 - 460, "Decision on Victims' Representation and Participation (hereinafter Ruto and Sang Decision)", para. 61.

② ASF Report, "Modes of Participation and Legal Representation", p. 29.

③ ICC, Prosecutor v. Lubanga, "Judgment pursuant to Article 74 of the Statute", ICC - 01/04 - 01/06 - 2842, 14 March 2012, para. 20.

④ ICC, Prosecutor v. Katanga and Ngudjolo, Order on the organisation of common legal representation of victims, ICC - 01/04 - 01/07 - 1328, 22 July 2009, p. 13.

混合任命制度。第一审判分庭的独任法官根据书记官长的建议，指派被害人公共律师办公室的律师作为被害人的共同法律代理人团队的主律师，由驻在科特迪瓦对案件以及对当地的情况很了解的院外律师予以协助。[①] 在“检察官诉威廉·鲁托等人案”中，法庭采用了与巴博案相反的混合代理人制度，指派的两名共同法律代理人应驻在肯尼亚当地，公共律师办公室的律师则作为共同法律代理人和分庭的中间联系人，被允许参加允许被害人参与的听讯，共同法律代理人指示公共律师办公室的律师代表他们在法庭上提意见。[②] 在恩塔甘达案的审判阶段，指派了两名被害人公共办公室的律师作为两组被害人的代理人，每组在当地有一名律师助理。[③]

在被害人公共律师办公室和院外律师混合代理制度中，鲁托等人案模式不易操作，院外律师作为主律师常驻在肯尼亚，由被害人公共律师办公室的律师协助院外律师并在法院出庭，由于海牙和肯尼亚当地的通信困难，被害人公共律师办公室的律师在法庭代为回应法官的问题有时就会发生困难。巴博案模式是以公共律师为主，并在法庭代表被害人提出意见，就不会发生上述困难。但是也有人对该种模式有疑问：院外律师仅为公共律师的助理，在以公共律师为主导的代理案中，院外律师究竟能在制定诉讼战略方面起多大的作用？[④]

在被害人参与诉讼方面，国际刑事法院的做法是，在诉讼的适当阶段允许被害人参与。被害人参与的主要方式是通过被害人的法律代理人，只有少数个别的被害人可以到法庭参与诉讼。从审判庭的空间、法院的资源以及对被告迅速审判的要求来看，成百上千的被害人都出庭参与是不现实，也是不可能的；因此，由被害人的律师代表他们参与是最合理的安排。更重要的是，被害人有权自由选择其法律代理人，法院在为被害人指

① ICC, Situation in the Republic of Côte d'Ivoire, "Decision on Victims' Participation and Victims' Common Legal Representation at the Confirmation of Charges Hearing and in the Related Proceedings", ICC-02/11-01/11-138, 4 June 2012, paras. 43-44.

② ICC, Prosecutor v. Ruto and Sang, ICC-01/09-01/11-460, 3 October 2012, para. 60.

③ ICC, Prosecutor v. Ntaganda, "Decision on Victims' Participation in Trial Proceedings" ICC-1/04-02/06-449, para. 51.

④ ASF Report, "Modes of Participation and Legal Representation", p. 31.

定律师时应充分征求被害人的意见。但在实践中，分庭有时忽视了这个规则。[①] 无国界律师组织指出，在卡汤加案中，法庭全面征求了被害人对指派法律代理人的意见。但在后来的案件中，就忽略了征求被害人的意见，有时完全不征求被害人的意见。在有些案件中，国际刑事法院干脆公开招聘被害人的律师。[②]

另一个被害人非政府组织认为书记官处应该与被害人进行有效和有益的磋商，询问被害人想选什么样的代理人，而且在协助被害人作出选择时应告知他们有关的规则。例如，被害人可以对书记官处选择的律师提出异议，《条例》里有具体的质疑机制。[③] 玛丽安娜·佩纳（Mariana Pena）等人指出，在被害人参与和选择被害人法律代理人方面应授权给被害人决定，而不是由其他人决定被害人如何做最好。[④]

另外，国际刑事法院关于选择共同的法律代理人的做法不时在变化。起初大都维持先期已帮助同案的被害人的律师。后来，有的分庭并不认为共同法律代理人先前的参与是非常重要的。在鲁托等人案中，由于原来的被害人律师不愿意一直驻在肯尼亚，她认为不驻在肯尼亚不妨碍她代表被害人，但是分庭认为她这样做会使被害人参与的新制度无法运作，因此终止了对她的任命，而任命了另一名符合条件的律师在该案审判阶段代表被害人。[⑤] 但是，艾波伊—欧苏吉（Eboe Osuji）法官认为该名律师有肯尼亚国籍、熟悉肯尼亚及其人民和环境、熟悉案件，已经长期代理了该案的被害人并愿意继续代理。分庭的多数法官应该多考虑一下这些因素，让她继续代理被害人参与审判，而不应该仅因为她不能全部时间驻在肯尼亚就终

① di Giuseppe Zago, "The Role of Victims at the International Criminal Court: Legal Challenges from the Tension between restorative and Retributive Justice", p. 11, http://www.penalecontemporaneo.it/upload/1415744172ZAGO_2014.pdf，最后访问日期：2017 年 6 月 12 日。

② ASF Report, "Modes of Participation and Legal Representation", p. 27.

③ Redress, "The Legal Representation of Victims before the ICC: Challenges and Opportunities", 26 November 2014, p. 2, http://www.redress.org/downloads/victims-legal-representation-at-the-icc-background-notenov2014.pdf，最后访问日期：2017 年 6 月 12 日。

④ Mariana Pena & Gaelle Carayon, "Is the ICC Making the Most of Victim Participation?", *The International Journal of Transitional Justice* 7 (2013): 534.

⑤ ICC, Prosecutor v. Ruto and Sang, "Decision on Appointing a Common Legal Representative of Victims", ICC-01/09-01/11-479, 23 November 2012.

止了她的工作。[①]

另外一些观点也认为，在诉讼的一个不同节点改变律师会阻碍法律代理人的连续性。在没有被害人如此要求而在诉讼中间决定更换代理人时，需要保证诉讼的效率，还需要考虑被害人能否理解这种决定和面临重新构建与新代理人的信任关系问题。法官应在被害人表达其观点和诉讼效率之间作出平衡，在执行这种改变之前应征求被害人和代理人的意见。[②]

二 被害人参与诉讼的方式

《规约》第 68 条第 3 款规定在法院认为合适的诉讼阶段，被害人可以参与诉讼。但是，《规约》并没有预先制定准许参与案件各阶段的被害人可行使的诉讼权利，即参与的方式，而是留给了分庭通过自由裁量予以决定。[③]

当有关分庭准许被害人参与案件预审阶段、审判阶段、中期上诉阶段或上诉阶段的诉讼后，在确定诉讼权利时，分庭不必对被害人的个人利益进行第二次评估。[④] 上诉分庭在卢班加案的判决中表明，上诉分庭不要求被害人证明他们的个人利益受到每一个上诉部分的诉讼活动或证据的影响；相反，上诉分庭主要评估被害人的个人利益是否受整体中期上诉的影响，也就是说每个中期上诉是上诉分庭的一个不同的独立的诉讼。[⑤] 如果每次一个自然人打算参与有关的诉讼活动，该人都要经过提出参与申请程

① ICC, Prosecutor v. Ruto and Sang, ICC－01/09－01/11－479, 23 November 2012.

② Redress, "The Legal Representation of Victims before the ICC: Challenges and Opportunities", p. 2.

③ ICC, The Prosecutor v. Germain Katanga and Mathieu Ngudjolo Chui, "Decision on the Set of Procedural Rights Attached to Procedural Status of Victim at the Pre-Trial Stage of the Case", ICC－01/04－01/07－474, 13 May 2008, para. 45; "Decision on Request for leave to appeal the 'Decision on the Requests of the OPCD on the Production of Relevant Supporting Documentation Pursuant to Regulation 86 (2) (e) of the Regulations of the Court and on the Disclosure of Exculpatory Materials by the Prosecutor'", ICC－02/05－11823 January 2008, p. 5.

④ ICC, The Prosecutor v. Germain Katanga and Mathieu Ngudjolo Chui, ICC－01/04－01/07－474, para. 45.

⑤ ICC, Situation in Darfur, Sudan, "Decision on the Requests for Leave to Appeal the Decision on the Application for Participation of Victims in the Proceedings in the Situation", ICC－02/05－121, 6 February 2008, p. 6.

序，由分庭在进行相关的具体诉讼活动或讨论相关证据之前对申请作出决定，法院的整体有效运作就可能会受到阻碍。同样，在案件预审阶段，用上述方法决定参与诉讼的被害人的诉讼权利，也会造成诉讼的重大延误，还会大大限制被害人在法院审理的刑事诉讼中所起的作用，导致被害人在参与诉讼时享有的诉讼权利存在更大的不确定性。①

因此，分庭的惯常做法是，明确确定那些被准许参加该案预审阶段或审判阶段诉讼的被害人可以行使的一套诉讼权利，当然必须确保以不损害被告人的权利或不违反被告人受公平、公正审判的方式确定这些诉讼权利。一旦分庭对案件预审阶段或审判阶段被害人的诉讼权利作出了决定，该权利就属于已被准许参与该诉讼和今后准许参与该诉讼的所有被害人，包括自然人和法人，而且始终适用于该诉讼期间，而不再在诉讼的不同时间作出很多的决定。但是，在预审阶段，所赋予的被害人的任何诉讼权利不能被回溯行使。这样，不仅向案件各当事方和参与人提供法律上的确定性，还旨在确保被准许参与该案预审阶段的被害人所起的作用。②

《规约》第 68 条第 3 款和《规则》第 91 条、第 92 条仅仅指明分庭有义务以不损害被告的权利和公平、公正审判的方式确定这些诉讼权利，没有明确规定准许参与案件各阶段诉讼的被害人的诉讼权利，而由各分庭规定对参与各自审理的案件的预审程序和审判程序的被害人的诉讼权利。虽然各分庭在这些权利的归类和表述上略有不同，例如在卡汤加案中，被害人在预审阶段的诉讼权利被分为六组，在“检察官诉盖乌达案”（The Prosecutor v. Bahr Idriss Abu Garda）中，被害人有四个方面的诉讼权利。其中有些规定是一致的，但也存在一些差别。被害人在预审阶段和审判阶段参加诉讼的权利也有所不同。

（一）被害人参加预审程序和审判程序相同的方式

被害人参加审判程序与参加预审程序大致相同的方式有以下几种。

---

① ICC，The Prosecutor v. Germain Katanga and Mathieu Ngudjolo Chui，ICC – 01/04 – 01/07 – 474，paras. 47，48.

② ICC，The Prosecutor v. Germain Katanga and Mathieu Ngudjolo Chui，ICC – 01/04 – 01/07 – 474，paras. 4，51，145.

1. 出席并参加听讯和提出书面意见[①]

根据《规则》第91条第2款的规定，被害人或其法律代理人有权根据分庭依《规则》第89条和第90条裁定的条件，出席和参加公开和不公开的听讯。当听讯必须是单方参加的，分庭会基于个案的具体情况评估是否应邀请被害人的法律代理人参加。在卡汤加案中，分庭准许法律代理人的介入一般应仅限于提交书面意见。检方和辩方必须有机会对被害人的法律代理人作出的口头或书面意见作出回应。[②] 在卢班加案中，分庭可以自行或经当事方或参与人的要求，视情况而决定是否允许被害人参加不公开的、单方面的听讯。每当被害人申请参加此类听讯时，分庭要在可能和必要的范围内征求当事方的意见。[③] 在班达等人案中，分庭准许被害人的法律代理人参加不公开的听讯或单方面听讯，如果被害人的个人利益有此需要。被害人的法律代理人与法庭达成明确的协议，不将分庭命令的保护措施中包括的任何信息透露给其代理的被害人。诉讼各方有权在任何阶段对被害人的法律代理人或其部分团队成员的参与或出现在特定的听讯提出不同的意见。此外，基于例外的情况，分庭可以允许单方面的、只有被害人参加的听讯，如果认为被害人的个人利益有此需要。[④]

2. 在审判中作开庭陈词和终结陈词

根据《规则》第89条第1款的规定，被害人被明确授权作出陈述。分庭一般都准许被害人的法律代理人在审判时作开庭陈词和终结陈词。[⑤]

---

① ICC, The Prosecutor v. Germain Katanga and Mathieu Ngudjolo Chui, "Decision on the Modalities of Victim Participation at Trial", ICC - 01/04 - 01/07 - 1788 - tENG, 22 January 2010, para. 68; ICC, Prosecutor v. Lubanga, "Decision on Victims' Participation", CC - 01/04 - 01/06 - 1119, 18 January 2008, para. 111; ICC, The Prosecutor v. Germain Katanga and Mathieu Ngudjolo Chui, ICC - 01/04 - 01/07 - 474, para. 140; ICC, Situation in Darfur, Sudan, "Decision on Victims' Modalities of Participation at the Pre-Trial Stage of the Case", ICC - 02/05 - 02/09 - 136, 06 October 2009, paras. 17, 20.

② ICC, The Prosecutor v. Germain Katanga and Mathieu Ngudjolo Chui, ICC - 01/04 - 01/07 - 1788 - tENG, paras. 69, 71.

③ ICC, Prosecutor v. Lubanga, ICC - 01/04 - 01/06 - 1119, para. 113.

④ ICC, The Prosecutor v. Abdallah Banda Abakaer Nourain, "Decision on the Participation of Victims in the Trial Proceedings", ICC - 02/05 - 03/09 - 545, 20 March 2014, para. 41.

⑤ ICC, The Prosecutor v. Germain Katanga and Mathieu Ngudjolo Chui, ICC - 01/04 - 01/07 - 1788 - tENG, para. 68; ICC, Prosecutor v. Lubanga, para. 117; The Prosecutor v. Germain Katanga and Mathieu Ngudjolo Chui, ICC - 01/04 - 01/07 - 474, paras. 141 - 143.

3. 询问证人、专家或被告人[①]

在审判中，被害人询问证人、专家或被告人是可能的，但不是绝对的权利。根据《规则》第91条第3款a项的规定，若被害人的法律代理人希望向证人、专家或被告人提问，他必须向审判分庭提出申请。在卡汤加案中，分庭可命令将问题以书面提出并告知检察官，以及适当的话，告知辩方以征得他们的意见。根据《规则》第91条第3款b项的规定，分庭要考虑诉讼的阶段，被告人的权利，证人的利益，公平、公正和迅速审判需要等各种因素，对该请求作出裁决。根据《规约》第64条规定的分庭的权力，该裁定可包括对提问的方式、提问的顺序以及文件的制作作出指示。分庭如果认为适当，还可以代表法律代理人向证人、专家或被告人提问。在审判分庭看来，这种询问必须是为了查明事实真相，因为被害人不是审判当事方，询问不是为了支持检察官。然而，鉴于被害人具有当地知识和社会文化背景，他们的干预可能使分庭能够更好地了解一些有关的问题。[②]

由于《规约》中缺乏有关的规定，卡汤加案中的审判分庭在有关《规则》第140条的决定中具体规定了诉讼方和参与人询问证人、专家或被告人的顺序，以及被害人的法律代理人询问的确切程序。[③] 法院现已经形成了处理被害人请求向证人提问的有效方法，在卢班加案中，代理人必须在有关证人作证的7天前提交询问的请求，因为到那时，要出示证据到何种程度和产生的问题都已经清楚，能使分庭作出适当的决定，使程序中断的时间减到最小，并便利审判的有效运行。[④]

班达等人案基本采取了卢班加案的做法，被害人的法律代理人应当充

---

① The Prosecutor v. Germain Katanga and Mathieu Ngudjolo Chui, ICC - 01/04 - 01/07 - 474, paras. 135 - 139; ICC, Situation in Darfur, Sudan, ICC - 02/05 - 02/09 - 136, 06 October 2009, paras. 23 - 24.

② ICC, The Prosecutor v. Germain Katanga and Mathieu Ngudjolo Chui, ICC - 01/04 - 01/07 - 1788 - tENG, paras. 72, 73, 75.

③ ICC, The Prosecutor v. Germain Katanga and Mathieu Ngudjolo Chui, "Directions for the Conduct of the Proceedings and Testimony in Accordance with Rule 140", ICC - 01/04 - 01/07 - 1665, 20 November 2009.

④ ICC, Prosecutor v. Bemba, "Corrigendum to Decision on the Participation of Victims in the Trial and on 86 Applications by Victims to Participate in the Proceedings", ICC - 01/05 - 01/08 - 807 - Corr, 12 July 2010, para. 37.

分提前提交书面申请且不迟于预计作证日期的 7 天前。申请书还应包括可能提问的范围和提问到何种程度，以及那些问题影响被害人的个人利益的理由，并应附上提问时要使用的有关文件的清单。在被害人的法律代理人提问前，当事双方都可以提出他们的口头意见。

关于被害人的法律代理人对证人的提问方式，各审判分庭的做法都一致。在控方提问完成后，允许被害人的法律代理人提问题，除非参与的被害人已向分庭提出该证据和分庭根据《规约》第 69 条第 3 款要求提交该证据。在这种情况下，被害人的法律代理人在检方提问之前提问题。一般来说，被害人的法律代理人应以中立的方式提问，[①] 不能使用引导或封闭式的问题，除非分庭另有授权。[②]

4. 获取机密文件和案件记录中的证据

根据《规则》第 121 条第 10 款的规定，书记官处应创建和保持分庭所有程序的全面和准确记录。被害人或其法律代理人，除受有关保密和保护国家安全信息的限制外，可以查阅该记录。[③] 因此，书记官长必须向法律代理人通知提交的请求、意见、动议和有关的其他文件，以及在其参与的阶段中法庭所作出的决定。为了促进被害人有效参与审判，法律代理人有权查阅案件记录中所有公开和保密的决定和文件，但归类为单方的文件除外。[④] 在班达等人案中，法律代理人获得的机密文件仅限于该文件的内容涉及其所代理的被害人的个人利益。[⑤] 卢班加案的审判分庭比较谨慎，认为由于案件记录内的机密文件往往包含有关国家安全、保护证人和被害人的敏感信息，以及检方的调查，因而被害人的法律代理人只可获得公开

---

① ICC, The Prosecutor v. Germain Katanga and Mathieu Ngudjolo Chui, ICC - 01/04 - 01/07 - 1788 - tENG, para. 78.

② ICC, The Prosecutor v. Abdallah Banda Abakaer Nourain, "Decision on the Participation of Victims in the Trial Proceedings", ICC - 02/05 - 03/09 - 545, paras. 32, 33.

③ ICC, The Prosecutor v. Germain Katanga and Mathieu Ngudjolo Chui, ICC - 01/04 - 01/07 - 1788 - tENG, para. 118; ICC - 02/05 - 03/09 - 545, para. 34; ICC, Prosecutor v. Lubanga, ICC - 01/04 - 01/06 - 1119, para. 105.

④ ICC, The Prosecutor v. Germain Katanga and Mathieu Ngudjolo Chui, para. 119; ICC, The Prosecutor v. Abdallah Banda Abakaer Nourain, "Decision on the Participation of Victims in the Trial Proceedings", ICC - 02/05 - 03/09 - 545, para. 35.

⑤ ICC, The Prosecutor v. Abdallah Banda Abakaer Nourain, "Decision on the participation of victims in the trial proceedings", ICC - 02/05 - 03/09 - 545, para. 36.

存档文件。然而，如果机密文件与参与诉讼的被害人的个人利益实质相关，应考虑向有关被害人提供此信息，只要它不会违反仍需保持的其他保护措施。①

法律代理人也被授权查阅当事方提供的材料。在卡汤加案中，分庭认为必须准许法律代理人至少在相关证人作证 3 天前查阅打算在询问检察官的证人时所使用的材料，有权获取预审阶段的机密案件记录。还准许法律代理人获取检察官制定的证明有罪的证据清单。另外，该案的当事方根据《规则》第 69 条的规定与被害人法律代理人签订了有关证据的若干协议，被害人的法律代理人要求获得这些证据。为了确保被害人有效参与审判，分庭同意被害人的法律代理人获得该等文件。②

根据《律师的专业行为守则》第 8 条第 4 款，被害人的法律代理人不得泄露受保护的被害人和证人的身份，或可能泄露其身份和下落的任何机密资料，除非经法庭授权这样做。法律代理人还必须遵守保密义务，在清单中所列的案件证据和书记官处保持的系统中登记的证据只限于他们自己获取，而不能扩大到其代理的被害人。③ 检察官根据《规约》第 54 条第 3 款第 5 项的规定的条件所取得的证明被告有罪的文件，不能让被害人的法律代理人获得。④

（二）参与审判阶段的其他方式

1. 提出有关被告有罪或无罪的证据和对证据的可采性或相关性提出质疑的权利

（1）提出有关被告有罪或无罪的证据

关于参与审判的被害人是否能够提出有关被告有罪或无罪的证据的问题，曾发生了争议。在卢班加案中，检察官、辩护律师和乔治斯·皮基斯

① ICC, Prosecutor v. Lubanga, ICC – 01/04 – 01/06 – 1119, para. 106.

② ICC, The Prosecutor v. Germain Katanga and Mathieu Ngudjolo Chui, ICC – 01/04 – 01/07 – 1788 – tENG, paras. 121, 122, 125.

③ ICC, The Prosecutor v. Germain Katanga and Mathieu Ngudjolo Chui, ICC – 01/04 – 01/07 – 1788 – tENG, paras. 120, 123.

④ ICC, The Prosecutor v. Germain Katanga and Mathieu Ngudjolo Chui, ICC – 01/04 – 01/07 – 1788 – tENG, para. 124.

（G. M. Pikis）法官都主张被害人不可以提出关于被告有罪或无罪的证据，[①]他们主张，首先，提出被告有罪或无罪的证据的权利专属于当事方，[②] 被害人不是当事方，他们的职能不同于检方和辩方的职能，按照《罗马规约》和《规则》，只有当事方才有披露的义务。允许没有披露义务的被害人提出关于被告有罪或无罪的证据对于适当的审判管理和辩方的权利都有严重的影响。《规约》第 66 条第 2 款明确规定，举证责任专属于检察官，允许被害人提出关于被告有罪或无罪的证据，将导致举证责任的转移，[③]而且意味着迫使辩方面对多个控方，这违反了公平审判的控辩平等原则。[④]此外，《规约》为检察官和辩方提供了收集这些证据的手段，特别是为他们参与这些活动的人员始终提供安全保障，《规约》对于被害人没有这种规定，因此如果允许他们收集和提出证据，他们的安全以及有风险人员的安全也会因收集到的信息而受到影响。[⑤]

其次，《规约》第 68 条第 3 款规定的提出“意见和关注”，不包括提出有罪或无罪的证据。[⑥]《规约》第 68 条第 3 款起草的历史可以证明这点，在初期规约草稿中包含一项规定，授权被害人法律代理人参与诉讼程序，以提出确定刑事责任的依据所需的其他证据，但在罗马谈判时这项规定被从《规约》中删除了。《规则》全面规定了被害人参与制度，其中没有提

① ICC, Prosecutor v. Lubanga, “Judgment on the Appeals of The Prosecutor and The Defence against Trial Chamber I's Decision on Victims' Participation of 18 January 2008”, ICC－01/04－01/06－1432－tCMN, 11 July 2008, paras, 69, 77；乔治斯·皮基斯法官的部分不同意见，第 5 段。

② ICC, Prosecutor v. Lubanga, “Prosecution's Document in Support of Appeal against Trial Chamber I's 18 January 2008 Decision on Victims' Participation”, ICC－01/04－01/06－1219, 10 March 2008, para. 30；ICC, Prosecutor v. Lubanga, “Defence Appeal Against Trial Chamber I's 18 January 2008 Decision on Victims' Participation”, ICC－01/04－01/06－1220－tENG, 10 March 2008, para. 46；ICC, Prosecutor v. Lubanga, ICC－01/04－01/06－1432－tCMN, paras. 71, 78；乔治斯·皮基斯法官的部分不同意见。

③ ICC, Prosecutor v. Lubanga, ICC－01/04－01/06－1219, para. 33；ICC, Prosecutor v. Lubanga, ICC－01/04－01/06－1432－tCMN, para. 72.

④ ICC, Prosecutor v. Lubanga, ICC－01/04－01/06－1220－tENG, para. 48；ICC, Prosecutor v. Lubanga, ICC－01/04－01/06－1432－tCMN, para. 78；乔治斯·皮基斯法官的部分不同意见。

⑤ ICC, Prosecutor v. Lubanga, ICC－01/04－01/06－1219, para. 34；ICC, Prosecutor v. Lubanga, ICC－01/04－01/06－1432－tCMN, para. 71.

⑥ ICC, Prosecutor v. Lubanga, ICC－01/04－01/06－1219, paras. 38－39；ICC, Prosecutor v. Lubanga, ICC－01/04－01/06－1432－tCMN, paras. 74, 78.

及被害人有权在审判中提出证据，有关规定实际上确认了只有当事方才有权提出证据。[①]

最后，《规约》第 64 条第 6 款第 4 项和第 69 条第 3 款规定的审判分庭的权力，不能被解释为被害人可以或应该提交被告有罪或无罪的证据。检方认为，审判分庭裁定允许被害人在分庭认为有助于查明事实的情况下提出和审查证据是“错误地将被害人的利益与检方的职能合二为一”。被害人只有在赔偿诉讼程序中，才可以向分庭提交材料以支持其主张。[②]

被害人的法律代理人认为，法院的文件间接授权被害人以两种形式提交关于被告有罪或无罪的证据，一种是根据《罗马规约》第 68 条第 3 款提出他们的意见和关注，另一种是根据《规则》第 91 条第 3 款规定的询问证人、专家和被告。另外，《规约》允许审判分庭根据《规约》第 76 条下令为判决的目的提交关于被害人的有关证据，其要求同审判时一样。[③]这些论点都未得到检察官的支持。[④]

（2）对证据的可采性或相关性提出质疑

关于被害人是否可以对证据的可采性或相关性提出质疑的问题，检察官认为，被害人不可以对证据的可采性或相关性提出质疑，因为根据《规约》第 64 条第 9 款，审判分庭有权“应当事方的申请”或自行裁定可采性。[⑤] 皮基斯法官认为，证明和推翻指控是诉讼中对抗双方的事，被害人对此没有发言权。司法利益由法庭来保障，法庭有责任确保在其审理的诉讼程序中只接受相关的和可采信的证据。无罪推定使得除检察官以外的任何人都不能在法庭审理的刑事诉讼程序中提出相反主张，并通过提出相关的、可采信的证据来加以证明。[⑥] 被害人的法律代理人提出，《规则》第 72 条第 2 款允许被害人在某些情况下对证据的相关性或可采性提出意见，

---

① ICC, Prosecutor v. Lubanga, ICC – 01/04 – 01/06 – 1220 – tENG, para. 50; ICC, Prosecutor v. Lubanga, ICC – 01/04 – 01/06 – 1432 – tCMN, para. 78.

② ICC, Prosecutor v. Lubanga, ICC – 01/04 – 01/06 – 1219, paras. 41 – 46; ICC, Prosecutor v. Lubanga, ICC – 01/04 – 01/06 – 1432 – tCMN, paras. 73 – 75.

③ ICC, Prosecutor v. Lubanga, ICC – 01/04 – 01/06 – 1432 – tCMN, paras. 80 – 81.

④ ICC, Prosecutor v. Lubanga, ICC – 01/04 – 01/06 – 1432 – tCMN, paras. 83 – 84.

⑤ ICC, Prosecutor v. Lubanga, ICC – 01/04 – 01/06 – 1219, para. 49; ICC, Prosecutor v. Lubanga, ICC – 01/04 – 01/06 – 1432 – tCMN, para. 76.

⑥ ICC, Prosecutor v. Lubanga, ICC – 01/04 – 01/06 – 1432 – tCMN; 乔治斯·皮基斯法官的部分不同意见，第 19 段。

足见《规则》并没有排除被害人在其他情况下对证据的可采性或相关性提出质疑。而且提出或拟提出的证据可能影响被害人获得赔偿的权利，也可能对他们产生直接的损害。[①] 检察官虽然承认被害人的个人利益可能在某些特殊情况下会受到证据的影响，但检察官仍表示，这不能导致被害人对每件证据的可采性或相关性提出质疑的一般权利。只有当一件证据的采信将影响被害人个人利益时，才允许被害人就该证据的可采性提出意见和关注。[②]

（3）法庭的裁定

审判分庭裁定，在适当情况下，分庭有权在被害人提交申请后，允许参与该案诉讼的被害人提出和审查证据。理由是在《罗马规约》框架内没有任何规定禁止审判分庭按照《规约》第68条第3款和第69条第4款这样做。[③]

但是上诉分庭并不完全支持审判分庭的裁定，上诉分庭认为，第一，在审判诉讼中提出被告有罪或无罪的证据和对证据的可采性或相关性提出质疑的权利，主要属于各当事方即检察官和辩护方所有。[④] 《规约》第69条第3款所述“当事各方可以依照第64条提交与案件相关的证据”，以及第64条第6款第4项规定，法庭有权“命令提供除当事各方已经在审判前收集，或在审判期间提出的证据以外的其他证据”，明确规定在审判期间，证据将由当事方提交。上诉分庭指出，《罗马规约》框架中包含众多支持这一解释的条款，例如《规约》第15条、第53条、第54条、第58条和第61条第5款，规定检察官的职权包括调查犯罪、形成指控，决定提出哪些与指控有关的证据。《规约》第66条第2款规定：“证明被告人有罪是

① ICC, Prosecutor v. Lubanga, ICC-01/04-01/06-1219, paras. 28-29; ICC, Prosecutor v. Lubanga, ICC-01/04-01/06-1432-tCMN, para. 82.

② ICC, Prosecutor v. Lubanga, ICC-01/04-01/06-1219, paras. 26, 28; ICC, Prosecutor v. Lubanga, ICC-01/04-01/06-1432-tCMN, para. 85.

③ ICC, Prosecutor v. Lubanga, ICC-01/04-01/06-1219, paras. 96, 108; ICC, Prosecutor v. Lubanga, ICC-01/04-01/06-1432-tCMN, paras. 86, 92,《规约》第68条第3款的有关部分规定：“本法院应当准许被害人在其个人利益受到影响时，在本法院认为适当的诉讼阶段提出其意见和关注供审议。被害人提出意见和关注的方式不得损害或违反被告人的权利和公平公正审判原则。……”《规约》第69条第4款的有关部分规定：“本法院可以……考虑各项因素，包括证据的证明价值，以及这种证据对公平审判，……可能造成的任何不利影响，裁定证据的相关性或可采性。”

④ ICC, Prosecutor v. Lubanga, ICC-01/04-01/06-1432-tCMN, para. 93.

检察官的责任。”因此，提出被告有罪的证据是检察官的职能。此外，《规则》第76至第84条规定的当事方的披露义务，是针对当事方而不是被害人的。

第二，尽管如此，这些规定并不排除被害人在诉讼程序中提出被告有罪或无罪的证据并对证据的可采性或相关性提出质疑的可能性。[①] 因为《规约》第69条第3款清楚地规定：“法院有权要求提交一切其认为必要的证据以查明真相。”检察官负有该责任的事实不能解读成排除了法庭的法定权力，因为法院“必须确信被告人有罪已无合理怀疑”。而且，在审判中提出的与被告有罪或无罪无关的证据，很有可能被视为不可采信和无关的证据。如果一般性地和在所有情况下都排除被害人提交关于被告有罪或无罪的证据和对证据的可采性或相关性提出质疑的可能性，那么他们参与审判的权利实际上就可能变得毫无意义。[②]

第三，根据对《规约》第69条第3款第2句、《规则》第68条第3款和第91条第1款的解释，分庭有权使被害人能够提出动议，请分庭要求提交其认为对查明事实有必要的所有证据。[③]

第四，被害人没有提出或质疑证据的无限制权利。条件是：（1）被害人必须证明他们的利益受到证据或问题的影响，法庭视具体情况，酌情裁定是否允许其参与；（2）审判分庭对每项申请作出裁决时，必须注意保护被告的权利；（3）如果审判分庭决定应当提交证据，它可以在允许提交该证据前决定披露该证据的适当形式和提出证据的方式，例如，命令某一当事方提交证据，或自行传唤证据，或命令被害人出示证据。[④]

关于被害人对证据的可采性或相关性是否有提出质疑的权利，上诉分庭指出，《规约》第69条第4款规定：“本法院可以依照《程序和证据规则》，考虑各项因素，包括证据的证明价值，以及这种证据对公平审判或公平评估证人证言可能造成的任何不利影响，裁定证据的相关性或可采性。”审判分庭有宣布任何证据为可采或相关的一般权利。该规定对哪些

---

① ICC, Prosecutor v. Lubanga, ICC -01/04 -01/06 -1432 - tCMN, paras. 94 -95.

② ICC, Prosecutor v. Lubanga, ICC -01/04 -01/06 -1432 - tCMN, para. 97.

③ ICC, Prosecutor v. Lubanga, ICC -01/04 -01/06 -1432 - tCMN, para. 98.

④ ICC, Prosecutor v. Lubanga, ICC -01/04 -01/06 -1432 - tCMN, paras. 99, 100.

人可对该证据提出质疑没有作出任何规定。[①] 根据《规约》第 64 条第 9 款，审判分庭有权自行对证据的可采性或相关性作出裁定。这两项条款没有排除审判分庭在收到被害人对被告人是否有罪的证据的意见后对证据的可采性或相关性作出裁定的可能性。

被害人是否可以对证据的可采性或相关性提出质疑，还必须参照关于被害人参与的规定，即原已确定被害人的利益会受到影响，而且是在被害人参与权的范围之内，那么在某些情况下，例如，如果一些证据的来源可能缺乏可信度，或者可能与确定其损害无关，采信证据将影响参与诉讼的被害人的个人利益。[②] 同样，有些证据可能违反了保密规则，对被害人的保护有影响；或是以违反被害人及其家人国际公认人权的手段获得的；或其提交可能危害被害人的安全或有损其尊严；或在性侵害的情况下，违反《规则》第 70 条和第 71 条有关性暴力案或性行为的证据规则；或违反根据《规约》第 54 条第 3 款第 4 项与被害人或其家人达成的协议。这些证据的提交有可能影响被害人的个人利益，对他们有可能获得赔偿的权利造成不利后果，或对他们有直接的损害。[③] 分庭也可以考虑允许被害人对这些证据的可采性或相关性提出质疑。

卢班加案的审判分庭还为允许被害人提出并审查证据制定了程序和范围。即他们的申请应当说明，他们拟提出的证据为什么与查明事实有关，以及它对查明真相有什么帮助。如果要求允许宣誓作证，申请必须在检察官的案件陈述完成前提出，并必须包含对他们拟提出证词的“全面摘要”。然后，应将该申请通报当事方，让当事方有 7 天时间进行答复。如果申请获得批准，经签名的拟提交证词的“全面摘要”将构成《条例》第 54 条第 6 款所指的披露。被害人还可以向分庭申请提出书面证据。拟提出的书面证据必须与申请一起提交，并通知诉讼程序的当事方和参与方。审判分庭指示，原则上，关于提出书面证据的申请应当尽快提交。[④] 上诉分庭肯

① ICC, Prosecutor v. Lubanga, ICC - 01/04 - 01/06 - 1432 - tCMN, para. 101.

② ICC, Prosecutor v. Lubanga, ICC - 01/04 - 01/06 - 1432 - tCMN, para. 102.

③ ICC, Prosecutor v. Lubanga, ICC - 01/04 - 01/06 - 1432 - tCMN, para. 103.

④ ICC, The Prosecutor v. Germain Katanga and Mathieu Ngudjolo Chui, “Judgment on the Appeal of Mr Katanga Against the Decision of Trial Chamber II of 22 January 2010 Entitled ‘Decision on the Modalities of Victim Participation at Trial’”, ICC - 01/04 - 01/07 - 2288, 16 July 2010, para. 19.

定了这种程序包括：单独的申请，通知当事方，证明受到具体诉讼程序影响的个人利益，遵守披露义务和保护令，确定其适当性，符合被告的权利和公平审判的原则。上诉分庭认为，实施安保措施后，给予被害人参与权，使其可以提出被告有罪或无罪的证据，并对证据的可采性或相关性提出质疑，与检察官证明被告有罪的义务并不冲突，也不妨碍被告的权利和公平审判原则。[①]

上诉分庭作出判决后，其他分庭遵从了上诉分庭的意见，本巴案的审判分庭允许被害人提出被告人有罪或无罪的证据，以帮助分庭寻找真相。[②] 卡汤加案的审判分庭承认法律代理人有提出书面证据和质疑证据可采性的可能，只要符合分庭制定的程序。[③] 班达等人案的审判分庭承认被害人的法律代理人可以提请分庭在审判中关注的证据，分庭将在逐案基础上作出裁决。分庭也可允许被害人就证据的相关性或可采性提出意见和关注。只有当被害人的个人利益受到影响，在适当时，分庭将要求被害人的法律代理人对证据的可采性提出意见。[④]

2. 被害人是否有披露证据的义务

（1）在审判开始前未预先通知的情况下提出证据

在卡汤加等人案中，该案的审判分庭同样允许被害人根据《规约》第 69 条第 3 款的规定，向审判分庭申请提出证据，[⑤] 但被告认为，该裁决隐含被害人法律代理人可以在审判开始前未预先通知的情况下，提出证据并传唤被害人就被告人的犯罪作证，包括提出有罪证据和证言，被告认为该裁决犯了法律错误。[⑥] 理由是：按照《规约》第 67 条第 1 款第 2 项，被告

---

① ICC, Prosecutor v. Lubanga, ICC - 01/04 - 01/06 - 1432 - tCMN, paras. 4, 104.

② ICC, Prosecutor v. Bemba, "Corrigendum to Decision on the Participation of Victims in the Trial and on 86 Applications by Victims to Participate in the Proceedings", ICC - 01/05 - 01/08 - 807 - Corr, 12 July 2010, para. 32.

③ ICC, The Prosecutor v. Germain Katanga and Mathieu Ngudjolo Chui, ICC - 01/04 - 01/07 - 1788 - tENG, paras. 98 - 101, 104.

④ ICC, The Prosecutor v. Abdallah Banda Abakaer Nourain, "Decision on the Participation of Victims in the Trial Proceedings", ICC - 02/05 - 03/09 - 545, paras. 28 - 30.

⑤ ICC, The Prosecutor v. Germain Katanga and Mathieu Ngudjolo Chui, ICC - 01/04 - 01/07 - 2288, 16 July 2010, para. 18.

⑥ ICC, The Prosecutor v. Germain Katanga and Mathieu Ngudjolo Chui, ICC - 01/04 - 01/07 - 2288, para. 17.

人享有充分的时间和便利以准备答辩的权利；根据《规约》第 64 条第 3 款第 3 项的规定，必须在审判开始前提前足够的时间披露以前未披露的任何信息；《规则》第 76 条第 1 款和第 2 款以及第 77 条规定，检察官应在审判开始前披露检察官掌握的控方证人姓名、证词及材料。对被告人的整个案件，包括支持案件的证据都必须在审判前明确告知，以便被告人能够充分准备并对抗该等证据。审判分庭既然允许被害人提出被告人有罪的证据，就应该确定被告人也有在审判开始前告知被告人这些证据的义务，除非在审判的后期阶段，可以允许提出未在审判前披露的新证据，前提是“审判分庭已竭尽全力，确保在审判前告知和披露了所有证据”。①

被害人和检察官有如下几点共识：第一，被害人在诉讼程序中的地位不同于当事人，因此在收集、提交和披露证据方面具有不同的权利和义务；第二，被害人提交任何证据的前提是，审判分庭行使其《规约》第 69 条第 3 款规定的权力；第三，由于是审判分庭传唤被害人提出证据，因此不能有在审判前披露所有证据的绝对要求。②

检察官指出，如果按照被告人所主张的所有证据都必须在审判前披露，审判分庭将无法行使《规约》第 69 条第 3 款规定的权力。这违反了其他法庭的惯例，对保护被告人的公平审判也是不必要的，而且还可能阻挠审判分庭查明真相。检察官认为，在遇到提交补充证据的申请时，审判分庭都可以决定采取必要措施，例如：排除证据；在权衡证据的重要性和其披露的时间后采信证据；决定证据是否“是查明真相所必需的”；以及拒绝在判决中考虑该证据，以确保被告人的公平审判权利。③

被害人认为，他们要提出证据需通过审判分庭的准许，审判分庭不会允许被害人提出的证据超越对被告人的已有指控范围。而且在审判分庭决定传唤证人时，都不要求必须在审判开始前，而是要求必须在证人作证前

① ICC, The Prosecutor v. Germain Katanga and Mathieu Ngudjolo Chui, ICC－01/04－01/07－2288, paras. 20－26.

② ICC, The Prosecutor v. Germain Katanga and Mathieu Ngudjolo Chui, ICC－01/04－01/07－2288, para. 35.

③ ICC, The Prosecutor v. Germain Katanga and Mathieu Ngudjolo Chui, ICC－01/04－01/07－2288, paras. 27－29.

提前足够的时间披露证词。[①]

实际上，根据国际刑事法院的要求，原则上，检察官应当在审判开始前披露。[②]《规约》第 61 条第 3 款和《规则》第 121 条第 3 款和第 5 款均规定，检察官必须在确认指控听讯前，披露拟在该听讯中使用的所有证据。根据《规约》第 64 条第 3 款第 3 项，在确认指控听讯后，审判分庭应“指令在审判开始以前及早披露此前未曾披露的文件或资料，以便可以为审判作出充分的准备”。《规约》、《规则》和《法院条例》也强调，分庭有责任确保检察官在审判开始前披露案件预审阶段未披露的任何证据。

如前所述，审判分庭可以依《规约》第 69 条第 3 款规定的权力要求被害人提交证据，属于审判分庭行使其授权要求提交“其认为必要的证据以查明真相”的制度范畴。由于审判分庭可能无法在审判之前知道哪些证据是查明真相所必需的，也无法预先知道被害人的个人利益是否受到影响，因此审判分庭有权命令在审判过程中出示该等证据。[③]

在某些情况下，审判分庭要求提交的证据可能无法在审判开始前通知被告人。正如检察官所主张的，坚持在审判开始前通知被告人，会导致审判分庭无法在听取当事方提交的证据之后判断需要什么来查明真相。因此，适用于检察官应在审判开始前披露证据的要求，不适用于应审判分庭要求根据《规约》第 69 条第 3 款提交的证据。[④]

卡汤加也承认，在某些情况下可以在审判中提交未在审判开始前披露的证据，但只有在例外情况下才可以允许在审判的后期阶段提交新证据。上诉分庭对此不予认同，因为《规约》第 69 条第 3 款和第 64 条第 6 款第 4 项的文本规定，“命令出示当事方在审判前已经收集和在审判期间提交的证据以外的证据”是法院的权力，[⑤] 不是例外。

---

① ICC, The Prosecutor v. Germain Katanga and Mathieu Ngudjolo Chui, ICC – 01/04 – 01/07 – 2288, paras. 31, 32.

② ICC, The Prosecutor v. Germain Katanga and Mathieu Ngudjolo Chui, ICC – 01/04 – 01/07 – 2288, para. 43.

③ ICC, The Prosecutor v. Germain Katanga and Mathieu Ngudjolo Chui, ICC – 01/04 – 01/07 – 2288, para. 44.

④ ICC, The Prosecutor v. Germain Katanga and Mathieu Ngudjolo Chui, ICC – 01/04 – 01/07 – 2288, para. 45.

⑤ ICC, The Prosecutor v. Germain Katanga and Mathieu Ngudjolo Chui, ICC – 01/04 – 01/07 – 2288, paras. 46, 47.

关于在审判中提出的所有证据是否必须在审判开始前向被告人披露，辩方称，允许在审判中提交未曾在审判开始以前向被告人披露的证据将侵犯被告人受到公平审判的权利，特别是“有充分时间和便利准备答辩”的权利。该案的上诉分庭认为，公平审判的概念意味着原则上审判的各当事方应有机会了解并评论提出的所有证据和意见以影响法庭的裁决，以及被告人必须能够充分查阅证据材料，以便他们能够对面临的指控进行有效辩护。国际性人权法院的实践没有显示，在审判开始后披露证据本身会导致侵犯被告人的人权。此外，法庭已有的披露审判分庭所要求证据的制度，为审判分庭确保被告人受到公平审判的权利得到尊重提供了充分的保障。在这种情况下，审判分庭将命令在审判中呈交证据前向被告人充分披露该证据，并采取其他必要的措施，确保被告人受到公平审判的权利，特别是“有充分时间和便利准备答辩”的权利。①

（2）被害人没有义务披露其持有的有罪和无罪的信息

在卡汤加案中，辩方主张被害人有义务披露其持有的有罪和无罪的信息，审判分庭认为《规约》和《规则》都没有对被害人施加这种义务，因为被害人参与诉讼是以预先批准为条件的，因此被害人没有理由承担一般义务，向当事方披露其掌握的有罪证据或无罪证据。卡汤加则认为，被害人起码有向被告人披露可证明无罪材料的义务，这是对被告人在犯罪中所起作用提供证词的必要条件。而且，对被害人施加一般披露义务，可以避免因在诉讼程序的后期阶段发现被害人掌握的无罪证据而需要重审的情况，有助于诉讼的从速进行。卡汤加因而向上诉分庭提起上诉。②

检察官认为，对被害人施加一般披露义务是没有依据的，对被害人不应施加这种义务。首先，《规约》和《规则》中的信息披露制度是为了“确保检察官在调查中的客观性原则在审判阶段产生有意义的效果”。既然被害人没有义务平等地调查有罪和无罪情形，也就没有必要对他们施加《规约》第54条对检察官施加的义务，即一般披露义务。其次，被害人缺乏评估向被告人披露信息可能带来的危险所需要的专业知识和资源，对被害人施加

① ICC, The Prosecutor v. Germain Katanga and Mathieu Ngudjolo Chui, ICC - 01/04 - 01/07 - 2288, paras. 50 - 52, 55.

② ICC, The Prosecutor v. Germain Katanga and Mathieu Ngudjolo Chui, ICC - 01/04 - 01/07 - 2288, paras. 58 - 61.

披露义务会导致对第三方的风险。最后，检察官质疑披露制度对被害人的可执行性，由于《规约》未曾预设对该义务违反的救济，违反有可能给诉讼程序带来深远的影响。[①]

被害人主张，《规约》和《规则》明文规定，披露义务仅针对当事方而不是针对被害人的。检察官之所以承担一系列披露义务，包括披露无罪证据的义务，是由于检察官在审判程序中的作用。被害人在诉讼程序中的作用有限，他们在审判中不完全等同于当事方，因而，对他们施加的义务也不可能等同于对检察官施加的义务。“既然没有授予他们必要的手段来支持对被告人的归罪，那么期望他们提出无罪材料就是不合逻辑的。”[②] 但是，卡汤加认为，由于在本案中被害人在提交和检查有罪证据方面发挥了一定的作用，他们没有披露义务显然是不公平的。[③]

上诉分庭支持了检察官和被害人的论点，[④] 并指出，根据《规约》第54条第1款第1项，检察官有责任平等地调查无罪和有罪情形。根据《规约》第54条第3款第2项，检察官可在调查中要求被调查人员、被害人和证人到场接受质询。所以，若被害人要求参与诉讼程序申请中的材料表明被害人可能持有无罪信息，检察官的调查理应扩展到发掘被害人掌握的该等信息。然后根据《规约》第67条第2款和《规则》第77条向被告人披露该等信息。因而不会影响被告人受公平审判的权利。[⑤]

至于被告人所称，如果允许被害人向分庭提交有罪证据，就应当要求他们披露将影响他们拟提证据的可信度或可靠性的任何信息。上诉分庭亦没有采信该论点，因为，审判分庭将仅允许“在被害人的介入对查明真相有适当帮助且不影响本法院诉讼程序的公平公正原则的情况下”提交证据。被害人的法律代理人受《律师职业行为准则》（以下简称《准则》）的约束，根据

① ICC, The Prosecutor v. Germain Katanga and Mathieu Ngudjolo Chui, ICC – 01/04 – 01/07 – 2288, paras. 63 – 65.

② ICC, The Prosecutor v. Germain Katanga and Mathieu Ngudjolo Chui, ICC – 01/04 – 01/07 – 2288, paras. 66 – 69.

③ ICC, The Prosecutor v. Germain Katanga and Mathieu Ngudjolo Chui, ICC – 01/04 – 01/07 – 2288, para. 70.

④ ICC, The Prosecutor v. Germain Katanga and Mathieu Ngudjolo Chui, ICC – 01/04 – 01/07 – 2288, paras. 72 – 77.

⑤ ICC, The Prosecutor v. Germain Katanga and Mathieu Ngudjolo Chui, ICC – 01/04 – 01/07 – 2288, para. 81.

该《准则》第24条第1款和第3款，代理人应采取一切必要措施确保其行为不危害正在进行的诉讼程序，并且不得蓄意误导法庭。所以，审判分庭不必对被害人施加一般披露义务以确保自己不会受到根据其要求提交的证据的误导。①

对于卡汤加强调的，如果允许被害人向审判分庭提交有罪证据，就必须要求他们披露其掌握的任何无罪证据，上诉分庭认为也无此必要，因为审判分庭在此方面有自由裁量权。它有权要求提交审判分庭认为是查明真相所必需的所有证据，可以要求被害人提交有罪证据，也可以要求被害人提交其掌握的无罪证据。在批准了提交证据的请求情况下，审判分庭还有权采取任何必要措施以确保被告人受到公平审判的权利。②

因此，上诉分庭支持审判分庭的裁定：没有理由对被害人施加披露其持有的所有有罪或无罪证据的一般义务。同时，上诉分庭认定，虽然不是必须对被害人施加一般义务，但在某些特殊情况下，例如，某当事方或诉讼参与人提请审判分庭注意存在该等信息，审判分庭认为该等信息是查明真相所必需的，审判分庭可以要求被害人向被告人披露其掌握的无罪证据。③

被害人没有披露无罪信息的一般义务也得到其他审判分庭的遵从。④

3. 在审判过程中提出部分有关赔偿的证据

一般，只有在被告被定罪后才进入赔偿程序，因此，在审判阶段，法庭主要审查的是被告是否有罪的证据。但是，关于在审判过程中是否可以提出部分有关赔偿的证据，按照《条例》第56条，审判分庭可以在审判的同时，询问证人和审查为作出赔偿裁决的证据。卢班加案的检方提出，审判时完全可以提出被告人有罪或无罪的证据和有关赔偿的证据。但是审判分庭不同意这样做，因为关于赔偿的有些方面的证据作为审判过程的一部分予以考虑是不合适的、不公平的或低效率的。在审判中提出有关赔偿

① ICC, The Prosecutor v. Germain Katanga and Mathieu Ngudjolo Chui, ICC - 01/04 - 01/07 - 2288, para. 83.

② ICC, The Prosecutor v. Germain Katanga and Mathieu Ngudjolo Chui, ICC - 01/04 - 01/07 - 2288, paras. 84 - 86.

③ ICC, The Prosecutor v. Germain Katanga and Mathieu Ngudjolo Chui, ICC - 01/04 - 01/07 - 2288, para. 71.

④ ICC, The Prosecutor v. Abdallah Banda Abakaer Nourain, "Decision on the Participation of Victims in the Trial Proceedings", ICC - 02/05 - 03/09 - 545, para. 40.

的证据是允许的，如果是为了个别证人或被害人的利益，或者它将有助于对可能出现的问题进行有效处理。然而，分庭强调，在任何时候都要确保这个过程不涉及对被告人有罪或无罪问题的任何预判。这一规定的目的是使分庭能够在整个诉讼过程的不同阶段考虑证据，以确保审判迅速有效的进行。如果在审判过程中出现提出的有关赔偿的证据可能对确定指控是可采信和有关的，分庭就需要考虑对被告人无罪或有罪作决定时考虑这一证据是否公平。当然，如果被告被判有罪，分庭并无困难将涉及指控的证据与仅仅涉及赔偿的证据分开，并将后者留到赔偿诉讼阶段，因此，分庭认为，《条例》第56条的规定并不损害被告人的权利和无罪推定。而且，这样也能够避免证人为再次作证而往来法院，以及由此带来的不必要困难或不公，还能保证分庭保全在诉讼的稍后阶段可能无法得到的证据。[①]

4. 被害人法律代理人传唤被害人或其他人作证

被害人可以亲自或通过代理人的方式提出其意见和关注，被害人宣誓作证可能有助于法庭对真相的确定，也是表示其意见的一种方式。被害人宣誓作证就使其成为一个具有被害人和证人双重地位的人。实际上，有两种方式会出现双重地位的人：（1）被害人被一方传唤为证人；（2）分庭经被害人法律代理人的要求或主动根据《规约》第69条第3款传唤被害人为证人。[②]

（1）被害人被一当事方传唤为证人

无论《规约》还是《规则》都没有禁止准许一个已经有检方或辩方证人地位的人同时有被害人的地位。同样，《规则》第85条也没有禁止一个已被赋予被害人地位的人随后为任一当事方提供证据。[③] 因此被害人可以被当事一方传唤为证人。然而，卡汤加的辩护律师提出，已经被分庭授权参加诉讼的一名被害人又被检方传唤作证，他可能需要调整其陈述的事实使其与检察官的意见兼容。这种风险主要来自他们被允许查阅检察官办公室记录中的文件和证据。[④] 审判分庭认为，在该案中，只有非匿名被害人

① ICC, Prosecutor v. Lubanga, ICC –01/04 –01/06 –1119, paras. 120 – 122.

② ICC, The Prosecutor v. Abdallah Banda Abakaer Nourain, "Decision on the Participation of Victims in the Trial Proceedings", ICC –02/05 –03/09 –545, para. 22.

③ ICC, The Prosecutor v. Germain Katanga and Mathieu Ngudjolo Chui, ICC –01/04 –01/07 –1788 –tENG, para. 110.

④ ICC, The Prosecutor v. Germain Katanga and Mathieu Ngudjolo Chui, ICC –01/04 –01/07 –1788 –tENG, para. 109.

的法律代理人才有查阅该案记录的机密部分和参加不公开的听讯的权利，非匿名的被害人无权查阅案件记录的机密部分和参加不公开的听讯，而且分庭禁止非匿名被害人的法律代理人将该案记录的保密部分所含有的文件或证据的副本以及不公开听讯的记录发送给其被代理人。[①] 虽然允许被害人的法律代理人有可能与其被代理人商量案件记录中的某些方面，那主要是为了保护证人的安全。而且，在与他们代理的被害人商量时，律师必须受《准则》的约束，必须确保不将影响或促使被害人改变他们的陈述的机密信息传递给证人。[②] 该案的检察官把被害人安排在最后出庭，其他检方证人在他之前可能已对同一问题作了证，这样就减少了他的证词的影响。[③] 分庭以此打消被告人的顾虑。

（2）被害人法律代理人或审判分庭传唤被害人宣誓作证

卢班加案和卡汤加案的审判分庭都允许法律代理人有机会传唤一个或多个被害人在审判时宣誓作证。[④] 分庭认为，如果排除高度相关和有证明力的证人证言的唯一理由是他们也是被授权参与诉讼的被害人，这将有悖分庭确立真相的义务。实际上，被害人宣誓作证本身就赋予了其证人的地位，可以受辩护方的盘问，如果他提供虚假证词，就要按照《规约》第 70 条第 1 款第 1 项对检方承担责任。[⑤]

听取法律代理人传唤的被害人作证的最合适时机是在检方出示证据后马上进行。[⑥] 因为在所有的证人和被害人提供了关于被告被指控的罪行以

---

① ICC, The Prosecutor v. Germain Katanga and Mathieu Ngudjolo Chui, ICC - 01/04 - 01/07 - 1788 - tENG, para. 111.

② ICC, The Prosecutor v. Germain Katanga and Mathieu Ngudjolo Chui, ICC - 01/04 - 01/07 - 1788 - tENG, para. 113.

③ ICC, The Prosecutor v. Germain Katanga and Mathieu Ngudjolo Chui, ICC - 01/04 - 01/07 - 1788 - tENG, para. 115.

④ ICC, The Prosecutor v. Germain Katanga and Mathieu Ngudjolo Chui, ICC - 01/04 - 01/07 - 1788 - tENG, para. 86; ICC, Prosecutor v. Lubanga, ICC - 01/04 - 01/06 - 1119, paras. 132 - 134.

⑤ ICC, The Prosecutor v. Germain Katanga and Mathieu Ngudjolo Chui, ICC - 01/04 - 01/07 - 1788 - tENG, para. 88.

⑥ ICC, Prosecutor v. Lubanga, "Order Issuing Public Redacted Version of the Decision on the Request by Victims a/ 0225/06, a/0229/06 and a/0270/07 to Express Their Views and Concerns in Person and to Present Evidence During the Trial", ICC - 01/04 - 01/06 - 2032, 9 July 2009, para. 1; ICC, The Prosecutor v. Germain Katanga and Mathieu Ngudjolo Chui, ICC - 01/04 - 01/07 - 1788 - tENG, para. 88.

及被告在犯罪中发挥的作用的证据后，辩方应有机会对这些证据作出回应。如果对被害人证词的可靠性有潜在的怀疑，分庭可以决定不授权被害人宣誓作证。[①]

卡汤加案的审判分庭曾裁定，可以允许诉讼代理人传唤一位或多位被害人就被告人在被指控犯罪中的作用等问题作证。[②] 卡汤加则认为，若允许被害人作证，也必须排除被害人提出的关于被告人行为和有罪行为的证据，否则，他们的参与将妨碍公平审判。[③]

检察官认为，关于被告人罪行的一般证据与特别涉及被告人行为的证据之间没有截然的区别。审判分庭可以命令被害人提交其他证据，只要该等证据不仅具有证明力和相关性，而且是“查明真相所必需的”，并且被害人提出的证据涉及他们的个人利益。由于被告人在被控犯罪中的作用是许多审判中争论的关键问题，审判分庭可考虑需要额外证据以查明真相。[④]

被害人同样强调，他们通过提供关于被告人行为的信息参与审判，这些信息是查明真相所必需的。审判分庭已经制定了一套制度，为诉讼程序的公正性提供了所有必要的保障，并且符合被告人的权利。卡汤加提出被害人不能就被告人的作用作证，是企图使被害人参与审判失去意义。[⑤]

上诉分庭支持检察官和被害人的意见，并认为被害人可以就包括被告人在其被控犯罪中的作用在内的事宜作证，其依据是《规约》第 69 条第 3 款规定的审判分庭拥有要求提供必要证据以查明真相的权力。被告人在被控犯罪中的作用是一个关键问题，它必须由审判分庭在审判结束时裁定。因此，与被告人的作用有关的证据原则上可能属于审判分庭认为是查明真相所必需的证据的范围。《规约》和《规则》中没有任何条款限制只有检察官才能提交与被告人行为有关的证据，也没有理由区别被害人可以提交

① ICC, The Prosecutor v. Germain Katanga and Mathieu Ngudjolo Chui, ICC – 01/04 – 01/07 – 1788 – tENG, paras. 88 – 91.

② ICC, The Prosecutor v. Germain Katanga and Mathieu Ngudjolo Chui, ICC – 01/04 – 01/07 – 1788 – tENG, para. 86.

③ ICC, Prosecutor v. Katanga and Ngudjolo, ICC – 01/04 – 01/07 – 2288 – tCMN, paras. 92 – 97.

④ ICC, Prosecutor v. Katanga and Ngudjolo, ICC – 01/04 – 01/07 – 2288 – tCMN, paras. 98 – 101.

⑤ ICC, Prosecutor v. Katanga and Ngudjolo, ICC – 01/04 – 01/07 – 2288 – tCMN, paras. 103 – 107.

的不同类别证据。所以，要求被害人就被告人在被控犯罪中的作用作证，不会让他们成为“案件中的补充检察官”。其本身并不违反被告人的权利和公平审判的理念。当然，审判分庭必须根据具体情况，逐案确保被告人受到公平审判的权利得到尊重。被害人就涉及被告人行为的事宜作证必须是影响被害人的个人利益，涉及案件的相关问题，有助于查明真相，以及符合被告人的权利，特别是有充分时间和便利准备辩护的权利以及受到公平公正审判的权利。[①]

（3）传唤其他的证人

如果其他证人可以提供有关影响被害人的利益问题的相关信息，法律代理人可以提请分庭注意，传唤他们作证。虽然这不能成为被害人参与审判的一项权利，但不能排除这种可能性。一旦辩方出示完他们的证据，当分庭准备考虑额外的证据或听取当事方传唤以外的证人时，被害人的法律代理人就有这样做的可能。[②] 如果经法律代理人要求分庭传唤了一名证人，分庭可以授权法律代理人在分庭询问前或后向证人提问。[③]

在国际刑事法院审判中传唤证人、出示证据的顺序是：第一阶段由检察官办公室出示对被告的证据，这个阶段结束后，被害人若有此愿望，可以请求法庭允许出庭作证。第二阶段是被告提出辩护。第二阶段结束时，分庭可以决定进一步传唤证人，包括被害人的法律代理人建议的证人。只有出示完所有这些证据后，分庭对这些证人的利益和相关性有了充分了解，才能对所出示的证据和意见进行评估。[④]

（四）匿名被害人的诉讼权利

被害人出于自身或家属的安全，在参与诉讼中不愿意透露其姓名，被分庭允许匿名参与，成为匿名的被害人。在卢班加案中，有 3 名被害人一

---

① ICC，Prosecutor v. Katanga and Ngudjolo，ICC－01/04－01/07－2288－tCMN，paras. 110－115.

② ICC，The Prosecutor v. Germain Katanga and Mathieu Ngudjolo Chui，ICC－01/04－01/07－1788－tENG，para. 94.

③ ICC，The Prosecutor v. Germain Katanga and Mathieu Ngudjolo Chui，ICC－01/04－01/07－1788－tENG，para. 97.

④ ICC，The Prosecutor v. Germain Katanga and Mathieu Ngudjolo Chui，ICC－01/04－01/07－1788－tENG，para. 95.

直坚持在确认指控前和确认指控中为其姓名保密。预审分庭考虑到 3 名被害人非常脆弱，生活在一个危险地区，刚果（金）的安全形势在恶化，影响了对被害人能够采取的保护措施的实施，认为给予他们匿名是当时对他们可执行的保护。只有保持他们匿名，他们才能有效参与确认指控的听讯。① 在卡汤加案中，预审分庭的法官基于卢班加案预审分庭同样的考虑，准许他们匿名参与预审阶段的程序。② 参加诉讼的匿名被害人会被分配一个号码，在法庭上和在有关文件中都只能称呼或显示他们的号码。

关于匿名被害人参与预审阶段的诉讼权利，两案的分庭都指出：被准许匿名的被害人不能增加任何事实或证据，他们也不能依《规则》第 91 条第 3 款规定的程序对证人提问。③ 如果允许他们那样做，就违反了不得匿名指控的基本原则。④ 匿名被害人被给予的诉讼权利有：（1）通知有关案件记录中所含的公开文件；（2）出席公开举行的情况会商，或部分情况会商；（3）出席公开的确认指控听讯；（4）在确认指控的听证会上作开庭和终结陈述。卡汤加案允许匿名被害人的法律代理人在作陈述时，也可以谈法律问题，包括在检方指控文件中包含的责任模式的法律特性；（5）若在情况会商时和在确认指控的公开听证会上要求表态，分庭将根据个案情况作出决定。⑤ 这些权利并非必定是全部的，两案的分庭都指出，这套诉讼权利在例外情况下可以扩大。⑥

关于被害人匿名参加审判的问题最早出现在卢班加案中。被害人公共

---

① ICC, Prosecutor v. Lubanga, "Decision on the Arrangements for Participation of Victims a001/06, a002/06 and a003/06 at the Confirmation Hearing", ICC - 01/04 - 01/06 - 462 - tEN, 22 September 2006, p. 6.

② ICC, Prosecutor v. Germain Katanga and Mathieu Ngudjolo Chui, "Decision on Victims' Requests for Anonymity at the Pre-Trial Stage of the Case", ICC - 01/04 - 01/07 - 628, 23 June 2008, p. 9.

③ ICC, Prosecutor v. Lubanga, ICC - 01/04 - 01/06 - 462 - tEN, p. 8; ICC, Prosecutor v. Germain Katanga and Mathieu Ngudjolo Chui, ICC - 01/04 - 01/07 - 628, p. 9; The Prosecutor v. Germain Katanga and Mathieu Ngudjolo Chui, ICC - 01/04 - 01/07 - 474, paras. 181, 182.

④ ICC, Prosecutor v. Lubanga, ICC - 01/04 - 01/06 - 462 - tEN, p. 7.

⑤ ICC, Prosecutor v. Lubanga, ICC - 01/04 - 01/06 - 462 - tEN, p. 8; ICC, Prosecutor v. Germain Katanga and Mathieu Ngudjolo Chui, ICC - 01/04 - 01/07 - 628, p. 9; The Prosecutor v. Germain Katanga and Mathieu Ngudjolo Chui, ICC - 01/04 - 01/07 - 474, para. 184.

⑥ ICC, Prosecutor v. Lubanga, ICC - 01/04 - 01/06 - 462 - tEN, p. 7; ICC, Prosecutor v. Germain Katanga and Mathieu Ngudjolo Chui, ICC - 01/04 - 01/07 - 628, p. 9.

律师办公室主张，被害人的参与不应有赖于他们身份的公开，因为《罗马规约》框架中含有匿名的条款（《规则》第81条和第87条）。此外，欧洲人权法院曾决定，在刑事诉讼中允许使用匿名证人，但受一些条件限制，最主要的是在被告人的权利和被传唤作证的证人或被害人之间的权利作出适当的平衡。然而，欧洲人权法院的有罪判决可能不完全根据匿名证人的证据。被害人公共律师办公室认为，基于有关证人的判例法，被害人匿名参加审判符合公平审判的要求，只要分庭采取充分的平衡措施。[①] 但是，检方和辩方均反对在审判期间被害人可以对被告人保持匿名。[②]

审判分庭驳回了当事方不允许匿名的被害人参加诉讼的意见，因为这些被害人特别脆弱，他们生活的地区正在发生冲突，难以保证他们的安全。然而，审判分庭认为，允许匿名被害人参加诉讼必须极为谨慎地对待被告人的权利。保护被害人的安全是法院的一项核心责任，但不能允许他们的参与破坏对公平审判的根本保证。审判分庭认为，被害人的身份最好向当事方透露，而且拟议参与的程度和重要性越大，分庭就越可能要求被害人表明自己的身份。[③]

在卡汤加案中，第二审判分庭不排除匿名被害人参与诉讼的可能性。但是，分庭强调，它不会授权希望对辩方保持匿名的任何被害人作证。如果他们被传出庭作证，他们必须放弃匿名。[④] 在本巴案中，除非分庭另有命令，第三审判分庭比照适用第一审判分庭和第二审判分庭采取的方法。[⑤]

结　论

《罗马规约》允许被害人参加诉讼程序。在法院的实践中，绝大多数被害人是通过代理律师参与诉讼的，只有少数个别的被害人可以亲自到法庭参与诉讼。不同的分庭对不同的案件采取了为被害人指派代理人的一些

---

① ICC, Prosecutor v. Lubanga, ICC－01/04－01/06－1119, para. 75.

② ICC, Prosecutor v. Lubanga, ICC－01/04－01/06－1119, para. 130.

③ ICC, Prosecutor v. Lubanga, ICC－01/04－01/06－1119, paras. 130, 131.

④ ICC, The Prosecutor v. Germain Katanga and Mathieu Ngudjolo Chui, ICC－01/04－01/07－1788－tENG, paras. 92, 93.

⑤ ICC, Prosecutor v. Bemba, ICC－01/05－01/08－807－Corr, para. 69.

不同做法。法院今后在为被害人指定律师时，应更注重被害人自由选择其法律代理人的权利，应充分征求被害人的意见，并应在被害人表达其观点和诉讼效率之间作出平衡。

《罗马规约》和《规则》没有规定被害人参加诉讼的具体方式，各分庭通过对各案的裁定，规定了被害人在参加诉讼的不同阶段享有的诉讼权利，它们除了些许差异外，基本是一致的，使得被害人在分庭的控制下有意义地参加诉讼，有助于法庭公正审判程序的进行。此外，分庭也通过判例，解决了对被害人参加诉讼的一些争议，澄清了被害人参加诉讼的一些理论问题，是对国际刑事司法的重要发展。

（责任编辑：何田田）

（本文原载于《国际法研究》2017 年第 4 期）

国家官员外国刑事管辖豁免问题最新进展述评*

邓　华**

一　引言

国家官员的外国刑事管辖豁免（Immunity of State Officials from Foreign Criminal Jurisdiction，下文简称“官员豁免”）是指一国特定官员在外国享有不受当地刑事管辖的外交特权。它不仅关涉国家官员能否顺利履行职责，而且关系到国家间的友好关系以及国际关系之稳定。在传统上，国家官员在外国法院享有刑事管辖豁免特权；但是，最近有一种呼声日益凸显，即对犯有严重国际罪行的国家官员，国际法应当剥夺其豁免权。这就使得“官员豁免”问题随之变得愈加复杂和敏感，国家间关于这一问题的争论也日益激烈。2007 年，在联合国国际法委员会（United Nations International Law Commission，下文简称“委员会”）第 59 届会议上，“官员豁免”问题被列入其工作方案，① 委员会也为这一专题任命了第一位特别报告员（Special Rapporteur）。此后，在两任特别报告员罗曼·阿纳托列维奇·科洛德金（Roman Anatolevich Kolodkin）先生和康塞普西翁·埃斯科瓦尔·埃

* 本文为“中国人民大学 2015 年度拔尖创新人才培育资助计划成果”。

** 邓华，中国社会科学院法学研究所博士后研究人员，原文发表时作者为中国人民大学法学院国际法学专业博士研究生。

① 联合国大会：《国际法委员会报告（第 59 届会议）》，A/60/10（2007），第 376 段。

尔南德斯（Concepción Escobar Hernández）女士[①]相继提交的7份报告[②]的基础上，委员会就有关官员豁免问题的起源、渊源、范围、例外和程序等进行了热烈的讨论。这一讨论一直持续至今，有关该专题的条款草案（draft article）也在陆续产生，迄今共有6项条款草案暂时得以通过。[③]

二 “官员豁免”问题之现状：渊源和判例

（一）法律渊源

在国际交往的实践中，一国通常会给予某些外国官员以刑事管辖豁免，使其免受外国的刑事管辖。尽管1961年《维也纳外交关系公约》、1963年《维也纳领事关系公约》、1969年《联合国特别使团公约》对外交代表、领事官员以及特别使团成员的特权与豁免作出了规定，但是上述条

① 科洛德金先生一共提交了3份报告。2012年，委员会第64届会议任命埃尔南德斯女士代替科洛德金先生担任特别报告员，科洛德金先生不再担任委员会委员。截至2015年第67届会议，埃尔南德斯女士一共提交了4份报告。

② 联合国大会：《国际法委员会（第60届会议）关于国家官员的外国刑事管辖豁免的初步报告（报告员：罗曼·阿纳托列维奇·科洛德金）》，A/CN. 4/601（2008）；联合国大会：《国际法委员会（第62届会议）关于国家官员的外国刑事管辖豁免的第二次报告（报告员：罗曼·阿纳托列维奇·科洛德金）》，A/CN. 4/631（2010）；联合国大会：《国际法委员会（第63届会议）关于国家官员的外国刑事管辖豁免的第三次报告（报告员：罗曼·阿纳托列维奇·科洛德金）》，A/CN. 4/646（2011）；联合国大会：《国际法委员会（第64届会议）国家官员的外国刑事管辖豁免的初步报告（报告员：康塞普西翁·埃斯科瓦尔·埃尔南德斯）》，A/CN. 4/654（2012）；联合国大会：《国际法委员会（第65届会议）国家官员的外国刑事管辖豁免的第二次报告（报告员：康塞普西翁·埃斯科瓦尔·埃尔南德斯）》，A/CN. 4/661（2013）；联合国大会：《国际法委员会（第66届会议）国家官员的外国刑事管辖豁免的第三次报告（报告员：康塞普西翁·埃斯科瓦尔·埃尔南德斯）》，A/CN. 4/673（2014）；联合国大会：《国际法委员会（第67届会议）国家官员的外国刑事管辖豁免的第四次报告（报告员：康塞普西翁·埃斯科瓦尔·埃尔南德斯）》，A/CN. 4/686（2015）。

③ 联合国大会：《国际法委员会（第65届会议）国家官员的外国刑事管辖豁免：起草委员会在国际法委员会第65届会议期间暂时通过的第1、第3和第4条草案条文》，A/CN. 4/L. 814（2013）；联合国大会：《国际法委员会（第66届会议）国家官员的外国刑事管辖豁免：起草委员会2014年7月15日暂时通过的第2条（e）项和第5条草案的案文》，A/CN. 4/L. 850（2014）；联合国大会：《国际法委员会（第67届会议）国家官员的外国刑事管辖豁免：起草委员会在第67届会议上暂时通过的条款草案案文》，A/CN. 4/L. 865（2015）。

约并没有对国家官员在外国的刑事管辖豁免问题作出一般性规定，也没有对在哪些具体情形之下以及哪一部分官员可以享有豁免作出明确规定。迄今为止，国际社会仍然没有一个普遍性的条约对“官员豁免”问题作出全面性的规定。

总体而言，目前大部分与“官员豁免”问题相关的规则都存在于习惯国际法当中。[①] 国家元首、政府首脑和外交部长——即俗称的“三巨头”（the Troikas）——在任时享有属人豁免（Immunity *Ratione Personnae*），卸任时享有属事豁免（Immunity *Ratione Materiae*），而其他国家官员在他们履行职能时享有属事豁免。属人豁免是一项古老的豁免，是指某类人员因为担任某种较高职位而在任职期间享有豁免，豁免持续时间从担任该职务时起算，至卸任时或卸任后一段合理时间内消失，它来自官员的地位及其在为政府工作时担任的职位，并来自官员在这个职位上需要为国家履行的职能。属事豁免，又被称为职权豁免或职能豁免，传统上是指相关人员在其行使职权的范围内，其行为豁免于刑事、民事或其他性质的诉讼，基于属事豁免的理念，习惯国际法上可以将相关人员的行为区分为“以官方身份从事的行为”（act performed in an official capacity）[②] 和“以私人身份从事的行为”（act performed in a private capacity）两类，即属事豁免仅适用于国

---

① 参见例如 H. Fox，“The Resolution of the Institute of International Law on the Immunities of Heads of State and Government”，*International and Comparative Law Quarterly* 51（2002）：119；H. Fox，*The Law of State Immunity*（Oxford：Oxford University Press，2002），p. 426；A. Watts，“The Legal Position in International Law of Heads of States，Heads of Government and Foreign Ministers”，*Recueil des Cours* 247（1994 – Ⅲ）：36；Y. Simbeye，*Immunity and International Criminal Law*（Surrey：Ashgate，2004），p. 94；M. A. Summers，“Diplomatic Immunity Ratione Personae：Did the International Court of Justice Create a New Customary Rule in Congo v. Belgium?”，*Michigan State Journal of International Law* 16（2007）：466；Malcolm N. Shaw，*International Law*（Cambridge：Cambridge University Press，7th edn.，2014），p. 536。

② 在法律实践和文献中，有许多短语被用来指称官员所从事的可能导致属事豁免的行为，例如“公务行为”、“代表国家的行为”、“以国家名义的行为”、“公行为”、“政府行为”、“国家行为”等，这些短语往往互换使用，并因此被视为同义。当然，应当指出，上述用语在使用中并不总是含义相同。但是，在法律文献中，“以公务身份从事的行为”或“以官方身份从事的行为”（act performed in an official capacity）这一表述似乎是最为常见的用语，同时这也是国际法委员会选择的用语，因此，本文亦统一采用“以官方身份从事的行为”这一表述。参见 A/CN. 4/686，para. 28。

家官员在其任职期间的“以官方身份从事的行为”。[①] 前南斯拉夫国际刑事法庭的上诉庭在“检察官诉蒂霍米尔·布拉什基奇案”的判决中指出，国家官员仅仅是作为国家的工具，因此他们以官方身份从事的行为就只能归责于国家。因为他们的行为并非私人性质，而是代表国家作出的，所以他们不能为此而成为受制裁或刑罚的对象。[②] 也就是说，即使官员代表国家作出了违法行为，这一违法后果也不能由官员自身承担，承担违法后果的主体是国家，而非官员个人。国际法院在“逮捕令案”的判决中就各方援引的文书指出，“这些公约对豁免问题的某些方面提供了有益的指导，但是，其中并未包含任何明确定义外交部长所享有豁免的条文，因此，法院必须根据习惯国际法来裁定本案中提出的关于外交部长豁免的问题”。[③] 而各国法院的司法裁判也承认，“官员豁免”规则的渊源是习惯国际法，如法国最高法院在“卡扎菲案”的裁决中指出，“如果没有对当事方具有约束力的与此相反的国际法规则，按照国际惯例，则不得在外国刑事审判机构对现任国家元首提起诉讼”。[④] 因此，委员会在对此专题进行编纂时认为有足够的依据可以申明：国家官员的外国刑事管辖豁免的来源不是国际礼让，它主要来自国际法，尤其是习惯国际法，习惯法是“这一领域的基本国际法渊源”。[⑤]

然而，以习惯国际法形式存在的“官员豁免问题”，仍然存在许多模糊点，譬如：“三巨头”是否享有绝对的豁免？针对他们上任前的行为是否可以主张豁免？其离任后针对他们在位期间的行为是否还可以主张豁免？除了“三巨头”，还有哪些国家高级官员可以享有豁免，而他们的豁

---

① 参见王秀梅《国家官员的外国刑事管辖豁免探析》，《西安交通大学学报》（社会科学版）2010 年第 4 期。

② *Prosecutor v. Tihomir Blaskic*, ICTY Appeal Chamber Judgment on the Request of the Republic of Croatia for Review of the Decision of Trial Chamber Ⅱof 18 July 1997, 29 October 1997, para. 38, http://www.icty.org/x/cases/blaskic/acdec/en/71029JT3.html，最后访问日期：2016 年 6 月 15 日。

③ *Arrest Warrant of 11 April 2000* (*Democratic Republic of the Congo v. Belgium*), Judgment, I. C. J. Reports 2002, para. 52.

④ “*Gaddafi*, France, Court of Cassation, Criminal Chamber, 13 March 2001”, in *International Law Reports*, Vol. 125 (Cambridge: Cambridge University Press, 2004), p. 509.

⑤ A/CN. 4/601, paras. 30 – 34; A/CN. 4/654, para. 26.

免范围又如何？“以官方身份从事的行为”如何具体界定？等等。[①] 这些问题至今仍存在很多不明朗之处，在各国的司法实践中也不甚统一，更是由于它的高度政治性，当一个内国法院涉及这一规则的适用时，便极有可能引起争议，有些案例已在国际社会上引起了很大的争议。因此，目前我们至多只能认为，国家官员的外国刑事管辖豁免规则作为一个整体以习惯国际法的形式存在，但进一步涉及上述更为详细的规则时，普遍统一的国家实践仍未形成，相关的习惯法规则仍在发展当中。

（二）司法实践

有关“官员豁免”问题最为经典的案例无疑是国际法院的“逮捕令案”。2001 年，比利时布鲁塞尔初审法院的调查法官依据比利时 1993 年《关于惩治严重违反国际人道法罪行的立法》在比利时法院起诉时任刚果民主共和国外交部长耶罗迪亚（Yerodia Ndombasi），理由是他犯有战争罪（war crimes）和危害人类罪（crimes against humanity）。布鲁塞尔初审法院的调查法官依据普遍管辖原则，签发逮捕令，要求逮捕耶罗迪亚；比利时政府通过国际刑警组织将此逮捕令发布到世界各国，在全世界范围内缉拿耶罗迪亚。但是，刚果民主共和国却认为，比利时在 1993 年国内立法的基础上发出的逮捕令违反了国际法上关于国家官员享有外国刑事管辖豁免的规则，并影响了其正常的外交活动，遂把比利时告到了国际法院。[②] 2002 年，国际法院在判决中指出，根据习惯国际法授予一国外交部长刑事管辖豁免是为了保证他在代表其国家时能够有效地履行其职责，而非为了其私人利益；考虑到外交部长在执行一国外交政策方面的重要性，也考虑到一国外交部长的行为会造成对其代表国和他国关系的影响，他所享有的地位与国家元首和政府首脑是相同的；因此，国际法院得出结论，即一国外交部长在任期间，对外国的刑事程序享有完全的豁免权利。[③] 那么，这是否意味着，“三巨头”在任期间的一切行为皆能援引管辖豁免？包括犯有严

① Malcolm N. Shaw, *International Law* (Cambridge: Cambridge University Press, 7th edn., 2014), p. 537.

② 参见朱文奇《现代国际法》，商务印书馆，2013，第 217—219 页；邵沙平主编《国际法院新近案例研究（1990—2003）》，商务印书馆，2006，第 445—474 页。

③ *Arrest Warrant of 11 April 2000 (Democratic Republic of the Congo v. Belgium)*, Judgment, I. C. J. Reports 2002, pp. 3, 20.

重国际刑事罪行的情形？国际法院在此案中给出了肯定的回答。[①] 事实上，当国际法院审理此案时，耶罗迪亚已经从外交部长转任为教育部长，不再属于“三巨头”之列，那此时比利时能否对其进行逮捕起诉？国际法院指出，当其不再担任外交部长的职务时，其他国家的法院可以就其任职前或任职后的行为，以及任职期间的私人行为进行起诉，[②] 这就意味着，对一国外交部长在任职期间的“以官方身份从事的行为”，外国法院无论在任何时候都不能起诉。同样是国际法院的案例，在2008年吉布提诉法国的“刑事事项互助问题案”中，国际法院采取了与在“逮捕令案”中的同一立场，认为属人豁免规则在本质上是绝对的，且没有任何的例外。[③]

著名的1998年“皮诺切特案”[④] 与“逮捕令案”极其相似，争议点都在于卸任的总统或外交部长对其任职期间所犯国际罪行能否享有豁免特权。但在“皮诺切特案”中，英国上议院认为，一国基于严重的国际罪行行使普遍管辖权时，行为人的官方身份也不能成为豁免的理由，遂判定皮诺切特（Augusto Pinochet）不享有豁免特权。[⑤] 2009年9月，英国一些律师代表16名巴勒斯坦人援引普遍管辖权向伦敦威斯敏斯特地区法院起诉时任以色列国防部长巴拉克（Ehud Barak），指控其在2008年12月的加沙冲突中犯下了战争罪，结果法院以巴拉克在职拥有外交豁免权为由予以驳回。[⑥] 2009年12月，英国一家法院受理了加沙地带巴勒斯坦人委托的一名律师的起诉，指控以色列前外交部长利夫尼（Tzipi Livni）犯有战争罪，英国法院签发了逮捕令，决定逮捕利夫尼，该案在英国和以色列之间也引起

---

① *Arrest Warrant of 11 April 2000* (*Democratic Republic of the Congo v. Belgium*), Judgment, I. C. J. Reports 2002, p. 24.

② *Arrest Warrant of 11 April 2000* (*Democratic Republic of the Congo v. Belgium*), Judgment, I. C. J. Reports 2002, pp. 25 - 26. 不过，奥恩·哈苏奈（Al-Khasawneh）法官对此有不同意见，他认为外交部长在任时也只享有有限的豁免特权，即执行职务时享有属事豁免权，参见 the Dissenting Opinion of Judge Al-Khasawneh, pp. 96 - 100.

③ *Case Concerning Certain Questions of Mutual Assistance* (*Djibouti v. France*), Judgment, I. C. J. Reports 2008, paras. 170, 174.

④ 参见周忠海主编《皮诺切特案析》，中国政法大学出版社，1999，第1—2页。

⑤ 参见朱文奇主编《国际法学原理与案例教程》（第三版），中国人民大学出版社，2014，第305页。

⑥《以色列防长访英险遭逮捕 借外交豁免权脱身》，环球网，http://world.huanqiu.com/roll/2009-09/592855.html，最后访问日期：2016年6月19日。

了轩然大波。[①] 可以说，随着国际刑法的发展，一国官员在外国被刑事起诉逐渐成为愈加多见之现象，在此难以逐一列举。尽管国际法院在“逮捕令案”和“刑事事项互助问题案”中都作出了维护传统豁免规则的裁判，但也遭到了极大的批评，被诟病为不利于人权保护，且迄今为止，各个国家的做法并不一致，仍然常常引发争议。而就在2016年6月，赤道几内亚又在国际法院提起诉讼，诉称法国侵犯了其负责国防和国家安全的第二副主席的刑事管辖豁免特权。[②] 关于此案的进一步发展，我们可密切关注，从中考察国际法院在“逮捕令案”和“刑事事项互助问题案”之后就“官员豁免”问题的立场是否会发生变化，以及它对这一问题相关规则又会否作出进一步的澄清和发展。

三 国际法委员会对“官员豁免”问题的编纂和发展

在这样的背景下，委员会在2007年把“官员豁免”问题列入其工作方案是对国际法实践的一种现实的和及时的回应。

（一）专题进展概况

如前所述，第一任特别报告员科洛德金先生一共提交了3份报告，其中确定了这一专题的审议范围，并分析了与“官员豁免”问题有关的实质性和程序性问题的各个方面。[③]

第二任特别报告员埃尔南德斯女士在2012年提交的初步报告实质上是一份“过渡报告”，其中设法帮助澄清了截至当时的辩论情况，并查明了仍然存有争议、委员会今后可以继续研究的要点，此外，该报告还确定了委员会需要审议的问题，建立了研究的方法依据，并阐述了本专题的审议

① 《英国法庭以战争罪向以色列前女外长发出逮捕令》，环球网，http://world.huanqiu.com/roll/2009-12/661015.html，最后访问日期：2016年6月19日。

② 参见 Press Release of the International Court of Justice, “The Republic of Equatorial Guinea Institutes Proceedings against France with Regard to the Immunity from Criminal Jurisdiction of Its Second Vice-President in Charge of Defence and State Security, and the Legal Status of the Building Which Houses its Embassy in France”, June 14, 2016, http://www.icj-cij.org/docket/files/163/19028.pdf，最后访问日期：2016年6月19日。

③ A/CN.4/601, A/CN.4/631, A/CN.4/646.

工作计划。[①]

2013 年，埃尔南德斯女士提交了第二份报告，其中审查了本专题及条款草案的范围、豁免和管辖的概念、属人豁免与属事豁免的区别，以及属人豁免的规范要素，该份报告载有 6 项拟议条款草案，分别述及条款草案的范围与定义，以及属人豁免的规范要素。[②]

2014 年，埃尔南德斯女士提交了第三份报告，其中首先分析了属事豁免的规范要素，特别是与主体要素有关的方面，随后详细审查了“国家官员”的一般概念，列出了在确定此类人员时应予考虑的标准；接着，报告还分析了属事豁免的主体范围，确定了哪些人可享有此类豁免；最后，考虑到在使用“国家官员”一词以及该词在其他语言版本中的对等词方面提出的术语问题，报告审查了最适合用来称呼享有豁免人员的词语，特别报告员提议使用更具普遍意义的“国家机关”一词。在第三份报告中，特别报告员根据对国家和国际司法实践、相关条约以及委员会以往相关工作的分析，列出了 2 项条款草案，分别关于“国家官员”一般概念和属事豁免的主体范围。[③]

2015 年，埃尔南德斯女士在其第四份报告中处理属事豁免的规范性要素时，首先强调了这类豁免的基本特性，即豁免是给予所有国家官员的，仅适用于“以官方身份实施的行为”，不受时间限制；至于属事豁免的规范性要素，如上所述，第三份报告已经处理了主体范围的问题，第四份报告侧重于实质和时间范围，[④] 重点提出了识别“以官方身份实施的行为”的标准，在相继分析了国际和国家司法实践、条约实践和委员会以往工作的基础上，特别报告员接着审视了由此得出的就外国刑事管辖豁免而言“以官方身份实施的行为”具有的三个特征，即行为的犯罪性质（criminal nature of the act）、行为归于国家（attribution of the act to the State）以及行使主权和实施行为过程中的政府权力要素（sovereignty and exercise of elements of the governmental authority）。[⑤]

---

① A/CN. 4/654.

② A/CN. 4/661.

③ A/CN. 4/673.

④ 联合国大会：《国际法委员会报告（第 67 届会议）》，A/70/10（2015），第 179 段。

⑤ A/CN. 4/686.

按照工作计划，特别报告员将在2016年提交给委员会的第五份报告中分析“官员豁免”的限制和例外问题，彼时将完成对这一专题的实质性问题研究；至于程序性问题，按计划则应在第六份报告中论述。①

（二）暂时通过的条款草案

截至2015年8月的第67届会议，② 委员会的起草委员会（Drafting Committee）一共暂时通过了有关此专题的6项条款草案及部分条款草案的评注，其中把豁免类型明确划分为属人豁免和属事豁免。③ 下文就这6项条款草案，结合所附评注，作进一步述评。

> 第1条　本条款草案的范围
>
> 1. 本条款草案适用于国家官员对另一国刑事管辖享有的豁免。
>
> 2. 本条款草案不妨碍依照国际法特别规则享有的刑事管辖豁免，特别是与外交使团、领馆、特别使团、国际组织和一国军事力量相关的人员所享有的刑事管辖豁免。④

第1条第1款涵盖了界定本专题宗旨的三个要素：谁能享受豁免（国家官员）；豁免影响哪些类型的管辖权（刑事管辖权）；这类刑事管辖权是在什么领域行使（另一国的刑事管辖权）。关于第一个要素，委员会将本专题限于代表一国的或为一国利益行事的人员可享有的外国刑事管辖豁免，而对“国家官员”的界定，则具体体现在第2条（e）款的定义中。关于第二个要素，本专题只处理刑事管辖方面的豁免问题，主要理由是在实践中这类管辖产生的问题最大，而对于界定本专题的范围而言，根据这一条款草案所附的评注，“凡提到外国刑事管辖，都应理解为是指一套与司法程序相关的行为，旨在确定一人是否负有刑事责任，包括在这方面可

---

① A/CN. 4/686, para. 139.

② A/70/10, paras. 171 - 243.

③ 有委员指出，虽然“属人豁免”和“属事豁免”的区分很重要，但是，这并不意味着这两者毫无交集，尤其当从更广义的角度考虑豁免的功能时——譬如这两者都体现了尊重国家主权平等原则 。参见 the Statements of Mr. Nolte in *Provisional Summary Record of the 3273rd Meeting*, 21 July 2015, A/CN. 4/SR. 3273。

④ A/CN. 4/L. 814.

对享受豁免者采取的强制行为”。[①] 关于第三个要素，本专题处理的刑事管辖豁免只限于外国国内法院的管辖问题，而不涉及国际刑事法庭或法院的管辖及豁免，因为后者主要由创立相关的国际刑事法庭或法院的条约来规范。[②] 总而言之，本专题不涉及国家官员的国际刑事法庭或法院管辖豁免、本国管辖豁免或民事豁免。而且，委员会将外国刑事管辖豁免视为程序性的。因此，外国刑事管辖豁免不能构成免除享有豁免的人按照刑法实质性规则所负刑事责任的手段，即追究实体责任的可能性被相应地保留了下来。[③]

第2款通过一项“但书”确立了本专题与其他所述特别制度之间的关系，根据这一“但书”，本专题的规定“不妨碍”特别制度的规定；但是，委员会有必要将已有的特别制度考虑在内，以确保豁免原则的协调和统一，以及国际法律秩序的一致性。[④] 此外，委员会认为，这些特别制度与本专题界定的制度是共存的，在两种制度产生冲突的情况下，适用特别制度。[⑤]

> 第2条 定义
>
> 为本条款草案的目的：
>
> ……
>
> (e)“国家官员”是指代表国家或行使国家职能的任何个人。
>
> (f)“以官方身份实施的行为”是指国家官员在行使国家权力时实施的任何行为。[⑥]

第2条是关于术语的定义，目前暂时通过的是（e）款“国家官员”和（f）款“以官方身份实施的行为”。

其中，（e）款对“国家官员”作出界定有助于理解豁免的规范性要素之一：享受豁免的个人，即“官员豁免”问题仅适用于个人。该款的评注指出，（e）款不应与界定谁享有每一类豁免的第3条和第5条的性质和目

① 联合国大会：《国际法委员会报告（第68届会议）》，A/68/10（2013），第49段。

② A/CN. 4/654, paras. 23 – 30.

③ A/68/10, para. 49.

④ 联合国大会：《国际法委员会报告（第67届会议）》，A/67/10（2012），第108段。

⑤ A/68/10, para. 49.

⑥ A/CN. 4/L. 850.

的相混淆，即享有属人豁免和属事豁免的人员都在“国家官员”的定义范围之内，这一定义对两类人员都适用。当然，“国家官员”或“官员”的概念在不同的国内法律制度中所指可能不同，而且国际法对此也没有统一的定义，因此，该项的“国家官员”必须理解为只是为本专题的目的而拟定的。至于属事豁免适用的“国家官员”，委员会认为无法明确列举一份详尽无遗的名单，因此，必须根据定义中所包含并表明国家与官员之间具体关系（即代表国家或行使国家职能——同时满足这两个要求或只满足其中一个要求）的标准逐案确定。一方面，“代表国家”，根据各个国家的法律制度，还可以适用于除“三巨头”之外的国家官员，即官员是否代表国家也需要逐案确定；此外，该款中单独提到“代表国家”也是为了将某些类别的个人诸如国家元首包含进来——他们通常不履行严格意义上的国家职能，但确实是代表国家。另一方面，“国家职能”必须从广义上理解，指国家开展的活动，包括国家履行的立法、司法、行政或其他职能。对界定“国家官员”的目的而言，重要的是个人与国家的联系，而联系的形式则具体取决于国家立法和每个国家的惯例，且官员职位高低与定义的目的无关。总而言之，“国家官员”的定义与豁免涵盖的行为种类毫无关系，“代表国家”和“行使国家职能”不能被解释为以任何方式界定了豁免的实质范围，“国家官员”的定义也不能被解释为包含对豁免例外情况的说明。①

对于（f）款，② 特别报告员承认，就本专题而言，沿用国际法院在“逮捕令案”中所使用的“以官方身份实施的行为”这一表述，目的是确保委员会内部术语的一致性。③ 在分析有关实践的基础上，特别报告员提出了识别“以官方身份实施的行为”的明确标准，进而概括出以下三个特征：是具有犯罪性质的行为；是代表国家实施的行为；涉及行使国家主权和政府权力要素。④ 在委员会内部，大部分委员赞同对“以官方身份实施

---

① 联合国大会：《国际法委员会报告（第66届会议）》，A/69/10（2014），第132段。

② A/CN. 4/L. 865.

③ 参见 the Statement of Ms. Escobar Hernánde in *Provisional Summary Record of the 3271st Meeting*, 16 July 2015，A/CN. 4/SR. 3271。

④ A/70/10，paras. 187 – 189.

的行为”这一提法的定义和理解；但是，也有部分委员认为没有必要在本专题中对此作出界定，因为法律概念往往是不确定的，并不总是能够形成精确的法律定义，在此前提下只需要与“以私人身份实施的行为”对比，逐案作出判断。[①] 在这一点上，笔者赞同特别报告员的主张，认为应该在考察国家实践的基础上赋予“以官方身份实施的行为”在此专题下的定义，因为，目前针对“以私人身份实施的行为”也没有一个确切的定义和统一的国家实践，所以，期望在司法程序中通过比照“以私人身份实施的行为”这一模糊的法律概念来澄清“以官方身份实施的行为”，更无助于法律的确定性；此外，定义“以官方身份实施的行为”亦体现了委员会对国际法的逐步发展。该款的评注预计在2016年第68届会议上审议。[②]

第3条　享有属人豁免的人员

国家元首、政府首脑和外交部长对外国行使的刑事管辖享有属人豁免。[③]

第3条规定了属人豁免的主体范围，“国家元首、政府首脑和外交部长对外国行使的刑事管辖享有属人豁免”，即属人豁免的主体仅限于“三巨头”。虽然传统上，习惯国际法一直都有区分“属人豁免”和“属事豁免”，但是，在应否赋予“三巨头”属人豁免这一问题上，委员会内部也产生了不同的观点。[④] 为什么赋予且只赋予“三巨头”属人豁免？除了“三巨头”之外，其他的高级别官员是否就不需要或者不能够享有属人豁免？如中国代表在第67届联合国大会第六委员会的发言中就指出，“国际社会的基本共识是，国家元首、政府首脑、外交部长有作为国家代表履行公共职能的需要，应享有属人豁免。基于同样的理由，议长、副总理、政府部长等其他高级官员，越来越多地直接参与国际交往并行使代表国家的

---

① A/70/10, paras. 204 - 205.

② A/70/10, para. 176.

③ A/CN. 4/L. 814.

④ A/CN. 4/654, paras. 44, 61 - 63.

职能，因此也应享有属人豁免。"[①] 根据该条款的所附评注，委员会认为，从代表和职能这两个方面看，有充分理由给予"三巨头"以属人豁免：一方面，国家元首享受属人豁免这一点在现行习惯国际法中已得到确认，对此没有争议，且在国际和国内的判例法中也得到承认；另一方面，政府首脑和外交部长享有属人豁免之所以得到承认是因为，根据国际法，其作为国家代表的职能接近于国家元首并且这一点得到了承认。至于其他类别的国家官员能否被列入属人豁免的人员清单，譬如一些委员建议的，国防部长或国际贸易部长或许可以享有属人豁免？委员会在考察了相关的国际和国家实践后认为，除了"三巨头"外，还难以确认可以被视为毫无争议地享有属人豁免的高级官员，且确认"高级官员"本身也很困难，因为这在很大程度上取决于国家的组织结构和赋予职能的方式，而国家之间在这方面各不相同。[②]

第 4 条　属人豁免的范围

1. 国家元首、政府首脑和外交部长仅在其任职期间享有属人豁免。

2. 国家元首、政府首脑和外交部长享有的此种属人豁免涵盖他们在任职之前或任职期间的所有行为，无论是私人行为还是公务行为。

3. 属人豁免的停止不妨碍关于属事豁免的国际法规则的适用。[③]

该条从时间和内容两个角度规定了属人豁免的范围。简而言之，"三

---

① 《中国代表李琳琳在第 67 届联大六委关于"国际法委员会第六十四届会议工作报告"议题的发言》，2012 年 11 月 5 日，中华人民共和国常驻联合国代表团网站，http://www.fmprc.gov.cn/ce/ceun/chn/lhghywj/fyywj/fayan2012/t988122.htm，最后访问日期：2016 年 3 月 1 日。此外，中国代表团在 2013 年和 2014 年再次重申了这一立场，参见《中国代表、外交部条法司司长黄惠康在第 68 届联大六委关于"国际法委员会第 65 届会议工作报告"议题的发言》，2013 年 10 月 30 日，中华人民共和国常驻联合国代表团网站，http://www.fmprc.gov.cn/ce/ceun/chn/lhghywj/fyywj/2013/t1095221.htm，最后访问日期：2016 年 3 月 23 日；《中国代表、外交部条法司司长徐宏在第 69 届联大六委关于"国际法委员会第 66 届会议工作报告"议题的发言》，2014 年 10 月 31 日，中华人民共和国常驻联合国代表团网站，http://www.fmprc.gov.cn/ce/ceun/chn/lhghywj/fyywj/2014/t1207043.htm，最后访问日期：2016 年 3 月 23 日。

② A/68/10，para. 49.

③ A/CN. 4/L. 814.

巨头”在任时享有全方位的绝对的属人豁免，虽然卸任后属人豁免即告结束且不能再被援引，但其仍享有属事豁免。这就意味着，第 4 条条款草案中规定的属人豁免是没有例外的，这与“逮捕令案”和“刑事事项互助问题案”的立场相一致。迄今各国法院的判决和国际法学会的决议亦持同样的主张，这也是学术界目前普遍的观点。[①] 当然，关于属人豁免的绝对性，委员会内部也一直都存在不同的声音，即认为应当排除违反强行法或可能被界定为严重国际犯罪的行为。[②] 那么，从保护人权和打击有罪不罚的角度来看，是否真的应该赋予“三巨头”属人豁免一种绝对性？在这一点上，委员会究竟是在编纂已经确立的习惯法，抑或逐渐发展了国际法？其在编纂或者发展国际法的同时，是否确切把握住了现代国际法的发展趋势？根据该条款的所附评注，虽然委员会在通过第 4 条第 2 款时没有涉及豁免的可能例外问题，但其声明该问题将在之后讨论，[③] 关于这一点，我们拭目以待。

第 5 条　享有属事豁免的人员

国家官员在以此种身份行事时，对外国行使的刑事管辖享有属事豁免。

该条规定了属事豁免的主体范围。[④] 同是规定主体范围，这一条与第 3 条是平行关系，它们具有相同的结构。一方面，第 5 条中使用的“国家官员”的定义应从第 2 条（e）款中寻找。另一方面，“以此种身份行事”指的是官员实施的行为具有公务性质，它强调了属事管辖的职能性，并确立了与属人豁免的区别。此外，根据第 4 条第 3 款，属事豁免也适用于“以国家官员身份行事”的前“三巨头”。当然，第 5 条亦不妨碍规定属事豁免的例外情形，依照特别报告员的计划，这些例外也将在之后讨论。[⑤]

---

① A/CN. 4/631, para. 55.

② A/CN. 4/654, para. 64.

③ A/68/10, para. 49.

④ A/CN. 4/L. 850.

⑤ A/69/10, para. 132.

第6条　属事豁免的范围

1. 国家官员只有在以官方身份实施的行为方面享有属事豁免。

2. 对以官方身份实施的行为的属事豁免在所涉个人不再担任国家官员后继续存在。

3. 根据第4条草案享有属事豁免的个人任期届满后，继续就任期内以官方身份实施的行为享有豁免。[①]

第6条规定了属事豁免的范围。同是规定豁免的范围，这一条与第4条是平行关系。此外，我们也可看到，第6条与第2条（e）（f）款、第4条、第5条都有紧密联系，需要相互指引。一方面，“以官方身份实施的行为”这一概念是整个专题的一个核心问题，其定义应从第2条（f）款中寻找，对于属事豁免具有特殊意义——即只有国家官员以官方身份实施的行为才属于外国刑事管辖豁免的范围。另一方面，属事豁免的时间要素在理论和实践上都没有争议，对这一类豁免的无限期性质存在广泛共识，即属事豁免可以适用于实施该行为后的任何时间，无论该官员是仍在职或已离职；不过，这里需要注意区分两个时间点，即可能产生豁免的行为实施的时刻和援引豁免的时刻，前者必须发生在国家官员任期内，后者则是在对行为人提起诉讼时出现。因此，属事豁免的时间要素在性质上与其说是有限制的，不如说是有条件的：如果产生豁免的行为实施的时刻发生在国家官员任期内这一条件得到满足，那么适用属事豁免根本没有限制——这有别于在本质上有限制的属人豁免的时间要素，根据第4条第1款，属人豁免在“三巨头”卸任时终止，且不能在卸任之后再援引。当然，对属事豁免和属人豁免的时间要素进行区分，并不意味着这两类豁免是相互排斥的，相反，属事豁免可以适用于任何国家官员。因此，如本条第3款所规定，“三巨头”在卸任后虽不再享有属人豁免，但仍然享有属事豁免，此时，上述属事豁免的时间要素亦适用于卸任后的“三巨头”。[②] 跟第2条（f）款一样，该款的评注预计在2016年第68届会议上审议。[③]

---

① A/CN. 4/L. 865.

② A/CN. 4/686, paras. 128 - 131.

③ A/70/10, para. 176.

四 “官员豁免”问题核心之争：豁免抑或豁免例外?

如前文所述，按照特别报告员的工作计划，其将在2016年提交的第五份报告中分析“官员豁免”的限制和例外问题。事实上，通过回顾两任特别报告员相继提交的7份报告，以及委员会在此基础上进行的辩论和评述，我们会发现，关于“官员豁免”问题的核心之争，仍在于豁免的限制和例外问题，进一步而言，委员会拟制订的条款草案，其在确认传统豁免规则的基础上，是否允许制定豁免规则的所有例外情形？即该条款草案的重点究竟应是进一步确认豁免抑或承认和界定豁免例外。

通说认为，国际法上给予国家官员豁免主要基于“代表说”和“职能说”这两种理论的综合。因为只有通过国家官员这一载体，“国家”这一抽象实体才能够有所作为，所以，作为其逻辑结果，由代表国家的国家官员所作出的行为就理应属于国家自身所作出的行为，并归责于国家。进一步而言，国际法上赋予国家官员的官方行为豁免实质上是赋予国家的豁免，这背后体现的正是国家主权平等原则。因此，国家官员不能因其官方行为而成为外国法院诉讼程序中的主体。[1] 但有争议认为，“官员豁免”规则，至少属事豁免规则，应该存在例外，譬如，当国家官员犯下了大规模的暴行和严重违反国际人权法时，他们就不能再享有豁免。[2] 对于享有属事豁免的在任和卸任国家官员的豁免例外存在各种理由。有观点认为，由国家官员作出的严重刑事犯罪行为不能被认为是国际法下的“以官方身份从事的行为”。[3] 如果国际犯罪不仅归责于国家，而且归责于作出这一行为的国家官员，那么，这一国家官员就不能再在刑事程序中援引属事豁免。也有争议认为，在针对某些严重国际犯罪时，普遍管辖原则排除了豁免规

---

① Andrea Bianchi, “Immunity Versus Human Rights: The Pinochet Case”, *European Journal of International Law* 10 (1999): 262 - 265.

② Huang Huikang, “On Immunity of State Officials from Foreign Criminal Jurisdiction”, *Chinese Journal of International Law* 13 (2014): 1 - 11.

③ Kaitlin R. O'Donnell, “Certain Criminal Proceedings in France (Republic of Congo v. France) and Head of State Immunity: How Impenetrable Should the Immunity Veil Remain”, *Boston University International Law Journal* 26 (2008): 416.

则的适用。[①]

在豁免规则究竟应否存在例外这一问题上，委员会的意见也发生了分歧。第一任特别报告员科洛德金先生在他提交的报告中指出，国家官员享有的豁免特权是国际法上确立的一项规则，而有关管辖例外的各种理由并没有充分的说服力，如果认为豁免例外已经成为国际法上确立的规则，那是不恰当的，因为豁免例外并不像豁免规则一样已经得到确信无疑的宣示。[②] 而在委员会内部，有一些委员则倾向于认为科洛德金先生的观点是过时的：因为他没有考虑到当今国际刑法和国际人权法的发展趋势，而对人权的保护是现今国际社会的首要价值，没有任何其他价值包括国家主权或国家豁免规则能够超越对人权的保护；此外，国际强行法严禁诸如严重侵犯人权的行为，在国际法的效力位阶中，国际强行法优先于豁免规则；有鉴于此，有委员主张，关于“官员豁免”这一专题应以制定“豁免例外规则”为重点，即限制对严重国际罪行授予豁免。[③]

笔者同意，从长远来看，随着国际社会的变迁和国际法的发展，“官员豁免”问题的相关规则亦会随之发生变化，以进一步契合国际法的人本化发展趋势，[④] 逐渐呈现出更多的维度和层次。但是，在目前这一阶段，笔者不同意“官员豁免”专题应以制定“豁免例外规则”为重点，针对这一问题，下文将主要从“豁免规则会否导致有罪不罚”，以及“豁免规则会否有碍人权保护”这两个角度就此作进一步探讨和厘清。

（一）豁免规则是否有违打击有罪不罚的世界潮流？

早在20世纪初，即有观点认为，对国家官员的豁免应当被限制在某些特定情形之下。战后，国际社会对“国家官员或军事官员应否对基于上级命令而犯下的严重罪行承担责任”这一问题展开了热烈的讨论。在纽伦堡

---

① “The Princeton Principles on Universal Jurisdiction, Principle 5 - Immunities”, University of Minnesota, http://www1. umn. edu/humanrts/instree/princeton. html，最后访问日期：2016年1月22日。

② A/CN. 4/631, paras. 90 - 93.

③ Huang Huikang, “On Immunity of State Officials from Foreign Criminal Jurisdiction”, *Chinese Journal of International Law* 13 (2014): 4 - 5; The Statements of Mr. Murase in International Law Commission, *Provisional Summary Record of the 3275th Meeting*, A/CN. 4/SR. 3275 (2015), pp. 9 - 12.

④ 参见曾令良《现代国际法的人本化发展趋势》，《中国社会科学》2007年第1期。

审判和东京审判中，“与官职无关”的归责原则被提了出来，根据这一原则，如果一个国家它自身的授权行为超出了国际法的许可范围，那么，国家官员即使得到了国家的授权，他或她也不能因为战争罪行等而得到豁免。[①] 随着一系列国际刑事法庭和国际刑事法院在20世纪90年代后相继建立，国际刑法在国际层面对灭绝种族罪、危害人类罪、战争罪和侵略罪等严重国际罪行的管辖方面迈出了很大的一步。在某种程度上，打击国际法上有罪不罚的现象已经成为当今的世界潮流。当然，对国际罪行的管辖是否能够延伸到国内层面，仍然是不确定的。那么，在世界情势已经发生了如此变化的前提下，一味地维护传统的豁免规则，是否会不利于打击有罪不罚的现象？是否会有逆当今世界之主流？

笔者认为，首先，豁免规则是中立的，它本身不会产生国际罪行，也不会鼓励有罪不罚。[②] 导致有罪不罚结果的因素有很多，因此需要通过一系列措施进行综合治理。作为一个程序性规则，“官员豁免”确实会对一国行使刑事管辖构成一定的障碍，但是，它并不因此就等于赦免了国家官员的罪行。国际法院在前述的“逮捕令案”的判决中就此问题提出了四种具体措施，包括：由享有豁免特权的国家官员的本国根据其国内法对其进行起诉；由享有豁免特权的国家官员的本国决定放弃豁免特权；在享有豁免特权的国家官员卸任后再对其进行起诉；由具有管辖权的国际刑事法庭进行起诉。[③] 事实上，从国际司法实践的角度来看，自第二次世界大战之

① Andrea Bianchi, “Immunity Versus Human Rights: The Pinochet Case”, *European Journal of International Law* 10 (1999): 259.

② 外交部条法司司长徐宏在第69届联合国大会第六委员会关于“国际法委员会第66届会议工作报告”议题的发言中亦指出，“由于国家官员豁免属于程序性规则，不免除其应承担的实体责任……因此豁免与有罪不罚没有必然联系”。参见《中国代表、外交部条法司司长徐宏在第69届联大六委关于“国际法委员会第66届会议工作报告”议题的发言》，2014年10月31日，中华人民共和国常驻联合国代表团网站，http://www.fmprc.gov.cn/ce/ceun/chn/lhghywj/fyywj/2014/t1207043.htm，最后访问日期：2016年3月23日。此外，中国代表团在2015年再次重申了上述立场，“官员豁免是基于国家主权平等原则，体现国家间的相互尊重，属于程序性规则，不应与有罪不罚联系起来”，参见《中国代表、外交部条法司司长徐宏在第70届联大六委关于“国际法委员会第67届会议工作报告”议题的发言》，2015年11月6日，中华人民共和国常驻联合国代表团网站，http://www.china-un.org/chn/hyyfy/t1327113.htm，最后访问日期：2016年3月23日。

③ *Arrest Warrant of 11 April 2000 (Democratic Republic of the Congo v. Belgium)*, Judgment, I. C. J. Reports 2002, paras. 60 - 61.

后，从纽伦堡审判和东京审判，到前南斯拉夫国际刑事法庭和卢旺达国际刑事法庭的建立，再到国际刑事法院的建立，国际社会对严重侵犯人权的行为和国际犯罪几乎采取了零容忍的态度。[①] 可以说，对犯下严重国际罪行的国家官员进行起诉的法律框架已基本建立起来。

其次，豁免规则作为程序问题，跟正当程序原则有关，它具有自身独特的价值，应被视为跟其他诸如反对有罪不罚和国际正义等价值具有同等地位。国际社会已经把灭绝种族罪、危害人类罪、战争罪等纳入了可以行使普遍管辖权的国际犯罪之范畴，但是，与国内法不同，在国际法层面，目前在不同的法律部门之间并没有等级之分，亦难以得出结论认为国际法上已经产生了在效力等级上高于豁免规则的程序性规则。实体正义的实现不能以牺牲正当程序为代价——这也是法治原则的内在本质。在"逮捕令案"的判决中，国际法院就指出，"虽然各种预防和惩罚严重国际罪行的公约赋予了国家或起诉或引渡的义务，并要求国家延伸它们的刑事管辖权，但是，在习惯国际法上，国家对刑事管辖权的延伸并不能影响豁免规则……同样地，法院认为，这种情形也并不能推导出在习惯国际法中存在任何对豁免规则的例外"。[②] 如前所述，在"刑事事项互助问题案"中，国际法院亦采取了与在"逮捕令案"中的同一立场。[③] 而在 2012 年"德国诉意大利案"的判决中，国际法院指出，国家豁免是一项程序性事项，它是一项不同于有关规定如种族灭绝罪或其他国际罪行的强行法的国际法规则，而违反国际强行法并不自动导致国家豁免的丧失。[④] 虽然这一案例主要处理国家豁免问题，但在理论上，国家官员的豁免亦起源于国家豁免理

① 如国际刑事法院于 2016 年 3 月 21 日作出的一项判决，判决刚果（金）前副总统本巴（Jean-Pierre Bemba）在 2002 年 10 月至 2003 年 3 月中非共和国冲突期间犯下的危害人类罪和战争罪成立。参见 ICC Press Release，"ICC Trial Chamber III Declares Jean-Pierre Bemba Gombo Guilty of War Crimes and Crimes against Humanity"，March21，2016，https://www.icc-cpi.int/en_menus/icc/press%20and%20media/press%20releases/Pages/pr1200.aspx，最后访问日期：2016 年 3 月 23 日。

② *Arrest Warrant of 11 April 2000*（*Democratic Republic of the Congo v. Belgium*），Judgment，I. C. J. Reports 2002，paras. 58 – 59.

③ *Case Concerning Certain Questions of Mutual Assistance*，Judgment，paras. 170，174；*Arrest Warrant of 11 April 2000*，Judgment，paras. 51，54，56，58.

④ *Case Concerning Jurisdictional Immunities of the State*（*Germany v. Italy*：*Greece Intervening*），Judgment，I. C. J. Reports 2012，paras. 92 – 97.

论，或从属于国家豁免理论，因此具有参考价值。

最后，豁免规则的适用由这一规则的内在标准决定，而非取决于国际罪行的严重性。有人认为，严重的国际犯罪并不能被认为是代表国家作出的行为。[①] 但是，当我们判断一个行为是否构成官方行为时，应该判断这一行为是不是国家官员在其任职期间的“以官方身份从事的行为”，而非该犯罪行为的严重性。事实上，大规模暴行通常都是由国家机构利用公共资源作出，并被纳入机制政策的一部分，这一类的罪行在本质上就是官方行为——这一观点目前也体现在了委员会暂时通过的条款草案中。同样值得注意的是，因为迄今还没有对严重国际罪行的范畴达成共识，所以，要在严重罪行和普通罪行之间划出一条清晰的界线，由此决定是否适用豁免规则，这也是非常困难的。[②]

此外，即使豁免例外规则在国际法层面确立了，但国内法院如果对外国官员行使管辖权的话，也很可能会引起一些难题，如证据的缺乏和司法协助的困难等。而且，如果在承认豁免例外的前提下制订过于宽泛的豁免例外规则，对别国官员在国内法院提起刑事诉讼的数量极有可能随之增多，那么这种做法将会很容易损害豁免规则，也违反了国际法上尊重他国主权的义务。

（二）豁免规则是否会导致人权保护的倒退？

第二次世界大战之后，基于对战争的反思，人权保护开始全面进入国际法领域。[③] 从 20 世纪下半叶开始，人权国际保护得到了越来越多的关注。为了实现对人权的保护，尤其在卢旺达大屠杀和其他大规模践踏人权的暴行发生之后，对严重侵犯人权的国家官职人员进行起诉便成为国际法上最重要的一个原则。有提议尝试建立普遍管辖权，声称国家官员应对他

---

① Kaitlin R. O'Donnell, "Certain Criminal Proceedings in France (Republic of Congo v. France) and Head of State Immunity: How Impenetrable Should the Immunity Veil Remain", *Boston University International Law Journal* 26 (2008): 416.

② Huang Huikang, "On Immunity of State Officials from Foreign Criminal Jurisdiction", *Chinese Journal of International Law* 13 (2014): 1 – 11.

③ 参见龚刃韧《关于人权与国际法若干问题的初步思考》，《中外法学》1997 年第 5 期；Malcolm N. Shaw, *International Law* (Cambridge: Cambridge University Press, 7th edn., 2014), pp. 197 – 199。

们所犯下的暴行负责，而不管他们的国籍和官职地位。也有观点认为，由于国家官员享有豁免特权，从而使得受害者诉诸法庭的权利被剥夺了，这本身也构成了对基本人权的违反。[①]

但是，直到今天，在国际法层面仍然还没有确立一国高级官员在外国法院的刑事豁免特权被剥夺这一规则。长久以来的事实证明，在国际政治生活中，国内法院起诉外国的国家官员在大多数情况下并非一个好的解决方案。几乎相反地，这种做法经常引起争端。[②] 不恰当的豁免例外会在某种程度上导致一些具有政治动机的起诉，譬如，无论一个国家的国家官员是否真正地违反国际人权法，他都有可能受到某些具有政治企图的外国法院的起诉，这种情形无疑损害了国家主权平等原则。它会对国家的内部稳定产生负面影响，同时也会有损国家之间的关系。

国际法是一系列价值的有机组合，它不仅致力于保护人权，同时也必须在主权原则和不干涉内政原则的基础上运行。因此，豁免特权和人权保护之间的关系就不仅仅是一个非此即彼的两面问题，它需要我们从更多的维度来进行探讨。从根源上说，豁免规则的背后体现了主权原则，而固守主权原则是否会导致人权保护的后退？这显然也不能简单地给出一个“是”或“否”的答案，而需要我们结合实际情况进行个案分析。事实上，委员会在编纂“官员豁免”问题时也没有无原则地固守豁免规则，从现在暂时通过的条款草案来看，尽管“三巨头”被赋予了绝对豁免，但针对其他高级国家官员，他们享有的仍然是有限度的豁免——即使豁免例外规则迄今没有成为这一专题的重点，但按照委员会的工作计划，它也将可能被纳入将来的条款草案中去。[③]

因此，如果我们在抽象的层面泛泛主张豁免规则和人权保护之间非此即彼的关系，其实际意义不大，正如涉及主权和人权之间关系的辩论一

---

① Huang Huikang, “On Immunity of State Officials from Foreign Criminal Jurisdiction”, *Chinese Journal of International Law* 13 (2014): 1－11.

② 如徐宏指出的“近年来，一国不顾外国国家官员所享有的刑事管辖豁免，滥用刑事起诉的案件时有发生，影响国家间交往的正常开展和国际关系的稳定……当前国际社会虽将种族灭绝、种族清洗、危害人类罪等确定为严重国际罪行，但没有形成排除官员享有豁免的习惯国际法规则。下一步委员会研究豁免例外时，应全面考察各国实践，谨慎处理豁免的例外问题”。参见《中国代表、外交部条法司司长徐宏在第69届联大六委关于“国际法委员会第66届会议工作报告”议题的发言》。

③ A/69/10, para. 131.

样。毫无疑问地，人权保护是当今世界的整体发展趋势，而主权原则则是整个现代国际法的基石；尽管人权理念根源于自然法，但人权国际法也是在“国家同意”的基础上发展起来的，现今我们适用的人权规则也是被实在法化了的规则。迄今为止，无论是豁免规则、豁免例外规则，还是人权保护规则，都是在“国家同意”的主权框架之内运行，在个案中进行规则之间的价值平衡和具体考量显得尤为重要和现实。

五 结语

“官员豁免”问题是国际法领域的一个传统议题，它根源于国家主权原则，历来受到习惯国际法的调整。随着国际刑法和国际人权法的发展，“官员豁免”问题也不断受到挑战和反思，具体体现在一系列的司法判例当中。从2007年开始，委员会把这一专题列入其工作方案，以实现“国际法之逐渐发展与编纂”。通过考察委员会关于此专题的报告和辩论，可以发现，“官员豁免”问题的核心之争仍在于，授予国家官员外国刑事管辖豁免究竟是一项原则性规范抑或一项例外性规范？即，在委员会的编纂成果里面，“官员豁免”专题的重点究竟是应该进一步确认授予国家官员外国刑事管辖豁免，抑或明确国家官员不能享有外国刑事管辖豁免的所有例外情形？结合上述分析，笔者认为，在主权国家仍作为国际法最主要主体的今天，为了国家间正常交往和国际关系之稳定，仍应以确认授予国家官员外国刑事管辖豁免为原则——事实上，这也是迄今为止委员会关于此专题的工作方法和最新进展之体现。

（责任编辑：何田田）

（本文原载于《国际法研究》2016年第4期）

投资者[*]

——国家争端解决机制的革新与国家的“回归”

朱明新[**]

政治风险是外国投资者从事跨国投资面临的重要风险，较之基于市场产生的商业风险，外国投资者应对由于东道国政府产生的政治风险要困难得多。以市场为基础的利益共同体机制、政府或私人保险机制、规定了可进行国际仲裁的投资合同机制以及国际投资条约机制均可以在一定程度上预防或降低这些政治风险。① 在上述应对投资政治风险的机制中，投资条约被认为是最为可靠的。投资条约中的投资者—国家仲裁程序虽然被认为是投资条约中最重要的创新，② 但是因其导致国家的管制权受到严格限制③以及将外国私人利益凌驾于内国公共利益之上而饱受争议。革新投资者—国家仲裁程序成为晚近学术研究的热点，诸如构建投资仲裁上诉机构，④

---

* 本文系江苏高校哲学社会科学研究项目（项目号：2015SJB530）的阶段性研究成果。

** 朱明新，苏州大学王健法学院讲师。

① Lauge N. Skovgaard Poulsen, *Bounded Rationality and Economic Diplomacy: The Politics of Investment Treaties in Developing Countries* (Cambridge: Cambridge University Press, 2015), pp. 6 – 7.

② 有学者认为投资者—国家仲裁并不是现代投资条约的创新，只不过是在投资条约化时代被具体化而已。Jason Webb Yackee, "The First Investor-state Arbitration? The Suez Canal Dispute of 1864 and Some Reflections on the Historiography of International Investment Law", in Stephan W. Schill, Christian J. Tams and Rainer Hofmann, eds., *International Investment Law and History* (Cheltenham: Edward Elgar Publishing Limited, 2018), pp. 70 – 101.

③ Aikaterini Titi, *The Right to Regulate in International Investment Law* (Baden-Baden: Beck/Hart, 2014), pp. 123 – 188.

④ Barton Legum, "Options to Establish an Appellate Mechanism for Investment Disputes", in Karl P. Sauvant, eds., *Appeals Mechanism in International Investment Disputes* (New York: Oxford University Press, 2008), pp. 231 – 239.

构建更一致性投资仲裁体制,[①] 强化国家在投资者—国家仲裁程序中的作用,[②] 重塑投资者—国家仲裁程序[③]以及重新控制投资条约体系[④]等。

通过对诸多改革方案的研究与分析，笔者认为，在一定程度上国家在投资条约缔结和争端解决程序中的“离开”，是当前国际投资法存在的缺陷之一。国家“离开”实质上“私人化”了投资仲裁程序，使得投资仲裁员控制了国际投资法的运作。[⑤] 投资条约缔结者已经意识到这一缺陷，并努力从实体待遇[⑥]和程序待遇两个层面寻求国家“回归”。本文以欧盟投资法院体系为视角，分析国家“回归”争端解决程序的路径。主要围绕以下问题展开：第一部分分析国家在投资争端解决程序中的“离开”以及投资者—国家争端解决（investor-state dispute settlement，以下简称 ISDS）的构建；第二部分分析以私法范式为基础的 ISDS 体制的运作及其诱发的过度保护投资者的偏好，国家管制权受到限制的投资条约缔结者开始改革，并寻求国家“回归”投资争端解决程序的路径；第三部分以欧盟投资法院体系为例，分析国家如何“回归”投资争端解决程序。结语部分指出，需要对国际司法机关的性质进行重新定位，承认国际司法机关的司法造法权，并利用缔约国在国际层面的政治立法权限制国际投资仲裁庭的恣意造法。

---

① Roberto Echandi and Pierre Sauvé, eds., *Prospects in International Investment Law and Policy* (United Kingdom: Cambridge University Press, 2013), pp. 389 – 456; Katharina Diel-Gligor, *Towards Consistency in International Investment Jurisprudence: A Preliminary Ruling System for ICSID Arbitration* (Leiden: Brill-Nijhoff, 2017), pp. 333 – 451.

② Shaheeza Lalani and Rodrigo Polanco Lazo, eds., *The Role of the State in Investor-State Arbitration* (*Leiden: Brill-Nijhoff*, 2014), pp. 241 – 349.

③ Jean E. Kalicki and Anna Joubin-bret, eds., *Reshaping the Investor-state Dispute Settlement System: Journeys for the 21st Century* (Leiden: Martinus Nijhoff, 2015), pp. 569 – 889.

④ 具体包括从投资程序方面、实体待遇方面以及投资政策与趋势方面构建国家重新控制投资条约体系的建议，参见 Andreas Kulick, “Reassertion of Control: An Introduction”, in Andreas Kulick, eds., *Reassertion of Control over the Investment Treaty Regime* (Cambridge: Cambridge University Press, 2017), pp. 3 – 29。

⑤ Pia Eberhardt & Cecilia Olivet, *Profiting from Injustice: How Law Firms, Arbitrators and Financiers are Fuelling an Investment Arbitration Boom* (Brussels/Amsterdam: Corporate Europe Observatory and the Transnational Institute, 2012), pp. 36 – 50.

⑥ 国家在实体待遇方面的“回归”主要表现为国际投资协定逐渐从第一代条约转向第二代条约。表现形式为通过采取详细定义加附件方式，制定投资实体待遇条款和限制相关条款适用范围，限制仲裁庭的自由裁量权。本文重在研究国家“回归”争端解决程序。

一 国家“离去”与ISDS构建

国际法框架下，针对个人（自然人和法人）遭受不法行为损害的救济大体经历了以下四个阶段：中世纪的私人报复救济规则；现代民族国家形成后的“炮舰外交学说”；第一次和第二次海牙和会创设的通过外交保护进行的和平解决争端模式；赋予私人直接诉诸国际法院或仲裁庭的创新模式。[①] 随着《联合国宪章》的生效与国际法诸领域的碎片化发展，和平解决争端框架下的外交保护和个人直诉国际司法机关的争端解决方式成为受不法行为侵犯的外国人可以选择的方案。第二次世界大战后，经济全球化的纵深发展使肇始自国家共存时期的“瓦特尔假设”，即外交保护学说及其实践已经不再适合国家间合作的国际法之需要，[②] 争端解决的去政治化和转向法律化成为主流趋势，虽然法律化方法固有其不足之处。[③]

（一）“去政治化”与国家“离去”

在国际关系逐渐法律化的大背景下，国际投资争端解决程序开始逐渐背离传统的国家间充满政治色彩的外交保护模式，走上了法律化的道路，以避免国家间由于外交保护可能引发的政治对抗。

1. 外交保护学说的缘起及其不足

外交保护学说有其根源，瓦特尔（Vattel）指出：不友好对待一国公民间接损害该公民之母国，该母国必须保护该公民。[④] 根据该学说，当外国违反了国际法义务，不恰当对待外国国民时，母国可以采取国际法非禁

---

① Berk Demirkol, *Judicial Acts and Investment Treaty Arbitration* (Cambridge: Cambridge University Press, 2018), pp. 7 – 12.

② Wolfgang Friedmann, *The Changing Structure of International Law* (London: Stevens & Sons, 1964), pp. 60 – 62.

③ 法律化方法并不能够解决所有的国家间争端，甚至有可能恶化争端，典型者如国际法院处理的美国与尼加拉瓜案件，最终导致美国撤销了依据《国际法院规约》第36（2）条作出的任择管辖声明。参见 Wade Mansell and Karen Openshaw, *International Law: A Critical Introduction* (Oxford/Portland, Hart Publishing, 2013), p. 12。

④ Emmerich De Vattel, *The Law of Nations* (Indianapolis: Liberty Fund, Inc., 2008), p. 298.

止之方式襄助本国国民之申诉。① 后经过常设国际法院在“巴勒斯坦特许权案”(Mavrommatis)② 的系统阐述和国际法委员会的编纂努力,③ 外交保护现在已经成为国际法的一个确定性原则。④ 通常而言,外交保护具有两大条件:持续国籍要求和用尽当地救济。就国际投资者而言,外交保护使投资者处于东道国和母国的双重专断(double arbitariness)之下。⑤ 具体表现为,一方面,用尽东道国当地救济是提起外交保护的前提条件;另一方面,外交保护权是母国的一项权利而非义务,国家对于是否襄助受损投资者享有自由裁量权,母国可能为了维护与施害国间良好的外交关系而拒绝受损投资者的请求;母国取代国民以自身名义提起针对施害国的外交保护程序,⑥ 受损投资者无参与权和决策权;即便母国成功行使外交保护权并获得赔偿,受损投资者是否能够获得赔偿完全取决于母国的自由裁量。⑦ 由于外交保护可能诱发国家间的政治对抗和受损投资者无法真正获得救

① Hersch Lauterpacht, eds., *Oppenheim's International Law*, vol. I (London: Longman, 8th, 1955), pp. 686 - 687.

② *Mavrommatis Case* (*Greece v. U. K.*), PCIJ Series A, No. 2, 1924, p. 12.

③ Art. 1 of the Draft Articles on Diplomatic Protection with Commentaries, ILC 2006, UN Doc. A/61/10, p. 29.

④ 有学者认为,外交保护学说同时包括母国襄助本国国民和本国国民遵守国际最低行为标准两个方面。国民请求母国进行外交保护时,必须无过错(clean hand)。但经过西方国际法学者的刻意选择后,外交保护学说强调母国保护,漠视本国国民遵守国际最低行为标准。Muin Boase, "A Genealogy of Censurable Conduct: Antecedents for an International Minimum Standard of Investor Conduct", in Stephan W. Schill, Christian J. Tams and Rainer Hofmann, eds., *International Investment Law and History* (Cheltenham: Edward Elgar Publishing Limited, 2018), pp. 321 - 366.

⑤ Andreas Kulick, "Narrating Narratives of International Investment Law: History and Epistemic Forces", in Stephan W. Schill, Christian J. Tams and Rainer Hofmann, eds., *International Investment Law and History* (Cheltenham: Edward Elgar Publishing Limited, 2018), pp. 54 - 55.

⑥ 现代观点认为母国主张具有双重属性,同时代表受损国民个人和母国利益。受损国民将法律申诉权转移给母国行使,但仍然保留裁决收益(award proceeds)的经济利益请求权。Jose Daniel Amado and Jackson Shaw Kern, *Arbitrating the Conduct of International Investors* (Cambridge: Cambridge University Press, 2018), pp. 45 - 47.

⑦ Stephan Hobe, "The Law Relating to Alien, the International Minimum Standard and State Responsibility", in Marc Bungenberg, Jorn Griebel, Stephan Hobe and August Reinisch, eds., *International Investment Law: A Handbook* (Baden-Baden/Munchen/Oxford/Portland: Beck/Hart, 2015), pp. 7 - 13; August Reinisch and Loretta Malintoppi, "Methods of Dispute Resolution", in Peter Muchlinski, Federico Ortino and Christoph Schreuer, eds., *The Oxford Handbook of International Investment Law* (New York: Oxford University Press, 2008), pp. 712 - 714.

济，国际社会开始采取“去政治化”方法解决投资争端，并最终选择了法律化的国际仲裁模式。①

2. 法律化仲裁模式与国家“离开”

二战后的去殖民化运动中，为应对发展中国家质疑外国人保护的习惯国际法、提出构建新国际经济秩序的运动，② 1959 年，原联邦德国与巴基斯坦签署了一个“偶然”（Inadvertently）条约，③ 通过模糊语言赋予了外国投资者实体性保护待遇，并最终改变了外国投资保护的轨迹。④ 面对发展中国家“破旧立新”的集体努力，时任世界银行总法律顾问的布罗奇斯（Aron Broches）提出程序先于实体（procedure before substance），先组建争端解决程序后制定实体法的设想。⑤ 在投资保护程序方面，《华盛顿公约》缔结和“国际投资争端解决中心”（ICSID）的成立，进一步强化了赋予外国投资者直接利用仲裁起诉东道国的国际司法机制。⑥ 这种投资仲裁体制实际上边缘化了国家，并赋权投资者绕过用尽当地救济规则，最终导致国家在投资争端解决程序方面被迫“离开”。投资实体待遇保护方面，先是以阿比斯—肖克罗斯法典（Abs-Shawcross Code）为蓝本的欧式投资条约获得了成功。随着美国实现了从友好、通商与航海条约（FCNs）向双边投资条约（BITs）的战略转移后⑦，以欧式和美式范本为基础缔结的双边投资

---

① Ibrahim F. I. Shihata, “Towards a Greater Depoliticization of Investment Disputes: The Roles of ICSID and MIGA”, *ICSID Review-Foreign Investment Law Journal* 1 (1986): 1 –25.

② Rudolf Dolzer and Christoph Schreuer, *Principles of International Investment Law* (Croydon: Oxford University Press, 2nd, 2012), p. 4.

③ 该条约第 11 条规定了临时的国家—国家仲裁程序和国际法院程序，没有规定投资者—国家仲裁程序。第一个规定无条件的投资者—国家仲裁程序的为意大利—乍得双边投资条约（1969）。参见 Andrew Newcombe and Lluis Paradell, *Law and Practice of Investment Treaties: Standards of Treatment* (Alphen aan den Rijn: Kluwer Law International, 2009), pp. 44 –45。

④ Farouk El-Hosseny, *Civil Society in Investment Treaty Arbitration: Status and Prospects* (Leiden: Koninklijke Brill, 2017), p. 295; Lauge N. Skovgaard Poulsen, *Bounded Rationality and Economic Diplomacy: The Politics of Investment Treaties in Developing Countries* (Cambridge: Cambridge University Press, 2015), p. xiii.

⑤ Rudolf Dolzer and Christoph Schreuer, *Principles of International Investment Law* (New York: Oxford University Press, 2008), p. 20.

⑥ 关于《华盛顿公约》缔结详情，参见 Antonio R. Parra, *The History of ICSID* (Croydon: Oxford University Press, 2012), pp. 1 –117。

⑦ 有学者认为美国 FCNs 其实就是最早的投资保护的双边条约，参见 Kenneth J. Vandevelde, *The First Bilateral Investment Treaties: U. S. Postwar Friendship, Commerce, and Navigation Treaties* (New York: Oxford University Press, 2017), pp. 27 –28。

条约体系塑造了国际投资保护的双边主义范式。[①] 投资条约实体待遇具有天生的模糊性与不确定性，很多表述诸如公平公正待遇和间接征收等常成为争议的焦点，并难以适用。这种模糊性给予外国投资者利用投资者—国家仲裁程序质疑东道国各种立法、司法[②]以及行政行为的机会。可以在一定程度上认为，投资条约条款的模糊性实质上将国家的政治缔约权转变成为国际司法机关手中的司法自由裁量权，意味着国家在国际层面的缔约程序中的退出。

（二）国家“离开”与 ISDS 私法塑形

国家在投资争端解决程序层面的被迫“离开”，在一定程度上促成了投资争端解决的“私人化”救济模式的塑形，并最终确立了以投资争端解决的私法模式为基础的投资者—国家仲裁机制。具体包括以下内容。

1. 国际法“父爱主义”转向“对角线学说”

国际法“父爱主义”的典型表现是外交保护学说，该学说认为国家—臣民利益具有一体化特征，[③] 臣民之损害视为国家之损害，国家可以襄助臣民获得救济。随着主权国家间缔结的国际条约赋予第三方以实体和程序权利，国际司法机关获得了免于国家控制的更多自治权。现代国际投资条约赋权国家代理人或第三方启动国际司法程序，这种发展趋势打破了传统条约法奉行的国家间约定必守的“双务性”机制，[④] 最终转向了条约赋权的第三方无须经由母国襄助，而直接在国际司法机关起诉条约另一方的“对角线学说”的塑形。[⑤] 这种转变实现了国际投资争端解决由国家主导的国际法“父爱主义”的公法范式向由私人主导的私法范式的转变，意味着

---

① 有学者认为当前的国际投资条约体制实际上是一种多边体制或双边基础之上的多边体制，参见 Stephan W. Schill, *The Multilateralization of International Investment Law* (New York: Cambridge University Press, 2009), pp. 65 - 117。

② Berk Demirkol, *Judicial Acts and Investment Treaty Arbitration* (Cambridge: Cambridge University Press, 2018), pp. 1 - 2.

③ Kate Miles, *The Origins of International Investment Law: Empire, Environment and the Safeguarding of Capital* (Cambridge: Cambridge University Press, 2013), pp. 33 - 42.

④ Valentina Vadi, *Analogies in International Investment Law and Arbitration* (Cambridge: Cambridge University Press, 2016), p. 63.

⑤ Valentina Vadi, *Analogies in International Investment Law and Arbitration* (Cambridge: Cambridge University Press, 2016), p. 63.

投资者母国在投资争端解决程序方面的退出。虽然《华盛顿公约》和国际投资条约预设了东道国起诉外国投资者的可能性，但限于反诉制度[①]和获得进行投资仲裁的投资者方同意的困难，东道国利用投资仲裁的能力受到了极大的影响。可以认为，正是东道国在投资条约中的自我限制，投资者一国家仲裁成为一种单车道程序。

2. 国际投资仲裁的私人驱动

对于投资仲裁是以商事仲裁为蓝本，还是源自国家间的公法仲裁，学界存有分歧。[②] 不可否认的是，从投资条约的缔结到仲裁裁决的最终执行，私人是最主要的驱动者。在仲裁程序启动方面，虽然理论上存在东道国提起申诉和反诉的可能性，但现实中则是绝大部分案件均由投资者启动。虽然不同投资条约可能规定不同的仲裁程序规则，但基本都规定仲裁员的选择奉行当事方选定原则。通常的做法是，争端方各自指定一名仲裁员，双方共同或其指定的仲裁员共同指定主任仲裁员。[③] 相较于国内法院法官的固定任期制，投资仲裁的仲裁员具有临时性，为增加自己被再次选任的机会，仲裁员可能更倾向于支持指定方的观点与利益，并形成了事实上所谓的"旋转门现象"。仲裁员的当事方选任机制和任期的临时性，使得指定方和仲裁员之间在某种程度上已经形成了利益共同体。甚至有些学者认为，在国际投资仲裁领域存在"白人男性俱乐部"。[④]

3. "视为国内最终裁决"的执行机制

国际法发展初期，无强制执行力是学者们质疑国际法存在的重要依

---

① Anne K. Hoffmann, "Counterclaims", in Meg Kinnear, Geraldine Fischer and JaraMinguez Almeida, eds., *Building International Investment Law*, *The First 50 Years of ICSID* (Alphen aan den Rijn: Kluwer Law International, 2016), pp. 505 – 520.

② H. H. A. Van Harten, *Investment Treaty Arbitration and Public Law* (New York: Oxford University Press, 2007), pp. 50 – 58; Eric De Brabandere, *Investment Treaty Arbitration as Public International Law: Procedural Aspects and Implications* (Cambridge: Cambridge University Press, 2016), pp. 17 – 21; Zachary Douglas, "The Hybrid Foundations of Investment Treaty Arbitration", *British Yearbook of International Law* 151 (2003): 151 – 155.

③ Jonathan Bonnitcha, Lauge N. Skovgaard Poulsen and Michael Waibel, *The Political Economy of the Investment Treaty Regime* (New York: Oxford University Press, 2017), pp. 62 – 65.

④ Sergio Puig, "Social Capital in the Arbitration Market", *The European Journal of International Law* 387 (2014): 388.

据,[①] 但路易斯·亨金（Henkin）认为，几乎所有的国家在几乎所有的时间里遵守了所有的国际法原则和义务。[②] 国际法的理性主义学派代表古兹曼（Guzman）提出了声誉、报复和互惠“3R 理论”解释国际法的执行机制。[③] 事实上，法律的有效性并不取决于不法行为被纠正或者加害方被处罚。在国际法发展过程中，某些领域，比如国际投资法已经发展出类似具有强制性的执行机制。投资仲裁裁决执行机制大体分为两种类型，分别是《华盛顿公约》规定了自成一体的、将仲裁裁决视为国内最终裁决的执行机制（这种机制已经被其他条约文件效仿）和将投资仲裁裁决视为商事仲裁裁决的《纽约公约》执行机制。[④] 这种执行机制为投资者提供了掌控仲裁裁决执行的可能性，某些投资者已经开始利用“国际投资争端解决中心”（ICSID）和 1958 年《纽约公约》的执行机制充公被诉方政府的财产。[⑤] 缔约方在国际层面构建功能优越的关于承认与执行仲裁裁决的法律框架，并将仲裁裁决视为国内法院作出的终局判决，最终在跨国经济关系中实现了私人正义的勃兴。[⑥]

二 ISDS 私法模式的运作机制与影响

国际投资法的两分模式——实体待遇方面的模糊赋权、程序待遇方面的强化投资者直诉权，外加近似强制性的执行机制，使得国家在投资争端解决中逐渐退出，最终导致投资仲裁机制具备了更强的私法模式。争端解

① Mary Ellen O'Connell, *The Power and Purpose of International Law* (New York: Oxford University Press, 2008), pp. 40 – 42.

② Louis Henkin, *How Nations Behave: Law and Foreign Policy* (New York: Columbia University Press, 2nd, 1979), p. 47.

③ Andrew T. Guzman, *How International Law Works: A Rational Choice Theory* (New York: Oxford University Press, 2010), pp. 33 – 48.

④ Jose Daniel Amado and Jackson Shaw Kern, *Arbitrating the Conduct of International Investors* (Cambridge: Cambridge University Press, 2018), p. 162.

⑤ Luke Peterson and Filip Balcerzak, "*Amidst Concerns about Prompt Payment of Arbitral Awards, Stays of Enforcement Are Lifted in Two ICSID Cases*", Investment Arbitration Reporter (1 April, 2014).

⑥ W. Kidane, *The Culture of International Arbitration* (New York: Oxford University Press, 2017), p. 285.

决程序创造了将投资条约中实体性待遇转变为现实权利的可能性，并塑造了一个非常强大的授予外国投资者前所未有的实体与程序权利相结合的国际法机制。这种机制的运作结果是将外国的私人利益凌驾于公共的国家利益之上，因而招致严厉批评，并引发了各种改革建议。

（一）确定管辖权的冒险

如何实现国际投资协定中规定的实体待遇，很大程度上取决于争端解决条款构建的国际司法机关的管辖权。[①] 通常观点将国际司法机关视为当事方选择的功能单一的争端解决机构，其合法性源自当事方的合意授权。[②] 在投资条约框架下，解决争端的当事方是身份不确定的私人投资者和身份确定的投资条约的缔约国，双方间并不存在解决投资争端的直接合意（仲裁协议或仲裁条款）。投资仲裁庭在仲裁实践中依据“自裁管辖权”原则，偶然（accidental）且创造性解释了“仲裁合意”，并形成了所谓的合同类比理论、无协议仲裁理论[③]和国家单方行为理论。其中，无协议仲裁理论和单方行为理论对投资仲裁庭扩大其管辖权影响甚大。

1. *要约承诺理论*

投资者—国家仲裁最普遍的解释是，东道国通过双边投资条约同意将与投资者的争端提交仲裁解决，投资者通过申请仲裁的行为接受了东道国的要约。[④] 这种解释的理论依据在于，投资者—国家仲裁在某些方面类似于合同关系。[⑤] 将投资者—国家仲裁视为一种合同类比受到了历史演进的影响，因为早期的投资者—国家仲裁事实上构建在国家和外国投资者之间

---

① Campbell McLachlan, Laurence Shore and Matthew Weiniger, *International Investment Arbitration: Substantive Principles* (New York: Oxford University Press, 2007), p. 45.

② 在解决外国投资争端的初级阶段，投资者与东道国间的争端常通过条约（比如“杰伊条约”）设立的临时委员会进行解决。19世纪至20世纪60年代，投资者和东道国间的争端常依据双方间达成的合同中的同意仲裁条款组建的司法机关解决。参见 Krista Nadakavukaren Schefer, *International Investment Law: Text, Cases and Materials* (Cheltenham: Edward Elgar Publishing Limited, 2013), pp. 369 – 370。

③ Jan Paulsson, “Arbitration Without Privity”, *ICSID Review Foreign Investment Law Journal* 232 (1995): 232.

④ *ICS Inspection and Control Services Limited (United Kingdom) v. The Republic of Argentina*, UNCITRAL, PCA Case No. 2010 – 9, Jurisdiction (Feb. 10, 2012), para. 270.

⑤ Andrea K. Bjorklund, “Contract Without Privity: Sovereign Offer and Investor Acceptance”, *Chicago Journal of International Law* 183 (2001): 183.

的合同承诺基础之上。[①]

2. 无协议仲裁理论

ICSID 仲裁历史上有一个常被忽视的革命性裁决，即“亚洲农产品公司诉斯里兰卡案”（AAPL v. Sri Lanka）。这个案件裁决完成了 ICSID 仲裁庭在确定管辖权方面的“静悄悄的革命”，开启了以国际投资协定为基础的投资仲裁程序时代，以至于有学者将这个案件视为国际投资法发展历史上的拐点案件。[②] 该案裁决在解释仲裁同意理论方面的做法如下：首先是将仲裁同意分为两个部分，投资条约缔约方在双边投资条约中表达的希望采取仲裁解决争端的意思表示，构成事先的同意，私人投资者在特定案件出现后，通过提示或请求进行仲裁的行为，表达了愿意采取仲裁解决争端的事后的同意，至此，争端方之间达成了进行仲裁的合意；其次，确立了私人投资者可以直接援引双边投资条约中规定的权利；最后，投资仲裁程序的准据法遵守当事方意思自治原则，在意思自治缺位时，适用双边投资条约。[③] 该案裁决和波尔森（Paulsson）发表在 ICSID 评论上的《无协议仲裁》论文，似乎为后续以投资条约为基础的投资者—国家仲裁程序铺平了道路。

3. 单方行为理论

根据联合国国际法委员会通过的《适用于可创设法律义务的国家单方声明的指导原则》，单方行为是指国家方作出并表明愿意受其创设的法律义务拘束的声明。[④] 单方行为通常包括独立行为和依据条约进行的行为。[⑤]

---

① 关于该理论以及优缺点的详细阐述，参见 Frederic Gilles Sourgens, *A Nascent Common Law: The Process of Decisionmaking in International Legal Disputes Between States and Foreign Investors* (Leiden: Brill-Nijhoff, 2015), pp. 35 – 48。

② Jan Paulsson, “Tipping Point”, in Meg Kinnear, Geraldine Fischer and Jara Minguez Almeida, eds., *Building International Investment Law: The First 50 Years of ICSID* (Alphen aan den Rijn: Kluwer Law International, 2016), pp. 85 – 94.

③ Joost Pauwelyn, “Rational Design or Accidental Evolution? The Emergence of International Investment Law”, in Zachary Douglas, Joost Pauwelyn and Jorge E. Vinuales, *The Foundations of International Investment Law: Bringing Theory into Practice* (New York: Oxford University Press, 2014), pp. 31 – 33.

④ *Guiding Principles Applicable to Unilateral Declarations of States Capable of Creating Legal Obligations*, in Reports of the International Law Commission, 58th session, May 1 – June 9, July 3 – Aug. 11, 2006, U. N. Doc. A/61/1; GAOR, 61st Sess., Supp. No. 10 (2006), p. 1.

⑤ 关于国际法上单方行为的详细研究，参见 Przemyslaw Saganek, *Unilateral Acts of States in Public International Law* (Leiden: Brill-Nijhoff, 2015), pp. 1 – 85。

独立行为常表现为国家官员通过合理的公开或外交方式作出的，且能够使该国受国际义务拘束的声明或行为。依据条约的行为指政府依据条约作出的行为，虽然行为是单方的，但相关环境表明这些行为承认且承担条约中规定的法律义务。[①] 在投资者—国家仲裁中，东道国通过国际条约同意采取仲裁方式解决其与投资者的争端，这种同意是一种条约义务，且是一个单方行为。[②] 通过这个单方行为，国家权力受到了拘束。目前，单方行为理论也逐渐成为投资条约仲裁庭偏好的确定自身管辖权的法律依据。

（二）解释实体待遇的能动性

国际投资条约运动是在发展中国家质疑西方国家关于外国人待遇保护的习惯国际法的背景下启动的，其目的之一便是将被质疑的非成文、模糊的习惯国际法转变为清晰具体的条约法。鉴于人类语言的局限性，在转变习惯法为条约法的过程中，国际投资条约中的某些待遇标准仍然模糊不清，甚至和原先的习惯法同样的不精确。投资条约条款表述方面的模糊性为投资仲裁庭的适用过程提供了宽泛的自由裁量空间，诱发了司法能动性。

1. 解释机关的非常设性

国际司法机关有常设和临时之区分，临时性使得这些司法机关更倾向于创新和冒进，并最终导致国际法的碎片化。[③] 对这些临时司法机关而言，采取传统观点并将自己置身于现存法律框架的刺激相对较弱。这些临时仲裁庭通过发布裁决创新或背离传统法律，特别是在其发展的早期。投资仲裁制度的典型特征之一便是临时性，所有投资仲裁庭均为遵循当事方意思自治原则临时组建，并具备通常临时司法机关具备的创新和冒进等共性。相对于常设性的司法机关，临时性司法机关都是为解决特定争端而组建，争端得到解决便意味着司法机关完成其职能并解散。这种功能定位的单一性使得临时司法机关是在“临床隔离状态”而非整个法律体系中作出裁

---

① Patrick Daillier and Alain Pellet, *Droit International Public* (Paris: Librairie générale de droit et de jurisprudence, 7th, 2002), pp. 361 - 364.

② Michael D. Nolan & Frederic G. Sourgens, “A Preliminary Comment—The Interplay between State Consent to ICSID Arbitration and Denunciation of the ICSID Convention: The (Possible) Venezuela Case Study”, *Transnational Dispute Management* 1 (2007): 28 - 29.

③ Philippa Webb, *Judicial Integration and Fragmentation in the International Legal System* (Croydon: Oxford University Press, 2013), p. 150.

决，无须承担法律一致性和可预期性的责任。

2. 解释对象的模糊性

虽然《国际法院规约》第38条被有的学者批评为形式主义，[①] 但无可否认的事实是，条约和习惯法仍然是国际法的最主要渊源。在国际投资法的渊源中最重要的当属国际投资条约，习惯国际法可在条约缺位时补充适用。[②] 处理投资争端的仲裁庭主要承担解释条约和习惯法，并将之适用于具体争端的任务。如果一个法律领域由详细且综合性的条约调整，这将会为国际司法机关的解释活动提供指南，并限制其自由裁量权。如果一个法律领域主要由习惯国际法调整，多样化的国家实践和主观性的法律确信将会事实上赋予国际司法机关更大的自由裁量空间。[③] 虽然今天的国际投资法体制由3000多个双边投资条约构成，但其中的某些待遇条款，如最惠国待遇条款、伞型条款、公平公正待遇和间接征收等条款，可能和习惯国际法一样模糊不清。[④] 投资仲裁庭在解释适用这些待遇条款时，常作出非一致甚至冲突裁决。比如"SGS系列案"、"Lauder/CME系列案"以及"非排除措施条款系列案"。

3. 解释过程缺乏先例与对话机制

《国际法院规约》第59条表明，在国际法体系中，并不存在所谓法律上的先例制度。具体到国际投资法领域，国际投资条约和国际投资仲裁庭的仲裁规则同样确认，国际投资仲裁领域不存在法律意义上的垂直先例制度。不可否认，在投资仲裁实践中发展出的所谓的事实先例或水平先例制度，但这种先例的适用取决于后续仲裁庭的自由援引。[⑤] 司法对话本质上

---

① Jean d'Aspremont, *Formalism and the Sources of International Law: A Theory of the Ascertainment of Legal Rules* (New York: Oxford University Press, 2013), pp. 12 – 29.

② 关于国际投资法渊源的介绍，参见 Christian J. Tams, "The Sources of International Investment Law: Concluding Thoughts", in Tarcisio Gazzini and Eric De Brabandere, *International Investment Law: The Sources of Rights and Obligations* (Leiden: Martinus Nijhoff, 2012), pp. 319 – 331; Jean d'Aspremont and Samantha Besson, eds., *The Oxford Handbook of the Sources of International Law* (New York: Oxford University Press, 2018), pp. 1069 – 1115。

③ Alan Boyle and Christine Chinkin, *The Making of International Law* (New York: Oxford University Press, 2007), p. 268.

④ 关于条约和习惯法之间的联系与区别，参见 Robert Kolb, *Theory of International Law* (Oxford: Hart Publishing, 2016), pp. 124 – 134。

⑤ Jeffery P. Commission, "Precedent in Investment Treaty Arbitration: A Citation Analysis of a Developing Jurisprudence", *Journal of International Arbitration* 129 (2007): 129 – 158.

是一种更加灵活的水平先例，不仅包括司法机关援引、适用和解释其他司法机关的案例，还包括非正式的信息交换、法院间联合会议以及人员交流等。其好处是司法机关在裁决时能够理解现存案例，从而更有效地解释和证明自己的推理，最终促进国际法渐进式发展。[①] 随着国际司法机关的持续运作，事实先例和司法对话机制能够在一定程度上促进国际投资法法理的发展。

（三）估算赔偿数额的激进

依据投资仲裁程序的三分法，仲裁程序可分为管辖权阶段、实体审理阶段和赔偿估算阶段。投资条约除规定充分赔偿这一基本原则外，很少就赔偿估算提供具体指南。仲裁庭在确定救济方法以及估算标准时，多数依据“霍茹夫工厂案原则”和联合国国际法委员会起草的 2001 年《国家对国际不法行为的责任条款草案》中的相关规则估算损害赔偿数额。在可选择的救济方式中，投资仲裁庭更偏爱裁决金钱赔偿，这增加了国内政府民主决策成本，并为相关商业机构通过第三方资助创造了谋求利润的空间。

1. 金钱赔偿模式

投资仲裁多采取金钱赔偿为主的模式，具体原因可能包括：恢复原状并不具有可行性、争端方可能认为恢复原状不是更优的救济方式以及投资仲裁庭缺乏明确条约授权裁决恢复原状或非金钱救济等。[②] 投资争端大致可分为征收、违反非征收外的投资条约条款以及违反合同等类型，投资条约或习惯国际法对这些违反类型规定了救济的不同法律原则。投资仲裁庭需要借助于各种估价技术将这些法律原则转变为具体的赔偿数额，这些估价技术大体可分为以收入为基础、以市场为基础以及以资产为基础的估价方法等。[③] 上述估价技术中，有些涉及对未来损坏的预测，这相当于投资

---

① Philippa Webb, *Judicial Integration and Fragmentation in the International Legal System* (Croydon: Oxford University Press, 2013), pp. 197 – 198.

② Meg Kinnear, “Damages in Investment Treaty Arbitration”, in Katia Yannaca-Small, eds., *Arbitration Under International Investment Agreements: A Guide to the Key Issues* (New York: Oxford University Press, 2012), p. 533.

③ Irmgard Marboe, *Calculation of Compensation and Damages in International Investment Law* (New York: Oxford University Press, 2009), p. 186.

仲裁庭实际上拥有了一个具有魔法功能的水晶球。[①] 根据相关学者的实证研究结果，虽然最终裁决的赔偿数额可能远低于申诉方请求的数额，但在多数仲裁裁决中，具体裁决的数额仍然可能异常巨大。[②] 比如"尤科斯诉俄罗斯案"（*Yukos v. Russia*），仲裁庭裁决的赔偿数额达 500 亿美元。[③]

2. 管制寒蝉效应（chilling effect）

面对巨额赔偿，多数国家出于维护良好的投资目标国形象而自愿执行。这种赔偿可能会对国家的管制权产生影响，并形成管制寒蝉效应。首先，在某些情况下，有些国内法允许的行为却被仲裁庭裁定违反了国际投资协定，并为此支付赔偿，这将会增加国内民主决策的成本。比如，在"瓦腾福诉德国案"（*Vattenfall AB and others v. Federal Republic of Germany*）中，汉堡市新参议院需要实施一项选举承诺，这将会增加对未来火力发电厂的生态环境要求，但原参议院却无此规定。为此，瓦滕福（*Vattenfall*）等公司提出了投资仲裁请求，并索赔 14 亿欧元。[④] 其次，在国家拒不支付赔偿时，这些国家在国际组织中的相关权利可能会受到限制，并最终影响这些国家参与国际立法和国际治理的权限。比如阿根廷在经济危机引发的系列仲裁案后，最初拒绝向美国公司支付赔偿。美国则暂停针对阿根廷的贸易减让，并阻止阿根廷从国际货币基金组织和世界银行获得国际贷款，最终双方和解，阿根廷为此支付了 5 亿美元。[⑤]

3. 第三方资助

这种现象最初起源于国内诉讼领域，后逐渐向仲裁领域扩张。受国际

① Hans van Houtte and Bridie McAsey, "Future Damages in Investment Arbitration—A Tribunal with a Crystal Ball?", in David D. Caron, Stephan W. Schill, Abby Cohen Smutny and Epaminontas E. Triantafilou, eds., *Practising Virtue: Inside International Arbitration* (New York: Oxford University Press, 2015), pp. 642 - 657.

② Susan D. Franck, "Review: The Public International Law Regime Governing International Investment by José E. Alvarez", *The American Journal of International Law* 890, p. 894 (2012); Matthew Hodgson, "Counting the Costs of Investment Treaty Arbitration", *Global Arbitration Review 1* (2014): 5.

③ Diana Rosert, *The Stakes Are High: A Review of the Financial Costs of Investment Treaty Arbitration* (Winnipeg: International Institute for Sustainable Development, 2014), p. 3.

④ *Vattenfall AB and others v. Federal Republic of Germany*, ICSID Case No. ARB/09/6, Request for Arbitration (30 Mar 2009), p. 24.

⑤ Lauge N. Skovgaard Poulsen, *Bounded Rationality and Economic Diplomacy: The Politics of Investment Treaties in Developing Countries* (Cambridge: Cambridge University Press, 2015), p. 6.

金融市场的不稳定性、投资仲裁费用以及裁决赔偿的数额巨大等因素影响，第三方资助开始延伸至投资仲裁领域。投资仲裁的第三方资助指由与案件争议无利害关系的资助者支付一方当事人的全部或部分仲裁费用，在受资助当事人胜诉后，资助者按预先约定比例（通常为 20%—50%），以裁决最终支持的数额为基数收取利益的一种安排。[①] 目前，国际社会存在 50 个以上专业的第三方资助公司。[②] 投资仲裁第三方资助可分为投资者资助和东道国资助类型，但投资者资助类型更为普遍。任何事物都具有两面性，投资仲裁的第三方资助在促进国际法治的同时，会引发消极的不利后果（比如“滥诉”问题），国家可能会面临越来越多的案件，[③] 最终使国际投资仲裁制度丧失公正性，并沦为第三方资助者牟利之工具。比如，在“泰因福案”（*Teinver S. A. , Transportes de Cercanías S. A and Autobuses Urbanosdel Sur S. A. v. The Argentine Republic*）中，第三方资助公司伯福德资本（Burford Capital）获得了 1.4 亿美元的回报。

简言之，投资者—国家仲裁已经背离其创立者预设的互惠愿景，成为投资保护的单车道程序。在众多改革建议中，强调国家特别是投资者母国“回归”在某种程度上成为一种共识。因此，国家如何“回归”则成为未来投资争端解决机制构建的关键，《里斯本条约》生效后的欧盟提出了投资法院体系的设想，并成为改革的新趋势。

三 国家的“回归”与欧盟投资法院方案

在现代国际投资法体制发展初期，欧洲国家主导的双边投资协定获得了巨大成功。20 世纪 70 年代末期，美国在经历政策反思期后实现了从 FCNs

---

① 关于第三方资助的研究，感兴趣的读者可以进一步阅读以下材料。Jonas von Goeler, *Third-Party Funding and its Impact on International Arbitration Proceedings* (New York: Wolters Kluwer, 2016); Lisa Bench Nieuwveld and Victoria Shannon Sahani, *Third-Party Funding in International Arbitration* (New York: Wolters Kluwer, 2017).

② 最新数据和详细清单参见 http://www.international-arbitration-attorney.com/third-party-funders，最后访问日期：2018 年 4 月 12 日。

③ Howard Mann, “Reconceptualizing International Investment Law: Its Role in Sustainable Development”, *Lewis and Clark Law Review* 521 (2013): 534.

模式向双边投资条约模式的转变,① 后来居上，成为塑造当前国际投资条约体制的主导力量。究其原因，很可能在于美国更早地意识到，当前投资条约体系不再是单车道程序，而是事实上的双边双向程序，并采取措施，在投资待遇界定和争端解决程序方面寻求国家的“回归”。② 欧盟在《里斯本条约》生效后，将成员国对外投资事项纳入共同商业政策［《欧盟运行条约》(TFEU) 第 207（1）条］，并获得了成员国授权的对外缔结投资条约的排他性权力。欧盟委员会开始了系列谈判，回顾且反思了投资者—国家仲裁的以往体验、批评以及经验教训,③ 提出在未来签署的投资协定中构建投资法院体系的设想。

欧盟—加拿大全面经济贸易协定（CETA）签署后，欧盟委员会认为该协定中的投资者—国家争端解决制度是与过去制度的一个最大决裂，是目前为止最具有进步意义的投资者—国家争端解决体系。④ 紧接着 2015 年 9 月欧盟委员会发布了《跨大西洋贸易与投资伙伴关系协定》(Transatlantic Trade and Investment Partnership，TTIP）投资章草案，将其主要挑战界定为达成投资者的保护与基于欧盟及其成员国权利和公共利益而进行的管制能力之间的恰当平衡，并认为投资者—国家仲裁体系显然不适合 21 世纪,⑤ 应当利用投资法院取代临时仲裁。本部分立足于 TTIP 投资法院体系的制度设计，分析国家在投资争端解决程序中的“回归”路径。

TTIP 作为一个更加政治化的文件，构建了投资法院体系。通过组建缔约方之间的贸易委员会，将裁判者由当事方指定原则修改为贸易委员会指定原则，修改一审终审制为初审与上诉审的两审终审制度以及并入类似于《华盛顿公约》规定的视为国内法院最终裁决的执行机制等，为国家在争

---

① 关于美国国际投资协定的历史演进，参见 Kenneth J. Vandevelde，*U. S. International Investment Agreements*（New York：Oxford University Press，2009），pp. 11 - 26。

② José E. Alvarez，“The Return of the State”，*Minnesota Journal of International Law* 223（2011）：223 - 264.

③ Armin von Bogdandy and Ingo Venzke，*In Whose Name?：A Public Law Theory of International Adjudication*（New York：Oxford University Press，2016），p. xliii.

④ European Commission，*Investment Provisions in the EU-Canada Free Trade Agreement*（*CETA*）（26 September，2014）.

⑤ Cecilia Malmstrom，*Investments In TTIP and Beyond-towards an International Investment Court*（5 May，2015）.

端解决程序方面的“回归”设计了路径。[①]

（一）利用缔约国政治立法权限制司法造法

作为针对投资仲裁庭可能的司法造法的回应，TTIP 投资章规定了更多的缔约国政治立法权介入国际投资条约运作的路径。首先，TTIP 投资章第二部分（“投资保护”）第 2（1）条明确规定了国家的管制权，国家在其领土内有权制定诸如保护公共健康、安全、环境保护和公共道德、社会或消费者保护以及文化多样性等必要措施。这意味着这些措施在国家管制权范围内，司法机关不得进行复审。其次，制定更加详细的待遇标准，比如采取一个封闭清单方式，列举可能构成违反公平公正待遇的要素，如 TTIP 投资章第二部分（“投资保护”）第 3（2）条列举了违反公平公正待遇的五种情况。对于间接征收、国民待遇条款、最惠国待遇条款引发的不确定性和不受欢迎的发展，也通过更加详细的方式加以界定。这种清晰且封闭的定义将会为司法机关的司法活动提供必要指南，并限制司法人员的自由裁量权。再次，TTIP 试图设立缔约方之间的政治机关，比如贸易委员会（trade commission）负责条约的解释。在出现关于本协议投资保护、投资争端解决以及投资法院体系部分的解释事项时，委员会可以通过决议解释这些条款，并对初审法院和上诉法院具有法律拘束力。最后，坚持投资法院体系的开放性。TTIP 投资章第三部分第 18 条规定了透明度义务，表明该部分的争端解决程序应当遵循联合国国际贸易法委员会透明度规则。第 22 条规定被诉方应将收到的文件（第 4—6 条所指文件）转交投资条约的非争端方，且非争端方有权参加听证会。第 23 条规定了第三方介入程序，法庭应当允许对争端解决结果具有直接或间接影响的自然人或法人作为第三方介入争端解决程序。通过上述条款的设计，TTIP 构建的争端解决程序不断强化条约缔约方的政治立法权，将原先由仲裁庭进行自由裁量的权限收归缔约方，必将进一步限制争端解决机关的司法造法。

---

① 参见 F. Baetens, “The European Union's Proposed Investment Court System: Addressing Criticisms of Investor-State Arbitration While Raising New Challenges”, *Legal Issues of Economic Integration* 367（2016），pp. 367 - 384。

（二）将争端方指定原则修改为缔约方委员会指定原则

欧洲议会希望利用一个由公开任命的法官主导，并遵守监控与透明度规则的新司法体系取代私人仲裁。[①] 法官的指定过程与传统仲裁明显不同，不再奉行当事方指定原则。传统仲裁庭的组建权在争端方手中，仲裁员更类似于代表当事方处理争端的代理机构，而不是代表公共利益的法官。[②] 在投资法院体系中，由条约方组建的贸易委员会具体负责法官的公开选任。

条约方组建的贸易委员会指定初审法院的 15 名法官［第 9（2）条］，人选来自条约双方各三分之一，剩下的来自第三国。与投资者—国家仲裁不同的是，投资者不能参加指定程序。涉及具体案件时，当事方无法决定由谁审理案件的，决议由仲裁庭主席作出，并确保组成的随机且无法预测，同时给予每一个法官平等的机会［第 9（7）条］。所有法官通过抽签方式从来自第三国的法官中选择主席［第 9（8）条］。常设上诉法院共有 6 名法官（第 10 条），选任办法和初审法院法官相同。

法官采取固定任期制，任期 6 年，可连任一次。法官任职资格要求并未采取高尚的道德标准，而是要求法官具备国际公法领域的知识，并力求避免利益冲突确保法官的独立性与公正性。比如第 11 条禁止法官担任任何未决或新投资争端的法律顾问，并采取附件方式详细规定了法官的行为准则。

（三）将一审终审制修改为初审和上诉两审机制

TTIP 投资章草案提议设立初审和上诉的两审机制，对于一审终审制度的现代投资法体系而言，这无疑是一个重大创新。

国际投资仲裁裁决已经明确，如果原先裁决构成合理预期，处理后案的仲裁庭具有正当性依据，甚至有义务参照原裁决，进而有利于国际投资法整体的协调发展。不可否认，在扁平化且去中心化的投资仲裁中，存在所谓的水平先例制度，但仲裁员更容易漠视或边缘化原先的裁决，其代价

---

① EU Parliament, *TTIP: Ease Access to Us Market, Protect EU Standards, Reform Dispute Settlement* (8 July 2015).

② Armin von Bogdandy and Ingo Venzke, *In Whose Name?: A Public Law Theory of International Adjudication* (New York: Oxford University Press, 2016), p. li.

就是丧失了投资仲裁的确定性和一致性，同时也降低了仲裁裁决对创设普遍国际投资法的贡献。

欧盟投资法院体系设立的上诉机制可能为投资争端解决的一致性注入新动力。在一个设立上诉机制的体系中，不仅可以允许对初审法院权威的审查，同时又增加了整体的司法权威。通过将两审终审制度与委员会指定法官的制度相结合，投资条约的缔约国可以强化对投资争端解决程序的控制。

（四）国家在裁决救济形式和裁决执行方面的控制权

国际投资协定并未规定仲裁庭可以采取的最终救济方式。多数情况下，投资仲裁庭裁定金钱赔偿。欧盟投资法院体系规定了不同的制度，目的在于强调国家对裁决形式与执行方面的控制和引导。首先，TTIP 投资章第 28 条规定投资法院可以裁决金钱赔偿、利息或恢复原状。其次，第 30（1）条规定了最终裁决应当具有拘束性，不能进行任何上诉、复审、撤销或任何其他救济。最后，第 30（2）条规定应当将金钱裁决部分视为国内法院最终裁决加以执行。这意味着在裁决执行方面，TTIP 实际上构建了类似于 ICSID 的强大执行机制。通过规定裁决形式、裁决终局性和视为国内法院最终裁决等设计，欧盟投资法院实现了国家在这些程序中的“回归”。

结　语

投资者—国家仲裁在确保外国投资者诉诸司法权、去政治化争端、支持投资保护的原则和标准以及促进国际法治方面发挥着重要作用，但投资者—国家仲裁应该同时确保东道国可以行使管制权，颁布服务于公共利益的措施。但当前的投资者—国家仲裁对于外国投资者—东道国模式[①]之外的利益相关者的合理预期漠不关心。为此，针对国际投资争端解决机制的

---

① Jose Daniel Amado and Jackson Shaw Kern and Martin Doe Rodriguez, *Arbitrating the Conduct of International Investors*（Cambridge: Cambridge University Press, 2018）, pp. 1 - 2.

不满与批评逐渐增多。[①] 本文分析表明，当前投资者—国家仲裁程序备受批评的原因之一是国家在投资争端解决程序中的“离开”，使得投资者—国家仲裁呈现出私人驱动与仲裁员主导的私法面向。在当前的改革建议中，欧盟投资法院体系为国家重新“回归”争端解决程序提供了一种可行的模式。欧盟投资法院体系的效果如何仍需要时间检验，但下述反思可能会对未来投资争端解决机制的发展有所裨益。

其一，国际司法机关的多功能性定位。国际司法的委托代理理论（principal-agent theory）认为，国际司法机关的权利源自当事方的授权，主要职责是解决双方间的争端。[②] 在投资争端解决的“去政治化”过程中，投资者—国家仲裁构建在当事方同意基础之上，负责解决当事方之间的争端。国际司法机关的公法理论认为，在现实中，除解决争端外，国际司法机关还具有司法造法、稳定法律预期以及控制或合理化其他公共机关行使公共权力的功能。[③] 原先的依据争端解决单一功能定位确立的投资者—国家仲裁的制度，显然无法匹配现实中司法机关的多功能性。

其二，国际司法机关裁决篡夺国家在国际层面的缔约权。在国际投资法的发展中，国家在逐渐“离开”。这种“离开”表现为，在程序方面，投资争端解决的对角线学说获得了青睐，边缘化了投资者母国，同时限制了投资者东道国（有限反诉和难以获得投资者的仲裁同意）。在实体待遇层面，国际投资协定中的某些条款具有模糊性，此外，还存在为达成特定目标而设置的建设性模糊条款。国家在程序待遇和实体待遇方面的“离开”，等同于将国家在国际层面的缔约权拱手让与私人主导的投资者—国家仲裁机制。

其三，国家通过国际条约行使政治立法权，限制国际司法机关的司法造法。国际司法机关因其专业性和高效性，最终获得了独立于政治机关的地位，但这种独立性并非绝对，政治机关仍然可以设计政治立法权进入国

---

① Michael Waibel, Asha Kaushal and Kyo-HwaChung, eds., *The Backlash against Investment Arbitration: Perceptions and Reality* (Alphen aan den Rijn: Kluwer Law International, 2010), pp. xxxvii – li.

② Anthea Roberts, "Power and Persuasion in Investment Treaty Interpretation: The Dual Role of States", *American Journal of International Law* 179 (2010): 186.

③ Armin von Bogdandy and Ingo Venzke, *In Whose Name?: A Public Law Theory of International Adjudication* (New York: Oxford University Press, 2016), pp. 9 – 17.

际司法机关的途径。就国际投资法而言，一方面，国家可以细化国际投资协定中的待遇条款，限制司法机关的能动性解释；另一方面，国家可以组建缔约方之间的政治机关，强化相互间对于条约的共识，并指导司法机关的实践。

（责任编辑：郝鲁怡）

（本文原载于《国际法研究》2018 年第 4 期）